PSYCHOLOGY
In Search of the Human Mind
THIRD EDITION

PSYCHOLOGY
In Search of the Human Mind
THIRD EDITION

ROBERT J. STERNBERG
Yale University

HARCOURT COLLEGE PUBLISHERS

Fort Worth   Philadelphia   San Diego   New York   Orlando   Austin   San Antonio

Toronto   Montreal   London   Sydney   Tokyo

Publisher	**EARL MCPEEK**
Acquisitions Editor	**BRADLEY J. POTTHOFF**
Market Strategist	**KATIE MATTHEWS**
Developmental Editor	**DIANE DREXLER**
Project Editor	**ELIZABETH CRUCE ALVAREZ**
Art Director	**BURL SLOAN**
Production Manager	**CYNTHIA YOUNG**

Cover image: Diana Ong/SuperStock.

ISBN: 0-15-506940-3

Library of Congress Catalog Card Number: 00-105040

Copyright © 2001, 1998, 1995 by Harcourt, Inc.

Address for Domestic Orders
Harcourt College Publishers, 6277 Sea Harbor Drive, Orlando, FL 32887-6777
800-782-4479

Address for International Orders
International Customer Service
Harcourt, Inc., 6277 Sea Harbor Drive, Orlando, FL 32887-6777
407-345-3800
(fax) 407-345-4060
(e-mail) hbintl@harcourtbrace.com

Address for Editorial Correspondence
Harcourt College Publishers, 301 Commerce Street, Suite 3700, Fort Worth, TX 76102

Web Site Address
http://www.harcourtcollege.com

Harcourt College Publishers will provide complimentary supplements or supplement packages to those adopters qualified under our adoption policy. Please contact your sales representative to learn how you qualify. If as an adopter or potential user you receive supplements you do not need, please return them to your sales representative or send them to: Attn: Returns Department, Troy Warehouse, 465 South Lincoln Drive, Troy, MO 63379.

Printed in the United States of America

0 1 2 3 4 5 6 7 8 9 032 9 8 7 6 5 4 3 2 1

Harcourt College Publishers

About the Author

Robert J. Sternberg is IBM Professor of Psychology and Education in the Department of Psychology at Yale University. He was graduated summa cum laude, Phi Beta Kappa, with a BA from Yale in 1972, receiving honors with exceptional distinction in psychology. He received the PhD in psychology in 1975 from Stanford University and an honorary doctorate from the Complutense University of Madrid in 1994. He will receive three more honorary doctorates in 2000–2001.

Sternberg has won several scholarships and fellowships, including a National Merit Scholarship to attend Yale, where he won the Wohlenberg Prize; a National Science Foundation Fellowship to attend Stanford, where he received the Sidney Siegel Memorial Award; and a Guggenheim Fellowship while a faculty member at Yale. He also has won several other awards, among them the James McKeen Cattell Award from the American Psychological Society; the Early Career and McCandless Awards of the American Psychological Association; the Outstanding Book, Research Review, Sylvia Scribner, and Palmer O. Johnson Awards of the American Educational Research Association; the Distinguished Career Contribution Award from the Connecticut Psychological Association; the Cattell Award of the Society of Multivariate Experimental Psychologists; and the International Award of the Association of Portuguese Psychologists. He is a Fellow of the American Psychological Association, American Psychological Society, the American Academy of Arts and Sciences, and the American Association for the Advancement of Science. Sternberg has taught introductory psychology for more than two decades. He has been a frequent contributor to *Teaching of Psychology* and has been a featured speaker at many conferences on the teaching of psychology. He is editor of *Teaching Introductory Psychology*.

Sternberg has been editor of the *Psychological Bulletin* and is currently editor of *The APA Review of Books: Contemporary Psychology*. He has been president of Divisions 1 (General Psychology), 10 (Psychology and the Arts), 15 (Educational Psychology), and 24 (Theoretical and Philosophical Psychology) of the American Psychological Association. He is the author of more than 800 books, book chapters, and articles, and has held more than $10 million in research grants and contracts.

Sternberg has two children, Seth and Sara, both of whom won the psychology prize at their high school. Seth is majoring in political science, and Sara is majoring in history.

PREFACE

The mission of *Psychology: In Search of the Human Mind* is to teach introductory psychology students to understand and to think about the field as psychologists do—to learn that, in the search for understanding of the human mind, psychology is both a product and a process. The text equally embraces biological, cognitive, developmental, social-psychological, and clinical approaches to demonstrate this balance. It also emphasizes the interactions among these different approaches. Psychology advances as a scientific discipline because psychologists are able to integrate ideas from diverse approaches.

Points of Change

The third edition of *Psychology: In Search of the Human Mind* has evolved in seven key ways, based on feedback received from professors and students who used the second edition.

1. **Psychological ideas flow from the mind to the lab to the everyday world and back again.** This concept is emphasized in the text in the following ways:

   • First, **Think About It** questions at the end of every chapter help students process as well as reflect analytically, creatively, and practically upon the material they have learned. Sample responses are provided for each question and students may try out their own answers online at the *In Search of the Human Mind* Web site (http://www.harcourtcollege.com/psych/ishm).

   • Second, **In the Lab of** . . . boxes represent first-hand accounts of some of the most exciting research currently being done in the field of psychology. Each box is written by a key investigator in the field of psychology, expressing in terms students can understand what research is being done, why the investigator finds it so exciting, and why the students should find it exciting too! These boxes show how higher order thinking is applied in the lab of the psychologist.

   • Third, **Psychology in Everyday Life** boxes show the links between higher order thinking and laboratory work, on the one hand, and the everyday world, on the other. Students see how psychologists' ideas and research can make a difference to the students' everyday lives.

   These three features are designed to emphasize for students the flow of ideas in the field of psychology, starting with the mind, proceeding to testing in the lab, and then out into the everyday world. The everyday world, in turn, provides the feedback that enables psychologists to fine-tune their ideas and to develop them further.

2. **The length and number of chapters have been reduced.** In order to transform the book into one

that can be more in harmony with the goals and requirements of both one- and two-term courses, the textual material has been reduced in length and the number of chapters has been reduced from 20 to 18. The previously separate chapters on Sensation and Perception have been combined, as have the chapters on Language and Thought. As a result, the book is more balanced among the areas of psychology.

3. **Placement of content.** There have been two major changes regarding placement of content: First, there has been a reordering of the major content of chapters 1 and 2. In response to requests from reviewers and users of the book, the material on the history of psychology now precedes rather than follows the material on research methods.

   Second, in response to reviewers' and users' comments that they prefer to teach motivation and emotion earlier in the course, the chapter on Motivation and Emotion now precedes the two chapters on social psychology rather than following these chapters.

4. **Currency of theory and research.** The explosion of knowledge in psychology in recent years has given rise to new theories, research, and paradigms that are reshaping the field. The third edition of *Psychology: In Search of the Human Mind* is totally current with respect to these new developments. Thus, the book contains over 500 new references, most of them from the middle to late 1990s.

5. **Parts.** Because every instructor has a preferred way of ordering the chapters, the part structure of the book has been eliminated. With the current format, instructors can decide for themselves how to structure the chapters into higher order units if, indeed, they wish to do so at all.

6. **Modified second edition features.** The use of three of the features from the second edition has been reworked in this edition.

   • First, the Psyche myth, which played a major role in the earlier editions, has been downplayed in this edition because many students simply did not relate to it. In its place each chapter now opens with a work of fine art and a quotation that captures some aspect of the themes covered in that chapter.

   • Second, analytical, creative, and practical thought questions, which previously were interspersed throughout each chapter, now only occur

at the end of each chapter as the Think About It questions. This change was made to provide a more unified and coherent presentation after the reader has covered the chapter material. In addition, sample answers are now provided for all questions.

   • Third, the theme of dialectical thinking continues in this edition, but has been integrated into the text without calling major attention to it. The goal is to teach students to think dialectically—realizing that science is constantly striving to redefine its questions and answers—without necessarily calling direct attention to this goal.

7. **Reading level.** Some students found the reading level of the previous editions of the text to be a bit higher than was ideal for them. In this edition, each sentence has been checked for readability. Where necessary, sentences have been reworked in order to increase their clarity and comprehensibility and to decrease their length. These modifications have been made without in any way affecting the integrity of the text or the depth with which the ideas are presented.

Points of Continuity

In addition, the third edition of *Psychology: In Search of the Human Mind* retains the most successful features of the second edition:

   • Psychology is presented as both a natural and a social science. Both natural-science and social-science viewpoints are presented and their interactions explored.

   • The third edition, like the second, emphasizes jointly how organisms and ideas evolve. This interweaving of two key evolutionary themes results in a text that is fully rather than partially evolutionary in its approach.

   • This edition embraces the use and expansion of fully integrated multicultural and cross-cultural material that will help students understand that these perspectives are not something separate from the core of psychology but an integral part of it.

   • An appendix demonstrates statistical methods by having students survey their classmates and analyze the data.

   • A glossary fully defines key terms from the text.

- A comprehensive reference list, as well as detailed name and subject indexes, make the book easy to use for study and reference.

In Conclusion: A Personal Journey

Many years ago, when my career was just starting, I was approached by another psychologist at Yale and asked to collaborate on an introductory psychology text that would emphasize an evolutionary approach to psychology. Committed then as I am now to an evolutionary approach, I agreed, and we commenced the collaboration. Unfortunately, the collaboration ended when we discovered that each of us meant something different by evolution—the other psychologist meant biological evolution and I meant the evolution of ideas. The other psychologist undertook a text focused on biological evolution, and I, some years later, undertook the first edition of *Psychology: In Search of the Human Mind* to focus on the evolution of ideas.

The second edition of *Psychology: In Search of the Human Mind* represented progress in my own thinking—synthesizing the evolution of organisms and of ideas in a single text. We can be grateful that biological evolution has advanced humans to the point where we can develop in our thinking through the evolution of ideas.

The third edition of *Psychology: In Search of the Human Mind* focuses on further progress in my thinking, particularly as it pertains to the teaching of psychology. Students need to understand the fundamental flow of ideas in psychology—from the mind to the lab to the everyday world and back again.

Ancillary Package

In support of *Psychology: In Search of the Human Mind*, the ancillary package builds on solid pedagogical theory to serve the needs of the introductory psychology student and instructor and to take full advantage of the latest in technology.

- The **Study Guide** by Bernard C. Beins (Ithaca College) provides practice at identifying, understanding, and integrating important psychological ideas presented in the main text. Students will learn to apply the concepts in creative, practical, and analytical ways. Each chapter lists specific goals and objectives, helps students review the material through a variety of questions, reinforces terminology with matching exercises, and encourages students to synthesize the information through short-answer questions of varying levels of difficulty. The Study Guide provides a progress test for each chapter and features a cumulative final exam to foster synthesis of the material. As an APA fellow and secretary of Division 2, Teaching of Psychology, Bernard Beins is involved extensively with the issues regarding the introductory psychology course. He has published numerous articles and has given various presentations on the subject of enhancing the learning experience.

- The **Instructor's Manual** by Ellen Pastorino (Valencia Community College) and Susann Doyle (Gainesville College) provides lecture outlines, a convenience for time-constrained professors, as well as creative ideas for class discussion, activities, outside resources, teaching tips, handouts, and writing exercises. Activities and exercises are integrated with the major themes of the main text: the flow of ideas from the mind to the lab to everyday life, and the evolution of ideas as well as organisms.

- Each chapter in the **Testbank** by Patrick Ackles and Patrick Conley (University of Illinois–Chicago) contains at least 180 convergent, multiple-choice items and 45 divergent, short-essay items. Two-thirds of the convergent items are conceptual (the remaining one-third are factual), and all are rated by difficulty and keyed to the section and page in the textbook where the concept is discussed. The divergent items ask students to answer questions in essay format to bring out different forms of thinking. Answer guidelines for essay questions give instructors key concepts to look for in the students' essays.

- **Computerized versions** of the Testbank are available in Windows and Macintosh formats. The Testbank software *EXAMaster+*™ offers three unique features to the instructor. EasyTest creates a test from a single screen in just a few easy steps. Instructors choose parameters, then either select questions from the database or let EasyTest randomly select them. FullTest offers a range of options that includes selecting, editing, adding, or linking questions or graphics; random selection of questions from a wide range of criteria; creating criteria; blocking questions; and printing up to 99 versions of the same test and answer sheet. *EXAMRecord*™ records, curves, graphs, and prints out grades according to criteria the instructor selects. Grade distribution displays as a bar graph or plotted graph.

For the instructor without access to a computer, or who has questions about the software, Harcourt College Publishers (800-447-9457) offers two services. RequesTest provides a software specialist who will compile questions according to the instructor's criteria and mail or fax the test master within 48 hours. The Software Support Hotline (800-447-9457) is available to answer questions Monday through Friday, 9 A.M. to 5 P.M., Central time.

• The **Overhead Transparencies** come in two packages: A supplementary package of illustrations and tables specially selected from *Psychology: In Search of the Human Mind* and the Harcourt Introductory Psychology package, which contains more than 200 transparencies. Each acetate, with accompanying guide, is in full color.

• **The Whole Psychology Catalog: Instructional Resources to Enhance Student Learning** by Michael B. Reiner, Kennesaw State College. Instructors can easily supplement course work and assignments with this manual. It has perforated pages containing experiential exercises, questionnaires, and visual aids. Each activity is classified by one of eight learning goals central to the teaching of psychology. Also included in this version is an informative section on using the Internet and the World Wide Web.

Multimedia and Interactive Software

• **PowerPsych CD-ROM** offers students an opportunity to learn the core concepts in *Psychology* in an interactive and fun environment. It contains exciting graphics, tutorials, and even a "Check Mastery" self-test section that accompanies each major feature. Use of virtual reality technology and 3D-rendered animations and simulations allow students to view and manipulate structures. For example, they may view the brain to study functions, such as ion movement during the action potential, and to review concepts, such as classical conditioning and systematic desensitization. This is all possible from different perspectives, and can be done at each student's pace and under his or her control.

• **The** *In Search of the Human Mind* **Web site** provides resources for both students and instructors. Students can test themselves with our self-assessment quizzes or learn more about introductory psychology concepts with our Web activities, Shockwave® animations, and our guide to psychology research. Instructors will find an electronic version of the Instructor's Manual, the Harcourt guide to using films in teaching introductory psychology concepts, overhead transparencies to print out, and teaching strategies. Instructors should contact their Harcourt sales representative for the password to the instructor's materials. (http://www.harcourtcollege.com/psych/ishm)

• *Psychology: In Search of the Human Mind* **PowerPoint® Presentation:** This PowerPoint® presentation follows the outline of the text and includes many of the graphs, tables, and photos from the text as well as additional videos to help enhance your lectures.

• **Dynamic Concepts in Psychology II,** a highly successful videodisc developed by John Mitterer (Brock University), covers every major concept of introductory psychology. Media include animated sequences, video footage, still images, and demonstrations of well-known experiments. A modular format allows instructors to tailor the program to their course. LectureActive presentation software (Windows, Macintosh) accompanies Dynamic Concepts in Psychology II. This software gives instructors the ability to preprogram classroom presentations as well as to import material from other multimedia sources, such as other videodiscs, CD-ROMs, or your own hard drive.

• **Psychology MediaActive™,** a CD-ROM-based psychology image bank to be used with commercially available presentation packages like PowerPoint® and Astound™, as well as Harcourt's LectureActive™ 2.0 for Windows and Macintosh.

• **The Harcourt College Publishers Multimedia Library** provides additional media for instructors to use in the classroom. The Library includes videos from Films for the Humanities and Sciences and Pyramid Films, as well as series such as *The Brain* teaching modules, *The Mind* video modules, *Discovering Psychology* telecourse, *Childhood*, *Seasons of Life*, and *Time to Grow*. Contact your Harcourt College Publishers representative for qualifying details and further information.

Acknowledgments

I am grateful to the following colleagues who provided helpful commentary in prerevision reviews and reviews of the third edition manuscript:

Ronald Baenninger, Temple University
Nan Bernstein Ratner, University of Maryland, College Park
Ellen Berscheid, University of Minnesota
John Borkowski, University of Notre Dame
Donald M. Burke, Minot State University
George A. Cicala, University of Delaware
David E. Clement, University of South Carolina
Dennis Cogan, Texas Tech University
Paul T. Costa, National Institute on Aging
Lawrence Fehr, Widener University
Michela Gallagher, Johns Hopkins University
Gary Gargano, St. Joseph's University
Thomas Gerstenberger, SUNY Potsdam
Harvey J. Ginsburg, Southwest Texas State University
Gary Greenberg, Wichita State University
R. W. Kamphaus, University of Georgia
Matthew Kinslow, Eastern Kentucky University
Karen Kopera-Frye, University of Akron
Stephen A. Maisto, Syracuse University
Arthur Markman, University of Texas, Austin
Johnmarshall Reeve, University of Iowa
Brian Oppy, California State University, Chico
Jesse E. Purdy, Southwestern University
Michael Raulin, State University of New York, Buffalo
Russell Revlin, University of California, Santa Barbara
Bret Roark, Oklahoma Baptist University
Henry Roediger, Washington University
Thomas Rowe, University of Wisconsin–Stevens Point
Juan Salinas, University of Texas, Austin
Thomas R. Scott, University of Delaware
Jerome Sehulster, University of Connecticut, Stamford
Robert S. Siegler, Carnegie Mellon University

Pawan Sinha, University of Wisconsin, Madison
Steven Smith, Texas A & M University
Shelley Taylor, University of California, Los Angeles
William Van Ornum, Marist College
Nancy J. Woolf, University of California, Los Angeles
Michael Zarate, University of Texas, El Paso

I would like to thank a number of individuals who were part of the team effort that produced this textbook. Earl McPeek, the publisher, supported this project in all of its phases. Leslie Carr and Diane Drexler, developmental editors, helped in developing all aspects of the book. Beth Alvarez paid careful attention to the book from the copyediting stage onward in her role as project editor. Cindy Young, production manager, oversaw the book's production. Burl Sloan is responsible for the artistic work on the book as its art director. Sue Howard and Sandra Lord, photo researchers, located many difficult to find photos, and Katie Matthews, the marketing strategist, helped to prepare a book that would be appropriate for and appealing to its intended market of students of introductory psychology. Finally, Sai Durvasala at Yale helped oversee many aspects of word processing and communication with the publisher. I was most fortunate to have such an outstanding team working together on this book.

I would like especially to thank my introductory psychology students for putting up with me over the years as I tried out the materials in class. My undergraduate advisor, Endel Tulving, and my graduate advisor, Gordon Bower, both profoundly affected how I think about psychology, as did Wendell Garner as a faculty mentor at Yale.

Finally, I thank my group of collaborators at Yale for the support they have always shown me in my work.

RJS

PSYCHOLOGY
In Search of the Human Mind
THIRD EDITION

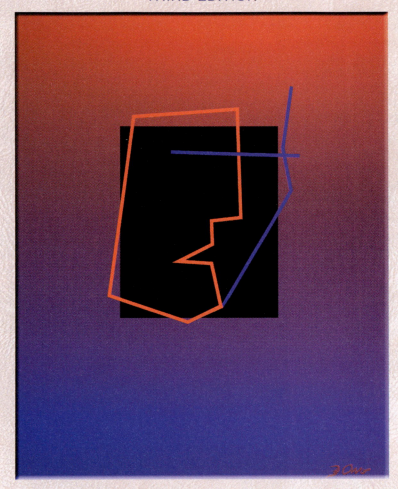

ROBERT J. STERNBERG

USING *PSYCHOLOGY:*
IN SEARCH OF THE HUMAN MIND
A Guide to Learning From Your Textbook

Psychology: In Search of the Human Mind, third edition, is designed to give you a thorough introduction to the principles of psychology and to illuminate and illustrate the many concepts, terms, and examples that will be presented in the psychology course.

As you set out on your search for the human mind, this book will prepare you to look at and think about psychology differently than you might now be doing—it will prepare you to think as a psychologist does, by examining the many faces of psychology. Among those faces are:

- psychology is both a natural and a social science;
- psychology is the process of evolution of ideas and behavior;
- psychology encompasses a variety of viewpoints and methods;
- psychology represents a balance between theory and research.

The following pages will introduce you to the many features of *Psychology: In Search of the Human Mind*, third edition, and show you how to use the learning aids provided to enhance your study of psychology.

Outlines, Vignettes, and Questions

Outlines assist you in your search by surveying the main topics to be discussed. Vignettes give multiple perspectives on the same topic. Questions teach you to think as a psychologist does.

Chapter Opening Photos: Each of the photos appearing at the beginning of every chapter in this text was chosen because of its ability to create new perspectives on the chapter topic.

In Search of . . . Questions: These questions help you ask the main question addressed in each section. By the end of the section, you should have a good idea of how psychologists have tried to answer this question.

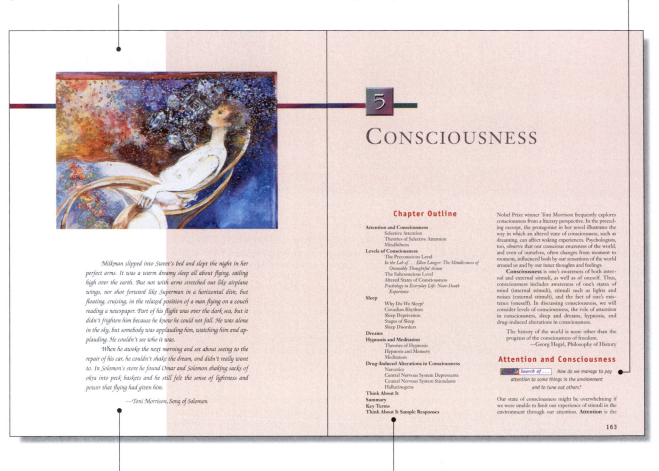

Milkman slipped into Sweet's bed and slept the night in her perfect arms. It was a warm dreamy sleep all about flying, sailing high over the earth. But not with arms stretched out like airplane wings, nor shot forward like Superman in a horizontal dive, but floating, cruising, in the relaxed position of a man flying on a couch reading a newspaper. Part of his flight was over the dark sea, but it didn't frighten him because he knew he could not fall. He was alone in the sky, but somebody was applauding him, watching him and applauding. He couldn't see who it was.

When he awoke the next morning and set about seeing to the repair of his car, he couldn't shake the dream, and didn't really want to. In Solomon's store he found Omar and Solomon shaking sacks of okra into peck baskets and he still felt the sense of lightness and power that flying had given him.

—Toni Morrison, *Song of Solomon*

5

CONSCIOUSNESS

Chapter Outline

Attention and Consciousness
 Selective Attention
 Theories of Selective Attention
 Mindfulness
Levels of Consciousness
 The Preconscious Level
 In the Lab of . . . Ellen Langer: The Mindlessness of Ostensibly Thoughtful Action
 The Subconscious Level
 Altered States of Consciousness
 Psychology in Everyday Life: Near-Death Experience
Sleep
 Why Do We Sleep?
 Circadian Rhythms
 Sleep Deprivation
 Stages of Sleep
 Sleep Disorders
Dreams
Hypnosis and Meditation
 Theories of Hypnosis
 Hypnosis and Memory
 Meditation
Drug-Induced Alterations in Consciousness
 Narcotics
 Central Nervous System Depressants
 Central Nervous System Stimulants
 Hallucinogens
Think About It
Summary
Key Terms
Think About It Sample Responses

Nobel Prize winner Toni Morrison frequently explores consciousness from a literary perspective. In the preceding excerpt, the protagonist in her novel illustrates the way in which an altered state of consciousness, such as dreaming, can affect waking experiences. Psychologists, too, observe that our conscious awareness of the world, and even of ourselves, often changes from moment to moment, influenced both by our sensations of the world around us and by our inner thoughts and feelings.

Consciousness is one's awareness of both internal and external stimuli, as well as of oneself. Thus, consciousness includes awareness of one's states of mind (internal stimuli), stimuli such as lights and noises (external stimuli), and the fact of one's existence (oneself). In discussing consciousness, we will consider levels of consciousness, the role of attention in consciousness, sleep and dreams, hypnosis, and drug-induced alterations in consciousness.

The history of the world is none other than the progress of the consciousness of freedom.
 —Georg Hegel, *Philosophy of History*

Attention and Consciousness

In Search of . . . How do we manage to pay attention to some things in the environment and to tune out others?

Our state of consciousness might be overwhelming if we were unable to limit our experience of stimuli in the environment through our attention. **Attention** is the

163

Chapter Opening Quotes: Each chapter begins with a quote that highlights the theme of the chapter and gives a fresh perspective.

Chapter Outline: A chapter outline previews the chapter material in an organized and consistent format.

Visual Summaries

Visual summaries present text information efficiently and creatively.

Tables and Figures: The liberal use of tables and figures assists you by giving a visual explanation of important information.

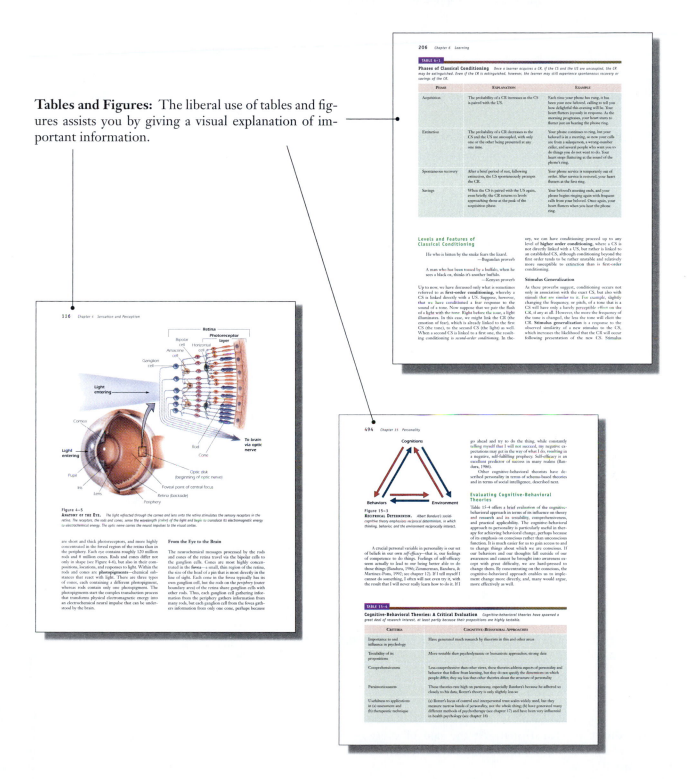

Variety of Viewpoints

The third edition of *Psychology: In Search of the Human Mind* shows how psychological ideas are created, analyzed, and applied to your everyday life.

In the Lab of . . . Boxes: These boxes, written by the foremost researchers in the field, show how real-life psychologists analyze ideas in their labs.

Psychology in Everyday Life Boxes: Psychology isn't just researched in a lab. It happens in our everyday lives. These boxes highlight practical applications of psychological concepts.

Think About It Questions: At the end of every chapter, you are invited to reflect on the concepts you have learned.

Figure 3–17
PICTURES VERSUS SYMBOLS. *Japanese schoolchildren study two forms of written language: kanji and kana. Kanji is based on Chinese ideographs and conveys an entire idea within each symbol; kana is based on phonetic syllables. In the 1970s, Japanese researchers studied whether the pictorial and phonetic forms are processed differently in the two hemispheres of the brain. Some concluded that the phonetic-based kana is processed in the left hemisphere, while the picture-based kanji is processed in both hemispheres.*

Cultural Diversity: Examples of how the ideas and thinking of another culture may be quite different from our own are integrated throughout the text and shed light on how psychological processes manifest themselves in different cultures.

Cultural and Contextual Models: Intelligence as a Cultural Invention

Figure 8–3
THE NINE-DOT PROBLEM. *How can you connect all nine dots without lifting your pencil from the paper and using just four straight lines? Psychologists study how people use insight to solve this and other ill-structured problems.*

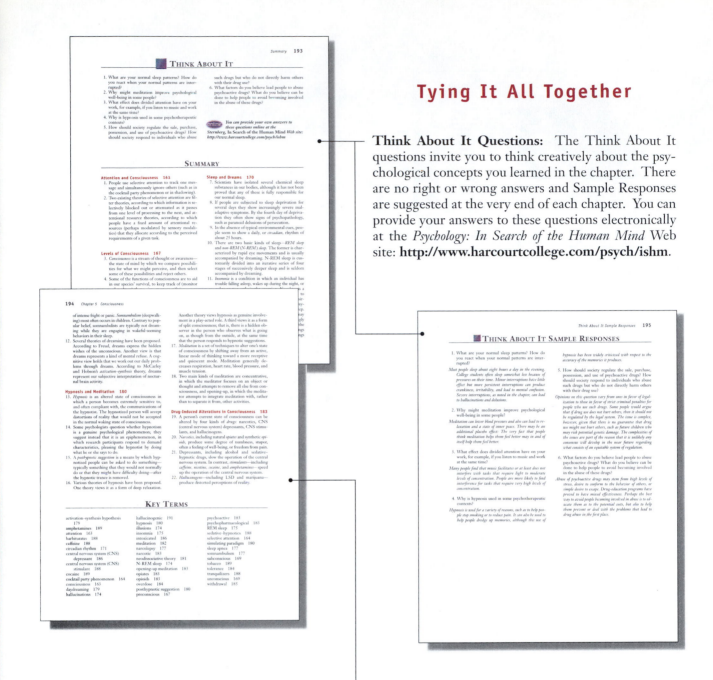

Tying It All Together

Think About It Questions: The Think About It questions invite you to think creatively about the psychological concepts you learned in the chapter. There are no right or wrong answers and Sample Responses are suggested at the very end of each chapter. You can provide your answers to these questions electronically at the *Psychology: In Search of the Human Mind* Web site: **http://www.harcourtcollege.com/psych/ishm**.

Summary and Key Terms: Designed to help you master the material presented in the text, these features provide a summary of the main points and a list of key words and concepts covered in the chapter with page references so you can easily refer back to the chapter.

Additional Study Aids

The statistical appendix, glossary, and extensive reference list will serve as useful study tools, as well as provide points for further learning. Additionally, Harcourt College Publishers offers the following study aids, which you can purchase through your local bookstore or at the Harcourt College Store on the Web at **http://www.harcourtcollege.com/store/**.

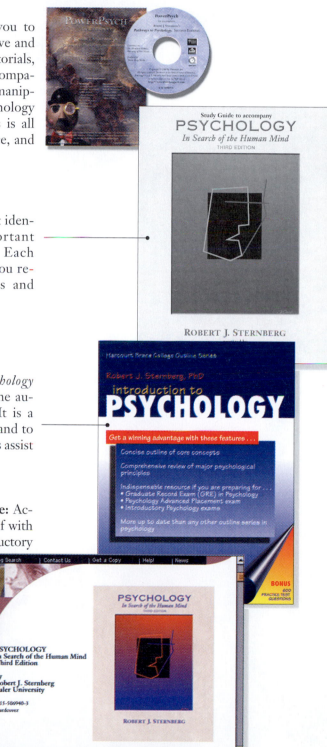

PowerPsych CD-ROM: This CD-ROM allows you to learn the core concepts in psychology in an interactive and *fun* environment. It contains exciting graphics, tutorials, and even a "Check Mastery" self-test section that accompanies each major feature. You will be able to view and manipulate graphics through the use of virtual reality technology and 3D-rendered animations and simulations. This is all possible from different perspectives, at your own pace, and under your control.

Study Guide: The Study Guide provides practice at identifying, understanding, and integrating important psychological ideas presented in the main text. Each chapter lists specific goals and objectives and helps you review the material through a variety of questions and exercises.

College Outline Series: The *Introduction to Psychology* edition of the College Outline Series is written by the author of *Psychology: In Search of the Human Mind*. It is a handy study tool to preview material, to use in class, and to use in reviewing before a test. The annotated outlines assist you in looking for the main points in the text.

***Psychology: In Search of the Human Mind* Web Site:** Access to the Web site is free. Here you can test yourself with our self-assessment quizzes or learn more about introductory psychology concepts with our Web activities, Shockwave® animations, and our guide to psychology research. Check it out at **http://www.harcourtcollege. com/psych/ishm**.

FEATURE BOXES

Contents in Brief

Contents

CHAPTER 7   **MEMORY   228**

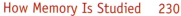

CHAPTER 15   PERSONALITY   478

The school psychologist entered the elementary-school classroom. I froze. I knew who she was. I knew why she was there. She passed out some booklets. She spoke to us, but I could hardly listen. Then she loudly said, "Go." I didn't. I couldn't. While my classmates were busily working, I sat there, still frozen, gaping at the test booklet. I knew the price I would have to pay: a low intelligence-test score. I had to know what had gone wrong—on that test and others. That's how I first became interested in intelligence and mental abilities—what I later came to know was just one aspect of the field of psychology. My anxiety during the test is also part of that field of study, as are concerns about the culture-fairness of the test I was taking. Because of this experience, I decided to study psychology and become a psychologist. How about you? What interests you about psychology? And what is psychology, anyway?

1

WHAT IS PSYCHOLOGY?

Psychology as a Natural Science and a Social Science

In Search of . . . *What is psychology, what do psychologists study, and how is psychology different from other fields that study the mind and behavior?*

To study **psychology**—the study of the mind, behavior, and the relationship between them—is to seek to understand how humans and other organisms think, learn, perceive, feel, act, interact with others, and even understand themselves. Although people are the predominant focus of psychological theory and research, many psychologists study a broad array of other organisms, from single-celled creatures to mammals. Sometimes, these studies are ends in themselves, and sometimes they are ways to investigate structures and phenomena that it would be impossible, impractical, or unethical to study in humans. For example, the study of animal physiology (such as the functioning of the eye or of nerve cells) and animal behavior (such as responses to various kinds of rewards) offers insights into possible analogies in human physiology and behavior. Because it encompasses both human and social issues as well as biological and physiological ones, psychology is categorized as both a natural and a social science.

As a *natural science*, psychology involves the study of the laws of nature. As a *social science*, psychology involves the study of the laws of the thoughts, feelings, and behavior of humans and other organisms. Some psychologists deal more with the natural–scientific aspects of psychology, studying, for example, the brain and its relations to behavior. Other psychologists deal more with the social–scientific aspects of psychology, studying, for example, how people interact in groups. Often, though, it is difficult to distinguish between the two aspects of psychology, because nature interacts bidirectionally in many ways with all living organisms. For example, climate affects the way people act. But people also have acted on the environment in ways that affect the climate, as through the rising temperatures of the greenhouse effect, for which humans are largely responsible. Many other natural scientists study human behavior: For example, *geneticists* study the influence of heredity on behavior, and *physiologists* study physical and biochemical influences on behavior.

Psychologists and other scientists view these various roads to understanding behavior as complementary, not as mutually exclusive. Indeed, psychologists profit from the insights into human behavior offered by disciplines such as biology and computer science.

Psychology also shares a focus on human behavior with other social–scientific disciplines, such as sociology and anthropology. Actually, the borders among these fields are fuzzy. The fields overlap considerably both in what they study and how they study it. Nonetheless, these disciplines each offer slightly different emphases and perspectives.

Consider, for example, the family. The focus of psychology is generally on the individual, whether alone or in interaction with others and the environment. A psychologist might study how the family affects the development of the child, or how the behavior of the child affects the family. *Sociology*, another social science, is concerned with larger aggregates of individuals, such as occupational, societal, economic, or ethnic groups. The sociologist might therefore be interested in how economic factors affect the cohesion of the family unit. *Cultural anthropologists* seek to gain insight into various cultures. Thus, a cultural anthropologist might be interested in how family units differ from one culture to another. *Physical anthropologists* study human evolution from simpler organisms. They might be interested in comparing the family unit among humans to that among, say, birds or monkeys.

Nonscientists also study human behavior. For example, we may gain insight into what people are like and how they act by reading poems or novels, philosophical treatises, historical analyses, or religious works. Works of art, such as paintings and sculptures, can also provide insight into human behavior. The difference between the psychological approach to the study of the human mind and the approach of the humanities is psychology's emphasis on scientific theory and methodology as its means for conceptualizing and empirically testing ideas. Science provides a unique set of methods for testing the validity of ideas and for replacing ideas that do not adequately account for empirical phenomena with new ideas that better capture these phenomena. These methods will be the subject of the next chapter.

This chapter is concerned with the general shape and development of the field of psychology. We will examine its history, the roots of contemporary psychology, by getting to know a little about the people and ideas that have shaped the field. Though looking back may not seem the best way to begin at first, the advantage of this approach is that the way we interpret contemporary ideas and determine what seems reasonable is shaped by our contemporary context and by the past ideas that have led up to the present ones. One key theme threading through this historical view is that ideas evolve in a cyclical way. For example, recent research (discussed in chapter 18) has begun to show the ways in which psychological stress

Psychology is both a natural and a social science. Psychologists may study ways to help children learn and recall information. They may also study the neural basis for memory.

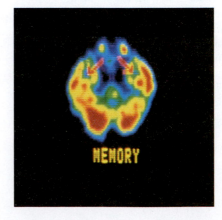

can produce physical illness, raising the level of compounds associated with a breakdown of immune system functioning. This idea, that the mind affects the body, was popular with the ancient Greeks, but not at all popular with many psychologists during the first half of the twentieth century, who were seeking to establish psychology's credentials as a science. It has come up again at the turn of this new century because modern scientific studies have provided evidence for it. During the course of this chapter, and this book, we will be looking at the evolution of some of these core ideas of psychology.

One of the reasons for this cyclical development of ideas is that often philosophers, psychologists, and others propose and believe strongly in one view for a while until a contrasting view comes to light. The most attractive or reasonable elements in each are melded into a new view, which then gains acceptance. This integrated view then serves as the springboard for a new contrasting view, and eventually yet another melding of views.

The Evolution of Ideas

In Search of ...

How do ideas evolve over time?

Georg Hegel (1770–1831), a German philosopher, referred to this evolution of thought as a **dialectic**—a continuing intellectual dialogue in which thinkers strive for increased understanding. First, thinkers strive to reach the truth by positing an initial **thesis** (statement of opinion). Other thinkers soon propose an **antithesis** (an opinion that takes a somewhat different perspective and often contradicts the original thesis). Eventually, another thinker later suggests a **synthesis** (selective combining of the two; Hegel, 1807/1931). This synthetic statement may then be considered a new thesis, for which there may then also arise an antithesis, and so on, as the evolutionary process of developing thought continues. The dialectical process is not entirely linear, in that scientists may find new problems with long-established theses. They also may find that long-discarded theses have new relevance. This dialectical evolution of thought is a primary characteristic of science and helps contribute to the attainment of scientific goals.

Dialectical progression depends on permitting current beliefs (theses) to be challenged by alternative, contrasting, and sometimes even *radically* divergent views (antitheses). These challenges then may lead to the origination of new ideas based on an integration of several features of the old ideas (syntheses). Western critical tradition is often traced back to the Greek philosopher Thales (624–545 B.C.), who invited his students to improve on his thinking, not an easy stance for any teacher to take. In addition, Thales did not hesitate to profit from knowledge accumulated in other parts of the world. He traveled around the Mediterranean and learned a great deal about astronomy, geometry, and other subjects from the Egyptians. Today, when we criticize the ideas of our predecessors, we accept Thales' invitation to make progress by building upon or springing away from old ideas.

Note that even when we reject outdated ideas, those ideas still move us forward, serving as valuable springboards for new ideas—the theses to our innovative antitheses. What are some of the early ideas that have been springboards for current thinking?

A Brief Intellectual History: Western Antecedents of Psychology

In Search of ...   *What are some of the early recorded ideas about the nature of the human mind?*

Where and when did the study of psychology begin? Arguably, historical records do not accurately trace the earliest human efforts to understand the ways in which we humans think, feel, and act. In fact, contemporary historians recognize that much of what we know—or think we know—about the past reflects the biases and prejudices of those who have written the accounts of history. All of us are shaped by the social context in which we live and view the world. We are guided in our thoughts by the thoughts of those persons who preceded us and of those persons who surround us.

Historians are not immune to the influences of the society in which they are writing their historical records. For example, because the historical documents that have reached us have been written primarily by Europeans, these records tend to highlight the contributions of Europeans and to downplay or ignore altogether the contributions of Asians, Africans, and others.

In this chapter, we trace our roots only as far back as ancient Greece. Actually, many highly sophisticated civilizations predated European civilization by centuries, and many technological advances occurred outside of Europe millennia before Europeans either imported them or invented them independently.

Centuries later the seeds of such intellectual endeavor reached the northern shores of the Mediterranean, where they took root and grew. On the Greek isles, some of our earliest records of the attempt to understand human psychology may be found in literature. Around the eighth century B.C., for example, the blind poet Homer wove his psychological insights into his epic poems about Greece, the *Iliad* and the *Odyssey*. Indeed, the study of psychology derives its name from the ancient Greek myth of *Psyche*. Psyche's name was synonymous with the vital "breath of life"—the soul—believed to leave the body at death.

Ancient Greece and Rome (600–300 B.C.)

Psychology traces its roots to two different approaches to human behavior: *philosophy*, a means of seeking to explore and understand the general nature of many aspects of the world, primarily through **introspection,** the self-examination of inner ideas and experiences; and **physiology,** the scientific study of living organisms and of life-sustaining functions and processes, primarily through observation. Actually, in ancient Greece, the approaches of these two fields did not differ much. Both used the more philosophical approach of introspective contemplation and speculation as a means of seeking to understand the nature of the body and the mind—how each works and how they interact. In ancient Greece, many philosophers and physiologists believed that understanding could be reached without having or even pursuing supporting observations.

Key Themes in the Evolution of Psychological Thinking

As the fields of philosophy and physiology diverged, they continued to influence the way in which psychology was to develop. Several important philosophical ideas served as precursors to modern psychological thought. These ideas will prove to be four major themes throughout the book.

1. Are the mind and body separate entities or are they united?

2. To what extent can we understand psychological phenomena through an understanding of biology, and to what extent must we understand such phenomena through the study of behavior?

3. To what extent is who we are and what we know the result of innate capabilities and to what extent is it acquired through experience?

4. To what extent are skills and knowledge general across domains (such as linguistic, mathematical, and artistic processing), and to what extent are they specific to such domains? (Knowledge and skills that are general across domains are referred to as *domain general*, whereas knowledge and skills that are specific to individual domains are referred to as *domain specific*.)

Hippocrates, Plato, and Aristotle

The origins of questions such as these go way back. The Greek physician (and philosopher) Hippocrates (ca. 460–377 B.C.), commonly known as the father of medicine, left his mark on both physiology and philosophy. During his time, these fields were highly overlapping. What sharply distinguished Hippocrates from archaic Greek philosophers and physicians was his unorthodox idea that disease is not a punishment sent by the gods. He also presaged modern psychology by speculating that biological malfunctions rather than demons cause mental illness, thereby turning away from divine intervention as a cause of human behavior.

Hippocrates also used what were then unorthodox methods—empirical observations—to study medicine. Contrary to the mode of the day, he studied animal anatomy and physiology directly, using both *dissection* (dividing cadavers into sections for purposes of examination) and *vivisection* (operating on living organisms, as a means of study). He was not entirely empirical in his methods, however. He often mistakenly assumed that what he had observed in animals automatically could be generalized to apply to humans (Trager, 1992).

Hippocrates was particularly interested in discovering the source of the mind. He saw the mind as a separate, distinct entity that controlled the body. This philosophical belief that the mind (or "spirit," or "soul") is qualitatively different from the body is termed **mind-body dualism.** According to this view, the body is composed of physical substance, whereas the mind is ethereal and is not composed of physical substance. Hippocrates proposed that the mind resides in the brain. He induced this conclusion by observing that when either side of the head was injured, spasms were observed in the opposite side of the body (D. N. Robinson, 1995).

Two younger contemporaries of Hippocrates also considered the location of the mind to be within the body: Plato (ca. 428–348 B.C.) agreed that the mind resides within the brain. Plato's student Aristotle (384–322 B.C.) located the mind within the heart. These two philosophers profoundly affected modern thinking in psychology and in many other fields. Of the many, far-reaching aspects of Platonic and Aristotelian philosophies, there are three key areas in which the dialectics between these two philosophers are particularly relevant to modern psychology: the relationship between mind and body, the use of observation versus introspection as a means for discovering truth, and the original source of our ideas.

Plato and Aristotle differed in their views of mind and body because of their differing views regarding the nature of reality. According to Plato, reality resides not in the concrete objects of which we are aware through our body's senses, but in the abstract forms that these objects represent. These abstract forms exist in a timeless dimension of pure abstract thought. For example, reality is not inherent in any particular chair we see or touch, but in the eternal abstract *idea* of a chair that exists in our minds. We reach truth not via our senses but via our thoughts. Aristotle, in contrast, believed that reality lies *only* in the concrete world of objects that our bodies sense. To Aristotle (a naturalist and biologist, as well as a philosopher), Plato's abstract forms—such as the idea of a chair—are only derivations of concrete objects.

Aristotle's concrete orientation set the stage for *monism*, a philosophy concerning the nature of the body and mind. This philosophy is based on the belief that reality is a unified whole, existing in a single plane, rather than being separated into physical substance versus nonphysical mind. According to monism, the mind (or soul) does not exist in its own right. Rather, it is merely an illusory by-product of anatomical and physiological activity. Thus, the study of the mind and the study of the body are one and the same. We can understand the mind only by understanding the body.

Observation and Experimentation: A Source of Knowledge or a Reduction of Realty?

Their differing views regarding the nature of reality led Plato and Aristotle also to disagree about how to investigate their ideas. Aristotle's belief that reality is based on concrete objects led him to research methods based on the observation of concrete objects and their actions. Today we would call Aristotle an **empiricist,** a person who believes that we acquire knowledge through **empirical methods,** obtaining evidence through experience, observation, and experimentation.

At the School of Athens, rationalist Plato disagreed with empiricist Aristotle regarding the path to knowledge. (Raphael Raffaello Sanzio, The School of Athens)

The Aristotelian view is associated with the empirical methods by which we conduct research—in laboratories or in the field—on how people think and behave. Aristotelians tend to *induce* general principles or tendencies, based on observations of many specific instances of a phenomenon. For example, empiricists might induce principles of how to learn about psychology from observations of psychology students engaged in learning.

For Plato, however, empirical methods have little merit because true reality lies in the abstract forms, not in the imperfect copies of reality observable in the world outside our minds. Observations of these imperfect, unreal objects and actions would be irrelevant to the pursuit of truth. Instead, Plato suggested a **rationalist** approach, one that asserts that knowledge is most effectively acquired through rational methods, using philosophical analysis to understand the world and people's relations to it.

Aristotle's view, then, leads directly to empirical psychological research, whereas Plato's view foreshadows theorizing that might not be grounded in extensive empirical observation. Each approach has merit. Rationalist theories without any connection to observations may have little connection to everyday events. But mountains of observational data without an organizing theoretical framework have little use.

In addition to differing both in their views of the relationship between mind and body and in their methods for finding truth, Plato and Aristotle differed in their views about the origin of ideas. Aristotle believed that ideas are acquired from experience. Plato, on the other hand, believed that ideas are innate and need only to be dug out from the sometimes hidden nooks and crannies of the mind.

The Renaissance *(1300–1600)* and the Beginnings of Science

During the Renaissance, science as we know it was born. Direct observation was established as the basis of knowledge.

In the Middle Ages, the dominant view was that thought and behavior should be guided by religious theory. In the Renaissance, however, this view came under attack. The British essayist, philosopher, and statesman Francis Bacon (1561–1626) proposed an antithesis to the medieval point of view: Scientific study must be purely empirical—not guided by theory at all. Bacon believed that theories color our vision and get in the way of our perceiving the truth. He therefore asserted that studies of nature and of humankind must be wholly unbiased and *atheoretical* (not based on or guided by any particular theoretical approach).

Today, many contemporary scientists seek to synthesize the two extreme views on the role of theory: Theory should guide and give meaning to our observations; yet our theories should be formed, modified, and perhaps even discarded as a result of our observations. As you will see as this chapter progresses, the progress of psychology as a science today is seen as depending on a continual interaction between theory and data. But during the beginnings of the modern period, many thinkers, such as Descartes and Locke, emphasized either theory or data, rather than their interaction.

The Beginnings of the Modern Period (1600–1850)

Is the Mind Separate From the Body? Debate Over Two Centuries: 1600–1800

The French philosopher René Descartes (1596–1650) continued the dialectic of theory versus data in the seventeenth century. Descartes agreed with Plato's rationalist belief that the introspective, reflective method is superior to empirical methods for finding truth. Also like Plato, Descartes (1662/1972) espoused the ideas both of *mind-body dualism*, believing that the

René Descartes (1596–1650)

John Locke (1632–1704)

mind and the body are separate and qualitatively different, and of innate (versus acquired) knowledge. According to Descartes, the dualistic nature of humans—combining the nonmaterial, incorporeal, spiritual mind and the material body—is what separates humans from animals. For humans, the mind and its powers are supreme: *Cogito ergo sum* (Latin for, "I think, therefore I am"). Although the mind generally has greater influence than the body, Descartes did believe the body still has some effect on the mind. Thus, Descartes is considered both *mentalistic*, because he viewed the body as subordinate to the mind, and *interactionistic*, in that he held that there is a two-way interaction between mind and body.

On the other side of this idea, the British empiricist philosopher John Locke (1632–1704) believed that the interaction between mind and body is a symmetrical relationship between two aspects of the same unified phenomenon. The mind depends on the body, specifically the experience of the senses, for its information. In contrast, the body depends on the mind to store processed sense experience for later use (J. Locke, 1690/1961). Locke believed that humans are born without knowledge—and must therefore seek knowledge through empirical observation. Locke's term for this view is *tabula rasa*, which means "blank slate" in Latin. Life and experience "write" knowledge upon us.

Kant *(1750–1850)*

In the eighteenth century, the debates about both dualism versus monism and empiricism versus rationalism had peaked. German philosopher Immanuel Kant (1724–1804) began the process of dialectical synthesis for these questions. He redefined the mind–body question by asking how mind and body are related, rather than whether the mind is in control (Kant, 1781/1987). Instead of phrasing the problem in terms of duality or unity, he proposed a set of *faculties*, or mental powers: the senses, understanding, and reason. He said that the faculties, working in concert, control and provide a link between mind and body, integrating the two.

Kant believed that the quest for understanding of mental faculties required use of both rationalism and empiricism working together. According to Kant's synthesis, understanding requires both experience-based knowledge (thesis) and innate concepts (antithesis), such as knowledge of the concepts of time and causality, which permit us to profit from our experiences. In this way, understanding evolves through both nature (innate concepts) and nurture (knowledge gained through experience).

Did Kant settle these debates once and for all? Certainly not. Questions probing the nature of thought and reality probably never will be settled for good. Scholars will always wrestle with aspects of these problems; that is, the nature of intellectual inquiry. Kant did, however, effectively redefine many of the issues with which philosophers before him had grappled. Kant's enormous impact on philosophy interacted with nineteenth-century scientific exploration of the body and how it works, producing profound influences on the eventual establishment of psychology as a discipline in the 1800s.

Psychological Perspectives: The 1850s and Beyond

In Search of ...   How did psychology emerge as a discipline, and what are some of the key ideas and schools of thought underlying it?

The Merging of Philosophy and Physiology Into Modern Psychology (1850–1900)

The issues confronted by philosophers, physicians, and psychologists have always been viewed as intertwined. Perhaps for this reason, when psychology was starting out as a field in the late 1800s, it was viewed by some as a branch of philosophy and by

Understanding Psychology's Public Image

Ludy T. Benjamin, Jr., *Texas A&M*

I am interested in the question of psychology's public image. My research has looked at this topic in the present, but because I chiefly do research in the history of psychology, most of my work has focused on the past. I am trying to understand how the public's image of psychology has evolved over the past 100 years since the emergence of the science of psychology.

In my work I have conceptualized public image as having two broad dimensions: understanding and popularity. Understanding refers to the public's knowledge of psychology, that is, what is believed to be true about psychology. Popularity refers to how the public feels about psychology and psychologists. Finally, we have looked at what people know about the field of psychology, by analyzing how it is presented in magazines and encyclopedias (Benjamin et al., 1997).

Psychologists today are often dismayed at the misconceptions people hold about their field. In fact, even undergraduate psychology students experience this when they hear comments such as, "Oh, you're studying psychology, I bet you can read my mind." In truth, the public's understanding of scientific psychology has never been very good (Benjamin, 1986). Long before there was a scientific psychology there was a popular psychology. For example, "getting your head examined" was big business in the 19th century. The phrase referred to the work of phrenologists, who measured the bumps and indentations on the skull to help people choose careers, employees, and marital partners. The public also equated psychology with psychic events such as extrasensory perception.

Since arriving on the scene in the last quarter of the 19th century, scientific psychology has tried to convince the public to give up its belief in the pseudopsychologies and to adopt what psychologists have viewed as the only legitimate psychology, one that is science-based. It hasn't worked. Our research (Wood, Jones, & Benjamin, 1986) and 24 other studies since 1948 show that the public still doesn't have a good understanding of the science of psychology or what psychologists do.

The popularity of psychology has waxed and waned with changes in American history. Psychology was especially popular in America in the 1920s, a time of generally great prosperity and social change, but was less popular in the 1930s, partly because of the Great Depression. Psychology gained in popularity again in the 1960s, when America was in turmoil over social issues. To evaluate the popularity of the field, we surveyed listings in the *Reader's Guide to Periodical Literature*, looking at the percentage of articles on psychology published in the popular literature (Benjamin, 1986, 1988).

Another way to gauge popularity across time is to see what popular media existed for the public. Our research has focused mostly on magazines because they have been in existence for the entire twentieth century. Through a lot of detective work, searching libraries, old book stores, and a few magazine directories, we found that the first popular psychology magazines in America appeared in the 1920s, exactly in the decade we would have predicted from our research. Two appeared in 1923 and a third in 1926. One of those was quite successful, but by the 1930s all were out of print (Benjamin & Bryant, 1997). A few other psychology magazines made brief appearances in the 1940s and 1950s, but they lasted only a few years. It was not until *Psychology Today* began publication in 1967 that such a magazine enjoyed popular success again.

So why do I study psychology's public image? Partly it is sheer intellectual curiosity; the subject is an inherently interesting one, and reading the old popular literature is entertaining as well as educational. But there is a more important purpose: For the public to gain access to psychological services it needs, it must understand the nature of scientific psychology and the practical services it can offer. For example, we know from contemporary surveys that many people who need mental health care will not seek it—inaction that is related to what is called the stigma of mental illness. A better understanding of what clinical/counseling psychology is and what those psychologists do could increase people's willingness to seek professional help when they need it and their ability to assess the quality of the help they are getting. A better understanding of public image can thus help psychology and, more importantly, the public that psychologists seek to serve.

References

Benjamin, Jr., L. T. (1986). Why don't they understand us? A history of psychology's public image. *American Psychologist, 41*, 941–946.

Benjamin, Jr., L. T. (1988). A history of teaching machines. *American Psychologist, 43*, 703–712.

Benjamin, Jr., L. T., & Bryant, W. H. M. (1997). A history of popular psychology magazines in America. In W. G. Bringmann, H. E. Luck, R. Miller, & C. E. Early (Eds.), *A pictorial history of psychology* (pp. 585–593). Carol Stream, IL: Quintessence.

Benjamin, Jr., L. T., Bryant, W. H. M., Campbell, C., Luttrell, J., & Holtz, C. (1997). Between psoriasis and ptarmigan: American encyclopedias portray psychology, 1880–1940. *Review of General Psychology, 1*, 5–18.

Wood, W., Jones, M., & Benjamin, Jr., L. T. (1986). Surveying psychology's public image. *American Psychologist, 41*, 947–953.

 Find out more about this topic at www.harcourtcollege.com/psych/ishm

others as a branch of medicine. Gradually, the psychological branches of philosophy and medicine diverged from the two parent disciplines. Psychology then increasingly became a distinct, unified, scientific discipline focused on the study of mind and behavior. However, the differing points of view that characterized psychology's intellectual roots continued to exert their influence, and still do today. In this chapter's In the Lab feature, researcher Ludy Benjamin describes how he and his associates have gone about tracing how psychology's public image has evolved during the twentieth century.

Psychology's Youth: A Study in Diverging Perspectives

The key themes in psychology and their evolution provide evidence for the idea that psychology has hosted a wide variety of intellectual perspectives on the human mind and how it should be studied. The predominant early psychological perspectives (summarized in Table 1-1) are discussed in this section. As you read, notice how different perspectives build on and react to those perspectives that came before them. The cyclical, dialectical process that appears throughout the early history of psychology also threads through modern psychology. This process starts with approaches that focus on mental structures and continues with approaches that focus on mental functions or on mental associations.

Structuralism, Functionalism, Pragmatism, and Associationism: Studying Behavior, Not Mental States

Structuralism: An Early Systematic, Scientific Exploration of the Mind

The goal of the proponents of **structuralism,** the first major school of thought in psychology, was to understand the *structure* of the mind—by analyzing the distinctive configuration of component elements of the mind, such as particular sensations or thoughts (see chapter 4). At the time when structuralism was a dominant school of psychological thought, scientists in other fields were similarly analyzing materials into basic elements and then studying combinations of these basic elements. Chemists were analyzing substances into their constituent chemical elements. Biologists were analyzing the biochemical constituents of cells. Physiologists were analyzing physiological structures. For example, German scientist Hermann von Helmholtz, who was trained as a physicist, was the first individual to measure the speed with which nerve impulses travel. Although structuralism is no longer a dynamic force in psychology, it is important for having taken the first steps toward making psychology a systematic, empirical science and for establishing some of the dialectics of contemporary psychology. An example of such a dialectic is that between the structuralists' molecular analysis of behavior and the global analysis of behavior.

A forerunner to structuralism was the perspective of German psychologist Wilhelm Wundt (1832–1920). Wundt was no great success in school, failing time and again and frequently finding himself subject to the ridicule of others. However, Wundt's stunning career shows that school performance does not always predict career success.

Wundt believed that psychology should focus on immediate and direct, as opposed to *mediated*, or interpreted, conscious experience. For example, suppose that you look at a green, grassy lawn. To Wundt, the concepts of *lawn* or even of *grass* would be irrelevant. Even your awareness of looking at a grassy lawn would not have particularly interested Wundt. These conceptually mediated experiences are too far removed from the mental elements of your experience. You infer these mental elements from the more important (to Wundt) immediate experience of seeing narrow, vertical, spiky, green protrusions of varying lengths and widths, amassed closely together on a two-dimensional surface. It was to these elementary sensations that Wundt gave his attention.

For Wundt, the optimal method by which a person could be trained to analyze these sensory experiences was a form of self-observation called *introspection*. This method involves looking inward at pieces of information passing through consciousness—a form of self-observation. Wundt and his associates tried to train observers to be as objective as possible in making their observations.

Wilhelm Wundt (1832–1920) established the first laboratory for psychological experimentation.

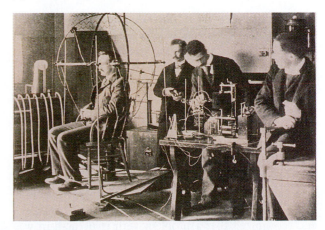

TABLE 1–1

Early Psychological Perspectives   *To this day, psychological research continues to reflect its roots in structuralism (focusing on basic psychological structures) and in functionalism (focusing on the processes of thinking and feeling).*

PERSPECTIVE	KEY EMPHASES	KEY METHODS OF ACQUIRING INFORMATION	KEY THINKERS INSTRUMENTAL IN DEVELOPMENT OF PERSPECTIVE	KEY CRITICISMS
Structuralism	The nature of consciousness; analysis of consciousness into its constituent components (elementary sensations)	Introspection (self-observation)	Wilhelm Wundt, Edward Titchener	Too many elementary sensations; lack of means for understanding the processes of thought; lack of application to the world outside the structuralist's laboratory; rigid use of introspective techniques
Functionalism (and its offshoot, pragmatism)	Mental operations; practical uses of consciousness; the total relationship of the organism to its environment	Whatever works best	William James, John Dewey	Too many definitions of the term *function*; overly flexible use of too many different techniques, resulting in lack of experimental coherence; overemphasis on applications of psychology; insufficient study of fundamental issues
Associationism	Mental connections between two events or between two ideas, which lead to forms of learning	Empirical strategies, applied to self-observation and to animal studies	Hermann Ebbinghaus, Edward Lee Thorndike, Ivan Pavlov	Overly simplistic; does not explain cognition, emotion, or many other psychological processes

Wundt's student Edward Titchener (1867–1927) went to Cornell University after studying with Wundt. Titchener was a full-blown structuralist with views generally similar but by no means identical to Wundt's. Like Wundt, Titchener (1910) believed that all consciousness could be reduced to elementary states.

During most of his life, Titchener was a strict structuralist. He used structuralist principles in his teaching, research, and writings. Toward the end of his life, however, Titchener eventually came to argue that psychology should study not merely the basic elements of sensation, but also the categories into which these sensations could be grouped (Hilgard, 1987). Titchener, like others, recognized that a problem with structuralism was

that it proposed too many elementary sensations, and that the number could increase without end. Structuralism also provided no means for understanding processes of thought. Furthermore, it probably was too rigidly tied to a single methodology, that of introspection.

Titchener's change of mind illustrates an important point about scientists in general, and psychologists in particular: Outstanding scientists do not necessarily adopt a particular viewpoint and then stick with it for the rest of their lives. They allow their thinking to evolve, often changing their views about things during this evolutionary process, the process that gave rise to the next major school of thought in psychology—functionalism.

Functionalism: An Emphasis on Active Processes

The roots of structuralism were in Germany, but its countermovement, **functionalism,** was rooted in America—the first U.S.-born movement in psychology. Functionalism focuses on active psychological processes, rather than on passive psychological structures or elements. The key difference between structuralists and functionalists lay not in the answers they found, but in the fundamentally different questions they asked. Whereas structuralists asked, "What are the elementary contents, the structures, of the human mind?" functionalists asked, "What do people *do*, and *why* do they do it?"

Another way of viewing the difference between structuralism and functionalism is to say that structuralists viewed humans and other organisms as largely passive in analyzing incoming sensations. Functionalists, in contrast, viewed humans and others as more actively engaged in processing their sensations and in formulating their actions. Some people have suggested that the American culture may have led to this more active kind of psychology.

Functionalists were unified by the kinds of questions they asked, but not necessarily by the answers they found or by the methods they used for finding those answers. We might even suggest that they were unified in believing that a diversity of methods could be used, as long as each method helped to answer the particular question being probed.

Functionalists' openness to diverse methodologies broadened the scope of psychological methods. Among the various approaches used by functionalists was animal experimentation. This approach was perhaps prompted by Charles Darwin's (1809–1882) revolutionary ideas on evolution. Darwin's theory is perhaps unique in its usefulness in an astonishingly wide variety of disciplines.

A leader in the functionalist movement was William James (1842–1910)—physician, philosopher, psychologist, and brother of author Henry James. The chief functional contribution of William James to the field of psychology was a single book: his landmark *Principles of Psychology* (1890b). James proved that one truly influential work, as well as the reputation of its author, can help shape a field. James is particularly well known for his pragmatic theorizing about consciousness, emphasizing that the function of consciousness is to enable people to adapt to the environment and to give them choices for operating within that environment. James was a leader in guiding functionalism toward *pragmatism*, a view of science and psychology asserting that knowledge is validated by its usefulness. In this view, then, the value of knowledge is in how useful it is.

William James (1842–1910)

Functionalism, like structuralism, did not survive as an organized school of thought. The term *function* lacked clear definition, and the result was that the school did not hold together. But the influence of functionalism remains widespread today in psychological specializations that stress flexibility of research methods or practical usefulness of potential results as a basis for choosing problems to study. The influence of functionalism is particularly apparent in a related strand of thought, associationism.

Associationism: Early Ideas About Learning

Associationism, like functionalism, was less a rigid school of psychology than an influential way of thinking. In general, the main interests of associationists are in the middle- to higher-level mental processes, such as those of learning. This focus on rather high-level mental processes runs exactly counter to Wundt's insistence on studying elementary sensations.

Associationism examines how events or ideas can become associated with one another in the mind, thereby resulting in a form of learning. For example, with repetition, concepts such as *thesis, antithesis,* and *synthesis* will become linked in your mind, because they are presented together so often that they become inextricably associated with one another. You will have learned that the dialectical process involves a thesis, an antithesis, and a synthesis. Learning and remembering thus depend on mental association.

An influential associationist, the German experimenter Hermann Ebbinghaus (1850–1909), was the first experimenter to apply associationist principles systematically. Ebbinghaus prided himself on using much more rigorous experimental techniques (such as counting his errors, recording his response times, etc.) than Wundt used during introspection. On the other hand, Ebbinghaus used himself as his only experimental *participant* (person, other organism, or other object of experimental study, also called a *subject*), just as Wundt had done. In particular, Ebbinghaus used his self-observations to study and quantify the relationship between *rehearsal*—conscious repetition—and recollection of material.

Interestingly, Ebbinghaus had no university appointment, no formal laboratory, no formal mentor, and none of the usual trappings of academe. He worked alone, yet he made a groundbreaking experimental discovery—that frequent repetition fixes mental associations more firmly in memory, and, by extension, that repetition aids in learning (see chapter 6). Great contributions do not require academic positions or complicated equipment.

Ebbinghaus's ideas were elaborated by Edwin Guthrie (1886–1959), who observed animals instead of himself. Guthrie proposed that two observed events (a stimulus and a response) become associated through their close *temporal contiguity*—their occurring very close together in time. In other words, the stimulus events and the response behaviors become associated because they continually occur at about the same time. In contrast, Edward Lee Thorndike (1874–1949) held that the role of "satisfaction," rather than of Guthrie's temporal contiguity, is the key to forming associations. Thorndike (1905) termed this principle the **law of effect:** Over time actions ("the *effect*") for which an organism is rewarded ("the *satisfaction*") are strengthened and are therefore more likely to occur again in the future, whereas actions that are followed by punishment tend to be weakened and are thus less likely to occur in the future.

In considering the methods of Ebbinghaus, Guthrie, and Thorndike, we see that the associationists followed the functionalist tradition of using various methods in their research. In fact, the work of Thorndike can be tied directly back to the work of his functionalist mentor, William James. James even encouraged Thorndike to conduct his experiments on animals, offering his own house as the locale for some of Thorndike's earliest studies of animals learning to run through mazes.

Associationism in its strictest form has not survived. The school of thought was overly simplistic and did not explain cognition, emotion, or many other psychological processes. Nevertheless, associationism made a contribution to much contemporary thinking in psychology, and associationism has been linked to many other theoretical viewpoints. Traveling backward in time, its principles can be traced directly to Locke's view that the mind and the body are two aspects of the same unified phenomenon, a view rooted in Aristotle's ideas. Traveling forward in time, subsequent views, such as behaviorism, described in the next section, were also founded on associationism. Clearly, it is difficult to categorize associationism as belonging strictly to one era.

Evolving Twentieth-Century Perspectives on Psychology

In Search of . . . *What are the main perspectives of the twentieth century on psychological thought?*

Perspectives of the twentieth century build on earlier perspectives at the same time that they add to these earlier perspectives new layers of sophistication. In fact, the history of psychology during the first half of the twentieth century is characterized by a series of competing perspectives, each new perspective giving rise to a countering school of thought. At the heart of the differences among these perspectives lay some of the central themes or questions first examined by the Greeks. By the end of the twentieth century, however, the idea one perspective or school of psychological thought would emerge as *the* explanation of all human behavior and mental life had itself evolved into a more inclusive and integrative view. Somewhat as a reaction against the competition among approaches that characterized psychology in the first half of the twentieth century, the second half began to see efforts to integrate approaches; an acceptance of the idea that behavior and mental states are most often a mix of biological, psychological, and social factors had gained momentum. Before all this could happen, however, the central themes of psychology were intensively debated, with new perspectives emerging frequently. Consider, for example, how associationism was transformed into behaviorism.

From Associationism to Behaviorism

Some contemporaries of Thorndike used animal experiments to probe stimulus–response relationships in ways that differed from those of Thorndike

Ivan Pavlov (1849–1936)

Behaviorism—A Search for Rigor and Reduction

Behaviorism was and is a theoretical outlook that emphasizes the idea that psychology should be scrupulously objective, focusing only on the relation between observable behavior, on the one hand, and environmental events or stimuli, on the other. Behaviorism was born as a reaction against the focus found in both structuralism and functionalism, as well as in psychodynamic theorizing (discussed below), on personal, subjective mental states. According to strict, "radical" behaviorists, any conjectures about internal thoughts and ways of thinking are nothing more than speculation. Although such conjectures might belong within the domain of philosophy, they have no place in psychology.

Watson's Groundwork

The individual usually acknowledged as the founder of radical behaviorism is American psychologist John Watson (1878–1958). As an innovative thinker, Watson drew on the thoughts of others, both those who preceded him and his own contemporaries. Watson had no use for internal mental contents or mechanisms. Still, although Watson disdained key aspects of

John Watson (1878–1958)

and his fellow associationists. These researchers straddled the line between associationism and the emerging field of behaviorism (see Table 1-2), which dealt with the most basic sort of association, that between a specific stimulus and an associated pattern of behavior. Some of these researchers studied responses that are voluntary, whereas others studied responses that are involuntarily triggered, in response to what appear to be unrelated external stimuli. The specifics of the relationship between stimulus and response are discussed in more detail below and in chapter 6.

In Russia, Nobel Prize–winning physiologist Ivan Pavlov (1849–1936) studied involuntary learning behavior of this sort, beginning with the observation that dogs salivated in response to the sight of the lab technician who fed them before the dogs even saw whether the technician had food. To Pavlov, this response indicated a form of learning, termed **classically conditioned learning** (whereby an originally neutral stimulus comes to be associated with a stimulus that already produces a particular physiological or emotional response), over which the dogs had no conscious control. In the dogs' minds, some type of involuntary learning was linking the technician with the food (Pavlov, 1955).

TABLE 1–2

Modern Psychological Perspectives
The various psychological perspectives offer complementary insights into the human psyche.

PERSPECTIVE AND ITS KEY DEVELOPERS	KEY EMPHASIS	KEY METHODS OF INVESTIGATION	KEY CRITICISMS
Behaviorism ■ John Watson ■ B. F. Skinner	Observable behavior	Experimental; strong focus on animal subjects	Ignores or does not address any internal causes of behavior; does not allow for social (observational) learning; doesn't explain many aspects of human behavior (e.g., the acquisition and use of language or the enjoyment and appreciation of music or other arts)
Gestalt psychology ■ Max Wertheimer ■ Kurt Koffka ■ Wolfgang Köhler	Holistic concepts, not merely as additive sums of the parts, but as emergent phenomena in their own right	Experimentation and observation (more emphasis on observing holistic data than on controlling variables)	Little data relative to the abundance of theory; lack of experimental control; lack of precise definitions and use of circular thinking
Cognitivism ■ Herbert Simon ■ George Miller ■ Ulric Neisser	Understanding how people think; how knowledge is learned, structured, stored, and used	Experimentation and naturalistic observation, primarily of humans and of other primates	Emotions, social interactions, and other aspects of human behavior are not investigated as enthusiastically as more obviously cognitive aspects of behavior; naturalistic observations reduce scientific rigor and control
Biological psychology ■ Roger Sperry ■ Eric Kandel	Biological interactions of the body and the mind, particularly the workings of the brain and nervous system	Experimentation; studies on humans, animals; neurophysiological and neurochemical examination of brains	Not all aspects of human behavior are now subject to investigation via biopsychological study; many aspects of human behavior may not now ethically be studied in humans, and animal investigations may not always generalize to humans
Evolutionary psychology ■ Leda Cosmides ■ David Buss	Evolutionary bases of human behavior	Plausible inference; experimentation; survey methodology	Views are difficult to falsify empirically; speculative quality
Psychodynamic psychology ■ Sigmund Freud	Personality development; psychotherapy; uncovering unconscious experience	Psychoanalysis, based on clinical case studies	Overemphasis on sexuality; over reliance on case-study research; overly comprehensive; not easily subject to scientific investigation; overly theory driven
Humanistic psychology ■ Abraham Maslow ■ Carl Rogers	Free will and self-actualization of human potential; conscious rather than unconscious experience	Clinical practice and case-study observations; holistic rather than analytic approach	Theories not particularly comprehensive; limited research base

functionalism, he clearly was influenced by the functionalists in his emphasis on what people do and on what causes their actions.

Watson's radical conception of behaviorism stated that any behavior can be shaped and controlled. This view is dramatized in a famous excerpt:

> Give me a dozen healthy infants, well-formed, and my own specified world to bring them up in, and I'll guarantee to take any one at random and train him to become any type of specialist I might select—doctor, lawyer, artist, merchant-chief and yes, even beggarman and thief—regardless of his talents, penchants, tendencies, abilities, vocations, and race of his ancestors. (J. B. Watson, 1930, p. 104)

Some psychologists disagreed with Watson's behaviorist view. For example, in a debate between Watson and psychologist William McDougall (1871–1938), McDougall said:

> I come into this hall and see a man on this platform scraping the guts of a cat with hairs from the tail of a horse; and, sitting silently in attitudes of rapt attention, are a thousand persons who presently break out into wild applause. How will the Behaviorist explain these strange incidents: How explain the fact that the vibrations emitted by the cat-gut stimulate all the thousand into absolute silence and quiescence; and the further fact that the cessation of the stimulus seems to be a stimulus to the most frantic activity? (J. B. Watson & McDougall, 1929, p. 63)

Behaviorism differed from previous movements in psychology in its emphasis on animal rather than human research participants. Historically, much behavioristic work has been (and still is) conducted with laboratory animals such as rats and pigeons. Watson himself preferred animal subjects. He believed that it was easier with animal subjects to ensure behavioral control and to establish stimulus–response relationships while at the same time minimizing external interference. Indeed, the simpler the organism's emotional and physiological makeup, the less the researcher needs to worry about any of the interference that can plague psychological research with humans as participants. Many nonbehavioral psychologists wonder whether results of animal research can be *generalized* to humans. In other words, can the results apply more generally to humans instead of just specifically to the animals that were studied? In response, some behaviorists would argue that the study of animal behavior is a legitimate pursuit in its own right. Virtually all behaviorists would assert that we can learn from such studies useful principles that generalize to a variety of species, including humans.

Hull's Synthesis With Pavlovian Conditioning

An American behavioral psychologist who tried to connect the involuntary learning studied by Pavlov with the voluntary learning studied by Watson and Thorndike was Clark Hull (1884–1952), whose work was ignored for a decade before its importance was recognized (Hilgard, 1987). Hull (1952) was particularly influential for his belief that the laws of behavior could be *quantified*—expressed in terms of numerical quantities—as are laws in other scientific disciplines such as physics.

Skinner's Experimental Analysis of Behavior

In modern times, radical behaviorism has seemed almost synonymous with the work of one of its most radical proponents, B. F. Skinner (1904–1990). Skinner, unlike Watson, was not an S–R (stimulus-response) psychologist (Skinner, 1953; Viney, 1993). Skinner (1953) distinguished between two kinds of learned behavior. *Respondent* behavior, the kind studied by Pavlov, is involuntary. It is elicited by a definite stimulus (such as food or even the sight of a lab technician). *Operant* behavior, on the other hand, is largely voluntary. It cannot be simply and certainly elicited, as can be involuntary behavior. The probability of an operant behavior occurring can, however, be increased if its emission is followed by an event referred to as a *reinforcer*. The reinforcer increases the likelihood that the operant behavior will occur again under similar circumstances.

For example, suppose we train a rat to press a lever or bar, reinforcing the bar-press with food only when a light comes on above the bar. Soon, the rat will learn to press the bar when the light comes on. According to Skinner, the light does not directly elicit the response. Rather, it enables the rat to discriminate a reinforcing situation from a nonreinforcing one. For this reason, Skinner referred to the light as a *discriminative stimulus*. In addition, the stimulus of the light is not inextricably linked with the response of bar-pressing. A rat that has a full stomach may end up not pressing the bar under any circumstance. The bar-pressing operant behavior in this case is voluntary. It thus is referred to as an *emitted* rather than as an elicited response.

The operant behavior observed in an experiment, such as the one with the light, is not a response, but rather a class of responses. The rat might press the bar with one paw (a response), or both paws (another response), or even with its head (still another response), for that matter. All of these individual responses represent the same operant because they are responses to the same discriminative stimulus, the light.

B. F. Skinner (1904–1990)

What two images do you see in this Gestalt reversible figure?

The radical behaviorist approach, by ignoring internal states, effectively limits itself. It has difficulty explaining many aspects of behavior, such as the acquisition and use of language and the enjoyment and appreciation of music or other arts. But in evaluating behaviorism we must remember that even critics agree that the overt behavior of a research participant is the object of study most accessible to observation. Despite many criticisms, such as those of the Gestalt psychologists considered next, behaviorism has had a great impact on the development of psychology as a rigorous science grounded in empirical evidence.

Gestalt Psychology: The Whole Is Different

Of the many critics of behaviorism, Gestalt psychologists may have been among the most vocal. Actually, this movement was not only a reaction against the early behaviorist tendency to break down behaviors into stimulus–response units, but also against the structuralist tendency to analyze mental processes into elementary sensations. According to **Gestalt psychology**, psychological phenomena are best understood when viewed as organized, structured wholes— that is, *holistically*—not when they are analyzed into myriad component elements.

The maxim "the whole is different from the sum of its parts" aptly sums up the Gestalt approach. The name of the approach comes from the German word **"Gestalt"** (distinctive totality of an integrated whole, as opposed to merely a sum of various parts). This term does not have an exact synonym in English, although its meaning is something close to "whole unitary form," "integral shape," or "fully integrated configuration" (D. Schultz, 1981). The movement originated in Germany, the fount of structuralism, and spread to the United States, the fount of behaviorism, and to other countries.

Gestalt psychology is usually traced to the work of German psychologist Max Wertheimer (1880–1943), who collaborated with compatriots Kurt Koffka (1886–1941) and Wolfgang Köhler (1887–1968) to form a new school of psychology. This new school placed its emphasis on understanding "wholes" in their own right. The Gestaltists applied this framework to many areas in psychology. For example, they proposed that problem solving cannot be explained simply in terms of automatic responses to stimuli or to elementary sensations. Instead, new insights often emerge in problem solving. People can devise entirely new ways of seeing problems, ways that are not merely recombinations of old ways of seeing problems.

The Gestalt perspective has been criticized on several grounds. It generated little data relative to the abundance of theory it provided. Studies conducted under the Gestalt approach tended to lack careful experimental controls. And the approach often used imprecise definitions of terms and even occasionally circular thinking. For example, an

In Sunday on La Grande Jatte *(ca. 1885), Georges Seurat demonstrated the Gestalt principle of the whole being different from the sum of its parts. See from the detail how the painting comprises only dots of paint.*

insight was viewed as a sudden "aha" experience, which in turn was viewed as an insight. But many psychologists now believe that the most fruitful approach to understanding psychological phenomena is to combine the holistic strategies tracing back to the Gestalt approach with more analytic strategies tracing back to associationist and behaviorist approaches. Cognitivists are among the many who use both of these strategies.

Cognitivism: Returning to Mental Acts

Cognitivism, a movement in psychology dating from the 1960s, emphasizes the importance of cognition as a basis for understanding much of human behavior, which can be understood if we first analyze how people think. This way of thinking was motivated, in part, by the failure of behaviorism to consider cognition as something even worthy of serious psychological study. The contemporary cognitivist examines the elementary structuralist contents of thought, the functionalist processes of thought, and the Gestaltist holistic results of thinking. The cognitivist, like the Gestaltist, may well conclude that, indeed, the whole is different from the sum of its parts. At the same time, however, cognitive psychologists attempt to analyze precisely which mental mechanisms and which elements of thought make that conclusion true. Cognitivists would study what we perceive as the Gestalt of a book chapter or of a Seurat painting, but they also would want to determine precisely how we perceive them.

Mary Whiton Calkins (1863–1930) may be considered a forerunner of cognitivism. In 1913, she wrote an article criticizing Watson's behaviorist approach of psychology and suggested that the study of the human mind was essential. (Calkins, 1913)

Early cognitivists (e.g., G. A. Miller, Galanter, & Pribram, 1960) argued that traditional behaviorist accounts of behavior are inadequate precisely because they ignore how people think. Subsequently, Allen Newell and Herbert Simon (1972) proposed detailed models of human thinking and problem solving from the most basic levels to the most complex (such as playing chess). Ulric Neisser's (b. 1928) book *Cognitive Psychology* (Neisser, 1967) was especially critical in bringing cognitivism to prominence. Neisser defined *cognitive psychology* as the study of how people learn, structure, store, and use knowledge.

The approach of the early cognitivists tended to emphasize exclusively *serial processing*, or step-by-step processing of information. For example, in solving a math problem, the problem solver might be seen as first reading the problem, then formulating a relevant equation, then solving the equation, and so on. Today, some cognitivists continue to emphasize such serial processing (e.g., J. R. Anderson, 1983, 1993; Newell, 1990), either alone or in combination with *parallel processing*, whereby multiple mental processes are viewed as occurring all at once (e.g., Rumelhart et al., 1986; W. Schwartz, 1990; Seidenberg, 1993). Parallel processing might occur, for example, in the way we respond to multiple aspects of a great painting simultaneously. We see it, consider it, and may have an emotional response to it all at the same time.

The cognitive approach has been applied in a variety of areas of psychology, ranging from thinking to emotion to the treatment of various psychological syndromes, including depression. In the functionalist tradition, cognitive psychologists use a variety of methods to pursue their goal of understanding human thought, including the study of reaction times, the study of people's subjective reports as they solve problems, and the formulation and implementation of computer simulations.

In the 1960s, cognitivism was just coming of age. Today, cognitivism is popular, and many fields within psychology have adopted a cognitive perspective. At the same time, it is important to remember that many aspects of behavior, such as emotion and social interaction, probably cannot simply be reduced to cognitive processing. Like all perspectives, the cognitivist perspective may someday fade in importance and yield to other perspectives. The dominant perspective of the future and even some of the psychological phenomena it seeks to explain may be unimaginable today. Psychology is a dynamic science precisely because it is ever-evolving in its perspectives on the puzzles of human behavior. Of course, not only perspectives on human behavior, but also, human behavior itself has evolved. This fact has motivated biological psychologists in general, and evolutionary psychologists in particular, to understand just how behavior may have evolved and may still be evolving.

Current Frontiers: Biological Psychology—The Brain and the Body Reunited (Sort Of)

Recent advances in technology and our understanding of the biochemistry underlying emotions and other psychological states have meant that one of the most dynamic areas of psychology today is a field that yields exhilarating discoveries almost daily. **Biological psychology** is less a school of thought than an area of psychology that attempts to understand behavior by carefully studying anatomy and physiology, especially of the brain (*neurobiology*). Its roots go back to Hippocrates, who observed that the brain seems to control many other parts of the body. By definition, *psychobiology* assumes that the mind and the body are interrelated, and perhaps indistinguishable. Certainly, the study of each one can yield information about the other. The psychobiological perspective is less an organized school of thought grounded in a particular place and time than an affirmation of biological theorizing and experimentation as desirable bases for studying psychological problems.

One psychobiological approach is to determine which specific regions of the brain are responsible for the origination, learning, or expression of particular behaviors, feelings, or kinds of thoughts. For example, Nobel Prize–winning American researcher Roger Sperry tried to determine what kinds of thinking occur in each of the two halves of the brain. Today, neuroscientists are isolating with great precision the locations in the brain where various cognitive operations take place (e.g., Hawkins, Kandel, & Siegelbaum, 1993; Kandel, 1991; Tulving, Kapur, Craik, Moscovitch, & Houle, 1994; Ungerleider & Haxby, 1994). Today, moreover, many psychological disorders, which once were studied and treated exclusively by psychological means, are being understood and treated, at least in part, by biological means.

Closely related to the biological approach is the study of **behavioral genetics,** which is an interdisciplinary field of study that attempts to account for behavior (and often particular psychological characteristics

"Oh, not bad. The light comes on, I press the bar, they write me a check. How about you?"

and phenomena, such as intelligence) by attributing behavior and underlying traits in part to the influence of particular combinations of genes as they express themselves in a given environment. A behavioral geneticist might attempt to identify, for example, genetic elements contributing to intelligence, creativity, or mental illness, as well as their relations to environmental influences. These and other insights into our minds and bodies—and the interactions between the two—fascinate scientists and laypeople alike (e.g., Plomin, Owen, & McGuffin, 1994).

Biopsychosocial Approaches: Trying to Integrate the Gains of Psychology in the Twentieth Century

The **biopsychosocial approach** to psychology seeks an understanding of the individual in terms of the various psychological, social, and biological factors that contribute to behavior. It is most often applied in psychology but really applies in all areas of psychology. This approach suggests that thought and behavior cannot be fully understood through any single view or perspective.

Evolutionary Psychology: Understanding the Adaptive Value of Certain Behaviors

In his theory of natural selection and evolution, Darwin (1859) sought to understand how behaviors such as facial expressions, mating rituals, or even emotions might have evolved from or be related to those in other species. Today, psychologists building on the integrative work of Darwin have created **evolutionary psychology** as a field in its own right (Buss, 1995; Buss & Kenrick, 1998; Cosmides & Tooby, 1987; Dennett, 1995; R. Wright, 1994). The goal of this new and exciting but controversial field is to explain behavior in terms of organisms' evolved adaptations to a constantly changing environmental landscape. For example, certain sex differences between women and men are explained in terms of the different challenges women and men have faced over evolutionary time and of how men and women might have adapted differentially to meet these challenges. Those individuals who met these challenges were more likely to survive long enough to reproduce and pass their genes (hereditary material) on to subsequent generations. As a result, individuals of the present epoch are likely still to show in their behavior the adaptations that worked for extended periods of time in the distant past. It is important to realize that, at least at the present time, evolutionary explanations often have a speculative quality to them and frequently are not directly confirmable or disconfirmable empirically.

During the twentieth century two other approaches to psychology developed specifically to understand and explain mental dysfunction as well as function. Both are quite broad, and each encompasses what are sometimes widely differing ideas and theories. Each of these approaches, the *psychodynamic* and the *humanistic*, is held together by a core belief. In the case of psychodynamic views, it is a belief in behavior and mental states as being influenced by processes that may be unconscious. Humanistic psychologists are united by their faith in humans' ability to exercise free will and desire to fulfill their individual potential.

Psychodynamic Psychology: Conscious Behavior as the Tip of the Iceberg

One of the oldest, most controversial, stimulating, and influential schools of psychology developed from the observations made in the clinical practice of a *neurologist* (a physician who treats disorders of the brain and nervous system) who incorporated many ideas from biology into his psychological theories. The neurologist was Sigmund Freud (1856–1939). When many people think of psychology, they may think of Freud's **psychodynamic theory,** a theory of human motivations and behavior. This theory emphasizes the importance of conflicting unconscious mental processes as well as the importance of early childhood experiences in affecting adult personality. People also may think about psychology in terms of **psychoanalysis,** a form of psychological treatment based on Freud's theory of motivations and behavior discussed in chapter 17.

In his theory of psychoanalysis, Freud (1949) proposed two levels of awareness of reality. The *conscious* is composed of mental states such as memories, of which we are aware. It is just the tip of the iceberg, according to Freud, who believed that the motivation for many of our actions is often outside our awareness. In contrast, the *unconscious* is composed of mental states of which we are unaware or to which we do not normally have access. According to Freud, the unconscious and conscious minds operate according to different governing principles. For example, the individual who vehemently opposes pornography at a conscious level may be attracted to it at an unconscious level.

In addition, Freud proposed three mental structures (the id, the ego, and the superego, discussed in chapter 15), each of which was proposed to operate according to different principles and to serve different functions. Freud also posited a multistage theory of development, which emphasizes the important role of early childhood experiences in the development of personality—and, when problems arise in this development, mental disorder.

Several valid criticisms have been leveled against psychoanalysis. For example, it probably overemphasized sexual explanations of phenomena and relied

Sigmund Freud (1856–1939) developed the first and most influential psychodynamic theory. His daughter, Anna Freud (1895–1982), also became an influential psychodynamic psychologist.

Humanistic Psychology

During the 1950s, one of several responses to psychodynamic theory in America (behaviorism was another) was the humanistic-psychology movement. In contrast to psychodynamic psychology, which tended to see humans as being somewhat at the mercy of developmental events in their individual lives, **humanistic psychology** emphasizes free will and the importance of human potential, as well as holistic, rather than analytic approaches to psychological phenomena. It also emphasizes conscious experience in personal development rather than unconscious experience. An *analytic* approach, such as Freud's, aims to break down a construct such as personality into its constituent components. A *holistic* approach to personality theory, however, seeks to avoid dividing the personality into smaller elements. It argues that the essence of the construct is lost through such divisions. These hallmarks of the Renaissance-era humanistic movement (from which modern humanism takes its name) thus contrast with the more deterministic view of Freud, according to which we are subject to a host of conflicting unconscious impulses.

A leading humanistic psychologist, Abraham Maslow (1908–1970), proposed that all people possess an innate drive for *self-actualization* (Maslow, 1970). People seek to *actualize* (make real through action) their

Abraham Maslow (1908–1970)

overly heavily on case-study research. Some of the case studies may have been interpreted in ways that overstated their fit to Freud's ideas. These ideas also have not been subjected to as much rigorous empirical testing as would be ideal. Nevertheless, Freud contributed greatly to the development of psychological theory. His insights have shown us the rich material that can be available through case-study research (see chapter 2).

Freud's is not the only version of psychodynamic theory. Several of Freud's disciples rebelled, formulating their own versions of the theory. These more recent psychodynamic theorists are often called "neo-Freudians." Their views have differed from Freud's in many and varied respects. One of the main differences has been in the neo-Freudians' greater emphasis on conscious as opposed to unconscious processing and on the profound influence key human relationships (such as those with our parents) can have on how we come to view the world. Freud's theories, as well as those of the neo-Freudians are discussed in detail in chapters 15 and 17.

potential as creatively as they can. Maslow believed that people differ in the extent to which they succeed in self-actualizing. Those who succeed have in common an objective view of reality, an acceptance of their nature, including both their strengths and their limitations. They also share a commitment to their work; a need for autonomy coupled with empathy for humankind; resistance to blind conformity; and a drive to be creative in their work and in their lives in general.

Carl Rogers (1902–1987), another humanistic psychologist, followed Maslow's emphasis on self-actualization. But Rogers (1961a) stressed the dependence of self-actualization on the relationship between mother and child. He believed that if the mother meets the child's need for unconditional love, the child will probably later develop in a well-adjusted way. Rogers argued that we need this love, which he termed *unconditional positive regard*, in infancy and childhood. Many of the problems we have later are due to the lack of it.

The humanistic approach has made a valuable contribution to our understanding of human nature. At the same time, it is important to realize that its theories tend to be somewhat less comprehensive than is the case for some alternative approaches. Moreover, the research base supporting this approach is somewhat limited.

Carl Rogers (1902–1987)

To conclude, a wide variety of approaches have been used to understand the nature of the human mind. By understanding these approaches, students of psychology can both learn from their predecessors

---

Psychology in Everyday Life

Psychology and Social Action

The history of psychology is filled with examples of how psychology has been used to make a difference in people's lives. There are many examples of such interaction between psychology and social policy.

In the United States, ability and achievement testing has a profound impact on people's lives, for better or worse. The testing industry is a multimillion dollar business that affects people's lives from early childhood through adulthood. Tests are and have been used for military recruitment and placement, school-based decisions, evaluation of job performance, and assessment of people's personal suitability for work in jobs that require great discretion, such as in

intelligence agencies.

Today, many attorneys hire psychologists to serve as jury consultants in order to select those juries that are most likely to render a favorable verdict for their clients. These consultants sometimes have proven to be quite accurate in their assessments of how potential jurors will vote. This accuracy is astonishing, given that the decisions must be made before the case is even presented to the future jury. In the case of the famous O. J. Simpson criminal trial, the defense relied heavily on jury consultants, whereas the prosecution scorned their advice. Although one cannot say why for sure, Simpson was acquitted.

A third area in which psy-

chology has had a profound influence on social policy is in the design of programs to help disadvantaged children achieve their maximum potential. Beginning in the 1960s, the United States started a massive series of interventions programs under the label of "Head Start" to help children, and especially disadvantaged children, reach their full potential. These programs are still going strong today.

In sum, the history of psychology cannot be divorced from the history of society. At all points, the two histories interact, and each shapes and is shaped by the other.

and hope to avoid their mistakes. Psychology students also can better understand the diversity of approaches that continue to be applied within the fields that exist in contemporary psychology.

Fields Within Psychology

In Search of . . .   *What are the principal specialized fields within psychology, and what are some of the career opportunities in these fields?*

The previous section was a sprint through the often cyclical history of psychology. This section is another sprint through the territory that the discipline of psychology has come to encompass. This territory is easily as vast and varied as the history of psychology might lead you to expect. Whereas a psychological **perspective** centers on a particular set of theories and beliefs based on the philosophical strands described early in this chapter, a **field** is a domain of study centered on a set of topics that have a common core of related phenomena. There are many fields within the field of psychology. The very names of these fields suggest the scope of their topics: educational psychology, personality psychology, developmental psychology, social psychology, and so on. Certainly, investigators within some fields are believers in one or more perspectives that define the field. For example, biological psychologists take a biological viewpoint. Still, a given field can provide the grounds for a multitude of perspectives. For example, among *clinical psychologists*—those who treat clients with psychological problems—you will find psychoanalysts, behaviorists, cognitivists, and others. Within each of the main fields of psychology, there are often several subfields. For example, within developmental psychology there is the study of infancy, social development, cognitive development, physical development as well as adolescence, adulthood and aging, to name but a few of the subfields in this one area. These fields and subfields will become more familiar as you move through the chapters of this text, for in many cases they serve as the topics of chapters. One of the most useful ways of understanding some of these different fields is to look at some of the questions with which they concern themselves.

Psychobiology, also termed *biological* or *physiological psychology,* deals with the biological structures and processes underlying thought, feeling, motivation, and behavior. In some cases, biological psychologists may work at the level of the biochemistry of cells or they may work on understanding the physical effects of emotions or on how the eye's structure affects perception. Some questions of interest to psychologists working in this area might be:

What neurochemicals are active in the brain when a person feels depressed?

What happens in the brain when we experience physical pleasure?

What brain structures are invoked when people perceive three-dimensional objects?

How does the brain receive messages from and send messages to the limbs?

Cognitive psychology deals with how people perceive, learn, remember, and think about information. Cognitive psychologists study how people use language, think, solve problems, and make decisions. Those working in this field might be concerned with:

How do people perceive depth?

Why do people remember some facts but forget others?

How do people think when they play chess or solve everyday problems?

What is insight? How is insight different from creativity?

Developmental psychology is the study of how people develop over time through processes of maturation and learning. As mentioned earlier, developmental psychologists may focus on particular ages (infancy, childhood, adolescence, adulthood and aging) and they also tend to focus on an aspect of development such as mental abilities or social skills such as peer relations. For example, a developmental psychologist might wonder:

Are there certain kinds of substance-abuse prevention messages that are likely to be particularly effective with an adolescent audience?

How do children form attachments to their parents?

How do people acquire an understanding of what others expect of them in social interactions?

At what age does it begin to be more difficult for a child to learn a second language?

Social psychology is concerned with how people interact, both as individuals and in groups. This field encompasses work on attraction, prejudice, persuasion, and conformity, to name just a few areas of research. Social psychologists might ask:

What situations encourage people to be violent or cruel?

What makes a message persuasive?

Do opposites attract?

How do people form stereotypes and prejudices?

Personality psychology focuses on the personal dispositions that lead people to behave as they do, and also on how these dispositions interact with situations to affect behavior. Personality psychologists may be concerned with trying to pinpoint or measure personality traits and they may be seeking answers to such questions as,

> Why do some people seem nervous and tense, even in apparently safe settings, whereas other people are easygoing and relaxed?

> What makes some people highly conscientious and others less so?

> How much does personality change over time?

Clinical psychology deals with the understanding and treatment of abnormal behavior. Clinical psychologists may offer therapy or do research on particular disorders or kinds of treatment. Some questions they might be concerned with include:

> What behavior is just a little out of the ordinary, and what behavior is truly abnormal?

> How could a person lose touch with reality and with rational thought?

> What causes people to engage in behavior that they themselves consider inappropriate and even abnormal and would like to stop if they could?

> What sorts of experiences seem linked to depression? Anxiety?

Notice that both physiological and clinical psychologists may be interested in depression. A biological psychologist will perhaps be seeking biochemical clues to this disorder, while the clinician may be using his or her therapeutic techniques to discover the roots of an individual's feelings of depression. Similarly, a social psychologist, a personality psychologist, and a clinical psychologist may all be concerned with substance abuse, but from different angles. The social psychologist may be interested in social situations contributing to drug use; the personality psychologist might be interested in personality types at risk for substance abuse; and the clinical psychologist might be interested in what makes an effective treatment program. There is often considerable overlap. The clinical psychologist studying the problems of adolescence, for example, is also likely to have a great deal of interest and background in developmental psychology.

Although the fields of psychology described above are the main ones covered in this book, they are by no means the only ones. New specialties of psychology are constantly evolving as old ones fade, although specialties rarely die out altogether. Current examples include:

- *Cultural psychology* extends the study of psychological topics to all cultures. Through it, mechanisms of mind and behavior can be studied and compared in multiple cultures. Researchers in cultural psychology endeavor to understand how culture and ethnicity affect human behavior. For example, do people of certain cultural groups show more of a predisposition to violence than people of other cultural groups, and why?

- *Health psychology* seeks to understand the reciprocal interaction between the psychological processes of the mind and the physical health of the body. For example, does a positive attitude in and of itself help people recover from physical illnesses?

- *Educational psychology* uses psychology to develop and improve curricula, school administration, and classroom teaching practices.

- *School psychology* uses psychology to diagnose psychologically-based problems of children in school and to recommend, where possible, means of correcting or at least coping with these problems.

- *Organizational psychology* applies psychology to understanding organizations and to decision making about employees and hiring in institutional settings, such as workplaces and businesses.

- *Engineering psychology* deals with human–machine systems and how instruments such as computers and automobile dashboards can be made more user-friendly.

When reading about some of the fields and specialties within psychology, you may find yourself drawn to considering a career in psychology. Table 1-3 lists some of the specific career paths available to psychology majors and describes the typical duties, the education required, and the work settings for various fields. A more detailed description of some of these careers, as well as others within psychology, can be found in *Career Paths in Psychology* (R. J. Sternberg, 1997a).

The list of careers within psychology is not static. Rather, as psychology is applied to more and more other disciplines, new specialties within psychology are appearing almost every year. Recent examples of this growth are health psychology and forensic psychology. With aging populations in many countries, gerontological psychology—the psychological study of the elderly—although not new, has become of more interest than ever before. Within just a few years' time, other specialties, as yet unheard of, may well have appeared. Psychology frequently draws on and contributes to other academic disciplines, which in turn continually stimulate and rejuvenate psychological thought. Just as psychological thought has evolved from diverse ideas in its past, it continues to develop through intersection and interaction with diverse fields and sources of information in the present. It will continue to develop in this way in the future. At the same time, the methods of investigation it uses will continue to develop. Old and new methods alike are discussed in chapter 2.

TABLE 1–3

Career Options for Psychologists   *The study of psychology can prove valuable for any career path. Here are some of the options available to persons who pursue degrees in psychology.*

CAREER	TYPICAL TRAINING	JOB DESCRIPTION
Academic psychologist	PhD	Works in a college or university teaching and conducting research; advises students, assists in educational administration
Clinical psychologist	PhD or PsyD	Diagnoses and treats patients for psychological problems; teaches, trains, and conducts research in a hospital, clinic, college, or university
Counseling psychologist	MA, EdD, or PhD	Counsels people about their problems, conflicts, or choices; often works in a school, office, hospital, or clinic
Engineering or human-factors psychologist	PhD	May work in an industrial setting; designs machines and workplace environments to maximize productivity and safety; often works with engineers and designers
Industrial or organizational psychologist	MA or PhD	Works in a business or industrial setting to help with hiring and firing, testing, interviewing, and placement; assists in developing more hospitable and effective workplaces
Consumer psychologist	MA or PhD	Works in a business, consulting, or advertising firm to generate ads that will sell products; supervises testing of ads and determines consumer preferences
Military psychologist	PhD	Works in the armed forces to deal with the interface between psychology and military life; involved in testing, counseling, designing, and implementing new procedures and requirements
Psychometrician	MA or PhD	Creates psychological tests, including aptitude, achievement, personality, attitude, and vocational preference tests; collects and analyzes test data
School psychologist	MA, EdD, or PhD	Works in a school setting to test and counsel students; identifies children with perceptual and learning disabilities, as well as gifted children
Consulting psychologist	MA, EdD, or PhD	Works for a consulting firm on a special for-hire basis to perform any of the various aforementioned services

 THINK ABOUT IT

1. If you were to accept Thales's invitation to participate in the critical tradition, what perspectives and ideas in this chapter would you criticize? Critique at least one of the views that has been expressed in this chapter.

2. Choose an early school of thought and a twentieth-century school of thought. In what ways did the older one pave the way for the newer one? (List both similarities and differences.)

3. Quickly jot down a description of your sensations as you believe a structuralist would describe them introspectively.

4. In *Walden Two*, B. F. Skinner describes a utopia in which behaviorist principles are applied to all aspects of life for people of all ages. Choose one of the schools of thought described in this chapter and briefly describe a utopian community being governed by psychologists from that school of thought.

5. In your everyday life, you confront many new situations. Describe a situation in which your theory of the nature of the situation (which may be entirely idiosyncratic) largely guided your responses.

6. What is one thing that your psychology professor—or the author of this book—could do to apply the notion of the dialectic to your current psychology course? Give a specific example of how you might apply this notion.

online *You can provide your own answers to these questions online at the* Sternberg, **In Search of the Human Mind** *Web site:* *http://www.harcourtcollege.com/psych/ishm*

SUMMARY

Psychology as a Natural Science and a Social Science   3

1. Psychology is the study of the mind, behavior, and the relationship between them.

2. Psychology is both a natural science and a social science.

The Evolution of Ideas   5

3. By studying views on certain issues in philosophy and *physiology*, as they have evolved over time, we can trace the history of the foundations of psychology. Some of the most important questions in the history of psychology are whether the mind and body are one or are two separate phenomena, to what extent psychology should focus on each of biology and behavior, to what extent behavior is a function of innate factors and to what extent it is a function of environmental factors, and the extent to which behavior is general or specific across domains.

4. A dialectic is a search for truth through the resolution of opposites; first, a thesis is proposed; then a countering antithesis; and eventually, a unifying synthesis. One such dialectic in psychology is about the role of theory in scientific research. Should research be wholly guided by theory, performed without regard to theory, or performed with both a theory in mind and a recognition that results may not fit into the proposed theoretical framework?

A Brief Intellectual History: Western Antecedents of Psychology   5

5. Psychology traces its roots back to archaic Greece. In fact, the word *psychology* (the study of the mind and behavior) is derived from the Greek word *psyche*, which means soul or breath of life.

6. The Greek physician Hippocrates (ca. 460–377 B.C.) believed that the source of the mind was in the brain. Hippocrates espoused an empirical approach to learning how the body works.

7. The work of the ancient Greek (ca. 428–322 B.C.) philosophers Plato and Aristotle aptly demonstrates the nature of dialectics. The issues raised in their work continue to be argued today. Plato emphasized the supreme power of the mind and thought, which made him a *rationalist*. Plato believed that knowledge is innate; that the search for truth can best be achieved through intellectual reflection; and that the mind and body are qualitatively different and separate, a concept known as *mind–body dualism*. Aristotle emphasized the world we can see and touch as the route to reality, truth, and knowledge, which made him an *empiricist*. In contrast to Plato, Aristotle believed that knowledge is learned through interactions with and direct observation of the environment. He also presaged monism, the view that the mind and body are essentially one.

8. During the Renaissance (1300–1600), science as we know it was born. Thinkers began to depend less on faith and more on empirical observation for proof of theories. Francis Bacon, perhaps in reaction against what he perceived as rigid adherence to and guidance by theory in medieval times, proposed that all science should proceed only from empirical observation; it should be completely free from the influence of any theory.

9. René Descartes, a rationalist philosopher, believed in mind–body dualism. In particular, he believed that the mind is the determiner of true existence—*Cogito ergo sum*. In opposition, the British empiricist school of philosophers (1600–1850), including John Locke, believed in the continuity and interdependence of mind and body.

10. Immanuel Kant sought to synthesize questions about mind–body dualism versus monism and innate versus acquired sources of knowledge. Kant's work in philosophy helped bring about the establishment of psychology as a discrete discipline, separate from both philosophy and medicine.

Psychological Perspectives: The 1850s and Beyond   9

11. Over time, psychologists have approached the study of the mind and behavior from different perspectives as manifested in different schools of thought. These perspectives, from functionalism through cognitivism, have often been in part reactions to what came before them. Modern perspectives in psychology are viewed, generally speaking, as those that originated in the twentieth century. New theories continue to evolve dialectically.

12. Structuralism was the first strictly psychological school of thought. *Structuralists* sought to analyze consciousness into its constituent components of elementary sensations, using *introspection*, a reflective self-observation technique. Structuralism emphasized the role of experience in behavior.

13. *Functionalists*, in reaction to structuralism, sought to understand what people do and why. Many functionalists were pragmatists, who looked at the applications of knowledge to practice.

Evolving Twentieth-Century Perspectives on Psychology   14

14. *Associationism* examines how events or ideas can become associated with one another in the mind to result in a form of learning. Associationism emphasized the role of experience over innate factors in behavior.

15. An offshoot of associationism, *behaviorism*, was a reaction to structuralism and is based on the belief that the science of psychology should deal only with observable behavior.

16. *Gestalt psychology* is based on the notion that the whole is often more meaningful than the sum of its parts; this perspective developed partly as a reaction against the extreme analytic perspectives of both structuralists and behaviorists.

17. *Cognitivism* is the belief that much of human behavior can be understood in terms of how people think. Some cognitivists emphasize the importance of innate factors in behavior, whereas others emphasize the role of environmental factors.

18. *Biological psychology* studies the ways in which human anatomy and physiology (especially of the nervous system, including the brain) interact with human behavior. Biological researchers emphasize the importance of the biological bases of behavior.

19. *Evolutionary psychology* seeks explanations of how behavior might have been adaptive for our ancestors in the environments they confronted.

20. The basis of *psychodynamic psychology* is the view that many of the thoughts and feelings that motivate behavior are unconscious, and that there is a continual tension among internal mental structures.

21. *Humanistic psychology* studies how people consciously actualize, or realize through action, their own great inner potential.

Fields Within Psychology   24

22. Many different *fields* appear under the umbrella of psychology. Some of the main fields are psychobiology, cognitive psychology, social psychology, personality psychology, clinical psychology, and developmental psychology. Some fields, such as clinical psychology, accommodate a variety of perspectives (cognitive, psychoanalytic, humanistic, etc.). New specialties are constantly evolving. The various fields in psychology have given rise to diverse career opportunities.

23. Psychologists in different specializations may study the same problem. But depending on the perspectives they use, they may organize information differently and use different methods of inquiry—in effect, approaching the same issue from different angles.

KEY TERMS

antithesis   5
associationism   13
behavioral genetics   20
behaviorism   15
biological psychology   20
biopsychosocial approach   21
classically conditioned
    learning   15
cognitivism   19
dialectic   5

empirical methods   7
empiricist   7
evolutionary psychology   21
field   24
functionalism   13
Gestalt   18
Gestalt psychology   18
humanistic psychology   22
introspection   6
law of effect   14

mind-body dualism   6
perspective   24
physiology   6
psychoanalysis   21
psychodynamic theory   21
psychology   3
rationalist   8
structuralism   11
synthesis   5
thesis   5

THINK ABOUT IT SAMPLE RESPONSES

1. If you were to accept Thales's invitation to participate in the critical tradition, what perspectives and ideas in this chapter would you criticize? Critique at least one of the views that has been expressed in this chapter.

You might critique any point of view. Perhaps the most important thing is to learn to critique not only the points of view with which you tend to disagree, but also the points of view with which you tend to agree. So I, as the author of this book, have tended to favor the cognitivist perspective in much of my work. But I realize that the perspective has limitations. Often cognitivists fail adequately to take into account individual differences, treating individual differences merely as sources of error rather than as important in their own right. Cognitivists also sometimes fail to take into account cultural differences, assuming that a finding that emerges in one culture automatically applies to all others. The important thing is to be as skeptical of your own preferred beliefs as you are of the beliefs of others.

2. Choose an early school of thought and a twentieth-century school of thought. In what ways did the older one pave the way for the newer one? (List both similarities and differences.)

British empiricism paved the way for behaviorism. Empiricism, like behaviorism, emphasized the importance of experience in determining behavior and placed little or no emphasis on innate dispositions. Indeed, Locke referred to the baby's mind as a blank slate. Empiricism also stressed the importance of observation for acquiring knowledge, as did behaviorism. Both schools of thought also emphasized the malleability of human behavior: Peoples' destinies are not predetermined. Rather, people can shape their own destiny, or their destiny can be shaped for them.

3. Quickly jot down a description of your sensations as you believe a structuralist would describe them introspectively.

Right now I am looking at a solid white, rectangular structure that is longer than it is wide and that is supported by metallic objects fastened to the structure and connected to another structure. The structure at which I am peering can swing back and forth toward or away from me. (It is what we call a "door.")

4. In *Walden Two*, B. F. Skinner describes a utopia in which behaviorist principles are applied to all aspects of life for people of all ages. Choose one of the schools of thought described in this chapter and briefly describe a utopian community being governed by psychologists from that school of thought.

In a Gestaltist utopia, people might be judged only as a whole in terms of their global contribution to the society. People might not much care whether they did one particular kind of thing or another, and people might not make distinctions according to single features like religion, ethnic group, a score on a test, or a grade-point average in a school. Rather, people might see others as wholes, and value them for their total personhood.

5. In your everyday life, you confront many new situations. Describe a situation in which your theory of the nature of the situation (which may be entirely idiosyncratic) largely guided your responses.

When I went on college-admissions interviews, as many students do, I went to one college expecting not to like it. I had heard some very mixed reviews of the place and was almost convinced it was not the place for me. My expectations were fulfilled, perhaps because I was seeking confirmation of my prior beliefs. I was dissatisfied with the people I met, with the physical layout of the place, and the weather was terrible to boot. I left the place and remember saying to myself, "Thank goodness I'll never have to visit that dump again." As it turned out, I went to college there and have been teaching there for over a quarter of a century. For the most part, I have been very satisfied. Sometimes life takes unexpected twists.

6. What is one thing that your psychology professor—or the author of this book—could do to apply the notion of the dialectic to your current psychology course? Give a specific example of how you might apply this notion.

When I took tests in my introductory psychology course, I was dissatisfied with them. The multiple-choice questions were objective, but often seemed to measure picky facts that seemed to me of little interest or importance to anyone. The essay questions on the tests, although dealing with larger questions, seemed to lend themselves only to very subjective grading. So I thought both means of assessment were inadequate. In a sense, then, I found both the thesis of multiple-choice questions and the antithesis of essay questions unsatisfactory. Then I realized that the professor of the course used both kinds of assessments precisely because he thought each, in itself, was inadequate. His synthesis was to combine them so that the strengths of each would compensate for the weaknesses of the other.

Nearly all of us consider ourselves at least somewhat expert at observing and understanding behavior. You may have heard talk-show guests offer tips about love and how you can improve your love life. He or she might say, "Two of the best predictors of happiness in a relationship are how you feel about your partner and how your partner feels about you." Hearing that, you may wonder why psychologists even bother to study such obvious and commonsensical "facts" about human behavior. Interestingly, this statement, that happiness in a relationship is best measured by the feelings of the two people involved, shows why psychologists do bother—because psychological research has proved that "obvious" statement to be wrong (Sternberg & Barnes, 1985).

2

RESEARCH METHODS IN PSYCHOLOGY

Here is another example of the fallibility of common sense. Many self-help programs emphasize how focusing upon our goals can help us attain those goals. The idea is that if we want to be rich, or professionally successful, or successful in love, we need to visualize the goal we wish to achieve, and think frequently about it. By focusing upon such goals, they are more likely to come true. Shelley Taylor and her colleagues (Taylor, Pham, Rivkin, & Armor, 1998) did a series of studies to test this idea. In her studies, she had people focus either on the goals they wished to attain or on the processes of attaining those goals, or not focus on anything in particular. She found that focusing on goals, if it did anything, actually interfered with goal attainment. Those who focused on nothing in particular were more likely to achieve their goals than those who focused on the goals themselves. However, focusing on the *means* of goal attainment did improve one's chances of attaining one's goals. Thus it is focusing on the means to goal attainment, rather than on the ends, that is more likely to get people where they wish to go.

In addition, what seems unmistakably clear to those in one culture may not be at all clear to persons elsewhere. Consider the following anecdote:

Once upon a time, an anthropologist was telling an English folk-fable to a gathering of the Bemba of Rhodesia. She glowingly described "a young prince who climbed glass mountains, crossed chasms, and fought dragons, all to obtain the hand of a maiden he loved." The Bemba were plainly bewildered, but remained silent. Finally an old chief spoke up, voicing the feelings of all present in the simplest of questions: "Why not take another girl?" he asked.

—M. M. Hunt, *The Natural History of Love*

In sum, psychology does not just restate what is apparent to all. It is more precise and thoughtful than common sense. Some psychological findings do confirm what we already suspected, but many of them surprise us. In fact, psychologists, like other scientists, expect to find results that surprise them. Surprises are common in science.

Characteristics of Scientific Findings

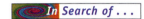 *In* Search of . . .

What are the main characteristics of scientific findings?

Scientists employ a particular set of methods as they strive to find the truth. These methods help scientists—whether they are biologists, chemists, or psychologists—ensure that the information (data) they gather and theories they develop are (a) verifiable and accurately reported, (b) made public, and (c) built on other verified findings. Of course, scientists cannot guarantee their data will have these characteristics, but by using the methods described in this chapter, they can ensure that they, as scientists, seek these characteristics to the best of their abilities, given their frailties and their biases, as well as their cultural contexts (see Table 2-1).

Scientific findings have several characteristics. These characteristics distinguish scientific findings from findings or ideas in fields that are outside the scope of science. What exactly are these characteristics?

Scientific Findings Are Verifiable

Scientific findings are **verifiable;** there must be some means of confirming the findings. For example, if one scientist conducts an experiment and draws conclusions, other scientists must be able to **replicate** the experiment—to repeat the original methods and produce the same results as were obtained by the first scientist. For example, suppose you were to investigate why, in the middle of a test, you cannot remember something you studied earlier. You suspect anxiety about time constraints was the cause of this difficulty.

To find out whether anxiety about time constraints is indeed the cause of being unable to think clearly while in a test situation, you must come up with a procedure that meets two criteria: The procedure must produce results that are both reliable and valid. If your experimental procedure produces results that are **reliable,** you and others can count on your procedure to produce the same results time after time.

Reliability is necessary for evaluation, but it is not sufficient. For example, suppose that you read about a researcher's attempt to investigate the effects of anxiety about time constraints on test performance. This researcher compared students' test performance in a room in which a clock loudly ticked with the passage of time to performance in a room in which no clock was present. Even if the results of this procedure could be tested again and again and could reliably show that test takers in the room without the clock performed better than did students in the room with the clock, the interpretation of those findings still might not be **valid**—that is, the investigation might not have shown what it was purported to show. Maybe the difference

---

| TABLE 2-1 | |

Three Characteristics of Science

Scientists use various methods for obtaining data and formulating theories, which have these three characteristics.

CHARACTERISTICS PRIZED BY SCIENTISTS	REASON FOR PRIZING THE CHARACTERISTIC
Verifiable	Researchers can evaluate whether the research outcomes are reliable and the conclusions are valid.
Public	Carefully reviewed research published in scientific journals informs scientists about existing research, so they may evaluate that research and build on it.
Cumulative	To move science forward, scientists build on past research.

in test performance was due to test takers' irritation with the noisy clock rather than to anxiety about time constraints. The results of the procedure might be deemed to be reliable, but the interpretation of those results in terms of anxiety might be considered invalid. Additional research would be needed in order to find out whether it was the anxiety about time constraints, irritation, or some other factor that had caused the difference in test performance.

The test-taking example shows the need for scientific findings to be *accurately reported*. Accurate reporting allows both the initial researcher and other researchers to assess the reliability and the validity of the research results.

Scientific Findings Are Public

Science is *public*. Regardless of how many interesting research studies are conducted, the results do not fully benefit science and society until they become public, usually through *scientific journals* (periodicals that report research results to the scientific community).

Scientists are motivated to write about their results for at least three reasons. First, the process of writing has helped many scientists interpret their own results and clarify the directions in which their experiments were taking them. For example, Sir Isaac Newton made discoveries about prisms and light while he was writing about his studies (Gorman, 1992).

Second, writing about research enables referees (people who evaluate articles submitted to scientific journals) and editors (people who decide which articles should be published in scientific journals) to scrutinize the relative scientific merits of the articles submitted for publication. The reviewers and editors evaluate the ideas, the research testing these ideas, and the interpretations of the research presented in the articles.

Third, publication of compelling results permits readers to learn of research findings that might lead to further research or to relevant applications in their field of interest. Fellow scientists have the opportunity to read, pause, reread, reflect, mull over details, and analyze the research, as well as to consider possible applications of the information. Once the scientific merits of the findings have been evaluated, reporters in the nonscientific news media also may consider broader publication of the findings, based on *news value*—the general appeal and popular interest of the findings. (Note that scientific value and news value often differ.)

This public aspect of science operated in the writing of this book and could help you in reading it. The articles and books used for investigating, documenting, and supporting the information in this book are *cited*—the last names of the authors as well as the year in which the book or study being cited was published—are placed in parentheses following the statement or statements for which the research provides evidence (see the Shelley Taylor study mentioned earlier). Citations show that the statements and claims in a work are based on previously published and accepted data. Citations also publicly credit other researchers for their work. Finally, citations identify a source of further information for readers. Whenever you see citations in this text and would like more information, you may look up the citations in the "References" section at the back of this textbook; these references can lead you to the original study, which in turn will have references to other, earlier research findings—another quality of scientific findings.

Scientific Findings Are Cumulative

In addition to being verifiable, the work of science is *cumulative*. Even revolutionary science that invents a new way of looking at problems builds on past work, perhaps using it as a basis for what not to do. When Albert Einstein revolutionized the way scientists view physics, he built on the foundation of Newtonian physics. Had Isaac Newton's previous work not existed, Einstein never could have formulated his general and special theories of relativity. Whether scientists embrace or reject the work of their intellectual ancestors, they profit from the earlier work. In designing your experiments for your hypothetical study of the factors affecting test performance, you would profit from your predecessors' work. You also would benefit from reading widely about other research on attention, memory, thinking, the effects of emotions on performance, and the ways in which physiological stress affects thinking, among other things. You are able to read about these things because scientists make the results of their work public.

Other factors also tend to characterize much, but not all, scientific work. For example, where possible, scientists typically prefer simpler rather than more complex explanations and they prefer explanations that account for as many different and diverse findings as possible. Having discussed some of the major characteristics of scientific work, we can begin to take a look at some of the misconceptions or myths surrounding it.

What Science Is Not

Part of scientific thinking is examining the assumptions one may be making in connection with a given area—such as the idea that it is the anxiety-producing presence of the clock and not its ticking that affects test scores. So, in considering what science is, it is helpful also to consider what it is not. Here are some of the

Psychology in Everyday Life

Is Psychology All Obvious?

Folk wisdom provides a way of guiding people in their everyday lives. The most common form of folk wisdom is the proverb. Are proverbs really useful guides to living? Robert Epstein (1999) has pointed out that the problem with proverbs is that they so often recommend contradictory courses of action. Examples of such contradictions are "Absence makes the heart grow fonder," "Out of sight, out of mind," "Haste makes waste," and "He who hesitates is lost."

To what extent does research support the recommendations of proverbs? Epstein decided to examine some key proverbs to determine whether they are supported by research.

Consider, for example, the proverb, "Confession is good for the soul." Generally research is supportive of this notion. People who self-disclose are likely to show better mental and physical health than people who do not disclose (Pennebaker, 1997). The research shows that self-disclosure is not uniformly helpful, however. Some kinds of disclosure, such as to individuals who are likely to be judgmental, may backfire (Kelly, 1999). Disclosures of having been the victim of child abuse also have produced mixed results (Sauzier, 1989).

Another proverb is "All work and no play makes Jack a dull boy." Research suggests that long working hours can slow down reaction times and reduce people's alertness (Knauth, 1996). In contrast, leisure activities tend to improve mood, relieve stress, and even boost the functioning of the immune system (Tinsley, Hinson, Tinsley, & Holt, 1993).

In sum, proverbs are a mixed bag. Sometimes they are supported, sometimes they are not, and sometimes they are supported under certain circumstances and not others. An advantage of psychology over conventional wisdom is that it seeks answers not merely from people's beliefs, but from research into human behavior.

misconceptions that frequently are associated with science, scientists, and scientific endeavors.

Misconception 1: Science Is Always Correct

Scientific accounts are not always correct. In fact, they are often wrong, or at least incomplete. Today, we view many of the beliefs of 19th-century and even early 20th-century psychology—such as the belief that thinking is always accompanied by some form of talking to oneself (J. B. Watson, 1930)—as quaint and curious. In the future, many of the views we hold dear today also will seem outdated and peculiar. To be of value, science must be dynamic and constantly evolving, as new theories continually take the place of old ones. But this evolution does not always occur in an idealized manner.

Misconception 2: Scientific Research Is Always Conducted in a Certain Way

Scientists, in general, and psychologists, in particular, rarely use the orderly, linear, scientific methods they learned in school. Almost all scientists make false starts from time to time and have to reconsider *why* they are doing *what* they are doing, or even what they should have done in the first place. Sometimes, they

have to revise their original hypotheses or fine-tune their research procedures in order to get them to work. Sometimes, research that starts off being about one thing ends up being about another. For example, studies of why children fail in school may begin by studying the children's abilities, but then end up also studying their motivations, personalities, and environments because they surface as more important to success than ability.

Misconception 3: Scientific Research Is Always Conducted With Perfect Objectivity

Scientists sometimes fail to reach their goal of being completely objective in deciding what to study, how to study it, and how to interpret the findings of their studies. Like their fellow humans, they can rationalize when they fall prey to errors in thinking. For example, people tend to seek to confirm rather than to refute existing beliefs (D. Halpern, 1995; Oakhill & Garnham, 1993; Sternberg & Ben-Zeev, 2001; Wason & Johnson-Laird, 1972), a tendency referred to as **confirmation bias.** When viewing new evidence, scientists, like anyone else, may seek an interpretation of the evidence that best fits what they already believe (Kuhn, 1970). For this reason and other reasons, scientists should actively seek to **disconfirm,** not just

An expectation that children in an environment such as this will have a more difficult time learning may result in a confirmation bias—a tendency to seek out information that confirms one's beliefs. It is better when studies are designed not just to show which ideas are useful, but also, which are not.

confirm, what they believe (Popper, 1959): Science often advances most effectively when studies are designed not just to show which ideas are useful, but also which ideas are not useful.

Values—preconceptions regarding what is valuable—also affect the way in which research is conducted. Whatever our values are, and however widely we share them, our values will influence the way we do research. For example, values influence what topics we deem worthy of study, how we believe that these topics should be studied, and how we interpret the results of those studies. For example, as life expectancies have increased and populations in various countries thus have increased in average age, the study of aging has come to seem more valuable to many people. Hence, increased attention has been devoted to it.

As this chapter has shown, science itself has values. These values include objectivity, the importance of empirically testing theories, accuracy, honesty, concise but illuminating public sharing of information, and openness to question and to verification. When these values are set aside, the effects can be disastrous. For example, occasional cases in which companies have hidden potentially disastrous side effects of drugs

have resulted in catastrophic results for the human guinea pigs who unwittingly took these dangerous drugs. Sometimes it is not even obvious that a drug is involved, as in the case of nicotine, a potentially deadly component of tobacco. Many of its harmful effects were known to officers of certain cigarette manufacturing companies well before the information about these effects became public. It would not be realistic—or perhaps even desirable—to aspire to have no values. A more realistic aspiration is to recognize our values and to try to keep them from biasing or otherwise interfering with the way in which we study human behavior.

Misconception 4: Science Is Merely a Collection of Facts

One of the cultural values that can color our view of science is an emphasis on products (such as facts) above processes (such as the pursuit of knowledge and understanding). This emphasis leads to what may be the most important misconception about science— that science is merely a collection of facts. But facts become part of the scientific enterprise only when they are presented in the context of a **theory,** a statement of some general principles explaining particular events. Theories are not merely opinions but are analyses of the relations among sets of facts. We need theories because science is not merely descriptive but also explanatory. Without theories, we still might be able to describe behavior, or at least to make some discrete observations about behavior, but we would not really understand it. In looking at human behavior, we would be able to investigate and find answers to *what* is happening, but not to *why*, and possibly not even to *how* it is happening.

Theories also play an important role in guiding observations and experimentation. For example, people typically think of illusions as problematical. Shelley Taylor and Jonathan Brown (1988) formulated a theory that postulated the reverse. They argued that certain illusions, such as the idea that you could become a professional basketball player, actually may help preserve rather than damage psychological well-being by increasing motivation. Their theory provided the impetus for them to review the literature and find that the available data in fact supported their theory. Their theory guided their thinking, determined what they were looking for, and led them to an important discovery.

Thus far, we have described the characteristics of science, including some of the erroneous assumptions made about it. Let us now begin to consider how scientists think about the things they study, and how they study those things.

Learning From the Errors of Early Researchers

Ray Hyman, *emeritus, University of Oregon*

Smart people sometimes goof. Some of the best and brightest scientists and scholars have occasionally blundered badly. In my work, I am interested in how the same person who has succeeded in intellectual pursuits can also fail badly in such quests. I also want to see how well contemporary psychological theory and research regarding cognition, or thought processes, can account for both the successes and failures of these smart people.

To answer these questions, I rely on historical research. I search through the history of science and biographies of outstanding scientists and scholars, and I look for cases that meet the following criteria:

1. The blunder involved was one that, as far as we can tell, could—and should—have been avoided given the resources and knowledge at the time it occurred.

2. The person who blundered was recognized by his or her peers as someone who had made important contributions to an area of science or other scholarly or artistic domain.

3. The person, at the time of the blunder, had no known mental disease, incompetence, or other defect.

4. Sufficient documentation exists concerning the details of the blunder and the life of the blunderer.

For each case, I try to provide a plausible reconstruction of the scholar's error in terms of contemporary cognitive psychology. Such a reconstruction does not have to correspond with the actual thought processes of the person under study. The goal is simply to see if we can create a plausible scenario regarding the lapse in thinking or reasoning that led to the mistaken idea using current theories of psychology. Although there are always a number of factors which contribute to the mistaken thinking in each case, I look for cases that can be explained in terms of one or two major psychological factors. I try to select my set of cases so that each one emphasizes a somewhat different psychological explanation.

For example, based on the information available, I can create a plausible scenario of how Blondlot, the physicist who "discovered" N-rays, came to believe in these nonexistent rays. He was working with what was known then regarding the structure of the eye and how the sensory system operates under conditions of very weak input. Similarly, to understand how Gall, the physician who discovered phrenology, came to believe that human faculties were correlated with the shape of the skull, requires a reconstruction involving cognitive factors that deal with how humans perceive correlations among events. A plausible scenario to account for how scientists falsely believed that Piltdown Man had a human cranium and an ape's jaw requires using social and cultural principles, such as national pride, along with such tendencies as confirmation bias.

In addition to exploring plausible explanations for how smart people can go wrong, I hope my project also will help find possible deficiencies in contemporary psychological theory and research. Some of these deficiencies might simply point to incompleteness, or they may provide hints about possible ways to extend psychological theory to cover certain cases. Others may suggest that a psychological theory is actually wrong.

One obvious problem in trying to apply the theories and findings of cognitive psychology to my cases is a problem of scale. Most of the models and research in cognitive psychology deal with processes that occur during a matter of seconds. The majority of data upon which psychological theory relies involves behavior that occurs in a range from a fraction of a second to several minutes. The historical cases in my project involve events that unfold over months and years— sometimes over a lifetime.

Contemporary psychological research and theory do very well in accounting for human errors and biases. However, many of these errors are easily detected and corrected by the persons committing them. When subjects fall prey to the stronger illusions—both perceptual and cognitive—they can be made aware that they have, indeed, made a mistake. The blunders that characterize my cases differ from these sorts of errors in that the person making the error never recognizes it as incorrect. Indeed, the most striking characteristic of these false beliefs by smart people is their persistence in the face of strong arguments and evidence against them.

Still, it is comforting to find that current psychological theory, in spite of its drawbacks, still provides useful insights into many of the blunders in my collection. This suggests that we do not necessarily need to replace current theories. Rather, we need to extend and add to the range of phenomena they encompass.

 Find out more about this topic at
www.harcourtcollege.com/psych/ishm

How Scientists Formulate and Solve Problems

In *Search of . . .* *What are the steps scientists follow in understanding and solving problems?*

Scientists have a set of methods to find the solutions to a variety of problems. But in science, today's solutions frequently become tomorrow's new scientific problems. Consider a problem: Do women prefer men with a more masculine or with a more feminine face? Some people might guess that they would prefer a more masculine face; others might guess the opposite. But neither option is correct. According to a recent report (Penton-Voak et al., 1999), whether women prefer a more masculine or a more feminine face depends on the stage they are in with respect to their menstrual cycle. According to the researchers, women near ovulation and hence more likely to conceive prefer faces that are more masculine, whereas women far from ovulation and hence less likely to conceive prefer more feminine faces. So one problem is solved, but other problems are raised. Why would women prefer different faces at different points in their menstrual cycle? An evolutionary interpretation might be that at time of ovulation, women look for the man most likely to produce the best possible offspring. But other problems arise as well. Is a man with a masculine face really more likely to contribute to producing the best possible offspring? Do men have similar time-bound preferences for women? And on the list of questions goes. Much problem solving proceeds in the same way as in this example. Solving one scientific problem or answering one question raises a set of other problems or questions.

Identifying the Problem

"Is there any point to which you would wish to draw my attention?"

"To the curious incident of the dog in the night-time."

"The dog did nothing in the night-time."

"That was the curious incident," remarked Sherlock Holmes.

—Sir Arthur Conan Doyle, "Silver Blaze," *The Memoirs of Sherlock Holmes*

The first step in problem solving is to identify the problem (Bransford & Stein, 1993; Sternberg & Ben-Zeev, 2001). You cannot study a problem unless you identify it as a problem. Also, some problems are more deserving of attention than are others. Harriet Zuckerman (1983) and other sociologists who study

science have claimed that a major distinction between greater and lesser scientists is in their taste in problems. Greater scientists identify and study more significant problems.

No one way of coming up with ideas works for everyone. If you are having difficulty thinking of ideas for your own studies, try simply watching people, including yourself. You are bound to find puzzles that intrigue you regarding the way people act.

One of the best ways to generate ideas is to become broadly educated. Many of the best problem identifiers are people who bring ideas from one field to bear on another. For example, Nobel Prize–winning cognitive psychologist Herbert Simon dramatically influenced psychology by introducing ideas he brought from computer science, such as comparing and contrasting how humans and computers solve problems. Other people have contributed ideas from far-flung disciplines to various areas of psychology as well. For example, psychologist Margaret Floy Washburn brought her extensive knowledge of animal behavior to bear on questions of sensation and movement (Furumoto & Scarborough, 1986; Hilgard, 1987). Psychologist Kenneth Clark imported ideas from sociology to help understand certain problems of African American children in schools. And psychologist George Miller used ideas from linguistics for his remarkable insights into memory.

Defining the Problem

Once we identify the existence of a problem, we still have to figure out exactly what the problem is. In other words, we have to define the nature of the problem. When defining a scientific problem, we may use an **operational definition,** a means researchers use to specify exactly how to test or measure the particular phenomena being studied. Operational definitions allow researchers to communicate how they conducted an experiment and how they came to particular conclusions.

For example, Laurel Furumoto and Elizabeth Scarborough (1986) were interested in investigating the ways in which early female psychologists contributed to the field of psychology. How could they possibly even start to study such a sweeping construct? They needed to find some way to pin down their study to a specific set of early female psychologists whose contributions they could study. Thus, they operationally defined the object of their study as the contributions to psychology made by "the 22 women who identified themselves as psychologists in the first edition of *American Men of Science*" (p. 35). The authors acknowledged that their study, by definition, did not include the work done by many other women who contributed significantly to the early development of psychology. Because these

Psychologist Kenneth Clark devoted a major portion of his career to studying how schools could be improved in ways that serve minority schoolchildren.

two researchers indicated their operational definition, other psychologists and historians who read about Furumoto and Scarborough's findings are able to interpret those findings in light of their definition.

One reason operational definitions are so important in psychology is that psychology often makes use of the **hypothetical construct**—an abstract concept that is not itself directly measurable or observable but that gives rise to measurable phenomena and patterns of data. For example, psychologists infer the existence of the hypothetical construct of *intelligence*, based on test scores and on particular kinds of behavior. Constructs, such as intelligence, are often the centerpieces of psychological theories.

Much of scientific research depends on how the problem is identified and defined. Most of us have much more experience in solving problems than we do in identifying and defining them (Bruer, 1993). To become good scientists, we need both kinds of experience.

Formulating Hypotheses

Once you have figured out the problem you wish to study, you may wish to formulate hypotheses. For example, British psychologists Michael Howe and his colleagues (Howe, Davidson, & Sloboda, 1998), building upon work by K. Anders Ericsson (1996) and others, hypothesized that the main difference between experts and novices in a given field such as music or art is in the amount of time they devote to *deliberate practice*—practice that is focused toward a goal and that is directed toward the correction of errors. They reviewed the literature in a wide variety of fields and found that, consistent with their expectations, deliberate practice seemed to be an excellent predictor of the level of expertise a person would obtain in a given endeavor. Their results were surprising because many people had assumed that differences in levels of attained expertise were due largely to differences in people's inborn levels of talent. Although these results do not rule out the importance of differences in inborn levels of talent, the results do suggest that dedicated effort may play a larger role in the attainment of expertise than previously had been believed. Often psychologists need not only formulate hypotheses but also revise them. For example, some psychologists have come to believe that although deliberate practice is important, it interacts with abilities to produce expert behavior (e.g., Sternberg, 1996, 1998).

Constructing a Strategy for Solving the Problem

Once you have determined what problem you wish to solve and have some hypotheses about what the solution to the problem is, you still need to figure out how you are going to test it (Nisbett, 1993). In many psychological investigations the preferred strategy is to conduct experimental research, but other methods may be more effective for solving problems that do not lend themselves to experimental manipulations on the part of the investigator. (Alternative strategies are discussed in greater detail in a subsequent section of this chapter.) There is no single ideal strategy for addressing every problem. Instead, the optimal strategy depends on both the problem and the investigator's personal taste in problem-solving methods.

For example, Robert Cialdini (1984) became interested in how he and other people are suckered into buying things they do not really want. Cialdini decided on a strategy of *participant observation*, whereby the person studying a phenomenon both observes it and participates. For a three-year period, Cialdini answered newspaper ads for sales trainees in various advertising, public-relations firms, and fund-raising organizations. While feigning to be in training for sales, he learned the techniques that organizations use for persuading people to buy products and services that the people do not necessarily want. Had Cialdini not been willing to become a participant in sales training, it is unlikely that the organizations would have informed him of their secrets for influencing people to

A study designed to test the hypothesis that the best predictor of expertise is the amount of time devoted to deliberate practice found that this was the case. Experts tend to spend more time practicing in a systematic way.

buy their products. Cialdini's distinctive strategy provided the basis for his developing a comprehensive model of influence.

Studies also show that expert problem solvers (and better students) tend to devote more of their mental resources to *global* (big-picture) strategy planning than do novice problem solvers. Novices (and poorer students) tend to allocate more time to *local* (detail-oriented) strategy planning than do experts (Larkin, McDermott, Simon, & Simon, 1980; R. J. Sternberg, 1981a). For example, better students usually spend more time in the initial phase of problem solving—deciding how to solve the problem—and less time actually solving it than do poorer students (Bloom & Broder, 1950). By spending more time in advance deciding what to do, good students are less likely to fall prey to false starts, winding paths, and all kinds of errors. By allocating more of their mental resources to planning on a large scale, they are able to save time and energy and to avoid frustration. Simi-

larly, in doing scientific research, it makes good sense to anticipate potential problems before you start. By thinking carefully at the outset, you are likely to avoid problems later on that could have been anticipated in advance.

Monitoring and Evaluating Problem Solving

You need to monitor your problem solving while you are in the process of solving a problem. In other words, you have to be asking yourself whether you are moving toward a solution of the problem you set out to study. It is for this reason that scientists often conduct *pilot studies,* or small-scale studies to determine whether the effects the scientists expect to see actually can be produced. The scientists do not proceed to their full-scale investigation until they have some confidence that they are likely to get the results they expect. For example, in studies of the effects of rewards on behavior, psychologists need first to know what their participants consider to be rewarding. The psychologists thus might wish to do pilot studies with different kinds of potential rewards in order to find just which ones their participants actually believe to be rewarding.

Then, when you are done with your problem solving, you need to evaluate your solution to the problem (Bryson, Bereiter, Scardamalia, & Joram, 1991; Halpern, 1995; Perkins, 1995a; Stanovich, 1994, 1996). Some of the evaluation may occur right away; the rest may occur a bit later, or even much later. As suggested, very few scientific questions—particularly questions about how people behave—are ever resolved once and for all. Rather, we reach an answer that seems right at a given time, or that is the best or most nearly complete answer we are able to find at that time. Later we may realize that the answer was incomplete or even incorrect. To a large extent, success in scientific problem solving depends on the researcher's ability to profit from feedback, both self-generated and from others.

The Goals of Scientific Research

In Search of . . .

What do scientists seek to accomplish in their work?

Thus far, we have addressed the *what* and the *how* of scientific research. We still must discuss the *why*. Why do scientists do what they do? What are their goals? In addition to the broad goal of advancing

TABLE 2–2

Four Primary Goals of Psychological Research
Psychologists seek to achieve one or more of the following goals by conducting research.

GOAL	QUESTIONS PSYCHOLOGISTS ASK WHEN TRYING TO REACH THIS GOAL
Description	What happens? When and where does it happen? How does it happen?
Explanation	Why does it happen?
Prediction	What will happen next?
Control	How can we influence this behavior or intervene in this situation?

scientific thought, we generally distinguish among four main goals for science: description, explanation, prediction, and control. (See Table 2-2 for a summary of these goals.)

Description

In psychology, **description** refers simply to characterizing what and how people think, feel, or act in response to various kinds of situations. Before we can begin to explain or to predict people's behavior, we need to describe their behavior. At first, description might seem trivial. Why would scientists need to describe behavior that people easily could see for themselves? Indeed, descriptive research often starts with people watching, and then wondering. Many of the most interesting ideas in psychology, such as those of Freud, emanated from observing and describing behavior.

Consider, for example, the following observations. Various studies have shown certain sex differences, on average, in abilities (A. R. Halpern, 1986, 1989; D. F. Halpern, 1997). One such difference is that women show better spatial-location memory than do men (Silverman & Eals, 1992). For example, they may find it easier to remember where they saw something than do men. Men, however, show better spatial-rotation ability than do women (Silverman & Eals, 1992). For example, they can more quickly and accurately state whether a given object is a rotated version of another object or is instead a mirror image of the first object. Thus, research can tell us at a descriptive level that both men and women show certain superiorities with respect to each other in aspects of

spatial ability. But why? To explain this phenomenon, we need to probe further.

Explanation

Explanation addresses why people think, feel, or act as they do. Were psychology only descriptive, people would almost certainly become disillusioned with it. Ideally, theories in psychology should be explanatory as well as descriptive. Theories need to answer the *why*, as well as the *what* and the *how* of psychological functioning (which are more dealt with by descriptive studies).

Let us return to the description of aspects of spatial ability. Why might men be superior in one aspect, women in another? One of the explanations put forward is an evolutionary one. Over the course of many generations, women may have developed superior spatial-location memory in order to aid them in gathering food, which in times past (and in some places, present) was their primary role in helping bring food to the table. Men may have developed superior spatial-rotation ability to aid them in hunting, where they would need to be able to estimate trajectories of moving objects. Although we cannot be certain these explanations are correct, they give a plausible account of how sex differences might have emerged (Buss, 1995; Silverman & Eals, 1992). They do not provide the only possible account, but they do make sense in terms of likely adaptations to the environment over many generations of human evolution. Bear in mind, however, that few explanations are definitive. As psychologists learn more and gather more data, these explanations will be elaborated, modified, and perhaps replaced altogether by explanations that seem better to fit the new information.

One of the most important explanatory studies in psychology was conducted by Rescorla and A. R. Wagner (1972; see chapter 6). Their data suggested that learning in animals (and by implication in humans) could be explained by higher order thinking processes that many scientists previously had doubted even existed in these laboratory animals.

Prediction

Psychologists often try to predict the outcomes of their research. **Prediction**—a declaration about the future based on observation, experience, or reasoning—can be very important in practice as well as in theory. For example, given the sex differences described earlier, one might predict that if men and women were asked to play certain video games their performances might differ. In one video game, people need to shoot at imaginary attacking invaders from another planet who are moving rapidly on a screen. In another game, people need to remember in what location in an imaginary jungle they have seen various kinds of creatures. We might predict that, on average, men would do better on the first task, women on the second. We therefore would give both men and women both game-based tasks and see whether, in fact, our prediction is supported by the data. It is important to remember, however, that these are only averages and thus do not apply to every individual case. Moreover, there is evidence that average sex differences in abilities may be decreasing over time (R. Feingold, 1988; A. R. Halpern, 1989).

Predictive information can be a double-edged sword. It can help in predicting behavior, but if overvalued, it can lead to erroneous judgments. Sometimes, it even can *affect* the outcomes it was originally supposed only to *predict*. Researchers tested this notion in one context by telling teachers that particular students in their classes were likely to be "late bloomers"—students whose performance was likely to start picking up and improving (Rosenthal & Jacobson, 1968). Later on, the students who had been thus identified did indeed improve scholastically. However, the teachers had been deceived. In reality, the "late bloomers" had been selected at random. They were initially no different in measured abilities from any of the other students. Although the teachers could recall no differential treatment of the "late bloomers," the teachers' expectations of improvement clearly had an effect (sometimes called a Pygmalion effect, based on a literary allusion) on their students. The results suggest that a prediction can become a *self-fulfilling*

prophecy. The very fact of predicting something about someone can make that thing come true. Although the Rosenthal–Jacobson study had some flaws (Elashoff & Snow, 1971; R. E. Snow, 1995), the phenomenon of the self-fulfilling prophecy seems fairly common. We need to be careful about making predictions, especially pessimistic ones, about people's behavior, because those predictions may contribute to bringing about that very behavior. Prediction, therefore, can end up not only anticipating but also exerting some control over future behavior.

Control

Control is the fourth goal of science. Scientists may seek to control behavior or to help people to control their own behavior. The idea of control can also have negative connotations, as one gathers from books such as George Orwell's *1984*, in which a government seeks to control all of people's thoughts and actions. In seeking control of behavior, psychologists always need to think in terms of helping people gain control over their own destinies rather than in terms of taking that control away from them. Many of us would like to be able to stop some of our bad habits or improve some aspect of our minds or behavior. Control of behavior is what enables us to change it. For example, people often seek **psychotherapy** (a remedial intervention that uses the principles of psychology in order to treat mental or emotional disorder) in order to get control of their lives. (The term *control* is also used in another sense—in experimental designs—as discussed later.)

People can control not only their behavior, but also their minds. Such control is a major goal of interventions to improve intellectual abilities, including spatial abilities, such as those discussed previously. Intellectual abilities are not fixed but rather are flexible and modifiable. For example, a number of educational programs are designed to help students develop their thinking skills (Bransford & Stein, 1993; Detterman & Sternberg, 1993; Feuerstein, 1980; R. J. Sternberg & Grigorenko, in press; W. Williams et al., 1996). When these programs are successful, they help students to take better control of their intellectual functioning and to develop and use their abilities more effectively.

The goals of science, then, as they apply to psychological theory, research, and practice help us describe, explain, predict, and control thoughts and actions. These goals are not mutually exclusive, and usually, psychologists seek some combination of them in their work. The goals often interact, so that achieving one helps us to achieve another. In the time that psychology has been an academic discipline, it has made great strides toward achieving these ends. It has done so through research using a variety of methods.

Research Methods in Psychology

In *Search of . . .*

How do scientists conduct research?

So far, this chapter has alluded to various reasons and ways that psychologists study problems without systematically considering the range of the methods they employ to do this. This section shows some of the specific methods psychologists can bring to bear on the problems that interest them: (a) naturalistic observation; (b) case studies; (c) tests, questionnaires, and surveys; and (d) experiments. These research methods are summarized in Table 2-3. In every form of research, empirical *data* are gathered by one means or another and analyzed. Because human behavior is sometimes best studied by naturalistic observation, **experimental methods,** those research designs investigating cause-effect relationships by controlling or carefully manipulating particular variables to note their effects on other variables, are not always practical ways of studying behavior because people tend to behave differently in the artificial settings in which experiments often take place. **Correlational methods,** those that assess the degree of relationship between two or more variables or attributes, are therefore often used instead. Although correlational methods are useful for identifying relationships between variables, they generally

---

TABLE 2–3

Research Methods
To achieve their goals, psychologists may use various methods of investigation.

METHOD	DESCRIPTION OF METHOD	FORM OF DATA OBTAINED	ADVANTAGES OF METHOD	DISADVANTAGES OF METHOD
Experiments	Study cause-and-effect relationships through the manipulation of variables	Quantitative ("hard data", statistical, verifiable by replication)	1. Precise control of independent variables 2. Usually, large numbers of participants allow results to be generalized	1. Usually, less intensive study of individuals 2. Ability to generalize to real-world behavior is sometimes limited
Tests, questionnaires, and surveys	Obtain samples of behavior, beliefs, or abilities at a particular time and place	Quantitative or qualitative ("soft data"; descriptive, practical)	1. Ease of administration 2. Ease of scoring and statistical analysis	1. May not be able to generalize results 2. Discrepancies between real-life behavior and test behavior
Case studies	Intensive studies of single individuals, which draw general conclusions about behavior	Qualitative	Highly detailed information, including the historical context	1. Small sample size compromises ability to generalize information 2. Reliability can be limited
Naturalistic observations	Observations of real-life situations	Qualitative	1. Wide applicability of results 2. Understanding of behavior in natural contexts	1. Loss of experimental control 2. Presence of observer may influence observed behavior

are not useful for establishing causal direction. For example, correlational methods could be used to determine a relationship between parental frustration and child abuse, but they could not well establish whether frustration leads to abuse, abuse leads to frustration, or both depend on some third higher-order variable. Child abuse is an example of a phenomenon that one could not study experimentally—at least not ethically. To do so, one would have to induce at least one (experimental) group of individuals to abuse children, a procedure that would be ethically unacceptable.

Naturalistic Observation

Naturalistic observation, also known as *field study,* involves going outside the laboratory or the clinical setting and into the community ("the field") to *observe* (listen to, watch, take note of) and record the behavior of people engaged in the normal activities of their daily lives. Naturalistic observation is particularly useful when the phenomenon being studied is strongly affected by the natural context in which it occurs. It includes the participant observation done by Cialdini (1984), whose work on persuasion was described earlier in this chapter. An impressive naturalistic observation in the behavioral sciences is of identity formation in inner-city youth (Heath & McLaughlin, 1993). Shirley Heath and Millbrae McLaughlin studied how organizations in which youngsters participate after school sometimes provide a sense of identity and purpose that the children are not able to find in the school setting. Their work has provided rich and fine-grained insights about identity formation that would be hard to obtain from laboratory experiments.

Naturalistic observation has several potential advantages, such as the usually wide applicability of the results and the understanding of behavior as it occurs

Jane Goodall uses naturalistic observations to study the behavior of chimpanzees.

in natural contexts. Potential disadvantages of this method, however, are the uncontrolled complexity of what is observed (and hence the difficulty of isolating causes of behavior) and the possibility that the presence of an observer may influence the behavior being observed.

Sometimes it may not be possible directly to observe those you would like to observe, for example, if they are deceased. In this event, another method may be called for, such as the case study.

Case Studies

In a **case study,** a psychologist conducts an intensive investigation of a single individual or set of individuals in order to draw general conclusions about behavior applying to the individual or individuals studied and perhaps to other individuals as well. Case studies, used in a variety of psychological pursuits, are particularly useful when the phenomenon being studied is relatively rare, such as in case studies of highly creative people or of people with unusual psychological disorders. For example, in **clinical** work, in which psychologists and psychiatrists deal directly with clients for purposes of therapeutic guidance, case studies are essential for understanding problems that people face both individually and collectively.

One of the better-known writings in the field of marriage and family therapy (see chapter 17, on psychotherapy) is Robert Weiss's (1975) analysis of marital separation. Called a *monograph* because it was written about one topic in depth, the report drew almost exclusively on case-study observations. Weiss's style was to find commonalities in case studies that suggested reasons marriages fail. For example, a recurrent theme in some of the accounts of failed marriages was that the marriage was wrong from the start. Often case studies are used in conjunction with other kinds of evidence in order to establish a point. For example, David Lykken (1998) drew upon a variety of kinds of evidence in order to make the point that the results of polygraph (lie-detector) tests are highly questionable and can have disastrous results for individuals and for society. Lykken presented a number of case studies, such as that of Mack Coker, who worked for a company that was experiencing thefts. First Coker lost his job as a result of a failed polygraph test even though no other evidence was offered to support the idea he was guilty of the thefts. He then became the object of vicious rumors in the community in which he lived. Lykken pointed out that Coker eventually got his job back, but that many others are not so lucky.

A potential advantage of case-study methodology is that it provides highly detailed information, including information about the historical contexts

Case studies, such as those developed in psychotherapy, are intensive investigations of a single individual or set of individuals. Though they provide highly detailed information, their findings are not generalizable.

in which behavior occurs. It provides a rich, three-dimensional portrait of the person and the circumstances for their behavior. A potential disadvantage of the method is that the sample size typically is small, which makes it hard to generalize the results. Moreover, the reliability of the information can be limited, given that the information is obtained in very particular settings.

Other things, such as abilities and attitudes, also evolve over many years, and these things are often studied through tests, questionnaires, and surveys.

Tests, Questionnaires, and Surveys

Early in the twentieth century, Alfred Binet, a French psychologist, was commissioned to develop a test to distinguish children who were genuinely mentally deficient from those who were capable of scholastic achievement but who had behavior problems that interfered with that achievement. A **test** is a procedure used to measure an attribute of one or more individuals at a particular time and in a particular place. Testers almost invariably key the responses to tests as being either right or wrong, or at least as being better (more accurate, more appropriate, more creative, and so on) or worse. Tests are used in many kinds of psychological studies. Test scores vary not only across people but also across time for a given person. Test results may vary because of an actual change in what is supposed to be measured or because of various factors that may affect performance

at the time of testing, such as ill health or ambient noise. Thus, tests can indicate only an approximation of a person's true abilities, personality, or whatever else the tests attempt to measure.

"That's the worst set of opinions I've heard in my entire life."

Psychologists also use in their research two other methods. The **survey** is a method of research in which the researcher seeks people's responses to questions regarding their beliefs and opinions. The **questionnaire** is the set of questions used in a survey or other questioning procedure. For example, questionnaires are frequently used to inquire into people's health practices, such as their eating, drinking, or smoking habits. Surveys and questionnaires are particularly useful when one wishes to obtain a large amount of information in a relatively short amount of time.

Unlike tests, surveys and questionnaires virtually never have right or wrong answers. They are typically measures of beliefs and opinions rather than of abilities or knowledge. For example, you might use a questionnaire or a survey to determine college students' attitudes toward campus regulations regarding alcohol, to gather their opinions regarding the usefulness of survey data, or to determine whether the students object to responding to questionnaires. Questionnaire and survey data are notorious for lending themselves to multiple interpretations. During political campaigns, you probably have heard the identical survey data be interpreted in entirely different ways by opposing candidates. Nonetheless, questionnaires and surveys are handy research tools for providing a means of quantifying beliefs and opinions.

A potential advantage of tests, questionnaires, and surveys is that they tend to be easily administered. They also typically are easy to score and to analyze. A potential disadvantage, however, is that unless the sample is fairly large and representative, it may be difficult to generalize the results to people who were not directly tested or surveyed. Sometimes, moreover, there are discrepancies between what people say or do in tests, questionnaires, and surveys, and how they behave in daily life.

Experiments

An **experiment,** in the strictest scientific sense, is an investigation that studies cause-effect relationships through the control and manipulation of **variables,** which are attributes or characteristics of a situation, person, or a phenomenon, which may differ or fluctuate across situations, across persons, or across phenomena. Experiments are particularly useful when it is possible to manipulate and thus gain control of the variables whose effects one wishes to study. Experimenters carefully manipulate one or more particular variables to note their outcome effects on other variables. An experiment provides a way to test some ideas about human behavior (or anything else) by constructing a set of operations to test these ideas. The construction of this set of operations is called *operationalization.*

Suppose you conduct an experiment in which students are given challenging mathematics problems

Critical thinking helps keep us alert to the informal fallacies to which we are all prone. For example, two of these candidates seem to be blaming each other, a classic ad hominem argument in which one tries to undermine the other's position simply by saying that he or she is wrong, rather than offering evidence.

that will require serious effort to solve. You want to see the effect of encouragement on the students' performance. So you tell some of the students that they can expect to do very well, whereas you give other students no encouragement at all. What are the elements of this experiment?

There are basically two kinds of variables in any given experiment. First, there are **independent variables,** which are aspects of an investigation that are individually *manipulated*, or carefully regulated, by the experimenter, while other aspects of the investigation are held constant (i.e., not subject to variation). Second, there are **dependent variables,** which are (usually quantified) outcome responses, the values of which depend on how one or more independent variables influence or affect the participants in the experiment. When you tell some student research participants that they will do very well on a task, but you do not tell the other student participants anything about how well they will do, the independent variable is the amount of information that the students are given about their expected task performance. That is, either they are or are not given information. The dependent variable is how well both groups of students actually perform the task.

Experiments often involve two different types of *conditions*, or aspects of an experimental design. Different conditions typically represent different manipulations of the independent variable. In the first type of condition, the **experimental condition,** participants are exposed to an experimental treatment, which is a carefully prescribed set of circumstances. For example, in this experiment, the participants were told that they would do very well on the task they were about to be given. The experimental condition is also described as the *treatment condition*. In the second type of condition, the **control condition,** the participants do not receive the experimental treatment but may receive an alternative treatment. In this experiment, the participants were not told anything about how they would do on the task they were about to be given. The goal of the experiment was to see whether the participants who were told that they would succeed actually performed better on the task than did those who were told nothing.

In fact, this particular manipulation can make a large difference in test scores. Claude Steele and Joshua Aronson (1995) found that African American children performed better on ability tests when they were told that on the particular test they were going to take there was no difference between African American and Caucasian racial groups. Similarly, Wendy Walsh (1997) found that when women were told that there would be no gender differences on a difficult mathematical problem-solving test, the women outperformed the men. But when the women were told that

there typically were gender differences on the test, the men outperformed the women.

Usually, two kinds of groups of participants are used: one for the experimental condition and the other for the control condition. When two or more groups of participants are used, the participants that receive the experimental treatment are the *experimental group*, and the participants who are used as a comparison group are the *control group*. The control group may receive some alternative (and usually irrelevant) treatment or no treatment at all. The results for the control group are included as a standard of comparison against which to judge the results of the experimental group(s) and also to control for irrelevant, confounding variables. Sometimes, there is more than one control group to control for multiple, confounding variables. Without a control group, it is usually hard to draw any conclusions at all. For example, if you told all of the participants that they would do well on a task they were about to be given, you would have no way of isolating and hence of knowing the effect of telling them about their expected performance. To evaluate the effects of telling participants how well they would do on a task, you need a control group of participants who are not told about their expected performance.

Ideally, the inclusion of the control group or groups would leave just one interpretation of the results. It can be difficult to reach this ideal in practice, however. Without any control groups at all, causal inference would be impossible.

Controlled experiments have several potential advantages as a research method. For one thing, they allow precise control of independent variables. For another, if they involve large numbers of participants, they may yield generalizable results. The method also has some potential disadvantages. First, individuals usually are not studied intensively, as they might be in case studies. Second, the ability to generalize to real-world behavior is limited if what people do in the lab or other experimental setting does not generalize to what the people do in their everyday lives.

Causal Inference in Psychological Research

In **Search of . . .** *How do scientists draw causal inferences from their research?*

The preceding section described four methods of research that psychologists can use. As mentioned, both the problem studied and the personal stylistic preferences of the investigator influence the researcher's choice of method. One remaining issue also influences the choice of research method. A major goal of psychological research is to draw **causal inferences** (conjectures about cause-and-effect relationships regarding behavior that seek to explain what causes a person to behave in a certain way). For example, we might ask if a particular independent variable (e.g., whether people are told that they will do well on a task) is responsible for particular variation in a given dependent variable (e.g., the number of items answered correctly on a mathematical problem-solving task). What kinds of circumstances enable investigators to draw conclusions about causality? In other words, what do we need in a research study in order to be able to conclude that "so-and-so" causes "such-and-such"?

As you may suspect, when it comes to human behavior, it is not always possible to detect a clear causal relationship between independent and dependent variables, for a variety of reasons. For one thing, our ability to draw causal inferences depends not only on the question we ask in our research, but also on how the research is designed. **Design** refers to how a given set of variables are chosen and interrelated, as well as to how participants are assigned to conditions.

Earlier, we defined *experiment* using the strictest definition. However, we can broaden the use of the term *experiment* to apply to investigations not as highly controlled by the experimenter. More loosely speaking, an experiment studies the effect of some variables on other variables. Now we explore three ways in which to design experimental research, including the strict, narrow definition used here and two other types of experimental design. We will consider three of the major kinds of designs in psychological research—controlled experimental, quasi-experimental, and correlational—and the kinds and degrees of causal inference that can be drawn from each. (See Table 2-4 for a summary of the similarities and differences among these designs.)

Controlled Experimental Designs

In a true **controlled experimental design,** the experimenter carefully manipulates or controls one or more independent variables in order to see the effect on the dependent variable or variables. To be sure the treatment (and not some other variables or even random variation) is producing the effect, the experimenter includes one or more control groups that do not receive the experimental treatment.

In a true controlled experimental design, participants must be randomly assigned to the experimental and the control groups. This *random assignment* is important because it ensures that later differences between the results for each group are not due to prior differences in the participants themselves. For example, if rats are randomly assigned to either an enriched environment or an impoverished one, the rats assigned to the enriched environment will develop better cognitive skills than the rats assigned to the impoverished environments (Tryon, 1940).

Evaluating and Interpreting Research Data

Representative Samples

A problem in all research, regardless of design, is that we never can be certain that our inferences are correct because we can never be absolutely sure that a difference between group results is not caused by chance—random fluctuations in the data—unless we test the entire population of people in whom we are interested. Unfortunately, it is rarely practical or even possible to test the whole population in which we are interested. So we may settle for testing what we believe to be a **representative sample** (a subset of the population, carefully chosen to represent the proportionate diversity of the population as a whole) of people. We may obtain representation by a wholly *random sample*, hoping that people chosen at random from the population will adequately represent the population. We actually have no guarantee that our participants do indeed accurately represent the entire population we would ideally like to test.

As you might imagine, some portions of the total population are more readily accessible to researchers,

Advertisers hope we will make the causal inference that their product has caused an athlete-spokesperson's success. But correlation is not causation.

TABLE 2–4

Experimental Designs   *Psychologists draw different conclusions from their research, depending on the type of research design they use for studying a given phenomenon.*

Type of Design	Definition	Advantages	Disadvantages
Controlled experimental	Experimenter manipulates one or more independent variables and observes the effects on the dependent variable or variables; participants are randomly assigned to control or treatment conditions.	Permits causal inference regarding the treatment variable or variables.	Might not apply to settings outside the laboratory; a sample may not truly represent the entire population of interest. May involve ethical concerns.
Quasi-experimental	Similar to experimental design, but participants are not randomly assigned; in some cases, there is no control group.	May be more convenient in some situations; may be permissible where ethical considerations prohibit random assignment of participants; may be conducted in a naturalistic setting, yielding more richly textured data. In the case of correlational data, the entire population (e.g., all voters) may sometimes be available for study.	Does not permit causal inferences regarding the treatment variable or variables. Also, sample data may not apply to the entire population.
Correlational	Researchers just observe the degree of association between two or more attributes that occur naturally. Researchers do not manipulate variables or randomly assign participants to groups.		

so they may be overrepresented in research. In addition, there may be other reasons why some people are under- or overrepresented in research samples. For example, women and persons of color are often understudied, whereas men, Caucasians, and college students are often overrepresented in research.

It is quite common for cross-cultural researchers to use *samples of convenience* (also called "bunch" or "grab" samples) because of the immediate availability of such samples (Lonner & Berry, 1986). This strategy is not restricted to research across cultures. Countless millions of students in U.S. colleges and universities have been included in such samples over the years. It is very common, for example, for researchers to solicit the participation of several hundred students from an introductory psychology class. Are such groups repre-

sentative of any population of interest? If so, what population do they represent?

Statistical Analysis of the Results

When we test participants, we are really interested in the results, not only for those participants in particular but also for the population as a whole from which the participants were drawn (e.g., all humans, all mothers, or all college students). Because the whole population is not tested, we use **sample statistics** (numbers that characterize the sample we have tested with regard to the attributes under investigation) as estimates of *population parameters* (numbers that would characterize everyone we conceivably might test who fit our desired description). Actual popula-

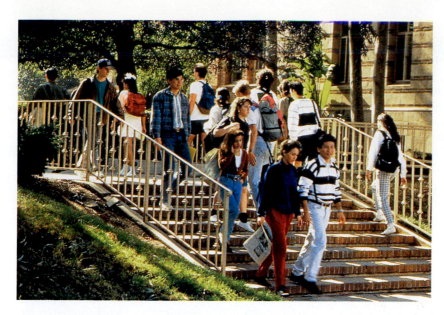

Is this a random sample? A good deal of psychological research has been done on college students, a sample of convenience, causing them to be overrepresented in research.

tion parameters are unknowable unless we have the whole population to test, and we almost never do. It is for this reason that we need to use samples of the population in order to estimate the characteristics of the population.

Because sample statistics are only estimates of the whole-population parameters, they vary to some degree from one sample to another. In general, researchers seek to include as large a proportion of the population as possible in the research sample. Although constraints of time and other resources limit the sizes of the samples we can actually test, proportionately larger samples help to average out random sources of error.

Statistical analysis helps researchers to minimize errors in two ways. First they help ensure accurate and consistent *description* of a sample from a population (for example, the average annual salaries reported by 30-year-olds in the sample). Second, they provide a consistent basis for the *inference* of characteristics of an entire population, based on the characteristics of only a sample. For example, if the average annual salaries of college graduates in the sample were far greater than the annual salaries of those who did not graduate, we could infer that, for the whole population, having graduated from college somehow enhanced the potential to earn larger annual salaries. Clearly, it is easier to be certain of the accuracy of the descriptions than it is to be certain of the accuracy of the inferences.

To increase the accuracy of our inferences, we use specially devised *inferential statistics*, which allow us to draw reasoned conclusions based on the implications of the descriptive data. Inferential statistics can help us decide whether the difference between a treatment group and a control group (or other group) is likely to be true of the population as a whole, or whether the difference is likely to be caused by chance fluctuations in the data. In research, we use the concept of **statistical significance**—a probability level agreed on by convention that helps us decide how likely it is that a result would be obtained were only chance factors in operation. To determine whether a result is statistically significant, we measure the probability that an obtained result would be obtained were only chance at work. If that probability reaches a particular preset point (usually 5% down to 1%), we consider the result statistically significant.

For example, we could determine whether clients in psychotherapy for a specified period of time improved more during this period than did individuals with comparable problems who did not receive psychotherapy. If our analysis of our experiment revealed that there was only a 5% chance that the results we found would have been obtained had only chance been operative, then we could say that our results were statistically significant at the "0.05" level. The 0.05 level of statistical significance corresponds to a 5% chance that results as unusual as those we obtained would have been obtained were only chance factors at work. If our results showed a 0.01 level of significance, there would be only a 1% chance that our findings would have been obtained were only chance factors at work. If clients in psychotherapy showed greater improvement than those without therapy, at a rate that was statistically significant at the 0.01 level, it means there was only a 1% chance that such unusual results would be obtained were only chance factors affecting the outcomes of the psychotherapy. The smaller the probability level, the greater is the level of statistical significance for the result. In fact, recent research overwhelmingly suggests that clients view themselves as having improved through psychotherapy (Seligman, 1995).

There are two important things to notice. First, although we can set our probability point as low as we want, we can never be absolutely certain that a difference is not due to the operation just of chance factors. We can be 99% confident (with a 0.01 level of significance), but never 100% confident (with a 0.00 level). Second, we can never prove beyond doubt the **null hypothesis,** the hypothesis of *no* difference between (or relation between) performance of groups. That is, we cannot prove that a particular variable has no effect or that there is no difference between two different groups of participants or among two or more different conditions. This limit holds whether we use the kind of controlled experimental design we have discussed here or the kind of quasi-experimental design to which we now turn.

For example, suppose a psychologist compares two kinds of psychotherapy and finds that the difference in average effects is not significant. The psychologist cannot therefore conclude with certainty that the two forms of psychotherapy are equally effective. It always is possible that, with a larger sample or with more careful measurements, a difference could emerge.

Quasi-Experimental Designs

Suppose that we wish to study the effect on students' learning of two methods for teaching introductory psychology. Ideally, we would establish two completely comparable colleges, with virtually identical instructors, to which we might randomly assign two groups of students. We then would offer the two groups of students different kinds of psychology courses, one at each college and each taught by a different method. This controlled experiment could never actually be done, however. Instead, we are likely to use a more convenient design. Students who already are enrolled in one college might serve as experimental participants (they receive the independent variable, the new curriculum), while students enrolled in a similar college might serve as control participants (and do not receive the new curriculum). In this case, participants are not randomly assigned to groups. Therefore, the design is not a true controlled experimental design. Instead, it is considered a **quasi-experimental design.** It has many of the features of a controlled experimental design, but it does not ensure the random assignment of participants to the treatment and the control groups. The study still will use the experimental method. Variables are manipulated, and cause–effect relations still are being sought. Nonetheless, its design is less precise and less experimenter-controlled than is a true experimental design. For this reason, we cannot draw a definite causal conclusion from a quasi-experimental design.

In the curriculum study, for example, we cannot draw causal conclusions. The reason is that it is possible that instead of the difference in results between the two college groups being caused by the experimental curriculum, some of the difference is caused by preexisting differences in the kinds of students who attend the two colleges or in other aspects of the two college environments. There are statistical methods for trying to control for differences between groups after the fact. However, we can never be certain that we are controlling for all relevant differences, and so nonrandom assignment of participants to groups precludes firm causal inferences.

Another form of quasi-experimental design involves a group that receives an experimental treatment, but in the absence of a control group. For example, a researcher might have students take a preliminary test (*pretest*) on their knowledge of introductory psychology and then have an instructor teach a curriculum covering introductory psychology. Finally, the students would take a concluding test (*posttest*) similar in content to the pretest, the purpose of which would be to measure student achievement and curriculum effectiveness.

This quasi-experimental design is surprisingly common in research on various kinds of curricula. The prevalence of this kind of design is surprising because no one can conclude that the curriculum caused any of the gains that might be observed. Why not? For one thing, perhaps students matured from pretest to posttest, independently of the curriculum, and thus scored higher on the posttest because of their maturation. They also might have learned something about psychology outside of class, between pretest and posttest, which helped them improve. Perhaps even the very experience of taking the pretest enabled them to test better the second time around. Such an effect could occur because the test information had become familiar, and the students therefore knew what to expect in the test situation. A parallel control group that received the pretest and the posttest without the curriculum (or better, with an alternative curriculum on some other topic) would have countered these alternative explanations. Without the use of a control group, however, no clear conclusions can be drawn.

Although quasi-experimental designs are less scientifically desirable than are controlled experimental designs, they are often unavoidable. In naturalistic observational settings that cannot be controlled by experimenters, we sometimes have to take what we are given or else take nothing at all. We gain the advantage of the naturalistic setting, but lose control.

Sometimes, the limitations on research are ethical constraints. For example, if we wish to study the effects of long-term alcohol addiction on psychological health, we are ethically bound to accept in the alcoholic group those who already have chosen to drink excessively and in the control group those who already have chosen not to do so. We cannot randomly assign people to one group or the other and then insist that those assigned to the drinking group become chronic alcoholics! Thus, quasi-experimental designs are used when controlled experimental designs simply are not feasible or ethically appropriate. But sometimes, even quasi-experimental designs are not feasible, in which case we may use correlational designs.

Correlational Designs

In a pure **correlational design,** researchers merely observe the degree of association between two (or more) *attributes* (characteristics of the participants, of the setting, or of the situation) that already occur naturally in the group or groups under study. In correlational designs, researchers do not directly manipulate the variables themselves, and they do not randomly assign participants to groups. Instead, researchers usually observe participants in naturally preexisting groups, such as particular students in two or more classrooms, or particular employees in two or more work settings. As with quasi-experimental designs, a correlational study is less scientifically desirable than a strict controlled experimental investigation, but frequently, it is unavoidable. As is the case with quasi-experimental designs, correlational designs generally do not permit us to infer causation.

When two attributes show some degree of statistical relationship to one another, they are *correlated.* **Correlation** is a degree of statistical relationship between two attributes, which usually is expressed as a number on a scale that ranges from −1 to 0 to 1. A correlation of −1 indicates a perfect **negative (inverse) correlation,** in which increases in the value of one attribute are associated with decreases in the value of another attribute, for example, the number of equal slices of a pizza eaten in relation to the number of slices remaining. A correlation equal to 0 indicates no relationship at all. For example, we would expect a 0 correlation between the frequency of eating pizza for dinner and undergraduate grade-point average. A correlation of 1 indicates a perfect **positive correlation,** in which increases (or decreases) in the value of one attribute are associated with increases (or decreases) in the value of another attribute. An example of a correlation of 1 would be the number of equal pepperoni slices consumed in relation to the amount of pepperoni pizza you eat. Numbers between 0 and 1 indicate some intermediate degree of positive correlation (e.g.,

0.7, 0.23, 0.01); numbers between 0 and −1 indicate some intermediate degree of negative correlation (e.g., −0.03, −0.2, −0.75). The closer a correlation is to being perfect (either 1 or −1), the stronger the relationship between the two items. A correlation close to 0 indicates a weak relationship. A correlation of −0.75, for example, indicates a stronger relationship between two things than does a correlation of 0.25. Perfect correlations of 1 and −1 are extremely rare. Usually, if two things are correlated, it is in some intermediate degree, such as the correlation between number of years of education and future income. Figure 2-1 shows how correlations appear in graphic form.

It is important to note that, for each kind of correlation (as shown in the examples), the direction of causality, if any causality exists at all, is not known. For example, we might give people a test of depression and a test of self-esteem in order to determine whether there is a connection between depression and self-esteem. Both self-esteem and depression are preexisting variables over which experimenters have no control. Suppose that we find a *correlation* between self-esteem and depression. We might expect it to be negative (inverse) in some degree, and it is. Those who have high self-esteem tend to be less depressed, and those with low self-esteem are more depressed. This correlation might mean that low self-esteem causes depression. Or it might mean that depression causes low self-esteem. Or it might even mean that both depression and low self-esteem depend on some third overarching variable, which we have not yet identified (e.g., rejection in childhood).

Figure 2−1

GRAPHIC REPRESENTATION OF A CORRELATION. *This graph shows a positive correlation between a pair of variables.*

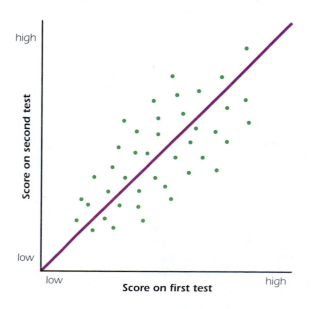

To conclude, then, correlational designs are useful in seeing whether relationships exist but cannot be used to specify exactly how a relationship works or what might cause it. The fact that the number of home electrical appliances is an excellent predictor of the use of contraceptives in Taiwanese households (Li, 1975; Stanovich, 1996) almost certainly does not imply a direct causal link between having electrical appliances and using contraception!

Critical Thinking in Psychological Research

In Search of . . .   *How is critical thinking relevant to psychological research?*

Critical thinking is the conscious direction of mental processes toward representing and processing information, usually in order to find thoughtful solutions to problems, make judgments or decisions, or to reason. When people do not think critically, they often fall into various traps, committing informal logical fallacies. What are some of these fallacies?

1. *Irrelevant conclusion.* We commit the fallacy of irrelevant conclusion when our conclusion is irrelevant to the line of reasoning that led to it. For example, Tom reads an experiment by Dr. Bailey. Tom is very upset that, in Bailey's experiment, rats are made hungry so that they will run mazes in order to seek a food reward. Asked about the experiment, Tom criticizes its results as invalid. Asked why, Tom says that he "would never trust the results of someone who starves animals."

2. *Composition.* We commit the fallacy of composition when we reason that what is true of parts of a whole is necessarily true of the whole itself. In fact, though, elements (such as members of a team) may interact in ways (such as through poor teamwork) that render untrue for the whole what is true for each part. For example, Jeannette reads an experiment by a team of five researchers led by Dr. Hawthorne, for whom Jeannette has very great respect. Later, Jeannette is asked what she thinks of the particular team of researchers that produced the article. Jeannette comments that "it is a great team," figuring that any team with Hawthorne on it must be a great team.

3. *Personalization.* If you see yourself as the cause of some event for which you were not primarily responsible, you have committed the fallacy of personalization. Taking personally a statement that is not directed toward you is also an inappropriate personalization. For example, in an exchange of opinions, Mrs. Dittman criticizes a particular statistic as yielding questionable results. Mrs. Fleming has used that statistic in her research. She decides that Dittman is criticizing her personally and attacks Dittman as ignorant and incompetent.

4. *False Cause.* The fallacy of false cause is committed when someone concludes from the fact that two events happened in rapid succession, or have tended to happen together, that the first event must have caused the second. For example, one day, Jack wears his fraternity T-shirt, and the results of his experiment come out. A couple of weeks later, Jack is again wearing his T-shirt, and his results again come out. Jack decides that it is probably a good idea to wear his fraternity T-shirt on days when he will find out if his results have worked out.

5. *Ad hominem argument.* In this type of argument, one attempts to attack an individual personally in order to undermine the individual's position. For example, Mr. Faver has been asked to comment on the research of Mr. Dunn. Faver has never liked Dunn and sees his chance to get back at what he perceives as injustices Dunn has committed toward him. Faver remarks that Dunn received his degree at a university that is not very well known and, therefore, people really should not trust Dunn's results.

Of course, there are other kinds of informal fallacies that can creep into our thinking. The important thing is to be on guard for these fallacies and to catch ourselves when we make them. In this way, we improve both our thinking and the conclusions we draw from it.

One more important issue remains before we leave this introductory discussion of psychological research methods and practices: the issue of researcher ethics.

Research Ethics

In Search of . . .   *What are the main ethical issues confronting psychologists in their work?*

A number of ethical issues arise in psychological research (as well as in medical and other research). Four of the main ones involve deception, pain, the ethics of research on animals, and confidentiality.

Deception

Sometimes, in order for a research study to work, participants must be kept unaware of the purpose of the study until the study is completed. For example, the deception involved in the Rosenthal-Jacobson "Pygmalion in the classroom" study discussed earlier probably would be considered benign. In some cases, however, psychologists have used extreme forms of deception, as did Stanley Milgram, who led participants to believe that they were delivering painful electric shocks to another person, when in fact they were not (Milgram, 1974). When Milgram carried out his studies, researchers were generally not required to obtain advance approval of their plans in order to conduct a psychological investigation. Another example of an ethical issue arises when researchers pay participants to indulge in a vice, as when researchers pay alcoholics to drink in order to study their drinking behavior (Jacob, Krahn, & Leonard, 1991). Today, virtually all institutions have a research-review process and require approval of investigations prior to their being carried out.

These boards are charged with protecting the rights of experimental participants, and they use two key methods for making sure that participants are protected. First, before participants begin their involvement in a study, they are required to give *informed consent* to participating in the research. In the informed-consent procedure, the individuals are told what kinds of tasks they may be expected to perform and what kinds of situations they may expect to encounter, with specific qualifications for use of deception (see chapter 17 for more on informed consent). Second, after the research is completed, the participants are fully *debriefed* about the research. They are told exactly the nature of the experiment, informed about any deception that may have been involved, and given the reason for the deception. Most research-review boards will allow minor deceptions if the value of the proposed research seems to justify the deception, if the deceptions are fully explained afterward, and if the deceptions are deemed necessary for the purpose of the experiment. Research-review boards sometimes also will allow minor amounts of pain to be administered.

Physical or Psychological Pain

In the past, it was not uncommon for experiments to involve mild electric shocks to participants. These shocks were slightly painful but not harmful. In addition, studies sometimes have had the potential for causing psychological damage. For example, many experiments are somehow stressful for participants. How stressful a study is often depends on the individual as much as on the experiment. What is difficult for one person may be relaxing for another and neutral for yet another. Still, researchers generally try to anticipate and to minimize distress (unless distress itself is the construct under study). Institutional review boards will generally not permit studies that are likely

to cause any long-lasting pain or harm. If participating in a study might cause short-term pain or stress, participants must be fully informed in advance regarding possible consequences, via the informed-consent procedure. Moreover, informed consent requires that participants be told that they are free to leave the experiment at any time without fear of any negative repercussions. Thus, if participants thought that they could tolerate the conditions of an experiment beforehand but then found in the course of it that they could not, they could leave at once.

Issues in Animal Research

The situation is murkier when animals—such as rats, pigeons, rabbits, dogs, or even simple multicelled organisms—are involved instead of people. Animals cannot sign informed-consent forms. Most institutions vigorously attempt to ensure that animals and their health are protected and that the animals have all they require in terms of food, shelter, and freedom from harm or discomfort. Furthermore, in recent years, government has increasingly regulated scientific research and the appropriate use of animals. However, animals sometimes have been exposed to painful or even harmful procedures. In such cases, review boards attempt to weigh the potential benefits of the research to humans against the potential harm to the animals.

Questions regarding how to guard animal rights are not easily answered. On the one hand, no scrupulous researcher actively wishes to cause harm to animals. On the other hand, some of our most important discoveries in both medicine and psychology have come from research in which animals were sacrificed in order to advance our knowledge about and our ability to help humans. Given the choice of testing new drugs that may be beneficial but whose side effects are unknown first on laboratory animals or first on people, society has opted for testing of laboratory animals. Those whose lives have been saved by such testing, or who have had relatives whose lives have been saved, understand at first hand why the testing has been approved by society. Review boards and policymakers attempt to weigh the costs and benefits involved in all research, whether it employs human or animal participants. Still, the controversy over use of animal participants is far from over. Fortunately, there is much less controversy regarding another ethical issue, that of confidentiality.

Confidentiality

The large majority of experiments in psychology are conducted on an anonymous basis—participants' names are not associated with their data. Occasionally, however, complete anonymity is not possible. For example, if an experimenter wants to compare students' scores on some standardized test of ability in relation to their freshman grades in college, the experimenter needs to have some means of identifying individual students. Only in this way can the experimenter associate individuals with their test scores and with their grades in order to correlate the scores and the grades. Even when participants cannot be anonymous, however, experimenters go to great lengths to ensure that the names of the participants are known only to the experimenters. Confidentiality can be a particularly important issue when researchers are studying basic characteristics of individuals, such as health status. One needs to ensure individuals that information about their health, for example, will not later be used against them, such as in employment situations.

The next chapter, concerning the biological bases of behavior, looks at how psychology intersects with one particular but very broad-ranging field, biology. In that chapter, we turn our focus to the body, the source of all biological and psychological activity. We also consider the evolutionary bases of behavioral adaptations to the environment. We further examine how the nervous system works, as well as how the body's functioning affects and interacts with the functioning of the mind—which you may view as a separate entity from the body or as an alternative perspective on a single phenomenon.

THINK ABOUT IT

1. For what kinds of psychological phenomena is *control* a suitable goal? What kinds of psychological phenomena should be off-limits in terms of control? (If you answer "none" to any question, tell why you say so.)
2. If you were in charge of an ethics committee deciding which experiments should be permitted, what questions about the experiments would you want to have answered?
3. Describe the steps you would take if you were systematically to observe members of a new and unfamiliar culture with the goal of learning what their customs are and why they have those customs.
4. If a psychologist from a distant planet were to observe television programs, what conclusions would the psychologist draw about our culture?

5. What is a challenging problem you have solved in your personal life? Compare the steps you took in solving your problem with the steps given in the problem-solving process described in this chapter.
6. Why should all psychological interventions in schools and communities have control groups of some kind?

 You can provide your own answers to these questions online at the **Sternberg, In Search of the Human Mind** *Web site:* *http://www.harcourtcollege.com/psych/ishm*

SUMMARY

1. Although much of what we learn from studying psychology is obvious, many psychological results are surprising.
2. Results that would seem surprising before we know what they are often seem more obvious after we become aware of what they are.

Characteristics of Scientific Findings   32
3. A scientific discipline has several characteristics: (a) ideas are accurately reported and can be *verified*; (b) researchers report findings publicly in scientific journals; and (c) work is cumulative with respect to past research.

4. It is important to recognize some misconceptions about science. Science (a) is not always correct, (b) does not always follow the orderly progression of steps students learned as "the scientific method," (c) is not always completely objective and value-free because it is practiced by human beings, and (d) is not merely a collection of facts.

How Scientists Formulate and Solve Problems   37
5. Scientific *problem solving* is a thought process. Typically, it occurs in several main steps: (a) identifying the problem, (b) defining the problem, (c) constructing a strategy for problem solution, and (d) monitoring and evaluating problem solving.

The evaluation of the solution often leads to the recognition of a new challenge and thus the repetition of the process. The steps of the process are not necessarily executed exactly in this order. Some problems are redefined as the process goes along, or new strategies are tried as old ones fail.

The Goals of Scientific Research 39

6. When addressing a problem, the goals of psychological research are (a) *description*, (b) *explanation*, (c) *prediction*, and (d) *control*.

Research Methods in Psychology 42

7. Psychologists employ various research methods, such as (a) *naturalistic observation;* (b) *case studies;* (c) *tests*, *questionnaires*, and *surveys;* and (d) *experiments*.
8. An experiment is a carefully supervised investigation in which a researcher studies cause-and-effect relations through the manipulation of one or more *independent variables* in order to observe their effects on one or more *dependent variables*. An experiment should include one or more control groups to ensure that differences in results are caused by the experimental treatment and not by irrelevant group differences.

Causal Inference in Psychological Research 46

9. Because we generally cannot conduct studies on whole populations, we use *sample statistics* (numbers that characterize the sample we have tested with regard to the attributes under investigation) as estimates of the *population parameters* (numbers that would characterize everyone we conceivably might test who would fit our desired description). The use of sample statistics is based on the assumption that the researcher has found a *representative sample* or a *random sample* of the population under study.

10. Although we are never able to prove the *null hypothesis* (which states that there is no difference between two groups under study), we can demonstrate that a particular difference has reached a level of *statistical significance*—that is, one unlikely to have occurred were the null hypothesis (of no difference) true.
11. Psychological researchers try to draw *causal inferences*, or conjectures about cause-and-effect relationships. Experimental designs are better suited to the drawing of such inferences than are *quasi-experimental designs*, which lack at least one experimental characteristic (usually random assignment of participants to groups), or *correlational designs*, which show associations between variables but not which variables cause which other ones.

Critical Thinking in Psychological Research 52

12. Critical thinking is of great importance to psychological research. When people do not think critically, they are likely to commit informal fallacies, such as the fallacies of irrelevant conclusion, composition, personalization, false cause, and ad hominem argument.

Research Ethics 52

13. Scientists, including psychologists, must address questions of ethical research procedures. Most questions center on whether participants—human or animal—are treated fairly. Research institutions today have standard policies that require informed consent by and debriefing of human participants. Most institutions have also set up boards of review to study and approve proposed research. Some government agencies also monitor research practices, especially as they pertain to animals.

KEY TERMS

case study 43
causal inferences 47
clinical 43
confirmation bias 34
control 41
control condition 46
controlled experimental design 47
correlation 51
correlational design 51
correlational methods 42
critical thinking 52
dependent variables 46
description 40

design 47
disconfirm 34
experiment 45
experimental condition 46
experimental methods 42
explanation 40
hypothetical construct 38
independent variables 46
naturalistic observation 43
negative (inverse) correlation 51
null hypothesis 50
operational definition 37
positive correlation 51
prediction 41

psychotherapy 41
quasi-experimental design 50
questionnaire 45
reliable 32
replicate 32
representative sample 47
sample statistics 48
statistical significance 49
survey 45
test 44
theory 35
valid 32
variables 45
verifiable 32

■ THINK ABOUT IT SAMPLE RESPONSES

1. For what kinds of psychological phenomena is *control* a suitable goal? What kinds of psychological phenomena should be off-limits in terms of control? (If you answer "none" to any question, tell why you say so.)

Control is a suitable goal for those thoughts, feelings, and patterns of behavior an individual wishes to change. The individual may wish to change these behaviors through expanded self-control, or through control established in collaboration with others, such as a psychotherapist. Control is not a suitable goal to change behavior that an individual does not wish to change, unless the individual is a danger to him- or herself or to others.

2. If you were in charge of an ethics committee deciding which experiments should be permitted, what questions about the experiments would you want to have answered?

You would wish to know the costs and benefits of the experiments. You should be particularly concerned with deceptions, breaches of confidentiality, and risks to potential participants' physical or psychological well-being. You would also wish to be assured that participants will give full informed consent. You also may seek assurance that potential participants will be adequately debriefed about the experiments after the participants have completed their assigned tasks.

3. Describe the steps you would take if you were systematically to observe members of a new and unfamiliar culture with the goal of learning what their customs are and why they have those customs.

You would first wish to have local informants who are familiar with the culture and speak the language of the culture. These informants would need to orient you to the culture and, ideally, teach you the language and as many of the customs as possible. It is important that you understand the culture from its own point of view, and not just your point of view as an outsider. You also would wish to observe the behavior of people in many different roles and in many different stations in life. It would be important that you not "take sides" but rather try to be as objective as possible. You would need to seek multiple points of view on your observations in order to sort out how different people in the culture themselves understand what is going on.

4. If a psychologist from a distant planet were to observe television programs, what conclusions would the psychologist draw about our culture?

The psychologist likely would view our planet as preoccupied by sex and violence. The psychologist also would be likely to view males as being assigned dominant roles. The psychologist further would be likely to conclude that a major goal of television, as important as or more important than entertainment, is to persuade people to buy products or services they do not need or even initially have no desire for. The psychologist might further conclude that the media seek to entertain people by appealing to a "lowest common denominator" in terms of people's intellectual sophistication.

5. What is a challenging problem you have solved in your personal life? Compare the steps you took in solving your problem with the steps given in the problem-solving process described in this chapter.

One problem that many people have confronted or will confront is the choice of a college major. They need first to identify the problem—namely, their need before some deadline to decide in what area of academic endeavor they wish to specialize. Then they need to define the problem. On what bases should they decide on a major? In terms of interest to them? Future income possibilities? Desire to please parents? Social prestige? Meaningfulness of the work? Or what? Next they need to formulate hypotheses about what might be good potential majors for them. Perhaps they will decide on one of the social sciences, such as psychology, anthropology, or sociology. Then they need to construct a strategy to make their decision. Perhaps they will decide to take at least two courses in each area in which they are potentially interested. Perhaps they will talk to faculty who teach in

the department of interest, or students who currently are pursuing a major in which they are interested. Finally, they will want to monitor and evaluate their judgment. If they start majoring in something and then come to regret their decision, they may wish to switch as soon as possible to an alternative major.

6. Why should all psychological interventions in schools and communities have control groups of some kind?

Without a control group, it is difficult to draw meaningful conclusions about interventions. Suppose, for example, that a group of students receives a special educational program designed to improve their school achievement. The group that receives the intervention does, in fact, improve. Can one conclude that the intervention caused the improvement? No, because the improvement may be improvement that resulted simply because of the passage of time between pretest and posttest. Or it may have resulted from instruction students would have received anyway, whether or not they had the intervention. In order to rule out alternative hypotheses, a control group is necessary for the experimental design to yield valid conclusions.

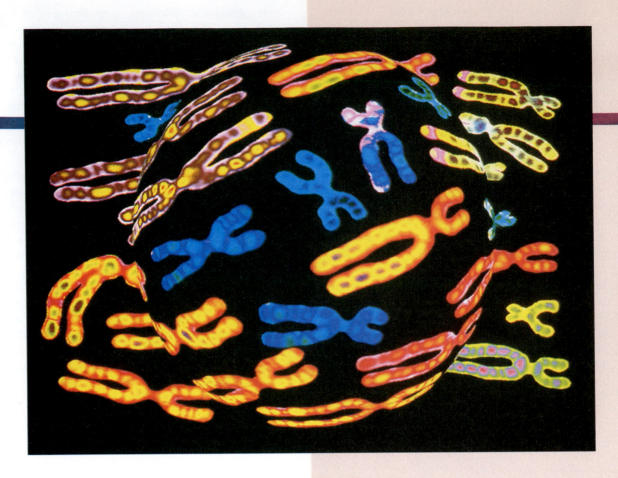

Dr. P. was a musician of distinction. . . . "What seems to be the matter?" I asked him at length.

"Nothing that I know of," he replied with a smile, "but people seem to think there's something wrong with my eyes."

"But you don't recognise any visual problems?"

"No, not directly, but I occasionally make mistakes."

It was while examining his reflexes—a trifle abnormal on the left side—that the first bizarre experience occurred. I had taken off his left shoe and scratched the sole of his foot with a key—a frivolous-seeming but essential test of a reflex—and then, excusing myself to screw my ophthalmoscope together, left him to put on the shoe himself. To my surprise, a minute later, he had not done this.

"Can I help?" I asked.

"Help what? Help whom?"

"Help you put on your shoe."

"Ach," he said, "I had forgotten the shoe," adding sotto voce, "The shoe? The shoe?" He seemed baffled.

"Your shoe," I repeated. "Perhaps you'd put it on?"

He continued to look downwards, though not at the shoe, with an intense but misplaced concentration. Finally his gaze settled on his foot. . . . "My eyes," he explained, and put a hand to his foot, "This is my shoe, no?"

"No, it is not. That is your foot. There is your shoe."

"Ah! I thought that was my foot."

—Oliver Sacks, The Man Who Mistook His Wife for a Hat

3

Biological Bases of Behavior

Chapter Outline

At the core of the way we think, feel, and act is the nervous system. The **nervous system** is the physiological network of intercommunicating nerve cells that form the basis of our ability to perceive, adapt to, and interact with the world. It is the means by which humans and other vertebrates receive, process, and then respond to messages from the environment and from inside our bodies. Dr. P's strange perceptions and behavior were rooted in a disruption in his brain caused, according to neurologist Oliver Sacks, by either a tumor or brain disease. Because of the seamless way the nervous system processes information and executes commands, the work it does is often most clearly seen when something goes awry, such as in the case of Dr. P., the musician. We take for granted that we know the difference between our feet and our shoes—until the ability to do so vanishes and reveals the highly integrated communication system on which such perceptions depend.

The discussion of the nervous system presented here takes a functional approach. We are concerned not only with the anatomical structures that are there, but also with what those structures do and why (the physiological functions). In describing the functions of our physiological communication systems, we often refer to various human-made inventions (e.g., telephones, televisions, computers) as models for understanding the communication systems within our bodies. However, nothing created by humankind even approaches the complexity, subtlety, and sophistication of the systems of communication within our bodies.

In discussing the nervous system, we first will consider its structures and subsystems. Then we will

The feedback our nervous system provides about body position helps make this possible.

examine how information moves through the nervous system—both within cells and among them. Finally we will examine in some detail the supreme organ of the nervous system—the brain—paying special attention to the cerebral cortex, which controls many of our thought processes.

The Organization of the Nervous System

In Search of . . .

How is the nervous system organized?

The Central Nervous System

The overall structure of the nervous system is shown in the diagram in Figure 3-1. The nervous system is divided into two main parts, the central nervous system and the peripheral nervous system. The **central nervous system (CNS)** consists of two parts: the brain and the spinal cord, both of which are encased in bone and further buffered from shocks and minor traumas (injuries) by a fluid that is secreted constantly in the brain. This *cerebrospinal fluid* circulates throughout the brain and the spinal cord. Although the clear, colorless cerebrospinal fluid probably does not provide nourishment (which is provided by the rich blood supply going to the CNS), it may play a role in help-

ing the CNS dispose of waste products. The CNS controls our senses and motor abilities as well as our reflexes and mental activity.

The Brain and the Spinal Cord

The **brain,** protected by the skull, is the organ in our bodies that most directly controls our thoughts, emotions, and motivations, as well as motor responses, and that responds to information it receives from elsewhere in the body. Textbook diagrams such as Figure 3-11 involving the brain and its interconnections must somewhat oversimplify structures in order to reveal their fundamental elements and relationships. Such diagrams may not show all of the interconnections between the brain and other organs, or between the central and peripheral nervous systems, but the connections are there, and they are what enable us to serve a tennis ball, thread a needle, solve a math problem, change a tire, or put on our shoes. Communication within the brain is two-way: Information is sent to the brain; the brain processes it; and then the processed information is sent from the brain with instructions on how to proceed.

A rough analogy to the way the brain and the entire nervous system work would be the events that take place on a football field during an active game. A quarterback gets ready to pass the ball to a teammate. The quarterback needs to decide what to do. But there are many complications. The quarterback is running. The teammate is running. An opponent is moving toward the quarterback to try to tackle him. The teammate is distracted by a different opponent, and meanwhile, other players are constantly in motion. The complexity of the system seems overwhelming, and yet the game goes on and yields sensible and coherent outcomes. Similarly, the brain and all the elements of the nervous system are able to work together in a coherent fashion, despite the astonishing level of complexity of the system as a whole, a level of complexity that would make the events on a football field look like the simplest of child's play.

If we start from your brain, we can follow a network of cells called **neurons,** individual cells that receive and transmit information within the nervous system to the spinal cord. The **spinal cord** is a slender, roughly cylindrical bundle of interconnected fibers, about the size of your little finger, which is enclosed within the spinal column and which extends through the center of the back, starting at the brain and ending at the lower end of the small of the back (see Figure 3-2). Inside the spinal column, invisible from the outside of the body, the spinal cord bulges slightly in two places to accommodate large bundles of connecting neurons. These bulges reflect the importance of their contents. Because the arms, hands, legs, and feet are required almost constantly to do important work, their control requires many neurons. One of the two bulges contains the neurons controlling the

Central nervous system

Brain   Spinal cord

Peripheral nervous system

Somatic
(sensory and
motor nerves,
voluntary)

Autonomic
(involuntary)

Sympathetic
(activates under
stress)

Parasympathetic
(maintains body
functions)

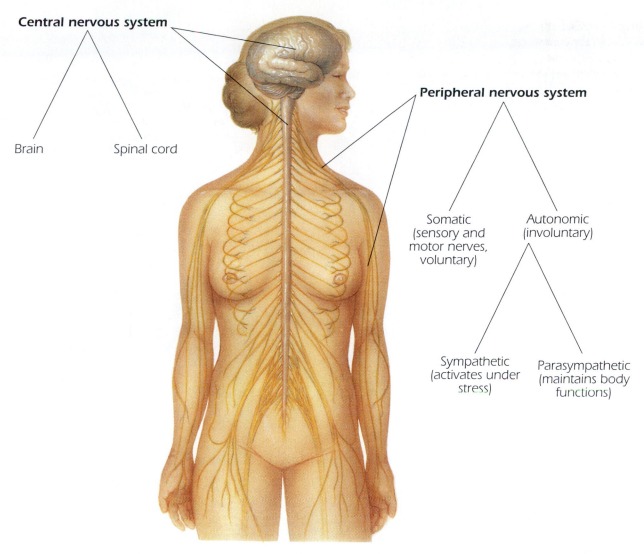

Figure 3–1
DIVISIONS OF THE NERVOUS SYSTEM.   *The central nervous system (CNS), protected by bone, comprises the brain and spinal cord. The peripheral nervous system (PNS), not protected by bone, comprises the nerves of the autonomic and somatic systems. The autonomic system transmits messages between the brain and internal organs, and the somatic system transmits messages between the brain and the sensory and motor nerves, which are linked to the skeletal muscles.*

sensations and movement of the arms and hands, and the other bulge contains the neurons controlling the legs and feet. After the bulges, the cord tapers gradually to a point in the lower portion of the back.

One function of the spinal cord is to collect information from the peripheral nervous system and transmit it to the brain, as well as to relay information back from the brain to the outlying neurons. The two-directional communication of the nervous system involves two kinds of neurons: **Sensory afferents** receive electrochemical *sensory information* from the outlying neurons of the body, such as those in the eyes, ears, and skin, and transmit that information back up through the spinal cord to the brain. More generally, an *afferent* of any kind is a neuron that brings information into a structure. **Motor efferents**

transmit *motor information* (e.g., movements of the large and small muscles) either from the brain through the spinal cord to the muscles (for voluntary muscle movements) or directly from the spinal cord to the muscles (in the case of reflexes), thus controlling bodily responses. More generally, an *efferent* is a neuron that carries information away from a structure.

Spinal Reflexes

The spinal cord plays a crucial role in routing sensory and motor information to and from the brain. Under some circumstances, however, the spinal cord transmits a message directly from sensory afferent neurons to motor efferent neurons, without routing the message through the brain prior to the bodily response to

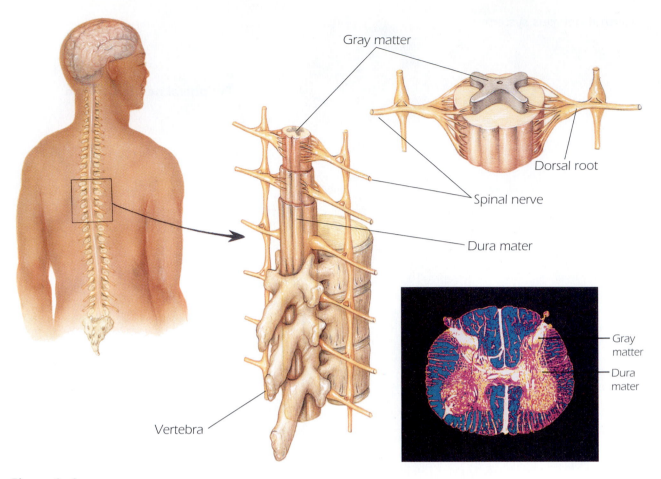

Figure 3-2
THE STRUCTURE OF THE SPINAL COLUMN.   *The spinal cord and its connecting nerves are protected by dura mater and vertebrae.*

the sensory information. The direct-connection responses are **reflexes** (see Figure 3-3), which offer much faster automatic physiological responses to an external stimulus than do voluntary responses. For example, it takes only about 50 milliseconds from the time the patellar tendon in your knee is tapped until your calf and foot jerk forward, compared with the many hundreds of milliseconds for you to move your knee in response to your being told to move it.

Indeed, 50 milliseconds is such a short span of time that normally you are not even aware of its passage. If you were as rapidly as you can to press the button on a stopwatch twice, once to start the stopwatch and once to stop it, you could never reach a time as short as 50 milliseconds with such a voluntary movement. Quick reflexes are adaptive because they allow the body to respond immediately to particular sensory information without its taking the time to route the information through the brain. For example, when you experience tissue damage, you reflexively withdraw from whatever causes the damage. Not only do reflexes minimize the pain that will be felt after they occur, but more importantly, they also minimize any tissue damage that might

result from potentially harmful stimuli such as fire. Thus, in both functional and evolutionary terms, our reflexes better enable us to survive.

The reflex response shows how the spinal cord has the power to act alone; yet it also demonstrates the brain's essential role in whether we consciously feel pain, pleasure, pressure, or temperature anywhere outside our heads. For example, suppose that a traumatic accident severed your spinal cord at the neck. You would be both paralyzed and without sensation below your neck, because your spinal cord would not be able to receive or send messages from or to your brain. This is not to say, however, that you could not move at all; your intact spinal reflexes would still jerk your hand away from a hot stove. You would never become consciously aware of pain, for your brain would not be able to get the sensory information via your spinal cord. Nor could you intentionally move your hand away from any impending danger that your brain recognized. To recognize your bodily sensations, or to move your body purposefully, your spinal cord must be able to communicate with your brain. This situation gives an interesting twist on the mind-body dilemma: When the brain is severed

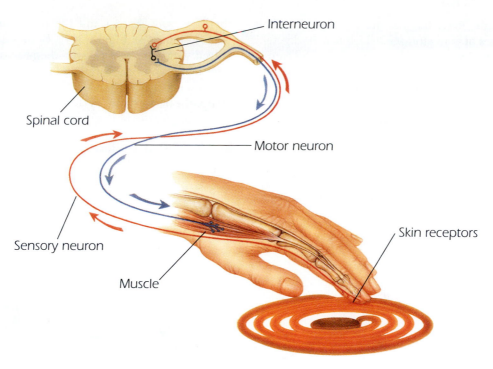

Interneuron

Spinal cord

Motor neuron

Sensory neuron

Skin receptors

Muscle

Figure 3–3

SPINAL REFLEX. *Reflexes enable us to remove ourselves immediately from danger by avoiding the time it would take for a message to go to and from the brain. In this example, the interneuron in the spinal column intercepts the "extreme heat" message from the sensory neuron and directs the motor neurons to contract the hand muscles, thereby pulling the hand away from the burner.*

from the spinal cord, events that happen in the body below the severance are not processed by the mind.

In sum, the body is an exceptionally well-organized system, with lower levels in the hierarchy of command capable of responding without intervention of the brain when the immediate need arises, but with higher levels in the hierarchy essential for full physical interaction with and perception of the world around us.

The Peripheral Nervous System

Below the level of the CNS in the hierarchy of command is the **peripheral nervous system (PNS)**, which comprises all of the neurons *except* the neurons of the brain and the spinal cord. *Peripheral* has two meanings: "auxiliary," because the PNS assists the CNS; and "away from the center," because the peripheral neurons are external to the CNS. Note that the PNS even includes the neurons of the face and head that are not a part of the CNS. The primary function of the PNS is to relay information between the CNS and the afferents and efferents lying outside of the CNS. The PNS connects with afferents in both our external sensory organs that receive information— such as skin, ears, and eyes—and with our internal body parts, like the stomach and the muscles. It also connects with efferents in parts of the body that produce movement, speech, and so on.

The PNS comprises two main parts: the somatic nervous system and the autonomic nervous system. The **somatic nervous system** is in charge of quick and conscious movements of our skeletal muscles. *Skeletal muscles* are those attached directly to our bones, and they allow us to walk, type, wave, and swim—in short, to move. The skeletal muscles are sometimes referred to as striated muscles because, under a microscope, they appear to have striations, or stripes. In general, we have voluntary control over the muscles served by neurons from the somatic system; whenever we want to control them, we can. The somatic nervous system usually can respond quickly to whatever the CNS asks of it—such as jumping out of the way of an oncoming bicycle.

The **autonomic nervous system** controls movement of our *nonskeletal muscles*, which include the striated cardiac (heart) muscles and the *smooth muscles*, which lack the striations found in the muscles of the somatic system. The smooth muscles include those of the blood vessels and of the internal body organs, or *viscera*, such as the muscles of the digestive tract. We have little and in some cases no voluntary control over these muscles. We are usually not even aware of their functioning. In fact, *autonomic* means "self-regulating." This system does not need our conscious attention.

To illustrate the two systems, suppose that you are writing at a word processor. You are controlling the striated muscular movements of your hands and fingers as they press the keys, but you are not directing the smooth muscles of your stomach, which may be digesting your dinner. In general, the responses of the autonomic nervous system are more sustained and less rapid than those of the somatic nervous system.

The autonomic nervous system is itself further divided into two intercommunicating parts: the sympathetic nervous system and the parasympathetic nervous system (see Figure 3-4). Both systems are involved with your *metabolism*—the processes by which your body captures, stores, and uses energy and material resources from food and eliminates waste. The **sympathetic nervous system** is concerned primarily with *catabolism*—the metabolic processes that *use* the

Figure 3–4
THE AUTONOMIC NERVOUS SYSTEM.   *Note how the two parts of the autonomic system, the sympathetic and parasympathetic systems, complement one another as they regulate the functions of the organs.*

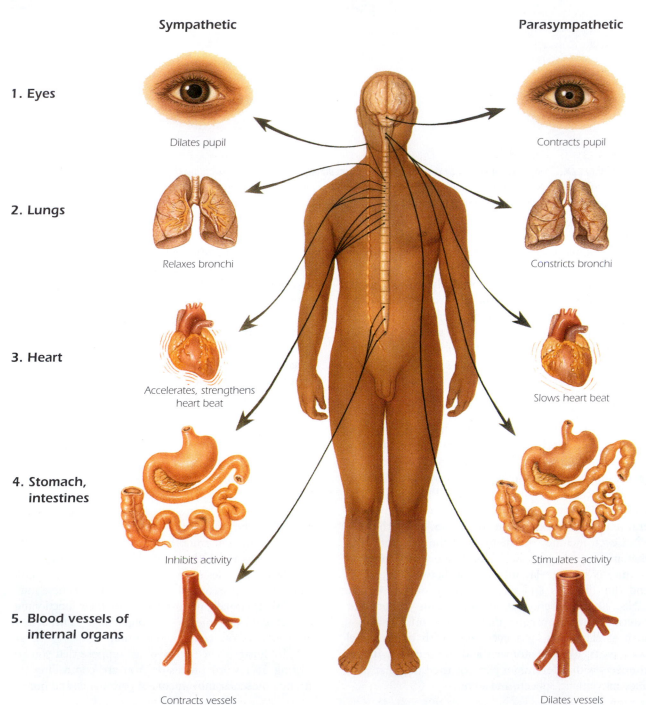

Sympathetic

Parasympathetic

1. **Eyes**

Dilates pupil

Contracts pupil

2. **Lungs**

Relaxes bronchi

Constricts bronchi

3. **Heart**

Accelerates, strengthens heart beat

Slows heart beat

4. **Stomach, intestines**

Inhibits activity

Stimulates activity

5. **Blood vessels of internal organs**

Contracts vessels

Dilates vessels

energy and other resources from the reserves stored in the body. The **parasympathetic nervous system** is concerned primarily with *anabolism*—the metabolic processes that *store* energy.

The sympathetic and parasympathetic systems often work in tandem, for example, in determining our metabolism through the storage and use of nutrients. In general, the sympathetic nervous system is activated by situations requiring arousal and alertness. At such times, this system increases heart rate and diverts blood flow to muscles, as needed for exercise or emergency. On the other hand, the parasympathetic nervous system becomes active when the body is conserving energy. It promotes the activity of the digestive system and also slows heart rate, thereby slowing the body and aiding in energy storage. Thus, the sympathetic and parasympathetic systems work in parallel, yet also in opposition to one another. If you have a heated argument right after dinner, your sympathetic system will be stirred up, readying you for a fight. Unfortunately, it will end up warring with your parasympathetic system, which will be trying to conserve body energy in order to digest your food. You may end up feeling drained, tired, and even sick to your stomach.

How do the components of the nervous system work? Let us start our examination of these components with a consideration of the most basic unit of the nervous system, the neuron.

Cellular Structures and Functions

[**In** *Search of...*] *What are the neurons, what are their parts, and how do they communicate?*

Neurons

To understand how the entire nervous system processes information, we first need to examine the structure of the cells—*neurons*—that constitute the nervous system. There are three main types of neurons, serving three different functions: sensory neurons, motor neurons, and interneurons.

Three Functions of Neurons

Sensory neurons receive information from the environment. They connect with *receptor cells* in the sensory organs that detect physical or chemical changes, including those in the skin, ears, tongue, eyes, nose, muscles, joints, and internal organs. Sensory neurons carry information away from the sensory receptor cells and *toward* the spinal cord or brain. **Motor neurons** carry information *away from* the spinal cord and the brain and toward the body parts that are supposed to respond to the information in some way. Both motor neurons and sensory

neurons are part of both the PNS as well as the CNS. For example, through the autonomic nervous system, motor and sensory neurons send information to and from the intestines and, through the somatic nervous system, to and from the toe muscles.

Interneurons, as the name implies, serve as intermediaries between sensory and motor neurons. They are all neurons that are neither afferent (originating from another source) or efferent (projecting to another structure). They *receive* signals from either sensory neurons or other interneurons, and they *send* signals either to other interneurons or to motor neurons. In complex organisms such as humans, the large majority of neurons are interneurons. In the spinal reflex discussed earlier in this chapter, an interneuron located in the spinal cord might act as an intermediary between the incoming sensory neuron, in essence carrying the message, "Burning hand on stove!" and the outgoing motor neuron, carrying the message, in essence "Move that hand!" Another interneuron sends the incoming message via the spinal cord to the brain, which interprets the incoming message as pain and more deliberately determines what to do about the situation.

Parts of the Neuron

Neurons vary in their structure, but almost all neurons have four basic parts, as shown in Figure 3-5: a soma, or cell body; dendrites; an axon; and terminal buttons. We discuss each part in turn, as well as the important junction between neurons—the synapse.

The **soma,** or body of the neuron, is responsible for the life of the cell. It contains the *nucleus*, the center portion. The nucleus performs metabolic and

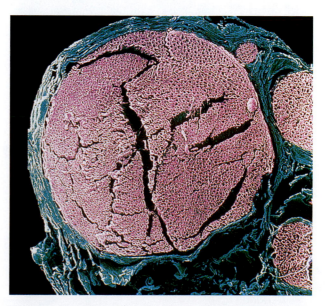

This photomicrograph shows the myelin sheath and nodes of Ranvier, the terminal buttons, and the glial cells of a neuron.

reproductive functions for the cell, and is responsible for the life of the neuron. The **dendrites** (branch-like parts of the neuron at the end of the soma) and the soma receive communications from other cells via distinctive receptors on their external membranes.

The **axon** is a long, thin tube, which can divide and branch many times at its *terminus* (end). The axon responds to the information received by the dendrites and soma; the axon can transmit the information

through the neuron until it reaches a place where it can be transmitted to other neurons through the release of chemical substances. A bundle of axons is called a **nerve.**

Axons are of two basic kinds, in approximately equal proportions in the human nervous system (see Figure 3-6). The key distinction between the two kinds of axons is the presence or absence of *myelin*, a white fatty substance. One kind of axon is *myelinated*, surrounded by a **myelin sheath,** which insulates and protects the axon from electrochemical interference from other neurons in the area. The myelin sheath also speeds up the conduction of information along the axon. In fact, the rate of transmission in myelinated axons can reach 100 meters per second (equal to about 224 miles per hour), or even more. Myelin is not distributed continuously along the axon, but rather in segments, which are broken up by **nodes of Ranvier**—small gaps in the myelin coating along the axon of myelinated neurons. A healthy diet in infancy, including a balanced set of nutrients, including fat, is important for proper development of the myelin sheath. Degeneration of the myelin sheath is associated with multiple sclerosis (MS), although the nature of the causal mechanism remains unclear. Impeded and tangled communication in the neurons results in progressive loss of motor function and, often, eventually in death.

The second kind of axon lacks the myelin coat altogether. Typically, these axons are smaller and shorter

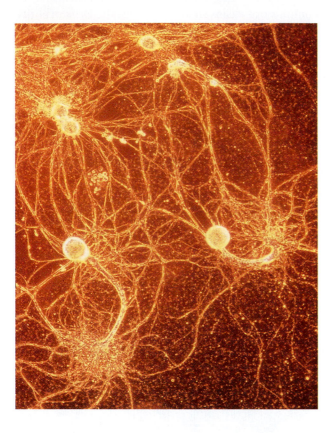

Figure 3–5

NEURONS. *The shape of a neuron is determined by its function. Each neuron, however, has the same structure: soma, dendrites, axon, and terminal buttons.*

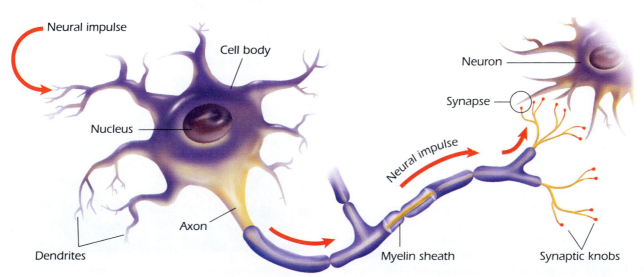

Neural impulse

Cell body

Nucleus

Axon

Dendrites

Myelin sheath

Neural impulse

Neuron

Synapse

Synaptic knobs

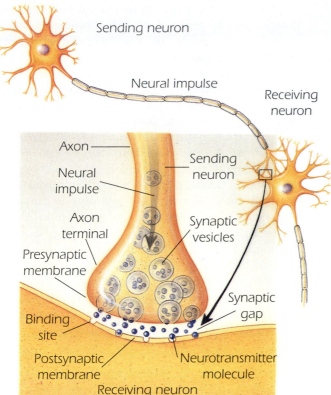

Sending neuron

Neural impulse

Receiving neuron

Axon

Neural impulse

Axon terminal

Presynaptic membrane

Binding site

Postsynaptic membrane

Sending neuron

Synaptic vesicles

Synaptic gap

Neurotransmitter molecule

Receiving neuron

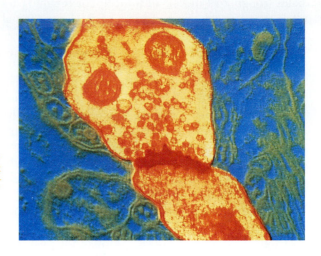

Figure 3–6

THE SYNAPSE. *Neurons relay electrochemical messages by releasing neurotransmitters that cross the synapse to the dendrites of the receiving neurons. This electron micrograph shows how densely packed the neurons are.*

than the myelinated ones, so they do not need the increased conduction velocity of a lengthy, myelinated axon. In unmyelinated axons, conduction is much slower, sometimes as relatively sluggish as 5 meters per second. (At the same time, most of us would be lucky to be able to run that fast!)

Myelin serves as an insulator and speeds up transmission of nerve impulses. In addition, conduction speed increases as the diameter of the axon increases. Motor neurons in control of supplying quick and constant power to arms and legs, for example, are generally thick and myelinated. On the other hand, neurons to the stomach muscles are mostly small in diameter and unmyelinated, because the digestive process usually does not require speed. Thus, form follows function. Ironically, part of the reason myelin helps speed up neural transmission is that there *are* gaps, the nodes of Ranvier, in the myelin sheath. That is, electrochemical impulses save time by leaping across the myelin sheath, to be reconstructed anew at each uncoated node of Ranvier.

The last part of the neuron to be mentioned are the **terminal buttons,** which are small knobby structures found at the ends of the branches of an axon. These terminal buttons play an important part in interneuronal communication, to be discussed later.

How many neurons are there? The number of neurons in the human nervous system is estimated at

more than 100 billion (100,000,000,000). If a team of scientists were to count 3 neurons per second, it would take the team more than 1,000 years to count them all. For the most part, these neurons are irreplaceable, at least in adults. Once the neuron's soma dies, the neuron is gone forever. However, as long as the soma continues to live, the remaining stumps of damaged but living neurons can sometimes regenerate new axons, although this regeneration process is more successful in the PNS than in the CNS. As a result, damage to the CNS is much more serious than is damage to the PNS because of the lower probability of full recovery of function when there is damage in the CNS.

Neuronal size is more difficult to quantify in absolute terms. The soma of the neuron ranges in diameter from about 5 to about 100 microns (thousandths of a millimeter, or millionths of a meter). Dendrites, too, are relatively small, generally a few hundred microns in length. Axons, however, can vary considerably in length. Some axons are as short as a few hundred microns (in fact, some neurons in the eye and elsewhere have virtually indistinguishable axons). The axons of some of the longer motor neurons, however, can extend all the way from the head to the base of the spinal cord, and from the spinal cord to the fingers and the toes. In relative terms, visualize an orange attached to a long wire stretching the length of over 200 football fields (roughly 14 miles). This metaphor roughly parallels the soma and axon of some of the longer spinal neurons.

Glial Cells

Neurons are not the only kind of cell in the nervous system. In fact, they constitute only about 10% of the cells in the CNS. In the CNS, the neurons are supported by the all-purpose **glial cells** (also termed *neuroglia*). Glial cells, in part, function as a kind of glue to hold the CNS together, and more specifically, to hold the neurons in their proper places, keeping them at optimal distances from one another and from other structures in the body. Thus, glial cells help ensure that signals do not get crossed. Some of the glial cells also assist in forming the myelin sheath. In fact, the nodes of Ranvier in the sheath are actually the gaps between glial cells.

Glial cells nourish and support the neurons of the CNS. They also destroy and eliminate neurons that have died either through injury or age. The dead neurons are then often replaced with new glial cells. Destruction of glial cells, which can be caused by disease, can result in serious breakdowns in communication within the nervous system. Messages become scrambled as they cross through uncharted territory: As the disease progresses and the insulating myelin sheaths deteriorate, dead neurons and other waste accumulate and clutter the neural landscape, and inadequate nourishment impedes normal cell function and repair of damaged tissue.

There are basically two kinds of neuronal communication: intraneuronal (communication of elements within the neuron) and interneuronal (communication between neurons). We consider intraneuronal communication (within neurons) first.

The Action Potential

Communication within the neuron is *electrochemical*—accomplished through interactions involving chemicals having positive or negative electrical charges. Each neuron contains electrically charged chemical particles called *ions*. If the concentrations of the various ions inside and outside the neuron always remained in a *static equilibrium* (a perfect balance, with no changes inside or outside the neuron), intraneuronal communication would never occur. In living organisms, however, change is constant. Ongoing electrical activity within the body stimulates changes in the concentrations of ions inside and outside the neuron, which in turn affects the functioning of the neuron (see Figure 3-7).

Because of the tremendous amount of fluctuating electrical activity going on in our bodies every moment of our lives, our neurons must be somewhat selective in reacting to the electrical activity. If our neurons reacted to every slight fluctuation, utter chaos would result. To avoid this pandemonium, electrical charges of most levels of intensity and frequency produce virtually no effect in the neuron at all. However, once a charge reaches or surpasses a certain level—the neuron's **threshold of excitation**—the neuron reacts quite differently (see Figure 3-8). At or above its threshold, an **action potential**—a brief change in the electrochemical balance inside and outside a neuron that occurs when electrochemical stimulation of the neuron reaches or exceeds the neuron's threshold of excitation. The specific threshold of excitation that is required for a given neuron's action potential differs for the various neurons. When an action potential occurs, the neuron "fires." It is the action potential that carries impulses, or messages, through the axon, from one end to the other. Action potentials are *all or none*. Either the electrical charge is strong enough to generate an action potential, or it is not. Once the threshold is reached, the charge will travel all the way down the axon without losing strength.

You might compare the firing of a neuron to a sneeze. In order to generate a sneeze, the membranes of your nose must be tickled beyond a certain point by some outside irritant. If you are like most people, once that tickle threshold has been crossed, you will definitely sneeze. It is an all-or-none process. Similarly, a neuron will definitely fire once its threshold level has been reached.

What, exactly, happens during the conduction of a neural impulse? Initially, the neuron is at rest. During this phase, it has a potential of −70 millivolts. When the neuron is stimulated and an action potential occurs, the voltage changes (see Figure 3-8), becoming positive. Gates that allow sodium to enter the axon open, with the result that positively charged sodium ions start to flow into the axon. As the action potential peaks, the sodium gates close, but different potassium gates open, allowing potassium ions to flow outward. This process can be repeated many times, with sodium gates opening, sodium ions flowing into the axon, potassium gates then beginning to open, sodium gates closing, potassium flowing outward, and finally, the potassium gates closing. At the end of this complex process, the neuron returns to its initial potential of −70 millivolts. The whole process then involves changes in the balance between sodium and potassium as conduction proceeds.

Now suppose that the neuron has just fired and that another strong electrical charge has again reached

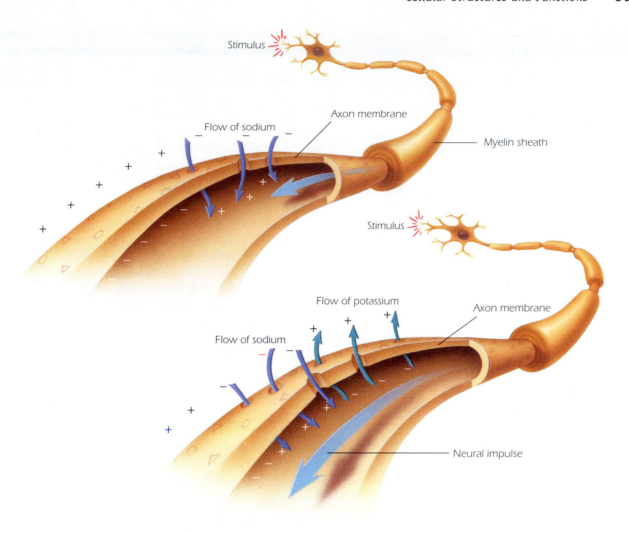

Figure 3–7
NEURAL IMPULSE.   *The neural impulse depends on the alternating flow of sodium and potassium ions.*

the axon. Will the neuron fire? It will not. As long as the dynamic equilibrium of the ions inside and outside the neuron has not yet returned to normal after firing, the neuron cannot reach its action potential again. At this point—the **absolute refractory phase**—no matter how strong the stimulus may be, the neuron cannot fire again. After the absolute refractory phase, some of the dynamic equilibrium of ions begins to return to normal, and the neuron reaches a **relative refractory phase,** in which the neuron can fire, but only in response to a stronger stimulus than would typically be necessary. Finally, after the dynamic equilibrium of ions has returned to normal, the neuron regains its usual sensitivity to electrochemical stimulation for reaching its action potential. Functionally, the refractory phases prevent the organism from overstimulation of individual neurons.

Consider the sneezing analogy again. A few sneezes are helpful. But if you were to continue sneezing again and again without interruption, the aversive effects of the sneezing gradually would start to outweigh the positive effects of clearing irritating particles from the nasal cavity.

To summarize, transmission of information occurs within a neuron through the propagation of all-or-none action potentials along an axon. The potentials are set off by an electrical current at or beyond the neuron's threshold of excitation. This process sets in motion a complex electrochemical reaction that transmits the message down the neuron. Propagation of impulses is especially rapid in myelinated axons. Once the impulse reaches the terminal buttons, it causes them to release their neurotransmitter chemicals.

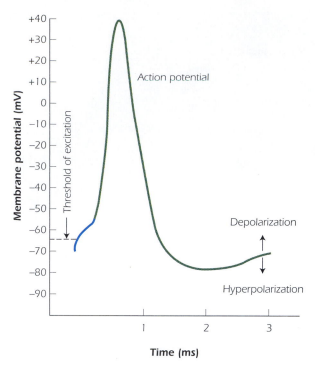

Figure 3–8
ACTION POTENTIAL.   *When electrochemical stimulation reaches a neuron's threshold of excitation, the neuron generates an action potential. During an action potential, ions swiftly cross the membrane of the neuron.*

Neural Transmission

Communication within neurons is essential for each neuron to work effectively, but the work of each individual neuron would be for naught if there were no way for neurons to communicate with one another. In other words, interneuronal communication is essential.

Interneuronal communication begins with the terminal buttons, introduced earlier. The terminal buttons of the axon do not directly touch the dendrites of the next neuron. Rather, a very small gap, the **synapse,** exists between the terminal buttons of one neuron's axon and the dendrites (or sometimes the soma) of the next neuron (see Figure 3-6). To send a message, the terminal buttons on the axon of the presynaptic neuron—the one sending the message— release a **neurotransmitter**—a chemical messenger— across the synaptic gap to the receptor sites of either the receiving dendrites or the soma of the postsynaptic neuron. The neurotransmitter then reaches one or more (usually more) neurons and continues the line of communication. There are a number of kinds of neurotransmitters operating at any given synapse. The receptor sites on the postsynaptic neuron are specialized and, as described below, are affected only by certain kinds of neurotransmitter.

We already know *where* (in the synapse) and *when* (whenever an action potential triggers release of a neurotransmitter) neurons communicate. We even know *what* (neurotransmitters) they use for communicating. We just need to know a little more about *how* they do so. Stated simply, here is how it works (see Figure 3-9):

1. One neuron ("Neuron A") releases a neurotransmitter from its terminal buttons.

2. The neurotransmitter crosses the synapse and reaches the receptors in the dendrites (or soma) of another neuron ("Neuron B").

3. The dendrites of Neuron B are stimulated by the neurotransmitters Neuron B receives from Neuron A until Neuron B reaches its own distinctive threshold of excitation. The effects of these neurotransmitters summate (add together), growing as their quantities increase.

4. At Neuron B's threshold of excitation, the Neuron B action potential travels down its axon.

5. When Neuron B's action potential reaches Neuron B's terminal buttons, Neuron B releases its own neurotransmitter into the next synapse (perhaps with Neuron C), and so on.

Figure 3–9
NEURAL TRANSMISSION.   *A neural impulse flows from the axon of a neuron to the axon's terminal buttons, instigating the release of neurotransmitter substances, which bind to specific receptor sites that provide a fit to them. The relationship is like that of a key opening only a specific kind of lock.*

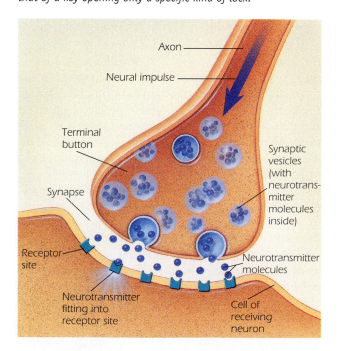

At any given synapse, there are usually multiple, often hundreds, of connections among neurons, with dendritic trees branching out to receive messages from many axons (see Figure 3-10). Furthermore, on the receiving membranes of each postsynaptic neuron are numerous receptor sites for neurotransmitters. Scientists have devised a descriptive metaphor for the interaction of neurotransmitters and receptors. Neurotransmitters and receptors operate somewhat like keys and keyholes. Each receptor has a somewhat different molecular shape. The distinctive molecular shape of a given receptor may be viewed as a keyhole, and the distinctive molecular shape of a given neurotransmitter may be viewed as a key. When the shape of the key matches the shape of the keyhole, the receptor responds.

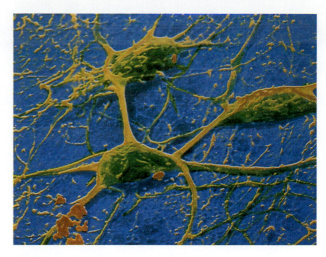

Figure 3–10

DENDRITES. *Dendrites are the primary structure by which neurons receive communications from other cells. They do this via distinctive receptors on their external membranes. The multibranched dendrites resemble tree branches and are named after the Greek word for "tree."*

Excitatory and Inhibitory Messages

Differing receptor sites respond distinctively to the messages of neurotransmitters. The message received can be of either two kinds: a message of excitation or one of inhibition. Many receptors are *excited* by the neurotransmitters they contact in the synapse, thereby *increasing* the likelihood that the postsynaptic (receiving) neurons will reach their own threshold of excitation. Other receptors, however, are actually *inhibited* by the neurotransmitters they receive, thereby *decreasing* the probability that the postsynaptic neurons will reach their threshold of excitation. That is, for a given neurotransmitter, certain receptor sites on some neurons may be excited, whereas certain other receptor sites on other neurons may be inhibited. Excitatory receptors on the postsynaptic neurons excite the neuron's response, and inhibitory receptors inhibit the neuron's response.

Neuromodulators

To make matters even more complicated, although each neuron is equipped to release only one particular neurotransmitter, the terminal buttons of some neurons also release other chemical substances, called **neuromodulators,** which serve to enhance or to diminish the responsivity of the postsynaptic neuron, either by directly affecting the axon or by affecting the sensitivity of the receptor sites.

To summarize, myriad presynaptic neurons are releasing neurotransmitters and neuromodulators into the synapse. Some of the receptors of the postsynaptic neuron are being excited, and others are being inhibited. Furthermore, the degree of excitation or inhibition is being influenced by the actions of the neuromodulators, which either enhance or diminish the responsivity of the postsynaptic neurons. In order for the postsynaptic neuron to fire, the overall balance of excitatory and inhibitory responses must reach the neuron's threshold level of excitation. When you think about all that is involved in getting one neuron to fire, it seems a miracle that any of us can think at all. In fact, however, the time it takes for a given message to cross the synapse can be as little as half a millisecond, or it can take as long as a second or more. As you process the words on this page, many thousands of interacting neurons are at work to help you understand just what it is that the text is telling you about these neurons.

Given the tremendous volume of neurotransmitters and neuromodulators spilling into each synapse, it makes sense that not all the chemical messengers released by axons can be neatly absorbed by the dendrites. What, then, happens to the unused transmitter chemicals? Fortunately, our bodies have mechanisms for dealing with this situation.

Reuptake

The first and more common mechanism is **reuptake,** in which neurotransmitters are removed from the synapse: The terminal button of an axon reabsorbs the chemical transmitter that it released into the synapse. The next cell is thereby spared excessive stimulation, and the neuron that released the substance can store it for future use. The second, less common, mechanism is *enzymatic deactivation;* in this process, an *enzyme* (a protein that *catalyzes,* or brings about, chemical reactions) breaks apart the neurotransmitter or neuromodulator, thereby making it inactive.

An additional kind of mechanism also may affect interneuronal processing. A certain kind of receptor called an *autoreceptor* sometimes can be found at the tip of the axon of the presynaptic neuron. An autoreceptor is sensitive to the neurotransmitter released by the axon. It appears that some of the transmitter substance can make its way back to the autoreceptor and provide negative feedback to it. This negative feedback possibly reduces further release of the neurotransmitter (Kalsner, 1990).

Common Neurotransmitters and Neuromodulators

Although scientists already know of hundreds of chemical substances involved in neurotransmission, it seems likely that we have yet to identify all of them. Medical and psychological researchers are working to discover and understand these chemical substances and how they interact with drugs, foods, moods, abilities, and perceptions. Although we know quite a bit about the mechanics of impulse transmission in neurons, we still know relatively little about how the nervous system's chemical activity relates to psychological states. Despite the limits on present knowledge, however, we have gained some insight into how several of these substances affect our psychological functioning.

The key neurotransmitters are often termed the "classical neurotransmitters" because they were among the first neurotransmitters to be discovered. They include acetylcholine, which is synthesized from the choline in our diet (and which often is classified as part of the Vitamin-B complex); dopamine, epinephrine, and norepinephrine, which are synthesized from dietary tyrosine; and serotonin, which is synthesized from dietary tryptophan. These classical neurotransmitters account for only a very small fraction of the transmission sites in the brain. The most common neurotransmitters are excitatory amino acids, glutamate, and GABA (discussed below).

In the brain, **acetylcholine (ACh)** excites the neuronal receptor sites. ACh has been found in the hippocampus, an area known to be involved in memory (Squire, 1987). Acetylcholine is thus believed to be involved in memory function. Researchers are currently trying to find out whether ACh is somehow blocked from action in the brains of people with *Alzheimer's disease*, an illness that causes devastating losses of memory. ACh is also found in various sites throughout the body, where it can excite the PNS to cause contraction of the skeletal muscles, leading to movement, or it can inhibit the neurons in the muscles of the heart.

Dopamine (DA) seems to influence several important activities, including movement, attention, and learning. Although most receptors for dopamine are inhibitory, some of the receptors are excitatory. In *Parkinson's disease*, a particular group of neurons that

produces dopamine degenerates; this degeneration is associated with tremors, rigidity of limbs, and difficulty in balance. Dopamine-producing neurons synthesize dopamine through enzyme actions: One enzyme adds a chemical ingredient to tyrosine, forming l-dopa, and then another enzyme removes a different chemical constituent from l-dopa, forming dopamine. There is no easy way to get dopamine to the brain; but physicians have been able to give Parkinson's sufferers synthetic l-dopa, which is rapidly converted by the remaining dopamine-producing neurons to produce more dopamine. Unfortunately, it also is possible to get too much of a good neurotransmitter: Schizophrenia appears to be associated with the release of too much dopamine. Similarly, overdoses of l-dopa in the treatment of Parkinson's disease can result in overproduction of dopamine, which can lead to symptoms of schizophrenia. Two other substances that can serve as neurotransmitters are produced by further synthesis of tyrosine: norepinephrine and epinephrine, which appear to be involved in the regulation of alertness.

Serotonin (5-HT) appears to be related to arousal and sleep, as well as to regulation of mood, appetite, and sensitivity to pain. Although serotonin has an excitatory effect on a few receptor sites, it is usually an inhibitory neurotransmitter, and its behavioral outcomes are generally inhibitory as well. Among other actions, serotonin acts to inhibit dreaming. The mood-altering drug lysergic acid diethylamide (LSD) inhibits the actions of serotonin; LSD can accumulate in the brain and overstimulate neurons, leading to feelings of well-being but also to hallucinations—in effect, waking dreams. Serotonin also is involved in anxiety. Mice lacking certain serotonin receptors (and hence who are unable to process serotonin) show reduced anxiety and are hyperactive during their entire life span (Brunner, Buhot, Hen, & Hofer, 1999).

Other primary neurotransmitters are glutamate (glutamic acid), aspartate, and glycine. Also included in this group is gamma-aminobutyric acid (GABA), which is synthesized from glutamate by the simple removal of one chemical constituent. These neurotransmitters are particularly interesting because they appear to have both a specific neurotransmission effect, when acting on specific neuronal receptor sites, and more general neuromodulating effects. For example, glutamate seems to have direct excitatory effects on the axons of postsynaptic neurons, thereby lowering the threshold of excitation. GABA seems to have direct inhibitory effects on axons, thereby increasing the threshold of excitation (point at which interneuronal communication is triggered). Imbalances in the amino-acid neurotransmitters, as this group is called, have been linked to seizures, Huntington's chorea (an inherited neurological disorder), and the fatal effects of tetanus.

Synaptic Bases for Learning and Memory

William T. Greenough, *University of Illinois, Urbana-Champaign*

As an undergraduate student I worked with Dr. James McGaugh, who was then at the University of Oregon. He had just made a major breakthrough—finding that long-term memory was not formed immediately upon learning but took time to form and could be manipulated during that time (for example, with drugs) to make it better or worse. This finding showed that memory was a process that took place over time and was amenable to study from a physiological perspective. Until then, the principal approaches had been to ask what parts of the brain were necessary for various types of memory—usually by destroying brain regions. This turning point allowed researchers to ask, "What happens in the brain when a memory is formed?" I decided to work on that problem, and, while I've made some progress, I haven't completely solved it, nor have the other researchers working on this issue, but we are gaining on it.

My work has shown that both the early brain organization that results from experience in development, and much of what we refer to as adult memory, involve changes in the number and structure of the *synapses* through which nerve cells communicate. My research was initially stimulated by findings showing that: (1) synapses in rats' visual cortices were altered when they first experienced patterned visual experience; (2) when rats were reared in groups in challenging, object-rich environments (EC, "environmental complexity" rats), regions of the cerebral cortex grew larger, compared to rats housed in ordinary laboratory cages (SC, "social cage" with another rat, or IC, "individual cage"); and (3) EC rats performed better than SC or IC rats on complex behavioral tasks such as maze learning.

Learning Electron Microscopy

With my first lab group at the University of Illinois, I began studying synapses with electron microscopy and nerve cells with optical microscopy in rats. We found that the dendrites, the parts of the nerve cell that receive most of its synaptic input, were more extensive in EC rat visual cortices and that EC rats had larger synapses than SC or IC rats in some parts of the visual cortex. Thus, we had evidence for formation of additional synapses (on the more extensive dendrites) and modification of synapses in the EC rats that had experienced a greater opportunity for learning. Later we confirmed that there was a greater number of synapses per neuron in EC rat visual cortices using electron microscopy, the "gold standard" for anatomical studies. The work on dendrites was done with Fred Volkmar, who then was an undergraduate student and now is a professor of psychiatry at Yale University.

To do this work I had to learn electron microscopy, one of many technical procedures that I have learned. It is important to be willing to learn whatever techniques are necessary to answer critical research questions and not be bounded by those techniques with which you are familiar. Training in psychology provides an enormous advantage because of its emphasis on rigorous experimental methods, balanced designs, and appropriate statistical analyses—areas that often receive less emphasis in other disciplines. Some disciplines, particularly the biological sciences, provide valuable measurement techniques that can be applied to psychological research questions.

Subsequently, we examined other types of tissue in the brain. We found that EC rats had more blood vessels and more supportive glial cells in the visual cortex. This indicated that *plasticity*, or the ability of cells to alter their characteristics in response to the way in which they are used, was a fairly general property of the tissues making up the brain and not just a special property of nerve cells. We also found that expansion of neuronal dendritic fields occurred in animals trained on mazes or taught motor skills such as reaching into a tube for food. When training was lateralized to one side of the brain, by using an opaque contact lens during maze learning or by reach training only one forepaw, the neuronal changes were appropriately lateralized in the brain, indicating that they arose from the brain activity of training and not because of some generally acting result of training, such as stress hormone action.

To make sure these neuronal changes reflected *learning* rather than simply activity—muscles grow larger with exercise, for example, but we do not usually think of such changes as "memories"—we compared rats that learned motor skills (a difficult elevated obstacle course) with animals that merely exercised (in an activity wheel or on a treadmill) with very little learning. We found that the learners formed additional synapses with no blood vessel increase, while the exercisers formed additional blood vessels with no synaptic increase. Thus, synapse formation was associated with learning and blood vessel formation was associated with stamina, or capacity for sustained activity.

Research Leads in New Direction

In the course of these studies, we observed that the cellular structures that synthesize protein were more common near synapses in EC than in SC or IC rats. Subsequently, we determined that one of the proteins synthesized near synapses was FMRP, the protein that is absent in fragile X mental retardation syndrome, the most common cause of inherited mental retardation. Currently we are investigating the role of this protein in the nerve cell and the neural correlates of the syndrome, both in autopsy material from human patients and in a genetic "knockout" mouse in which the gene for FMRP has been inactivated.

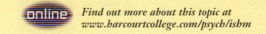

Find out more about this topic at
www.harcourtcollege.com/psych/ishm

Although many neurotransmitters pass through brain tissue, a *blood–brain barrier* prevents most other substances from passing from the body to the brain. The purpose of this barrier is to prevent potential toxins from destroying brain tissue. Evolutionarily, organisms with such a barrier would be at an advantage over organisms without such a barrier in their potential for survival and reproduction.

The preceding description—as complex as it may seem—drastically oversimplifies the intricacies of the neuronal communication that constantly takes place in the nervous system. Much of this communication takes place in the brain, and it is to the brain we turn next.

The Brain: Structure and Function

In Search of ... *How does the brain and its various parts function to produce feelings, thoughts, and behaviors?*

Throughout this chapter, we have mentioned from time to time the brain and its importance to almost all that we do. What does a brain actually look like? Figure 3-11 shows several views of a brain. Upcoming figures and simplified schematic diagrams point out in greater detail some of the main features of the brain.

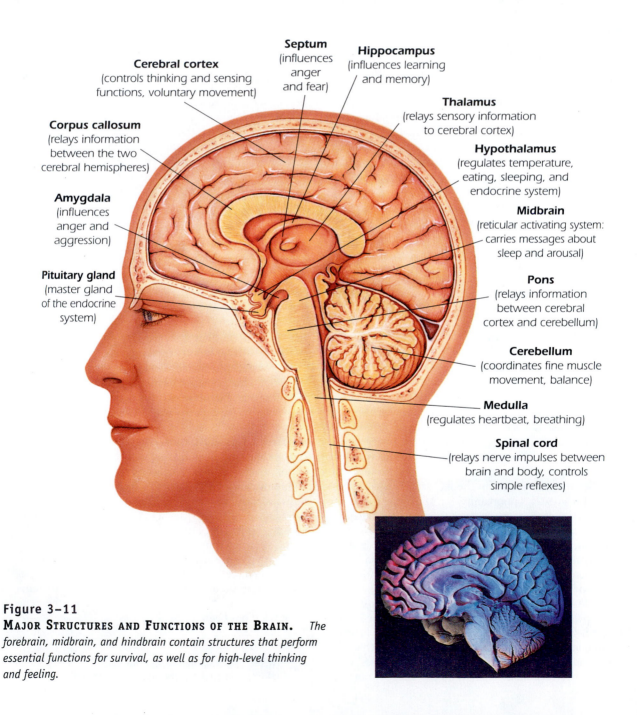

Septum
(influences anger and fear)

Hippocampus
(influences learning and memory)

Cerebral cortex
(controls thinking and sensing functions, voluntary movement)

Thalamus
(relays sensory information to cerebral cortex)

Corpus callosum
(relays information between the two cerebral hemispheres)

Hypothalamus
(regulates temperature, eating, sleeping, and endocrine system)

Amygdala
(influences anger and aggression)

Midbrain
(reticular activating system: carries messages about sleep and arousal)

Pituitary gland
(master gland of the endocrine system)

Pons
(relays information between cerebral cortex and cerebellum)

Cerebellum
(coordinates fine muscle movement, balance)

Medulla
(regulates heartbeat, breathing)

Spinal cord
(relays nerve impulses between brain and body, controls simple reflexes)

Figure 3–11
MAJOR STRUCTURES AND FUNCTIONS OF THE BRAIN. *The forebrain, midbrain, and hindbrain contain structures that perform essential functions for survival, as well as for high-level thinking and feeling.*

The brain is the most complex internal biological system of which we are aware, and yet, we could hold a brain in our hands if we so chose.

The brain can be divided into three major regions: hindbrain, midbrain, and forebrain. These labels do not correspond exactly to their locations in an adult's or even a child's head, because the terms come from the front-to-back physical arrangement of these parts in a developing embryo's nervous system, which is formed from the neural tube: The **hindbrain** is farthest back, near the back of the neck. The **midbrain** is next in line, located between the forebrain and the hindbrain. The **forebrain** is the farthest forward, toward what becomes the face.

The remainder of the neural tube becomes the spinal cord (see Figure 3-12a). In development, the relative orientations change, so that the forebrain becomes almost a cap on top of the midbrain and hindbrain. Nonetheless, the terms are still used to designate areas of the fully developed brain. Figure 3-12a, b, c shows the changing locations and relationships of the hindbrain, the midbrain, and the forebrain over the course of development of the brain, starting from an embryo a few weeks after conception and proceeding to a fetus of seven months. We now consider each of these major regions in turn, starting from the hindbrain and working our way roughly upward and forward.

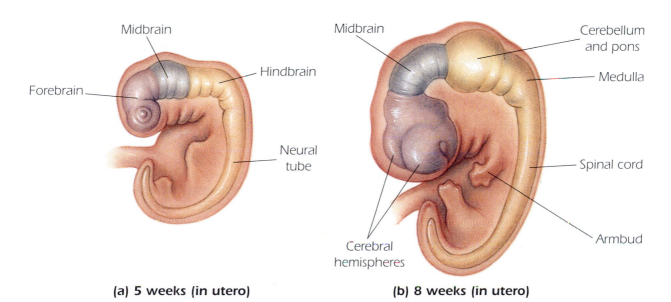

(a) 5 weeks (in utero)

(b) 8 weeks (in utero)

(c) 7 months (in utero)

Figure 3–12
NEURAL DEVELOPMENT. *Over the course of embryonic and fetal development the brain becomes more highly specialized; the locations and relative positions of the hindbrain, midbrain, and forebrain change from conception to full term.*

The Hindbrain

The hindbrain is the site of some of the most primitive and basic functions that the brain controls. It comprises the medulla oblongata, the pons, and the cerebellum. The **medulla oblongata** is an elongated interior structure of the brain, located at the point where the spinal cord enters the skull and joins with the brain, that helps to keep us alive by entirely controlling heart rate and largely controlling breathing, swallowing, and digestion. The medulla oblongata is a part of the reticular activating system (discussed later in this chapter), a midbrain structure that actually extends into the hindbrain. The medulla is also the place at which neurons from the right side of the body cross over to the left side of the brain, and neurons from the left side of the body cross over to the right side of the brain. (We examine the functional significance of this crossover shortly.)

The **pons** serves as a kind of relay station, containing neurons that pass signals from one part of the brain to another. Its name, which means "bridge," was given to it because many axons in the pons cross from one side of the brain to the other side. The pons also contains a portion of the reticular activating system, as well as neurons serving parts of the head and face. The **cerebellum** controls bodily coordination, balance, and muscle tone. If the cerebellum is damaged, movement becomes jerky and disjointed, posing a challenge for the function of the midbrain.

The Midbrain

The midbrain is more important in nonmammals than in mammals because in nonmammals it is the main source of control for visual and auditory information. In mammals these functions are mostly taken over by the forebrain, but the midbrain does help to control eye movements and coordination. Table 3-1 lists several structures and functions of the midbrain, but by far the most important of these is the **reticular activating system (RAS),** a network of neurons essential to the regulation of consciousness (sleep, wakefulness, arousal, and even attention, to some extent), as well as to such vital functions as heart rate and breathing (see Figure 3-13).

As mentioned, the reticular activating system actually extends into the hindbrain and includes the medulla and pons. Together, the midbrain, the hindbrain, and the thalamus and hypothalamus, both located in the forebrain, form the **brain stem,** which connects the brain to the spinal cord.

Brain stem function is central to life. Indeed, physicians make a determination of brain death based on the function of the brain stem. But even more central to our experiencing of life is the functioning of the forebrain.

The Forebrain

The forebrain is the region located toward the top and front of the brain (see Table 3-1 and Figure 3-11). It comprises four parts: the limbic system, the thalamus, the hypothalamus (which is often viewed as part of the limbic system), and the cerebral cortex. The most complex mental processing take place here. The forebrain is also the largest area of the brain and encompasses a number of structures and systems.

The Limbic System: A Center of Emotion

The **limbic system** is a system of brain structures important to emotion, motivation, and learning. Animals such as fish and reptiles, which have relatively undeveloped limbic systems, respond to the environment almost exclusively by instinct. Mammals, especially humans, have relatively more developed limbic systems, which seem to allow us to suppress instinctive responses (such as the impulse immediately to strike at someone who accidentally causes us pain). Our limbic systems make us better able to adapt our behavior flexibly in response to our changing environment.

The limbic system involves three central interconnected cerebral structures: the hippocampus, the amygdala, and the septum. The **hippocampus** plays an essential role in memory formation. People who have suffered damage to or removal of the hippocampus can still recall existing memories (for example, they can recognize old friends and places), but they are unable to form new memories after the time of the brain damage. You could converse with such a person every day for a year, and each time the two of you met you would be entirely unfamiliar to this person (Squire, 1987).

The **amygdala** is located somewhat below the hippocampus (see Figure 3-11). It plays a role in anger and aggression, and the **septum** is involved in anger and fear. Studies of monkeys have revealed some of these physiological functions. For example, monkeys with *lesions* (damage due to pathology or injury) in some areas of the limbic system seem to lack inhibition and are easily enraged. Monkeys with damage to other areas of the limbic system cannot be provoked to anger even when attacked; their hostility seems to have been erased. The amygdala also may modulate long-term storage of memories carried out in other parts of the brain (Bianchin, Mello e Souza, Medina, & Izquierdo, 1999).

The Thalamus: A Gateway

Most of the sensory input into the brain passes through the **thalamus,** a two-lobed structure located in about the center of the brain, at about the level of the eyes, just beneath the cerebral cortex. The thalamus relays the incoming sensory information to the appropriate region

TABLE 3–1

The Three Major Regions of the Brain
The brain has three major regions, each with distinct structures and functions.

REGION OF THE BRAIN	MAJOR STRUCTURES WITHIN THE REGIONS	FUNCTIONS OF THE STRUCTURES
Hindbrain	■ **Cerebellum**	■ Essential to balance, coordination, and muscle tone
	■ **Pons** (also contains part of the RAS)	■ Involved in consciousness (sleep/arousal); bridges neural transmissions from one part of the brain to another; involved with facial nerves
	■ **Medulla oblongata**	■ Juncture at which nerves cross from one side of the body to opposite side of the brain; involved in cardiorespiratory function, digestion, and swallowing
Midbrain	■ **Superior colliculi** (on top)	■ Involved in vision (especially visual reflexes)
	■ **Inferior colliculi** (below)	■ Involved in hearing
	■ **Reticular activating system** (also extends into the hindbrain)	■ Important in controlling consciousness (sleep, arousal), attention, cardiorespiratory function, and movement
	■ **Gray matter, red nucleus, substantia nigra, ventral region**	■ Important in controlling movement
Forebrain	■ **Cerebral cortex** (outer layer of the cerebral hemispheres)	■ Receiving and processing sensory information, thinking, other cognitive processing, and planning and sending motor information

	■ **Limbic system**
	    Hippocampus
	    Amygdala
	    Septum
		■ Learning, emotions, and motivation
		    Learning and memory
		    Anger and aggression
		    Anger and fear

	■ **Thalamus**	■ Primary relay station for sensory information coming into the brain; transmits information to the correct regions of the cerebral cortex
	■ **Hypothalamus** (sometimes viewed as part of the limbic system)	■ Controls the endocrine system (described later in this chapter); controls the autonomic nervous system, internal temperature regulation, including appetite and thirst regulation, and other key functions; involved in regulation of behavior related to species survival; plays a role in controlling consciousness (see reticular activating system); involved in emotions, sexual response, pleasure, pain, and stress reactions

of the cortex through its *projection fibers*, which are neurons that project from one part of the brain to another. To accommodate all the types of information that must be sorted out, the thalamus is divided into groups of neurons with similar functions, called *nuclei*. The nuclei receive sensory information and project it to the cerebral cortex. For example, one nucleus, called the lateral geniculate nucleus, receives information from the visual

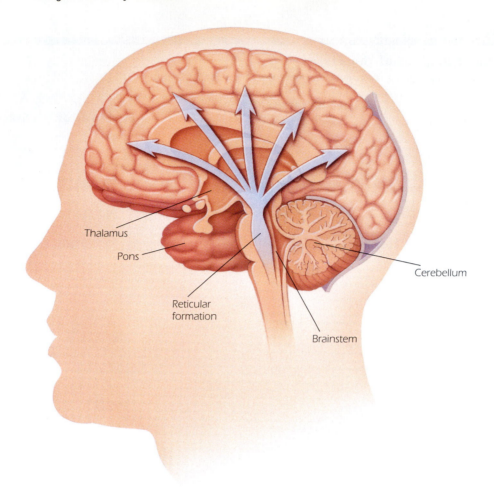

Figure 3–13
RETICULAR ACTIVATING SYSTEM. *The reticular activating system is important in regulating sleep and waking, and arousal in general.*

receptor neurons via the optic nerves and projects the information to the visual cortex, permitting us to see. The thalamus also helps in the control of sleep and waking. Both the thalamus and the reticular activating system are essential to our having any conscious awareness of or control over our existence.

The *basal ganglia* constitute a set of structures close to the thalamus. In conditions where there is deterioration of the basal ganglia, such as Parkinson's disease and Huntington's disease, individuals show diverse symptoms, including impaired movement, attention disorders, and memory and thinking deficits.

The Hypothalamus, Regulating Biological Systems

The **hypothalamus** is a structure located at the base of the forebrain, beneath the thalamus. The hypothalamus is roughly the size of a kidney bean. The small size of this structure belies its important function: It controls water balance in the tissues and

bloodstream, as well as many other functions of the autonomic nervous system (see Table 3-1 for more information). The hypothalamus, which interacts with and is often viewed as part of the limbic system, also regulates behavior related to species survival: fighting, feeding, fleeing, and mating. It makes sense, therefore, that the hypothalamus is also active in regulating emotions and reactions to stress. Mild electrical stimulation in particular areas of the hypothalamus causes pleasurable sensations, whereas stimulation in nearby areas causes sensations of pain. The hypothalamus also plays an important role in regulating the hormonal, or endocrine system, discussed later in this chapter.

The Cerebral Hemispheres and the Cerebral Cortex

The *cerebral cortex* forms the outer layer of the cerebral hemispheres (the right and left halves of the brain) and plays such a vital role in our thinking and other mental processes that it merits a special section. The cerebral hemispheres and the cerebral cortex together make up the *cerebrum*, that essential part of the human brain that sets us apart from other members of the animal kingdom by allowing us a greater range of psychological functioning.

The **cerebral cortex** is a 2-millimeter-deep layer on the surface of the brain. The cortex enfolds the brain, somewhat like the bark of a tree wraps around the trunk. In human beings, the cerebral cortex is highly *convoluted*, containing many folds. The purpose of these folds is to increase the surface area of the cortex; if the wrinkly human cortex were smoothed out, it would take up about 2 square feet. The cortex comprises 80% of the human brain. The cerebral cortex is responsible for our being able to plan, coordinate thoughts and actions, perceive visual and sound patterns, use language, and in general, to think.

The surface of the cerebral cortex is grayish because it primarily contains the gray neurons that processes the information that the brain receives and sends. The cerebral cortex is sometimes referred to as the *gray matter* of the brain. In contrast, the underlying *white matter* of the brain's interior comprises mostly white-colored neurons, which conduct information. The white matter comprises axons covered with myelin, whereas the gray matter comprises axons that are not so covered. Both the white and the gray matter are essential to cognitive abilities such as reasoning and decision making.

The cerebral cortex is actually the outer layer of the two rounded halves of the brain, the **left** and **right cerebral hemispheres.** Although the two hemispheres look quite similar on visual inspection, they function quite differently. The left hemisphere is specialized for some kinds of activity, the right for other kinds. Much information transmission travels from one side of the body (e.g., the left) to the part of the brain on the opposite side (e.g., the right). Note that not all information transmission is *contralateral*, occurring or appearing on the opposite-side. Some same-side, or *ipsilateral*, transmission occurs as well (see Figure 3-14).

Despite this general tendency for contralateral specialization, the hemispheres do communicate with each other. The **corpus callosum,** a dense body of nerve fibers, connects the two cerebral hemispheres (see Figure 3-15). Once information has reached one hemisphere, the corpus callosum allows that information to travel across to the other hemisphere without difficulty. Research shows that when the corpus callosum is severed, cognitive functioning, such as learning and memory performance, is impaired (Jha, Neal, Baynes, & Gazzaniga, 1997).

How did psychologists find out that the two hemispheres have different responsibilities? Chapter 2 mentioned brain-hemisphere research in general

terms; we now look more closely at the kinds of research that led to the discovery of specialized functioning in each hemisphere, a key feature of brain function.

Hemispheric Specialization

A major figure in the study of hemispheric specialization was Paul Broca. At a meeting of the French Society of Anthropology in 1861, Broca noted that a patient of his with *aphasia*, a loss of speech as a result of brain damage, was shown later to have a lesion in the left cerebral hemisphere of the brain. Despite an initially cool response to his ideas, Broca soon became a central figure in the heated controversy over whether functions, particularly speech, are indeed localized in particular areas of the brain, rather than generalized over the entire brain. By 1864, Broca was convinced that the left hemisphere of the brain is critical for speech. This was a view that others before him had proposed, and a view that has held up over time. In fact, the specific area Broca identified as contributing to speech is today referred to as Broca's area (see Figure 3-21 at the conclusion of this section). (Curiously, although people with lesions in Broca's area cannot speak fluently, they can use their voices to sing or shout.) Another important early researcher, German neurologist Carl Wernicke (1848–1905), studied language-deficient patients who could speak, but whose speech made no sense. He also traced language ability to the left hemisphere, though to a different precise location, now known as Wernicke's area (see Figure 3-21, p. 87).

Others continued in this tradition, studying problems such as *apraxia*, the inability to perform movements upon request, and *agnosia*, the inability to recognize familiar objects, often faces. In addition to Broca's and Wernicke's case-study research and postmortem examination of brains, other researchers (e.g., Penfield & Roberts, 1959) have used techniques, such as stimulation by electrodes, to map specific functions to particular areas of the brain. For example, following the stimulation of the speech area of the human brain, people experience temporary aphasia.

Despite these valuable early contributions, the individual most responsible for modern theory and research on hemispheric specialization is Nobel Prize–winning American psychologist Roger Sperry. Sperry (1964a, 1964b) argued that each hemisphere behaves in many respects like a separate brain. In a classic experiment that supports this contention, Sperry and his colleagues (Sperry, 1964a) severed the corpus callosum connecting the two hemispheres of a cat's brain. They then showed that information presented visually to one cerebral hemisphere of the cat was not recognizable to the other hemisphere.

Split-Brain Studies

Some of the most interesting information about how the human brain works, and especially about the respective roles of the hemispheres, has emerged from studies of humans with epilepsy in whom a severed corpus callosum prevents epileptic seizures from spreading from one hemisphere to the other, thereby greatly lessening their severity. This procedure also results in a loss of communication between the two hemispheres. It is as if the person had two separate specialized brains processing different information and performing separate functions.

People who have undergone such operations are termed *split-brain* patients. Although split-brain patients behave normally in many respects, in a few ways their behavior is bizarre. Instances have been reported

Figure 3–14

VISUAL INPUT TO A SPLIT BRAIN.   *Input received from the left visual field reaches the right side of each eye and is transmitted to the right hemisphere of the brain. Input received from the right visual field reaches the left side of each eye and is transmitted to the left hemisphere of the brain. Typically, information is shared between the two hemispheres. In split brain patients, however, the corpus callosum connecting the two hemispheres has been severed, so that sharing of information is not possible. Thus, information can be presented by an experimenter to one hemisphere without its being shared by the other hemisphere.*

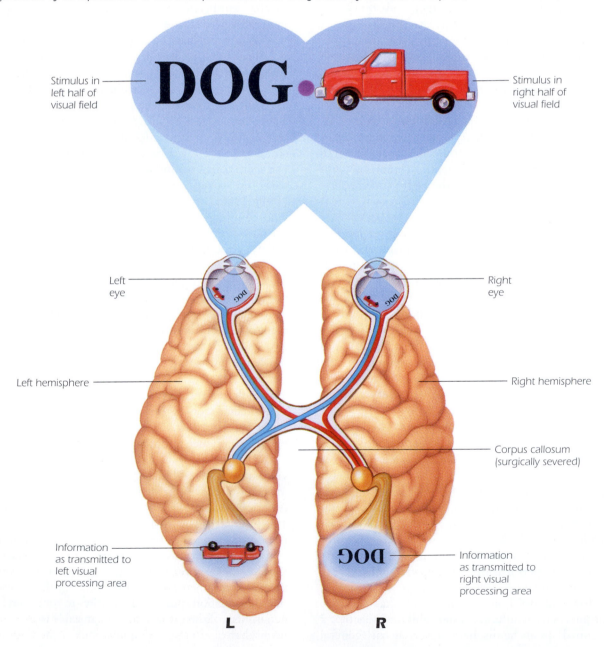

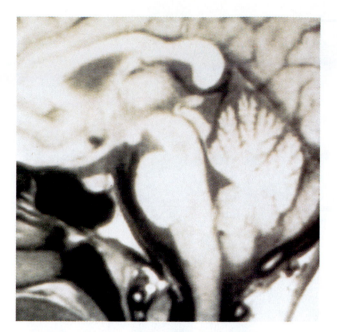

Figure 3–15

CORPUS CALLOSUM. *This dense network of fibers, shown from the base of the brain, provides a fundamental communication link between the two cerebral hemispheres.*

of a person's left hand struggling against the right hand in order to accomplish a task such as putting on pants. A patient, angry at his wife, reached to strike her with his left hand while his right hand tried to protect her and stop his left one (Gazzaniga, 1970). Split-brain patients almost literally have two separate minds of their own.

Split-brain research reveals fascinating possibilities regarding the ways we think. Many investigators in the field have argued that language is completely localized in the left hemisphere, and that *visuospatial* ability, a set of skills involving aspects of visual and spatial orientation and perception, is localized in the right hemisphere (Farah, 1988a, 1988b; Gazzaniga, 1985; Zaidel, 1983). For example, the ability to understand this sentence would be localized in the left hemisphere, but the ability to imagine what a car would look like if it were rotated 180 degrees would be localized in the right hemisphere. Jerre Levy (one of Sperry's students) and colleagues (Levy, Trevarthen, & Sperry, 1972) have probed the link between the cerebral hemispheres and visuospatial versus language-oriented tasks, using participants who have undergone split-brain surgery.

In one kind of study, the participant is asked to focus his or her gaze on the center of a screen. Then a *chimeric face* (a face showing the left side of the face of one person and the right side of another) is flashed on the screen. The participant is asked to identify what he or she saw, either verbally or by

pointing to one of several normal (not chimeric) faces (see Figure 3-16).

Typically, split-brain patients are unaware that they saw conflicting information in the two halves of the picture. When asked to give an answer in words about what they saw, they say that they saw the right half of the picture. Bearing in mind the contralateral association between hemisphere and side of the body, it seems that the left hemisphere controls their verbal processing of visual information—their speaking about what they saw. In contrast, when asked to use their fingers to point to what they saw, participants chose the image from the left half of the picture. This finding indicates that the right hemisphere appears to control spatial processing, or pointing out, visual information. Thus, the task that the participants are asked to perform is crucial in determining what image the participant thinks was shown.

How Distinct Are the Two Hemispheres?

Are the two sides of the brain really so distinct in their functioning? Additional split-brain research supports the view that visuospatial processing occurs primarily in the right hemisphere (Gazzaniga, 1985; Gazzaniga & LeDoux, 1978) and language processing primarily in the left hemisphere, although some researchers hold that the right hemisphere may have some role in language processing. Michael Gazzaniga (1985; Gazzaniga, Ivry, & Mangun, 1998) has argued that the brain, especially the right hemisphere, is organized into relatively independent functioning units that work in parallel. According to Gazzaniga, the many discrete units of the mind operate relatively independently of the others, often outside of conscious awareness. While these various independent and often subconscious operations are taking place, the left hemisphere tries to assign interpretations to these operations. Even when the left hemisphere perceives that the individual is behaving in a way that does not intrinsically make any particular sense, it still finds a way to assign some meaning to that behavior.

Some biopsychological researchers have also tried to determine whether the two hemispheres think in ways that differ from one another. Levy (1974) found some evidence that the left hemisphere tends to process information *analytically* (piece by piece, usually in a sequence) and the right hemisphere to process it *holistically* (as a whole, all at once). In another study, Schiffer, Zaidel, Bogen, and Chasan-Taber (1998) have found that the right hemisphere of a split-brain patient appeared to be more disturbed than the left hemisphere by childhood memories of the individual's being bullied. At present, the specific distinctions between the right and left hemispheres are subject to alternative explanations of the findings.

Figure 3–16

CHIMERIC FACES. *Research on split-brain patients reveals that each hemisphere of the brain processes images and other information distinctively. (a) A composite photograph of two different faces is flashed before a split-brain participant. (b) When shown a group of photographs and asked to pick out the person shown in the composite, the participant will say it is the face from the right half of the composite. (c) However, if asked to point out which one the participant originally saw, she will indicate the picture from the left side of the composite. (After Levy, Trevarthen, & Sperry, 1972)*

As always, alternative scientific interpretations of the same data make science both frustrating and exciting.

Thinking in Pictures and Symbols

Cross-cultural research offers yet another way of looking at the contrasting localizations of visuospatial and sound-based language symbols. In school, Japanese children study two forms of written language: *kanji*, which is based on Chinese ideographs and conveys an entire idea within each symbol, and *kana*, which is based on pho-

netic syllables and can be used for writing foreign words such as scientific terms (see Figure 3-17). In the 1970s, Japanese researchers started wondering whether the pictorial versus the phonetic forms might be processed differently in the two hemispheres of the brain. Some concluded that Japanese children and adults process the phonetic-based *kana* entirely in the left hemisphere but the picture-based *kanji* in both the left and the right hemispheres (Shibazaki, 1983; Shimada & Otsuka, 1981; Sibitani, 1980; Tsunoda, 1979). It seems that to explore and understand the diverse abilities

Figure 3-17
PICTURES VERSUS SYMBOLS. *Japanese schoolchildren study two forms of written language:* kanji *and* kana. Kanji *is based on Chinese ideographs and conveys an entire idea within each symbol;* kana *is based on phonetic syllables. In the 1970s, Japanese researchers studied whether the pictorial and phonetic forms are processed differently in the two hemispheres of the brain. Some concluded that the phonetic-based* kana *is processed in the left hemisphere, while the picture-based* kanji *is processed in both hemispheres.*

and functions of the human brain, researchers must study the rich diversity within the human community.

Lobes of the Cerebral Hemispheres and Cortex

Hemispheric specialization is only one way to view the various parts of the cortex. Another way to look at the cortex is to divide it into four *lobes:* frontal, parietal, temporal, and occipital (shown in Figure 3-21). These lobes are not distinct units but rather arbitrary anatomical regions, named for the bones of the skull lying directly over them. We are able to distinguish some local specializations among the lobes, but the lobes also interact. Roughly speaking, higher thought processes, such as abstract reasoning and motor processing, occur in the **frontal lobe,** *somatosensory* processing of the sensations in the skin and muscles of the body in the **parietal lobe,** auditory processing in the **temporal lobe,** and visual processing in the **occipital lobe.**

Sensory processing occurs in the **projection areas** where the neurons containing sensory information from the eyes, ears, lips, tongue, nose, and skin senses go to the thalamus, from which they are projected to the appropriate area in the relevant lobe. Similarly, the projection areas relay motor information downward through the spinal cord, via the PNS, to the appropriate muscles to direct their movement. When sensory information reaches the lobes of the brain, what happens? Consider first what happens in the frontal lobe.

Frontal Lobe

The frontal lobe is located toward the front of the head. It contains the **primary motor cortex,** which specializes in the planning, control, and execution of movement, particularly movement involving any kind of delayed response. If your motor cortex were electrically stimulated, you would react by moving a corresponding body part, depending on where in the motor cortex your brain had been stimulated.

As with the hemispheres in general, control of body movements is located contralaterally on the primary motor cortex. A similar inverse mapping occurs from top to bottom, with the lower extremities of the body represented on the upper side of the motor cortex, toward the top of the head, and the upper part of your body represented on the lower side of your motor cortex. Information going to neighboring parts of the body also comes from neighboring parts of the motor cortex. Thus, the motor cortex can be mapped to show where and in what proportions different parts of the body are represented in the brain. Such a map is often called a *homunculus,* which means "little person" (see Figure 3-18). Motor functioning works in conjunction with the sensory functioning, largely controlled by the parietal lobe.

Parietal Lobe

The three other lobes are located farther away from the front of the head. These lobes specialize in various kinds of sensory and perceptual activity. For example, in the parietal lobe, the **primary somatosensory cortex,** located right behind the frontal lobe's primary motor cortex, receives information from the senses about pressure, texture, temperature, and pain. If your somatosensory cortex were electrically stimulated, you would probably report feeling as if you had been touched. The parietal lobe is also involved in attention. As with the primary motor cortex in the frontal lobe, a homunculus of the somatosensory cortex can

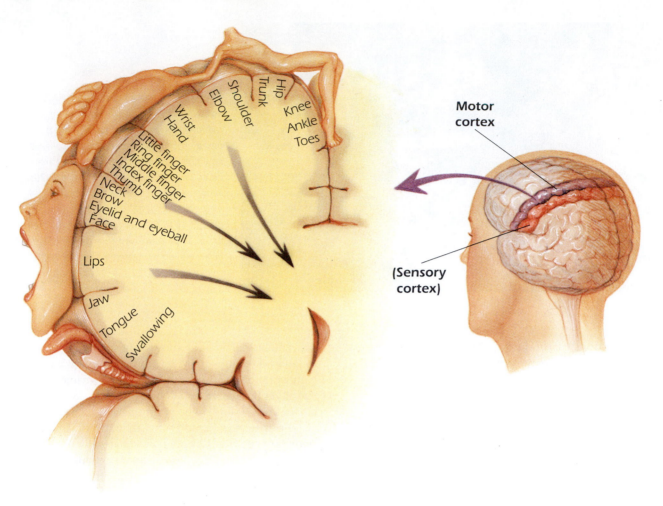

Figure 3–18
HOMUNCULUS OF THE MOTOR CORTEX. *The proportion of information received from the body's parts and sent to them can be mapped in the motor cortex of the frontal lobe.*

be used to map the parts of the body from which it receives information (see Figure 3-19).

From looking at the motor and sensory homunculi, you can see that the relation of function to form applies in the development of the motor and somatosensory cortex regions: The more need we have for use, sensitivity, and fine control in a particular body part, the larger the area of cortex that is generally devoted to that part. It appears that the brain has evolved such that its form relates to its function, including the auditory function, considered next.

Temporal Lobe

The region of the cerebral cortex pertaining to hearing is located in the temporal lobe. This lobe, located just above the ear, performs complex auditory analysis, as is needed in understanding human speech or in listening to a symphony. Damage to parts of the temporal lobe can cause impaired comprehension of speech, in particular, and of language, in general.

The temporal lobe is specialized: Some parts are more sensitive to sounds of higher pitch, others to sounds of lower pitch. The auditory region, like the other regions we have discussed, is primarily contralateral, with processing on one side of the auditory cortex depending mostly on sensory information from the ear on the opposite side. However, both sides of the auditory area have at least some representation from each ear. If your auditory cortex were stimulated electrically, you would report having heard some sort of sound. Hearing must be coordinated with vision, controlled in the brain by the occipital lobe. Without such coordination, you would be unable to understand movies, television, or even everyday conversations where you combine auditory and visual cues.

Occipital Lobe

The visual region of the cerebral cortex is primarily in the occipital lobe, at the back of the head. Some neurons carrying visual information travel ipsilaterally

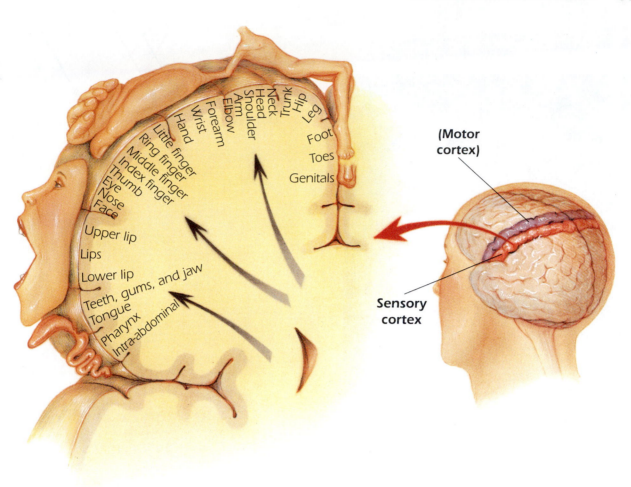

Figure 3–19

HOMUNCULUS OF THE SOMATOSENSORY CORTEX. *As with the motor homunculus, the proportion of sensory information received from the parts of the body can be mapped in the somatosensory cortex of the parietal lobe.*

from the left eye to the left cerebral hemisphere and from the right eye to the right cerebral hemisphere. Other neural fibers cross over the **optic chiasma** and go contralaterally to the opposite hemisphere (see Figure 3-20). In particular, neurons go from the left side of the visual field for each eye to the right side of the visual cortex; complementarily, the neurons from the right side of each eye's visual field go to the left side of the visual cortex. Electrical stimulation of the visual cortex results in the perception of random patterns of light, much like when you close your eyes and gently rub across your eyelids. (See Figure 3-21 for a summary of the cortical locations of the various lobes.)

Association Areas

It is in the interconnections among our senses, body movements, and thought processes that the brain is working at some of its most complex levels. It therefore is not surprising that a great deal of the brain would be devoted to areas that handle associations among various areas and functions of the brain. The areas of the lobes that are not part of the somatosensory, motor, auditory, or visual cortices are **association areas,** which make up roughly 75% of the cerebral cortex, although in most other animals the association areas are much smaller. It used to be thought that the association areas of the cortex are primarily responsible for linking the activity of the sensory and motor cortices. It now appears, however, that the association areas are best viewed as processing sensory information more elaborately than do the primary sensory areas of the brain (Van Hoesen, 1993). For example, it is estimated that more than 50% of the cortex in the primate brain is used for visual processing. Thus, the association cortex adjacent to the primary visual cortex is responsive to visual information, rather than being used to "associate" visual information to motor information. Moreover, input to the association areas does not come exclusively from primary sensory areas of the cortex. It

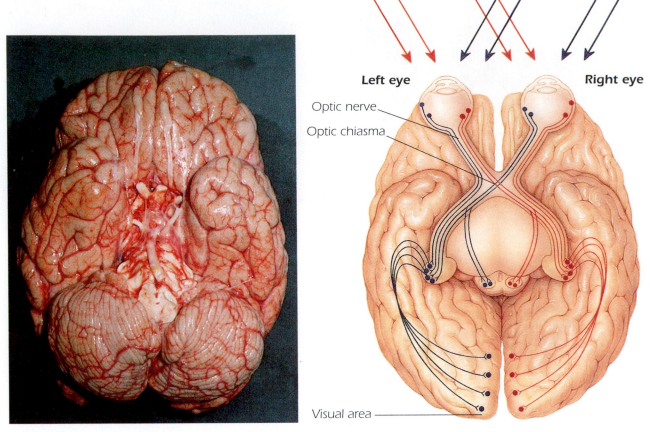

Figure 3–20
OPTIC NERVES AND OPTIC CHIASMA. *Some nerve fibers carry visual information ipsilaterally from each eye to each cerebral hemisphere; other fibers cross the optic chiasma and carry visual information contralaterally to the opposite hemisphere.*

can come from sensory areas of the thalamus too (Diamond, 1979, 1983). Thus, association cortex is now viewed as used for elaborated sensory processing rather than for "association," per se. In fact, there does not appear to be any one area of the brain that "associates." Association functions appear to be diffused throughout the brain.

The frontal association area in the frontal lobe seems to be crucial to problem solving, planning, judgment, and personality. In a situation calling for escape from danger, for example, people with a damaged frontal lobe know that they ought to run away. Paradoxically, however, they may stand still, incapable of initiating flight. Broca's and Wernicke's speech areas, mentioned earlier in this chapter, are also located in association areas. Although the roles of association areas in thinking are not completely understood, these areas definitely seem to be places in the brain in which a variety of intellectual abilities are seated.

Given all the activities of the brain, it may not surprise you to learn that although the brain typically makes up only 2.5% (one-fortieth) of the weight of an adult human body, it uses about 20% (one-fifth) of the circulating blood, 20% of the available *glucose* (the blood sugar that supplies the body with energy), and 20% of the available oxygen. It is now technologically possible to watch the brain and its use of some of these substances. These research methods are greatly expanding our understanding of the location and integration of brain functions. The Psychology in Everyday Life box, Seeing Inside the Brain, describes some of the methods used to view the structure and functioning of the brain.

Measuring Electrical Activity

The electrical activity of the entire living brain can be measured by the tried-and-true method of using electrodes to obtain an **electroencephalogram**—an **EEG.** To obtain EEG recordings, electrodes establish contact between the brain and a device that sums the effects of brain activity over large areas containing

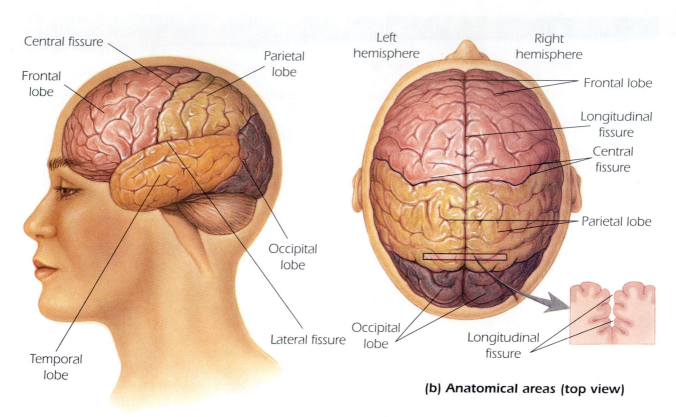

(a) Anatomical areas (left lateral view)

(b) Anatomical areas (top view)

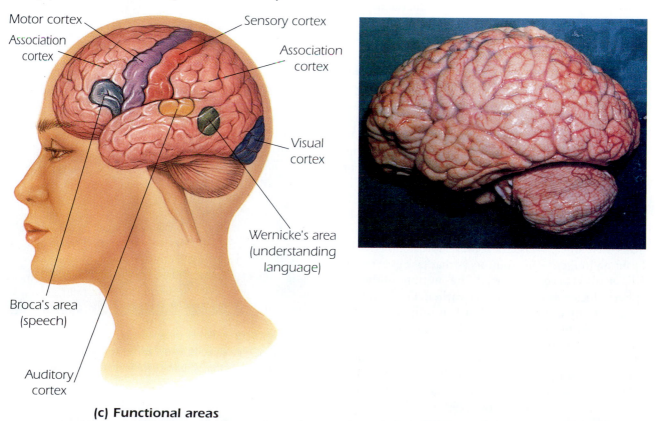

(c) Functional areas

Figure 3–21
LOBES OF THE CEREBRAL CORTEX. *The cortex is divided into the frontal, parietal, temporal, and occipital lobes. The lobes have specific functions but also interact to perform complex processes.*

Psychology in Everyday Life

Seeing Inside the Brain

When Marta Koopmans hit a crack in the pavement in the dark and was thrown from her bike, the doctors at the emergency room were concerned about a possible head injury. She had been riding without a helmet, and admitted she had "blacked out a little" for what she thought was a minute or two. She had a serious cut requiring stitches above her left eye. Brain trauma can cause swelling of the brain or bleeding in the *dura mater*, the tough membrane which is the outermost covering of the brain and spinal cord, that can put pressure on the brain. Either can result in brain damage. For centuries, the only means available for seeing the brain was through surgery or autopsy. As valuable as such studies have been and continue to be, scientists are not content merely to study the state of dead brains. As Marta's example illustrates, an organ characterized by constant dynamic activity seems to cry out for methods to study it *in vivo* (within living organisms) and noninvasively. Contemporary microscopic and biochemical techniques developed in the last half century allow scientists to study dissected portions of the brain at increasingly precise levels of detail. The images these methods yield can help doctors pinpoint problems and injuries and also have enabled researchers to understand more about the areas of the brain where certain mental functions, such as listening to music or thinking about a math problem, take place.

many neurons. Usually, electrodes are attached directly to the scalp; sometimes, however, microelectrodes are inserted into the brain. The former technique is used with humans, the latter with animals. In either case, the minute quantifiable fluctuations of electrical activity picked up by the electrodes are amplified, and an oscilloscope displays the amplified electrical activity as up or down fluctuations of waves. (Often, now, computer screens are used instead of oscilloscopes.) The patterns of electrical waves indicate different levels and kinds of brain activity (see Figure 3-22).

The use of EEG measurement has been particularly helpful for the study of mental functioning, especially sleep, awareness, and brain disease. For example, there appears to be an overall decrease in the extent of cortical activation as measured by EEG after practice on various kinds of cognitive tasks (Smith, McEvoy, & Gevins, 1999). This result suggests that once a task becomes more familiar, the brain no longer needs to process that task as actively. EEGs also have supported the notion of hemispheric localization discussed earlier. For example, more activity occurs in the left hemisphere during a verbal task, more in the right hemisphere during a spatial task (Kosslyn, 1988; Springer & Deutsch, 1985). Different patterns of EEG also have been found in individuals with different personality-related emotional responses to faces (Pizzagalli, Koenig, Regard, & Lehmann, 1999).

EEG measurement is problematic, however, because it is a *hash recording*. The EEG measures the electrical activity of many large areas in the brain at once, so it is hard to sort out exactly where particular wave forms

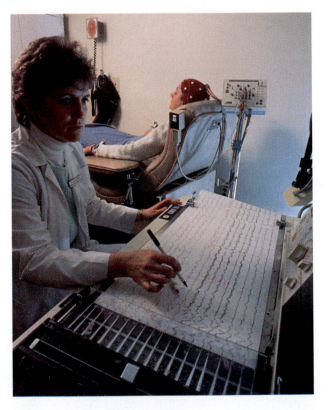

Figure 3-22
ELECTROENCEPHALOGRAMS (EEGS).   *EEGs record electrical activity and translate the data into wave patterns.*

are originating. For this reason, investigators have turned to the use of **event-related potentials (ERPs),** which are measured by averaging wave forms on successive EEG recordings. In other words, an ERP is an

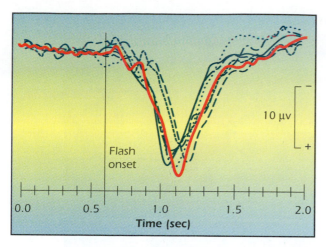

Figure 3–23
EVENT-RELATED POTENTIAL (ERP). *An ERP is a series of EEG recordings in which the variability of electrical interference has been averaged out of the data. The colored line here is averaged from the many recordings shown beneath it.*

EEG recording with respect to a specific stimulus event in which at least some of the electrical interference has been averaged out of the data (see Figure 3-23). Note that ERPs are brain responses that always are linked to a particular stimulus event. Event-related potentials have been used to map which parts of the brain are active and to what degree, in response to familiar and unfamiliar stimuli. For example, Helen Neville (1998) has studied people who were born deaf, and by using ERPs, she has discovered that their brains have an organization that is different from that of hearing people. In particular, visual ERPs are substantially larger in deaf than in hearing people, suggesting that parts of the brain that are used for auditory processing in hearing people are used for expanded visual processing in deaf people.

Despite many intriguing EEG and ERP findings, the EEG and the ERP provide only a limited understanding of various structures of the brain. We need some way of getting a picture of how a living, functioning person's brain is working. Fortunately, advances in technology have made it possible to observe the functioning of the brain with little discomfort to the patient. The photos and illustrations in this section show several of the many ways of viewing the brain.

X Rays

For most of the twentieth century, *neuroscientists* (psychologists and other scientists interested in studying the nervous system) have been able to take various kinds of snapshots of the living brain. The first of these techniques uses *X rays*, a type of electromagnetic radiation capable of passing through

solids. This technique yields a two-dimensional picture of the varying densities of the structures that have been scanned. Unfortunately, however, the density of most portions of the brain is roughly the same, so X-ray photos of the head are useful for showing skull fractures but little else that would be of concern to psychologists.

Angiograms are essentially X-ray pictures that have been enhanced to provide some visual contrast by injecting special dyes into the blood vessels of the head. Angiograms are most frequently used to study the functioning of the heart. Angiograms also often are used to assess *vascular* diseases (diseases of the blood vessels, which may lead to strokes) and to locate particular kinds of brain tumors, but they can also indicate which parts of the brain are active when people perform different kinds of listening, speaking, or movement tasks (see Figure 3-24a). Thus, angiograms provide dynamic information about the living brain, although this information focuses mostly on the blood vessels.

Brain Scans

As you might infer from the brain's extraordinarily great use of the nutrients and oxygen in the blood, any disturbance in the blood supply is dangerous. Impairment of the blood supply, whether due to clots, narrowed vessels, or hemorrhage, leads to stroke. Stroke, in turn, usually causes immediate

A lab technician gives a patient a CAT scan.

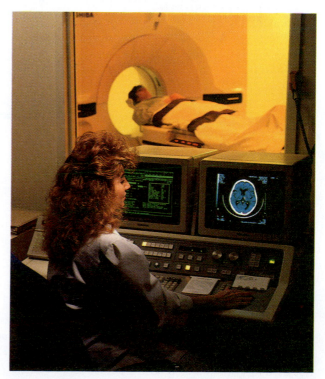

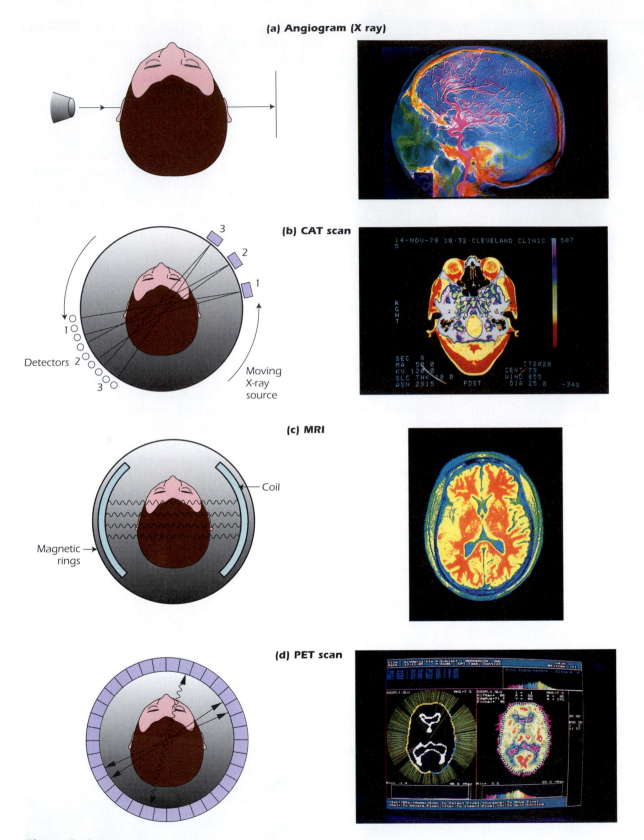

Figure 3–24

IMAGES OF THE BRAIN. *Researchers and physicians use various techniques to identify and diagnose the structures and processes of the brain. (a) A brain angiogram highlights the blood vessels of the brain. (b) CAT-scan images show a three-dimensional view of brain structures. (c) A rotating series of MRI scans show a clearer three-dimensional picture of brain structures than do CAT scans. (d) PET scans permit the study of brain physiology.*

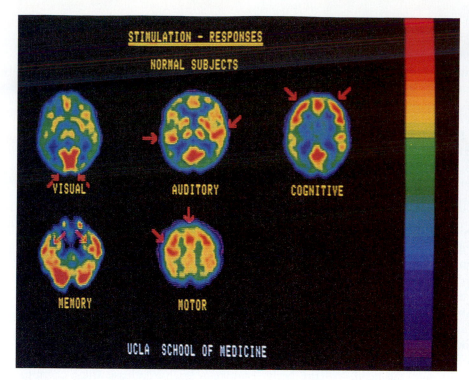
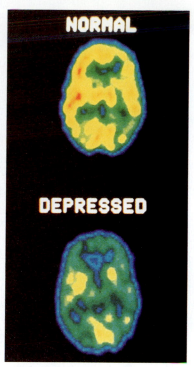

Figure 3–25
PET SCAN IMAGES. *Images from PET scans show different metabolic processes in reaction to different activities and stimuli, as well as different mental states.*

changes in consciousness. If the blood supply is impaired for any length of time, the surrounding tissue begins to die. The potentially devastating implications of stroke depend on the duration of the stroke and the area of the brain affected.

When clinicians and researchers try to detect strokes or other physiological bases for disorders, they often use a highly sophisticated X-ray-based technique for viewing the brain: the **computerized axial tomogram (CAT)** or *CAT scan.* The picture a CAT scan generates shows a cross-sectional slice of the brain (see Figure 3-24b). In this procedure, a patient lies on a table with his or her head in the middle of a doughnut-shaped ring that takes and analyzes X-ray pictures. The ring takes the pictures as it rotates 360 degrees around the patient's head. Thus, small amounts of X rays penetrate the head from many angles. Opposite the sources of the X rays in the ring are detectors recording the amount of X-ray radiation reaching them. This amount is determined by the density of tissue at various locations in the head. The more dense the material through which the X rays must pass, the smaller the amount of X-ray radiation reaching the detectors. A computer then analyzes the amount of radiation reaching each of the detectors and thereby constructs a three-dimensional X-ray picture of a cross-section of the brain, which is far more revealing than would be obtained if the pic-

tures were being taken from a single position only (see Figure 3-24b). CAT scans are often used to detect blood clots, tumors, or brain diseases, but they are also used by neuropsychologists to study how particular types and locations of brain damage affect people's behavior.

An even more sophisticated technique for revealing the structure of the brain is **magnetic resonance imaging (MRI),** also sometimes termed NMR, for nuclear magnetic resonance. The MRI scanner resembles a CAT scanner and reveals much of the same information, except that it uses no radiation, and its pictures are clearer and more detailed. With the patient lying down, an extremely strong magnetic field, which changes the orbits of nuclear particles in the molecules of the body, is passed through the part of the body being studied. The bursts of energy associated with these changes are registered over time and analyzed by computer. Different molecules in the body react differently to the magnetic field as a result of their composition and environments. The computer then generates a highly precise, three-dimensional picture based on the molecular variations (see Figure 3-24c).

Several types of MRI scans are now available. Structural MRI looks at static, anatomical images, whereas functional MRI (also called fMRI) measures changes in the magnetic state of the blood as a function of the blood's degree of oxygenation (Gabrieli et al., 1996; Ogawa, Lee, Nayak, & Glynn, 1990). Functional MRI has been used to identify regions of the brain active in many areas, such as vision (Engel et al., 1994), movement (S. G. Kim et al., 1993), language (McCarthy, Blamire, Rothman, Gruetter, & Shulman, 1993), attention (J. D. Cohen et al., 1994), and memory (Gabrieli et al., 1996; Squire et al., 1992; Tulving et al., 1994). For example, fMRI has been used to show that the lateral prefontal cortex is essential for working memory (see chapter 7), a part of memory that is used to process information that is actively in use at a given time (McCarthy et al., 1994).

Another breakthrough is **positron emission tomography (PET),** a scan that enables us to see the brain in action. A mildly radioactive form of glucose is injected into a patient and is absorbed by cells of the body. The amount of glucose absorption in the brain indicates the degree to which a given cell is metabolically active. While the irradiated glucose is going to the person's brain, the person's head is placed in a ring similar to that of the CAT scanner, and a beam of X rays is passed through the head. The radioactive substance is detected by the scanners. A computer then determines which portions of the brain have absorbed the most radioactive glucose, thereby determining the areas that are the most active (see Figure 3-24d). PET scans have been used to show which parts of the brain are active in such tasks as listening to music, playing computer games, speaking, and moving parts of the body (see Figure 3-25, p. 91). PET scans also have shown that dreaming during certain stages of sleep engages areas of the brain that are involved in language processing and other aspects of cognition (Gottschalk, Buchsbaum, Gillin, Wu et al., 1991). Because the PET scan shows the physiological functioning of the brain, not just its anatomical structure, this technique offers dynamic insights into the brain previously offered only by cruder techniques, such as the EEG and the angiogram. PET scanning has been used in many psychological studies attempting to localize function. For example, it has been used to show that attention to features of stimuli such as color, form, and movement occurs in a particular area of the brain called the extrastriate visual cortex (Corbetta, Miezin, Dobmeyer, Shulman, & Petersen, 1991; Corbetta, Miezin, Shulman, & Petersen, 1993).

New technology for viewing the brain is being developed. One of the latest techniques is *optical imaging*, which uses fiber-optic light and a special camera attached to a surgical microscope. The many imaging techniques that are becoming available shed new light on the brain, both literally and metaphorically.

The Endocrine System

In *Search of...* *What are the basic elements of the endocrine system and its functioning?*

Under most circumstances, the nervous system does an excellent job of communicating sensory information to our brains and motor information from our brains to our muscles. The nervous system is particularly effective in communicating specific information speedily, so that we can respond immediately to our environments. Sometimes, however, our bodies use an alternative mode of communication. This other communication network, which complements the nervous system, is the **endocrine system.** (Endocrine means *secreting or releasing inside.* Our bodies also have an *exocrine system,* by which some glands can secrete substances, such as tears or sweat, through *ducts* to outside the body.) The endocrine system operates by means of **glands,** groups of cells that secrete chemical substances for use elsewhere in the body. Endocrine glands release their chemical products directly into the bloodstream. The blood carries the secreted substances to the target organ or organs.

Hormones and the Brain

The chemical substances secreted by endocrine-system glands are **hormones,** which foster the growth and proliferation of cells. Hormones play an important part in growth and general human development and especially sexual development. In some cases, hormones affect the way a receptive cell goes about its activities. Hormones perform their work either by interacting with receptors on the surfaces of target cells or by entering target cells directly and interacting with specialized receptor molecules inside the cells. Some parallels exist between neurotransmitters and hormones: Hormones are chemical substances operating within a communications network, which are secreted by one set of cells (in the case of hormones, the glands), and then communicate a message to another set of cells (in this case, the target organ or organs). Also, the specific actions of the chemicals are largely determined by the nature of the receptors that receive the chemicals. For example, the same hormones that speed the heart can slow the digestive organs.

Thus, hormones, like transmitter substances, are key aspects of communication within the body. Indeed, some of the same substances that serve as transmitter substances in the nervous system also can serve as hormones in the bloodstream.

The whole endocrine system largely operates without our conscious control, and hormones are released reflexively. A stimulus from either inside or outside the body brings about a change in neural activity, which prompts secretion of one or more hormones. The body monitors the levels of a given hormone and the activities that the hormone affects through a *negative-feedback loop*, diagrammed in Figure 3-26. When the particular hormonal function has been accomplished or the hormone levels in the bloodstream have reached a desirable level, a message is sent to the brain (or to a more local command center), and the secretion is discontinued.

What are some of the major endocrine glands of the body, their major physical effects, and their psychological significance? Some of the major glands are depicted in Figure 3-27.

Endocrine Glands

Adrenal Glands

Each of the adrenal glands, which are located above the kidneys, consists of two parts: the adrenal *medulla* (inner part of an anatomical structure) and the adrenal *cortex* (outer part). These glands are very important in mood, energy level, and reaction to stress. The **adrenal medulla** secretes two hormones: epinephrine (also called "adrenaline") and norepinephrine (also called "noradrenaline"). When in the nervous system, epinephrine and norepineph-

rine can serve as neurotransmitters, but they can also serve as hormones when they are in the bloodstream. As a neurotransmitter, norepinephrine plays a more important role than epinephrine. For example, norepinephrine affects wakefulness. When the two substances function as hormones, both epinephrine and norepinephrine are intimately involved in sudden arousal reactions, such as increasing your heart rate and blood pressure and reducing the flow of blood to your digestive system, which can lead to a *fight-or-flight response:* When you feel a surge of energy in response to a crisis requiring confrontation or escape, the surge comes from adrenal arousal.

The *adrenal cortex* alone produces more than 50 hormones, which perform various functions, many of which are vital to physiological survival or to our sexual differentiation and reproductive function. Disturbing the complex balance of hormones can lead to unwanted consequences. For example, high doses of anabolic steroids—synthetic forms of the natural male sex hormones produced in the adrenal cortex—have been linked to extreme aggression, severe mood swings, and mental instability, as well as to sterility and other physiological damage or disease (Pope & Katz, 1988). Malfunction of another endocrine gland, the thyroid gland, can also have serious physiological and behavioral consequences. Baseball home-run star Mark McGwire dosed himself with a commercially available preparation (which was legal

Figure 3–26
NEGATIVE-FEEDBACK LOOP. *Through a negative-feedback loop, an endocrine gland monitors the levels of hormones in the bloodstream. If the monitoring processes yield negative responses (feedback), indicating the need for a higher level of a given hormone, the hormone secretion continues.*

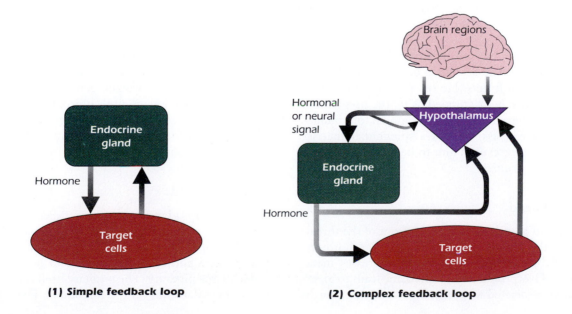

(1) Simple feedback loop

(2) Complex feedback loop

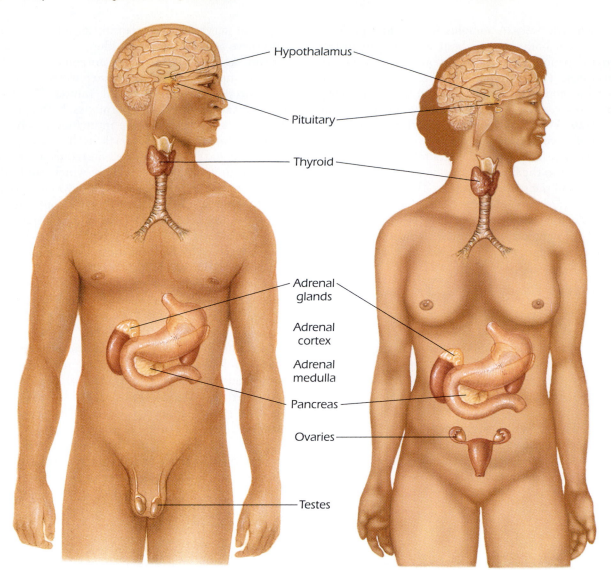

Figure 3–27
MAJOR ENDOCRINE GLANDS OF THE BODY. *The adrenal glands, thyroid gland, and pituitary gland are among the most important of the endocrine glands, but other glands also carry out important physiological functions.*

for use in baseball but not in most other sports) during the 1998 baseball season in order to increase his muscle mass and fitness. He set a home-run record. In the 1999 season, he stopped using the preparation because he believed it to set a bad model for younger people. Nevertheless, he had a splendid home-run season. Whatever caused him to be a home-run star, it was not the drug.

Thyroid Gland

The **thyroid gland,** located at the front of the throat, regulates the metabolic rate of cells. The hormone produced by the thyroid, *thyroxine,* increases metabolic rate. Overproduction of thyroxine leads to *hyperthyroidism,* associated with high blood pressure, weight

loss, and muscular weakness. Not enough thyroxine causes *hypothyroidism,* associated with slowed metabolism and consequent weight gain and sluggishness. Often, when physicians are confronted by patients who feel fatigued or depressed, they check the patients' thyroid function before making a referral for psychological counseling.

Pituitary Gland

The **pituitary gland,** sometimes called the master gland, is of central importance to the endocrine system. It controls many other endocrine glands, which release their hormones in response to hormones released by the pituitary. The pituitary itself is controlled by the hypothalamus (in the forebrain). The pituitary

In 1998 Mark McGuire used a legal form of anabolic steroids to build his muscle mass and thus improve his hitting. He stopped using the preparation in 1999 because he said he believed it set a bad example for young athletes.

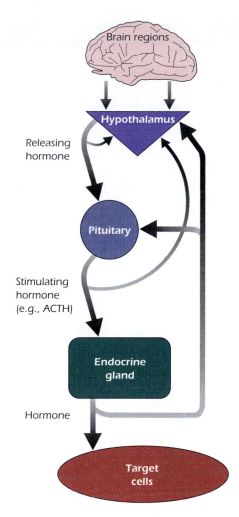

Figure 3-28
ACTION LOOP. *The physiological interaction of the pituitary gland and the hypothalamus provides a crucial link between the nervous system and the endocrine system.*

gland (located above the mouth and underneath the hypothalamus, to which it is attached) releases hormones that both directly and indirectly affect other physiological functions.

The pituitary also provides a direct link from the endocrine system to the nervous system. When the nervous system signals a stressful situation to the brain, neurons in the hypothalamus stimulate it to act on the pituitary. In response, the pituitary secretes *adrenocorticotropic hormone (ACTH)*, the primary stress hormone of our bodies. The bloodstream carries ACTH to various other organs, most notably the adrenal glands, which secrete, among other hormones, the fight-or-flight hormones of epinephrine and norepinephrine. This action loop is diagrammed in Figure 3-28.

Thus, the endocrine system provides a means of activating responses in the body via hormones in the bloodstream. The endocrine system is in some ways self-directing, but it is also subject to control by the nervous system via the hypothalamus. Nonetheless, both the endocrine system and the nervous system are an integral part of the fabulous network of the human body; both play important, but not yet fully understood, roles in defining the elusive relationship of the mind to the body.

Genetic Bases of Behavior

In Search of . . . *What is evolutionary theory, and how does it apply to psychology?*

To understand the influence of biology on psychologists' thinking, we need to understand the influence of evolutionary theory on biologists' thinking. Because psychologists are interested in behavior, and biological psychologists are interested in the interaction of the body and behavior, evolution is a good place to start.

Evolutionary Theory

The Nature of Evolutionary Theory

Evolutionary theory, which describes the ways our bodies and behaviors change across many generations of individuals, is usually credited to English naturalist Charles Darwin (1809–1882). In his book *The Origin of Species* (1859), Darwin proposed the notion of **natural selection,** the evolutionary principle describing a mechanism by which organisms have developed and changed, based on what is commonly called the "survival of the fittest." In this view, organisms show a great deal of biological variation. At a given time, some individual organisms will be better able to adapt to the given environmental conditions than will others. They will thereby have an advantage for survival and will eventually produce a larger number of viable offspring. Over generations, their progeny will become more prevalent. These individuals will have been selected by nature for survival—hence, the term *natural selection.* On average, those individuals that are not as well able to adapt will reproduce less successfully (where reproductive success is viewed in terms of number of viable offspring that will themselves eventually be able to reproduce). It is important to remember that as environmental conditions change, so potentially does the adaptability of each individual organism. Adaptability can be assessed only relative to a particular set of environmental conditions.

For example, during the Industrial Revolution in late 19th-century England, a particular dark-colored moth became more prevalent than a related light-colored moth. Why? Industrial pollution had blackened the forests, improving the darker moth's camouflage against predators such as birds. The light-colored moth became too visible to predators to survive. Recently, however, with restrictions on air pollution, the light moth is making a comeback. Thus, natural selection is a constantly shifting process, influenced not only by an organism's biology but also by the interaction of that biology with environmental conditions.

How have Darwin's ideas about natural selection come to influence psychology and the study of behavior? As humans have evolved, an increasing percentage of our behavior has come under voluntary control by the brain; our actions are more self-directed and less instinctual than those of many other animals whose brains are less developed (Pinker, 1998). Thus, biopsychologists study the nervous system to pinpoint its influence on our moods, feelings, drives, thought processes, and behavior. Others in fields related to psychology have also attempted to apply evolutionary principles of natural selection to human behavior, although using approaches very different from the biopsychological approach. It is important to remember that, from an evolutionary standpoint, the adaptive success of an organism depends on its fit to an environmental niche. If, for example, there were major climatic changes in the

world, the organisms that would survive would be those that were able to adjust to the changes, whether or not they are complex in the sense of having well-evolved brains or anything else.

Evolutionary theory is important not only for the concept of natural selection, but also for its embodiment of the philosophy of *functionalism*, discussed in the previous chapter: Just as early functionalists in psychology sought to understand *why* people behave as they do, functionalists who have studied evolution have sought to explain *why* organisms change and evolve as they do. What purpose does a particular evolutionary change serve for the organism undergoing the change? From a functionalist standpoint, we seek to understand natural selection in terms of what enables some individuals to adapt and reproduce more successfully than do others.

According to evolutionary theory as it was originally posed, evolution through natural selection has been gradual. Recently, however, some theorists have proposed an alternative viewpoint: punctuated equilibrium. According to the viewpoint of *punctuated equilibrium*, organisms remain relatively stable for long periods of time, with such periods of stability punctuated by relatively brief periods (on an evolutionary scale) of rapid change (e.g., Gould, 1981). Stephen Jay Gould and others agree with Darwin that natural selection is the key to evolution. They merely disagree with him regarding the timing of evolutionary processes.

The Uses and Limitations of Evolutionary Theory in Psychology

Evolutionary theory provides a wonderful, unified framework for understanding many and diverse phenomena in psychology. Just as we seek to understand the evolution of ideas in order to appreciate how psychologists and others have come to think the way they do (see chapter 2), we can seek to understand the evolution of organisms in order to appreciate how they have come to be the way they are.

Sometimes, evolutionary theory provides us with a basis for understanding phenomena that are difficult to explain in any other way. For example, Leda Cosmides (1989) found that in a certain type of reasoning task, people reason better if the content of the task pertains to people being cheated than if it pertains to other things. Why would people be at an advantage when the problem deals with cheating behavior? Because, according to Cosmides, we have evolved in a way that makes us particularly sensitive to cheating. Our ancestors who were not sensitive to being cheated were at a disadvantage in adapting to their environments, and by letting themselves be taken advantage of, they had fewer opportunities to reproduce. For example, they may have let themselves be cheated out of reproductive opportunities or perhaps the food they needed to stay alive and reach the point when they could reproduce. Whatever the case, people who were good "cheater detectors" were at an adaptive advantage and more likely to have been our ancestors than those who were poor cheater detectors.

In this book, we will see in every chapter at least some reference both to the evolution of organisms and to the evolution of ideas. Is there any relation between the two kinds of evolution? Perhaps. Richard Dawkins (1989) has speculated that essentially the same laws of evolution that apply to organisms may apply to cultural artifacts, including ideas. And a number of psychologists have suggested that ideas may evolve along the lines of a mechanism whereby the "fittest" survive, namely, those that are best adapted to the cultural milieu in which they are proposed and diffused (D. T. Campbell, 1960; Lumsden, 1998; Perkins, 1995b; Simonton, 1995, 1998). On the one hand, we need to recognize that ideas are not living organisms in the same way that people are. On the other hand, we can also recognize that ideas, like organisms, can fit more or less well into an environmental niche. Their fit does not render them true: Cultures have accepted, over the years, many ideas that are demonstrably false, such as the idea that a mysterious (and, in fact, nonexistent) substance called phlogiston (the hypothetical principle of fire regarded formerly as a material substance) causes fire or that the soul leaves the body temporarily when one sneezes. Evolutionary theory does not provide any kind of code of truth or ethics. Neither organisms nor ideas that fit a given environment are in any real sense better than others in an absolute sense. Rather, they are simply organisms or ideas that are well adapted to a given time or place.

Although evolution provides a useful framework for understanding many psychological phenomena, we need to be careful not to push this or any other framework too far. We can end up in a position where we take whatever phenomenon we observe and then, after the fact, construct an evolutionary "explanation" for it, just as we would have if we had found the opposite phenomenon. In such cases, evolutionary interpretations cannot be refuted, because they are created after the fact to account for whatever is found. The evolutionary framework, like all others, is useful if we realize that it can provide a way of understanding some phenomena, but that it is no more a panacea than is any other single framework. No one framework will provide the answers to all the questions we might ask in psychology.

A final aspect of our consideration of the biological bases of behavior is even more minute than the neurons described earlier. Inside each cell, our **genes** provide the basic physiological building blocks for the hereditary transmission of our **biological traits**—the distinctive characteristics or behavior patterns that are genetically determined. We receive our genes, and hence our traits, from our parents at the time of our conception. Though no one doubts that genes influence behavior, the degree to which our genes influence behavior is a matter of ongoing research and debate in the field of psychology. **Behavioral genetics** is a branch of psychology that attempts to attribute behavior and certain psychological characteristics at least in part, to particular combinations of genes.

Genetics

Modern genetic theory dates back to the research of an Austrian monk and botanist, Gregor Mendel (1822–1884), who performed breeding experiments on common varieties of the garden pea. Mendel observed some interesting effects in the inheritance of attributes of the pea. For example, if true-breeding tall pea plants (ones that always produce tall offspring) are crossed with true-breeding dwarf pea plants (ones that always produce small offspring), the offspring of the tall and the dwarf plants will always be tall. Mendel referred to the stronger attribute that appeared in this first generation of offspring as the **dominant trait** (here, tallness). He called the weaker trait, which did not appear, the **recessive trait** (here, dwarfism).

Next, if you interbreed all of the tall members of the first generation of offspring, the second generation of offspring will have both tall and short plants, in a ratio of about three tall plants to every one short plant. How can we account for this odd potpourri of results? Today, we know that these results are due to genes.

To make this example simple, suppose that the height of a plant is controlled by exactly two genes, one from each parent. Both inherited genes may be for tallness, both may be for dwarfism, or one may be for tallness and one for dwarfism. If we represent tallness by T and dwarfism by d, then the possible gene combinations—the possible **genotypes** (the pair of genes on a given chromosome pair, which is inherited from each parent and *not* subject to environmental influence—except in cases of genetic mutation)—for height in the plant are TT, Td, dT, or dd. Now we need to know just one principle: Whenever a dominant gene is paired with a recessive gene, even though both genes are present, the *observable result*—the **phenotype** (expression of an inherited trait, based on the dominant trait in the genotype and also subject to environmental influence)—will be the dominant trait. Mendel determined that tallness was dominant because a plant with TT, Td, or dT gene combinations shows up as tall, whereas only a plant with a dd gene combination shows up as short.

Now we can account for Mendel's results in the varied heights of his pea plants in different generations. In the first generation, all offspring were hybrids, meaning that they contained mixed gene patterns (Td and dT). Because tallness (T) is the dominant trait, all offspring appeared tall. In the second generation of offspring, however, equal numbers of TT, Td, dT, and dd offspring existed. In this generation, three of the genotypes (TT, Td, dT) produce the phenotype of tall plants, and only one of the genotypes (dd) produces the phenotype of a short plant. (See Figure 3-29 for a chart of Mendel's results.)

One Genotype, Widely Varying Phenotypes

In humans, the expression of a single genotype can give rise to a fairly wide range of phenotypes, because the science of genetics is not as simple as what we have just seen. For example, a person's height is largely genetically controlled, but a range of actual phenotypic heights may be reached, depending on other factors such as nutrition, hormones (described in regard to the endocrine system, later in this chapter), and immune-system efficiency. Thus, the expression even of traits that are genetically based is not completely controlled by genetics. Genes do help to determine phenotypes, but so do other influences, such as the environment.

The environment that is ideal for one genotype may not be ideal for another. For example, the ideal environment for the white moth is different from the ideal environment for the gray moth. Which set of genes (those for whiteness or those for grayness) will thrive will depend on the environment in which the set of genes is expressed. As another example, the sickle-cell trait conveys an advantage to humans who live in malaria-prone regions, because it makes it harder for the malaria parasite to infect the body. But this same trait can cause health problems, especially for someone living at high altitudes (where the mosquitoes that cause malaria are not to be found). Thus, whether the sickle-cell trait is advantageous or not depends on the environment in which the individual lives.

Consider a psychological trait, such as musical ability. A child is born, say, with a set of genes that provides him or her with a basis to develop tremendous musical talent. But will the child ever develop this talent, or will the child ever become a first-rate musician? If the child is brought up in a home where musical instruction is valued, perhaps. But even given these opportunities, other factors will come

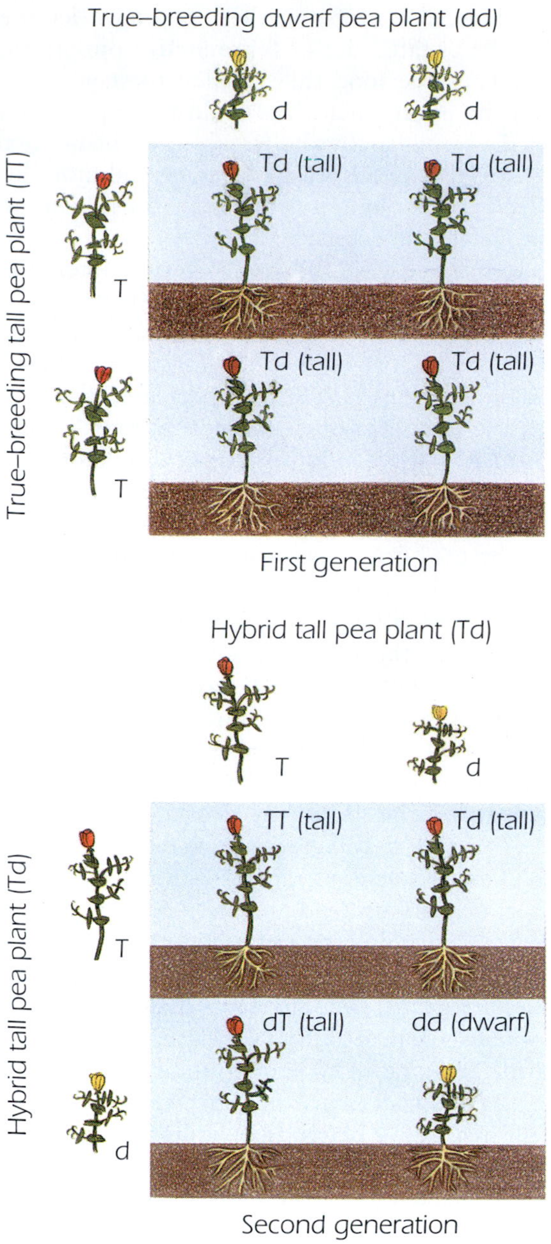

Figure 3–29
GENETIC CHART OF PEA TRAITS. *By studying the characteristics of successive generations of peas, Gregor Mendel discovered the fundamental process of genetic inheritance.*

into play, such as sheer persistence and luck, for example, in having his or her talent recognized by the music world. But suppose the child is brought up in a home where music is frowned upon. Perhaps musical expression is contrary to the parents' religion, or perhaps the parents view music as a frivolous pursuit. In such cases, no one may even know that the child had the potential to be a great musician, including the child himself or herself. The potential is left unexpressed, much as the potential for reading is left unexpressed in a preliterate culture.

The Genome Project

Efforts are under way to do *genetic mapping*, which is the determination of the location as well as the chemical sequence of specific genes located on specific chromosomes. A 15-year international project called the *Human Genome Project* is attempting to map the entire human genome, or configuration of genes on chromosomes. Given that the number of genes in humans is estimated to be about 100,000, the workers in this project have their work cut out for them. But even if they succeed, it is important to remember that the result will be nothing like total prediction of behavior. Behavior is a function of the interaction of the genes with the environment.

The information gleaned from the *Human Genome Project* will allow scientists to better understand the genes that cause or contribute to diseases and ultimately will help scientists devise more effective pharmaceutical treatments for some of these diseases. The information also may enable us to better understand how people are similar to and different from one another genetically. Some people are concerned about possible unethical uses of the database. But any scientific discovery ultimately can be used for good or ill, and it is the responsibility of a society to turn scientific knowledge to prosocial rather than antisocial uses.

How do we assess the strength of genetic and of environmental influences?

Heritability

It is possible to measure genetic influence, but only in a limited way. **Heritability** is a technical term that refers to the proportion of variation among individuals that is due to genetic causes. It is important, however, to distinguish genetic influence on a trait from the heritability of that trait. For example, height is highly heritable because who will be taller and who will be shorter can be predicted on the basis of inheritance from parents; but if there is little or no variability in a trait, it is genetic but not heritable. For example, the fact that we are born with two hands is genetic but would not be reflected in measures of heritability, because almost everyone is born with two hands.

This distinction becomes particularly important in the case of traits that a given society may value highly, such as intelligence. In concentrating on individual differences among people, we can forget the ways in which people are highly similar genetically and the ways that have made it possible for them to

be intelligent as a species. For example, one of the most impressive human accomplishments, the ability to speak, is made possible through a variety of complex genetic (as well as environmental) mechanisms, but because virtually all humans speak, we are unlikely to find a test of the ability to speak on a test of intelligence. Nor will the ability to speak be reflected in measures of heritability, precisely because almost everyone has it.

In interpreting measures of heritability, you need to keep several things in mind (Plomin, DeFries, McClearn, & Rutter, 1997; Wahlsten & Gottlieb, 1997; Sternberg & Grigorenko, 1999). First, heritability is always estimated with respect to a given trait in a given population at a given time. It does not apply to single individuals. How heritable a trait is estimated to be will depend in part on the source of variation in the trait in the population. For example, in a society that forces children to write with their right hand, the heritability of observed handedness in writing in the society will be quite low. However, it could be quite high in some other society where there was no environmental pressure to write with the right hand. We need also to remember that even highly heritable traits can be subject to environmental modification. For example, although height is highly heritable, heights have risen substantially in recent generations due to better nutrition. Human intelligence, as measured by conventional tests of abilities, also increased during most of the years of the 20th century, despite some level of heritability of intelligence (see Neisser, 1998). Finally, we need to remember that relatively few traits are controlled by a single gene. Rather, traits are quite often caused by multiple genes. We will never find "the" gene for intelligence, for example, because there is no single gene that controls intelligence. Moreover, genes interact, in part through their relations to chromosomes.

Chromosomes and Chromosomal Abnormalities

Genes are parts of **chromosomes,** rod-shaped bodies that contain many genes. Different species have different numbers of chromosomes, which come in pairs. Humans, for example, have 23 pairs of chromosomes, for a total of 46. Most of the cells of our bodies have each of these 23 pairs of chromosomes. One of each pair was received at conception from each of the mother and the father, so that half of each person's heredity can be traced to each parent.

Chromosomes are composed, in part, of the biological material that provides the mechanism for transmission of genetic information: **deoxyribonucleic acid—DNA.** Chromosomes govern everything from our eye color to our blood type and sex. Two specific

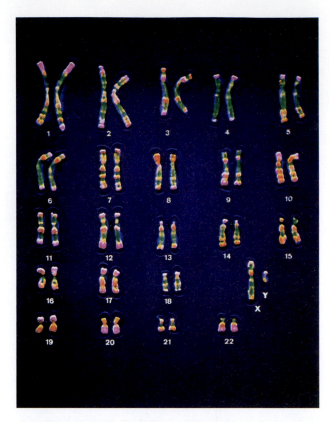

Humans have 23 pairs of chromosomes, including the pair that determines each person's sex.

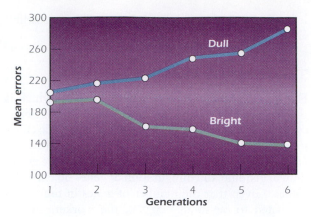

Figure 3–30
SELECTIVE BREEDING IN RATS. *Successive generations of rats were bred for their ability to run particular mazes. However, this ability did not generalize to other aspects of intelligence—or even to other kinds of mazes. (After Thompson, 1954)*

chromosomes are crucial in determining sex: the X and Y chromosomes, which appear as the twenty-third pair in each set. Females receive an X chromosome from both parents. Their sex-chromosome pairing is thus XX. Males receive an X chromosome from their mothers and a Y chromosome from their fathers. Their sex-chromosome pairing is thus XY. Can we influence the hereditary material that passes from one generation to another? People have tried to exert such influence.

Selective Breeding

If we can breed for height in peas, we might expect that we could breed for other traits as well. Indeed, race horses often become breeding studs once they are retired, with their owners commanding high prices for granting the opportunity to mate mares with them. In fact, many sophisticated reproductive options (e.g., artificial insemination, in vitro fertilization, surrogacy) are in use among animal breeders. If we can breed racing ability, how about learning ability, emotionality, resistance to alcohol dependency, or even intelligence? All of these selective breeding experiments have actually been done;

here, we focus on an experiment involving the breeding of rats for intelligence.

Various rats were tested for their ability to run a maze and then were bred in successive generations to be more or less able to run the maze (Tryon, 1940). Results were mixed. On the one hand, it was possible to breed rats that were more or less able to run the maze, as you can see in Figure 3-30. On the other hand, the rats' abilities turned out to be astonishingly specific. Even changes in the nature of the maze eliminated the significant difference in maze-running ability between groups. Clearly, the relation of genes to environment, in this case, that of the maze, is more complex than it might have seemed to be.

A Key Theme: The Relative Contributions of Nature and Nurture

In Search of . . .

Are heredity and environment opposing forces?

The best way to conduct a controlled experimental investigation of genetic influences on underlying traits and on behavior in the environment is by using genetically identical twins. Identical twins show similarities in intelligence and other characteristics, even if they have been raised separately in different environments.

This is not to say, however, that our genes inalterably determine everything about us. There is no question that our upbringing, our parents' personalities, our schooling, our physical surroundings—in short, our environments—greatly affect who we become. How much? No clear answer to this question is available. In fact, throughout this book, in discussions of mental disorders, personality, cognitive abilities and temperament, you will read of efforts to try to uncover the relative contributions of nature and nurture—of the degree to which who we are is determined by one's environment and genetics. Today nature and nurture are seen as interacting, rather than in opposition. For example, one may have a genetic predisposition to anxiety by being genetically predisposed to be more easily arousable (Kalin, 1993), but the environment one lives in, including one's neighborhood, economic situation, family life and social network may play a big role in how this genetic predisposition plays out (Plomin, DeFries, McClearn, & Rutter, 1997).

Another example of how nature and nurture may interact is in the expression of *handedness*, the preference a person shows for using the right hand, the left hand, or both, as in the case of ambidextrous individuals. There is substantial evidence in support of a genetic basis for handedness, but genetic factors alone cannot adequately account for variations in handedness across cultures (J. W. Berry, Poortinga, Segall, & Dasen, 1992). For example, although left-handedness apparently occurs in 5% to 10% of individuals in populations that do not restrict the use of either hand, socialization processes in some societies use selective pressures to force the use of the right hand and not the left, as mentioned earlier. In some of these more right-selective societies, the left hand is often used to achieve personal cleanliness and is therefore associated with dirtiness. Thus, cultural factors may influence rates of handedness. Intelligence (see chapter 9) and many other traits appear to be greatly affected by a highly complex and incompletely understood interaction of genetic and environmental factors. Even sensation and perception, the topics of the next chapter, represent a complex interaction between genes and environment.

THINK ABOUT IT

1. What ethical issues would be involved in tinkering with humans' genetic material?
2. Compare and contrast the ways in which people you know respond to new information that casts doubt onto existing beliefs. How might people improve their ways of responding?
3. If you were designing the human brain, what, if anything, would you do differently in order to render humans more adaptive to their environments?
4. Imagine beings who evolved on another planet and who differed from humans in ways that led them never to have wars. What differences in brain structure might be associated with such a course of evolution?
5. Karl Spencer Lashley, a pioneering neuropsychologist in the study of brain localization, suffered from migraine headaches, the specific nature of which still puzzles neuropsychologists. Many scientists have personal reasons for their intense curiosity about particular psychological phenomena or special fields of study. What is an aspect of human behavior that particularly puzzles you? Which area or areas of the brain might you wish to study to find out about that behavior? Why?
6. What is a circumstance in which you find it particularly difficult to think as clearly or as insightfully as you would like? If you were a biological psychologist trying to determine the physiological factors that contribute to this circumstance, how might you investigate these factors?

online *You can provide your own answers to these questions online at the* Sternberg, **In Search of the Human Mind** *Web site:* http://www.harcourtcollege.com/psych/ishm

SUMMARY

1. Biological psychology is the study of how biology affects behavior. Examination of the nervous and endocrine systems—in particular, the brain—helps psychologists answer questions about the interaction of mind and body.

Organization of the Nervous System 60

2. The nervous system is divided into two main parts: the *central nervous system*, consisting of the brain and the spinal cord, and the *peripheral nervous system*, consisting of the rest of the nervous system (e.g., the nerves in the face, legs, arms, and viscera).

3. *Afferents* are structures that receive something; afferent neurons receive sensory information (e.g., sensations in the eyes, ears, and skin) from the outlying nerves of the body and transmit that information back up through the spinal cord to the brain. *Efferent* transmit motor information (e.g., movements of the large and small muscles) from the spinal cord (and usually from the brain) about how the body should act in response to the information it receives.

4. A *reflex* is an automatic, involuntary response to stimulation that does not require input from the brain. The brain, however, assigns conscious meaning to stimuli that elicit reflexes.

5. The peripheral nervous system is divided into two parts: the *somatic nervous system*, which controls voluntary movement of skeletal muscles, and the *autonomic nervous system*, which controls the involuntary cardiac and smooth muscles.

6. The autonomic nervous system is divided into two parts: the *sympathetic nervous system* and the *parasympathetic nervous system*. The former is concerned primarily with expending energy, especially in situations requiring arousal and alertness. The latter is involved in storing energy.

Cellular Structures and Functions 65

7. A *neuron* is an individual nerve cell. *Nerves* are bunches of neurons. There are three functional types of neurons. Some neurons are *sensory neurons*, by which the CNS receives information from the environment; others are *motor neurons*, which carry information away from the CNS toward the environment; and still others are *interneurons*, which transmit information between sensory and motor neurons.

8. The *soma* (cell body) of a neuron is responsible for the life of the nerve cell. The branchlike *dendrites* are the means by which neurons receive messages, either from bodily receptors or from other neurons. *Axons* are the means by which neurons transmit messages. Some axons are covered by segments of a white, fatty substance termed *myelin*, which increases the speed and accuracy of transmitting information down the neuron. Axons often branch at their ends. *Terminal buttons* are knobs at the end of each branch of an axon; each of these buttons releases a chemical *neurotransmitter*. The small gap between the terminal buttons of one neuron and the dendrites of the next neuron is the *synapse*.

9. *Glial cells* serve as supportive structures for the neurons, holding them in place, isolating them from the rest of the body, and getting rid of dead neurons and other waste.

10. A rapid increase in the membrane potential (electrical charge) of a *neuron*, followed by a quick decrease, is an *action potential*. It provides the means by which intraneuronal communication takes place. Action potentials are all-or-none, occurring only if the electrical charge of the neuron has reached a *threshold of excitation*.

11. After a neuron fires, it goes through an *absolute refractory phase*, during which it absolutely cannot fire again, and a brief subsequent *relative refractory phase*, during which its susceptibility to firing is diminished.

12. The effects of neurotransmitters on the receptors located on the dendrites of postsynaptic neurons can be either excitatory (stimulating an increased likelihood of firing) or inhibitory (suppressing the likelihood of firing).

13. An excess of neurotransmitters at the synapse can be absorbed by *reuptake* back into the terminal buttons or by enzymatic deactivation, whereby the transmitter substance is chemically decomposed.

14. The classic neurotransmitters include *acetylcholine (ACh)*, *dopamine (DA)*, and *serotonin*. Newer neurotransmitters include glutamate and gamma-aminobutyric acid (GABA).

The Brain: Structure and Function 74

15. In the *hindbrain*, the *medulla oblongata* controls the heartbeat and largely controls breathing, swallowing, and digestion. The medulla oblongata also routes the sensory and motor neurons contralaterally from one side of the body to the opposite side of the brain. The *pons* contains nerve cells that pass signals from one part of the brain to another. The *cerebellum* controls bodily coordination.

16. The *midbrain* is involved in eye movements and coordination. Its relative importance is greater in animals of lesser brain complexity. The *reticular activating system*, which is responsible for arousal and sleep, extends from the midbrain to the hindbrain. The midbrain, the hindbrain, and part of the forebrain together compose the *brain stem*, the good health of which is vital to survival as an independent human being.

17. In the *forebrain*, the *thalamus* serves as a relay station for input into the cerebral cortex. The *hypothalamus*, which controls the autonomic nervous system and the endocrine system, is involved in activities such as regulation of temperature, eating, and drinking. The *limbic system*, also in the forebrain, is involved in emotion, motivation, and learning; in particular, the *hippocampus* is involved in memory.

18. The highly convoluted *cerebral cortex* surrounds the interior of the brain. It is the source of humans' ability to reason, think abstractly, and plan ahead.

19. The cerebral cortex covers the left and right hemispheres of the brain, which are connected by the *corpus callosum*. In general, each hemisphere contralaterally controls the opposite side of the body.

20. Based on extensive split-brain research, many investigators believe that the two hemispheres are specialized (perform different functions). In most people, the left hemisphere seems to control language; the right hemisphere seems to control certain aspects of spatial and visual processing. The two hemispheres may process information differently.

21. Another way to divide the brain is into four lobes. Roughly speaking, higher thought and motor processing occur in the *frontal lobe*, sensory processing in the *parietal lobe*, auditory processing in the *temporal lobe*, and visual processing in the *occipital lobe*.

22. The *primary motor cortex*, in the frontal lobe, governs the planning, control, and execution of movement. The *primary somatosensory cortex*, in the parietal lobe, is responsible for the sensations in our muscles and skin.

23. *Association areas* appear to link the activity of the motor and sensory cortices.

24. *Electroencephalograms (EEGs)* measure and record electrical activity in the brain. Because many processes are measured at once through EEG techniques, wave forms are often averaged to increase the stability of the readings. Averaged wave forms are referred to as *event-related potentials (ERPs)*.

25. X-ray pictures of the brain are taken by passing electromagnetic radiation through the tissues of the head. *Angiograms* are X-ray pictures taken after injection of special dyes that increase the visibility of specific structures, such as blood vessels.

26. A *computerized axial tomogram (CAT scan)* uses computer analysis of X-ray pictures taken from a variety of locations to construct a more revealing picture of the brain than is possible through X-ray pictures taken from a stationary device.

27. *Magnetic resonance imaging (MRI)* provides pictures of the brain by creating a very strong magnetic field that changes the orbits of nuclear particles, which emit energy bursts; these bursts are picked up by the scan.

28. *Positron emission tomography (PET scan)* enables psychologists, physicians, and other scientists to see the brain in action. X rays trace the passage of an injected radioactive substance through various parts of the brain.

The Endocrine System   93

29. The *endocrine system* is a means by which *glands* can secrete their products directly into the bloodstream. The secretions of the endocrine system are *hormones*, and their release is regulated by a negative-feedback loop (which feeds information back to the gland regarding the level of a hormone in the bloodstream).

30. One of the major endocrine glands is the *adrenal medulla*, which secretes epinephrine and norepinephrine, both of which increase heart rate and blood pressure; both hormones also reduce the flow of blood to the digestive system.

31. The nervous and endocrine systems are to some extent parallel, in that both are communication systems and both use chemical substances as messengers: neurotransmitters and hormones, respectively. The brain also has some control over the endocrine system, just as hormones can influence the brain.

Genetic Bases of Behavior   95

32. Darwin's view of **natural selection** holds that individuals tend to have reproductive success as a function of their ability to adapt to the environment, with more adaptable individuals producing, on average, a larger number of viable offspring. The concept of natural selection has been applied to ideas as well as to organisms, although this application remains speculative.

33. A *mutation* occurs when the genetic message that would normally be passed on from parents to offspring is altered, resulting in a new organism with a genetic code not predictable from the genetic material of the parents.

34. Punctuated equilibrium refers to the view that evolutionary change proceeds in bursts rather than through smooth, gradual transitions.

35. *Genes* are the biological units that contribute to the hereditary transmission of traits. Genes are located on *chromosomes*, which come in pairs. Humans have 23 chromosome pairs, the 23rd of which is responsible for determining male versus female sex.

36. A *genotype* is the genetic code for a trait. A *phenotype* is the actual visible expression of the trait in offspring. A given genotype may produce a variety of phenotypes.

37. *Heritability* is a measure of genetic contribution to individual differences in a trait. Heritability is distinct from modifiability and can vary across time and place.

KEY TERMS

absolute refractory phase   69

acetylcholine (ACh)   72

action potential   68

adrenal medulla   93

amygdala   76

angiograms   89

association areas   85

autonomic nervous system   63

axon   66

behavioral genetics   97

biological traits   97

brain   60

brain stem   76

central nervous system (CNS)   60

cerebellum   76

cerebral cortex   79

cerebral hemispheres (left and right)   79

chromosomes   99

computerized axial tomogram (CAT)   91

corpus callosum   79

dendrites   66

deoxyribonucleic acid (DNA)   99

dominant trait   97

dopamine (DA)   72

electroencephalogram (EEG)   86

endocrine system   92

event-related potential (ERP)   88

forebrain   75

frontal lobe   83

genes   97

genotypes   97

glands   92

glial cells   68

heritability   99

hindbrain   75

hippocampus   76

hormones   92

hypothalamus   77

interneurons   65

limbic system   76

magnetic resonance imaging (MRI)   91

medulla oblongata   76

midbrain   75

motor efferents   61

motor neurons   65

myelin sheath   66

natural selection   96

nerves   66

nervous system   59

neuromodulators   71

neurons   60

neurotransmitter   70

nodes of Ranvier   66

occipital lobe   83

optic chiasma   85

parasympathetic nervous system   65

parietal lobe   83

peripheral nervous system (PNS)   63

phenotype   97

pituitary gland   94

pons   76

positron emission tomography (PET)   91

primary motor cortex   83

primary somatosensory cortex   83

projection areas   83

recessive trait   97

reflexes   62

relative refractory phase   69

reticular activating system (RAS)   76

reuptake   71

sensory afferents   61

sensory neurons   65

septum   76

serotonin   72

soma   65

somatic nervous system   63

spinal cord   60

sympathetic nervous system   64

synapse   70

temporal lobe   83

terminal buttons   67

thalamus   76

threshold of excitation   68

thyroid gland   94

THINK ABOUT IT SAMPLE RESPONSES

1. What ethical issues would be involved in tinkering with humans' genetic material?

A number of issues are involved. One issue is whether humans—any humans—have the right to tinker with the genetic material of other humans. A second issue is how one can possibly know, in a complex system such as the genetic one, whether the costs may be greater than the benefits. For example, certain desirable traits may be obtained at the cost of other, negative ones. A third issue is what even constitutes a "positive" change. A change that one individual might view as positive, another might view as negative. A fourth issue is whether changes might be made for nefarious purposes, such as to breed assassins or warriors without a conscience.

2. Compare and contrast the ways in which people you know respond to new information that casts doubt onto existing beliefs. How might people improve their ways of responding?

Some people respond to such new information defensively. They seek to maintain their prior beliefs at any cost. The cost of such an attitude is that they tend to maintain old beliefs even in the face of evidence that contradicts these beliefs. People can improve their responding by pledging to themselves that they will be ever-vigilant regarding their beliefs and open to changing these beliefs as new information arrives. In this way, they can continue to grow intellectually not just during the years when they are students, but during all the years of their lives.

3. If you were designing the human brain, what, if anything, would you do differently in order to render humans more adaptive to their environments?

It is always hard to know whether changes one would make actually would improve functioning or degrade it. But one change that some people might view as desirable would be a lesser tendency for people to form stereotypes about or prejudices against other people. Stereotypes and especially prejudices bias our thinking about others and lead us to see flaws where they may not exist, as well as to refuse to see strengths that may be staring us in the face.

4. Imagine beings who evolved on another planet and who differed from humans in ways that led them never to have wars. What differences in brain structure might be associated with such a course of evolution?

Such individuals might have amygdalas that are less susceptible to certain kinds of negative emotions, particularly, emotions related to anger.

5. Karl Spencer Lashley, a pioneering neuropsychologist in the study of brain localization, suffered from migraine headaches, the specific nature of which still puzzles neuropsychologists. Many scientists have personal reasons for their intense curiosity about particular psychological phenomena or special fields of study. What is an aspect of human behavior that particularly puzzles you? Which area or areas of the brain might you wish to study to find out about that behavior? Why?

Everyone has to answer this question for himself or herself, of course. In my own case, I started studying intelligence because, as a child, I performed poorly on IQ tests. For much of my career, I have tried to figure out why! A wonderful feature of psychology is that it can enable us to answer questions we always have had about ourselves and others.

6. What is a circumstance in which you find it particularly difficult to think as clearly or as insightfully as you would like? If you were a biological psychologist trying to determine the physiological factors that contribute to this circumstance, how might you investigate these factors?

People often find it difficult to think clearly when they are under great stress. A biological psychologist might seek to relate quantities of stress-related hormones in the body to the quality of thinking people show when they solve insightful-thinking problems, such as crossword puzzles or brain-teasers.

Where Am I?

She could see nothing. . . . It was not black, but . . . gray . . . like a night cloud reflecting the city lights of Moscow, featureless, but somehow textured. She could hear nothing, not the rumble of traffic, not the mechanical sounds of running water or slamming doors. . . . She turned her head, but the view remained the same, a gray blankness, like the inside of a cloud, or a ball of cotton, or—

She breathed. The air had no smell, no taste, neither moist nor dry, not even a temperature that she could discern. She spoke . . . but incredibly she heard nothing. . . .

Is this hell?

—Tom Clancy, *The Cardinal of the Kremlin*

4

SENSATION AND PERCEPTION

Chapter Outline

Not hell, but sensory deprivation. In Tom Clancy's novel *The Cardinal of the Kremlin*, Svetlana Vaneyeva has been purposely deprived of all sensory stimulation to extract a confession from her. First she panics, later she hallucinates, and eventually she willingly confesses everything. Sensory deprivation can have such effects on people, but, interestingly, it is also used by some people for relaxation and stress reduction. The paradoxical effects of sensory deprivation illustrate both the importance of sensations from the world around us and the importance of occasionally being free of some sensations. Psychologists study sensation because our thoughts, feelings, and actions are largely a reaction to what our senses do—or do not—take in. The senses provide all our contact with the external world. Without the senses, you would have no contact whatsoever with the world outside yourself.

Generally speaking, psychologists define a **sensation** as a message regarding physical stimulation of a sensory receptor that our brains receive from our senses. A **sense** is a physical system for receiving a particular kind of physical stimulation and translating that stimulation into an electrochemical message the brain can understand. This neural language of the brain is primarily electrochemical (see chapter 3). Thus, for example, you might collect information about a steaming, circular, flat, tangy-smelling, red and white object via your eyes and nose, then somehow translate this information and send it racing to your brain via sensory neurons. You would have yet to make sense of these sensations.

When your brain receives these various sensations, it organizes, integrates, processes, and interprets the sensory information, so that you then might say, "Ah! Pizza for dinner!" This high-level processing of information is *perception*, which takes up roughly where sensation leaves off. What is perception? **Perception** is the set of mental processes that organize and interpret sensory information that has been transmitted to the brain. Perception usually refers to the cognitive processes in the brain through which we interpret the messages our senses provide. Perception involves synthesizing and assigning meaning to sensations by taking into account our expectations, our prior experiences, and sometimes our culture. The boundary between sensation and perception is not clear-cut, however, because what we sense can also be affected by our prior experiences. When a background noise (e.g., a fan or other motor noise) is so common that we get used to its presence, for example, we may say that we "don't hear" it any more.

Many cross-cultural psychologists are intrigued by the extent to which the physiological structures and processes of the brain can be affected by culture. Although culture is known to have a profound effect on perception, there appears to be little variability in the various sensory domains that can be traced directly to culture (Poortinga, Kop, & van de Vijver, 1990). That is, the more closely a psychological phenomenon is tied to strictly physiological processes, the less variability we should expect to find among humans, regardless of culture. Conversely, the more closely the phenomenon is tied to the environment and to social processes, the more cultural (and, of course, environmental) variation we can expect to find. For example, there is likely to be more variation in the way people across cultures perceive distant points of light in the sky than in the way they sense them. The moon may look like a desolate wasteland to us and like an inhabited heavenly body to someone else.

Biology is critical to sensory processing and, to some extent, to perceptual processing. The importance of biology becomes clear when we consider the adaptive value of sensory processing from an evolutionary standpoint. We are sensitive to only a very small proportion of the various kinds of stimulation that exist in the environment. For example, our eyes cannot detect the large majority of wavelengths in the electromagnetic spectrum, and our ears cannot hear many pitches that are of very high or very low frequencies. Are there advantages to not being able to detect certain stimuli? Yes—we are protected from drowning in a sea of irrelevant stimulation. At the same time, certain forms of stimulation must be detected. For example, although few people enjoy pain, an organism that did not experience pain would be in grave danger, because of its lack of awareness of damage to bodily tissue. As another example, after awhile, we stop noticing certain stimulation that is constant in the environment. The

adaptive advantage is that we thereby become more ready to detect changes, including ones that are potentially hazardous. In short, we have evolved in ways that tune in to the most relevant information in the physical environment and that detect changes from constant levels of this information. These adaptations help us optimize our fit to our environments. Psychologists study sensory systems not only in humans, but also in other organisms. In this way, they are better able to understand both universal constraints on sensory systems across species and also adaptations of sensory systems of particular organisms for their own particular ecological niches.

This chapter describes how our senses provide us with the sensations of light, color, sound, taste, scent, pressure, temperature, pain, balance, and motion. It also describes how visual sensations are converted into perceptions. Before we examine each sense individually, however, we should explore two areas relevant to the study of all kinds of sensation and perception. First, we investigate how the senses are studied and measured. Second, we probe some biological properties common to all our senses.

Psychophysics

In Search of . . . *What are the relations between various forms of psychophysical stimulation and the psychological sensations they produce?*

Psychophysics is the systematic study of the relationship between the *physical* stimulation of a sense organ and the *psychological* sensations produced by that stimulation. A psychophysical experiment, for example, might measure the relationship between the rate at which a light flashes and your ability to detect individual flashes.

Measurements of psychophysical relationships can be put to many practical uses in everyday life. When you have your vision checked, the eye doctor needs to determine how large the letters must be for you to see them clearly. The audiologist who checks your hearing needs to determine how faint a tone you can hear. Psychophysics is also relevant in human factors and engineering psychology, as in the design of instrument panels. How brightly should an automobile's dashboard gauges be illuminated in order to be visible, but not distracting, at night? In the development of products, consumer psychologists tackle questions such as how strong a perfume can be without becoming overpowering. All of these answers can be found with psychophysical techniques. Psychophysics also deals with several basic problems related to perception: detection, measurement error, and discrimination (Coren, Ward, & Enns, 1994).

Detection and Thresholds

Detection is awareness of the presence of a sensory stimulus. In sensory-detection studies, researchers ask how much light, sound, taste, or other sensory stimulation is needed in order for our senses minimally to detect it. The hypothetical minimum amount of physical energy of a given kind—scent, sound, pressure, and so on—that an individual can detect is the **absolute threshold** for that kind of energy. We cannot sense the stimulus below the absolute-threshold level, and we can consistently sense the stimulus above that level. Table 4-1 shows some approximations of the absolute thresholds of different senses.

A simple way for an experimenter to determine an absolute threshold is to start with an extremely weak stimulus, such as a faint beep, and ask the person being assessed whether he or she can detect it. The beep should be so weak that detection is impossible. The experimenter then increases stimulus intensity until the person hears the beep. Ideally, the dividing line between when the person can and cannot hear the stimulus is his or her absolute threshold for hearing that sort of sound. In practice, however, factors such as fatigue, distractions, or a cold can affect when people begin to notice the stimulus. To account for such differences, psychologists operationally define (that is,

Computer software makers must take psychophysics into account when they design the complex functions of games such as this one. They must design the visual images on the screen to be optimally detectable.

define in terms of measurement operations) the absolute threshold *as the level at which a stimulus is first detected 50% of the time* (see Figure 4-1). But there are still factors, such as a person's patterns of guessing, that can distort sensory measurements.

The traditional method of determining an absolute threshold does not fully take into account factors that can distort sensory measurements, such as response bias and background noise. For example, when a signal, such as a doorbell, is very faint, we sometimes cannot be sure whether we hear anything or not. In this situation, some people are inclined to guess "yes," saying they heard the bell. Others say they heard the bell only when they are quite confident of having heard it, responding "no" otherwise. This predisposition to guess one way or another is *response bias*. A further confounding problem is that of background noise. Background-noise problems occur when people truly think they hear a signal but actually are just picking up background sounds in the environment or even within themselves.

A more systematic method for measuring detection takes into account these and other distortions of the measurement process. This method, *signal-detection analysis*, provides both an important approach to psychophysics and ingenious insights into the processes of decision making. The key advantage of this method is that it allows the experimenter to separate out true sensitivity to a stimulus from distorting factors like response bias or background noise.

According to **signal-detection theory (SDT)**, four possible combinations of stimulus and response exist. Suppose you are asked to detect the flicker of a light. One possibility is that the *signal*, or stimulus (in this case, the flicker of the light), is present, and your response is to detect it correctly; this pairing is a *hit*. Another

---

TABLE 4–1

Absolute Sense Thresholds   *Here are some approximations of the absolute thresholds for the senses. (After Galanter, 1962)*

Sense	Minimum Stimulus
Vision	A candle flame seen at 30 miles on a dark, clear night
Hearing	The tick of a watch at 20 feet under quiet conditions
Taste	One teaspoon of sugar in 2 gallons of water
Smell	One drop of perfume diffused into the entire air volume of six rooms
Touch	The wing of a fly falling on your cheek from a distance of 1 centimeter

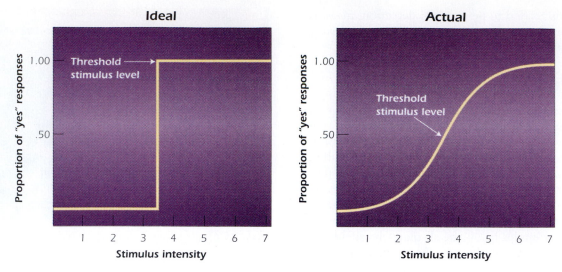

Figure 4–1

IDEAL AND REAL ABSOLUTE THRESHOLDS. *Because it is virtually impossible to identify an ideal absolute threshold, psychologists define an absolute threshold as the level of stimulation that an individual can detect.*

possibility is a *miss:* The light flickers, but you do not detect it. A third possibility is a *false alarm:* The light does not flicker, but you think that you see it flicker. The fourth possibility is a *correct rejection:* The light doesn't flicker, and you don't think that it does. These combinations of stimuli and responses are summarized in Table 4-2. Thus, SDT allows for hits and misses, like traditional psychophysical threshold measurement, but also allows for false alarms and correct rejections (Green & Swets, 1966; Swets, Tanner, & Birdsall, 1961).

According to SDT, we do not merely *report* objectively whether we *do* or *do not* detect a signal; rather, we *decide*—taking into account the background noise, emotional context, and personal expectations—how

likely it is that a sensation has been caused by a signal. For example, have you ever been at home alone at night, when your senses detected odd noises or shadows? Compare the sensations you would probably notice in such a situation with those sensations that you would probably experience were you walking down a main street in broad daylight.

By comparing the percentage of responses that fall into each of the four categories, psychologists determine whether people tend to have a response bias toward giving more "yes" answers or toward giving more "no" answers in situations in which they have to guess. Knowing about any response bias or other distorting effects can help researchers reach more nearly correct threshold measurements.

TABLE 4–2

Outcomes of a Signal-Detection Experiment

Signal-detection theory allows four possible combinations of stimulus and response, thereby allowing psychologists to consider the expectations of the person sensing the stimulus.

SIGNAL	RESPONSE	
	Yes (Color A)	*No (Color B)*
(Color A) Present	Hit	Miss
(Color B) Absent	False alarm	Correct rejection

Discrimination: Difference Threshold and the Just Noticeable Difference

Being able to detect a single stimulus is certainly crucial in many circumstances. Often, however, the problem is not how strong or intense a stimulus must be in order for a person to detect it, but rather how easily one stimulus can be distinguished from another. This psychophysics problem involves **discrimination:** the ability to ascertain the difference between one stimulus and another. For example, in your everyday life you might need to discern whether the color of one piece of clothing matches (or clashes with) that of another piece of clothing. Or in listening to a concert, you might observe that an instrument is out of tune and that its notes are not harmonious with those of other instruments.

The JND

The minimum amount of difference that can be detected between two sensory stimuli is the *difference threshold*, or the **just noticeable difference (jnd).** Just as our absolute thresholds for detecting stimuli vary, so do our responses to differences between stimuli. The resulting variation causes measurement error. For this reason, psychologists average data from multiple trials aimed at measuring difference thresholds. In practical terms, the operational definition of the jnd is the difference between two stimuli that can be detected 50% of the time. In a typical jnd experiment, a researcher asks a participant to make many comparisons between pairs of a particular kind of stimulus that vary in just one respect. For example, you could be asked to lay your hand on two otherwise identical surfaces that might differ in temperature; you would then have to say whether the two surfaces feel as though they are the same temperature or different. The degree of difference that you could detect exactly 50% of the time would be your jnd for temperature.

Sensory-difference thresholds are important in everyday life and even in some professions. A coffee taster must be able to taste and smell the differences among various blends, grinds, and roasts of bean. Musicians must be able to hear whether their instruments are just a fraction of a note off-key.

There is no single jnd that applies to all senses equally. In addition to variations in jnds from person to person, the human species as a whole also varies in its responses to different types and magnitudes of sensory stimulation. For all senses, however, the jnd usually increases proportionately and consistently with increases in the magnitude of the original stimulus. For example, if you were holding a 10-ounce bag of cherries, and the grocer added half an ounce more to your bag, you would probably notice the weight difference. If you were holding a 10-pound bag of cherries, however, and the grocer added a half-ounce more, you probably would not detect the weight difference. The reason that you would sense the extra half-ounce the first time but not the second is that as the stimulus intensity (here, the weight of the bag before the grocer began adding more cherries) increases, the amount of change needed to produce a jnd also increases. You need a greater amount—probably at least 3 or 4 ounces—added to the 10-pound bag for you to sense the difference.

Weber's Law

The fact that the change needed to cause a jnd increases proportionately with increases in the magnitude of the stimulus was first noticed in 1834 by Ernst Weber, a German physiologist. Weber noted that a jnd is not a constant fixed amount, but rather a constant proportion of the stimulus, and this conclusion is now known as **Weber's law.** According to this law, the greater the magnitude of the stimulus, the larger a difference needs to be in order to be detected as a difference.

The relative amount of change needed for a given type of stimulus to produce a jnd is termed the *Weber fraction*. The actual fraction varies for different sensory experiences. The Weber fraction for weights is about 0.02. For example, for a 10-pound bag, you would just notice a difference of as little as one-fifth pound, 2% of 10 pounds. For the 10-ounce bag, you would need only a difference of a fifth of an ounce. However, for a 50-pound bag, you would need a difference of 1 pound in order to detect the difference. We are much better able to detect differences in amounts of electric shock (low Weber fraction of 0.01) than we are able to detect differences in taste (high Weber fraction of 0.2). Table 4-3 shows Weber fractions for a variety of types of sensory stimulation. The smaller the fraction, the more sensitive we are to differences in that sensory *mode* (e.g., vision or hearing), and the higher the fraction, the less sensitive.

Now that we have explored some of the techniques and theories psychologists use when assessing sensory functioning, we can find out what psychologists have discovered by using those techniques. The following section describes some of the biological properties common to all the senses. Many of these

TABLE 4-3

Weber Fractions for Various Types of Stimuli *Because people show different degrees of sensitivity to distinct kinds of sensations, the Weber fractions for various kinds of stimuli differ. (After Teghtsoonian, 1971)*

Type of Stimulus	Weber Fraction
Electric shock	.01
Heaviness	.02
Length	.03
Vibration (fingertip)	.04
Loudness	.05
Odor	.05
Brightness	.08
Taste (salt)	.2

If one bucket has 2 ounces more water in it, will the difference be noticeable?

properties, such as the action potential, were introduced to you in chapter 3, and now we can apply them specifically to the study of physical sensation.

Biological Properties Common to All Senses

In Search of . . .

How do we sense physical stimuli?

Receptor Cells and Transduction

Every sensation—whether it is the color of a lawn, the smell of a rose, or the experience of a breeze felt on our skin, starts when our sensory organs are stimulated at specialized **receptor cells,** cells which have evolved to detect particular kinds of energy, such as mechanical, electromagnetic, or chemical energy. Each receptor cell receives messages from a specific area of the external world.

When sensory receptors in our eyes, ears, or other sense organs are stimulated by a form of energy, they must relay that information in electrochemical form to the brain. Because the information is not initially in electrochemical form, the sensory receptors must first convert, or **transduce** this energy received from the environment into the electrochemical form of energy that is meaningful to the nervous system. Although the task of transduction is common to all the senses, the method for doing this task is different for each sense. Each sense has a set of specialized receptors for transducing its own kind of stimulus energy.

Sensory Coding

A bright red floodlight does not look the same as a dim blue night light. The trill of a flute does not sound like the wail of an electric guitar. **Sensory coding** is a physiological form of communication through which sensory receptors convey a range of information about stimuli within the nervous system. Receptors and neurons use an electrochemical language to signify shades of meaning in their messages.

Each sensory stimulus has both *intensity*, the amount of physical energy that is transduced by a sensory receptor and then sensed by the brain (such as the degree of spiciness we taste in a food); and *quality*, the nature of the stimulus that reaches a sensory receptor and is then sensed in the brain (for example, whether the food is salty or sweet). Sensory neurons encode aspects of the physical properties of a stimulus via special *patterns* of neural firing—the action potentials described in the preceding chapter—that specifically identify those properties to the brain. One way to measure the firing patterns of individual neurons is **single-cell recording,** a recording of one nerve cell (neuron) in the brain. Single-cell recording is a technique that lets researchers determine exactly which neurons are activated by exactly which kinds of stimuli. Once researchers know which neurons are active, they can then look for firing patterns.

Single-cell recording techniques have vastly increased our knowledge about how neurons perform sensory coding, especially regarding stimulus intensity. Two aspects of neuronal firing indicate stimulus intensity: the neuron's *rate of firing*, measured in terms of how many times the neuron fires within a given period, and the neuron's *firing-pattern regularity*. The less intense the stimulus, the less frequently and the less regularly the neuron will fire. The more intense the stimulus, the more frequently and the more regularly the neuron will fire. This relation between the intensity of the stimulus and the rate and pattern of neuronal firing makes sense intuitively because a more intense stimulus would more frequently and more regularly cause a neuron to reach its threshold of excitation, stimulating its action potential. (See Figure 4-2 for an illustration of coding intensity.)

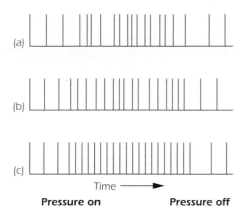

(a)

(b)

(c)

Time ⟶

Pressure on   **Pressure off**

Figure 4–2
NEURAL RATES OF FIRING.   *Neurons fire at varying rates, according to the types of stimuli that prompt the neural activity. Responses of three different neurons are shown.*

Sensory Adaptation

As explained in the description of absolute and jnd thresholds, our senses are designed to detect *changes* in stimulus energy. From a functional and evolutionary standpoint, this reaction reflects our need to pay attention to what is new and strange in order to determine whether it is—literally or figuratively—friend or foe. When stimulus energy changes, the receptor cells fire more vigorously, alerting the brain to the change. A physiological mechanism, sensory adaptation, helps us adjust to changes in stimuli.

Sensory adaptation is a temporary physiological response to a sensed change in the environment; it encompasses the temporary gradual decrease in sensitivity that occurs when a sensory system is stimulated for a period of time, and the temporary increase in sensitivity that occurs when a sensory system is not stimulated for a period of time. Because it is generally not subject to conscious manipulation or control, it does not usually depend on previous experience with the given type of environmental change (e.g., changes in temperature or other changes in intensity). For example, without any conscious effort, our vision adapts to changes in light intensity (to darkness or to increased brightness). Similarly, our sense of smell, or olfaction, adapts to having a particular odor in the environment. A smell that is horrendous in the first minute may be barely detectable after a few minutes. You need no training or previous experience to make these sensory adaptations, and you will make the sensory adaptations just about exactly the same way the first time and every time thereafter. (There is some decrement in our ability to adjust to darkness due to aging, however.) The degree of sensory adaptation required relates directly to the intensity of the stimulus in the environment, not

to the number of times you were previously exposed to the stimulus or to the length of time between your last exposure and your present one. Furthermore, when the environment returns to its former state, your physiological mechanisms for adaptation return to their former states.

For example, if you have adapted to a stimulus, such as cold ocean water on your body, then you will eventually find that the water does not seem as cold as it originally did. You have thus shifted to a new adaptation level (Helson, 1964). The **adaptation level** is the reference level of sensory stimulation against which an individual may judge new stimuli or changes in existing stimuli. Once your body has adapted to the cold water, an ice cube will feel less cold to you than it would have before you went swimming; conversely, hot sand will feel hotter. However, as soon as you get out of the water and spend some time sunning on the sand, your body will adapt again to the change in temperature, reaching a new adaptation level for this warmer temperature. Regardless of how many times you repeat this process, or how long you wait between jumping into or out of the water, your body will go through approximately the same adaptation response that it went through the very first time you adapted to the change in temperature. Furthermore, you generally have little conscious control over how quickly

Water that feels icy cold upon entering gradually seems less so as your body adapts to the reference level of sensory stimulation.

your body adapts to the change in temperature, or to other types of changes, such as in levels of light. Your ability to adapt to light depends on your vision.

Vision

In Search of . . . *What are the sensory and perceptual mechanisms that enable us to see?*

Have you ever awakened to utter darkness? You get out of bed and stumble over the shoes you left out in the middle of the floor. The light switch on the wall—somehow, it seems not to be there when you cannot see it. You appreciate your vision then in a way that you cannot when you see well, and in a way that a blind person might like to be able to do. To understand how vision is possible, we need to know something about light, about the structure of the eye, and about how the eye interacts with light to enable us to see. We consider each of these topics in turn.

The Physical Properties of Light

Light is the form of electromagnetic energy that the receptors of our eyes are distinctively designed to receive. Our eyes detect only a very narrow band of the electromagnetic spectrum of radiation. The **electromagnetic spectrum** is a range of energy of varying wavelengths (see Figure 4-3), and human eyes are receptive only to the narrow wavelength range from about 350 to 750 *nanometers* (nm; billionths of a meter). White light, such as the light from the sun, consists of all of the visible wavelengths combined. Other visible wavelengths of light are seen as different colors. Other species differ from humans in what they can see. Some animals can see electromagnetic radiation that is invisible to us. For example, humans cannot see wavelengths in the infrared and ultraviolet bands of the spectrum that other animals can see. The wavelengths organisms see first are detected through their eyes. The ability to detect different wavelengths depends not only on the wavelengths, but on contextual factors. For example, sensitivity is reduced in the

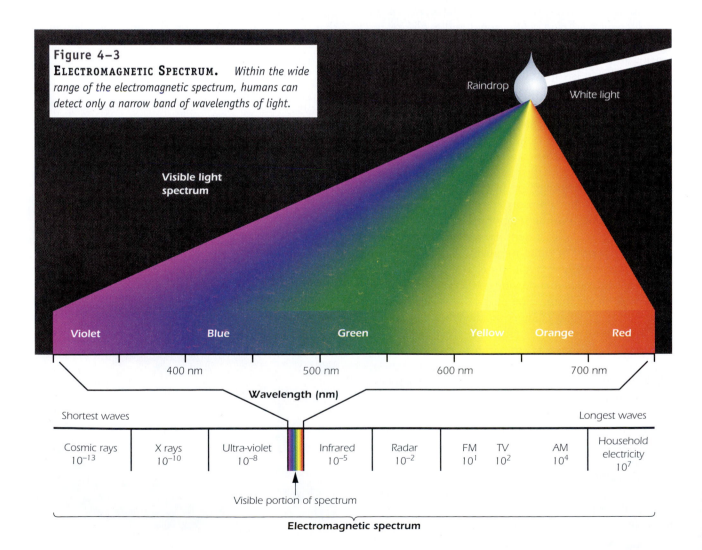

Figure 4-3
ELECTROMAGNETIC SPECTRUM. *Within the wide range of the electromagnetic spectrum, humans can detect only a narrow band of wavelengths of light.*

Raindrop
White light

Visible light spectrum

Violet   Blue   Green   Yellow   Orange   Red

400 nm   500 nm   600 nm   700 nm
Wavelength (nm)

Shortest waves   Longest waves

| Cosmic rays 10^{-13} | X rays 10^{-10} | Ultra-violet 10^{-8} | Infrared 10^{-5} | Radar 10^{-2} | FM 10^{1} | TV 10^{2} | AM 10^{4} | Household electricity 10^{7} |

Visible portion of spectrum

Electromagnetic spectrum

presence of a bright, uniform background (Freeman & Badcock, 1999).

The Functional Organization of the Eye

As illustrated in Figure 4-4, light beams enter the eye via the **cornea,** which bulges slightly to form a clear, dome-shaped window. The cornea serves as a curved exterior lens that gathers and focuses the entering light. The cornea is actually a specialized region of the *sclera* of the eye (the external rubbery layer that holds in the gelatinous substance of the eye). The entire sclera, and particularly the cornea, is very sensitive to touch. When a foreign substance comes in contact with the sclera, your body almost instantaneously initiates a series of protective responses, as you know from experiences with having had dust, lashes, or any other particles touch your eye.

Upon penetrating the cornea, the light beam passes through the **pupil,** a hole in the center of a circular muscle, the **iris.** The iris reflects certain light beams outward and away from the eye, giving our eyes their distinctive colors. When light coming into the eye is very bright, the iris reflexively causes the pupil to become constricted to limit the amount of light entering the eye. The pupil can reach a diameter of as little as 2 mm. When light is dim, the pupil becomes dilated to as much as 8 mm to collect more light. (The 4-fold increase in diameter equals about a 16-fold increase in area, so the eyes are actually quite adaptive.) As we age, however, our pupils become less able to dilate. This decreased ability leads to more difficulty with vision in dim lighting.

Figure 4-4
HOW THE EYE ADJUSTS TO FOCUS VISUAL IMAGES.
The cornea and lens refract light through the pupil to focus the light on the retina at the back of the eye.

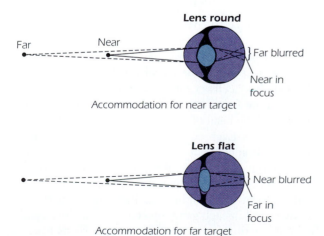

Slower pupillary reflexes also make it harder for older persons to adapt to rapid changes in light and dark, such as those encountered driving at night on a busy two-way street.

After entering the pupil, light bends as it passes through the curved interior **lens** of the eye. Because the curvature of the cornea does most of the gross *refraction* (bending of light waves), the lens does mostly fine tuning, adjusting its own amount of curvature to get the focus just right. The process by which the lens changes its curvature to focus on objects at different distances is termed *accommodation.* Figure 4-4 shows how the changes in curvature of the cornea and the lens adjust the focus of objects at different distances; a flatter lens bends the light less and focuses more distant objects, whereas a more curved lens focuses closer objects more clearly. Figure 4-5 shows the anatomy of the entire eye, including the cornea and the lens.

The Retina

The refracted light focuses on the **retina,** a network of neurons extending over most of the back (posterior) surface of the interior of the eye. The retina is where electromagnetic light energy is transduced into neural electrochemical impulses. Even though the retina is only about as thick as a single page in this book, it nevertheless consists of three main layers of neural tissue, as shown in Figure 4-5.

The first layer of neuronal tissue—closest to the front, outward-facing surface of the eye—is the layer of **ganglion cells,** whose axons constitute the optic nerve. The second layer consists of three kinds of interneuron cells. **Amacrine cells** and **horizontal cells** make single lateral connections among adjacent areas of the retina in the middle layer of cells. **Bipolar cells** make dual connections forward and outward to the ganglion cells, as well as backward and inward to the third layer of retinal cells.

The Photoreceptors

The third layer of the retina contains the **photoreceptors,** which transduce light energy into electrochemical energy that can then be transmitted by neurons to the brain. It is this transmission that enables the eye to detect visual stimulation. Ironically, the photoreceptor cells are the retinal cells farthest from the light source; light must pass through the other two layers first, and messages are passed back outward toward the front of your eye before traveling to the brain. There are two kinds of photoreceptors. The **rods** are long and thin photoreceptors, and more highly concentrated in the periphery of the retina than in the foveal region of the retina and the **cones**

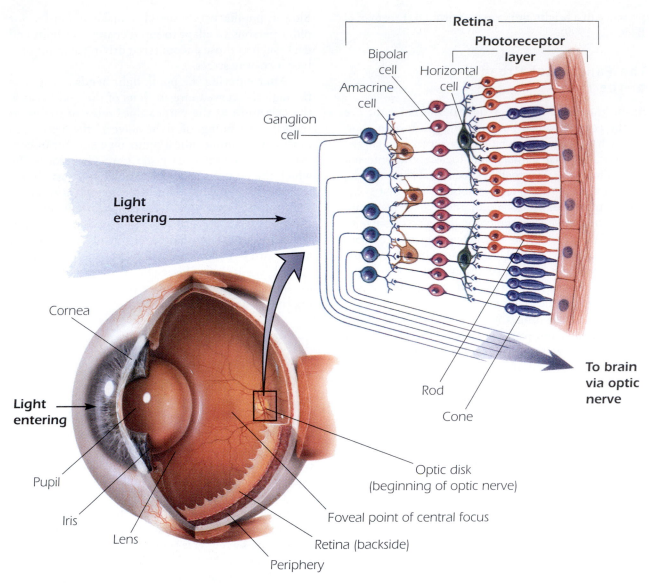

Figure 4-5
ANATOMY OF THE EYE.   *The light refracted through the cornea and lens onto the retina stimulates the sensory receptors in the retina. The receptors, the rods and cones, sense the wavelength (color) of the light and begin to transduce its electromagnetic energy to electrochemical energy. The optic nerve carries the neural impulses to the visual cortex.*

are short and thick photoreceptors, and more highly concentrated in the foveal region of the retina than in the periphery. Each eye contains roughly 120 million rods and 8 million cones. Rods and cones differ not only in shape (see Figure 4-6), but also in their compositions, locations, and responses to light. Within the rods and cones are **photopigments**—chemical substances that react with light. There are three types of cones, each containing a different photopigment, whereas rods contain only one photopigment. The photopigments start the complex transduction process that transforms physical electromagnetic energy into an electrochemical neural impulse that can be understood by the brain.

From the Eye to the Brain

The neurochemical messages processed by the rods and cones of the retina travel via the bipolar cells to the ganglion cells. Cones are most highly concentrated in the **fovea**—a small, thin region of the retina, the size of the head of a pin that is most directly in the line of sight. Each cone in the fovea typically has its own ganglion cell, but the rods on the *periphery* (outer boundary area) of the retina share ganglion cells with other rods. Thus, each ganglion cell gathering information from the periphery gathers information from many rods, but each ganglion cell from the fovea gathers information from only one cone, perhaps because

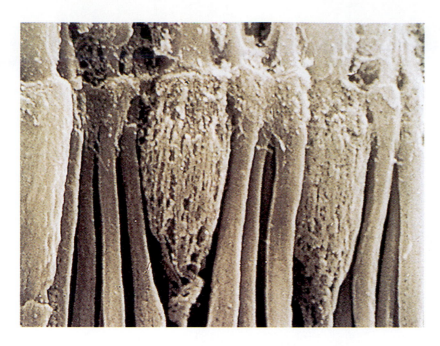

Figure 4–6
PHOTORECEPTORS. *An electron microscope photo of photoreceptors shows the distinct shape and length of the rods and the cones.*

of the more complex function of cones with regard to the processing of color.

As noted earlier, the axons of the ganglion cells in the eye collectively form the optic nerve for that eye. The optic nerves of the two eyes join at the base of the brain, to form the optic chiasma. At this point, the ganglion cells from the inward, or nasal, part of the retina—the part closer to your nose—cross through the optic chiasma and go to the opposite hemisphere of the brain. The ganglion cells from the outward, or temporal, area of the retina, closer to your temple, go to the hemisphere on the same side of the body. The lens of each eye naturally inverts the image of the world as it projects the image onto the retina, so that the message sent to your brain is literally upside-down and backward (see Figure 4-7).

After being routed via the optic chiasma, the ganglion cells then go to the thalamus. From the thalamus, neurons carry information to the primary visual cortex in the occipital lobe of the brain. The visual cortex contains several processing areas, each of which handles different kinds of visual information relating to intensity and quality, including color, location, depth, pattern, and form.

How We See: Rods and Cones

There are two separate visual systems. One system, responsible for vision in dim light, depends on the rods. The other, responsible for vision in brighter light, depends on the cones.

What evidence supports the existence of two separate visual systems? Evidence comes both from psy-chophysical tests and from people who lack either rods or cones. Although such people are rare, they can be found, and they were first studied by German physiologist J. A. von Kries. Von Kries (1895) found that people with no (or nonfunctioning) rods suffer from night blindness. From twilight onward, and without artificial light, they cannot see.

Individuals without functioning cones, in contrast, exhibit day, or bright light, blindness. Whereas they can see relatively well when light is dim, they find normal sunlight or bright artificial light painful, and they have very poor visual *acuity* (keenness of sensation) in such light. People without working cones are also completely color-blind, because the cones receive color, but the rods do not. It is for this reason that for all of us, in dim light, objects appear only in various shades of gray (see Figure 4-8). Our night vision is *achromatic*, or lacking color.

The rods and the cones are unequally distributed in the eye, as shown in Figure 4-9. The cones are highly concentrated in the fovea, which makes it the area of clearest vision. In fact, when you look straight at an object, your eyes rotate so that the image falls directly onto the fovea. The visual receptive field of the fovea is approximately as big as the size of a grape held at arm's length. The rods, in contrast, are spread throughout the retina, except for two locations—the fovea and the blind spot.

The **blind spot** is the small area on the retina where the optic nerve pushes aside photoreceptors to exit the eye. Because you lack photoreceptors in the blind spot, you are unable to see any images that happen to be projected onto that spot. You are not normally aware of the

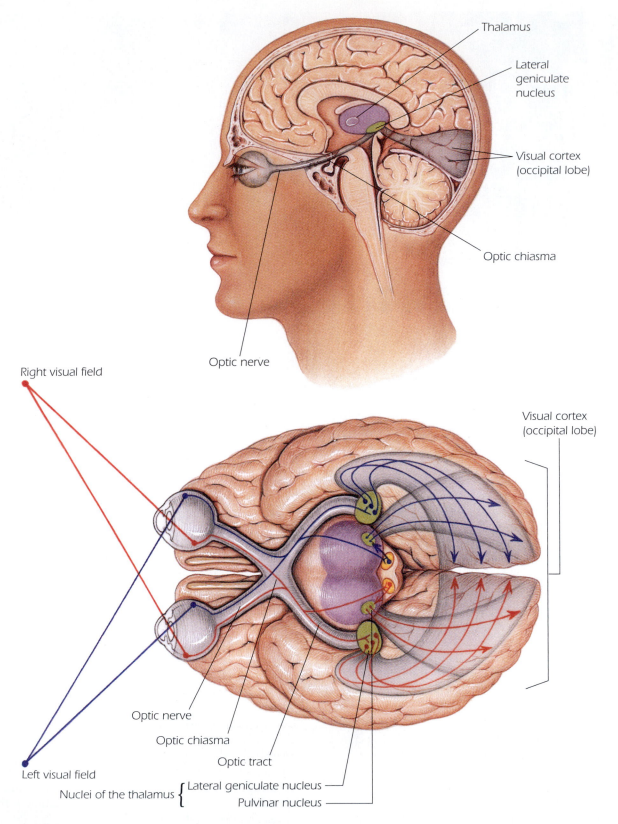

Figure 4–7
NEURAL PATHWAYS FROM THE EYE TO THE BRAIN.   *From the photoreceptors in the retina, the ganglion cells travel to the optic nerve of each eye. The impulses from each side of the eye then route via the optic nerve through the optic chiasma to the thalamus. The thalamus organizes the visual information and sends it to the visual cortex in the occipital lobe.*

Figure 4–8
COLORFUL CONES AND MONOCHROMATIC RODS. *During the day, in bright light, our cones enable us to see vivid colors. As the sun sets, limiting the amount of light, our rods enable us to see the same image but in monochromatic shades—that is, in shades of gray.*

blind spot, in part because the blind spot of one eye is in the normal visual field of the other eye, and your brain uses the complete information from each eye to compensate for the blind spot in the complementary eye (see Figure 4-10).

Your day vision, as you have probably already noticed, is better when you look at objects directly in front, rather than off to the side, of you. Your rod-based night vision is better for objects in your peripheral vision than in your central line of vision (see Figure 4-11). Thus, at night, you can see a star more clearly if you look just to the side of it. One star may appear to us as brighter than another. How do we detect brightness and differences in brightness?

How We See Brightness

Light has the physical dimensions of intensity and *wavelength* (the distance from the crest of one wave to the crest of the next wave). It also has the corresponding psychological dimensions of brightness and color, which result from how our bodies and minds process the physical information we take in through our receptors. The physically quantifiable amount of light that reaches our eyes from an object is termed the *retinal illuminance*. *Brightness*, however, refers not to an actual quantifiable light intensity, but to our *impression* of light intensity, based on lightwave *amplitude* or "height." Brightness is thus a psychological rather

Figure 4–9
RETINA OF THE EYE. *In the fovea, the center of the retina, the concentration of cones is greater. In the periphery of the retina, the concentration of rods is greater. Why are these photoreceptors distributed as they are?*

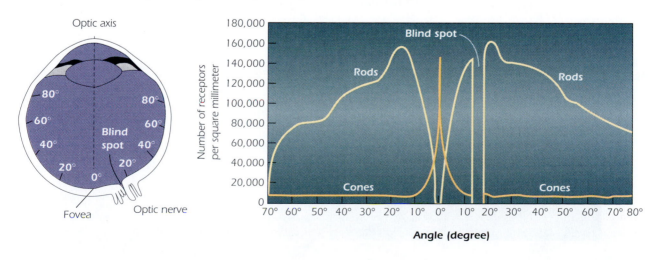

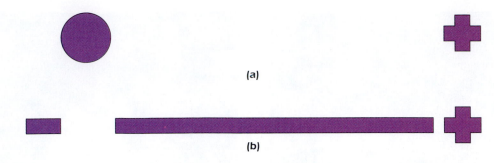

Figure 4–10
BLIND SPOT.   *To find your blind spot, hold this page about 12 inches from your face and close your right eye. Staring at the cross in the upper right corner, gradually move the page toward and away from your face until the circle on the left disappears. You can do the same to the cross and the bar, until the bar seems solid.*

Figure 4–11
VISUAL ACUITY.   *In dim light, look directly at these converging lines and mark with your finger where the lines begin to blur together. Then look slightly to the side and again mark where the lines begin to blur. Which condition showed greater acuity? Why?*

than a physical quantity (see Figure 4-12). Our sensation of brightness is not directly related to the actual intensity of light reflected by an object. Rather, the relationship is curvilinear: An increase of one physical unit decreases in its impact as the intensity of the light increases. (We saw this principle earlier in the discussion of psychophysics.)

We sense brightness partly because of the physical structure of the eye—that is, perceived brightness depends in part on the retinal location of the image of a stimulus. The rods, the more light-sensitive photoreceptor cells, are concentrated in the periphery of the retina, and are more sensitive to brightness than are the cones. As a result, we are more sensitive to brightness in the periphery of our visual field than at its center. Habituation (discussed further below) and sensory adaptation also affect our sensation of brightness.

As mentioned previously, our senses help us adapt to environmental changes. When you walk from a dark room into bright sunlight, you probably have to squint, and you may even have to close your eyes for a moment. Your eyes are experiencing *light adaptation*—adjustment to an increase in light intensity. Similarly, when you go from the bright outdoors into a dim or dark room, at first you will have difficulty seeing anything at all. It may take 30 minutes, or even more, for your eyes to adapt fully. Here, you are experiencing *dark adaptation*—adjustment to a decrease in light intensity. Interestingly, in dark adaptation, although your pupil area may increase by a factor of only as much as 16, your visual sensitivity to light may increase by a factor of as much as 100,000—quite a difference. The time course of dark adaptation, as measured by absolute thresholds, does not progress uniformly, as shown by the oddly shaped

Figure 4–12
BRIGHTNESS AS A PSYCHOLOGICAL PHENOMENON.   *Which gray area in the center appears to be brightest? Why?*

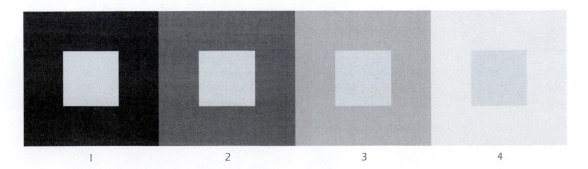

| 1 | 2 | 3 | 4 |

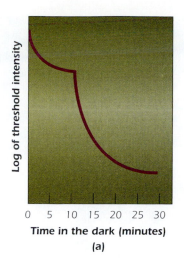  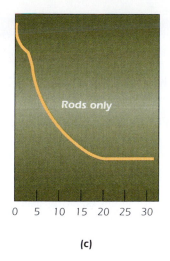

Figure 4–13

DARK ADAPTATION CURVE. *After participants have adapted to a bright light, they are placed in darkness and become increasingly sensitive to light. The sharp break in the curve at about 10 minutes is known as the rod-cone break.*

curve in Figure 4-13. What might generate this oddly shaped curve for the time course of dark adaptation?

The appearance of a discontinuity in a curve often suggests that two or more processes underlie the function represented by the curve. As you may have guessed, the two mechanisms involve the cones and the rods. The cones adapt quickly, but the rods take up to 30 minutes to reach maximum sensitivity. Because these mechanisms enter the process of dark adaptation at different times, they generate an irregular curve.

How We See Color

An area of psychological research about which there is considerable controversy is color vision. Look at Figure 4-14. Can you see the shapes embedded in it? If so, it is likely you have normal color vision. Some people, who are wholly or partially color-blind, do not see red or green. Rather, they may see either or both of these colors as shades of gray. Before we address color-blindness and its causes, however, we

Figure 4–14

PSYCHOPHYSICAL TESTS FOR COLOR-BLINDNESS. *What shapes can you see when you look at these circles? These and other psychophysical tests are used to diagnose various kinds of red-green color-blindness.*

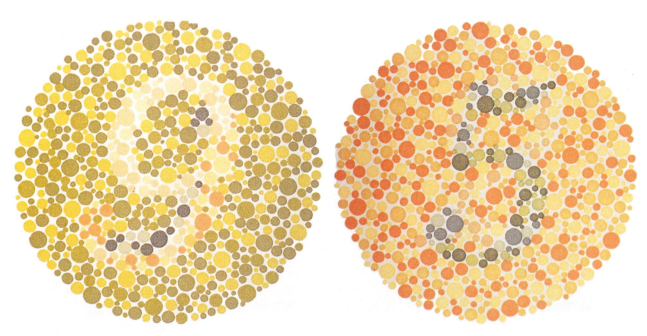

should look at how a person with normal vision senses color.

Physical Properties of Light and Psychological Sensations of Color

Wavelength produces the most basic quality for us—hue. *Hue* corresponds quite closely to what we call "color." Those of us with normal color vision see light waves of a variety of hues within the visible electromagnetic spectrum. The shortest wavelengths we can see are violet (starting at a wavelength of about 350 nm), and the longest are reddish (up to a wavelength of about 750 nm). Colors are not inherent in the objects we see as colored. They are not even inherent in the light reflected from objects. Rather, colors are a reaction of our nervous systems to particular wavelengths of the visible spectrum. The sensation of color, then, lies in the interaction between light and the nervous system.

A second property of color, also determined by spectral wavelength, is the color's saturation. *Saturation* refers to how vivid, vibrant, or rich the hue appears. A highly saturated hue will seem to be bursting with color, with no hint of paleness, whereas a weakly saturated one will seem to be washed out. The third property of color, *brightness*, was described earlier in terms of the way we see visible light. Brightness is caused by the amplitude of the light wave and refers to the amount of light that we see as emanating from the hue. (See Figure 4-15 for illustrations of these properties.)

Relationships Among Colors

We know that the colors we see correspond to spectrum intensities that increase from violet (the shortest visible wavelength) to red (the longest). Yet, psychologically, violet and red do not appear to be as different from each other as, say, do violet and green, or red and green. Somehow, the way that we perceive colors to be related psychologically is not the way that they are related in terms of physical wavelengths on the spectrum you saw back in Figure 4-3.

Within the visible spectrum, we see approximately 150 hues, but most of the hues we see are not pure. *Purity* refers to the extent to which a hue cannot be analyzed in terms of a combination of other hues. It is by combining hues that we obtain the vast majority of the hues that we see. Given that hues can also have brightness and saturation, we can discriminate more than 7 million colors of varying hue, intensity, and brightness. It turns out that these hues can be mixed to produce other hues in two ways.

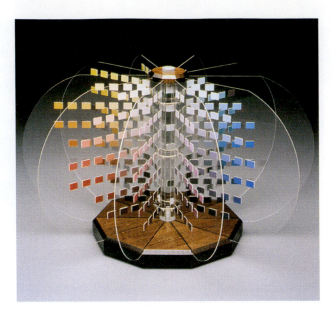

Figure 4-15
COLOR SOLID.   *The color solid shows the three dimensions of color vision: hue (around the circumference), saturation (along the horizontal axis), and brightness (along the vertical axis).*

Mixtures of Colors

Colors can be mixed either additively or subtractively, two processes that work quite differently and result in different colors. When light waves of varying wavelengths are mixed or blended, as when aiming spotlights of different colors toward one point, we obtain an **additive color mixture.** Each light wave *adds* its wavelength to the color mixture, and the resulting sum of the wavelengths is what we see. Figure 4-16a shows what happens when red light, blue light, and green light are mixed in different combinations. The additive mixture of all three colors, or indeed, of all colors, of light will produce white light.

Unless you have worked as a lighting technician, you are probably more familiar with **subtractive color mixture,** which is the remaining wavelengths of light that are reflected from an object after other wavelengths of light have been absorbed by that object. Most colored objects do not generate light. Rather, they reflect it. That is, an apple appears red to us not because it generates red light, but because it absorbs all wavelengths other than red, subtracting those colors from our sight. It reflects only red light. Therefore, when light-reflecting colors (such as those found in paint pigments) are mixed, the combination of pigments *absorbs*, or *subtracts* from our vision, more wavelengths of light than each pigment does individually. The more light that is subtracted, the darker the result

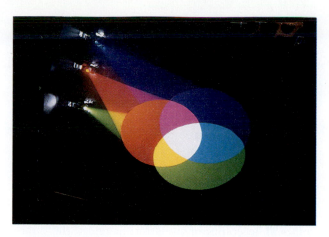

Figure 4-16

COLOR MIXTURES. *Additive color mixtures (a, left) combine lights; when all light colors are mixed together, the result is white. Subtractive color mixtures (b, right) combine pigments; when the three primary pigments are mixed together, the result is black.*

looks. Figure 4-16b shows what happens when sub-tractively mixing together pigments that are yellow, *cyan* (greenish blue as a pigment, but deep blue when used as an additive color), and *magenta* (purplish red).

Theories of Color Vision

Scientists who wish to propose a theory of color vision must address the question of how we can see more than 150 hues and many thousands of colors that dif-fer in saturation and brightness, as well as in hue (Coren, Ward, & Enns, 1994). Almost certainly, we could not have a different kind of receptor for each conceivable hue.

Trichromatic Theory. One possible mechanism draws on our understanding of the notion of *primary colors* (red, green, and blue), which can combine additively to form all other colors. If primary colors can generate all of the different hues, then perhaps different receptors are somehow attuned to each of the primary colors. Imagine, for example, that there are just three kinds of receptors, one especially sensitive to red, one to green, and one to blue. Each receptor is a different type of cone (each of which functions via a different kind of photopigment). The idea, then, is that three different photopigments exist, one of which is activated primarily on exposure to what we see as red, one to what we see as green, and one to what we see as blue. We see the full range of colors by the combination and the amount of activation of the pigments by which each of the three kinds of cones operates. Figure 4-17 shows how cones respond to different wavelengths of light. This theory was originally proposed by Thomas Young (1901/1948) and revived by Hermann von Helmholtz (1909/1962).

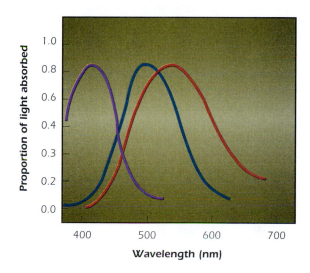

Figure 4-17

TRICHROMATIC THEORY. *According to the trichromatic theory, our cones are particularly receptive to light of specific relative wavelengths. Each cone absorbs lightwaves that are ei-ther short, medium, or long. Light of relatively short wave-length is violet or blue, light of medium wavelength is green and yellow, and light of relatively long wavelength is orange or red. (After Wald & Brown, 1965)*

Young and Helmholtz worked solely from behavioral data, rather than studying the anatomy of the eye. Today, their theory is known as the Young–Helmholtz theory, or the **trichromatic theory of color vision,** one of two proposed mechanisms for explaining how color vision occurs.

Support for the trichromatic theory can be found by studying people whose cones are defective. Most people who have such defects are only selectively color-blind. They can see some colors, but not others. The trichromatic theory suggests that people who are selectively color-blind will have trouble seeing red, or green, or blue, or combinations thereof. This prediction is, in fact, confirmed by empirical observations (C. H. Graham & Hsia, 1954). In addition, the genes that direct the cones to produce red-, green-, or blue-sensitive pigments have been found (Nathans, Thomas, & Hogness, 1986), lending further support to the trichromatic approach.

Opponent-Process Theory. The other major theory of color vision is the **opponent-process theory of color vision,** proposed originally by psychophysiologist Ewald Hering (1878/1964) and formalized by Leo Hurvich and Dorothea Jameson (1957). The opponent-process theory is based on the notion of opposing processes in human vision, each of which contrasts one color with another. It specifies two sets of two opposed colors—four colors altogether. The four opposed colors, according to the opponent-process theory, are blue and yellow, and red and green. Hurvich and Jameson also count black and white as a third opposing set of achromatic primaries that are perceived in much the same way as are the other opposing pairs.

Hering noted that we virtually never combine the opposing primaries, referring, say, to a yellowish blue or a reddish green. Hering's suggestion was that a single neuron handles both colors in an opponent color pair. The activity of the neuron either increases or decreases, depending on which color in the pair is presented. For example, the activity of a red–green opponent-pair neuron would increase with exposure to red and decrease with exposure to green. If you detected red at a particular point on your retina, you would be physiologically unable also to detect green at that same point, which explains why you cannot see greenish red. Red–green and yellow–blue neurons interact to produce sensations of other colors.

There is both psychological and physiological evidence to support the opponent-process theory. When people select what they think are the essential colors, they choose the four primaries postulated by the opponent-process theory. Furthermore, neurophysiological excitation of a red receptor does seem to inhibit the sensation of green, and vice versa. The same applies for blue and yellow (Hurvich & Jameson, 1957). Opponent-process theory also explains and is explained by afterimages (see Figure 4-18). If you stare at a colored picture for a prolonged period and then look away at a white blank space you will see an afterimage of the same picture in different colors. The colors of the afterimage are the opponent colors of opponent-process theory.

The trichromatic and opponent-process theories appear both to be correct, but at different levels of analysis. The trichromatic theory accounts for aspects of color vision at the level of receptors. The opponent-process theory accounts for aspects of color vision at the higher level of the ganglia. Thus, the trichromatic theory is correct with regard to the existence of three types of cones in the retina. But this theory does not explain complementary colors and afterimages. To understand these phenomena, we need to turn to opponent-process theory. Thus, each of the two theories seems to capture different aspects of the phenomenon of color vision (Hurvich, 1981).

Visual Perception

Sensation receives psychological meaning through perception. But sometimes the meaning it receives is illusory. Humans have been pondering perception for millennia, as indicated by the **optical illusions**—visual images that prompt distortions of visual perceptions—used in the construction of the Parthenon (Figure 4-19). What factors affect perception and whether we see optical illusions?

Figure 4–18
AFTERIMAGES. *Stare at the center of this flag for about 30 seconds, then look at a blank white page. What do you see? How would the opponent-process theory explain the afterimage that you see?*

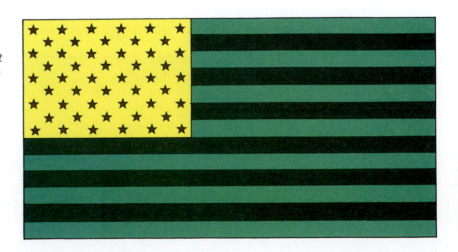

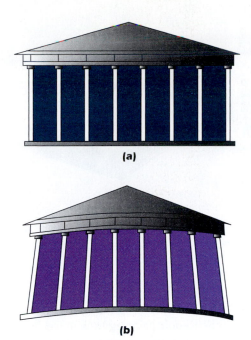

Figure 4–19

THE PARTHENON. *Ictinus and Callicrates, designers of the Parthenon, were keenly aware of optical illusions—that is, how the immense facade would appear to people standing at its base. To make the facade look rectilinear (a), they raised the center of the base to offset the illusion (b).*

Perceptual Constancies

Picture yourself walking across campus to your psychology class. Suppose that a student is standing just outside the door as you approach. As you get closer to the door, the amount of retinal space devoted to the student increases. Yet, despite this clear sensory evidence that the student is becoming larger, you know that the student has remained the same size. Why is that?

Your classmate's apparent consistency in size is an example of perceptual constancy. **Perceptual constancy** is the perception that stimuli remain the same even when immediate sensations of the stimuli change. There are several kinds of perceptual constancies.

Size Constancy

Size constancy is the perception that an object maintains the same size despite changes in the size of the proximal stimulus on the retina. The size of an image on the retina directly depends on the distance of that object from the eye. That is, the same object at two different distances projects different-sized images on the retina. Size constancy is illustrated nicely by *Le Moulin de la Galette*, a painting by French Impressionist Pierre-Auguste Renoir (1841–1919), shown in Figure 4-20. The characters in the background are much smaller than the ones in the foreground, but we are

not led to believe that the background characters are midgets or the foreground characters, giants. Rather, we perceive all of the characters as being about the same size because of size constancy.

Size constancy is learned through experience. A classic example of how experience helps us interpret

Figure 4–20

THE ROLE OF SIZE CONSTANCY IN ART. *French Impressionist Pierre-Auguste Renoir's* Le Moulin de la Gallette *relies on our perception of size constancy to know that the people in the background are similar in size to those in the foreground.*

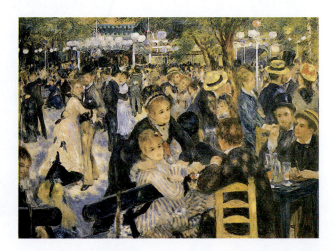

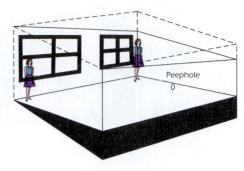

Figure 4–21
PERCEPTUAL CONSTANCY.   *When we view the boy and dog through a hole in the wall, we perceive impossible relative sizes. When we see a sketch of the room, however, we see that its shape is actually quite distorted.*

perceptions comes from C. Turnbull's (1961) ethnographic account of the pygmies of the Iturbi forest. Turnbull told of a pygmy who once accompanied him out of the forest. At one point, the two saw some cows grazing in the distance. Although most pygmies frequently have seen cows at close range in the forest, few have ever seen cows at a distance. Much to Turnbull's surprise, his travel companion thought that he was looking at ants.

Our ability to use size constancy can be fooled when we experience novel stimuli, such as the distorted room shown in Figure 4-21. More often,

though, we encounter situations such as that shown in Figure 4-20. We observe that the persons in the foreground of the Renoir painting back in the figure are of roughly the same height with respect to the bench as the persons in the background. Hence, the contextual information provided by the bench tells us that all the people are of roughly the same height.

Some striking illusions can be achieved when our perceptual apparatus is fooled by the very same information that usually helps us to experience size constancy. For example, in Figures 4-22a and b, we perceive the top line and the top log as being longer

Figure 4–22
PONZO ILLUSION.
Which log is larger? Measure the logs. The principle of size constancy leads us to believe that the log farther from us is larger.

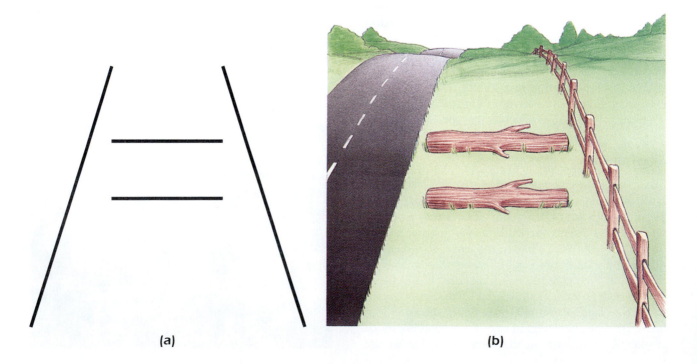

(a)   (b)

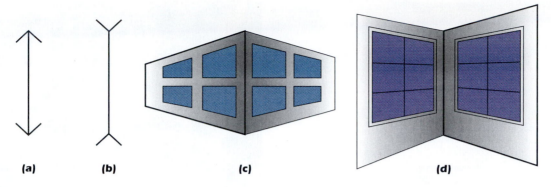

(a)   (b)   (c)   (d)

Figure 4–23
MÜLLER-LYER ILLUSION.   *Which of the line segments (a or b, c or d) is longer? Measure them. The principle of depth constancy may lead us to perceive the inward-facing angles as being larger, as if they represent the "far" corner of the room instead of the "near" corner of the wall.*

than the bottom line and the bottom log, respectively, even though the top and bottom figures are identical in length. We do so because in the real three-dimensional world, the top line and log would be larger. This effect, called the **Ponzo illusion,** stems from the depth cue provided by the converging lines.

Another illusion, which you may have seen elsewhere, is the **Müller–Lyer illusion,** illustrated in Figure 4-23. In this illusion, too, we tend to view two equally long line segments as being of different lengths. In particular, the vertical line segments in panels a and c appear shorter than the line segments in panels b and d, even though all the line segments are of the same length. Psychologists are not certain why such a simple illusion occurs. One explanation is that the diagonal lines at the ends of the vertical segments in panels a and b serve as implicit depth cues similar to the ones we would see in our perceptions of the exterior and interior of a building (Coren & Girgus, 1978; Gregory, 1966).

When considering this and other illusions, remember that such illusions are relatively rare occurrences in our lives and often have to be contrived quite carefully to work. The large majority of the time our perceptual apparatus enables us to perceive things, such as size, in ways that are surprisingly accurate, even in the face of potential distortions (such as varying degrees of fog or rain). Our perceptual apparatus also enables us to perceive shape constancy.

Shape Constancy

Shape constancy refers to our perceiving an object as retaining its shape, even when the shape of its retinal image changes. For example, in Figure 4-24, you see a rectangular door and door frame, with the door closed, slightly opened, or half-opened. Of course, the

door does not seem to take on a different shape in each panel. It would be odd, indeed, if we perceived a door to be changing shape as we opened it. Yet, the shape of the image of the door is different in each panel and the image of the door on the retina does change as we open the door.

Lightness Constancy

Lightness constancy refers to our perception that an object is evenly illuminated, despite differences in the actual amount of light reaching our eyes. In fact, we are remarkably capable of compensating for differences in the actual amount of light that is reflected at a given moment. For example, observe how Jan Vermeer used lightness constancy to advantage in his painting *Woman Holding a Balance,* shown in Figure 4-25. The wall in the background is illuminated by a brilliant ray of light, as is part of the face of the woman weighing gold. Nonetheless, we see the whole wall as blue and the gold-weigher's face as white, despite the fact that the shadings of light on the wall and her face are varied. Similarly, if you observe this page with different shading caused by different amounts of background illumination, the page will always appear white and of roughly the same shade.

An interesting way of viewing perception and the phenomena associated with it is to consider evolutionary theory. That is, how does perceptual constancy aid us in surviving and being able to reproduce? We are indeed more adaptive because of the way our brains work to create the constancies described here. In fact, we would not survive long in this world if we were unable to experience perceptual constancies. You could not even have located this book on your desk—let alone opened the book and positioned it for reading—if you were incapable of perceptual constancy. Without such

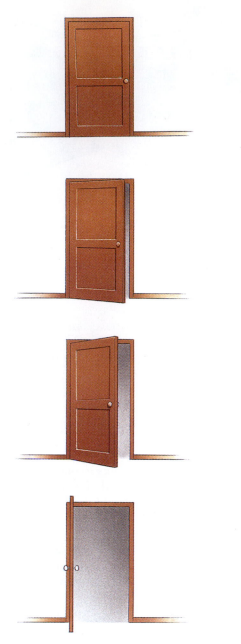

Figure 4–24
SHAPE CONSTANCY. *When we look at a door, we perceive it always to have the same shape, even though our sensations of the shape change as the door opens and closes. (After Gibson, 1950)*

constancy, you could not recognize the book as the same object, despite changes in retinal illumination with changes in room lighting or changes in the shape of the book's image on the retina with changes in the book's position on the desk. Without perceptual constancies, you would be lost in the world and your survival would be at risk.

Another important survival skill, for both humans and animals, is the ability to perceive depth, which we will discuss next.

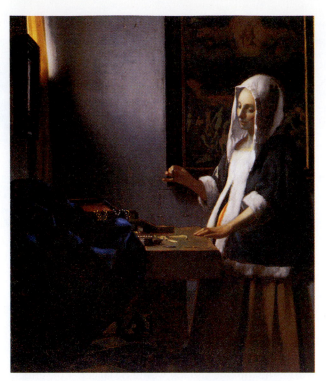

Figure 4–25
LIGHTNESS CONSTANCY. *In* Woman Holding a Balance, *painted about 1657, Dutch artist Jan Vermeer uses the principles of lightness constancy to manipulate our perception of the people and the room. We perceive his use of highlighting and shadowing as changes in illumination, not as changes in the perceived lightness of the room.*

Depth Perception

Before you read this section, look at the engraving by William Hogarth in Figure 4-26. List the perceptual cues in Hogarth's picture that are consistent with other such cues and those that are not consistent with other cues. (For example, notice some oddities about the sign hanging in front of the building.)

As you move, you constantly look around and visually orient yourself in three-dimensional space. As you look forward into the distance, you look into the third dimension of *depth*, or distance from a surface (usually using your own body as that reference surface). Whenever you transport your body, reach for or manipulate objects, or otherwise position yourself in your three-dimensional world, you must make judgments regarding depth.

You even make judgments regarding depth and distances that extend beyond the range of your body's reach. When you drive, you judge depth to assess the distance of an approaching automobile. When you decide to call out to a friend walking down the street, you determine how loudly to call according to how far

Figure 4-26
FALSE PERSPECTIVE.   *At first, the engraving of English artist William Hogarth (1697–1764) seems realistic, but closer inspection reveals conflicting perceptual cues. As Hogarth explained, "Whoever makes a design, without the knowledge of perspective, will be liable to such absurdities as are shown in this print."*

away you perceive your friend to be. If you decide to jump into water, you use depth cues to ascertain whether you are about to land with a thud in shallow water or to plunge freely into deep water.

As can happen with size constancies, we can also be taken in by optical illusions of depth. An everyday example of such an illusion is our belief that two-dimensional representations actually have depth when we enjoy television and movies. Generally, depth cues are either monocular (one-eyed) or binocular (two-eyed). We consider each of these kinds of cues in turn.

Monocular Depth Cues

One way of judging depth is through **monocular depth cues,** which can be represented in just two dimensions, as in a picture. These depth cues are referred to as "monocular" because one eye is sufficient to perceive them, in contrast to depth cues (considered later) that require two eyes to be perceived. Refer to Figure 4-27, *The Annunciation,* which illustrates the following monocular depth cues.

Relative size is the perception that things farther away (such as the rear tiles on the floor or the trees in

the background) are smaller; the farther away an object is, the smaller its image is on the retina. When you look down from an ascending airplane, the automobiles look like toys, and the people, if you can still see them, look like midgets. Our ability to perceive depth, using relative size as a cue, is related to our ability to perceive size constancy.

Texture gradient is a change in both the relative sizes of objects and the densities in the distribution of objects—distances among particles, components, or objects—when viewed at different distances. Consider the floor tiles again. At a distance, the floor tiles appear much more densely packed than when viewed from up close.

Interposition occurs when an object perceived to be closer partially blocks the view of an object perceived to be farther away. That is, the blocking object, such as the angel in Figure 4-27, is perceived to be in front of the blocked object, in this case the columns and the wall.

Figure 4-27
MONOCULAR DEPTH CUES IN ART.   *Giovanni di Paolo's* The Annunciation, *painted in 1481, illustrates several monocular depth cues: texture gradients, relative size, interposition, linear perspective, location in the picture plane, and aerial perspective.*

Linear perspective helps us make judgments about distance based on the perception that parallel lines, such as the lines along the sides of the corridor walls in Figure 4-27, or the rails of a railroad track as you stand on it, appear to converge as they move farther into the distance. In some pictures, the lines extend all the way toward the horizon, where we can see the so-called vanishing point. At the *vanishing point*, the lines appear to converge, becoming indistinguishable, and then to disappear entirely at the horizon.

Location in the picture plane indicates depth, in that objects farther from the horizon are more distant. When the objects we look at are below the horizon, the objects that are higher in the picture plane appear to be more distant (such as the location of the door at the end of the corridor, compared with the figures of Mary and the angel kneeling in the cubicle to the foreground). When the objects we look at are above the horizon, higher objects appear to be closer. In other words, the closer the object is to the plane of the horizon, the farther it is perceived to be from the viewer. Try noticing this phenomenon for yourself, either by looking out the window or by drawing a horizon and then drawing two birds, one higher and one lower in the picture plane. Then notice which bird appears to be closer to you.

Aerial perspective enables people to use the relative distribution of moisture and dust particles in the atmosphere as a means of judging distance. Objects closer to us are relatively unaffected by these particles and therefore appear clear. But, at increasing distances, larger numbers of these particles make objects appear hazier and less distinct. Notice how clear the two figures in the foreground appear in comparison to the mountains visible through the doorway at the end of the corridor. The effect of aerial perspective is particularly dramatic on foggy, smoggy, or otherwise hazy days, when objects can appear farther away than they actually are because of the unusually high concentration of water droplets or dust particles in the air. On a particularly clear day, objects may appear closer than they actually are, due to the near-absence of such particles. On a clear day, a mountain range that is a day's drive away can look as though it can be reached in a couple of hours.

Glance back at Hogarth's *False Perspective* (Figure 4-26) and your list of perceptual cues and miscues. How many cues did you miss before that you can find now? One final monocular depth cue is not shown clearly in either *The Annunciation* or Hogarth's engraving: motion parallax.

Motion parallax is the apparent difference in the speed and direction of objects when seen from a moving viewpoint. Because motion parallax is the result of movement, it cannot be shown in a two-dimensional, static picture. You have observed the phenomenon before, however. Imagine going for a ride in a train and watching the passing scenery through a side window. Parallax is created by motion as you move from one point to another and apprehend stationary distant objects from changing points of view. If you look through the window and fixate on one given point in the scene, objects closer to you than that point will appear to be moving in the direction opposite to your direction, while objects beyond the fixation point will appear to be moving in the same direction as you are. You thereby obtain a depth cue by ascertaining which objects are moving in which direction. Moreover, the objects that are closer to you (either before or after your focal point) appear to be moving (toward you or with you) more quickly than do objects that are farther away (see Figure 4-28).

Motion parallax is more visually complex than the other monocular cues because it requires movement and therefore cannot be used to judge depth in a stationary image, such as a picture. Another level of complexity involves binocular depth cues, which are based on disparities in perception between the two eyes. Table 4-4 summarizes some of the monocular and binocular cues used in perceiving depth.

Binocular Depth Cues

Binocular depth cues capitalize on the fact that each eye views a scene from a slightly different angle; this disparity of viewing angles provides information about

Figure 4-28
EFFECTS OF MOTION PARALLAX.   *When we are moving through a (relatively) stationary environment, the objects we see will appear to move in the direction opposite to the direction of our own actual movement.*

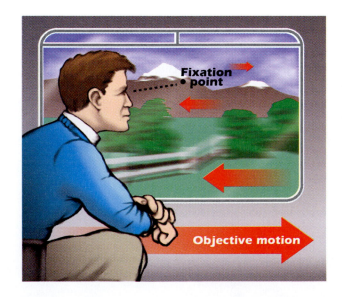

TABLE 4–4

Monocular and Binocular Cues for Depth Perception *Various perceptual cues help us perceive the three-dimensional world. We can observe some of these cues with only one eye and others with both eyes.*

CUES FOR DEPTH PERCEPTION	APPEARS CLOSER	APPEARS FARTHER AWAY
Monocular Depth Cues		
Texture gradients	Larger grains, farther apart	Smaller grains, closer together
Relative size	Bigger	Smaller
Interposition	Partially obscures other object	Is partially obscured by other object
Linear perspective	Apparently parallel lines seem to diverge	Apparently parallel lines seem to converge
Aerial perspective	Images seem crisper, more clearly delineated	Images seem fuzzier, less clearly delineated
Location in the picture plane	Above the horizon, objects are higher in the picture plane; below the horizon, objects are lower in the picture plane	Above the horizon, objects are lower in the picture plane; below the horizon, objects are higher in the picture plane
Motion parallax	Objects closer to you than the fixation point appear to be moving in the direction opposite to your direction	Objects beyond the fixation point appear to be moving in the same direction as you
Binocular Depth Cues		
Binocular convergence	Eyes feel a tug inward toward nose	Eyes relax outward toward ears
Binocular disparity	Huge discrepancy between image seen by left eye and image seen by right eye	Minuscule discrepancy between image seen by left eye and image seen by right eye

depth. The term for three-dimensional perception of the world through the use of binocular (two-eyed) vision is *stereopsis*. With stereo sound, you hear slightly different sounds coming to each ear, and you fuse those sounds to form realistic auditory perceptions. With stereopsis, you receive slightly different visual images in each eye, and you fuse those two images to form realistic visual perceptions. You rely on this fusion of the images from each eye to give you a coherent visual representation of what you are viewing. Not all parts of a visual image actually fuse, although you are not normally aware of seeing two images. Under extraordinary circumstances—after a serious blow to the head, for example—your eyes may go out of alignment, and you may become uncomfortably aware of *diplopia*, or double vision. Now consider two binocular depth cues.

Binocular Convergence. Because your two eyes are in slightly different places on your head, when you rotate your eyes so that an image of an object that is in front of you falls directly on each fovea, each eye must turn inward slightly to register the same image. The closer the object you are trying to see, the more your eyes must turn inward, as illustrated by Figure 4-29. Our brains receive neural information from the eye muscles about the convergence of the eyes, and they assume that the more the eyes converge, the closer the perceived object must be.

Binocular Disparity. Because the two eyes are in different places, each has a slightly different view of the world (see Figure 4-29). Because of this binocular disparity (slight discrepancy in the viewpoint of each eye), the brain must integrate two slightly different sets of information from each of the optic nerves to make decisions about depth, as well as about height and width.

The closer an object is to us, the greater the disparity is between each eye's view of the object. You can test these differing perspectives by holding your finger about an inch from the tip of your nose. Look at it first with one eye covered, then with the other eye covered. Your finger will appear to jump back and forth. Now do the same for an object 20 feet away, then 100 yards away. The apparent jumping, which indicates the amount of binocular disparity, will decrease with distance. If something is askew in our depth perception, we are seriously impaired in our ability to function in a three-dimensional world. Another aspect of vision seems to be at least as important as depth perception and appears to be far less complex than depth perception does at first glance: form perception.

Form Perception

Form perception is what enables us to distinguish one form from another. Principles of form recognition are important not only in understanding human perception, but also in constructing machine-based perceptual systems, such as those that recognize fingerprints and faces. Our discussion of form perception is divided into two main parts: (1) how we recognize forms, and (2) how we recognize forms that fall into patterns, such as letters and numbers.

Two of the main attributes of form are size and shape. How, exactly, do we perceive size and shape? Let's consider the Gestalt and the feature-detector approaches to form perception.

The Gestalt Approach to Form Recognition

The **Gestalt approach** is based on the notion that the whole is different from the sum of its individual parts (see chapter 2). Gestalt principles are particularly relevant to understanding how we perceive an assembly of forms; they account for much of our ability perceptually to organize the world (Palmer, 1992). One of the key Gestalt ideas is that of figure and ground.

When you walk into a familiar room, you perceive that some things, such as faces in photographs or posters, stand out and that other things, like undecorated walls and floors, fade into the background. A **figure** is any object perceived as being highlighted, almost always against, or in contrast to, some kind of receding, unhighlighted (back)**ground.**

Figure 4-30 illustrates the **figure–ground** concept. It shows **reversible figures,** in which each of a given pair of adjacent or even interconnecting figures

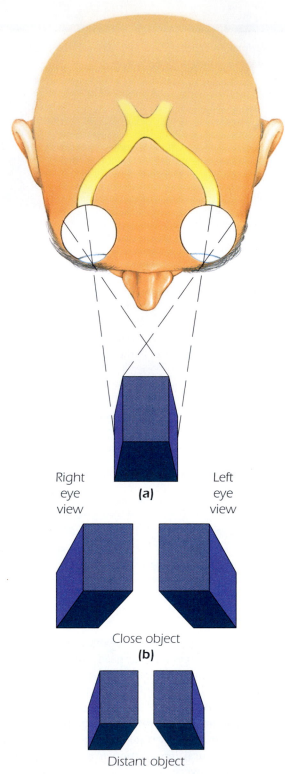

Right eye view   **(a)**   Left eye view

Close object
(b)

Distant object

Figure 4–29
BINOCULAR CONVERGENCE AND DISPARITY. *To focus on an object, our eyes converge—that is, they adjust to have the image fall on each retina (a). Because our eyes are separated, they see a slightly different angle of the object. This disparity in the view from each eye is greater for objects that are closer to us (b). Our brains use the convergence and disparity information as depth cues.*

can be seen as either figure or ground. In one, you can see a white vase against a black background; in the other, two silhouetted faces peer at each other against the ground of a white screen. Note, however, that it is impossible to see both sets of objects simultaneously. Although you may switch rapidly back and forth between the vase and the figures, you cannot see them both at the same time. A natural example in which figure–ground is important is that of camouflage: Soldiers wearing camouflage uniforms hope to blend in with the background—that is, to make it more difficult for the enemy to distinguish figure from ground.

Table 4-5 summarizes and defines a few of the Gestalt principles of form perception, including figure–ground perception: (a) proximity—elements that are close to each other are grouped together; (b) similarity—elements that resemble each other are grouped together; (c) closure—gaps in what otherwise would be viewed as a continuous border are ignored; (d) good continuation—those segments of intersecting lines that would form a continuous line with minimal change in direction are grouped together; (e) symmetry—elements are grouped together so as to form figures that comprise mirror images on either side of a central axis; and (f) common movement—elements moving in the same direction and at the same velocity are grouped together (see Figure 4-31).

The Gestalt principles of form perception are remarkably simple, yet they characterize much of our perceptual organization. It is important to realize, however, that these principles are descriptive rather than explanatory. The Gestalt perspective cannot be categorized as taking either a "top-down" constructivist

Figure 4-30
A GESTALT GIFT. *The figure shows a reversible figure-ground picture, in which one way of perceiving the picture brings one object to the fore as the figure, and another way of perceiving the picture brings out a different figure and relegates the former foreground to the background. Is this a light vase against a dark ground or the light-silhouetted profiles of Queen Elizabeth II and Prince Philip against the background? The vase was a gift to the queen on her silver jubilee.*

Figure 4-31
GESTALT PRINCIPLES OF VISUAL PERCEPTION.
The Gestalt principles of figure-ground, proximity, similarity, good continuation, closure, and symmetry aid in our perception.

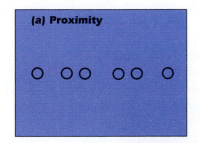

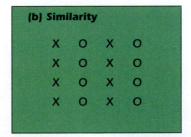

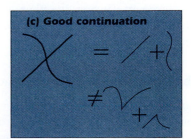

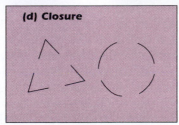

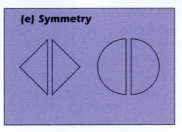

TABLE 4–5

Gestalt Principles of Form Perception

Gestalt psychologists proposed a number of principles regarding how we perceive form.

GESTALT PRINCIPLES	PRINCIPLE	FIGURE ILLUSTRATING THE PRINCIPLE
Figure–ground	When perceiving a visual field some objects (figures) seem prominent, and other aspects of the field recede into the background (ground).	Figure 4-30 shows a reversible figure–ground picture, in which one way of perceiving the picture brings one object to the fore as the figure, and another way of perceiving the picture brings out a different figure and relegates the former foreground to the background.
Proximity	When we perceive an assortment of objects, we tend to see objects that are close to each other as forming a group.	Figure 4-31a shows six circles, which we tend to see as forming groups rather than six separate circles.
Similarity	We group objects on the basis of their similarity.	Figure 4-31b shows four rows of letters. We see alternating rows of Xs and Os.
Good continuation	We tend to perceive smoothly flowing or continuous forms rather than disrupted or discontinuous ones.	Figure 4-31c shows crossed lines, which we perceive as a straight line bisecting a curved line, rather than two angles, one atop the other.
Closure	We tend perceptually to close up or complete objects that are not, in fact, complete.	Figure 4-31d shows only disjointed, jumbled line segments, which we close up in order to see a triangle and a circle.
Symmetry	We tend to perceive forms that comprise mirror images about their center, based on limited sensory information.	Figure 4-31e shows two triangles and two hemispheres, which we perceive as a diamond and a circle each split into two symmetrical parts.

approach or a "bottom-up," direct-perception approach. Merely labeling a phenomenon does not, in itself, account for how the phenomenon occurs. One contemporary approach to form perception better explains how we perceive forms.

The Feature Detection Approach

A more recent approach attempts to link the perception of form to the functioning of neurons in the brain. This psychophysiological method, the **feature-detector approach,** is an approach to form perception based on observing the activity of the brain in which specific neurons of the visual cortex respond to specific features detected by photoreceptors. This approach is the result of the pioneering work of Nobel laureates David Hubel and Torsten Wiesel (1979). Using single-cell recording techniques with animals, these researchers carefully traced the route of neurons

from the receptors in the retina, through the ganglion cells and the thalamic nucleus cells, to the visual cortex. Their research showed that specific neurons of the visual cortex respond to varying stimuli that are presented to the specific retinal regions connected to these neurons. Each individual cortical neuron, therefore, can be mapped to a specific receptive field on the retina, with a disproportionately large amount of the visual cortex devoted to neurons mapped to receptive fields in the foveal region of the retina.

Surprisingly, most of the cells in the cortex do not respond simply to spots of light, but rather to "specifically oriented line segments" (Hubel & Wiesel, 1979, p. 9). What's more, these cells vary in the degree of complexity of the stimuli to which they respond. In general, the size of the receptive field increases—as does the complexity of the stimulus required to prompt a response—as the stimulus proceeds through the visual system to higher levels in the cortex. More

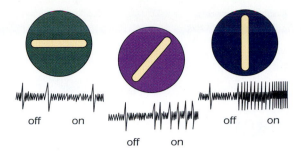

Figure 4–32
FEATURE DETECTORS. *David Hubel and Torsten Wiesel discovered that cells in our visual cortex become activated only when they detect the sensation of line segments or particular orientations. The illustrations above show the firing pattern of a cell sensitive to vertical lines.*

specifically, Hubel and Wiesel isolated three kinds of visual cortex neurons (see Figure 4-32): (1) simple cells, (2) complex cells, and (3) hypercomplex cells.

Primitive cortical cells chiefly relay information to the appropriate simple cells. These *simple cells* then fire in response to lines in the receptive field. Each of these cells seems to be most excited by lines that are located in particular parts of the receptive field, and that are of particular widths oriented at a particular optimal angle. The simple cells feed into complex cells. Each *complex cell* fires in response to lines of particular orientations anywhere in the receptive field of that cell's group of simple cells. Complex cells appear to be insensitive to the particular type of light–dark contrasts of a line segment, as long as the segment is oriented appropriately. *Hypercomplex cells* respond to particular lengths of stimulus lines. These kinds of cells may provide the basis for perceiving patterns.

Approaches to Pattern Recognition

The forms we perceive fall into patterns of various kinds. One of the more interesting problems that psychologists have tried to address is how people recognize such patterns as letters, numbers, or faces. The problem is tricky. Although it is possible to specify in a reasonably complete way the features of a letter or number, it is exceedingly difficult to specify completely the features of a face. What you may take for granted—for example, the ability to recognize the face of your friend—is not something everyone does easily.

How do you know the letter A when you see it? You may be thinking it is an A because it looks like an A. What makes it look like an A, though, instead of like an H? Just how difficult it is to answer this question becomes apparent when you look at Figure 4-33. What subjectively feels like a simple process of pattern recognition is almost certainly quite complex.

How do we connect what we sense in the environment to what we have stored in our minds? The problem posed by this question is shown in Figure 4-33, where two identical perceptual forms evoke different letter names. What explanations account for how we make the connection between what we perceive and what we know? Two main approaches to pattern recognition are template matching and feature matching.

Template-Matching Approaches. A template-matching theory posits that we have stored in our minds templates, or prototypes, which are best examples that represent each of the patterns we might potentially recognize. We recognize a pattern by matching it to the template that best fits what we see (Selfridge & Neisser, 1960). We see examples of template matching in our everyday lives. Fingerprints are matched in this way, and machines rapidly process imprinted numerals on checks by comparing them to templates. However, the theory of template matching has some obvious difficulties, as suggested by its inability to explain our perception of the words in Figure 4-33.

Feature-Matching Approaches Plausible explanations of pattern recognition that fit the Hubel and Wiesel findings are **feature-matching** theories, according to which we attempt to match features of an observed pattern to features stored in memory. One such feature-matching model is Oliver Selfridge's (1959) "pandemonium" model, based on the notion that metaphorical "demons" with specific duties receive and analyze the features of a stimulus, as shown in Figure 4-34.

Compare Selfridge's model with Hubel and Wiesel's description of the hierarchically arranged visual system. Selfridge's model describes "image demons" (much like the subcortical parts of the visual system), which pass on a retinal image to "feature demons." The feature demons behave like the simple and complex cells described by Hubel and Wiesel. Selfridge did not specify exactly what such features might be, but Hubel and Wiesel's feature detectors respond

Figure 4–33
PATTERN RECOGNITION. *When you read these words, you probably see a capital H and a capital A in the middle of each respective word. Look more closely at them though. Do any features differentiate the two letters? If not, why did you perceive them as different? (After Selfridge, 1955)*

THE CAT

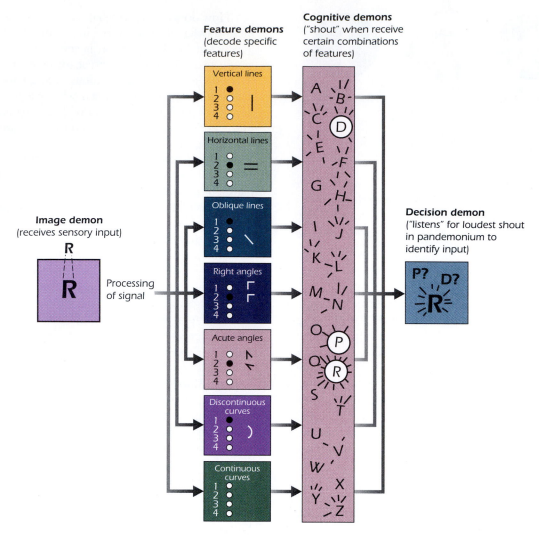

Figure 4-34

PANDEMONIUM. *According to the feature-matching model, we recognize patterns by matching observed features already stored in memory. We recognize the patterns for which we have found the greatest number of matches. (After Selfridge, 1955)*

to such features as orientation of lines, angles of intersecting lines, shapes, and so on.

At this point, the parallel ends, because Hubel and Wiesel left it to future research to trace the higher levels of cortical processing. Selfridge's model continues, suggesting that at a higher level are "cognitive [thinking] demons," which "shout out" possible patterns stored in memory that conform to one or more of the features processed by the feature demons. A "decision demon" listens to the pandemonium of the shouting cognitive demons and decides what has been seen, based on which demon is shouting the most frequently (i.e., which has the most matching features).

Although Selfridge's pandemonium model specifies neither exactly what the elementary features are, nor how to go about determining what they might be, Hubel and Wiesel supplied some of the missing information, based on how the brain really works. However, no one would argue that lines of various lengths and orientations can account for the richness of all our visual perception.

Irving Biederman (1987) has proposed a more comprehensive set of elementary components—*geons*—which are variations of the shape of a cylinder. Figure 4-35 shows how a small number of geons can be used to build up basic shapes and then basic objects. A small set of geons comprising as few as 36 elements can generate myriad three-geon objects. The idea, then, is that the perceptual system builds up a representation of what it sees by combining geons. Other theorists have taken a similar tack (e.g., Guzman, 1971; Marr, 1982). Thus, it seems within our grasp to construct a feature-matching theory that specifies the simple features that together compose complex objects; as of yet, however, no theory is definitive.

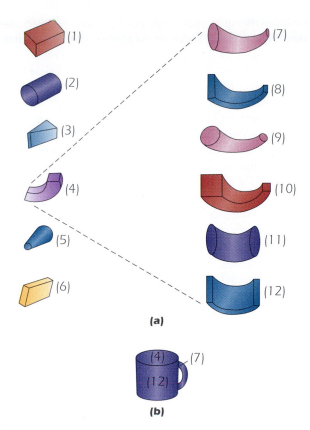

(a)

(b)

Figure 4–35

GEONS. *Irving Biederman amplified feature-matching theory by proposing a set of elementary shapes (a) that can be combined to become more sophisticated objects (b). (After Biederman, 1987)*

Problems for Theories of Pattern Perception. Neither template nor feature theories can account fully for some remaining difficult problems. One of the problems that current models still do not fully explain is the influences of the surrounding environment on cognition, *context effects*, as demonstrated when we perceived "THE CAT" correctly even though what we perceived as two different letters are actually physically identical. Clearly, some "top-down," higher order processes must be at work for us to be able to read two identical stimuli as constituting different letters.

Context effects can be demonstrated experimentally. In one study, people were asked to identify objects after they had viewed them in either an appropriate or an inappropriate context (Palmer, 1975). For example, research participants might have viewed a scene of a kitchen followed by stimuli such as a loaf of bread, a mailbox, and a drum. Objects that were appropriate to the established context, such as the loaf of bread in this example, were more rapidly recognized than were objects inappropriate to the established context.

Perhaps even more striking is a context effect known as the *word-superiority effect*, which results in

letters being more easily read when they are embedded in words than when they are presented either in isolation or with letters that do not form words. This effect again demonstrates top-down, higher order processing. The first report of this effect dates back to James McKeen Cattell (1886), who observed that it takes people substantially longer to read unrelated letters than to read letters that form a word. Further demonstrations of the effect were offered by Gerald Reicher (1969) and Daniel Wheeler (1970), and so it is sometimes called the "Reicher–Wheeler effect."

To summarize, neither template nor feature-matching approaches can explain all of the phenomena we encounter in the study of form and pattern perception. Given the complexity of the form-perception process, it is impressive that we understand as much as we do. Nevertheless, a comprehensive theory still eludes our grasp.

In addition to the challenge of explaining how we perceive forms and patterns, another challenge for perceptual theories is explaining movement. How do we know when the forms and patterns we see are moving, or when they are standing still?

Motion Perception

Through the perception of motion, we can make inferences about the forms and patterns of what we see that we could not make if we perceived objects only in stationary states. For example, Gunner Johanssen (1975) attached a small light bulb to each of the major joints of a person's body and then filmed the person walking and performing various actions so that only the lights and not the person could be seen. When people saw just a single frame—a still—they did not know what they were seeing. But even two frames of the film—a mere 1/10 second of viewing time—were sufficient for most people to recognize that they were seeing a person walking. The same paradigm with lights attached to both men and women reveals that people often judge the sex of the moving figure by the patterns of motion (Cutting, Proffitt, & Kozlowski, 1978; Runeson & Frykholm, 1986).

Our perception of motion does not depend exclusively on the motion of the object being observed. Recent research suggests that moving stimuli of higher visual contrast appear to be moving faster than stimuli of lower contrast, even when they are not actually moving faster (Gegenfurtner, Mayser, & Sharpe, 1999).

To put motion perception into context, we must note that not all psychologists agree there really is such a thing as motion perception. According to some psychologists, we do not perceive actual motion; all we see is an object first in one place, then in another. According to this view, then, motion perception is nothing more than a subconscious inference drawn from observing two static states.

Stroboscopic Motion

Through the study of stroboscopic motion, Gestalt psychologists found evidence inconsistent with the idea that motion is only inferred. **Stroboscopic motion** (termed "apparent motion" in the descriptions of Gestalt psychology in chapter 2) is the perception of motion produced by a stroboscope—an instrument that intermittently flashes an alternating pair of lights against a dark background. If the lights are flashed at an appropriate distance apart and at appropriately timed intervals (within milliseconds), it appears that a solitary light has moved. If the time interval is too short, the lights appear to flash simultaneously; if the interval is too long, the lights appear to flash in succession, and the observer does not sense the apparent motion. Given just the right timing, the experience of apparent motion indicates that the viewer actually perceives motion and does not merely make an inference from two static states (Wertheimer, 1912).

Movies and cartoons use the principle of stroboscopic motion. Similar to the stroboscope, movies are merely rapidly displayed sequences of individual frames, or single still pictures, shown at the rate of 24 frames per second. We see the same effect in signs that appear to be flowing cascades of moving lights. The apparently flowing lights are merely rapid linear sequences of individual bulbs flashing on and off.

In sum, perception can be of many different kinds of things. Recent work on visual perception has identified separate neural pathways in the cerebral cortex for processing different aspects of the same stimuli (De Yoe & Van Essen, 1988; Köhler, Kapur, Moscovitch, Winocur, & Houle, 1995), termed the "what" and the "where" pathways. The "what" pathway descends from the primary visual cortex in the occipital lobe toward the temporal lobes, and is mainly responsible for processing the color, shape, and identity of visual stimuli. The "where" pathway ascends from the occipital lobe toward the parietal lobe and is responsible for processing location and motion information. Thus, feature information feeds into at least two systems for identifying objects and events in the environment.

Deficits in Perception

Certain kinds of deficits in visual perception, as mentioned in chapter 3, are referred to collectively as *agnosias*. These severe deficits in the ability to perceive sensory information can be of different kinds. For example, people with *visual-object agnosia* can sense all parts of the visual field, but the objects they see do not mean anything to them. For example, one agnosic patient, upon seeing a pair of eyeglasses, noted first that there was a circle, then that there was another circle, then that there was a crossbar. He finally guessed that he was looking at a bicycle, which does, indeed, comprise two circles and a crossbar (Luria, 1973). In *prosopagnosia*, people have a severe deficit in their ability to recognize human faces, even though they may be able to recognize other kinds of faces, such as those of farm animals. This disorder is a hot topic of recent research (Farah, Levinson, & Klein, 1995; Farah, Wilson, Drain, & Tanaka, 1995; Haxby, Ungerleider, Horwitz, Maisog, Rappaport, & Grady, 1996).

Although most of us rely on vision as our primary means of sensing the world around us, our life experiences would be impoverished if we were deprived of our other sensations. Chief among our nonvisual senses is our sense of hearing.

Hearing

How do we hear stimuli in the environment?

The ability to hear sounds can be both a blessing and a curse. It can enable many of us to hear what goes on in the world around us. At the same time, those of us who can hear often wish we could turn down the volume, or eliminate many sounds altogether. To understand hearing, you need to know about the structures and processes that permit us to hear: the nature of sound, the functional organization of the ear, and the distinctive interactions between sound and the ear.

Physical Properties of Sound

Sound results from mechanical pressure on the air. When you pluck the string of a guitar or clap your hands together, you are pushing on air molecules. The disrupted air molecules momentarily collide with other air molecules, which then collide with still other air molecules, resulting in a three-dimensional wave of mechanical energy. The air particles themselves do not move much—it is the wave of pressure that covers the distance. Compare this effect to a line of cars waiting at a stoplight. Along comes a speeder who fails to stop in time, rear-ending the last car in line. That car then hits the car in front of it, and so on. The mechanical pressure spreads in a wave forward through the line of cars, but the car that started the wave does not move much at all. You can observe the same phenomenon with billiard balls.

We are accustomed to thinking of sound as traveling through air, but it can also result from mechanical pressure being applied to another medium, such as water. Thus, if there is no medium, such as in an airless vacuum, there is no sound. For sound to occur, there must be some particles through which the pressure wave can pass. Therefore, you can see light but not hear sound in a vacuum.

Sound also travels much more slowly than does light, which is why you see a distant lightning bolt before you hear the thunder, even though the lightning and thunder occur almost simultaneously. In addition, the speed of sound depends on the density of the medium. Somewhat surprisingly, sound generally moves more quickly through more densely packed molecules. This phenomenon is not completely counterintuitive when you think about it in terms of the car-crash analogy. The more densely packed the cars, the more rapidly the wave of crashing cars proceeds. Sound travels approximately 340 meters per second (750 miles per hour) in air, but it travels 1,360 meters per second (3,000 miles per hour) in water, which is why sounds are amplified under water.

Corresponding Physical and Psychological Properties of Sound Waves

Sound waves have three physical properties that affect how we sense them and process them psychologically. The first two are familiar: the amplitude and the wavelength. Sound amplitude (intensity) corresponds to our sensation of loudness. The higher the amplitude, the louder the sound. The usual unit of measurement for the intensity of sound is the *decibel (dB)*. The absolute threshold for normal human hearing is at zero decibels. Sound that is comfortably audible to humans ranges from about 50 to 100 decibels in amplitude and from about 20 to 20,000 hertz in frequency. For us to sense sounds above 20,000 hertz, they must have increasingly higher amplitude. Table 4-6 shows the decibel levels of various common sounds.

Sound waves also vary in frequency, which produces our sensation of *pitch*—how high or low a tone sounds. Actually, for sound, we usually speak in terms of the *frequency* of the wave, conventionally measured as the number of *cycles* (crest-to-crest

---

TABLE 4–6

Decibel Table   *This table shows the intensities of some common sounds and indicates how dangerous to our receptors certain levels of sound can become.*

DECIBEL LEVEL	EXAMPLE	TIME TO DAMAGE HEARING WITHOUT EAR PROTECTION
0	Lowest sound audible to human ear (threshold)	
30	Quiet library, soft whisper	
40	Quiet office, living room, bedroom away from traffic	
50	Light traffic at a distance, refrigerator, gentle breeze	
60	Air conditioner at 20 feet, conversation	
70	Busy traffic, noisy restaurant (constant exposure)	Critical level begins with constant exposure
80	Subway, heavy city traffic, alarm clock at 2 feet, factory noise	More than 8 hours
90	Truck traffic, noisy appliances, shop tools, lawn mower	Less than 8 hours
100	Chain saw, boiler shop, pneumatic drill	2 hours
120	Rock concert in front of speakers, sandblasting, thunderclap	Immediate danger
140	Gunshot blast, jet plane	Any exposure is dangerous
180	Spacecraft launch	Hearing loss inevitable

progressions of sound waves) per second, rather than in terms of wavelengths. A frequency of one cycle per second is called 1 *hertz (Hz)*, after the German physicist Heinrich Hertz. Humans can generally hear sound waves in the range from about 20 to 20,000 Hz, whereas many other animals can hear sound waves of much higher frequencies. Frequency and wavelength are inversely related. This inverse relationship makes sense because a short wavelength would crest over and over again more frequently than would a long one within the same space or time interval. Thus, a high-pitched sound has a high frequency and a short wavelength, and a low-pitched sound has a low-frequency sound and a long wavelength (see Figure 4-36).

The third psychological dimension of sound is timbre (pronounced "tamber"). *Timbre* is the quality of sound; it allows us to tell the difference between an A flat played on a piano and an A flat played on a harmonica. It corresponds to the visual sensation of color saturation. When you play a note on a musical instrument, you generate a complex series of tones. The single tone produced by the note itself is the *fundamental frequency*, but at the same time, the instrument produces distinctive tones—harmonics—multiples higher than the fundamental frequency. Different musical instruments produce different harmonics, resulting in the distinctive sounds of the instruments. When additional sound waves are irregular and unrelated, we

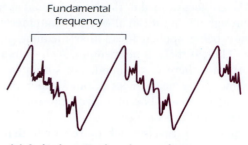

Fundamental
frequency

(a) A single note played on a piano

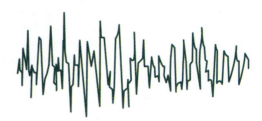

(b) Explosion (noise)

Figure 4–37
SOUND WAVES: MUSIC VERSUS AN EXPLOSION. *As you look at these two sets of sound waves, how would you explain the differences in our sensation of a single note played on a piano versus an explosion?*

hear *noise*—confusing, nonsensical, and often unpleasant combinations of sounds. (Figure 4-37 shows the contrast between the pleasant sounds of harmonics and the random dispersal of noise.) What are the parts of the ear that work together to enable us to hear noise, or anything else?

The Functional Organization of the Ear

When sound waves enter the ear, they pass through three regions: the outer ear, the middle ear, and the inner ear (see Figure 4-38a). Sound waves are collected by the **pinna,** the visible outer part of the ear. From the pinna, the sound waves move down the auditory canal toward the **eardrum** (also termed the *tympanum*), a physiological structure of the outer ear that vibrates in response to the sound waves. The higher the frequency of the sound, the faster the vibrations of the eardrum.

The eardrum vibrations pass into the middle ear, where a sequence of three tiny bones passes these vibrations to the inner ear. The three bones—the *malleus, incus,* and *stapes*—normally amplify the vibrations transmitted by the eardrum and then transmit those vibrations to the cochlea. Interestingly, though, for extremely intense sounds that could damage the inner ear, the angle of the stapes against the inner ear

Figure 4–36
PROPERTIES OF SOUND WAVES. *What we sense of sound consists of waves of compressed air. Sound waves are measured in amplitude (what we sense as loudness) and frequency (what we sense as pitch).*

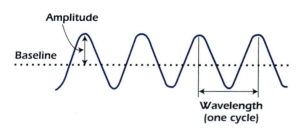

(a) Long-wavelength (low-frequency) sound

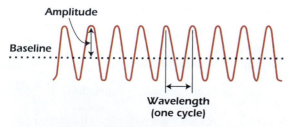

(b) Short-wavelength (high-frequency) sound

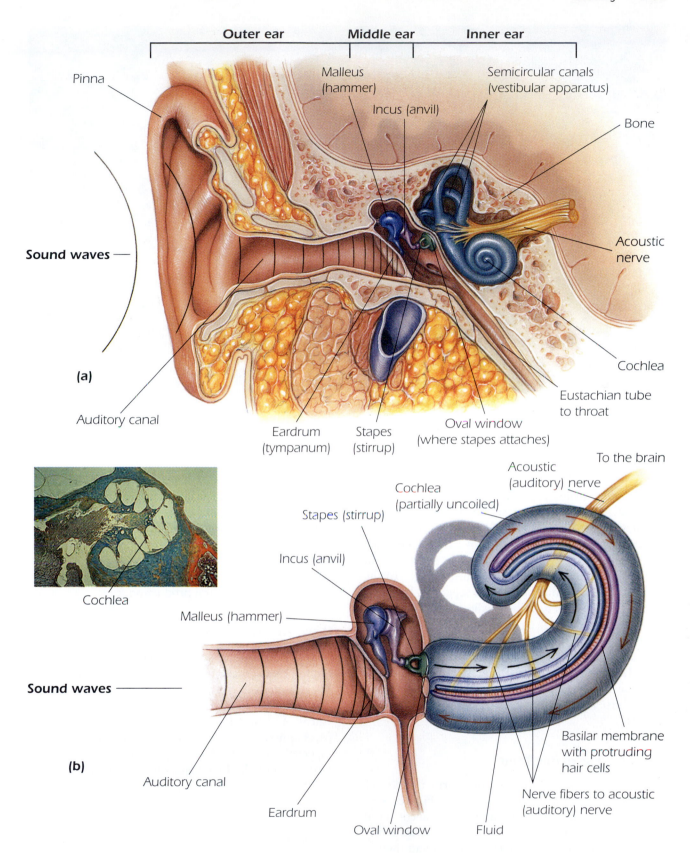

Outer ear   **Middle ear**   **Inner ear**

Pinna

Malleus
(hammer)

Incus (anvil)

Semicircular canals
(vestibular apparatus)

Bone

Sound waves

Acoustic
nerve

(a)

Cochlea

Eustachian tube
to throat

Auditory canal

Eardrum
(tympanum)

Stapes
(stirrup)

Oval window
(where stapes attaches)

To the brain

Acoustic
(auditory) nerve

Cochlea
(partially uncoiled)

Stapes (stirrup)

Incus (anvil)

Cochlea

Malleus (hammer)

Sound waves

Basilar membrane
with protruding
hair cells

(b)

Auditory canal

Nerve fibers to acoustic
(auditory) nerve

Eardrum

Oval window   Fluid

Figure 4–38
ANATOMY OF THE EAR.   *The ear comprises three parts: the outer, middle, and inner ear. The inner ear contains the cochlea (see detail and photograph), which includes the auditory receptors as well as the vestibular system.*

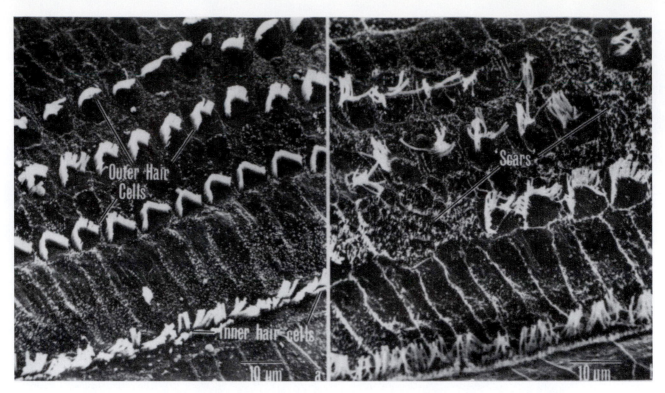

This electron micrograph shows healthy and scarred hair cells, which were damaged by prolonged exposure to loud noises.

changes, decreasing the vibration and protecting the ear—another adaptive function of our physiology.

The stapes normally rests on the **oval window,** the first part of the inner ear. As Figure 4-38b shows, the oval window is at one end of the **cochlea,** the coiled and channeled main structure of the inner ear. Three fluid-filled canals run the entire length of the cochlea. The fluid-filled canals are separated by membranes, one of which is the **basilar membrane.** On the basilar membrane are thousands of **hair cells,** which function as our auditory receptors. Specialized hairlike appendages, or offshoots, of the hair cells are moved by the vibration of the stapes. The hair cells transduce the mechanical energy into electrochemical energy that is transmitted via the sensory neurons to the brain.

From the Ear to the Brain

The axons of the sensory neurons form the *acoustic nerve* (also called the auditory nerve; see Figures 4-38 and 4-39). The specific route of information conveyed along the acoustic nerve is quite complex, involving relay stops first in the medulla oblongata and then in the midbrain. The information is finally relayed through the thalamus to the auditory cortex in the temporal lobes of the brain. The cortex seems to map out the relationships among frequencies of the auditory field in a way that roughly approximates the way the visual cortex maps out spatial relationships in the visual field. Also, although the contralateral connections are the strongest ones, some information from both ears reaches both cerebral hemispheres. In the brain, the auditory cortex is connected to our areas for language perception and production.

How We Hear

Just as we can only see intermediate wavelengths of the full electromagnetic spectrum, we are most sensitive to sounds in the middle range of audible frequencies, roughly corresponding to the range of human voices. As you might expect from our discussions of psychophysics and evolutionary adaptability, we are especially sensitive to changes in sounds, such as changes in pitch. Two major theories of how we sense pitch have been proposed: place theory and frequency theory.

Place Theory

Helmholtz (1863/1930), whose ideas on color have been seen in our discussion of vision, proposed a theory of how we hear called place theory. **Place theory**

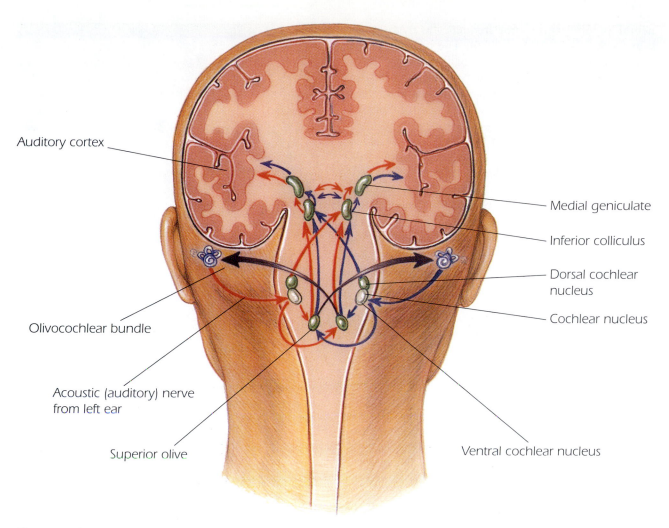

Auditory cortex

Medial geniculate

Inferior colliculus

Dorsal cochlear nucleus

Cochlear nucleus

Olivocochlear bundle

Acoustic (auditory) nerve from left ear

Superior olive

Ventral cochlear nucleus

Figure 4–39
NEURAL PATHWAYS FROM THE EAR TO THE BRAIN. *The auditory receptors on the basilar membrane of the cochlea join to form the acoustic nerve, which routes through the medulla oblongata to the thalamus. The thalamus organizes the electrochemical impulses and sends them to regions of the auditory cortex in the temporal lobes.*

posits that we hear each pitch as a function of the location in the basilar membrane that is stimulated. The hair cells at different places on the basilar membrane vibrate in response to different pitches, and in the process they excite different neurons. Each neuron is therefore sensitive to the specific frequencies that originally stimulated the basilar membrane. In fact, prolonged exposure to a very loud sound of a particular frequency damages the hair cells at a specific spot on the basilar membrane, causing hearing loss for sounds of that pitch.

Georg von Békésy (1960) did Nobel Prize–winning research that led him to similar conclusions. He cut tiny holes in the cochleas of guinea pigs and as pitches of different frequencies were played, he observed the guinea pigs' basilar membranes with a

microscope. Low-frequency tones stimulated the hair cells at the wider end of the basilar membrane (farthest from the oval window), and high-frequency tones stimulated the cells at the narrower end (closest to the oval window). Unfortunately, not everything Békésy saw fit in perfectly with place theory. Low-frequency tones also stimulated the cells along the whole basilar membrane, and even tones of intermediate frequencies sometimes stimulated wide areas of the membrane.

Frequency Theory

Instead of relying on location to explain pitch, **frequency theory** suggests that the basilar membrane reproduces the vibrations that enter the ear, triggering neural impulses at the same frequency as the original sound wave (E. G. Wever, 1970). The pitch we sense is determined by the frequency of the impulses that enter the auditory nerve connecting the ear with the brain. A tone of 500 Hz produces 500 bursts of electrical responses per second in the auditory nerve, and so on.

Frequency theory handles well the broader stimulation associated with the sensation of low-frequency tones that place theory does not fully explain. However, frequency theory cannot account for all of the phenomena associated with pitch at the high end of the frequency scale. The problem with frequency theory is that a single neuron can conduct a maximum of only about 1,000 impulses per second (corresponding to a 1,000 Hz sound), but humans can hear frequencies of up to 20,000 Hz. We are not capable of a high enough rate of neuronal conduction to mirror the vibrations of high-frequency pitches. So once again, one theory does not provide all the answers.

Keeping frequency theory alive is the **volley principle** (E. G. Wever, 1970), according to which auditory neurons are able to cooperate. That is, neurons can fire not just singly, but in alternating groups. While one neuron is resting, a neighboring neuron can fire. This neighbor can cooperate similarly with other neurons, as well. Thus, although no one neuron can fire at a fast enough rate to simulate the vibrations of the higher frequencies, a group of neurons can. Think of a group of rifle-wielding sharpshooters, each of whom must reload after each shot. If the sharpshooters cooperate so that some of them fire while others reload, the group can fire volleys much faster than can any one sharpshooter alone.

Nonetheless, we must account for some findings that still support place theory. As a result, the most widely accepted current view on the hearing of pitch is **duplicity theory,** according to which both place and frequency play some role in hearing pitch. The details of duplicity theory have not yet been worked out, however. A similar dialectic occurred in vision research, with the trichromatic and opponent-process theories of color vision. Theories that incorporate elements of competing theories are popular ways of resolving problems because they use the best features of each of the competitors (Kalmar & Sternberg, 1988). The final word in theories of pitch has yet to be heard. Psychologists have more definitive ideas, however, about how people locate sounds.

Locating Sounds

How do we determine where sounds are coming from? The fact that we have two ears roughly 6 inches apart on opposite sides of the head is the key.

People who use power tools or work in other loud environments, from construction sites to rock concerts, now frequently use protective earphones.

When a sound comes from our right, it has less distance to travel to reach the right ear than the left ear. Granted, the time difference between arrival at the right and left ears can be minuscule, but it is enough for us to sense and process. In fact, we can detect time differences as brief as 10 microseconds (Durlach & Colburn, 1978). Another way we process location is by comparing the differences in the intensities of the sounds reaching our ears; the farther ear receives a sound of lesser intensity than the closer ear because our heads absorb some of the sound going to the farther ear. It seems that the *time-difference method* works best for low-frequency sounds, and the *intensity-difference method* works best for high-frequency sounds (see Figure 4-40).

What if a sound comes from a source equidistant from our ears, so that it arrives at both ears simultaneously? In such cases, we are easily confused. You have heard sounds for which you were not able immediately to pinpoint the location. In an attempt to locate the source, you probably (and almost unconsciously) rotated your head in order to receive two slightly different messages in your ears. Then, using either the time- or intensity-difference method, you located the source of the sound.

Hearing, together with seeing, provides us with much of our input from the outside world. But if we could only see and hear, we would never have the

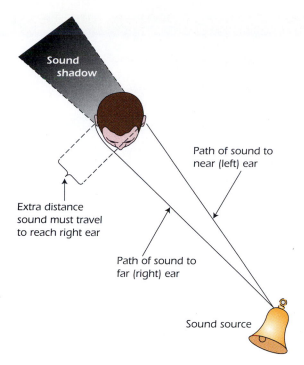

Figure 4-40
DETERMINING THE SOURCE OF A SOUND. *We locate the source of a sound by using two methods: We deduce that the sound is coming from the direction of the ear that either heard the sound first or sensed the greater volume.*

pleasure of tasting a delicious chocolate cake, smelling a freshly baked pizza, or feeling our back be massaged. Other senses are important to our enjoyment of life, and sometimes, such as in the case of pain, to our survival.

Taste, Smell, and the Other Senses

In *Search of . . .* *How do we experience stimuli through senses other than vision and hearing*

What kinds of sensations do we experience beyond those of seeing and hearing?

Taste

We are able to see objects and hear events that occur at some distance from our bodies. To do so, we transduce the energy waves that we receive from those objects and events into the electrochemical energy of neural transmission. In contrast, to use our sense of taste, we must come into physical contact with the particular chemical makeup of the things we taste. In

fact, what we taste has already entered our bodies. Just how does this highly intimate sensory system work? To answer this question, we explore the physical and psychological properties of taste, the anatomy of taste both in the tongue and in the nervous system, and the specific mechanisms of taste.

Physical and Psychological Properties in the Sense of Taste

For us to taste a stimulus, the stimulus must contain chemical molecules that can dissolve in saliva, and we must have sufficient saliva in our mouths to dissolve those chemicals. From these chemicals, we detect the four primary psychological qualities of saltiness, bitterness, sweetness, and sourness (Bartoshuk, 1988). Sweet tastes typically come from *organic molecules*, which contain varying amounts of carbon, hydrogen, and oxygen. Bitter-tasting substances tend to contain some amount of nitrogen; sour substances are usually acidic; and salty-tasting substances tend to have molecules that break down into electrically charged particles (ions) in water. Other tastes are produced by combinations of the four primary tastes, much as colors can be produced by a combination of the three primary colors. For example, a grapefruit is both sour and bitter and is also sometimes sweet. The distribution of tastes on the tongue is shown in Figure 4-41.

Our sensitivity to taste changes as we age: Children are hypersensitive to taste, as you may have noticed if you have ever eaten with young children. The total number of taste buds on the tongue, however, decreases as we grow older, resulting in a decrease in our sensitivity to tastes. Although most people's absolute thresholds for taste are fairly low, the jnd's for taste are rather high, with Weber fractions ranging from 0.1 to 1.0. These relatively high jnd thresholds mean that, in order for us to perceive differences in intensities, we must add at least 10% more taste, and possibly 100% more, depending on the flavor! Taste is probably our least finely tuned sensory system. Processing of taste is possible by means of the structure and functioning of the tongue.

Anatomy of the Tongue. As tasty substances enter the mouth, they land on the tongue, where they are detected by one or more of roughly 10,000 **taste buds,** clusters containing taste-receptor cells located inside the small visible protrusions on the tongue, the **papillae.** Taste buds are clustered all over the tongue and also in the back of the throat. The cells within the taste buds last only about 10 days, after which they typically are replaced (Pfaffmann, 1978). In the center of each taste bud is

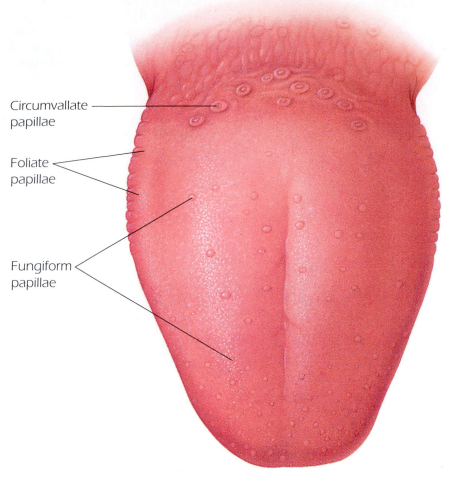

Circumvallate papillae

Foliate papillae

Fungiform papillae

Figure 4–41

THE TONGUE AND OUR SENSE OF TASTE. *Taste buds cluster around tiny bumps on the tongue. These bumps are called papillae. There are three types of papillae: circumvallate papillae, foliate papillae, and fungiform papillae. The taste buds located in each of the types of papillae show somewhat different levels of sensitivity to each of the four basic tastes, as shown in the figure. (Adopted from Bartoshuk, 1993)*

a pore, out of which grow microvilli (extremely small, fingerlike projections) through which chemicals from food and drink are sampled. Contact with these chemicals activates the taste buds, thereby beginning the transduction process. The receptors for taste (and for smell) transduce chemical energy into electrochemical energy; the taste receptors seem specially tailored to receive particular kinds of chemicals (e.g., salts or acids) and then send the message about the chemicals through the electrochemical system of neuronal conduction. Sensitivity to the various tastes is distributed unevenly across the various parts of the tongue, but the pattern of distribution is quite complex so that it is not possible completely to localize a particular kind of taste

to a particular portion of the tongue (Bartoshuk, 1993).

From the Tongue to the Brain. Three nerves are devoted to carrying information from the taste bud receptors on different regions of the tongue to the medulla oblongata. From the medulla oblongata, the information is transmitted to the thalamus. In the thalamus, the information is routed to an area of the cortex, alongside the portion of the cortex where areas of the face are mapped, primarily in the parietal lobe and also in the temporal lobe (see Figure 4-42). Some of the gustatory (taste) information, however, gets sidetracked from the thalamus to the nearby hypothalamus and to parts of the limbic system.

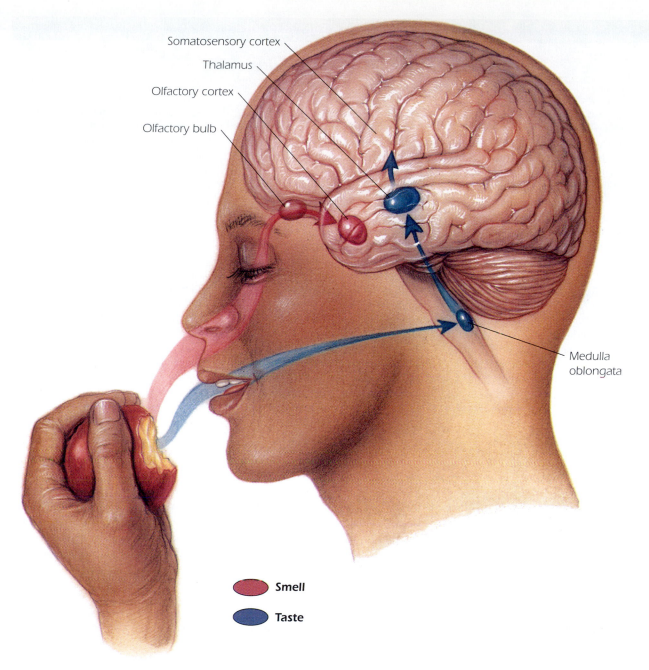

Somatosensory cortex

Thalamus

Olfactory cortex

Olfactory bulb

Medulla oblongata

● **Smell**

● **Taste**

Figure 4–42
NEURAL PATHWAY FROM THE TONGUE TO THE BRAIN. *From the taste receptors on the tongue, three nerves carry electro-chemical impulses to the medulla oblongata, which transmits most of the information through the pons to the thalamus. The thala-mus organizes and then routes the impulses to the somatosensory cortex. Some of the information goes to the hypothalamus and to parts of the limbic system.*

How We Taste

What might account for our ability to distinguish the four primary tastes? The most widely accepted theory of taste (Pfaffman, 1974) posits that although the sensory receptors on the tongue do not each respond uniquely to a single taste, different receptors do respond more strongly to certain taste sensations than to others (see Figure 4-43). It appears that taste buds interact to produce the wide variety of tastes that we sense.

Thus far, we have indicated that taste embraces only four fundamental sensations. What about all the other nuances of taste we enjoy? Much of what we refer to as the distinctive taste of food is actually its smell.

Psychology in Everyday Life

Do Ideas Evolve as Organisms Do?

We know that organisms evolve. Ideas also evolve. Is there any relationship between the two? Perhaps. Richard Dawkins (1989) has speculated that essentially the same laws of evolution that apply to organisms may apply to cultural artifacts, including ideas. And a number of psychologists have suggested that ideas may evolve along the lines of a mechanism whereby the "fittest" survive, namely, those that are best adapted to the cultural milieu in which they are proposed and diffused (D. T. Campbell, 1960; Perkins, 1995b; Simonton, 1995, 1999). On the one hand, we need to recognize that ideas are not living organisms, in the same way that we are. On the other hand, we can also recognize that ideas, like organisms, can fit more or less well into an en-

vironmental niche. Their fit does not render them true: Cultures have accepted, over the years, many ideas that are demonstrably false, such as the idea that a mysterious (and, in fact, nonexistent) substance called phlogiston (the hypothetical principle of fire regarded formerly as a material substance) causes fire. Evolutionary theory does not provide any kind of code of truth or ethics. Neither organisms nor ideas that fit a given environment are in any real sense better than others in an absolute sense. Rather, they are simply organisms or ideas that are well adapted to a given time or place.

Consider, for example, the notion that we love the taste of pizza, coconut, peaches, or whatever food we happen to love. For generation after generation, the idea that

we love certain kinds of tastes and dislike others has remained with us. We all speak this way, despite the fact that it is, strictly speaking, incorrect. What we love is the smell. There are only four basic tastes—sweet, sour, bitter, and salty—and this fact has been known for a long time. Most of what we refer to as taste is really smell. So why doesn't the idea of "how foods taste" go away? This puzzle points out that many ideas survive that are wrong, and that they survive even after society, or at least scientists, know they are wrong. It is for this reason that you must be especially careful before accepting what you are told. Many ideas that have made their way into our common ways of thinking are, quite simply, wrong.

Smell

Many of us discover the importance of smell when we have a bad cold: Our food seems virtually tasteless because our nasal passages are blocked. Thus, two foods that are equally sweet but that smell quite different (and hence are described casually as "tasting" differ-

ent) may taste the same unless we can also smell them. The temperature of food can also affect our sensation of smell because heat tends to release aromas. For some of us, color and texture are also quite important to our enjoyment of food and drink.

As is the case with vision and hearing, humans depend on their sense of smell for survival and for infor-

Figure 4–43
THE IMPORTANCE OF SMELL TO PERCEIVED TASTE. *Many foods are much less easy to identify when they cannot be smelled.*

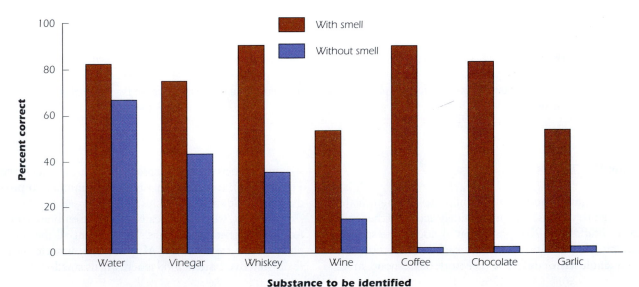

mation gathering, but not nearly as much as do other animals. In fact, humans have only 10 million smell receptors, whereas dogs have about 200 million. Nonetheless, odors and fragrances interact powerfully with our emotions, instantaneously calling up memories of past times and places.

Odors are important not only for our enjoyment of food and fragrance, but for other reasons as well. For example, odors are becoming increasingly important to humans for security purposes. Because the human nose is not particularly sensitive, machines have been created that can sniff out drugs and explosives. Sometimes, too, trained dogs are used for these purposes because their sensitivity to odors so far exceeds that of humans.

Physical and Psychological Properties in the Sense of Smell

The sense of smell, **olfaction,** enhances our ability to savor food, but also, of course, it functions on its own, independent of taste. Like taste, smell is a chemically activated sense. Airborne molecules that can dissolve in either water or fat are candidates for sensation by our olfactory system.

Once our olfactory system detects scent-bearing molecules, we sense the odor. Researchers have tried to define *primary smells* to parallel the basic psychological qualities of the other sense systems we have studied. One such attempt divided smells into flowery, foul, fruity, burnt, resinous, and spicy, leaving room for combinations of smells (Henning, 1915). The relationships and differences among smells, however, have proven very hard to define systematically. To get an idea of the problem, think of five things you enjoy smelling. Now, describe those smells without using any similes (i.e., "it smells like . . ."). For some reason, our vocabulary for smells is limited unless we compare or contrast one substance with a distinctive odor to another substance. Thus, although we know that smell is active in our psychological functioning in the recall of memories, there is still no satisfactory way of characterizing what we sense when we detect a smell.

Absolute thresholds for smell are difficult to study because the nasal receptors are somewhat inaccessible. In addition, different substances have different thresholds for detection, as do the smell receptors of different people. In fact, some people are *odor-blind*—unable to detect one or more specific scents. It is also extremely difficult to control the concentrations of odors and to eliminate interference from body, clothing, and environmental odors.

The olfactory system seems to be more sensitive than the gustatory (taste) system in discriminating between stimuli. Weber fractions for jnd's in smell intensity can be as low as 0.05—that is, differences in scent intensity of only 5% can be detected about half the time (Cain, 1977). One of the most interesting

topics in the study of smell is **pheromones,** chemical substances secreted by animals, which trigger specific kinds of reactions in other animals, usually of the same species. These reactions include mutual identification of parent and child, sexual signals, territorial-boundary markers, and both limits on and prompts toward aggression. However, there is some disagreement as to whether pheromones operate in the human species in a way that triggers sexual attraction (Quadagno, 1987)

Research shows that people react psychologically to smell. For example, evidence indicates that within the first few weeks of life, breast-fed infants can identify their mothers by smell (Cernoch & Porter, 1985). Women who have at least weekly contact with male underarm secretions (e.g., through intimate contact) appear to have more regularly timed menstrual cycles, and women who have regular contact with other women (or with their underarm secretions) tend to have synchronized menstrual cycles (Cutler et al., 1986). The link between smell and sexual attraction is less clear, but women seem to find male odors more attractive than do other men. In any case, women seem more sensitive to odors (in absolute terms) and more responsive to odors (in terms of their self-reports and other behavior) than are men. In addition, smells have been known to evoke distant memories, including the emotions pertaining to the remembered events.

From the Nose to the Brain

Airborne scent molecules are drawn up and into the nose by the force of a person's inhalation (see Figure 4-44). They pass up through the nasal cavity to a point below and behind the eyes, where they encounter the **olfactory epithelium** (the "smell skin") in the nasal *mucosa,* the membranes that secrete protective mucus. There, the particles contact the olfactory receptor cells that detect smells and initiate the transduction of the chemical energy of the odors into the electrochemical energy needed for neural transmission. Smell receptors are notable for being among the few kinds of neurons that can fully regenerate in adult mammals. It is a good thing they do, because they die after 4 to 8 weeks.

The receptors in the olfactory epithelium are also unique among sensory systems in that their axons actually penetrate the skull and combine directly to form each of the two olfactory nerves. Each of the olfactory nerves terminates at one of the two **olfactory bulbs,** where its neurons communicate with other neurons in complex arrangements. From an olfactory bulb, smell impulses primarily bypass the thalamus (unlike other sensory neurons) and go eventually into the olfactory cortex in the temporal lobe or to the limbic system (especially the hypothalamus). The hypothalamus and the limbic system may be involved in whether we accept or reject a food, based on its smell.

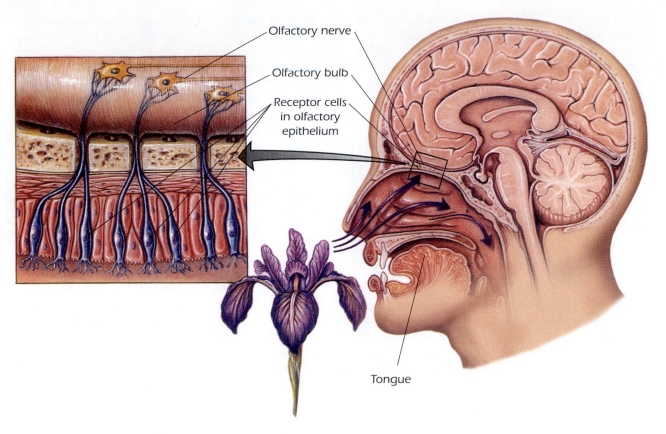

Olfactory nerve

Olfactory bulb

Receptor cells
in olfactory
epithelium

Tongue

Figure 4–44
NASAL CAVITY.   *Airborne molecules are inhaled into the nasal cavity. Receptor cells in the olfactory epithelium transduce the chemical energy of smell into the electrochemical energy of the nervous system.*

How We Smell

We sense an odor when molecules are released from a substance and carried through the air into the nasal cavity and up to the olfactory receptors in the olfactory epithelium. How, exactly, do those receptors work? Many of the specifics are not understood, although we do know that each smell receptor can respond to a number of odors (Keverne, cited in Klivington, 1989). Because there is a constant turnover of smell receptors, it may be advantageous to have each receptor respond to more than one distinctive odor. Although the smell receptors do not respond to one odor alone, each receptor does seem to have a unique pattern of chemical responses to different odors.

As with the other senses, there are wide individual differences in sensitivity to smells. Most people have lost most or all of their sense of smell at one time or another, as when their nasal passages are blocked by mucus, preventing any external access to the olfactory receptors. The sense of smell also decreases with age. Many people over age 70 report a serious loss in their sensitivity to smells (Rabin & Cain, 1986), perhaps because as their nasal receptor cells die, the receptors are not regenerated as much or as quickly.

Skin Senses

Many talk-show hosts and perfume sellers suggest that smell plays a powerful role in our sexual and other interpersonal behavior. Although psychologists may question this conclusion about smell, few doubt that touch plays such a role.

Often, we call the sense of touch the fifth sense. The term "touch," however, insufficiently characterizes the various sensations of pressure, temperature, and pain. A better term may be the "skin senses," because there are so many sensations we receive through our skin. The formal term for the various means by which we become sensitive to pressure, temperature, and pain stimulation directly on the skin is the *haptic* senses.

Thus far, we have discussed the way in which our sensory systems respond to sensory information that reaches us from outside our bodies. These *exteroceptive* systems receive external stimulation. In addition, we have *interoceptive* systems, which receive internal stimulation from within our bodies, such as feeling flushed, feeling a stomachache, feeling dizzy, or feeling how our bodies are positioned in space. Some also refer to interoception as *proprioception* (receiving information about your own body). The haptic senses largely include exteroceptive systems but some, such as the sense of pain, can offer us proprioceptive information as well.

Some research indicates the importance of touch to humans. For instance, although researchers clearly would not introduce severe touch deprivation to human infants, medical professionals and developmental psychologists have noticed that tactile stimulation seems to enhance the physiological stability of preterm infants and to promote their weight gain (a crucial factor in the health and vitality of such infants). Touch even seems important to the early development of visual perception (T. G. R. Bower, 1971). Some research on adults shows positive effects of touch as well. For example, touching or stroking a pet seems to lower the heart rate of the person doing the petting.

Physical and Psychological Properties in the Skin Senses

Our skin can respond to a variety of external stimuli. The way we sense these physical stimuli results in a psychological interpretation of the sensation as pain, warmth, and so on. Objects pressed against the skin change the skin's shape, causing the sensation of pressure. When even a single tiny hair on our skin is displaced, we feel pressure from its movement. The temperature of an object against the skin results in a sensation of warmth or cold. Slight electrical stimulation of our skin usually results in a sensation of pressure and perhaps of temperature. Too much of any kind of stimulation generally results in pain. Intense stimulation from inside the body, or tissue damage either inside or outside the body, can result in the sensation of pain as well. The bodily response that culminates in pain often begins with sensations detected in the skin.

Anatomy of the Skin. We can feel through our skin because its layers are permeated with sensory receptors (see Figure 4-45). Our various skin senses have different kinds of sensory receptors for touch, pain, pressure, and temperature. Our specialized receptors for touch have distinctive globular ("corpuscular") swellings at their dendritic endings. These corpuscular cells are located at different levels of the skin and are sensitive to different types of touch (pinpoint surface pressure, broad-region surface pressure, deep pressure, movement, and vibration). Suppose you were blindfolded and then touched by three different objects, each of which had a 1-inch-square surface that was pressed against your skin: a cube of absorbent cotton, then a stiff brush, and then a polished metal cube. Even with the blindfold, you could probably tell the differences among them. If the brush or another object were vibrated, even if it were not moved otherwise, you would be able to detect the vibration, too. Our skin also contains specialized sensory receptors

for noticing when a hair follicle is bent, for noticing pain, and for noticing temperature. These receptors, called **free nerve endings,** are noncorpuscular. They lack the globular swellings of touch receptors. Sensations travel from them, eventually reaching the brain.

From the Skin to the Brain. From the skin, two kinds of sensory neurons travel to the spinal cord, where they pass impulses to other neurons that travel to the brain. The sensory neurons are either fast-conducting myelinated neurons, which usually travel over relatively long distances to reach the spinal cord, or relatively slow-conducting unmyelinated neurons, which usually have to travel only short distances to reach the spinal cord. Once the sensory neurons reach the spinal cord, the two kinds of neurons take different routes, via two different kinds of nerves in the spinal cord.

The first kind of spinal-cord nerve collects the information from the myelinated neurons, ascends the spinal cord, crosses over to the other half of the brain at the medulla oblongata, goes to the thalamus, and then to the somatosensory cortex, where it is mapped, as described in chapter 3. This kind of nerve responds mostly to the sense of pressure and also to movement.

The second kind of spinal nerve collects information from the unmyelinated sensory neurons in the skin. In the spinal cord, these unmyelinated sensory receptor neurons can also make local connections with motor effector neurons to produce reflexive reactions. This second kind of nerve provides information about pain to the brain. This kind also carries information about temperature and pressure. These nerves travel up the spinal cord and then divide into two bundles at the medulla oblongata. One bundle conveys information about diffuse, dull, or burning pain, and the other information about localized, sharp, or piercing pain. Both bundles cross over contralaterally, so that pain in the right side of the body is related with activity in the left side of the brain, and vice versa. The nerve bundles stop at the thalamus and the limbic system, important for emotion and memory, and then go to the somatosensory cortex. We sense temperature, pressure, pain, and movement information that travels this route with less precise localization than we do our sensations that travel via the faster route. Let us consider how we process these various kinds of information.

How We Feel Pressure

The skin sense of pressure allows us to feel physical stimuli that contact the exterior of the body. We are able to sense heaviness, vibration, and location of pressure. Our absolute thresholds for pressure differ widely across various parts of the body. For example, the cheek is more sensitive than the palm of the hand (Weinstein, 1968). Absolute thresholds are usually

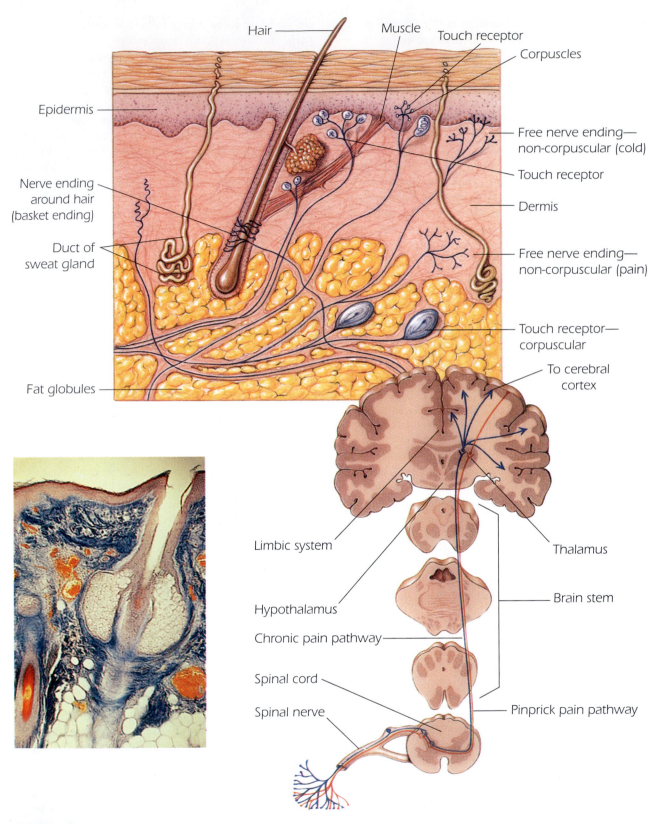

Figure 4–45

SKIN RECEPTORS.   *Our skin contains sensory receptors for pain, pressure, and temperature, each of which serves a different function and provides distinctive sensory information. (See the magnified photo.) As we saw in the discussion of reflex movement in chapter 3, if the receptors detect a sudden, strong feeling of pain (or pressure or extreme temperature), the neural impulse normally sent to the brain may be rerouted at the spine to create a sudden muscular movement that removes the body from the source of the pain. If the strong pain continues, the neural impulses it creates go directly to the cerebral cortex; chronic pain is routed through the limbic system to the cortex.*

tested by touching different locations on the skin with a small bristle or vibrating stimulus, using various amounts of force (see Figure 4-46).

How We Feel Temperature

Maintaining a consistent body temperature is essential to our survival, and two kinds of nerve fibers (bundles of neurons) in the skin enable us to sense warmth and cold via their patterns of firing. *Cold fibers*, as you might imagine, respond to cooling of the skin by increasing their rate of firing relative to the rate at which they fire when at rest. *Warm fibers* respond analogously to warming of the skin (in the range of 95–115 degrees Fahrenheit [35–46 celsius]; Hensel, 1981). The two types of fibers are not equally distributed across the body. Even across a small patch of skin area, different portions may be differentially responsive to cold and warmth.

Because the two types of fibers are highly responsive to changes in temperature, what we sense as cold or warm depends on our adaptation level. When we start off cold, what we sense as warm may be quite a bit colder than what we sense as warm when we start off hot. Consequently, it is very difficult to quantify absolute thresholds in measurement of temperature, so research has focused largely on adaptation and, to a

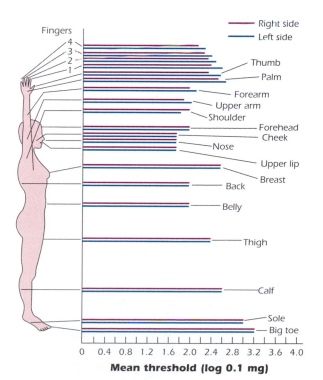

The pressure receptors in their skin enable these children to sense touching and being touched.

lesser extent, on jnd's. When our skin is at a normal temperature, we can detect greater warmth of 0.72 degree Fahrenheit (0.4 celsius) and increased coolness of 0.27 degree Fahrenheit (0.15 celsius; Kenshalo, Nafe, & Brooks, 1961).

How We Feel Pain

Intense stimulation, as well as any resulting damage to tissues, can lead to pain. When tissue is damaged, it releases a neurotransmitter, which starts an impulse on its way to the central nervous system.

Different parts of the body are differentially susceptible to pain. The back of the knee, for example, is much more susceptible than the sole of the foot. Moreover, people differ widely in their apparent sensitivity to pain. In extreme cases, some individuals feel no pain at all (see Sternbach, 1963). Although such insensitivity might seem to be an ideal state, many of these individuals die early deaths due to accidental injury. For instance, such persons might lose an enormous amount of blood before even noticing they had been injured, particularly in cases of internal bleeding. Pain is unpleasant, but it serves a functional, evolutionary purpose. It prompts us to remove ourselves from dangerous or stressful situations or to seek a quick remedy for injuries. Stomachache, earache, intestinal cramps, injured joints or bones, and other kinds and sources of proprioceptive pain (i.e., pain whose source arises from within the body) alert us to internal assaults on our bodies, which may at least help us to avoid future insults to our systems, even if we cannot escape the immediate one.

It is important to recognize, however, that factors that go beyond the individual's mere sensory physiology, such as cultural influences, personal expectations, and adaptation levels, seem to affect how much pain a person experiences. Needs, beliefs, expectations, and practices characteristic of one culture may serve either to

Figure 4-46

ABSOLUTE THRESHOLDS FOR PRESSURE. *Different regions of the body have differing degrees of sensitivity to pressure. How would an evolutionary psychologist explain this varying amount of sensitivity?*

raise or to lower thresholds in contrast with other cultures. For example, Asians report more pain than Caucasians and other groups in response to having their ears pierced (V. J. Thomas & Rose, 1991; for more information on pain, its psychological consequences, social and demographic factors contributing to it, and therapeutic treatments of it, see chapter 18). Needs and expectations can also affect the functioning of the body senses.

Body Senses

Pain is not the only proprioceptive sense that serves us. You probably do not remember when you learned to walk, but that moment was a triumphant one for your sense of kinesthesis and your vestibular sense, or equilibrium. We are not typically conscious of the functioning of these senses, which help us to move, stand upright, and generally feel physically and spatially oriented. Our lack of awareness does not imply that these senses are unimportant, however. If you question the importance of the body senses, try spinning yourself around and around, as you probably did

The kinesthetic receptors in this girl's skeletal muscles combine with her vestibular sense to make her aware of the swiftly changing position of her body as she leaps through space.

when you were a child, and then see whether you can walk a straight line. Now let us consider the two body senses of kinesthesis and equilibrium.

Kinesthesis

Kinesthesis is the sense that helps us to ascertain our skeletal movements and positioning: Where are the various parts of our body in respect to one another, and how (if at all) are they moving? Kinesthetic receptors are in the muscles, tendons, joints, and skin. When these receptors detect changes in positions via pressure, they transduce this mechanical energy into neural energy, which codes information about the speed of the change, the angle of the bones, and the tension of the muscles. This information is sent up the spinal cord, where it eventually reaches the brain and is shifted contralaterally in the brain to the somatosensory cortex and to the cerebellum, which is responsible for automatic processes and motor coordination (see chapter 3).

Equilibrium: The Vestibular Sense

The vestibular sense—roughly speaking, the sense of balance or equilibrium—is determined by the orientation of the head relative to the source of gravity, as well as by the movement and acceleration of our bodies through space. We tend not to be aware of our vestibular sense unless it is overstimulated—perhaps on a bumpy airplane flight or on a carnival ride that is a bit too wild. You probably know the results: dizziness and nausea. Video games and virtual reality simulations can also cause a form of motion sickness known as cybersickness. Research on reducing these unwanted effects is the subject of our In the Lab box.

The receptors for equilibrium are located in the inner ear (see Figure 4-47). The **vestibular system** is a sensory system that comprises the vestibular sacs and semicircular canals, both of which contain a fluid that moves when the head rotates. The movement in turn causes the hair cells inside the sacs and canals to bend. This mechanical energy is then transduced into electrochemical impulses in the nerves. The impulses travel, via the auditory nerve, to the cerebellum and the cortex of the brain, carrying information about the rate of acceleration of the head, as well as about its direction of movement and its relative orientation. Motion sickness can result when the brain has to integrate incompatible information from various sensory systems. For example, picture yourself riding in a moving vehicle but being unable to see outside (much as a young child might be in a car or a below-deck passenger might be on a boat). What you would see (the inside of the vehicle) would not be moving, but your body would still feel vestibular and kinesthetic movements. As you might guess, we generally feel better when our visual information agrees

Part of the thrill of amusement park rides is feeling the rapidly changing sensations from our vestibular system.

with our vestibular and kinesthetic information than when it disagrees.

Vestibular sensations are welcomed by more than just sensation-seekers who crave speed and motion. The countless rocking chairs that have been used for ages attest to the lulling effects of vestibular stimulation. Perhaps you have gone for a drive or for a walk when troubled, seeking to be soothed.

We are tremendously lucky to have the resources of our sensory and perceptual systems available to us. When they are damaged, or lacking, life as we know it is radically different. Our senses are our gateways to thoughts, feelings, and ideas—our bridges from the external world, through our bodies, to our minds. Consciousness, considered in the next chapter, enables us to keep track of our sensations and perceptions.

Figure 4–47

VESTIBULAR SYSTEM. *Movement of fluid in the semicircular canals in the inner ear enables us to sense shifts in the orientation of our head in relation to gravity.*

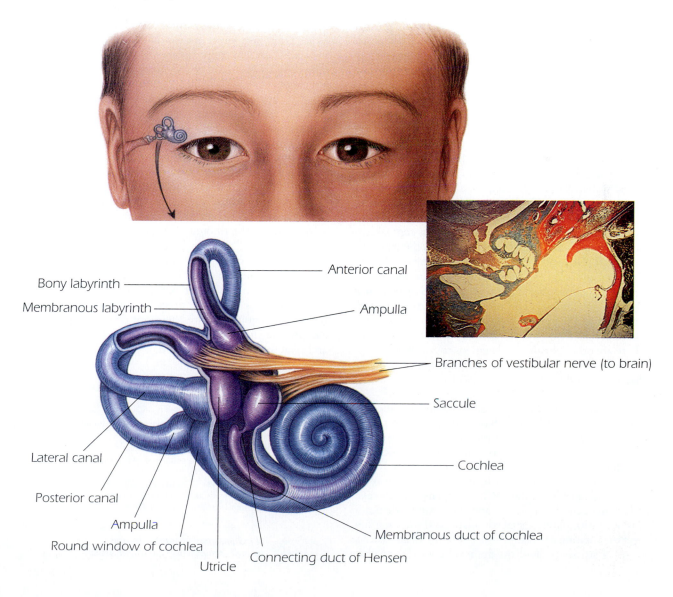

Virtual Reality and Motion Sickness

James G. May, *University of New Orleans*

Computer technology now makes possible virtual environments that really make you feel as if you are there. A computer is fed information from a movement sensor (e.g., a head-tracking device) and responds by systematically changing the scene, so it appears that you are looking around a three-dimensional space. This technology has generated an explosion of applications far beyond mere video games. It is now used in driving and flying simulators, architecture, and surgical training. But there are still some problems and the most compromising is *cybersickness* (Kennedy, Lanham, Drexler, & Massey, 1997).

With even short exposures to many virtual environments many people experience a form of motion sickness that appears to be visually induced. My lab has been interested in understanding the causes of cybersickness and how we can prevent it. We think that any sort of nausea and vomiting is a protective mechanism that has evolved to empty the gut of toxic material. Why does motion result in this response? One notion is that the effects of toxic poisoning have early effects on the eye muscles, resulting in eye muscle imbalance and diplopia (double vision). This creates a mismatch between two sensory signals and in turn results in activation of a part of the brainstem that causes vomiting. This general mismatch idea has been elaborated into the sensory conflict theory of motion sickness (Benson, 1984). This theory takes into account the fact that in many situations, the senses do not agree with regard to whether you are moving or not, or in which direction. Below deck on a ship, your vestibular system responds to ship motion, but the visual system sees no environmental motion because the eyes are moving with the cabin. In an IMAX theater, the vestibular system senses little motion because you are sitting in a stationary chair, but the visual system takes in the movement of the video scene that fills the whole visual field. Generally, in the real world, the whole field does not move on the retina unless you are moving, so there is a compelling illusion of self-motion or *vection*. This is the situation one often has in virtual environments, and the cybersickness that results can be even more severe than sickness evoked by real motion. But there are other possible explanations to consider.

Look at the X on the next line and move your head back and forth.

X

Your head moved but your eyes remained stationary. Right? WRONG! Your eyes had to rotate in the sockets in precisely the opposite direction and at exactly the same velocity as that of your head movement. This mechanism is called the vestibuloocular reflex (VOR) and it allows us to keep an image stable on the retina while the head is moving. What happens with the eyes when the head is stationary and the sense of vection is induced with purely visual stimulation? If we seat a subject on a stationary chair inside a rotating drum that has vertical stripes painted on the inside, we can produce the illusion of self-motion (circular vection) (Dichgans & Brandt, 1973). The eyes begin to smoothly pursue a point on the drum, but when they reach a certain point in the sockets, they snap back to the center to compensate for this reflex following response. So, *when the whole visual field is moved, eye movements are elicited*.

Some researchers have suggested that certain eye movement patterns are what give rise to motion sickness (Ebenholtz, Cohen, & Linder, 1994). Feedback signals associated with eye movements are sent to the vestibular nuclei in the brainstem, which may be relayed to the cerebellum and ultimately to the "poison" center.

Have you ever watched people play VR video games? They are rarely stationary. It may be that these compensatory head and body movements are attempts to create congruity between the visual and vestibular senses. So, we are left with several factors that may lead to cybersickness: *real or illusory motion can lead to bodily movements; bodily movements can lead to head movements; head movements can lead to eye movements; and the perception of self-motion without head or body movement can lead to eye movements*.

To begin to figure out what is behind cybersickness, we use VR scenarios that provoke cybersickness in sensitive subjects. We record eye and head movements along with the signs (pallor and vomiting) and symptoms (e.g., nausea, stomach awareness, dizziness, drowsiness, etc.) of cybersickness. Within such scenarios we impose restrictions on head movements (with the use of a bite bar to stabilize the head) and eye movements (with the use of a central fixation point). We also ask subjects to rate the amount of vection experienced under each condition. This basic design will tell us whether we get more or less cybersickness when the head or eyes are more active; whether vection is a necessary condition for cybersickness; and whether certain patterns of head or eye movements (or both) precede cybersickness. This research is ongoing, but we have hope that this approach will provide knowledge about what causes cybersickness and what we can do to prevent it.

References

Benson, A . J. (1984). *Motion sickness*. In M. R. Dix & J. D. Hood (Eds.), *Vertigo*. New York: John Wiley & Sons, Ltd.

Dichgans, J., & Brandt, T. (1973). Optokinetic motion sickness and pseudo-Coriolis effects induced by moving visual stimuli. *Acta Otolaryngology—Stockholm*, 76(5), 339–348.

Ebenholtz, S. M., Cohen, M. M., & Linder, B. J. (1994). The possible role of nystagmus in motion sickness: a hypothesis. *Aviation, Space and Environmental Medicine*, 65(11), 1032–1035.

Kennedy, R. S., Lanham, D. S., Drexler, J. M., & Massey, C. J. (1997). A comparison of cybersickness incidences, symptom profiles, measurement technique, and suggestions for further research. *Presence, 6*, 638–644.

 Find out more about this topic at **www.harcourtcollege.com/psych/ishm**

THINK ABOUT IT

1. What are the main limitations of template-matching theories of visual perception?

2. Why are objects closer than they visually appear on a foggy day?

3. Hubel and Wiesel have noted that their discoveries and their research were possible because of the technologies available to them. What current technology do you find not only pleasant but also even important to your ability to perform a task you do often? How would your life be different without that technology? (It does not have to be a complex or "high-tech" item.)

4. Try eating your next meal (or a snack) while keeping your eyes closed. Briefly describe how the other senses work together in helping you prevent yourself from ingesting bad food.

5. In what ways have you noticed that smells affect the way you feel about particular people, particular kinds of food, and particular situations or settings?

6. If you had to memorize a long list of terms and definitions, would you be better off trying to remember them by seeing them (e.g., reading printed flashcards) or by hearing them (e.g., having someone drill you by saying the words aloud)? Do you seem to be able to remember material better if it is presented visually (e.g., in a book) or vocally (e.g., in a lecture)? How do you tailor your studying to your sensory preferences?

online *You can provide your own answers to these questions online at the* **Sternberg, In Search of the Human Mind** *Web site: http://www.harcourtcollege.com/psych/ishm*

SUMMARY

Psychophysics 108

1. A *sensation* is a message that the brain receives from a sense. A *sense* is a physical system that collects information for the brain and transduces it from one form of energy into the brain's electrochemical energy.

2. *Perception* is the set of processes by which we recognize, organize, and make sense of stimuli in our environment.

3. *Psychophysics* is the study of the relationship between physical stimulation and its psychological effects.

4. *Detection* refers to the ability to sense a stimulus. The minimal amount of physical energy of a given kind that can be sensed (detected) exactly 50% of the time is operationally defined as the *absolute threshold*.

5. *Signal-detection theory (SDT)* analyzes responses in terms of *hits* (true positive responses), *misses* (false negatives), *false alarms* (false positives), and *correct rejections* (true negatives). SDT is also used for explaining how we determine the likelihood that a sensation is caused by a particular signal.

6. *Discrimination* involves ascertaining the distinction between one stimulus and another. The *just noticeable difference (jnd)* is the minimum amount of difference that can be detected between two stimuli 50% of the time. The jnd provides a way of measuring the difference threshold.

7. *Weber's law* states that a jnd is a constant proportion of the stimulus. The Weber fraction is a measure of the ratio of change in stimulus intensity to intensity.

Biological Properties Common to All Senses 112

8. All of the senses share particular biological properties, such as psychophysical thresholds, *transduction, sensory coding,* and *sensory adaptation*.

9. Each sense has specialized sensory *receptor cells*, which take in a particular form of energy and transduce it so that sensory neurons can transmit the sensed information to the brain. Impulses from most sensory receptors go via the sensory neurons to the thalamus, which then relays information to the cerebral cortex.

10. The contralateral shift enables sensory neurons from the left side of the body to cross over to the right hemisphere of the brain, and vice versa.

11. Through sensory coding, sensory receptors convey a range of information, such as intensity (amplitude) and quality (e.g., wavelength) of a stimulus. Sensory neurons encode these physical aspects through neural firing, which can be measured by *single-cell recording*. Stimulus intensity is coded by rate of firing and firing-pattern regularity.

12. When our senses detect changes in energy, receptor cells fire vigorously to alert the brain. *Sensory adaptation* is the temporary physiological response to a change in the environment; it varies according to the intensity of the change in the stimulus.

Vision 114

13. We can see because the receptors of our eyes receive and transduce the electromagnetic radiant energy of a very small portion of the electromagnetic spectrum of light.

14. The black round opening in the center of the *iris* is the *pupil*, which becomes dilated or contracted in response to the amount of light entering it. The *lens* of the eye refracts light and focuses it on the retina, enabling us to see objects clearly at varying distances from us. The *retina* transduces the electromagnetic radiant energy in light into electrochemical impulses.

15. People have two separate visual systems, one of which is used primarily for vision in the dark (*rods*), and the other of which is used primarily for vision in light (*cones*).

16. Brightness refers to our impression of light intensity. It is a psychological, rather than a physical, phenomenon.

17. Three properties of color are hue, which is what we usually refer to as "color"; saturation, which is the vividness, vibrancy, or richness of a color; and brightness, reflected from the color.

18. The *trichromatic theory of color vision* posits that we see color through the actions and interactions of cone receptors for three primary colors—red, green, and blue.

19. The *opponent-process theory of color vision* states that we see color through the opposing actions of receptors for red versus green and blue versus yellow.

20. Perceptual constancies result when our perceptions of objects tend to remain constant even as the stimuli registered by the sensory apparatus change. Examples are size, shape, and lightness constancies. Two size-constancy illusions are the *Ponzo illusion* and the *Müller–Lyer illusion*, both of which may be related to the way we interpret monocular depth cues. Shape constancy, too, may be tied to our interpretation of depth cues (e.g., in the observation that parallel lines appear to converge as they recede into the distance). Lightness constancy appears to be affected by context cues.

21. Depth perception is made possible in part by monocular depth cues, which can be noted by just a single eye. Examples of monocular depth cues are relative size, texture gradients, interposition, linear perspective, location in the picture plane, aerial perspective, and motion parallax. Artists manipulate many of these cues to create illusions of depth on two-dimensional surfaces.

22. Binocular depth cues, those used by the two eyes in conjunction, also facilitate space perception. Binocular convergence cues depend on the degree to which our two eyes must turn inward toward each other as objects get closer to us. Binocular disparity cues capitalize on the fact that each of the two eyes receives a slightly different image of the viewed object.

23. According to the Gestalt approach, the whole is different from the sum of its parts. Gestalt principles of form perception—such as figure–ground, proximity, similarity, closure, good continuation, and symmetry—characterize how we perceptually group together various objects and parts of objects.

24. According to the feature-detector approach to form perception, various cortical neurons can be linked to specific receptive fields on the retina. Differing cortical neurons respond to different kinds of forms, such as line segments or edges in various spatial orientations. Visual perception seems to depend on three levels of complexity in the cortical neurons; each successive level of complexity seems to be further removed from the incoming information received by the sensory receptors.

25. Two of the main theoretical approaches to pattern perception are template matching, according to which we recognize a pattern by matching it to a corresponding form (prototype) in our minds, and feature matching, according to which we recognize a pattern by comparing the features or aspects of the pattern to features stored in our memories. Neither template-based nor feature-based models of pattern perception, however, can fully account for context effects, or influences of the situation in which perception occurs.

26. Stroboscopic motion is the appearance of motion produced by the precisely timed intermittent and alternating flashing of two lights positioned at precise locations against a dark background.

27. Various deficits in visual perception fall under the category of agnosias.

Hearing 138

28. The cochlea, the main structure of the inner ear, has within it the basilar membrane. The hair cells of the basilar membrane transduce the mechanical energy of sound waves into electrochemical energy that can be processed by the brain.

29. According to *place theory*, we hear each pitch as a function of the location that is stimulated in the

inner ear. According to *frequency theory*, the vibrations in the inner ear reproduce the vibrations of the sounds that enter the ear. According to the *volley principle*, neurons cooperate in reproducing these vibrations. *Duplicity theory* holds that both place and frequency contribute to hearing.

30. There are two methods for locating the source of a sound: The time-difference method works best for low-frequency sounds, and the intensity-difference method works best for high-frequency sounds.

Taste, Smell, and the Other Senses 145

31. We are able to taste because of interactions between chemical substances and *taste buds*, sensory receptors on our tongues. According to a widely accepted theory of taste, the various sensory receptors in the tongue are differentially sensitive to various combinations of the four primary tastes: sweet, sour, bitter, and salty.

32. We are able to smell because of interactions between chemical substances and sensory receptors in our nasal cavities.

33. Some skin-sense nerves respond to the sense of pressure and movement; others convey two kinds of pain information (one dull, the other sharp), as well as temperature and pressure information.

34. *Cold* and *warm nerve fibers* in the skin enable us to sense temperature through their patterns of firing. Our response to temperature depends on our existing adaptation level.

35. Pain results when damaged tissue stimulates release of a neurotransmitter, which sends an impulse to the central nervous system. Different parts of the body have differing sensitivity to pain. People also differ in their sensitivity to pain.

36. *Kinesthesis* is the sense whereby we ascertain whether we are moving or stationary, where our various body parts are, and how (if at all) the parts are moving. The receptors for kinesthesis are in the muscles, tendons, joints, and skin.

37. Receptors of the *vestibular system*, located in the inner ear, allow us to maintain our balance, also termed *equilibrium*. Inputs from the vestibular, kinesthetic, and visual systems converge in the cerebral cortex.

KEY TERMS

absolute threshold   109
adaptation level   113
additive color mixture   122
amacrine cells   115
basilar membrane   142
binocular depth cues   130
bipolar cells   115
blind spot   117
cochlea   142
cones   115
cornea   115
detection   109
discrimination   110
duplicity theory   144
eardrum   140
electromagnetic spectrum   114
feature-detector approach   134
feature matching   135
figure   132
figure–ground   132
fovea   116
free nerve endings   151
frequency theory   143
ganglion cells   115
Gestalt approach   132
ground   132

hair cells   142
horizontal cells   115
iris   115
just-noticeable difference (jnd)   111
kinesthesis   154
lens   115
lightness constancy   127
monocular depth cues   129
Müller–Lyer illusion   127
olfaction   149
olfactory bulbs   149
olfactory epithelium   149
opponent-process theory of color vision   124
optical illusion   124
oval window   142
papillae   145
perception   108
perceptual constancy   125
pheromones   149
photopigments   116
photoreceptors   115
pinna   140
place theory   142
Ponzo illusion   127

psychophysics   108
pupil   115
receptor cells   112
retina   115
reversible figures   132
rods   115
sensation   107
sense   107
sensory adaptation   113
sensory coding   112
shape constancy   127
signal-detection theory (SDT)   109
single-cell recording   112
size constancy   125
stroboscopic motion   138
subtractive color mixture   122
taste buds   145
transduce   112
trichromatic theory of color vision   123
vestibular system   154
volley principle   144
Weber's law   111

■ THINK ABOUT IT SAMPLE RESPONSES

1. What are the main limitations of template-matching theories of visual perception?

These theories do not deal well with the fact that symbols such as letters or numbers can come in various forms and still be recognized. For example, two letters in different fonts (f, f) are both recognizable as the same letter, even though their appearances are different. These theories also do not well explain context effects, that is, effects of the surrounding context on perception, as illustrated by the word-superiority effect.

2. Why are objects closer than they visually appear on a foggy day?

On a foggy day, many particles of moisture are suspended in the air. The amount of intervening particulate matter in the air is usually a cue to distance: The hazier objects appear, the more distant they are. We do not automatically adjust to the greater amount of particulate material in the foggy air. Hence we tend to believe the objects are at a distance that would be appropriate for a less foggy day, that is, at a farther distance.

3. Hubel and Wiesel have noted that their discoveries and their research were possible because of the technologies available to them. What current technology do you find not only pleasant but also even important to your ability to perform a task you do often? How would your life be different without that technology? (It does not have to be a complex or "high-tech" item.)

There are many examples of technologies that make our lives easier. One is the use of computers in word processing. With computers, it is possible to erase unwanted letters, words, paragraphs, or even pages at the flick of a button or two. This process greatly speeds up writing. When I was young, for example, every typewriting mistake would have to be erased, with an eraser, by hand, consuming enormous amounts of time. For most writers, such time-consuming erasures are a relic of the past.

4. Try eating your next meal (or a snack) while keeping your eyes closed. Briefly describe how the other senses work together in helping you prevent yourself from ingesting bad food.

You generally see the food, which helps you decide whether it is fresh and whether it has an appealing appearance. Then you insert it in the mouth and immediately begin to taste and smell it. If either the taste or smell is "off," you may stop eating the food and even spit it out. In this way, you protect yourself from poisons. You can also feel its texture, and if the texture is different from what it is supposed to be (e.g., crunchy food that is softened), you may decide that the food is old and should not be eaten. You also even can hear yourself consuming the food, and again, the process of eating a food that is crunchy should produce a certain sound. If it does not, something may be wrong with the food.

5. In what ways have you noticed that smells affect the way you feel about particular people, particular kinds of food, and particular situations or settings?

The multi-million dollar perfume industry is so successful because people are attracted to certain kinds of personal smells. The deodorant industry succeeds because people find other kinds of personal smells unappealing. Simi-larly, going into a town that has a bad smell (as from an industrial complex) can predispose people not to like the town.

6. If you had to memorize a long list of terms and definitions, would you be better off trying to remember them by seeing them (e.g., reading printed flashcards) or by hearing them (e.g., having someone drill you by saying the words aloud)? Do you seem to be able to remember material better if it is presented visually (e.g., in a book) or vocally (e.g., in a lecture)? How do you tailor your studying to your sensory preferences?

Each individual has to answer this question for him or herself. Many people find that they have distinct sensory preferences. I would rather read something than hear it, but I know many people who would rather hear it than read it. Some people profit from engaging with learning material kinesthetically—they seek some kind of bodily movement. We maximize our learning when we come to understand how we learn best.

Milkman slipped into Sweet's bed and slept the night in her perfect arms. It was a warm dreamy sleep all about flying, sailing high over the earth. But not with arms stretched out like airplane wings, nor shot forward like Superman in a horizontal dive, but floating, cruising, in the relaxed position of a man flying on a couch reading a newspaper. Part of his flight was over the dark sea, but it didn't frighten him because he knew he could not fall. He was alone in the sky, but somebody was applauding him, watching him and applauding. He couldn't see who it was.

When he awoke the next morning and set about seeing to the repair of his car, he couldn't shake the dream, and didn't really want to. In Solomon's store he found Omar and Solomon shaking sacks of okra into peck baskets and he still felt the sense of lightness and power that flying had given him.

—Toni Morrison, *Song of Solomon*

5

CONSCIOUSNESS

Nobel Prize winner Toni Morrison frequently explores consciousness from a literary perspective. In the preceding excerpt, the protagonist in her novel illustrates the way in which an altered state of consciousness, such as dreaming, can affect waking experiences. Psychologists, too, observe that our conscious awareness of the world, and even of ourselves, often changes from moment to moment, influenced both by our sensations of the world around us and by our inner thoughts and feelings.

Consciousness is one's awareness of both internal and external stimuli, as well as of oneself. Thus, consciousness includes awareness of one's states of mind (internal stimuli), stimuli such as lights and noises (external stimuli), and the fact of one's existence (oneself). In discussing consciousness, we will consider levels of consciousness, the role of attention in consciousness, sleep and dreams, hypnosis, and drug-induced alterations in consciousness.

> The history of the world is none other than the progress of the consciousness of freedom.
> —Georg Hegel, Philosophy of History

Attention and Consciousness

In *Search of . . .* *How do we manage to pay attention to some things in the environment and to tune out others?*

Our state of consciousness might be overwhelming if we were unable to limit our experience of stimuli in the environment through our attention. **Attention** is the link between the enormous amount of information that assails our senses and the limited amount of information that we actually perceive. As you read these words, you are probably paying attention to the words (figure) on the text page and disregarding all the other visual sensations (ground) reaching your retina. If you paid attention to all the sensory information available to you at any one time, you would never be able to concentrate on the important and ignore the unimportant. As you read this page, you may be vaguely aware of the ways your skin is being touched by your clothes, of the ambient sounds surrounding you, or even of some internal cues such as hunger or fatigue. What allows you to dismiss most of this sensory information and to concentrate on reading? Pay attention and find out.

Attention involves mostly the interaction of diverse areas of the brain, with no specialized areas fully responsible for specific attentional functions (Cohen, Romero, Servan-Schreiber, & Farah, 1994; Farah, 1994). Certain areas of the brain do appear to be partly responsible for certain kinds of attention, however. Michael Posner (1995) has suggested that the frontal lobe tends to be activated during tasks requiring the paying of attention to verbal stimuli, and that the parietal lobe tends to be activated during tasks requiring the paying of attention to visual and spatial stimuli.

Selective Attention

Suppose you are at a banquet. It is just your luck to be seated next to this year's winner of the "Most Boring Conversationalist" award. As you are talking to this blatherer, who happens to be on your right, you become aware of the conversation of the two diners sitting on your left. Their exchange is much more interesting, so you find yourself trying to keep up the semblance of a conversation with the bore on your right while tuning in to the dialogue on your left.

This vignette describes a naturalistic experiment in **selective attention,** in which you attempt to track one message and to ignore another. This very phenomenon inspired the research of E. Colin Cherry (1953), who was interested in how we follow one conversation in the face of the distraction of other conversations. Cherry referred to this phenomenon as the **cocktail party phenomenon,** based on his observation that cocktail parties provide an excellent setting for observing selective attention.

Cherry did not actually study conversations at cocktail parties, but rather conversations in a more carefully controlled experimental setting. He used shadowing, in which each of the ears listens to a different message, and the person is required to repeat back the message going to one of the ears as soon as possible after hearing it. In other words, the person is to follow one message (think of a detective "shadow-

ing" a suspect) but ignore the other. This form of presentation is often referred to as dichotic presentation, meaning that each ear receives a different message. (When the two ears receive the same message, it is referred to as binaural presentation.)

Cherry's work prompted additional work in this area. For example, Anne Treisman (1964a, 1964b) noted that people shadowing the message presented to one ear heard almost nothing of the message presented to the other ear. They were not, however, totally ignorant of the other message. They could hear, for example, if the voice in the unattended ear was replaced by a tone or if a man's voice was replaced by a woman's voice. Moreover, if the unattended message was identical to the attended one, every research participant noticed it, even if one of the messages was temporally out of synchronization with the other. When this delay effect was studied systematically, people typically recognized the two messages to be the same when the shadowed message was either as much as 4.5 seconds ahead of the unattended one, or as far as 1.5 seconds behind the unattended one (Treisman, 1964a, 1964b). In other words, it is easier to recognize the unattended message when it follows, rather than precedes, the attended one. Treisman also observed that, when people who were fluently bilingual were studied, some of them noticed the identity of messages if the unattended message was the translated version of the attended one. Various theories have been proposed to account for selective attention, such as that displayed in shadowing studies.

Selective attention can be influenced by various kinds of psychological disorders. One such disorder is obsessive-compulsive disorder. People with obsessive-compulsive disorder (see chapter 16) tend to be preoccupied with thoughts they cannot get out of their minds and behaviors they are unable to control. Such people show decreased ability selectively to attend to stimuli to which they wish to attend and to screen out other stimuli they wish to ignore (Clayton, Richards, & Edwards, 1999).

Before you read about psychologists' theories of selective attention, think about your own present understanding of attention. What do you think explains why you attend to some things and not to others? Why do you think that you sometimes find it difficult to choose how to focus your attention?

Theories of Selective Attention

Theories of selective attention differ primarily in terms of whether or not they propose that we somehow filter, and thus sort out, the stimuli to which we pay attention. If the theories do propose a filter, disagreements arise over when filtering occurs and what it affects. Figure 5-1 summarizes the main theories.

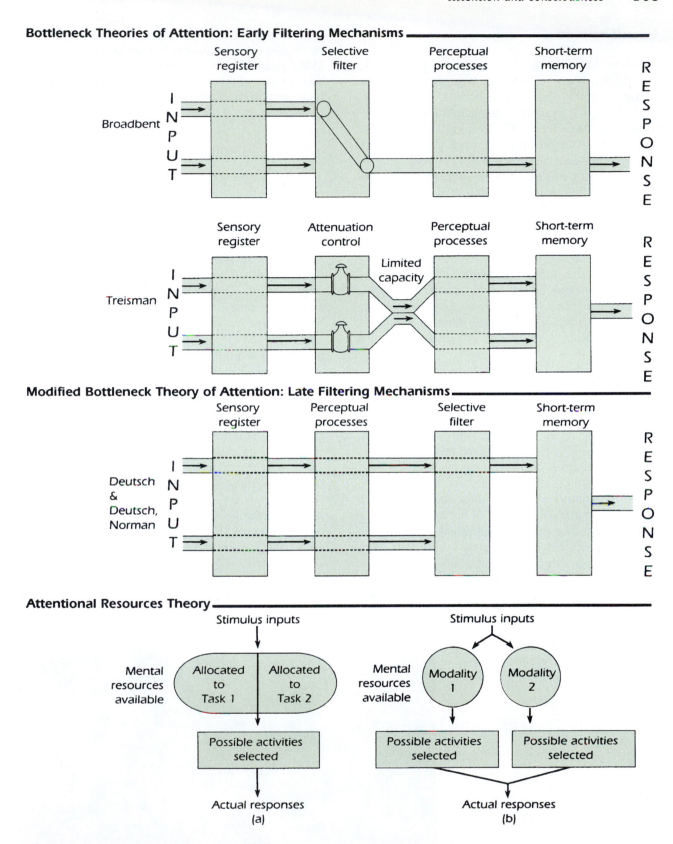

Figure 5–1

COMPARISON OF THEORIES OF ATTENTION.   *Various mechanisms have been proposed suggesting a means by which incoming sensory information passes through the attentional system to reach high-level perceptual processes. According to some cognitive psychologists, the attentional filtering mechanisms follow, rather than precede, preliminary perceptual processes. Attentional resources may involve either a single pool or a multiplicity of modality-specific pools. Although attentional resources theory has been criticized for its imprecision, it seems to complement filter theories in explaining some aspects of attention.*

Filter Theories

An early theory of selective attention, proposed by Donald Broadbent (1958), suggested that we filter information right after it is registered at the sensory level. Thus, we filter out irrelevant stimuli almost as soon as we hear them. These stimuli never receive any top-down, higher order processing. Subsequent research, however, indicated that Broadbent's model must be wrong. For example, participants in shadowing studies will hear one particular stimulus in the unattended ear, regardless of when it occurs: the sound of their own name (Moray, 1959). If we are able to recognize our own names in this way, then some higher level processing of the information must be occurring and reaching the supposedly unattended ear. If such processing were not occurring, we would not recognize the familiar sounds. That is, if the incoming information were being filtered out at the level of sensation, we would never perceive it in order to recognize it.

This kind of finding led some investigators to adopt a theory that places the filter later in the perceptual process, after some top-down, higher order conceptual analysis of input has taken place (Deutsch & Deutsch, 1963; D. A. Norman, 1968). This later filtering would allow us to recognize the meaning of information entering the unattended ear (such as the sound of our own names).

An alternative to both of these theories suggests that a filter may take the form of a signal-attenuating mechanism rather than of a signal-blocking mechanism (Treisman, 1964b). According to this view, information is not totally blocked out at any level; rather, it is weakened. We receive some of the information that is transmitted, but in a degraded form. The filter lets through some information, but not other information. What gets through is determined by a series of tests that decides whether the information is more likely to be important (such as our names) or more likely to be unimportant (such as idle prattle).

Attentional Resource Theories

More recent theories have moved away from the notion of filters and toward the notion of attentional resources. The idea is that people have a fixed amount of attention, which they can choose to allocate according to what the task requires. Our attention has a single pool of resources that can be divided up, say, among multiple tasks (Kahneman, 1973). For example, suppose that you were dividing your total attention among the acts of talking to a friend, reading your textbook, and drawing a doodle in the margin of your textbook. The amount of attention you could devote to each task would depend on how you allocated your single pool of attentional resources to each task. In this model, allocating attention to one task always takes away attention from all other tasks.

The single-pool model, however, now appears to be an oversimplification because people are much better at dividing their attention when competing tasks are in different perceptual modalities (e.g., one task requiring seeing, the other, hearing). Multiple-pool resource models specify that at least some attentional resources may be specific to the modality in which a task is presented. Thus, it is more likely that two visual tasks will interfere with each other than it is that a visual task will interfere with an auditory one. Competition for resources also can occur as a result of overlap

Attention is what enables us to focus on some stimuli and block out others. However, sometimes our attention may wander.

in the content type. For example, words heard on a radio are more likely to interfere with your reading of words than is instrumental music heard on the radio.

In sum, current models of selective attention emphasize that we bring to bear multiple attentional resources, using more than one sensory modality, on tasks that require divided attention.

Mindfulness

A construct related to selective attention is that of *mindfulness* (Langer, 1989, 1997), which is one's deliberate and considered attention to the immediate situation at hand. Lack of mindfulness is mindlessness. Ellen Langer (1989) gave an example of mindlessness. In 1982, a pilot and copilot went through a routine checklist prior to takeoff, mindlessly noting that the anti-icer was "off"—as it should be under most circumstances, but not under the icy conditions in which they were preparing to fly. The flight ended in a crash that killed 74 passengers. Fortunately for most of us, our mindlessness usually has far less lethal consequences, as when we may pour a glass of milk and then start to put the carton of milk in the cupboard rather than the refrigerator. Attention is generally a quite purposeful application of our consciousness, however, as in the above example, consciousness also operates automatically and at a number of different levels.

Levels of Consciousness

In *Search of . . .*

What is consciousness and what forms does it take?

According to British philosopher John Locke (1632–1704), a major function of consciousness is to help us form a sense of personal identity by linking past and present events to ourselves. It is the means by which we define who we are. British philosopher David Hume (1711–1776), in contrast, believed that our sense of personal identity is a myth, but it is not something we can empirically establish through any of our senses. All consciousness can do is reveal a succession of states of the world. It can never connect them. An analogy would be the successive frames of a film strip. We provide the connections between what are really large numbers of rapidly moving static frames. We only imagine them to be linked together.

A contemporary philosopher, Daniel Dennett (1995), believes, like Locke, that we have a sense of identity. But Dennett believes our sense of identity stems not from high-level consciousness, but from low-level processing. Basing his notions on Darwin's (1859) theory of evolution, Dennett argues that our senses of self and of intentionality (what we want to

do) are a product of countless simple molecular processes going on within us simultaneously. These myriad processes, rather than any unitary consciousness, combine to give us feelings of self and intentionality.

Whether or not consciousness establishes a sense of personal identity, it clearly serves two main purposes: monitoring and controlling (Kihlstrom, 1984). By *monitoring*, the individual keeps track of internal mental processes, personal behavior, and the environment, in order to maintain self-awareness in relation to the surrounding environment. By *controlling*, the individual plans what to do, based on the information received from the monitoring process. These two functions seem to operate, in one way or another, at various levels of consciousness. Normally, we see ourselves as being at a fully conscious level of awareness. Sometimes people seek to achieve a "higher" level of consciousness, through practices such as meditation or drug use, which we discuss later in the chapter. However, various lower levels of consciousness exist as well, classified as either preconscious or subconscious.

The Preconscious Level

The **preconscious** level of consciousness comprises information that could become conscious readily but that is not continuously available in awareness. For example, if prompted, you could remember what your bedroom looks like, but obviously, you are not always thinking about your bedroom. Also stored at the preconscious level are *automatic behaviors*, those requiring no conscious decisions regarding which muscles to move or which actions to take, such as dialing a familiar telephone number or driving a car to a familiar place via empty roads.

Perhaps our most common experience of preconsciousness is the tip-of-the-tongue phenomenon, which occurs when we are trying to remember something we already know but cannot quite retrieve. For example, if a man needs a new wallet, he might try to remember the name of the store where he bought the wallet he has. But the store is not one he patronizes frequently so the name does not immediately come to mind. He remembers the name of the store begins with a "C" and an image of a cow comes into his mind. Eventually he remembers the name of the store is "Cowley's." This phenomenon indicates that particular preconscious information, although not fully accessible, is still available in conscious thinking.

Researchers have demonstrated preconscious processing (Marcel, 1983). Research participants were shown words for just 10 milliseconds, after which the word was replaced by a visual mask. The rate of presentation was so rapid that observers were generally unaware that they had even seen a word. When the

In the Lab of . . .   Ellen Langer

Mindlessness of Ostensibly Thoughtful Action

Ellen Langer, *Harvard University*

Before the airport in Provincetown, Massachusetts, was renovated, a large glass wall looked out over the runway. While waiting for a friend to arrive, I asked the person behind the check-in counter when the flight from Boston was expected. She said it should be on time. There was no one else either at that gate or in the surrounding area, and I was less than two feet from the check-in counter when the plane arrived in full view. Rather than just lean over and tell me that was the plane, she announced the arrival over the public address system filling the empty room with the information. Not infrequently I have noticed that smart people were not paying attention to the information available to them.

My work has focused on understanding how mindlessness comes about and how pervasive it may be. When we are mindless, we are not consciously processing new information. Instead of mindfully attending to change and novelty, when we are mindless, we hold things still and treat the present as though it is an exact replica of the past. In our experiments assessing mindlessness, we've found that it comes about in two ways: either through repetition or on a single exposure to information. The first case is the more familiar. Most of us have had the experience, for example, of driving and then realizing, only because of the distance we have come, that we made part of the trip on "automatic pilot," as we sometimes call mindless behavior. Another example of mindlessness through repetition is when we learn something—like riding our bike home—by practicing it so that it becomes like "second nature" to us. We try to learn the new skill so well that we don't have to think about it. The problem is that if we've been successful, it won't occur to us to think about it even when it would be to our advantage to do so. We expect the route to be the same (because we traversed it so often), and we may not even notice a new path that may be shorter and more scenic, or a new hole in the pavement that it would have been good to avoid.

We also become mindless when we hear or read something and accept it without questioning it. Most of what we know about the world or ourselves we have mindlessly learned in this way. An example I'm particularly fond of is of my own mindlessness that I wrote about in *The Power of Mindful Learning*. I was at a friend's house for dinner and the table was set with the fork on the right side of the plate. I felt like some natural law had been violated, because the fork "goes" on the left side! I knew this was ridiculous. Who cares where the fork is placed? It is actually easier for right-handed people to reach it on the right. I thought about how I had learned this. One day as a child, my mother simply said to me that the fork goes on the left. I became trapped without any awareness that the way I learned the information would stay in place in the future. Whether we become mindless over time or on initial exposure to information, we unwittingly lock ourselves into a single understanding of that information.

When we are mindful, we are actively drawing novel distinctions, rather than relying on distinctions drawn in the past. This makes us sensitive to context and perspective. When we are mindless, our behavior is governed by rule and routine. Essentially we freeze our understanding and become oblivious to subtle changes that would have led us to act differently, if only we were aware of them. In contrast, when mindful, our behavior may be guided rather than governed by rules and routines, but we are sensitive to the ways the situation has changed. Thus if we're biking mindfully, we would avert the danger not yet arisen and avoid the new pothole.

With this understanding of the difference between mindlessness and mindfulness, the next step was to understand the costs of being mindless. While pursuing these thoughts, I was conducting research on the importance of perceived control with elderly people in nursing homes. It was a short step to ask myself about mindlessness with respect to this population. Were the elderly suffering because of mindlessness? After all, the older we get, the more opportunity we have for repetition and to learn "perspective-free" facts. We can only perceive control if we are mindful. If the elderly were experiencing excessive mindlessness, would encouraging mindfulness help? In several experimental investigations in nursing homes we found that increasing mindfulness, by having residents attend to novelty, had clear health benefits, not the least among them an increase in longevity. Twenty-five years of research has revealed that mindlessness may be very costly. In these studies, conducted in hospitals, schools, and places of business, we have found that an increase in mindfulness results in an increase in competence, health and longevity, positive affect, creativity, charisma, and reduced burnout, to name a few of the findings (Langer 1989, 1997). We have found ways of increasing mindfulness and ways of preventing mindlessness, but ways to "cure" it are more difficult and need more investigation.

References

Langer, E. (1989). *Mindfulness*. Reading, MA: Addison Wesley.

Langer, E. (1997). *The Power of Mindful Learning*. New York: Perseus.

 Find out more about this topic at ***www.harcourtcollege.com/psych/ishm***

Have you ever thought you heard someone call your name in a crowded room? Selective attention is also known as the cocktail party phenomenon.

research participants were shown a second word for a longer period of time, this new word was recognized more quickly if it was related to the first word than if it was unrelated. For example, *doctor* and *nurse* would be considered to be related words, whereas *doctor* and *oven* would be considered to be unrelated. Some kind of recognition of the rapidly presented word must have taken place—the recognition was clearly preconscious. This *subliminal perception*, a kind of preconscious processing of information that is thus below the level of conscious awareness of that information, suggests that people have the ability to detect information without being aware they are doing so. However, situations in which subliminal perception occurs appear to be quite limited and the effects are small. For example, Krosnick, Betz, Jussim, and Lynn (1992) studied the effects of a subliminal intervention on attitudes. Participants were shown slides designed to arouse either positive emotions (e.g., a bride and groom) or negative emotions (e.g., a skull). The exposure durations of the slides were extremely short, however, a mere $^{13}/_{1000}$ of a second. Participants then viewed a series of slides showing an individual engaged in ordinary, everyday activities. The question was whether the subliminally presented slides would affect people's attitudes toward the individual in the slides. Krosnick and his colleagues obtained small but statistically significant effects, suggesting that the subliminal intervention was having some effect in the expected direction, but that the effect was a small one.

One effect that appears to be totally absent is for subliminal tapes. Indeed, a careful study of such tapes renders it questionable whether they really contain any subliminal messages at all. Even if they are there, but well-hidden, they do not work (Greenwald, Spangenberg, Pratkanis, & Eskenazi, 1991), although many par-

ticipants believe they work. Thus, any effect they have is likely to be a *placebo effect*, whereby people's belief in the efficacy of a treatment results in an improvement in behavior, health, or whatever an intervention is supposed to affect.

To summarize, automatic behaviors, tip-of-the-tongue phenomena, subliminal perception, and other forms of preconscious knowledge are outside the view of our conscious minds, but they are available to our conscious minds under many circumstances.

The Subconscious Level

Unlike knowledge stored at the preconscious level, information stored at the **subconscious** or **unconscious** level is not easily accessible. The subconscious level involves less awareness than full consciousness and is either synonymous with the *unconscious* level (according to many theorists) or slightly more accessible to consciousness than the *unconscious* level (according to a few theorists). For our purposes, we make no distinction. In general, however, the term *unconscious* is usually preferred by followers of Sigmund Freud, the founder of psychoanalysis (see chapter 15).

According to Freud, material that we find too anxiety-provoking to handle at a conscious level is often *repressed*—that is, never admitted to consciousness, lest it make us feel distressed. Freud believed that many of our most important memories and impulses are unconscious. They are unavailable to us consciously, but nonetheless they have a profound effect on our behavior. For example, the person who experienced a sense of rejection by one of his or her parents (or both) is more likely to be extremely sensitive to rejection in all areas of life than someone who had no such early experience. However, the person may be unaware of the reason why he or she is more sensitive to and afraid of rejection than others because he or she repressed the original feelings of rejection. The existence of a process of repression is open to debate, however, and has not been conclusively documented.

Altered States of Consciousness

There are many different states of consciousness. What constitutes a "normal" state and what constitutes an "altered" state is a matter of some debate. One way to view "altered states" is as those other than our normal, waking state. In an altered state of consciousness, such as sleep and dreaming (discussed below), awareness is somehow changed from our normal, waking state. Each state of consciousness involves qualitative changes, which include the differing degrees of alertness and awareness associated with each state.

Altered states of consciousness have several common characteristics (Martindale, 1981). First, cognitive processes may be more shallow or uncritical than usual. For example, during sleep, you accept unrealistic dream events as being real, although you would never accept those events as realistic while awake. Sec-

ond, perceptions of self and of the world may change from what they are during wakefulness. Under the influence of hallucinogenic drugs, for example, objects may appear to take on bizarre forms, or objects that do not exist may be clearly perceived. Third, normal inhibitions and the level of control over behavior may weaken. People under the influence of alcohol, for example, may do things they normally would not do in a sober state. The remainder of this chapter looks at consciousness through the lens of altered states of consciousness such as sleep and dreaming and hypnosis and meditation, as well as chemically induced altered states.

Sleep

In Search of . . .   *Why do we sleep and what are the mechanisms involved in producing sleep?*

The cycle of sleep and waking is one of the most basic in humans as well as other organisms. In humans, the part of the brain most relevant to sleep is the reticular

---

Psychology in Everyday Life

Near-Death Experience

Near-death experience is an experience in which an individual either comes extremely close to dying or is actually believed to be dead and then is revived before permanent brain death occurs. During this time, some people undergo unusual psychological experiences.

Near-death experiences have been reported in writings throughout history and in the lore of cultures as disparate as those of the ancient Greeks, Buddhists, and North American Indians. A variety of researchers have reviewed accounts of people claiming to have had near-death experiences (e.g., Blackmore, 1993; Serdahely, 1990; Zaleski, 1987). A large number of people of differing ages and cultural backgrounds report similar near-death sensations. They often feel peace or intense joy. Some feel that they have left their bodies or have looked at their own bodies

from the outside. They often report traveling through a dark tunnel and seeing a brilliant light at the end of it. Some speak of reunions with deceased friends or relatives and others report contact with a being that encourages them to return to life. Some report rapidly reviewing many or all of the events of their lives.

Not all of the people who have the near-death experience are equally likely to experience all of these phenomena. The frequency and intensity of these experiences tend to be greatest for people who are ill, lowest for people who have attempted suicide, and in between for accident victims. Interestingly, few people have reported any negative experiences.

Although there are many explanations for near-death experiences, recent thinking has converged on attempts to explain these experiences in terms of

events produced by the brain (Blackmore, 1993; Persinger, 1999; Persinger & Richards, 1995). For example, the experience of seeing or walking through a tunnel may result from activation of the medial occipital cortexes due to insufficient blood supply, which then causes contrast between the peripheral and central visual fields, or the experiencing of a tunnel. Although such explanations are plausible, they have yet to be proven, and so near-death experience remains something of a mystery. Perhaps the most interesting thing to come out of near-death-experience research is that people who have such experiences typically say that their lives have changed for the better. They are less afraid of death, more appreciative of what they have, and more determined to live their lives to the fullest.

formation (see chapter 3). In particular, the *ascending reticular activating system* contributes to the alternating cycle of sleep and wakefulness. Other areas of the brain are involved as well, however, so that this one area cannot be seen as "responsible for" sleep. A number of neurotransmitters, including norepinephrine, dopamine, and GABA are involved in sleep, although their exact roles remain to be determined (Jones, 1994). Thus, there is no one neurotransmitter that is responsible for sleep either.

Why Do We Sleep?

During sleep, people become relatively, but not totally, unaware of external sources of stimulation (Antrobus, 1991). Despite centuries of inquiry, scientists have yet to reach a consensus about exactly why people need to sleep. Two possibilities, which are not mutually exclusive, are a preservation and protection theory and a restorative theory.

The Preservation and Protection Theory of Sleep

According to this theory, sleep serves an adaptive function: It protects the individual during that portion of the 24-hour day in which being awake, and hence roaming around, would place the individual at greatest risk. In order to feed themselves and meet other necessities, animals do not require 24 hours. From the standpoint of adaptation, therefore, they are best off staying out of harm's way. There is some evidence to support this theory (Allison & Cicchetti, 1976; Webb, 1982). The amount of time various species sleep tends to vary with the amount of time required to find the food they need to stay alive and how well they can hide themselves when they sleep. Moreover, they sleep at times that maximize their safety, given their physical capacities and their habits. For example, animals that tend to be prey for other animals guided primarily by vision tend to sleep during the day (when they would most likely be seen if they were roaming about), often in obscure places.

The Restorative Theory of Sleep

A second view as to why we sleep is that we sleep to restore depleted resources and to dissipate accumulated wastes. In other words, a restorative theory of sleep posits that there may be chemical causes of sleep. One way that psychologists study the restorative theory of why people sleep is to search specifically for sleep-causing chemicals produced in our bodies. Several substances seem to be associated with sleep, although none of them has been shown conclusively to cause sleep. One experiment was designed to see whether chemicals in the brains of sleep-deprived goats would induce sleep in rats (Pappenheimer, Koski, Fencl, Karnovsky, & Krueger, 1975). One group of goats was deprived of sleep for several days, while a control group was allowed to sleep normally. Then cerebrospinal fluid (see chapter 3) from each group of goats was injected into rats. Rats injected with fluid from the first group of goats slept more than did rats who received fluid from the control group. What was in the sleep-deprived goats' cerebrospinal fluid that caused the rats to sleep more? It was a small peptide made up of five amino acids, including muramic acid. This acid was recognized to be the sleep-producing compound that may have built up in the central nervous systems of the sleep-deprived goats.

Another sleep-producing compound, SPS (sleep-promoting substance), has been isolated (Inoue, Uchizono, & Nagasaki, 1982), as has been a third sleep-producing substance, DSIP (delta-sleep–inducing peptide; Schroeder-Helmert, 1985).

Circadian Rhythms

Biological cycles lasting about 24 hours in humans and various other species are called **circadian rhythms.** In humans, circadian rhythms show variations related to age, as well as individual and cultural factors.

Usually, infants alternate frequently between sleep and wakefulness, for a total of about 17 hours of sleep per day. Within the first 6 months, however, their sleep patterns change to about two short naps and one long stretch of sleep at night, for a total of about 13 hours per day. By 5 to 7 years of age, most of us have adopted what is basically an adult pattern of sleep (Berger, 1980), in which we sleep about 8 hours each night and remain awake about 16 hours each day. Regardless of the average, the actual range of sleep

According to the preservation and protection theory of sleep, day-sleeping animals maximize their safety by remaining hidden and asleep during the hours when their predators are awake.

French geologist Michel Siffre was shielded from all time cues in this underground cavern for 6 months. When people have no external time cues, their natural circadian rhythms shift from a 24-hour day to a 25-hour day. When they return to a normal environment, their circadian rhythms return to a 24-hour day, cued by clocks and the daily cycle of the sun.

needed varies widely across individuals, with some people requiring as little as an hour of sleep each day and others requiring 10 to 12 hours of sleep per day. Studies of long sleepers (people who regularly sleep more than 9.5 hours per day) and short sleepers (who regularly sleep less than 4.4 hours per day) show no differences in their average relative health. People differ not only in how much they sleep, but also in when they prefer to sleep. Research has shown that our intuitions that people differ in the time of day when they are most alert and aroused—that there are "day people" and "night people"—have proven to be correct (B. Wallace, 1993). Culture can also affect people's circadian rhythms. For example, people's sleep schedules can be affected by a variable as simple as the typical hour for dinner, which in the United States is 3 to 5 hours earlier than in Spain.

Sunlight and Sleep Cycles

Despite individual and cultural differences, the usual sleeping–waking pattern for most people roughly corresponds to our planet's cycle of darkness and light. Humans experience physiological changes that can be measured according to their daily rhythm, such as a lowering of body temperature at night, as well as changes in various hormone levels. The rhythm is controlled by the hypothalamus (Ralph, Foster, Davis, & Menaker, 1990).

Several investigators have studied circadian rhythms (see Hobson, 1989; R. A. Wever, 1979). Participants in one study were placed in a specially built underground living environment in which they were deprived of all cues normally used for telling the time of day—the rising and setting of the sun, clocks, scheduled activities, and so on (R. A. Wever, 1979). For one month, these participants were told that they could create their own schedules. They could sleep whenever they wished, but they were discouraged from napping.

The results were striking and have since been replicated many times (e.g., Mistlberger & Rusak, 1994; Welsh, 1993). As people acclimated to an environment without time cues, their subjective days became longer, averaging about 25 hours. Typically, they would go to bed a little bit later each night that they spent in isolation and eventually drifted toward a point where they were spending slightly more awake time than they had when there were time cues. Participants showed stable individual rhythms, although the rhythms differed somewhat from person to person. When returned to the normal environment, however, the participants reestablished a 24-hour cycle.

Anything that changes our circadian rhythm can interfere with sleep. Many of us have experienced *jet lag*, which is a disturbance in circadian rhythm caused by altering the light–dark cycle too rapidly or too slowly when we travel through time zones. Even if you have never flown out of your own time zone, you may have experienced a mild case of jet lag if you have changed to and from daylight savings time. Think about how you feel that first Sunday morning after setting your clocks forward an hour in the spring.

It sometimes is easier to adjust one's circadian rhythm when flying in one direction rather than another. Suppose someone travels from Los Angeles to New York. When it is 8:00 PM for native New Yorkers, it is only 5 PM for native Californians, so the westerners may be less tired than the easterners. As an example, one study found that visiting teams in basketball performed 4 points better, on average, when they traveled west to east rather than east to west, thereby almost nullifying the home-court advantage of the home team (Steenland & Deddens, 1997). The reason for the difference may be, at least in part, that people tend to have a natural sleep-waking cycle of 25 rather than 24 hours, so that it is easier for them to have to go to sleep later than to go to sleep earlier.

Neurochemicals and Sleep Cycles

Sleeping–waking cycles appear to be controlled in part by the pineal gland, which also secretes certain sleep-producing substances. Recently, there has been a great deal of interest in *melatonin*, a natural hormone secreted by the pineal gland, which appears to play an important role in regulating waking–sleeping cycles (Lewy, Ahmed, Jackson, & Sack, 1992; Reppert, Weaver, Rivkees, & Stopa, 1988). Small doses of melatonin—as little as a fraction of a milligram—appear to be capable of restarting the bodily clock and, especially, of helping travelers who cross time zones to adjust to the changes in the clock (Arendt, Aldhous, & Wright, 1988; Tzischinsky, Pal, Epstein, Dagan, & Lavie, 1992). Melatonin supplements are now available commercially and without a prescription, but people taking such supplements need to exercise caution because there can be some side effects (such as drowsiness in the morning),

and the long-term effects of high dosages are unknown. *Tryptophan*, an amino acid that is a precursor to the neurotransmitter serotonin, also has sleep-inducing properties. Light levels also affect the sleeping–waking cycle. For example, bright lights have been used to help people get over jet lag (D. Dawson, Lack, & Morris, 1993). Computer software is now available to calculate optimal amounts of bright light to use for a large number of different flight paths, so that it is possible to individualize the dosage of light to the actual trip an individual takes (Houpt, Boulos, & Moore-Ede, 1996).

Although some chemicals that *can* cause sleep have indeed been found, the assumption in this work—that sleep actually *is* induced chemically—has not been proved. Indeed, the restorative theory presumably would predict that people who are more active on a given day would sleep more than when they are not active. A related prediction would be that people who are active in general would sleep more. But these predictions have not been upheld. Researchers have thus sought other ways to study why we sleep, such as studying the effects of not sleeping.

Sleep Deprivation

In sleep-deprivation experiments (e.g. Borbely, 1986; Dement, 1976), research participants usually have few problems after the first sleepless night, and they appear to be relaxed and cheerful. They have more difficulty staying awake during the second night, however, and usually are severely tired by 3 a.m. of the second day. If they are given long test problems to solve, they will fall asleep but will often deny having done so.

By the third day, the participants appear tense. They become increasingly apathetic and are irritable

Athletes who travel to competitions in different time zones must adjust their sleep schedules carefully to maintain peak performance.

when disturbed. Although they may follow the instructions of the experimenter, they do so with little energy. Their moods swing wildly. By the third night, they are unable to stay awake without special intervention. By this time, periods of *microsleep* are observed: People stop what they are doing for periods of several seconds and stare into space. During these periods, their EEGs (electroencephalograms; see chapter 3) show brain-wave patterns typical of sleep. People deprived of sleep for this long may start to experience visual **illusions,** distorted perceptions of objects and other external stimuli, as well as **hallucinations,** or perceptions of sensory stimuli in the absence of any actual corresponding external sensory input from the physical world. They commonly experience auditory hallucinations, such as hearing voices in the sound of running water.

Things really start to fall apart after four days. Research participants typically become paranoid, sometimes believing the experimenters are plotting against them. It is possible to keep sleep-deprived people awake for longer than four days, but clearly, prolonged sleep deprivation is serious business and of questionable ethical justification.

Although research has not determined conclusively why we need to sleep, studies of circadian rhythms help us understand when and how much most people need to sleep.

Stages of Sleep

When studying circadian rhythms and other aspects of our sleeping–waking cycles, psychologists often examine people's brain-wave patterns, using electroencephalograms (EEGs). EEG recordings of the brain activity of sleeping people have shown that sleep occurs in stages common to almost everyone. During relaxed wakefulness, we exhibit an *alpha-wave* EEG pattern, as shown in Figure 5-2. As we doze, the alpha-wave rhythm of the EEG gives way to smaller, more rapid, irregular waves. This pattern characterizes *Stage 1* sleep, which represents a transitional state between wakefulness and sleep. If we are brought back to full consciousness from Stage 1 sleep, we may observe that our thoughts during this period did not make much sense, even though we may have felt fully or almost fully awake.

In *Stage 2* sleep, the stage in which we spend more than half of our sleeping time, the EEG pattern changes again. Larger EEG waves appear, and they overlap with *sleep spindles* (bursts of rapid EEG waves) and occasionally with *K-complexes* (large, slow waves). Muscle tension is markedly lower in Stage 2 than in the waking state.

In the next stages, the EEG pattern changes to *delta waves,* which are larger and slower than alpha

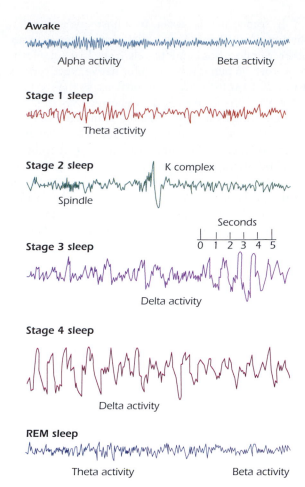

Figure 5–2

EEG Patterns Showing the Stages of Sleep.
These EEG patterns illustrate changes in brain waves, which reflect changes in consciousness during REM sleep and during the four stages of N-REM sleep. (a) Alpha waves typify relaxed wakefulness. (b) More rapid, irregular brain waves typify Stage 1 of N-REM sleep. (c) During Stage 2, large, slow waves are occasionally interrupted by bursts of rapid brain waves. (d) During Stages 3 and 4, extremely large, slow brainwaves (delta waves) predominate. When delta waves are 20% to 50% of all EEG waves, the sleeper is in Stage 3, whereas when delta waves are more than 50% of all EEG waves, the sleeper is in Stage 4. (e) During REM sleep, the brain waves look very much like those of the awake brain.

waves. Delta waves characterize *delta sleep,* or deep sleep, which comprises both Stages 3 and 4. The distinction between Stages 3 and 4 is the proportion of delta waves. When delta waves represent 20% to 50% of the EEG waves, the sleeper is in *Stage 3;* when delta waves represent more than 50% of the EEG waves, the sleeper is in *Stage 4.*

These first four stages of sleep make up **N-REM sleep** (non-rapid eye movement sleep). They are not characterized by rapid eye movements and are

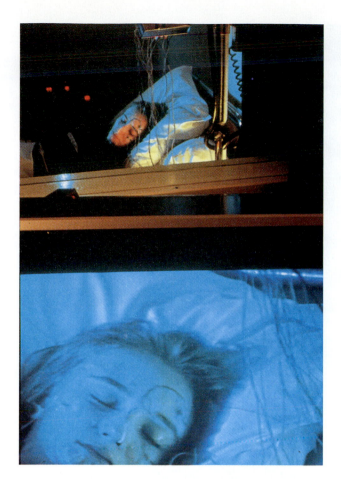

Sleep researchers monitor the patterns of brain-wave activity throughout the sleep cycles of research participants.

frequently associated with dreaming. During these four stages, as the name "N-REM" implies, our eyes are not moving very much. During the next stage, however, our eyes roll around in their sockets (Kleitman, 1963). If sleepers are awakened during this eye-rolling stage of sleep, they usually report being in the midst of a dream (Dement & Kleitman, 1957). This fifth stage has become known as **REM sleep**, the distinctive kind of sleep that is characterized by rapid eye movements (REMs) and is frequently—although not exclusively—associated with dreaming. Dreaming may also occur during N-REM sleep, although dreams from N-REM sleep are generally less clearly remembered upon waking than are the dreams from REM sleep.

EEG patterns become extremely active during REM sleep, which begins about an hour after Stage 1. The EEG of REM sleep somewhat resembles the EEG of the awake brain (see Figure 5-2), although it is usually difficult to awaken a person from REM sleep. Because this stage of sleep is, at the same time, both the most like wakefulness in terms of people's EEG patterns and the hardest from which to wake people, REM sleep is sometimes called "paradoxical

sleep." This term is also used because at the same time that the brain is very active, the body's capacity for movement is greatly diminished.

The stages of N-REM and REM sleep alternate throughout the night, roughly in 90-minute cycles. As the night progresses, the duration and sequence of the sleep stages may vary, as shown in Figure 5-3.

Sleep Disorders

Although circadian rhythms and sleep cycles normally vary somewhat from person to person, extreme variations from the normal sleep patterns can wreak havoc on a person's life. Sleep disorders that cause problems for many people include: lack of sleep, known as insomnia; sudden uncontrollable sleep, called narcolepsy; breathing difficulties during sleep, or sleep apnea; and sleepwalking, also termed somnambulism.

Insomnia

Insomnia, or lack of sleep, is a condition that afflicts millions. Insomnia is characterized by various disturbances of sleep, which include difficulty falling asleep, waking up during the night and being unable to go back to sleep, or waking up too early in the morning, and which may vary in intensity and duration. People may experience temporary insomnia because of stress or prolonged bouts of insomnia because of poor sleeping habits. Somewhat surprisingly, most people who suffer from insomnia usually sleep for at least a few hours, although they may not even be aware of having slept. Laboratory studies have also shown that insomniacs usually overestimate the amount of time it takes them to fall asleep.

Figure 5–3
SEQUENCES OF STATES AND STAGES OF SLEEP.   *The sequence of REM and N-REM stages of sleep cycles alternates throughout the night. The repetitions of the REM stage are identified in red. (After Hartman, 1968)*

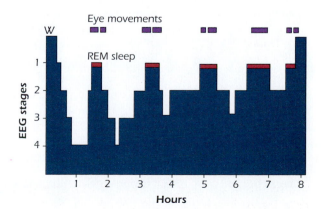

About 15% of adults experience insomnia, which encompasses a number of sleep disturbances.

Although almost everybody has trouble falling asleep occasionally, in one survey, 6% of adult respondents said that they had sought medical attention because of sleeplessness. Roughly 15% of adults report serious insomnia and another 15% report milder levels of insomnia or occasional insomnia (Bootzin, Manger, Perlis, Salvio, & Wyatt, 1993). Insomnia, and most other sleep disorders, are more common among women and the elderly (Borbely, 1986; Mellinger, Balter, & Uhlenhuth, 1985). Sleeping pills may help temporarily, but their side effects are troublesome, and they often eventually exacerbate the insomnia. Prescription sleep-ing pills interfere with the natural sleep cycle, usually decreasing REM sleep. This interference ultimately can result in the pills' disrupting the sleeping cycle rather than helping the individual establish a more regular pattern of sleep. Moreover, sedatives often continue to work during the day, impairing cognitive and motor functions while the sedative user is awake. Sedatives are also habit-forming, and people who rely on them may find it hard to sleep without taking medicine. For all of these reasons, physicians often recommend that their patients take the steps listed in Table 5-1 to avoid the need to take medicine (Borbely, 1986).

TABLE 5–1

How to Get a Good Night's Sleep *The following recommendations have been suggested by numerous experts in the field of sleep research. (After Atkinson, Atkinson, Smith, & Bem)*

Do	Don't
Set a regular bedtime Get up at the same time every morning	Change schedule on the weekends
Drink alcohol only in moderation	Have caffeine for 5–6 hours before bedtime
Try warm milk or a *light* snack before bedtime	Eat heavily just before bedtime
Establish a relaxing evening ritual	Take sleeping pills; they can disrupt sleep cycles and leave you "hung over"
Exercise regularly	Attempt to "wear yourself out" with exercise before bedtime or when sleep won't come
Stay in bed and try to relax if having problems sleeping	

Some people believe that they suffer from insomnia when they do not. What they are showing is a form of pseudo-insomnia, or *sleep state misperception.* Many of us have had the experience of thinking that we are up for hours, only to check the clock and to discover that our tossing and turning was for much less time than we thought. Others have had the experience of being certain that they did not sleep all night, only to have someone who observed them tell them that they actually slept for several hours. In each case, people believe their sleep is severely disrupted, when, at worst, it is only mildly disrupted. Indeed, 5% of individuals who go to insomnia clinics may suffer from pseudo-insomnia (Hauri, 1994).

Narcolepsy

In contrast to insomnia, **narcolepsy** is a disturbance in the pattern of wakefulness and sleep, in which the narcoleptic experiences an uncontrollable urge to fall asleep periodically during the day and as a result loses consciousness for brief periods of time (usually 10 or 15 minutes), thereby putting the narcoleptic in grave danger if the attacks occur when the person is driving or otherwise engaged in activities in which sudden sleep might be hazardous. Narcolepsy actually is more accurately described as a disorder of the waking state than as a sleep disorder, although narcoleptics frequently experience disturbed nighttime sleep as well. Narcoleptics usually fall into REM sleep immediately; a person with normal sleep patterns rarely (if ever) does so. This observation has led some scientists to suggest that, for narcoleptics, REM sleep may be insufficiently differentiated from the waking state. Narcolepsy affects 1 or 2 people in every 1,000 (Borbely, 1986). Although the cause of narcolepsy is unknown, the disorder seems to run in families, which suggests that it may be inherited. Fortunately, medication can usually control the symptoms of this disorder.

Sleep Apnea

Another disorder with unknown etiology and possible hereditary involvement is **sleep apnea,** a breathing disorder that occurs during sleep in which the sleeper repeatedly (perhaps hundreds of times per night) stops breathing. The episodes usually last only a few seconds, but they may last as long as two minutes in severe cases. Sleep apnea is potentially dangerous because it deprives the body of oxygen. It most often afflicts overweight men over 40 years of age. It also seems to be associated with alcohol consumption. The disorder is difficult to treat in adults, although weight loss sometimes helps.

Sleep apnea is also found frequently in prematurely born infants. Infants generally outgrow the disorder, but it may be life threatening if the breathing patterns of young infants at risk are not closely monitored. It has also been suggested that there may be a link between sudden infant death syndrome (SIDS) and sleep apnea. Maternal smoking has also been linked to SIDS, as has the baby's sleeping on its stomach (J. A. Taylor & Sanderson, 1995). It is therefore particularly important that parents not expose their baby to smoke (even in utero) and also that they place their baby in a position other than on the stomach for sleeping.

Sleepwalking

Somnambulism (sleepwalking) combines aspects of waking and sleeping, with the sleepwalker able to see, walk, and perhaps even talk, but usually unable to remember the sleepwalking episodes. For many years, scientists believed that sleepwalkers were merely acting out their dreams. In fact, however, sleepwalking usually begins during Stage 3 or Stage 4 of N-REM sleep and typically is not accompanied by dreaming. If the sleepwalking episode is short, sleepwalkers may stay in the deep sleep of Stages 3 and 4; if the episode is lengthy, EEG patterns begin to resemble either those of Stage 1 of N-REM sleep or those of the waking state.

Sleepwalking varies in severity. Some people may experience episodes in which they simply sit up in bed, mutter a few words, and then lie down again. Such episodes are no cause for concern. Other people may get out of bed, get dressed, walk around, and even leave their homes. Although sleepwalkers' eyes are open (usually with a rigid facial expression), and they can see, their perception is often impaired, and they can injure themselves by mistaking one thing for another, such as a window for a door.

Most sleepwalkers do not remember their episodes of sleepwalking when they awaken the next morning, and they may even be surprised to find

"Wait! Don't! It can be dangerous to wake them!"

themselves asleep in some place other than in their beds. Scientists have not found a cause or a cure for sleepwalking, although sleepwalking is known to be more common in children than in adults, and it usually disappears as children grow older.

Dreams

In Search of . . .   Why do we dream, and what are some of the main theories of dreaming?

People have always been fascinated with dreams. Dreams have been used to predict the outcomes of battles and have caused people to change religions. Indeed, dreams fill our heads with fantastic ideas—sometimes pleasant, sometimes frightening. Some people have experienced breakthrough insights or other creative ideas while dreaming or in a dreamlike state of mind. What is it about dreaming that may facilitate such breakthroughs?

All of us have dreams every night, whether or not we remember them (Ornstein, 1986). Dreams often occur in the form of strange fantasies that we accept as true while we sleep, yet would dismiss if we were awake. Common dreams among college students are shown in Table 5-2.

Why do we dream? Consider several theories. Perhaps the best-known theory of dreaming was proposed by Sigmund Freud (1900/1954). According to Freud, dreams allow us to express unconscious wishes in a disguised way. Freud called dreams the "royal road to the unconscious" because they are one of the few ways we have of allowing the contents of the unconscious to be expressed. However, he also postulated that the contents of the unconscious would be so threatening if expressed directly and clearly that we might awaken every time we dreamed. Thus, according to Freud, we dream in symbols that both express and disguise our unconscious wishes. Because these wishes are disguised, they do not shock us into wakefulness. The empirical support for this theory is weak. Other theorists, however, have suggested that dreams represent everyday concerns expressed in a language that is peculiar to dreams (Foulkes, 1990), or even that dreams have no particular meaning at all (Crick & Mitchison, 1983)—that they represent a kind of mental housekeeping that has no deep psychological meaning whatsoever.

If dreams do indeed have meaning, sometimes the disguises of dream content are rather thin (Dement, 1976). For example, in a study of the dreams of people who were deprived of liquid, a number of the dreams

TABLE 5–2

Common Dreams Among College Students

TYPE OF DREAM	PERCENTAGE OF STUDENTS
Falling	83
Being attacked or pursued	77
Trying again and again to do something	71
School, teachers, studying	71
Sexual experiences	66
Arriving too late	64
Eating	62
Being frozen with fear	58
A loved one's death	57
Being locked up	56
Finding money	56
Swimming	52
Snakes	49
Being inappropriately dressed	46
Unable to breathe	44
Being nude	43
Fire	41
Failing a test	39
Flying	34
Unable to move	30

SOURCE: Griffith, Miyago, and Tago (1958)

were found to involve liquid consumption (p. 69): "Just as the bell went off, somebody raised a glass and said something about a toast. I don't think I had a glass."

Some theorists take a cognitive perspective on dreaming. In particular, a *problem-solving view* of dreaming suggests that dreams provide a way for us to work out problems we have in our lives (Cartwright,

1977; Cartwright & Lamberg, 1992). For example, women going through a divorce are likely to dream about problems related to divorce. In fact, women who dream about divorce-related problems seem better able when they are awake to adjust to the problems of divorce than are those who do not frequently dream about it (Cartwright, 1991).

Another proposed perspective on dreaming is the **activation–synthesis hypothesis** (McCarley & Hobson, 1981), which states that dreams are the result of subjective organization and interpretation (synthesis) of neural activity (activation) that takes place during sleep. According to theorists Robert W. McCarley and J. Allan Hobson, our acceptance of bizarre occurrences in dreams is caused by changes in brain physiology. That is, just as our brains work to organize sensory information during wakefulness, our brains also strive to organize sensory information during sleep. Thus, the brain may interpret the neural activity that occurs during dreaming and that blocks motor commands as a sensation of our being chased. Our sleeping brains may interpret neural activity in the vestibular system (which controls balance; see chapter 4) as the sensation of floating, flying, or falling.

Although the biological purpose or reasons for dreaming may someday be discovered, it is unlikely that scientists will ever devise a definitive model of dream interpretation or for decoding the contents of dreams. Dreams are highly personal, and to say that you could prove why people dream what they dream, you would have to be able to predict the content of a specific dream at a specific time (Hobson, 1989). Such prediction is not likely to occur.

Psychoanalysts, such as Sigmund Freud and Carl Jung, looked for universal symbols that would mean the same things in every person's dreams. Because dreams are personal, however, many people freely interpret their own dreams within the context of their current lives and past memories, drawing conclusions that seem appropriate to them. Some people find analyzing their dreams merely entertaining, and some believe the messages they find in their dreams are useful in solving the problems of waking life. Occasionally, dreams can be terrifying

Nightmares are anxiety-arousing dreams that may lead to a person's waking up, sometimes seemingly in order to avoid some threat that emerges in the nightmares. People who have nightmares often remember them if asked to recount them immediately after waking. Nightmares tend to increase during periods of stress, although some people seem to be more susceptible to them than others. For example, children are more susceptible, on average, than are adults. Nightmares generally require no special action unless they are unusually severe or common, or the same nightmare keeps repeating itself again and again.

Night terrors are sudden awakenings from N-REM sleep that are accompanied by feelings of intense fright or panic. These awakenings are characterized by intense arousal of the autonomic nervous system, including greatly accelerated heart rate. People can experience night terrors at any age, but they are especially common in children roughly in the age range from 3 to 8 years. Often people will wake up suddenly and may scream or suddenly sit upright. They usually do not remember any specific coherent nightmare, although they may recall a frightening image or thought. Often people who experience night terrors find that their sense of panic quickly fades and that they are able fairly rapidly to fall back asleep.

No discussion of dreaming would be complete without mentioning **daydreaming**—a state of consciousness somewhere between waking and sleeping that permits a shift in the focus of conscious processing toward internal thoughts and images and away from external events. Daydreaming can be useful in cognitive processes that involve the generation of creative ideas, but disruptive—as anyone knows who has ever been questioned while daydreaming in class—in cognitive processes requiring focused attention on environmental events. Another state of mind often associated with creative, unrestrained thought is the state of consciousness that results from hypnosis.

Daydreaming can help us to creatively contemplate the information we have been studying.

Hypnosis and Meditation

In Search of . . .   *What is hypnosis and why does it occur, and what is meditation and how is it produced?*

Hypnosis is viewed by most (but not all) psychologists as an altered state of consciousness that usually involves deep relaxation and extreme sensitivity to suggestion and appears to bear some resemblance to sleep. For example, hypnotized people may imagine that they see or hear things when they are prompted to do so (Bowers, 1976). They may also receive a **posthypnotic suggestion,** in which instructions are given to an individual during hypnosis to be implemented after having wakened from the hypnotic state. Participants often have no recollection of having been given the instructions or even of having been hypnotized (Ruch, 1975). Hypnotized persons also may not sense things that they otherwise would sense; for example, a person may not feel pain when dipping an arm into very cold water. Hypnotized persons also may be induced to remember things they had seemingly forgotten.

Despite what has been found about the hypnotized state, many psychologists wonder whether hypnotism is a genuine psychological phenomenon. Historically, even the man credited with introducing hypnotism as a psychological phenomenon, Franz Anton Mesmer (1734–1815), did not recognize the phenomenon as hypnotism. Mesmer came to be viewed as a fraud, largely because he made claims for his techniques that he could not scientifically support (see Figure 5-4).

Since Mesmer's time, scientists have continued to investigate hypnotism. One way to determine whether hypnotism is genuine is to use the **simulating paradigm**

Figure 5–4

MESMERISM.   *Franz Anton Mesmer, one of the first to experiment with hypnotism, believed that animal magnetism could cure illnesses. His patients would sit around the "magnetized" tub, wrap themselves with cord, and hold onto bent iron bars. "Magnetizers," Mesmer's helpers, would rub the patients' afflicted parts to hasten the cure. Mesmer and his method were discredited.*

(Orne, 1959), a research technique for determining the true effects of a psychological treatment in which one group of participants is subjected to the treatment (hypnotized) and another group (a control group) is not. The control participants are then asked to behave as though they had received the treatment (in this case, been hypnotized). People must then try to distinguish between the behavior of the treatment group and the behavior of the control group.

As it turns out, simulators are able to mimic some, but not all, of the behavior of hypnotized participants (Gray, Bowers, & Fenz, 1970). Also, hypnotized participants in simulation experiments provide very different reports than do simulators of their subjective experiences. Simulating participants report themselves as actively faking, whereas hypnotized participants report the behavior as more or less just happening to them. Moreover, simulating participants try to figure out what the hypnotist expects from them, whereas hypnotized participants claim to be uninfluenced by the experimenter's expectations of them (Orne, 1959). Thus, hypnotized people do not appear to be faking (Kinnunen, Zamansky, & Block, 1994; Spanos, Burgess, Roncon, Wallace-Capretta, & Cross, 1993).

Theories of Hypnosis

If we accept the phenomenon of hypnosis as genuine, we still need to determine exactly what goes on during hypnosis. We discuss here only the more credible theories. One such theory holds that hypnosis is a form of deep relaxation (Edmonston, 1981). This theory builds on the idea of hypnosis as a form of sleep, as suggested earlier this century by Ivan Pavlov, a Russian physiologist (see also chapter 6). We now know that EEG patterns shown during hypnosis are different from EEG patterns shown during sleep. Nevertheless, there may still be a close connection between hypnosis and the deep relaxation that sometimes precedes or resembles sleep.

A second theory suggests that hypnosis is an *epiphenomenon*, a phenomenon that exists only as a secondary outcome of another phenomenon. Two psychologists who have taken this position are Theodore Barber (1979, 1986) and Nicholas Spanos (1986; Spanos & Coe, 1992). According to this view, hypnosis is a form of role playing in response to experimenter demands. In attempting to fulfill the role set out by the experimenter, a person may act in particular ways. This view seems similar to the view that the behavior of hypnotized people is merely a sham, but the two views are not the same. According to this view, the person in a situation involving hypnosis is believed to become so genuinely caught up in the role that he or she unwittingly enacts the role of a hypnotized person

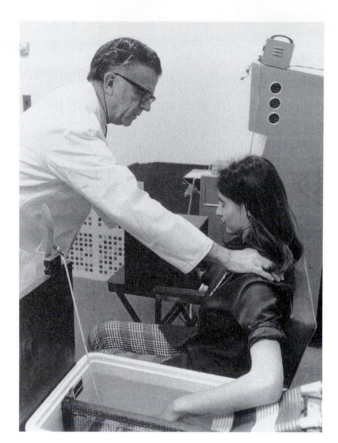

Hypnotists are able to induce a state of deep relaxation in susceptible individuals. Here, Ernest Hilgard conducts an experiment to determine the effects of hypnosis.

for a brief period of time. Advocates of this position point out that individuals can be quite successful in faking many of the phenomena attributed to hypnosis. More recently, it has become increasingly apparent that many of the memories seemingly miraculously retrieved under hypnosis are instead after-the-fact constructions emanating from the suggestions of the hypnotist (McConkey, 1992; see also chapter 7). In other words, hypnosis resulted not in people's being able to perform an astounding feat of memory, but in their constructing memories that they may have believed the hypnotist wanted them to construct.

Perhaps the most widely accepted view among scientists who believe that hypnosis is a genuine phenomenon is Ernest Hilgard's (1977) **neodissociative theory.** According to this view of hypnosis, some individuals are capable of separating one part of their conscious minds from another part (*dissociation*). In one part of the mind the individual responds to the hypnotist's commands. In the other part of the mind, the individual becomes a hidden observer who simultaneously observes and monitors the events and actions taking place. These events and actions include some of those events and actions that the hypnotized participant appears not to be processing in the part of the conscious mind that is engaging in the actions (Hilgard, 1977).

For example, studies of pain relief through hypnosis have found that while participants respond to a hypnotist's suggestion that they feel no pain and behave in ways that seem to show they are not in pain, they nevertheless are also able to describe how the pain feels. In other experiments, participants can be made to write down messages while unaware that they are doing so because they are actively engaged in another task at the same time (see Kihlstrom, 1985; Knox, Crutchfield, & Hilgard, 1975; Zamansky & Bartis, 1985). Thus, it seems that part of the person's consciousness is unself-consciously involved in the hypnosis, while another part observes and thereby knows, at some level, what is taking place.

People differ in their susceptibility to hypnosis (Hilgard, 1965), with some people readily becoming deeply hypnotized, others less so, and still others appearing invulnerable to hypnotism. Highly hypnotizable people tend to be highly susceptible to suggestion, whether or not they are hypnotized. Unsurprisingly, hypnosis is more successful as a clinical treatment with highly hypnotizable individuals. Today, hypnosis is used in clinical settings to control smoking and to treat a variety of health-related problems, such as asthma, high blood pressure, and migraine headaches. The effects of hypnosis, however, appear to be temporary. For this reason, hypnotism generally is used in conjunction with other therapeutic techniques. Still, hypnosis appears to have an effect that goes beyond other treatment techniques, whether in relieving pain or in changing behavior. Other uses of hypnosis appear rather dubious, such as its use for recovering lost memories.

Hypnosis and Memory

Some psychologists have become convinced that hypnosis can be used to dredge up old memories of events that otherwise would appear to be forgotten, even memories of past lives! For example, in one study, a full third of the hypnotized college students who were instructed to remember events from previous lives were able to do so (Spanos, DuBreuil, & Gabora, 1991). While they were recalling these past lives, they were asked questions about their lives and surrounding events. Their recall cast serious doubt on the validity of their assertions. One student, for example, recalled his life as Julius Caesar in A.D. 50, when he was emperor of Rome. Caesar died in 44 B.C. and was never crowned emperor of Rome.

The evidence suggests that people under hypnosis are highly suggestible and that at least some of their recall may be inadvertently induced by their

hypnotists (L. S. Newman & Baumeister, 1994). For example, hypnotists' questions about events during reported abductions by extraterrestrial aliens often contain suggestions, which are then picked up by the hypnotized individual and "recalled" as having happened. An example is being asked whether one was injected with a needle by the extraterrestrials, and then "remembering" that one was, indeed, injected (Fiore, 1989).

Some recollections under hypnosis may be correct (Geiselman, Fisher, MacKinnon, & Holland, 1985). But the current weight of the evidence is that recollections made under hypnosis need to be treated with skepticism and that corroborating sources of evidence for these recollections should be obtained before they are accepted as true memories. Hypnosis not only seems to be questionable as a technique for inducing recall of memories from the intermediate and distant past, but also as a technique for inducing recall of very recent memories. When memory for recently learned stories was compared for participants who either were or were not hypnotized, the hypnotized participants actually showed worse recall of the stories than did the nonhypnotized participants (Muzur, Fabbro, Clarici, Braun, & Bava, 1998).

The verdict on hypnosis is not yet in. Although persuasive evidence suggests that hypnosis is more than a crass simulation, psychologists have not reached consensus regarding what hypnosis is, or even whether it is a genuine phenomenon.

Meditation

A set of techniques that may be related to hypnosis come under the label of meditation. **Meditation** is a set of techniques used for altering consciousness through contemplation, by "a shift away from the active, outward-oriented, linear mode and toward the receptive and quiescent mode, and often, a shift from an external focus of attention to an internal one" (Ornstein, 1977, p. 159). Brain-wave patterns, as well as experiences of the world, can be altered during meditation. Some of the different kinds of meditation are described here. Meditation is viewed as slightly exotic in many Western cultures but is a more regular part of life in some Eastern cultures.

Concentrative meditation is a form of contemplation in which the meditator focuses on an object or thought and attempts to remove all else from consciousness. Concentrative meditation is performed in various ways. For example, meditators might focus on the whole process of breathing—to think about the movement of the air as it reaches the nose, permeates the lungs, remains in the lungs, and then is finally expelled. The idea is to focus on a simple, repetitive, and rhythmic activity.

At another time, the meditator might contemplate the answer to a *koan*—a riddle or paradox, such as "What is the sound of one hand clapping?" or "What is the size of the real you?" These questions have no logical answers, which is just the point. You can think about the questions time and again without coming to a conclusion.

Opening-up meditation is the second of the two main forms of contemplation, in which the meditator integrates meditation with the events of everyday life, seeking to expand awareness of everyday events, rather than to separate meditation from mundane existence. Yoga can take an opening-up form, as well as a concentrative one. In one form of opening-up yoga, the individual learns to observe him or herself as though he or she were another person. In another form of opening-up meditation, the person performs everyday actions slightly differently from the customary way, in order to become more aware of the routine of his or her life.

What happens during meditation, and what value, if any, is there in the various forms of meditation? In general, respiration, heart rate, blood pressure, and muscle tension decrease (D. H. Shapiro & Giber, 1978; R. K. Wallace & Benson, 1972). Some evidence indicates that meditation can help patients with bronchial asthma (Honsberger & Wilson, 1973) and that it can decrease blood pressure in patients who are hypertensive (Benson, 1977). It may reduce insomnia in some people (Woolfolk, Carr-Kaffashan, McNulty, & Lehrer, 1976) and some symptoms of psychiatric syndromes in others (Glueck & Stroebel, 1975). EEG studies suggest that concentrative meditation tends to produce an accumulation of alpha waves, the type of brain wave associated with a state of relaxation and the beginning stages of sleep (Fenwick, 1987). Thus, concentrative meditation seems to relax people, which is of value in its own right. In addition, many practitioners of meditation believe that it enhances their overall consciousness and moves them toward a more enlightened state of consciousness. Users of various drugs also sometimes seek such a state, more often than not with negative, and sometimes even life-threatening, results.

Drug-Induced Alterations in Consciousness

In Search of . . . **What are the main psychoactive drugs, and what are their psychological consequences?**

Drugs introduced into the body may destroy bacteria, ease pain, or alter consciousness. In this chapter we are concerned only with **psychoactive** drugs, those that produce a **psychopharmacological** effect affecting behavior, mood, and consciousness. Psychoactive drugs can be classified into four basic categories (Seymour & Smith, 1987): narcotics, central nervous system depressants, central nervous system stimulants, and hallucinogens. (See Table 5-3 for a summary of drugs in each category.) We consider each of these four kinds of drugs in turn, starting with the potent analgesics (pain relievers) known as narcotics. It is important to realize that sometimes different kinds of drugs are used in combination, such as a "speedball," which combines a stimulant (cocaine) with a narcotic (heroin). The use of such combinations is more likely to be seriously toxic or deadly than is the use of single drugs.

Narcotics

Narcotic, from the Greek term for "numbness," originally referred only to *opium* and to drugs derived from opium, such as heroin, morphine, and codeine. Narcotics can be either naturally or synthetically produced to create the numbing, stuporous effects of opium and can lead to addiction (see Table 5-3). Narcotics derived from the opium poppy pod are **opiates.** Drugs that have a similar chemical structure and set of effects to those of opiates, but that are made synthetically through combinations of chemicals, such as meperidine or methadone, are called **opioids.** When used illegally, opiates and opioids are usually injected intravenously, smoked, or inhaled. When used medically, they are either swallowed or injected intravenously. Narcotics lead to a reduction in pain and an overall sense of well-being.

Drug Actions

Narcotics are highly addictive and are usually either regulated by prescription or banned outright. Narcotics are sometimes prescribed for very brief periods to reduce postsurgical pain, and, in very low doses, to relieve diarrhea. They have a constipating effect because narcotics also depress other physiological systems, including metabolic processes.

Narcotics primarily affect the functioning of the brain and of the bowel. They bring about pain relief, relaxation, and sleepiness. They also help to suppress coughs (hence their use in the form of *codeine* prescription cough medicines) and can stimulate vomiting. Users typically notice impairment in their ability to concentrate and experience a sense of mental fuzziness or cloudiness. For these reasons, driving under the influence of narcotics is extremely dangerous, and doing cognitively intensive work (such as studying) while one is affected by them is likely to be unproductive. Side effects of narcotics include contraction of the pupils, sweating, nausea, and depressed breathing.

TABLE 5–3

Four Basic Categories of Drugs

Psychoactive drugs can be sorted into four basic categories, each of which produces distinctive psychoactive effects.

CATEGORY	EFFECT	DRUGS IN THIS CLASS
Narcotics	Produce numbness or stupor, relieve pain	■ Opium and its natural derivatives: morphine, heroin, and codeine ■ Opioids (synthetic narcotics): meperidine (Demerol®), propoxyphene (Darvon®), oxycodone (Percodan®), methadone
CNS depressants ("downers")	Slow (depress) the operation of the central nervous system	■ Alcohol ■ Sedative–hypnotics Barbiturates: secobarbital (Seconal®), phenobarbital (Dilantin®) Tranquilizers (benzodiazepines): chlorpromazine (Thorazine®), chlordiazepoxide (Librium®), diazepam (Valium®), alprazolam (Xanax®) ■ Methaqualone (Quaalude®) ■ Chloral hydrate
CNS stimulants ("uppers")	Excite (stimulate) the operation of the central nervous system	■ Caffeine (found in coffee, teas, cola drinks, chocolate) ■ Amphetamines: amphetamine (Benzedrine®), dextroamphetamine (Dexedrine®), methamphetamine (Methedrine®) ■ Cocaine ■ Nicotine (commonly found in tobacco)
Hallucinogens (psychedelics, psychotomimetics)	Induce alterations of consciousness	■ LSD ■ Mescaline ■ Marijuana ■ Hashish ■ Phencyclidine (PCP)

Tolerance and Dependency

Another danger of narcotic use over time is the possibility of an eventual **overdose,** an ingestion of a life-threatening or lethal dose of drugs. Narcotics users develop **tolerance,** a consequence of prolonged use of psychoactive drugs, in which drug users progressively experience less of a drug's effects for a given amount of the drug. Tolerance often prompts drug users to seek increasing amounts of a given drug to achieve the same desired effect. Actually, most narcotics users find that the euphoria they felt when initially using the drug disappears after prolonged use. Rather, they must continue to use drugs in order to keep from feeling ill from withdrawal of the drugs.

This dependency occurs because, like many other drugs, narcotics mimic neurotransmitters in the way they act at synapses (see chapter 3 and Figure 5-5). The molecular composition of opiates resembles that of endorphins, which are *endogenous morphines,* the body's naturally produced painkilling neurotransmitters (see also chapter 18). Initial use of narcotics prompts pain relief and some of the euphoria that normally accompanies the natural release of endorphins. Prolonged use of narcotics apparently causes a drop in the body's natural production of particular endorphins. Interestingly, some activities produce an increase in the production of endorphins. For example, long-distance running may cause pain, which triggers the release of endorphins, which in turn results in a

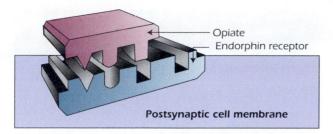

Figure 5–5

MOLECULAR SIMILARITY OF OPIATES AND ENDORPHINS. *Opiates and endorphins have very similar structures, which is why narcotics easily fit the receptor sites for endorphins.*

feeling of exhilaration or a "natural high" (Harte, Eifert, & Smith, 1995).

As a drug replaces the body's natural painkillers, people can develop *drug dependence,* a state in which an individual must continue to use a drug to satisfy intense physical, mental, or emotional cravings for the drug. In the past, it was common to distinguish between physical dependence, in which a person continues to use a drug to avoid physical symptoms, and psychological dependence, in which a person continues to use a drug to avoid mental or emotional symptoms. Today, however, many psychologists believe that the distinction between the two kinds of dependence is so fuzzy as to render it futile (Koob & Bloom, 1988; Ray & Ksir, 1990). Dependence increases and tolerance develops because more narcotic is needed to do the job that the body gradually ceases to perform. **Withdrawal** symptoms are the temporary discomforts (which may be extremely negative, much like a severe case of intestinal flu, accompanied by extreme depression or anxiety) associated with a decrease in dosage or a discontinuation altogether of a psychoactive drug. During withdrawal, the drug user's physiology and mental processes must adjust to an absence of the drug. Typical narcotic withdrawal symptoms are chills, sweating, intense stomach cramps, diarrhea, headache, and repeated vomiting. These symptoms may occur individually or in various combinations.

Treatment of Narcotic Abuse

Once a user has formed narcotic dependence, the form of treatment differs for *acute toxicity* (the damage done from a particular overdose) versus *chronic toxicity* (the damage done by long-term drug addiction). Acute toxicity is usually treated with naloxone. Naloxone (as well as a related drug, naltrexone) occupies opiate receptors in the brain better than the opiates themselves occupy those sites; thus, it blocks all effects of narcotics (see Figure 5–6). In fact, naloxone has

such a strong affinity for the endorphin receptors in the brain that it actually displaces molecules of narcotics already in these receptors and then moves into the receptors itself. Naloxone is not addictive, however, because even though it binds to receptors, it does not activate them. Although naloxone can be a lifesaving drug for someone who has overdosed on opiates, its effects are short-lived, making it a poor long-term treatment for drug addiction.

Maintenance and detoxification are the primary methods of treating chronic toxicity caused by prolonged drug addiction. *Maintenance* controls an addict's use of the drug. In a maintenance program, the addict is still given the drug or a substitute, but in a controlled manner. The goal is to substitute a more controllable, less lethal, addiction—a goal considered

Figure 5–6

MOLECULAR SIMILARITY OF OPIATES, METHADONE, AND NALOXONE. *The nonnarcotic drug naloxone fits the receptor sites for endorphins so well that it can push out opiates and block them from reentering those sites, as shown in panel (c). Hence, naloxone can be used as effective temporary treatment for narcotic overdose, although its effects are short-lived. For long-term treatment, methadone is often substituted for heroin. It also fits the endorphin receptor sites, as shown in panel (b) and can reduce heroin cravings and withdrawal symptoms.*

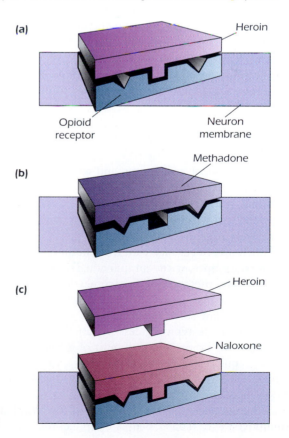

controversial by many. *Detoxification* seeks to break the addiction both by weaning an addict off the drug to break the habit and by restoring good health habits. In narcotic detoxification, methadone is substituted for the narcotic (typically, heroin). Methadone binds to endorphin receptor sites in a similar way to naloxone (see panel (b) of Figure 5-6) and reduces the heroin cravings and withdrawal symptoms of addicted persons. After the substitution, gradually decreasing dosages are administered to the patient until he or she is drug-free.

Central Nervous System Depressants

Drug Actions

Another highly addictive class of psychoactive drugs is the **central nervous system (CNS) depressant** drugs (e.g., alcohol and the sedative–hypnotics), which slow the operation of the CNS and are often prescribed in low doses to reduce anxiety and in relatively high doses to combat insomnia. Alcohol is readily available for purchase by adults in most countries around the world. Sedative–hypnotics are usually prescribed. CNS depressants can be ingested orally or injected. They usually elevate mood, reduce anxiety and guilt, and relax normal inhibitions. However, people **intoxicated** (characterized by stupefaction because of the effects of toxins) by depressants may also find themselves susceptible to sudden shifts in mood, so that their relaxation and euphoria quickly give way to *increased* anxiety and irritability. High doses of depressants can cause slow reflexes, unsteady gait, slurred speech, and impaired judgment. Overdoses can slow physiological responses so much that they cause death.

Alcohol

Alcohol is the most well known and widely used CNS depressant. The natural result of the fermentation of fruits and grains, alcohol is so widely promoted and consumed that people tend to ignore the fact that it is an addictive psychoactive drug.

Alcohol's effects vary with the amount consumed, rate of consumption, and an individual's body weight, tolerance, and metabolism. Someone who sips a drink over the course of an evening is less likely to become intoxicated than someone who gulps it, and a 300-pound person is typically less affected than a 100-pound person by the same amount of alcohol. However, a frequent drinker usually builds up a tolerance (similar to narcotics tolerance), and this tolerance can lead to increased consumption.

When concentrations of alcohol in the blood are around 0.03% to 0.05%, people often feel relaxed and

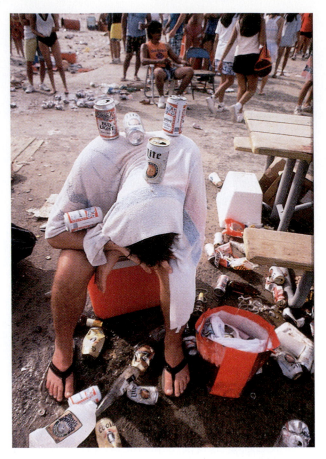

Although party-goers often drink alcohol to relax and reduce inhibitions, prolonged or excessive drinking can cause stupor, damage to the brain and nervous system, and sometimes death. Is this person having fun yet?

uninhibited, and they have a general sense of well-being. At a blood-alcohol level of 0.10%, sensorimotor functioning is markedly impaired. Many states consider people to be legally drunk at this level. Some states use a lower level of 0.08%. People may exhibit slurred speech and grow angry, sullen, or morose. At a concentration of 0.20%, people show grave dysfunction. With concentrations of 0.40% or more, there is a serious risk of death.

Most dosages of alcohol decrease the effectiveness of the neurotransmitter *dopamine* (see chapter 3), reducing motor abilities and attention. Alcohol also appears to interfere with the activities of other neurotransmitters (Hittner, 1997). At first, alcohol often appears to increase people's level of arousal, apparently because it first depresses the effects of synapses that release inhibitory neurotransmitters in the brain. Because the inhibiting neurotransmitters are depressed, they do not inhibit neurotransmission as much. Thus, even though synaptic activity is being depressed and there is less activity overall, people initially may feel more excited because inhibitory activity is slowed and excitatory transmissions predominate. Soon, however, alcohol depresses the effects of excitatory synapses as well, causing a general decrease in sensorimotor functioning.

Treatment of Alcohol Abuse

Alcoholism, a tendency to abuse alcohol to a degree that leads to social, cognitive, or occupational dysfunction, is one of the most common afflictions in the United States. Alcoholics have great difficulty abstaining from alcohol and controlling their drinking once they start. Roughly two-thirds of adults in the United States report that they use alcohol. An estimated 10% of these people have problems related to alcohol use, and 5% of them are alcoholics, with physical as well as psychological dependence. Probably at least 10 million adults in the United States suffer from alcohol dependence (Seymour & Smith, 1987), and an estimated 90% of all assaults, 50% to 60% of all homicides, and more than 50% of rapes and of sexual attacks on children are alcohol related. The costs to society of alcohol abuse are probably double those of all other types of drug abuse combined (Segal, 1988).

Chronic alcoholics may sustain permanent damage to the nervous system, pancreas, liver, and brain cells. Heavy drinking can also lead to suppression of the immune system, nutritional deficits, and general failure to be careful about health matters. These problems can eventually lead to many other unfortunate consequences, including increased risk of cancer (Herity, Moriarty, Daly, Dunn, & Bourke, 1982; Heuch, Kvale, Jacobsen, & Bjelke, 1983). For these and other reasons, alcoholics generally have their life expectancy cut short by an average of 10 to 12 years. Alcoholics also may experience blackouts, loss of memory, cardiac arrest, psychosis, and alcohol-induced death. They are at risk for *Korsakoff's syndrome*, a brain disorder in which learning and other cognitive functions are impaired. Alcohol use by pregnant women, even in moderate amounts, can result in *fetal alcohol syndrome*, which may produce permanent mental retardation, as well as facial deformities, in the children who must endure this toxic prenatal environment.

The National Institute on Alcohol Abuse and Alcoholism has developed a list of seven questions for self-diagnosis of alcoholism (see Table 5-4). An affirmative answer to even one question may suggest that alcohol is a problem, and affirmative answers to several questions should be taken as an indication that you may be an alcoholic. Most of these questions boil down to a central issue: Is your use of alcohol creating problems in other areas of your life?

Heavy drinkers experience withdrawal symptoms when they stop drinking alcohol. For withdrawal from chronic (long-term) intoxication, symptoms are severe, including the possibility of severe convulsions, hallucinations, tremors, agitation, and even death (Seymour & Smith, 1987). Chronic alcoholism can be treated through medical intervention, through a counseling program such as Alcoholics Anonymous, or through a combination of treatments.

TABLE 5-4

Are You an Alcoholic?   *If you answer yes to any of these questions, developed by the National Institute on Alcohol Abuse and Alcoholism, alcohol may be a problem in your life. If you answer yes to several of the questions, you may be an alcoholic.*

IF YOU CAN ANSWER YES TO EVEN ONE OF THESE QUESTIONS, CONSIDER SEEKING ADVICE ABOUT YOUR USE OF ALCOHOL
1. Has someone close to you sometimes expressed concern about your drinking?
2. When faced with a problem, do you often turn to alcohol for relief?
3. Are you sometimes unable to meet home or work responsibilities because of drinking?
4. Have you ever required medical attention as a result of drinking?
5. Have you ever experienced a blackout—a total loss of memory while still awake—when drinking?
6. Have you ever come in conflict with the law in connection with your drinking?
7. Have you often failed to keep the promises you have made to yourself about controlling or cutting out your drinking?

For withdrawal from acute intoxication, typical symptoms are headache, loss of appetite, nausea, and shakiness—in short, a hangover. Detoxification for a hangover is simply a matter of time. As time passes, the body will metabolize the alcohol, and the symptoms will dissipate. Drinking coffee does not reduce the effects of alcohol. Instead, it creates a wide-awake, stimulated drunk. Drinking a lot of nonalcoholic liquids can help, as can moderate exercise. Drinking more alcohol to reduce the effect of a hangover does little good, and it can lead to increased alcohol dependence.

Tranquilizers and Barbituates

Sedative–hypnotics are the second of the two primary CNS depressants used for calming anxiety and relieving insomnia (see Table 5-3; see also chapter 17). The most widely used sedative–hypnotic drugs are classified as **barbiturates,** which are antianxiety drugs prescribed to reduce anxiety through physiological inhibition of arousal. When used properly, barbiturates are effective sedative–hypnotics. In low doses, barbiturates calm the user. Higher dosages inhibit neurons in arousal centers in the brain, causing sleep. Still higher dosages can cause respiratory failure. As is true of nearly all psychoactive drugs, the addictive properties of barbiturates encourage rampant abuse; chronic use leads to increased tolerance, so that the user takes more and more of the drug to achieve the same effect. Increased dosages can misfire in several ways, however. For one thing, because the user may fall asleep or be groggy in situations demanding full attention, accidents can result and lead to injury or even death. As well, the user may ingest a lethal dosage in a desperate attempt to fall asleep.

Following the development of tranquilizers (benzodiazepines, listed in Table 5-3), physicians shifted away from prescribing barbiturates as sedatives and moved toward prescribing them primarily as sleep inducers. **Tranquilizers** are another class of the sedative–hypnotic drugs used for combating anxiety and considered to be safer than barbiturates, because of the lower dosages required and the reduced likelihood of drowsiness and respiratory difficulties, although the potential for addiction remains a problem. Even so, they are the second most commonly prescribed drugs in the United States (Seymour & Smith, 1987). Clearly, the potential for abuse exists.

Treatment of Depressant Abuse

Treatment for addiction or overdose varies according to the sedative–hypnotic drug, but both psychological and physiological dependence must be addressed.

Chronic toxicity may be treated through a counseling and support program, or, in the case of barbiturates, through maintenance via gradual phenobarbital substitution. Whereas withdrawal from narcotic drugs is extremely uncomfortable but usually not life threatening, withdrawal from sedative–hypnotic drugs can be both painful and life threatening. Withdrawal symptoms can include anxiety, tremors, nightmares, insomnia, anorexia, nausea, vomiting, fever, seizures, and delirium (Seymour & Smith, 1987).

Central Nervous System Stimulants

Drug Actions

Stimulants, like the other drugs we have considered, have been around for centuries. **Central nervous system (CNS) stimulants** are drugs (e.g., caffeine, amphetamines, cocaine, and nicotine—found in tobacco) that arouse and excite the central nervous system, either by stimulating the heart or by inhibiting the actions of natural compounds that depress brain activity (in other words, they act as "double-negatives" on brain stimulation; see Table 5-3). Short-term effects of relatively low doses include increased stamina and alertness, reduced appetite, exuberance, and euphoria. Stronger doses may cause anxiety and irritability. Problems with tolerance and addiction are linked with long-term use, and problems with sensitization are tied to intermittent use. Societally, illegal stimulants, most notably cocaine, have overtaken narcotics as the greatest drug problem in the United States.

Caffeine

Caffeine is probably the mildest stimulant, and it creates fewer problems than the other drugs in this category. Caffeine is found in a number of drinks that come close to being "national drinks"—coffee in the United States, tea in the United Kingdom, *guarana* in Brazil, *maté* in Argentina. Chocolate and cola drinks are also sources of caffeine. An ounce of coffee typically contains 11–29 mg of caffeine, whereas tea typically contains 5–17 mg. Cola and other soft drinks vary widely in caffeine content, depending on the brand.

Caffeine increases neural activity, stimulating tension in the heart and skeletal muscles. Caffeine stimulates the CNS partly by suppressing the effects of *adenosine*, a naturally occurring depressant (inhibitory chemical) in the brain. High doses of caffeine can cause anxiety, nervousness, irritability, tremulousness, muscle twitching, insomnia, rapid heart beat, hyperventilation, increased urination, and gastrointestinal disturbances. Very high levels of caffeine also can increase blood pressure and possibly contribute to coronary heart disease (Lane & Williams, 1987; D. Shapiro, Lane, & Henry, 1986), although it appears that caffeine is dangerous for most people only in very large amounts. Thus, someone who drinks seven or eight cups of coffee a day may be at risk, but someone who drinks a cup or two of coffee a day is not.

Caffeine is addictive. Caffeine addiction is not a major societal problem, but the indications of addiction are similar to those of other, more destructive drugs. These indications include compulsive behavior, loss of control, and continued drug use despite adverse consequences (Seymour & Smith, 1987). Some people, for example, continue to ingest high doses of caffeine, despite symptoms such as noticeable increases in heart rate, nervousness, and difficulties sleeping at night after drinking coffee or tea. Symptoms of withdrawal from caffeine include lethargy, irritability, difficulties in working, constipation, and headache.

Amphetamines

Amphetamines are a type of synthetic CNS stimulant and are usually either swallowed or injected. Short-term effects include increased body temperature, heart rate, and endurance. They are sometimes used by people whose jobs require long hours and sustained attention and are also used in some diet pills to reduce appetite. In the brain, amphetamines stimulate the release of neurotransmitters such as *norepinephrine* and *dopamine* (see chapter 3) into brain synapses, creating a euphoric "high" and increasing alertness. Amphetamines may further increase the levels of these neurotransmitters by preventing their reuptake from the synaptic gaps (Ray & Ksir, 1990). The resulting higher-than-normal concentrations of these neurotransmitters lead to increased arousal and motor activity. At very high levels, amphetamines also affect transmission of *serotonin*. When taken over long periods of time, the levels of serotonin and other neurotransmitters in the brain may start to decrease, thereby producing damage to the neural communication system within the brain.

As is true of many other drugs, prolonged use of amphetamines creates tolerance and a resulting need for higher doses. In sufficiently large doses, amphetamines can produce odd behavior, such as repetitive searching and examining, prolonged staring at objects, chewing, and moving an object back and forth (Groves & Rebec, 1988). Overdoses produce intoxication, paranoia, confusion, hallucinations, and may lead to death caused by respiratory failure or wild fluctuations in body temperature. Withdrawal symptoms include extreme fatigue and depression. Rare or occasional use of amphetamines also seems to produce the paradoxical phenomenon of *sensitization*, in which an intermittent user of a drug demonstrates heightened sensitivity to low doses of the drug.

Cocaine

Cocaine, a CNS stimulant and probably the most powerful natural stimulant, was used in religious ceremonies by the Incas in pre-Columbian times. For centuries, South Americans have chewed the leaves of the coca plant to increase their physical stamina in their rugged environment. Cocaine, commonly known as "coke," is highly addictive, especially when smoked in the form of "crack." Physiologically, cocaine increases body temperature and constricts peripheral blood vessels. It also produces spurious feelings of increased mental ability and can produce great excitement. If consumed in sufficient quantity, cocaine can cause hallucinations and seizures. Like amphetamines, cocaine appears to increase the transmission of *norepinephrine* and *dopamine* across synapses and to inhibit the reuptake of both these neurotransmitters and of *serotonin*. Increased concentrations of these neurotransmitters result in the heightened arousal and motor activity associated with amphetamines. Initially, at least, cocaine also seems to stimulate acute sexual arousal, but prolonged use diminishes sexual arousability and performance (Wade & Cirese, 1991). Prolonged use also leads to lower levels of neurotransmitters and difficulties in neural transmission similar to those associated with prolonged amphetamine use.

Recovering cocaine addicts crave the drug intensely. Their prolonged use has diminished their natural brain-stimulant mechanisms, so they feel great anxiety, loss of control, depression, and lethargy.

Tobacco

Tobacco is a plant product containing nicotine, a CNS stimulant, and is legally available to adults in a variety of forms. Nevertheless, stop-smoking campaigns, widespread publicity about the health dangers, and reports of the harmful effects of inhaling *secondary smoke*, exhaled by smokers or otherwise released into the air by burning tobacco, have led to increasingly restrictive laws prohibiting smoking in public places. Laws also have restricted accessibility of tobacco to young people, although even preadolescent children often can find means to gain access to tobacco products.

The tobacco leaf is grown throughout the world and is usually smoked, but it is also often chewed. *Nicotine*, the stimulant substance in tobacco, is absorbed through the respiratory tract, as well as the oral and nasal mucosa and the gastrointestinal tract. Most of the inhaled nicotine is absorbed by the lungs.

Nicotine is one of the most highly addictive substances known. Because so many methods to stop smoking are readily available, the opportunities and support for people who wish to quit smoking are greater than ever.

Nicotine activates nicotinic receptors located on nerve cells and on skeletal muscles. These receptors use *acetylcholine*, and their activation thereby increases the neurotransmission of acetylcholine.

Tobacco has complex effects on the body. It can increase respiration, heart rate, and blood pressure, but decrease appetite. Intoxication is characterized by euphoria, light-headedness, giddiness, dizziness, and a tingling sensation in the extremities (Seymour & Smith, 1987). Tolerance and dependence develop relatively quickly, so that the intoxication effect is typically experienced only by initiates to smoking. People who habitually use tobacco usually stabilize at some point that becomes a maintenance dosage for them.

Tobacco is now believed to be among the most addictive substances in existence, and 9 out of 10 people who start smoking become addicted (as com-

pared with 1 in 6 people who try crack cocaine and 1 in 10 people who experiment with alcohol). In 1996, the Food and Drug Administration recommended that nicotine be classified as a controlled substance. Smoking by pregnant women has been linked to both premature birth and unusually low birth weight, grave risk factors for newborns. Most of the long-term adverse effects of tobacco occur after prolonged use. They include heart disease, cancers of various sorts (especially lung and mouth cancers), gum disease, eating disorders, emphysema, gastrointestinal disease, and brittleness of bones. Secondary smoke has been linked with many of these ailments as well. Nicotine is highly poisonous and is even used as a potent insecticide. Tobacco smoke contains a number of potentially harmful by-products in addition to nicotine, including tar, carbon monoxide, and hydrogen cyanide. During the 1980s, 5 million people are believed to have died because of tobacco use, compared with 1 million who died from alcohol-related causes and 350,000 who died from other addictions. Actually, nearly all of the stimulant drugs discussed here can cause death if taken in sufficient quantities. Abuse can and should be treated before it is too late.

Treatment of Stimulant Abuse

Acute toxicity from stimulants must be treated medically. The exact treatment depends on the drug that was taken. For example, a massive amphetamine overdose may call for inducing bowel movements in people who are conscious and for stomach pumping in individuals who have lost consciousness. Overdoses of cocaine may be treated with tranquilizers and may require hospitalization.

The most common treatment for chronic addiction to stimulants is individual or group psychotherapy. Stimulant abusers need to become drug-free, develop a lifestyle that will enable them to stay drug-free, understand what got them addicted in the first place, and find ways to stay off drugs. Education about the dangers of cocaine abuse and support groups are, for now, the best methods of overcoming cocaine addiction. Organizations dedicated to helping people get off drugs include Narcotics Anonymous, which helps with stimulant abuse as well, and Cocaine Anonymous.

Drug-substitution therapy is generally not used except in the case of nicotine. For acute nicotine withdrawal, nicotine gum and epidermal patches appear to be effective when used in combination with some other form of therapy. Without additional supportive treatment, users run the risk of becoming addicted to

"Don't worry. If it turns out tobacco is harmful, we can always quit."

the substitute. Numerous stop-smoking programs (such as those offered by the American Lung Association) use a wide array of techniques, including hypnosis, acupuncture, *aversion therapy* (overdosing people with smoke or nicotine to render it repulsive), group support, and education (see chapter 17 for more information on these treatments).

Finally, let's consider the remaining major class of psychoactive drugs: hallucinogens.

Hallucinogens

Drug Actions

Hallucinogenic drugs are a type of psychoactive drug (e.g., mescaline and LSD) that alter consciousness by inducing hallucinations and affecting the way the drug-takers perceive both their inner worlds and their external environments. *Hallucinations* are experiences of sensory stimulation in the absence of any actual corresponding external sensory input. These drugs are often termed *psychotomimetics* (and are also known as "psychedelics") because some

clinicians believe these drugs mimic the effects produced by psychosis; others suggest that these hallucinations differ in kind from those produced by psychosis (see Table 5-3).

People react in very different ways to hallucinogenic drugs, and their reactions appear to be determined partly by situational factors. Physiologically, most hallucinogenic drugs, such as LSD, work by interfering with the transmission of *serotonin* in the brain (Jacobs, 1987). Serotonin-releasing neuronal systems begin in the brain stem (see chapter 3) and progress to nearly all parts of the brain; the fact that hallucinations can seem so real on so many different sensory levels may be connected to this widespread cerebral interference. Some suggest that a way to think of this mechanism is that serotonin normally blocks us from dreaming when we are awake, so the inhibition of serotonin during wakefulness allows the hallucinations associated with dreams to occur. Serotonin interference is not characteristic of marijuana, mescaline, or phencyclidine (PCP), however. The mechanisms of action for these hallucinogens are still uncertain, although stimulation of norepinephrine neurotransmission may be a factor.

LSD

The hallucinogenic effects of *lysergic acid diethylamide* (LSD, first synthesized in 1938) were discovered in 1943, when a chemist working for Sandoz Pharmaceuticals in Switzerland accidentally ingested some. LSD typically causes physical symptoms such as dizziness, creeping or tingling of the skin, nausea, and tremors; perceptual symptoms such as hallucinations and an altered sense of time; affective, or emotional, symptoms such as rapid mood swings, ranging from severe depression to extreme agitation and anxiety; and cognitive symptoms, such as the feeling of having learned things that would have been impossible to learn without the drug (Groves & Rebec, 1988; Jacobs & Trulson, 1979).

Yet, LSD can also cause people to become anxious at their inability to control the drug experience or "trip." The most dangerous time in a bad reaction to LSD occurs during hallucinations. Users may try to flee the hallucinations, which can put them into physical danger. Even LSD users who enjoy the experience can be at risk; people have jumped out of windows, thinking they could fly! Occasionally, users who forgot they had ingested LSD or people who were given the drug without their knowledge panic, afraid the hallucinations will go on forever.

Marijuana

The most commonly used hallucinogen, *marijuana*, is produced from the dried leaves and flowers of the cannabis plant. *Hashish* is a stronger form of marijuana, made from a concentrated resin derived from the plant's flowers. Most users of marijuana or hashish either smoke the drug or ingest it as an ingredient in food.

People under the influence of marijuana typically experience a disconnected flow of ideas and altered perceptions of space and time. Some people become extremely talkative, others inarticulate. Users may experience intense food cravings and may become impulsive. Very high doses can even lead to hallucinations, although typical use of the drug does not.

Even moderate use of marijuana appears to lead to impairment in some short-term learning and memory processes (C. F. Darley, Tinklenberg, Roth, Hollister, & Atkinson, 1973). There is disagreement about the long-term effects of marijuana use. Some investigators claim that it damages nerve cells and the reproductive system; other researchers have failed to replicate such findings (V. Rubin & Comitas, 1974). Because marijuana is usually smoked, however, daily use has been conclusively shown to contribute to mouth and lung cancer.

Phencyclidine

Phencyclidine (PCP) is popular among young adolescents in some communities because of its modest price and easy accessibility. PCP somehow profoundly alters the relationship between the body's physical experiences and the mind's perceptual experiences, causing extreme cognitive and perceptual distortions. Its effects work particularly on receptors that play a role in learning, and its potential for causing serious cognitive deficits is great. Thus, use of the drug should be treated as soon as possible. Another popular drug with similar effects is MDMA, known commonly by its street name, Ecstasy.

Treatment of Hallucinogen Abuse

Acute overdoses of hallucinogens are normally treated by having a therapist attempt to talk to the user in order to reduce anxiety reactions and to make the user feel as comfortable as possible ("talking the user down"). Tranquilizers are also sometimes used, with a final alternative being antipsychotic drugs. Chronic use of hallucinogens can lead to prolonged psychotic reactions, severe and sometimes life-threatening depression, a worsening of preexisting psychiatric problems, and flashbacks of past drug experiences without further ingestion of the drug (Seymour & Smith, 1987). Scientists do not understand how flashbacks occur because they have not yet found any physiological mechanism that can account for them.

With all the problems associated with drug use, you may wonder why anybody uses drugs. The answers are as varied as are people themselves. Some people take drugs to experiment, feeling confident that they are personally immune to addiction or that they will not get addicted in the short amount of time that they plan to take the drugs. Others feel so unhappy in their daily lives that the risks seem worth it.

In sum, consciousness is our means for monitoring and evaluating the environment. Through consciousness, we come to experience the world in our own terms. Altered states of consciousness enrich our lives, and some of them, such as sleep, seem to be necessary to our survival. Others of these altered states, however, are produced by addictive substances that ultimately may have considerable addictive potential. Whatever the reasons for taking addictive psychoactive drugs, people need to learn that the harmful outcomes generally outweigh any perceived benefits. Learning is the topic of the next chapter.

THINK ABOUT IT

1. What are your normal sleep patterns? How do you react when your normal patterns are interrupted?
2. Why might meditation improve psychological well-being in some people?
3. What effect does divided attention have on your work, for example, if you listen to music and work at the same time?
4. Why is hypnosis used in some psychotherapeutic contexts?
5. How should society regulate the sale, purchase, possession, and use of psychoactive drugs? How should society respond to individuals who abuse such drugs but who do not directly harm others with their drug use?
6. What factors do you believe lead people to abuse psychoactive drugs? What do you believe can be done to help people to avoid becoming involved in the abuse of these drugs?

online   *You can provide your own answers to these questions online at the* **Sternberg,** *In Search of the Human Mind Web site:* *http://www.harcourtcollege.com/psych/ishm*

SUMMARY

Attention and Consciousness   163

1. People use selective attention to track one message and simultaneously ignore others (such as in the cocktail party phenomenon or in shadowing).
2. Two existing theories of selective attention are filter theories, according to which information is selectively blocked out or attenuated as it passes from one level of processing to the next, and attentional resource theories, according to which people have a fixed amount of attentional resources (perhaps modulated by sensory modalities) that they allocate according to the perceived requirements of a given task.

Levels of Consciousness   167

3. *Consciousness* is a stream of thought or awareness—the state of mind by which we compare possibilities for what we might perceive, and then select some of these possibilities and reject others.
4. Some of the functions of consciousness are to aid in our species' survival, to keep track of (monitor and evaluate) the environment, to sift important from unimportant information, and to facilitate memory and planning.
5. John Locke believed that consciousness is essential to establishing a sense of personal identity.
6. Consciousness occurs on multiple levels. The *preconscious* level is immediately prior to or just outside of consciousness. The *unconscious* level is deeper, and we normally can gain access to it only with great difficulty or via dreams.

Sleep and Dreams   170

7. Scientists have isolated several chemical sleep substances in our bodies, although it has not been proved that any of these is fully responsible for our normal sleep.
8. If people are subjected to sleep deprivation for several days they show increasingly severe maladaptive symptoms. By the fourth day of deprivation they often show signs of psychopathology, such as paranoid delusions of persecution.
9. In the absence of typical environmental cues, people seem to show a daily, or *circadian*, rhythm of about 25 hours.
10. There are two basic kinds of sleep—*REM sleep* and *non-REM (N-REM) sleep*. The former is characterized by rapid eye movements and is usually accompanied by dreaming. N-REM sleep is customarily divided into an iterative series of four stages of successively deeper sleep and is seldom accompanied by dreaming.
11. *Insomnia* is a condition in which an individual has trouble falling asleep, wakes up during the night, or wakes up too early in the morning. *Narcolepsy* is a syndrome characterized by the strong impulse to sleep during the day or when it is otherwise undesirable to do so. *Sleep apnea* is a syndrome in which oxygen intake is temporarily impaired during sleep. *Nightmares* are anxiety-arousing dreams that may lead to a person's waking up, sometimes seemingly in order to avoid some threat that emerges in the nightmares. *Night terrors* are sudden awakenings from NREM sleep that are accompanied by feelings

of intense fright or panic. *Somnambulism* (sleepwalking) most often occurs in children. Contrary to popular belief, somnambulists are typically not dreaming while they are engaging in wakeful-seeming behaviors in their sleep.

12. Several theories of dreaming have been proposed. According to Freud, dreams express the hidden wishes of the unconscious. Another view is that dreams represents a kind of mental refuse. A cognitive view holds that we work out our daily problems through dreams. According to McCarley and Hobson's *activation–synthesis* theory, dreams represent our subjective interpretation of nocturnal brain activity.

Hypnosis and Meditation   180

13. *Hypnosis* is an altered state of consciousness in which a person becomes extremely sensitive to, and often compliant with, the communications of the hypnotist. The hypnotized person will accept distortions of reality that would not be accepted in the normal waking state of consciousness.

14. Some psychologists question whether hypnotism is a genuine psychological phenomenon; they suggest instead that it is an epiphenomenon, in which research participants respond to demand characteristics, pleasing the hypnotist by doing what he or she says to do.

15. A *posthypnotic suggestion* is a means by which hypnotized people can be asked to do something— typically something that they would not normally do or that they might have difficulty doing—after the hypnotic trance is removed.

16. Various theories of hypnosis have been proposed. One theory views it as a form of deep relaxation.

Another theory views hypnosis as genuine involvement in a play-acted role. A third views it as a form of split consciousness; that is, there is a hidden observer in the person who observes what is going on, as though from the outside, at the same time that the person responds to hypnotic suggestions.

17. *Meditation* is a set of techniques to alter one's state of consciousness by shifting away from an active, linear mode of thinking toward a more receptive and quiescent mode. Meditation generally decreases respiration, heart rate, blood pressure, and muscle tension.

18. Two main kinds of meditation are concentrative, in which the meditator focuses on an object or thought and attempts to remove all else from consciousness, and opening-up, in which the meditator attempts to integrate meditation with, rather than to separate it from, other activities.

Drug-Induced Alterations in Consciousness   183

19. A person's current state of consciousness can be altered by four kinds of *drugs:* narcotics, CNS (central nervous system) depressants, CNS stimulants, and hallucinogens.

20. *Narcotics,* including natural *opiates* and synthetic *opioids,* produce some degree of numbness, stupor, often a feeling of well-being, or freedom from pain.

21. Depressants, including alcohol and sedative–hypnotic drugs, slow the operation of the central nervous system. In contrast, *stimulants*—including *caffeine, nicotine, cocaine,* and *amphetamines*—speed up the operation of the central nervous system.

22. *Hallucinogens*—including LSD and marijuana— produce distorted perceptions of reality.

KEY TERMS

activation–synthesis hypothesis
    179
amphetamines   189
attention   163
barbiturates   188
caffeine   188
circadian rhythm   171
central nervous system (CNS)
    depressant   186
central nervous system (CNS)
    stimulant   188
cocaine   189
cocktail party phenomenon   164
consciousness   163
daydreaming   179
hallucinations   174

hallucinogenic   191
hypnosis   180
illusions   174
insomnia   175
intoxicated   186
meditation   182
narcolepsy   177
narcotic   183
neodissociative theory   181
N-REM sleep   174
opening-up meditation   183
opiates   183
opioids   183
overdose   184
posthypnotic suggestion   180
preconscious   167

psychoactive   183
psychopharmacological   183
REM sleep   175
sedative–hypnotics   188
selective attention   164
simulating paradigm   180
sleep apnea   177
somnambulism   177
subconscious   169
tobacco   189
tolerance   184
tranquilizers   188
unconscious   169
withdrawal   185

■ THINK ABOUT IT SAMPLE RESPONSES

1. What are your normal sleep patterns? How do you react when your normal patterns are interrupted?

Most people sleep about eight hours a day in the evening. College students often sleep somewhat less because of pressures on their time. Minor interruptions have little effect but more persistent interruptions can produce crankiness, irritability, and lead to mental confusion. Severe interruptions, as noted in the chapter, can lead to hallucinations and delusions.

2. Why might meditation improve psychological well-being in some people?

Meditation can lower blood pressure and also can lead to relaxation and a state of inner peace. There may be an additional placebo effect: The very fact that people think meditation helps them feel better may in and of itself help them feel better.

3. What effect does divided attention have on your work, for example, if you listen to music and work at the same time?

Many people find that music facilitates or at least does not interfere with tasks that require light to moderate levels of concentration. People are more likely to find interference for tasks that require very high levels of concentration.

4. Why is hypnosis used in some psychotherapeutic contexts?

Hypnosis is used for a variety of reasons, such as to help people stop smoking or to reduce pain. It can also be used to help people dredge up memories, although this use of hypnosis has been widely criticized with respect to the accuracy of the memories it produces.

5. How should society regulate the sale, purchase, possession, and use of psychoactive drugs? How should society respond to individuals who abuse such drugs but who do not directly harm others with their drug use?

Opinions on this question vary from ones in favor of legalization to those in favor of strict criminal penalties for people who use such drugs. Some people would argue that if drug use does not hurt others, then it should not be regulated by the legal system. The issue is complex, however, given that there is no guarantee that drug use might not hurt others, such as future children who may risk potential genetic damage. The complexities of the issues are part of the reason that it is unlikely any consensus will develop in the near future regarding what consists of an equitable system of regulation.

6. What factors do you believe lead people to abuse psychoactive drugs? What do you believe can be done to help people to avoid becoming involved in the abuse of these drugs?

Abuse of psychoactive drugs may stem from high levels of stress, desire to conform to the behavior of others, or simple desire to escape. Drug-education programs have proved to have mixed effectiveness. Perhaps the best way to avoid people becoming involved in abuse is to educate them as to the potential costs, but also to help them prevent or deal with the problems that lead to drug abuse in the first place.

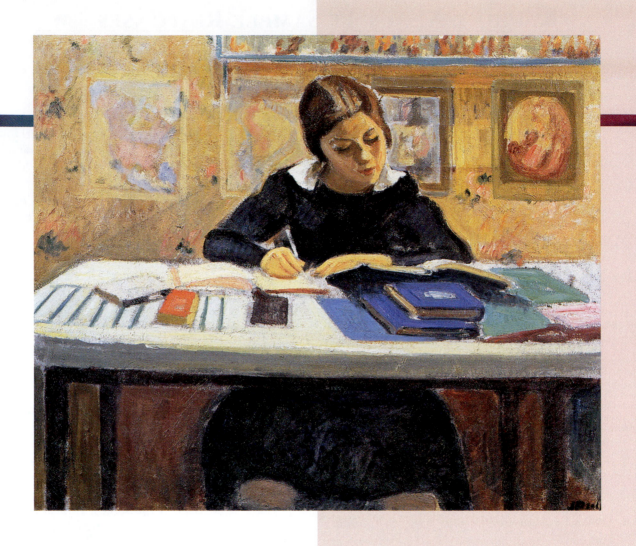

Personally, I'm always ready to learn, although I do not always like being taught.

—*Winston Churchill*

6

LEARNING

Psychologists generally define **learning** as any relatively permanent change in the behavior, thoughts, and feelings of an organism—human or other animal—that results from prior experience. From an evolutionary point of view, learning plays an important role in the adaptation of the individual to the environment. If all behavior were instinctive or otherwise preprogrammed, organisms might come to be very well adapted to a given fixed set of environmental circumstances; but unless they were able to learn, to adapt to changes in these circumstances, changes in the environment might wreak havoc. Learning is what enables individuals, as well as species, to remain flexible and to adapt to the ever-changing circumstances in which they find themselves (see Johnston & Pietrewica, 1985). One type of learning is classical conditioning.

Classical Conditioning

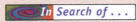 *In Search of . . .*

What is classical conditioning and how does it occur?

It is beyond a doubt that all our knowledge begins with experience.
    —Immanuel Kant, *The Critique of Pure Reason*

Does the scent of particular foods make your mouth water? Does the sound of barking or growling dogs make your heart pound? Each of these common responses results from **classical conditioning**, the

197

learning process in which an originally neutral stimulus, such as the food or the dogs, becomes associated with a particular physiological or emotional response that the stimulus did not originally produce by being paired with a stimulus that originally produced this response or, in many cases, a similar or related response. For example, the pleasurable experience of eating chocolate chip cookies may become associated with the smell of chocolate or the sight of cookies in general, causing you to feel hungry, or at least your mouth to water when you walk by a bakery.

The Discovery of Classical Conditioning

The mechanisms of classical conditioning were originally studied by Ivan Pavlov (1849–1936), who accidentally noticed a phenomenon of learning while he was studying digestive processes in dogs. A meticulous investigator, Pavlov conscientiously avoided allowing extraneous factors to interfere with his research on digestion. However, one particularly annoying factor continually hampered his work. He had devised a means of collecting dogs' salivations in a container in which he measured the amount of saliva the dog

produced when it smelled food (meat powder, in this case; see Figure 6-1). The dogs would start salivating even *before* they smelled the powder, in response to the sight of the lab technician, or even to the sound of the lab technician's footsteps. At first, Pavlov (1928) tried to invent ways to keep this irritating phenomenon from interfering with his important research on digestion.

Happily for psychology, however, Pavlov was open to new discoveries and was able to see the startling implications that any number of other scientists conducting the same research might well have let pass. As Louis Pasteur once said, "Chance favors only the prepared mind."

Pavlov realized that some kind of associative learning must have taken place. The response (the salivation) that was originally connected to receiving the food was now being elicited by stimuli associated with the food. This form of learning has come to be called *classical conditioning*, or *Pavlovian conditioning*. Having made his serendipitous discovery, Pavlov set out to study classical conditioning systematically. First, he needed to show that dogs would naturally and spontaneously salivate at the sight or other sensation of food but would not naturally salivate in

Figure 6–1

PAVLOV'S APPARATUS.   *Ivan Pavlov used specialized equipment to measure the amount of saliva that dogs produced when they smelled food. During this work, he noticed that the dogs started to salivate even before they smelled the food. This observation led him to figure out the principles of classical conditioning.*

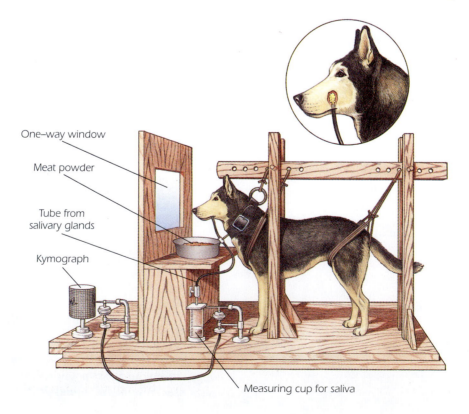

One–way window

Meat powder

Tube from salivary glands

Kymograph

Measuring cup for saliva

After using a buzzer in his first experiments, Pavlov went on to investigate whether other sound cues and even cues to other senses, such as sight and touch, could be manipulated systematically to prompt associative learning in his dogs. His creative exploration of alternative stimuli illustrates the scientific method at work.

response to a nonfood stimulus, such as a buzzer. He experimentally confirmed that a dog, indeed, would salivate in response to meat powder being placed on its tongue, but that it would not salivate in response to the sound of the buzzer alone.

Once the original pattern of stimuli and responses was established, Pavlov started the second phase of the experiment. He sounded the buzzer and then immediately placed the meat powder on the dog's tongue. After he repeated this procedure a number of times, he sounded the buzzer without the meat powder following it. The dog still salivated. It had been conditioned to respond to the originally neutral stimulus of the buzzer through the pairing of the buzzer with the food. (Figure 6-2 illustrates this experiment.) What are the components of this conditioning process?

The Components of Classical Conditioning

Although the content of the stimuli and responses used in classical conditioning can vary, the basic structure of the paradigm does not. If you were to create a classical conditioning experiment, you would proceed as follows:

1. Start with a stimulus (such as Pavlov's meat powder) that elicits an automatic, unlearned physiological or emotional response—that is, determine the **unconditioned stimulus (US)**.

2. Note your participant's automatic, unlearned physiological response to this stimulus—the **unconditioned response (UR)**. (For Pavlov's dogs the UR was salivation.)

3. Choose a stimulus (like the buzzer Pavlov used) that is originally neutral but that will later elicit the desired response through its pairing with the unconditioned stimulus. This originally neutral stimulus becomes the **conditioned stimulus (CS)**.

4. Pair your CS and your US, so that the CS and the US become associated. Eventually, you obtain from this CS a **conditioned response (CR)**, a learned pattern of behavior that typically is similar or identical to the UR, except that it is elicited from the CS rather than from the US. (In Pavlov's studies, the salivation response came to be elicited from the buzzer.)

Timing and Classical Conditioning

Stand-up comics, actors, musicians, ventriloquists, dancers, and magicians all appreciate the value of timing. Psychologists involved in classical conditioning, too, have observed the importance of timing.

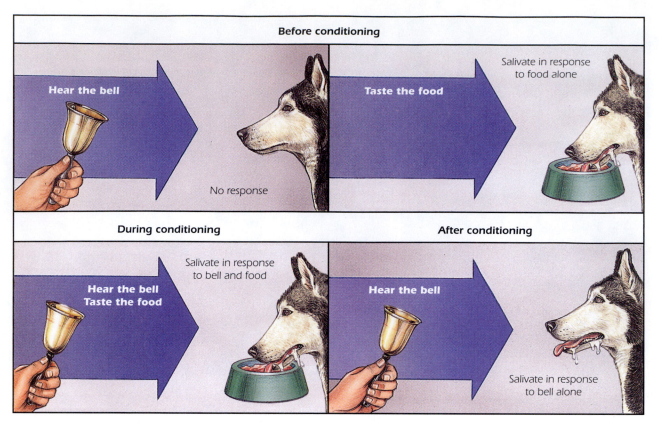

Figure 6-2

PAVLOV'S CLASSIC EXPERIMENT. *Before the experiment, the sound yielded no response from the dog, whereas tasting the food (US) made the dog salivate (UR). During the experiment, Pavlov paired the sound (CS) with the food (US) to prompt the dog to salivate (UR). After many repetitions, the sound (CS alone) prompted the dog to salivate (CR).*

The effects of timing in classical conditioning are shown in Figure 6-3. Panel a of Figure 6-3 shows the standard classical conditioning paradigm, with the onset of the CS almost immediately preceding the onset of the US. For example, a child starts to learn that every time his father comes home from work with a certain kind of a smile the child soon will receive a present. The child learns to associate that smile with an upcoming present. In this example, the unconditioned stimulus is the present. The conditioned stimulus is the smile shown by the father. The unconditioned response is the happiness experienced upon receiving the present. The conditioned response is the happiness experienced upon seeing the certain kind of smile shown by the father. What happens if this classical timing is changed?

Panel b shows **delay conditioning,** which introduces a long delay between the onset of the CS and the onset of the US. **Trace conditioning** is similar to delay conditioning, except that the CS is terminated for a while before the US begins. In the example of the child and the father as applied to trace conditioning, the father would come home from work with a smile. Then the smile would vanish. And at some point thereafter, the child would receive a present. What is the result of delay or trace conditioning? Initially, conditioning re-

sults are similar to those for the standard paradigm. Eventually, however, the animal learns that there will be a long delay from the onset of the CS to the onset of the US, with the result that the CR does not appear until the CS has been in effect for some length of time.

Panel c shows an even more obvious example of conditioning responsive to time intervals—**temporal conditioning.** In this procedure, the CS is a fixed time interval between US presentations, so that the animal learns that the US—say, food—will occur at a given, fixed time. The result is that the animal begins to show a CR right before the presentation of the US. In effect, it has learned that when a certain amount of time has passed, the food will be presented. In the above example, the child might learn that her father will give her a present every seven days. Thus the seven-day interval serves as the conditioned stimulus for learning when the present will be forthcoming.

Contingency: Why Does Conditioning Occur?

Psychologists—and most other scientists—are rarely satisfied merely with noting their observations of phenomena. Many of the most intriguing investigations

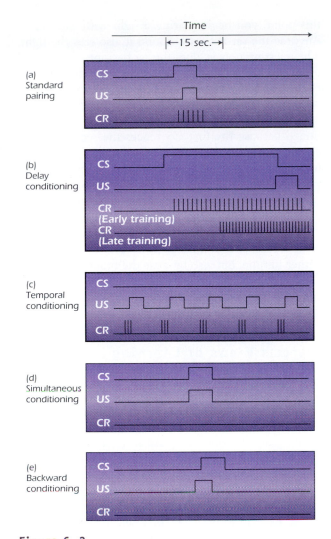

Time

|←15 sec.→|

(a) Standard pairing — CS, US, CR

(b) Delay conditioning — CS, US, CR (Early training), CR (Late training)

(c) Temporal conditioning — CS, US, CR

(d) Simultaneous conditioning — CS, US, CR

(e) Backward conditioning — CS, US, CR

Figure 6–3

SOME COMMON PAVLOVIAN CONDITIONING PROCE-
DURES. *Various classical conditioning procedures yield differing outcomes. Stimulus starts when line rises and stops when it falls.*

attempt to discover why particular phenomena occur. Several explanations have been proposed to explain why classical conditioning takes place.

An obvious explanation is *temporal contiguity*—that is, the mere proximity in time between the CS and the US is sufficient to explain conditioning. However, although simple contiguity is necessary for learning—if too long a time period passes between the offset of the CS and the onset of the US, conditioning will not take place—it is by no means sufficient for learning to take place because the organism will not associate one stimulus (the CS) with the other (the US).

A now classic study by Robert Rescorla (1967) suggests that what is needed for conditioning to take place is not just temporal contiguity, but **contingency,** the dependent relationship between the occurrence of an unconditioned stimulus and the occurrence of a conditioned stimulus. Rescorla designed an experi-

ment to test the notion that contingency analysis underlies classical conditioning. In the experiment, the CS was a tone, and the US was a painful shock. Rescorla conducted the experiment with four different groups of dogs. In all four groups, he was looking to see whether the physiological and emotional responses of pain and fear (the URs) would become associated with the tone (thereby becoming CRs). The four conditions were as follows:

1. *Condition A.* The dogs received the standard pairing of the CS with the US. In other words, shock consistently followed the presentation of a tone. The prediction was that classical conditioning would take place, as usual.

2. *Condition B.* The dogs received the same number of CSs and USs as in Condition A, except that they were explicitly unlinked; that is, the CS was disassociated from the US—they were never presented together. In other words, the CS (tone) predicted the *absence* of the US (shock).

3. *Condition C* (a control group). The dogs again received the same number of CSs and USs, but now there was a random association between the US and the CS: Sometimes, the CS (the tone) predicted the US (the shock); other times, it did not. Any pairings that occurred were strictly by chance, so the CS was a worthless predictor of the US.

4. *Condition D.* The CS and the US were again paired only at random, with one exception. Whenever the random pairing indicated delivery of the US (shock) more than 30 seconds after the most recent CS (tone), the US was canceled. Thus, the US never occurred more than 30 seconds after the CS. Therefore, although the number of accidental pairings between the US and the CS would be the same in Group D as in Group C, the shock was more likely to occur within 30 seconds following the tone than to occur in the absence of the tone. Thus, the animals should learn to associate shock with the tone because there is a contingency, albeit an imperfect one.

The results of Rescorla's experiment confirmed the contingency point of view. Fear conditioning took place in Conditions A and D, where there was a positive contingency between the tone and the shock. No conditioning took place in Group C, because although the tone and the shock were sometimes paired, the pairing was random and hence not contingent. In Group B, the tone actually became an inhibitor of fear. The dogs learned to associate the tone with safety. Thus, they learned a *negative contingency*, whereby the CS (a tone) would predict the absence of the US (a shock).

In his experiment, Rescorla showed that contingency rather than contiguity seems to establish classical conditioning. He suggested that the mechanism underlying classical conditioning is more cognitive—that is, more sophisticated and thoughtful in terms of the functioning of the mind—than would seem possible for such a simple form of learning. According to Rescorla, humans and other animals try to make sense of the stimuli in their environments that affect them. The initial presentation of the US is unexpected and is therefore surprising. This element of surprise sets the stage for optimal learning in order to make subsequent presentations of the US more predictable and thus less surprising—thereby making the environment more comprehensible. When a CS contingently predicts the occurrence of the US, learning occurs easily and rapidly. More generally, animals appear to have some kind of mental representation of both the conditioned and the unconditioned stimuli (Domjan, 1997; Roitblat & von Fersen, 1992; Rescorla, 1988).

The results of Rescorla's experiment apply to humans. Suppose that every time you see a certain friend who lives in your dormitory, he has something nice to say about you—perhaps about the way you look, or about the way you think, or about the way you act. Soon you may find yourself having a warmly positive feeling the moment you see this individual, before he even says anything. The friend represents a contingency for you—a prediction of a positive remark soon to be made.

A cognitive interpretation of classical conditioning is bolstered by a phenomenon first observed by Leon Kamin (1969). Suppose you condition a rat to behave in a certain way whenever it hears a particular sound. The sound thus becomes a reliable conditioned stimulus that leads to a particular conditioned response. At this point, you begin pairing a light with the sound: Anytime the rat hears the sound it also sees the light. The question now is, does the rat become conditioned to the light? The answer is no. The prior conditioning to the sound, in effect, *blocks* conditioning to the light. A cognitive interpretation of this **blocking effect** (the failure of a second CS to become classically conditioned because the first CS blocks the second one in eliciting a CR) is that the rat has already become able to predict the unconditioned stimulus (such as a shock) via the sound. The light is completely redundant. Because the light provides no new predictive information, conditioning to it does not occur.

In sum, humans and other animals learn not simply because two stimuli happen to occur close together in time, but also because the first stimulus predicts the second. Temporal proximity, in which one stimulus does not predict the other, by itself will not establish systematic learning.

Systems Views of Learning

In understanding conditioning, it is important to understand not only how conditioning is represented cognitively, but also how it occurs in natural contexts. Michael Domjan (1997) has noted that many animal-learning theorists currently are seeking to understand how animals learn within the context of an adaptive behavior system. Systems views place learning in the context of the animal's natural history. They require an examination of the organism's individual experiences, its evolutionary history, its genetics, and its physiological states. Examples of the use of such an

approach are the analysis of foraging behavior in rats (Timberlake, 1993) and the analysis of animal responses to predators (Fanselow & Lester, 1988).

One study of Norway rats examined social influences on food choices. These investigators found that prior interaction with a rat eating a certain diet tended to influence the Norway rats to choose the diet preferred by the rat with which they had interacted (Galef & Whiskin, 1998; Galef, Whiskin, & Bielavska, 1997). Thus the Norway rats were open to social influences, a topic discussed in chapter 14. Once they started eating this diet, the diet was made successively more unpalatable by changing its flavor. For example, the amount of cayenne paper in a cayenne-pepper-flavored diet would be increased until the food became unpalatable. Under these circumstances, the rats *decreasingly* chose the cayenne-pepper-flavored food. In sum, the rats were socially influenced up to a point, but after that point, palatability took over as the more important factor in their food choices. This study shows the complexity of the system of variables that can be involved in a behavior as basic as food choice. Both biologically based and social factors, as well as food availability, of course, can influence decisions regarding what an organism decides to eat at a given time.

Another example of the importance of context is shown by work on *hierarchical learning*. Researchers provided rats with two types of trials (R. T. Ross, 1983; R. T. Ross & Holland, 1981). In the first type of trial, rats received a presentation of a light for five seconds, followed by a 5-second delay. This delay was followed by a 5-second tone and then food was delivered. During the second type of trial, the rat received the 5-second tone followed by no food. The two types of trials were randomly distributed during a day's session. The researchers found that the rats came to respond to the tone, but only in the presence of the light. They argued that the light "set the occasion" for the tone-food relationship. They suggested that this kind of occasion-setting represented a new form of learning, one that is cognitive in nature and that is affected by the contextual setting in which the learning takes place (P. C. Holland, 1992; Rescorla, 1985).

Influences on Rate of Conditioning

Pavlov had long established that classical conditioning takes place over a series of learning trials, not all at once (although exceptions to this rule are described later in this chapter). Rescorla and his colleague, Allan Wagner, observed the process of learning over successive learning trials. Then, building on the suggested mechanism of contingency, they proposed a quantitative theory to specify precisely the rate at which learn-

ing would take place (Rescorla & Wagner, 1972; A. R. Wagner & Rescorla, 1972).

The two researchers found that learning tends to increase at a rate that actually *slows down* as the amount of learning increases. In this pattern of *negative acceleration*, a gradual reduction in the amount of increase occurs in successive conditioning trials. The more learning that has taken place, the slower the pace of the subsequent learning. If you think about your own learning curve, when learning a new sport for example, you will probably recognize this phenomenon. The reason they suggest for this slowing of the rate of learning is that as learning progresses the relative unpredictability of the US declines. As the US becomes more predictable, the need to notice the contingent relationship between the US and the CS declines. According to this theory, if we were to plot graphically the trials linking the US and the CS, the curve would start rising quickly. But as it went up, the curve would level off and eventually reach an *asymptote*, the most stable level of response (usually graphed as a curve), where the degree of learning levels off. This pattern is shown in the idealized learning curve of Figure 6-4.

Consider again the example of the friend who always says something nice about you. Most of your learning will occur after the first few remarks. Thereafter, if the friend maintains his behavior, you may find that the increase in your positive feelings starts to slow down as no new learning is taking place, at least with respect to the friend's offering of compliments. Eventually, you reach an asymptote in your response.

Figure 6–4

IDEALIZED LEARNING CURVE. *According to Robert Rescorla, the rate of learning slows down as the amount of learning increases, until eventually learning peaks at a stable level.*

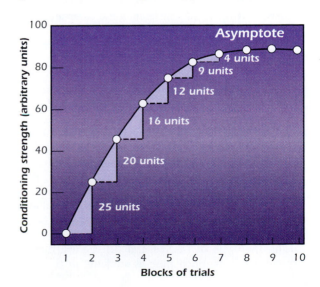

Students Get Better Grades When Tested Frequently in Class

Bruce W. Tuckman, *The Ohio State University*

I had been doing research on enhancing students' academic engagement and performance in college and had begun to suspect that many students who performed poorly were actually knowledgeable about study skills and self-regulation strategies, but simply didn't use them. Low achievers did not seem to spend the necessary time and effort to get the information they were learning in their classes into their heads.

I had come to the conclusion from my own work and that of others that achievement required aptitude and motivation, and motivation required a combination of attitude, strategy, and drive. In my research I had been able to improve both attitude and strategy, but had not found a way to increase drive. I began to think about what it might be that finally motivated a student to learn, or at least to get information into long-term memory. And then it hit me: *tests!* As much as we all dread them, tests motivate us because they present us with a situation in which, if we want to achieve success or avoid failure, we have to learn material in such a way as to be able to recall it. In that way, tests provide an incentive to learn.

I had to find a way to test the hypothesis that tests prompted better achievement, and that they did so because they motivated students to get what they were being taught into their "heads" (or long-term memories). If I could show that, then it would also imply that they already knew appropriate learning skills and strategies.

I was teaching a large lecture course that had a number of sections, all of which covered the same material, used the same textbook, and included the same examinations. This was ideal, since I felt that academic motivation and performance could only be studied in real classes involving real grades, rather than in a laboratory, where student behavior would not have the same consequences. I constructed a series of studies where I manipulated a variable in the environment and studied its effects, rather than examining outcomes after the fact, where it would be difficult to draw conclusions about cause and effect.

Frequent Testing Versus Homework

In experiments it is necessary to control variables other than those you are attempting to study. I needed something to which I could compare frequent testing to see if frequent testing led to higher grades. I decided to compare frequent testing with required homework. The required homework assignment was to outline each chapter by identifying the 20 most important concepts and provide a textbook definition and elaboration (i.e., a description in one's own words) of each. This would (a) teach the students the study skill of using this type of outline and (b) require that they spend about as much time as students in the testing condition who were given a test on each chapter.

I did essentially the same study three times:

> On a 5-week segment of the 15-week course, in which I also included a third group that got neither tests nor homework;

> On the whole course, where I included only tests and homework conditions and required all students to keep a log of time spent on coursework, which I then used to compare the results for high-, middle-, and low-GPA students;

> On exactly the same group as the second set of conditions above except that I measured students' tendency to procrastinate (using a scale I had developed), and compared results for high, middle, and low procrastinators.

The Results

This is what I found: In all three studies, students in the frequent testing condition earned higher grades than students in the homework condition (and in the control condition in the first experiment). The difference ranged from a whole grade (a B compared to a C) to a third of a grade (a B– compared to a C+).

What was considerably more dramatic and revealing were the results for students at different GPA levels and different degrees of procrastination. Students with high (3.6–4.0) or middle (2.9–3.5) GPAs showed no differences in examination grades between frequent tests and homework conditions. However, students with low GPAs (2.0–2.8) in the class given frequent tests averaged B– on the grade scale across the three tests, while those who just did homework averaged a C–, a difference of 10% on a 100-point scale. In fact, the low-GPA students given frequent tests did so well they outscored the middle GPA students in both the homework and frequent testing conditions.

For procrastination level, the findings were even more dramatic. High procrastinators in the frequent test condition not only outscored high procrastinators in the homework condition (by over a full grade), they outscored both middle and low procrastinators in both homework and test conditions.

The overall results clearly showed that frequent tests worked better than homework in improving achievement. Even if your professors don't give frequent tests, test yourself on a regular basis to ensure that you are getting what you learn into long-term memory.

 Find out more about this topic at www.harcourtcollege.com/psych/ishm

Rescorla and Wagner further noted that success of conditioning depends on at least two variables: the salience of the stimuli and the maximum level of conditioning that can be achieved for a given US. As the *salience*—degree of conspicuousness or obviousness—increases, so does the rate of learning. For example, a strong *emetic* (chemical that causes vomiting) is likely to be a very salient US, whereas a barely noticeable electric shock is likely to be much less salient and to result in a slower *rate* of learning. In addition, according to the theory, different USs support different maximum levels of conditioning. A strong emetic is likely to lead to a higher stable level of learning than is a very weak shock. Thus, the second variable is the particular *maximum* stable level of learning (shown on a graph as the distinctive asymptote of the learning curve) that can be achieved for a given CS–US pairing. If we were to plot curves graphing the trials linking the US and the CS for different stimuli, each stimulus would have a distinctive curve. Some of these curves would yield higher asymptotes than others.

Phases of Classical Conditioning

Acquisition

Although the *rate* of learning may *decrease* over learning trials, the *probability* of a given performance reflecting learning—that is, the likelihood of the occurrence of a CR—*increases* over learning trials. For example, if students nod their heads when a teacher shows a certain behavior, the teacher's learning will be reflected by the fact that the likelihood of that certain behavior probably will increase. The phase of learning during which a CR strengthens and the occurrence of the response increases in likelihood is the **acquisition** phase. Eventually, as shown in the work of Rescorla and others, the CR reaches its asymptote—its most stable probability of occurrence.

Extinction

Suppose that the CS were to continue to be presented, but in the absence of the US. For example, a buzzer that previously had preceded shock would no longer precede shock. Gradually, the probability of the occurrence of the CR decreases, eventually approaching zero. This phase of learning is the **extinction** phase. The curve and asymptote for extinction would show a decrease in the number of responses over time, with the response level eventually reaching zero.

Spontaneous Recovery

The term *extinction* may be somewhat misleading, however. A casual observer of an extinguished CR might assume that because the CR was extinguished, it was gone forever, as if the CR had never existed at all. That is not quite the case. The CR may be extinguished, but the memory of the learning has not been completely erased, and the behavior can still be elicited. In fact, an interesting phenomenon occurs after an individual is given a series of extinction trials and is then allowed to rest; surprisingly, a resumption of extinction trials after the rest period will result in a higher level of responding than has occurred just before it. This phenomenon is **spontaneous recovery,** in which a CR reappears without any environmental prompting. The individual seems to recover some level of responding spontaneously during the rest period, even though the CS was already absent before the rest.

New views of extinction suggest that it is relatively context-specific. If the conditioned response of an animal is extinguished in one context (e.g., a particular maze), it may not be extinguished in a novel context (e.g., a completely different maze or other environment). Thus, extinction appears to involve the inhibition of a particular learned response in a particular context rather than any kind of true forgetting (Bouton, 1991, 1993).

Consider again your friend who pays you compliments. You have now been conditioned to react favorably immediately upon seeing him. You have reached asymptotic response. But then your friend has a personal crisis that embitters him toward you and others. You continue to see him, but he no longer pays you compliments. Over time, the positive response you once felt upon seeing him starts to fade. You are experiencing extinction. Eventually the two of you drift apart and when you see him, you feel pretty much nothing at all. The positive response you once had has been completely extinguished. Then he changes dormitories and you stop seeing him altogether. In fact, you do not see him again until graduation, at which time you see him only in the distance. Upon seeing him again after all this time, you are surprised to experience a bit of the positive feeling you once felt toward him. You now realize that your positive feelings never disappeared entirely. You have experienced spontaneous recovery of your learned feelings toward him.

Note that in spontaneous recovery, the CS is presented again, without the US. Spontaneous recovery is not quite the same as *savings*, which occurs when for a period of time the CS and the US are not linked, and then the CS is presented again in the presence of the US. In conditioning involving savings, when the CS is again paired with the US, even if only briefly, the CR returns to levels approaching those at the asymptote (stable peak of the learning curve) of the acquisition phase. Table 6-1 illustrates these phases.

TABLE 6–1

Phases of Classical Conditioning   *Once a learner acquires a CR, if the CS and the US are uncoupled, the CR may be extinguished. Even if the CR is extinguished, however, the learner may still experience spontaneous recovery or savings of the CR.*

PHASE	EXPLANATION	EXAMPLE
Acquisition	The probability of a CR increases as the CS is paired with the US.	Each time your phone has rung, it has been your new beloved, calling to tell you how delightful this evening will be. Your heart flutters joyously in response. As the morning progresses, your heart starts to flutter just on hearing the phone ring.
Extinction	The probability of a CR decreases as the CS and the US are uncoupled, with only one or the other being presented at any one time.	Your phone continues to ring, but your beloved is in a meeting, so now your calls are from a salesperson, a wrong-number caller, and several people who want you to do things you do not want to do. Your heart stops fluttering at the sound of the phone's ring.
Spontaneous recovery	After a brief period of rest, following extinction, the CS spontaneously prompts the CR.	Your phone service is temporarily out of order. After service is restored, your heart flutters at the first ring.
Savings	When the CS is paired with the US again, even briefly, the CR returns to levels approaching those at the peak of the acquisition phase.	Your beloved's meeting ends, and your phone begins ringing again with frequent calls from your beloved. Once again, your heart flutters when you hear the phone ring.

Levels and Features of Classical Conditioning

He who is bitten by the snake fears the lizard.
—Bugandan proverb

A man who has been tossed by a buffalo, when he sees a black ox, thinks it's another buffalo.
—Kenyan proverb

Up to now, we have discussed only what is sometimes referred to as **first-order conditioning**, whereby a CS is linked directly with a US. Suppose, however, that we have conditioned a fear response to the sound of a tone. Now suppose that we pair the flash of a light with the tone. Right before the tone, a light illuminates. In this case, we might link the CR (the emotion of fear), which is already linked to the first CS (the tone), to the second CS (the light) as well. When a second CS is linked to a first one, the resulting conditioning is *second-order conditioning*. In the-

ory, we can have conditioning proceed up to any level of **higher order conditioning**, where a CS is not directly linked with a US, but rather is linked to an established CS, although conditioning beyond the first order tends to be rather unstable and relatively more susceptible to extinction than is first-order conditioning.

Stimulus Generalization

As these proverbs suggest, conditioning occurs not only in association with the exact CS, but also with stimuli that are similar to it. For example, slightly changing the frequency, or pitch, of a tone that is a CS will have only a barely perceptible effect on the CR, if any at all. However, the more the frequency of the tone is changed, the less the tone will elicit the CR. **Stimulus generalization** is a response to the observed similarity of a new stimulus to the CS, which increases the likelihood that the CR will occur following presentation of the new CS. Stimulus generalization thus results in an expansion of the range of stimuli that produce the CR, such that stimuli that resemble a CS can also elicit the CR.

A famous experiment involving stimulus generalization was conducted by John B. Watson (see chapter 1) and Rosalie Rayner (1920). Their study examined generalization of conditioned fear in an infant of 11 months of age who has come to be called "Little Albert." Initially, Little Albert was unafraid of a living white rat. Watson and Rayner paired the presentation of the white rat with the presentation of a loud and startling gong that did evoke fear in Little Albert. After just seven pairings of the rat with the gong, the rat came to elicit fear. Then, five days later, Watson and Rayner exposed Little Albert to other, similar stimuli, including a white rabbit, a white dog, and a white fur coat, among other things. The fear response generalized to these other white furry things, and even generalized to Watson's whitening hair.

Unfortunately, Little Albert was removed from the hospital setting where the research was conducted before Watson and Rayner had an opportunity to extinguish the fears they had created. We thus have no idea of what eventually happened to Little Albert. Perhaps the fears gradually became extinguished over time as Little Albert learned that

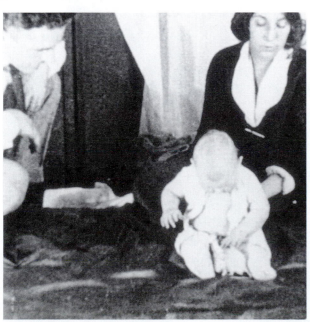

John Watson and Rosalie Raynor with Little Albert before he was conditioned to fear the rat. Today such an experiment would be considered unethical, but Watson and Raynor's proof that fears can be conditioned is a good example of stimulus generalization.

not all white furry things are dangerous. Perhaps Little Albert became phobic of white furry things for the rest of his life. Watson and Rayner were criticized in subsequent years for failing to ensure that Little Albert's fear was extinguished. But at the time, the kind of stringent institutional review of experiments that now exists was not available, and so such fiascoes may have happened more often than we can know.

Stimulus Discrimination

As the observed difference between a new stimulus and the original CS increases, it becomes increasingly less likely that the CR will occur. This mechanism, whereby the CR becomes less probable as the new stimulus increasingly differs from the old one, is **stimulus discrimination** (the ability to ascertain the difference between one stimulus and another). The more different the new stimulus is from the old one, the lower the probability of the new stimulus eliciting the CR. In discrimination-learning experiments, the experimenter helps produce learning by reinforcing responses to one stimulus but not reinforcing responses to another, similar stimulus, or perhaps to a set of similar stimuli.

For example, the proverbial Bugandan who fears lizards, which somewhat resemble snakes, would be less likely to feel afraid of a long, thin but furry mammal, such as a weasel or a mink, and would be highly unlikely to fear pigs, elephants, or buffalo. However, the fabled Kenyan who fears both the buffalo and the black ox might feel mildly anxious at the sight of a pig or an elephant but would be fearless at the sight of a snake, a lizard, or a weasel. Thus, for the snake-shy Bugandan, the fine gradations of discrimination center on the stimulus's similarity to the snake; for the buffalo-fearing Kenyan, being able to discriminate among animals that resemble the buffalo determines his likelihood of experiencing fear.

Preparedness

An interesting follow-up to this story is that although fears may be learned, predispositions to have certain fears may be innate. In particular, research suggests that rhesus monkeys do not innately fear snakes, but that they do have an apparent predisposition to fear snakes (Cook & Mineka, 1990). Organisms appear to have a *preparedness* to learn. They learn some associations more easily than others (Seligman, 1971). For example, phobias of some things, such as spiders and snakes, are much more common than phobias of other objects, such as flowers and rain. Many investigators believe that these differences in preparedness reflect evolutionary programming: Spiders and snakes *are* more likely to be dangerous to humans than are flowers and rain.

The Qualitative Relationship Between the Stimulus and the Response

Up to now, we have described conditioned and unconditioned stimuli that bear only an arbitrary relationship to each other—for example, a tone and an electric shock. Does the nature of the CS and the US ever make any difference? Apparently, it does, although this relationship was not appreciated until the 1960s. In fact, the discovery of a relationship we now consider "obvious" was not at all obvious prior to its discovery. Psychologists used to think that the nature of the relation between the CS and the US was irrelevant to the rate at which conditioning would take place.

In an experiment by John Garcia and Robert Koelling (1966), whenever a group of experimental rats licked a drinking spout, the rats tasted some flavored solution, heard a clicking sound, and saw a flash of light. That is, whenever the rats licked the spout, they sensed three conditioned stimuli: the taste of flavored solution, the sound of a click, and the sight of a flash of light. Subsequent to licking the spout, some of the rats were mildly poisoned and other rats were shocked. After a number of learning trials for both the poisoned rats and the shocked rats, a new procedure was introduced: The CS of the flavoring was separated from the combined CS using the sound and the light. Thus, for each group of rats, on one day, when the rats licked the spout, the rats tasted the flavored solution without seeing the light or hearing the noise. On another day, when the rats licked the spout, they saw the light and heard the noise, but tasted only regular tap water instead of the flavored solution.

The critical finding was that for the rats who were exposed to poison as the US, taste was a more effective CS than was the combination of light and noise. In contrast, when electric shock was the US, the bright, noisy water was a more effective CS than was the flavored solution. In other words, there was a natural association between taste and poison, on the one hand, and between electric shock and the combination of the light and sound, on the other (see Figure 6-5). As we will see in the next section, the most effective timing of the stimulus is also influenced by the type of physiological response.

Garcia and Koelling's finding of an association between the CS and the US surprised the scientific community, given the then-prevalent view that the choice of CS was arbitrary. Garcia had yet another surprise for fellow psychologists that was even more counterintuitive to the prevailing perspective: Conditioning could occur after only a single learning trial. Garcia found that if rats were subsequently poisoned, they demonstrated a CR to the flavored solution after just one exposure to it. Because his finding so strongly conflicted with the prevailing views at that time, Garcia had a great deal of difficulty getting his research published. People just did not believe—and did not want to believe—Garcia's results, precisely because his results differed sharply from what people thought they knew about learning.

Conditioned Emotional Responses

We have discussed classical conditioning theory primarily in the context of experiments with animals, but the principles of classical conditioning are very relevant to the lives of humans as well. Consider just a few examples: fear and other conditioned emotional reactions, neuroses, and addictions. An understanding of

John Garcia found that conditioning can occur after only a single learning trial. His work on taste aversion was not at first accepted by fellow psychologists because it ran counter to what was known about learning.

Modality of CS		Modality of US		Classical-Conditioning Response
Taste		Poisoning		Easily paired; apparent predisposition to classical conditioning
Light and noise	click	Poisoning		Not easily paired; apparent resistance to classical conditioning
Taste		Electric shock		Not easily paired; apparent resistance to classical conditioning
Light and noise	click	Electric shock		Easily paired; apparent predisposition to classical conditioning

Figure 6–5

SICKENING TASTES AND SHOCKING SIGHTS AND SOUNDS. *John Garcia and Robert Koelling surprised the scientific community when they found that some pairs of stimuli and responses were more easily formed than were others. Taste was a more effective CS for learning a CR to poisoning, and a pairing of bright light and noise was a more effective CS for learning a CR to electric shock.*

these phenomena already has led to some treatments and may lead to others.

Fear, a feeling about a particular object, and *anxiety*, a more generalized feeling about a situation or experience, are both emotions that we can become conditioned to feel. Classical conditioning also accounts for many of our other emotional responses. Most of these **conditioned emotional responses** (classically conditioned feelings that an individual experiences in association with particular stimulus events; sometimes called CERs) are linked to distinctive physiological reactions. Partly because of their potent physiological associations, emotional responses appear to be very susceptible to classical conditioning. For example, most of us have experienced the *Garcia effect*, in which

we avoid eating a particular food because its taste and perhaps its associated smell remind us of a past unpleasant association disgusting us and possibly making our stomachs feel queasy.

CERs need not be negative. For example, as you see your loved one approach, you may feel joyful, tingling from head to toe, because of previous pleasurable experiences with that individual. Television advertisers are experts in classically conditioning our positive emotions. They know how to use classical conditioning to appeal to our appetites for food and for sexual gratification, leading us to associate satisfaction with new cars, perfumes, cosmetics, and foods of every shape, texture, and color. Just what are you expected to learn about a product by sensing the

Chances are her fear of dogs is the product of social learning. Unless she was once attacked, that is.

high-pitched acceleration of a flashy red car as a sexy driver zips around a narrow road on a cliff overlooking the ocean?

The *process* of becoming conditioned to experience particular emotions appears to be universal. However, the *content* of the conditioning can vary widely across both individuals and cultures. For instance, many U.S. students and instructors have learned to feel annoyed when other people talk during lectures, because in this culture, total silence means rapt attention; students and educators elsewhere may respond differently. In India it is fairly common for students to talk among themselves during lectures. The Indian professor typically interprets classroom chatter as an affirmation that he or she is stimulating students to talk about the topic. In fact, for many Indian instructors, silence in the classroom may be a classically conditioned stimulus that might arouse in the instructors a fear that the students may have lost interest in the lecture (W. Lonner, personal communication, December 1993). Thus, classical conditioning can arouse either positive or negative feelings, a point that becomes even more clear when we consider classically conditioned experimental neuroses.

Experimental Neurosis

In addition to discovering and investigating classical conditioning in dogs, Pavlov explored how dogs reacted to an unusual *discrimination-learning procedure,* in which subjects learned to recognize the differences between at least two stimuli. At the start of the procedure, one neutral stimulus was linked to an unconditioned stimulus, whereas another neutral stimulus was not. In one experiment, a picture of a circle was accompanied by food, whereas a picture of an ellipse was not (Pavlov, 1928). Over repeated trials, Pavlov changed the conditioned stimuli, gradually making the circle more like the ellipse and the ellipse still more like the circle. Eventually, the two stimuli became virtually indistinguishable. Pavlov observed that the dogs subjected to this conditioning procedure became extremely agitated, barking and howling and attempting to escape from the situation. Pavlov referred to this conditioning procedure as having induced an *experimental neurosis*—a maladjustment in behavior or cognitive processing, in which the discriminative stimulus is so ambiguous that it is virtually impossible to discern whether a particular response is appropriate or inappropriate. What at first seems like a clear choice becomes less and less clear, leading to conflict on the part of the learner.

It is possible that some disorders (maladjustments in living) develop as a result of a classical conditioning procedure similar to the one Pavlov used in his laboratory. Pavlov's idea that his discoveries regarding exper-

imental neurosis in animals apply to humans is not as widely accepted as are his discoveries about classical conditioning overall; still, it is easy to see how such disorders might develop.

Sometimes, it is very difficult to tell which stimuli are associated with which responses. For example, some people make us feel both excited with passion and frustrated with anger. Some situations strike fear in our hearts, yet thrill us with the possibility of tremendous rewards. In each of these cases, it is not clear whether the relevant stimulus is aversive or delightful, with the result that we find ourselves agitated when exposed to it. Like Pavlov's dogs, we may be experiencing a neurosis induced through classical conditioning. We can also become addicted to harmful substances through the mechanisms of classical conditioning, as well as other mechanisms.

Addictions

Addictions—persistent, habitual, or compulsive physiological or at least psychological dependencies on one or more psychoactive drugs—are extremely complex, which is one reason why they are so hard to break (see chapter 5). At least in part, however, addictions appear to be classically conditioned. Consider, for example, the consumption of alcoholic beverages. Many people find the state of intoxication induced by the alcohol to be pleasant, so that this state (or the emotion associated with the anticipation of it) becomes the US. Unfortunately, over time, it takes more and more of a given drug to produce the same effect. This phenomenon tends to lead to drug abuse. The need for more of the drug to produce the same effect, however, is partly driven by the environmental context. If the drug user abuses a drug in a novel environment, the amount of drug needed may decrease greatly. The result is that the drug has a much larger effect, resulting in a major overdose and potential death of the user.

Classical conditioning also has important implications for treating addictions. Simply to stop drinking—or to stop smoking, to consider another addiction—will not break the addiction (B. Schwartz, 1989). Extinction does not result from simple discontinuation of the CS. Rather, the addict has to break the pairing of the CS with the US. Effective procedures for overcoming addictions break this association (see chapter 17).

One way of breaking addictions is through the procedure of **counterconditioning,** a technique in which the positive association between a given US and a given CS is replaced with a negative one by substituting a new US, which has a different UR. For example, some specific drugs can cause violently aversive reactions to the consumption of alcohol (or of tobacco). The idea is that the addict is thereby counterconditioned to avoid rather than to seek out the addictive substance. A less aggressive procedure is to elicit extinction simply by removing the desirable properties of the addictive substance. Thus, the recovering addict might start drinking nonalcoholic beer or smoking cigarettes with little or no nicotine. In such cases, the idea is to achieve extinction by removing the association between the CS and the US. Regardless of the procedure, the strategy involves using principles of learning to fight the addiction.

Clearly, classical conditioning offers many practical applications. An entirely different type of conditioning also offers a vast array of practical applications. This alternative means of associative learning—operant conditioning—holds similar potential for improving people's lives when it is understood and applied appropriately.

Operant Conditioning

What is operant conditioning and how does it occur?

He who learns and runs away will live to learn another day.

—Edward Lee Thorndike

An alternative to classical conditioning is called **operant conditioning** (or *instrumental conditioning*). In operant conditioning, learning occurs as a result of stimuli that either strengthen (through reinforcement) or weaken (through punishment or lack of reinforcement) the likelihood of a given behavioral response. Much everyday learning occurs through random trial-and-error reactions to the environment. Operant conditioning deals with the kind of learning that takes place in such situations.

Suppose that there is a vending machine on your dormitory floor. On the machine is a sign saying "1 dollar" for a can of soda. You put in a dollar's worth of change, and nothing comes out. You trying shaking the machine, but still nothing happens. There is a number to call to get a refund but you do not want to bother. You leave the machine, feeling angry. A week later, you are thirsty and pass by the machine. You decide to give it one more try. In goes your dollar, and out comes nothing. You mutter something under your breath and go to a local convenience store. You never use the soda machine again. You have learned something about the machine, not through classical conditioning, but through operant conditioning. This kind of learning was first shown in a very different kind of context.

The study of operant conditioning is usually viewed as originating with Edward Lee Thorndike. Through experiments with cats in puzzle boxes, Thorndike (1898, 1911) discovered this distinct type of learning. Consider the hungry cat in the puzzle box shown in Figure 6-6. The door to the *puzzle box* is held tightly shut by a simple latch, which opens easily when a fastening device located inside the cage is triggered, usually by a button, a loop, or a string. The cat inside the cage can see a delicious-looking piece of fish in a dish just outside the cage. The cat first tries to reach the fish by extending its paws through the slats; then it starts scratching, bumping, and jumping around the cage. Eventually, it accidentally releases the latch, simply through trial and error. When the latch gives way, the door to the cage opens, and the cat runs to get the fish. Later, the cat is placed again in the cage, and the whole procedure is repeated. This time, the scratching and jumping around do not last very long. As Thorndike (1898) explained, "After many trials, the cat will, when put in the box, immediately claw the button or loop in a definite way" (p. 13) to release the latch, thereby opening the cage, to get the fish.

Law of Effect

It is a process of selection among reactions . . . by eliminating the unsuitable reaction directly by discomfort, and also by positively selecting the suitable one by pleasure. . . . It is of tremendous usefulness.

—Edward Lee Thorndike

Figure 6–6
THORNDIKE'S PUZZLE BOX. *Edward Lee Thorndike's puzzle box demonstrates operant conditioning—that is, how an animal (including a human) can learn a behavior by interacting with its environment. In this case, a cat put in the box learns how to release the latch, which will enable it to get out of the box and eat the fish placed nearby.*

Thorndike proposed a behavioristic principle to account for operant conditioning, which he termed the *law of effect*. Occasionally, our actions result in a reward—an outcome with pleasurable consequences. At other times, our actions result in a punishment—an outcome with aversive consequences. The law of effect states that over time those actions ("the effect") that are rewarded ("the satisfaction") are strengthened and therefore are more likely to occur again, whereas actions that are punished tend to be weakened and are thus less likely to occur in the future.

The main difference between classical and operant conditioning is in the role of the individual. In classical conditioning, the individual has less control over what happens during learning: Behavior is elicited. The experimenter or the environment controls the reinforcement schedule—for example, by repeatedly pairing a CS with a US. In operant conditioning, the individual has more control. The individual operates on the environment to create reinforcement: Behavior is emitted, meaning that it is executed voluntarily rather than executed largely automatically in response to a particular stimulus. In classical conditioning, the crucial relationship for conditioning is between the CS and the US; in operant conditioning, the crucial relationship is between an emitted behavior and the environmental circumstances that it creates.

In operant conditioning, acquisition occurs as a result of the reinforcement of certain emitted behaviors. Extinction occurs when these behaviors stop being reinforced. Generalization of behavior can occur if a wider and wider range of behavior is reinforced, and discrimination if the range of behavior that is reinforced becomes successively narrower. The laws of operant conditioning have been elucidated through the experimental analysis of behavior.

Experimental Analysis of Behavior

Possibly the most influential of modern behaviorists was B. F. Skinner, who developed the theory and methods for what he called the "experimental analysis of behavior." For Skinner (1974), the *experimental analysis of behavior* meant that all behavior should be studied and analyzed in terms of specific behaviors emitted as a function of environmental contingencies; Skinner particularly prized observation of animal behavior as a means of understanding behavior in humans. Containers in which an animal undergoes conditioning experiments are often called **Skinner boxes,** in Skinner's honor.

Skinner believed that the principles of conditioning could be applied widely in life. What mattered to him were the reinforcement contingencies that produce various patterns of behavior, regardless of what might go on inside the head. Notice that by defining the problem of understanding human behavior totally in terms of emitted behavior as a function of environmental contingencies, Skinner essentially created a mission for the field of psychology different from the mission that people typically follow now, a mission he believed was highly relevant to people's everyday lives.

Operant conditioning is of great importance in our lives, literally from the day we are born. Parents reward some actions and punish others, exploiting the laws of operant conditioning to socialize their children. In this way, parents hope to strengthen their children's adaptive behavior and to weaken the children's maladaptive behavior. The same mechanisms are used in school. Some kinds of behavior are rewarded by nods, approbation, or good grades, whereas other kinds of behavior result in isolation from other students, trips to the principal's office, and so on. Operant conditioning, like classical conditioning, can be sensitive to the context in which it takes place. It is also subject to the kind of occasion setting described earlier for classical conditioning (Colwill & Delameter, 1995). Next we examine these mechanisms in more detail.

Reinforcement

In the study of operant conditioning, the term *operant* refers to a kind of behavior that operates on or has some effect on the world. Asking for help, drinking a glass of water, threatening to hurt someone, kissing your lover—all of these are operants. Operant conditioning results in either an increase or a decrease in the probability that these operant behaviors will be performed again.

A **reinforcer** is a *stimulus* that increases the probability that a given operant behavior associated with the stimulus (which usually has occurred immediately or almost immediately before the reinforcing stimulus) will be repeated. Reinforcers can be either positive or negative.

A **positive reinforcer** is a reward, a pleasant stimulus that follows an operant and strengthens the associated response. Examples of positive reinforcers (for most of us) are a smile or a compliment from a teacher following a correct answer or a candy bar released by a vending machine after we put in the required change. When a positive reinforcer occurs soon after an operant response, we refer to the pairing of the positive reinforcer with the response as **positive reinforcement.**

"Remember, every time he gives you a pellet, reinforce that behavior by pulling the lever."

A **negative reinforcer** is a (usually unpleasant) stimulus whose removal or cessation increases the probability that the type of behavior that preceded it will be repeated in the same type of situation. **Negative reinforcement** refers to the process whereby the removal of the unpleasant stimulus results in an increased probability of response. For example, the removal of electric shock would serve as a negative reinforcement if the reward of its removal increased the probability that the type of behavior that preceded it would be repeated in the same type of situation. If putting up an umbrella stops cold rainwater from trickling down the back of your neck, you might be more likely to open your umbrella in the future because you have been negatively reinforced for doing so.

Punishment

> Do not call to a dog with a whip in your hand.
> —Zulu proverb

Unlike the various forms of reinforcement, which increase the probability of an operant response, **punishment** is a process that *decreases* the probability of an operant response. (It should not be confused with negative reinforcement, despite its somewhat unpleasant-sounding name and associations with aversive stimuli, which *increases* the likelihood of a response.) **Positive punishment** is the application of an unpleasant stimulus. Examples of positive punishment include being hit, humiliated, or laughed at, or receiving a failing grade in a course or a negative evaluation from a work supervisor. **Negative punishment** (also sometimes called a *penalty*) is the removal of a pleasant stimulus. Being restricted from enjoyable activities such as tele-

vision viewing or social interactions with friends are examples of negative punishment.

One way of looking at the difference between reinforcement and punishment is that reinforcement captures and to some extent controls behavior, whereas punishment blocks behavior. Reinforcement has fairly predictable consequences and punishment does not. Punishment is thus a less effective way of controlling behavior than is reinforcement.

Punishment must be used with care because it can sometimes lead to several unintended consequences (Bongiovanni, 1977). First, a person may find a way to circumvent the punishment without reducing or otherwise changing the operant behavior. Second, punishment can increase the likelihood of aggressive behavior on the part of the person being punished. That is, the person being punished may imitate the punishing behavior in other interactions. The stereotypical example of this pattern is when the boss yells at the parent, the parent goes home and screams at the child, the child wails at the dog, and the dog snarls at the cat. Third, the punished person may be injured. Punishment becomes child abuse when the child is damaged, physically or psychologically—an unfortunately common occurrence. Fourth, sufficiently severe punishment may result in extreme fear of the punishing person and context, rendering the punished individual incapable of changing the behavior that is being punished. For example, screaming at a child who scored poorly on a test because of test anxiety is more likely to increase than to reduce the child's anxiety. Fifth, even if behavioral change is achieved, the change may damage the punished person's self-esteem. This cost may be greater in the long run than was the cost of the operant behavior that prompted the punishment.

Behaviorists have studied how to make reinforcement and punishment more effective in producing behavioral change. To correct errant behavior, punishment works best under the following circumstances (Parke & Walters, 1967; G. C. Walters & Grusec, 1977) and is useful for parents:

1. Make alternative responses available to replace those that are being punished. A Kenyan proverb suggests the intuitive wisdom of this strategy: "When you take a knife away from a child, give him a piece of wood instead."

2. Complement the punishment technique by using positive reinforcement to foster the desired alternative operant behavior.

3. Make sure that the individual being punished knows exactly what behavior is being punished and why.

4. Implement the punishment immediately after the undesirable operant behavior.

5. Administer a punishment that is sufficiently intense to stop the undesirable behavior, but that is no greater and of no longer duration than necessary.

6. Try to ensure that it is impossible to escape punishment if the operant behavior is demonstrated.

7. Use negative punishment or penalties—removal of pleasant stimuli—rather than physical or emotional pain as a punisher.

8. Take advantage of the natural predilection to escape from and to avoid punishment; use punishment in situations in which the desired alternative operant behavior involves escape from or avoidance of a dangerous situation (e.g., teaching a child to seek escape from dangerous places or to avoid dangerous objects).

Punishment can be used in operant conditioning, termed **aversive conditioning.** In it, the individual is encouraged to avoid a particular behavior or setting as a consequence of punishment in association with the given behavior or setting, and which has as its goal **avoidance learning,** whereby an individual learns to refrain from a particular behavior or keep away from a particular stimulus. For example, rats can learn to avoid a particular behavior (such as scratching at a door latch) by being aversively conditioned (such as through shocks) to avoid that behavior. Note that the aversive conditioning that leads to avoidance learning may also lead to some classical conditioning, in that the object or situation that the individual is being conditioned to avoid may also serve as a conditioned stimulus for a fear response. For example, in the case of rats that learn to avoid scratching at a latch, the rats also may learn to feel fearful of the latch or even of the area near the latch. Operant conditioning through the use of punishment leads to the behavioral outcome of avoidance, and the classical conditioning that may accompany it leads to an emotional and physiological response of fear. Thus, the two forms of learning may interact complementarily to strengthen the outcome.

Discriminating Between Reinforcement and Punishment

To summarize, reinforcement *increases* the probability of some future response; punishment *decreases* it. Reinforcement can involve the presentation of a rewarding stimulus (positive reinforcement) or the removal of an aversive stimulus (negative reinforcement), just as punishment can involve the presentation of an aversive stimulus (positive punishment) or the removal of a rewarding one (negative punishment, or penalty). In other words, both forms of reinforcement (positive or negative) teach the person what to do, whereas both forms of punishment teach the learner what *not* to do. Table 6-2 summarizes these differences.

TABLE 6–2

Summary of Operant Conditioning   *For a given operant behavior, reinforcement increases the probability of its future recurrence, whereas punishment reduces the likelihood that it will be repeated in the future. How might you use these principles to shape the behavior of persons in your environment?*

Operant-Conditioning Technique	Stimulus Presented in the Environment as an Outcome of Operant Behavior	Effect of Stimulus on Operant Behavior
Positive reinforcement	Presentation of *positive reinforcer*—Pleasant stimulus that is introduced follows desired behavior	Strengthens and increases the likelihood of the operant behavior
Negative reinforcement	Presentation of *negative reinforcer*—Unpleasant stimulus that is removed following desired behavior	Strengthens and increases the likelihood of the operant behavior
Positive punishment	Presentation of unpleasant stimulus	Weakens and decreases the likelihood of the operant behavior
Negative punishment (penalty)	Removal of pleasant stimulus	Weakens and decreases the likelihood of the operant behavior

These children are learning some skills and information about things in their environment. Perhaps more importantly, however, they are learning that when they work hard and try to gain skill and knowledge, they gain both smiles of approval and companionship from their parents.

What Makes a Stimulus a Reinforcer?

Thus far, we have discussed reinforcement without explicitly discussing the problem of what makes a stimulus reinforcing, both in general and in particular circumstances. David Premack studied this problem.

The Premack Principle

In 1959, Premack offered children a choice of two activities: playing with a pinball machine or eating candy. Not surprisingly, some children preferred one activity, others the alternative activity. What was more interesting was that, for children who preferred eating candy, the rate of playing with the pinball machine could be increased by using candy as a reinforcer; for the children who preferred playing with the pinball machine, the amount of candy eaten could be increased by using pinball-machine playing as a reinforcer. Thus, the more preferred activity served to reinforce the less preferred one, whichever may have been the more or less preferred activity for a given child.

This research led to what is termed the **Premack principle:** (a) More preferred activities reinforce less preferred ones, and (b) the specific degree of preference is determined by the individual who holds the preference. According to Premack, all individuals have a reinforcement hierarchy, so that (a) reinforcers higher in the hierarchy are more likely to trigger operant behaviors than are reinforcers lower in the hierarchy, and (b) activities higher in the hierarchy reinforce those lower in the hierarchy. Using this principle, we can reinforce someone's operant behavior by offering as a reward something the person prefers more than the activity we wish to rein-

force. Thus, candy will reinforce playing of a pinball machine if candy is the preferred stimulus. Playing pinball will reinforce eating candy if playing the pinball machine is the preferred stimulus.

Primary and Secondary Reinforcers

Primary reinforcers are those reinforcers that are immediately rewarding, such as food, sexual pleasure, and other immediately satisfying or enjoyable rewards. As you may recall from the earlier discussion of the levels of classical conditioning, second-order conditioning sometimes develops, based on first-order conditioning. Similarly, **secondary reinforcers** are rewarding stimuli that are less immediately satisfying and perhaps also less tangible than primary reinforcers. They include money, good grades, and high-status objects that may gain reinforcing value through association with primary reinforcers. Thus, when a primary reinforcer is not immediately available or is inconvenient to administer, secondary reinforcers can fill the gap.

A common type of secondary reinforcer used extensively in designing operant conditioning is the *token*, a tangible object (such as a metal disc or a token) that has no intrinsic worth but that can be exchanged for something of worth to the person whose behavior is subject to operant conditioning. *Token economies*, or systems in which token-based reinforcement is systematically used to change behavior, have shown some success in facilitating language development and behavioral control in autistic persons, who are otherwise out of touch with their environments (Lovaas, 1968, 1977). Researchers and clinicians have become interested in using similar reward systems with normal children. A danger of such systems, however, is that under some circumstances they can undermine children's natural interest in performing the behaviors that are being reinforced (Eisenberger & Cameron, 1996; Lepper, Greene, & Nisbett, 1973). Just how do reinforcements work at the physiological level?

Physiological Considerations in Reinforcement

Most of the reinforcers we consider, and the large majority of reinforcers that have been studied in the laboratory, are either objects or activities. However, research suggests that the brain itself offers even more fundamental reinforcement. Reinforcement can come through direct stimulation of specific regions of the brain. About four decades ago, James Olds and Peter Milner (1954) were investigating rat brains via the use of microelectrodes. During their studies of mammal brains, Olds and Milner implanted an electrode in an area of the brain near the hypothalamus. Much to the surprise of these investigators, the animals sought the electrical stimulation. When the rats were given a chance to press a bar that would produce stimulation to this same area of the brain, the rats pressed at phenomenal rates, in excess of 2,000 times per hour for as long as 15 to 20 hours. Indeed, the rats kept pressing until they collapsed through sheer exhaustion. Subsequent research has shown that similar behavior can be generated in other species. Moreover, whereas the stimulation in this research was pleasurable, stimulation in other areas of the brain can be aversive and thus punishing. In short, it is possible to produce learning not only through reactions to external objects and activities, but also through reactions to direct internal stimulation of the brain.

The physiological processes of learning continue to be a dynamic area of psychological research. Other physiological factors internal to the individual also influence learning (see Table 6-3).

The Gradient of Reinforcement: Effects of Delays

As well as the physiological processes, another important consideration in establishing, maintaining, or extinguishing operant conditioning is the **gradient of reinforcement**—the length of time that occurs between the operant response and the reinforcement that affects the strength of the conditioning. This principle is important both for establishing and for suppressing behavior. For example, one of the difficulties people face when trying to stop smoking is that the positive reinforcement for smoking comes soon after lighting up the cigarette, whereas the punishment is not certain and, in any case, is usually perceived as occurring far in the future.

Similarly, in the age of casual sexual relationships and AIDS, couples know that they should use condoms for protection against the deadly disease, and yet many couples continue not to use them. For these couples, the immediate reinforcements of not using condoms (e.g., not wishing to interrupt the flow of sexual communion) take psychological precedence over the perception of a less immediate and less predictable danger. For all that we know about the dangers of smoking and unprotected intercourse, even very intelligent people engage in these dangerous behaviors because reinforcement principles can be so strong that they overpower rational thinking.

The effectiveness of reinforcement generally declines rapidly with the passage of time, because

---

TABLE 6–3

Physiological Considerations in Learning
Physiological conditions can affect rate and level of learning.

PHYSIOLOGICAL CONSIDERATIONS	EXAMPLES
Behavioral predispositions	It is much easier to train a seal to perform stunts such as leaping into and out of the water than to train a kangaroo to do so.
Maturational considerations	It is easier to toilet train a 30-month-old child than an 18-month-old because the 30-month-old is maturationally ready for bowel and bladder control.
Trauma and acute physiological factors	An injured leg might hamper the ability to jump over a hurdle. Also, fatigue and other temporary physiological conditions affect performance and the conditioning experience. The effects of physiological need (e.g., hunger) on the salience of stimuli (e.g., food) are well known.

the link between the reinforcement and the behavior it reinforces rapidly becomes less clear. The father who tells the child that she will be sorry for her misbehavior when her mother comes home is reducing the effect of the punishment by having the child wait for hours. Similarly, it would be ineffective to reward children for desirable behavior long after the behavior occurs; immediate reinforcement would produce far more potent results. The principle applies to all species.

Shaping Behavior

Sometimes, of course, we wish to create a behavior, not suppress one. For example, we may wish to teach an elephant to stand on a small platform or to encourage a significant other to do the laundry. How can we create behavior when we cannot realistically expect it to occur by chance? **Shaping** is a means of operant conditioning for behavior that is unlikely to be generated spontaneously through a series of **successive approximations** (the stimulation of a sequence of operant behaviors to be reinforced during shaping of a desired behavior). Shaping is used for training animals in circuses, aquatic shows, and the like. To implement this method, you first reward a crude approximation of the behavior of interest. Once that rather rudimentary behavior has been established, you begin to look for a somewhat closer approximation to the desired behavior, and you reward only those closer approximations. You continue with this procedure until the desired behavior is reached.

Parents use the method of shaping on their children all the time. For example, parents usually expect their children to show certain table manners. The parents do not expect these table manners to appear all at once, however. At first, the parents may reward their children just for keeping the places where they eat reasonably neat. Then the parents may expect the children to learn properly to use each of the pieces of silverware. By raising the stakes for what kinds of behavior they will reinforce, parents try to shape behavior that will be acceptable for the children to display later when the children become adults.

Extinction

Applied to operant conditioning, *extinction* refers to the gradual weakening and eventual disappearance of an operant because that operant is no longer followed by a reinforcer. For example, behavior that once brought a food pellet to a rat may no longer bring the food pellet to the rat. Often, there is an increase in the behavior before there is a decrease in that behavior. Parents of infants often have to decide how to extin-

Often when we think of trained animals, we think of amazing stunts performed at circuses or other shows. More commonly, trained animals perform much more important—and perhaps even heroic—work, such as enabling their owners to hike the entire Appalachian Trail.

guish crying behavior in their infants. Newborns cry periodically during the night in order to be fed. The parents typically get up, feed the infant, and then go back to sleep. But after some number of months, the behavior of the infant may continue past the point where it is desirable for either infant or parents. The infant has reached a point where he or she could sleep through much or all of the night, but has become accustomed to frequent feedings. The parents typically decide at some point to stop going in to feed the infant. At first, the infant is likely to cry more. But eventually, when reinforcement is not forthcoming, the infant cries less.

Infants differ in the amount of resistance they show to extinction. Some may stop crying after just a few nights, whereas others may cry for a week or more. In this case, resistance to extinction is a burden to the parents and to the infant as well. But there are other cases in which resistance to extinction may be viewed as a blessing rather than a burden. Parents typically try to instill in their children a prosocial set of values, such as honesty, sincerity, and desire to help others in need. But inevitably, there are times in their children's lives when these values are challenged—when honesty, sincerity, or the desire to help others do not seem to be paying off. At these times, parents hope that the values and behaviors they have taught their children will resist extinction—that they will endure despite periods in which they do not seem to pay off.

Schedules of Reinforcement

When and how regularly reinforcement is given affects its effectiveness in producing a desire behavior. The child who always receives a dollar for reading a book may cease to value the dollar as a reward. When we think of reinforcement, we need to think of it as a phenomenon that can be administered on various **schedules of reinforcement**—that is, patterns of operant conditioning, which determine the timing of reinforcement following the operant behavior.

Up to now, we have assumed **continuous reinforcement,** whereby a reinforcement always and invariably follows a particular operant behavior. A continuous schedule of reinforcement is fairly easy to establish in a laboratory but is actually quite rare in everyday life. In normal everyday life, we are much more likely to encounter a schedule of **partial reinforcement** (also termed *intermittent reinforcement*), whereby a given type of operant response is rewarded some of the time, but not all of the time. Partial reinforcement schedules are of two types: ratio schedules and interval schedules. In a **ratio schedule,** a proportion (ratio) of operant responses is reinforced, regardless of the amount of time that has passed. In an **interval schedule,** reinforcement occurs for the first response after a certain amount of time has passed, regardless of how many operant responses have taken place during that time.

Ratio Schedules

There are two basic types of ratio schedules: fixed ratios and variable ratios. In a **fixed-ratio reinforcement** schedule, reinforcement always occurs after a certain number of operant responses, regardless of the amount of time it takes to produce that number of responses. Many factory workers and cottage-industry artisans get *piecework wages*, meaning that they get paid a flat rate for completing a set number of tasks or crafting a set number of products. In a **variable-ratio reinforcement** schedule, reinforcement occurs, *on average*, after a certain number of operant responses, but the specific number of responses preceding reinforcement changes from one reinforcement to the next. The classic example of a variable-ratio reinforcement schedule in the real world is provided by the slot machine. Gamblers are reinforced by winning coins or tokens after a varying number of pulls on the handle, with each machine set to require a certain number of pulls, on average, before it "pays off."

Interval Schedules

Just as there are fixed- and variable-ratio schedules, so are there fixed- and variable-interval reinforcement schedules. In a **fixed-interval reinforcement** schedule, reinforcement always occurs for the first response after the passage of a fixed amount of time, regardless of how many operant responses have taken place after that time interval. Many aspects of our lives are tied to fixed-interval reinforcements. In most salaried and wage-based jobs, workers are reinforced with paychecks at regular intervals. Similarly, you may study your school assignments in anticipation of fixed-interval reinforcement—such as high grades on final examinations. In a **variable-interval reinforcement** schedule, reinforcement occurs for the first response after the passage of an average interval of time, regardless of how many operant responses have taken place after that time interval. In this type of reinforcement, the specific amount of time preceding reinforcement changes from one reinforcement to the next. For example, in some countries that are undergoing economic turmoil, workers are supposed to be paid on a fixed-interval schedule but actually are paid on a variable-interval schedule. They are eventually paid the amount they are owed, but the paychecks do not have anything like the regularity they are supposed to have. In Russia, for example, many state workers are paid their salaries, but at variable intervals rather than on the days they may expect to be paid.

Comparison and Contrast of Reinforcement Schedules

What effects can we expect from the four kinds of partial-reinforcement schedules? How do they compare with each other and with a continuous-reinforcement schedule? Perhaps the most important point is that partial reinforcement is generally more effective than continuous reinforcement at maintaining a long-term change in behavior. If we want to establish or maintain a long-lasting behavior, we will be more successful if we partially reinforce it. This result seems paradoxical. Why should partial reinforcement be more effective than continuous reinforcement in maintaining behavior? With continuous reinforcement, cessation of reinforcement is obvious and easy to recognize. For example, when people notice that a vending machine (which supplies continuous reinforcement for depositing money) has stopped dispensing the items being purchased, individual purchasers stop depositing their quarters into the machine almost immediately. With partial reinforcement, it is often difficult to distinguish the cessation of reinforcement from merely a prolonged interval within a partial-reinforcement schedule. For example, people often do not immediately stop putting their quarters into a slot machine for gambling even when the machine has not provided any reinforcement for quite a while.

Figure 6-7 shows the patterns of behavior that tend to be produced by the various schedules of reinforcement. These patterns appear to apply to all organisms, including humans. Note that the patterns of behavior produced by the various schedules are different. Although the rate of extinction is greater for continuous reinforcement, the onset of the operant behavior is also faster for this schedule; that is, on this schedule, behavior starts quickly and stops quickly. For the intermittent-reinforcement schedules, ratio schedules generally produce more operant behavior than do interval schedules; that is, fixed-ratio schedules produce higher rates of operant behavior than do fixed-interval schedules, just as variable-ratio schedules produce higher rates than do variable-interval schedules. Note that for the fixed schedules, the operant ceases for a period after each reinforcement. Variable schedules maintain a more constant rate of responding.

In everyday life, reinforcement schedules may be complex, with the ratio or interval of reinforcement changing with the time and the circumstances. Moreover, what starts out as one kind of schedule may change to another (e.g., variable ratio to variable interval).

Clinical Implications of Operant Conditioning: Learned Helplessness

Some types of conditioning, particularly of punishment, may lead to a far more serious consequence: the phenomenon of learned helplessness. **Learned helplessness** occurs when an individual is conditioned to emit no behavior to escape aversive conditions. Consider an example. In a classic experiment, Martin Seligman and S. F. Maier (Seligman, 1975; Seligman & Maier, 1967) placed dogs in a chamber where they received painful (but not harmful) electric shocks. The dogs were unable to escape the shock. Later, the chamber was divided into two parts, so the dogs could escape the shock simply by jumping over a barrier that separated the electrified part from the nonelectrified part. Because the dogs had previously learned that they could not escape, however, they made no effort to escape; instead, they just whined.

In contrast, consider the behavior of a second group of dogs, which did not have the previous experience of being unable to escape. These dogs were placed in the cage, and the shock was turned on. At first, the dogs ran around frantically. Eventually they saw the barrier and jumped it, escaping the shock. On subsequent trials, when the shock was turned on, they quickly jumped the barrier, minimizing the time that they felt pain. Thus, it is evident the first group of dogs' feelings of helplessness rendered them unable to learn.

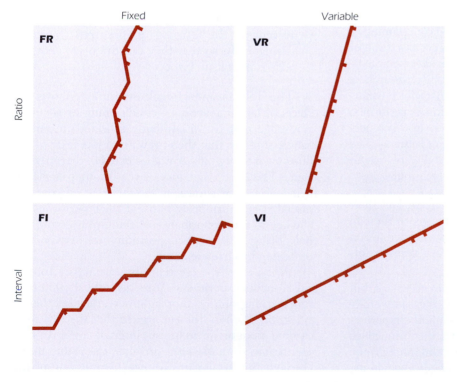

Figure 6–7

TYPICAL PATTERNS OF RESPONSE TO REINFORCEMENT. *Each of the four kinds of reinforcement schedules leads to a different characteristic pattern of response. In general, variable schedules lead to more stable patterns of response (as shown by straight lines) than do fixed schedules (as shown by zig-zag lines), and ratio schedules produce higher levels of response than do interval schedules.*

Psychology in Everyday Life

Learned Helplessness

Alas, humans are not invulnerable to learned helplessness, which appears to be a fairly pervasive phenomenon. We try something; we fail. Maybe we try again and fail again. Soon we have learned to believe that we cannot perform that task or master that skill, so we never try again. The child who fails in school, the adult who fails on the job, the lover who fails to sustain a lasting romantic relationship—all of these people are susceptible to learned helplessness. Our conditioning may tell us that we cannot succeed. Some people stop accepting challenges because they feel sure that they cannot cope with them.

It is worthwhile to analyze our own behavior in terms of learned helplessness. For example, in my own case, I was only a middling French student and was becoming convinced that I simply did not have the ability to learn a foreign language adequately. One day my French teacher confirmed my impression by telling me that she could tell from the kinds of mistakes I made that I had little foreign-language learning ability. This comment confirmed my impression. I stopped even trying hard in the course, which just confirmed the futility of my efforts. I was convinced I was unable to master foreign languages, and I never took another foreign-language course during my school years. As an adult, my work required me to learn Spanish, and I learned it quite easily as a result of its being taught by a method that better fit my learning style than the way I had been taught French. I realized that I had falsely learned to feel helpless about my skills. With dedication and a style of teaching that fit my needs, I could learn a new language.

Ask yourself whether there are opportunities you are missing out on just because you have convinced yourself that you cannot take advantage of them. You may find, as I did, that you really can do "impossible" things if you only set your mind to it.

By now, you may be feeling greatly challenged by the similarities and differences between classical and operant conditioning. At this point, it may be helpful to summarize briefly the features of each, as shown in Table 6-4.

Up to this point, we have described conditioning in terms of the observable changes that occur as a result of learning. However, what we learn is not always immediately evident. In 1930—long before other researchers acknowledged internal mechanisms that affect conditioning—Edward Tolman and C. H. Honzik performed an elegant experiment to illustrate a way in which performance may not be a clear reflection of learning. The investigators were interested in the ability of rats to learn a maze. Rats were divided into three groups:

Group 1. The rats had to learn the maze, and their reward for getting from the start box to the end box was food. Eventually, these rats learned to run the maze without making any wrong turns or following blind alleys.

Group 2. The rats were also placed in the maze, but they received no reinforcement for successfully getting to the end box. Although their performance improved over time, they continued to make more errors than did the reinforced group. These results are hardly surprising; we would ex-

pect the rewarded group to have more incentive to learn.

Group 3. The rats received no reward for 10 days of learning trials. On the 11th day, however, food was placed in the end box. With just one reinforcement, the learning of these rats improved dramatically, so that they ran the maze about as well as the rats in Group 1.

The Tolman and Honzik experiment shows the effects of **latent learning**—conditioning or acquired knowledge that is not presently reflected in performance. It seems that the unrewarded rats learned the route, even though it was not reflected in their performance. Once they were given a reward, they displayed their learning, as shown by the fact that just one rewarded trial enormously boosted their performance. The key to the performance of the Group 3 rats was their being given the opportunity to display that something had been learned.

What, exactly, were the rats learning in Tolman and Honzik's experiment? It seems unlikely that they were learning simply "turn right here, turn left there," and so on. Rather, Tolman argued that the rats were learning a **cognitive map**—an internal cognitive representation of a pattern, in this case, the maze. Through this argument, Tolman became one of the

TABLE 6–4

Comparison of Classical and Operant Conditioning *Both classical and operant conditioning are processes of association by which individuals learn behavior, but the two processes differ in several key ways.*

CHARACTERISTICS	CLASSICAL (OR PAVLOVIAN)	OPERANT (OR INSTRUMENTAL)
Key relationship	Environment's CS and Environment's US	Organism's operant and Environment's contingencies (reinforcement or punishment)
Organism's role	Elicited behavior: little or no control over learning situation	Emitted behavior: more control over learning situation
Sequence of events	Initiation of conditioning: CS→US→UR	Operant response→Reinforcer→Increase response
	Peak of acquisition phase: CS→CR	Operant response→Punishment→Decrease response
Schedules of conditioning	Standard classical conditioning, delay conditioning, trace conditioning, temporal conditioning	Continuous reinforcement, fixed ratios, variable ratios, fixed intervals, and variable intervals of reinforcement
Extinction techniques	Uncouple the CS from the US, repeatedly presenting the CS in the absence of the US	Uncouple the operant behavior from the reinforcer or punishment; repeatedly fail to reinforce or to punish the operant behavior

earliest cognitive theorists, arguing for the importance not only of behavior, but also of the mental representations that give rise to the behavior.

Note that the work of Tolman was a beginning of a cognitive tradition for understanding learning, rather than being strictly in the behaviorist tradition. Tolman's work thus provides a bridge between strictly behaviorist approaches and the more cognitive approaches to learning considered in subsequent chapters.

The Biological Bases of Learning

In Search of . . .

What are some of the main biological bases of learning?

The neurobiological basis of learning has been studied extensively in Aplysia, a type of sea snail. Recent work suggests that the gill withdrawal reflex in this sea animal exhibits the principles of classical conditioning, including second-order conditioning (Hawkins, Greene, & Kandel, 1998). What mechanism underlies this learning? Research suggests that increases in the sensitivity of the synapse, referred to as *potentiation*, occur at the sensory-motor neuron synapses and may partly underlie the classical conditioning of the gill withdrawal reflex in the Aplysia (Bao, Kandel, & Hawkins, 1998). In other words, conditioning can be linked directly to neural events. Moreover, many of the molecular and structural changes that accompany potentiation at the synapse have been determined in Aplysia (Bailey, Alberini, Ghirardi, & Kandel, 1994).

Wise men learn by others' mistakes, fools by their own.

—Henry George Bohn

When you follow in the path of your father, you learn to walk like him.

—Ashanti proverb

All of the research discussed so far has involved learning through classical or operant conditioning. In our everyday lives, however, not all of our learning derives from direct participation. Consider, for example, the effect on a child of seeing an older sibling punished for something that she herself did just the day before or the effect on a drug addict of seeing a fellow addict die of an overdose of drugs.

Social Learning

In Search of . . .

What is social learning and how does it take place?

Social learning, sometimes called *observational* or *vicarious learning,* is learning that occurs by observing the behavior of others as well as of the environmental outcomes of their behavior. Is there empirical evidence for this kind of learning?

Albert Bandura (1965, 1969) and his colleagues have performed numerous experiments demonstrating that vicarious social learning is an effective way of learning. In a typical study, preschool children were shown a film featuring an adult who punched, kicked, and threw things at an inflatable punching doll, also called a Bobo doll. The adult even hit the doll with a hammer. The film ended in different ways, depending on the group to which a particular child viewer was assigned. In one group, the adult model was rewarded for the aggressive behavior; in a second group, the adult model was punished; and in a third (control) group, the adult model was neither rewarded nor punished. When, after the film, the children were allowed to play with a Bobo doll, those children who had seen the adult model rewarded for aggressive behavior were more likely than the controls to behave aggressively with the doll, whereas those who had observed the adult model punished were less likely than the controls to behave aggressively with the doll. Clearly, observational learning had taken place.

Other studies show that reinforcement contingencies are not needed for social learning to take place. In another experiment (Bandura, Ross, & Ross, 1963), preschool children watched an adult model either sit quietly next to the Bobo doll or attack it. No rewards or punishments went to the adult. When children were later left alone with the doll, those who had observed aggressive behavior were more likely to behave aggressively.

What conditions are necessary for observational learning to occur? There appear to be four of them (Bandura, 1977b):

1. *Attention* to the behavior on which the learning might be based;

2. *Retention* of the observed scene when the opportunity arises later to exploit the learning;

3. *Motivation* to reproduce the observed behavior;

4. *Potential reproduction* of the behavior—in other words, you need to be able to do what you saw being done.

In numerous experiments, Albert Bandura has shown that children learn to imitate the behavior of others. By observing a movie of a woman behaving aggressively toward a Bobo doll (top), this boy and girl learned to punch the doll.

Also, generalization and discrimination play important roles in the effectiveness of learning and in the applicability of learning to a particular context.

Each of these four factors has several contributing factors. For example, several factors enhance the salience of a model, although these factors are not necessary for social learning to take place: (a) The model stands out in contrast to other competing models; (b) the model is liked and respected by the observer (or by others in the environment); (c) the observer perceives a similarity between herself or himself and the model; (d) the model's behavior is reinforced.

Observational learning is not limited to scenes with Bobo dolls, of course. Many children, as well as adults, spend countless hours in front of televisions watching violent behavior. Considerable evidence supports the contention that exposure to violent activity on television leads to aggressive behavior (e.g., Friedrich-Cofer & Huston, 1986; Huesmann, Lagerspetz, & Eron, 1984; Parke, Berkowitz, Leyens, West, & Sebastian, 1977).

Observational learning is important not only in identifying behavior typically considered to be unde-

sirable, such as highly aggressive behavior, but also in identifying and establishing who we are. For example, gender identification and gender-role development (discussed in chapter 11) clearly rely heavily on observational learning; children's observations of same-sex parents, as well as of same-sex peers, are particularly influential (S. K. Thompson, 1975).

In sum, observational learning is important to both children and adults. We are not always aware of its occurrence, but it is always consequential for us— whether beneficial or harmful. Those of us who are loath to practice what we preach especially need to be aware: Children are more likely to learn and remember by imitating what we practice than by listening to what we preach. The many factors that influence our later recollection of what we observe are the subject of the next chapter.

THINK ABOUT IT

1. In what kinds of situations does learning tend to be advantageous? In what kinds of situations might learning be disadvantageous?
2. What are the main similarities and differences between classical and operant conditioning?
3. Prescribe a counterconditioning program for a specific phobia or addiction.
4. Suppose you worked for a company and wanted people to buy a particular product you believe they need. How could you use some of the principles of conditioning to encourage people to buy this product?
5. What is something (a skill, a task, or an achievement) that you think is worthwhile but that you

feel a sense of learned helplessness about successfully accomplishing? How could you design a conditioning program for yourself to overcome your learned helplessness?
6. Given the powerful effects of social learning, how might the medium of television be used as a medium for *lowering* the rate of violent crimes in our society?

online *You can provide your own answers to these questions online at the* **Sternberg, In Search of the Human Mind** *Web site:* **http://www.harcourtcollege.com/psych/ishm**

SUMMARY

Preparation for Learning, Reflexes, Instincts, and Imprinting   197

1. An organism (including a human) *learns* when it makes a relatively permanent change in its behavior, thoughts, or feelings as a result of experience.

2. Learning serves an important evolutionary function, enabling organisms to adapt to ever-changing environments.

Classical Conditioning   197

3. Pavlov identified *classical conditioning* when he was trying to conduct experiments on digestion. After noting that his dog drooled when it anticipated meat powder, he realized that he could condition or teach the dog to have the same reaction to a sound, something that it would not do otherwise.

4. *Classical conditioning* teaches an organism to pair a neutral stimulus with a stimulus that produces an unconditioned physiological or emotional response.

5. The dog's salivation in response to the meat powder was the *unconditioned response (UR)*, the meat powder was the *unconditioned stimulus (US)*, the buzzer (an originally neutral stimulus) became the *conditioned stimulus (CS)*, and the salivation (originally the UR) in response to the buzzer became the *conditioned response (CR)*.

6. In the standard classical conditioning paradigm, the CS precedes the onset of the US by a brief interval of time. Other timing arrangements include *delay conditioning, temporal conditioning, and trace conditioning.*

7. Temporal contiguity appears not to be sufficient for classical conditioning to occur; rather, a *contingency* must be established between the stimulus and the response if conditioning is to occur.

8. If we plotted the rate of learning, the curve would rise quickly but then level off at the asymptote. The rate of learning shows a negative acceleration over time.

9. The probability of learning is highest in the *acquisition* phase. If the US is not presented in conjunction with the CS, the learned response is *extinguished*. However, the learned behavior will *spontaneously recover* if the CS is presented once again. If the US is presented once again with the CS, then *savings* will occur and the CR will be almost as strong as during the *asymptote*.

10. In *first-order conditioning*, a CS is linked to a US. In second-order conditioning, a second CS is linked to the first CS, and so on analogously for *higher order conditioning*.

11. When we show a CR to a stimulus that is similar to the CS, we experience *stimulus generalization*. However, when the new stimulus increasingly differs from the CS, to the point where we are unlikely to show the CR, we experience *stimulus discrimination*.

12. We seem to be predisposed toward making some associations and not others. For example, for rats that were exposed to poison as the US, taste was a more effective CS than the combination of light and noise as the CS.

13. Classical conditioning applies to more than just animal experimentation. Many of our *conditioned emotional responses*—such as fear, anxiety, or even joy—are linked to distinctive physiological feelings. When we experience conflicting stimuli, we may experience a neurosis. *Addictions* also appear to be partly classically conditioned, although they can be broken by *counterconditioning*.

Operant Conditioning   211

14. *Operant conditioning* is learning produced by the active behavior (an *operant*) of an individual. According to the law of effect, operant actions that are rewarded will tend to be strengthened and thus will be more likely to occur in the future, whereas operant actions that are punished will tend to be weakened and thus will be less likely to occur in the future.

15. B. F. Skinner believed that all behavior should be studied and analyzed into specific emitted behaviors emanating from environmental contingencies.

16. A *reinforcer* is a stimulus that increases the probability that the operant associated with it will happen again. A *positive reinforcer* is a reward that strengthens an associated response; *positive reinforcement* pairs the positive reinforcer with an operant. A *negative reinforcer* is an unpleasant stimulus, relief from which also strengthens an associated response; *negative reinforcement* pairs an operant with the discontinuation of an unpleasant stimulus.

17. *Punishment* is a process that decreases the probability of a response. *Positive punishment* provides an unpleasant stimulus that is introduced after an undesired response. *Negative punishment* is the removal of a desired stimulus. Punishment differs from negative reinforcement, which increases the probability of a response. Punishment should be administered carefully because it can lead to many unintended consequences.

18. *Avoidance learning* occurs when an individual learns to stay away from something. Under some

circumstances, avoidance learning can occur after just a single trial of *aversive conditioning*.

19. According to the *Premack principle*, more-preferred activities can serve to reinforce less-preferred activities.

20. When *primary reinforcers* (e.g., food or sexual pleasure) are not available, *secondary reinforcers* (e.g., money, gifts or good grades) can provide reinforcement if they are associated with primary reinforcers.

21. Reinforcement can be administered directly to the brain. Reinforcement to some areas of the brains of animals can cause them to seek repeated stimulation until they drop from exhaustion.

22. The *gradient of reinforcement* refers to the fact that the longer the time interval is between the operant behavior and the reinforcement, the weaker the effect of the reinforcement will be.

23. When *shaping* behavior, such as training an animal or changing a person's behavior, the method of successive approximations reinforces operant behaviors that are successively closer to the desired behavior.

24. Operant conditioning is extinguished when an operant that once was reinforced stops being reinforced.

25. In operant conditioning, behavior can be *reinforced continuously* or *partially*. Partial reinforcement has four forms: *fixed-ratio reinforcement*, *variable-ratio reinforcement*, *fixed-interval reinforcement*, and *variable-interval reinforcement*.

26. Animals or people display *learned helplessness* when they feel there is no way to escape a painful or aversive stimulus. The original experimental demonstration of this phenomenon was via dogs who learned that they could not escape electric shocks. People often display this behavior when they have repeated failures.

27. We do not always display in our behavior what we have learned; this nonobservable learning is termed *latent learning*. Edward Tolman showed that mental representations, such as are provided by a *cognitive map*, are the foundation for behavior.

The Biological Bases of Learning   221

28. Many of the effects of conditioning can be traced to changes that occur at neuronal synapses.

Social Learning   222

29. When we watch the behavior of others and the outcomes of that behavior, we learn the behavior vicariously; we engage in *social learning*. A classic example of this kind of social learning is shown in Bandura's experiment with children who watched and mimicked aggressive behavior with a Bobo doll.

30. *Social learning* is important because it helps us identify desired behavior and establish our identities.

KEY TERMS

◼ THINK ABOUT IT SAMPLE RESPONSES

1. In what kinds of situations does learning tend to be advantageous? In what kinds of situations might learning be disadvantageous?

Learning tends to be advantageous in situations in which we use experience to figure out how to deal with a relatively novel task or situation. Learning can be disadvantageous if we apply it in situations in which it turns out not to apply, for example, when we behave toward a teacher in a way that we learned is appropriate for our peers but that is not in fact appropriate in interactions with a teacher. It also can be disadvantageous in situations where an extremely rapid response is necessary, for example, when one is burned by touching an extremely hot object. In this case, a reflex reaction likely will be more adaptive than will be one processed by the brain.

2. What are the main similarities and differences between classical and operant conditioning?

In classical conditioning, behavior is elicited. The organism has little or no control over the learning situation. In operant conditioning, the behavior is emitted, with the organism typically having more control over the learning situation. In classical conditioning, the sequence of events typically begins with the initiation of a conditioned stimulus. In operant conditioning, the sequence of events typically begins with the initiation of an operant response, which either is or is not reinforced (or punished). Extinction of classical conditioning occurs when the CS is uncoupled from the US, which can occur by repeatedly presenting the CS in the absence of the US. Extinction of operant conditioning occurs when the operant behavior is uncoupled from the reinforcer or punishment.

3. Prescribe a counterconditioning program for a specific phobia or addiction.

Counterconditioning to alcohol is sometimes achieved by prescribing a drug that produces extreme distress in the individual if that individual consumes alcohol. The idea is that the alcohol then becomes associated with an adverse experience.

4. Suppose you worked for a company and wanted people to buy a particular product you believe they need. How could you use some of the principles of conditioning to encourage people to buy this product?

You might believe that couples should purchase condoms in order to reduce the risks of unwanted pregnancies or to prevent the spread of venereal disease. Thus you would want to provide some kind of reward to people who buy condoms. One kind of reward might be to design condoms that enhance the pleasure of sexual experience (e.g., condoms of unusual colors or shapes). Another kind of reward might be a money-back offer or the assurance of sex without undue risk.

5. What is something (a skill, a task, or an achievement) that you think is worthwhile but that you feel a sense of learned helplessness about successfully accomplishing? How could you design a conditioning program for yourself to overcome your learned helplessness?

Each person needs to answer this question for him or herself. In my own case, I wanted to lose weight at various points in my life but had not had much success. I decided that the reason was that I was setting unrealistic goals. I wanted to lose a lot of weight fast, and when I did not succeed in doing so, I viewed myself as having failed. I then decided I needed to work out a reinforcement schedule whereby I would reward myself for small weight losses. I did just that. I allowed myself to engage in an activity I looked forward to when I lost small amounts of weight (2 pounds). This reinforcement schedule enabled me to attain realistic goals and to lose weight slowly but surely.

6. Given the powerful effects of social learning, how might the medium of television be used as a medium for *lowering* the rate of violent crimes in our society?

Television shows might provide nonviolent rather than violent role models. At the very least, the proportion of nonviolent to violent shows could be greatly increased. Shows could be constructed so that nonviolence led to more positive results, violence to less positive or negative ones.

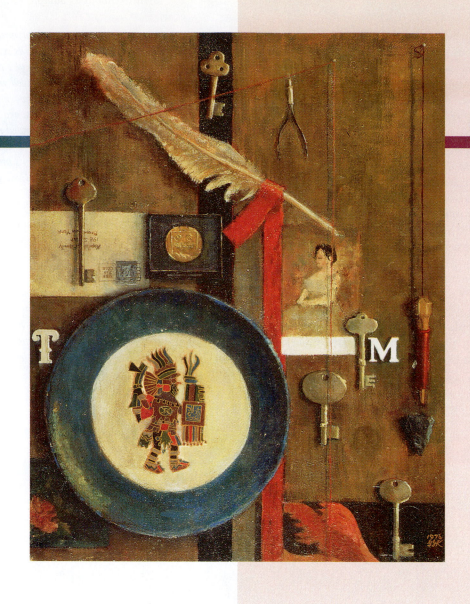

No Passenger was known to flee—
That lodged a night in memory—
That wily—subterranean Inn
Contrives that none go out again—

—Emily Dickinson, Poem 1406

7

MEMORY

Chapter Outline

We use our memories almost constantly—to remember phone numbers, people's faces, names of people we once knew. Sometimes a sound or an odor can bring back the memory of an experience we had many years before, complete with a recollection or even a reexperiencing of the feelings we had at the time.

Sometimes what we need to remember is material we purposely learned. Many of us have had the experience of memorizing large amounts of information for a test, only to discover that we seem to have forgotten it a short time thereafter. Sometimes we do not even seem to remember the information for a long enough time to recall it when we take the test. This kind of incident illustrates two points.

First, we can memorize or think we are memorizing material, but unless we process the material in a way that renders it memorable, we later may remember nothing of what we have memorized (or thought we have memorized). This issue is addressed in the section on long-term memory. Second, if we wish to memorize material for the long term, the conventional study techniques many students use in college may not be adequate. This issue is addressed throughout the chapter and especially in the discussions of encoding specificity and mnemonics. In addition, we consider the answers to several important questions about memory: What, exactly, is memory? How does memory work? Are there different kinds of memory, and if so, what are they? How is each kind of memory organized? How are different kinds of memories related?

How can we measure memory, and how can we improve it? To answer these questions, we first explore what memory is and how it is measured.

A major theme of this chapter is that when we remember things, we are constructing an account of the past rather than merely dredging up information from some kind of mental storage bin. Because memory involves such constructive processing, it can play tricks on us. In one commentary, President Ronald Reagan reminisced and remembered his role in World War II, except that what he was remembering was a part he had played in a movie rather than anything he actually did in the war. Thus, there is no guarantee that what people remember actually happened or is even close to anything that happened.

How Memory Is Studied

How can we assess people's memories?

Memory refers to the process by which past experience and learning can be used in the present. We draw upon our memory of the past to help us understand the present.

In studying memory, researchers have devised various tasks that require research participants to remember arbitrary information, such as numerals, in different ways. Because this chapter includes many references to these tasks, it is useful to have an *advance organizer*—a basis for organizing the information to be given—so that you will know how memory is studied. Refer back to this description of memory tasks if you forget some of the details about the purposes of various tasks.

Recall and Recognition

Memory tasks can involve recall, recognition, or a combination of the two. If you were given a task requiring **recall memory,** you would be asked to produce facts, words, or other items from memory. Fill-in-the-blank tests require that you recall items from memory. For example, "Who is the author of this textbook?" is a recall question (if you don't peek at the answer). However, if you were given a memory task requiring **recognition memory,** in which an individual is asked just to recognize as correct (not to produce) a fact, a word, or other item from memory, you would have to select or identify an item as being one that you learned previously. Multiple-choice and true–false tests typically involve recognition, although they may require other processes, such as reasoning, as well. For example, "Is Robert J. Sternberg the author of this

textbook?" requires you to recognize whether the given information is correct. If you are asked, "Fill in the missing letters in the last name of the author of this book—"S_e_n_e_g"—then you are being asked to recall the letters, but are being given some of the letters of the name, which may help you recognize who the author is. This last task, combining elements of both recall and recognition, is sometimes called **cued recall,** whereby a participant must recall something by using a cue, or prompt, provided by an experimenter or other individual.

The types of recall tasks typically used in experiments are serial recall, free recall, and paired-associates recall. A simple way to assess recall is through **serial recall,** which is measured by a memory task in which you are presented with a list of items and are asked to repeat the items in the exact order in which the items were presented. Occasionally, research participants are asked to repeat the list they heard, but backward, as on the Wechsler intelligence scales (see chapter 9). Serial recall can be done with other kinds of stimuli besides digits, of course, such as letters or words.

In **free recall,** as in serial recall, you are presented with a list of items and are asked to repeat the items in any order you prefer. When there are multiple trials, items are usually presented in a different random order on each trial.

In **paired-associates recall,** you are presented with a list of paired (and often related) items, which you are asked to store in memory; then, you are presented with one item in each pair and are asked to provide the mate of each given item. For example, if you learn the list of pairs *time–city, mist–home, switch–paper, credit–day, fist–cloud, number–branch,* when you are later given the stimulus *switch,* you will be expected to say *paper.* Again, the task may be presented either in a single-recall trial or in multiple trials.

In each of these tasks, you need to produce an item from memory. In a recognition memory task, however, the experimenter produces an item, and your job is to indicate whether it is one that you have learned in the context of the experiment. For example, if you receive the list *time, city, mist, home, switch,* you may be asked later if the word *switch* appeared on the list. The paired-associates recall task described above may be viewed as a form of cued recall, because the experimenter provides a cue, or prompt, and the research participant, who has to recall something, uses that cue to bolster recall.

Although there are some exceptions, recognition memory is usually much better than recall. For example, Lionel Standing, Jerry Conezio, and Ralph Haber (1970) found that people could recognize close to 2,000 pictures in a recognition-memory task. Recall from chapter 6 the discussion of the relationship between learning and performance. Your performance on a memory task would often seem to indicate different levels of learning, depending on whether you were asked to recall or simply to recognize what you had learned. (For this reason, you may prefer multiple-choice over fill-in-the-blank questions when you are less confident of your knowledge in a particular subject.)

Typically, research participants are aware that they are performing a memory task, but not always. Memory researchers often distinguish between explicit and implicit memory tasks. In an implicit-memory task, participants are not aware they are performing a memory task.

Explicit Versus Implicit Memory Tasks

Each of the preceding tasks involves **explicit memory,** a form of memory in which an individual consciously acts to recall or recognize particular information—for example, words from a prior list. Psychologists also find it useful to understand the phenomena of **implicit memory** (Graf & Schacter, 1985), in which an individual recalls or recognizes information without consciously being aware of doing so. Every day, you engage in many tasks that involve your recollection of information without your being aware of being engaged in recall. As you read this book, for example, you are remembering the meanings of particular words, some of the psychological concepts you read about in earlier chapters, and even how to read, without your being aware of your doing these things. Memory researchers also distinguish between **procedural memory,** a recognition and awareness of how to perform particular tasks, skills, or procedures—"knowing-how" skills, such as how to ride a bicycle—and those that involve **declarative memory,** a recognition and understanding of factual information—"knowing-that," such as the terms in a psychology textbook.

In the laboratory, experimenters sometimes study implicit memory by studying people's performance on word-completion tasks, which involve implicit memory. In a word-completion task, the research participant is presented with a word fragment, such as the first three letters of a word, and is asked to complete it with the first word that comes to mind. For example, suppose that you were asked to supply the missing five letters to fill these blanks and form a word: imp_ _ _ _ _. Because you had recently seen the word *implicit*, you would be more likely to provide the five letters l-i-c-i-t for the blanks than would someone who had not recently been exposed to the word. In general, research participants perform better when the word is one they have seen on a recently presented list. Even though they have not been explicitly instructed to remember words from the earlier list, their

Riding a bicycle requires the encoding, storage, and retrieval of procedural knowledge. Prior to storing this knowledge, the boy must work hard to try to remember how to move his muscles in the right ways at the right times. With a little rehearsal, however, he will master these skills so well that he will be able to remember them the rest of his life.

improved performance on the word-completion tasks shows they may have remembered implicitly.

Implicit memory encompasses a number of types of phenomena. For example, memory for how to do things—*procedural memory*—is typically implicit. When you ride a bicycle, you are not typically aware of recalling how to mount, how to steer, how to use the brakes, and so on. You just do it. The same is true when you write a paper for a course. You are not aware, typically, of recalling a set of procedures— first I need a title, then I need an opening sentence, then I need to make sure that sentence has a subject and a verb and that it ends with a period, and so on. Again, you just do it. Another typically implicit memory phenomenon is **priming,** the activation of one or more existing memories by a stimulus, as in the example above where you probably filled in the blanks with the word "implicit" because you had recently seen this word. Memories appear to be of several types, not just one type. What are the types of memories?

You are likely to remember your parents' names forever. When you are introduced to someone new at a party, however, you may forget that person's name almost immediately. Why and how do we remember some things and not others? To understand, it is necessary to learn about different types of memory, as well as how information is placed into, retained in, and later extracted from memory.

The Classic Conceptualization of Memory: The Atkinson-Shiffrin Multiple-Store Model

In Search of ... *What are the stores of memory in the "standard" memory model?*

The prevailing model of memory in psychology was originally proposed by Richard C. Atkinson and Richard Shiffrin (1968), who conceptualized memory in terms of three memory stores (functional storage locations): (1) a brief, fleeting sensory memory; (2) a somewhat larger but still very limited store of actively conscious memory; and (3) a store of information that is of virtually limitless capacity, which requires effective retrieval to bring it into active memory. This metaphor of memory stores is not the only way to conceptualize memory, and alternative models, using different metaphors, are discussed later in the chapter, but variants of the Atkinson–Shiffrin model are still commonly used by psychologists.

Three Memory Stores

As mentioned, memory theorists often distinguish among three memory stores: (1) the **sensory store,** which has the smallest capacity for storing information and has the shortest duration for memory storage; (2) the **short-term store,** or short-term memory (STM), which has a modest capacity and has a duration for storing information of only a number of seconds; and (3) the **long-term store,** or long-term memory (LTM), which has a greater capacity than both the sensory store and the short-term store; it can store information for very long periods of time, perhaps even indefinitely.

These three stores are not distinct physiological structures. Rather, they are hypothetical constructs embracing sets of processes. For example, the processes used for long-term memory are thought to be somewhat different than those used for short-term memory. The processes of long-term memory result in the storage of information that can be held essentially indefinitely whereas the processes of short-term memory result in information that is stored only briefly. Figure 7-1 shows a simple information-processing model of these stores, which typifies models proposed in the 1960s and 1970s (e.g., R. C. Atkinson & Shiffrin, 1971).

Figure 7–1

THE THREE-STORES VIEW. *In Richard Atkinson and Richard Shiffrin's model of memory, information flows from sensory to short-term to long-term memory stores. Their metaphor for memory long served as the basis for research on memory processes. (After R. C. Atkinson & Shiffrin, 1971)*

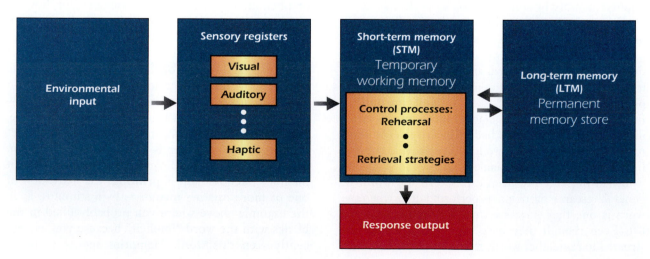

The Mechanisms of Memory: Encoding, Storage, and Retrieval

All three memory stores process information similarly; they encode, store, and retrieve it. Each operation represents a stage in memory processing. **Encoding** refers to the process by which a physical, sensory input, such as a word or a sound or even an odor, is transformed into a representation that can be stored into memory. **Storage** refers to moving encoded information into a memory store and to maintaining the information. **Retrieval** refers to recovery of stored information from a memory store and moving the information into consciousness for use in active cognitive processing. Encoding, storage, and retrieval are sequential stages, whereby we first take in information, then hold it for a while, and later pull it out. However, the processes interact with each other and are interdependent. For example, when you study, you need first to encode information, and then to store it. When you are tested, you need to retrieve some of that information. How well you retrieve the information will depend upon how well you encoded and then stored it.

The three stages of memory can be illustrated with reference to the object pictured in Figure 7-2. Suppose that you see a photo of this animal while you are leafing through a magazine. You are in a hurry and do not have time to read the accompanying article. You do not know what the animal is and, as a result, find the creature difficult to fathom. Later, you go back to the magazine and learn that the animal is a large African mammal that feeds on insects, especially ants and termites: an *aardvark*. You have heard of this animal before but have never actually seen one, either in life or in a picture. Now,

knowing what the animal is, you find yourself encoding features in the picture, such as the animal's powerful claws, large ears, and heavy tail. You also encode the animal's name, as well as an image of what it looks like. Although you do not make any particular effort to remember what an aardvark looks like, the visual information has been stored in your memory because the verbal label has made it meaningful to you. Several years later, on a visit to a zoo, you see an animal and immediately recognize it as an aardvark. You have retrieved from memory the representation you stored earlier without even being fully aware you were doing so.

The example of the aardvark illustrates an interesting property of memory—namely, that having a verbal label (such as a name) to attach to something can often help us make sense of that something, even though it is, indeed, only a label. In this case, the verbal label helped us organize information about an animal shown in a picture. Verbal labels also can help us encode, store, and retrieve information that is presented in text. See if you can figure out what is going on in the passage below:

> The procedure is actually quite simple. First you arrange items into different groups. Of course one pile may be sufficient depending on how much there is to do. If you have to go somewhere else due to lack of facilities that is the next step; otherwise, you are pretty well set. It is important not to overdo things. That is, it is better to do too few things at once than too many. In the short run this may not seem important but complications can easily arise. A mistake can be expensive as well. At first, the whole procedure will seem complicated. Soon, however, it will become just another facet of life. It is difficult to foresee any end to the necessity for this task in the immediate future, but then, one can never tell. After the procedure is completed one arranges the materials into different groups again. Then they can be put into their appropriate places. Eventually they will be used once more and the whole cycle will then have to be repeated. However, that is part of life.

If you are given the title of this passage, "Washing Clothes," this procedure is considerably easier to recall and understand than it is without the title (Bransford & Johnson, 1972, cited in Bransford, 1979, pp. 134–135). The verbal label helps us to encode, and therefore to remember, a passage that otherwise seems incomprehensible.

Now that we have mapped out an overview of memory processes and of the three memory stores, we can more deeply probe each memory store, starting with the sensory store.

Figure 7-2
What is this?

Sensory Memory

The sensory store, which is the initial repository of much information that eventually enters the short- and long-term stores, may take two forms: the iconic store for visual memories and the echoic store for auditory memories.

Excellent evidence indicates the existence of a sensory register for the fleeting storage of discrete visual images, the **iconic store** (so called because information is believed to be stored in the form of *icons*, visual images that represent something). Visual information appears to enter our memory system through an iconic store that holds the visual information for very short periods of time. George Sperling (1960) showed people 12 letters in a 3 × 4 grid for 50 msec. Experimental participants then were asked to report the identity and location of a part of the grid. Sperling found that people could hold about eight items in iconic memory after a tenth of a second. Most of the information is gone after half a second, and almost all of it after a whole second. In the normal course of events, this information may be either transferred to another store or erased if other information is superimposed on it before there is sufficient time for the transfer of the information to another memory store. If you have ever "written" your name with a lighted sparkler on the Fourth of July, you have experienced the persistence of a visual memory; that is, you have briefly "seen" your name, even though the sparkler left no physical trace. This *visual persistence* is an example of the type of information held in the iconic store.

Short-Term Memory

Our short-term store holds information for matters of seconds and, occasionally, for up to a minute or two. Even though you might look at something you re-

The persistence of visual memory is what makes "writing" with a sparkler possible.

member after a day as involving only recall over the short term, for psychologists the *short-term* store is responsible for the storage of information only for much briefer periods of time (up to a couple of minutes). When you look up a phone number in the phone book and try to remember it long enough to enter it you are using the short-term store. Why do we forget such simple information so easily, and how can we keep ourselves from forgetting it? In discussing the short-term store, we consider next the encoding, storage, and retrieval of information.

Encoding of Information in Short-Term Memory

When you need to remember a phone number, you may say it back to yourself, perhaps even several times. What you are trying to do is encode the information in the phone number into your short-term memory. When you encode information into short-term memory, what kind of code do you use? A landmark experiment by R. Conrad (1964) successfully addressed this question. Conrad presented research participants visually with several series of six letters at the rate of 0.75 second per letter. The letters used in the various lists were B, C, F, M, N, P, S, T, V, and X. Participants had to write down each list of six letters, in the order given, immediately after the letters were presented. Conrad was interested particularly in the kinds of recall errors people made. The pattern of errors was clear. Despite the fact that letters were presented *visually*, errors tended to be based on *acoustic confusability*. In other words, instead of recalling the letters they were supposed to recall, people in the study substituted letters that sounded like the correct letters. Thus, they were likely to confuse F for S, T for C, B for V, P for B, and so on. In an experiment based on acoustically similar and dissimilar words versus semantically similar and dissimilar words (words that have similar or different meanings), Alan Baddeley (1966) clinched the argument that short-term storage relies primarily on an acoustic rather than a *semantic code*. However, information can also be stored over the short term in other forms, such as through visual images (Baddeley, 1992) or even through a semantic code (Shulman, 1970).

Short-Term Storage and Forgetting

Why does information retained in the short-term store not remain there indefinitely? How do we keep it in and how do we lose it? We consider in turn what we know about the answers to each of these questions. Although psychologists may disagree about how we forget information from the short-term store, they have reached fairly widespread consensus as to how we retain it. One strategy we use for keeping information in short-term

Need to remember that number the operator just gave you? You will use short-term memory encoding strategies.

memory, or for moving information into long-term memory, is by repeating the information over and over, a process known as **rehearsal.** (We discuss transferring information into long-term memory later in this chapter.) Rehearsal can be of two types. In *maintenance rehearsal,* one merely repeats words over and over to oneself, without giving much thought to these words. In *elaborative rehearsal,* one attempts to reflect mindfully on the words and their meanings as one repeats them. For example, one might form interactive images relating the words to each other (e.g., if two words are *table* and *food,* by imagining food sitting on a table).

Rehearsal comes naturally to almost all of us as adults—so much so that we may believe we have always done it. We have not. The major difference between the memory of younger and of older children (as well as adults) is not in basic mechanisms, but in learned strategies, such as rehearsal (Flavell & Wellman, 1977). In particular, younger children, and especially preschoolers, lack *metamemory skills*—that is, understanding and control of their own memory abilities. Older children and adults understand that to retain words in the short-term store they need to rehearse; younger children do not understand this fact. Another consideration is that for rehearsal to be effective, the person must be actively engaged in the process of trying to encode and store the information; mere repeated exposure to words does not constitute effective rehearsal (Tulving, 1966).

Interference.   Rehearsal strategies enable us to retain information; what processes lead us to forget? Why do we forget a phone number or the names of people at a

party after a brief period of time? Several theories have been proposed as to why we forget information from the short-term store. The two most well-known theories are interference theory and decay theory. **Interference** refers to information that competes with the information an individual is trying to store in memory, thereby causing the individual to forget that information. **Decay** refers simply to forgetting that occurs as a result of the passage of time.

One of the most famous experimental paradigms in the study of human memory is called the Brown–Peterson paradigm, after its originators, John Brown (1958) and Lloyd Peterson and Margaret Peterson (1959). Both the Brown and the Peterson and Peterson studies were taken as evidence for the existence of a short-term store and also for the **interference theory** of forgetting, according to which information is forgotten because it is displaced by competing information, which disrupts and displaces the information that the individual had tried to store in memory originally. Consider the experiment of Peterson and Peterson (1959).

The Petersons asked their research participants to recall strings of three letters, called *trigrams,* at intervals of 3, 6, 9, 12, 15, or 18 seconds after the presentation of the last letter. The Petersons used only consonants, so that the trigrams would not be easily pronounceable—for example, "K-B-F." Figure 7-3 shows percentages of correct recalls after the various intervals of time. Why does recall decline so rapidly? Because after the oral presentation of each trigram, the Petersons asked their participants to count backward

Figure 7–3
PERCENTAGE OF RECALL FROM SHORT-TERM MEMORY.
In the study by Lloyd Peterson and Margaret Peterson, research participants were unable to use rehearsal to keep information in short-term memory. As a consequence, their ability to recall three consonants (a trigram) rapidly declined as the delay between presentation and recall increased from 3 to 18 seconds. Some have suggested that retroactive interference may have caused the rapid decline in recall.

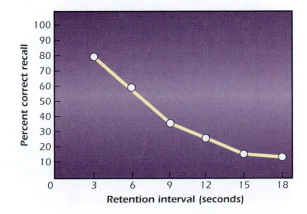

by threes from a three-digit number spoken immediately after the trigram. The purpose of having the participants count backward was to prevent them from rehearsing during the *retention interval*—the time between the presentation of the last letter and the start of the recall phase of the experimental trial. Clearly, the trigram is almost completely forgotten after just 18 seconds if participants are not allowed to rehearse it.

At least two kinds of interference figure prominently in memory theory and research: retroactive interference and proactive interference. **Retroactive interference** (or retroactive inhibition) occurs when interfering information is presented *after*, rather than *before*, presentation of the information that is to be remembered. An example of retroactive interference would be studying for a psychology test, then studying for a biology test, and then taking the psychology test. One might find, to one's dismay, that biology facts kept coming to mind but that the psychology facts did not! **Proactive interference** (or proactive inhibition) occurs when the interfering information is presented *before*, rather than *after*, presentation of the information that is to be remembered. (See Figure 7-4.) An example of proactive interference would be studying for a biology test, then studying for a psychology test, then taking the psychology test. One might find, in this case, that the studying for the biology test interfered with one's recall of the material for the psychology test. Or, as described in this chapter's In the Lab of . . . box, violent television

programming may actually interfere with memory for the message advertisers are trying to get across.

Decay. **Decay theory** asserts that information is forgotten because it gradually disappears over time, rather than because the information is displaced by other information. Thus, whereas interference theory views one piece of information as knocking out another, decay theory views the original piece of information as gradually disappearing unless something is done to keep it intact. There is some evidence for decay (Reitman, 1974).

Decay theory is exceedingly difficult to test because it is difficult to prevent research participants from intentionally or even inadvertently rehearsing—and thereby maintaining in memory the given information. If participants are prevented from rehearsing, however, the possibility of interference arises: The task used to prevent rehearsal may interfere retroactively with the original memory (Reitman, 1971, 1974). Try, for example, not to think of white elephants as you read the next page. When instructed not to think about them, it is actually quite difficult not to, even if you try to follow the instructions.

To conclude, evidence exists for both interference and decay in the short-term store. The evidence for decay is not airtight, but it is certainly suggestive. The evidence of interference is rather strong, but at present, it is unclear as to the extent to which the interference is retroactive, proactive, or both.

We have discussed how information gets encoded into short-term memory, how it can be kept there, and how it may be lost. But what about the information that is kept in short-term memory? How much information can we hold in the short-term store? How can we retrieve it?

The Capacity of the Short-Term Store

Try to remember this string of 21 digits: 101001000100001000100. It is extremely difficult to hold so many single digits in short-term memory. Now try chunking the digits into larger units, such as 10, 100, 1000, 10000, 1000, and 100. You will probably find you can easily reproduce the 21 digits as 6 items. In a classic article, George Miller (1956) noted that our short-term memory capacity appears to be about 7 items, plus or minus 2. An item can be something simple such as a digit, or something more complex, such as a word. Remembering more complex units, or **chunks** (a collection of separate items into a single grouping), effectively increases the amount of total information we can hold, despite the seven-item limit.

Of course, as the preceding discussion has suggested, our seven-item capacity can be limited still

Figure 7–4
PROACTIVE INTERFERENCE AND SHORT-TERM MEMORY.
Geoffrey Keppel and Benton Underwood demonstrated that proactive interference also affects recall, as shown by the decline in recall after increasing numbers of trigrams were presented. The effect of proactive interference increased over increasingly long retention intervals.

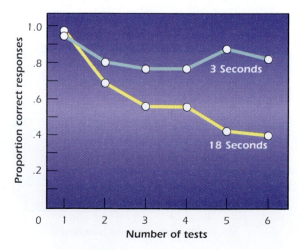

Television Violence and Memory for Advertisements

Brad Bushman, *Iowa State University*

As a researcher who had conducted research on the harmful effects of TV violence, I was concerned that none of the data uncovered in research on the perils of TV violence had affected network and cable programmers' attitudes about putting violent content on the air. So, I decided to approach the topic from a different angle—by seeing how violent content on television affected memory for advertised products.

About 60% of the programs shown on television contain violence.[1] By the time the average American child graduates from elementary school, he or she will have seen more than 8,000 murders and more than 100,000 other assorted acts of violence on network television (Huston et al., 1992).

CBS programming chief Jeff Sagansky hit the nail on the head when he said: "The number one priority in television is not to transmit quality programming to viewers, but to deliver consumers to advertisers. We aren't going to get rid of violence until we get rid of advertisers. The advertiser wants something exciting with which to get the audience" (Kim, 1994). However, advertisers not only want to draw a lot of viewers, they also want viewers to remember their ads.

There is a large body of research evidence indicating that mood can affect memory and that viewing violence makes people angry. I knew of at least two reasons why anger might impair memory. First, the angry mood induced by violent TV programs might prime or activate aggressive thoughts that interfere with rehearsal of the ads. Second, angry people might try to repair their bad moods, which takes a lot of effort. During the time that advertisers hope viewers are absorbing ads, viewers might actually be focusing on themselves, trying to calm the anger brought on by what they have just seen. They might think of more positive things, talk to others, eat, or drink.

How We Set Up the Study

Many violent TV programs are exciting, arousing, action-adventure programs. It is difficult to know whether violence, arousal, or both influence memory. To get around this confounding problem, I selected violent and nonviolent TV programs that were equally exciting and arousing. From a pool of 52 videotaped TV programs, I chose 10 programs (5 violent, 5 nonviolent) that did not differ in how exciting, boring, arousing, and involving people thought they were. I showed some of the programs to a separate group of participants while we measured their blood pressure and heart rate. No differences were found between the violent and nonviolent programs on any of the variables we measured. The ads were for products with broad market appeal (i.e., laundry detergent, mouth rinse, glue). The same ads were embedded in violent and nonviolent programs.

I conducted three studies involving a total of 720 participants (360 men, 360 women) (Bushman, 1998). The procedure was similar in the three studies. Participants were told that the purpose of the study was to rate TV programs for a National Consumer Research Project. By random assignment, participants watched either a violent or nonviolent TV program. After watching the TV program, they completed a mood questionnaire and then rated the TV program. Next, participants received a surprise memory test. They tried to recall the brand names of the products advertised and everything they could remember about the ads. For each product (e.g., laundry detergent), participants also saw six slides—one showed the advertised brand (e.g, Wisk) and the other five showed distracter brands (e.g., Cheer, Fab, Gain, New Era, Tide). They had to choose which of the six brands was in the ad.

Participants also reported the number of hours per week they spent watching various types of television programs, including violent ones. We included this measure because we wanted to know if preferences for TV violence influenced the results.[2]

Our Results

In all studies, TV violence impaired memory for ads. If the ads were embedded in a violent program, people recalled fewer brands, recalled fewer details from the ads, and recognized fewer brands from the slides than if the ads were embedded in a nonviolent program. The violent programs made people angry. The more angry people were, the less they remembered about the ads.

References

Bushman, B. J. (1998). Effects of television violence on memory of commercial messages. *Journal of Experimental Psychology: Applied, 4,* 291–307.

Huston, A. C., Donnerstein, E., Fairchild, H., Feshbach, N. D., Katz, P. A., Murray, J. P., Rubinstein, E. A., Wilcox, B. L., & Zuckerman, D. (1992). *Big world, small screen: The role of television in American society.* Lincoln, NE: University of Nebraska Press.

Kim, S. J. (1994, April). "Viewer discretion is advised": A structural approach to the issue of television violence. *University of Pennsylvania Law Review, 142,* 1383–1441.

 Find out more about this topic at
www.harcourtcollege.com/psych/ishm

[1] This estimate was obtained from three very large content analyses: (a) National Television Violence Study (1996). *National television violence study* (Vol. 1). Thousand Oaks, CA: Sage; (b) National Television Violence Study (1997). *National television violence study* (Vol. 2). Studio City, CA: Mediascope; and (c) National Television Violence Study (1998). *National television violence study* (Vol. 3). Santa Barbara, CA: The Center for Communication and Social Policy, University of California, Santa Barbara.
[2] Participants also reported whether they had seen the film from which the clip had been taken, and whether they had seen the commercials imbedded within the film clip. However, neither of these measures influenced the results.

further by any delay or any interference in recall. Cognitive psychologists have sought a way to measure the degree to which delay and interference can limit this seven-item capacity. One method for estimating the capacity of the short-term store under delay or interference conditions draws inferences from a **serial-position curve,** which represents the probability that each of a series of given items will be recalled, given the order in which the items were presented in a list, or their respective *serial positions.*

Suppose you are presented with a list of words and are asked to recall them. For example, say the following list of words once to yourself, and then, immediately thereafter, try to recall all the words in any order, without looking back at them: *table, cloud, book, tree, shirt, cat, light, bench, chalk.* If you are like most people, you will find that your recall of words is best for items at and near the end of the list, second best for items near the beginning of the list, and poorest for items in the middle of the list. A typical serial-position curve is shown in Figure 7-5.

Superior recall of words that occur at or near the end of a list of words is a **recency effect.** Superior recall of words that occur at or near the beginning of a list of words is a **primacy effect.** Recall of words from the beginning and middle of the list is due primarily to the effects of the long-term store, considered later in this chapter, and recall of words from the end of the list is due primarily to the effects of the short-term store. The recency effect is due to the participants' dumping out the contents of their short-term store just as soon as they are given the signal to recall. The serial-position curve, incidentally, makes sense in terms of interference theory. Words at the end of the list are subject to proactive but not to retroactive interference; words at the beginning of the list are subject to retroactive but not to proactive interference;

and words in the middle of the list are subject to both. Thus, recall would be expected to be poorest in the middle of the list, as indeed it is.

Another way of broadening our understanding of short-term memory is to consider also the cultural contexts within which people are immersed. For example, Rumjahn Hoosain and others have shown that Hong Kong undergraduates have a mean digit span of 9.9. That is, they can store 9.9 numerals in their short-term memory. This span is a little more than two digits greater than the span reported for speakers of several Western languages. Before we infer any far-reaching conclusions regarding the arithmetic abilities of Asians, however, it may be important to consider a property of the Chinese language. Readers can read numerals more quickly in Mandarin than in German, for example, and speakers can pronounce numbers in Cantonese more rapidly than in English (M. H. Bond, 1986; Hoosain & Salili, 1987). The linguistic differences may affect encoding.

Retrieval

Once we encode and store information in the short-term store, how do we retrieve that information? A classic series of experiments on this issue was done by Saul Sternberg (1966). The phenomenon he studied is short-term **memory scanning,** whereby an individual checks what is contained, usually in short-term memory.

Sternberg's basic paradigm was simple. He gave participants a short list, containing from one to six digits, which they were expected to be able to hold in short-term storage. After a brief pause, a test digit was flashed on a screen, and participants had to say whether this digit had appeared in the set they had been asked to memorize.

Psychologists use information-processing models to specify the stages of processing a person must go through from start to finish when undertaking a task such as the one Sternberg proposed. In the case of retrieval from the short-term memory store, a fundamental question when building such a model is whether items are retrieved all at once or sequentially. If we retrieve the items sequentially, the question then arises, do we retrieve all of the items, regardless of the task, or do we stop retrieving items as soon as an item seems to accomplish the task?

Parallel processing refers to cognitive manipulation of multiple operations simultaneously, so that the items stored in short-term memory are retrieved all at once, not one at a time. **Serial processing** refers to the cognitive manipulation of operations, in which each operation is executed one at a time in a series. In the digit-recall task, the digits would be retrieved in succession, rather than all at once. If information

Figure 7–5

IDEALIZED SERIAL POSITION CURVE. *Most people recall items at the end of a list (greatest recall) and at the beginning of a list (second-greatest recall) much more easily than items in the middle of a list (least recall).*

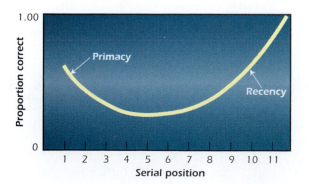

processing is serial, then there are two ways to gain access to the stimuli: exhaustive or self-terminating processing. *Exhaustive serial processing* implies that the individual seeks to retrieve an item stored in memory by checking the item being sought against all of the possible items that are presented, even if a match is found partway through the list. Here, the person always checks the test digit against *all* digits in the positive set, even if a match is found partway through the list. *Self-terminating serial processing* implies that the individual seeks to retrieve a particular item stored in memory by checking each of the items that is presented against the item being sought until the individual reaches the item being sought. Here, the person checks the test digit against only those digits that are needed in order to make a response. Sternberg (1966) found his data supported an exhaustive serial model of comparisons, and that comparisons took roughly 38 milliseconds (0.038 seconds) apiece. Subsequent research, however, has presented alternative interpretations of the data (e.g., Townsend, 1971).

Long-Term Memory

When we talk about memory in our everyday interactions, we are usually talking about the long-term store, which is where we keep memories that stay with us over long periods of time, sometimes indefinitely. How does information get from the short-term store to the long-term store? One method is through rehearsal of information. Another is by deliberately attempting actively to understand information. Perhaps an even more important way that we accomplish this transfer is by making connections or associations between the new information and what we already know and understand—by integrating the new data into our existing stored information. As we did for the short-term store, we will examine the three processes of encoding, storage, and retrieval in the long-term store.

Forms of Encoding in Long-Term Memory

Information in the long-term store seems to be primarily *semantically encoded*—that is, encoded by the meanings of words. However, we can also hold visual and acoustic information in the long-term store. Thus, there is considerable flexibility in the way we store information in long-term memory. One way to show semantic encoding is to use test words that bear a semantic relationship to other test words. William Bousfield (1953), for example, had research participants learn a list of 60 words that included 15 animals, 15 professions, 15 vegetables, and 15 names of people. The words were presented in a random order, so that members of the various categories were thoroughly

Once we have stored information in long-term memory, that information can be recalled again many years later. Through long-term memory, this teacher can vividly describe many of her childhood experiences to her students, such as the hardships she faced when she had to walk 10 miles uphill to school.

intermixed. After participants heard the words, they were asked to recall the items in any order they wished. Bousfield then analyzed the order of output of the recalled words. The participants recalled successive words from the same category more frequently than would be expected by chance. It thus appears that people were remembering words by grouping them into categories.

Encoding of information also can be achieved visually. Nancy Frost (1972), for example, presented participants with 16 drawings of objects, including four items of clothing, four animals, four vehicles, and four items of furniture. Frost manipulated not only the semantic category, but also the visual category. The drawings differed in visual orientation, with four angled to the left, four angled to the right, four horizontal, and four vertical. Items were presented in random order, and participants had to recall them freely. Participants' output orders showed effects of both semantic and visual categories, suggesting that people were encoding visual as well as semantic information.

Even acoustic information can be encoded in the long-term store (T. O. Nelson & Rothbart, 1972). Given all the different ways in which information can be encoded in long-term memory, under what circumstances do we use each form of encoding?

Circumstances of Encoding

We store memories both verbally and visually in ways that are complementary (Paivio, 1971, 1986). The form of representation used depends on both the form of presentation (verbal or nonverbal) and the imagery value of the stimuli to be remembered. Some words are highly concrete and also high in imagery value, such as *bluejay*, *lemon*, *radio*, and *pencil*. They lend themselves to visual representation, even if presented verbally. In contrast, words such as *truth*, *kindness*, and *joy* are less likely to be stored visually, simply because we have no images that we more or less uniformly associate with these words.

Encoding Meaning.   What about the meaning underlying a relationship among concepts? John Anderson and Gordon Bower (1973) proposed a *propositional* view, according to which both images and verbal statements are stored in terms of their *deep meanings*—that is, as propositions, not as specific images or statements. Herbert Clark and William Chase (1972) asked their participants to compare verbal representations of situations (e.g., "The star is above the plus") to pictorial representations of these situations (i.e., a picture of a star above the plus). Half the time, the verbal and pictorial representations corresponded, and half the time they did not (e.g., the picture would show a plus above a star rather than the verbally depicted star above the plus). Clark and Chase found that people were able to do such comparisons very efficiently. On the basis of their data, Clark and Chase proposed a fairly simple model of how both the verbal form of the statement and pictorial form could be encoded into a deeper propositional form. Colin MacLeod, Earl Hunt, and Nancy Mathews (1978) obtained persuasive evidence suggesting that we can use either a propositional or an imaginal representation.

Representing Images.   Stephen Kosslyn has done a number of experiments to demonstrate the use of imaginal representations in memory. In one of the more interesting experiments (Kosslyn, Ball, & Reiser, 1978), research participants were shown a map of an imaginary island, which you can see in Figure 7-6. The participants studied the map until they could reproduce it accurately from memory, placing the locations of each of the six objects in the map no more than a quarter of an inch from their correct locations. Once the memorization phase of the experiment was completed, the critical phase began.

Research participants were instructed that, upon hearing the name of an object read to them, they should picture the map, mentally scan directly to the mentioned object, and press a key as soon as they arrived at the location of the named object. This procedure was repeated a number of times, with the participants mentally moving between various pairs of objects on successive trials. The experimenter kept track of response times on each trial—how long it took to scan from one object to the next. An almost perfect linear relation was found between the distance separating successive pairs of objects in the mental map and the amount of time it took people to press

Figure 7-6
IMAGE-BASED ENCODING IN LONG-TERM MEMORY.
This map of an imaginary island shows six target objects, such as a hut, a tree, and a lake. Research participants learned to draw such maps from memory, accurately placing each of the six objects within one-quarter inch of their correct locations.

the button. In other words, people seem to have encoded the map in the form of an image and actually to have scanned that image as needed.

Kosslyn (Kosslyn & Koenig, 1992) has also found some intriguing effects of image size. Look at the rabbit and the honeybee in Figure 7-7. Now close your eyes and picture them both in your mind. Now imagine only the honeybee and determine the color of its head. Do you notice yourself having to take time to zoom in to "see" the detailed features of the honeybee? Now look at the rabbit and the elephant and picture them both in your mind. Now close your eyes and look only at the elephant. Imagine walking toward the elephant, watching it as it gets closer to you. Do you find there comes a point when you can no longer see all of the elephant? Most people find that the image of the elephant seems to overflow the size of their image space.

People also may use mental images to store geographical information in memory (Stevens & Coupe, 1978). For example, many people have stored in memory a rough map of the United States. Which city is farther west: Reno, Nevada, or San Diego, California? Most people believe San Diego to be west of Reno. Their map looks something like that in Panel A

Figure 7–7

IMAGE SIZE.   *Particpants in Stephen Kosslyn's study tested the limits of their mental imagery by picturing the rabbit with the honeybee and then imagining the rabbit with the elephant. When picturing the rabbit and the bee, research participants had to zoom in to see details of the honeybee. When picturing the rabbit and the elephant, the image of the elephant overflowed their mental image space as they imagined approaching it.*

of Figure 7-8. Actually, however, Reno is west of San Diego, as shown in the correct map in Panel B of the figure. The kinds of errors people make in this task suggest the use of imaginal representations.

As these studies show, we seem to encode information in memory by using both propositional and imaginal representations. *Dual-trace theory* captures this dual representation, although other theories explain it in different ways. The question we presently need to address is when we use which representation.

We rely heavily on our long-term store, in which we keep the information we need to function in our daily lives. We have seen how we encode information, but how do we store it?

Storage and Forgetting in LTM

Many factors affect our ability to store or to forget information, including the pace at which the information is learned, rehearsal strategies, organization of information, and both retroactive and proactive interference.

Time and Pace During Learning.   Suppose you have to study vocabulary words for a French test. You have 240 vocabulary words to learn, and you can allocate 4 hours to study. You could budget your time in several ways. One would be to study each word once for 1 minute. Another would be to study each word twice for 30 seconds each time. What strategy will help you remember the words best?

If your four available hours are all in one block of time, it does not matter which strategy you use. According to the **total-time hypothesis,** which is widely accepted as an assumption (at least in a limited form by many researchers), the degree to which a person is able to learn information by storing it in memory depends

Figure 7–8

ACCURACY OF IMAGES IN STORED MEMORY.   *Maps locating Reno, Nevada, and San Diego, California: Most people believe San Diego to be west of Reno, so their mental map looks something like the map in Panel A. Actually, however, Reno is west of San Diego, as shown in the correct map in Panel B.*

(a)

(b)

on the total amount of time spent studying the material in a given session, rather than on the way in which the time is apportioned within a given session.

If you distribute your time across a series of sessions, however, it becomes another matter, because the temporal pacing of learning can affect storage or forgetting of information. Harry Bahrick and Elizabeth Phelps (1987) found an important principle of memory while studying people's long-term recall of Spanish vocabulary words learned 8 years earlier. People tend to learn better when they acquire knowledge via **distributed learning** (i.e., learning that is spaced across sessions over time) rather than via **massed learning** (i.e., learning that is crammed together all at once). The greater the distribution of learning trials over time, the more people remembered. This principle is important to remember in studying. You will recall more, on average, if you distribute your learning of subject matter, rather than trying to mass or cram it all into a short period of time.

No matter how you divide your study time, one of the strategies you will probably use to memorize class information is rehearsal. Does the quality of your rehearsal also affect the effectiveness of your memory?

Rehearsal. In the discussion of short-term memory, we saw that rehearsal clearly helps maintain information in memory. Rehearsal also seems to facilitate the transfer of information from short-term to long-term memory. How you rehearse the information, though, influences how effectively you retain it. Going back to the example of studying Spanish vocabulary words, you could simply repeat the items over and over again, or you could elaborate the items in a way that makes them more meaningful to you. That is, you could relate the items to what you already know or connect them to one another and thereby make them more memorable. (Recall the effects of chunking, in which a person can chunk many smaller units of information into larger units of integrated information in order to remember the information more easily.) Elaborating information during rehearsal, rather than merely repeating it, can greatly increase the effectiveness of the rehearsal, especially when one studies for a test. One way to elaborate information is to organize it.

Organization of Information: Semantic and Episodic Memory

How do we organize information in memory? Probably the most illuminating studies addressing this question have looked at information in **semantic memory,** which is our general world knowledge—our memory for facts that are not unique to us and that are not recalled in any particular temporal context (Tulving, 1972). For example, my knowledge that the long cylindrical object outside my window is a tree trunk or

that Napoleon was a French general are examples of information stored in my semantic memory. Semantic memory is distinguished from **episodic memory,** the memory of personally experienced events or episodes, which is the kind of memory we use when we learn meaningless lists of words. For example, if I need to remember that I saw Hector Gonzalez in the lunchroom yesterday, I must draw on an episodic memory; however, if I need to remember the name of the person I now see in the lunchroom again today ("Hector Gonzalez"), I must draw on a semantic memory. There is no particular time tag associated with the name of that individual as being Hector, but there is a time tag associated with my having seen him at lunch yesterday. It is not clear that semantic and episodic memory are two distinct systems, although they do appear to function, at times, in different ways.

Semantic memory operates on **concepts**—ideas to which various characteristics may be attached and to which various other ideas may be connected. People mentally organize concepts in some way, and researchers have tried to make memory processing more readily understood by envisioning an organizational structure of memory. Psychologists often use the term **schema** to describe a cognitive framework for organizing associated concepts, including information and ideas, based on previous experiences. For example, a schema for having lunch at a nice restaurant might associate all the things you have personally experienced regarding lunch at such a restaurant, as well as what you have learned from other people and from other information sources regarding lunch. The schema might include things like entering through the door, having a host or hostess seat you, having your water glass filled up, being handed a menu, being told the day's specials, and so forth.

Interference in the Long-Term Store

We have seen that interference affects short-term memory; it also plays an important role in long-term memory. Recall that *retroactive interference* is caused by activity that occurs *after* we try to store something in memory, but before we try to retrieve that thing from memory. In contrast, *proactive interference* occurs when the interfering material occurs *before* the learning of the material.

In other situations, however, prior learning can cause *positive transfer*—that is, old information's causing greater ease of learning and remembering of new information. For example, the prior experience of learning to drive a standard-shift car may offer positive transfer when we are learning to drive an automatic-shift car; most of the skills and knowledge of the former aid in learning the latter. Often, prior learning helps in some ways and hurts in others. When it hurts, it results in *negative transfer*—that is, the experiencing

*"Waiter, I'd like to order, unless I've eaten,
in which case bring me the check."*

of old information's producing interference in learning and remembering new material. For example, someone who has learned first to drive a standard-shift car may put his foot on the brake in an effort to shift gears, nearly putting everyone in the front seat through the windshield.

Once we learn to drive a standard-shift, we will probably remember the skill for years, maybe the rest of our life. The remarkable duration of long-term memory suggests the following questions: How much information can we hold in the long-term store, and how long does the information last?

The Capacity of the Long-Term Store

Psychologists do not know the capacity of long-term storage, nor do they know how they would find out. Although they can design experiments to tax the limits of the short-term store, they do not know how to tax the limits of the long-term store and thereby find out its capacity. Some theorists have suggested that the capacity of the long-term store is infinite, at least in practical terms (Hintzman, 1978).

It turns out that the question of how long information lasts in the long-term store is not very easily answerable either because, at present, psychologists have no proof that there is an absolute outer limit to how long information can be stored. Researchers have found evidence in support of the durability of long-term memories. An interesting study on memory for names and faces was conducted by Harry Bahrick, Phyllis Bahrick, and Roy Wittlinger (1975). They tested research participants' memories for names and photographs of their

Prior learning can help us learn new things more easily, but sometimes negative transfer occurs. Memory for these training wheels may make learning to ride without them more difficult for a while.

high school classmates. Even after 25 years, people tended to recognize names as belonging to classmates rather than to outsiders, and recognition memory for matching names to graduation photos was quite high.

As you might expect, recall of names showed a higher rate of forgetting. Names appear to be harder to retrieve than are faces. What, in general, makes some memories harder to retrieve than others? Let's now consider retrieval of information from memory.

Retrieval

> But this mysterious power that binds our life together has its own vagaries and interruptions. It sometimes occurs that Memory has a personality of its own, and volunteers or refuses its information at its will, not at mine.
> —Ralph Waldo Emerson,
> *Natural History of Intellect*

If, as some believe, nothing is ever lost from long-term memory, then why do we sometimes have trouble remembering things? It is important to distinguish between **availability,** the existence of given information in long-term memory, and **accessibility,** the ease of gaining access to information that has been stored in long-term memory. Memory performance depends on the accessibility of the information to be remembered.

The phenomenon of availability versus accessibility of memories becomes particularly important in the case of a phenomenon that has recently become among the most controversial in psychology—the recovery of repressed memories, particularly adults' memories of sexual abuse suffered as children. The main controversy is whether the phenomenon is a genuine one, and if so, how frequently it occurs.

Problems of sexual abuse of children have always been with us. For the most part, the occurrence of such abuse has been considered to be more or less rare. Recently, some books have been published—largely for the mass market rather than for psychologists—arguing that such abuse is much more common than anyone thought. According to these books, the reason that abuse has been so little reported is that many victims repress their memories of it—in other words, memories are available, but largely inaccessible. Using a variety of techniques, some therapists have claimed that they are able to help clients recover these repressed memories. But the validity of these memories remains in serious doubt (Bowers & Farvolden, 1996; Ceci & Loftus, 1994; Lindsay & Read, 1994; Loftus & Ketcham, 1994; Pennebaker & Memon, 1996).

Studies of retrieval from the long-term store are often dated back to Hermann Ebbinghaus (1902, 1885/1964), who tested his own memory using nonsense syllables. The idea of using such syllables was that they would have no meaning attached to them, which should have made it possible to study pure recall phenomena without the influence of prior associations and meanings. There are two problems with this logic, however. The first is that people sometimes make up their own associations. The second is that, arguably, we should be interested in how people learn material of the kind they actually need to recall in their everyday lives, not material that they will never have any occasion to learn.

Cue Effectiveness and Encoding Specificity. The way information is presented can make a difference in how likely a person is to recall information. Associations, or cues of any kind, can substantially aid recall, especially if the cues are meaningful to the individual. Timo Mantyla (1986) found that when research participants created their own retrieval cues, they were able to remember, almost without errors, lists of up to 500 and even 600 words. For each word on a list, the participants were asked to generate another word (the cue) that, to them, was an appropriate description or property of the target word. Later, they were given a list of their cue words and were asked to recall the target word. Mantyla found that cues were most helpful when they were both *compatible* with the target word and *distinctive*, in that they would not tend to generate a large number of related words. For example, if you are given the word *coat*, then *jacket* might be both compatible and distinctive as a cue; however, if you came up with the word *wool* as a cue, it might make you think of a number of words, such as *fabric* and *sheep*, which were not the target word.

The associations we assign to material we remember are not always generated entirely by the material itself. External contexts may also affect our ability to recall information. We appear to be better able to recall information when we are in the same context as we were when we learned the material. For example, we are likely to do better on a test if we are tested in the same room that we learn material than if we are tested in a different room. In one experiment, 16 underwater divers were asked to learn a list of 40 unrelated words, either while they were on shore or while they were 20 feet beneath the surface (Godden & Baddeley, 1975). Later, the divers were asked to recall the words either when in the same environment as where they had learned them or in the other environment. Recall was better when it occurred in the same place as the learning. In another study (Butler & Rovee-Collier, 1989), researchers have found that even infants demonstrate context effects on memory. When given an opportunity to kick a mobile in the same context as that in which they first had learned to kick it or in a different context, they kicked more strongly in the same context.

Even our moods and states of consciousness may provide a context for encoding and later retrieving memories. That is, those things that we encode during a particular mood or state of consciousness we may retrieve more readily when we are in the same state again (Baddeley, 1989; G. H. Bower, 1983). For example, Baddeley (1989) has suggested that a factor in maintaining depression may be that the depressed person can more readily retrieve memories of previous sad experiences, which may further the continuance of the depression. (For other cognitive views of depression, see chapter 17.) If psychologists or others can intervene to prevent this vicious cycle, the person may begin to feel happier, leading to retrieval of happier memories, thus further relieving the depression, and so on. Perhaps the folk wisdom to "think happy thoughts" is not entirely unfounded.

The results of the various experiments on retrieval suggest that the way in which items are encoded has a strong effect on the way items are retrieved and how well items are retrieved. Endel Tulving and Donald Thomson (1973) have referred to this relation as **encoding specificity**—that is, the specific way of representing information as it is placed into memory as it affects the specific way in which the information may be retrieved later. To summarize, retrieval interacts strongly with encoding. If you study for a test and want to recall the information well at the time of testing, organize the information you are studying in a way that will help you to recall it.

The Constructive Nature of Memory

It appears that we recall meaningful information more readily than meaningless information, and that sometimes we even create the meaning that we later recall. In fact, it appears that memory is not just **reconstructive,** whereby the individual stores in memory some information about events or facts exactly as the events or facts took place; it is also **constructive,** whereby the individual actually builds memories based on experience and expectations, such that existing schemas may affect the way in which new information is stored.

Frederick Bartlett (1932) was an early researcher interested in whether memory for material is affected by previous (e.g., culturally based) understandings. Bartlett had his participants in Great Britain learn what was to them a strange and difficult-to-understand North American Indian legend called "The War of the Ghosts." The text is depicted in its entirety in Figure 7-9a. He found that people distorted their recall to make the story more understandable. In other words, their prior knowledge and expectations had a substantial effect on their recall. Bartlett suggested that people bring into a memory task their already existing schemas, which affect the way they recall what they learn. This result has recently been replicated (Bergman & Roediger, in press). Figure 7-9b shows a typical student's recall of The War of the Ghosts.

Some later cross-cultural work (Tripathi, 1979) also illustrates the importance of schemas as a framework for constructive memory. For example, Indian children were asked to read several stories from *The Panchatantra*, a collection of ancient Hindi fables and folk tales. The stories contain quaint names and unusual settings that are unfamiliar to contemporary Indian schoolchildren. Subsequently, the children were asked to recall the stories. Over time, the children added words and sentences not originally presented in the stories, and their reconstructions generally modified the stories from unfamiliar to more familiar forms, as well as from complex to simple forms.

When we are recalling a given experience, we often associate the degree to which the remembered experience seems vivid and richly detailed with the

Psychology in Everyday Life

Flashbulb Memories

An important factor that seems to increase the likelihood that we will recall a particular experience over other experiences is the emotional intensity of that experience. Unfortunately, however, such intensity does not ensure the accuracy of our recall either. An oft-studied form of vivid memory is the **flashbulb memory**—a recollection of an event that is so emotionally powerful that the recollection is highly vivid and richly detailed, as

if it were indelibly preserved on film (R. Brown & Kulik, 1977). Memories of the assassination of President John F. Kennedy, as well as memories of the attack on Pearl Harbor or even of the explosion of the space shuttle *Challenger*, have been studied as examples of common flashbulb memories. Flashbulb memories may be preferentially recalled because their recall is mediated by the hormones that are released in response to arousal.

Thus, the experiencing of strong emotion when viewing important events may enhance later recall of these events. Surprisingly, although people feel certain of their memories of the events, and the vividness and detailed texture of their memories seem to support their accuracy, it turns out that these remembered events are often recalled inaccurately (D. Schacter, 1996).

(a) Original Indian myth

The War of the Ghosts

One night two young men from Egulac went down to the river to hunt seals, and while they were there it became foggy and calm. Then they heard war-cries, and they thought: "Maybe this is a war-party." They escaped to the shore, and hid behind a log. Now canoes came up, and they heard the noise of paddles, and saw one canoe coming up to them. There were five men in the canoe, and they said:

"What do you think? We wish to take you along. We are going up the river to make war on the people."

One of the young men said, " I have no arrows."

"Arrows are in the canoe," they said.

"I will not go along. I might be killed. My relatives do not know where I have gone. But you," he said, turning to the other, "may go with them."

So one of the young men went, but the other returned home.

And the warriors went on up the river to a town on the other side of Kalama. The people came down to the water, and they began to fight, and many were killed. But presently the young man heard one of the warriors say: "Quick, let us go home; that Indian has been hit." Now he thought: "Oh, they are ghosts." He did not feel sick, but they said he had been shot.

So the canoes went back to Egulac, and the young man went ashore to his house, and made a fire. And he told everybody and said: "Behold I accompanied the ghosts, and we went to fight. Many of our fellows were killed, and many of those who attacked us were killed. They said I was hit, and I did not feel sick."

He told it all, and then he became quiet. When the sun rose he fell down. Something black came out of his mouth. His face became contorted. The people jumped up and cried.

He was dead.

(b) Typical recall by a student in England

The War of the Ghosts

Two men from Edulac went fishing. While thus occupied by the river they heard a noise in the distance.

"It sounds like a cry," said one, and presently there appeared some in canoes who invited them to join the party of their adventure. One of the young men refused to go, on the ground of family ties, but the other offered to go.

"But there are no arrows," he said.

"The arrows are in the boat," was the reply.

He thereupon took his place, while his friend returned home. The party paddled up the river to Kaloma, and began to land on the banks of the river. The enemy came rushing upon them, and some sharp fighting ensued. Presently someone was injured, and the cry was raised that the enemy were ghosts.

The party returned down the stream, and the young man arrived home feeling none the worse for his experience. The next morning at dawn he endeavoured to recount his adventures. While he was talking something black issued from his mouth. Suddenly he uttered a cry and fell down. His friends gathered round him.

But he was dead.

Figure 7–9

BARTLETT'S LEGEND.   *Quickly read the following legend, then turn over the page and write all that you can recall from it. Turn back to the legend and compare what you wrote with what the legend describes.*

degree to which we are accurately remembering the experience. Ulric Neisser (1982) and others have questioned that association. Apparently, we cannot distinguish constructive from reconstructive memory based on the vividness of our recall.

Some of the strongest evidence for the constructive nature of memory has been obtained by those who have studied the validity of eyewitness testimony.

Eyewitness Memory

A survey of U.S. prosecutors estimated that about 77,000 suspects are arrested each year after being identified by eyewitnesses (Dolan, 1995). Studies of more than 1,000 known wrongful convictions have pointed to errors in eyewitness identification as being "the single largest factor leading to those false convic-

tions" (Wells, 1993, p. 554). What proportion of eyewitness identifications are mistaken? The answer to that question varies widely ("from as low as a few percent to greater than 90%"; Wells, 1993, p. 554), but even the most conservative estimates of this proportion suggest frightening possibilities. Consider the story of a man named Timothy.

In 1986, Timothy was convicted of brutally murdering a mother and her two young daughters (Dolan, 1995). He was then sentenced to die, and for 2 years and 4 months, Timothy lived on death row. Although the physical evidence did not point to Timothy, eyewitness testimony placed him near the scene of the crime at the time of the murder. Subsequently, it was discovered that a man who looked like Timothy was a frequent visitor to the neighborhood of the murder victims, and Timothy was given a second trial and was acquitted.

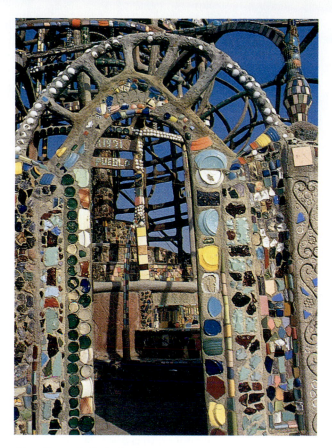

When Simon Rodia built the Watts Towers in East Los Angeles (c.1921–1954), he assembled it from fragments of realistic objects, according to his own preexisting ideas. Similarly, we construct our memories from fragments of realistic events, according to our own preexisting schemas.

Experiments by Elizabeth Loftus and her colleagues (e.g., Loftus, 1975, 1977) have demonstrated we are highly susceptible to distortion in eyewitness accounts. In one study, Elizabeth Loftus, David Miller, and Helen Burns (1978) showed people a series of 30 slides in which someone drove a red car down a street, stopped at a stop sign, turned right, and then knocked down a pedestrian crossing at a crosswalk. As soon as the people finished seeing the slides, they had to answer a series of 20 questions about the accident. One of the questions contained information that was either consistent or inconsistent with what they had been shown. Half of the research participants were asked: "Did another car pass the red car while it was stopped at the stop sign?" The other half of the participants received the same question, except with the word *yield* replacing the word *stop*. In other words, the information in the question given this second group was inconsistent with what the people had seen.

Later, after an unrelated *interpolated*, or inserted, activity, all people were shown two slides and asked

which they had seen. One had a stop sign, the other a yield sign. Accuracy on this task was 34% better for people who had received the consistent question (stop sign question) than for people who had received the inconsistent question (yield sign question). Although this distortion may be due to phenomena other than just constructive memory, it does show that we can easily be led to construct a memory that differs from what really happened.

Loftus (e.g., Loftus & Ketcham, 1991) has been instrumental in pointing to the potential problems of wrongful conviction when using eyewitness testimony as the sole or even the primary basis for convicting accused persons of crimes. She further notes that eyewitness testimony is often a powerful determinant of whether a jury will convict an accused person. The effect is particularly pronounced if eyewitnesses appear highly confident of their testimony, even if the eyewitnesses can provide few perceptual details or offer apparently conflicting responses. People sometimes even think they remember things simply because they have imagined or thought about them (Garry & Loftus, 1994). Indeed, having people repeatedly imagine doing something increases their confidence that they actually have done what they only have imagined doing (Goff & Roediger, 1998). It has been estimated that as many as 10,000 people per year may be convicted wrongfully on the basis of mistaken eyewitness testimony (Cutler & Penrod, 1995; Loftus & Ketcham, 1991).

John Brigham, Roy Malpass, and others (e.g., Bothwell, Brigham, & Malpass, 1989; Brigham & Malpass, 1985; Shapiro & Penrod, 1986) have pointed out that eyewitness identification is particularly weak when identifying persons of a race other than the race of the witness. Astonishingly, even infants seem to be influenced by postevent information when recalling

The jurors in this courtroom are counting on the reconstructive memory of an eyewitness account; however, this lawyer is arguing that such accounts are unreliable. Hard evidence shows that eyewitness accounts are often built using constructive memory, based partly on what actually happened and partly on what the individual assembles from various fragments of recollections.

an experience, as shown through their behavior in operant-conditioning experiments (Rovee-Collier, Borza, Adler, & Boller, 1993). Not everyone views eyewitness testimony with such skepticism, however (e.g., see McKenna, Treadway, & McCloskey, 1992; Zaragoza, McCloskey, & Jamis, 1987), so the issue regarding the validity of such testimony is still open.

A study that suggests how easy it is for people to manufacture memories was conducted by Henry Roediger, III, and Kathleen McDermott (1995). These investigators asked people to memorize lists of words with extremely high associates to target words, such as *sleep*. Thus, words like *dream* and *bed* would appear on the list to be memorized. But the word *sleep* would not appear on the list. To the researchers' surprise, people were as likely to remember having heard the nonpresented word (*sleep*) as they were to remember words actually presented on the list! In other words, people can believe they have heard something they have not heard with the same confidence they remember something they have heard. This result has been replicated multiple times (McDermott, 1996; D. Schacter, Verfaellie, & Pradere, 1996).

Why are people so weak in distinguishing what they have heard from what they have not heard? One possibility is a *source-monitoring error*, which occurs when a person attributes a memory derived from one source to another source. Research by Marcia Johnson and her colleagues (Johnson, 1996; Johnson, Hashtroudi, & Lindsay, 1993; Lindsay & Johnson, 1991) suggests that people frequently have difficulties in *source monitoring*, or figuring out the origins of a memory. They may believe they read an article in a prestigious newspaper, such as the *New York Times*, when in fact they saw it in a tabloid on a supermarket shelf while waiting to check out. When people hear a list of words not containing a word that is highly associated with the other words, they may believe that their recall of that central word is from the list rather than from their minds.

Children's Memories

Children's recollections are particularly susceptible to distortion, especially when the children are asked leading questions, as in a courtroom setting. Stephen Ceci and Maggie Bruck (1993, 1995) have reviewed the literature on children's eyewitness testimony and come to a number of conclusions. First, the younger the child is, the less reliable the testimony of that child can be expected to be. In particular, children of preschool age are much more susceptible to suggestive questioning that tries to steer them to a certain response than are children of school age or adults. Second, when a questioner is coercive or even just seems to want a particular answer, children can be quite susceptible to providing the adult what he or she seems to

want to hear. Given the pressures involved in court cases, such forms of questioning may be unfortunately prevalent. Third, children may believe that they recall observing things that others have said they observed. In other words, they hear a story about something that took place, and then believe that they have observed what allegedly took place. Perhaps even more than eyewitness testimony from adults, the testimony of children must be interpreted with great caution.

Steps can be taken to enhance eyewitness identification (e.g., using methods to reduce potential biases, to reduce the pressure to choose a suspect from a limited set of options, and to ensure that each member of an array of suspects fits the description given by the eyewitness, yet offers diversity in other ways; described in Wells, 1993). In addition, some psychologists (e.g., Loftus, 1993a, 1993b) and many defense attorneys believe that jurors should be advised that the degree to which the eyewitness feels confident of her or his identification does not necessarily correspond to the degree to which the eyewitness is actually accurate in her or his identification of the defendant as being the culprit. At the same time, some psychologists (e.g., Egeth, 1993; Yuille, 1993) and many prosecutors believe that the existing evidence, based largely on simulated eyewitness studies rather than on actual eyewitness accounts, is not strong enough to risk attacking the credibility of eyewitness testimony when such testimony

Children's memories are particularly susceptible to distortion. Kelly Michaels was accused of sexually abusing some of the children left in her care. Her conviction was overturned because the children's testimony was found to be unreliable.

might send a true criminal to prison, preventing the person from committing further crimes. Still others (e.g., Bekerian, 1993; described also in LaFraniere, 1992) suggest that there are no typical eyewitnesses and that conclusions based on an average case should not necessarily be applied to all other cases.

Thus far, we have discussed several ways that psychologists disagree about some of the specific mechanisms of memory, within the context of the three-store model of memory. Next, we consider whether there is a plausible alternative way to view what we know about memory.

Alternative Models of Memory

In Search of . . .

What are alternatives to the traditional model of memory?

In previous chapters, we have seen how different psychologists interpret identical data in different ways. Memory is another area in which what we know can be interpreted in more than one way. The core differences arise from the choice of metaphor used for conceptualizing memory (Roediger, 1980). Metaphors often serve an important function in organizing ideas, aiding researchers to conceptualize a phenomenon well enough to investigate it. As research progresses, the metaphor may be modified to accommodate new data, or other researchers may propose alternative metaphors.

Levels of Processing

A later model, that of Craik and Lockhart (1972), proposed that rather than there being separate stores, memories occur along a continuum depending on depth of processing of information. In this *levels-of-processing framework*, storage varies along a continuous dimension in terms of depth of encoding. In other words, there are theoretically an infinite number of levels of processing at which items can be encoded, with no distinct boundaries between one level and the next. Craik and Lockhart found that they could manipulate the alleged level of processing to which a word was encoded by the kind of question they asked when a word was presented. For example, asking whether the word was presented in all capital letters would result in a relatively superficial level of encoding, whereas asking the meaning of the presented word would result in a relatively deep level of encoding.

This framework has an immediate, practical application. In studying, the more elaborately and diversely you encode material, the more readily you are likely to recall it later. Just looking at material again and again in the same way is likely to be less productive for learning the material than is asking oneself meaningful questions about the material and finding more than one way to learn it.

Working Memory

Some psychologists (e.g., Baddeley, 1990a, 1990b; Baddeley & Hitch, 1994; J. Cantor & Engle, 1993; Daneman & Tardif, 1987; Engle, 1994; Engle, Carullo, & Collins, 1992) view short-term and long-term memory from yet a different perspective. Table 7-1 contrasts the traditional Atkinson–Shiffrin model with this alternative perspective. You may note the semantic distinctions, the differences in metaphorical representation, and the differences in emphasis for each view. The key feature of the alternative view is the emphasis on **working memory,** which is the activated portion of long-term memory that moves activated elements of information into and out of short-term memory.

Working memory consists of three main elements: the phonological loop, the visuospatial sketchpad, and the central executive. The *visuospatial sketchpad* briefly holds some visual images. The *phonological loop* briefly holds inner speech for verbal comprehension, as well as for acoustic rehearsal (without which acoustic information decays after about 2 seconds). The *central executive* coordinates attentional activities and governs responses. Baddeley also has proposed that there are probably a number of other "subsidiary slave systems" that perform other cognitive or perceptual tasks.

Some support for a distinction between working memory and long-term memory comes from neuropsychological research. Neuropsychological studies have shown abundant evidence of a brief memory buffer (used for remembering information temporarily), which is distinct from long-term memory. Furthermore, some promising new research using PET techniques (see chapter 3) has found evidence for distinct brain areas involved in the different aspects of working memory. The phonological loop, maintaining speech-related information, appears to involve bilateral activation of the frontal and parietal lobes (Cabeza & Nyberg, 1997). Interestingly, the visuospatial sketchpad appears to activate slightly different areas, depending on the length of the retention interval. Shorter intervals activate areas of the occipital and right frontal lobes, whereas longer intervals activate areas of the parietal and left frontal lobes (Haxby, Ungerleider, Horwitz, Maisog, Rapoport, & Grady, 1995). Finally, the central executive functions appear to involve activation mostly in the frontal lobes (Roberts, Robbins, & Weiskrantz, 1996). Although these findings are interesting and exciting, they should be taken as somewhat speculative until more research has been done to confirm them.

TABLE 7–1

Traditional Versus Nontraditional Views of Memory   *The traditional three-stores view differs from a contemporary alternative view in terms of the choice of terms, of metaphors, and of emphasis.*

	TRADITIONAL THREE-STORES VIEW	ALTERNATIVE VIEW OF MEMORY*
Terminology	*Working memory* is another name for short-term memory, which is distinct from long-term memory.	*Working memory* (active memory) is the part of long-term memory that comprises all the knowledge of facts and procedures that has been recently activated in memory, including the brief, fleeting short-term memory and its contents.
Relationships of stores	Short-term memory is distinct from long-term memory, perhaps either alongside it or hierarchically linked to it.	Short-term memory, working memory, and long-term memory are concentric spheres, in which working memory contains only the most recently activated portion of long-term memory, and short-term memory contains only a very small, fleeting portion of working memory.
Movement of information	Information moves directly from long-term memory to short-term memory, and then back; it is never in both locations at once.	Information remains within long-term memory; when activated, information moves into long-term memory's specialized working memory, which would actively move information into and out of the short-term memory store contained within it.
Emphasis	Distinction between long- and short-term memory.	Role of activation in moving information into working memory and the role of working memory in memory processes.

*Examples of studies proposing this view: Baddeley, 1990a, 1990b; J. Cantor & Engle, 1993; Daneman & Tardif, 1987; Engle, 1994; Engle, Carullo, & Collins, 1992.

Based partly on the use of computer models of memory processes, including simulations of memory used in artificial intelligence, many cognitive psychologists now prefer a *parallel-processing model* to describe many phenomena of memory, particularly in terms of working memory as the activated portion of long-term memory. This view implies that working memory contains the simultaneously activated (parallel), yet perhaps widely distributed, portions of long-term memory. Thus, the new metaphor also broadens the debate between serial and parallel processes in memory function, encompassing use of long-term memory in addition to the ramifications for short-term memory discussed earlier.

Some people's memories seem to work much worse or better than the rest of ours. Let's consider the extremes of memory.

Extremes of Memory

What is exceptional memory and what are its causes?

Some people have exceptional memories. They may either remember poorly or extremely well. Let's consider both extremes.

Memory Deficiencies: Amnesia

That sacred Closet when you sweep—
Entitled "Memory"—
Select a reverential Broom—
And do it silently. . . .

—Emily Dickinson, *Poem 1273*

We usually take for granted the ability to remember, much as we do the air we breathe. However, just as we become more aware of the importance of air when we do not have enough to breathe, we are less likely to take memory for granted when we observe people with serious memory deficiencies.

Amnesia is loss of explicit memory. Amnesia victims perform extremely poorly on many explicit memory tasks but they show normal or almost normal performance on word-completion tasks involving implicit memory (Baddeley, 1989). When asked whether they have previously seen the word they just completed, however, they are unlikely to remember the specific experience of having seen the word. These data suggest that the effects of amnesia are on explicit, rather than on implicit, memory.

Amnesia victims also show paradoxical performance in tasks that involve *procedural memory* versus those that involve *declarative memory*. For example, amnesia victims may perform extremely poorly on traditional memory tasks requiring recall or recognition memory of declarative knowledge. However, they may demonstrate improvement in performance due to learning—remembered practice—when engaged in tasks that require procedural memory, such as solving puzzles, learning to read mirror writing, or mastering motor skills (Baddeley, 1989).

Psychologists study amnesia patients in part to gain insight into memory function in general. One of the general insights gained by studying amnesia victims who perform tasks involving procedural memory and implicit memory, like those described, is that the ability to reflect consciously on prior experience, which is required for tasks involving explicit memory of declarative knowledge, seems to differ from the ability to demonstrate remembered learning in an apparently automatic way, without conscious recollection of the learning (Baddeley, 1989).

One of the most famous cases of the severe memory loss known as amnesia is the case of H. M., reported by William Scoville and Brenda Milner (1957; Milner, Corkin, & Teuber, 1968). Following an experimental surgical treatment for uncontrollable epilepsy, H. M. suffered severe **anterograde amnesia**—the inability explicitly to recall events that occurred *after* whatever trauma caused the memory loss. However, H. M. had full recollection of events that had occurred before his operation. Although his postsurgical intelligence test score was 112, which is above average, his score on the memory test was 67, which is much below average (see chapter 9). Moreover, shortly after taking a test from the memory scale, he could not remember that he had taken it. Had he been given the test again, it would have been as though he were taking it for the first time. H. M. once remarked on his situation: "Every day is alone in itself, whatever enjoyment I've had, and whatever sorrow I've had" (Scoville

& Milner, p. 217). H. M. all but lost his ability to form new explicit memories, so he lived suspended in an eternal present in which he was unable to create any explicit memories of the time following his operation.

> Without [memory] all life and thought [are] an unrelated succession. As gravity holds matter from flying off into space, so memory gives stability to knowledge; it is the cohesion which keeps things from falling into a lump, or flowing in waves.
>
> —Ralph Waldo Emerson,
> *Natural History of Intellect*

Another type of memory loss is **retrograde amnesia,** the inability explicitly to recall events that occurred *before* the trauma that caused the memory loss. W. Ritchie Russell and P. W. Nathan (1946) reported a case of severe retrograde amnesia following a physical trauma: A 22-year-old greens keeper suffered serious memory loss following a motorcycle accident. By 10 weeks after the accident, however, he had recovered his explicit memory for most events, starting with the events in the most distant past and gradually progressing up to more recent events. Eventually, he was able explicitly to recall everything that had happened up to a few minutes prior to the accident. As is often the case, the events that occurred immediately before the trauma were never recalled.

Yet another form of amnesia is one that all of us experience: **infantile amnesia,** the inability to recall events that happened during early development of the brain. Generally, we can remember little or nothing that has happened to us before the age of about 5 years, and it is extremely rare for someone to recall any memories before the age of 3 years. The reports of childhood memories usually involve memories of significant events, such as the birth of a sibling or the death of a parent (see Fivush & Hamond, 1991). Presumably, these emotional memories last because they make a very strong impression. However, they are not always accurate (D. Schacter, 1996).

People with various forms of amnesia show reduced memory functioning. Some people, however, show exceptionally high levels of memory functioning, among whom are mnemonists.

Outstanding Memory: Mnemonists

A **mnemonist** is a person who uses memory-enhancing techniques for greatly improving his or her memory or who has a distinctive sensory or cognitive ability to remember information, particularly information that is highly concrete or can be visualized readily. The mnemonist's ability shows us what we might long to have, especially when, as students, we wish we had photographic memories for material we need to remember when taking exams.

Perhaps the most famous of mnemonists was a man called "S.," who was described by Alexander Luria, a celebrated Russian psychologist. Luria (1968) reported that one day a man employed as a newspaper reporter appeared in his laboratory and asked to have his memory tested. Luria tested him and discovered that the man's memory appeared to have virtually no limits. S. could reproduce series of words of any length whatsoever, regardless of how long ago the words had been presented to him. Luria studied S. over a period of 30 years and found that even when his retention was measured 15 or 16 years after a session in which S. had learned words, S. could still reproduce the words.

What was S.'s trick? How did he remember so much? Apparently, he relied heavily on the mnemonic of visual imagery. He converted material that he needed to remember into visual images. For example, he reported that when asked to remember the word *green*, he visualized a green flowerpot, whereas for the word *red*, he would visualize a man in a red shirt coming toward him. Even numbers called up images. For example, *1* was a proud, well-built man, and so on. S.'s heavy reliance on imagery created difficulty for him when he tried to understand abstract concepts, such as *infinity* or *nothing*, which did not lend themselves well to visual images.

His excellent memory also caused S. other problems. He could not forget things even when he wanted to forget them, and at times, images would come into his consciousness and interfere with his ability to concentrate and even to carry on a conversation. Eventually, S. became a professional entertainer, dazzling audiences with his memory feats, not so much because he wanted to entertain, but because he found himself unable to succeed in other pursuits.

The story of S. is a good example of how memory and all other cognitive functions represent an evolutionary compromise. Often, as we improve in one function, other functioning can suffer as a result. For example, S.'s superior memory interfered with his ability to adapt in other spheres of life. Similarly, in the physical domain, someone who builds up an extraordinarily muscular frame may lose agility. In eons past, such a person might have been at an advantage in some forms of hand-to-hand combat, but might have had some difficulty making a quick escape in the force of overwhelming odds against a stronger, possibly nonhuman predator. Thus, when we complain about being forgetful or even less strong than we might like to be, we should remember that our minds and physiques as well represent evolutionary compromises that may not optimize on any one function, but that may optimize (or close to it) on a delicate balance of functions.

Another mnemonist, S. F., studied by K. Anders Ericsson, William Chase, and Steve Faloon (1980),

remembered long strings of numbers by segmenting them into groups of three or four digits each, and encoding them as running times for different races. An experienced long-distance runner himself, S. F. was familiar with the times that would be plausible for different races. S. F. did not enter the laboratory as a mnemonist; rather, he was selected to represent the average college student in terms of intelligence and memory ability. S. F.'s original memory for a string of numbers was about seven digits, average for a college student. After 200 practice sessions distributed over a period of two years, S. F. had increased his memory for digits more than tenfold and could recall up to about 80 digits. His memory was only average, however, when the experimenters purposely gave him sequences of digits that could not be translated into running times. The work with S. F. by Ericsson and his colleagues suggests that a person with a fairly typical level of memory ability can be converted into one with quite an extraordinary memory, at least in some domains, with a great amount of concerted practice.

Exceptional mnemonists offer some insight into the processes of memory. For example, mnemonists generally recode arbitrary, abstract, meaningless information into more meaningful or sensorially concrete information, which aids recall from long-term memory, as we saw earlier. In the next section, we consider how to use mnemonic devices to improve our own memory abilities. These devices rely on similar kinds of recodings that add meaning to otherwise meaningless information. Although most people will never perform at the level of these extraordinary mnemonists, we can all improve our memories by using mnemonics.

The Biological Underpinnings of Memory

In Search of . . .   *What are the neural and other mechanisms underlying memory functioning?*

Psychologists have been able to locate many cerebral structures involved in memory, such as the hippocampus and other nearby structures (Squire, 1987). A great deal of our information on the brain structures involved in memory originally came from the study of people who had sustained some sort of brain damage. Memory is volatile and may be disturbed by a blow to the head, a disturbance in consciousness, or any number of other injuries to, or pathologies of, the brain. Studies of such brain-injured patients are

I AM PACK and Other Techniques for Improving Memory

There are two kinds of memory: The natural memory is that memory which is imbedded in our minds, born simultaneously with thought. The artificial memory is that memory which is strengthened by a kind of training and system of discipline.
—Cicero, *Ad Herennium*

The memory performance of mnemonists is quite rare, but you can use several similar mnemonic devices to improve your learning of new material. **Mnemonic devices** comprise a variety of specific techniques for aiding in the memorization of various isolated items by adding meaning or imagery to an otherwise arbitrary listing of isolated items that may be difficult to remember. Of the many mnemonic devices available, the ones described here rely on organization of information into meaningful chunks—such as *categorical clustering, acronyms,* and *acrostics;* or on visual images—such as *interactive images,* a *pegword system,* the *method of loci,* and the *keyword system.*

In **categorical clustering,** various items are grouped into categories in order to facilitate recall of the items. For example, if you need to remember to buy apples, milk, grapes, yogurt, Swiss cheese, and grapefruit, try to memorize the items by categories: *fruits*—apples, grapes, grapefruit; *dairy products*—milk, yogurt, Swiss cheese.

Acronyms are another type of memory device, where a set of letters forms a word or phrase, in which each letter stands for a certain other word or concept (e.g., U.S.A., IQ, and laser). For example, you could try to remember the names of these mnemonic devices by using the acronym I AM PACK: **I**nteractive images, **A**cronyms, **M**ethod of loci, **P**egwords, **A**crostics, **C**ategories, and **K**eywords.

Acrostics, on the other hand, are the initial letters of a series of items that are used in forming a sentence, such that the sentence prompts the recall of the initial letters, and the letters prompt the recall of each of the items. Music students use the acrostic "**E**very **G**ood **B**oy **D**oes **F**ine," to memorize the notes on lines of the treble clef.

When using **interactive images** to enhance memory, you can link a set of isolated words by creating visual representations for the words and then picturing interactions among the items. For instance, if you needed to remember a list of unrelated words such as *aardvark, table, pencil,* and *book,* you could imagine an *aardvark* sitting on a *table* holding a *pencil* in its claws and writing in a *book.*

A system that uses interactive images is the **pegword system.** With a pegword system, memorization of a familiar list of items can be linked (via interactive images) with unfamiliar items on a new list. Using a pegword system, you might take advantage of this nursery rhyme: One is a bun, two is a shoe, three is a tree, four is a door, five is a hive. Then you imagine, say, an aardvark ready to be eaten on a bun, a shoe resting on a table, a tree that has pencils for branches, and a large book serving as a door, complete with doorknob and hinges.

Still another method, the **method of loci,** consists of visualization of a familiar area with distinctive landmarks that can be linked (via interactive images) with items to be remembered. In using this method, you could mentally walk past each of the landmarks and visualize an image incorporating a new word and a landmark. For example, you could envision an *aardvark* digging at the roots of a familiar tree, a *table* sitting on a familiar sidewalk, and a *pencil*-shaped statue in the center of a familiar fountain. To remember the list, you take your mental walk and pick up the words you have linked to each of the landmarks along the walk.

A **keyword system** for learning isolated words in a foreign language forms an interactive image that links the sound and meaning of the foreign word to the sound and meaning of a familiar word. For instance, to learn that the French word for *butter* is *beurre,* you might note that *beurre* sounds like *bear.* Next, you would associate the keyword *bear* with butter in an image or sentence, such as a bear eating a stick of butter. Later, *bear* would provide a retrieval cue for *beurre.*

Of the many mnemonic devices available, the ones described here rely on two general principles of effective recall that we covered earlier. Categorical clustering, acronyms, and acrostics involve organizing information into meaningful chunks, which we have seen can help with both short-term and long-term memory. Storing memory as visual images can help with retrieval from long-term memory and is the basis of mnemonic techniques such as interactive images, the pegword system, the method of loci, and the keyword system. What happens in the brain when we store memories?

informative, offering distinctive insights not previously observed in people with normal brain function, such as the insights into declarative versus procedural knowledge, gained through the study of amnesia victims. In addition, although studies of brain-injured people do not necessarily provide conclusive evidence regarding localization of function, such studies may still indicate that a particular structure at least participates in a given function (Kosslyn & Koenig, 1995).

Brain Structures Involved in Memory

For example, some studies show preliminary findings regarding the specific structures involved in various kinds of memory, such as procedural versus declarative memory. In particular, procedural memory seems to depend on the basal ganglia (Mishkin & Petri, 1984). However, the hippocampus seems to play a crucial role in complex learning (McCormick & Thompson, 1984), particularly in regard to the encoding of declarative information (Kolb & Whishaw, 1990; Zola-Morgan & Squire, 1990). The hippocampus also appears to be involved in the consolidation of encoded information in the long-term store, perhaps as a means of cross-referencing information stored in different parts of the brain (Squire, Cohen, & Nadel, 1984). In addition, the cerebral cortex appears to play a minor but important role in long-term memory, particularly declarative memory (Zola-Morgan & Squire, 1990). Another form of memory is the classically conditioned response, in which the cerebellum seems to play a key role (R. F. Thompson, 1987). For example, when dogs are classically conditioned to salivate at the sight of those who bring them food, we can expect activation in the cerebellum.

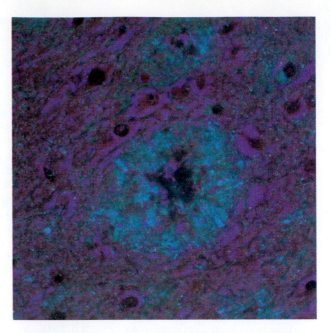

This photomicrograph shows Alzheimer's plaques, which may interfere with memory. Alzheimer's patients show severe loss of the brain tissue that secretes acetylcholine, a neurotransmitter that seems to enhance neural transmission associated with memory.

The Neurophysiology and Neurochemistry of Memory

In addition to these preliminary insights into whatever macro-level structures of memory may exist, we are beginning to understand the micro-level structure of memory. For example, we know that repeated stimulation of particular neural pathways tends to strengthen the likelihood of firing; that is, at a particular synapse, there appear to be physiological changes in the dendrites of the receiving neuron, which make the neuron more likely to reach the threshold for firing again.

We also know that some neurotransmitters disrupt memory storage, and other neurotransmitters enhance memory storage. Both serotonin and acetylcholine seem to enhance neural transmission associated with memory, and noradrenaline may also do so. High concentrations of acetylcholine have been found in the hippocampus of normal persons (Squire, 1987), but low concentrations are found in victims of Alzheimer's disease—a disorder causing severe memory loss. In fact, Alzheimer's patients show severe loss of the brain tissue that secretes acetylcholine. Despite intensive research in this area, scientists have yet to pin down the specific causes of Alzheimer's disease. Researchers have been better able to track down the cause of another form of memory dysfunction, alcohol consumption, which disrupts the activity of serotonin, thereby impairing the formation of memories (Weingartner, Rudorfer, Buchsbaum, & Linnoila, 1983).

How might neurotransmitters affect memory? Consider the case of acetylcholine. Some evidence suggests that dendritic changes may be induced by this neurotransmitter. During memory formation, there is a breakdown of the protein called MAP-2 (a microtubule-associated protein that normally stabilizes dendrite structure and regulates branching of the dendrites). This breakdown occurs particularly in the cortical and hippocampal pyramidal cells that contain receptors to acetylcholine (Woolf, 1998). A relationship between dendrite structure and acetylcholine is also apparent in experiments with transgenic mice (mice that have genes taken from other organisms). Transgenic mice with too much acetycholinesterase (the protein that breaks down acetylcholine) show poor spatial memory as adults. Their cortical dendrite branches are no further developed than those of normal mice that are 5 weeks of age (Beeri et al., 1997).

The neurophysiology of memory is somewhat different from the neurophysiology of learning because the changes that accompany long-term memory storage have to endure longer than the changes in synaptic effectiveness that occur in learning could possibly last. After all, memories can endure for a person's entire lifetime. Relatively permanent structural alterations can occur in dendrites that correlate with memory consolidation in mammals or with other mental abilities in these mammals. A type of neuron that appears to be important for memory is called a *pyramidal neuron*, which is a neuron that has a cell body shaped like a pyramid, and that generally has a long axon (see chapter 3). The large pyramidal cells in the cerebral cortex and hippocampus appear to be critical in memory. The dendrites of these large cells become increasingly structured over the life span, with alterations and additions occurring mainly at the outermost branches. One key structural element underlying the shape and branching pattern of the dendrite is the *microtubule* (extremely small tube-like structure) and the proteins associated with it. Microtubules transport materials to and from the cell body.

Ultimately, memory-related changes in dendritic structure would affect the number and distribution of synapses, which would in turn affect overall patterns of neural activity. Thus, we might become conscious of a particular memory when particular synapses are activated. Alternatively, it may be that various states of excitation can develop in dendritic microtubules and that it is this excitatory phenomenon that is the basis of consciousness and conscious recall (Hameroff, 1994; Hameroff & Penrose, 1995; Penrose, 1994).

This chapter has shown that although we have learned a great deal about how memory works, much remains unknown. As researchers engage in increasingly sophisticated studies of the cognitive and physiological mechanisms of memory, we will understand memory much more profoundly. We are also rapidly approaching the day when we can use physiological means to help people who have pathological deficits of memory. Perhaps we will even be able to expand our normal memory capacities through neuropsychological intervention. For now, however, we must be content to use mnemonic devices and other external aids to enhance our memories.

One of the key ways we remember information is the use of language. Language aids memory by offering us external aids such as written lists and by making isolated bits of information meaningful through the organization of the information and through the use of mnemonic devices such as acrostics and acronyms. The many facets and uses of language form the topic of the next chapter.

THINK ABOUT IT

1. How did the Atkinson–Shiffrin model shape both the questions asked about memory and the methods used to find answers to those questions?
2. It is often said that Alzheimer's patients eventually lose their personalities and their distinctive identities when they lose their memories. How does your memory serve as the basis for your unique personality and identity?
3. Why might people sometimes think they remember events that never in fact have happened?
4. Describe one means by which a researcher could study the relation between perception and memory.

5. Cognitive psychologists frequently study patterns of errors when they investigate how a particular cognitive process works. What is a pattern of errors in memory tasks you have performed?
6. What have you learned that has led to both positive transfer and negative transfer when you were learning something else? Explain the effects of each.

online   *You can provide your own answers to these questions online at the* Sternberg, **In Search of the Human Mind** *Web site:* *http://www.harcourtcollege.com/psych/ishm*

SUMMARY

How Memory Is Studied   230

1. *Memory* is the process by which past experience and learning can be used in the present.

2. Four of the main kinds of tasks used to study memory are (1) *serial recall*, in which a person needs to remember items according to the order in which they are presented; (2) *free recall*, in which the person can remember items in any order; (3) *paired-associates recall*, in which a person needs to remember the second member of two paired words; and (4) *recognition*, in which a person must indicate whether a presented word is one that has been learned previously. Cued recall has aspects of both recall and recognition tasks.

3. In addition, memory researchers study *explicit memory*, in which people are asked to make a conscious recollection, as well as *implicit memory*, in which task performance is characterized by a recollection that we are not conscious of making. *Declarative memory* is memory for static knowledge, whereas *procedural memory* is memory for how to do things.

Conceptualizations of Memory: The Atkinson-Shiffrin Model   232

4. In a model proposed by Richard Atkinson and Richard Shiffrin, memory is often conceived of as involving three stores: (1) a *sensory store*, capable of holding relatively limited amounts of information for very brief periods of time; (2) a *short-term store*, capable of holding small amounts of information for somewhat longer periods of time; and (3) a *long-term store*, capable of storing large amounts of information virtually indefinitely.

5. Three operations that occur in all three of the suggested memory stores are (1) *encoding*, by which information is placed into the store; (2) *storage*, by which information is maintained in the store; and (3) *retrieval*, by which information is pulled into consciousness from the store.

Sensory Memory   234

6. The *iconic store* refers to visual sensory memory.

Short-Term Memory   234

7. Encoding of information in the *short-term store* appears to be largely, although not exclusively, acoustic, as shown by the susceptibility of information in the short-term store to acoustic confusability—that is, errors based on sounds of words.

8. We retain information mainly by *rehearsing* it. Two of the main theories of forgetting are (1) *interference theory*, which hypothesizes that information is forgotten when a new memory trace competes with an old one; and (2) *decay theory*, which postulates that information is lost when it remains unused for a long period of time. These theories apply to both short-term and long-term memory.

9. Interference theory distinguishes between (a) *retroactive interference*, caused by activity occurring *after* we learn the stimulus material to be recalled; and (b) *proactive interference*, caused by activity occurring *before* we learn the stimulus material to be recalled.

10. The capacity of the short-term store is about 7 plus or minus 2 items. We often form *chunks* of bits of information if the items are lengthy or complex. The *serial-position curve* shows our level of learning as a function of where a particular item appears in a list. The curve typically shows elevated recall at the beginning (*primacy effect*) and the end (*recency effect*) of a list, although experimental conditions can be constructed to reduce or eliminate these effects.

11. Processing of information in the short-term store may be in the form of either (a) *parallel processing*, which refers to multiple operations occurring simultaneously; or (b) *serial processing*, which refers to just a single operation occurring at a given time.

12. *Serial processing* can be characterized as either (a) *exhaustive*, implying that a person always checks all information on a list; or (b) *self-terminating*, implying that a person checks only that information on a list that is necessary for a particular comparison to be made.

The Long-Term Store   239

13. Information in the long-term store appears to be encoded primarily in a *semantic* form, so that confusions tend to be in terms of meanings rather than in terms of the sounds of words.

14. Theorists disagree as to whether all information in the long-term store is encoded in terms of propositions (the meaning underlying a particular relationship among concepts or things) or in terms of both propositions and images (mental pictures).

15. We tend to remember better when we acquire knowledge through *distributed learning* (learning that is spaced over time), rather than through *massed learning* (learning that occurs within a short period of time). To learn material gradually over the term of a course would be an example of distributed learning, whereas to cram for an examination would be an example of massed learning.

16. How we *rehearse* information influences how well we retain it. If we elaborate the items—that is, if we relate them or connect them to something we already know—then we are far more likely to remember them.

17. Some theorists distinguish between (a) *semantic memory*, our memory for facts not recalled in any particular temporal context; and (b) *episodic memory*, our memory for facts having some kind of temporal tag associated with them. Our memory for the meaning of a word is normally semantic; we do not remember when or where we learned that meaning. In contrast, our memory for the words on a list to be learned is normally episodic; we are likely only to recall words from some list just learned and not from other lists that may be in the long-term store.

18. *Encoding specificity* refers to the fact that what is recalled depends largely on what is encoded: How information is encoded at the time of learning will greatly affect how it is later recalled. The context and the category of information also influence how we encode information.

19. Memory appears to be not only *reconstructive* (a direct reproduction of what was learned) but also *constructive* (influenced by attitudes and past knowledge). Constructive memories can present special problems if they interfere with eyewitness testimony in court.

Alternative Models of Memory   249

20. Some theorists conceive of memory not in terms of fixed stores, but in terms of a potentially infinite number of levels of processing.

21. *Working memory* usually is defined as being part of long-term memory and also comprises short-term memory; from this perspective, working memory holds only the most recently activated portion of long-term memory, and it moves these activated elements into and out of short-term memory. Instead of this view, some psychologists define working memory as being the same as short-term memory.

Extremes of Memory   250

22. Severe loss of memory is referred to as *amnesia*. *Anterograde amnesia* refers to difficulty in explicitly remembering events occurring after the time of trauma, whereas *retrograde amnesia* refers to severe difficulty in explicitly remembering events occurring before the time of trauma. *Infantile amnesia* is our inability to remember events that occurred to us before about age 5.

23. A *mnemonist* relies on special techniques, such as imagery, for greatly improving his or her memory; anyone can use these techniques.

Techniques for Improving Memory   251

24. *Mnemonic devices* are used to improve recall. Examples of such devices include *categorical clustering*, *acronyms*, *acrostics*, *interactive imagery*, and *keywords*.

The Biological Underpinnings of Memory   252

25. Although they have yet to identify particular locations for particular memories, researchers have been able to learn a great deal about the specific structures of the brain that are involved in memory. In addition, researchers are investigating the biochemistry of neural processes involved in memory, such as the role of some specific neurotransmitters (e.g., serotonin and acetylcholine) and hormones.

KEY TERMS

■ THINK ABOUT IT SAMPLE RESPONSES

1. How did the Atkinson–Shiffrin model shape both the questions asked about memory and the methods used to find answers to those questions?

This model assumed that memories are stored in relatively static receptacles. Thus the goal of research became to understand how these static receptacles are used in the encoding, storage, and retrieval of information. Later theorists began to question whether memory storage truly is so static and whether the model of "receptacles" accurately captures the nature of memory storage.

2. It is often said that Alzheimer's patients eventually lose their personalities and their distinctive identities when they lose their memories. How does your memory serve as the basis for your unique personality and identity?

Through our memory, we remember the experiences that have made us who we are. In making decisions in life, we also think back to past experiences and events and

use them as a guide. We may think about not only our own past experiences, but those of others. Without memory, we would not have our unique knowledge base on which to draw. And it is this knowledge base, as it guides our actions, that is part of what makes us who we are.

3. Why might people sometimes think they remember events that never in fact have happened?

Research shows that people often have difficulty distinguishing between events they have imagined and events that actually have happened to them. Moreover, even when people remember events, they often remember them incorrectly, despite their belief they remember them correctly. If people are interrogated, leading questions can result in the people thinking they remember things that never happened. It is for this reason that interrogations to be used for legal purposes must be scrupulously fair in avoiding questions asked in a way that might lead people to believe things happened that, in fact, never occurred.

4. Describe one means by which a researcher could study the relation between perception and memory.

There are many means by which this relation could be studied. One means would be to have people either form strong images of pictures they perceive or not form strong images. One would then compare people's recall under the two conditions to investigate the extent to which actively forming strong images of what is perceived influences later recall.

5. Cognitive psychologists frequently study patterns of errors when they investigate how a particular cognitive process works. What is a pattern of errors in memory tasks that you have performed?

In short-term memory tasks, people tend to show a primacy effect and a recency effect. For example, if you try to remember a phone number that you look up in the phone book or hear from telephone directory assistance, you are more likely to remember the first few digits and the last few digits than all the rest of the digits.

6. What have you learned that has led to both positive transfer and negative transfer when you were learning something else? Explain the effects of each.

Often people show both positive and negative transfer when they are learning a second language. On the one hand, the first language often helps them learn the second language. For example, knowing the English word maternal *may help a person learn the word* madre (mother) *in Spanish. But knowing the English word* deception *may actually hurt a person in learning that the word* decepcionado *in Spanish means* disappointed. *The words are so-called false cognates: They look like they should mean roughly the same thing, but they do not.*

In Through the Looking Glass, Alice talks with Humpty Dumpty, who points out that there is only one day in a year when people receive birthday presents, as opposed to 364 when they can receive unbirthday presents. He remarks:

"There's glory for you!"

"I don't know what you mean by 'glory,'" Alice said.

Humpty Dumpty smiled contemptuously. "Of course you don't—till I tell you. I meant 'there's a nice knockdown argument for you.'"

"But 'glory' doesn't mean 'a nice knockdown argument,'" Alice objected.

"When I use a word," Humpty Dumpty said in rather a scornful tone, "it means just what I choose it to mean—neither more nor less."

"The question is," said Alice, "whether you can make words mean so many different things."

"The question is," said Humpty Dumpty, "which is to be master—that's all."

—Lewis Carroll, Through the Looking Glass

8

LANGUAGE AND THOUGHT

Chapter Outline

Language is the use of an organized means of combining words in order to communicate. For language to be meaningful, words and other features of language must have meanings at least somewhat common to us all. Humpty Dumpty shows some unusual thinking through his use of language. Much of our thinking occurs through language. For this reason, the first part of this chapter reviews some of what psychologists know about language, and the second part reviews some of what psychologists know about thought and how it uses language. Both language and thought build upon a large knowledge base that is stored in our long-term memories, so it makes sense that a chapter on language and thought would follow directly after a chapter on memory.

Although there is some disagreement about what qualities are key to defining language, some consensus exists regarding six properties that many psychologists would accept as distinctive of language (e.g., R. Brown, 1965; H. H. Clark & Clark, 1977; Glucksberg & Danks, 1975). Some psychologists also add a seventh property.

Key Properties of Language

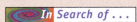

What are the important properties of language?

Language has six and perhaps seven key properties. What are these properties?

First, language is communicative. Despite being the most obvious feature of language, it is the most important. The notion that I can write what I am thinking and feeling so that you may read and understand my thoughts and feelings is the basis for all uses of language.

Second, language is arbitrary. Human language involves a shared system of *arbitrary symbolic reference*, symbols (images, sounds, or objects that represent or suggest other things) that are selected arbitrarily as a means of representing particular things, ideas, processes, relationships, and descriptions. A particular combination of letters or sounds may be meaningful to us, but the particular symbols do not themselves lead to the meaning of the word. Shakespeare aptly described the arbitrary nature of language when he wrote, "What's in a name? That which we call a rose, by any other name would smell as sweet" (*Romeo and Juliet*, act 2, scene 2). With the rare exceptions of *onomatopoeia*, in which a word sounds like what it describes (e.g., *buzz, hiss,* and *hum*), the sound combination is arbitrary. For example, the word for *tree* in Spanish is *arbol*. Neither the English nor the Spanish word is particularly evocative of anything intrinsic about a tree.

Third, language is meaningfully structured or rule governed. Structure makes possible this shared system of communication. Particular patterns of sounds and of letters form meaningful words, and particular patterns of words form meaningful sentences, paragraphs, and discourse. Although individual languages may vary in the particular structures that are deemed acceptable, all require some sort of structure. For example, adding *-s* to an English-language singular noun typically serves to convert that noun into its plural form.

Fourth, language has multiplicity of structure. Any meaningful utterance can be analyzed at more than one level. Particular patterns of words can have more than one meaning, as illustrated by a sign seen in a New York drugstore: "We dispense with accuracy" (Lederer, 1987, p. 63), and a particular basic idea can be expressed by more than one pattern of words. For example, "The student chewed the pencil" is fundamentally the same as "The pencil was chewed by the student."

Fifth, language is productive. We can use language to produce an infinite number of unique sentences and other meaningful combinations of words. Language is inherently creative, precisely because it would never be possible for any of us previously to have heard all the sentences we are capable of producing. Moreover, any language has the potential to express any idea that can be expressed in any other language, although the ease, clarity, and succinctness of expression of a particular idea may vary greatly from one language to the next. For example, "I lost the key" is often said "Se me

olividó la llave" ("The key was lost to me") in Spanish. The Spanish expression may seem awkward to an English speaker but it also differs in its connotation, seemingly removing some of the responsibility from the person who lost the key.

Sixth, language is dynamic. It constantly evolves. New words, phrases, and meanings make their way into common usage every day.

An additional property that is sometimes added to this list is that language (at least, a first language) is spontaneously acquired. In other words, children learn to speak their first language without any special effort on their behalf. Children learn their first language in their interactions with parents and peers, without seeming to make any great effort to do so. Given these characteristics of language, how are we to think about communication in animals?

Do Animals Use Language?

In Search of ... *What is the evidence for and against language use in nonhuman animals?*

The philosopher René Descartes suggested that language is what qualitatively distinguishes human beings from other species. Was he right? Before we get into the particulars of language in nonhuman species, we should underscore again the distinction between communication and language. Few would doubt that nonhuman animals communicate in one way or another. What is at issue is whether they do so through what reasonably can be called a language. Whereas *language* is the specific use of an organized means of combining words in order to communicate, *communication* more broadly encompasses not only the exchange of thoughts and feelings through language, but also nonverbal communication, such as through gestures, glances, distancing, and other contextual cues.

Primates—especially chimpanzees—offer our most promising insights into nonhuman language. Perhaps the most internationally well known investigator of chimpanzees in the wild has been Jane Goodall. She has studied many aspects of chimp behavior, including chimps' vocalizations, many of which she considers to be clearly communicative, although not necessarily indicative of language. For example, chimps have a specific cry indicating that they are about to be attacked and another vocalization for calling together their fellow chimps. Nonetheless, their repertoire of communicative vocalizations seems to be small, nonproductive (new utterances are not produced), limited in structure,

Although primates definitely communicate in their natural environments, they do not spontaneously use language. Attempts to teach nonhuman primates to use language have been successful to varying degrees.

lacking in multiplicity of structure, and relatively nonarbitrary. It also is not spontaneously acquired. The chimps' communications thus do not satisfy our criteria for a language.

By using sign language, the researchers R. Allen and Beatrice Gardner were able to teach their chimp, Washoe, rudimentary language skills (R. Brown, 1973), although her development never went beyond the stages of language a human toddler could reach. Subsequently, David Premack (1971) had even greater success with his chimpanzee, Sarah, who picked up a vocabulary of more than 100 words of various parts of speech and who showed at least rudimentary linguistic skills.

A less positive view of the linguistic capabilities of chimpanzees was taken by Herbert Terrace (1979), who raised a chimp named Nim Chimpsky, a takeoff on the name of the eminent linguist Noam Chomsky. Over the course of several years, Nim made more than 19,000 multiple-sign utterances in a slightly modified version of ASL. Most of his utterances consisted of two-word combinations.

Terrace's careful analysis of these utterances, however, revealed that the large majority of them were repetitions of what Nim had seen. Terrace concluded that, despite what appeared to be impressive accomplishments, Nim did not show even the rudiments of syntactic expression (discussed below): The chimp could produce single- or even multiple-word utterances, but not in a syntactically organized way. For example, Nim would alternate signing "Give Nim banana," "Banana give Nim," and "Banana Nim give," showing no preference for the grammatically correct form. Moreover, when Terrace studied films showing other chimpanzees supposedly producing language, he came to the same conclusion for them that he had reached for Nim. His position, then, is that although

chimpanzees can understand and produce utterances, they do not have linguistic competence in the same sense that even very young humans do. They lack structure and particularly multiplicity of structure.

Susan Savage-Rumbaugh and her colleagues (Savage-Rumbaugh, McDonald, Sevcik, Hopkins, & Rubert, 1986; Savage-Rumbaugh et al., 1993) have found the best evidence yet in favor of language use among chimpanzees. Their pygmy chimpanzees have spontaneously combined the visual symbols (such as red triangles, blue squares, etc.) of an artificial language the researchers taught them. They even appear to have understood some of the language spoken to them. One pygmy chimp in particular (Greenfield & Savage-Rumbaugh, 1990) seems to possess remarkable skill, even possibly demonstrating a primitive grasp of language structure. It may be that the difference in results across groups of investigators is due to the particular kind of chimp tested or to the procedures used. It also is not clear that the chimp's language meets all the constraints posed by the properties of language described at the beginning of the chapter. For example, it is not clear that the language used by the chimps is spontaneously acquired. At this point, we just cannot be sure if the chimps truly show the full range of language abilities.

Whether or not species other than the human one can use language, it seems almost certain that the language facility of humans far exceeds that of other species we have studied. Noam Chomsky (1991) has stated the key question regarding nonhuman language quite eloquently:

> If an animal had a capacity as biologically advantageous as language but somehow hadn't used it until now, it would be an evolutionary miracle, like finding an island of humans who could be taught to fly.

What is it about the human brain that enables our language abilities? How does the brain produce and understand language, and where in the brain do production and comprehension of language occur? These questions are considered next.

Language and the Brain

What are the brain mechanisms underlying language?

Researchers interested in the brain's role in language have devised increasingly sophisticated techniques to study the brain. Some of our earliest insights into brain localization are related to an association between specific language deficits and specific organic damage to the brain, as first discovered by Paul Broca and Carl Wernicke (see chapters 2 and 3). Broca's aphasia and Wernicke's aphasia are particularly well documented instances in which brain lesions affect speech (see chapter 3). Since the time of Broca and Wernicke, doctors and researchers have found that lesions in certain areas of the brain are often related to specific observed language deficits in patients who are brain injured. Through methodical studies of brain-injured patients, researchers have learned a great deal about the relations between particular areas of the brain and particular linguistic functions. Although lesion studies are valuable, researchers also investigate brain localization of linguistic function via other methods, such as by evaluating the effects on linguistic function that follow electrical stimulation of the brain (e.g., Ojemann, 1982; Ojemann & Mateer, 1979). Through stimulation studies, researchers have found that stimulation of particular points in the brain seems to yield discrete effects on particular linguistic functions (such as the naming of objects) across repeated, successive trials. However, across individuals, these particular localizations of function vary widely. Yet another avenue of research involves the study of the metabolic activity of the brain and the flow of blood in the brain during the performance of various verbal tasks. Figure 8-1 shows brain scans relevant to the production of language.

Relying mainly upon lesion studies, scientists have been able to determine many of the locations of the brain that are involved in both normal language activities and disruptions in language. For example, we can broadly generalize that many linguistic functions are primarily located in the areas identified by Broca and Wernicke, although it is now believed that damage to Wernicke's area, in the back area of the cortex, entails more grim consequences for linguistic function than does damage to Broca's area, closer to the front of the brain (Kolb & Whishaw, 1990). Also, lesion studies have shown that linguistic function is governed by a much larger area of the posterior cortex than just the area identified by Wernicke, and that other areas of the cortex also play a role, such as other association-cortex areas in the left hemisphere, and a portion of the left temporal cortex, as well as some subcortical structures. Studies of brain metabolism have also contributed to research describing the location of language functions in the brain. For example, preliminary metabolic and blood-flow studies of the brain (e.g., Petersen, Fox, Posner, Mintun, & Raichle, 1988) have indicated that more areas of the brain are involved in linguistic function than we would have determined without having these studies available.

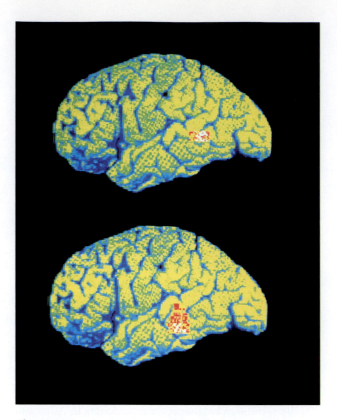

Figure 8–1
PET SCANS OF BRAIN ACTIVITY DURING SPEECH.
The various methods of studying the brain support the view that for all right-handed, and most left-handed, individuals, the left hemisphere of the brain is clearly implicated in syntactical aspects of linguistic processing, and it is clearly essential to speech.

Hemispheric Differences in Processing

In addition to being more widespread than early researchers might have thought, language functions seem to be differentially specialized in the two hemispheres of the brain. The various methods of studying the brain support the view that for all right-handed individuals and most left-handed persons, the left hemisphere of the brain is clearly implicated in syntactical aspects of linguistic processing, and it is clearly essential to speech (Cabeza & Nyberg, 1997). The left hemisphere also seems to be essential to the ability to write, whereas the right hemisphere seems capable of quite a bit of auditory comprehension, particularly in terms of semantic processing, as well as of some reading comprehension. The right hemisphere also seems to be important in several of the subtle nuances of linguistic comprehension and expression, such as understanding and expressing vocal inflection and gesture, as well as comprehending metaphors and other nonliteral aspects of language, such as those used in jokes and sarcasm (Kolb & Whishaw, 1990). Damage to the major left hemisphere areas responsible for language functioning can sometimes lead to enhanced involvement of other areas as language functioning recovers—as if previously dormant or overshadowed areas take over the duties left vacant (Cappa et al., 1997; Weiller et al., 1996).

Sex Differences

From her studies of brain-injured men and women, Doreen Kimura (1987) has observed some intriguing sex differences in terms of the ways in which linguistic function appears to be localized in the brain. The men she studied seemed to show more left-hemisphere dominance for linguistic function than the women showed; women showed more bilateral, symmetrical patterns of linguistic function. Further, the brain locations associated with aphasia seemed to differ for men and women. Most aphasic women showed lesions in the anterior region, although some aphasic women showed lesions in the temporal region. In contrast, aphasic men showed a more varied pattern of lesions, and they were more likely to show lesions in posterior regions (toward the back of the head) rather than in anterior regions (more toward the front of the head).

One interpretation of Kimura's findings is that the role of the posterior region in linguistic function may be different for women than it is for men. Another interpretation is that because women show less lateralization of linguistic function, the brains of women may be better able than those of men to compensate for any possible loss of function due to lesions in the left posterior hemisphere by making increased use of the right posterior hemisphere. The possibility that there also may be subcortical sex differences in linguistic function further complicates the ease of interpreting Kimura's findings.

Related evidence comes from another lab that further suggests that men and women appear to process language differently, at least at the phonological level (Shaywitz et al., 1995). An fMRI (functional magnetic resonance imaging) study of men and women asked participants to perform one of four tasks: (1) indicate whether a pair of letters were identical; (2) indicate whether two words have the same meaning; (3) indicate whether two words rhyme; (4) compare the lengths of two lines (a control task). The researchers found that when both male and female participants were performing the letter-recognition and word-meaning tasks, they showed activation in the left temporal lobe of the brain. When they were performing the rhyming task, however, only the inferior (lower) frontal region of the left hemisphere was activated for men, whereas the inferior frontal region of both the left and right hemispheres was activated in women. These results suggested that men localized their phonological processing more than did women.

Aspects of Language

In Search of . . .

What are the different aspects of language and its use?

How do we study this vehicle that lets us engage in flights of communication with our fellow humans? The smallest distinguishable unit of all possible human speech sounds is the *phone*, of which there are more than 100. No known language uses all of the possible phones, however. Each distinct language uses only a subset of these possibilities; the particular speech sounds the users of a specific language can identify are **phonemes**. In English, phonemes are generally identifiable as vowel or consonant sounds, such as the *b*, *i*, and *t* sounds in *bit*. Linguists sometimes travel to remote villages in order to observe, record, and analyze different languages, some of which are dying as members leave tribal areas in favor of more urban areas (e.g., Ladefoged & Maddieson, 1996).

A **morpheme** is the smallest unit of sound that denotes meaning within a particular language. For example, the word *talked* has two morphemes: *talk* and the suffix *–ed*. Thus, some morphemes are words, and others are word-building components, such as *–ed*.

Linguists use the term **lexicon** to describe the entire set of morphemes in a given language or in a given person's linguistic repertoire. The average English-speaking high school graduate has a lexicon of about 60,000 root morphemes, and most college students have lexicons about twice that large (G. A. Miller, 1990). By combining morphemes, most adult English speakers have a **vocabulary**, or repertoire of words, in the hundreds of thousands. For example, by affixing just a few morphemes to the root content morpheme *study*, we have *student*, *studious*, *studied*, *studying*, and *studies*. One reason English has more words than any other language is the relative ease with which its vocabulary can be expanded by combining existing morphemes in novel ways. Some suggest that a part of William Shakespeare's genius lay in his talent for creating words by combining existing morphemes. Shakespeare is alleged to have coined more than 1,700 words (8.5% of his written vocabulary) as well as countless expressions—including the word *countless* itself (Lederer, 1991). Other words attributed to Shakespeare include *accommodation*, *assassination, critical, dexterously, eyesore, horrid, initiated, pedant,* and *premeditated.*

For linguists, the next level of analysis after the analysis of phonemes, morphemes, and lexicon is *syntax,* which refers to the way users of a particular language put words together in sentences. Linguists consider the study of syntax to be fundamental to understanding the structure of language, and the syntactical structure of language is specifically addressed later in this chapter.

The final and most comprehensive level of linguistic analysis is that of **discourse,** which encompasses language use at the level beyond the sentence, such as in conversation, in paragraphs, articles, chapters, and entire books. (Figure 8-2 summarizes various aspects of language.) The goal of discourse is generally to communicate some message or meaning. The paragraph you are reading, for example, is part of the discourse in a chapter designed to teach you about language and thought. How do you understand the meaning of the discourse in this chapter? Theories of meaning are discussed next.

You probably do not remember the moment that words first came alive to you, but your parents surely do. In fact, one of the greatest joys of being a parent is to watch a child's discovery that words have meanings.

Semantics

Semantics is the study of the meanings of words. Linguists, philosophers, and psychologists have long contemplated just what the word *meaning* means and have proposed several theories over the years.

Componential theory, also termed *definitional theory,* claims that the meaning of a word (or concept) can be understood by disassembling the word (or concept) into a set of *defining features,* which are essential elements of meaning that are singly necessary and jointly sufficient to define a word (or concept; J. J. Katz, 1972; J. J. Katz & Fodor, 1963). Consider, for example, the word *bachelor.* A bachelor can be viewed as comprising three components: male, unmarried, and adult. Because the components are each singly necessary, even the absence of one component makes the word inapplicable. Thus, an unmarried male who is not an adult would not be a bachelor.

The **prototype theory** claims that the meaning of a word (or concept) can be understood by describing the concept in terms of a prototype, which is the best representation of a given concept and which comprises a set of *characteristic features* that tend to be typical of most examples of the concept (Rosch & Mervis, 1975; see also E. E. Smith & Medin, 1981). Whereas a defining feature is possessed by every instance of a concept, a characteristic feature need not be. Instead, many or most instances would possess a characteristic feature. Thus, the ability to fly is typical of birds, but it is not a defining feature of a bird, because some birds, such as ostriches, cannot fly. For example, a robin seems more prototypically birdlike than an ostrich because it has many features that match most people's prototype of a bird, including the fact that a robin can fly. Some theorists (e.g., Erickson & Kruschke, 1998; B. H. Ross & Makin, 1999; B. H. Ross & Spalding, 1994; E. E. Smith, Patalano, & Jonides, 1998) have

Figure 8-2
SUMMARY DESCRIPTION OF LANGUAGE. *All human languages can be analyzed at many levels.*

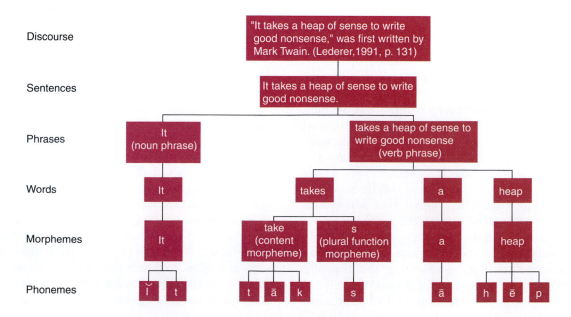

suggested that instead of using a single prototype for deriving the meaning of a concept, we use several **exemplars**—several typical representatives of a particular concept or of a class of objects. For example, in considering birds, we might think of not only the prototypical songbird, which is small, flies, builds nests, sings, and so on, but also of exemplars for birds of prey, for large flightless birds, for medium-sized waterfowl, and so on. If we have multiple exemplars, when we see an instance of a bird, we can more flexibly match this instance to an appropriate exemplar than to a single prototype. To understand concepts fully we also have to understand their roles in sentences, that is, their syntactic usage.

Syntax

As mentioned earlier, an important part of the psychology of language is known as **syntax,** which is the systematic structure through which words can be combined and sequenced to make meaningful phrases and sentences. Syntax begins with the study of the grammar of phrases and sentences.

Psycholinguists use the term **grammar** to refer to the study of regular patterns in language that relate to the functions and relationships of words in a sentence, extending as broadly as the level of discourse and as narrowly as the pronunciation and meaning of individual words. In your English courses, you may have been introduced to **prescriptive grammar,** which is the formulation of various rules dictating the preferred use of written and spoken language, such as the functions, structures, and relationships of words in a sentence. For example, it is grammatically correct to say, "The student loves the book," not "The student love the book." Of greater interest to psycholinguists is **descriptive grammar,** which is the description of language patterns that relate to the structures, functions, and relationships of words in a sentence (Pinker, 1994). There are several kinds of descriptive grammars.

Phrase-structure grammars analyze sentences in terms of the superficial sequence of words in sentences, regardless of differences or similarities of meaning. Also termed *surface-structure grammars*, these grammars deal with syntax at a surface level of analysis. Basically, any sentence in the English language can be analyzed according to a phrase-structure grammar. Consider the following:

1. Susie greedily ate the hungry crocodile.
2. The hungry crocodile was eaten greedily by Susie.

A phrase-structure grammar would not show any particular relation at all between sentences 1 and 2. Yet in terms of meaning, the two sentences differ only in voice, with the first sentence expressed in the active voice and the second in the passive voice. According to *transformational grammar*, the underlying meaning of the two sentences is the same, so the structural difference between the two sentences centers on *attitude*—that is, the stance that the speaker is taking toward the events or items being described.

Linguist Noam Chomsky (1957) proposed that sentences can be analyzed both at a surface-structure level, as is done with phrase-structure grammars, and at a **deep-structure level,** described as the underlying meaning of a sentence which gives rise, through *transformations*, to alternative surface structures. For example, the two sentences about Susie and the crocodile have the same deep-structural representations, even though their surface-level phrase-structural representations are quite different. Chomsky posited a way to derive surface structures from deep structures and to interrelate different surface structures. Chomsky's grammar is termed **transformational grammar** because it centers on the operations used to transform deep structures into surface structures. Not all psychologists agree with all aspects of Chomsky's theories. Many particularly disagree with his emphasis on syntax (form) over semantics (meaning) (e.g., Bock, Loebell, & Morey, 1992; Garrett, 1992; Jackendoff, 1991). In any case, syntax is only part of the story of meaning; we also need to look at pragmatics.

Pragmatics

Traditionally, linguistic studies have focused on how people understand language at the phoneme, morpheme, word, and sentence levels, giving little attention to the broader range of discourse. Psycholinguistic research (research on the psychology of language) has followed suit. In recent decades, however, students of language have become increasingly interested in **pragmatics,** the study of how people use language, and *sociolinguistics*, the study of how people use language in the context of social interaction.

Some sociolinguists also study the ways in which people use nonlinguistic elements in conversational contexts. For example, sociolinguists and psycholinguists interested in observing your language use in context would be interested in your use of gestures and vocal inflections, as well as your use of *proxemics*, the relative distancing and positioning of you and your fellow conversants. Under most circumstances, you usually unself-consciously change your language patterns and nonlinguistic elements to fit different contexts, such as a first date versus a classroom context.

To get an idea of how you change your own use of language in different contexts, suppose that you and your friend are meeting right after work. Something comes up and you must call your friend to change the time or place for your meeting. When you call your friend at work, your friend's supervisor answers and offers to take a message. Exactly what would you say to your friend's supervisor to ensure that your friend will know about the change in time or location? Suppose, instead, that the 2-year-old son of your friend's supervisor answers. Exactly what would you say in this situation? Finally, suppose that your friend answers directly. How has your language for each context been modified, even though your purpose in all three contexts was the same?

Scripts

Maxims and turn-taking strategies may help to guide us through almost any conversational context. For example, we are expected to wait for a person to finish what he or she is saying before we take our turn. In some situations, however, in order to communicate effectively, the parties to the communication must have a shared understanding about the situation being discussed. Some researchers suggest, in such situations, that we may use scripts to help us fill in the gaps that often appear in actual conversations. Roger Schank and Robert Abelson (1977, p. 41) defined a **script** as a predetermined, stereotyped sequence of actions that defines a well-known situation. Common examples of scripts would be going to a doctor's office or to a fast-food restaurant. In the latter case, typical elements of the script would be entering, standing in line, ordering, paying, and sitting down to eat.

Various empirical studies have tested the validity of the script notion. For instance, Gordon Bower, John Black, and Terrence Turner (1979) presented research participants with various brief stories describing common situations. The participants were then asked either to recall as much as they could of each of the stories or to discern which of several sentences had been included in the stories. The critical result was that people in the studies showed a significant tendency to recall elements and sentences that were not actually in the stories, but that were parts of the scripts that the stories represented. That is, scripts seem to guide what people recall and recognize.

Slips of the Tongue

Until now, this chapter has focused on how people use—or at least attempt to use—language correctly. It is only fair, in a discussion of pragmatics, to talk about how people use language incorrectly. One of the most obvious errors is **slips of the tongue**—inadvertent semantic or *articulatory* (related to the production of language sounds) errors in what is said. Slips of the tongue show that we produce language via a plan rather than just one word at a time, with one word serving as the stimulus for the next word. Among the first psychologists to study

slips of the tongue was Sigmund Freud. In fact, his description of this phenomenon led us to term particular instances of such errors *Freudian slips*, which are those slips that seem to reveal hidden (repressed) motivations and sentiments. For example, a businessperson might encounter a business rival and say, "I'm glad to beat you," instead of saying, "I'm glad to meet you."

In contrast to the psychoanalytic view, psycholinguists and other cognitive psychologists are intrigued by slips of the tongue because of what the errors may tell us about how language is produced. In speaking, we have a mental plan for what we are going to say. Sometimes, however, this plan is disrupted when our articulatory mechanism does not cooperate with our cognitive one. Slips of the tongue may be taken to indicate that we have a language of thought that differs from the language through which we express our thoughts (Fodor, 1975). We have the idea right, but its expression comes out wrong. Sometimes, we are not even aware of the slip until it is pointed out to us because in the language of the mind, whatever it may be, the idea is right, even though the expression is inadvertently wrong.

Sometimes, slips of the tongue can be fortuitously opportune, creating **spoonerisms,** in which a reversal of the initial sounds of two words produces two entirely different words, usually yielding a humorous outcome. The term is named after the Reverend William Spooner, who was famous for reversals. One of his choicest slips was "You have hissed all my mystery lectures." As you might have guessed, many slips of the tongue provide insights not only into how people use language, but also into how people think. The interaction of language and thought is the topic of the next section.

The Relation of Language to Thought

The relationship between language and thought pervades the study of language. Almost everything written about language implies that thought and language interact. The language we hear and read shapes our thoughts, and our thoughts shape what we say and write. For example, hate mongers tend to dehumanize their targets by referring to them with derogatory words, such as *insect* or *vermin*. The use of such language is designed to instill negative thoughts and feelings toward the victims so characterized. Studies comparing and contrasting differing languages and the expressions within them are one way to explore how language and thought are intertwined.

> "This rain is very strong," I said in Chinyanja. The word I used for rain, *mpemera*, was very precise. It meant the sweeping rain driven into the veranda by the wind.
>
> —Paul Theroux, *My Secret History*

Linguistic Relativity and Linguistic Universals

Different languages use different lexicons and syntactical structures that reflect the physical and cultural environments in which the languages arose and developed. For example, the Garo of Burma distinguish among many kinds of rice, which is understandable, because they are a rice-growing culture. Nomadic Arabs have more than 20 words for camels. These peoples clearly conceptualize rice and camels more specifically and in more complex ways than do people outside their cultural groups. The question is whether, as a result of these linguistic differences, the Garo think about rice differently from the way we do. Also, do the Arabs think about camels differently from the way we do?

The syntactical structures of languages differ, too. Almost all languages permit some way in which to communicate actions, agents of actions, and objects of actions (Gerrig & Banaji, 1994). What differs across languages is the range of grammatical inflections and other markings that speakers are obliged to include as key elements of a sentence. For example, in describing past actions in English, we indicate whether an action took place in the past by so indicating in the verb form (e.g., walk*ed*). In Spanish and German, the verb further must indicate whether the agent of action was singular or plural and is being referred to in the first, second, or third person. In Turkish, the verb form must indicate past action, singular or plural, and the person, and it must indicate whether the action was witnessed or experienced directly by the speaker or was only experienced indirectly. Do these differences and other differences in obligatory syntactical structures influence—perhaps even constrain—the users of these languages to think about things differently because of the language they use while thinking?

Linguistic relativity theory asserts that the language you speak influences the way you think and the cognitive systems you develop. Consequently, people with different languages will think quite differently about the world. Thus, according to the relativity view, the Garo might think about rice differently from the way we do. For example, the Garo might develop more cognitive categories for rice than would their English-speaking counterparts. When the Garo contemplated rice, they could purportedly view it differently—and perhaps with greater complexity of thought—than would English speakers, who have only a few words for rice. Thus, language would, at least in part, shape thought (Lucy, 1997).

The linguistic relativity hypothesis is sometimes referred to as the *Sapir–Whorf hypothesis*, after the two men who most assertively propagated it. Edward Sapir (1941/1964) said that "we see and hear and otherwise experience very largely as we do because the language habits of our community predispose certain choices of interpretation" (p. 69). Benjamin Lee Whorf (1956) said it even more strongly:

> We dissect nature along lines laid down by our native languages. The categories and types that we isolate from the world of phenomena we do not find there because they stare every observer in the face; on the contrary, the world is presented in a kaleidoscopic flux of impressions which has to be organized by our minds—and this means largely by the linguistic systems in our minds. (p. 213)

The Sapir–Whorf hypothesis has been one of the most widely mentioned ideas in all of the social and behavioral sciences (Lonner, 1989). However, some of its implications appear to have reached mythological proportions. For example, it would make sense, in terms of the Sapir–Whorf hypothesis, for Eskimos to have many words for snow, which would allow the Eskimos to think about the snow in the many ways that their constant encounters with snow require. Many social scientists have, in fact, warmly accepted and gladly propagated the notion that Eskimos have multitudinous words for the single English word *snow*. In direct refutation of the myth, however, anthropologist Laura Martin (1986) has shown that Eskimos do *not* have numerous words for snow. According to G. K. Pullum (1991), "no one who knows anything about Eskimo (or more accurately, about the Inuit and Yupik families of related languages spoken from Siberia to Greenland) has ever said they do" (p. 160).

The Limits of Linguistic Relativity

Thus, it appears that we must exercise caution in our interpretation of linguistic relativity when we observe nouns such as *rice* and *camel*. In fact, such relativity becomes even more interesting when we actually go beyond nouns to consider other syntactical elements of language. For example, Spanish has two forms of the verb *to be*—*ser* and *estar*. However, they are used in different contexts (see Sera, 1992). In general, *ser* is used for permanent or at least long-term states of being. For example, I might say, "Soy profesor," which uses the first-person singular form of *ser* to communicate that I am a professor. *Estar* is used for temporary states of being. I would say "Estoy escribiendo," using the first-person singular form of *estar*, to express that I am temporarily engaged in writing. The psychological question is whether native Spanish speakers have a more differentiated sense of the temporary and the permanent than would native English speakers who would use the same verb form to express both senses of *to be*. Thus far, based on the existing literature in linguistic relativity and crosscultural analyses, this question can be answered with unequivocal certainty: We do not know.

Curt Hoffman, Ivy Lau, and David Johnson (1986) came up with another intriguing experiment designed to assess the possible effects of linguistic relativity. In Chinese, a single term, *sh ì gù*, specifically describes a person who is "worldly, experienced, socially skillful, devoted to his or her family, and somewhat reserved" (p. 1098). English clearly has no comparable single term to embrace these diverse characteristics. Hoffman and colleagues composed text passages in English and in Chinese describing various characters, including the *sh ì gù* character. The researchers then asked individuals who were bilingual in Chinese and English to read the passages either in Chinese or in English and then to rate various statements about the characters, in terms of the likelihood that the statements would be true of the characters. Their results seemed to support the notion of linguistic relativity, in that the research participants were more likely to rate the various statements in accord with the *sh ì gù* stereotype when they had read the passages in Chinese than when they had read the passages in English. Similarly, when participants were asked to write their own impressions of the characters, their descriptions conformed more closely to the *sh ì gù* stereotype if they had previously read the passages in Chinese. These authors do not suggest that it would be impossible for English speakers to comprehend the *sh ì gù* stereotype, but rather that having that stereotype readily accessible facilitates its mental manipulation.

Linguistic Universals?

Some research addresses **linguistic universals**—characteristic patterns of language that apply across all of the languages of various cultures—and relativity. Much of this research has used color names. At first glance, these words seem to be an ideal focus of research because they provide an especially convenient way of testing the hypothesis. People in every culture can be expected to be exposed, at least potentially, to pretty much the same range of colors. Yet it turns out that different languages name colors quite differently (Berlin & Kay, 1969; Kay, 1975). It appears that people see colors in particular, and the world in general, in pretty much the same way, regardless of the language they use (Davies, 1998; Davies & Corbett, 1997). But do people see the world the same way, regardless of their level of cognitive and linguistic development? Let us consider next how language develops.

Language Acquisition

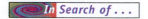

How do people acquire language?

Stages of Language Acquisition

Within the first years of life, we go from listening and responding to language to being able to produce it ourselves. All people seem to accomplish this feat in just about the same way, by following the same sequence of steps. Humans progress through the following stages to acquire their primary language:

1. prenatal responsivity to human voices
2. postnatal cooing, which comprises all possible phones
3. babbling, which comprises only the distinct phonemes that characterize the primary language of the infant
4. one-word utterances
5. two-word utterances
6. telegraphic speech
7. basic adult sentence structure, which is present by about age 4

Prenatal Influences

Some studies suggest that language acquisition begins before birth. Fetuses can hear their mothers' voices in the watery prenatal environment, and within days after birth, newborns show clear preferences for their mothers' voices over the voices of other women (DeCasper & Fifer, 1980). They also seem to prefer hearing their mother read stories they heard her read *in utero* to stories she never read aloud before their birth (DeCasper & Spence, 1986). The results of these studies seem to show that newborns already have gained some familiarity with their mothers' voices and so are becoming prepared to pay attention after birth to the mothers' voices. Interestingly, infants prefer to listen to someone speaking in what will be their native language over a future non-native language, possibly focusing on the rhythmic structure of the language as their means of identification (Bertoncini, 1993; Mehler, Dupous, Nazzi, & Dehaene-Lambertz, 1996). After birth, in addition to responding preferentially to their mothers' voices, newborns seem to respond motorically—to move—in synchrony with the speech of the caregivers who are interacting with them directly (T. Field, 1978; J. A. Martin, 1981; Schaffer, 1977; C. E. Snow, 1977; D. Stern, 1977). Furthermore, the emotional expression of infants responds to and matches that of their caregivers (Fogel, 1992).

Perhaps because they have heard their mother's voice from within the womb, newborns tend to respond preferentially to that voice and seem to move in relation to the speech of caregivers.

Cooing and Babbling

Infants also produce sounds of their own; most obviously, the communicative aspect of crying—whether intentional or not—works quite well to get attention or food, or to signal distress in general. In terms of language acquisition, however, it is the cooing of infants that most intrigues linguists. **Cooing** is the infant's oral expression that explores the production of all the phones that humans can possibly produce. The cooing of infants around the world, including deaf infants, is practically identical.

During the cooing stage, hearing infants can also discriminate among all phones, not just among the phonemes characteristic of their own language. For example, during the cooing stage, both Japanese and American infants can discriminate the /l/ from the /r/ phone (Eimas, 1985). However, as infants move into the next stage (babbling), they gradually lose this ability to distinguish the phones, and by 1 year of age,

Japanese infants—for whom the distinction does not make a phonemic difference—can no longer make this discrimination (Eimas, 1985).

At the babbling stage, deaf infants no longer vocalize, and the sounds produced by hearing infants change. **Babbling** is the infant's preferential production of only those distinct phonemes characteristic of the babbler's own language (J. L. Locke, 1994; Petitto & Marentette, 1991). Thus, although the cooing of infants around the world is essentially the same, infant babbling reflects the language the infant is acquiring. As suggested, the ability of the infant to perceive, as well as to produce, nonphonemic phones recedes during this stage.

Holophrasic Speech—One Word Utterances

Eventually, that first magnificent word is uttered, followed shortly by one or two more, and soon after yet a few more. The infant uses these one-word utterances—termed *holophrases*—to convey intentions, desires, and demands. Usually, the words are nouns describing familiar objects that the child observes (e.g., *car, book, ball, baby, nose*) or wants (e.g., *Mama, Dada, juice, cookie*). By 18 months of age, children typically have vocabularies of 3 to 100 words (Siegler, 1986). Because the young child's vocabulary cannot yet encompass all that the child wishes to describe, the child quite deftly overextends the meaning of words in his or her existing lexicon to cover things and ideas for which a new word is lacking. For example, the general term for any man may be "Dada"—which can be quite distressing to a new father in a public setting—and the general term for any kind of four-legged animal may be "doggie." The term for this overapplication of the meaning of a given word to more things, ideas, and situations than is appropriate for the denotation and the defining features of a word is **overextension error.**

Why do overextension errors occur? A *feature hypothesis* suggests that children form definitions that include too few features (E. V. Clark, 1973). Thus, a child might refer to a cat as a dog because of a mental rule that if an animal has the feature of four legs, it is a "doggie." An alternative *functional hypothesis* (K. Nelson, 1973) suggests that children base their initial use of words on the important purposes (functions) of the concepts represented by the words, and children then make overextension errors because of their confusion regarding the functions of the objects being identified. Lamps give light, and blankets make us warm. A dog and a cat both do similar things and serve the same purposes as pets, so a child is likely to confuse them. Although the functional hypothesis has usually been viewed as an alternative to the feature hypothesis, it seems entirely possible that both mechanisms are at work in children's overextensions. As is often the case, perhaps neither position is completely right, and the truth as best we can know it is a synthesis of both views.

Telegraphic Speech

Gradually, by about 2½ years of age, children begin to combine single words to produce two-word utterances. Thus begins an understanding of syntax. These early syntactical communications lead to speech that seems more like telegrams than conversation because articles, prepositions, and other function morphemes are usually left out. Hence, linguists refer to these rudimentary syntactical communications of two words or more as **telegraphic speech.** Examples of telegraphic speech are "Up Mama," to indicate the child wants to be picked up by his or her mother, or "Daddy cup," to point out a father's drinking glass. In fact, the term *telegraphic speech* can be used to describe three-word utterances and even slightly longer ones if they have these same characteristic omissions of some function morphemes. Vocabulary expands rapidly, more than tripling from about 300 words at about age 2 to about 1,000 at about age 3.

Almost incredibly, by age 4 children acquire the foundations of adult syntax and language structure. By age 5 most children also can understand and produce quite complex and uncommon sentence constructions, and by age 10 children's language is fundamentally the same as that of adults. The aspects of language that are difficult for children at this point—things like dealing with passives, ambiguity, and abstractions—are also difficult for adults. In the next section, we will examine some of the possible explanations of the processes that work to allow humans to acquire language.

Explanations of Language Acquisition

A major theme in psychology and in this book is whether nature or nurture molds who we are and what we do. This debate continually resurfaces in new forms, particularly in regard to language acquisition. On one hand, exposure to language—nurture—influences language development. On the other hand, there appears also to be a biologically determined window of opportunity for learning language, suggesting that we are "wired" for language by nature. Few psychologists (if any) have asserted that language is entirely a result of nature. Both the diversity of languages in the world and the observations of children acquiring language appear to dispute this possibility. In contrast, some researchers and theoreticians have suggested that children acquire language largely because of the environment to which they are exposed. Two mechanisms for this phenomenon have been proposed: imitation and conditioning.

Imitation

One proposed mechanism for acquiring language is imitation. Even amateur observers notice that children's speech patterns and vocabulary reflect those of persons in their environment. In fact, parents of very young children seem to go to great lengths to make it easy for children to attend to and to understand what they are saying. Almost without thinking, parents and other adults tend to use a higher pitch than usual, to exaggerate the *vocal inflection* of their speech (i.e., more extreme raising and lowering of pitch and volume), and to use simpler sentence constructions when speaking with infants and young children. This characteristic form of speech that adults use has been termed *motherese*, but it is also perhaps more accurately termed *child-directed speech*. Through child-directed speech, adults seem to go out of their way to make language interesting and comprehensible to infants and other young children.

Indeed, infants do seem to prefer listening to child-directed speech more than to other forms of adult speech (Fernald, 1985). These exaggerations seem to gain and hold infants' attention, to communicate emotion-related information, and to signal to the infants when to take turns in vocalizing. Across cultures, parents seem to use this specialized form of speech, further tailoring it to particular circumstances: using rising intonations to gain attention; falling intonations to comfort; and brief, discontinuous, rapid-fire explosions of speech to warn against prohibited behavior (Fernald et al., 1989).

Parents even seem to model the correct format for verbal interactions. Early caregiver–child verbal interactions are characterized by *verbal turn-taking*, in which the caregiver says something and then uses vocal inflection to cue the infant to respond; the infant babbles, sneezes, burps, or otherwise makes some audible response; the caregiver accepts whatever noises the infant makes as valid communicative utterances and replies; the infant further responds to the cue; and so on for as long as they both show interest in continuing. Parents also seem to work hard to understand children's early utterances, in which one or two words, such as *ma* or *pa*, might be used for conveying an entire array of concepts. As the child grows older and more sophisticated and acquires more language, parents gradually provide less linguistic support and demand increasingly sophisticated utterances from the child. It is as if they initially provide a scaffolding from which the child can construct an edifice of language, and as the child's language develops, the parents gradually remove the scaffolding.

The mechanism of imitation is quite appealing in its simplicity; unfortunately, it does not explain many aspects of language acquisition. For example, if imitation is the primary mechanism, why do children universally begin by producing one-word utterances, then two-word and other telegraphic utterances, and later complete sentences? Why not start out with complete sentences? The most compelling argument against imitation alone is the phenomenon of **overregularization,** which commonly occurs during language acquisition, in which the novice language user has gained an understanding of how a language usually works and overapplies the general rules of the language to exceptional cases for which the rule does not apply. For example, instead of imitating the parent's sentence, "The mice fell down the hole, and they ran home," the young child might overregularize the irregular forms and say, "The mouses falled down the hole, and they runned home." An alternative explanation of language acquisition is thus needed.

Conditioning

The proposed alternative mechanism of conditioning is also exquisitely simple: Children hear utterances and associate those utterances with particular objects and events in their environment. They then produce those utterances and are rewarded by their parents and others for having spoken. Initially, their utterances are not perfect, but through successive approximations, they come to speak just as well as native adult speakers of their language. The progression from babbling to one-word utterances to more complex speech would seem to support the notions that children begin with simple associations and that their utterances gradually increase in complexity and in the degree to which they approximate adult speech.

As with imitation, the simplicity of the proposed conditioning mechanism does not suffice to explain actual language acquisition. For one thing, parents are much more likely to respond to the truth or falsity of the child's statement than to the relative pronunciational or grammatical correctness of the speech (R. Brown, Cazden, & Bellugi, 1969). In addition, even if parents did respond to the grammatical correctness of children's speech, their responses might explain why children eventually stop overregularizing their speech but not why they ever begin doing so. Perhaps the most compelling contradiction relates to productivity: the observation that children constantly employ novel utterances, for which they have never previously been rewarded and which they never heard uttered before. Children consistently apply the words and language structures they already know to novel situations and contexts for which they have never before received reinforcement. Clearly, some other process or predisposition must be involved in children's acquisition of language.

Critical Periods

If neither nature nor nurture alone adequately explains all aspects of language acquisition, just how might nature facilitate nurture in the process? Linguist Noam Chomsky proposed (1965, 1972) a hypothetical construct of an innate human predisposition to acquire language, a *language-acquisition device (LAD)*. That is, we humans seem to be mentally prewired or biologically preconfigured to be ready to acquire language. In fact, there seems to be a *critical period*—a time of rapid development, during which a particular ability must be developed if it is ever to develop adequately—for acquiring language. During such periods, the environment plays a crucial role. For example, the cooing and babbling stages seem to be a critical period for acquiring a native speaker's discrimination and production of the distinctive phonemes of a particular language; during this critical period, the child's linguistic context must provide those distinctive phonemes.

Evidence for a general critical period in language development comes from studies of "wild children." For example, in 1970, a social worker in California discovered that a woman and her husband had kept their 13-year-old daughter locked up in nearly total isolation during the years of her childhood. The girl, Genie, could neither speak nor stand erect. Unclothed, she had been tied to a child's potty seat for her entire childhood, and was able to move only her hands and feet. At night Genie was put into a sort of straightjacket and placed in a crib with wire mesh sides and a covering that turned it into a cage. Any kind of noise that Genie made resulted in her father's beating her, and the father communicated with her only through growling at her (Rymer, 1992). After her discovery, attempts were made to teach Genie basic skills (Curtiss, 1977), including language, but Genie never has been able to produce sentences of more than two or three words, and the sentences lack basic elements of grammar. Cases such as Genie suggest that if language is not acquired by a certain age, it may never be acquired. At the same time, given the traumatic environment in which Genie was raised, her case presents so many confounding variables that it is hard to know whether her later failure to acquire language was truly a result only of her lack of exposure to language during childhood.

There seems to be a critical period for acquiring a native understanding of a language's syntax, too. Perhaps the greatest support for this view comes from studies of adult users of American Sign Language (ASL). Among adults who have signed ASL for 30 years or more, researchers could discernibly differentiate among those who acquired ASL before age 4, between ages 4 and 6, and after age 12. Despite 30 years of signing, those who acquired ASL later in childhood showed less profound understanding of the distinctive syntax of ASL (Meier, 1991; Newport, 1990). Studies of linguistically isolated children seem to provide additional support for the notion of the interaction of both physiological maturation and environmental support. Of the rare children, like Genie, who have been linguistically isolated, those who are rescued at younger ages seem to acquire more sophisticated language structures than do those who are rescued when they are older.

There also seems to be a critical period for accent: If children learn a second language early enough, they will not show an accent that reflects their language, whereas adults who learn a second language almost always show an accent that reflects their first language.

Given the complex neurophysiology of other aspects of human perception and thought, it is not unreasonable to consider that we may be neurophysiologically predisposed to acquire language. Several observations of humans support this notion. For one thing, human speech perception is quite remarkable. In addition to noting our rapid phonemic specialization (mentioned in regard to babbling), consider our amazing ability to discern from a continuous flow of

There seems to be a critical period for acquiring a native understanding of a language's syntax. Perhaps the greatest support for this view comes from studies of adult users of American Sign Language (ASL). Despite 30 years of signing, those who acquired ASL later in childhood showed less profound understanding of the distinctive syntax of ASL.

auditory stimuli the distinct places where one word ends and another word begins. Note also that all children within a broad normal range of abilities and environments seem to acquire language at an incredibly rapid rate.

Evolutionary Processes

Some theorists, including Noam Chomsky (1980) as well as Steven Pinker (1994), have argued that the pattern of language acquisition must be innate. Moreover, because it follows a common path across many cultures (Pinker, 1994), it appears to be an evolutionary adaptation. For example, children all around the world (a) pass through the same stages of language acquisition, (b) generate combinations of words that adults would never produce (an argument against imitation), and (c) acquire more or less correct syntax despite infrequent correction of errors by parents and other adults. Moreover, (d) even children of relatively low intelligence acquire language. Although Pinker and others do not deny the role of the environment in language acquisition (e.g., in that language is acquired), they believe that evolutionary processes have set us up to acquire language in a certain way, which proceeds except in cases of severe environmental deprivation.

Thus it seems that neither nature nor nurture alone determines language acquisition. An alternative postulate, *hypothesis testing*, also suggests an integration of nature and nurture: Children acquire language by mentally forming tentative hypotheses regarding language and then testing these hypotheses in the environment. It has been suggested (Slobin, 1971, 1985) that the way in which children implement this process follows several operating principles. In forming hypotheses, young children look for and attend to (a) patterns of changes in the forms of words; (b) morphemic inflections that signal changes in meaning, especially suffixes; and (c) sequences of morphemes, including both the sequences of affixes and roots and the sequences of words in sentences.

In addition, children learn to avoid exceptions to the general patterns they observe and to avoid interrupting or rearranging the noun phrase and the verb phrase in sentences. Because children seem to follow these same general patterns of hypothesis testing, regardless of the language they acquire or of the context in which they acquire it, some psychologists believe that children must be naturally predisposed to hypothesis testing. Although not all linguists support the hypothesis-testing view, the phenomena of overregularization (using and sometimes overapplying rules) and of language productivity (creating novel utterances based on some kind of understanding of how to do so) seem to support it.

The bottom line, therefore, is that the old debate of nature versus nurture does not well represent the current state of knowledge. Rather, psychologists now attempt to discover what abilities are innately given, and how these abilities are tempered by the environment of the child—a process aptly termed "innately guided learning" (Jusczyk, 1997). Nature and nurture always interact in language development. They also interact in all human thought, the topic considered next.

The Nature of Thought

What is thought?

Thinking involves the representation and processing of information in the mind. Thought can be represented and processed with words, images, mental maps, concepts, and many other kinds of elements.

Because thinking is so important to almost everything we do, it is one of the most active areas of psychological research (Hunt, 1999). One way in which we view thought is to consider **critical thinking,** the conscious direction of mental processes toward representing and processing information, usually in order to find thoughtful solutions to problems. Critical thinking can be contrasted with noncritical thinking, in which we routinely follow customary thought patterns, without consciously directing how we think. Psychologists have observed that critical thinking may be directed to *analysis*, which involves breaking down wholes into component elements and which may be viewed as a process that complements *synthesis*, a process that involves integrating component parts into wholes. Critical thought may also involve generating many ideas, known as *divergent thinking*, or focusing on (converging toward) one idea from an assortment of possible ideas, called *convergent thinking*. Analysis and synthesis can be complementary processes, as can divergent and convergent thinking (see Table 8-1).

TABLE 8–1

Kinds of Critical Thinking *Critical thinking can be viewed both in terms of analysis and synthesis and in terms of divergent thinking and convergent thinking.*

KIND OF THINKING	DESCRIPTION	EXAMPLE
Analysis	Breaking down large, complex concepts or processes into smaller, simpler forms	Suppose that you were asked to write a term paper. You might break down the whole big project into the smaller steps: (1) choose a topic, (2) research the topic, (3) write a first draft, (4) revise, and so on.
Synthesis	Combining or integrating two or more concepts or processes into a more complex form	In writing a psychology term paper, you might combine some examples from your literature or your history class showing how poor judgment affected various literary or historical figures and then integrate the examples with psychological theories of decision making and judgment.
Divergent thinking	Generating a diverse assortment of possible alternative solutions to a problem	To discover topic ideas for a term paper, you might try to come up with as many ideas as possible in order to find interesting research topics that can be investigated and reported within a single semester.
Convergent thinking	Proceeding from various possible alternatives to converge on a single, best answer	From the many ideas you generated, you might try to converge on a single research topic.

In fact, cognitive psychologists often categorize problems according to whether the problems have clear paths to a solution. **Well-structured problems** are problems for which a clear path to the solution is known, although it may still be very difficult to implement (such as "How do you find the area of a parallelogram?"). **Ill-structured problems** are those problems for which a clear path to the solution is not known (such as "How do you succeed in the career of your choice?"). Of course, in the real world of problems, these two categories may represent more a continuum of clarity in problem solving than two discrete classes with an unambiguous boundary between the two. Nonetheless, the categories are useful in understanding how people solve problems. We next consider each of these kinds of problems in turn.

Psychologists have studied thinking in terms of four domains of inquiry: problem solving, judgment and decision making, reasoning, and creativity. The goal of **problem solving** is to move from a problem situation (e.g., not having enough money to buy a new car) to a solution, overcoming obstacles along the way. The goal of **judgment and decision making** is to select from among choices or to evaluate opportunities (e.g., choosing the used car that would please you the most for the amount of money you have). The goal of *reasoning* is to draw conclusions from evidence (e.g., reading consumer-oriented statistics to find out the reliability, economy, and safety of various cars). The goal of **creativity** is to produce something original and valuable (e.g., a fuel-efficient engine design, a distinctive marketing idea for the car, or a story to tell your parents as to why you need a car). Accordingly, this part of the chapter is divided into four subparts, each of which corresponds to one of these four domains of inquiry.

Strategies and Obstacles in Problem Solving

In Search of . . . | *How do people solve problems and what difficulties do they encounter in problem solving?*

We engage in problem solving when we need to overcome obstacles in order to answer a question or achieve a goal (Holyoak, 1995). Successful problem solving may occasionally involve tolerating some ambiguity regarding how best to proceed.

Solving Well-Structured Problems: Heuristics and Algorithms

People seeking to solve well-structured problems rely on a set of **heuristics**—informal, intuitive, speculative strategies, which sometimes work for solving problems and sometimes do not. For example, you might try several routes to your early morning class in order to find the fastest one, so that you can sleep as late as possible. Here you would be employing a simple *trial-and-error heuristic.* Heuristics are often contrasted with **algorithms,** formal paths for reaching a solution that involve one or more successive processes that usually lead to a correct solution. For example, an algorithm to find a book on your book shelf is to start with the first book at the left corner on the top shelf and then to proceed left to right, top to bottom, until you encounter the book.

Why would anyone ever use a heuristic, which does *not* guarantee a solution, instead of an algorithm, which does guarantee a solution? For one thing, often there is no obvious algorithm for solving a problem. In chess, for example, it is usually not obvious to us what algorithm, if any, would guarantee our winning the game. Later in this chapter, we discuss judgment and decision making, for which we may be able to apply heuristics in some situations, but for which it is rare to find a surefire algorithm. For another thing, it may be that an available algorithm would take so long to execute that it just is not practical to use it. For example, an algorithm for cracking a safe would be to try all possible combinations, but this algorithm is generally not practical for the safecracker in a hurry!

Many problems can be solved in more than one way. Often, the way in which we view a problem is shaped by our cultural contexts. For example, suppose that you want to sail from one island to another.

If you are a native Westerner, you will probably plan to use your charts and navigational equipment. However, some natives of particular islands in the South Pacific would probably scoff at such technicalities, and they might be puzzled by the idea of "going to" another island. Instead, these natives use the concept of the "moving island" to navigate vast expanses of ocean (Gladwin, 1970). That is, in their view, each island is adrift, floating along in the ocean. To get from one floating island to another, they do not "go" anywhere in the usual sense. Rather, they sit in their small boats, watch the changes in the currents and the color of the water, and then "catch" the island as *it* drifts by. As this alternative view of figuring out how to get from one island to another suggests, many problems may be solved in various ways, and some of these methods may seem more obvious to us than others. When the apparently obvious means of solving a problem does not seem to be working, it may be valuable to try to view the problem from a different perspective. Sometimes the means to solving a problem are not obvious because the problem is ill structured, as considered next.

Solving Ill-Structured Problems: The Nature of Insight

Before reading on, treat yourself to a little quiz (R. J. Sternberg, 1986a). Be sure to try both of the following problems before you read about their solutions.

1. Figure 8-3 shows a picture of nine dots arrayed three by three. Your task is to connect all nine dots with a set of line segments. You must never lift your pencil off the page, you must not go through a dot more than once, and you must not use more than four straight line segments. See whether you can connect the nine dots with a series of line segments without ever taking your pencil off the page.

2. A woman was putting some finishing touches on her house and realized she needed something she did not have. She went to the hardware store and asked the clerk, "How much will 150 cost me?" The clerk in the hardware store answered, "They are 75 cents apiece, so 150 will cost you $2.25." What did the woman buy?

Both of these problems are *ill-structured* problems. These particular ill-structured problems are termed *insight problems*, that is, they require **insight**—novel reconceptualization of the problem—in order to reach a solution. Insight provides a distinctive and apparently sudden understanding of a problem or a sudden realization of a strategy that aids in solving a problem. Insight often involves

Figure 8-3
THE NINE-DOT PROBLEM.   *How can you connect all nine dots without lifting your pencil from the paper and using just four straight lines? Psychologists study how people use insight to solve this and other ill-structured problems.*

reconceptualizing a problem or a strategy for its solution in a totally new way. To solve each problem you need to see the problem differently from the way you would probably see it at first, and differently from the way you would probably solve problems in general (Davidson, 1995). Frequently, an insight emerges through the detection and combination of relevant old and new information to gain a novel view of the problem or of its solution. Insight can be involved in solving well-structured problems, but it is more often associated with the rocky and twisting path to a solution that characterizes ill-structured problems. Although insights may feel sudden, they are often the result of much prior thought and hard work, without which the insight would never have occurred.

To understand insightful problem solving, it is useful to know the solutions to the two preceding insight problems. The solution to Problem 1, the nine-dot problem, is shown in Figure 8-4.

Most people find the problem extremely difficult to solve, and many never solve it. One hindrance is the common assumption that the lines must be kept within the confines of the square implicitly formed by the nine dots. In fact, the problem can be solved only by going outside those confines.

With regard to Problem 2, the woman might have been buying house numbers. Her house number is 150, so she needs three numerals, for a total cost of $2.25. From this point of view, this problem can be solved only if it is recognized that the "150" in the problem may refer to the three separate digits, rather than to the number 150. "House numbers" is not the only possible answer. For example, the woman might

Children's Cognitive Strategies

Robert S. Siegler, *Carnegie Mellon University*

During the past decade, great progress has been made in understanding the way in which children learn and think, especially math and science, the areas on which I will focus. Two basic concepts to keep in mind are *cognitive variability* and *adaptive choice*.

Cognitive Variability

First consider cognitive variability. Until recently, children's thinking was thought of as something like a staircase, in which children would first use one approach to solve problems, then adopt a more advanced approach, and later adopt an even more advanced approach. For example, descriptions of children's basic arithmetic indicated that when starting school, they added by counting from one; sometime during first grade, they switched to adding by counting from the larger addend; and by third or fourth grade, they added by retrieving the answers to problems.

More recent studies, however, have shown that children's thinking is far more variable than such staircase models suggest. Rather than adding by using the same strategy all of the time, children use a variety of strategies from early on, and continue to use both less and more mature approaches for many years. Thus, even early in first grade, the same child, given the same problem, will sometimes count from one, sometimes count from the larger addend, and sometimes retrieve the answer.

This is a spontaneous feature of children's thinking. Efforts to change it do not usually meet with much success. My research and that of a number of others has shown that pupils' use of strategies such as counting fingers actually helps them learn. On the surface, it seems as if the opposite would be true. After all, older students and those better at math don't use their fingers, and younger and less-apt students do. However, children actually learn better when they are allowed to use whatever strategies they want. Immature strategies usually fade naturally when students have enough knowledge to answer accurately without them. Even basic strategies such as counting fingers allow students to generate correct answers, while forbidding use of the strategies would lead to many errors. Further, students who use a greater variety of different strategies for solving problems also tend to learn better. This is in part because the greater variety leads the students to cope with whatever kinds of problems they encounter, rather than just being able to cope with a narrow range.

Adaptive Choice

A second concept that has emerged as important for understanding children's thinking and learning is *adaptive choice*. Children who know a variety of strategies for solving a given kind of problem must constantly choose which one to use on each particular occasion. To choose adaptively, they must adjust both to situational differences and to differences among problems. Situational variables include time limits, instructions, and the importance of the task. For example, if children need to solve as many simple addition problems as possible within a minute, it is adaptive for them to state answers quickly, even if they aren't absolutely sure of them. Similarly, if it's important to be correct in the particular situation, then checking the correctness of answers becomes more worthwhile.

Adaptive choice also involves adjusting the cognitive strategy one uses to the characteristics of particular problems. Adaptive choice involves using quick and easy strategies when they are sufficient and using increasingly effortful ones when they are necessary to be correct.

Substantial individual differences exist in both cognitive variability and the kinds of strategy choices that children make. My research has revealed that as early as first grade, children can be divided into three groups on the basis of their strategy choices in arithmetic and reading: good students, not-so-good students, and perfectionists. Good students and not-so-good students differ in all the ways that would be expected from the names. The good students are faster, more accurate, use more advanced strategies, and perform better on standardized IQ and achievement tests.

The differences between the perfectionists and the other two groups are more interesting. The perfectionists are just as accurate as the good students. They also have just as high IQs and just as high math and reading achievement. However, in terms of their strategy choices, they choose a higher proportion of slow and effortful strategies. Unless they are very sure of the answer, they don't rely on memory, preferring instead to use such strategies as counting from one or from the larger addend.

Socioeconomic Differences

Our work on strategy choice also has revealed some surprising similarities and differences in the performance of children from different socioeconomic groups. My research indicates that children from low-income backgrounds seem to lack adequate factual knowledge about the answers to academic problems. This in turn seems to be due to less practice in solving problems, and perhaps to less good execution of strategies, rather than to any deficiency in their high-level thinking. The findings indicate that greater practice and instruction in how to execute strategies may be the most useful approach to improving their academic skills.

 Find out more about this topic at www.harcourtcollege.com/psych/ishm

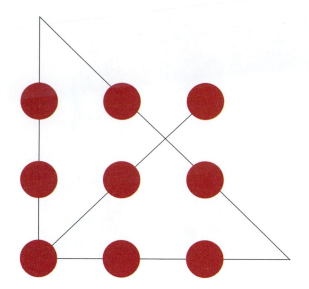

Figure 8-4
SOLUTION TO THE NINE-DOT PROBLEM.
How did you approach the task of solving this problem?

have been buying boxes of nails, whereby one box (of 50 nails) would cost 75 cents, and 150 nails (three boxes) would cost $2.25. With the solution involving nails, the problem can be solved only if we realize that the units have changed from nails to boxes of nails. Whether the problem is defined as one of house numbers or of nails (or something else bought in quantity), the terms of the problem are not what they originally appear to be. Sometimes, problems that appear to be about one thing really turn out to be about another, as was the case here.

Psychological Perspectives on Insight

Insight problems such as the preceding ones have intrigued psychologists for decades. The first psychologists to explore such problems in great depth, however, were Gestalt psychologists (see chapter 1). According to the Gestaltists, insight problems require problem solvers to go beyond associations among various parts in order to perceive the problem as a whole. Gestalt psychologist Max Wertheimer distinguished between *productive thinking* (Wertheimer, 1945/1959), which involves insight that goes beyond the bounds of existing associations identified by the thinker, and *reproductive thinking*, in which the thinker makes use of existing associations involving what the thinker already knows. According to Wertheimer, insightful, productive thinking differs fundamentally from associationistic, reproductive thinking. It does not just extend associationistic thinking to novel kinds of problems. In solving the preceding insight problems, you had to break

away from your existing associations and see each problem in an entirely new light. Productive thinking also can be applied to well-structured problems, as shown in Figures 8-5 and 8-7. (Before looking at Figure 8-7, try to solve the problem in Figure 8-5.)

Wertheimer's Gestaltist colleague, Wolfgang Köhler (1927), studied insight by observing a chimpanzee confined in a cage with two sticks. Outside the cage, out of his reach and out of the reach of either stick, was a banana. After trying to grab the banana with his hand and each stick, the chimp took to tinkering with the sticks. Suddenly, he realized that the sticks could be attached to one another to form a new tool: one long pole that he could then use to roll the banana into range. In Köhler's view, the chimp's behavior illustrated insight and showed that insight is a special process, involving thinking that differs from normal information processing. (Figure 8-6 illustrates a chimp engaged in a similar insight task.)

Gestalt psychologists provided and described many other examples of insight and speculated on a few ways in which insight might occur: It might result from (a) extended unconscious leaps in thinking, (b) greatly accelerated mental processing, or (c) some kind of short-circuiting of normal reasoning processes (see Perkins, 1981). Unfortunately, the Gestaltists did not provide convincing evidence for any of these views, nor did they specify just what insight is (see Weisberg, 1992).

Insights can startle us with their brilliance but still be wrong. Many of the great insights of history have seemed right at the time but were later proved wrong or at least partial. For example, the physical principle proposed by Sir Isaac Newton represented brilliant insights, but were later shown by Albert Einstein to be based on an incomplete understanding of the nature of the physical universe. No matter how convinced we may be of the validity of our own or someone else's insights, we need to be open to the possibility that the insights may later seem to be incorrect. On the other hand, we should not casually dismiss our insights just

Figure 8-5
AREA OF PARALLELOGRAM PROBLEM. *What is the area of this parallelogram? According to Gestaltist Max Wertheimer, you will need to engage in productive thinking, not reproductive thinking, to solve it.*

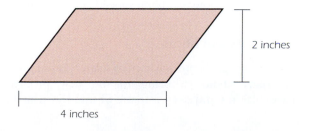

2 inches

4 inches

Figure 8-6

A DEMONSTRATION OF INSIGHT BY A CHIMPANZEE.   *In one of Wolfgang Kohler's experiments, the chimp demonstrated insightful problem solving to retrieve the bananas hanging from the top of the enclosure. According to Gestaltists, insightful problem solving is a special process that differs from ordinary information processing.*

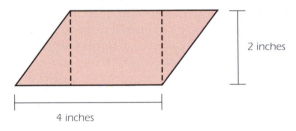

Figure 8-7

SOLUTION TO AREA OF PARALLELOGRAM PROBLEM.
To solve the problem posed by Wertheimer, you may have to re-frame the problem, as suggested by the lines shown in this fig-ure. Once the problem is reframed, you can see that it is similar to finding the area of a rectangle.

because they seem improbable at first glance. (Figure 8-8 demonstrates the different artistic insights of two landscape painters.)

Hindrances to Problem Solving

There are several common potential hindrances to problem solving, which can occur singly or in combina-tion: mental sets and fixation, and functional fixedness. Each sheds light on how our problem-solving processes operate and the potential blind spots that can occur.

Mental Sets and Fixation

Many insight problems are hard to solve because prob-lem solvers tend to bring to the new problem a particular **mental set**—a frame of mind in which a

problem solver is predisposed to think of a problem or a situation in a particular way (sometimes termed "en-trenchment"), often leading the problem solver to focus or fixate on a strategy that normally works. A mental set may be helpful in solving some (or perhaps even most) problems, but it still may not work in solv-ing a particular problem. For example, in the nine-dot problem, we may fixate on strategies that involve draw-ing lines within the dots; in the house-numbers prob-lem, we may fixate on strategies involving 150 items.

Abraham Luchins (1942) exquisitely demonstrated the phenomenon of mental set in what he called "water-jar" problems. In these problems, participants are asked how to measure out a certain amount of water, using different jars, with each jar holding a dif-ferent amount of water. The jars have no graduated measurements on their sides. Table 8-2 shows the problems used by Luchins. You need to use the jars to obtain the required amounts of water (measured in numbers of cups) in the last column. Columns A, B, and C show the capacity of each jar. The first problem, for example, enables you to get 20 cups of water from just two of the jars, a 29-cup one (Jar A) and a 3-cup one (Jar B). Easy: Just fill Jar A and then empty out 9 cups from this jar by taking out 3 cups three times, using Jar B. Problem 2 is not too hard either. Fill Jar B with 127 cups, then empty out 21 cups using Jar A, and then empty out 6 cups, using Jar C twice. Now try the rest of the problems yourself.

If you are like many people solving these problems, you will have found a formula that works for all but one of the remaining problems (which one?): You fill up Jar B, then pour out the amount of water you can put

Figure 8–8
EXAMPLES OF INSIGHT IN ART.   *Excellent examples of insights include Claude Lorrain's keen awareness of the natural beauty of landscapes in* II Tramonto (The Sunset, *left) and Paul Cezanne's observations of diffuse, warm light in* Mont Saint-Victoire Seen From Les Lauves *(right). Each artist selected the key relevant visual elements from the vast array of visual information.*

into Jar A, and then twice pour out of it the amount of water you can put into Jar C. The formula, therefore, is B – A – 2C (Figure 8-9). However, Problems 7 through 11 can be solved in a much simpler way, using just two of the jars. For example, Problem 7 can be solved by A – C, Problem 8 by A + C, Problem 9 by A – C but *not* by B – A – 2C, Problem 10 by A + C, and Problem 11 by A – C. People who are given Problems 1 through 6 to solve generally continue to try to use the B – A – 2C

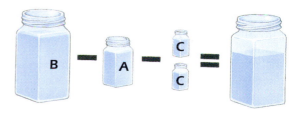

Figure 8–9
LUCHIN'S WATER-JAR SOLUTION.   *This figure shows an algorithm for solving most of the water-jar problems shown in Table 8-2. Although the algorithm solves most of the problems given, is there an easier way to solve some of them? (From Luchins, 1942)*

formula in solving Problems 7 through 11. However, people who go from Problem 2 immediately to Problem 7 generally see the simpler formula: They have no established mental set that interferes with their seeing things in a new and simpler way.

Functional Fixedness

A particular type of mental set involves **functional fixedness,** in which the problem solver is unable to recognize that something that is known to be used in one way, for one purpose, may also be used for performing other functions, perhaps even through use in another way. Functional fixedness prevents us from using old tools in novel ways to solve new problems. Overcoming functional fixedness is what first allowed people to use a reshaped coat hanger to get into a locked car, and it is what first allowed thieves to pick simple spring-door locks with a

| TABLE 8-2 |

The Water-Jar Problems   *What is the most effective way of measuring out the correct amount of water using Jars A, B, and C? (From Luchins, 1942)*

PROBLEM NUMBER	JARS AVAILABLE FOR USE			REQUIRED AMOUNT (CUPS)
	A	B	C	
1	29	3		20
2	21	127	3	100
3	14	163	25	99
4	18	43	10	5
5	9	42	6	21
6	20	59	4	31
7	23	49	3	20
8	15	39	3	18
9	28	76	3	25
10	18	48	4	22
11	14	36	8	6

credit card. It is also what might allow you to think of an introductory psychology textbook as a resource for criminal ideas!

Functional fixedness may be influenced by cultural context in a way that might surprise some Westerners. Some early writers hypothesized that there are higher and lower levels of mental development across cultures, and that these levels influence the depth or quality of cognitive processes. French anthropologist Claude Levi-Strauss (1966; see also Cole & Scribner, 1974) rejected this highly ethnocentric hypothesis. Instead, he maintained that the human mind works in essentially the same way across cultures and across time. The only difference between the thought systems employed by persons in nonindustrialized versus industrialized, highly specialized societies might be in the strategies people use. Levi-Strauss noted that scientific thinkers and problem solvers in nonindustrialized societies are generally *bricoleurs* (jacks-of-all-trades). A *bricoleur* has a bag of tools that can be used to fix all sorts of things, whereas the focused expert of an industrialized society might be effective only in thinking about and solving problems within a narrow area of expertise. One extension of this line of thinking is that persons who live in less specialized, nonindustrialized societies may be less subject to functional fixedness than their more specialized, industrialized counterparts.

Transfer

Transfer refers to prior learning that affects one's ability to solve a problem. It may help or hinder problem solving (Gick & Holyoak, 1980, 1983). For example, when you learn a second language, your knowledge of the first language can help you learn the new language, because it may share many of the same word roots and grammatical principles. But in trying to recall words in the new language, words from the old language may keep popping into your mind, hindering your recall. In this sense, transfer can be a form of functional fixedness. However, if you allow yourself to apply or transfer knowledge from one domain to another ("I know I passed that store near the end of the bike race, so if I just retrace my steps starting at the finish line, I'll find it"), you can expand on your own experiences.

Incubation

Sometimes we get stuck on a problem that requires an insight. The insight just does not seem to come to us. A useful process in solving insight problems is **incubation**—a process by which a problem solver discontinues intensive work on solving a problem, stops focusing conscious attention on solving the problem

for a while, and permits problem solving to occur at a subconscious level for a period of time. For example, if you find that you are unable to solve a problem, and none of the strategies you can think of seem to work, try just setting the problem aside to incubate for a while. During incubation, you do not consciously think about the problem. Still, the problem may be processed at a level beneath that of full consciousness. Although no one knows exactly why incubation works, some researchers believe it is because as time passes, new stimuli—both internal and external—may activate new perspectives on the problem, weakening the effects of old mental sets (Bastik, 1982; Yaniv & Meyer, 1987). People who are prepared to receive relevant new information from the environment are particularly likely to incubate successfully (Seifert, Meyer, Davidson, Patalano, & Yaniv, 1995).

For example, when you write a paper for a course and you find that you just cannot seem to organize the paper effectively, it may help just to let the problem incubate for a while. A few days later, you may come across some new ideas or otherwise find that what seemed like an insoluble problem is now more easily solved. Using this strategy means, of course, that you need to start thinking about the paper enough in advance of the deadline so that you have time for incubation.

Sometimes we get stuck on a problem. The insight needed to solve it just won't come; for example, when you write a paper for a course and just can't seem to figure out how to organize it effectively. In such cases, it may be best to allow the problem to incubate for a while, as time permits.

Expertise: Knowledge and Problem Solving

Thus far, this chapter has discussed various strategies we all use for solving problems. If these strategies are available to all of us, why can experts solve problems in their field more effectively than can novices? What do experts know that makes the problem-solving process more effective for them than for novices in a field?

Studies have shown that much of what distinguishes experts from novices is the extent and organization of the knowledge base. William Chase and Herbert Simon (1973), following up on work by Adrian de Groot (1965), set out to find what experts know and do by determining what distinguishes expert from novice chess players. In one of their studies, Chase and Simon had expert and novice players briefly view a display of a chessboard with the chess pieces on it and then recall the positions of the chess pieces on the board. In general, the experts did quite a bit better than did the novices—but only if the positions of the chess pieces on the board made sense in terms of an actual game of chess. If the pieces were randomly distributed around the board, experts did not recall the positions of the pieces any better than did the novices.

According to Chase and Simon, the key difference between groups was that chess experts (but not novices) could call on their knowledge of tens of thousands of board positions, each of which they could remember as an integrated, organized chunk of information. For a random pattern of pieces on the board, however, the knowledge of the experts offered them no advantage over the novices. Like the novices, they had to try to memorize the distinctive interrelations among the many discrete pieces and positions.

After the Chase and Simon work, a number of other investigators conducted extensive studies of large numbers of experts in different domains (e.g., see Chi, Glaser, & Farr, 1988; Ericsson, 1996; Frensch & Funke, 1995; R. J. Sternberg & Frensch, 1991). Although several characteristics were found to distinguish experts from novices, what most clearly differentiated the two groups was the amount of existing knowledge, and how well the existing information was organized. It also has been found that deliberate, systematic practice is one of the best ways to become an expert in a wide variety of endeavors (Ericsson, 1996), although such practice is more effective if supplemented by a talent for the endeavor one pursues (Shiffrin, 1996; Wagner & Stanovich, 1996). Micheline Chi and her colleagues (e.g., Chi, Feltovich, & Glaser, 1981), further studying experts versus novice performance in physics, asked people to sort physics problems into groups of problems that "belonged together." Chi found that the experts tended to sort problems by the underlying principles of physics involved, whereas novices tended to sort the problems in terms of surface features of the problems, such as whether the problems involved pulleys. Alan Lesgold and his colleagues studied radiologists and found several other differences between experts and novices (Lesgold, 1988; Lesgold et al., 1988). For example, they found that experts tend to spend more time than do novices in representing problems, and that experts are better at using new evidence than are novices.

Whereas problem solving involves inventing or discovering strategies in order to answer a complex question, other forms of thinking may involve simply (but not necessarily easily) choosing among alternatives or evaluating opportunities. The next section deals with how we make these choices and judgments.

Judgment and Decision Making

In *Search of . . .*

How do we make judgments and decisions?

In the course of our everyday lives, we are constantly making judgments and decisions. One of the most important decisions you may have made is that of whether and where to go to college. Once in college, you need to choose the courses you will take and, eventually, your major field of study. You make decisions about friends, about how to relate to your parents, and about how to spend money. How do you go about deciding on possible options and then making these decisions?

Decision Theory

The earliest models of decision theory assumed that decision makers operate in ideal circumstances and make optimal decisions. Although we may now see these assumptions as unrealistic, a great deal of economic research has been and still is based on this model. Subsequent models of decision making have recognized that we humans may not face ideal circumstances, but these models have asserted that we nevertheless strive to make optimal decisions. For example, according to *utility-maximization theory*, the goal of human action is to maximize pleasure (*positive utility*) and to minimize pain (*negative utility*). Utility-maximization theorists suggest that we can predict what people will do by assuming that they will seek the highest possible utility—in other words, whatever decision maximizes pleasure and minimizes pain. Suppose, for example, that you are deciding whether to buy a desktop computer. You do not like the fact that such a computer is not portable and cannot be taken on trips. This factor can be viewed as a negative utility. At the same time, you like the large screen and the rapid processing speed of the machine. These factors provide positive utilities. Whether you buy the desktop computer will depend on whether the positive utilities outweigh the negative ones in your mind.

Although it is certainly appealing to come up with objective, mathematical models for decision making, in practice, it is very difficult to assign objective utilities to decisions, and models based on such assignments are likely to produce inaccurate representations of reality. As a result, cognitive psychologists interested in decision theory introduced *subjective-utility theory*, which acknowledges that each individual may have a distinctive understanding regarding the various utilities for a given action, based on the idiosyncratic hopes, fears, and other subjective motivations of the individual. For example, being turned down for a date may be extremely negative for one person, and only slightly negative for another.

Satisficing

Principles of economics are often based on the notion that decision makers have unlimited rationality and use it in making their decisions. The decision makers decide what criterion to maximize or minimize and then make the optimal decision for doing so. Even in the 1950s, however, some psychologists were beginning to recognize that we humans do not always make ideal decisions, that we usually include subjective considerations in our decisions, and that we are not entirely and boundlessly rational in making decisions.

The most well-known challenge came from Herbert Simon (1957), who went on to win the Nobel Prize in economics. Simon did not suggest that we humans are irrational, but rather that we exhibit **bounded rationality**—the limits within which humans demonstrate reasoned behavior. Simon suggested one of the most typical decision-making strategies: satisficing. In **satisficing,** the decision maker considers options one by one, immediately selecting the first option that appears to be satisfactory—just good enough, rather than considering all of the possible options and then carefully computing which of the entire universe of options will maximize gains and minimize losses. Thus, we will consider the minimum possible number of options to arrive at a decision that we believe will satisfy our minimum requirements. For example, you may use satisficing when considering research topics for a term project or paper; of the countless possible topics, you may consider a few, and then settle on the first satisfactory or even pretty good topic you think of, without continuing your exploration.

The trend that led from fully rational models of decision making to models of bounded rationality involved the increasing recognition that people are not perfect decision makers. We make decisions in less than ideal circumstances, given inadequate or incomplete information, and using limited objectivity and rationality. Often, we are even willing to settle for the first acceptable option that becomes available, fully aware that other options may be better. What additional human frailties have researchers discovered in the study of decision making?

Heuristics and Biases in Decision Making

In the 1970s, Amos Tversky and Daniel Kahneman found even more evidence of the boundaries of human rationality. Tversky, Kahneman, and their colleagues investigated several heuristics and biases we often use when making decisions and other judgments (see Shafir & Tversky, 1995); some of these heuristics and biases—such as representativeness, availability, and some of the other phenomena involving judgment—are described in the following section.

Representativeness

Before you read a definition of representativeness, try out the following problem (Kahneman & Tversky, 1971):

> All the families having exactly six children in a particular city were surveyed. In 72 of the families, the exact order of births of boys (B) and girls (G) was G B G B B G. What is your estimate of the number of families surveyed in which the exact order of births was B G B B B B?

Most people judging the number of families with the B G B B B B birth pattern estimate the number to be less than 72. Actually, the best estimate of the number of families with this birth order is 72, the same as for the G B G B B G birth order. The expected number for the second pattern would be the same because the gender for each birth is independent (at least, theoretically) of the gender for every other birth, and for any one birth, the chances of a boy (or a girl) are one out of two. Thus, any particular pattern of births is equally likely, even B B B B B B or G G G G G G.

Why do people believe some birth orders to be more likely than others? Kahneman and Tversky suggest that it is because they use the **representativeness heuristic,** a judgment regarding the probability of an uncertain event according to (a) how obviously the event is similar to or representative of the population from which it is derived, and (b) the degree to which the event reflects the salient features of the process by which it is generated (such as randomness). For example, people believe that the first birth order is more likely because first, it is more representative of the number of females and males in the population, and because second, it looks more random than does the second birth order. In fact, of course, either birth order is equally likely to occur by chance.

Similarly, if asked to judge the probability of flips of a coin yielding the sequence—H T H H T H—people will judge it as higher than they will if asked to judge the sequence—H H H H T H. Thus, if you expect a sequence to be random, you tend to view a sequence that "looks random" as more likely to occur. Indeed, people often comment that the ordering of numbers in a table of random numbers "doesn't look random," because people underestimate the number of runs of the same number that will appear wholly by chance.

In order fully to understand the representativeness heuristic, it helps to understand the concept of **base rate**—the prevalence of an event or characteristic within its population of events or characteristics. People often ignore base-rate information, even though it is important to effective judgment and decision making. In many occupations, the use of base-rate information and the representativeness heuristic are essential for adequate job performance. For example, if a doctor were told that a 10-year-old girl is suffering chest pains, the doctor would be much less likely to worry about an incipient heart attack than if told that a 50-year-old man has the identical symptom. Why? Because the base rate of heart attacks is much higher in 50-year-old men than in 10-year-old girls. It is also easier to recall cases of people of roughly 50 years of age who have had heart attacks: Such instances are more available, which leads us to the next heuristic.

Availability

Fewer than 1 in 250,000 plane flights has even the most minor of accidents; fewer than 1 in 1.6 million scheduled flights ends in fatalities (L. Krantz, 1992); the odds were 1 in 2.2 million of being killed in an airplane crash in 1988 (Shook & Shook, 1991). Although the chances of dying during any given car trip (however brief) are low, more than 1 in 125 Americans will die in a car-related accident (L. Krantz, 1992). Intoxicated 18-year-old men driving without seat belts are 1,000 times more likely to die in a car crash than are sober 40-year-old drivers, either male or female, who are wearing their seat belts (Shook & Shook, 1991).

Why is it that so many more people are afraid of flying in airplanes than of riding in cars, despite the fact that the probability of being injured or dying in a car crash is much higher? One reason is the **availability heuristic** (Tversky & Kahneman, 1973), an intuitive strategy for making judgments or inferences, or for solving problems, on the basis of the ease with which particular examples or ideas may be called to mind, without necessarily considering the degree to which the particular examples or ideas are relevant to or suitable for the given context. Newspapers and television give much more play to plane crashes than to car crashes, and it is usually easier to call to mind grim instances of plane crashes than of car crashes. Hence, unequal coverage may be one reason (of many) that people tend to fear riding in planes more than they fear riding in cars. Similarly, politicians spend a lot of time on fund-raising to buy advertising because they know that the media exposure that makes their names more readily available to voters than the names of their competitors can be critical in their winning elections.

Sometimes, availability and representativeness work together to lead to a less than optimal conclusion. Take, for example, the following true story, which is

Which of these accidents has the higher base rate? How does the availability of some information (and the unavailability of other information) influence our perceptions and decisions?

similar to a story used in the research of Tversky and Kahneman.

> A high school senior has thoroughly checked out two colleges. Call them College A and College B. He has looked in guide books and spoken to people who are well acquainted with each college. On the basis of all the available information, College A looks better. Yet, when he visits, he likes his host at College B more than his host at College A. The class he attends at College B also is more interesting than the one he attends at College A. Moreover, on the day he visits College B, the weather is excellent, whereas on the day he visits College A, the weather is terrible. He even gets paint on his raincoat at College A. He finds it hard not to prefer College B. The actual visits to the colleges seem more representative in their information about the colleges than does second-hand information, and the information from the visits is also more readily available. Yet, College A is probably the better choice because it is almost certainly a mistake to judge two colleges on the basis of a single host, a single class, and the weather on the day of the visit.

(This very set of events happened to me. I chose College A despite it all, and I am happy I did.)

It is important to realize that heuristics such as representativeness and availability do not always lead to wrong judgments. Indeed, we use them because they are so often right. For example, in buying a computer, you may decide to buy from a company for which the company name is readily available in memory, based on the view that you are taking a bigger risk in buying from a company that is relatively unknown. The known company does not necessarily make a better computer, but because the computer is a large purchase, you may not want to take the risk of buying from an unknown manufacturer.

Other Decision-Making and Judgment Phenomena

There are other oddities in people's judgments (see Osherson, 1995). One is **overconfidence**—an excessive valuation of skills, knowledge, or judgment, usually applied to a person's valuation of his or her own abilities or decisions. Baruch Fischhoff, Paul Slovic, and Sarah Lichtenstein (1977) gave people 200 two-alternative statements, such as "*Absinthe* is (a) a liqueur, (b) a precious stone." People were asked to choose the correct answer and to give the probability that their answer was correct. People were strangely overconfident. For example, when people were 100% confident of their answers, they were right only 80% of the time! (Absinthe is a licorice-flavored liqueur.)

Kahneman and Tversky (1979) asked people questions such as "I feel 98% certain that the number of nuclear plants operating in the world in 1980 was more than _____ but less than _____." Despite stating that they were almost certain they were correct, people were in fact often wrong. Nearly one third of the time, the correct answer to questions such as these was outside the range that people gave (in this case, there were exactly 189 nuclear plants operating at that time). Due to overconfidence, people often do things that are dangerous or bad for them. One example of overconfidence is the belief held by many smokers that, although lung cancer and heart disease may strike other people, they themselves are not likely to be struck by these diseases. It is not clear why we tend to be overconfident in our judgments; one simple explanation is that we prefer not to think about being wrong (Fischhoff, 1988).

Another common error is **gambler's fallacy,** an intuitive and fallacious inference that when a sequence of coincidental events appears to be occurring in a nonrandom pattern, subsequent events are more likely to deviate from the apparent pattern than to continue in the apparent pattern. Actually, the probability of each event continues to be exactly the same at each occurrence. In other words, just by the nature of things, eventually, a person's luck is bound to change. Thus, the gambler who loses in five successive bets may believe that a win is more likely the sixth time. In truth, of course, the gambler is no more likely to win on the sixth bet than on the first—or on the 1,001st! Of course, luck *can* change. Often, however, it changes only when we make our own luck.

Much of the work on judgment and decision making has focused on the errors people make. As Jonathan Cohen (1981) and Gilbert Harman (1995) have pointed out, however, people do act rationally in many instances. (For example, you have made the rational decision to read the textbook in order to do well on the examinations in your psychology course—as well as to learn about psychology.) Nonetheless, the research of Tversky and Kahneman, as well as of others, shows that our rationality is limited. It is as much a part of being human not to be rational at times as it is to be rational at other times.

Reasoning

How do we reason?

We have seen that judgment and decision making involve evaluating opportunities and selecting one choice above any others. A more formal kind of thinking, familiar to students in logic courses, is reasoning. **Reasoning** involves drawing conclusions from evidence (Wason & Johnson-Laird, 1972). It is often divided into two types—deductive and inductive reasoning. **Deductive reasoning** is the process of drawing conclusions from evidence involving one or more general **premises**—statements of fact or assertions of belief on which a deductively reasoned argument may be based—to reach a logically certain, specific conclusion. In contrast, **inductive reasoning** is the process of drawing general explanatory conclusions based on evidence involving specific facts or observations. Inductive reasoning permits the reasoner to draw well-founded or probable conclusions but not logically certain conclusions. We will now examine each of these two types of reasoning. Some theorists believe that humans have two systems of reasoning, one that is largely logical, and the other that is largely alogical or experiential (e.g., Sloman, 1996, 1999). Moreover, even when people are trying to be rational, their preconceptions can have a strong effect on their reasoning (Bassok, Wu, & Olseth, 1995). In any case, people do not show the same skill in reasoning in all domains. For example, they might be strong verbal reasoners but not as strong in mathematical reasoning (Frensch & Buchner, 1999).

Deductive Reasoning

Deductive reasoning proceeds from a set of general premises to a specific, logically certain conclusion. It is the process of reasoning from what is already known to reach a new conclusion. One specific type of problem often used to illustrate deductive reasoning is the syllogism. **Syllogisms** are deductive arguments that permit conclusions to be drawn, based on two premises, in which each of the two premises contains two terms, at least one term of which is common to both premises. Although it is possible to specify rules for solving syllogisms, some psychologists believe that problem solvers do not use formal rules, but rather, model the problems by imagining concrete terms of the problems (Johnson-Laird, 1999). For example, they would think of the following syllogism in terms of concrete psychology students, pianists, and athletes:

All psychology students are pianists.
All pianists are athletes.
Therefore, all psychology students are athletes.

Various theories have been proposed as to how people solve syllogisms. Philip Johnson-Laird and Mark Steedman (1978) have proposed a theory (see also Johnson-Laird & Byrne, 1991) based on the notion that people solve syllogisms using mental models; that is, they manipulate in their minds actual exemplars of elements of the syllogisms, trying to find what the correct

solution should be. In contrast, Lance Rips (1994, 1995) has suggested that we solve such problems using a set of mental rules for combining premises.

A different approach to deductive reasoning has been suggested by Leda Cosmides (1989; Cosmides & Tooby, 1992). According to Cosmides, psychologists should take an evolutionary view of cognition and should consider what kinds of thinking skills would provide a naturally selective advantage for humans in adapting to our environment across evolutionary time. To gain insight into human cognition, we should look to see what kinds of adaptations would have been most useful to human hunters and gatherers during the millions of years of evolutionary time that predated the relatively recent development of agriculture and the very recent development of industrialized societies.

Cosmides has suggested that one of the distinctive adaptations shown by human hunters and gatherers was in the area of social exchange, as occurs in any kind of a deal between two people, such as a barter or sale. Two of the kinds of inferences that people should be well equipped to make are those related to cost–benefit relationships and those related to the detection of cheating in a social exchange. Thus, you will reason better if a reasoning problem involves detection of your being cheated than if it involves, say, a procedure for washing clothes. The idea is that people in earlier times who were not skilled in assessing costs and benefits of a deal with someone and in determining when they were being cheated would have been at a disadvantage in adaptation, and they would have been less likely ultimately to have descendants. Over a series of nine experiments, Cosmides found that the predictions of her social-exchange theory better fit the data from people's performance on deductive-reasoning tasks than did the predictions of either permissions-related schemas or of abstract deductive-reasoning principles.

It is also important to keep in mind that deductive reasoning with abstract kinds of terms is an activity that is practiced and rewarded in some cultures but not others. Individuals in some cultures may find such problems confusing and rather pointless (Cole, Gay, Glick, & Sharp, 1971; Luria, 1976).

> "Alas, Adso, you have too much faith in syllogisms! What we have, once again, is simply the question. . . ."
> I was upset. I had always believed logic was a universal weapon, and now I realized how its validity depended on the way it was employed.
> —Umberto Eco, *The Name of the Rose*

In inductive reasoning, considered next, the reasoner cannot reach a logically certain conclusion; she or he can only hope to determine the strength, or probability, of a conclusion.

Inductive Reasoning

Suppose that you are not given a neat set of premises from which you can draw a conclusion. Instead, you are given a set of observations. For example, suppose that you notice that all of the persons enrolled in your introductory psychology course are on the dean's list (or honor roll). From these observations, you could inductively reason that all students who enroll in introductory psychology are excellent students (or at least earn the grades to give that impression!). However, unless you can observe the grade-point averages of all persons who ever have, or ever will, take introductory psychology, you will be unable to prove your conclusion. Further, a single poor student who happened to enroll in an introductory psychology course would disprove your conclusion. Still, after many observations, you might conclude that you had made enough observations to make an inductive inference.

In this situation and in many others requiring reasoning, you were not given clearly stated premises or obvious, certain relationships between the elements, by which you would be able to deduce a surefire conclusion. In this type of situation, you simply cannot deduce a logically valid conclusion. An alternative kind of reasoning is needed. Inductive reasoning involves reasoning from specific facts or observations to a general conclusion that may explain the facts (Bisanz, Bisanz, & Korpan, 1994). For example, you may try to remember where you placed your lost keys on the basis of plausible inferences, such as where you usually put the keys, where you have recently been, and so forth. None of these considerations guarantees a solution to the problem, but your inductive reasoning may help you find the keys. An important feature of inductive reasoning, which forms the basis of the empirical method discussed in chapter 2, is that we cannot reasonably leap from saying, "All observed instances of X are Y" to "Therefore, all X are Y." For example, suppose that a child has seen many kinds of birds flying in the sky. She may reasonably conclude, "All birds fly." However, when she visits the zoo and encounters penguins and ostriches for the first time, she can see that her inductive conclusion is false. Like other empiricists, she can thereby find that her inductive conclusions, based on many observations, can be disproved by just one contradictory observation. Furthermore, regardless of the number of observations or the soundness of the reasoning, no inductively based conclusions can be proved. Such conclusions can only be supported, to a greater or lesser degree, by available evidence. Thus, the inductive reasoner must state any conclusions about a hypothesis in terms of likelihoods, such as "There is a good chance of rain tomorrow," or "There is a 99% probability that these findings are not a result of random variability."

For example, suppose that in Jason's mental model of a college campus, he originally formulated a rule that "people on college campuses are either students or professors." Later, after Jason had a few encounters with administrative personnel, librarians, service personnel, and others on campus who are neither students nor professors, he realized that his rule had to be modified. He then modifies his rule to be "people on college campuses are students, professors, or paid staff members."

To conclude our discussion of reasoning, it seems that despite our occasional lapses and distortions, we often reason pretty well. Still, even the most enlightened reasoning cannot create something from what appears to be nothing. To do that, we need creativity.

Creativity

In Search of . . . *What is creativity and what are the characteristics of creative people?*

Creativity is the process of producing something that is both original and valuable. The *something* could be a theory, a dance, a chemical, a process or procedure, or almost anything else (Figure 8-10).

Just what does it mean for that something to be *original?* Almost everything we do is based on the ideas and the work of those who have come before us. Creative individuals, even if they learn from the techniques, styles, and ideas of predecessors, are those who analyze or synthesize this information in a novel, unconventional, and valuable way. Value is another important idea in the definition of creativity. What makes something valuable is that it is significant, useful, or worthwhile in some way, to some segment of the population or some field of endeavor. Sometimes, people do not appreciate the value of the creative work until long after the creator dies.

Characteristics of Creative Thinking

What does it take to create something original and worthwhile? What characteristics do psychologists notice in creative individuals? Although we have yet to develop a method for detecting highly creative individuals at a glance, psychologists have found that highly creative individuals seem to share a few intrinsic characteristics. Psychologists who take a *psychometric* approach, such as Joy Guilford (1950), have emphasized performance on tasks involving specific aspects of creativity, such as *divergent production*, which involves the generation of a diverse assortment of appropriate responses to a problem

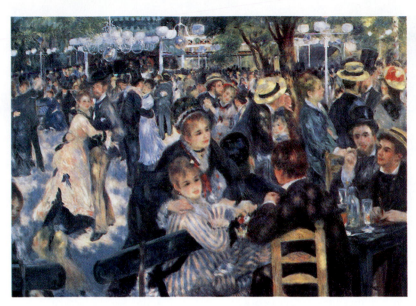 

Figure 8–10

CREATIVITY IN ART. *Highly creative individuals, such as Vincent van Gogh, whose* Landscape With Cypress and Star *is shown on the right, often lead a revolutionary movement away from the contemporary mode, illustrated by the Impressionist painting* Le Moulin de la Galette *by Pierre-Auguste Renoir, shown on the left.*

question or task. For example, coming up with ideas for a term paper involves divergent production.

Creativity may vary in its manifestation at different points in life. Howard Gardner (1993a; Policastro & Gardner, 1999), using case studies, has suggested that earlier contributions by individuals tend to be more radically creative, and later ones, more integrative with past work in their expression of creativity. It also seems that differing forms of literary creativity surface at different ages. For instance, a survey of 420 literary creators both across cultures and across vast expanses of time supports the notion that people write more creative poetry during their youth, but better prose when they are older (Simonton, 1975). These data suggest that powerful poetry draws on the idealism, romanticism, passionate love, and whimsical moods that often come with youth. On the other hand, it appears that outstanding prose (such as that in epic novels) requires the depth, wisdom, and understanding that age provides.

Internal and External Factors

Teresa Amabile and others (e.g., Amabile, 1996; Hennessey & Amabile, 1988) have still further expanded our understanding of creativity. They have noted the importance of motivation. Amabile and others differentiate *intrinsic motivation*, which is internal to the individual, from *extrinsic motivation*, which is external to the individual; for example, intrinsic motivators might include sheer enjoyment of the creative process or

personal desire to solve a problem, whereas extrinsic motivators might include a desire for fame or fortune. According to Amabile, the former is essential to creativity, but the latter may actually impede creativity under many circumstances.

In addition to these intrinsic characteristics of creative individuals, some researchers focus on the importance of external factors that influence creativity (e.g., Csikszentmihalyi, 1996, 1999; Feldman, 1999). For example, according to Mihaly Csikszentmihalyi (1988, p. 325), "we cannot study creativity by isolating individuals and their works from the social and historical milieu in which their actions are carried out. . . . [W]hat we call creative is never the result of individual action alone." Dean Simonton (1988, 1999) goes beyond the immediate social, intellectual, and cultural context to embrace the entire sweep of history. In Simonton's view, multiple internal and external factors contribute to highly creative work. Thus, a highly creative individual must be the right person, exploring the right ideas, in the right social, cultural, and historical setting. Who knows what Einstein would have contributed had he grown up during the Middle Ages?

These contextual considerations may be the reason why so few women gained recognition in art and science in earlier times. Until the latter half of the 19th century, few women were encouraged—or even permitted—to nurture their intellects; most young women were expected to prepare to nurture others instead. Even women who were permitted to gain an education or to develop their talents were discouraged later from

Psychology in Everyday Life

Increasing Creativity

Although some researchers believe that only a few rare persons can be creative, most believe that anyone can become more creative by working to become so. Quite a few also believe that many more of us could become exceptionally creative if we wished. For example, you could increase your own creativity by taking these steps:

1. Find something you love to do. People do their most creative work when they are excited about the work they are doing.
2. Listen to feedback, but do not mindlessly follow the crowd. Creative people forge their own paths; at the same time they profit from others' advice.
3. Deeply believe in the value and importance of your creative work; do not let others discourage you or dissuade you from pursuing your work. On the other hand, you should monitor and criticize your own work, seeking always to improve it.
4. Carefully choose the problems or subjects on which you will focus your creative attention (remembering the importance of problem selection and definition); find problems that appeal to your own sense of aesthetics. Creative people often generate ideas that are undervalued, underappreciated, and even scorned by their contemporaries—that is, ideas that are initially considered ugly and unappealing by others.
5. Use the processes, such as seeing analogies, that characterize insight, as well as divergent-thinking processes. At the same time, realize that creative work always takes tradition into account, even if it is to disagree with it.
6. Choose associates who will encourage you to take sensible risks, to go against convention, and to try new ideas and methods.
7. Acquire as much of the available knowledge as possible in your chosen field of endeavor. In this way, you can avoid "reinventing the wheel" or producing the same old stuff being produced by others in your field. Then try to go beyond the boundaries of this knowledge.
8. Commit yourself deeply to your creative endeavor.

There is some consensus that each of the preceding suggestions may play a role in creative productivity. However, many psychologists and other researchers might dispute one or more of these factors, and many creative individuals deviate from this general pattern. In fact, we might say that as a group, creative people are characterized by their deviations. There are many other factors in the study of creativity about which psychologists have not reached consensus.

One additional factor seems to show a consistent relationship to creativity: above-average intelligence. Surprisingly, beyond a given level of intelligence, further increases in intelligence do not necessarily correlate with increases in creativity. Thus, to be creative, an individual must be bright but not necessarily brilliant.

---

using them. For example, Felix Mendelssohn's older sister, Fanny, was sometimes viewed as being a finer musician and composer than her brother—or was considered at least comparable in talent. Yet her family, including her younger brother, would not permit her to publish her compositions under her own name and would not allow her to perform in public (Forbes, 1990). Once society allowed women to be productive outside of the family, outstanding women came to the fore, such as writers Maya Angelou, Nelly Bly, the Brontë sisters, Emily Dickinson, Toni Morrison, Gertrude Stein, Alice Walker, and Virginia Woolf; artist Frida Kahlo; poet and politician Sojourner Truth; and scientists Rachel Carson (biology), Marie Curie (physics and chemistry), Rosalind Franklin (DNA structure), Sophie Germain (mathematics and physics), Margaret Mead (anthropology), and Helen Taussig (medicine), among countless others.

Robert Sternberg and Todd Lubart (1995, 1996, 1999) have synthesized several of these approaches by suggesting that multiple individual and environmental factors must converge for creativity to occur. That is, in addition to having a suitable environmental context, the creative individual must possess adequate knowledge, intellectual processes, personality variables, and motivation, as well as an intellectual style to facilitate creativity. Sternberg and Lubart call their theory the *investment theory of creativity* because the theme unifying the various factors is that the creative individual buys low and sells high. That is, the creative individual focuses attention on an idea that is undervalued by contemporaries ("buys low"), then develops that idea into a meaningful, significant creative contribution. Once the creator has convinced other people of the worth of his or her idea, this creator moves on to the next idea ("sells high"). Creativity is viewed as

An evolutionary view of how our reasoning abilities have developed emphasizes social exchange, and the adaptive value of being able to tell if one is being cheated is at the root of reasoning. In fact, in some cultures, the Western model of deductive reasoning with abstract terms is not practiced or rewarded.

an attitude toward life and one that can be taught (R. J. Sternberg & Williams, 1997). The Psychology in Everyday Life box, "Increasing Creativity," describes some of the steps you can take to foster your creativity.

Evolutionary Influences

David Perkins (1995b) and Dean Simonton (1995) have suggested that evolutionary principles may be applied, at least to some extent, to the understanding of human creativity. According to these investigators (see also D. T. Campbell, 1960), new ideas are generated more or less at random, much as are genetic mutations. But these ideas, like mutations, undergo a selection process. Most of the ideas serve no particularly useful purpose and are quickly discarded. But a few ideas may be not only novel, but also useful, and those ideas are selected by a society as ones of value. They then become a part of the society's ways of thinking, much as useful mutations can become part of humanity's genetic makeup.

THINK ABOUT IT

1. Many language lovers enjoy the dynamic quality of language and relish each new nuance of meaning and change of form that arises. In contrast, others believe that to cherish a language is to preserve it exactly as it is at present—or even exactly as it was at some time in the past. Give the pros and cons of both welcoming and resisting change in language.

2. Assuming that some animals can be taught rudimentary language or languagelike skills, what distinguishes humans from other animals?

3. What steps can nonnatives take when studying another culture in order to understand the breadth and depth of that culture with minimal distortion from their own biases?

4. How do advertisers (and other propagandists) use invalid reasoning to influence people? Give some specific examples of ads you have seen or experienced with salespersons or other persuaders.

5. If you were the head of a problem-solving team, and your team members seemed to be running into a block in their approach to the problem being addressed, what would you have the team members do to get around the block?

6. What is a particularly challenging ill-structured problem that you now face (or have recently faced)? What strategies do you find (or did you find) most helpful in confronting this problem?

 You can provide your own answers to these questions online at the Sternberg, **In Search of the Human Mind** *Web site:* *http://www.harcourtcollege.com/psych/ishm*

SUMMARY

Key Properties of Language 261

1. *Language* is the use of an organized means of combining words in order to communicate.
2. There are at least six properties of language: (1) Language permits us to communicate with one or more persons who share our language. (2) Language creates an arbitrary relationship between a symbol and its referent—an idea, a thing, a process, a relationship, or a description. (3) Language has a structure; only particularly patterned arrangements of symbols have meaning. Different arrangements yield different meanings. (4) The structure of language can be analyzed at more than one level (e.g., phonemic and morphemic). (5) Despite having the limits of a structure, language users can produce novel utterances; the possibilities for creating new utterances are virtually limitless. (6) Languages constantly evolve. In addition, a first language typically is acquired spontaneously.

Do Animals Use Language 262

3. Animals can clearly communicate with each other, although debate exists over whether this communication constitutes animal language—that is, communication exhibiting all the properties of language shown in human language.

Language and the Brain 263

4. Several linguistic functions in the brain have been localized, largely from observations on what happens when a particular area of the brain is injured or is electrically stimulated.

Aspects of Language 265

5. The smallest semantically meaningful unit in a language is a *morpheme*.
6. *Semantics* is the study of meaning.
7. Several alternative theories of meaning exist. The three main alternatives are the *componential theory* (meaning can be understood in terms of components, or basic elements, of a word), the *prototype theory* (meaning inheres in "best examples" of a concept), and the *exemplar theory* (meaning inheres in our use of exemplars of a concept).
8. *Syntax* is the study of linguistic structure at the sentence level.
9. Alternative kinds of grammars have been proposed to understand the structure of sentences: (a) *Phrase-structure grammars* analyze sentences in terms of the order in which words appear in phrases and sentences; and (b) *transformational grammars* analyze sentences in terms of deep (propositional meaning) structures that underlie surface (word-sequence) structures.
10. *Pragmatics* is the study of how language is used.
11. Sociolinguists, who study the relationship between social behavior and language, have observed that people engage in various strategies to signal turn taking in conversations.
12. In order to communicate effectively, parties must have a shared understanding about the situation being discussed; these shared understandings are called *scripts*.
13. *Slips of the tongue* refer to inadvertent semantic or articulatory errors in things we say.
14. *Linguistic relativity* asserts that cognitive differences resulting from a given language cause people who speak that language to perceive the world uniquely.
15. *Linguistic universals* are properties of language that are common across all languages.

Language Acquisition 270

16. Humans seem to progress through the following stages in acquiring language: (a) prenatal responsivity to human voices; (b) postnatal *cooing*, which comprises all possible phones; (c) *babbling*, which comprises only the distinct phonemes that characterize the primary language of the infant; (d) one-word utterances; (e) two-word utterances; (f) *telegraphic speech*; (g) basic adult sentence structure (present by about age 4).
17. During language acquisition, children engage in *overextensions*, in which they extend the meaning of a word to encompass more concepts than the word is intended to encompass.
18. Neither nature alone nor nurture alone can account for human language acquisition. The mechanism of *hypothesis testing* suggests an integration of nature and nurture: Children acquire language by mentally forming tentative hypotheses regarding language and then testing these hypotheses in the environment. They are guided in the formation of these hypotheses by an innate *language-acquisition device (LAD)*, which facilitates language acquisition.

The Nature of Thought 275

19. Thinking involves the processing of mental representations.

Strategies and Obstacles in Problem Solving 276

20. *Problem solving* involves mental work to overcome obstacles that stand in the way of answering a question.

21. Problems with well-defined paths to solution are referred to as *well-structured*.

22. *Ill-structured problems* are problems for which there is no clear, readily available path to solution.

23. *Heuristics* are informal, intuitive, speculative strategies for solving problems; they sometimes work and sometimes do not. Heuristics are often contrasted with *algorithms*, which are paths to an accurate solution.

24. Insightful problem solving involves the subjective feeling of a sudden realization of the solution to a problem.

25. *Mental set* refers to the use of a strategy that has worked in the past but that does not necessarily work for a particular problem that needs to be solved in the present. A particular type of mental set is *functional fixedness*, which involves the inability to see that something that is known to have a particular use may also be used for performing other functions.

26. *Incubation*, which follows a period of intensive work on a problem, involves laying a problem to rest for a while and then returning to it, so that subconscious work can continue on the problem while consciously the problem is being ignored.

27. Experts differ from novices in both the amount and the organization of knowledge that they bring to bear on problem solving in the domain of their expertise.

Judgment and Decision Making   283

28. *Utility-maximization theory* assumes that the goal of human action is to seek pleasure and to avoid pain. A refined form of this theory is *subjective-utility theory*, which acknowledges that utilities cannot always be objectified.

29. *Satisficing* involves selecting the first acceptable alternative that comes to mind.

30. A person using the *representativeness heuristic* judges the probability of an uncertain event by the degree to which that event is essentially similar to the population from which it derives and by the degree to which it reflects the salient features of the processes by which it is generated.

31. A person using the *availability heuristic* makes judgments on the basis of how easily she or he is able to call to mind what are perceived as relevant instances of a phenomenon.

32. People often exhibit *overconfidence*, judging that the probability of their correctness in reaching a solution to a problem is substantially higher than it actually is.

33. *Gambler's fallacy* refers to the belief that a person's luck is bound to change, just by the nature of things.

Reasoning   286

34. *Reasoning* refers to the process of drawing conclusions from evidence.

35. *Deductive reasoning* is involved when a person seeks to determine whether one or more logically certain conclusions can be drawn from a set of premises.

36. *Inductive reasoning* involves reasoning from specific facts or observations to reach a general conclusion that may explain the specific facts. Such reasoning is used when it is not possible to draw a logically certain conclusion from a set of premises.

Creativity   288

37. *Creativity* involves producing something that is both original and valuable.

38. Many factors characterize highly creative individuals, such as extremely high motivation to be creative in a particular field of endeavor and nonconformity in questioning conventions.

KEY TERMS

■ THINK ABOUT IT SAMPLE RESPONSES

1. Many language lovers enjoy the dynamic quality of language and relish each new nuance of meaning and change of form that arises. In contrast, others believe that to cherish a language is to preserve it exactly as it is at present—or even exactly as it was at some time in the past. Give the pros and cons of both welcoming and resisting change in language.

An advantage of preserving a language in all its features is that people can better continue to understand and appreciate records from the past and literature that has been preserved over time. A disadvantage is the loss of flexibility. Often new words and expressions are needed in order to keep up with changes in the world. For example, a word such as Internet *may not have been useful 100 years ago, but it certainly is useful now.*

2. Assuming that some animals can be taught rudimentary language or languagelike skills, what distinguishes humans from other animals?

What most distinguishes humans from animals appears to be complexity of thinking. Research suggests that humans are capable of solving problems and making decisions that are considerably more complex than the problems solved or decisions made by other animals.

3. What steps can nonnatives take when studying another culture in order to understand the breadth and depth of that culture with minimal distortion from their own biases?

It is important when learning about a culture to learn the language of that culture, if possible. First, this enables one to communicate firsthand with people of that culture. This is especially important because translations can distort what people say. Second, it may enable one to read the literature without translation. Third, informants often will reveal things to people who speak their language that they will not reveal to those who do not speak it. Fourth, the people will appreciate your attempt to learn their language, and may return the "favor" by telling you more.

4. How do advertisers (and other propagandists) use invalid reasoning to influence people? Give some specific examples of ads you have seen or experiences you have had with salespersons or other persuaders.

Advertisers frequently try to associate products with certain states people would like to enjoy. For example, advertisers for cigarettes are likely to show young, happy, apparently healthy, "with it" people enjoying smoking. The idea is to get you to believe that you, too, will share these attributes if you smoke. Needless to say, the inductive inference the advertisers want you to make is invalid.

5. If you were the head of a problem-solving team, and your team members seemed to be running into a block in their approach to the problem being addressed, what would you have the team members do to get around the block?

One of the best things you can encourage them to do is to incubate. They might put the problem aside for a few days, and then come back to it with a new perspective or from a fresh angle.

6. What is a particularly challenging ill-structured problem that you now face (or have recently faced)? What strategies do you find (or did you find) most helpful in confronting this problem?

Obviously, everyone has to answer this question for him or herself. But an example of an ill-structured problem is studying for an exam. One of the best strategies is to start studying well in advance, because we know (see chapter 7) that distributed learning results in better retention than does massed learning.

Two sophomores are hiking in the woods. One of them "aced" her freshman-year courses, getting straight A's. Her college entrance test scores had been phenomenal and she was admitted to college with a special scholarship reserved for the brightest entering students. The other student barely made it through her freshman year. Her college entrance test scores were marginal and she just squeaked by even getting into college. Nonetheless, people say of her that she is shrewd and clever—her teachers call her "street-smart." As the friends are hiking, they encounter a huge, ferocious, obviously hungry grizzly bear. Its next meal has just come into sight and they are it. The first student calculates that the grizzly bear will overtake them in 27.3 seconds. At that point, she panics, realizing there is no escape. She faces her friend, the fear of death in her eyes. To her amazement, she observes that her friend is not scared at all. To the contrary, her friend is quickly but calmly taking off her hiking boots and putting on jogging shoes. "What do you think you're doing?" the first hiker says to her companion, "You'll never be able to outrun that grizzly bear." "That's true," says the companion, "but all I have to do is outrun you."

9

INTELLIGENCE

Chapter Outline

Both students in this obviously fictional story are intelligent, but it is clear that they are intelligent in different ways. Indeed, the story raises the issue of just what it means to be intelligent, because although the first student would typically be labeled as such, it is the second student who would come out of the crisis alive. The story exemplifies the following definition of the concept of intelligence: **Intelligence** is goal-directed adaptive behavior. Actually, there are perhaps as many definitions of intelligence as there are intelligence researchers and theoreticians. In fact, much of intelligence research is dedicated to trying to answer such questions as "What is intelligence?" and "How can we even find out what it is" (Mackintosh, 1998; Sternberg, 2000)?

One thing that is clear is that intelligence draws on many of the skills that have been discussed previously in this book, including perceptual, learning, memory-based, language-based, and thinking skills.

The question regarding the nature of intelligence is not some abstract academic issue of interest only in psychology courses. Many children in the United States and in other countries take tests of intelligence, the results of which are used for academic placement, admissions to special academic programs, and making high-stakes decisions about a child's future. Tests that are not called "intelligence tests" but that contain problems similar to those on intelligence tests are used for college, university, graduate school, and professional-school admissions in the United States and elsewhere. With some societies so heavily invested in the use of these tests, it is crucial we understand what intelligence is (Ramey, 2000). If, for example, the second sophomore in the woods is intelligent but the type of intelligence she has is not measured by conventional tests, then societies may be missing out on one or more important aspects of intelligence when they make crucial decisions about children's futures. So what, then, is intelligence?

Definitions of Intelligence

In Search of ...

How have experts and others defined intelligence?

In 1921, 14 famous psychologists made explicit their implicit views on the nature of intelligence (see "Intelligence and its measurement: A symposium," 1921). Although their responses varied, two common themes ran through many of their responses: Intelligence comprises (1) the ability to learn from experience and (2) the ability to adapt to the surrounding environment. These common themes are important. Ability to learn from experience implies, for example, that smart people can indeed make mistakes; however, smart people learn from their mistakes, and they do not keep making the same ones again and again. Adaptation to the environment means that being smart goes beyond getting high scores on tests: It includes how you perform in school, handle a job, get along with other people, and manage your life in general.

Sixty-five years after the initial symposium, 24 different experts were asked to give their views on the nature of intelligence (R. J. Sternberg & Detterman, 1986). Once again, the experts noted the themes of learning from experience and adapting to the environment. However, contemporary experts also put more emphasis on the role of metacognition—people's understanding and control of their own thinking processes (such as during problem solving, reasoning, and decision making)—than did earlier experts. Contemporary experts also more heavily emphasized the role of culture, pointing out that what is considered intelligent in one culture may be considered stupid in another. In the study of intelligence, and many other psychological phenomena, the questions scientists ask in large part determine their answers. Two of the earliest psychologists who started asking questions about intelligence lived many years ago.

To understand current thinking about intelligence, we must go back to the late 19th and early 20th centuries to peek at the work of two intellectual giants: Francis Galton and Alfred Binet. These men started two largely opposing traditions for measuring, and to some extent understanding, intelligence:

Galton the psychophysical tradition, Binet the judgmental. Galton and Binet did not agree about much, but they did agree about one thing—that it is possible to understand and to measure intelligence scientifically (Brody, 2000).

Francis Galton and the Measurement of Psychophysical Performance

The publication of Charles Darwin's *The Origin of Species* (1859) profoundly affected many areas of scientific endeavor. One of these areas was the investigation of human intelligence and its development. Darwin suggested that human capabilities are in some sense continuous with those of lower animals and, hence, can be understood through scientific investigations like those conducted on animals. By studying individual human development, he argued, we might better understand the evolution of the human species and vice versa.

The development of intelligence can be seen as one of the crowning achievements of evolution. But it is difficult to track the evolution across species. For example, Stanley Coren (1994) noted that when we compare the intelligence of different kinds of dogs, we are comparing them in terms of what we may value in dogs, which may be only a rather limited aspect of what is truly adaptive for them. In short, comparisons of intelligence across species are fraught with hazards because what leads to successful adaptation in different species can be so different (Zentall, 2000).

Darwin's cousin, Sir Francis Galton, was probably the first to explore the implications of Darwin's book for the study of intelligence. Galton's (1883) theory of the "human faculty"—intelligence—and its development proposed two general qualities that distinguished the more gifted from the less so; energy, or the capacity for labor, and sensitivity to physical stimuli. Galton was also a believer in *eugenics*, the notion that careful breeding of organisms (including humans) can be used to increase the overall intelligence (or other abilities) of the population. Severe misuses of these notions, as in the horribly misguided exterminations practiced in Nazi Germany, have rendered the application of eugenics to societies a highly questionable practice.

James McKeen Cattell brought many of Galton's ideas from England to the United States. As head of the psychology laboratory at Columbia University, Cattell was in a good position to publicize the *psychophysical approach* to the theory and measurement of intelligence, which emphasized measurement of physical and sensory skills. Cattell (1890) proposed a series of 50 psychophysical tests, such as dynamometer pressure (greatest possible squeeze strength of a hand), rate of arm movement over a distance of 50 cm, the threshold for distance on the skin by which two points need to be separated for them to be felt separately, and the span of letters that could be recalled from memory. Underlying all of these tests was the assumption that these psychophysical tests measure mental ability.

The idea that psychophysical measures reflect intelligence was discredited when one of Cattell's own students, Clark Wissler (1901), found that scores on Cattell's tests were related neither to each other nor to undergraduate grades at Columbia. He and others interpreted the results as suggesting that whatever Galton's tests measured, it was not intelligence. Despite these disappointing findings, psychologists did not give up hope of understanding and measuring intelligence. An alternative approach to understanding and measuring it was beginning to lead to greater success.

Alfred Binet and the Measurement of Judgment

In 1904, the Minister of Public Instruction in Paris named a commission to find a means to differentiate truly mentally "defective" children from those who were unsuccessful in school for other reasons. The commission was to ensure that no child suspected of retardation be placed in a special class without first being given an examination "from which it could be certified that because of the state of his intelligence, he was unable to profit, in an average measure, from the instruction given in the ordinary schools" (Binet & Simon, 1916, p. 9). Alfred Binet and his collaborator, Theodore Simon, devised tests to meet this placement need. Thus, unlike theory and research in the tradition of Galton and Cattell, which grew out of pure scientific concerns, theory and research in the tradition of Binet grew out of practical educational concerns.

Binet and Simon's conception of intelligence and of how to measure it differed substantially from that of Galton and Cattell, whose tests they labeled "wasted time." Binet cited the example of Helen Keller as someone of known extraordinary intelligence whose scores on psychophysical tests would be notably inferior and yet who could be expected to perform at a very high level on tests of judgment. To Binet and Simon (1916), the core of intelligence is "judgment, otherwise called good sense, practical sense, initiative, the faculty of adapting one's self to circumstances. To judge well, to comprehend well, to reason well, these are the essential activities of intelligence" (pp. 42–43). How might these qualities be measured?

Helen Keller, who was blind and deaf, performed poorly on psychophysical tests of intelligence and was thought to be retarded until she learned how to use sign language and, eventually, to speak. Alfred Binet cited her as an example of how limited the early psychophysical measures of intelligence were. To him, the core of intelligence was "judgment, otherwise called good sense, practical sense, initiative, the faculty of adapting one's self to circumstances. To judge well, to comprehend well, to reason well, these are the essential activities of intelligence."

Mental Age and the Intelligence Quotient

To this day, schools usually segregate children according to their physical age, also called chronological age. In conjunction with his theory of intelligence based on judgment, Binet suggested that we might assess children's intelligence based on their **mental age**—a score indicating the chronological age of persons who typically perform at the same level of intelligence as a test taker. If, for example, a person performs on a test at a level comparable to that of an average 12-year-old, the person's mental age will be 12, regardless of the person's chronological age. Suppose, for example, that José is 10 years old, but his performance on a test of intelligence is equal to that of the average 12-year-old. Then his mental age would be 12. Mental age also conveniently suggests an appropriate school placement for a child according to mental, rather than chronological, level.

William Stern, a German psychologist, noted that mental age is of doubtful usefulness for comparing levels of intelligence of children who differ in chronological age. Stern (1912) suggested instead that we

measure intelligence by using an intelligence quotient (IQ): a ratio of mental age (MA) divided by chronological age (CA), multiplied by 100. This ratio can be expressed mathematically as follows:

$$IQ = (MA/CA) \times 100$$

Thus, if Anita's mental age of 5 equals her chronological age of 5, then her intelligence is average, and her IQ is 100, because (5/5)(100) = 100. People whose mental age equals their chronological age always have IQs of 100 because the numerator of the equation equals the denominator, giving a quotient of 1. If Bill's mental age of 4 is only half of his chronological age of 8, then his IQ is 50, because the quotient is ½, and half of 100 is 50. Subsequent investigators have suggested further modifications of the IQ, so Stern's conception of expressing intelligence in terms of a ratio of mental age to chronological age, multiplied by 100, is now termed a **ratio IQ.**

Unfortunately, the concept of mental age proved to be a weak link in the measurement of intelligence, even when used for calculating a ratio IQ. First, increases in measured mental age slow down at about the age of 16 years. Compare what you knew and how you thought when you were 8 years old with what you knew and how you thought when you reached 12 years old. Quite a difference! Now think about someone who is 30 years old, and compare how you imagine that person's knowledge and thought processes to be with what you imagine they will be at age 45. You probably do not picture as much of a difference in this case, even though the difference in age is much

greater. It might make sense to say that an 8-year-old who performs at the level of a 12-year-old has an IQ of 150. But it makes no sense at all to say that a 30-year-old who performs at the level of a 45-year-old has an IQ of 150 because the intellectual performance of a typical 45-year-old usually differs only minimally from that of a typical 30-year-old. Indeed, in older age, scores on some kinds of mental tests actually may start to decrease. When measuring across the whole life span, it seems less than effective to base the calculation of intelligence on mental age.

Score Distributions

Normal Distributions. Subsequent measurements of IQ have turned away from the construct of mental age across the life span and have focused instead on the way in which intelligence is believed to be distributed within the human population at a given age or range of ages. In measurements of large human populations, we find that measurement values often show a roughly normal distribution. In a **normal distribution,** most values congregate around the **median,** the middle score or other measurement value (100 on IQ tests), within a distribution of values with the measured values rapidly declining in number on either side of the median, and then tailing off more slowly as scores get more extreme. Also, in a normal distribution, the median is approximately the same as both the **mean,** the average score within a distribution of values, computed by adding all the scores and then dividing by the number of scores; and the **mode,** the most frequent score or other measurement value within a distribution of values. Like other measurements of large populations, IQ scores at a given age or range of ages show a roughly normal distribution. Figure 9-1 shows a picture of a normal distribution as it applies to IQ.

Percentiles. Graphs of measurements forming normal distributions are valuable in helping us to visualize the distribution of those measurements within a given population. For individual scores, however, it is less helpful to try to describe the score in terms of a graph than in terms of a **percentile**—the proportion of persons whose scores fall below a given score, multiplied by 100. For example, if 50% of the people who take a test receive scores of less than 25, then the percentile equivalent of the score of 25 is 50. In this case, 25 would be the **raw score**—the actual total sum of points obtained by a given test taker for a given test, which often equals the actual number of items answered correctly on the test—and 50 would be the percentile. If Rosa's raw score is 30, and 75% of the people taking the test scored below her score, then her percentile would be 75. Percentiles allow for relatively easy comparison of an individual's score with the

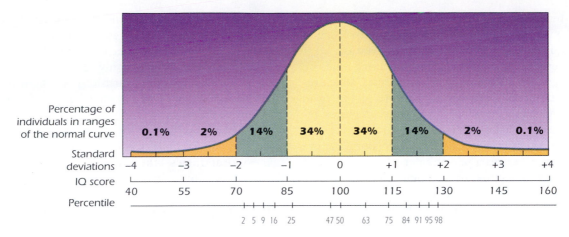

Figure 9–1

NORMAL DISTRIBUTION OF IQs.   *Normal distributions result from many measurements of large populations. Most college students have IQ scores above the middle score. Does that mean that most college students are smarter than most people who never attended college? Why or why not?*

scores of others in the population. As Figure 9-1 shows, percentiles can also be calculated for IQ. A person who scores 105 on an IQ test has scored better than 63% of the population and therefore has a percentile of 63. More commonly, however, the raw scores obtained on intelligence tests are translated into more comprehensible form by using a different means of comparison.

Deviation IQs.   Commonly, scores for many psychological tests—including intelligence tests—are calculated such that the average score is set to 100. In a normal distribution of IQ scores for a large population, roughly two-thirds of the scores are set to fall between 85 and 115, and about 95% of the scores to fall between 70 and 130. In contrast to ratio IQs, which are derived from an actual quotient (mental age divided by chronological age), such **deviation IQs,** based on deviations from the average score, are not, strictly speaking, IQs, because no quotient is involved.

Intelligence Tests

In a strange way, tests of intelligence have influenced the definition of intelligence. These tests and the number results they produce, frequently stand in for what intelligence is. Intelligence becomes a score. As we will see later in the chapter when we discuss more modern models of intelligence, this is perhaps too simplistic. A number of tests of intelligence measure various kinds of cognitive skills (Daniel, 1997, 2000; Kaufman, 2000). These tests are based largely on the notion that intelligence is a function of judgments of a fairly academic kind. You may recognize the names of some of the tests but wonder what one finds on these tests.

The Stanford-Binet Intelligence Scales

The preceding progression of methods for comparing relative levels of intelligence was reflected in the actual progression of intelligence tests. For example, Binet and Simon's original intelligence test calculated mental age alone, but the next major developer of intelligence tests—Lewis Terman, a professor of psychology at Stanford University—used ratio IQs for comparing intelligence across different individuals. Terman rewrote Binet and Simon's test in English, added some of his own ideas for items, and restructured the scoring so that it reflected ratio IQs instead of mental age, thereby constructing the earliest version of what has come to be called the Stanford-Binet Intelligence Scales (Terman & Merrill, 1937, 1973; R. L. Thorndike, Hagen, & Sattler, 1986). These tests measure a variety of skills, but perhaps they fail to do justice to the wide range of judgmental and other skills that, according to Binet, constitute intelligence.

An alternative set of scales, constructed by David Wechsler, has become the preeminent set of scales of this type for measuring intelligence.

The Wechsler Scales

The Wechsler intelligence scales include the third edition of Wechsler Adult Intelligence Scale—(WAIS-III), the third edition of the Wechsler Intelligence Scale for Children (WISC-III), and the Wechsler Preschool and Primary Scale of Intelligence (WPPSI). Scores are expressed as deviation IQs. The Wechsler tests yield three scores: a verbal score, a performance score, and an overall score. The verbal score is based on tests such as vocabulary and verbal similarities, in which the test taker has to say how two things are similar. The vocabulary test is a measure of knowledge of word meanings, whereas the similarities test is a measure of verbal reasoning skills. The performance score is based on tests such as picture completion, which requires identification of a missing part in a picture of an object, and picture arrangement, which requires re-arrangement of a scrambled set of cartoon-like pictures into an order that tells a coherent story. Picture completion measures a person's perceptual speed and acuity, whereas picture arrangement measures a person's ability to plan and understand how to organize events into a coherent structure. The overall score is a combination of the verbal and the performance scores. Figure 9-2 shows the types of items in each of the Wechsler adult-scale subtests, which you may wish to compare with those of the Stanford-Binet.

Wechsler, like Binet, had a conception of intelligence that went beyond what his own test measured. Although Wechsler clearly believed in the worth of attempting to measure intelligence, he did not limit his conception of intelligence to test scores. To Wechsler (1974), intelligence affects our everyday life. We use our intelligence not just in taking tests and in doing homework but also in relating to people, in doing our jobs effectively, and in managing our lives in general. And in fact, intelligence tests predict performance in a variety of real-world pursuits, such as in education (R. Mayer, 2000) and in the work force (Schmidt, Ones, & Hunter, 1992; Wagner, 1997).

Aptitude and Achievement Tests

Galton and Binet, and later Terman and Wechsler, were enormously influential in starting a tradition of testing for intelligence. Today, hundreds of intelligence tests are in everyday use. Some of them, like the Stanford-Binet and the Wechsler, are administered to people individually by highly trained psychologists. Others are group tests, which can be administered to large numbers of people at once by someone without extensive training.

Not all tests of cognitive performance assess intelligence. For example, some cognitively oriented tests measure aptitudes—the potential ability to accomplish something, to attain a level of expertise on performance of a task or a set of tasks, or to acquire knowledge in a given domain or a set of domains, such as musical aptitudes, athletic aptitudes, or fine eye–hand coordination aptitudes. These aptitudes may or may not involve intelligence.

You are probably quite familiar with another widely used test that includes content often considered to reflect intelligence: the Scholastic Assessment Test (SAT), administered by the College Board. The SAT contains items such as those shown in Table 9-1. Formerly titled the Scholastic Aptitude Test, the SAT was renamed to acknowledge that it measures both **aptitude** and **achievement**—an accomplishment or an attained level of expertise on performance of a task, or an acquired base of knowledge in a domain or a set of domains. Today, the test publisher usually refers to the test simply as the SAT.

Designing a suitable test of intelligence requires a lot of careful planning and trial-and-error testing. The following section of this chapter describes some of the *psychometric*—psychological measurement— properties of psychological tests and some of the ways in which test developers work to create the most suitable tests possible.

On both the WAIS-III (for adults) and the Wechsler Intelligence Scale for Children (WISC-III), test takers are asked to arrange simple cartoonlike pictures into a logical time sequence that tells a story. In the WISC-III, the sequences involve fewer pictures and simpler stories than the sequences in the WAIS-III.

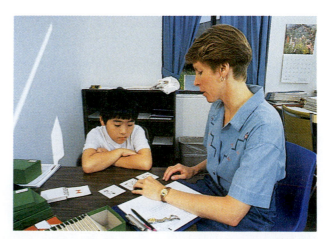

Figure 9–2
THE WECHSLER ADULT INTELLIGENCE SCALE–III (WAIS-III).
The Wechsler scales are based on deviation IQs. Items shown here are illustrative and are not found on the actual test.

Content area	Explanation of tasks/questions	Example of a possible task/question
Verbal scale		
Comprehension	Answer questions of social knowledge	What does it mean when people say, "A stitch in time saves nine"? Why are convicted criminals put into prison?
Vocabulary	Define the meaning of a word	What does **persistent** mean? What does **archaeology** mean?
Information	Supply generally known information	Who is Vladimir Putin? What are six New England states?
Similarities	Explain how two things or concepts are similar	In what ways are an ostrich and a penguin alike? In what ways are a lamp and a heater alike?
Arithmetic	Solve simple arithmetical-word problems	If Paul has $14.43, and he buys two sandwiches, which cost $5.23 each, how much change will he receive?
Digit span	Listen to a series of digits (numbers), then repeat the numbers either forward or backward or both	Repeat these numbers backward: "9, 1, 8, 3, 6."
Performance Scale		
Object assembly	Put together a puzzle by combining pieces to form a particular common object	Put together these pieces to make something. 
Block design	Use patterned blocks to form a design that looks identical to a design shown by the examiner	Assemble the blocks on the left to make the design on the right. 
Picture completion	Tell what is missing from each picture	What is missing from this picture? 
Picture arrangement	Put a set of cartoonlike pictures into a chronological order, so they tell a coherent story	Arrange these pictures in an order that tells a story, and then tell what is happening in the story. 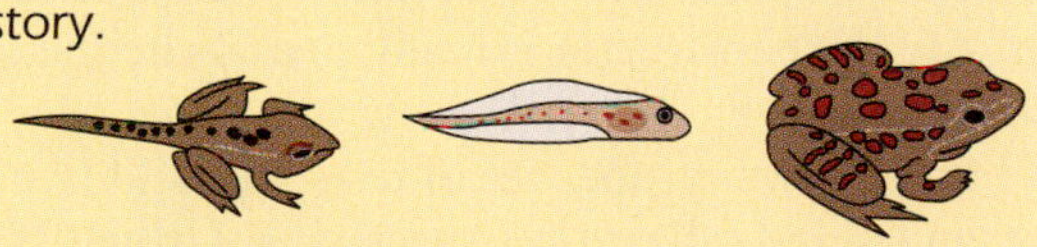
Digit symbol	When given a key matching particular symbols to particular numerals, copy a sequence of symbols, transcribing from symbols to numerals, using the key	Look carefully at the key. In the blanks, write the correct numeral for the symbol below each symbol.

TABLE 9–1

The Scholastic Assessment Test *In the early 1990s, the full name of the SAT was changed from Scholastic Aptitude Test to Scholastic Assessment Test, in recognition of the fact that the test assesses not only aptitude but also achievement. Which of the following questions or types of questions more clearly assess achievement and which more clearly test aptitude?*

CONTENT AREA	EXPLANATION OF TASK/QUESTION	EXAMPLE TASK/QUESTION
Verbal		
Vocabulary	Show knowledge of words and their definitions	Choose the word or set of words that best fits into the whole sentence.
Comprehension	Demonstrate understanding of a text passage	Correctly answer multiple-choice questions reflecting understanding of a text passage.
Quantitative		
Quantitative skills	Make calculations involving arithmetic, algebra, geometry, and so on	Choose the correct answer from among several possible answers.

Assessment Issues

In Search of . . . *How can intelligence be assessed, and what kinds of problems are encountered in assessment?*

The usefulness of tests of intelligence or tests of anything else depends on how well the tests are constructed. Any *assessment instrument* (i.e., way of measuring intelligence or anything else) needs to measure what it is supposed to measure and do so accurately. It is important to determine that the results of a test mean what they are supposed to mean. Recall, for example, how Galton's and Cattell's psychophysically based tests of intelligence failed rather miserably to measure what they were supposed to measure. The first step in test construction is for the test constructor to decide what is to be measured and how. Next, the test constructor must figure out what kinds of test items will assess the psychological characteristics he or she wishes to measure. Then, the test constructor is ready to evaluate the quality of the test.

Three critical properties of tests are validity, reliability, and standardization (Anastasi & Urbina, 1997; Millsap, 1994).

Validity

Validity indicates the extent to which a given form of measurement assesses what it is supposed to measure. For example, a test of musical aptitude would be valid to the extent it predicted success in musical endeavors. Several kinds of validity exist (Anastasi & Urbina, 1997; Messick, 1995; Messick & Jungeblut, 1981; Moss, 1994). **Construct-related validity** is the degree to which a test or other measurement actually reflects the hypothetical construct that the test or other measurement is designed to assess. That is, a test designer tries to design a test that reflects a given theory. For example, a test of intelligence is construct valid to the extent that it really measures intelligence and not some other construct, such as visual or auditory acuity. **Predictive validity** is the extent to which a test or other measurement predicts some kind of performance outcome (the criterion performance), which is to be measured well after the test or other measurement has been taken. For example, the SAT is designed to predict freshman grades in college. The higher the relation between the test scores and the student's performance in college, the more predictively valid the test is said to be.

In assessing the predictive validity of a test, we must be careful about the inferences we make. Consider, for example, the finding reported by Herrnstein and Murray (1994) that natural forces in the environment have created what the authors refer to as a "cognitive elite," in which people with higher IQs tend to end up in high-prestige, high-paying, cognitively rewarding jobs, and people with lower IQs tend to end up in lower prestige, low-paying, less cognitively rewarding jobs. The authors view this finding as evidence for the fact that cognitively rewarding jobs require high IQ and as support for the predictive validity of conventional ability tests. But we must be careful in using data about group differences to draw conclusions, because the tests themselves were used to select people for the access routes to the highly demanding jobs. This selection process may raise the correlation between test scores and being in demanding jobs. If one does not do well on those tests, it is very difficult even to become, say, a lawyer, a doctor, or academic scholar, because admission to graduate programs in these areas requires the individual to do quite well on an abilities-based admissions test. People who do not test well have great difficulty gaining the access routes to these occupations. Using the tests as we do guarantees that there will be a correlation between the test scores and occupational placement, much as selecting tall people to play on basketball teams guarantees a correlation between height and entrance into the world of professional basketball players (see R. J. Sternberg, 1995b, 1995c, 1996b). A number of other arguments have been advanced against Herrnstein and Murray's arguments as well (see, e.g., Fraser, 1995; Jacoby & Glauberman, 1995). Some of these arguments have been well-reasoned, others less so.

In **content-related validity,** experts judge the extent to which the content of a test measures all of the knowledge or skills that are supposed to be included within the domain being tested. If a general mathematics achievement test included only algebra, the test would not be content valid. Finally, in **face validity,** test takers judge the extent to which the content of the test measures all of the knowledge or skills that are supposed to be included within the domain being tested. For instance, students who do better in high-school courses than their standardized test scores would predict might not consider the SAT to be face valid in assessing their aptitude for performing well in college. The difference between content-related validity and face validity is in who does the judging. In the case of content-related validity, experts judge the quality of a test. In the case of face validity, the people taking the test make this judgment.

Reliability

Whereas validity assesses how well a test measures what it is supposed to measure, **reliability** indicates the dependability of a measurement instrument (e.g., a test), indicating that the instrument consistently assesses the outcome being measured. High reliability is indicated, for example, when the people who score relatively well (or poorly) in one administration of a test also score relatively well or poorly in a second administration of the test. In other words, reliability assesses how consistently a test measures whatever it is that it actually measures.

A test can be perfectly reliable and yet totally invalid if it consistently measures something that is irrelevant to what the test is supposed to measure. For example, it would be possible to develop a highly reliable measure of the length of college applicants' index fingers, but we would not expect any significant validity of this measure in predicting performance in college. Both reliability and validity are important in test construction.

There are four main kinds of reliabilities (Reynolds, 1994). **Test–retest reliability** is the degree to which people's test scores when taking the test on one occasion dependably predict their test scores if they take exactly the same test again some time later. Of course, the problem with this kind of reliability is that if people take exactly the same test twice, their performance on the second test may be enhanced merely because they are already familiar with the material. **Alternate-forms reliability** is the degree of relationship between test scores when people take one form of a test and the test scores when they take an alternate, parallel form of the same test some time later; the parallel form is comparable in content and difficulty but has different test items from the original test. Alternate-forms reliability is often used instead of test–retest reliability. **Internal-consistency reliability** is the extent to which all items on a test measure the same thing. Finally, **interrater reliability** is the extent to which two or more raters of a given response would rate the response in the same way. For example, when the College Board includes an essay on its English Composition achievement test, it typically has more than one person score the test. The interrater reliability here is the correlation between the ratings of the people evaluating the essay.

Standardization and Norms

Most tests are standardized prior to being administered. **Standardization** ensures that the conditions for taking tests are the same for all test takers. For example, it would be important that all students taking a test have a quiet place to work. To ensure that the conditions for taking the test are the same for all test takers, environmental distractors (such as interruptions) should be kept to a minimum. In addition, the instructions given before and during the test should be uniform, and the amount of time available for making responses should be identical. It is also important that the materials available should be consistent across test sessions.

Part of the standardization procedure ensures that those who administer the tests do so consistently, including the same wording, the same emotionality of expression (typically as little as possible), and so on, thereby minimizing the possibility of environmental influences affecting the scores. For group tests administered with paper and pencil, the requirements for standardization are relatively simple because interpersonal contact is kept to a minimum. For individual tests administered by a trained psychologist to an individual test taker, the test developers must create rigorous standardized test protocols—procedures for implementing the tests. The developers may also require that the psychologists who administer the tests receive specialized training to ensure that the test is implemented according to the standardized protocols.

A test that has been standardized can be administered to an enormous number of individuals, so that it becomes possible to determine scaled scores based on the scores of the large number of test takers. **Normative scores** (sometimes called simply **norms**) translate raw scores into scaled equivalents (normative scores) that reflect the relative levels of performance of various test takers. What kinds of scaled scores might test developers use?

Test developers can use any scale they choose. The IQ, for example, is a standard score that centers on a score of 100. Raw scores on various subscales are also typically converted into standardized equivalents centered on 100, thus facilitating comparisons among individuals. The College Board uses a different standard scale, with an average of 500 and a standard deviation of 100. The range is from a low of 200 to a high of 800. (See Figure 9-3, comparing the normal distributions for the SAT and for the WAIS.) The tests that yield these scores are based on experts' conceptions of what should be measured.

Figure 9–3

NORMAL DISTRIBUTION OF SCORES ON THE WAIS AND THE SAT. *Both the WAIS and the SAT are given to large numbers of individuals, so normal distributions of scores may be obtained. For both tests, raw scores are translated into standard (normative) scores, with a mean value of 100 for the WAIS and 500 for the SAT. The WAIS and the SAT are administered to different populations, and hence an IQ of 100 does not correspond to a SAT score of 500. On the WAIS, only 16% of the test takers score above 115. Should decisions regarding college admission, employment, or other opportunities be based on using tests such as these for screening applicants?*

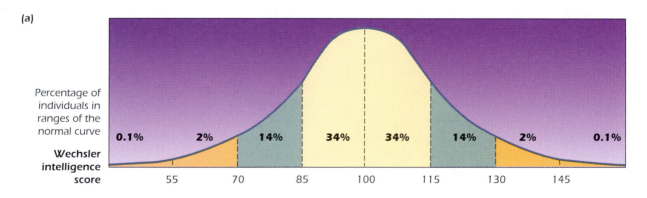

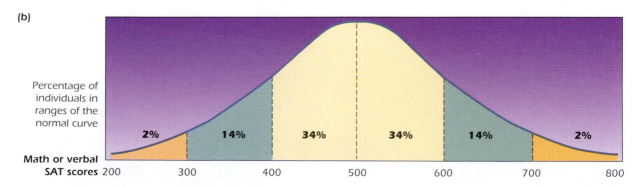

Theories of the Nature of Intelligence

In *Search of . . .*

What are the major theories of the nature of intelligence?

Psychometric Models: Intelligence as a Measurement-Based Map of the Mind

The view of intelligence as a map of the mind extends back at least to the 1800s, when phrenology was in vogue. During the first half of the 20th century, the model of intelligence as something to be mapped dominated theory and research. The psychologist studying intelligence in this way was both an explorer and a cartographer, seeking to chart the innermost regions of the mind. Like other explorers, psychologists who studied intelligence needed tools; in the case of research on intelligence, a useful tool appeared to be **factor analysis**, a method of statistical decomposition that allows an investigator to infer distinct hypothetical constructs, elements, or structures (called factors) that underlie a phenomenon. In this case, some intelligence researchers have believed that these factors form the basis of individual differences in test performance. The actual factors derived, of course, depend on the particular questions being asked and the tasks being evaluated. This approach continues to be used actively today (e.g., J. B. Carroll, 1993; see Brody, 2000; Embretson & McCollam, 2000).

Among the many competing factorial theories of intelligence, the main ones have been of a single general factor that dominates intelligence; of multiple, equally important abilities constituting intelligence; and of a hierarchy of abilities contributing to intelligence. Figure 9-4 visually contrasts three of these theories.

Figure 9–4

COMPARISONS AMONG SOME OF THE PSYCHOMETRIC MODELS OF INTELLIGENCE. *Although Spearman (a), Thurstone (b), and Carroll (c) all used factor analysis to determine the factors underlying intelligence, they all reached different conclusions regarding the structure of intelligence. Which model most simply, yet comprehensively, describes the structure of intelligence as you understand it? How do particular models of intelligence shape our understanding of intelligence?*

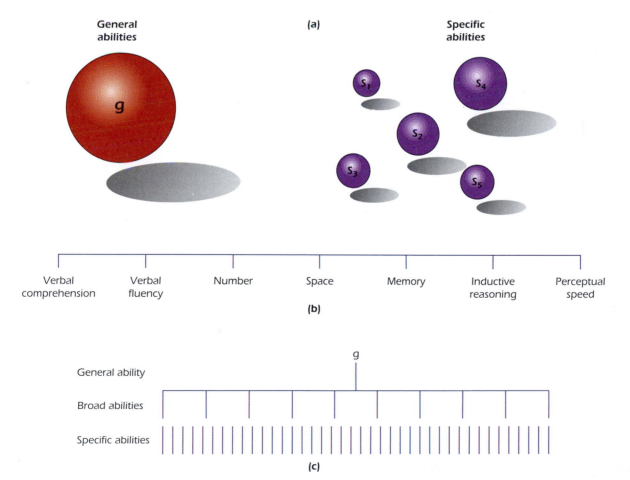

The g Factor

Charles Spearman is usually credited with inventing factor analysis. Using factor-analytic studies, Spearman (1927) concluded that intelligence could be understood in terms of both a single general factor (g) that pervades performance on all tests of mental ability and a set of specific factors (s), each involved in performance on only a single type of mental-ability test. (An example of a specific ability might be arithmetic computation.) In Spearman's view, the specific factors are of only casual interest, due to the narrow applicability of these factors. The general factor, however, provides the key to understanding intelligence. Spearman believed that g derives from individual differences in mental energy. The view that there is a general factor of intelligence persists among many contemporary psychologists (e.g., Jensen, 1998), although other psychologists furiously debate this issue (Sternberg, 1999).

Primary Mental Abilities

In contrast to Spearman, Louis Thurstone (1938) concluded that the core of intelligence resides not in one single factor but in seven factors of equal importance, which he referred to as primary mental abilities. According to Thurstone, the primary mental abilities and typical measures of them are (1) verbal comprehension—vocabulary tests; (2) verbal fluency—tests requiring the test taker to think of as many words as possible that begin with a given letter, in a limited amount of time; (3) inductive reasoning—tests such as analogies and number-series completion tasks; (4) spatial visualization—tests requiring mental rotation of pictures of objects; (5) number—computation and simple mathematical problem-solving tests; (6) memory—picture and word-recall tests; and (7) perceptual speed—tests that require the test taker to recognize small differences in pictures or to cross out the A's in strings of various letters.

Hierarchical Models

A more parsimonious way of handling a number of factors of the mind is through a hierarchical model of intelligence. One such model, developed by Raymond Cattell (1971), proposes that general intelligence comprises two major subfactors: fluid intelligence and crystallized intelligence. **Fluid intelligence** represents the acquisition of new information, or the grasping of new relations and abstractions regarding known information, as required in inductive reasoning tests such as analogies and series completions. **Crystallized intelligence** represents the accumulation of knowledge over the life span of the individual and is mea-

sured, for example, in tests of vocabulary, of general information, and of achievement. Subsumed within these two major subfactors are more specific factors. An intelligence test based on this model is the Kaufman Adolescent and Adult Intelligence Test. A more detailed hierarchical model, based on a reanalysis of many data sets from studies, has been proposed by John Carroll (1993). At the top of the hierarchy is general ability; in the middle of the hierarchy are various broad abilities (including learning and memory processes and the effortless production of many ideas). At the bottom of the hierarchy are many narrow, specific abilities such as spelling ability and reasoning speed. But how does one actually produce ideas, or spell, or reason? Computational models address this question.

Computational Models: Intelligence as Information Processing

Unlike the psychometric models, which map the structure of human intelligence, computational models strongly emphasize the processes underlying intelligent behavior. In particular, theorists using these models are interested in studying how people engage in **information processing**—that is, operations by which people mentally manipulate what they learn and know about the world. The ways in which information-processing investigators study intelligence differ primarily in terms of the complexity of the processes being studied. One way in which to study the relation between intelligence and information processing is to examine the simple information processing, as occurs when one must make rapid judgments about which of two lines is longer.

Simple Information Processing and Intelligence

Ian Deary and Laura Stough (1996) have proposed that a low-level psychophysical measure, inspection time, may provide us with insights into the fundamental nature of intelligence (see also Deary, 2000). The basic idea is that individual differences in intelligence may derive, in part, from differences in rate of intake and processing of simple stimulus information. In the inspection-time task, a person looks at two vertical lines of unequal length, and simply has to say which line is longer. Inspection time is the length of time of stimulus presentation an individual needs in order to discriminate which of two lines is longer. Investigators have found that more intelligent individuals can discriminate the lengths of the lines with lesser stimulus duration (inspection) times.

Complex Information Processing and Intelligence

Another computational approach considers complex information processing as occurs in tasks such as analogies, series problems (e.g., completing a numerical or figural series), and syllogisms (Lohman, 2000; Pellegrino & Glaser, 1980; Snow, 1980; R. J. Sternberg, 1977, 1984). The goal of this approach has been to find out just what it is that makes some people more intelligent processors of information than others. The idea is to take the kinds of tasks used on conventional intelligence tests and to isolate the components of intelligence—the mental processes used in performing these tasks. Examples of such processes are translating sensory input into a mental representation, transforming one conceptual representation into another, or translating a conceptual representation into a motor output.

In general, more intelligent people take longer during global planning—encoding the problem and formulating a general strategy for attacking the problem (or set of problems)—but they take less time for local planning—forming and implementing strategies for the details of the task (R. J. Sternberg, 1981a, 1982). The advantage of spending more time on global planning is the increased likelihood that the overall strategy will be correct. For example, the brighter person might spend more time researching and planning for writing a term paper, but less time actually writing it. This same differential in time allocation has been shown in other tasks as well, including solving physics problems (Larkin, McDermott, Simon, & Simon, 1980). Whereas information-processing investigators study such differences at the level of hypothesized mental processes, biological investigators seek to understand the origins of such differences in the functioning of the brain.

Biological Models: Intelligence as a Physiological Phenomenon

Biological approaches seek to understand intelligence by directly studying the brain and its functioning rather than by studying primarily products or processes of behavior (Jerison, 2000; Vernon, Wickett, Bazana, & Stelmack, 2000). As previous chapters have suggested, early studies, like those by Karl Lashley (1950) and others seeking to localize biological bases of intelligence and other aspects of mental processes, were a resounding failure. As tools for studying the brain have become more sophisticated, however, we are beginning to see the possibility of finding physiological indications of intelligence. Some researchers (e.g., Matarazzo, 1992) believe that we soon will have clinically useful psychophysiolog-

ical indices of intelligence although widely applicable indices will be much longer in coming. In other words, it may be possible in the future to use psychophysiological measurements to assess individuals for characteristics such as mental retardation. For now, some current studies offer appealing possibilities. Another biological approach examines the genetic influences on intelligence. The methods for studying heritability and some of the findings those methods have yielded are discussed later in this chapter.

Electrophysiological Evidence

Laboratory research has found that complex patterns of electrical activity in the brain, which are prompted by specific stimuli, correlate with scores on IQ tests (Caryl, 1994; Barrett & Eysenck, 1992). Also, several studies suggest that the speed of conduction of neural impulses may correlate with intelligence as measured by IQ tests (e.g., McGarry-Roberts, Stelmack, & Campbell, 1992; Reed & Jensen, 1992; P. A. Vernon & Mori, 1992), although the evidence is mixed. Some investigators (e.g., Jensen, 1997; P. A. Vernon & Mori, 1992) suggest that this research supports a view that intelligence is based on neural efficiency.

Metabolic Evidence

Additional support for neural efficiency as a measure of intelligence can be found by using a different approach to studies of the brain: studies of how the brain metabolizes glucose, a simple sugar required for brain activity, during mental activities. (This process is revealed in PET scans. See chapter 3, regarding brain-imaging techniques.) Richard Haier and his colleagues (Haier, Siegel, Tang, Abel, & Buchsbaum, 1992) cite several other researchers to support their own findings that higher intelligence correlates with reduced levels of glucose metabolism during problem-solving tasks—that is, smarter brains consume less sugar (meaning that they expend less effort) than do less smart brains doing the same task. Further, Haier and colleagues found that cerebral efficiency increases as a result of learning in a relatively complex task involving visuospatial manipulations (such as in the computer game *Tetris*). As a result of practice, more intelligent individuals show not only lower cerebral glucose metabolism overall but also more specifically localized metabolism of glucose. In most areas of their brains, smarter persons show less glucose metabolism, but in selected areas of their brains (thought to be important to the task at hand), they show higher levels of glucose metabolism. Thus, more intelligent people may have learned how to use their brains more efficiently. But do

Solving Practical Problems

Richard K. Wagner, *Florida State University*

Why is it that individuals with the highest grade-point averages in high school lead unremarkable lives thereafter, while those with only mediocre success in school are often the most successful individuals in a wide variety of career pursuits? What explains discrepancies between performance in school and in careers thereafter?

Obviously there are multiple causes. Motivation can change. Luck probably plays a role. However, it also is the case that the academic problems found in school (and on IQ tests) differ in important ways from the practical problems found in everyday life, including career pursuits (Wagner, 2000).

Academic problems tend to (a) be well defined, (b) come with all information necessary for solution, (c) be formulated by someone else such as a teacher or test maker, (d) have one correct answer, and (e) have one or at most a few methods of obtaining the correct answer. Practical problems, on the other hand, tend to be so ill defined that it may not be apparent that there even is a problem. Then, once the existence of a problem is suspected, it must be formulated by the problem solver. Because practical problems typically are incomplete, the problem solver will have to gather additional information, and determining what kind of information is required may be difficult. In addition, rather than having a single correct answer like the problems posed in academic settings, there are likely to be a number of possible courses of action.

To determine whether differences between academic and practical problems might partially explain differences between success in and out of school, we developed measures of practical problem solving. The measures presented scenarios from various domains describing everyday problems and asked respondents to rate the quality of possible actions. Responses were scored by comparing them to those of experts in that domain. For example:

You and a coworker jointly are responsible for completing a report on a new product by the end of the week. You are uneasy about this assignment because he has a reputation for not meeting deadlines. The problem does not appear to be lack of effort. Rather, he seems to lack certain organizational skills necessary to meet a deadline and also is a perfectionist. As a result, too much time is wasted coming up with the "perfect" idea, product, or report.

Your goal is to produce the best possible report by the deadline at the end of the week. Rate the quality of the following strategies for meeting your goal on a 1 (extremely bad) to 7 (extremely good) point scale.

- Divide the work to be done in half and tell him that if he does not complete his part, you obviously will have to let your immediate superior know that it was not your fault.
- Politely tell him to be less of a perfectionist.
- Set deadlines for completing each part of the report, and accept what you have accomplished at each deadline as the final version of that part of the report.

- Ask your superior to check up on your progress on a daily basis, after explaining why.
- Praise your coworker verbally for completion of parts of the assignment.
- Get angry with him at the first sign of getting behind schedule.
- As soon as he begins to fall behind, take responsibility for doing the report yourself to meet the deadline.
- Point out firmly, but politely, how he is holding up the report.
- Avoid putting any pressure on him because it will just make him fall even more behind.
- Offer to buy him dinner at the end of the week if you both meet the deadline.
- Ignore his organizational problem so you don't give attention to maladaptive behavior.

In addition to this measure for business management, similar measures of practical problem solving were created for the careers of academic psychology and sales. In a series of studies, the practical problem-solving measures were given to groups of individuals with differing amounts of experience and success (Sternberg, Wagner, Williams, & Horvath, 1995). For example, the business management measure was given to a nationwide sample of top executives, graduate students in MBA programs, and undergraduates with little or no experience in business management. Four important results emerged. First, more experienced groups scored higher on the measures than less experienced groups. Second, performance on measures of practical problem solving were more highly predictive of career success than were traditional IQ and employment tests. Third, there was little or no correlation between performance on the measures of practical problem solving and IQ. Fourth, performance on a practical problem-solving measure for one domain was related to performance on a practical problem-solving measure for another. What these results suggest is that with experience, individuals develop practical problem-solving skills that are common to different career pursuits yet are distinct from IQ.

References

Sternberg, R. J., Wagner, R. K., Williams, W. M., & Horvath, J. A. (1995). Testing common sense. *American Psychologist, 50,* 912–927.

Sternberg, R. J., & Horvath, J. (1999). (Eds.). *Tacit knowledge in professional practice: Researcher and practitioner perspectives.* Mahwah, NJ: Erlbaum.

Sternberg, R. J., Forsythe, G. B., Hedlund, J., Horvath, J. A., Wagner, R. K., Williams, W. M., Snook, S. A., & Grigorenko, E. L. (2000). *Practical intelligence in everyday life.* New York: Cambridge University Press.

Wagner, R. K. (2000). Practical intelligence. In R. Sternberg (Ed.), *Handbook of Human Intelligence* (pp. 380–395). New York: Cambridge University Press.

Wagner, R. K. (1997). Intelligence, training, and employment. *American Psychologist, 52,* 1059–1069.

 Find out more about this topic at **www.harcourtcollege.com/psych/ishm**

they use their brains efficiently as a function of their context or culture? Anthropological models seek to answer this question.

Cultural and Contextual Models: Intelligence as a Cultural Invention

We have seen how psychometric, computational, and biological psychologists view intelligence as something basically residing inside the head. In contrast, **contextualist** theorists of intelligence theorize about a psychological phenomenon (e.g., intelligence) largely in terms of the context in which an individual is observed and suggest that the phenomenon cannot be understood—let alone measured—outside the real-world context of the individual (Serpell, 2000; Suzuki & Valencia, 1997). These theorists study how intelligence relates to the external world. In fact, they view intelligence as so inextricably linked to culture that they believe intelligence to be something that a culture creates, at least in part. The purpose of this creation is to define the nature of adaptive performance and to account for why some people perform better than others on the tasks that the culture happens to value (see Suzuki & Valencia, 1997).

Cultural Influences on Perceived Intelligence

People in different cultures may have quite different ideas of what it means to be smart. One of the more interesting cross-cultural studies of intelligence was performed by Michael Cole and his colleagues (M. Cole, Gay, Glick, & Sharp, 1971; Glick, 1975). These investigators asked adult members of the Kpelle tribe in Africa to sort terms. In Western culture, when adults are given a sorting task on an intelligence test, more intelligent people will typically sort hierarchically. For example, they may sort names of different kinds of fish together, and then the word "fish" over that, with the name "animal" over "fish" and "birds," and so on. Less intelligent Westerners will typically sort functionally. They might sort "fish" with "eat," for example, because we eat fish, or "clothes" with "wear," because we wear clothes. Members of the Kpelle tribe generally sorted functionally—even after investigators tried indirectly to encourage the Kpelle to sort hierarchically.

Finally, in desperation, one of the experimenters directly asked one of the Kpelle how a foolish person would do the task. When asked to sort in this way, the Kpelle had no trouble at all sorting hierarchically. He and the others had been able to sort this way all along; they just had not done so because they viewed it as foolish—and they probably considered the questioners rather unintelligent for asking such foolish questions. Why would they view functional sorting as in-

To a member of the Kpelle tribe in Africa, categories are functional. Rather than sorting hierarchically (as in placing all fish together and putting this group under the heading of fish and then animals), they would put fish into the category of eat. Such cultural differences may also be operating in the varied performances on intelligence tests of people of different backgrounds.

telligent? Simple. In ordinary life, we normally think functionally. When we think of a fish, we think of catching or eating it; when we think of clothes, we think of wearing them. However, in Western schooling, we learn what is expected of us on tests. The Kpelle did not have Western schooling and had not been exposed to intelligence testing. As a result, they solved the problems the way Western adults might do so in their everyday lives but not on an intelligence test. The Kpelle people are not the only ones who might question Western understandings of intelligence. Work by Robert Serpell (1993, 1994) in Zambia shows that Zambians also have conceptions of intelligence quite different from those of North Americans and research shows that there are many other such differences around the world (Berry, 1974; Sternberg & Kaufman, 1998).

A study by Seymour Sarason and John Doris (1979) provides a closer-to-home example regarding the effects of cultural differences on intelligence, particularly on intelligence tests. These researchers tracked the IQ scores of an immigrant population: Italian Americans. Less than a century ago, first-generation Italian American children showed a median IQ of 87, which is considered to be in the low average range, even when nonverbal measures were used and when so-called mainstream American attitudes were tested.

Some social commentators and intelligence researchers of the day pointed to heredity and other nonenvironmental factors as the basis for the low IQs—much as they do today for other minority groups. For example, a leading researcher of the day, Henry Goddard, pronounced that 79% of immigrant Italians were "feeble-minded." He also asserted that about 80% of immigrant Hungarians and Russians were similarly unendowed with intelligence (Eysenck & Kamin, 1981). Goddard (1917) also asserted that moral decadence was associated with this deficit in intelligence; he recommended that the intelligence tests he used be administered to all immigrants and that all those with low scores be selectively excluded from entering the United States.

Yet, today Italian American students who take IQ tests show slightly above-average IQs; other immigrant groups that Goddard denigrated have shown similar "amazing" increases (Ceci, 1996). Even the most fervent hereditarians would be unlikely to attribute such remarkable gains in so few generations to heredity.

Cultural assimilation, including integrated education and adoption of American definitions of intelligence, seems a much more plausible explanation. At various times, and in various places, not all children have been encouraged to pursue an education, as the following excerpt from *Black Boy* shows.

> Whenever I brought a book to the job, I wrapped it in newspaper—a habit that was to persist in other cities and under other circumstances. But some of the white men pried into my packages when I was absent and they questioned me.
> "Boy, what are you reading those books for?"
> "Oh, I don't know, sir."
> "That's deep stuff you're reading, boy."
> "I'm just killing time, sir."
> "You'll addle your brains if you don't watch out."
>
> —Richard Wright, *Black Boy*

Group Differences

Cultural and societal analyses of the concept of intelligence render it particularly important to consider carefully the meaning of group differences in measured IQ (Fischer et al., 1996; Loehlin, 2000). For ex-

Research suggests that intelligence tests are not biased in a narrow sense, but because they measure only one kind of intelligence—the ability to get good grades—the bias may lie in the entire system of prediction upon which they are based.

ample, on average, African Americans score somewhat lower than Caucasians on conventional standardized tests of intelligence (Herrnstein & Murray, 1994); but remember, Italian American scores used to be considerably lower than they are now. Scores of African Americans have been showing an increasing pattern over time, just as have scores for other groups. Available evidence to date suggests an environmental explanation for these group differences (Mackintosh, 1998; Nisbett, 1995). Moreover, differences between groups in societal outcomes, such as likelihood of graduating from high school or going on welfare, cannot really be attributed simply to differences in IQ, as some people have tried to do, because after equating for IQ (and thus removing IQ as a source of group differences), African Americans are still considerably more likely than Caucasians to be born out of wedlock, born into poverty, and be underweight at birth (Herrnstein & Murray, 1994; see R. J. Sternberg, 1996b). Group differences may thus originate from a number of factors, many of which change over time. The result is that group differences are not immutable: A group that scores, on average, lower than another group at one given time may score, on average, lower, the same, or even higher at another time.

Sex Differences. An example of a change in the nature of group differences is that with regard to sex. Overall, males and females do about the same on cognitive ability tests, although differences have been noted on specific ability tests. Analyses of trends over time suggest that sex differences in scores on these cognitive-ability tests have been shrinking over the years (Feingold, 1988). Nevertheless, there do appear to be some differences that remain. In particular, males, on average, tend to score higher on tasks that require visual and spatial working memory, motor skills that are involved in aiming, and certain aspects of mathematical performance. Females tend to score higher on tasks that require rapid access to and use of phonological and semantic information in long-term memory, production and comprehension of complex prose, fine motor skills, and perceptual speed (Halpern, 1997). These differences refer only to averages, and there are many individuals of one sex who do better than individuals of the other sex, regardless of the particular skill measured by a given test. In any case, these score differences are not easily interpretable. Claude Steele (1997), for example, has found that when boys and girls take difficult mathematical tests, boys often do better. But when the two groups are told in advance that a particular test will show no difference, on average, scores of boys and girls converge, with girls' scores increasing and boys' scores actually decreasing.

Racial Differences. Another group difference is between African Americans and whites. As mentioned earlier, African Americans tend to score lower than do white Americans on conventional tests of intelligence. The available evidence is largely consistent with an environmental explanation of this difference (Nisbett, 1995). For example, in one study, offspring of American servicemen born to German women during the Allied occupation of Germany after the Second World War revealed no significant difference between IQs of children of African American versus white servicemen (Eyferth, 1961). This result suggests that given similar environments, the children of the two groups (African American and white) of servicemen performed equally on tests of intelligence. Another study found that children adopted by white families obtained higher IQ scores than did children adopted by African American families, again suggesting environmental factors contributing to the difference between the two groups (Moore, 1986). Another way of studying group differences has been through trans-racial adoption studies, in which white parents have adopted African American children (Scarr & Weinberg, 1976; Scarr, Weinberg, & Waldman, 1993; Weinberg, Scarr, & Waldman, 1992). The results of these studies have been somewhat difficult to interpret, in that both white and African American children who were adopted in the study showed decreased IQ in a 10-year follow-up on their performance.

There are a number of mechanisms by which environmental factors such as poverty, undernutrition, and illness might affect intelligence (Sternberg et al., 2000). One mechanism is through resources. Children who are poor often do not have the resources in the home and school that children from more affluent en-

vironments have. Another mechanism is through attention to and concentration on the skills being taught in school. Children who are undernourished or ill may find it hard to concentrate in school, and therefore they may profit less from the instruction they receive. A third mechanism is the system of rewards in the environment. Children who grow up in economically deprived environments may note that the individuals who are most rewarded are not those who do well in school, but rather those who find ways of earning the money they need to survive, whatever these ways may be. It is unlikely that there is any one mechanism that fully explains the effects of these various variables. It is also important to realize that whatever these mechanisms are, they can start in utero, not just after birth. For example, fetal alcohol syndrome results in reduced IQ and has its initial effects prenatally, before the child even enters the world outside the mother's womb.

Culture-Fair Testing

The preceding arguments with respect to culture and group differences may make it clear why it is so difficult to come up with what everyone would consider a **culture-fair test**—a test that is equally appropriate for members of all cultures and that comprises items that are equally fair to members of all cultures. If members of different cultures have different ideas of what it means to be intelligent, then the very behaviors that may be considered intelligent in one culture may be viewed as unintelligent in another. Consider, for example, the concept of mental quickness. In mainstream U.S. culture, quickness is usually associated with intelligence. To say someone is "quick" is to say that the person is intelligent, and indeed, most group tests of intelligence are quite strictly timed, as I have found out the hard way myself when I have failed to finish all the items on some of them.

There can be no doubt that sometimes it is important to be fast. When you have not yet started writing a paper that is due the next day, it is definitely adaptive to be quick. If you are an air-traffic controller, you had better be fast if you value the lives of the passengers on the airplanes you are monitoring. In many cultures, however, quickness is not at a premium. In these cultures, people may believe that more intelligent people do not rush into things. In fact, early in the 20th century, a leading psychometric theoretician of intelligence, Louis Thurstone (1924), defined intelligence as the ability to withhold an instinctive response. In other words, the smart person is someone who does not rush into action but thinks first. Even in our own culture, no one will view you as brilliant if you decide on a marital partner, a job, or a place to live in the 20 to 30 seconds you might normally have to solve an intelligence-test problem. So, is it culturally fair to include a speed or timing component in an intelligence test?

Almost everyone would like to construct only culture-fair tests. Unfortunately, there exist no perfectly culture-fair tests of intelligence. Even among the tests devised to date, performance on those tests that have been labeled as "culture fair" seems to be influenced in some degree by cultural factors, such as years of schooling and academic achievements (e.g., Ceci, 1996). In sum, one must be careful about drawing conclusions regarding group differences in intelligence (Greenfield, 1997; Loehlin, 2000) that may appear to be justified on the surface but that represent only a superficial analysis of group differences.

The development of culture-fair tests based on each culture's own definition of intelligence may be an unrealistic goal, but it is possible to provide culture-relevant tests. **Culture-relevant tests** employ skills and knowledge that relate to the cultural experiences of the test takers. Content and procedures are used in testing that are appropriate to the cultural context of the test takers.

For example, 14-year-old boys performed poorly on a task when it was couched as a cupcake-baking task but performed well when it was framed as a battery-charging task (Ceci & Bronfenbrenner, 1985). Brazilian maids had no difficulty with proportional reasoning when hypothetically purchasing food but had great difficulty with it when hypothetically purchasing medicinal herbs (Schliemann & Magalhües, 1990). Brazilian children whose poverty had forced them to become street vendors showed no difficulty in performing complex arithmetic computations when selling things but had great difficulty performing similar calculations in a classroom (Carraher, Carraher, & Schliemann, 1985; Ceci & Roazzi, 1994; Nuñes, 1994).

Systems Models of Intelligence

Two contemporary theorists have proposed theories of intelligence that attempt to be fairly encompassing in dealing with both the internal and the external worlds. These theories, that of multiple intelligences and that of the triarchic nature of abilities, view intelligence as a complex system (Davidson & Downing, 2000; Sternberg, 1990b).

Multiple Intelligences

Howard Gardner (1983, 1993b, 1999) does not view intelligence as just a single, unitary construct. However, instead of speaking of multiple abilities that together constitute intelligence, as have some other theorists, Gardner has proposed a **theory of multiple intelligences,** in which eight distinct intelligences function somewhat independently of one another, but may interact to produce intelligent behavior (see Table 9-2): linguistic, logical-mathematical, spatial, musical, bodily-kinesthetic, interpersonal, intrapersonal, and naturalist. Gardner (1999) has also speculated on the possible existence of existential and spiritual intelligences. Each intelligence is a separate system of functioning, although these systems can interact to produce what we see as intelligent performance. For example, novelists would rely heavily on linguistic intelligence but might use logical-mathematical intelligence in plotting story lines or checking through their stories for logical inconsistencies. Measuring these intelligences separately might give schools and individuals a profile of a range of skills that is broader than would be obtained, say, from just measuring verbal and mathematical abilities. This profile could then be used to facilitate educational and career decisions.

In order to identify these particular intelligences, Gardner has used converging operations, gathering evidence from multiple sources and types of data. The base of evidence used by Gardner includes (but is not

According to Howard Gardner's theory of multiple intelligences, this young gymnast is showing gifted levels of bodily-kinesthetic intelligence.

TABLE 9–2

Gardner's Eight Intelligences *On which of Howard Gardner's eight intelligences do you show the greatest ability? In what contexts can you use your intelligences most effectively? (After H. Gardner, 1983, 1993b, 1999)*

TYPE OF INTELLIGENCE	TASKS REFLECTING THIS TYPE OF INTELLIGENCE
Linguistic intelligence	Reading a book; writing a paper, a novel, or a poem; understanding spoken words
Logical-mathematical intelligence	Solving math problems, balancing a checkbook, doing a mathematical proof, logical reasoning
Spatial intelligence	Getting from one place to another, reading a map, packing suitcases in the trunk of a car
Musical intelligence	Singing a song, composing a sonata, playing a trumpet, appreciating the structure of a piece of music
Bodily-kinesthetic intelligence	Dancing, playing basketball, running a mile, throwing a javelin
Interpersonal intelligence	Relating to other people, such as when we try to understand another person's behavior, motives, or emotions
Intrapersonal intelligence	Understanding ourselves—who we are, what makes us tick, and how we can change ourselves
Naturalist intelligence	Understanding patterns in the natural world

limited to) the distinctive effects of localized brain damage on specific kinds of intelligences, distinctive patterns of development in each kind of intelligence across the life span, evidence from exceptional individuals (from both ends of the spectrum), and evolutionary history.

Gardner's view of the mind is modular. Modularity theorists believe that different abilities—such as Gardner's intelligences—can be isolated as emanating from distinct portions or modules of the brain. Thus, a major task of existing and future research on intelligence would be to isolate the portions of the brain responsible for each of the intelligences. Gardner has speculated as to at least some of these relevant portions, but hard evidence for the existence of the separate intelligences has yet to be produced.

There may be multiple kinds of intelligence beyond those suggested by Gardner. For example, Peter Salovey and John Mayer (1990; see also J. Mayer, Salovey, & Caruso, 2000) have suggested the existence of *emotional intelligence*, which involves the ability to understand and regulate one's emotions (see also Goleman, 1995), and which appears to be relatively distinct from intelligence as it is conventionally conceived.

Others have discussed a concept of *social intelligence*, which is a form of intelligence used in interacting effectively with other people (N. Cantor & Kihlstrom, 1987b; M. E. Ford, 1994; Kihlstrom & Cantor, 2000). Other investigators have suggested a concept of *practical intelligence*, or the ability to function effectively in everyday life (Sternberg et al., 2000; Wagner, 2000). Clearly, our concepts of intelligence are becoming much broader than they were just a few years ago. At the same time, not all psychologists accept these broader conceptions.

The Triarchic Theory

Whereas Gardner emphasizes the separateness of the various aspects of intelligence, Sternberg tends to emphasize the extent to which they work together in his **triarchic theory of human intelligence** (R. J. Sternberg, 1985a, 1988b, 1996b, 1999). According to the triarchic theory, intelligence comprises three aspects, which deal with the relation of intelligence (a) to the internal world, (b) to experience, and (c) to the external world. Intelligence draws on three kinds of information processing components: (1) metacomponents—

executive processes used to plan, monitor, and evaluate problem solving; (2) performance components—lower-order processes used for implementing the commands of the metacomponents; and (3) knowledge-acquisition components—the processes used for learning how to solve the problems in the first place. The components are highly interdependent.

Suppose you were asked to write a term paper. To succeed you would need all three types of components. You would use metacomponents to decide on a topic, plan the paper, monitor the writing, and evaluate how well your finished product succeeds in accomplishing your goals. You would use knowledge-acquisition components for research to learn about the topic. You would also use performance components for the actual writing. In practice, the three kinds of components do not function in isolation. Before actually writing the paper, you would first have to decide on a topic and then do some research. Similarly, your plans for writing the paper might change as you gathered new information. It might turn out there just was not enough information on particular aspects of the chosen topic, forcing you to shift your emphasis. Your plans also might change if particular aspects of the writing went more smoothly than did others.

These three kinds of components all contribute to three relatively distinct aspects of intelligence, as shown in Figure 9-5. In this "triarchy" of intelligence, analytical abilities are used to analyze, evalu-

Figure 9–5
STERNBERG'S TRIARCHIC THEORY OF INTELLIGENCE.
According to Robert Sternberg, intelligence comprises analytic, creative, and practical abilities. In analytical thinking, we try to solve familiar problems by using strategies that manipulate the elements of a problem or the relationships among the elements (e.g., comparing, analyzing). In creative thinking, we try to solve new kinds of problems that require us to think about the problem and its elements in a new way (e.g., inventing, designing). In practical thinking, we try to solve problems that apply what we know to everyday contexts (e.g., implementing, using).

ate, critique, or judge, as when you decide whether a certain argument you or someone else has made is a logical argument. A metacomponent, such as that of planning, might be used analytically to devise a strategy for solving a geometry problem. Creative abilities are used to create, invent, discover, and imagine, as when you come up with new ideas for a paper topic or an idea for a scientific experiment. The metacomponent of planning might be used here to create a poem. Practical abilities are used to apply, utilize, and implement ideas in the real world, as when you decide that your psychology professor would probably rather read a term paper on something to do with psychology than on the geological formation of the Himalayas. Mapping a route for climbing the Himalayas could be a practical use of the metacomponent of planning. Research suggests that the three types of abilities—analytical, creative, and practical—are statistically relatively independent (Sternberg, 1985a; Sternberg et al., 2000; Sternberg, Grigorenko, Ferrari, & Clinkenbeard, 1999; Sternberg & Lubart, 1995).

Practical abilities serve three functions in real-world contexts: adapting ourselves to our existing environments, shaping our existing environments to create new environments, and selecting new environments. You use adaptation when you learn the ropes in a new environment and try to figure out how to succeed in it. For example, when you started college, you probably tried to figure out the explicit and implicit rules of college life and how you could use those rules to succeed in the new environment. You also shaped your environment, deciding what courses to take and what activities to pursue. You even might have tried to shape the behavior of those around you. Finally, if you were unable either to adapt yourself or to shape your environment to suit you, you might have considered selecting another environment—transferring to another college.

According to the triarchic theory, people may apply their intelligence to many kinds of problems. For example, some people may be more effective in the face of abstract, academic problems, whereas others may be more intelligent in the face of concrete, practical problems. The theory does not define an intelligent person as someone who necessarily excels in all aspects of intelligence. Rather, intelligent persons know their own strengths and weaknesses and find ways to capitalize on their strengths and either to compensate for or to correct their weaknesses. For example, a person strong in psychology but not in physics might choose as a physics project the creation of a physics aptitude test (which I did when I took physics!). The point is to make the most of your strengths and to find ways to improve upon, or at least to live comfortably with, your weaknesses. Some people are extreme in their strengths and weaknesses, and we consider such people next.

Extremes of Intelligence

In Search of . . . *What constitute extremes of intelligence and what do they tell us about human potentials?*

Every theory of intelligence must deal with the issue of extremes. Although most people fall within the broad middle range of intellectual abilities, there are, of course, people at both the upper and the lower extremes. Different theorists conceive of the extremes in different ways. People at the upper extreme are usually labeled intellectually gifted, whereas those at the lower extreme are often labeled mentally retarded. We consider next each of the two extremes.

Intellectual Giftedness

Psychologists differ in terms of how they define the intellectually gifted (Callahan, 2000; Winner, 1997). Some use an exclusively IQ-based criterion. For example, many programs for the gifted screen largely on the basis of scores on conventional intelligence tests, taking children in perhaps the top 1% (IQ roughly equal to 135 or above) or 2% (IQ roughly equal to 132 or above) for their programs. Others also supplement the assessment of IQ as a basis of giftedness with other criteria, such as school or career achievements or other measures of gifted performance.

Probably the most well-known studies of gifted individuals were conducted by Lewis Terman. Terman conducted a *longitudinal study*, research that followed particular individuals over the course of their life spans (Terman, 1925; Terman & Oden, 1959). The study has continued even after Terman's death. In his sample of the gifted, Terman included children from California under age 11 with IQs over 140, as well as children in the 11- to 14-year age bracket with slightly lower IQs. The mean IQ of the 643 research participants selected was 151; only 22 of these participants had IQs lower than 140.

The accomplishments in later life of the selected group were extraordinary by any criterion. For example, 31 men from the study were listed in *Who's Who in America*. There were numerous highly successful businessmen, as well as individuals who were successful in all of the professions. The sex bias in these references is obvious. Most of the women became housewives, so it is impossible to make any meaningful comparison

between the men (none of whom were reported to have become househusbands) and the women. As with all correlational data, it would be difficult to assign a causal role to IQ in accounting for the accomplishments of the successful individuals in the study. Many factors other than IQ could have contributed to the success of Terman's sample, among the most important of which is familial socioeconomic status and the final educational level achieved by these individuals.

Today, many, if not most, psychologists look to more than IQ for the identification of the intellectually gifted. (See R. J. Sternberg & Davidson, 1986, and Winner, 1996, for descriptions of a variety of theories of giftedness.) For example, Joseph Renzulli (1986) believes that high motivation, or commitment to tasks, and high creativity are important to giftedness, in addition to above-average (although not necessarily outstanding) intelligence. Perhaps gifted people are persons who are good at something—sometimes just one thing—but who find a way of capitalizing on that something to make the most of their capabilities (R. J. Sternberg, 1985a). All of these theorists are in agreement that there is more to giftedness than a high IQ. Indeed, I argue that people can be creatively or practically gifted, and not even show up as particularly distinguished at all on an IQ test.

In one set of studies, high school students from all around the United States and some other countries were identified in terms of analytical, creative, and practical giftedness (R. J. Sternberg, 1997b; R. J. Sternberg & Clinkenbeard, 1995; R. J. Sternberg, Ferrari, Clinkenbeard, & Grigorenko, 1996). In many cases, students who were gifted in one of these kinds of abilities were not gifted in others. The identified students were then taught a college-level course that emphasized either analytical, creative, or practical forms of instruction. Some students were in an instructional condition that matched their pattern of abilities. Other students were taught in a way that mismatched their pattern of abilities. Students' achievement was also evaluated in all three ways. We found that students achieved at higher levels when they were taught in a way that matched their pattern of abilities (see also Sternberg, Torff, & Grigorenko, 1998).

These findings raise a potentially important issue. Research suggests that intelligence tests are not *biased* in a narrow statistical sense: They do not tend, on average, falsely to predict criterion performance for particular groups (Mackintosh, 1998). For example, lower intelligence test scores tend to be associated with lower school achievement for people from a variety of groups. But if intelligence tests measure a somewhat narrow set of skills and schools also tend to value this narrow set of skills, then there is a possibility that both the predictor (such as an intelligence test) and the criterion (such as school grades) share the same bias. Statistical analyses would fail to detect bias because both the predictor and the criterion that is predicted share the same bias. The bias is not in the predictor (the test), per se, but in the entire system of prediction (the test, the measure of achievement, and their interrelation). Perhaps if intelligence tests and schools both valued creative and practical abilities as well as analytical abilities, children now identified as relatively lacking in intelligence would be viewed as more intelligent.

In sum, the tendency today is to look beyond IQ to identify intellectually gifted individuals. There are many ways to be gifted and scores on conventional intelligence tests represent only one of these ways. Indeed, some of the most gifted adult contributors to society, such as Albert Einstein or Thomas Edison, were not top performers either on tests or in school during their early years. Einstein did not even speak until he was 3 years old, and many other remarkably gifted persons have even shown particular characteristics that some have regarded as indicating mental retardation. We might then wonder how we can identify truly retarded intellect.

Mental Retardation

Mental retardation refers to low levels of intelligence, including low adaptive competence (Detterman, Gabriel, & Ruthsatz, 2000; Detterman & Thompson, 1997). Simple enough. Much less simple is determining how we should conceive of mental retardation and whom we should label as being mentally retarded. Different viewpoints lead to different conclusions.

The Role of Adaptive Competence

The American Association on Mental Retardation (1992) includes within its definition of mental retardation two components: low IQ and low adaptive competence, the latter of which refers to how a person gets along in the world. In other words, to be labeled as retarded, an individual not only would have to perform poorly on an intelligence test but also would have to show problems adapting to the environment. A child whose performance was normal in every way except for low IQ would not, by this definition, be classified as mentally retarded. Table 9-3 illustrates some of the ways in which particular IQ scores have been related to particular adaptive life skills. Adaptive life skills are judged in a variety of domains, such as communication (as in talking to someone or writing them a letter), self-care (as in dressing oneself or using the toilet), home living (as in preparing meals), and social interaction (as in meeting the expectations of others).

It is not always easy to assess adaptive competence, however, as the following example (Edgerton, 1967) shows. A retarded man (who had scored low on tests of intelligence) was unable to tell time—an indication of some kind of cognitive deficit. However, the man employed a clever compensatory strategy. He wore a nonfunctional watch, so that whenever he wanted to know the time, he could stop, look at his watch, pretend to notice that his watch did not work, and then ask a stranger (who would have observed his behavior) to tell him the correct time. How should we assess this man's adaptive competence—in terms of his strategy for determining the time or in terms of his inability to tell time by looking at a watch? Was the man mentally retarded, and if so, why do you think so?

Cognitive Bases of Mental Retardation

Edward Zigler (1982; see also Hodapp, 1994) believes that some mentally retarded individuals simply develop mentally at a slower rate than do individuals with normal intelligence. Most investigators, however, seek not only to look at quantitative differences in rates of development but also at qualitative differences in performance. A key qualitative difference centers on metacognitive skill. There is fairly widespread agreement that mentally retarded individuals have difficulties with the executive processes of cognition, such as planning, monitoring, and evaluating their strategies for task performance (Campione, Brown, & Ferrara, 1982). An example would be their planning to rehearse lists of words they are asked to memorize (A. L. Brown, Campione, Bray, & Wilcox, 1973). To what extent might such difficulties be based on hereditary factors and to what extent on environmental factors?

Hereditary and Environmental Impairments of Intelligence

Both environmental and hereditary factors may contribute to retardation (Grigorenko, 2000; Sternberg & Grigorenko, 1997). Environmental influences before birth may cause permanent retardation—for example, retardation resulting from a mother's inadequate nutrition or ingestion of toxins such as alcohol during the individual's prenatal development (Olson, 1994). A child exposed to an impoverished environment or denied opportunities for even basic instruction in the home might display retardation. Even a brief trauma, such as from a car accident or a fall, can injure the brain, causing mental retardation.

Although we do not understand the subtle influences of heredity on intelligence very well at present, we do know of several genetic syndromes that clearly cause mental retardation. For example, one of the more common genetic causes of mental

TABLE 9–3

Levels of Mental Retardation   *Contemporary views of mental retardation de-emphasize IQ scores and more strongly underscore the ability of the individual to show the skills needed for adapting to the requirements of self-care and to societal expectations.*

DEGREE OF RETARDATION	RANGE OF TYPICAL IQ SCORES	ADAPTIVE LIFE SKILLS	LIVING REQUIREMENTS
Mild (≈ 85% of retarded persons; about 2% of general population)	50–70	With adequate training and appropriate environmental support: ■ Academic skills at or below the sixth-grade level ■ Social and vocation-related skills	Independent living and occupational success can be achieved.
Moderate (≈ 10% of retarded persons; 0.1% of the general population)	35–55	■ Academic tasks at or below the fourth-grade level if given special education ■ Unskilled or possibly highly routinized semi-skilled vocational activities ■ Many personal self-maintenance activities	Sheltered home and work environments, in which supervision and guidance are readily available, often work well.
Severe (≈ 4% of retarded persons; ≈ 0.003% of the general population)	20–40	■ Speech, or at least some manner of communication, possible ■ Simple tasks required for personal self-maintenance (including toileting) ■ Possibly some limited vocational activity	Some custodial services may be required, in addition to a carefully controlled environment.
Profound (<2% of retarded persons)	Below 25	■ Limited motor development and little or no speech ■ Some self-maintenance activities (not including toileting) possible	Constant supervision and assistance in a custodial setting are required.

retardation is Down's syndrome, once called "mongolism." This syndrome results from the presence of extra material on one of the chromosomes. The extra material disrupts the normal biochemical messages and results in retardation and other features of this syndrome.

Sometimes, hereditary factors interact with environmental ones to produce mental retardation. Although we cannot yet prevent the inheritance of these diseases, we can try to block the environmental contribution to the retardation. For example, we now know how to minimize the likelihood of mental retardation in phenylketonuria (PKU), a rare hereditary disease that results in mental retardation if environmental intervention is not imposed. Essentially, children with this disease do not produce an enzyme needed for properly metabolizing the amino acid phenylalanine. As a result, if PKU is not quickly discovered after birth, and the infant consumes foods containing complete proteins or other sources of phenylalanine, byproducts of the incomplete metabolism of this amino acid will accumulate in the bloodstream. These byproducts will cause progressively more severe brain damage and permanent retardation. In PKU, the interactive roles of nature and nurture are clear, and we can specify clearly these roles.

The Heritability of Intelligence

In Search of . . .

To what extent is intelligence inherited?

The ancient nature–nurture controversy continues in regard to intelligence (Sternberg & Grigorenko, 1997). However, today, the large majority of psychologists and *behavior geneticists*—those who study the effects of genes on behavior—believe that differences in intelligence result from a combination of hereditary and environmental factors. The degree to which heredity contributes to intelligence is often expressed in terms of a **heritability coefficient,** a number on a scale from 0 to 1, such that a coefficient of 0 means that heredity has no influence on variation among people, whereas a coefficient of 1 means that heredity is the only influence on such variation. This coefficient can be applied to intelligence or to any other trait, such as height or weight.

It is important to remember that the coefficient indicates variation in measured intelligence. The heritability coefficient can tell us only about genetic effects that result in individual differences among people. It tells us nothing about genetic effects when there are no, or only trivial, differences. For example, both how tall you are and how many fingers you have at birth are in large part genetically preprogrammed. But we can use the coefficient of heritability only to assess genetic effects on height, where there are large individual differences. We cannot use the coefficient to understand number of fingers at birth because there is so little variation across people.

It is also important to realize that heritability tells us nothing about the *modifiability* of intelligence. A trait can be heritable and yet modifiable. For example, height is highly heritable, with a heritability coefficient greater than .9 in most populations. Yet heights of Europeans and North Americans increased by over 5 cm between 1920 and 1970 (Van Wieringen, 1978). Consider, as another example, attributes of corn. Many attributes of corn, including height, are highly heritable. But if one batch of corn seeds were planted in the fertile fields of Iowa, and another similar batch were planted in the Mojave desert, the batch planted in Iowa undoubtedly would grow taller and thrive better, regardless of the heritability of the attributes of the corn. In this case, environment would largely determine how well the corn grew (Lewontin, 1975).

Current estimates of the heritability coefficient of intelligence are based almost exclusively on performance on standard tests of intelligence. The estimates can be no better than the tests and we have already seen that the tests define intelligence somewhat narrowly. How can we estimate the heritability of intelligence (at least that portion of it measured by the conventional tests)? Several methods have been used. The main ones are studies of separated identical twins, studies of identical versus fraternal twins, and studies of adopted children (Mackintosh, 1998; R. J. Sternberg & Grigorenko, 1997).

Separated Identical Twins

Identical twins have identical genes. No one knows exactly why identical twinning occurs, but we do know that identical twins result when a sperm fertilizes an egg and the newly formed embryo splits in two, resulting in two embryos with identical genes. Suppose that a set of identical twins is born, and then one of the twins is immediately whisked away to a new environment, chosen at random, so that no relationship exists between the environments in which the two twins are raised. The two twins would have identical genes, but any similarity between their environments would be due only to chance. If we then created a number of such twin pairs, we would be able to estimate the contribution of heredity to individual differences in intelligence by correlating the measured intelligence of each individual with that of his or her identical twin. The twins would have in common all their heredity but none of their environment (except any aspects that might be similar due to chance).

Although, of course, purposely creating such a group of separated twins is unethical, sometimes real-life circumstances have created instances in which twins have been separated at birth and then raised

These identical twins were separated at birth and were not reunited until they were 31 years old, when the two firefighters met and discovered striking similarities in their personal habits and interests. Studies of twins reared apart reveal a great deal about how much of our intelligence is due to our nature and how much is due to our nurture.

separately. In studies of twins reared apart, the various estimates tend to fall within roughly the same heritability-coefficient range of 0.6 to 0.8 (e.g., Bouchard & McGue, 1981; Juel-Nielsen, 1965; H. H. Newman, Freeman, & Holzinger, 1937; Shields, 1962).

These relatively high figures must be interpreted with some caution, however. In many cases, the twins were not actually separated at birth, but at some point afterward, giving the twins a common environment for at least some time. In other cases, it becomes clear that the supposedly random assortment of environments was not truly random. Placement authorities tend to place twins in environments relatively similar to those the twins had left. These tendencies may inflate in some degree the apparent contribution of heredity to variation in measured intelligence, because variation that is actually environmental is included in the correlation that is supposed to represent only the effect of heredity.

Identical Versus Fraternal Twins

Another way to estimate heritability is to compare the correlation of IQs for identical versus fraternal twins. The idea is that, whereas identical twins share identical genes, fraternal twins share only the same genes as would any brother or sister. On average, fraternal twins share only 50% of their genes. To the extent that the identical and fraternal twin pairs share similar environments due to age, we should not get environmental differences due merely to variations in age among sibling pairs. If environments are nearly the same for both twins, differences in the correlation of intelligence scores between fraternal and identical twins should be attributable to heredity. According to a review by Thomas Bouchard and Matthew McGue (1981), these data lead to a heritability estimate of about 0.75, again suggesting a high level of heritability. More recent estimates are similar, although quite variable (Mackintosh, 1998).

These data may be affected by the fact that fraternal twins often do not share environments to the same extent that identical ones do, particularly if the fraternal twins are not same-sexed twins. Parents tend to treat identical twins more nearly alike than they do fraternal twins, even to the extent of having them dress the same way. Moreover, the twins themselves are likely to respond differently if they are identical, perhaps seeking out more apparent identity with their twin. Thus, once again, the contribution of environment may be underestimated to some extent.

Adoption

Yet another way to examine hereditary versus environmental contributions to intelligence is by comparing the correlation between the IQs of adopted children with those of their biological parents, on the one hand, and their adoptive parents, on the other. Biological parents provide adopted children with their genes, and adoptive parents provide the children their environments. So, to the extent that heredity matters, the higher correlation should be with the intelligence of the biological rather than the adoptive parents; to the extent that environment matters, the higher correlation should be that with the intelligence of the adoptive rather than the biological parents. In some families, it is also possible to compare the IQs of the adopted children to the IQs of either biological or adoptive siblings.

Many psychologists who have studied intelligence as measured by IQ believe the heritability of intelligence to be about 0.5 in children and somewhat higher in adults (Mackintosh, 1998; Plomin, 1997), for whom the early effects of the child-rearing environment have receded. However, there probably is no one coefficient of heritability that applies to all populations under all circumstances. Indeed, changes in distributions of genes or in environments can change the estimates. Moreover, even if a trait shows a high heritability, we could not say that the trait cannot be developed. For example, the heritability of height is very high—about 0.9—yet we know that over the past several generations, heights have been increasing. We can thus see how better environments can lead to growth, physical as well as intellectual. This possibility of making the most of our intelligence brings us to the topic explored in Psychology in Everyday Life: Improving Intelligence.

Although heredity does play a role in intelligence, some research shows that the emotional and verbal responsivity of caregivers, appropriate play materials, avoidance of punishment, and variety in daily stimulation predict IQ scores more effectively than do socioeconomic status or family structure variables.

Psychology in Everyday Life

Improving Intelligence

At one time, it was believed that intelligence was fixed, and that we were stuck with whatever level of intelligence we have at birth. Today, many researchers believe that intelligence and the thinking skills associated with it are malleable, that these skills can be shaped and even increased through various kinds of interventions (Bransford & Stein, 1993; Detterman & Sternberg, 1982; Grotzer & Perkins, 2000; D. F. Halpern, 1996; R. Mayer, 2000; Perkins & Grotzer, 1997; R. J. Sternberg, 1996b). For example, the Head Start program was initiated in the 1960s as a way of giving preschoolers an edge on intellectual abilities and accomplishments when they started school. Long-term follow-ups have indicated that by mid-adolescence, children who participated in the program were more than a grade ahead of matched controls who were not in the program (Lazar & Darlington, 1982; Zigler & Berman, 1983). Children in the program also scored higher on a variety of tests of scholastic achievement, were less likely to need remedial attention, and were less likely to show behavioral problems. Although such measures are not truly measures of intelligence, they show strong positive correlations with intelligence tests. A number of other programs have also shown some success in environments outside of the family home (e.g., Adams, 1986).

Support for the importance of home environment was found by Robert Bradley and Bettye Caldwell (1984) in regard to the development of intelligence in young children. These researchers found that several factors in the early home environment, before children start school, may be linked to high IQ scores: emotional and verbal responsivity of the primary caregiver and the caregiver's involvement with the child, avoidance of restriction and punishment, organization of the physical environment and activity schedule, provision of appropriate play materials, and opportunities for variety in daily stimulation. Further, Bradley and Caldwell found that these factors more effectively predicted IQ scores than did socioeconomic status or family-structure variables. Note, however, that the Bradley–Caldwell study pertained to preschool children, and children's IQ scores do not begin to predict adult IQ scores well until about age 4. Moreover, before age 7, the scores are not very stable (Bloom, 1964).

Perhaps the best evidence for the modifiability of intelligence comes from research by James Flynn (1987; see also Neisser, 1998). This research suggests that ever since record keeping began early in the 20th century, IQ scores have been increasing roughly 9 points per generation (every 30 years). This result is sometimes referred to as the *Flynn effect*. From any point of view, this increase is large. No one knows exactly why such large increases have occurred, although the explanation must be environmental, because the period of time involved is too brief for genetic mutations to have had an effect. If psychologists were able to understand the cause of the increase, they might be able to apply what they learned to increasing the intellectual skills of individuals within a given generation.

Altogether, evidence now indicates that environment, motivation, and training can profoundly affect intellectual skills. Heredity may set some kind of upper limit on how intelligent a person can become. However, we now know that for any attribute that is partly genetic, there is a **reaction range**— the broad limits within which a particular attribute can be expressed in various possible ways, given the inherited potential for expression of the attribute in a particular individual. Thus, each person's intelligence can be developed further within this broad range of potential intelligence. We have no reason to believe that people now reach the upper limits in the development of their intellectual skills. To the contrary, the evidence suggests that, although we cannot work miracles, we can do quite a bit to help people become more intelligent.

THINK ABOUT IT

1. Does it make sense to speak of "overachievers"? Why or why not?
2. To what extent are people's achievements—including your own—an accurate reflection of their aptitudes? What other factors beside aptitudes affect achievement?
3. Create a test question that assesses a particular skill or topic of knowledge. Tailor that question to the following persons: (a) a 9-year-old homeless boy who supports himself by whatever means he finds available, (b) a 20-year-old college student, and (c) a 70-year-old retired plumber.

4. Many museums now include specifically child-oriented experiences and exhibits. Think of an exhibit at a museum you have visited or have heard about. How might you enhance the learning experience of a 10-year-old to help the child profit from the exhibit?

5. Are there things you could do to increase your own abilities? If so, what?

6. Are there aspects of your abilities that you could use better? If so, how might you better use them?

You can provide your own answers to these questions online at the **Sternberg,** *In Search of the Human Mind Web site:* *http://www.harcourtcollege.com/psych/ishm*

SUMMARY

Definitions of Intelligence   298

1. Two common themes that run through the definitions of *intelligence* proposed by many experts are the ability to learn from experience and the ability to adapt to the environment.

2. Two traditions in the study of intelligence are those of Francis Galton and of Alfred Binet. The tradition of Galton emphasizes psychophysical acuity, and that of Binet emphasizes judgment.

3. *Mental age* refers to a person's level of intelligence, as compared with the "average" person of a given chronological age. Because of conceptual and statistical problems, the mental age construct is rarely used in testing today.

4. The intelligence quotient (IQ) originally represented the *ratio* of mental age to chronological age, multiplied by 100. It was intended to provide a measure of a person's intelligence, relative to his or her age-mates.

5. A *percentile* refers to the proportion of people whose scores fall below a given level of performance, multiplied by 100. Thus, a percentile of 75 on a test would refer to a score at or above the score of 75% of the other persons taking the same test.

6. Today, IQs are typically computed so as to have a *median* (middle score) of 100 and a standard deviation (which measures dispersion of scores) of 15 or 16. IQs computed in this way are *deviation IQs.*

7. Two of the most widely used individually administered intelligence tests are the Stanford-Binet Intelligence Scales and the Wechsler Adult Intelligence Scale-III (as well as the third edition of the Wechsler Intelligence Scale for Children).

Assessment Issues   304

8. Test *standardization* refers to the process whereby the administration of the test in a given way ensures that the conditions for taking the test are the same for all test takers. *Normative scores* are standardized scores representing a translation of *raw scores* into scaled equivalents that reflect the relative performance of individual test takers, thereby permitting comparison.

9. Test *validity* is of several kinds. *Construct-related validity* is the extent to which a test measures the construct it is supposed to measure. *Predictive validity* is the extent to which a test predicts some kind of performance measured long after the test was taken. *Content-related validity* refers to the extent to which experts judge the content of a test to represent the universe of material that it is supposed to sample. *Face validity* is the same judgment made by the people who take the test or by other laypersons.

10. Test *reliability* is also of several kinds. *Test–retest reliability* refers to the degree of relation between two administrations of the same test. *Alternate-forms reliability* refers to the degree of relation between two administrations of parallel (comparable) forms of a test. *Internal-consistency reliability* is the extent to which a test measures a single (homogeneous) construct. *Interrater reliability* refers to the extent to which two or more raters of a given product or set of products rate the same products the same way.

Theories of the Nature of Intelligence   307

11. One approach to intelligence, the psychometric approach, involves the use of *factor analysis*, a statistical technique that may enable the user to identify latent sources of individual differences in performance on tests. Some of the main factor models of the mind are the two-factor model of Spearman, the primary-mental-abilities model of Thurstone, and the hierarchical models of Cattell and Carroll.

12. An alternative approach to intelligence, the computational approach, involves the analysis of *information processing*—the mental manipulation of symbols. Information-processing theorists have sought to understand intelligence in terms of constructs such as speed of lexical access or of components of reasoning and problem solving.

13. A third approach is the biological model, which can involve sophisticated means of viewing certain kinds of activity within the brain.

14. A fourth approach to understanding intelligence (based on an anthropological model) is a contextual approach, according to which intelligence is viewed as wholly or partly determined by cultural values. *Contextual* theorists differ in the extent to which they believe that the meaning of intelligence differs from one culture to another.

15. What is considered to be intelligent behavior is, to some extent, culturally relative. The same behavior that is considered to be intelligent in one culture may be considered to be unintelligent in another culture.

16. Because members of different cultures have different conceptions of what constitutes intelligent behavior, it is difficult, perhaps impossible, to create a test of intelligence that is *culture fair*—that is, equally fair for members of different cultures. Tests may be *culture relevant*, however.

17. A fifth approach to understanding intelligence is based on a systems model. Gardner's theory of multiple intelligences specifies that intelligence is not a unitary construct, but rather that there are multiple intelligences, each relatively independent of the others. Sternberg's *triarchic theory of human intelligence* conceives of intelligence in terms of information-processing components, which are applied to experience to serve the functions of adaptation to the environment, shaping of the environment, and selection of new environments.

Extremes of Intelligence 317

18. Intellectual giftedness refers to a very high level of intelligence and is often believed to involve more than just IQ—for example, high creativity and high motivation.

19. The American Association on Mental Retardation includes within its definition of *mental retardation* two components: low IQ and low adaptive competence, the latter of which refers to how a person gets along in the world.

20. Mental retardation appears typically to be caused by both hereditary and environmental factors, often in interaction.

21. Down's syndrome results from the presence of extra chromosomal material, and it usually results in some degree of mental retardation.

Heritability of Intelligence 320

22. The heritability of intelligence refers to the proportion of individual-differences variation in intelligence tests that is inherited within a given population. Heritability can differ both across populations and within populations, and across different times and places. Heritability measures only those genetic effects that produce individual differences.

23. Heritability can be estimated in several ways. Three of the most common are through the study of separated identical twins, by comparisons of identical versus fraternal twins, and by adoption studies that compare IQs of adopted versus biological siblings raised by a given set of parents to IQs of both the biological and the adoptive parents.

KEY TERMS

achievement 302
alternate-forms reliability 305
aptitude 302
construct-related validity 304
content-related validity 305
contextualist 311
crystallized intelligence 308
culture-fair test 313
culture-relevant test 314
deviation IQs 301
face validity 305
factor analysis 307
fluid intelligence 308

heritability coefficient 320
information processing 308
intelligence 297
internal-consistency reliability 305
interrater reliability 305
mean 300
median 300
mental age 299
mental retardation 318
mode 300
normal distribution 300
normative scores (norms) 306

percentile 300
predictive validity 304
ratio IQ 300
raw score 300
reaction range 322
reliability 305
standardization 305
test–retest reliability 305
theory of multiple intelligences 314
triarchic theory of human intelligence 315
validity 304

■ THINK ABOUT IT SAMPLE RESPONSES

1. Does it make sense to speak of "overachievers"? Why or why not?

It really does not make sense to speak of "overachievers" because someone cannot achieve at a level that is higher than his or her capabilities. If the person seems to be achieving at a higher level, it is because the predictive assessment of capabilities missed some capabilities that are instrumental to success. There are abilities besides those measured by conventional tests that are very important to success in school and in life.

2. To what extent are people's achievements—including your own—an accurate reflection of their aptitudes? What other factors beside aptitudes affect achievement?

Other factors that affect achievement include luck, determination, willingness to work hard, belief in one's ability to succeed, willingness to surmount obstacles, and willingness to take sensible risks.

3. Create a test question that assesses a particular skill or topic of knowledge. Tailor that question to the following persons: (a) a 9-year-old homeless boy who supports himself by whatever means he finds available, (b) a 20-year-old college student, and (c) a 70-year-old retired plumber.

(a) Where can you find food for free without stealing it?

(b) What is the difference between studying for a multiple-choice test and studying for an essay test?

(c) How long does a Social Security pension last?

4. Many museums now include specifically child-oriented experiences and exhibits. Think of an exhibit at a museum you have visited or have heard about. How might you enhance the learning experience of a 10-year-old to help the child profit from the exhibit?

One of the best things an exhibit can do is not only provide information but also show the children why they should care about the information. Exhibits tend to be more informative when people can relate them to their lives.

5. Are there things you could do to increase your own abilities? If so, what?

Research suggests that schooling in itself increases abilities. So just by being in and profiting from school, you are increasing your abilities. Another thing you can do is to adopt an attitude that learning is a lifelong endeavor. You should view learning as something you do inside and outside of school, for the duration of your life span.

6. Are there aspects of your abilities that you could use better? If so, how might you better use them?

Many people fail to use their abilities fully because they doubt they have them. For example, they are convinced that they cannot write well, so they do not try. Or they are convinced that they cannot succeed in physical activities (such as jogging or tennis), so they never try to develop expertise. The first step to better using abilities is to accept that abilities can be best used when one believes one has them.

The baby, assailed by eyes, ears, nose, skin, and entrails at once, feels that all is one great blooming, buzzing confusion.

—William James, Principles of Psychology

10

PHYSICAL AND COGNITIVE DEVELOPMENT

Chapter Outline

Does a baby really start life thinking that all is one blooming, buzzing confusion? Psychology's interest in how our mental, physical, and social abilities develop from birth onward stems from the fact that all play a big role in who we become. The 2-year-old, 10-year-old, and 25-year-old all have different physical, mental, and social abilities as a result of their differing points in **development**—similarity and difference as they emerge over time—as well as their different life experiences. **Developmental psychology** is the study of the differences and similarities among people of different ages, as well as the qualitative and quantitative psychological changes that occur across the life span. Developmental psychologists are interested in all aspects of the developing person, including physical, cognitive, and social development. Psychologists who study physical development want to know what physical changes occur in the organism over time, as well as what aspects of the organism remain relatively the same. Psychologists who study cognitive development want to know how and why people think and behave differently at different times in their lives. Psychologists who study social development are interested in the various ways we interact with other people as we develop throughout our life span.

This chapter will focus on physical and cognitive development. In this chapter, we first discuss some of the basic issues of *physical development*—that is, the biological bases of development. Next we discuss issues in **cognitive development,** the study of how mental skills build and change with increasing physiological maturity and experience. Next we consider some of the research methods that are used in the study of development. Then we present some theories of how cognition develops and consider the growth of cognition in specific domains, such as perception and reasoning. Finally, we look briefly at the development of adult cognition and at the principles that unify the field of cognitive development. Because much of social development depends on various cognitive developments, we will cover social development in the next chapter, the first of a trio of chapters on social psychology.

One of the most obvious features of development in humans is its notable dependence on other human beings. Children live with their parents for many years and go to school for many years as well. In today's society, a newly emerging doctor, for example, may have had 20 years of schooling or more. We are accustomed to such levels of dependence on parents and other adults, but this long period of dependence is unique among species. Why, if humans are so smart, do they take so long to become independent and set out on their own? Evolutionarily, longer periods of dependence are associated with greater, not lesser cognitive abilities. In most species, a far greater proportion of day-to-day behavior is instinctive, more than in humans. Because the behavior is preprogrammed, it does not need to be taught to younger individuals by older individuals. Humans are more flexible and have greater potential for adaptation to diverse environmental challenges. But the cost of such greater flexibility is a longer period of learning how to use the talents we have. With age, we learn more and more about how successfully to adapt.

At first glance, it might seem that differences across the life span are due only to **growth**—quantitative linear increases in amounts in physical, cognitive, and social skills. However, development involves much more than growth. Development also encompasses qualitative changes in complexity, often accompanied by quantitative increases in size or amount.

Just as social development depends, to some extent, upon a person's level of cognitive development, so is the person's cognitive development, in part, dependent on his or her level of physical development. A quick look at the how our brains and bodies develop will demonstrate some of the connections between physical and cognitive growth and development. But first we need to clarify the basic questions researchers confront when they study physical and cognitive development.

Basic Questions in the Study of Physical and Cognitive Development

In Search of . . . *What are some basic questions we need to answer about cognitive development?*

Five broad kinds of questions stand out in the field of physical and cognitive development: (1) What physical cognitive-processing capabilities does the newborn have? (2) At what ages do infants, children, and adults first demonstrate various kinds of competencies, and what do these competencies tell us about the individual as a whole? Are there critical periods for the acquisition of these competencies in which learning of a skill must be accomplished in order for it to be accomplished at all (e.g., learning to speak a second language without an accent reflecting one's first language)? It is important to remember that answers to this question are averages and do not necessarily apply to each individual. (3) What causes progressive, developmental changes in cognition, and what causes individual differences in these developments? What are the relative roles of maturation (nature) and learning (nurture) in physical and cognitive development? (4) To what extent is development stagelike and discontinuous, and to what extent is it smooth and continuous—an uninterrupted, gradual progression? (5) To what extent is development domain general, and to what extent is it domain specific?

The last three questions above have often been the subject of great controversy among developmental psychologists. Often, the questions have been phrased in ways that suggest an either-or answer, such as "Which is more important: nature or nurture?" (see Bouchard, 1997; Grigorenko, 1999; Loehlin, Horn, & Willerman, 1997; Plomin, 1999; Plomin, Fulker, Corley, & DeFries, 1997; R. J. Sternberg & Grigorenko, 1997; R. J. Sternberg & Okagaki, 1989; Scarr, 1997). When phrased as either-or questions, they seem to require a single, definitive answer. Simplistic questions tend to promote simplistic answers. Unfortunately, development—like so many other aspects of psychology—is not that simple. The questions we ask and the ways we define problems, in general, determine how we go about seeking answers—and whether we will find them. If we are to understand human development, we must phrase these questions in ways that encourage us to find realistic—and therefore possibly complex—answers.

The Respective Roles of Maturation and Learning

Two main concepts in development are maturation and learning (see Bornstein, 1999). **Maturation** is any relatively permanent change in an individual that occurs strictly as a result of the biological processes of growing older. *Learning* is any relatively permanent change in thought or behavior as a result of experience (see chapter 6). Maturation is preprogrammed; it will happen regardless of the environment. For example, an infant's ability to suck appears and then disappears at preprogrammed ages, almost entirely without regard to the influences of the environment. In contrast, learning will take place only if the individual has particular experiences. For example, recognizing your own name when it is spoken is almost exclusively a function of learning; it will not happen if you have never heard your name spoken.

Maturation and learning typically interact and so it often is difficult to separate their effects. For example, one should not assume that reflexes are all wholly preprogrammed biologically. Esther Thelen (1995), for example, has suggested that at least some reflexes (discussed below), such as the stepping reflex, which once was assumed to be wholly preprogrammed, may be the result of gene-environment interaction.

The stepping reflex is shown when newborn infants perform a well-coordinated, steplike pattern of movement when they are held upright with their feet resting on a supporting surface. The reflex disappears mysteriously within the first few months of life and then reappears when children start to stand and walk.

Thelen has suggested that the disappearance is due to rapid gains in body fat that make the infants unable to show the reflex, which actually is still available to them. Their legs just are too heavy to show the stepping reflex. Then when the baby fat disappears, the infants once again show the reflex. Thelen showed this phenomenon in a simple way: When the infants who appear to have lost the stepping reflex have their legs submerged in water, which lightens their legs, they again show the reflex.

Fundamentally, the maturation versus learning question is the age-old philosophical and psychological debate over nature versus nurture. Today, almost all psychologists believe that both maturation and learning influence development as interactive processes. We may be born with a particular genetic capacity, such as the capacity to play a musical instrument. But the extent to which our performance develops to meet this capacity will depend to a large extent on the environment. An example is whether we are given an opportunity to play an instrument or even to be exposed to various forms of music. One environment might bring out skills that another might not. A child with extraordinary musical talent might never discover this talent if raised in a nonmusical home.

Another controversy regarding development depends on the way we interpret the data we find: Does development occur in a series of discrete stages or does it occur in a single, continuous progression that gradually unfolds (Amsel & Renninger, 1997; Bennett, 1999)?

Continuity Versus Discontinuity

First, exactly what is a stage? John Flavell (1971) has suggested four key criteria for stages.

First, stages imply *qualitative changes.* As children grow older, they improve not only at doing what they already did, but also at doing new things. Thus, when children are in particular stages, they can think and reason only in particular ways. They develop the ability to think and reason in those ways only when in that stage and not before. For example, according to the late Swiss developmental theorist Jean Piaget (1954), young children tend to see things only from their own point of view (thereby exhibiting *egocentrism*). Later they come to see things in a qualitatively different way, seeing these things from the points of view of others as well as themselves.

Second, stages imply that a number of different new skills appear simultaneously. Thus, the child not only starts to see the relation between, say, addition and multiplication, but also other kinds of new relations as well that the child previously had been unable to grasp.

Third, the transitions between stages are fairly abrupt. The new abilities appear in a sudden surge rather than in tiny steps spread out over time.

Fourth and finally, in a new stage, the child does not just add a skill here and a skill there, but rather, reorganizes large amounts of information at the same time. The child comes to see the world in a new way.

Stages occur in an invariable sequence (Beilin, 1971; Kurtines & Greif, 1974). For example, in terms of physical development, children almost always creep on their bellies before they crawl on hands and knees, and they generally do both before they walk. Children also seem to show language development in an invariably sequenced progression (see chapter 8).

Given these criteria (the invariable sequence and the set of qualitatively distinct cognitive structures), does development actually exhibit stagelike properties? As with so many questions in psychology, the answer depends on whom you ask. Piaget (1969, 1972) deeply believed in the discontinuously phased nature of development. Charles Brainerd (1978) remained unconvinced that development is discontinuous. In Brainerd's view, too many findings do not meet the criteria for classifying development into discrete stages. Some theories of development (such as Piaget's) posit stages, but others (such as learning theories) do not. Moreover,

Maturation is preprogrammed. It will happen regardless of environment. Learning, however, takes place only if the child has particular experiences.

even those theorists who propose discontinuous stages of development recognize that the stages are rarely clear-cut. For example, Piaget (1972) conceded that achievements within a given stage do not appear to occur for every task in every domain all at once. Thus, children are able to recognize countable items as the same in number despite changes in their appearance before they can recognize volume as the same despite changes in appearance.

Such variations in a single child's abilities are at the base of the third of the major controversies in development, whether development is domain general or domain specific.

Domain Generality Versus Domain Specificity in Development

Throughout the first half of the twentieth century, theories of cognitive development emphasized *domain generality*, the notion that comparable development of a skill tends to occur in multiple areas simultaneously. For example, if memory ability were general, children would develop the ability to remember letters at the same time as they developed the ability to remember numbers. Some contemporary researchers continue to study domain-general processes of development. For example, many information-processing theorists point to several ways in which children's information processing becomes generally more sophisticated with age.

Since the 1970s, however, theorists have placed more emphasis on *domain specificity*, the notion that development of skills can occur in specific areas without comparable development in other areas (Frensch & Buchner, 1999). Much of this emphasis can be traced back to studies of chess masters (mentioned in chapters 7 and 8) which showed that experts recall chessboard positions better than do chess novices only if the positions they need to remember make sense in terms of their prior experience (Chase & Simon, 1973; de Groot, 1965). Chess masters have better memories only within their domain of expertise, and then only if what they need to remember fits their schemas for that domain.

This finding has been replicated not only with experts and novices but also with adults and children. Countless experiments have shown that adults remember better than do children (see Keil, 1989). However, the domain in which memory is tested can affect this finding. Children who were experts on chess, for example, performed better than did adults at remembering chess-board positions (Chi, 1978). The children's memory is not better overall, but it is superior in their domains of expertise (see Figure 10-1).

Figure 10–1

THE DOMAIN OF BIOLOGICAL KNOWLEDGE.   *Development influences children's biological knowledge. Between ages 4 and 11, children's knowledge of the animal world becomes restructured, as novices reorganize their knowledge when they become experts. When D. D. Richards and Robert Siegler asked children to name things that are alive, the responses depended on the children's level of development. For instance, although even younger children realize that eating, breathing, and reproduction apply to all animals, not until they get a little older do children understand that people are animals, too. (After data from Richards & Siegler, 1984)*

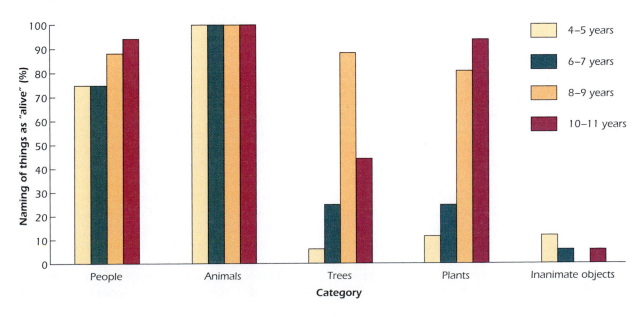

Thus, children's conceptual development appears to be largely (although not entirely) domain specific.

We probably pose an unanswerable question if we ask whether development is domain general or domain specific. It appears to be both. Those who argue for domain generality have to account for why development is not uniform across content domains within a given stage. At the same time, those who argue for domain specificity are hard-pressed to account for obvious uniformities in children's development, starting with those uniformities we observe at birth.

Of the five questions posed as key issues in development, the second one has prompted the most speculation and the most research: At what ages do infants, children, and adults demonstrate various kinds of thought and behavior? When there are serious problems in children's development, we need to know the normal progression of developmental milestones and the normal age ranges for these milestones. Researchers and theorists also need data about the basic accomplishments of different ages in order to construct theories of what underlies such achievements (see Table 10-1).

Methodological Issues

Various methods are used to study development. The methods discussed in chapter 2 are all used, but, because a key component of research on development is time, two types of studies dominate. One method involves **cross-sectional studies,** research that investigates a diverse sampling of persons of various ages at a given time. In contrast, **longitudinal studies,** which follow a particular group of individuals over the course of their life spans, or at least many years, tend not to show comparable evidence of decline (e.g., Bayley & Oden, 1955).

It is hard to say that one or the other kind of study is more likely to be an accurate indication of ability, because each type of study has limitations. Cross-sectional studies are susceptible to **cohort effects,** which are the distinctive effects of a particular group of participants having lived through a particular time in history. It would be difficult to compare the cognitive performance of current 80-year-olds to current 30-year-olds, for example, because the two cohorts of individuals have lived in very different eras, with different educational systems, opportunities, and values. For instance, many of those who grew up during the Great Depression had to drop out of school to support their families, regardless of their school performance. Differences among cohorts may reflect not ability differences, but also cultural and historical differences in terms of their opportunities.

On the other hand, longitudinal studies are not perfect either. Longitudinal studies are susceptible to dropout. Over time, people inevitably will disappear from the study sample. Some move away; others decide that they no longer want to participate. Still others die. Unfortunately, the selection process for dropping out is not entirely random, so neither those people who drop out nor those people who remain are a random sample of the group as a whole. For example, in a study of abilities, perhaps those with lower abilities will be less likely to continue in the study because they feel embarrassed or otherwise unmotivated to continue. Perhaps people who die young or who move frequently, and thus disappear, are cognitively different from those who live longer or whose lives are more stable. Today, many scholars believe that both cross-sectional and longitudinal designs are necessary, separately or in combination, to draw more accurate conclusions about cognitive development.

Physical and Neural Development

In Search of... *How do developmental changes in the brain and body affect cognitive development?*

Prenatal Development

All humans start as a single cell, the product of a union of just one sperm and one egg. This single cell contains all of the genetic information that, in combination with environmental forces, makes a person the adult he or she becomes.

Some students believe that genes and environment work independently and that genetic or other biological forces somehow determine what the brain's capacity will be. This belief is incorrect. On the contrary, brain development is *not* rigidly determined by genetic programming (Johnson, 1999; C. A. Nelson & Bloom, 1997). During the prenatal period as well as thereafter, the neural circuits in the cerebral cortex are constantly being modified in reaction to the input they receive from the environment.

Human brains contain no structures that are unique to the human. What differentiates the human brain from the brains of other animals is the greater volume of the brain, particularly the cerebral cortex, and the much slower and more extended period of development of the brain after the individual's birth. This slower development of the human brain renders humans more open to influences in interaction with the environment than is the case for other organisms (Johnson, 1997).

The period of life before birth is called the *prenatal* period. This period is commonly divided into

TABLE 10-1

Characteristic Progression of Cognitive Development
The various theories of cognitive development offer complementary information regarding how cognitive development progresses from birth through adolescence.

Theorists	Birth to 1 Year	1 to 2 Years	2 to 4 Years	4 to 6 Years	6 to 8 Years	8 to 10 Years	10 to 12 Years	12 to 16 Years
Bayley, Gesell	Sensorimotor alertness and abilities; social imitation and then verbal and motor imitation	Persistence; verbal labeling, comprehension, fluency, and syntax	Abstract reasoning ability emerges. Cognitive abilities increase (e.g., manipulation of language, emergence of reading and writing skills, quantitative skills)					
Piaget	Sensorimotor: builds on reflexive actions and acts to maintain or repeat interesting sensations (major accomplishment: object permanence)		Preoperational: intentional experimentation on physical objects, increasingly thoughtful planning, and internal representations of physical objects (major accomplishments: language and conceptual development)			Concrete operations: increasingly sophisticated mental manipulations of the internal representations of concrete objects (major accomplishment: conservation of quantity)		Formal operations: abstract thought and logical reasoning (major accomplishment: systematic abstract reasoning)
Fifth-stage theorists	Sensorimotor (see Piaget)		Preoperational (see Piaget)			Concrete operations (see Piaget)		Formal operations (see Piaget) followed by postformal thinking; the ability to handle ambiguities and contradictions in solving problems
Vygotsky	Increasing internalization and increasing abilities within the zone of proximal development							
Information-processing theorists	Increasingly sophisticated encoding, combination, knowledge acquisition, self-monitoring, use of feedback; increasing ability to distinguish appearances from reality, increasing verbal fluency and comprehension, increasing grasp of quantity; increasing knowledge of and control over memory; increasing control over strategies for solving problems; increasing ability to reason deductively and inductively							

three stages. The first stage is the *germinal* stage, which lasts for just about two weeks after conception. The main accomplishment of this time is simply for the fertilized egg to become firmly implanted in the uterus of the mother. The second stage, the *embryonic* stage, lasts from about the third to the eighth week after conception. During this stage, the central nervous system starts to form, as do major organs such as the heart and parts of the body, such as the arms, legs, eyes, and ears. During this stage, the embryo becomes recognizable as human in form. During the *fetal* stage, which lasts from about nine weeks after conception until birth, the fetus develops to the point of being able to sustain its own life. Muscular development proceeds rapidly, as does development of the brain. By 38 weeks (9 months), the fetus is typically ready for birth.

The importance of the prenatal period to later development can hardly be overstated. Good health and nutrition on the part of the mother are essential to proper prenatal development. Toxins ingested by the mother can severely damage the developing person. For example, ingestion of alcohol by the mother is strongly discouraged because of the risk of **fetal alcohol syndrome,** an assemblage of disorders, chief among which are impaired motor development, permanent and irreparable mental retardation and facial deformities, including deformed limbs, and malformed genitals (Julien, 1995). At one time it was thought that moderate drinking by the mother during pregnancy was safe, but the current recommendation is that expectant mothers ingest no alcohol whatsoever, as even small amounts of drinking have been linked to impaired development and signs of fetal alcohol syndrome (Hunt, Streissguth, Kerr, & Olsen, 1995). At the same time, such links are inferred from large samples, and may or may not emerge in individual cases. Learning disabilities and behavioral problems can also result (Streissguth et al., 1984; Streissguth, Sampson, & Barr, 1989) from alcohol consumption during pregnancy. Exposure to drugs (Griffith, Azuma, & Chasnoff, 1994; Lester et al., 1991) as well as dangerous chemicals in the environment, such as PCBs (polychlorinated bipheryls), can also cause damage that will affect development after birth (Jacobson, Jacobson, & Humphrey, 1990; Jacobson, Jacobson, Padgett, Brunitt, & Billings, 1992).

But now, let's look at what a healthy newborn can do.

Capabilities of the Newborn

Our views regarding the capabilities of the **neonate,** or newborn, have changed radically over time. Aristotle and the 17th-century English philosopher John Locke believed that the mind of the infant is a *tabula rasa,* a blank slate, on which the infant's experiences will be written. In contrast to these proponents of *nurture*—of the role of the environment in learning—Plato argued that learning brings into consciousness what we already know. In the 18th century Jean-Jacques Rousseau advocated the *nativist* position—that our nature dictates our course of development. According to this view, whether we will

Is this infant seeing "one great blooming, buzzing confusion," or is this infant already starting to scan the environment to find the most interesting sights? The more sophisticated we become in our observations of infants, the more we are amazed by their capabilities.

become friendly or antagonistic, open-minded or closed-minded, or any of a number of other things depends on our heredity.

Perceptual Abilities

Just what can newborns do? To start with, although newborns are very nearsighted, they can see, contrary to former belief. For roughly the first month of life, the infant's eyes have virtually no ability to accommodate to distances that vary from about 19 centimeters (the approximate distance from the infant to his mother's face while being breast-fed—see also chapter 4). Images that are closer or farther than the optimal 19 centimeters appear to be blurred (Teller & Movshon, 1986). Thus, infants cannot see small objects well, but they can see large ones close up. During early infancy, the lens of the eye reaches approximately normal flexibility with respect to accommodation.

Psychologists have deduced that infants seem to have a set of inborn rules that guides their scanning of the environment (Haith, 1979, 1994). For example, infants seem to have a general rule to scan the environment broadly, but to stop scanning and explore in depth if they see an edge, which is more likely than an uninterrupted surface to contain interesting information.

Infants also have a preference for looking at objects characterized by a high degree of complexity (preferring, for example, many somewhat narrow stripes to a few wide ones), many visual contours (showing a preference for edges and patterns over solid regions of color), curved contours rather than straight ones, high contrast between light and dark (such as preferring black and white to gray), and frequent movements (see Banks & Salapatek, 1983). Quite conveniently, every parent has available a highly stimulating object that perfectly matches these criteria: a human face. In one study, infants as young as 4 days of age were shown three different patterns—a standard face, a face with its features scrambled, or a bull's-eye pattern (Fantz, 1958, 1961). The babies showed a small but consistent preference for the sensible face over the scrambled one, and a much larger preference for both faces over the bull's-eye. Some researchers have suggested that infants' preference for faces might be some built-in biological imperative, but others question this notion.

Although fetuses can hear, the amniotic fluid may impede their hearing. Nevertheless, their hearing is pretty good: One study had expectant mothers read aloud Dr. Seuss's book *The Cat in the Hat* once a day during the final six weeks of pregnancy. After their birth, the infants listened to a recording of their mother either reading that story or an unfamiliar one. The infants exposed to the Dr. Seuss book while in utero showed recognition of *The Cat in the Hat* story (through sucking behavior) but not of the unfamiliar story (DeCasper & Spence, 1986).

Within just a few days after birth, any residual amniotic fluid has drained or evaporated from their ear canals, and infants can hear voices and distinguish musical notes just one tone apart. Neonates preferentially attend to the human voice, particularly the child-directed speech sometimes called "motherese" that characterizes the way in which adults communicate with infants. Newborns particularly respond also to the "clicks, kisses, and clucks" often used by their caregivers (Blass, 1990). Some researchers have found that newborns also seem to have almost a reflexive response for imitating a caregiver's smile, pout, open-mouthed expression of surprise, or tongue protrusion (e.g., T. G. R. Bower, 1989; T. M. Field, 1989; Meltzoff & Moore, 1989; Reissland, 1988). Newborns seem custom-designed to elicit and encourage the attention—perhaps even the love—of their caregivers, both because of their preprogrammed reflexes and because of their sometimes unpredictable but delightful behavior, such as smiling at unexpected moments.

Reflexes

In normal infants, many reflexes are present at or before birth. Some reflexes, for example, the breathing reflex, stay with us throughout the life span, and other reflexes, such as the rooting reflex, disappear during infancy. Table 10-2 shows some of the key reflexes that physicians and psychologists look for in normal infants. Deviations from the broad normal range may indicate some form of damage to the central nervous system.

A reflex of interest to some psychologists is the *orienting reflex*, a series of preprogrammed responses that are prompted by a sudden change in the environment, in which infants (and others) reflexively orient themselves in response to these sudden changes. The orienting reflex never disappears; when a bright light flashes, we pay attention to it reflexively. Developmental psychologists are interested not only in reflexes, but in motor behavior more generally.

Motor Development

The development of various other abilities also has been studied. For example, *The Bayley Scales of Mental and Motor Development (Revised)* (Bayley, 1993) specify the ages at which various physical, **motor** tasks, involving movements of the muscles, are typically accomplished by infants (see Figure 10-2). Some psychologists have even devoted their careers to specifying what skills (e.g., walking) and task performances (e.g., using thumb and forefinger to grasp a cube or other small object) can be expected to develop when. Perhaps the most notable of these psychologists was Arnold Gesell (1928; Gesell & Ilg, 1949), who meticulously specified a calendar of expected childhood accomplishments in a number of domains, including motor skills and language achievements.

As with the development of most reflexes discussed earlier in this chapter, the ages at which children develop particular motor skills bear little relation to their cognitive development or their future intelligence, *unless* the development of these skills falls far outside the normal range. For example, if particular 6-month-olds cannot lift their heads at the shoulders, 18-month-olds cannot crawl, or 4-year-olds cannot walk—and these children have no known motoric reason for this impairment—then they may have serious impairments of the nervous system. Such impairments can have grave implications for children's cognitive development. In addition, although particular motor accomplishments do not directly correlate with particular cognitive changes, they do alter the way the child can interact with the environment, and these interactions may facilitate cognitive development, discussed shortly.

Puberty

Up to about the age of 10, boys and girls grow at about the same rates. Then, from about 10 to 12 years of age, girls grow more quickly, becoming taller than their male counterparts. Boys show a comparable growth spurt typically around 12 to 14 or 15 years of age, during which they often then become taller, on

TABLE 10–2

Reflexes Present in Newborns   *Infants come well equipped with the reflexes they need for basic physiological survival; for eliciting help, affection, and care from their parents; and for subsequent development of conscious control over their bodies.*

REFLEX	STIMULUS FOR REFLEX	INFANT'S RESPONSE	ADAPTIVE FUNCTION
Rooting (birth to around 1 year)	Gentle touch on infant's cheek	Turns toward the source of the stroking	Turns the infant's head toward the nipple for feeding
Sucking (present at birth)	Insertion of a nipple or finger into the infant's mouth	Sucks on the object inserted	Draws out the fluid from a nipple
Swallowing (present at birth)	Putting fluid on the back of the infant's mouth (e.g., through a nipple)	Swallows the fluid	Ingests breast milk
Eliminating (present at birth)	Feed the infant and wait for the outcome	Urinates and defecates	Removes waste products from infant
Crying (present at birth)	Hunger	Cries	Gets the attention of a caregiver; lays down the neural pathways for more subtle psychological reasons for crying
Breathing (starts at full-term birth)	Birth or pat on back	Inhales and exhales	Oxygenates the blood
Eyeblink (present at birth)	Puff of air or bright light in eye	Closes eyes	Protects eye from foreign matter
Withdrawal (present at birth)	An aversive stimulus, such as a pin-prick	Flexes the legs, cries, and also may flex the arms or twist the body, depending on the location of the stimulus	Protects the infant from the stimulus and gets the attention of the caregiver to offer further protection

average, than do girls. By age 16, growth for both boys and girls has slowed considerably.

Somewhere between the ages of 11 and 13, on average, children enter **puberty,** the stage of development at which they begin to become capable of reproduction. Girls start to experience the growth of breasts, appearance of pubic hair, and soon after often have their first menstruation, called **menarche.** Boys experience appearance of pubic hair, enlargement of the genitals, and then their first ejaculation of sperm.

It is at puberty that the difference between two kinds of sexual characteristics becomes important. *Pri-*

mary sex characteristics make sexual reproduction possible. For girls, such sexual characteristics include the presence of the vagina, uterus, fallopian tubes, and ovaries. For boys, they include the penis, scrotum, testes, prostate gland (which manufactures seminal fluid), and seminal vesicles. *Secondary sex characteristics* refer to features that are sex stereotypical but not associated directly with reproduction, such as enlarged breasts for women and notable deepening of the voice in men.

Although girls become capable of reproduction before adolescence, their reproductive systems are

Figure 10-2

LANDMARKS OF MOTOR DEVELOPMENT. *Although the ages at which infants achieve various psychomotor tasks may differ across individuals, the sequence of achievements hardly varies.*

	MOTOR BEHAVIOR	HAND-EYE COORDINATION
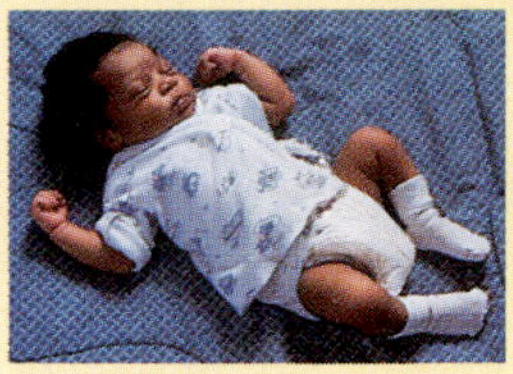	**1 Month** ■ Prefers to lie on back ■ Cannot hold head erect; head sags forward ■ Hands usually tightly fisted	■ Looks at object held directly in line of vision ■ Grasps reflexively if object is placed in hand ■ Eyes begin to coordinate
	2–3 Months ■ When lying on stomach, can lift head 45° and extend legs ■ Head-bobbing gradually disappears; may hold head erect	■ Follows objects visually within limited range ■ Looks at object but can grasp only by reflex
	**4 Months** ■ Can roll from back to side ■ When lying on stomach, can lift head 90°, arms and legs lift and extend ■ Can sit propped up for 10–15 minutes	■ Follows objects with eyes through an arc of 180° ■ When presented with object, may touch or grasp it ■ Brings any object grasped to mouth
	5–6 Months ■ Can roll from back to stomach ■ May "bounce" when held standing	■ Grasps small block using palmar grasp; little use of thumb or forefingers ■ Scratches at tiny objects but cannot pick them up ■ May hold own bottle with one or two hands
	**7–8 Months** ■ When lying on back, can lift feet to mouth ■ Can sit erect for a few minutes ■ May crawl ■ Can stand supporting full body weight on feet—if held up	■ Can grasp a small block, or may transfer block from hand to hand ■ Likes banging objects to make noise
	9–10 Months ■ Creeps on hands and knees ■ Can sit indefinitely ■ Can pull self to standing position and may "cruise" by moving feet ■ By 10 months may be able to sit down from standing position	■ Pokes at objects with forefinger ■ Can play pat-a-cake ■ May uncover toy he or she has seen hidden
	**11 Months** ■ Pulls self actively to feet and "cruises" along table or crib ■ May stand momentarily without support ■ Can walk if one hand is held; may take a few steps alone	■ Can grasp small objects in a pincer grasp; can grasp larger objects using thumb opposition ■ May try to stack two blocks
	12 Months ■ Can get up without help and may take several steps alone ■ Can creep up stairs on hands and knees ■ May squat or stoop without losing balance ■ Can throw ball	■ Helps turn pages of book ■ Can stack two blocks ■ Can find toy under box, cup, or cloth ■ Enjoys putting objects into containers and taking them out

immature until about the age of 15 (Garn, 1980). As a result, when younger girls become pregnant, whether through desire or, as is often the case, coercion, their infants are at risk of premature birth, as well as of low birth weight. These problems do not occur for women who become pregnant during adulthood.

Physical Development in Adulthood

Increases in height typically end by mid-to-late adolescence, although weight increases may continue for the entirety of the life span. Increase in weight is a typical but not necessary consequence of aging through the middle-aged years (except, obviously, during pregnancy), and can put a person's health at risk. Exercise becomes more and more important as people enter their 30s, and then 40s and 50s, in order to maintain cardiovascular fitness and muscle mass. At the same time, people have to be sensible in their exercising to avoid needless injuries. Women experience an additional physical change with age: **menopause,** which spells the end of the menstrual cycle. The average age of menopause in the West is 51 (Bailey, 1991), although there is considerable variation among women. Men's reproductive capacities also change. Men typically experience decreased sperm counts as they enter their later years.

Now let's go back and consider neural development, from the time of birth, onward.

Neural Development

The physiological development of the brain and neural apparatus is crucial to all other aspects of development (Johnson, 1999). At birth, the brain stem is almost fully developed, but the cerebral cortex is still largely immature (see chapter 3). The areas of the brain to develop most rapidly after birth are the sensory and motor cortexes, and subsequently, the association areas relating to problem solving, reasoning, memory, and language development. This pattern of neural development parallels the physical and cognitive development detailed in this chapter.

The neural networks of interconnections in the brain become increasingly complex during the first two years after birth. After that time, the rate of neural growth and development declines dramatically. In fact, 90% of neural growth is complete by age 6 years. Between our peak of neural development in early adulthood and about age 80 years, we typically lose about 5% of our brain weight. Nonetheless, our continually increasing neural connections (as long as we remain mentally active) help to compensate for our cell loss (Coleman & Flood, 1986).

Another area of physiological investigation has yielded some intriguing findings. A study (Thatcher, Walker, & Giudice, 1987) of the EEG patterns of 577

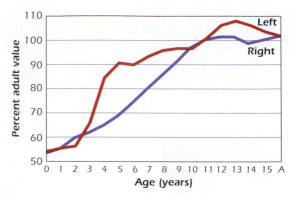

Figure 10-3
DEVELOPMENTAL CHANGES IN EEG PATTERNS. *This graph of developmental changes in EEG patterns shows increasing electrical activity in both cerebral hemispheres. Note, however, that whereas the course of development in the left hemisphere is discontinuous, showing bursts and plateaus, the course of development in the right hemisphere is continuous. (After Thatcher, Walker, & Giudice, 1987)*

people ranging in age from 2 months to early adulthood shows different patterns for each of the two cerebral hemispheres. In the right hemisphere, which is associated with more holistic processing of information, there appear to be continuous, gradual changes in EEG patterns associated with age. In the left hemisphere, which is associated with more analytic processing of information, there appear to be abrupt shifts in the EEG patterns, at least up through the time of early adulthood (see Figure 10-3). Thus, different kinds of cognitive processing may show different developmental progressions. Possibly, development results in part from changes in the electrical activity in the frontal lobe of the brain, the part of the brain most associated with problem solving (Case, 1992; Thatcher, 1992). (See also chapter 3 for more on EEGs and other aspects of physiological psychology over the course of the life span.) Now let's consider some basic questions about cognitive development.

Cognitive Development

In Search of... *What are the major mechanisms and milestones of cognitive development?*

As infants develop physically, they also develop mentally. One of the first indicators of an infant's cognitive development is his or her preference for novelty. This apparent preference for novelty is associated with the *moderate-discrepancy hypothesis*, according to which infants prefer stimuli that are moderately discrepant, or different, from what they already know (McCall, Kennedy, & Appelbaum, 1977). Preference for novelty is a predictor of later intelligence.

The preference for novelty explains why infants learn about things only when they are ready to learn about them. They do not waste their time attending to completely familiar things or to things so new that they are overwhelming. Indeed, it may be that infants who prefer some degree of novelty are more intelligent than are those who do not (M. H. Bornstein & Sigman, 1986; Lewis & Brooks-Gunn, 1981). Joseph Fagan (1984, 1985; Fagan & Montie, 1988) and Marc Bornstein (1989) have found that infants who show stronger preferences for novelty at ages 2 to 6 months are more likely to have high scores on intelligence tests at ages 2 to 7 years. Thus, new methods of measuring intelligence in infants show that infant intelligence may predict later intelligence (Colombo, 1993; McCall & Carriger, 1993; Rose & Feldman, 1995).

No single theory has yet explained all aspects of cognitive development. For example, it is difficult to explain in the context of a single theory how both perceptual skills and mathematical skills develop. The theories included here represent psychological theorists' best attempts to explain how human cognition develops. The theories described below are representative of a conversation that has been going on for hundreds of years between rationalists and empiricists (see chapter 1). Some of the theories, such as Piaget's, take a more rationalist stance, emphasizing inborn potentials and how they unfold over the course of the lifetime. Others of the theories, such as Vygotsky's, take a more empiricist stance, emphasizing the role of experience. The ongoing conversation challenges theorists of all kinds to develop and improve their theories in response to the inadequacies pointed out by those holding other positions.

We now turn to the cognitive-developmental work of Jean Piaget and the "neo-Piagetians," Lev Vygotsky, and the information-processing theorists. After looking at these theorists' work, we briefly summarize how each would respond to the questions that opened this chapter. (For a brief outline of how each of the theories describes the characteristic progression of cognitive development, refer to Table 10-1 as you read.)

The Cognitive-Developmental Theory of Jean Piaget

It would be hard to overestimate the importance of Swiss psychologist Jean Piaget to developmental research. His theory is generally considered to be the

Jean Piaget (1896–1980) learned a great deal about how children think by observing children and by paying detailed attention to what appeared to be errors in their reasoning.

most comprehensive theory of cognitive development. Although aspects of Piaget's theory have been questioned, and in some cases have been disconfirmed, the theory is still enormously influential. Indeed, the contribution of his theory, like that of others, is shown more by its influence on further theory and research than by its precise accuracy.

Piaget first entered the field of cognitive development when, working as a graduate student in Alfred Binet's psychometric laboratory (see chapter 9), he became intrigued with children's wrong answers to intelligence-test items. Piaget reasoned that researchers could learn as much about children's intellectual development from examining their incorrect answers to test items as from examining their correct answers. Through his repeated observations of children, including observations of his own children, and especially through investigation of their errors in reasoning, Piaget concluded that coherent logical systems underlie children's thought. These systems, he believed, differ in kind from those that adults use. If we are to understand development, we must identify these systems and their distinctive characteristics. In this section, we first consider some of Piaget's general principles of development and then look at the stages of development he proposed.

Equilibration, Assimilation, and Accommodation

Piaget believed that the function of cognitive development in general and intelligence in particular is to aid in adaptation to the environment. He rejected the distinction proposed by the Gestaltists (see chapter 1) and others between "intelligent acts," which require insight or thought, and "nonintelligent acts," which are habits and reflexes (Piaget, 1972; see R. J. Sternberg & Powell, 1983). Instead, Piaget preferred to think of a continuum of increasingly complex responses to the environment (Piaget, 1972). He further proposed that both intelligence and its manifestations become differentiated with age.

Piaget believed that development occurs in stages that evolve via **equilibration,** a process of cognitive development in which children seek a balance (equilibrium) between the information and experiences they encounter in their environments and the cognitive processes and structures they bring to the encounter, as well as among the cognitive capabilities themselves. In other words, equilibration involves a balance between what the environment offers in an encounter and what the person brings to the encounter. Equilibration involves two processes: assimilation and accommodation.

In some situations, the child's existing mode of thought and existing mental frameworks, or *schemas,* are adequate for confronting and adapting to the challenges of the environment The child is thus in a state of equilibrium. At other times, however, information that does not fit with the child's existing schemas creates cognitive disequilibrium. The imbalance comes from shortcomings in thinking as the child encounters new challenges, and disequilibrium is more likely to occur during periods of stage transition. The child consequently attempts to restore equilibrium through **assimilation**—the process of trying to restore cognitive equilibrium by incorporating new information into existing schemes. For example, a very young child, seeing a cat for the first time, might call it a "doggie," thinking that all pets are "doggies." If new information will not fit into existing schemas, Piaget would suggest that the child would modify the existing schemas through **accommodation**—the process of responding to cognitively disequilibrating information about the environment by modifying relevant schemas, thereby adapting the schemas to fit the new information and reestablishing equilibrium. An older child, recognizing that the cat does not fit the schema for dogs, might create a modified conceptual schema in which cats and dogs are viewed as distinct kinds of pets. Together, the processes of assimilation and accommodation result in a more sophisticated level of thought than was previously possible. In addition, these processes reestablish equilibrium and offer the individual higher levels of adaptability.

Piaget's Stages of Development

According to Piaget, the equilibrative processes of assimilation and accommodation account for all of the changes associated with cognitive development. Although Piaget posited that these processes go on throughout childhood as we continually adapt to our environment, he also considered development to involve discrete, discontinuous stages. In particular, Piaget (1969, 1972) divided cognitive development into four main stages: the sensorimotor, the preoperational, the concrete-operational, and the formal-operational.

The Sensorimotor Stage. The first stage of development (from birth to about age 2 years) is the **sensorimotor stage.** During this stage, the child builds on reflexes and develops the first mental representations of things that are not being sensed at the moment. In the first month after birth, the infant responds primarily reflexively, such as through the reflexive schemas for sucking, grasping, orienting toward noises and other novel stimuli, and so on. According to Piaget, infants gradually modify these reflexive schemas as they adapt to their environments to accomplish purposeful action. During the next few months, infants repeat interesting effects they produce, such as a gurgling noise.

From ages 4 through 12 months, new actions involve repetitive behavior, but now the outcomes also may involve objects other than the child's own body. For example, the infant might play with a ball or a mobile and watch what it does, again and again. Still, even these actions are largely a means of capitalizing on interesting events that happen by chance.

From 12 to 18 months, however, the infant actively searches for novel ways of relating to objects. The infant no longer waits for interesting things to happen by chance but rather makes them happen. Although the child repeats actions, he or she may modify them to achieve some desired effect, as in getting a mobile to swing in a certain preferred way. During this time, infants also actively experiment with the objects in their environments, just to see what *might* happen.

Children in this stage have surprisingly good memories. If a 3-month-old encounters a mobile twice within three days, the infant will better recall five to seven days later how kicking of the mobile affects the mobile than if the infant saw the mobile only once previously (Rovee-Collier, Evancio, & Earley, 1995).

Throughout these early phases of cognitive development, infant cognition seems to focus only on what the infants can immediately perceive through their senses. They do not conceive of anything that is not immediately perceptible to them. According to Piaget, infants do not have a sense of **object permanence,** the cognitive realization that objects may continue to exist even when thy are not currently being perceived. For example, before about 9 months of age, infants who observe an object being hidden from view will not seek the object once it is hidden from view. If a 4-month-old were to watch you hide a rattle beneath a blanket, the 4-month-old would not try to find the rattle beneath the blanket, whereas a 9-month-old would (Figure 10-4).

To have a sense of object permanence requires some internal, mental representation of an object even when the object is not seen, heard, or otherwise perceived. By 18 to 24 months of age, in fact, children begin to show signs of **representational thought**—the thinking that involves mental images, such as images of tangible objects, or other forms of representation (such as propositions). In this ending of the sensorimotor stage, which is a transition to the preoperational stage, the children start to be able to think about objects and people who are not necessarily immediately perceptible.

The Preoperational Stage. The **preoperational stage** is Piaget's second stage of development (from about 2 years until about 7 years), during which the child develops language and concepts about physical objects. However, the communication is largely egocentric. A conversation may seem to have no coherence at all. Children say what is on their minds, pretty much without regard to what anyone else has said. As children develop, however, they increasingly take into account what others have said when forming their own comments and replies.

In a study of representational thinking, Judith DeLoache (1987) showed a scale model of a room to children of 30 and 36 months of age. They were then shown a small toy being hidden in the scale model of the room. Next the children were asked to find the toy in an actual life-sized version of that room. So, for example, the children might see the experimenter hiding "Little Snoopy" in the scale version of the room. Then they would be asked to find "Little Snoopy" in the full-sized room. At age 30 months (2½ years), children showed an error rate of over 80 percent. At age 36 months (3 years), children showed an error rate of less than 30 percent.

Why did the younger children have difficulty with the task? A control condition showed that the problem was not one of memory. The children did remember where the object was hidden. Continued research suggested that the problem was not exactly one of a difference in representational thinking either, as Piaget's theory would suppose. Rather, it appears that the younger children found the scale models interesting in their own right and, as a result, they did not think of them simply as scale models but rather as objects of interest in themselves. The older children, less interested in the scale models in their own right, were more willing to see them as representative of the more interesting larger room (De-Loache, 1991, 1995).

As children grow older, they become less egocentric—here **egocentrism** refers to a cognitive characteristic (not a personality trait) in which children's

Figure 10-4

OBJECT PERMANENCE.   *Before about 9 months of age, infants do not yet realize that objects continue to exist even when they cannot be seen or heard. To this infant, once the turquoise monkey is out of sight, it no longer exists, so the infant loses all interest in it. An older infant would try to pursue the monkey behind the barrier.*

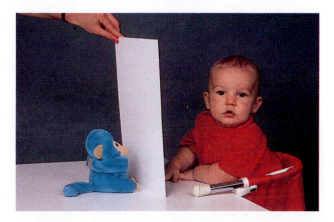

mental representations are focused solely on their point of view and experiences, making it difficult for them to grasp the viewpoint of others. For example, early mental representations of preoperational children involve only the child. The child cannot imagine how a scene, say, of a mountain range, would look when viewed from another perspective (e.g., from the top versus the bottom of the mountain range). Piaget viewed this early trend as indicative of a broader trend for children of all ages to become increasingly aware of the outer world and of how others perceive that world. (The effect of egocentrism on the child's interpersonal interactions is discussed in chapter 11.)

Many developmental changes occur during the preoperational stage. Children's active, intentional experimentation with language and with objects in their environments results in tremendous increases in conceptual and language development. These developments help to pave the way for the next stage of cognitive development.

The Concrete-Operational Stage. In Piaget's third stage of cognitive development called **concrete operations,** from roughly ages 7 until 12 years, children can mentally manipulate internal representations of tangible (concrete) objects. For example, children can imagine a top spinning without actually seeing it spin. Children now not only have thoughts and memories of objects, but they also can perform mental operations on these thoughts and memories. However, they can do so only in regard to concrete objects, thoughts and memories of cars, food, toys, and other tangible things.

Initially, children rely on their immediate perceptions of how things appear to be. Gradually, they begin to formulate internal rules regarding how the world works. Eventually, they use these internal rules to guide their reasoning, rather than appearances alone. Some of the most dramatic evidence of the change from preoperational thought to the representational thought of the concrete-operational stage is seen in Piaget's classic experiments (1952, 1954, 1969) on conservation.

Perhaps the most well-known Piagetian conservation experiment uses two beakers, demonstrating *conservation of liquid quantity* (Figure 10-5). The experimenter shows the child two short, stout beakers with liquid in them. The experimenter has the child verify that the two beakers contain the same amounts of liquid. Then, as the child watches, the experimenter pours the liquid from one beaker into a third beaker, which is taller and thinner than the other two. In the new beaker, the liquid in the narrower tube rises to a higher level than in the other still-full shorter beaker. When asked whether the amounts of liquid in the two full beakers are the same or different, the preoperational child says that there is now

Figure 10–5
CONSERVATION OF LIQUID QUANTITY. *This young boy is participating in the classic Piagetian liquid conservation task. The researcher measures out equal quantities of liquid into two identical short, stout beakers, then pours from one of the beakers into a tall, thin beaker. In the final photo, the boy asserts that the tall, thin beaker contains more liquid than the short, stout beaker. Still in the preoperational stage, he does not recognize that the quantity is conserved, despite superficial changes in the appearance of the amount. Once he reaches the stage of concrete operations, the boy will readily conserve.*

Studying Early Cognitive Development

Susan Gelman, *University of Michigan*

Most children ask a lot of questions from a young age. Some of these are deep questions about how the world works, questions that also occupy the minds of scientists and philosophers. For example: "Where do babies come from?" "What is God?" "What makes boys different from girls?" "What are the stars made of?" These questions show that children are working hard to understand the larger world of which they are a part.

In my research, I am trying to uncover the rudimentary "theories" that children construct about the world, especially as they understand biological categories (such as "Where do babies come from?" or "What makes boys different from girls?"). All people (indeed, all animals) have to divide experience into categories. We couldn't survive if every object we came across was considered wholly new and different from everything we had experienced before. If we know what the category *fruit* is, we will probably not be thrown by seeing a new kind of fruit we have never seen before. We do this so automatically that we're usually not even aware that we're doing so.

It used to be thought that children think about categories in qualitatively different ways from adults, and that children can't even form categories in the sense that adults do. The Swiss psychologist Jean Piaget's famous set of studies, known as the "conservation" experiments, are an example of this. In my own work, I have challenged the notion that children are qualitatively different from adults in the categories they form. In contrast, young children form categories from a young age and, most importantly, draw extensive inferences on the basis of knowing to what category something belongs. In some respects young children seem even *more* aware of categories and category boundaries than are adults. What most distinguishes my work from that of others who came to different conclusions is that we rely on different kinds of experimental tasks to uncover children's understanding.

In a typical experiment, I present the child with a set of questions in a gamelike format, questions which (unbeknownst to the child) are aimed at uncovering a specific issue. For example, in one series of studies I reexamined Piaget's claim that children's categories are strictly based on "superficial" cues (such as the size, shape, or color of an item). Instead, I asked whether children—like scientists—appreciate that for categories, appearance is not always reality. We asked the question indirectly, focusing on categories with which children have a great deal of experience: biological categories of animals and people.

We presented children with a series of sets of three pictures ("triads") that posed an appearance–reality conflict: for example, a stegosaurus (dinosaur), a pterodactyl (dinosaur that looks like a bird), and a blue-jay (bird). After learning what kind of animal each item depicted, children were asked to make an inference about a biological property (e.g., whether the pterodactyl will have the same kind of blood as a stegosaurus or as a bluejay). The results showed that young children (all preschoolers and in some studies no more than 2½ years old) extended inferences on the basis of category membership (for example, generalizing from the stegosaurus to the pterodactyl) rather than outward appearances (generalizing from the bluejay to the pterodactyl).

In another set of studies, we probed children's beliefs about the *sources* of category differences. Having found that children do expect categories to capture important properties that are more than superficial appearances (such as internal parts and typical behaviors), we sought to ask how malleable or flexible children consider such properties to be. For example, are the typical properties that a cow displays (mooing, straight tail) due to fixed inborn potential, or can they be modified under different environmental conditions? My colleagues and I examined this issue by asking young children what sound, for example, would a cow make if it were raised by pigs: Would it moo or would it oink? In contrast to the messages often provided by children's fiction (e.g., the movie *Babe*, or Dr. Seuss's *Horton Hatches an Egg*), preschool children emphasized the animal's nature, rather than nurture, reporting that animals have certain inborn properties that emerge even under unfavorable environmental conditions.

There are three general motivations for doing this work. The first motivation is a scientific one: I think we have an excellent opportunity to discover general cognitive biases by studying how beliefs form in early childhood. I hope that some day my studies of children's categorization will shed light on the question of why people stereotype and how to reduce stereotyping in adults as well as children. The second motivation is a practical consideration: I believe that the more we understand the complexities of children's thought processes, the better we can educate and parent young children. The final motivation is purely selfish: It is fascinating and great fun to listen to children as they try to figure out answers to important questions. I have enormous respect for the intellectual work that even preschool children are doing when thinking about the questions I pose in my experiments, but also am amused by the many charming things children tell me along the way.

 Find out more about this topic at
www.harcourtcollege.com/psych/ishm

more liquid in the taller, thinner beaker because the liquid in that beaker reaches a perceptibly higher point. The preoperational child does not conceive that the amount is conserved despite the change in appearance. The concrete-operational child, on the other hand, says that the beakers contain the same amount of liquid, based on the child's internal schemas regarding the conservation of matter.

What can the concrete-operational child do that the preoperational child cannot? The concrete-operational child can manipulate internal images, mentally conserving the notion of amount and concluding that despite different physical appearances, the quantities are identical. Moreover, concrete-operational thinking is *reversible*. If the experimenter poured the liquid back into the small beaker, the concrete-operational child would still recognize it as the same amount. Remember, however, that the operations are concrete—that is, the mental operations act on mental representations of actual physical events. The final stage of cognitive development, according to Piaget, involves going beyond these concrete operations and applying the same principles to abstract concepts.

Although children in the stage of concrete operations can readily grasp the principle of conservation when it is applied to concrete objects, they may encounter more difficulty when trying to manipulate mathematical concepts that are more abstract. The following excerpt from Norton Juster's children's classic, *The Phantom Tollbooth*, illustrates some of the difficulties a young child might experience when trying to conserve distances, in this case, length, as measured in various units of measurement:

> Up ahead, the road divided into three [and] an enormous road sign, pointing in all three directions, stated clearly:
>
> Digitopolis
>
> 5 Miles
>
> 1,600 Rods
>
> 8,800 Yards
>
> 26,400 Feet
>
> 316,800 Inches
>
> 633,600 Half inches
>
> "Let's travel by miles," advised the Humbug; "it's shorter."
>
> "Let's travel by half inches," suggested Milo; "it's quicker."

In the formal-operational stage, children would not make this mistake.

The Formal-Operational Stage. Piaget's fourth stage of development, the **formal-operational stage** of cognitive development, occurs from roughly 11 or 12 years of age onward. In this stage, the child becomes able to manipulate abstract ideas and formal relationships (Inhelder & Piaget, 1958). During the stage of concrete operations, children begin to be able to see the perspective of others if the alternative perspective can be concretely manipulated. During formal operations, however, children are finally fully able to take perspectives other than their own, even when they are not working with concrete objects. Furthermore, those in the formal-operations stage purposefully seek to create a systematic mental representation of situations they confront.

According to Piaget (1972), during the formal-operational stage, people first become able to conceive of *second-order relations*—that is, relations between relations. For example, in the stage of formal operations, children realize that not only do they have parents (first-order relationships) but that all children have parents (second-order relationships—I am to my parents as other children are to their parents). Eventually, they become able to see second-order relations in the mathematical domain as well, such as being able to draw a parallel between the inverse relations of addition and subtraction, on the one hand, and multiplication and division, on the other. They can now see not only how two individual objects are related, but also how two sets of objects are related (as in reasoning by analogy; see Table 10-1 for a summary of Piaget's stages).

In sum, Piaget's theory of cognitive development involves stages that occur in a fixed order. Stages occur at roughly the same ages for different children, and each stage builds on the preceding stage. Piaget also believed progress through the cognitive developmental stages is irreversible: Once a child enters into a new stage, he or she never regresses. Other theorists would disagree with this view; among other things, observations of some elderly persons seem to discredit the view that regression never occurs. Indeed, in evaluating the current status of Piaget's theory, we find there are several specific areas on which theorists and researchers disagree with Piaget's conclusions.

Evaluation of Piaget's Theory

Piaget contributed enormously to our understanding of cognitive development. His work continues to have great influence on psychology. His major contribution was in prompting us to view children in a new light and to ponder the way children think. As a scientist, Piaget knew his work would not be an endpoint of investigation, but rather a beginning of an entire field of investigation. Others who have followed him have profited from his work and his insights, although their investigations have led them to question many of his specific conclusions and even some of his observations. To give you a richer perspective on Piaget's place in the field of developmental psychology, we must consider a few of the major criticisms of Piaget's theory.

First, as suggested earlier, many developmental theorists question Piaget's fundamental assumption that development occurs in discontinuous stages. Many believe that development is at least partly continuous (e.g., Brainerd, 1978; Siegler, 1998). Second, theorists have questioned Piaget's view of what causes difficulty for children in particular tasks (as discussed further later in this chapter). Third, theorists have questioned the accuracy of Piaget's estimates of the ages at which particular accomplishments can first be made. In general, the trend has been toward demonstrating that children can do things at ages earlier than Piaget had thought (Ahn, Kalish, Medin, & Gelman, 1995; Baillargeon, 1987; R. Gelman & Baillargeon, 1983; Huttenlocher, Newcombe, & Sandberg, 1994; Kotovsky & Baillargeon, 1994; Oakes & Cohen, 1995). For example, infants as young as 3½ months, if tested appropriately, have been shown to behave as though they can remember things they cannot see. In other words, they show signs of object permanence (Baillargeon & DeVos, 1991).

A fourth criticism of Piaget has been that his work largely centered on children in Western cultures, so it is difficult to know whether his findings would apply to children in non-Western cultures. Although the sequence of the early Piagetian stages seems to be confirmed by cross-cultural research, the specific age ranges hypothesized for many of the stages may vary across cultures. There is also some question as to whether adults, even in advanced societies, typically display formal reasoning (Byrnes, 1988; Kuhn, Garcia-Mila, Zohar, & Andersen. 1995).

Most cross-cultural psychologists attribute the disparities in achievement to environmental, experiential differences, rather than to hereditary differences. In addition, some researchers have questioned the universality of Piaget's later stages. For example, in some non-Western cultures, neither adolescents nor adults seem to demonstrate the cognitive characteristics of Piaget's stage of formal operations, and some adults do not even demonstrate mastery of the relatively symbolic aspects of the Piagetian stage of concrete operations (see Dasen & Heron, 1981). In 1972, Piaget modified his own theory to acknowledge that the stage of formal operations may be more a product of an individual's domain-specific expertise, based on experience, rather than on the maturational processes of cognitive development. Some theorists, however,

Cross-cultural research shows that children may pass through the Piagetian stages of cognitive development at different ages, perhaps due to variations in environment. Nonetheless, some researchers believe that all children pass through the same sequence of stages and show the same patterns of cognitive development, as shown by the cross-cultural similarity of many children's games (e.g., jumping rope or acting out the rhythmic patterns of chants).

draw on Piaget, but believe that cognitive development does not quite take the form proposed by Piaget.

Neo-Piagetian Theorists

Neo-Piagetian theories are based on a broad understanding of Piaget's theory of cognitive development. These theorists do not fully accept Piaget's theory, but have decided to modify and build upon the theory rather than reject it (e.g., Case & Okamoto, 1996; Demetriou, Efklides, & Platsidou, 1993; Fischer & Grannott, 1995; Halford, 1995). Although each neo-Piagetian researcher is different, most (a) accept Piaget's broad notion of developmental stages of cognitive development; (b) concentrate on the scientific or logical aspects of cognitive development (often observing children engage in much the same tasks as those used by Piaget); and (c) retain some ties with the notion that cognitive development occurs through equilibration. Of the many neo-Piagetian theorists, we briefly consider here only a few, namely, those proposing a fifth stage of development beyond formal operations, one of dialectical thinking.

Several psychologists, such as Deirdre Kramer (1990), Gisela Labouvie-Vief (1980, 1990), Juan Pascual-Leone (1984, 1990), and Klaus Riegel (1973) have asserted that after the stage of formal operations follows a stage of **postformal thinking,** in which individuals recognize the constant unfolding and evolution of thought (the dialectic originally proposed by philosopher Georg Hegel). In this stage, individuals can manipulate mentally various options for decisions and diverse alternative answers to questions. As described earlier in this book, through **dialectical thinking,** individuals recognize that humans seldom find final, correct answers to the important questions in life, but rather, pass through a progression of beliefs comprising some kind of thesis, a subsequent antithesis, and then a synthesis, which then serves as the new thesis for the continuing evolution of thought. Postformal, or dialectical thought, allows adults to manipulate mentally the vagaries and inconsistencies of everyday situations, in which simple, unambiguous answers are rarely available. Through postformal thinking, we can consider and choose among alternatives, recognizing that other alternatives may offer benefits not obtainable from the chosen one. An alternative and beneficial theory of cognitive development is that of Lev Vygotsky.

The Cognitive-Developmental Theory of Lev Vygotsky

In 1934, cognitive-developmental theorist Lev Vygotsky died of tuberculosis at age 37. Despite his early demise, the importance of this Russian psychologist has increased in recent years, and today, Vygotsky's stature in developmental psychology is comparable to that of Piaget. Whereas Piaget dominated developmental psychology in the 1960s and 1970s, Vygotsky was rediscovered in the late 1970s and 1980s and continues to be influential. Although Vygotsky had many fertile ideas, two of them are particularly important for us to consider here: internalization and the zone of proximal development.

Some neo-Piagetians propose a fifth stage of cognitive development, in which individuals recognize that many real-life situations pose multiple problems and opportunities for which there will not be one clear answer. Often, what is needed is to consider various alternatives and then to choose what seems to be the best option for the situation, recognizing that other possibilities may have offered other benefits. In deciding which route to take, these hikers must figure out which route offers them the best combination of advantages, realizing that they may miss some appealing landmarks or other benefits along the route not traveled.

Many of the ideas about how children think that were proposed by cognitive-developmental theorist Lev Vygotsky (1896–1934) have been important not only to psychologists but also to educators.

Internalization, Development from the Outside In

In Piaget's theory, cognitive development proceeds largely "from the inside out" through maturation. Environments can foster or impede development, but Piaget emphasized the biological, and hence the maturational, aspect of development. In contrast to Piaget's inside-out approach, Vygotsky (1962, 1978) emphasized the role of the environment in children's intellectual development. He posited that development proceeds largely from the outside in, through **internalization**—a process of absorbing information from a given social environmental context. Thus, social rather than biological influences are key in Vygotsky's theory.

Every day, at home, in school, and on the street, children listen to what people say and how they say it, and watch what people do and why they do it. For example, they see how their parents treat the service people they come in contact with—the teachers and gas station attendants, the waitpersons, the store clerks. Then they internalize what they see, making it

their own. They re-create within themselves the kinds of conversations and other interactions they see in their world. According to Vygotsky, then, much of a child's learning occurs through his or her interactions within the environment, which largely determine what the child internalizes.

The Zone of Proximal Development

Vygotsky's (1962, 1978) second major contribution to educational and developmental psychology is his construct of the **zone of proximal development,** or **ZPD** (sometimes termed the *zone of potential development*). The ZPD is the range between the developed abilities that a child clearly shows and the latent capacities that the child might be able to show, given the appropriate environment to do so. When we observe children, what we typically observe is the ability that they have developed through the interaction of heredity and environment. To a large extent, however, we are truly interested in what children are capable of doing—what their potential would be if they were freed from the confines of an environment that is never truly optimal. Before Vygotsky, people were unclear as to how to measure this latent capacity.

Vygotsky argued that we need to reconsider not only how we think about children's cognitive abilities but also how we measure them. Typically, we test children in a *static assessment environment*, in which an examiner asks a series of questions, offering no hints or guidance if the test taker makes incorrect responses and usually not even signaling whether the test taker has answered correctly or incorrectly—the examiner simply moves on to the next item in the test. Vygotsky recommended instead that we test in a *dynamic assessment environment*, in which the interaction between the test taker and the examiner does not end when the test taker gives an incorrect response. In dynamic assessment, when the child gives a wrong answer, the examiner gives the child a sequence of guided and graded hints to facilitate problem solving. In other words, the examiner serves as both teacher and tester. The examiner is particularly interested in the child's ability to use hints. The ability to use hints is the basis for measuring the ZPD because this ability indicates the extent to which the child can expand beyond her or his observable abilities at the time of testing. Several tests have been created to measure the ZPD (e.g., A. L. Brown & French, 1979; Campione, 1989; Campione & Brown, 1990; Grigorenko & Sternberg, 1997), the best known of which is Israeli psychologist Reuven Feuerstein's (1979) *Learning Potential Assessment Device.*

The ZPD is one of the more exciting concepts in cognitive-developmental psychology, because it enables us to probe beyond a child's observed performance.

Moreover, the combination of testing and teaching appeals to many psychologists and educators. Educators, psychologists, and other researchers have been captivated by Vygotsky's notion that we can extend and facilitate children's development of cognitive abilities.

Feuerstein (1980) has extended Vygotsky's work by highlighting the role of parents in facilitating their children's learning through *mediated learning experiences*, or MLE (see chapter 9). Through such experiences, an adult may introduce a child to an interesting environment (such as a museum) or task (such as how to cook) and then enhance the child's ability to learn by interpreting the experience through language the child understands. An alternative to MLE is *direct instruction*, in which the adult directly tells the child specific information that the child is to learn. Although mediation may be given either by adults or other children, mediation by adults tends to be more effective because the adults better understand how children learn than other children do (Rogoff, 1990). As a result, adults typically can construct better learning experiences for the children (Rogoff, Mistry, Goncu, & Mosler, 1993).

The power of Piaget and Vygotsky lay in their interest in probing beneath the surface to try to understand why children behave and respond as they do. As is true of almost any significant contribution to science, the ideas of Vygotsky and of Piaget are measured more by how much they prompt us to extend our knowledge than by the extent to which they have represented a complete, final understanding of a concept. Perhaps the most we can ask of a theory is to be worthy of further exploration, and we now explore the information-processing theories of cognitive development.

Information-Processing Theories and Research in Cognitive Development

Information-processing theorists seek to understand the ways in which various people perform mental operations on information, (i.e., decode, encode, transfer, combine, store, and retrieve information), particularly when solving challenging mental problems. Information-processing theorists do not claim to provide as comprehensive an explanation of cognitive development as did Piaget, but they do consider the entire range of mental processes that persons of all ages use to manipulate information. Any mental activity that involves noticing, taking in, mentally manipulating, storing, combining, retrieving, or acting on information falls within the purview of information-processing theory.

Information-processing analysis offers several advantages. First, it allows more precise analyses of the mental processes underlying cognition than do alternative approaches. Second, it allows more specific attention to the question of exactly how change occurs. Third, it lends itself to analysis of learning in specific areas, such as reading and arithmetic. In such areas, information-processing analysis enables the investigator to model quite precisely how the students are learning and thinking (Siegler, 1998).

When we turn the focus of information-processing theory to the topic of cognitive development, we ask, how do our processes, strategies, or ways of representing and organizing information change over time, if at all? If there are changes, what might cause the changes? Let us consider several domains of information processing.

Conceptual Understanding

Even in infancy, children show remarkable skill at understanding the world around them. To learn about the world, infants need to know where and how to pay attention to stimuli. They seem to be surprisingly competent in doing so.

Furthermore, these perceptual abilities develop rapidly to enable babies to learn a great deal about the world. For example, in one study, children as young as 4 months were shown two movies (Spelke, 1976). In one, a woman was playing and saying "peek-a-boo." In the other film, the child saw a hand holding a stick and rhythmically striking a wooden block. The catch was that the baby was shown the film either with its corresponding sound track or with the other movie's sound track. Infants spent more time looking at the picture if the sound corresponded to it. In other words, even at 4 months, children can match visual and auditory stimuli. This skill is important to all of us in our making sense of the world through our integration of sensory inputs.

Information-processing researchers also have been interested in the perceptual skills of older children, such as their perceptions of appearance and reality. For example, children of 4 and 5 years of age were shown imitation objects, such as a sponge that looked exactly like a rock (Flavell, Flavell, & Green, 1983). The researchers encouraged the children to become thoroughly familiar with the objects. Children then had to answer questions about the objects. Afterward, the children were asked to view the objects through a blue plastic sheet and to make color judgments about the objects; they also were asked to make size judgments while viewing the objects through a magnifying glass. The children were fully aware that they were viewing the objects through these intermediaries.

The children's errors formed an interesting pattern. They made two fundamental kinds of errors. On the one hand, when asked to report the reality (the way the object actually was), the children would sometimes report the appearance (the way the object looked).

Conversely, when asked to report the appearance of the objects, they would sometimes report the reality. In other words, they did not yet clearly perceive the distinction between appearance and reality (Flavell, Green, & Flavell, 1995).

Memory

As you might expect, memory is better in older children than in younger children (see Kail, 1990). The differences in gross memory capacity are obvious, but factors other than physiological ones may also play a role in children's performance on memory tasks. For example, the way we organize information plays a powerful role in memory (see chapter 7). In particular, we know that when we are knowledgeable about an area, and we can collect many small bits of information into larger chunks, we can more easily recall the information.

Although many information-processing theorists and other researchers have been interested in the effects of content knowledge on cognitive development, some of the most fascinating work has focused more on the strategies children use in regard to memory. In trying to learn new material, young children are more likely to resort to very simple strategies, such as rote repetition, whereas older children are more likely to use elaborative rehearsal strategies such as visual imagery and semantic categorization (Alexander & Schwanenflugel, 1994; Hasselhorn, 1990).

One particular line of memory-development research has sparked great interest: **metamemory**, which involves knowledge and understanding of memory abilities and ways to enhance memory abilities (Flavell, 1976, 1981; Flavell & Wellman, 1977; T. Nelson, 1996). It is a special case of *metacognition*, or understanding and control of one's own cognitive functioning (T. Nelson, 1999). For example, preschool children seriously overestimate their ability to recall information and they rarely spontaneously use rehearsal strategies when asked to recall items. That is, young children seem not to know about many memory-enhancing strategies. In addition, even when they do know about strategies, they do not always use them. For example, when trained to use rehearsal strategies in one task, most young children do not transfer the use of that strategy to other tasks (Flavell & Wellman, 1977). Thus, it appears that young children lack not only the knowledge of strategies but also the inclination to use them when they do know about them. Children improve in metamemory skills with age, although generally, metamemory is not a particularly good predictor of memory skills (Flavell, 1985; Flavell & Wellman, 1977). More generally, children's knowledge about their minds and their mental states increases dramatically between the ages of 2 and 5 years (Astington, 1993; B. Bower, 1993; Perner, 1999).

Cross-cultural comparisons of Western and non-Western children support the thesis that culture, experience, and environmental demands affect the use of memory-enhancing strategies. For example, Western children, who generally have more formal schooling than non-Western children, are given much more practice using rehearsal strategies for remembering isolated bits of information. In contrast, Guatemalan children and Australian aboriginal children generally have many more opportunities to become adept at using memory-enhancing strategies that rely on spatial location and arrangements of objects (Kearins, 1981; Rogoff, 1986).

Verbal Comprehension and Fluency

Chapter 8 described language acquisition in detail, so we only summarize it briefly here. Recall that *verbal comprehension* is the ability to comprehend written and spoken linguistic input, such as words, sentences, and paragraphs. *Verbal fluency* is the ability to produce such materials. In general, children's ability to process information efficiently, their verbal comprehension, increases with age (e.g., Hunt, Lunneberg, & Lewis, 1975; Keating & Bobbitt, 1978; K. Nelson, 1999). Older children also demonstrate greater verbal fluency than do younger children (e.g., Siegler, 1998; Sincoff & Sternberg, 1988). Much of what develops is not just verbal ability but also the ability to generate useful strategies, such as comprehension monitoring.

Research on comprehension monitoring has been an interesting aspect of research on strategies of verbal comprehension (E. M. Markman, 1977, 1979, 1992). *Comprehension monitoring* involves the individual's observing whether the information being processed is being understood, contains internal contradictions, or contains other problematic features that require attention for their resolution. Consider a typical experiment. Children between the ages of 8 and 11 years heard passages containing contradictory information. This description of how to make the dessert Baked Alaska is an example:

> To make it they put the ice cream in a very hot oven. The ice cream in Baked Alaska melts when it gets that hot. Then they take the ice cream out of the oven and serve it right away. When they make Baked Alaska, the ice cream stays firm and does not melt. (E. M. Markman, 1979, p. 656)

Note that the passage contains a blatant internal contradiction, saying both that the ice cream melts and that it does not. Almost half of the young children who saw this passage did not notice the contradiction at all. Even when they were warned in advance about problems with the story, many of the youngest children still did not detect the inconsistency. Thus, young children are not very successful at comprehension monitoring, even when cued to be aware of inconsistencies in the text they read. Some young children also find quantitative problems to be a challenge.

Quantitative Skills

Several lines of cognitive-development research have studied the quantitative skills of young children. One line of research has dealt with simple number understanding (as shown by counting) and arithmetic computation. The ability to count objects—and thereby to conserve number—is one of the earliest indications of children's quantitative skills and their conceptions of number. Piagetian descriptions of the numerical abilities of young children to have generally underestimated those abilities (Gelman & Gallistel, 1978; Siegler, 1996; Wynn, 1995). They conclude that many 2- and 3-year-olds may not be able to count more than three or four items, but nevertheless, they can differentiate when making judgments about unknown quantities. For example, toddlers may not be able to count to 100, but they know that 100 cookies are more than 20 cookies. Thus, even very young children have some rudimentary counting abilities not considered in Piagetian accounts. Moreover, Brazilian street vendors between the ages of 9 and 15 who could not solve certain mathematics problems in school could solve problems that were formally identical if the problems were presented to them in the context of their sales activities on the streets (Carraher, Schliemann, & Carraher, 1988; Nuñes, Schliemann, & Carraher, 1993). Such activities require active problem solving.

Problem Solving

Many psychologists have worked on problem solving in children. Here, we focus on one particularly interesting line of research, on balance-scale problems (Inhelder & Piaget, 1958; Siegler, 1976, 1978, 1996).

In the balance-scale task, children see a balance scale with four equally spaced pegs on each side. The arms of the balance scale can fall down to the left or right, or they can remain even, depending on the distribution of weights. The child's task is to predict which (if either) side of the balance scale will descend if a lever that holds the scale motionless is released (see Figure 10-6).

At first, children consider only the number of weights, not the distance from the fulcrum, in their predictions. Gradually, children use more complex rules as they grow older, with more complex rules defined as those that take into account more information than is present in the problem situation (e.g., discerning a relationship between the distance from the fulcrum and the weight). Use of information is also important in deductive reasoning (Siegler, 1976).

In general, children are less able to formulate and solve scientific problems than are adults, often because, as in the balance-scale task, they see situations too simplistically. For example, children are less likely than adults to design experiments in which they hold all but one variable constant. As a result, their experiments often have multiple interpretations of the data (Klahr, Fay, & Dunbar, 1993; Kuhn, Schauble, & Garcia-Mila, 1992). They also often do not conduct all the experimentation they need to reach a conclusion (Klahr, Fay, & Dunbar, 1993; Kuhn, Garcia-Mila, Zohar, & Andersen, 1995).

Inductive Reasoning

Inductive reasoning involves inferring general principles from specific observations. It does not lead to a single, logically certain solution to a problem, but only to solutions that have different levels of plausibility (see chapter 8).

Children even as young as 3 years of age seem to induce some general principles from specific observations, particularly those principles that pertain to categories for animals (S. A. Gelman, 1985; S. A. Gelman & Markman, 1987; S. A. Gelman & Wellman, 1991). For example (S. A. Gelman & Kremer, 1991), preschoolers were able to induce principles

Figure 10–6

BALANCE-SCALE PROBLEMS. *Balance-scale problems similar to these are used in some particularly interesting studies of the development of problem-solving skills. Which way do you predict the scales shown here will tip?*

Problem *A*   Problem *B*

that correctly attribute the cause of phenomena such as growth to natural processes rather than to human intervention. Preschoolers also were able to reason correctly that a blackbird was more likely to behave like a flamingo than like a bat because blackbirds and flamingos are both birds (S. A. Gelman & Markman, 1987). Note that in this example, preschoolers are going against their perception that blackbirds look more like bats than like flamingos, basing their judgment instead on the fact that bats are not birds (although the effect is admittedly strongest when the term *bird* is also used in regard to both the flamingo and the blackbird). In addition, a supportive context for induction can greatly enhance children's ability to induce appropriate principles (Keil, 1989, 1999).

To summarize these findings, it once again appears that early developmental psychologists may have underestimated the cognitive capabilities of young children. Nonetheless, there does appear to be a developmental trend as we get older toward increasing sophistication in inducing general principles from specific information and toward increasing reliance on more subtle features of the information on which such inductions are based.

Considering the Four Perspectives

The preceding theories of cognitive development (Piagetian, neo-Piagetian, Vygotskyan, and information-processing theories) are all influential in psychology. They are not mutually exclusive, however; some have been pursued simultaneously, some have evolved as reactions to others, and some are offshoots of others. Table 10-3 summarizes some of the ways these theories relate to one another. Theories of cognitive development, and of other important issues in psychology, all contribute to the ongoing dialectical process of understanding how and why we humans think, feel, and behave as we do.

Adult Development

What kinds of development occur in adults?

Thus far, this chapter has focused primarily on cognitive development in children. Psychological development, however, does not stop at adolescence. Many psychologists study **life-span development**—the developmental changes in characteristics that occur over the course of a lifetime. Before we close this chapter, we look at adult and life-span cognitive development.

Fluid intelligence tends to decline with age, and other cognitive abilities also seem to decline in many individuals. For example, performance on many information-processing tasks appears to be slower, particularly on complex tasks (Bashore, Osman, & Hefley, 1989; Cerella, 1985; Poon, 1987; Schaie, 1989, 1995, 1996). Similarly, for older adults, performance on some problem-solving tasks appears not to be as effective (Denny, 1980), although even brief training appears to improve their scores on problem-solving tasks (Willis, 1985).

Our views of memory and aging also may be confounded because when we hear about the devastating memory losses associated with aging, such as those associated with Alzheimer's disease, we may tend to think that such dementia is widespread among the elderly. In fact, devastating memory loss is uncommon even among the most elderly of us (see Figure 10-7). The elderly population as a whole shows much more diversity of abilities than does the population of young adults.

The evidence of intellectual decline has come under question, however (Schaie, 1974, 1995, 1996). For one thing, not all cognitive abilities decline. For example, some investigators (Schaie & Willis, 1986) have found that particular learning abilities seem to increase, and other investigators (Graf, 1990; Labouvie-Vief & Schell, 1982; Perlmutter, 1983) have found that the ability to learn and remember meaningful skills and information shows little decline. Also, even in a single domain, such as memory, decreases in one kind of performance may not imply decreases in another. For example, although short-term memory performance seems to decline (Hultsch & Dixon, 1990; West, 1986), long-term memory (Bahrick, Bahrick, & Wuttlinger, 1975) and recognition memory (Schonfield & Robertson, 1966) remain quite good.

Principles of Adult Development

Although the debate continues about intellectual decline with age, positions have converged somewhat. For example, three basic principles of cognitive development in adulthood have been suggested (Baltes, 1997; Dixon & Baltes, 1986). First, although fluid abilities and other aspects of information processing may decline in late adulthood, this decline is balanced by stabilization and even advancement of well-practiced and pragmatic aspects of mental functioning (crystallized abilities; Horn & Hofer, 1992; Salthouse, 1992, 1996). Thus, when adults lose some of their speed and physiology-related efficiency of information processing, they often compensate with other knowledge- and expertise-based

TABLE 10–3

Summary of Theories of Cognitive Development *How do the theories presented in this chapter address the issues of nature versus nurture, continuity versus discontinuity, domain generality versus domain specificity, and the nature of the developmental process?*

THEORY	NATURE OR NURTURE?	CONTINUOUS OR DISCONTINUOUS (STAGES)?	DOMAIN GENERAL OR DOMAIN SPECIFIC?	PROCESS BY WHICH DEVELOPMENT OCCURS?
Piaget	Biological maturation is crucial; environment plays a secondary but important role	Discontinuous; development occurs in four stages	Development largely occurs simultaneously across domains, although some domains may show change slightly ahead of others	Equilibrative processes of assimilation and accommodation
Neo-Piagetians	May emphasize role of the environment somewhat more than Piaget did	Discontinuous; may add a fifth stage; may question the ages for particular stages suggested by Piaget	Same as Piaget	Same as Piaget
Vygotsky	Social and physical environments play crucial roles; maturational readiness may provide the broad parameters (zone of proximal development) within which the social environment determines development	Continuous	The zone of proximal development may apply to many domains, but the environment may provide sufficient support for development only in specific domains	Internalization that results from interactions between the individual and the environment, occurring within the individual's zone of proximal development
Information-processing theorists	Nature provides the physiological structures and functions (e.g., memory capacity), and nurture provides the environmental supports that allow the individual to make the most of the existing structures and functions	Continuous	Some theorists have been interested in processes that generalize across all domains; others have focused their research and theories on specific domains	Internal changes in cognitive processing, as a result of physiological maturation, environmental events, and the individual's own shaping of cognitive processes

information-processing skills (see Salthouse & Somberg, 1982). Second, despite the age-related decline in information processing, sufficient reserve capacity allows at least temporary increases in performance, espe-

cially if the older adult is motivated to perform well. Third, other investigators (Baltes & Willis, 1979) have further argued that at all times throughout the life span, there is considerable **plasticity**—modifiability—

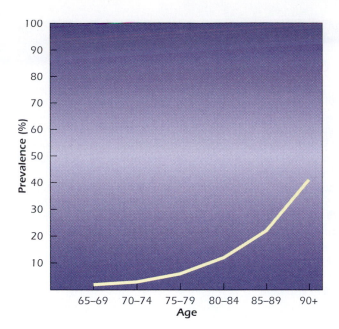

Figure 10-7

PREVALANCE OF DEMENTIA. *Studies conducted in Japan, Australia, New Zealand, the United Kingdom, Sweden, and Denmark show that the actual rate of dementia (such as that caused by Alzheimer's disease) does not meet our preconceptions of memory loss among the elderly until people reach very late adulthood. (After data from Preston, 1986)*

of abilities. None of us is stuck at a particular level of performance: Each of us can improve.

Many researchers have come to believe that not only does adult cognition not decline, it actually continues to develop and improve. Recall, for example, the characteristics of postformal thought described in regard to some of the neo-Piagetian fifth-stage theorists. Those who support the notion of postformal thought indicate several ways in which older adults may show a kind of thinking that differs qualitatively from the thinking of adolescents and perhaps even of young adults. Although older adults generally do not demonstrate the same speed of information processing shown in younger adults, they may show instead the benefits of taking time to consider alternatives and to reflect on experience before making judgments—a skill often termed *wisdom* (Baltes & Staudinger, in press; Sternberg, 1998). According to one theory, wise people are those who use their intelligence not just to further their own ends, but also, to advance the common good. They do so by making judgments that take into account their own interests, but also the interests of others and of institutions, such as society at large (Sternberg, 1998).

This chapter has described a number of different theories and approaches for studying cognitive de-

velopment. After viewing these diverse approaches, can we find any unifying principles that transcend the particular theory or method being used? In other words, regardless of the particular theoretical approach—whether Piagetian, Vygotskyan, or information processing—what basic principles crosscut the study of cognitive development and tie it together?

As we review the data, we find some possible answers (Lutz & Sternberg, 1999; Sternberg & Powell, 1983). First, over the course of development, we seem to gain more sophisticated control over our own thinking and learning. As we grow older, we become capable of more complex interactions between thought and behavior. Second, we engage in more thorough information processing with age. Older children encode more information from problems than do younger children, and they are therefore more likely to solve problems correctly. Third, we become increasingly able to comprehend ideas of successively greater complexity over the course of development. Finally, over time, we develop increasing flexibility in our uses of strategies or other information. As we grow older, we become less bound to using information in just a single context and we learn how to apply it in more and more contexts. We may even gain greater wisdom—insight into ourselves and the world around us (Baltes & Staudinger, in press; R. J. Sternberg, 1990, 1998).

The fact that these conclusions are confirmed by a wide variety of theoretical and experimental approaches strengthens them. The next chapter, on social development, offers an even greater diversity of perspectives. Will the diverse perspectives on social development similarly yield a harvest of conclusions regarding human development?

Many researchers have come to believe that not only does adult cognition not decline, it actually continues to develop and improve.

Psychology in Everyday Life

Use It or Lose It

Is cognitive growth never-ending? Do scores on cognitive-abilities tests continue to increase indefinitely? Available data suggest they may not. There is a difference between *fluid intelligence*—the ability to perform mental operations, such as the manipulation of abstract symbols, as in mathematics—and *crystallized intelligence*—specific knowledge tied to a particular cultural and historical milieu (see chapter 9). Although crystallized intelligence is often higher for older adults than for younger adults, fluid intelligence is often higher for younger adults than for older ones (Horn, 1994; Horn & Cattell, 1966). In general, crystallized cognitive abilities seem to increase throughout the life span, whereas fluid cognitive abilities seem to increase until the 20s, 30s, or even 40s, and slowly decrease thereafter (Salthouse, 1996). The rate and extent of decline vary widely (Mackintosh, 1998). However, the greatest decline in fluid abilities appears to be, on average, in the last 10 years of a person's life. Moreover, there are enormous individual differences in rate of decline. Some people show steep declines in these abilities, whereas others show hardly any declines at all. It appears that the lesson is that brain power is like muscle power: Use it or lose it. The best thing to prevent loss of brainpower is continuously to use the brainpower you have.

THINK ABOUT IT

1. What steps should researchers take to avoid interpreting their own limitations as investigators as being limitations in the cognitive abilities of children?
2. How does Piaget's notion of equilibration through assimilation and accommodation relate to Vygotsky's concept of the zone of proximal development?
3. What might you suggest as a possible "fifth stage" of cognitive development?
4. What skills might a child in a remote village in Kenya have that a child in a city in a highly developed country might not have?

5. How have you developed cognitively in the past 3 years? In what ways do you think differently from before?
6. What principal aspects of your parents' or your teachers' behavior have you internalized over the years?

 You can provide your own answers to these questions online at the **Sternberg,** In Search of the Human Mind *Web site:* **http://www.harcourtcollege.com/psych/ishm**

SUMMARY

Basic Questions in the Study of Physical and Cognitive Development 328

1. Learning refers to any relatively permanent change in thought or behavior as a result of experience; *maturation* refers to any relatively permanent change in thought or behavior that occurs simply as a result of aging, without regard to particular experiences.
2. Today, almost all psychologists believe that both maturation and learning play a role in cognitive development and, moreover, that the two processes interact.
3. Two criteria proposed for determining that cognitive development occurs in discontinuous stages are that development occurs in an invariant sequence and that each stage involves a distinctive set of thinking skills.
4. Much of children's conceptual development appears to be domain specific—occurring at different rates in different domains—although some

appears to be domain general—occurring in all domains at about the same rate.

5. Researchers use both cross-sectional and longitudinal designs in the study of development.

Physical and Neural Development 332

6. Infants possess many more physical and perceptual capacities than was once believed to be the case.

7. Reflexes provide an important mechanism whereby infants adapt to their environments.

8. Neural networks of the brain show their greatest growth during the first 6 years of a child's life. The brain areas to develop most rapidly are the sensory and motor cortexes, followed by the association areas relating to problem solving, reasoning, memory, and language development. Studies suggest, however, that development throughout the brain is not uniform. EEG patterns indicate that while the right cerebral hemisphere undergoes continuous, gradual changes, the left hemisphere shows more abrupt, discontinuous changes.

Cognitive Development 338

9. Jean Piaget proposed that cognitive development occurs largely through two processes of *equilibration: assimilation*, whereby the child incorporates new information into the child's existing cognitive schemas, and *accommodation*, whereby the child attempts to modify his or her cognitive schemas to fit relevant aspects of the new environment.

10. Piaget posited four stages of cognitive development: the *sensorimotor stage*, in roughly the first two years of life; the *preoperational stage*, from roughly 2 years to 7 years of age; the *concrete-operational stage*, from roughly 7 years of age to 12 years of age; and the *formal-operational stage*, from 11 or 12 years onward.

11. As children grow older, they become less *egocentric*—that is, less focused on themselves and more able to see things from the perspective of others.

12. At the end of the sensorimotor stage, children start to develop *representational thought*—cognitions about people and objects that the child cannot see, hear, or otherwise perceive.

13. Children start to show conservation in the concrete-operational stage. They can recognize that two quantities remain the same, despite transformations on them that may change their appearance.

14. Despite the valuable contribution of Piaget's theory to our understanding of cognitive develop-

ment, most scholars now believe that it inadequately estimates the ages at which children first become able to perform various tasks.

15. Some theorists have posited a fifth stage beyond Piaget's original four. Such a *postformal* stage might involve a tendency toward dialectical thinking. In *dialectical thinking*, beliefs tend to incorporate disparate, sometimes seemingly contradictory elements, with the recognition that many problems have no one right answer.

16. Lev Vygotsky's theory of cognitive development stresses the importance of (a) *internalization*, whereby we incorporate into ourselves the knowledge we gain from social contexts, and (b) the *zone of proximal development*, which is the range of ability between a child's existing undeveloped potential ability and the child's actual developed ability.

17. Reuven Feuerstein has emphasized the importance of mediated learning experiences, whereby an adult interprets, or mediates, for the child the potential opportunities for learning offered by experiences in the environment.

18. *Information-processing theorists* seek to understand cognitive development in terms of how children at different ages process information. Some theorists formulate general theories of how information processing works, and others study information processing within specific domains.

19. Over the course of development, children learn to engage in comprehension monitoring—the tracking of their own understanding of what they read and learn, more generally.

20. Young children appear to fail on some transitive-inference problems, apparently not due to a lack of reasoning ability but rather to a lack of memory of the terms and relations in the problems.

Adult Development 351

21. It appears that although some cognitive abilities, such as fluid abilities—involved in thinking flexibly and in novel ways—start to decline at some point in later adulthood, the decline is balanced by stability and perhaps increases in other abilities, such as crystallized abilities—represented by the accumulation of knowledge.

22. Some principles of cognitive development appear to transcend specific theories or perspectives. With age, people develop more sophisticated thinking strategies, their information processing becomes more thorough, their ability to comprehend more complex ideas develops, and they become increasingly flexible in their uses of strategies for problem solving.

KEY TERMS

accommodation 340
assimilation 340
cognitive development 327
cohort effects 332
concrete operations 342
cross-sectional studies 332
development 327
developmental psychology 327
dialectical thinking 346
egocentrism 341
equilibration 340
fetal alcohol syndrome 334

formal-operational stage 344
growth 328
information-processing theorists 348
internalization 347
life-span development 351
longitudinal studies 332
maturation 329
menarche 336
menopause 338
metamemory 349
motor 335

neonate 334
object permanence 341
plasticity 352
postformal thinking 346
preoperational stage 341
puberty 336
representational thought 341
sensorimotor stage 340
zone of proximal development (ZPD) 347

■ THINK ABOUT IT SAMPLE RESPONSES

1. What steps should researchers take to avoid interpreting their own limitations as investigators as being limitations in the cognitive abilities of children?

It is important to word questions to children in a variety of ways, to make sure that children's answers reflect their inability to answer, not their failure to understand what is being asked. It is also important to have the questions asked by a variety of examiners to make sure that failures to respond or wrong answers truly reflect lack of knowledge or skill rather than poor rapport with the examiner.

2. How does Piaget's notion of equilibration through assimilation and accommodation relate to Vygotsky's concept of the zone of proximal development?

Equilibration can tell us about the level of cognitive development a child has achieved. The zone of proximal development can tell us about the level of cognitive development a child is just about ready to achieve, but has not yet quite achieved. It is important to know both where the child is in terms of cognitive development and where the child is ready to go.

3. What might you suggest as a possible "fifth stage" of cognitive development?

Possible fifth stages might be finding important problems to solve, wisdom, thinking dialectically, and understanding how to achieve one's goals in a way that helps others in addition to oneself.

4. What skills might a child in a remote village in Kenya have that a child in a city in a highly developed country might not have?

The child in Kenya might have skills pertaining to agriculture and fishing that the urban child would not have. The Kenyan child would also be likely to know a number of herbal remedies for illnesses that the urban child in the developed world would not know.

5. How have you developed cognitively in the past 3 years? In what ways do you think differently from before?

Some theorists believe that students in college, particularly, gain sophisticated skills in the ability to see issues from a multitude of perspectives. Indeed, one of the main purposes of a college education is to develop these skills. Hence you might be substantially better at understanding multiple points of view now than you were a few years ago.

6. What principal aspects of your parents' or your teachers' behavior have you internalized over the years?

Answers will be different for different people. Students often internalize codes of moral and ethical behavior, ways of behaving toward other people, and attitudes toward intellectual tasks.

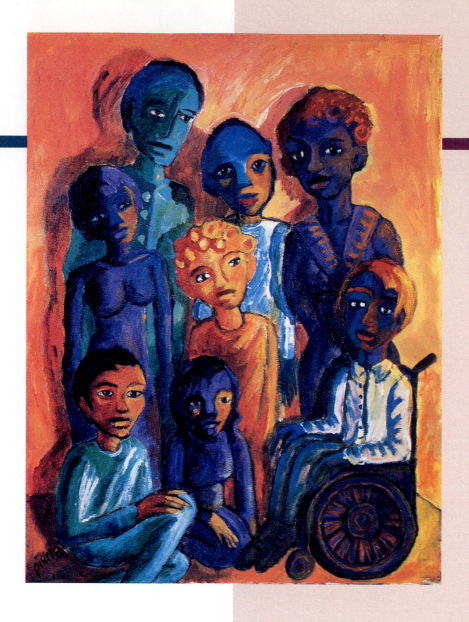

I do not remember having ever told a lie, . . . either to my teachers or to my school-mates. I used to be very shy and avoided all company. My books and my lessons were my sole companions. To be at school at the stroke of the hour and to run back home as soon as school closed, that was my daily habit. I literally ran back, because I could not bear to talk to anybody. I was even afraid lest anyone should poke fun at me.

—Mohandas Gandhi, *Gandhi's Autobiography*

11

SOCIAL DEVELOPMENT

The preceding chapter described developmental changes across the life span in terms of how we develop physically and how we think, reason, make judgments, and otherwise perceive and use information. Many of the changes associated with cognitive development affect the ways we think and feel about ourselves and the ways we interact with others. For example, 4-year-olds may be unable to take the perspectives of others in disagreements not because they do not want to, but because they are cognitively unable to. In this chapter, we directly consider the broad topic of **social development**—the process by which people learn to interact with other people and learn about themselves as human beings.

Social development encompasses several aspects of human development: emotional, personality, interpersonal, and moral development. These areas of study certainly cover a lot of psychological territory, but they are so highly interrelated that, at times, it seems quite difficult to assign developments to particular areas of study. For example, is the special feeling an infant or young child has toward its mother—or other primary caregiver—an emotion (love), a personality trait (dependence), or an interpersonal interaction (attachment)? Is the way we treat our beloved based on our moral development, our interpersonal development, our personality development, or our emotional development? For example, do we treat our beloved based on our sense of what is right and wrong, our ideas about how to interact with others, our personal predispositions to behave in some ways rather than others, or our tendency to feel certain ways but not others about people? Psychologists who study social development often consider all these aspects of development when studying a particular psychological phenomenon (see Figure 11-1).

Emotional Development

In Search of . . .

How and why do we develop emotions?

An *emotion* is a subjective conscious experience accompanied by bodily arousal and by typical overt expressions, such as smiling when one is happy. Thus, an emotion has a cognitive component (the subjective conscious experience), a physiological component (the bodily arousal), and a behavioral component (the overt expression). We will be discussing emotions themselves in more detail in the next chapter. Here, our focus is on how and when emotions develop. Researchers show a surprising degree of consensus about when emotions develop (Brazelton, 1983; Izard, 1991; Izard, Kagan, & Zajonc, 1984; Sroufe, 1979). It is a long road from the emotional world of the infant to the emotional world of the adult. The stages of emotional development are summarized in Table 11-1. Some of our earliest and most basic emotions, the infant's social smiles and **separation anxiety,** a generalized fear of being separated from a primary caregiver or other familiar adult appear to be common across cultures and occur at roughly the same ages, as shown in Figure 11-2.

Infant boys seem to express emotions somewhat differently from infant girls (Brody, 1996). For example, 6-month-old boys displayed more positive

Figure 11–1
SOCIAL DEVELOPMENT. *Across the life span, social development encompasses aspects of emotional development (such as expressing anguished desolation), interpersonal development (such as enjoying the company of friends), personality development (such as being shy versus outgoing), and moral development (such as beginning to internalize the dictates of societal authorities).*

TABLE 11-1

Emotional Development *The following characteristics of emotional development and the ages of their appearance are based largely on the observational data obtained by Alan Sroufe. As is the case with most data on development, the ages are approximations and suggest only a general sequence of developments, not a certain timetable of the developmental process.*

AGE (MONTHS)	CHARACTERISTICS
0–1	Infants show emotions, usually by crying or thrashing around. Their options for emotional expression are limited, so they express multiple emotions—grief, discomfort, anger—in a single way, such as by crying.
1–3	Infants begin to react to others. They develop a *social smile*, smiling when they see others smiling at them. They show stern or sad faces when they see sad faces on those around them. By about 2 months of age, they also smile in response to nonsocial stimuli, such as toys they have enjoyed playing with before.
3–6	Infants show high amounts of positive emotional reactions, smiling when they see their caregivers. By about 4 months, infants also laugh. At about 4 or 5 months, they begin to produce tears to accompany their crying.
6–9	Infants actively participate in and even initiate interactions. Social interactions are primarily physical. Infants start to fear strangers and unknown places. They may have difficulty eating or sleeping in unfamiliar environments and may actively avoid such situations. Infants also exhibit *separation anxiety*, fear of being separated from their mothers or other familiar adults. Infants begin to show anger.
9–12	Babies become increasingly effective at conveying emotional states to others. Infants become highly attached to their primary caregivers, and they seem possessive, wanting other people to stay away from their caregivers. Their fear of strangers, if anything, grows.
12–18	Infants explore the inanimate environment more. The close attachment to their primary caregivers now gives the infants greater confidence. As infants become increasingly inquisitive, their fear of strangers generally drops off.
18–36	Toddlers become more aware of themselves as individual people. They begin to develop differentiated self-concepts, realizing they play different roles (daughter, sibling, playmate) in different situations. At one moment, they want to assert their independence, and at the next moment, they want to cling to their caregivers. By the end of this stage, children also begin to show signs of empathy, sharing the joys and sorrows of others.

emotions (e.g., happiness) than did girls, but also displayed more negative emotions (e.g., anger) than did the girls (Weinberg, 1992). Boys also cry more when they feel frustrated and take longer to recover when they are distressed than do girls (Kohnstamm, 1989).

Stages of Emotional Development

Some investigators believe that there is a curvilinear pattern (shaped like a hill or an inverted U) in emotional response to stimuli (Kagan, Kearsley, & Zelazo, 1978), as shown in Figure 11-3. This view is based on a discrepancy hypothesis proposed by Jerome Kagan. On first presentation, a child may show no particular emotional reaction to an unfamiliar stimulus. Then, when something happens to violate the child's expectations, the child attends to, and perhaps interacts with, the unfamiliar stimulus, and an emotional reaction ensues (the upward arc of the curve). Finally, to use Jean Piaget's terms, when the child has either assimilated the situation into existing expectations or accommodated his or her existing schemas by forming new expectations (see chapter 10), the situation no longer provokes much interest or emotion (the downward arc of the curve).

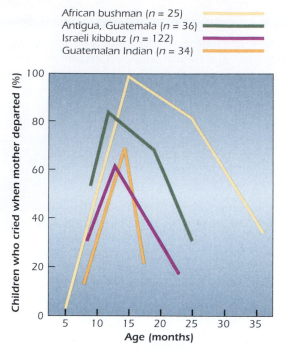

Figure 11–2

SEPARATION ANXIETY. *At about 8 months of age (give or take a month or two), infants start to show separation anxiety—a fear of being separated from their mothers or other familiar adults. Despite the universality of separation anxiety, some cross-cultural differences affect the intensity, the age of onset, and the duration of this phenomenon. When infants later acquire a concept of object permanence, they seem to be better able to cope with their anxiety about being separated from their primary caregivers. (After Kagan, 1984)*

Figure 11–3

KAGAN'S DISCREPANCY HYPOTHESIS. *According to Jerome Kagan and others, children respond to novel stimuli in a characteristic curvilinear emotional response pattern. The upward arc of the curve represents an infant's response to a stimulus that is moderately discrepant from the stimuli with which the infant is already familiar. Once the infant has become sufficiently familiar with the stimulus (via assimilation or accommodation), the infant loses interest in the stimulus, as shown by the downward arc of the curve. (After Kagan, Kearsley, & Zalazo, 1978)*

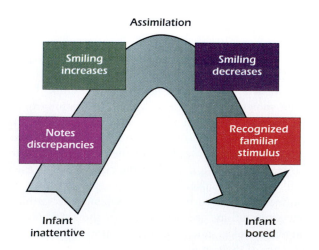

Children handle emotions differently at different points in development. For example, the appearance of a stranger can cause anxiety to an infant, an emotion sometimes referred to as *stranger anxiety*. Research suggests that infants of different ages handle their emotions in response to strangers differently. Six-month-olds confronted with a stranger often look away or become fussy, but 18-month-olds are more likely to use self-soothing and distraction to cope with the anxiety potentially aroused by a stranger (Mangelsdorf, Shapiro, & Marzolf, 1995).

Theories of Emotional Development

Numerous theories of emotional development have been proposed to account for how infants, who have very little experience, grow into adults with a wide range of emotional responses and experiences. All of these theories acknowledge an interaction between nature and nurture in the development of emotions. Here, we consider three theories of emotional development: differentiation theory, discrete-emotions theory, and cognitive-evolutionary theory.

Some theories of emotional development deal with when we develop various kinds of emotions.

Differentiation theory (Sroufe, 1979, 1996) posits that we are born with a single, generalized state of arousal and that this emotional state gradually becomes differentiated into the various emotions we feel as adults. Thus, just as cognitive abilities may become more specialized over time, so may emotions.

Whereas differentiation theory construes emotions as specializing over time, **discrete-emotions theory** asserts that the human neural system is innately predisposed to feel various discrete emotions, given the appropriate situation in which to express those emotions (Izard, 1977, 1991, 1994; Izard, Kagan, & Zajonc, 1984; Izard, Fantauzzo, Castle, Haynes, & Slomine, 1995). The emotions are generated by specific neural patterns in our brains, and each emotion appears when it first acquires value to the infant in adapting to the environment. For example, distress becomes relevant when the infant wants to learn to summon the parent: The infant becomes upset, and his or her crying summons the parent's attention. The innate predisposition may be part of our neural physiology.

Other psychologists (Campos, Barrett, Lamb, Goldsmith, & Stenberg, 1983) have recognized the *evolutionary adaptive functions* of emotions in animals—that is, emotions help an organism adapt to its own changing needs, as well as to changing circumstances in the environment. For example, feeling fear can be adaptive when one needs to run away from a source of danger. The emotions people develop at different times depend on their goals and needs as they interact with events. A child may feel upset when the babysitter knocks at the door, but the parent may feel relieved.

This evolutionary approach proposes five basic emotions: joy, anger, sadness, fear, and interest. Each occurs because of different perceptions of a situation. *Joy* results from believing we are about to achieve a goal, *anger* from the perception that we are or will be confronted by a hindrance. *Sadness* results when we come to see a goal as unattainable, and so on. Different emotions also engender different behavior. Anger often leads to actions designed to eliminate obstacles, such as an aggressive response to someone who tries to interfere with what you wish to do. In contrast, *fear* often results in flight or withdrawal from the fear-producing stimulus. *Interest* derives from moderate novelty and perceived possible relevance to one's life.

Each person's range of emotions and tendencies for expressing them contribute to the unique personality of that individual. How we develop our personality and become more aware of our selves is the topic of the next section.

Personality Development

[**In** *Search of . . .*] What changes occur in personality over time and why do they occur?

Personality and personality development are covered in more detail in chapter 15. Here, we consider the develoment of personality as it bears on a person's sense of being a unique individual in his or her social landscape. What is it that makes us sense who we are? Of the many aspects of personality development, this chapter covers only a few. (See chapter 15 for more on personality, especially regarding Sigmund Freud's views on the development of aspects of personality.)

Erikson's Theory of Personality and Identity Development

Because personality development is so multifaceted, is it possible to capture its many aspects within a single theory of discontinuous development? Erik Erikson (1950, 1968) attempted to do so in his **psychosocial theory** of personality development, which deals with how social factors interact with personality throughout the entire life span. One's identity—or sense of who one is—continues to develop throughout one's entire life. Today, the majority of developmental psychologists agree that personality development continues throughout the life span, so a stage-based theory of personality development such as Erikson's, with stages for the whole of the life span, now seems quite natural. Erickson's theory is not as strictly linked to age levels as some other theories. Rather, it is closely linked to predictable crises that occur in one's personal development. The manner in which a person resolves each crisis results in progress in the formation of personality, in general, and self-concept, in particular.

When Erikson first proposed the theory in 1950, however, the idea of a stage-based theory continuing into adulthood was a novelty. Until then the vast majority of stage theories had ended at adolescence or even earlier. Psychologists viewed any developmental processes that might exist thereafter as trivial and uninteresting. Even today, a gap persists between *child psychologists*, who study development only in children, and *life-span psychologists*, who study development throughout people's lives.

Erikson's theory of psychosocial development is still one of the most widely used and accepted. Each stage represents a developmental challenge that the psychologically healthy person meets. According to Erikson's theory, the unhealthy person fails to meet one or more challenges and must continue throughout life trying to cope with the conflicts that emerge because of this failure. The eight stages are as follows.

Stage 1—Trust versus mistrust (birth to 1 year). Infants learn either to trust or to mistrust that their needs will be met. They come to view the world as either basically friendly or basically hostile. Successful passage through this stage leads to the development of a *hopeful* attitude toward life and what can be gleaned from it.

Stage 2—Autonomy versus shame and doubt (ages 1–3). Children learn to exist within the expanded horizons of the environment. Those who do not master this stage doubt themselves and feel shame about themselves and their abilities in general. Those who do master the challenge become self-sufficient in walking, talking, eating, going to the toilet, and so on. Successful passage through this stage leads to the development of the *will*—a sense of control and mastery over their own emotions, thoughts, and behaviors. (Recall the emotional developments related to the developing sense of autonomy.)

Stage 3—Initiative versus guilt (ages 3–6). Children learn how to take initiative and to assert themselves in socially acceptable ways. However, children whose independence leads to excessive or unresolved conflict with authority figures may feel guilty and may have difficulty in taking initiative. Successful passage through this third stage engenders a sense of *purpose* in life.

Stage 4—Industry versus inferiority (ages 6–12). Children learn a sense of capability and of industriousness in their work. Those who do not develop this sense develop feelings of incompetence and low self-worth; they may feel unable to do many things well. The child who successfully passes through this stage develops a sense of *competence.*

Stage 5—Identity versus role confusion (adolescence). Adolescents try to figure out who they are, what they value, and who they will grow up to become. They try to integrate intellectual, social, sexual, ethical, and other aspects of themselves into a unified self-identity. Those who succeed develop a sense of *fidelity* to themselves. Those who do not remain confused about who they are and what to do with their lives.

Stage 6—Intimacy versus isolation (early adulthood). The emerging adult tries to commit him- or herself to a loving intimate relationship. The adult who succeeds learns how to *love* in a giving and nonselfish way. The adult who fails develops a sense of isolation and may fail to connect with the significant others in his or her life.

Stage 7—Generativity versus stagnation (middle adulthood). Adults try to be productive in their work and to contribute to the next generation, whether through ideas, products, raising children, or some combination. This productivity is termed *generativity.* Adults who do not succeed in passing through this stage become stagnant and possibly self-centered as well, leaving no lasting mark for having been alive.

Stage 8—Integrity versus despair (old age). People try to make sense of the lives they have led and, in particular, of the choices they have made. They may not feel as though every decision was right, in which case they must come to terms with their mistakes. Adults who succeed in this stage gain the *wisdom* of older age. Adults who fail may feel a sense of despair over mistakes or lost opportunities.

Do these stages actually exist? It is hard to say because no one has yet proposed a test that would clearly disconfirm the model. Certainly, these conflicts emerge at the ages specified in many people. Whether they are the primary conflicts is an open question. Clearly, the theory does not address cultural generality. For example, is our culture's emphasis on generativity really something that must characterize every human life? Are there not alternatives to the development of typical intimate sexual love relationships in early adulthood? Must those who cannot accept past mistakes fall into permanent despair? Probably no theory of psychosocial development will fully encompass every conflict for every person in every culture. Erikson's theory, however, does quite a commendable job of clarifying some of the main personal conflicts in Western society.

Marcia's Theory: The Achievement of a Personal Identity

Erikson's theory deals with attempts to form and re-form identity. Is it possible to specify in more detail the kinds of personal identities an adolescent, and ultimately an adult, can achieve? James Marcia (1966, 1980) has proposed that four kinds of identities can emerge as a result of conflicts and decision making. Note that these identities add another dimension to Erikson's theory, not a separate series of stages. These four identities are *identity achievement, foreclosure, identity diffusion,* and *moratorium* (see Table 11-2). People who have reached identity achievement would move beyond Erikson's stage of development for identity, but those with any of the other three identities would be blocked from progressing beyond that stage.

As an example of how psychological theories are intertwined with and even determined by the times, Marcia added a fifth identity during the Vietnam War. *Alienated achievement* characterizes the individual who considers the values of mainstream society to

TABLE 11–2

Marcia's Achievement of Personal Identity   *You can assess your own personal identity by asking yourself the two key questions in this table. Note that this matrix does not show the possible fifth identity, alienated achievement.*

		DO YOU MAKE COMMITMENTS (E.G., TO A CAREER, TO A MATE, TO YOUR VALUES)?	
		Yes	*No*
HAVE YOU ENGAGED IN A PERIOD OF ACTIVE SEARCH FOR IDENTITY?	*Yes*	You have reached *identity achievement*, having a firm and relatively secure sense of who you are. You have made conscious and purposeful commitments to your occupation, religion, beliefs about sex roles, and the like. You have considered the views, beliefs, and values held by others in achieving this identity, but you have branched out to achieve your own resolution.	Your identity is in *moratorium*, and you are currently having an identity crisis (turning point). You do not yet have clear commitments to society or a clear sense of who you are, but you are actively trying to reach that point.
	No	Your identity is in *foreclosure*; you have committed yourself to an occupation and various ideological positions, but you show little evidence of having followed a process of self-construction. You have simply adopted the attitudes of others, without serious searching and questioning; you have foreclosed on the possibility of arriving at your own unique identity.	You are experiencing *identity diffusion*, essentially lacking direction. You are unconcerned about political, religious, moral, or even occupational issues. You go your own way, not worrying about why others are doing what they are doing.

be inappropriate, or even bankrupt, and who rejects identification with that society. The individual does not respect the direction society has taken, and so separates him- or herself from it.

Like Erikson's theory of personality development as a whole, Marcia's theory may be culturally bound. Also, his theory has not generated much evidence either to confirm or to disconfirm it. Still, Marcia's theory provides an interesting way to view identity development, and each of us can probably think of persons who fall into each of his categories. The category into which one falls is likely to affect both how others see us and how we see ourselves. This latter issue, of how we see ourselves, brings us to the issue of self-concept.

A Developing Sense of Self: Self-Concept

Self-concept can be defined as an individual's view of her- or himself, which may or may not be realistic or even perceived similarly by other persons. A more

specific, culturally relevant definition of self-concept is one that includes our sense of *independence*, or autonomy and individuality, and our sense of *interdependence*, the feeling of belonging and collectivity (see, e.g., Markus & Kitayama, 1991). Although both of these aspects of self are important, the influence of culture determines how independence and interdependence combine to characterize a specific individual. For example, some Asian societies, such as those in China and Japan, tend to socialize individuals to be interdependent and collectivistic, whereas most Western societies tend to foster independence and emphasize individualism. Misunderstandings can arise between people of different cultures when the priorities with which they grew up come into conflict. For example, an adolescent from an individualistic culture may have trouble understanding why an adolescent from a collectivistic culture places so much emphasis on pleasing his or her parents and family.

Most research in developmental psychology emphasizes two other aspects of the self-concept:

self-understanding and self-esteem. Self-understanding is mainly cognitive, and self-esteem is mainly emotional.

Self-Understanding

Self-understanding refers to the way individuals comprehend themselves, including the various roles and characteristics that form a part of the individual's identities—as good students, as superathletes, as nice persons, as political activists, and so on. William Damon and Daniel Hart (1982, 1992) have presented an integrative model of the development of self-understanding. According to this theory, each of us has four aspects of the self: the *physical self*—our name, body, and material possessions; the *active self*—how we behave and are capable of behaving; the *social self*—the relationships we have with others; and the *psychological self*—our feelings, thoughts, beliefs, and personality characteristics.

At different ages, different aspects of self take precedence in the self-concept. During the first 2 or 3 years of life, a sense of self-awareness starts to emerge. The first signs of emergence relate to the physical self (see Bertenthal & Fischer, 1978; L. E. Levine, 1983). During the first year, infants develop an awareness of the babies they see in the mirror, come to have expectations about what they look like, and recognize their own names. During the second year, toddlers can say their own names, identify their own gender and age, and clearly recognize their own possessions: "mine." Another aspect of self-understanding also emerges during the preschool years: a sense of mastery (Kagan, 1981). When 2-year-olds cannot succeed at doing something they want to do, they appear clearly frustrated, and when they can succeed, they appear obviously pleased with themselves (recall Erikson's stages of autonomy versus shame and doubt and of initiative versus guilt). Lev Vygotsky (1934/1962) pointed out that at about 3 to 4 years of age, children begin to differentiate between the speech they direct toward themselves (e.g., while playing alone) and the speech they direct toward others (e.g., when talking to a parent). Eventually, inner-directed speech becomes internal and silent; it becomes thought. Despite these accomplishments, preschool-aged children largely emphasize their physical selves; what they look like constitutes who they are.

During the elementary school years, children increasingly focus on their active selves. Children emphasize what they can *do*—dance, play soccer, achieve high grades. In early adolescence, children concentrate on their social selves, paying special attention to developing peer relations. Finally, in late adolescence, teens turn their attention to their psychological selves and to an understanding of who they are as persons. They consider their beliefs, values, thoughts, and atti-

tudes important to who they are. Damon and Hart's model stops in adolescence, as do many developmental models, but development of the self continues throughout adulthood, as shown by Erikson's models.

The Damon and Hart model, like many developmental models, seems to be one of *successive differentiation*—as we develop, generalized concepts of ourselves become more highly differentiated and more specialized in terms of the aspects of the self. In addition, just as we become increasingly aware of how we differ from other people, we also come to realize more and more the ways we are bound up with others, through the institutions of culture and society, through the organizations we participate in, and through the choices we make. Humans are highly interdependent, and to some extent, our context influences the way we perceive ourselves. Damon and Hart's research was based on American children, and children in other cultures may well place more emphasis on their social selves, rooted in a social context and defined partly by the society with which they interact. In Western societies, self-understanding in adults may also be more differentiated according to our social context. We may think of ourselves as psychologically well-adjusted at home but not at work, or vice versa. Such differences in self-perception can lead to a complex picture of self-esteem, the construct to which we now turn.

Self-Esteem

Self-esteem refers to the degree which a person values him- or herself. According to research by Susan Harter (1990), our self-concepts become increasingly differentiated over the course of development; as we explore our abilities and learn more skills, our self-esteem also becomes more differentiated—we may think highly of ourselves in one area, but not in another.

Harter's differentiation hypothesis posits that between ages 4 and 7, children can make reliable judgments about themselves in four personal domains: cognitive competence, physical competence, social competence, and behavioral conduct (Harter & Pike, 1984). However, the younger the children are, the more likely their self-evaluations will show a *halo effect*—a high self-evaluation rating in one capacity that leads to a high self-evaluation rating in others as well.

Between the ages of 8 and 12 the four domains of the early years become further differentiated into five separate areas of self-esteem, which Harter categorizes somewhat differently: scholastic (rather than cognitive) competence, athletic (rather than physical) competence, peer social acceptance (rather than social competence), behavioral conduct, and physical appearance. During adolescence, even more areas of self-esteem emerge, including close friendship, romantic appeal, and job competence.

Where does self-esteem come from? William James believed it was based on a weighted average of our perceived competencies, with those qualities we feel most important carrying the most weight. An alternative view is that our self-esteem is based mostly on the social judgments of other people. There is evidence that both internal evaluation and others' judgments play a role in how we see ourselves.

By adulthood, 11 areas of competency emerge as aspects of self-worth: intelligence, sense of humor, job competence, morality, athletic ability, physical appearance, sociability, intimacy, nurturance, adequacy as a provider, and household management (Messer & Harter, 1985).

Where does self-esteem come from? According to William James (1890b), overall self-esteem involves more than merely averaging our perceived competencies; instead, we consider the importance of each competency and form a weighted average. For example, if a boy does not think much of his physical abilities, but he also does not place much weight on physical competence, then his overall self-esteem may still be quite high. By contrast, another boy might heavily weigh the same skill and would therefore feel less good about himself if he believed that he was not athletic.

An alternative view of self-esteem (Cooley, 1982) is that for each of us, our self-esteem is largely determined by other people's social judgments of us. As we absorb and integrate their evaluations, their cumulative evaluations eventually become our own self-evaluations. Evidence exists, however, to support a synthesis of the two positions (Harter, 1985). On the one hand, we do have internal evaluations, and we do not weigh equally the dimensions along which we evaluate ourselves. On the other hand, others' judgments of us

affect our judgment of ourselves. Once again we find that theoretical stances originally proposed as alternatives may ultimately be more complementary than contradictory. A synthesis can incorporate the best aspects of the thesis and its antithesis.

Generally, children's perceptions of their abilities become both more modest and more accurate as the children grow older (Eccles, Wigfield, Harold, & Blumenfeld, 1993; Frey & Ruble, 1987; Phillips & Zimmerman, 1990; Stipek, 1984). However, when self-perceptions are too modest and therefore inaccurate, problems result. Teachers and parents cannot neglect the importance of self-perceptions, especially because even inaccurate self-perceptions guide how children handle both schoolwork and life outside of school (Phillips, 1984, 1987). Self-evaluations of low ability lead to motivational problems, especially in older children (Rholes, Jones, & Wade, 1980). Children who underestimate their abilities also seem to seek out less challenging tasks than do more realistic children (see Harter, 1983). In addition, children who seriously underestimate themselves have low expectations for their success, believe that respected adults also take a dim view of their abilities, are reluctant to sustain effort in difficult tasks, and are more anxious about being evaluated than are other children (Phillips & Zimmerman, 1990).

Gender Differences in Self-Esteem

Research has suggested that differences in false or illusory perceptions of low competence are affected by gender, as determined by the difference between children's self-evaluations and their achievement-test scores. At the third and fifth grades, no gender differences exist, but at the ninth-grade level, virtually all those who wrongly believe themselves academically incompetent in particular areas are girls (Phillips & Zimmerman, 1990). Other investigators (e.g., Entwistle & Baker, 1983) have found differences as early as first grade, again with girls more than boys tending to believe themselves less competent in particular subjects.

A report by the American Association of University Women (AAUW) Education Foundation has found that girls who enter school roughly equal in abilities and self-esteem tend to leave school deficient in mathematical ability and in self-esteem, as compared with boys (AAUW, 1992). Why does this change occur? Research has shown that girls receive less attention from teachers, and that curricula in schools emphasize almost exclusively male achievements (C. Nelson, 1990; Sadker & Sadker, 1984). It appears also that early adolescence is a particularly difficult period for girls. Researchers Annie Rogers and Carol Gilligan (1988) have found that young girls are extremely self-confident until age 11 or 12 years, after which they become more conflicted about themselves and their roles in the world. In later adolescence, girls often have to cope with a negative body image, low self-esteem, and depression. Some researchers point to the inequality in society as a cause of adolescent inner turmoil in girls (AAUW, 1992) and so recommend policy changes in education.

Some of the differences between boys and girls may develop because of gender-related messages children receive in school (Ruble & Martin, 1998). The power structure in many schools is predominantly male, and in some elementary schools, perhaps the only male member of the faculty may be the principal. Teachers also often pay more attention to boys than to girls, with the result that girls may become successively more likely to show underachievement as they grow older (Eccles et al., 1993; Eccles, Wigfield, & Schiefele, 1998).

Our understandings and evaluations of ourselves become more complex and differentiated and more psychological and abstract across the life span. Also, throughout childhood and adolescence, we increasingly consider what others think and say about us and how they behave toward us, and we may internalize what we perceive others to believe about us. In adulthood, we continue to consider our perceptions of how others feel about us, but we also measure ourselves against our own internalized criteria for ourselves, giving more weight to some aspects of ourselves than to other aspects. One thing that may affect how others feel about us is our temperament.

Temperament

Some people get angry easily but get over it quickly. Others are slow to anger but have more difficulty recovering. Still others rarely get angry at all. Differences such as these are ones of **temperament**—a person's distinctive tendency to show a particular mood and a particular intensity and duration of emotion. Temperament is relatively consistent across situations and over time (Rothbart & Bates, 1998) and is affected by both genetic and environmental factors (Caspi, 1998). Temperament influences the development of personality and of relationships with other people (Thompson, 1999). Some of the most well-known and well-regarded work on temperament was done by A. Thomas and Stella Chess in a longitudinal study with children, starting at their birth and continuing until their adolescence (e.g., A. Thomas & Chess, 1977, 1987; A. Thomas, Chess, & Birch, 1970).

The study described three types of temperament in babies. *Easy babies,* who constituted roughly 40% of the sample, were playful, adaptable, and regular in their eating and other bodily functions. They were interested in novel situations and responded moderately to them. *Difficult babies,* by contrast, who constituted

10% of the sample, were irritable and not very adaptable. They avoided unfamiliar situations and reacted intensely to them. *Slow-to-warm-up babies,* 15% of the sample, had relatively low activity levels and showed minimal responses to novelty. They avoided new situations and in general needed more time than other babies to adapt to them. Even though more than one in every three babies, the remaining 35%, could not be classified according to these criteria, the categories have proven helpful in understanding temperament.

To what extent do the differences in infant temperament remain stable throughout development? There is some evidence for stability. Several studies (Kagan & Moss, 1962; Kagan, Reznick, Clarke, Snidman, & Garcia-Coll, 1984) have found consistency in temperament over time. In one study, children identified either as highly inhibited or essentially fearless at 21 months showed related patterns at age 4. In particular, three-fourths of the inhibited children remained inhibited, and none of the children who had been fearless had become inhibited. Calkins and Fox (1994) also found that inhibited behavior in childhood was predicted by temperamental characteristics in infancy.

How Temperament Affects Social Development

At first glance, temperament research seems only to state the obvious. Is it really surprising that two categories of babies are "easy" and "difficult"? Could these categories really change the way we look at babies? Yes. In fact, Thomas and Chess's work profoundly changed the way we view the *person-environment interaction*—the individual fit between a particular person and the environment in which the individual develops and interacts with others. Prior to the work of Thomas and Chess, researchers and practitioners in child development tended to ask, "What is the single best environment for infants and young children?" Countless books were written telling parents what constitutes a good or a bad environment for children, conceiving of "children" as a generic unit. The Thomas and Chess work, however, suggested that this question, as posed, is unanswerable. Rather, they showed, we ought to ask, "Which environment is best for which baby?" Clearly, not all babies are the same; different environments can provide the right nurturing atmosphere for different children.

The same basic idea applies to adults. Some people thrive on stressful and changeable environments where there is a new and difficult challenge almost every day; others require more stable settings in which they perceive less threat to their well-being. The true gift of this research was the idea that each individual needs to discover the optimally suitable environment.

Evaluating the Influence of Temperament

The ideas of Thomas and Chess have not been universally accepted (e.g., Kagan, 1982; Wasserman, Di Basio, Bond, Young, & Collett, 1990). For example, Thomas and Chess suggested that difficult children are essentially unmodifiable and that attempts by parents to change these children would only result in increased difficulty. These parents, according to the researchers, need patience more than anything else. However, consider some of the implications of this notion. One is that some babies are, in a sense, preferable to others. The terms *easy* and *difficult* almost certainly involve value judgments, and the danger is that parents with "difficult" children might think that their children are inferior.

A second implication is that parents should not blame themselves for difficult children—that is just the way the children are. To the extent that parents may have felt guilty about their children's behavior, perhaps this implication is constructive. However, there are grave dangers associated with the self-fulfilling prophecy. Once people perceive a child as "difficult," rightly or wrongly assigning the label and all that it implies, they may start to treat the child accordingly. Eventually, the child may make the prophecy come true by behaving according to the expectations. Even worse, the misbehaving child may then become a candidate for abuse (Starr, Dietrich, Fischoff, Ceresnie, & Zweier, 1984).

When we talk about "easy" or "difficult" children, or "friendly" versus "unfriendly" people, we are clearly placing value judgments on certain types of personality or other attributes. But there is no one "better type" of person from an evolutionary point of view. The adaptiveness of different personality attributes can differ from time to time, place to place, and person to person. In fact, few people are merely of a single type. Genes that might have committed people to being of just one type probably would have lost out evolutionarily to genes that provided a more flexible personality (Trivers, 1971; Wright, 1994). In personality and temperament, as in other attributes, the individual is at greatest advantage who is flexible in his or her pattern of behavior.

Psychosexual Development and Theories of Gender Typing

Psychosexual development refers to increasing self-identification with a particular gender and changing self-perceptions about sexuality. Obviously, adolescence is a period of rapid psychological and sexual growth but most developmental psychologists believe that psychosexual development starts much earlier than adolescence. In fact, children form gender identifications by the age of 2 or 3 (R. F. Thompson, 1975). **Gender typ-**

If this toddler is labeled as having a "difficult" temperament, how might that label affect the way her father and other people treat her?

ing, the process of acquiring the roles and associations related to the social and psychological distinction as being male or female, begins early, too. From ages 2 to 7, children seem to have rather rigid sex-role stereotypes; by the end of this period, they develop **gender constancy**—the realization that a person's gender is stable and cannot be changed by changing superficial characteristics or behaviors, such as hairstyle or the carrying of a purse. What are some of the main theories of sex-role acquisition and gender development?

Biological and Sociobiological Theories

Biological theories of sex-role acquisition (e.g., Benbow & Stanley, 1980) hold that boys and girls acquire different sex roles because they are genetically predisposed to do so. Likewise, sociobiological theories (Kenrick & Trost, 1993) hold that evolution determines or at least guides social behavior, in this case, sex-role differences (Buss, 1996). Obviously, many differences between the sexes have their bases in biological factors. The anatomies and physiologies of men and women are simply different. Still, why do people tend to perceive men as more dominant than women or as more likely to be interested in athletic activities? Are such personality and interest patterns biological or are they the result of *socialization,* whereby we learn ways of feeling, thinking, and acting by observing and imitating parents, siblings, peers, and other role models?

Social-Learning Theory

In contrast to sociobiological and biological theories, social learning theory (Bandura, 1977b) accounts for psychosexual development in terms of role models and rewards in the external environment. In this view, gender typing is no different from other kinds of social learning. Adults and peers reward boys for behavior considered masculine and punish them if they depart too far from what is considered gender appropriate. Similarly, adults and peers reward girls for emulating female role models and punish them if they go too far afield. Thus, each generation repeats the sex-role patterns of the past, albeit with some modification. Boys act like boys, or girls like girls, simply via imitation of what they perceive to be appropriate role models.

Observational learning clearly plays an important role in the establishment of gender identity. In addition, parents bolster these observations by encouraging gender-specific behaviors. For example, parents are more likely to encourage independence, competitiveness, and achievement in boys, and sensitivity, empathy, and trustworthiness in girls (Archer & Lloyd, 1985; Block, 1980, 1983; A. C. Huston, Carpenter, Atwater, & Johnson, 1986). Whereas boys are more encouraged to be independent, girls are more encouraged both to request help from others and to provide help to them (A. C. Huston, 1983).

Role modeling is important throughout life and in arenas other than gender. Perhaps the most important time for role modeling is during high school, college, and early adulthood. During these years, young adults cast around for models to emulate. Often, the role-modeling function of a respected adult is more important than what he or she may have directly to teach or to show. Role modeling becomes especially important as an individual tries to figure out what it means to be a professional in a given field. For example, students may learn from their teachers the importance of explaining difficult concepts to children in terms these children can understand. Workers new to a job often try to emulate those above them on the organizational ladder, hoping eventually to fill the niches of those superiors. Role modeling is not just an abstract psychological idea but rather an active process by which we develop into the kind of person we wish to become. Part of who we become depends on our schemas.

Schema Theory

Sandra Bem (1981, 1993) proposed a more cognitively based theory, **schema theory,** which holds that organized mental systems of information (i.e., *schemas*) help people both to make sense of their experiences and to shape their interactions, particularly in terms of their gender-relevant schemas for how males and females demonstrate differing sex-role-relevant behaviors and attitudes. We have gender schemas that differ for boys and girls and for men and women. The schema view suggests that we acquire sex roles by following the gender-appropriate schemas we have conceived. Individuals are seen as socially constructing their gender concepts with the help of those around them (Beall & Sternberg, 1993, 1995). We acquire our schemas through interactions with the environment but they also guide our interactions. In other words, we learn gender typing from the world, and then these gender-typing ideas guide how we behave in the world, as well as how the world responds to our behavior. For example, a man who learns that acting tough is part of being "male" may act tough toward others, leading others to respond to the man in particular ways—perhaps unsympathetically—that reflect the way they are treated. In general, schema theories tend to focus on specific concepts that individuals may incorporate into their schemas rather than on the developmental sequence of an integrated, global concept of gender.

Conclusions About Gender-Role Development

Gender theories typically deal with masculinity and femininity as opposite ends of a continuum, but it is important to note that this view is by no means universally accepted. Some theorists do not see masculinity and femininity as mutually exclusive constructs (S. L. Bem, 1981). Instead, they suggest that it is possible to conceive of someone as being masculine and feminine simultaneously. Some theorists have argued that theories of gender typing also need to take into account the concept of *androgyny,* which can refer either to a person high in both masculinity and femininity or to a person for whom stereotypically masculine and feminine behavior simply are not very relevant. Using the schema theory, we would say that an androgynous person does not have very strong sex-based schemas. Rather, he or she acts in ways that seem appropriate to the situation, regardless of stereotypes about how people of a particular gender should act.

Although nature clearly plays a role in sex differences, nurture also plays an important role. Our own schemas for boys and girls may influence the way we perceive our children of each sex, and these perceptions may in turn influence the way our children respond to us. Quite simply, there is no foolproof way to extricate the effects of pure biology from the effects of environment.

Thus far, this chapter has focused on intrapersonal development—development within a person—

as exemplified by emotional and personality development. We have yet to discuss the particular ways our interpersonal interactions both affect and are affected by our own development as individuals.

Interpersonal Development

In *Search of . . .*

How do people develop interpersonal skills?

As they grow up, children become increasingly aware of others and increasingly consider the perspectives of others throughout childhood and adolescence. This section considers specifically the ways we interact directly with others, starting with our early attachment to our parents and progressing ever outward into the wider community of other children and adults.

Attachment

Attachment refers to a strong and relatively long-lasting emotional tie between two humans (Bowlby, 1969). Our first attachment begins at birth (although some mothers contend that it begins even earlier) and is usually fully cemented within several years. Babies form long-term emotional attachments to their parents, especially their primary caregivers—usually their mothers. As mentioned at the beginning of the chapter, separation anxiety is a very early and common emotional expression. Mary Ainsworth and her colleagues (Ainsworth, Bell, & Stayton, 1971; Ainsworth, Blehar, Waters, & Wall, 1978) conducted some of the best-known work on attachment. In particular, Ainsworth and her colleagues have studied attachment by using a research paradigm known as the **strange situation:** In this paradigm, the research participants are usually a toddler, 12 to 18 months of age, and the toddler's mother. The mother and her infant enter a room containing a variety of toys. The mother puts down the infant and sits in a chair. A few minutes later, an unfamiliar woman enters the room, talks to the mother, and then tries to play with the child. While the stranger is trying to engage the child, the mother quietly walks out of the room, leaving her purse on the chair to indicate that she will return. Later, the mother returns. An observer positioned behind a one-way mirror records the child's reactions to the mother's return. Still later, the mother leaves yet again, but this time the child is left alone. The mother returns once more, and the observer records the child's reactions again. (See Figure 11-4.)

Figure 11–4
STRANGE SITUATION. *In the "strange situation," researchers observe the attachment of children to their mothers by noting how each child reacts to the mother's departure and her return.*

Ainsworth noticed that children's reactions tend to fit one of three different patterns: avoidant, secure, and resistant. In the **avoidant attachment pattern** ("Type A"), the child generally ignores the mother while she is present, and the child shows minimal distress when the mother leaves. If the child does show distress, the stranger is about as effective as the mother in providing comfort.

In the **secure attachment pattern** ("Type B"), the child generally shows preferential interest in—but not excessive dependence on—the attention of the mother while she is present. The child shows some distress when the mother leaves but can be calmed and reassured by her when she returns, usually through holding and hugging. The secure child is friendly with the stranger but shows an obvious preference for the mother.

In the **resistant attachment pattern** ("Type C"), the child generally shows ambivalence toward the mother while she is present, seeking both to gain and to resist physical contact with her when the mother returns after being gone a short time. For example, the child might run to the mother when she returns, but then, when held, tries to extricate him- or herself.

A further type of attachment pattern has also been proposed, which is related to the avoidant and resistant attachment patterns. This pattern is sometimes called a *disorganized attachment pattern* (Main & Solomon, 1990). When babies with this attachment pattern are reunited with their mothers, they seem confused and disoriented. Sometimes they look dazed or as though they are not sure what is happening to them.

Evaluating Attachment Theory

Just how much credence can we give to attachment theory, as measured in the strange situation? Researchers differ in their views, and some are skeptical (e.g., Kagan, 1986). For example, there are a number of possible limitations to the strange situation. First, an infant's attachment pattern appears not to be highly stable, at least as the strange situation has measured it. In one study, for example, roughly half of the infants classified one way at age 12 months were classified another way at age 18 months (R. A. Thompson, Lamb, & Estes, 1982). Second, the strange situation may measure temperament at least as much as attachment. Highly independent infants might be classified as avoidant, whereas infants classified as ambivalent or resistant might be those who are upset by almost any new situation, regardless of whether it involves the mother. Third, the procedure itself is brief, requiring typically only 6 to 8 minutes. How much can we tell about infants, or anyone, in

such a short span of time? Fourth, interpretation is somewhat more complex, in that the implied value judgments in the terms used for classification are open to question. Finally, it is important to remember that a number of factors can affect attachment pattern, such as societal norms and cultural mores (Colin, 1996; Thompson, 1998). Thus, attachment patterns valued in one culture may be less valued in another, as discussed below.

Socioeconomic status and environment also seem to play roles in attachment patterns. Ainsworth worked primarily with American middle-class children from stable homes during the 1970s, and she found that about 20% to 25% of children were avoidant, roughly 65% were secure, and approximately 12% were resistant. However, researchers have found different patterns among children in other cultural and socioeconomic contexts. For example, children in nonstable, nonintact American families of lower socioeconomic status are more likely to be considered avoidant or resistant (Egeland & Sroufe, 1981; Vaughn, Gove, & Egeland, 1980). Studies of other cultures have shown more avoidant children among Western Europeans and more resistant children among Israelis and the Japanese (Bretherton & Waters, 1985; Miyake, Chen, & Campos, 1985; Morelli, Rogoff, Oppenheim, & Goldsmith, 1992). If German children, who are more likely to show avoidant attachment behavior, are encouraged to be independent at an early age, why should we categorize such an independent pattern as somehow less than secure? Clearly, values regarding attachment patterns differ across cultures (Thompson, 1998).

Do attachment patterns have any long-term consequences? If so, what are they? John Bowlby (1951, 1969) claimed that an infant's attachment pattern has long-term effects on the child's development, and some evidence supports this claim. For example, infants who are securely attached at age 12 or 18 months approach problems when they are age 2 with greater interest and enthusiasm than do avoidant or resistant children (Matas, Arend, & Sroufe, 1978). Similarly, securely attached children in nursery school tend to be more active, more sought out by other children, and rated by their teachers as more eager to learn (Waters, Wippman, & Sroufe, 1979). In other words, secure attachment in infancy predicts a number of advantages in both cognitive and social adaptation later on.

Attachment to Fathers

Attachment research originally focused on the role of the mother in the life of the infant but later turned to studying the role of the father, and others as well (Ricks, 1985). Infants do become attached to fathers, protesting separations beginning at about 7 months of age (Lamb, 1977a, 1977b, 1979, 1996). At home, the infants approach fathers, smile at them, and seek contact with them. Fathers feeding their 3-month-old children can show the same sensitivity to cues as do mothers, but fathers rarely use this skill, usually yielding the feeding function to the mother (Parke & Sawin, 1980; Parke & Tinsley, 1987).

When the father substitutes for the mother in the strange situation, the child uses the father as a haven. Children prefer fathers to a strange female as well. In addition, infants who are cared for by their fathers while their mothers are at work are more likely to show secure attachment than are infants who are cared for outside the home (Belsky & Rovine, 1988).

Fathers seem to provide a different kind of care from mothers. They tend to have a more physical approach in playing with their children (Clarke-Stewart, Perlmutter, & Friedman, 1988; Parke, 1981, 1996) and engage in more novel games than do mothers (Lamb, 1977b). One study found that two-thirds of toddlers prefer playing with their fathers to playing with their mothers (Clarke-Stewart, 1978). Also, the relationship between toddlers and their fathers may be more instrumental than their relationships with their mothers in helping the infants to widen their social contacts and to interact sociably with persons outside their families (Bridges, Connell, & Belsky, 1988).

Adult Attachment

Attachment does not end in childhood. Robert Weiss (1982) has noted that adults, like children, tend to attach themselves to others. Attachment is crucial to the establishment of intimacy. Indeed, one of the main purposes of intimate relationships is to give adults someone to comfort them in times of need and to provide them with something resembling the closeness they once had with a childhood attachment figure. Although we still lack sufficient hard data to assert unequivocally that the quality of our early attachments to our parents affects the quality of our attachments as adults, some evidence suggests this relationship between early and later attachments (Feeney & Noller, 1990; Hazan & Shaver, 1994; Main, Kaplan, & Cassidy, 1985; Scharfe & Bartholomew, 1994).

Adults who have secure styles of attachment tend to be comfortable about, and to speak freely about, their relationship with their parents. People with a resistant style appear to be ambivalent about, and sometimes anxiously preoccupied with, their relationship with their parents. People with an avoidant style tend to try to dissociate themselves from feelings of attachment toward their parents,

Attachment does not end in childhood; it is crucial to the establishment of intimacy. One of the main purposes of intimate relationships is to give adults someone to comfort them in times of need.

thereby avoiding anxiety about their relationship (Dozier & Kobak, 1992).

Attachment Gone Awry

Children become attached to both mothers and fathers, and research has shown that members of the family or extended family can help compensate for an infant's inadequate attachment to the mother (Parke & Asher, 1983). But what happens when children are deprived of love and warmth from both father and mother and attachment processes either cannot form or go utterly awry? No scientist would conduct an experiment purposely exposing children to inadequate or distorted attachment; however, two research methods offer a way to examine such processes. One is the unfortunate instance in which naturalistic observation of extremely deprived children is possible, and the other is controlled experimentation with animals.

In one case of extreme deprivation, a girl named Genie (Curtiss, 1977) had been isolated in a small room, strapped to a potty chair, from roughly ages 2 to 13. Genie's only contact with humans was when a family member entered the room to give her food. When found at age 13, Genie could not walk, talk, stand up straight, or eat solid food, nor was she toilet-trained. Eventually, Genie did learn to speak a bit, but she never progressed beyond the level of a 4- to 5-year-old. Initially, Genie showed exciting improvements, and an onslaught of social scientists and social workers of all kinds descended on her. Genie now lives in an institution for retarded adults (Angier, 1993; Rymer, 1993). Although we must be wary of the conclusions we reach based on anecdotal evidence—

however rich the case material—we can clearly conclude that Genie was severely and permanently harmed by her lack of contact with loving or caring humans.

The other kind of research, controlled experimentation with animals, enables researchers to study attachment processes more directly (Harlow, 1958, 1962; Harlow & Harlow, 1965, 1966). In a series of experiments, Harry Harlow, Margaret Harlow, and other researchers raised infant monkeys with either or both of two substitute mothers—a wire mesh cylinder and a cylinder covered with soft terrycloth. Either "mother" could be set up with a bottle providing milk. Even when only the wire mother could provide milk, however, the monkeys still clung to the cloth mother, suggesting that comfort through physical contact was more important than nourishment. The monkeys also showed other signs of attachment to the cloth mother, but not to the wire mother. For example, when a frightening, noisy, bear-monster

doll was placed next to the monkeys, those raised with the cloth mother would run to it and cling, but later they would investigate the monster. The monkeys raised with the wire mother, however, just clutched themselves and rocked back and forth (see Figure 11-5).

Although the cloth mother but not the wire mother fostered attachment and security, ultimately neither surrogate proved adequate for fostering normal social development. Monkeys reared with either of the surrogate mothers were socially and sexually incompetent. Females who themselves later had children were poor mothers. Live, interactive attachment processes, therefore, appear to be crucial for the development of later social and familial competence, both in humans and in animals.

In sum, attachment is an essential part in development, and it continues to play a role throughout our lives. Although the patterns themselves may not yet be understood fully, their influence is clear. In addition to

Figure 11–5

"Mother Love" in Primates. *Harry Harlow's revolutionary research on the importance of "contact comfort" revealed that infant rhesus monkeys would become attached to—and seek comfort from—a cloth "mother" rather than from a wire "mother." Even when the wire mother provided milk, and the cloth mother did not, the infants would cling to the cloth mother most of the time. (After Harlow Primate Lab, University of Wisconsin)*

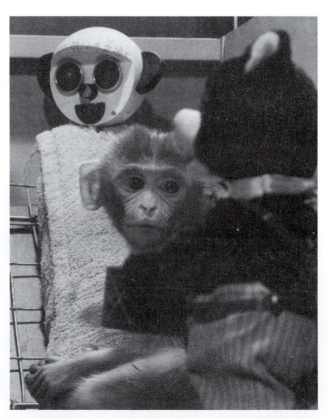

Psychology in Everyday Life

Parenting Styles

We know that large individual differences exist among parents in how they bring up children, differences that occur not only across individuals, but also across levels of education and socioeconomic status. For example, parents of lower levels of education and socioeconomic status are more likely to value obedience to authority and are more likely to use physical punishment. Parents of higher socioeconomic status and education levels are more likely to explain their actions and to let children make decisions for themselves (M. L. Kohn, 1976).

Research by Diana Baumrind (1971, 1978) suggests that parental styles of caring for children can be better understood if we view the styles in terms of three categories of parenting: authoritarian, permissive, and authoritative. **Authoritarian** mothers and fathers exhibit a style of parenting in which they tend to be firm, punitive, and generally unsympathetic to their children. These parents believe in the importance of their authority, and they value their children's obedience. They see

children as willful and in need of disciplining to meet parental standards. Authoritarian parents are somewhat detached from their children and tend to be very sparing with praise. **Permissive** mothers and fathers exhibit a style of parenting in which they tend to give their children a great deal of freedom, possibly more than the children can handle. These parents tend to be lax in discipline and to let children make their own decisions about many things that other parents might find inappropriate. **Authoritative** mothers and fathers exhibit a style of parenting in which they tend to encourage and support responsibility and reasoning in their children, explain their reasoning for what they do, and establish firm limits within which they encourage children to be independent, and which they enforce firmly but with understanding.

Research on 186 cultures (Rohner & Rohner, 1981) showed that the authoritative parenting style seemed to be the most common. Nonetheless, there are wide variations in the degrees of nurturance and control exhibited by par-

ents, and the cultural expression of nurturance and control may differ greatly. For example, Japanese mothers, whose interactions tend to foster warm and close relationships with their children, may exert firm behavioral control over their children by merely suggesting indirectly how the child's behavior may affect the quality of the relationship (Azuma, 1986).

As you might expect, differing parental styles lead to differing outcomes for the children (Baumrind, 1971, 1978, 1991). Children of authoritarian parents tend to be unfriendly, distrustful of others, and somewhat withdrawn in their social relationships. Children of permissive parents tend to be immature and dependent, seeking aid even for minor difficulties. They also tend to be unhappy in their lives in general. Children of authoritative parents seem to be the most well adapted. They tend to be friendly, generally cooperative, and relatively independent, showing a sense of responsibility in their social relations with others.

---

the quality of attachment patterns, other aspects of the child–parent relationship are important to the development of later social competence. One such aspect is the parents' style of caregiving. The Psychology in Everyday Life box on Parenting Styles describes what research has found about how different approaches to parental authority can affect how children come to see themselves in relation to others and the implications this can have on their lives.

An entirely different avenue of research suggests that being away from parents for a portion of the day may also affect children's social competence. Children who attend child-care programs seem to be more likely to interact spontaneously with other children than do those who do not attend. Participation in child care is not unequivocally beneficial, however, as the following section explains.

Effects of Child Care on Children's Development

Given the importance of the child's attachment to the parents and the importance of parental style, how does child care affect children of various ages in their social development? An estimated three-fourths of the mothers with children ages 6 to 17 work outside the home, and almost 58% of the mothers with children less than 6 years of age do so (H. A. Scarr, 1994). Given that more than half of infants under the age of 12 months are experiencing care from someone other than their mothers on a routine basis (National Institute of Child Health and Human Development, 1996), it is important to understand the effects of child care.

A summary of five studies of children's responses to the strange situation revealed that 74% of infants who participated in child care fewer than 20 hours per week were securely attached, whereas 57% of infants who participated in child care more than 20 hours per week were securely attached (Belsky & Rovine, 1988). Without considering again the merits of determining attachment based on the strange situation, it appears that increased participation in child care is associated with a decreased likelihood of being securely attached. Note, however, that the majority of infants in the studies were still securely attached.

Other factors influence the outcomes of infants' participation in child care. A mother's stress level will affect her behavior toward her child. For example, mothers who work part-time rather than full-time may feel less stress (L. W. Hoffman, 1989), and mothers who can cope more successfully with their employment are more likely to have securely attached infants (Belsky & Rovine, 1988). Another stress reducer for mothers is the participation of fathers in child care and in household chores (L. W. Hoffman, 1989).

An extensive body of research (Andersson, 1989; Belsky, 1990; Clarke-Stewart, 1989, 1993; T. Field, 1990; Gottfried & Gottfried, 1988; L. W. Hoffman, 1989) regarding preschoolers and school-aged children yields mixed results. For example, some research indicates some benefits of early child care, such as sociability and greater academic success (Andersson, 1989; T. Field, 1990). Other research indicates some drawbacks of early child care, such as increased aggressive behavior and increased desire for approval by peers, when specific efforts to curb such behaviors were not implemented in the child-care setting (Clarke-Stewart, 1989, 1993).

Perhaps the best lesson from this research is the importance of evaluating and considering the quality of the specific child-care program. Children in high-quality daycare are better self-regulated, more task-oriented, more considerate, less distracting toward other children, and less hostile than children in low-quality daycare (Howes, 1990). Many factors influence the quality of the program, but the single most important factor is the amount and quality of the attention given to children. As you might expect, caregivers are more likely to provide more high-quality attention to each child when they are in charge of fewer children. This is particularly important for infants and toddlers. In addition, the professional qualifications of the caregivers (S. Scarr, Phillips, & McCartney, 1990) and the stability of the center's work force affect the quality of the program. These facts are especially understandable when one considers that annual turnover of 50% is the average for these poorly paid professionals (Wingert & Kantrowitz, 1990). Highly qualified professionals who are motivated to remain in the program can provide child-centered activities that are appropriately challenging to children's needs for open-ended, creative, hands-on exploration of a wide array of materials. What seems to matter most is not whether children are in a child-care program, but which child-care program they are in.

An additional consideration in evaluating high-quality child-care programs must be the kinds of social relationships and social behaviors the caregivers encourage among the children. Friendships and play are the next subjects we address.

Peer Interactions: Friendship and Play

An important aspect of interpersonal development is learning how to interact with peers and learning to form friendships. Indeed, social rejection by peer groups is one of the best predictors of school failure and dropout (Rubin, Bukowski, & Parker, 1998; Rubin, Coplan, Nelson, Cheah, & Lagace-Seguin, 1999). Relationships with peers during childhood are important not only for the child's well-being but, eventually, for the well-being of the adult that the child will become.

Children's friendship patterns show increases with age in the degree of interaction among the children. In other words, as children grow older, they become more intensely involved in their interpersonal interactions. During early infancy, the only social exchange between very young infants seems to be that they are more likely to cry if they see and hear another infant crying. By about 3 or 4 months, they reach toward and even touch one another when they can (Vandell & Mueller, 1980). Their interactions increase somewhat over time, and they often smile at one another, but until 1 year of age, their exchanges usually are limited to one overture and one response. During the next couple of years, play interactions increase, and children learn gradually to cooperate, share, and play with one another. Friendships appear to teach children conflict-resolution techniques, and indeed, friends are more likely than nonfriends to resolve conflicts effectively (Hartup, 1996; Newcomb & Bagwell, 1995). Preschoolers show quite stable friendship patterns, often keeping the same friend for more than a year (Howes, 1988).

Play continues to be at the center of friendships during most of childhood (Gottman, 1983, 1986; Howes, 1988). According to John Gottman (1983), friendships among children ages 3 to 9 gradually show a sharing of thoughts and feelings, an exchange of information, an establishing of common ground, conflict resolution, positive reciprocity (the friends please each other), and self-disclosure (the friends reveal intimate details about themselves).

These aspects of friendship also apply to friendships among adults.

Although parents may be in the background, they contribute to children's friendships in three ways (Parke & O'Neil, 1997, 1998). First, they can serve as interactive partners who help children acquire the skills the children need to form friendships. Second, they can serve as coaches and educators in the development of friendships. Third, they can facilitate their children's social interactions with other children.

Gender Differences in Friendships

During childhood and adolescence, the friendships of boys and of girls seem to go through rather different stages. Children of both sexes seem to prefer same-sex friends throughout this period, and early friendships usually center on shared activities and other interests. The interests and activities of girls and boys differ, however, with boys more likely to be involved in groups and in competitive activities, and girls more likely to prefer cooperative activities involving just two people.

Adolescent girls' friendships progress through three stages (Douvan & Adelson, 1966). From roughly ages 11 to 13, the emphasis is on joint activities. A friend is someone with whom to do fun things. From roughly ages 14 to 16, friendships pass through an emotional stage, with an emphasis on sharing secrets, especially about other friends, both male and female. Trust is a critical element of friendship at this stage. Actually, across the life span, females show greater emotional closeness and shared intimacies in their friendships than do males (Berndt, 1982, 1986; K. H. Rubin, 1980). This pattern may be changing, however, as young men and women, particularly the well-educated, now show fewer sex differences regarding self-disclosure (Peplau, 1983). In late adolescence (age 17 years and beyond), the emphasis shifts to compatibility, shared personalities, and shared interests. During mid-adolescence, girls may transfer some of the possessiveness of their earlier friendships with females to their relationships with males.

In contrast, boys' friendships are oriented toward joint activities throughout adolescence. For boys, achievement and autonomy are important not only in their development as individuals but also in their friendships. Perhaps it is therefore no surprise that adult males typically report having far fewer close friends than do adult females.

Changes in Social Awareness in Adolescence

Although adolescents are well able to consider the thoughts and feelings of friends and others in their interpersonal relationships, they still show forms of ego-centrism, much as do younger children (Elkind, 1967, 1985). A common form of egocentrism in adolescents is the *personal fable*, in which adolescents believe that they—as opposed to other persons—are somehow unique and destined for fame and fortune. They also exhibit an *invincibility fallacy*, by which they believe that they are somehow not vulnerable to the kinds of ill fortune that can befall others. Adolescents are therefore at great risk for dangers ranging from automobile accidents to AIDS because of their belief in their own invincibility. They also often believe in what is known as an *imaginary audience:* the unfounded belief that other people are constantly watching or otherwise paying attention to, as well as judging, them.

Whatever our age and sex, we need to have someone (or ones) in whom we can confide, on whom we can depend for support, and to whom we are important, special, and needed as givers of support and as recipients of revealing self-disclosures. Across the life span, we improve in our skill at showing friendship toward our friends, a skill that plays a role in helping us cultivate that special relationship that becomes marriage, our next topic.

Marriage and the Family

Marriage provides an opportunity for intimacy that often is difficult to obtain in other ways. Most people get married, sooner or later, although in recent

Although adolescents can consider the thoughts and feelings of others in interpersonal relationships, they may still exhibit egocentric thinking by believing that they are invincible.

Bullying in School

Anthony D. Pellegrini, *University of Minnesota*

I became interested in studying bullying and victimization because I was working on boys' transitions to middle school and early adolescence, around ages 11 to 13. I was finding that some boys consistently engaged in a physically rough and vigorous form of play on the playground at recess—rough-and-tumble play (R&T), or play fighting. The boys who initiated these R&T bouts tended to be rated as dominant, or "tougher," by the peers who also said they liked them. The boys who were the targets of these R&T initiations were, according to teachers' ratings, boys who were "victimized" or "picked on." Some of these kids who were picked on hit back and others just took it.

The way in which R&T was used by adolescent boys—to exhibit or establish their dominance—was very different from what I and others had observed in younger boys, those, say, 10 or 11 or under. At this point I wondered why these bullies were aggressive and why, counter to my expectations, they would also be popular with some of their peers. Younger aggressive children are rejected by their peers. I also wondered why some victims hit back and others did not. It also seemed, at first blush, that the bullies were very systematic and Machiavellian in their use of aggression. They seemed to choose specific targets, but they were not randomly aggressing against all their peers. The victims who hit back, on the other hand, used aggression in reaction to provocation. These youngsters from whom bullies seek a reaction seem to have "hot temperaments" and lack self-control. At this early point I wondered how these different types of aggression were used by boys in their peer groups.

My interest in this topic corresponded to the time in American history when excess violence was occurring in American schools. The beginnings of the tragic series of shootouts in American schools, from Mississippi and Georgia to Colorado and Oregon, were just beginning to appear. Thus, the topic of bullying was both of scientific interest and a topic of great social relevance. I decided to begin the systematic study of bullying and victimization in middle schools to contribute what I could to our understanding of some of the roots of these tragedies.

While aggression and bullying occur from preschool through adulthood (for example, bullying and intimidation in the workplace), boys tend to become more physically aggressive as they move from primary to middle school. My idea was that boys bullied their peers in order to reestablish their status as they moved into their new peer group. In my work I distinguished between bullies who used aggression proactively to achieve some end and their peers who used aggression reactively in a less calculating and less instrumental way, such as after provocation or a loss of temper.

Building on the pioneering work of Dan Olweus in Scandinavia that used self-report methodology, (e.g., Do you think it's fun to make trouble for other students? Have you been bullied by more than one student?), we complemented self-report measures with other methods, such as diaries, peer nominations, direct observations, and teacher questionnaires. Youngsters in the study completed monthly diaries and were asked at a set time using standardized questions (e.g., Did you hit or tease anyone today? If so, who?) and a series of standardized responses (e.g., How did you feel? Happy, sad, nothing).

In the peer nomination measure we presented small groups of youngsters with the names of all of their classmates and read the names aloud. The youngsters are then asked to nominate three classmates meeting the criteria for each questions asked, such as "Name kids who start fights." We also have teachers complete a questionnaire on each child, after having them in class for three to four months, and rate the children on dimensions of dominance.

Lastly, we observe youngsters across the school-day for the whole year. This is a time-consuming process because aggression doesn't occur frequently and not usually in front of adults.

In our research we have found first that using a multi-method approach increased the validity of our findings. We also found that as boys make the transition from primary to middle school, the instances of bullying and aggression (across all measures) increase and then decrease during the second half of the year. We also found that bullies used proactive aggression, or aggression to achieve some end, while reactive aggression was used by provocative victims. The increase in aggression early in the year corresponded to bullies' sense of a decrease in their dominance. It appears that bullies used aggression and bullying deliberately to establish dominance with their peers. After their dominance status was established during the first year, aggression decreased, possibly because everyone knew their place in the peer hierarchy. After bullies used aggression to establish dominance, they were considered to be more friendly and popular by their peers (both boys and girls), and leaders by their teachers.

In short, some adolescent boys use aggression to establish peer status, and they are considered to be leaders by both peers and teachers. Future research should address how bullies reestablish their positive status with peers.

 Find out more about this topic at *www.harcourtcollege.com/psych/ishm*

years, the trend has been toward later. More and more people have postponed marriage into the late twenties, early thirties, or even later (Sporakowski, 1988). There are multiple reasons for the tendency toward postponement, including the increasing need and desire of women to support themselves in the workforce, the increasing acceptability of being single for longer periods of time, and the tendency even among the earlier married to postpone child-bearing.

Satisfaction in marriage tends to be greatest in the early years, to fall during the raising of children, and then to increase again in the later years when children grow older and, especially, when they start their own lives away from their families. Thus, the **empty-nest syndrome,** whereby parents adjust to having their children grow up and move out of the family home, can be partially offset by their own newfound happiness with each other.

What makes a happy marriage? According to Gottman (1994), the key is in the way a couple resolves the conflicts that are inevitable in any marriage. Gottman has found that three styles can succeed for resolving conflict. In a *validating marriage*, couples compromise often and develop relatively calm ways of resolving conflicts. In a *conflict-avoiding marriage*, couples agree to disagree and avoid conflicts to the extent possible. In a *volatile marriage*, couples have frequent conflicts, some of them very antagonistic. Any one of these styles can work, as long as the number of positive moments the couple has together is at least five times as great as the number of negative moments. What destroys a marriage, according to Gottman, are (a) attacking the partner's personality or character, rather than his or her particular behavior; (b) showing contempt for a partner; (c) being defensive in response to constructive criticism; and (d) stonewalling—failing to respond at all to the concerns of the partner.

Clifford Notarius and Howard Markman (1993) have also suggested that there are several keys to happiness in a relationship. For example, one really negative act can erase the effects of 20 acts of kindness. Moreover, it is not the differences between partners that cause problems but rather how the differences are handled. Notarius and Markman have found that they can predict with more than 90% accuracy whether a couple will stay married solely on the basis of how the couple handles conflict. They have devised a questionnaire that assesses conflict-resolution skills, including statements such as "I sometimes nag at my partner to get him/her to talk" and "It is very easy for me to get angry at my partner" (Notarius & Markman, 1993, p. 41). "True" answers to these statements tend to be associated with marital unhappiness.

The World of Work

Marriage and family responsibilities are part of many adults' lives. Work is another responsibility. Work can provide a way to achieve not only the money necessary to survive, but also the satisfaction that comes from a job well done. As we discuss in the next chapter, individuals tend to be satisfied with their work to the extent that it is both *intrinsically rewarding*, meaning that the person enjoys the work he or she is doing, and *extrinsically rewarding*, meaning that the person is well-compensated in various ways, including financially, for the work.

According to Donald Super (1985), there are five main stages of career development. In the *growth stage*, from ages 0 to 14, the individual learns about and acquires the ability to pursue a vocation. In the *exploration stage*, from roughly ages 15 to 24, the individual makes a tentative vocational choice and may enter a first job. In the *establishment stage*, from roughly ages 25 to 44, the individual seeks entry into a permanent occupation. In the *maintenance stage*, from roughly 45 to 65, the individual is usually established in the occupation, and continues in it. Finally, in the *decline stage*, from roughly age 65 to death, the individual adapts to leaving and then ultimately retires from the workforce. Whereas 30 years ago, this pattern would have applied almost exclusively to men, today it applies to large numbers of men and women alike.

Similar to many of the topics discussed so far, moral development, the final aspect of social development considered in this chapter, reflects a progressive development in understanding how our friends and other people might think, feel, and behave.

Moral Development

In Search of . . . *What are the stages in the development of moral reasoning and how, if at all, do they differ between males and females?*

An important aspect of social development is moral development. As children shift away from a more egocentric orientation toward life, they are better able to understand others' points of view and to formulate moral standards (Eisenberg & Fabes, 1998; Harter, 1998). Children view strictly moral issues as different from social issues (Bersoff & Miller, 1993; Helwig, 1995), recognizing that issues of morality tend to be universal whereas social conventions vary from one culture to another. For example, children as young as 6 years of age believe it is wrong to steal, but they recognize that children in different countries play different games (Turiel, 1998). These distinctions are probably learned through interaction with family and community members (Nucci & Weber, 1995). Parents are delegated by society to serve as authorities in moral matters, and even teenagers who reject many aspects of their parents' teachings recognize the parents' societally designated role as moral authorities (Smetana, 1995, 1997; Smetana & Asquith, 1994).

Theories of moral development must address a number of questions. How do children of different ages perceive their moral responsibilities to others and to themselves? How do these perceptions change, and why? Two major views of moral development are those of Lawrence Kohlberg and of Carol Gilligan. Kohlberg has proposed a model that emphasizes conceptions of justice. Gilligan has argued that Kohlberg's model may apply to men, but that it does not apply well to women, for whom caring is often more important than some abstract concept of justice.

Kohlberg's Model

Heinz's Dilemma

Kohlberg developed a number of scenarios to assess children's moral development. One of the most famous scenarios involves a man, Heinz, who is faced with a serious moral dilemma:

> In Europe, a woman was near death from a rare form of cancer. The doctors thought that one drug might save her: a form of radium a druggist in the same town had recently discovered. The drug was expensive to make, but the druggist was also charging ten times his cost; having paid $400 for the radium, he charged $4,000 for a small dose. The sick woman's husband, Heinz, went to everyone he knew to borrow the money, but he could collect only $2,000. He begged the druggist to sell it more cheaply or to let him pay the balance later, but the druggist refused. So, having tried every legal means, Heinz desperately considered breaking into the drugstore to steal the drug for his wife. (Adapted from Kohlberg, 1963, 1984)

Suppose that you are Heinz. Should you steal the drug? Why or why not? These and similar scenario-related questions form the basis for measuring the development of moral reasoning according to Lawrence Kohlberg's influential theory. According to Kohlberg, your answers will depend on your level of moral rea-soning, which passes through six specific stages, embedded within three general levels. Your solutions do not determine your stage of moral reasoning. Rather, the kinds of reasons you give to justify either stealing or not stealing the drug determine your moral stage. Your ability to produce various kinds of reasons depends critically on your ability to take on other perspectives—to see your actions as others see them (Turiel, 1998).

Levels in Kohlberg's Theory

Level I (ages 7–10).   Represents **preconventional morality,** in which moral reasoning is guided by punishments and rewards. In the first stage of this level, *punishment* and *obedience* guide reasoning. Stage 1 children think that it is right to avoid breaking rules because punishment may follow. Obedience to authority is desirable for its own sake. This stage is egocentric in that children do not really consider others' interests. Children simply assume that the perspective of authority figures is correct because the authority figures will punish the children otherwise.

In Stage 2 of preconventional morality, children's orientation shifts to *individualism* and *exchange.* Stage 2 children follow rules, but only when it is to their benefit. Children serve their own interests, but they recognize that other people may have different interests. They therefore strike deals to meet everyone's interests. In this stage of the first level, what children consider to be morally right is relative, depending on whatever they will be rewarded for doing.

Level II (ages 10–16 or beyond).   Involves **conventional morality,** in which moral reasoning is guided by *mutual interpersonal expectations* and *interpersonal conformity.* Upon reaching this level, the individual moves into Stage 3, in which societal rules have become internalized, and the individual conforms because it is right to do so. Stage 3 children live up to what others, who are important in their lives, expect of them. To be good is to have good motives behind their actions and to show concern for other people. They live by the Golden Rule, doing unto others what they would have done unto them. In this stage, children want to maintain rules and authority systems that support conventionally appropriate behavior. They recognize that the needs of the group take primacy over their individual interests.

In Stage 4 of the second level, teens become oriented toward *conscience,* and they recognize the importance of the *social system.* In general, they obey laws and fulfill their duties, except in extreme cases when those duties conflict with higher social obligations.

Right consists of contributing to and maintaining the society or institutions of which they are a part. They need to think of the consequences if everyone behaves as they do. In this stage, teens distinguish the point of view of society from that view taken in agreements between individuals. Even if two people agree that something is right, the Stage 4 individual may still consider it wrong from the standpoint of society as a whole.

Level III (ages 16 and beyond). Comprises **postconventional morality.** When a person reaches this level the individual moves on to Stage 5. An individual in Stage 5 recognizes the importance of (a) *social contracts* and (b) *individual rights:* (a) People hold a wide variety of values and opinions, most of which are essentially relative, but which should be upheld because they are part of a social contract to which people have agreed; (b) a few values and rights, such as the rights of life and liberty, should be protected and safeguarded regardless of the opinion of the majority of individuals or authority figures in a given society (interestingly, this assertion is in itself a moral judgment). Persons in Stage 5 define right in terms of a sense of obligation to the law. People need to abide by laws to protect everyone and bring about the greatest good for the greatest number of people. Sometimes, moral and legal points of view conflict with each other, however, with no easy resolution. About one fifth of adolescents reach Stage 5.

In Stage 6, which Kohlberg believes few people reach, individuals are oriented toward *universal principles of justice.* They believe that it is right to follow universal ethical principles, which they have chosen after considerable thoughtful reflection. Most laws and social agreements are valid because they follow such principles, but if laws violate these principles, Stage 6 individuals believe that they must act according to their principles. They seek to uphold universal principles, and they are personally committed to them, whether others adhere to those principles or not. See Table 11-3 for a summary of Kohlberg's theory.

Developmental changes seem to plateau in early adulthood, but college education seems to facilitate continued development. For those who attend college, the onset of the plateau occurs later and generally at a higher level than for those who do not attend college (Rest & Thoma, 1985; see also Finger, Borduin, & Baumstark, 1992; see Figure 11-6).

Evaluation of Kohlberg's Model

The evidence in favor of Kohlberg's theory is decidedly mixed. Some research has been supportive, but the theory is clearly nowhere near as general as

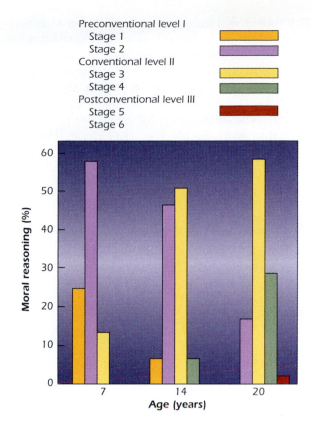

Figure 11-6
DEVELOPMENTAL CHANGES IN MORAL REASONING.
The percentages of children and adolescents (ages 7 through 16 years) who responded in terms of Kohlberg's preconventional, conventional, and postconventional moral levels are summarized graphically here. Clearly, preconventional reasoning sharply increases and postconventional reasoning slightly increases across the span of childhood and adolescence. Stage 6 is extremely rare, representing an ideal, not a common occurrence. (After Colby, Kohlberg, Gibbs, & Liberman, 1983)

Kohlberg thought. On one hand, other psychologists also have found that complexity of moral reasoning increases with age roughly along the lines Kohlberg suggested (e.g., Rest, 1983). Moreover, research with members of other cultures in places such as Turkey (Nisan & Kohlberg, 1982) and Israel (Snarey, Reimer, & Kohlberg, 1985a, 1985b) has been rather supportive of Kohlberg's theory.

Despite this supporting evidence, however, Kohlberg's theory has been highly controversial. First, the theory has been criticized because Kohlberg's moral dilemmas do not adequately represent situations commonly confronted by children and adolescents (Yussen, 1977). Second, Kohlberg's scoring is very subjective. Furthermore, interview-based scoring is quite difficult, and Kohlberg's highly detailed criteria complicate matters even further.

A third criticism is about the fixed-stage progression that Kohlberg's theory postulates (Kurtines & Greif, 1974). For one thing, people's responses may differ depending on which scenario is used for the assessment. Some people may skip stages (Holstein, 1976), and others may regress to earlier stages (Kohlberg & Kramer, 1969). For example, students who had previously gone beyond Stage 2 were in some cases found to return to it in college, in part perhaps because of the highly competitive nature of the environment. Kohlberg argued that such students still understood higher levels of morality, even if they did not act on them. Even adults placed in a sufficiently harsh

---

TABLE 11–3

Kohlberg's Theory of Development of Moral Reasoning
How did you respond to the dilemma and on what basis did you reach your answer?

LEVEL/STAGE	BASIS FOR REASONING	WHY YOU (AS HEINZ) SHOULD STEAL	WHY YOU (AS HEINZ) SHOULD NOT STEAL
Level I: Preconventional Morality (Ages 7–10)			
Stage 1 (Do not get caught.)	Egocentric consideration of whether the behavior leads to punishment or to reward. Might makes right, so people should obey authority.	If you do not steal the drug, your wife will be very angry with you, which would be painful. She might even die, which also would be painful.	You might get caught, and if you were caught, you would be punished (and your wife would not get the drug anyway).
Stage 2 (What is in it for me?)	Give-and-take exchanges guide behavior. Recognition that others have their own interests and considerations. Tries to strike deals that serve both parties' interests.	The druggist is making it impossible to make a deal that will work out okay for everyone, so the druggist is forcing you to find another solution. If you can get away with stealing the drug, your wife would be very happy with you for getting the medicine.	If you cannot work out a deal with the druggist, then work out a deal with your wife. She knows that it would not be reasonable to expect you to figure out how to steal the drug without getting caught. Besides, even with the drug, she might die anyway, so you would go to jail for no reason.
Level II: Conventional Morality (Ages 10–16 Years, and Usually Beyond)			
Stage 3 (I am being good/nice.)	Rules of behavior become internalized. Individuals perceive themselves as behaving in ways that are good, appropriate, or nice. Individuals conform to particular behaviors to please others.	Good people take care of the people they love. Even if it means breaking the law, to be a good person you must steal the drug for your wife. If you steal it, people will think you are very kind to your wife.	Good people do not steal. Even if it means that your wife will die, you must not steal. If you steal the drug, people will think you are a bad person, but if you do not steal it, they will think you are a good person.

continued

environment may sometimes regress to cope with the challenges they face. Still, regressions suggest that development need not be unidirectional, even if it occurs loosely in stages.

As the preceding criticism implies, a fourth criticism concerns the tenuous relation between thought and action (Kurtines & Greif, 1974). It is possible for someone to understand a given level of moral reasoning and even to answer test questions accordingly, but then to behave in a way that does not reflect this level. The test of morality perhaps shows how well the test taker plays the game rather than whether the test taker actually behaves according to moral principles. However, Kohlberg never claimed that understanding was tantamount to action. In general, research suggests that the measured moral

---

TABLE 11–3

Kohlberg's Theory of Development of Moral Reasoning   *continued*

LEVEL/STAGE	BASIS FOR REASONING	WHY YOU (AS HEINZ) SHOULD STEAL	WHY YOU (AS HEINZ) SHOULD NOT STEAL
Stage 4 (Preserve the social order.)	Societal rules form the basis of moral reasoning. Development of conscience and recognition of the importance of the social system guide moral reasoning.	You must steal the drug because when you married you made a promise to do all you could to ensure your wife's well-being. Not to steal the drug would be to break your promise.	You must not steal the drug because stealing violates the rules and laws of society. To steal the drug would be to break society's rules.
Level III: Postconventional Morality (Ages 16 and Beyond)			
Stage 5 (What ensures the rights and well-being of each person?)	Social contracts and individual rights form the basis of moral reasoning.	You must steal the drug because the individual's right to live exceeds society's right to impose laws regarding property.	You must not steal the drug because the life of one individual should not cause you to act in ways that rupture the fabric of society. If you steal, you ultimately harm everyone, even your wife.
Stage 6 (What is best from the point of view of each person involved, including the broadest ramifications of the individual actions?)	An orientation toward universal principles of justice guides moral reasoning.	You should steal the drug because the principle of preserving life takes precedence over the law against stealing the drug. Even the druggist would be better off because he would not be a party to your wife's death. If you were caught, your case might bring attention to the problems of paying for expensive drugs, so others might benefit even if your wife did not.	You should not steal the drug because your feelings for your wife should not take precedence over the well-being of others. If you steal the drug, others who need it may be deprived. The druggist may even raise the price of the drug. Others who are thinking about developing drugs may decide not to because the drugs might be stolen.

Do men and women develop differently when it comes to their sense of moral reasoning? Kohlberg's model didn't seem to take into account the way women approached Heinz's dilemma. Gilligan's alternative view, that men tend to take a more competitive view of moral issues, while women construe them cooperatively, may also be too narrow.

stage does predict behavior, but only imperfectly (Blasi, 1980; Rest, 1983).

Finally, Kohlberg's theory has been criticized for having been based on the study of a small sample of white, middle-class, American boys under 17 years of age. Do Kohlberg's findings really apply to persons not fitting into all of these categories? John Snarey (1985) has reviewed more than 45 cross-cultural studies of Kohlberg's theory and has generally found support for Kohlberg's view. Nonetheless, Snarey points out some cultural limitations in the range of stages and in the applicability of all of Kohlberg's stages across cultures. For example, even Snarey's studies in collaboration with Kohlberg revealed some cross-cultural differences. In particular, the communal kibbutz lifestyle of Israel encourages greater emphasis on community and collective happiness than is found in the individualistic lifestyle of the United States (Snarey et al., 1985b).

Since Snarey's review, other researchers have similarly found that the theory has some cross-cultural support, within limits (e.g., studies in South Africa [Maqsud & Rouhani, 1990], Iceland [Keller, Eckensberger, & von Rosen, 1989], and Poland [Niemczynski, Czyzowska, Pourkos, & Mirski, 1988]). For example, in China, the first three stages apply well, but the last three stages are less well supported and require modification to work well within traditional Chinese thought (Ma, 1988). In fact, probably no universal set of stages of morality can apply without modification across cultures. Still, Kohlberg's theory has shown some strength in this area, as previously noted.

Carol Gilligan, a student of Kohlberg's, had been coding interviews of moral dilemmas when she began noticing that many of the women's responses did not fit neatly into any of Kohlberg's categories. In fact, many of their apparent responses seemed to reflect an entirely different approach to moral dilemmas. In 1977, Gilligan proposed an alternative view of moral development in women.

Gilligan's Alternative Model

According to Gilligan (1982; Gilligan, Hamner, & Lyons, 1990), although women are as capable of conceiving morality as men, they tend to have a different conception. Men tend to focus on abstract, rational principles such as justice and respect for the rights of others, while women tend to see morality more as a matter of caring and compassion. They are more concerned about general human welfare and relationships that contribute to it. Women focus on the special obligations of their close relationships, and they resolve moral issues with sensitivity to the social context. Whereas men are more likely to be competitive, women are more likely to be cooperative. Gilligan proposed that women pass through three basic levels of morality, although not all women reach the third level. The first level involves the individual's concern only for herself. The second level involves self-sacrifice, in which concern for others predominates. And the third level involves integrating responsibilities to both self and others.

Others (e.g., Baumrind, 1986; J. C. Gibbs, Arnold, Ahlborn, & Cheesman, 1984) have found similar sex differences in responses to moral dilemmas. Gilligan and J. Attanucci (1988) have since confirmed these differences. L. Walker (1989) replicated Gilligan and Attanucci's procedures, using a larger sample, and found that most men and women, as well as girls and boys, used considerations of both caring and justice in their responses to moral dilemmas. However, although women were more likely than men to express a caring orientation, girls were not more likely than boys to do so. Perhaps a synthesis of both perspectives will eventually be suggested.

In conclusion, social development is a lifelong process encompassing emotional, personality, interpersonal, and moral development. Social development is inextricably intertwined with the environment, which largely dictates what people consider appropriate social development and social behavior for a child. We have seen this interweaving in many of the research studies discussed in this chapter, such as the work on attachment patterns in children, in which proportions of the various attachment patterns

TABLE 11–4

Summary of Social Development: Birth to Age 3

The first 3 years of a child's life are surprisingly eventful in terms of various aspects of social development.

ASPECT OF DEVELOPMENT: THEORIST	AGE (MONTHS)							
	0–1	*1–2*	*2–3*	*3–6*	*6–9*	*9–12*	*12–18*	*18–36*
Emotional: Sroufe	Emotions are undifferentiated; insensitive to the emotions of others	Social smile develops; facial expressions reflect others' expressions; smile in response to things		Highly positive emotions; smile and laugh with caregivers	Participate in emotional exchanges; begin to show anger	Communicate emotional states effectively; focus on caregivers; possessive; fear strangers	Explore wider world beyond caregivers; secure attachment; less fear of strangers	Differentiation of themselves from others, including self-concept; ambivalent impulses to assert independence and seek reassurance
Personality: Erikson	Trust versus mistrust						Autonomy versus shame and doubt	
Attachment: Ainsworth	Preattachment; nondifferentiated responses to people	Attachment in the making; respond more to familiars than to strangers; increasingly seek contact with primary caregivers; anxious around strangers			Clear-cut attachment; prefer primary caregivers; differentiated response to strangers; separation anxiety		Mature relationships	
Self-understanding: Damon and Hart	Emerging self-awareness; focus on the physical self						Understand own gender, age, and possessions; emerging feelings of mastery	
Self-esteem: Harter	Undifferentiated self-concept and evaluations of self-worth							
Friendships: Vandell, Mueller	May cry if another infant cries			May smile at another infant; may reach toward or even touch another infant			Interactions increase as does positive affect; frequent playmates may be recognized with positive affect	
Moral: Piaget, Kohlberg	Premoral							

differ across countries. Social development is also clearly linked to cognitive development, in that a child cognitively processes the perceptions and conceptions that influence his or her socialization. Tables 11-4, 11-5, and 11-6, summarize the key aspects of social development in infants, children, and adults, respectively.

In the next chapter we will explore how motivation and emotion contribute to social development and social behavior.

TABLE 11–5

Summary of Social Development: Preschool Through Adolescence
From preschool through adolescence, the child undergoes tremendous changes in terms of various aspects of social development.

ASPECT OF DEVELOPMENT: THEORIST	AGE (YEARS)							
	3–5	5–7	7–9	9–11	11–13	13–15	15–17	17+
Emotional: Sroufe	Social smile; festivities important; fears of unknown and strangers		Less distinctive events also important; fears include fantastic creatures or unrealistic beliefs		School and after-school activities, peer relationships are key to happiness		Relationships, self-improvement, recreation, and travel are key to happiness	
	Anger becomes focused	Anger includes consideration of others' intentions						
Personality: Erikson	Initiative versus guilt	Industry versus inferiority			Identity versus role confusion			
Self-understanding: Damon and Hart	Emerging self-awareness based on physical self; differentiate inner-directed versus other-directed speech	Self-understanding based on active self, on personal achievements and skills			Self-understanding based on social self and peer relations		Self-understanding based on psychological self and personal beliefs, thoughts, attitudes, and values	
Self-esteem: Harter	Self-esteem based on cognitive, physical, and social competence, and behavioral conduct		Self-esteem based on scholastic and athletic competence, peer social acceptance, behavioral conduct, and physical appearance		Self-esteem based on job, scholastic, and athletic competence; close friendship; romantic appeal; peer social acceptance; behavioral conduct; and physical appearance			
Play interactions: Parten	Play becomes increasingly social and interactive with peers							
Friendships: Gottman	Prefer same-sex friends; friendships center on shared activities; boys more likely to engage in competitive activities, autonomy, and achievement; girls more likely to prefer a cooperative pair, emotional closeness, and shared confidences						Boys do not show much change from earlier bases for friendships; girls increasingly emphasize shared personalities, interests, compatibility, turn their attention to boys	
Moral: Kohlberg			Preconventional morality		Conventional morality		Possible postconventional morality	

TABLE 11–6

Summary of Social Development: Adulthood   *Psychologists have developed theories of personality, identity, self-esteem, life structure, and morality for all three stages of adulthood.*

Aspect of Development: Theorist	Early Adulthood	Middle Adulthood	Late Adulthood
Personality: Erikson	Intimacy versus isolation	Generativity versus stagnation	Integrity versus despair
Identity: Marcia	Identity achievement, foreclosure, identity diffusion, or moratorium (or possibly alienated achievement)		
Self-esteem: Harter	Self-esteem based on intelligence, sense of humor, job competence, morality, athletic ability, physical appearance, sociability, intimate relationships, nurturance, adequacy as a provider, and household management		
Life structure: Levinson	Evaluate the nature of the world and one's place in it; eventually establish family and career; attempt to build a better life	Evaluate accomplishments to date; sometimes change marital status, career, or attitudes; begin to consider retirement and old age	Awareness of changing physical and mental abilities; must stay connected to family, friends, interests; come to terms with mortality
Moral: Kohlberg	Conventional morality (and, in rare cases, postconventional morality)		

THINK ABOUT IT

1. Describe a moral dilemma and tell how someone at Kohlberg's postconventional level of morality might respond to the dilemma. Give the rationale for the individual's response.
2. How do the development of the self-concept and interpersonal development interact?
3. Design an experience that would help children broaden their views regarding the range of behaviors that are appropriate for boys and for girls, helping them avoid being narrowly constrained by rigid sex-role stereotypes.
4. Suggest some criteria to be used in assessing the quality of child care for children less than 5 years of age.

5. How do your emotions influence your behavior?
6. Give examples of your own gender-role development. In what ways do you conform to traditional gender roles, and in what ways have you departed from traditional gender roles?

 You can provide your own answers to these questions online at the Sternberg, **In Search of the Human Mind** *Web site:* **http://www.harcourtcollege.com/psych/ishm**

SUMMARY

Emotional Development   360

1. *Social development* encompasses four areas of personal growth: emotional development, personality development, interpersonal development, and moral development.

2. Infants change from being egocentric, with limited emotional expression, to being fully functioning, independent, empathic, and responsive explorers of the world around them. On the way, they pass through *separation anxiety*.

3. Researchers do not agree as to how people develop emotions. Sroufe posits that we are born with one general form of emotional arousal, which later differentiates into various specific emotions (differentiation theory). Others (e.g., Izard) say that discrete emotions are generated by specific neural patterns in our brains.

4. An evolutionary theory of emotional development posits that we can understand how human emotions develop by understanding the adaptive requirements emotions serve.

Personality Development   363

5. Erikson's theory of *psychosocial development* was originally considered revolutionary because it traces development all the way through adulthood, not stopping at adolescence. The theory comprises eight stages. Those who successfully complete the stages develop hope, will, purpose, competence, fidelity, love, care, and wisdom.

6. Your sense of identity can be categorized, according to Marcia, as being in a state of *identity achievement*, if you have made your own decisions and have a firm sense of who you are; *foreclosure*, if you have chosen your path with little thought; *moratorium*, if you are still seeking an identity; *identity diffusion*, if you lack direction or commitment; or *alienated achievement*, if you have decided to opt out of society.

7. *Self-concept* consists of self-understanding, which is your definition of who you are, and self-esteem, which is your sense of self-worth.

8. According to Damon and Hart, *self-understanding* involves different aspects of the self, such as physical attributes, behavior, social relationships, and inner psyche. According to Harter, *self-esteem* is based on self-judgments about your worth in various domains of differing importance. Older children see themselves as functioning in more domains than do younger children. By adulthood, people function in 11 different domains. People also base their self-esteem on other people's judgments of them.

9. Children who underestimate their abilities tend to have more problems in school and social life than children who do not. Girls are more likely than boys to underestimate their abilities.

10. *Temperament* refers to individual differences in the intensity and duration of emotions. According to A. Thomas and Chess, babies may be easy, difficult, or slow-to-warm-up. Temperament must be taken into account when looking for the best fit between a person and his or her environment.

11. *Psychosexual development* is the growth of self-perceptions about sexuality and gender identifications. *Gender typing* is the acquisition of specific gender-related roles.

12. Our perceptions of sex roles and gender identification may be acquired through socialization, genetic predisposition, evolution, role modeling, or cognitive schemas.

Interpersonal Development   371

13. *Attachment* is the long-lasting emotional tie that results from bonding. It does not end in childhood, and indeed, patterns of childhood attachment seem to be repeated in adult life, especially in romantic relationships.

14. *Strange situation* research examines attachment patterns by studying how children react when left alone in an unfamiliar room with an unknown person and then when their mother returns. According to *attachment patterns*, *avoidant* children seem distant emotionally in the strange situation; *secure* children are more outgoing but need comforting; *resistant* children seem both aloof and in need of closeness. These labels seem to be culturally bound.

15. Infants can become attached to fathers and other caregivers, just as they do to mothers. Fathers play more games with young children than do mothers.

16. Young humans and animals that are deprived of natural nurturing and attachment do not grow up to be fully functional adults.

17. Parental disciplinary style affects the development of social skills in children. *Authoritarian* (very strict) parents tend to raise unfriendly and distrustful children. *Permissive* parents tend to raise immature and dependent children. *Authoritative* parents, who provide more of a balance, tend to raise well-adjusted children. The authoritative style is the most common across cultures.

18. Child care is a controversial issue. Research results on its effects are somewhat contradictory, although the majority of studies indicate that good-quality child care does children little harm and may offer some benefits. The most important consideration for parents, therefore, is the quality of the program they choose.

19. Learning how to make friends is important to a child's development. Theories of friendship development point to effective personal interaction, exchanging information, establishing common ground, resolving conflicts, positive reciprocal regard, and free self-disclosure as steps in learning how to be a friend. Girls' and boys' friendship patterns differ somewhat, with girls placing a greater emphasis on compatible feelings and outlooks, and boys on compatible activities.

20. Studies of couples show that several types of marriages can be successful. Unsuccessful marriages are characterized by personal attacks, contempt, defensiveness, and stonewalling.

21. People are most satisfied in their work when it is both intrinsically and extrinsically rewarding.

People pass through several different stages of career development, including growth, exploration, establishment, maintenance, and decline.

Moral Development 379

22. Kohlberg's stage theory of moral development and reasoning is the most widely accepted of such theories, although it has its detractors. In the *preconventional morality* level, children behave to avoid punishment and to seek self-interest; in the *conventional morality* level, older children and adolescents behave according to family and social rules; and in the *postconventional morality* level, adults behave according to shifting social needs but also according to universal ethical requirements.

23. There is some evidence in support of Kohlberg's theory, but on the whole, support is mixed.

24. Gilligan has suggested an alternative series of moral development levels for women, involving an orientation toward caring relationships more than toward an abstract notion of justice. This theory has little empirical evidence to support it.

KEY TERMS

attachment 371
authoritarian 375
authoritative 375
avoidant attachment pattern 372
conventional morality 380
discrete-emotions theory 363
empty-nest syndrome 379
gender constancy 369

gender typing 369
permissive 375
postconventional morality 381
preconventional morality 380
psychosexual development 369
psychosocial theory 363
resistant attachment pattern 372
schema theory 370

secure attachment pattern 372
self-concept 365
self-esteem 366
self-understanding 366
separation anxiety 360
social development 359
strange situation 371
temperament 368

■ THINK ABOUT IT SAMPLE RESPONSES

1. Describe a moral dilemma and tell how someone at Kohlberg's postconventional level of morality might respond to the dilemma. Give the rationale for the individual's response.

An example of a moral dilemma would be a bribe a government official receives to award a government contract to a particular firm. The individual offering the bribe points out that his company will do just as good a job as any other contractor, and quite possibly, a better job. Thus only good ends will come out of awarding the contract to his firm. He points out that no one will be hurt because the job will get done, it will get done well, and you, as the government official, will benefit at no one's expense. Should you accept the bribe and award the contract to the company whose official is attempting to bribe you? Someone at the postconventional stage of morality would certainly recognize that the bribe should not be accepted. First, it is not true that no one is hurt. Honest companies not offering bribes are being hurt if their honesty causes them to lose business. Eventually, they may go out of business or conclude that they need to offer bribes. Second, the taxpayers get hurt. The money for the bribe has to come from somewhere. Most likely it will be factored into the cost of the contract and, ultimately, taxpayers will pay. Third, accepting the bribe is dishonest, regardless of who gains and who loses.

2. How do the development of the self-concept and interpersonal development interact?

Your self-concept will affect the way you interact with other people. If you think poorly of yourself, you are likely to show this to others, who will then respond to your poor self-concept. They may agree or disagree, but the way they treat you will be affected by your own opinion of yourself. If you think well of yourself (but not unreasonably so), people may accept your positive view. Often they can then move on to the more important aspects of interpersonal interactions rather than concentrating on dealing with your opinion of yourself.

3. Design an experience that would help children broaden their views regarding the range of behaviors that are appropriate for boys and for girls, helping them avoid being narrowly constrained by rigid sex-role stereotypes.

Many boys believe that being sensitive to people's feelings is a "feminine" activity. Yet it is important for everyone to be sensitive to the feelings of others as well as of themselves. An activity children can do is to relate an event in their lives that left a strong emotional impression on them, positive or negative. The event, but not the feelings of the moment, should be described orally. Children in the classroom, including boys, then will be invited to comment on how the child must have felt when he experienced the event he describes.

4. Suggest some criteria to be used in assessing the quality of child care for children less than 5 years of age.

Some criteria to be used might include (a) number of caretakers, (b) past experience of the caretakers, (c) caretakers' training in working with children, (d) average longevity on the job of the caretaking staff, (e) number of toys and books available for children to use, and (f) quality of nutrition being offered in the program.

5. How do your emotions influence your behavior?

Emotions influence everyone's behavior. For example, when they are angry, people often look for outlets through which to express their anger. When they are happy, they do the same. When people are sad, sometimes they become withdrawn or they may seek the comfort others have to provide.

6. Give examples of your own gender-role development. In what ways do you conform to traditional gender roles, and in what ways have you departed from traditional gender roles?

Everyone must answer this question for him or herself. If you conform very strongly to your traditional gender role, you might consider trying out some activities that would render you more androgynous, that is, more flexible in the role you carry out.

"If at first you don't succeed, try, try again."

"Where there's a will there's a way."

MOTIVATION AND EMOTION

The English language contains large numbers of proverbs emphasizing the importance of motivation and initiative to success. What is motivation, and how important is it? And how does it relate to emotions? These are questions we will consider in this chapter.

Intuitively, the way we describe our motivations and our emotions is similar: "I feel like having a hamburger," "I feel like dancing." Both motivations and emotions are feelings that cause us to move or to be moved. Both seem to erupt within us in response to events or to thoughts and we often feel both as physiological sensations: "When I heard his footsteps behind me again, I panicked—I started shaking, my heart pounded, my throat swelled shut, my palms sweated, and I turned to ice." Motivation and emotion are inextricably linked.

The Nature and Characteristics of Motivation

In Search of . . . *What is motivation and what are some of the major theories of motivation?*

A **motive** is an impulse, desire, or need that leads to an action. *Motivation* involves processes that give behavior its energy and its direction. Psychologists study *why* or *how* we are motivated to act. More specifically, psychologists ask four questions (Houston, 1985): First, what *directions* do our actions move us in? That is, what attracts us, and what repels us? Second, what motivates us to *initiate* or start taking action to pursue a particular goal? That is, why do some people initiate action whereas others contemplate an action but never actually go ahead and act? Third, how *intensely* do we pursue those actions? Fourth, why do some people *persist* for longer periods of time in the things that motivate them, whereas other people flitter from one pursuit to another?

Early theories of motivation focused on the evolutionary and biological aspects of motives, chiefly, instincts and drives.

Motivation as Instinctive Behavior

Instinctive behavior has three main characteristics. First, it is *inherited*; we are born with all the instincts we ever will have. Thus, the desire for sexual union or the fear of a predator is innate, not learned. Second, it is *species specific*; that is, salmon return upriver to their place of birth, but tuna do not; bees do a certain kind of dance, but humans do not. Third, it is *stereotyped*; we engage in a behavior automatically in response to a particular stimulus. For example, running from a ferocious predator is automatic, and fortunately so. Charles Darwin (1859, 1965) was a major proponent

*"I don't sing because I am happy.
I am happy because I sing."*

of the instinctual point of view and believed that much of an animal's behavior is inherited, species specific, and automatic. Instinctive behavior, from an evolutionary point of view, is one of the keys not only to individual survival, but also to survival of the species. For example, without the instinct or instincts that motivate copulatory behavior, mammalian species would likely be doomed.

William James, the father of much of modern psychological thinking, suggested a list of 20 physical instincts, such as sucking and locomotion, as well as an additional 17 mental instincts (James, 1890a). The mental instincts included cleanliness, curiosity, fearfulness, jealousy, parental love, and sociability. A generation later, William McDougall (1908) proposed a further list of instincts, including the desire for food, the desire to have sex, the desire to dominate, and the desire to make things. The list of proposed instincts gradually grew to 10,000 (Bernard, 1924). Whereas James believed that instincts are *important* in behavior, McDougall argued that instincts are *necessary* for behavior. Without them, people would be totally passive, unmoved to action by anything.

Instinct theory, however, like many other psychological theories, became ponderous, cumbersome, and circular (Kuo, 1921). Behaviors were explained by instincts, which in turn were explained by the behaviors. For example, mothering behavior might be "explained" by a mothering instinct, which in turn would be "explained" by the behavior it supposedly generated. The arguments against instincts led people to lose interest in them as a basis for theorizing. Theorists sought new ways to explain motivation. As the aesthetic appeal of instinct theory waned, drive theory became increasingly attractive.

Drive Theory

Drive theory derives many of its principles, and many of its backers, from learning theory. There have been different versions of drive theory. The theory was first proposed by Robert Woodworth (1918), but the most well known version was proposed by Clark Hull. Hull (1943, 1952) believed that people have a number of basic physiological needs: the needs for food, water, sleep, and so on. To survive, we must satisfy all of these physiological needs. The hypothesized composite source of energy related to these physiological needs is known as **drive,** a hypothesized composite source of energy, which humans and other animals try to reduce. To reduce drive, we eat, drink, sleep, and otherwise satisfy our needs. Animals and humans alike are impelled to reduce drive.

Like instinct theory, drive theory fell out of favor because the assumptions underlying it proved not to be particularly well founded (White, 1959). Empirical support for the theory simply was inadequate. As drive paradigms began to yield diminishing returns, other paradigms seemed to be more fruitful. So researchers studying motivation moved on.

Contemporary Views of Motivation

In Search of . . .   *Why and how has motivation been studied by psychologists?*

Physiological Approaches

What prompted psychologists to start exploring the relationship between the central nervous system (particularly, the brain) and the psychological and behavioral phenomena of motivation? Actually, the physiological approach gained support almost by accident. Researcher James Olds misplaced an electrode in a portion of a rat's brain. When the rat was stimulated, it acted in ways to suggest that it wished more stimulation. Olds and Peter Milner (1954) then designed an experiment to test whether the rat was indeed seeking further stimulation. When electrodes were planted in a part of the limbic system, rats spent more than three-quarters of their time pressing a bar to repeat the stimulation. Olds had inadvertently discovered a

"pleasure center" of the brain. Other researchers showed that cats would do whatever they could to *avoid* electrical stimulation in another part of the brain (Delgado, Roberts, & Miller, 1954). Three theories for understanding the relationship between motivation and the physiology of the brain are considered here: arousal theory, opponent-process theory, and homeostatic-regulation theory.

Arousal Theory

Suppose that three students of equal intelligence and subject knowledge are about to take an important test. The first student does not care either about the test or about how well she will do on the test. The second student wants to do well but is not anxious about his performance. He knows that even if he were to do poorly, his life would not be changed inalterably for the worse. The third student is extremely nervous about the test, and she believes that her grade on this test will largely determine her future. Which student do you think is most likely to do best on the test?

These three students vary in their amount of **arousal**—the state of alertness, wakefulness, and activation caused by nervous-system activation. Arousal is caused by the activity of the central nervous system, including the brain. The relationship between arousal and efficiency of performance is shown in Figure 12-1.

The inverted U-shape shown in Figure 12-1 represents the *Yerkes-Dodson Law* (Yerkes & Dodson,

Figure 12–1
THE YERKES–DODSON LAW.   *In the hill-shaped linear relationship between arousal and performance, performance is at its peak when arousal is moderate, and performance levels are lower at both the low and high extremes of arousal. (After Yerkes & Dodson, 1908)*

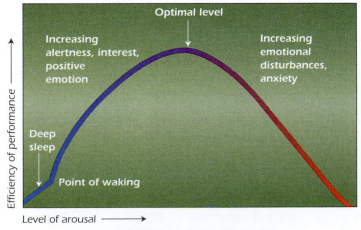

(a) General relationship between performance and arousal level

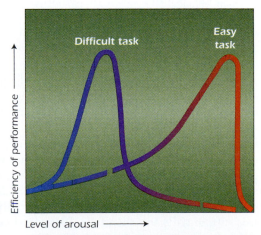

(b) Relationship between performance and arousal level on difficult vs. easy tasks

1908), which states that organisms will perform most efficiently when their level of arousal is moderate. According to this law, the second student, who is both motivated and relaxed, will do best. People generally also feel at their best when their level of arousal is moderate (Berlyne, 1967). At low levels of arousal, people feel bored, listless, and unmotivated. At high levels of arousal, people feel tense or fearful.

The optimal level of arousal appears to vary both with the task and with the individual. For relatively simple tasks, the optimal level of arousal is moderately high, whereas for difficult tasks the optimal level of arousal is moderately low (Bexton, Heron, & Scott, 1954; Broadhurst, 1957). If we need to perform a fairly repetitive and mindless task, a high level of arousal may help us get through and may motivate us to be efficient. If we have to perform a complex task, however, a low level of arousal may help us avoid becoming anxious, which would hamper our ability to start working on the task. One way to raise arousal is through certain kinds of substances, which, in large quantities, can often be addictive.

Opponent-Process Theory

The *opponent-process theory*, proposed by Richard Solomon (1980; Solomon & Corbit, 1974), addresses the cycle of emotional experience connected to addiction—whether to caffeine, nicotine, alcohol, or other substances. (This theory has nothing to do with the opponent-process theory of color vision.) What happens when we acquire and then try to get rid of a motivation (see Figure 12-2)? Originally, we are at a neutral state, a *baseline*, in which we have not acquired the motivation to act (e.g., to drink coffee), and thus the stimulus (coffee) is irrelevant to us. Then we drink the first cup of coffee, experience a "high," and our emotional state becomes positive. We feel the high because of the positive effect of the stimulus—often a chemical—on receptors of the brain. Regardless of the source, however, we feel good because of the stimulus, and thus we have an *acquired motivation* to seek out more of the stimulus.

According to Solomon, the brains of mammals always seek out emotional neutrality sooner or later. This pursuit of emotional neutrality means that when a motivational source impels us to feel emotions, whether positive or negative, we then come under the influence of an opposing motivational force—an *opponent process*—that acts to bring us back to the neutral baseline. Notice in Figure 12-2 that our emotional state after drinking a cup of coffee first rises substantially but then falls. It starts to go down when the opponent process begins to oppose the

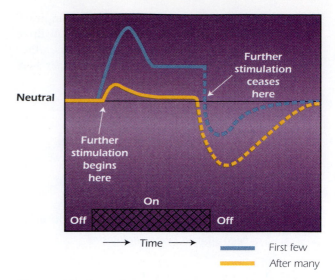

Figure 12–2
ACQUIRED MOTIVATION.   *In the beginning of the process of physiological addiction, the addictive stimulus elevates us above our neutral baseline level of response. At this point, if we stop using the addictive substance, we first drop below and then return to our neutral baseline level. However, once addicted, our responses to the substance act only to keep us in a steady state, which serves as our current neutral level of response. If we then abstain from the addictive substance, our responses will cause us to fall further below our neutral level of response for a longer time, and we will experience withdrawal. (After R. Solomon & Corbit, 1974)*

original process. Maybe we enjoyed the "buzz" from the coffee to start with but then found it made us too jittery to think straight. In other words, what was initially pleasurable now starts to become less so. Eventually, the effect of the stimulus wears off, and we reach a *steady state* of response to the stimulus. The original motivating force stops because the stimulus now only keeps us at our baseline level; it no longer elevates us above the baseline. In the coffee example, the body may have metabolized all the caffeine.

After using the stimulus for a long time, we find its effect on us to be quite different from what it was originally, as the figure shows. Once we *habituate* to the stimulus (see chapters 4, 5, and 6), it no longer gives us the boost above our baseline level. Maybe one cup of coffee no longer makes us jittery; now it only arouses us to the "barely awake" level. Unfortunately, the opponent process, which was slower to start, is also slower to stop. When the effect of the stimulus wears off, the effect of the opponent process remains, and so we quickly go into a state of *withdrawal*. We now feel worse than we did before: irritable, headachy, cranky, tired, sad, or upset. We may then seek out

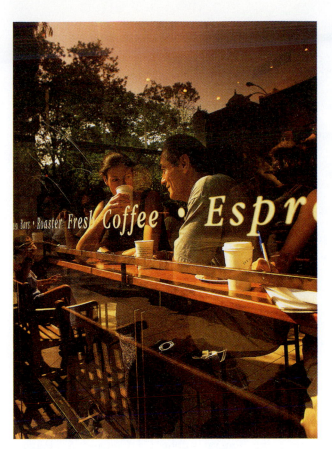

The tendency of the body is toward a state of equilibrium. According to opponent process theory, the pleasant buzz we at first get from just one cup of coffee will eventually be diminished by the body's efforts to counterbalance the jittery feeling, leaving us needing more coffee over time to produce the same effect.

more of the stimulus to relieve the withdrawal symptoms. Ironically, then, what starts off as a habit to achieve a high becomes a habit to avoid a low. We may drink coffee to avoid withdrawal symptoms. Fortunately, if we are able to ride out the withdrawal the symptoms will eventually end.

Arousal theory explains why we seek to explore and to master our environments, and opponent-process theory explains why we are motivated to seek substances to which we are addicted. However, neither theory satisfactorily addresses why we eat, drink, or satisfy our other basic physiological needs. Yet another theory is needed to explain these motivations.

Homeostatic-Regulation Theory

Consider a typical sequence of behavior during the morning. You wake up. After some time, you start to feel hungry and thirsty. You eat and drink. Now, no

longer hungry or thirsty, you begin your morning activities. After a while, you begin to notice sensations of hunger and thirst again. Maybe you have other things to do and just grab a drink instead of eating. The hunger pangs intensify. Finally, you decide that you really want to have lunch, so you eat again.

Homeostatic regulation is the tendency of the body to maintain a state of equilibrium. When the body lacks something, it sends signals that prompt the individual to seek the missing resource. When the body is satiated, it sends signals to stop obtaining that something. We regulate the need for food and liquid, as well as the control of body temperature, through homeostatic systems. These systems operate via a **negative-feedback loop,** a physiological mechanism whereby the body monitors a particular resource. The loop finds a way to increase the levels of the resource when levels are low, and then signals to find a way to decrease the levels of the resource when levels are high (see chapter 3). The systems work to negate the difference between the actual and ideal states. Most people stop eating around the time they no longer feel hungry, stop drinking when they no longer feel thirsty, or stop sleeping when they no longer feel tired.

Homeostatic regulation is not limited to the body. Most home heating systems, like the bodily heating system, work on the basis of homeostatic regulation. When the thermostat records temperatures below the preferred setting, the heater turns on. It stays on until the thermostat reaches the set point— the desired temperature. Once the thermostat registers a temperature at or above the set point, the heater turns off.

In the body, negative feedback is graded, rather than all-or-none. For example, suppose that you have had a very active day and arrive at dinner famished. At first, you are likely to eat and drink rapidly, but your rate of eating and drinking will decrease as you complete the meal because you are receiving feedback indicating that your needs are satisfied (L. Spitzer & Rodin, 1981). The body signals to you well before you have finished the meal that you are reaching satiation. If you eat fast, however, the signal is not so clear, which is why one dieting tactic is to have people eat more slowly so as to give their bodies time to signal satiety before they've overeaten.

Homeostatic regulation sounds like drive theory, but the emphases are different. In drive theory, a need supplies energy, which seeks to satisfy the need and to reduce the drive. The focus is on avoiding deficits. In homeostatic-regulation theory, the emphasis is on the need to maintain equilibrium. Both

TABLE 12–1

Physiological Approaches to Motivation   *There are three theories of motivation that are based on physiology: arousal theory, opponent-process theory, and homeostatic-regulation theory.*

THEORY	EXPLANATION
Arousal theory (Yerkes–Dodson law)	We feel relaxed and motivated when we are moderately aroused and we perform at optimum level. We feel bored when minimally aroused and anxious or tense when highly aroused.
Opponent-process theory (Solomon)	We seek emotional neutrality. When we feel emotions, an opposing motive brings us back to the neutral baseline.
Homeostatic-regulation theory	The body (brain) tries to maintain a state of equilibrium. When the brain senses that the body lacks food, the brain signals the body to seek food; when the brain senses that the stomach is full, it signals the body to stop eating.

deficits and surpluses are to be avoided. Table 12-1 briefly summarizes the physiological approaches.

Although we may not fully understand all of the mechanisms that prompt us to satisfy our physiological needs, we do not question our motivation to engage in behavior to satisfy those needs. In the next chapters, we explore what motivates us to conform to our culture's norms. Can all of our behaviors be understood in terms of the motivation to meet our physiological needs? What else motivates human behavior?

Clinical Approaches to Motivation

Clinical approaches to motivation consider physiological needs, but they are based on aspects of the personality and on case studies of patients and clients rather than on physiological data. For example, people are motivated differently. Some will stand for hours in all kinds of weather for a ticket to a concert that others would not accept money to attend.

Murray's Theory of Needs

Henry Murray (1938) believed that needs are based in human physiology and that they can be understood in terms of the workings of the brain. He saw needs as forming the core of a person's personality. Some of the 20 needs that Murray postulated have prompted a great deal of research—a measure of Murray's importance in the field. For example, much research has been done on Murray's constructs of the need for affiliation and the need for power. People who rank high in the need for affiliation like to form close connections with other people and to be members of groups. They avoid arguments (Exline, 1962), as well as competitive games (Terhune, 1968). They also tend to be-

come anxious when they feel they are being evaluated (D. Byrne, 1961).

People who rank high in the need for power seek to control others (Burger, 1992). They try to make the world conform to their own image of what it should be. In groups, they want to be recognized (Winter, 1973). They are also concerned with their visibility among the general public (McClelland & Teague, 1975). People ranking high in the need for power tend to be aggressive and are more likely to seek out occupations in which they can influence others (Winter, 1992, 1993; Winter & Stewart, 1978).

Murray also proposed that each of us has a need for achievement. This need has been extensively investigated by many other researchers, as we see next.

McClelland's Need for Achievement

David McClelland and his colleagues have been particularly interested in the need for achievement (McClelland, 1961; McClelland, Atkinson, Clark, & Lowell, 1953; McClelland & Koestner, 1992; McClelland, Koestner, & Weinberger, 1992; McClelland & Winter, 1969). According to McClelland (1985), people who rank high in the need for achievement are people who seek out moderately challenging tasks, persist at them, and are especially likely to pursue success in their occupations. Many entrepreneurs show high need for achievement. Why would these people seek out tasks that are only moderately challenging? These are the tasks in which they are likely both to succeed and to extend themselves. They do not waste time on tasks so challenging that they have little probability of accomplishing them, nor do they waste time on tasks so easy that they pose no challenge at all.

People are especially likely to develop high need for achievement if they experience achievement pressure from their parents (McClelland & Franz, 1992). Research has shown that perception of reality, rather than reality per se, is the more powerful predictor of how people, and especially children, react to demands for achievement (Phillips, 1984). In other words, people are motivated not by pressures that objectively exist, but rather, by their perceptions of these pressures. For example, a guitarist in a successful band may still feel the need to achieve to become as good as he perceives his musical idol to be, despite his own objective success.

Gender Differences. Unfortunately, girls often perceive their competence to be lower than do boys, particularly as they grow older, and the result may be that they expect less of themselves in terms of achievement than do boys (Phillips & Zimmerman, 1990). In particular, girls may view themselves as not well able to survive in a competitive environment, whereas boys may perceive themselves as being able to do well in such an environment (Spence & Helmreich, 1983). The effect appears to begin to emerge as early as kindergarten (Frey & Ruble, 1987).

Cultural Differences. The achievement motive, which involves competition with an internalized standard of excellence, is present in every culture and has been the focus of dozens of cross-cultural studies (Maehr & Nicholls, 1980; Markus & Kitayama, 1991, 1994). Because increases in the achievement motive may be linked to increases in productivity, several projects in various cultures have been done to increase levels of this motive among workers and managers. In one such project, investigators assessed the effectiveness of attempts by Indian business owners to encourage their employees to emulate the achievement motive shown

by many Western businessmen and women. Toward this end, the Indian employees participated in an intense series of seminars designed to teach them to become achievement-oriented business people. The project was modestly successful (McClelland & Winter, 1969).

One of numerous studies of the achievement motive in China found that Chinese parents place great emphasis on achievement, but their focus is different from that of American parents (Ho, 1986). The children, too, differ in their focus. Whereas American children are motivated to achieve for the purpose of being independent, Chinese children are motivated to please the family and the community.

The difference between American and Chinese children points out the importance of the distinction made by Harry Triandis (1990, 1994) and others between individualist and collectivist cultures. Individualist cultures, like that of the United States and Great Britain, stress individuality and the achievement of personal goals; collectivist cultures like China, Japan, and Venezuela place more emphasis on meeting the needs of the group. In general, collectivist cultures (comprising about 70% of the world's population) have lower rates of crime, alcoholism, and suicide than do individualist cultures. Apparently, feeling oneself to be an integral part of a group reduces the kinds of stress that lead to these maladaptive patterns of behavior.

Maslow's Need Hierarchy

Abraham Maslow (1943, 1954, 1970) viewed needs as forming a hierarchy (see Figure 12-3). Once we have satisfied needs at lower levels, we seek satisfaction of needs at higher levels of the hierarchy.

Figure 12-3
MASLOW'S HIERARCHY OF NEEDS.
According to Abraham Maslow, we must satisfy our more basic needs before we strive to meet the higher level needs.

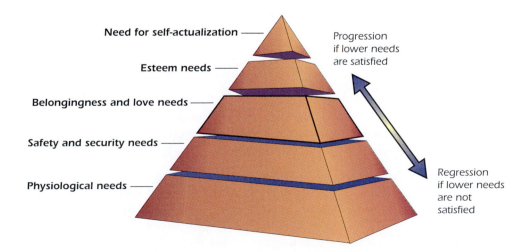

At the survival or first level are our basic survival or *physiological* needs, such as for food, water, and oxygen. Even in affluent countries many people live in poverty and struggle daily to meet this most basic level of needs. The second level addresses the needs for *safety and security*, for shelter and protection. The third level is the need to *belong*, to feel that other people love and care about us and to be part of a meaningful group, such as a family. The bond between children and their parents shows how important this need is. The fourth level is the need for *self-esteem*, to feel worthwhile. The highest level is the need for *self-actualization*, to fulfill our own potential.

Maslow's hierarchy is not a rigid one. Many people have given their lives in pursuit of causes fundamental to human dignity and self-esteem. But however the hierarchy is conceived, the empirical evidence in favor of this theory of motivation is weak to nonexistent. Table 12-2 summarizes clinical approaches to motivation.

Cognitive Factors Affecting Motivation

Cognitive theorists are especially interested in the cognitive, or thinking, processes underlying why people behave as they do.

Intrinsic and Extrinsic Motivators

Psychologists frequently describe motivation as being either intrinsic or extrinsic. **Intrinsic motivators** are rewards that come from within an individual, such as the desire to satisfy one's curiosity whereby the person engages in behavior because the person enjoys doing so. **Extrinsic motivators** are the rewards that come from outside the motivated individual. We can act on the basis of intrinsic reasons, extrinsic reasons, or combinations of the two. For example, we might study hard in a given subject because we are really excited about the material and want to learn it (intrinsic motivation), because we want to get an A in the course (extrinsic motivation), or because of both factors.

Society has created many extrinsic rewards to ensure that people accomplish what is in society's interests. Much of our system of education is based on grades, diplomas, and various other pieces of paper that attest to what we have and have not accomplished. These extrinsic rewards are examples of how society acknowledges the value of completing an educational program. How much weight do we as individuals give to extrinsic rewards?

People do their most creative work when they are intrinsically motivated (Amabile, 1983, 1985, 1996; see also R. J. Sternberg & Lubart, 1995, 1996). If we look at the most creative writers, artists, scientists, or workers in any other field, they are almost invariably people who have done their work largely for the enjoyment of it. This is not to say that these people were oblivious to extrinsic rewards, such as money or fame. Rather, they were task focused. They did what they did for the love of their work, with the money, fame, or other extrinsic rewards a pleasant by-product.

Extrinsic motivators can sometimes undermine intrinsic motivation (Deci, Koestner, & Ryan, 1999a, 1999b; Kohn, 1993; Lepper, 1998; Lepper,

---

TABLE 12–2

Clinical Approaches to Motivation   *Clinical psychologists have put forth three theories of motivation: that needs are the basis of our personalities, that we need to achieve, and that needs can be categorized in five different levels.*

THEORY	EXPLANATION
Theory of needs (Murray)	Needs form the core of our personalities. Among many other needs, we seek affiliation, power, and achievement.
Need for achievement (McClelland)	The need to achieve motivates us to be productive. People who have an intense need to achieve seek out moderately difficult tasks because they are most likely to succeed at those tasks while still being challenged by them.
Hierarchy of needs (Maslow)	We have five levels of needs (physiological, safety, belonging, self-esteem, and self-actualization). We need to fulfill the needs of one level before we can proceed to the next level.

Keavney, & Drake, 1996; Lepper & Henderlong, in press; Lepper, Henderlong, & Gingras, 1999; Tang & Hall, 1995). Janet Spence and Robert Helmreich (1983) have studied the motivational patterns and achievements of thousands of college students, scientists, pilots, business people, and athletes. They concluded that intrinsic motivation produces high achievement, and that extrinsic motivation often does not. Spence and Helmreich identified and assessed three facets of intrinsic motivation: people's quest for mastery, their drive to work, and their competitiveness. They found that, despite similar abilities, people oriented toward mastery and hard work typically achieve more. However, those who were *most* competitive, thereby showing a more extrinsic orientation, often achieve *less*. People driven by a desire for mastery and work achieved more if they were not also highly competitive.

Edward Deci and his colleagues (Deci, Koestner, & Ryan, 1999a, 1999b; Deci & Ryan, 1995; Deci, Vallerand, Pelletier, & Ryan, 1991; Rigby, Deci, Patrick, & Ryan, 1992; Vallerand, Fortier, & Guay, 1997) have suggested that people need to feel competent, autonomous, and securely and satisfyingly connected to other people. According to Deci, we are all powerfully motivated to meet these three innate needs.

This emphasis on self-determination helps explain extrinsic versus intrinsic motivation. Intrinsically motivated activities satisfy both our need for competence and our need for autonomy. In contrast, many extrinsically motivated activities can undermine our sense of autonomy because we attribute the control of our behavior to sources outside ourselves, rather than to internal ones. In such cases, the lack of control may lead us to feel less competent.

Characteristics of Effective Rewards

Fortunately, not all extrinsic rewards have a negative effect. Four critical factors seem to determine whether an extrinsic motivator will undermine intrinsic motivation (Cameron & Pierce, 1994; Eisenberger & Armeli, 1997; Eisenberger & Cameron, 1996). The first factor is *expectancy*. The extrinsic reward will undermine intrinsic motivation only if the individual expects to receive the award contingent on performing the tasks. The second factor is the *relevance* of the reward. The reward must be something important to the individual. If you are told that you will receive a spool of thread as a reward for performing a task, and a spool of thread is not of any interest to you, yet you engage in the task anyway, the nominal reward will probably not undermine your intrinsic motivation. Indeed, you may

well forget about it (R. Ross, 1975). The third factor is whether the reward is *tangible* (e.g., a certificate, a prize, money, candy, a grade) as a motivating factor. Whereas tangible rewards tend to undermine intrinsic motivation, intangible rewards—such as praise or a smile—do not seem to undermine it (Deci, 1971, 1972; Deci, Koestner, & Ryan, 1999a, 1999b; Reeve & Deci, 1996; Swann & Pittman, 1977). The fourth and final factor is whether the reward is *noncontingent*. Tangible rewards are contingent and thus require engaging in a task or completing the task in a high-quality way (Deci, Koestner, & Ryan, 1999a).

Explanatory Style

One of the best ways to remain intrinsically motivated is to adapt what Martin Seligman (1991) refers to as an *optimistic explanatory style*. People with such a style tend to attribute their successes to their own abilities and their failures to the environment. They motivate themselves by telling themselves that they have the ability to overcome the obstacles in their environment. People with a *pessimistic explanatory style*, in contrast, attribute their successes to the environment but their failures to their own lack of ability. They have greater difficulty motivating themselves because they believe that, as they lack the ability to succeed, it is scarcely worth trying (Peterson, Maier, & Seligman, 1993).

Other intrinsic motivators may include human beings' natural tendencies to seek out novelty and challenges and to control things that happen to us. These three motivators are discussed next.

Curiosity and Challenge

What makes people curious about some things and not others? We tend to be curious about things that are moderately novel to us and moderately complex, relative to our existing understanding (Berlyne, 1960; Heyduk & Bahrick, 1977; Loewenstein, 1994). This makes sense. If something is totally familiar to us, we ignore it; we have nothing to learn from it. Similarly, if something is wholly novel, we have no basis for understanding it. However, if we encounter something that is novel, but within our realm of understanding, it piques our interest; we become curious and explore it.

Even in everyday activities, we seek some degree of intrinsic motivation and challenge. We and our fellow primates seek to be active, to observe and explore our surroundings, to manipulate aspects of and objects in our environments, and to gain mastery over our environments (White, 1959).

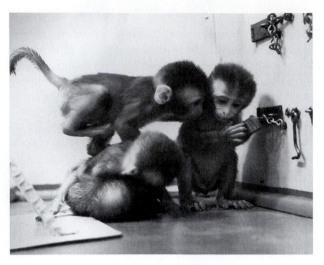

Primates of all species appear to show curiosity, exploring their surrondings for the sheer joy of doing so. For example, monkeys will learn to perform tasks, such as opening latches, just to have something to do. (Harlow, Harlow, & Meyer, 1950)

We also actively seek self-determination, rather than determination by outside forces (deCharms, 1968). We are often unhappy when we feel controlled, whether it is by another person or even by a substance (as in an addiction). We are generally unhappy when we feel like pawns—that our futures are predetermined, or that others are controlling our actions. We are motivated to be—and to feel—in charge of our own destiny.

Self-Efficacy Theory

How does our sense of competence affect the likelihood that we will attain our particular goal? Our expectations of **self-efficacy**—people's beliefs in their own competence to master the environment and reach personal goals—can derive from a number of sources: direct experience, our interpretation of the experience of others, what people tell us that we are able to do, and our assessment of our own emotional or motivational state. If we have a higher degree of self-efficacy, we are more likely to attain the outcomes we desire (Bandura, 1977a, 1986, 1995, 1996). However, there are no guarantees: Certain kinds of environments (e.g., repressive dictatorships) can make attainments difficult, regardless of people's self-efficacy.

Our level of self-efficacy can lead to self-fulfilling prophecies. When we believe we are able to do something, we are more likely to put in the effort and resources to do it, and therefore to achieve the outcome. One success leads to another, and we see ourselves as continually successful in maintaining the

outcomes we desire. In contrast, if we have a low sense of self-efficacy, we may believe that we are unable to succeed and, as a result, will hardly even try. The result, of course, is failure, which leads to the expectation of future failure, which then becomes the basis for more failure. One way to enhance our self-efficacy in reaching our goals is to set for ourselves a set of realistic, highly specific goals, and then to devise plans for meeting those goals. For example, if you have a goal of doing well in this course, you will do well to tell yourself that you have the ability to do well in the course, and then to set up a concrete, well-specified plan for studying that will enable you to succeed. People's sense of self-efficacy can be increased by setting goals. Psychological theorists have long recognized that setting goals can be effective both in motivating people and in helping them get done what they need to get done (Ames, 1992; Dweck, 1992; E. A. Locke & Latham, 1985, 1990; Meece & Holt, 1993; Urdan & Maehr, 1995; Tolman, 1932, 1959). Goals help us to focus our attention, mobilize our resources, and develop ways of getting things done, even in the face of obstacles.

The importance of goals is shown particularly well in work comparing children with learning versus performance goals. Carol Dweck (1999) has distinguished between goals that emphasize the importance of learning new information (learning goals) and those that emphasize the importance of showing oneself to be smart, regardless of whether one is really learning much (performance goals). Children who emphasize learning goals tend to be more willing to take on difficult courses and challenges than are children who emphasize performance goals. Moreover, when they encounter very challenging tasks, children who emphasize learning goals are much less likely to become frustrated and fall apart than are children who emphasize performance goals.

In sum, cognitive theories of motivation emphasize the role of thought processes in motivating behavior. Such approaches (summarized in Table 12-3) complement the other kinds of approaches that have been discussed.

It seems that no single motivational theory can explain everything. Physiological, clinical, and cognitive theories all have strengths and weaknesses in explaining behaviors. The theories generally work well to explain some motivations but not others. As in many other areas of psychology, perhaps the kinds of theories are complementary, each offering a partial explanation of a complex behavior. The next section considers in more detail two primary motivations that are more complex than they seem to be at first: hunger and sexual desire. As you read, consider what each of the theories discussed so far might have to say about why people eat and why they want sex.

The Ups and Downs of Intrinsic Motivation

Edward L. Deci, *University of Rochester*

Think for a moment about an activity that you love, something you happily do for no reward other than the interest and enjoyment you experience while doing it. Perhaps it is skateboarding, reading a novel, or playing softball. Psychologists would describe you as intrinsically motivated when you do the activity: The motivation is within you and is self-sustaining. Intrinsic motivation stands in contrast to extrinsic motivation in which you behave to attain a desired outcome, such as earning money, avoiding a reprimand, or winning a trophy.

Now imagine that your uncle wants to encourage you to do your favorite activity—let's say it's playing softball—so he offers you $20 for each game your team wins. How do you suppose the extrinsic rewards will affect your intrinsic motivation for softball?

That is exactly the question I set out to answer in an experiment 30 years ago (Deci, 1971). I had college students come into the laboratory one at a time, and I asked them to work on four interesting, building-block puzzles. I already knew the puzzles were intrinsically interesting because I had pilot-tested them with several students. I treated all the participants in the study exactly the same, except for one thing. I told half of them that they would earn a dollar for each puzzle they solved, but I said nothing about money to the other half.

All the students worked on the same puzzles, but only half of them earned rewards for each one they solved. Subsequently, they all had an opportunity to work on more puzzles, but this time there were no rewards for anyone. The idea was to see how much time, if any, they would choose to work on the puzzles when there was no reason for doing them other than the students' level of interest in the task itself. If the rewards had enhanced participants' intrinsic motivation, the rewarded group would spend more of this free-play time working on the puzzles than the non-rewarded group, but if the rewards had undermined intrinsic motivation, the rewarded group would spend less time with the puzzles.

In fact, the results showed that the previously rewarded group did spend significantly less time with the puzzles, indicating that the extrinsic rewards were undermining participants' intrinsic motivation. Since that study, more than 100 experiments, using different tasks, different-aged participants, and different types of rewards, have confirmed that overall, tangible, extrinsic rewards do, indeed, undermine intrinsic motivation.

Many years ago, Richard Ryan and I proposed that the reason rewards undermine intrinsic motivation is that people come to view rewards, rather than their interest, as the reason for doing the behavior.

Ryan and his colleagues subsequently suggested that although rewards often feel controlling, it should be possible to use them in a way that is experienced as providing positive feedback or expressing appreciation for a job well done. The researchers did an experiment to test this and found that when the language and style used to administer tangible rewards seemed controlling, the rewards were undermining, but when the language and style supported participants' initiative and acknowledged their good performance, the rewards were not detrimental (Ryan, Mims, & Koestner, 1983).

Ryan, our associates, and I then headed into schools and work organizations. We used questionnaire methods to investigate the same phenomena, within ongoing interactions, that we had observed in the lab.

We began by focusing on the degree to which different elementary school teachers were oriented toward controlling students' behavior (e.g., by using rewards as controls) versus supporting students' autonomy. We found that students whose teachers were *autonomy supportive* reported more intrinsic motivation for learning and had higher self-esteem than students whose teachers were controlling, thus indicating that the autonomy supportive teachers used rewards in ways that were less controlling and more informative (Deci, Schwartz, Sheinman, & Ryan, 1981).

We then moved on to a major multinational corporation where we found that subordinates of managers who were oriented toward supporting employees' autonomy felt less pressured, had a higher level of trust, and were more satisfied with their jobs than subordinates of managers who were more controlling (Deci, Connell, & Ryan, 1989).

It seems, then, that the same effects we produced in the laboratory do occur in the real world. That is, the use of rewards to motivate or control people's behavior tends to undermine their intrinsic motivation and related feelings such as satisfaction and trust. But when the people who administer rewards work to build and maintain meaningful relationships with the people they reward, the rewards are less likely to be detrimental.

References

Deci, E. L. (1971). Effects of externally mediated rewards on intrinsic motivation. *Journal of Personality and Social Psychology, 18,* 105–115.

Deci, E. L., Connell, J. P., & Ryan, R. M. (1989). Self-determination in a work organization. *Journal of Applied Psychology, 74,* 580–590.

Deci, E. L., Schwartz, A. J., Sheinman, L., & Ryan, R. M. (1981). An instrument to assess adults' orientations toward control versus autonomy with children: Reflections on intrinsic motivation and perceived competence. *Journal of Educational Psychology, 73,* 642–650.

Ryan, R. M., Mims, V., & Koestner, R. (1983). Relation of reward contingency and interpersonal context to intrinsic motivation: A review and test using cognitive evaluation theory. *Journal of Personality and Social Psychology, 45,* 736–750.

 Find out more about this topic at www.harcourtcollege.com/psych/ishm

TABLE 12–3

Cognitive Approaches to Motivation *Cognitive psychologists have proposed different theories of motivation: that we respond to internal and external motivators, that we are motivated by curiosity and control, and that we are motivated by our belief in ourselves.*

APPROACH	DESCRIPTION
Intrinsic and extrinsic motivators	Our interests motivate us intrinsically; rewards or threats of punishment motivate us extrinsically. Usually our behaviors are the result of a combination of intrinsic and extrinsic motivations, although we are most creative when we are mainly motivated intrinsically.
Curiosity, challenge, and control	We are most curious about things that are moderately new and complex because they challenge us without boring or confusing us. We can become totally absorbed in a task (Maslow). We always seek to understand and control our environments, to be competent (White, deCharms), and to be part of a group (Deci).
Self-efficacy theory (Bandura)	Our beliefs about whether we can attain a goal greatly influence our ability actually to attain it.

Biological Bases of Motivation

 *In Search of . . .*

What are the biological bases of motivation?

Hunger

Scientists used to think that the regulation of hunger was very simple: We felt hunger when our stomach contracted (Cannon & Washburn, 1912). However, research has shown, both in rats (C. T. Morgan & Morgan, 1940) and in humans (M. I. Grossman & Stein, 1948), that if the nerve responsible for carrying messages between the stomach and the brain is severed we still feel hunger. Even more persuasive is the finding that after people's stomachs are surgically removed (for medical reasons) they continue to feel hunger (Janowitz, 1967; Wangensteen & Carlson, 1931). Clearly, there is more to hunger than just the empty feeling in the stomach.

Of course, the stomach participates in the regulation of hunger (McHugh & Moran, 1985). In all mammals, the stomach empties at a constant rate; for humans, the rate is slightly over 2 calories per minute. (Note that it is caloric content, rather than the volume of food, that determines how fast the food leaves the stomach. A large bowl of lettuce with no dressing may leave you feeling hungry more quickly than a small piece of cake, because the stomach will empty itself of the lower-calorie lettuce more quickly.) As the stomach contracts, we feel more and more hungry. Usually, we start feeling hunger when the stomach is roughly 60% empty, and we feel very hungry when the stomach is 90% empty (Sepple & Read, 1989).

If the stomach is not the only organ responsible for hunger, then maybe other organs play a role in signaling us to eat. One of the most important organs in the body, the brain, is certainly involved in hunger.

The Role of the Brain in Hunger

The brain, particularly the hypothalamus, is very important in regulating hunger (refer back to Figure 3-11 for the location of the hypothalamus). If the ventromedial hypothalamus (VMH) in an animal has a lesion, that animal will overeat and eventually become obese (Hetherington & Ranson, 1940; Teitelbaum, 1961; but see Valenstein, 1973; see Figure 12-4). The VMH, therefore, appears to regulate hunger and, in particular, serves as a source of negative feedback. When the organism is satiated, the VMH signals that it is time to stop eating. In animals with a destroyed VMH, the satiation signal never is sent.

Lesions in the lateral hypothalamus (LH) have exactly the opposite effect of VMH destruction (Anand & Brobeck, 1951). An animal that has a lesion in the LH simply does not eat, which leads to starvation and death. Thus, in effect, the LH is an on switch for eating, and the VMH is an off switch.

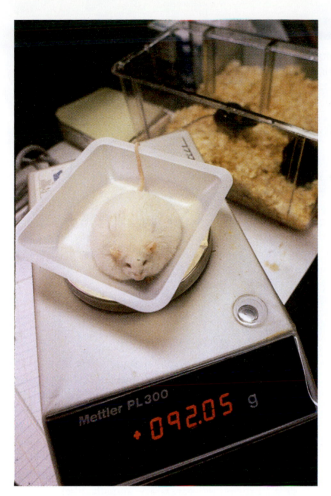

Figure 12–4

OBESE RAT.   *When a lesion is created in the ventromedial hypothalamus (VMH) of a rat brain, the rat becomes obese. Lesion studies led researchers to conclude that the VMH is involved in regulating the detection of when to stop feeling hunger. Are alternate explanations of this finding possible? If so, what are they? If not, why?*

Theories of the Regulation of Hunger

In order for the VMH and LH to regulate eating behavior, they need information from the body. What signals hunger or satiety (fullness)? Two major hypotheses present possible explanations, although they may not be mutually exclusive. According to the *glucostatic hypothesis*, levels of *glucose* (a simple body sugar) in the blood signal the body regarding the need for food (M. I. Friedman & Stricker, 1976). A person will feel hungry when the level of glucose in the body falls below a certain point. The term *glucostatic* refers to the stability of glucose levels in the body and the brain.

Some findings cannot be accounted for by this hypothesis (Cotman & McGaugh, 1980), which has led to the development of an alternative explanation for understanding hunger, the *lipostatic hypothesis*. This hypothesis suggests that the levels of *lipids* (fats) in the blood signal the body regarding the need for food. As the proportion of fats in the body decreases, hunger increases (Hoebel & Teitelbaum, 1966). According to this theory, eating is a way of maintaining adequate reserves of energy via body weight. Indeed, the body monitors these signs of fat cells on a fairly constant basis (Faust, Johnson, & Hirsch, 1977a, 1977b). When body fat gets too low, people eat, and when it gets too high, they stop eating (Keesey, Boyle, Kemnitz, & Mitchell, 1976; Keesey & Powley, 1975).

Recent evidence suggests that a hormone called *leptin* may be involved in food-seeking behavior. Obesity may be associated with lack of regulation of hunger by this hormone (Figlewicz et al., 1996; Rohner-Jeanrenaud,Cusin, Sainsbury, Zahrzewska, & Jeanrenaud, 1996; Tomaszuk, Simpson, & Williams, 1996; White & Martin, 1997).

The lipostatic hypothesis led Richard Keesey, Terry Powley, and their colleagues to formulate the **set-point theory,** according to which each person has a preset body weight that is biologically determined either at birth or within the first few years following birth, based on the fat cells in the body, which may increase but not decrease in number over the course of the life span (Grilo & Pogue-Geile, 1991; Keesey, 1980). People with more fat cells tend to have greater body weight. Although the number of fat cells can increase, it does not naturally decrease across the life span. What varies with weight is the size of the fat cells. When the person eats less, the size of the cells shrinks, and the person feels hungry. When the person eats more, the size of the cells increases, and the person feels full.

Set-point theory predicts that it will be very difficult for a person to lose weight because the tendency of the body will always be to return to the set point, the point at which the variably sized fat cells are of a normal size. If we diet, our bodies respond as though we were in a prolonged state of starvation, storing as much food energy as possible. Thus, the less we eat, the more our bodies work to help us overcome our starved condition, struggling to keep us as fat as possible despite our low intake of calories. In addition, overeating for a long time can raise the set point (Keesey & Powley, 1986). Statistics on weight loss seem to support set-point theory: More than 90% of weight-losing dieters eventually gain weight back. (See Table 12-4 for a summary of these theories.) Certain research (Safer, 1991; Seraganian, 1993) indicates that the combination of exercise and low-fat, low-calorie dieting may be more effective in achieving weight loss than are dietary restrictions alone and that both should be part of the treatment of the problem of obesity, which is considered next.

TABLE 12–4

Theories of the Regulation of Hunger *Three prominent theories of the regulation of hunger are based on the level of glucose in the blood, the level of fats in the blood, and the number of fat cells in the body.*

THEORY	EXPLANATION
Glucostatic hypothesis	The VMH and LH in the brain monitor the level of glucose in the blood to determine the need for food.
Lipostatic hypothesis	The VMH and LH in the brain monitor the level of lipids (fats) in the blood to determine the need for food.
Set-point theory	We each have a preset body weight, determined by the number of fat cells in the body. The fat cells expand when we gain weight and contract when we lose weight. If we try to lose weight, it will be difficult to go below the set point; our bodies interpret the diet as starvation and respond by storing as much food as possible. If we gain weight over time, the set point can increase.

Obesity and Dieting

People often are highly motivated to lose weight, yet fail. What are the factors that lead to success or failure in losing weight, especially when one starts off as obese?

To be considered obese, a person must be at least 20% over the normal range for a given height and weight (see chapter 18). In the United States, about 24% of men and 27% of women are considered to be obese. Many of those people, plus even more people who do not meet the definition of obesity, subject themselves to diets. Dieting often fails, however, because people become more susceptible to binge eating when they are dieting than when they are not (Polivy & Herman, 1983, 1985, 1993). When subjected to anxiety, depression, alcohol, stress, high-calorie foods, or other factors, dieters seem to drop the restraints that have kept them from eating and many start to binge (Polivy, Herman, & McFarlane, 1994). Those who are not dieting do not exhibit comparable behavior; this finding seems to give further support to set-point theory.

Polivy, Herman, and McFarlane (1994) have shown how attempts to diet or otherwise control weight through restrained eating can backfire. They classified a group of 96 female college students as either restrained eaters (trying to control weight by regulating food intake) or unrestrained eaters. Members of one group of participants were told they would have to give a speech which would give a measure of their abilities. Members of a second group were told they would be asked about perceptions of fabrics as a function of how the fabrics felt when touched. The goal of the manipulation was to introduce feelings of anxiety in the first group, but not in the second. Prior to this manipulation, however, participants were asked to take part in a study of taste perception, in which they were allowed to eat as many cookies as they wished before passing judgment on their taste. The critical finding was that restrained eaters increased their consumption of cookies when they were anxious, whereas unrestrained eaters decreased their consumption. These results suggest that restrained eaters, when confronted with the normal anxieties of life, are susceptible to binge eating, whereas unrestrained eaters are actually likely to decrease food consumption when feeling anxious.

Research (Brownell & Rodin, 1994; Brownell & Wadden, 1992; Lissner et al., 1991) also suggests that fluctuations in weight are more damaging to health than is being overweight. In other words, you may do yourself more harm by engaging in a constant cycle of losing and regaining weight than by just leaving your weight alone.

Other factors seem to contribute to obesity as well. For example, people tend to eat more when presented with a wide variety of foods (Rolls, 1979; Rolls, Rowe, & Rolls, 1982). People also tend to eat more in the presence of others (S. L. Berry, Beatty, & Klesges, 1985; deCastro & Brewer, 1992).

Cultural Factors in the Perception of Obesity

Some cross-cultural psychologists emphasize external factors in explaining wide individual differences in weight. Such differences can be observed across both cultures and time. For example, in Samoa, Fiji, Tonga, and other Pacific islands, it is not uncommon for males and females to weigh more than 300 pounds. In contrast, in Japan, very heavy people, such as well-fed Sumo wrestlers, clearly stand out in a crowd as violating societal norms. In the United States, J. Fuchs and his colleagues (1990) noted the relative infrequency of obesity among the Amish and attributed this distinction to the healthful characteristics of the lifestyle in that culture. Norms and expectations regarding what is considered to be an ideal weight also can be observed across time by viewing the historical collections in an art museum. In many masterworks by European artists, the bodies of nude females are quite ample by modern European or American standards. The contemporary trend toward ever more slender physiques has been documented by noting the increasing prominence of slim models in popular women's magazines in various countries (Silverstein, Peterson, & Perdue, 1986). Perhaps, as might be suggested by clinically based motivation theorists, people are motivated to satisfy their self-esteem or affiliation needs by achieving their culture's definition of the ideal weight.

Anorexia Nervosa

Being overweight is a serious problem for many people, but some people tend to be chronically underweight either because they metabolize food very quickly and inefficiently or because they have a hormonal imbalance. A minority of underweight people suffer from **anorexia nervosa,** an eating disorder in which a person undereats potentially to the point of starvation, based on the extremely distorted belief that she (usually) or he is overweight. People who suffer from anorexia perceive themselves to be fat and so put themselves on severe diets (Heilbrun & Witt, 1990). They are diagnosed as anorexic when they weigh less than 85% of their normal body weight, but nevertheless are intensely afraid of becoming fat (DSM-IV, 1994). In fact, up to 30% of anorexics ultimately die from the damage the disorder causes (Szmukler & Russell, 1986), such as to the heart. The vast majority (95%) of anorexics are females between ages 15 and 30 (Gilbert & DeBlassie, 1984). The high value that American society places on slimness helps explain why mainly young women suffer from this disorder. Interestingly, the incidence of anorexia has increased in other societies as well, such as Denmark and Japan (Nielsen, 1990; Suematsu, Ishikawa, Kuboki, & Ito, 1985).

No one knows what causes anorexia. Some evidence indicates that the roots of the disorder may be in dysfunctional family relationships (Bruch, 1973), particularly those in which perfectionism and control are highly valued. Other evidence indicates that the roots may be physiological (Gwirtsman & Germer, 1981). The treatments of the disorder reflect the possible causes. Anorexics may undergo psychotherapy, drug treatment, and in severe cases, hospitalization to treat the psychological and physical problems (F. E. Martin, 1985).

More common than anorexia is *bulimia*, a disorder characterized by eating binges followed either by

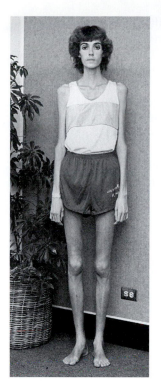

The photo on the right shows that this woman was fortunate to have recovered from the life-threatening disorder of anorexia nervosa. Astonishingly, like other anorexics, at the time the photo on the left was taken, this woman was starving herself to death because she perceived herself to be overweight and flabby.

vomiting or by other means of purging, such as the use of laxatives. This disorder, like anorexia, is primarily a disorder of adolescence and young adulthood. Bulimia, too, is far more common in women than in men, and it is especially common in adolescent girls (Striegel-Moore, Silberstein, & Rodin, 1993). Like anorexia, it is difficult to treat, but also like anorexia, it usually can be treated successfully with psychotherapy and, where appropriate, drugs.

Adolescents' (and adults') concerns over body image may be a reflection of a larger preoccupation that many Western societies seem to have—sex.

Sex

How much do people think about sex anyway? According to Michael, Gagnon, Laumann, and Kolatu (1994), people think about sex a lot, especially if they are male. As many as 54% of men and 19% of women think about it at least once a day.

Sexual motivation obviously differs in certain key respects from hunger motivation. For one thing, although very few people try to make themselves hungry or thirsty, most do seek sexual arousal. People also tend to enjoy sexual arousal more than they enjoy hunger. Perhaps the key difference relates to individual survival. People can survive without sexual gratification, but they cannot survive without food or water; you might therefore conclude that sexual motivation is in a category wholly different from that of hunger. In at least one sense, this conclusion would be incorrect. Sexual motivation is as important to the ultimate survival of humanity as is hunger motivation. If people do not satisfy their sexual wants, humanity will disappear just as certainly as it will from starvation.

The hypothalamus, which plays a role in hunger motivation, also plays an important role in sexual motivation. The role, however, is indirect. The hypothalamus stimulates the pituitary gland, which in turn releases hormones that influence the production of sex hormones (see chapter 3). There are two main kinds of sexual hormones: androgens and estrogens. Although both males and females have both androgens and estrogens, androgens predominate in the male, estrogens in the female. Without these hormones, sexual desire disappears—abruptly in many species, but only gradually among most humans (Money, Wiedeking, Walker, & Gain, 1976).

Sexual desire serves an important evolutionary function, in that it is key to the survival of many kinds of organisms. David Buss (1994) suggests men and women have rather different sexual strategies. Males can impregnate several women in relatively short succession, and so their optimal strategy for the spreading of their genes might lead them, evolutionarily, to have relatively lower standards for whom they impregnate. In theory, and too often in practice, they can impregnate a woman and quickly be gone. Women, who can be impregnated no more often than once every 9 to 12 months or so, perhaps can be expected evolutionarily to have higher standards. If they choose the wrong man, they are left with the consequences for not only the 9 months of pregnancy, but usually for the upbringing of the child as well.

Sexual Scripts and Social Norms

Sexual desire always occurs in the company of cognitive processing. One may feel strongly attracted to someone, but even blind attraction is accompanied by thoughts of how desirable the person is. One way to describe the cognitive processes that accompany sexual response is in terms of *sexual scripts* (Gagnon, 1973; W. H. Simon & Gagnon, 1986), which are mental representations of how sequences of sexual events should be enacted. For example, most of us—whether or not we have ever engaged in sexual intercourse—probably could describe some kind of sexual script, particularly if we have read racy novels, seen romantic television shows, or watched sexy movies. Most of us have many sexual scripts that we may use, depending on the person we are with—or

whether we are with another person at all. Although the desire for sexual consummation is largely a physiological need, scripts also reflect social influences.

An example of a sexual script "gone bad" is *date rape*, which occurs when someone is forced to have sexual intercourse in the context of a social engagement. Date rape is most likely to occur when men believe in a sexual script in which they see their role as one of overcoming resistance, in whatever way, on the part of a woman. If a woman has a script in which she believes she should offer token resistance and then give in, date rape is even more likely. According to Murnen, Peroit, and Byrne (1989), over half of college women report having experienced unwanted sexual activity. Clearly, both men and women need to recognize the adverse consequences of the maladaptive sexual scripts that allow or even foster date rape.

Every society attempts to regulate the sexual behavior of its members. For example, all societies impose a taboo against *incest*—sexual contact between biologically related members of the immediate family. Similarly, most societies attempt to regulate sexual behavior through cultural norms regarding modesty, masturbation, premarital intercourse, marital intercourse, extramarital intercourse, and homosexuality. For example, norms of modesty determine the regions of the male and the female body that should be covered or exposed, decorated or unadorned. Although the specific regions that are to be covered or exposed differ widely from one culture to another, all cultures seem to impose some standards of modesty, at least on one of the sexes, typically on females.

Homosexuality

In American culture, most sexual scripts are heterosexual but homosexual scripts are also common. **Homosexuality** is a tendency to direct sexual desire toward another person of the same sex. Although we speak of homosexuality and heterosexuality as though the two are discrete and mutually exclusive, perhaps it is best to consider them as aspects of a continuum. At one end are those who are exclusively homosexual; at the other end are those who are exclusively heterosexual; many others fall in between. People who identify themselves as directing their sexual desire to members of both sexes are referred to as **bisexual.** Most researchers in this field have found that about 10% of men and a slightly smaller proportion of women identify themselves as having predominantly homosexual orientations (e.g., see Fay, Turner, Klassen, & Gagnon, 1989; S. M. Rogers & Turner, 1991).

What causes homosexuality or bisexuality—or heterosexuality, for that matter? Various explanations exist, some more scientific than others (Biery, 1990). Of the several theories proposed (see Table 12-5), the greatest

TABLE 12–5

Reasons Underlying Homosexual Versus Heterosexual Orientation   *Over the years, psychologists have posited various reasons for sexual orientation. Most recently, biological reasons seem to be the most plausible, but additional research in this area is sorely needed.*

Reason	Related Motivational Theory	Description	Critique
Biological	Physiological	Sexual orientation is, in part, a result of biological processes.	There is some support for this view. A small region of the hypothalamus may be less than half the size in homosexual men than it is in heterosexual men (LeVay, 1991). If one of a pair of genetically identical male twins is homosexually oriented then the other will be almost three times more likely to have the same orientation as when the twins are not identical (J. M. Bailey & Pillard, 1991).
Weak father, strong mother	Clinical	Homosexuals had weak fathers or overly strong mothers.	Not well supported by data. There are far too many exceptions to this generalization and this view is not widely accepted today.
Arrested development	Clinical	Homosexuals become fixated in a homosexual phase of psychosexual development.	This view implies that all heterosexuals pass through a homosexual phase. There is no empirical evidence to support this point of view.
Personal choice	Cognitive, self-determination, control	People simply choose their sexual orientations.	Whatever attracts one person to another rarely is a matter solely of conscious choice.
Social learning	Cognitive, extrinsic motivation	Homosexuals were rewarded for homosexual leanings and punished for heterosexual ones.	Mainstream U.S. society (among others) gives few rewards for a homosexual orientation, and few children are likely to be exposed to overtly homosexual role models. Of those who are, about the same proportion become heterosexual or homosexual as in the mainstream population.
Gender nonconformity	Cognitive	Members of the same sex are seen as more exotic and hence more attractive than members of the opposite sex.	Evidence is very preliminary.

evidence seems to support a biological explanation, although the verdict is by no means in (R. Byrne, 1995). Until quite recently, many psychiatrists and psychologists believed that homosexuality was a form of mental illness. However, no inherent association between maladjustment or psychopathology and homosexuality has been found (Hooker, 1993).

Even if there is a biological basis for homosexuality, however, whether this predisposition is actually expressed in behavior may well depend on social learning and other environmental factors. For example, D. J. Bem (1996) has suggested that homosexual behavior results when the child views members of the same sex as more unfamiliar and exotic than members of the opposite sex. The child soon becomes attracted to members of the same sex. We view homosexuality and sexual orientation according to our culture's prescriptions and proscriptions (Wade & Cirese, 1991). We are unlikely to find a single cause of homosexual orientation. Rather, it is more likely that a combination of factors leads people one way or another.

As we have just seen, what at first may seem like a simple matter of satisfying a physiological need, whether for food or for sex, can actually be affected by a tangle of different motivational processes all interacting at once. In the next half of the chapter, we will see that our emotions are also quite complex.

Emotions and Their Characteristics

In Search of . . .

What are the major emotions and how do they function?

Having considered the nature of motivation, we now turn to emotion. An **emotion** is a psychological feeling, usually accompanied by a physiological reaction (see J. G. Carlson & Hatfield, 1992). For example, happiness and sadness are emotions.

Emotions can be either preprogrammed (genetic) or learned and they can be manifested in various ways, such as by facial expressions, tone of voice, and actions that reflect the emotions. Furthermore, they can be caused either by stimuli impinging on us from the outside or by things that happen within our body (Ekman & Davidson, 1994). For example, you may react differently to a missing set of car keys, depending on whether you have just had a large mug of black coffee or have just finished a large meal. Emotion and motivation are very closely linked and often it is difficult to distinguish them. In general, for motives the stimulus is unobserved whereas for emotions it often is apparent. Motives are also more likely to occur cyclically

(e.g., recurring hunger) than are emotions. Motives are further experienced as desires to attain something, whereas emotions are experienced as feelings. Just what are the major emotions?

Happiness, fear, anger, sadness, and disgust are the five emotions most often regarded as being basic to all humans. As we will see, these emotions have emerged as universal: They are experienced and recognized readily by individuals living in diverse cultures. To these emotions, some would add surprise (which is much less commonly recognized across cultures), guilt (private sense of culpability), and shame (public humiliation; see, for example, Figure 12-5 for various shadings of emotions). The five most widely recognized emotions have been researched more than most others. We now examine each.

Happiness or Joy

Happiness, the feeling of joy or at least contentment, is usually considered a fundamental emotion. When people describe what they experience when they feel *happy*, they say that they feel a warm inner glow, or feel like smiling, or feel a sense of well-being and of harmony and peace within themselves. Not everyone defines *happiness* in quite the same way. For some people, happiness is achieved with

Figure 12–5

PLUTCHIK'S EMOTION WHEEL. *Robert Plutchik posits eight basic emotions, which occur in four pairs that are opposite each other in the circle. Emotions that are adjacent to one another combine to create a composite emotion (e.g., joy combined with acceptance yields love). (After Plutchik, 1980)*

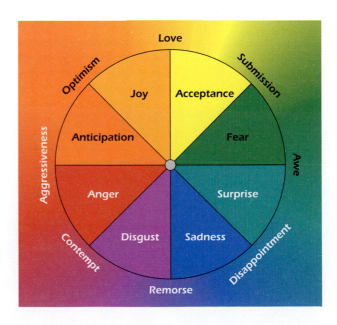

pleasure, almost without regard to the cost, whereas for others, happiness is essentially the absence of problems in their lives (Bradburn, 1969; Bradburn & Capovitz, 1965).

Although we tend to think of happiness as a temporary state, it may also have some of the aspects of an enduring trait. When people rate their happiness, the mean rating is about 6 on a 10-point scale (Wesman & Ricks, 1966). Moreover, ratings for a given person are remarkably constant from one day to the next. Married people generally tend to be happier than never-married people, and except in very poor countries, personal wealth is not predictive of happiness (D. Myers & Diener, 1995). There may also be differences in people across cultures. In a study of happiness in 13 countries, the proportion of people who described themselves as "very happy" varied from one country to the next. The percentages ranged from a low of 34% in South Korea to a high of 52% in Italy (Hastings & Hastings, 1982). The difference is obviously substantial.

Fear and Anxiety

Fear is an emotion characterized by being afraid of a specific threat of danger or harm, focused on a particular object or experience. From an evolutionary point of view, fear serves a protective function because it motivates us to avoid or to flee from the things that might cause us harm. **Anxiety** is a generalized feeling of dread or apprehension that is not focused on or directed toward any particular object or event. Thus, the difference between fear and anxiety is in the identification of the cause of distress. In fear, we can point to the cause; in anxiety, we cannot. When anxious, we feel apprehensive without knowing exactly why. In addition, anxiety is generally more pervasive and diffuse and it tends to last longer. Although almost everyone feels simple anxiety at one time or another, anxiety disorders are more serious (see chapter 16).

Anger

Anger can be activated by feeling frustrated or otherwise restrained from pursuit of a goal. We are most likely to be angry at another person when we believe that we have suffered unjustified and intentional insult or injury (Averill, 1983). If we believe that someone's behavior is either accidental or unavoidable, or justified, we are much less likely to get angry. Although we believe that we are likely to feel anger toward those whom we dislike or detest, in fact, we are most likely to feel anger toward the people closest to us. Consider some (rounded) percentages. About 29% of our overt expression of anger is directed toward people we love, 24% toward people we like, 25% toward acquaintances, and only 8% toward people we actively dislike (Averill, 1980, 1983). Only 13% of our expression of anger is directed toward strangers.

At one time, the prevailing belief was that the best way to rid oneself of anger is to express it and get it out of one's system. Recent research shows this advice to be incorrect. Expressing the anger often increases it and may lead to ill health, problems in interpersonal relationships, and even greater amounts of anger as the anger feeds on itself (Deffenbacher, 1994; Tavris, 1989; R. B. Williams, 1989). The advice to count to 10—or 100—before sounding off is generally good advice.

Sadness and Grief

Sadness is a relatively mild, shallow, and usually relatively brief emotion of sorrow, and *grief* is a sharp, deep, and usually relatively long-lasting emotion of great sorrow, often associated with a loss. Sadness and grief tend to be caused by an involuntary, often permanent, separation. Some of the typical causes of sadness are making a mistake, doing something to hurt others, or being forced to do something against your will (Izard, 1977). Although virtually no one enjoys feeling sad, sadness can have an adaptive function. For one thing, it can encourage people to change their lives (Izard, 1977; Tomkins, 1963). If, for example, we feel sad that we hurt another person, our sadness may motivate us to make amends. Sadness can also be a cue for other people to help us. When others see that we are sad, they may come to our aid, even if we have not explicitly said how we feel.

Disgust

Disgust is associated with a response to objects or experiences deemed to be repulsive due to their nature, origin, or social history (see Rozin & Fallon, 1987). Disgust serves an adaptive purpose by motivating us to remove ourselves from what might be harmful, such as putrid meat or other contaminated products. The item is offensive and is labeled "disgusting." This definition of disgust as a form of rejection is supported by experimentation (Rozin, 1996; Rozin, Millman, & Nemeroff, 1986). Disgust has a psychological origin, and, indeed, things that may seem disgusting in one culture (such as eating termites or cockroaches) may not seem disgusting in another.

Are There Basic Emotions?

Not all psychologists believe that the five emotions described here, or any other emotions, can be viewed as truly "basic" in any meaningful sense. For example, Phillip Shaver and his colleagues have pointed out that

The similarity of facial expressions across cultures exemplifies the communicative function of emotion. We have a good idea of what she is feeling because we can "read" her expression.

emotions considered "basic" by one culture may not be considered basic by another, or may not even be experiences identified as emotions at all (P. Shaver, Schwartz, Krison, & O'Connor, 1987; P. Shaver, Wu, & Schwartz, 1992). For example, "sad love," which involves feelings of unrequited love combined with infatuation and sorrow, was considered a basic emotion in the People's Republic of China, but would not even be considered a single emotion in the United States. Moreover, it is not even clear that some emotions that are considered "basic" in some theories, such as disgust, are so considered by the people who experience them. Clearly, the question of whether any emotions are truly "basic" remains an open one. One way in which it might be addressed is through an evolutionary perspective.

The Evolutionary Value of Emotions

Emotions have both a *physiological aspect*, in which we physically react in distinctive ways in each emotion, and a *cognitive aspect*, in which we interpret how we feel. Both aspects are essential to our survival. From an evolutionary perspective, there may be good reasons for emotions (Plutchik, 1983). Some emotions, such as anger and fear, can help prepare us to behave in particular ways in particular situations. Anger can prepare us to fight an aggressor whom we have a pretty good chance of defeating and fear can prepare us to flee from an aggressor who might conquer us. Survival depends on organisms knowing when to fight a beatable foe and when to flee from an unbeatable enemy. Disgust can also aid survival, steering us away from poisonous substances. Judicious reliance on

emotional reactions to danger may mean the difference between life and death.

Other emotions have evolutionary value also. Consider, too, the love parents feel for their children. Obviously, this love brings happiness to both parents and children. From the perspective of evolutionary survival, however, the love that bonds parents and children together helps ensure that the parent will watch over the child's safety, health, and survival while the child remains dependent on the parent. Perhaps parents exhibit a kind of emotional intelligence in caring for their children.

A possible adaptation is **emotional intelligence,** discussed in chapter 9, which is the ability to perceive accurately, appraise, and express emotion; the ability to access and/or generate feelings when they facilitate thought; the ability to understand emotion and emotional knowledge; and the ability to regulate emotions to promote emotional and intellectual growth (J. D. Mayer & Salovey, 1995). The concept was introduced by Salovey and Mayer (J. D. Mayer & Salovey, 1993; Mayer, Salovey, & Caruso, 2000; Salovey & Mayer, 1990), and popularized and expanded upon by Goleman (1995).

There is some evidence, although still tentative, for the existence of emotional intelligence. For example, J. D. Mayer and Gehr (1996) found that understanding the emotions of characters in a variety of situations correlates with SAT scores, with empathy, and with emotional openness. At the same time, Davies, Stankov, and Roberts (1998) found that the emotional-intelligence construct does not hold together psychologically. Full validation of the construct, therefore, appears to be needed, which in turn requires good measurement tools and techniques.

Emotions have evolutionary value. Anger can prepare us to fight an aggressor and the love that bonds parents and children helps ensure that the parent will watch over the child's safety.

Measuring Emotions

In *Search of* . . .

How are emotions measured?

How do we know when people feel emotion and how much of an emotion they experience? One way of finding out is simply to ask them. Such measures of psychological attitudes, feelings, opinions, or behaviors are **self-report measures,** which are obtained simply by asking people to state their responses to questions regarding those psychological processes and products. Often, researchers find it difficult to quantify people's spontaneous self-reported expressions, so alternative self-report measures have been devised.

One such measure of the psychological aspects of emotion is a **Likert scale,** which asks respondents to choose which of several options best describes the extent to which they are experiencing an emotion (or anything else). For example, people might be given a set of statements, such as "I feel tense," and then be expected to rate each of these statements on a 4-point scale, where "0" means that they do not feel tense at all, "1" means that they feel slightly tense, "2" that they feel moderately tense, and "3" that they feel very tense (see e.g., Spielberger, Gorsuch, & Lushene, 1983). A person's feelings of anxiety would then be the average (or sum) of the numbers checked for the various self-report items.

Various psychophysiological measures also register emotion, including heart rate, respiration rate, blood pressure, and galvanic skin response (GSR), which tracks the electrical conductivity of the skin. Conductivity increases with perspiration, so a person under emotional stress will perspire and thus increase his or her GSR (see Figure 12-7 in the next section). It is this physiological fact, and the belief that the body cannot lie, that is the basis for the art, and perhaps science, of lie detection, as discussed in the Psychology in Everyday Life box.

Expressing Emotions

The expression of emotion enables us to communicate our feelings to other people and also regulates how other people respond to us (Izard, 1989, 1991, 1993). For example, mothers respond in different ways, depending on their babies' expressions (Huebner & Izard, 1988). Facial expressions play a big role in the expression of emotion.

The similarity of facial expressions across cultures exemplifies the communicative function of emotion. Researchers studied the ability of tribal New Guineans to recognize facial expressions in photographs of Westerners (Ekman & Friesen, 1975). Both adults and

---

Psychology in Everyday Life

Detecting Lies

One controversial measure that has been used to ferret out emotions is the so-called lie detector—the **polygraph.** The polygraph provides a method of assessing the accuracy of self-report measures, by assessing various physiological processes, such as reactivity of heart rate, GSR, and respiration. The idea, of course, is to provide an objective measure of whether people are feeling emotional stress. In fact, because the polygraph measures only stress reactions, it also records stress reactions for reasons other than lying, and it does not record as lies responses made by people who feel no stress when telling lies.

A common format for polygraph testing is that the polygraph operator asks a series of questions and compares psychophysiological responses to innocuous questions ("In what city were you born?") with answers to potentially threatening questions ("Did you murder your professor?"). A more effective format for the use of polygraphs involves questions that assess whether a person possesses information that only a guilty person would know (Bashore & Rapp, 1993).

How accurate are polygraphs? The results of controlled studies are not terribly encouraging. Although professional interpreters of polygraphs have been found to be correct in identifying guilty parties 76% of the time, they have also labeled as guilty 37% of the innocent people they tested (Kleinmuntz & Szucko,

1984). A review of more than 250 studies of the validity of interpretation of polygraph results shows similar findings (Saxe, Dougherty, & Cross, 1985; see also Ben-Shakhar & Furedy, 1990). Thus, these studies suggest that interpreters of results are fairly good at recognizing guilty parties but also classify disturbing numbers of innocent people as guilty. In the language of signal-detection theory (see chapter 4), the hit rate is high, but so is the rate of false alarms. Results such as these indicate that polygraph tests, as they are now interpreted, are far from reliable, and some scientists question whether they are reliable at all (Lykken, 1998). At present, polygraph results should be interpreted only with the greatest of caution.

children were quite accurate in recognizing expressions of happiness, sadness, anger, disgust, surprise, and fear. Americans also were fairly accurate in recognizing New Guinean expressions. In all cases, accuracy was greatest for happiness and lowest for fear. This work was extended by showing identical photographs to people in the United States, Brazil, Chile, Argentina, and Japan (Ekman, 1984, 1992a, 1992b). Once again, there was a remarkable consensus across cultures, although there is some dispute over the interpretation of these results (Ekman, 1994; J. A. Russell, 1994). As in the study in New Guinea, consensus was greatest for happiness and lowest for fear. The high level of agreement across cultures suggests that facial expressions for emotions may be an innate part of our physiological makeup. In the case of the New Guineans, at least, the tribe members had virtually no contact with Westerners, and yet their facial expressions and judgments of facial expressions were very similar to those of people in the United States (see Figure 12-6).

Facial-Feedback Hypothesis

Normally, we would believe that the expression of emotion follows the experiencing of that emotion. Silvan Tomkins (1962, 1963) has taken the opposite point of view by suggesting the **facial-feedback hypothesis,** whereby we feel emotion as a result of feedback from the face. In other words, the facial expression of an emotion leads to the experiencing of that emotion.

A strong version of the facial-feedback hypothesis suggests that simply manipulating your face to show a certain emotion would lead you to feel that emotion. Thus, smiling would make you happy; puckering up your face in disgust would make you feel disgusted. The data on the strong version of the facial-feedback hypothesis are mixed. It does appear that creating a facial expression produces particular changes in psychophysiological reaction, but it is unclear that these changes are the same as experiencing the emotion itself (Ekman, Levenson, & Friesen, 1983; Levenson, Ekman, & Friesen, 1990; Tourangeau & Ellsworth, 1979; see Figure 12-7).

A weaker version of the facial-feedback hypothesis suggests merely that facial feedback can affect the intensity of an emotion but does not actually produce an emotion. The weaker version of the hypothesis has received fairly uniform support (e.g., M. Zuckerman, Klorman, Larrance, & Speigel, 1981).

Honest Faces

Is it possible to detect insincere facial expressions of emotion or to tell from facial expressions when people are lying? Apparently, it is possible (Ekman, 1992a, 1992b; Ekman, Friesen, & O'Sullivan, 1988). Genuine

Figure 12–6
CULTURAL AGREEMENT REGARDING FACIAL EXPRESSIONS. *Cross-cultural agreement regarding facial expressions of emotions appears highest for happiness and disgust and lowest for anger and fear. The greatest disagreements with others was shown by New Guineans, who have not had extensive contact with persons from other cultural groups. What are some possible implications of this finding? (After Ekman & Ericson, 1984)*

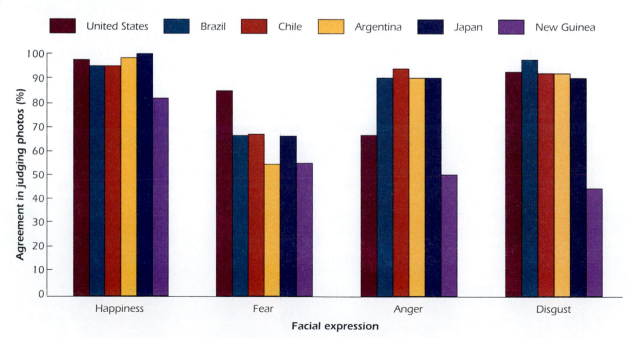

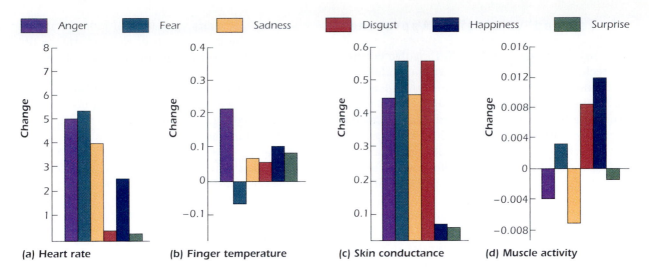

| Anger | Fear | Sadness | Disgust | Happiness | Surprise |

(a) Heart rate (b) Finger temperature (c) Skin conductance (d) Muscle activity

Figure 12–7

PHYSIOLOGICAL CHANGES CAUSED BY FACIAL EXPRESSION. *Some evidence indicates that when we change our facial expressions to show given emotions, our bodies respond through physiological changes in heart rate, circulation (as shown in finger temperature), sweating (as shown in skin conductance), and muscle activity. Do these changes necessarily mean that we are experiencing the emotions shown on our faces? (After Levenson, Ekman, & Ericson, 1990)*

expressions of emotions tend to be symmetrical, whereas false ones are likely to be asymmetrical (see Figure 12-8). In addition, if lying arouses emotion in a person, we may be able to detect whether the person is lying on the basis of facial expressions. If a person actually believes his or her own lies, however, it is very difficult to figure out whether the truth is being told. Also, experienced liars, such as criminals, may be quite able to convey deceptively honest-looking expressions. Of the people who are supposed to be skillful in detecting lies (police officers, members of the Federal Bureau of Investigation, and members of the Secret Service), members of the Secret Service seem to be the only group able to detect the emotional expressions that identify people as liars (Ekman, 1992a, 1992b). What are the approaches we might use to understand the emotions of liars or of anyone else?

Approaches to Understanding Emotions

In Search of . . .

What are the major approaches to understanding emotion?

Just as the approaches to, and suggested explanations of, motivation are diverse, so, too, are the approaches to understanding human emotions. As you read about psychophysiological, cognitive, structural, and cross-cultural approaches in this chapter, note that many of

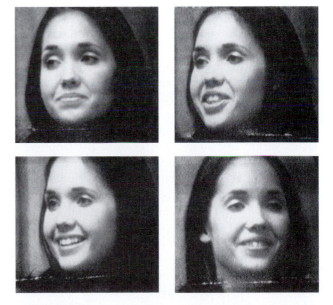

Figure 12–8

SINCERE SMILES. *Which of these smiles is genuine? According to Paul Ekman, most of us—including police officers and FBI agents—are not very good at determining when someone is lying simply by observing her or his facial expressions. Do not try to deceive a Secret Service agent, though; these agents can detect lies through facial expressions at better than chance levels. (After Ekman, Friesen, & O'Sullivan, 1988)*

these aspects are complementary rather than contradictory. Each approach offers insight into how and why we feel emotions as we do.

Early Psychophysiological Approaches

Today, psychophysiological studies involve cutting-edge technologies, state-of-the-art methodologies, and dynamic revolutions in theoretical understandings. Oddly, psychophysiological approaches to understanding emotions are also the most ancient approaches. Ancient Greek and Roman physicians believed that emotional states could be understood in terms of the physiology of the body and thus they foreshadowed the modern psychophysiological approach.

The earliest modern theory of emotion was proposed by William James (1890a). Because a Danish physiologist, Carl Lange, had a similar theory, the point of view that they jointly proposed is often called the James-Lange theory of emotion. The James-Lange theory turned common notions about emotion on their heads. The common-sense view of emotion is that first we perceive some event in the environment and that event evokes some kind of emotion within us. James and Lange proposed that exactly the reverse is true (Lange & James, 1922). We first sense the events in the environment. Next, according to James and Lange, we experience bodily changes in reaction to the events, and those physiological changes produce the emotion, rather than the other way around.

Ironically, James's son-in-law, Walter Cannon (1929), became the foremost critic of the James-Lange theory. Cannon argued that the James-Lange theory could not be right. First, different emotions are associated with identical psychophysiological states within the body. The identical psychophysiological states could not cause the different emotions. Second, Cannon argued, the organs of the body are not very sensitive. They could never provide the subtle differentiating information that people need in order to experience one emotion as opposed to another. Fear and excitement, for example, cause a similar adrenaline rush. Moreover, many of the organs of the body typically react slowly, whereas emotions are often felt immediately after a stimulus is perceived. Third, if researchers produce the changes in the body associated with a given set of emotions, in the absence of the normal provoking stimuli, people do not feel the emotion that corresponds to those physical reactions. For example, exposing people to onions and making them cry does not make them feel sad. Cannon proposed instead that the brain, in particular the thalamus, and not bodily reactions (such as crying or clenching your fist) controls emotional behavior. Philip Bard (1934) later elaborated on this view, and so it is sometimes called the Cannon–Bard theory of emotion.

There is merit in both positions. Cannon was correct in his recognition of the importance of the brain in the experiencing of emotion. Several parts of the limbic system, such as the hypothalamus and the amygdala, have been closely linked with emotional experience (see chapter 3). James and Lange were also correct, however, in asserting that people feel emotions in part by observing changes in the functioning of their bodies. (See Figure 12-9 for a comparison of these theories.) Just what is going on inside their bodies?

Modern Psychophysiological Approaches

The Central Nervous System

Joseph LeDoux (1986, 1992, 1993, 1995; LeDoux, Romanski, & Xagoraris, 1989) has suggested that arousal of the autonomic nervous system (ANS; see chapter 3) may not be all-or-none, as it is typically thought to be. Rather, there may be multiple patterns of ANS arousal and different emotions may correspond to different patterns of ANS activity. Other investigators (Cacioppo, Klein, Berntson, & Hatfield, 1993; Cacioppo & Petty, 1983; Derryberry & Tucker, 1992; Ekman, Levenson, & Friesen, 1983) have also suggested that different emotions may be characterized by different patterns of physiological response.

The Endocrine System

In contrast, others (Henry & Stephens, 1977) have emphasized the role of the *endocrine system* in emotion. They have argued that different emotions can be linked to different relative concentrations of hormones. For example, anger seems to be associated with increased levels of norepinephrine (noradrenaline), fear with increased levels of epinephrine (adrenaline), and depression with increases in adrenocorticotropic hormone (ACTH; see chapter 3). Elation, in contrast, is marked by decreases in ACTH and other hormones. Aggression is associated with increased levels of testosterone (Floody, 1983). What is exciting about this approach is its linking of moods and emotions with concentrations of hormones. The approach does not establish causality, however. Whether changes in hormone concentrations cause the emotion, or the emotions cause the changes in hormone concentrations, or whether—most likely—both are dependent on other things, has yet to be resolved. Conceivably, one of these other things might be cognitions.

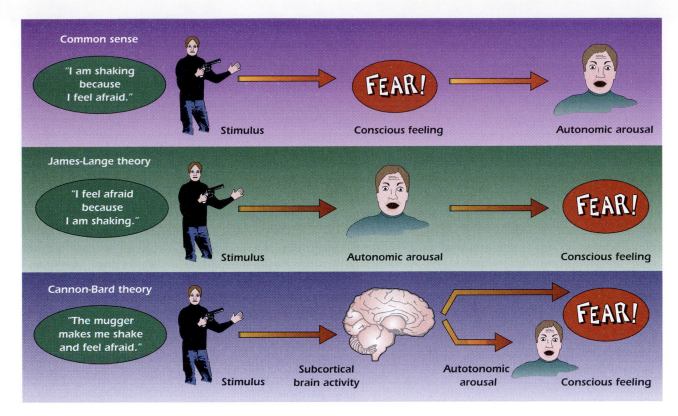

Figure 12–9
Psychophysiological Theories of Emotion.   *Various theories of emotion account for the physiological, affective, and cognitive components of emotions in different ways. Each theory accounts for some, but not all, of the phenomena of emotions.*

Cognitive Approaches

Cognitive approaches emphasize the role of cognition in leading to emotion. In response to an experiment showing that how we label arousal seems to determine the emotions we experience, Stanley Schachter and Jerome Singer (1962) developed a **two-component theory of emotion.** The first component is *physiological arousal*, which can be caused by any number of things, such as drugs or situational stimuli (e.g., a sudden surprise). The emotion we feel, according to Schachter and Singer, depends on the second component—how we *label* that physiological arousal. Thus, people who are aroused and who believe that the appropriate emotion is happiness will feel happy; people who are aroused and who believe that the appropriate emotion is anger will feel anger. All that distinguishes the various emotions is how we label our arousal. The arousal is the same in every case.

As a result of follow-up research, we now know that Schachter and Singer were not completely correct (see, e.g., Leventhal & Tomarken, 1986; G. D. Marshall & Zimbardo, 1979). For example, as previ-

ously mentioned, physiological differences exist in the kinds of arousal experienced for different emotions. Still, the classic work of Schachter and Singer instigated a great deal of important theory and research, including work by Richard Lazarus and Robert Zajonc.

Lazarus's and Zajonc's Temporal-Sequence Theories

When addressing the question of whether cognitions precede emotions or are simultaneous with them, Magda Arnold (1960, 1970) proposed that it is in part our thinking about a situation that leads us to feel emotions, and her point of view has been championed and elaborated upon by Richard Lazarus (1977, 1984, 1991, 1993; R. S. Lazarus, Kanner, & Folkman, 1980). According to Lazarus, we appraise a situation in stages. First, in *primary appraisal*, we determine the potential consequences of what is about to happen. For example, is the scruffy, dirty figure approaching us about to ask us for money, rob us, or start up a conversation? Second, we have to engage in *secondary appraisal*, meaning that we have to decide what to do.

Given our decision about the character approaching us, how should we act? Later we may need to *reappraise* the situation, as events develop. According to Lazarus, each of our appraisals of a situation determines what emotion or emotions we feel. Thus, cognition precedes emotion.

In contrast, Robert Zajonc (1980, 1984, 1998; Zajonc, Pietromonaco, & Bargh, 1982) has argued that cognition and emotion are basically separate. He believes that emotion is basic and does not require prior cognition. In fact, he argues, as do others, that emotions preceded thinking in evolutionary history, and so it does not make sense that cognitions would have to precede emotions. Lower animals know to fear predators or to attack potential food without going through complex thought processes. Zajonc therefore believes that we, as humans, often know how we feel long before we know what we think about a situation.

According to Lazarus and Zajonc's theories, our appraisal of a situation leads to how we feel about it. Is this swan a threat or not? The answer will affect the way this child feels.

Cross-Cultural Approaches

Batja Mesquita and Nico Frijda (1992) have conducted an extensive review of the anthropological literature and have developed a cross-cultural theoretical framework for understanding emotion, based in part on theories by others (such as Lazarus). In their view, when we seek to understand emotions, we must consider the following components: *antecedent events* (events that came before the emotional reaction), *event coding* (interpretation of the event), *appraisal* (evaluation of the event and its possible outcomes), *physiological reaction pattern* (emotion-related changes in the body), *action readiness* (preparedness to respond to the emotion-arousing event), *emotional behavior* (actions following the experience of the emotion), and *regulation* (degree to which the individual tries to make the emotion reaction stronger or weaker). Each of these elements may be influenced by cultural context.

An alternative cross-cultural approach has been suggested by James Russell (1991). Russell, too, conducted an extensive review of ethnographic literature, but from a slightly different view. He studied the way people categorize emotions, in terms of (a) the words they choose to use to describe their emotions, (b) the words they assign to given facial expressions of emotions, and (c) the dimensions (pairs of characteristics, such as aroused/unaroused, positive/negative, dominant/submissive) people use in judging the categories for emotions.

As a result of his study, Russell drew two conclusions. *First*, not all people sort their emotions according to the basic categories often used by English speakers and other speakers of Indo-European languages. That is, not all cultures recognize the same basic emotions; other cultures may include additional emotions. *Second*, despite these cross-cultural differences, many similarities exist across cultures in the emotions people identify, particularly in regard to emotions associated with particular facial expressions (e.g., Ekman, 1971, 1993; Ekman & Oster, 1979) and vocal expressions (e.g., Bezooijen, Otto, & Heenan, 1983). Although the range of expression for emotions and the boundaries between various emotions may differ, there appears to be a great deal of overlap in the ways distinctive cultures describe human emotions.

In this chapter, we have considered motivation, emotion, and some of the links between the two. These two constructs are linked very closely to the social contexts in which they are exhibited. These contexts are considered in chapters 13 and 14.

THINK ABOUT IT

1. Why is disgust a key emotion from an evolutionary standpoint?
2. Why are negative-feedback loops important to the homeostatic regulation of temperature in the body?
3. What strategies could you use to help a child increase his or her motivation to do homework?
4. How might you expect people's motivation to succeed economically to vary across cultures?
5. What goal can you set for yourself that would satisfy your need for achievement and that would enhance your sense of competence, autonomy, and self-efficacy? Devise a specific plan for reaching your goal, including the specific subtasks and subgoals you would need to accomplish.

6. When advertisers want you to buy their products or services, they seek to tap into some of the fundamental human emotions. Describe a recent advertisement you have seen or heard and explain how the advertiser was trying to manipulate your fundamental emotions to persuade you to buy the advertised product or service.

online *You can provide your own answers to these questions online at the* **Sternberg,** In Search of the Human Mind *Web site:* http://www.harcourtcollege.com/psych/ishm

SUMMARY

The Nature and Characteristics of Motivation 393

1. The study of motivation considers questions of direction, initiation, intensity, and persistence.
2. Darwin, James, and McDougall saw motivations as instincts. However, their theories became too complex and obscure to be useful.
3. Drive theory replaced instinct theory. According to Hull, *drive* is a composite source of energy, which animals and humans are impelled to reduce. Drive theory was discredited, however, because motivation can exist without physiological needs and even can be biologically maladaptive.

Contemporary Views of Motivation   395

4. Physiological approaches to motivation (arousal, opponent-process, and homeostatic-regulation theories) study how motivation relates to the brain.
5. According to the Yerkes–Dodson Law, people perform most efficiently and creatively when their level of *arousal* is moderate. The optimal level varies with both task demands and personal characteristics. High levels are helpful for simple tasks; lower levels are better for complex tasks.
6. Opponent-process theory, proposed by Solomon, explains how an addictive drug or habit, started in order to achieve a high, becomes a habit to avoid a low. When we feel the effects of a motivational source we then experience an opposing force—slower to start, slower to terminate—that tends to bring us back to baseline.

7. *Homeostatic regulation* is the tendency of the body to maintain equilibrium. A *negative-feedback loop* operates like a thermostat, telling us when we need food, drink, or sex and when those needs are satisfied.
8. Clinical approaches to motivation (e.g., Murray's theory of needs) emphasize personality theory. McClelland has studied in depth three needs that emerge from Murray's theory: the needs for achievement, power, and affiliation. A highly influential theory is Maslow's hierarchy of needs. These needs include physiology, safety and security, belonging and love, self-esteem, and self-actualization.
9. Cognitive approaches show that people are most creative when intrinsically motivated; *extrinsic motivators* tend to undermine *intrinsic motivators*. In addition, moderately novel phenomena are more motivating than are either totally familiar or wholly novel ones. We also need to feel in control of our environment.
10. Ultimately, motivation may lie in our belief of whether or not we can attain a goal (*self-efficacy theory*).

Biological Bases of Motivation   404

11. The brain is essential to the experience of hunger. The ventromedial hypothalamus (VMH) serves as an off switch for eating, the lateral hypothalamus (LH) as an on switch.

12. The glucostatic hypothesis holds that levels of glucose in the body signal the hypothalamus about the need for food. An alternative (perhaps complementary) explanation is the lipostatic hypothesis, which holds that the brain detects when lipids drop below a certain homeostatic level and hunger increases.

13. According to *set-point theory*, weight is biologically determined at birth by the number of fat cells. Successful weight loss is difficult because the body interprets dieting as starvation and so resists efforts to shrink the fat cells.

14. Sexual motivation is rooted in the hypothalamus, which stimulates the pituitary gland to release hormones that influence the production of androgens and estrogens.

15. Human sexual behavior is controlled partly by sexual scripts.

16. There are various theories of *homosexuality*. Current views tend to emphasize the role of biological factors.

Emotions and Their Characteristics   410

17. Distinct from but closely linked to motivation is *emotion*, the predisposition to respond experientially, physiologically, and behaviorally to certain internal and external variables. Current theories suggest the importance of the autonomic nervous system in emotional arousal.

18. Emotions serve an evolutionary function. For example, they may lead us to fight or to flee in the face of an attack, depending upon how the danger is perceived and which course of action is more likely to lead to survival.

19. Major emotions include happiness (joy), fear and *anxiety*, anger, sadness and grief, and disgust. They can be charted to show relationships among them.

20. *Emotional intelligence* is involved in control and regulation of emotions.

Measuring Emotions   413

21. We can measure emotional experience through *self-reporting* and/or through psychophysiological means; the *polygraph* is not a highly reliable measure of veracity, however.

22. The expression of emotion enables us to communicate feelings, regulates how others respond to us, facilitates social interaction, and encourages prosocial behavior.

23. The *facial-feedback hypothesis* holds, in its strong form, that (1) the facial expression of emotion leads to the experience of emotion, or, in its weak form, that (2) the facial expression affects an emotion's intensity. Facial expressions can also help somewhat to detect when someone is lying, particularly if the person doing the detecting has been highly trained to do so.

Approaches to Understanding Emotions   415

24. The James–Lange theory claims that bodily changes lead to emotion, rather than the reverse. Cannon and Bard disagreed, claiming that the brain controls emotional behavior.

25. Cognitive theories differ in details and sometimes in substance, but they all hold that emotion and cognition are linked closely. According to the Schachter–Singer *two-component theory of emotion*, we distinguish one emotion from another strictly by how we label our physiological arousal.

26. Emotions and cognitions are linked, but we do not yet know which comes first. Lazarus believes that cognition precedes emotion, but Zajonc does not.

27. Cross-cultural studies of emotions analyze emotions in terms of antecedent events, event coding, appraisal, physiological response patterns, action readiness, emotional behavior, and regulation. Although not all people categorize emotions in the same way, many similarities still exist across cultures in the ways that people express and identify emotions.

KEY TERMS

■ THINK ABOUT IT SAMPLE RESPONSES

1. Why is disgust a key emotion from an evolutionary standpoint?

We tend to be disgusted by substances that are poisonous. Disgust can be very important because it tends to prevent us from ingesting poisons.

2. Why are negative-feedback loops important to the homeostatic regulation of temperature in the body?

Negative-feedback loops tell the body when temperature has gone under or over the acceptable range. The body then takes steps to restore its temperature to an acceptable level.

3. What strategies could you use to help a child increase his or her motivation to do homework?

One strategy is to try to turn the homework into a game or otherwise render it fun. A related strategy is to try to make it more interesting in some other way. Another strategy is to emphasize the importance of the homework to the child's understanding of the material he or she is learning. A strategy that is risky is to offer an extrinsic reward: The child may then become dependent on extrinsic rewards, or find his or her interest in the homework activity undermined by the reward.

4. How might you expect people's motivation to succeed economically to vary across cultures?

In some cultures, monetary success is viewed as very important. The United States tends to be that way. In other cultures, enjoyment of life or personal fulfillment may be viewed as far more important. For example, many people in developing cultures (and developed ones as well) are skeptical of those who place a great emphasis on monetary success. Because money is a secondary reinforcer, people have no innate desire for it. The desire is learned, and that learning takes place in a cultural context.

5. What goal can you set for yourself that would satisfy your need for achievement and that would enhance your sense of competence, autonomy, and self-efficacy? Devise a specific plan for reaching your goal, including the specific subtasks and subgoals you would need to accomplish.

Everyone must answer this for him- or herself. In my own case, I quit playing the cello when I was in college. In recent years, I began seriously to regret this decision and became more and more motivated to return to playing the cello. I finally decided that I was not too old to restart, and so I did. I set as a goal having a weekly lesson and practicing at least a half-hour a day. Now I play the cello regularly and hope soon to join an amateur orchestra.

6. When advertisers want you to buy their products or services, they seek to tap into some of the fundamental human emotions. Describe a recent advertisement you have seen or heard and explain how the advertiser was trying to manipulate your fundamental emotions to persuade you to buy the advertised product or service.

Advertisements for luxury products often emphasize how happy these products will make you. You are encouraged to buy these products to achieve happiness. It is a safe bet that none of these products will truly bring you happiness!

The presence of others, other people, excite and rattle him, force him into an endless, frenzied, social chatter, a veritable delirium of identity-making and -seeking; the presence of plants, a quiet garden, the nonhuman order, making no social demands upon him, allow this identity-delirium to relax, to subside.

—Oliver Sacks, The Man Who Mistook His Wife for a Hat

13

SOCIAL PSYCHOLOGY: PERSONAL PERSPECTIVES

In the opening quotation, an individual who is mentally ill cannot well tolerate the presence of others. Most of us not only tolerate others well, but even seek out others. **Social psychology** is the study of how the presence of others affects each person's thoughts, feelings, and behaviors, even if that presence is only implied or imagined. Given this definition, what can we conclude about the nature of social psychology?

The Nature of Social Psychology

In Search of . . .

What is social psychology?

First, social psychology deals with both the *cognitive* (intellectual) and *affective* (emotional) sides of a person, as well as the *behavior* that results from and is influenced by thoughts and emotions. For example, when we look at how a car salesman tries to persuade us to buy a car, we must look at this attempt at persuasion as a multifaceted phenomenon. The salesman tries to convince us cognitively, with rational arguments, that the car is a good buy. He tries to make us long for the car—to develop some kind of emotional

Relationships with others are important to survival. Each person we encounter represents a source of help or harm to us. Perhaps this is why humans are often characterized as the most social creatures in the animal kingdom.

attachment to it. Ultimately, his behavior usually results in one of two behaviors on our part: Either we buy or do not buy, based in part on how effective he has been in attempting to persuade us to buy the car.

Second, social psychology is oriented toward how behavior is affected by either the presence or the idea of other people. For example, we may meet someone to whom we are attracted and with whom we might consider becoming further involved were it not for our prediction of our significant other's negative reaction to such an additional involvement. The significant other may not be physically present, but we may react to the person to whom we are attracted as though the significant other were there.

Third, social psychology usually takes a process-oriented, or *functionalist*, approach (see chapter 1). It deals not only with *what* people do but also with *how* and *why* they do it. Why do we seek to have friends and how do we choose our friends? How do we communicate and why do we need to do so?

Because social psychology addresses such compelling questions, this textbook includes two chapters on this field of study. The present chapter addresses issues in social cognition. **Social cognition** refers to the thoughts and beliefs we have about ourselves and other people, based on how we perceive and interpret information that we either observe directly or learn from other people (see Fiske, 1995; Fiske & Taylor, 1991). What do we think about ourselves? What do we think about other people? How are our thoughts and feelings influenced by our interactions with these other people? Whereas objects typically remain relatively stable (e.g., the lamp on my desk just stays there

in one of two states—off or on), people seem constantly to be changing, and hence cognitions about people inevitably gain a complexity and richness often absent from cognitions about objects (see Kenny, 1994; Kenny & DePaulo, 1993).

Social cognition is intertwined with such topics as emotion, motivation, and personality, but its particular focus is on thought processes in social interactions. It deals with (a) the ways in which we think and feel about others and about ourselves, and (b) the ways in which we behave because of our thoughts and feelings toward and about other people and ourselves. Among the topics covered by personal perspectives are how and why we form and change our attitudes; the ways in which we perceive ourselves, as shaped by the ways we think others perceive us; how we internally explain our own behavior and the behavior of others; and how and why we are attracted to, like, and even love other people. The common thread among these topics is that internal, personal processes both influence and are influenced by our interactions with other people.

Much of social psychology is built around the study of social relationships of various kinds. People believe such relationships to be of paramount importance in their lives. They are right: People with good social relationships live longer and have better health than people without them (Berscheid & Reis, 1998).

Relationships are important as well because it is so difficult for humans to survive independently of one another (Berscheid, 1999). Each person we encounter represents a potential source of help or harm to us. Perhaps this is why humans are so often characterized as the most social creatures in the animal kingdom. Moreover, it appears that, over evolutionary time, we have been "hard-wired" with biological equipment that facilitates our interactions with others. Those of our ancestors who could not get along with others for defense, food gathering, and reproductive purposes did not survive to contribute to evolutionary heritage of human beings (Reis, Collins, & Berscheid, in press).

One aspect in the study of social cognition is the study of attitudes.

The Nature and Functions of Attitudes

What are attitudes and how do they change?

What is an attitude? There are a variety of popular definitions of attitude, but for psychologists, an **attitude** is a learned, stable, and relatively enduring evaluation of a person, object, or idea that can affect an individual's behavior (Allport, 1935; Eagly & Chaiken, 1992,

1998; Petty & Cacioppo, 1981). Attitudes are a bit more substantial than impressions. Both, however, are aspects of social cognition. This definition makes several points. First, we are not born with the attitudes we have. We acquire them through the experiences we have, especially in interacting with others. Second, attitudes tend to be stable and relatively enduring. They tend not to change easily. Third, attitudes typically are evaluative. They are a means by which we judge things positively or negatively, and in varying degrees. Some issues may not concern us much one way or the other, whereas other issues may engender strong opinions. Finally, attitudes can influence behavior, such as when they cause people to act—to vote, protest, work, make friends, and so on—as a result of their attitudes.

At one time, it was believed that simply understanding people's attitudes toward things would help psychologists predict people's behavior with great accuracy, but this view turned out to be an oversimplification. Sometimes attitudes predict behavior, but other times they do not (Berscheid, 1999).

Some psychologists view attitudes as having cognitive, behavioral, *and* affective components: Your attitude toward someone or something depends on what you think and feel about the person or thing, as well as on how you act toward the person or thing, based on your thoughts and feelings (D. Katz & Stotland, 1959). Thus, attitudes are central to the psychology of the individual.

For example, suppose you meet Jacques, who is introduced to you as being from France. You have always had a good impression of France. You like French food, have admired French culture, and what you have learned about France has struck you as showing the country to be highly civilized and pleasant. As a result, you are eager to get to know Jacques. Your attitude toward France has already colored your attitude toward Jacques. Had Jacques come from a country about which you had a less favorable attitude, you might have been less eager to get to know Jacques and what he is like.

Why do we even have attitudes in the first place? According to Daniel Katz (1960), attitudes serve at least four functions. They (a) help us get what we want and avoid what we do not want, (b) help us avoid internal conflicts and anxieties, (c) help us understand and integrate complex sources of information, and (d) reflect our deeply held values.

Attitude Formation

Where do attitudes come from? As is often the case, the best answer is actually a synthesis of various approaches. Given that we are not born with particular attitudes and that specific attitudes do not naturally unfold during physiological maturation, we are left with various forms of learning theory to explain attitude formation. Three kinds of learning can contribute

to this process: classical conditioning, operant conditioning, and observational learning (see chapter 6).

The *classical-conditioning* view is that we learn attitudes when a concept or object toward which we have no particular attitudes (an unconditioned stimulus) is paired with a concept or object toward which we already have an attitude (a conditioned stimulus; Staats & Staats, 1958). For example, eating a food one likes while reading a passage has been shown to lead to the development of a favorable attitude toward the views presented in the passage (Janis, Kaye, & Kirschner, 1965). In another study, participants liked a television commercial more if it was embedded in a television program that was upbeat than if it was embedded in a program that was sad (Mathur & Chattopadhyay, 1991).

In *operant conditioning*, rewards can strengthen positive associations, just as punishments can strengthen negative associations (e.g., Insko, 1965). Attitudes that are rewarded are more likely to be kept and those that are punished are more likely to be changed or discarded. For example, if you are rewarded for showing positive attitudes toward the political party in power (e.g., by being praised) and punished for showing negative attitudes (e.g., by being thrown in jail, which in fact happens in some countries), you are more likely to develop positive than negative attitudes toward the party in power. As various dissident movements around the world make clear, however, this is not the only way attitudes are learned, or, changed.

In *observational learning* (where learning occurs as a result of observing both the behavior of others and the environmental outcomes of the behavior observed, as seen in chapter 6), children learn many of their attitudes by observing the attitudes being voiced and acted out by the important adults and children in their environments. In addition, children may learn some of their attitudes from television and other media.

One set of attitudes that may be learned from the media pertains to the roles of males and females in society. Stereotypes portrayed on television are not as bad as they once were, but they persist around the world (Furnham & Skae, 1997; Mwangi, 1996). For example, children's television programs show more male roles than female roles. Males are more likely to be shown as the doers who make things happen and who are rewarded for their actions. Females are more likely to be the recipients of actions. The females who do take action are more likely than males to be punished for their activity (Basow, 1986). On action-adventure shows (in which the heroic, bold, intrepid adventurer undertakes insurmountable challenges, struggles against unbeatable odds, and then deftly conquers all), 85% of the major characters are males. Of the leading characters on prime-time television, 65% to 75% are white males. The occupational and familial roles strongly reinforce gender and racial stereotypes. Just in case viewers selectively choose programs that minimize stereotypes, commercials still provide a whopping dose of stereotyped roles for viewers to observe (Gilly, 1988): Women are more often shown as preoccupied with their personal appearance, their household chores, and concerns about their families; men are usually shown engaged in working, playing, or being nurtured by women. Even music videos as portrayed on MTV show conventional male-female stereotypes (Gan, Zillmann, & Mitrook, 1997; Signorielli, McLeod, & Healy, 1994).

On a more positive note, when programs are designed to diminish sex-role stereotypes, both children (Eisenstock, 1984) and adults (Reep & Dambrot, 1988) express fewer stereotyped views. We might guess that the same would be true regarding other stereotype-based attitudes. Also, in addition to the television set, another obvious source of observational learning can be found in the home: the people who live there. Examine your parents' attitudes about religion, politics, and other social issues. How do they compare and contrast with your own? Young people are often surprised—sometimes unpleasantly—to realize how many of their own attitudes they have absorbed from their families. In more ways than one, education begins at home.

There clearly is evidence to support use of each of the three kinds of learning, so each probably contributes to the ways in which we form the attitudes we have. What about when we change attitudes we have already formed? Do these same processes underlie the means by which, and the reasons for which, we change our attitudes, or do other processes influence our changes in attitude?

Attitude Change

Have you ever noticed in yourself an attitude that you wanted to change? What about the attitudes held by people with whom you interact? Have you ever wanted to change the attitudes of other people? If you did want to change someone's attitudes, how might you go about doing so? Probably by persuading the person to think differently. Easier said than done, you say. Nonetheless, advertisers, politicians, political activists, charitable organizations, and any number of other people have spent a lot of time, money, and effort trying to figure out how to change people's attitudes. Governments have also been very interested in issues relating to attitude change.

Scientists do not conduct research in isolation from society. Attitude research aptly exemplifies the interaction of contemporary societal issues and psychological research. The origins of this research date back to World War II. During the war, the U.S. government needed information about attitudes and attitude change, and it needed the information fast. Japanese radio broadcaster "Tokyo Rose" was trying to break

Interest in attitudes and attitude change surged during World War II. As this war propaganda poster indicates, this interest was not purely academic.

the morale of the U.S. troops overseas with innuendoes about unfaithful spouses, unconcerned citizens at home, and treacherous political and military leaders. Various German-American "friendship organizations" were attempting to drum up support for Hitler in the United States. Were such measures turning both soldiers and civilians against the war effort? How could the U.S. government counter the influence of such propaganda? Government officials needed to know how to make the American people more resistant to those influences that might seek to change people's attitudes in ways that would disfavor the war effort.

At the same time, these government officials wanted to institute their own propaganda campaign, to change the attitudes of anyone who might not fully support the war effort. Suddenly, attitude research, which had been dormant, sprang to life. The goal of such research was to understand people's attitudes more fully and to figure out how and why people change their attitudes.

Because many individuals and organizations work to change your attitudes, you may wish to learn when to accept and when to resist such efforts. For example, how can you more effectively resist the attempts to change your attitudes by persons who do not necessarily have your best interests at heart? By examining various kinds of persuasive communications, researchers have discovered some variables likely to influence attitude change. These variables can be categorized into three groups: characteristics of the recipient of the attitude-change message (e.g., the recipient's motivation and expertise), characteristics of the message itself (e.g., balance and familiarity due to repetition), and characteristics of the source of the message (e.g., credibility and likability). Understanding these variables can help us to evaluate, and when appropriate, to resist attempts through persuasion to change our attitudes.

Characteristics of the Recipient

How easily we are persuaded by a message may depend largely on our own characteristics as recipients of the communication. Richard Petty and John Cacioppo (1981; Cialdini, Petty, & Cacioppo, 1981; Petty & Wegener, 1998) have proposed that the effectiveness of various persuasive techniques depends on specific characteristics of the person receiving the persuasive message. These researchers note two routes to persuasion. The first is the *central route to persuasion,* which emphasizes thoughtful arguments related to the issue about which an attitude is being formed. When the recipient is both motivated to think about the issue and able to do so, the central route is the most effective. The second is the *peripheral route to persuasion,* which emphasizes tangential, situational features of the persuasive message, such as the appeal of the message sender, the attractiveness of the message's presentation, or rewarding features of the message or its source. The peripheral route may be more effective than the central route when the recipient is not strongly interested in the issue or is unable to consider the issue carefully for various reasons, such as lack of skill in thinking about the issue, lack of expertise in the area related to the issue, or any number of other limitations on the individual's ability.

Although the investigators found that strong arguments were always more persuasive than weak arguments, this effect was augmented in those who were highly motivated to think about the issue (Cacioppo & Petty, 1986). In other words, the good arguments may have been partly wasted on those who were not really thinking about them, but such arguments were influential for those who were actively analyzing and interpreting them. Thus, when preparing to persuade others to your point of view, it helps to know your audience and to know which route to persuasion will be most effective. As you might guess, attitude change that is reached through the central route is much more stable and enduring. Attitude change reached through the peripheral route is more volatile and subject to subsequent change in the opposite direction.

Characteristics of the Message

In addition to the quality or forcefulness of the arguments, what other characteristics of your message might affect its persuasiveness? Two characteristics of the message have prompted a great deal of research: balanced presentation of arguments and familiarity due to repeated exposure. A key question in attitude research has been whether the *balanced presentation of viewpoints*—a presentation of both favorable (pro) and unfavorable (con) perspectives on a given issue—helps or hinders the process of changing someone's attitudes. There appears to be no significant difference between the effects of one-sided and two-sided messages on attitude change in a group comprising some people predisposed to agree and other people predisposed to disagree with the speaker's message (Lumsdaine & Janis, 1953). However, when listeners are exposed to both sides of an issue, they are more resistant to later persuasion from the opposing camp than are people who have heard only their own side of the issue.

Another way to change people's attitudes is simply to expose them repeatedly to the desired attitude. On average, repeating an argument enhances its effectiveness. Indeed, simply exposing people to a stimulus many times tends to increase people's liking for that stimulus (Arkes, Boehm, & Xu, 1991). This positive effect on attitudes that results from repeated exposure to a message supporting the attitude, or even just exposure to the stimulus about which the attitude is being formed or modified, is usually termed the **mere exposure effect** (Zajonc, 1968). For example, many people find that their liking for a piece of music, a work of art, or even a kind of food increases with repeated exposure, which is why we often call these preferences "acquired tastes."

However, if the repetition becomes boring or annoying, it can backfire, decreasing the likelihood of liking or of attitude change (Cacioppo & Petty, 1979, 1980). For example, if someone keeps telling you how wonderful he is you may simply become annoyed with him rather than convinced of his wonderful qualities. Thus, repetition is useful in order to make sure people get the message, but after a point, it may hurt your case.

Characteristics of the Source

Characteristics of the source of the persuasive message may also affect the effectiveness of the message in eliciting attitude change. Two key characteristics of the source are credibility and likability.

Credibility.   People are more likely to believe a communication if the source is rated high rather than low in *credibility,* that is, in believability (Hovland & Weiss, 1951). The effect of source credibility is greatest right after receiving the persuasive message. Over time, the effect of the credible source decreases. For example, the power of golfer Tiger Woods's endorsement of a particular product is likely to diminish in a person's mind as time marches on.

Likability. People also are more likely to be persuaded by messages from people whom they like than by messages from people whom they do not like (Chaiken & Eagly, 1983). Moreover, this **likability effect** is especially important if you are trying to persuade people to take a position that they initially resist or otherwise find unappealing (Eagly & Chaiken, 1975, 1992). The magnitude of this effect, however, depends on the medium for the message. The likability effect is greater in videotaped than in audiotaped messages and is inconsequential in written messages (see Figure 13-1). This difference probably occurs because we get a broader range of visual and auditory information from a videotape than we do from either an audiotape or written material. When we can see the persuader's facial expressions, clothing, and appearance, and also hear the persuader's voice, intonation, and actual words, we have a lot of sensory information with which to decide whether we find the person appealing. It is for this reason that some of the best radio announcers do not succeed when they try to switch to television: The personal impression they make diminishes when people not only hear them, but see them as well and discover that they do not look much different from or more believable than anyone else.

The Link Between Attitudes and Behavior

Implicit in the study of attitudes is the assumption that our attitudes are somehow linked to our behavior. However, have you ever noticed occasions when you observed a discrepancy between people's attitudes and their behavior? For example, do you always assume that the way a salesperson behaves toward you genuinely indicates that person's feelings toward you? Have you ever acted cruelly, carelessly, or unsympathetically toward someone about whom you care deeply? Clearly, people's behavior does not necessarily reflect their attitudes accurately. At the least, there may be several alternative explanations for the behavior we observe. However, our beliefs and attitudes are not entirely separate from our behaviors. Several factors increase the likelihood that our attitudes will be shown in our behaviors (see Brehm & Kassin, 1990; Eagly & Chaiken, 1992):

1. *Attitude strength:* Stronger attitudes are more clearly tied to behavior than are weaker ones.

2. *Amount of information and experience supporting the attitude:* Attitudes based on more information and more experience are more clearly linked to behavior than are other attitudes.

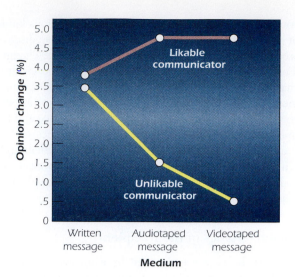

Figure 13-1

THE INTERACTION BETWEEN THE MEDIUM OF THE MESSAGE AND THE LIKABILITY OF THE MESSAGE SENDER. *Although likable message senders generally have a positive effect on attitude change, the positive effect is enhanced by using audiotaped or videotaped messages, rather than written ones. However, when the message sender is not likable, attitude change is even less likely to occur when the message sender uses audiotaped or videotaped messages.*

3. *Attitude specificity:* More highly specific attitudes are more clearly tied to behavior. For example, you are more likely to vote in favor of a proposition to increase property taxes in order to increase the availability of student loans if you have a positive attitude toward that specific use of funds than if you have a generally positive attitude toward having a well-educated citizenry.

4. *Situational factors:* Your current situation may affect whether you behave in accord with your attitudes. For example, if you win the lottery on the morning of the election, you may completely forget to go to the polling booth to vote for student loan funding. If, however, your parents call you and tell you that they have just declared bankruptcy, you will probably recruit a few extra voters to vote for the student-loan funding.

Another factor that influences both our attitudes and our behavior is the broad cultural context in which we live. For example, the terms *monochronic* (one time) and *polychronic* (many times) have been used to describe cultural variations in the perception of time (Hall, 1966). In a *monochronic culture*, time is precious, and its regulation is precise. In such a culture, people are more likely to have attitudes that prize time and to show behavior that reflects a rigid orientation toward time. On the other hand, in a *polychronic culture*, people place much less emphasis on the clock, and the measurement of time is much more fluid. In a polychronic culture, people may be expected to behave in ways that might be considered tardy or even irresponsible (because of the lack of attention to time) in a monochronic culture. Thus, behavior (such as being habitually late) that in one culture might engender very negative attitudes in another culture might be viewed as quite acceptable or even desirable.

Although we live in a largely monochronic culture, there are advantages to living in a polychronic culture. In a cross-cultural study (R. V. Levine & Bartlett, 1984), the monochronic emphasis on time has been linked to coronary heart disease. Some might conclude that if we pay less attention to the time we have, we may end up having more time to live.

Cognitive Consistency

Imagine that you are participating in an experiment in which the experimenter asks you to perform two mind-numbingly simple tasks of eye–hand coordination: repeatedly emptying and refilling a tray containing spools of thread for half an hour, then repeatedly turning an array of pegs one-quarter turn each for another half hour. After you have performed these excruciatingly dull tasks for a full hour, the experimenter mercifully tells you that you may stop. As far as you know, that is the end of the experiment on eye–hand coordination.

Now, as is customary after a psychological experiment, the experimenter debriefs you, explaining that the purpose of the experiment was to investigate the effects of psychological mind set on task performance. You were in the control group, so you were given no prior indication of whether the tasks would be interesting. In the experimental group, on the other hand, participants are told in advance that the tasks will be enjoyable. The experimenter goes on to tell you that the next participant, waiting outside, has been assigned to the experimental group, and that a research assistant will arrive soon to tell her how great the task will be.

Then the experimenter leaves the room for a moment and returns, worried because his research assistant has not yet arrived. Would you be willing to salvage the experiment by serving as a paid research assistant just for this one participant? Persuaded, you tell the next participant how much fun the experiment was. She replies that she had heard from a friend that it was a bore. You assure her, however, that it was pure entertainment, and then you depart. As you leave, a secretary in the psychology department interviews you briefly and asks you to rate just how much fun and how interesting the experiment really was.

Have you guessed the true point of this experiment? The independent variable was not whether you were told in advance that the experiment was fun and interesting. In fact, you and all the other participants who believed you were in the "control" condition were actually in the experimental condition. In the genuine control condition, participants merely performed the boring tasks and later were asked how interesting the tasks were.

In the true experimental condition in this classic study by Leon Festinger and J. Merrill Carlsmith (1959), the "participant" waiting outside was a confederate of the experimenter. There never was any other research assistant: The plan had always been to get you to convince the next "participant" that the experiment was a delight. The crucial manipulation was the amount of payment you received for saying that the experiment was interesting. The independent variable actually was that some participants were paid only $1; others were paid $20. The dependent variable was the experimental participant's rating of the interest level of the tasks when questioned by the secretary. The goal was to find out whether a relationship existed between the amount of money a person was paid for lying about the tasks and how interesting the person later reported the dull tasks to be. In other words, how did lying about tasks affect people's attitudes toward those tasks?

Participants who were paid $1 rated the boring experiment as much more interesting than did either those who were paid $20 or the control participants, as shown in Figure 13-2. When this result was discovered, it came as a great shock to the field of psychology, because the existing *incentive-motivation theory* predicted that individuals in the $20 group would have much

Figure 13–2
THE CLASSIC EXPERIMENT ON COGNITIVE DISSONANCE.
This graphic display of Festinger and Carlsmith's findings show the unambiguous, although quite surprising, results. To the astonishment of many psychologists, the participants who received $1 for feigning the enjoyment of the task later expressed some enjoyment when asked to give their candid views. In contrast, the control group emphatically expressed their extreme boredom during the task, and even the participants who received $20 for simulating the appearance of enjoyment later asserted that the task was boring.

more incentive to change their attitude toward the experiment than would individuals in the $1 group because $20 was a much greater reward than $1. Hence, this theory predicted that people in the $20 group would be much more motivated to show, and actually would show, more attitude change (Hovland, Janis, & Kelley, 1953). Consider two alternative explanations as to why people in the $1 group showed more attitude change—the explanations of cognitive-dissonance theory and of self-perception theory.

Cognitive Dissonance

Festinger and Carlsmith explained the counterintuitive results by suggesting that participants' responses could be understood in terms of the participants' efforts to achieve **cognitive consistency**—that is, a match between a person's thoughts and his or her behaviors. The fundamental importance of cognitive consistency was first pointed out by Fritz Heider (1958), who recognized that when people's cognitions are inconsistent with each other, the people strive to restore consistency. For example, cognitive consistency is extremely important to our mental well-being. Without it, we feel tense, nervous, irritable, and even at war with ourselves.

For example, suppose you meet someone you like a lot but then hear from others that your "new friend" is saying nasty things about you behind your back. The person you liked now has become a threat to your well-being, and you almost certainly will experience cognitive inconsistency. It is adaptive for you to feel very uncomfortable. The world no longer makes sense and your well-being is in jeopardy. Your discomfort is likely to lead you to check whether the rumors are really true, and if they are, to distance yourself from or set yourself in opposition to the false friend.

Now, reconsider the Festinger and Carlsmith experiment: The participants who were paid $20 performed an extremely boring task and then encouraged someone else to believe that the task was interesting. They were well compensated for doing so, however. They achieved cognitive consistency easily. Saying that a dull task was interesting but getting paid well for saying so allowed these participants to match their thoughts and beliefs to their behavior.

Now consider the plight of the participants who were paid $1. They not only performed a boring task but also lied about it by trying to convince someone else that it was interesting. Furthermore, they were paid poorly for their efforts. These participants were experiencing **cognitive dissonance**—a person's disquieting

How is this smoker achieving cognitive consistency? What strategies for reducing dissonance would be the most effective for the smoker who is aware of the hazards of smoking, both to the smoker and to other people near the smoker?

perception of a mismatch between his or her attitudes and his or her behavior.

Justification of effort—a means by which an individual rationalizes the expenditure of energy—is one route to achieving cognitive consistency. Most of us need to feel that we have good, logical reasons for why we do what we do, but how could the poorly paid experimental participants justify their efforts on the task? The only apparent justification was to decide that perhaps it was not really so bad. After all, it would have been embarrassing to admit that not only had they not liked the task, but also that they had lied about it to someone else and then had been paid a small amount of money for doing so. How much easier it must have seemed to decide that maybe it was all worth it and that it was even interesting and enjoyable. Thus, these latter participants achieved cognitive consistency by deciding that the task was perfectly acceptable. Another way of saying this is that the participants rid themselves of cognitive dissonance. They made sense of the lies they had told the confederate by deceiving themselves and changing their attitude toward the boring task.

We now look more closely at the conditions under which cognitive dissonance occurs. It appears that dissonance is most likely to occur when (a) you have freely chosen the action that causes the dissonance; (b) you have firmly committed yourself to that behavior, and the commitment or behavior is irrevocable; and (c) your behavior has significant consequences for other people. For example, suppose that a couple is very unhappily married, they have children, and they both devoutly believe that divorce is morally wrong, especially when a couple has children. This is a classic situation likely to generate cognitive dissonance.

In contrast, you are less likely to experience cognitive dissonance if you are forced into an action, if you still have the option of not continuing to perform the action, or if your behavior has consequences for no one but you. Someone who is coerced into marriage or who has no children to think about may have less compunction about filing for divorce. (See Figure 13-3 for a look at the conditions affecting dissonance.)

The preceding discussion has interpreted the results of the Festinger and Carlsmith (1959) experiment in terms of cognitive-dissonance theory, but this interpretation is not the only one possible. Consider now the rather different analysis of self-perception theory, which describes another route to cognitive consistency.

Self-Perception Theory

If questioned about the connection between our beliefs and our behavior, most of us would probably say that our behavior is caused by our beliefs. **Self-perception theory** (D. J. Bem, 1967, 1972) suggests essentially the opposite—that when people are not sure of what they believe, they *infer* their beliefs *from* their behavior, perceiving their own actions much as an outside observer would, and thereby drawing conclusions about themselves, based on their actions.

Consider a self-perception theory interpretation of the Festinger and Carlsmith (1959) experiment. As you find yourself explaining to another participant how enjoyable the experiment was, you wonder, "Why in the world am I doing this?" If you are not sure why, then how can you understand your own behavior? If you have been paid $20, the explanation is easy: You are doing it for the money. However, if you have been paid only $1, you cannot be doing it for the money. So, looking at the situation objectively, a logical interpretation is that you must have liked the task.

Examples of self-perception can occur in many other circumstances as well. For example, suppose you are trying to figure out whether you are interested in becoming more involved with a significant other. You are not sure how you feel toward that other. Then you realize that you have been spending large amounts of time with the person, have been buying the person expensive gifts, and have been spending much less time with friends with whom you used to spend time so that you could spend the time with the significant other. You infer on the basis of your behavior that you must really care a great deal about your significant other. You therefore decide you are ready for a deeper commitment.

Self-perception theory might seem somewhat contrary to both rationality and intuition—after all, don't you already know best what you like and dislike? Not always. For example, suppose that you "know" about yourself that you hate a particular type of food—such as brussels sprouts—that you have not even tried to taste for years. Now suppose that you are a guest in the home of someone whom you want very much to please. The only appetizer being served is tender brussels sprouts, marinated in a vinaigrette sauce and served icy cold. No choice—you have to try it and appear to be pleased. After your token helping, you find yourself reaching for more. How would you explain your behavior to yourself? Would you be open to changing your view of yourself enough to allow yourself to like something you previously "knew" you did not like?

It can be advantageous sometimes to consider whether our entrenched self-perceptions may be unnecessarily limiting our options. People change; preferences change; fears change. According to self-perception theory, when we behave in a way that conflicts with our existing self-perceptions, we have a chance to look at ourselves again from a fresh perspective. We may just shake up our self-perceptions and change how we perceive ourselves.

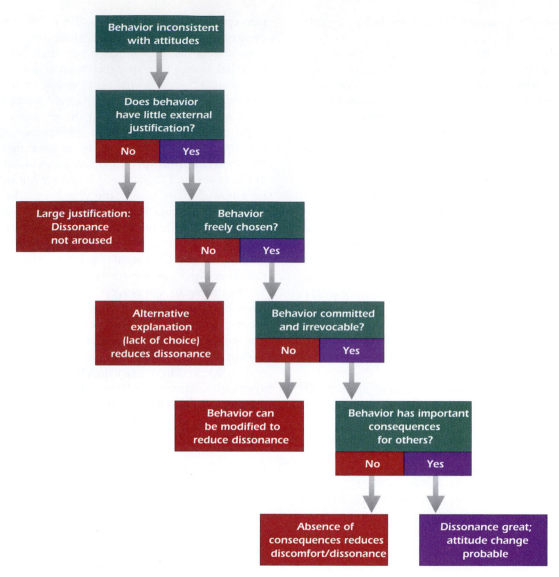

Figure 13–3
QUALIFYING CONDITIONS FOR COGNITIVE DISSONANCE. *In cognitive dissonance, people's behavior appears inconsistent with their attitudes, so they become intellectually confused and uncomfortable. This flowchart demonstrates the qualifying conditions for determining whether cognitive dissonance would be likely to lead to attitude change. A "no" answer at any point would mean that alternative outcomes—that is, other than attitude change—would be more likely.*

Researchers have conducted experiments to determine whether cognitive dissonance or self-perception theory better explains behavior that contradicts prior beliefs (e.g., D. J. Bem, 1967; J. Cooper, Zanna, & Taves, 1978). It appears that dissonance theory applies better when people behave in ways that do not follow at all their usual beliefs or attitudes. If you have always been a staunch Democrat, but a friend convinces you to attend meetings of a Republican policy group, which you then find persuasive, your lack of cognitive consistency might be a job for dissonance theory. Thus, dissonance theory seems better to explain *attitude change*, particularly when the change is dramatic and the original beliefs and attitudes are obvious and well defined. Self-perception theory applies better when people behave in ways that are only slightly discrepant from their normal patterns, particularly when the attitudes are vague, uncertain, and not fully formed. If you think that you do not like brussels sprouts, although you have never really tried them, but you find yourself happily eating them one night at dinner, self-perception theory might help you to achieve cognitive consistency. Self-perception theory seems better to explain *attitude formation*, when the person's attitudes are still ambiguous (Fazio, Zanna, & Cooper, 1977).

Attributions: Explaining and Interpreting Behavior

In Search of . . .

What are attributions and how do they explain behavior?

One of the ways in which we may achieve cognitive consistency is to make an **attribution**—a mental explanation that points to the cause of a person's behavior, including the behavior of the person making the attribution. For example, in self-perception theory, to explain our newfound fondness for brussels sprouts, we may make an *attribution* in our perceptions of ourselves, telling ourselves that we are among those people who like brussels sprouts, based on our observations of our own behavior. Attributions are important because they help us understand both our own behavior and the behavior of others. They can become matters of life and death. If a driver picks up a hitchhiker, for example, the driver is attributing the hitchhiking to the individual's need for a ride. If the driver's attribution is wrong and the hitchhiker's need is instead to rob or to kill the driver, the mistaken attribution will have proven to be costly indeed.

The Nature of Attributions

Because self-perception theory focuses on making attributions, it belongs to a broader class of social-psychological theories termed *attribution theories*, which address how people explain not only their own behavior but also the behavior of others. People make attributions to themselves, others, or situational variables so that they can understand their social world and can answer questions such as, "Why did I act that way?" and "Why did she do that?"

The origins of attribution theory are often traced to Fritz Heider (1958), who held that we humans are inclined to observe, classify, and explain (by making causal attributions) both our own behavior and the behavior of others. We then often base our own subsequent behavior on the earlier assumptions we have made in our causal attributions. For example, people living through difficult circumstances, such as economic deprivation or war, often seek scapegoats on which to pin the causes of their misfortune: They seek to attribute their misfortune to external causes.

Heider pointed out that people make two basic kinds of attributions in particular. **Personal attributions** or dispositional attributions, are mental explanations pointing to the causes of human behavior as lying within the individual who performs the behavior and hence are internal (e.g., "My stubbornness got us into this argument"). **Situational attributions** are mental explanations pointing to the causes of human behavior as lying outside the individual who performs the behavior and hence are external, such as the settings, events, or other people in the environment of the person engaging in a given behavior (e.g., "If they hadn't held the examination in that overheated room, I probably would have been more alert and achieved a better grade."). When there are several possible causal attributions for a particular event, we are less likely to attribute the event to any one particular cause (Morris & Larrick, 1995).

Attribution Heuristics and Biases

Up to this point, we have spoken about how people process various factors that influence causal attributions (whether praise, blame, or whatever) almost as if people were efficient computers, mechanistically measuring each possible causal factor. Actually, none of us carefully weighs every factor each time we make an attribution. Instead, we sometimes use *heuristics*—shortcut rules—to help us make decisions (see chapter 8 for more on heuristics). Unfortunately, these shortcuts sometimes lead to biases and other distortions in our thinking, such as in our thinking about the causes of behavior. For example, people sometimes scapegoat others simply because it is easier to look for scapegoats than to seek the often complex causes of personal or even national misfortunes. We now turn to some of the common heuristics and biases that affect how people make their causal attributions: social desirability, the fundamental attribution error, actor–observer effects, self-serving biases, and self-handicapping.

Social Desirability. Some research has indicated that in trying to infer the dispositions of people, we tend to give undeservedly heavy weight to socially undesirable behavior (Jones & Davis, 1965). In fact, we may focus so much attention on the socially undesirable behavior that we fail to notice even highly socially desirable behavior. For example, someone who belches, snorts, drools, and gags at the dinner table is likely to make a bad impression, despite the person's witty, insightful, thought-provoking conversation. This person may also be a kind and gentle humanitarian, but she or he will be hard-pressed to negate the effect of this socially undesirable behavior in other people's minds.

The Fundamental Attribution Error. The **fundamental attribution error** occurs when an individual tends to overemphasize internal causes and personal responsibility and to deemphasize external causes and situational influences when observing the behavior of other people (L. Ross, 1977). This error is called "fundamental" because it appears to be so generalized and so basic: In viewing the behavior of others, we see responsibility as residing within these others. For example, if a boss

Psychology in Everyday Life

The Culture of Honor

Do you feel that if someone mistreats a member of your family, you must uphold the family honor? Whether or not you do depends partially on whether you have grown up in what has come to be called a *culture of honor*. In such a culture, people emphasize the importance of honor, social status, and of aggression viewed as necessary to preserve honor and social status. In such cultures, even minor perceived slights to the honor of an individual or a family can lead to major confrontations and death.

Richard Nisbett and Dov Cohen (1996) have studied one culture of honor, the South of the United States. They have compiled evidence showing that rates of violence in the South are consistently higher than in other regions of the United States. Ever since records first started being kept, the South has led all other regions in rates of homicide. Why? Nisbett and Cohen have suggested that part of the answer lies in the self-perceived need of Southerners to uphold a culture of honor.

Why should such a culture have emerged in the South and not in other parts of the United States? Nisbett and Cohen have speculated that the needs of early settlers in the South were somewhat different from needs of settlers in other parts of the country. Settlers in the South were more likely to come from herding cultures characterized by inadequate enforcement of the law. In order to protect their flocks, the herders felt a need to take the law into their own hands. Settlers in the North, in contrast, were more likely to be farmers and to be more accustomed to the rule and enforcement of law.

Nisbett and Cohen have presented evidence that southerners are more likely than northerners to agree that a person has a right to kill in order to defend his family and home. They are more likely to agree to violence, so long as it is honor-related. In one set of experiments (Cohen, Nisbett, Bowdle, & Schwarz, 1996), white male students became involved in an encounter in a narrow hallway. A confederate of the experiments' passed a given participant and did not give way to the participant. The confederate bumped into the participant and then insulted him. The data showed that southerners were more likely than northerners to feel that their masculine reputations had been threatened. They showed more physiological signs of upset (e.g., rise in testosterone level). And subsequently, they engaged in more aggressive behavior, such as being unwilling to yield to another confederate who passed them in the narrow hallway.

These kinds of behavior are not limited to the South. Members of gangs in all parts of the country can be very touchy about the kinds of "respect" shown to them. People have been killed for not showing the proper "respect." Clearly, how people react to threats to their sense of honor are socialized by the kind of environment in which they grow up.

---

mistreats employees, we are more likely to attribute the boss's behavior to something about the boss's nature than to something about the situation. A person who often does favors for others is more likely to be judged as intrinsically helpful than as pressured by circumstances to do favors.

Actor–Observer Effect. Edward Jones and Richard Nisbett (1971) expanded on the notion of the fundamental attribution error in their hypothesized **actor–observer effect.** In this effect, people attribute the actions of other persons whom they observe to the stable dispositional characteristics of other persons, but they attribute their own actions to the momentary characteristics of the situation. In the latter, we are the actors (who must consider the relevant situational factors), and in the former, we are the observers (who notice the dispositions of

other people)—hence, the name of the effect. If I kick a dog, it is because the dog was about to bite. However, if I see someone else kick a dog, the action shows just how mean and nasty that person really is.

The actor–observer effect may even extend to groups of which we either do or do not identify ourselves as a part. Islam and Hewstone (1993), studying Hindu and Muslim students in Bangladesh, found that students tended to attribute positive behavior of members of the group with which they identified as due to the group members' good dispositions, and bad behavior as due to the situation. They made the reverse attribution for members of the group with which they did not identify.

Self-Serving Biases. Another bias in our attribution processes is that we tend to be generous—to ourselves—when interpreting our own actions (S. Epstein,

1992). For example, when students study for examinations and do well, they are likely to take credit for the success. But when students study and do poorly, they are more likely to attribute the low grade to the examination ("That test was unfair!") or to the professor ("His grading is so strict!"; Whitley & Frieze, 1985). In another study of self-serving biases (Kunda, 1987), students were found to be aware that the divorce rate in the United States hovers close to 50%, but these same students believed that their own chances of ever personally divorcing their future spouses were only around 20%. The occurrence of self-serving bias may differ across cultures, however (Markus, Kitayama, & Heiman, 1996). Markus and Kitayama (1991) have suggested, for example, that it seems to be more common among American than among Japanese students. Self-serving biases can perform at least one constructive function in our lives: They give us necessary self-confidence. This confidence in ourselves is often a first step toward achieving the goals we value, whether in personal relationships, in school, or on the job.

Self-Handicapping. In *self-handicapping*, people take actions to sabotage their own performance so that they will have excuses in case they fail to perform satisfactorily (Berglas & Jones, 1978). Uncertain of their ability to perform well, they create a situation in which they *cannot* perform well and then blame their poor performance on the situation, without acknowledging their role in creating that situation. For example, a student might not make the time to study for a test, and when she does badly on it she might attribute the failure to not being able to study.

We have surveyed a number of the heuristics and biases people use in making attributions. It is important to know not only the bases of attributions, but also the problems and prejudices inherent in attributions. Probably no one can see a situation clearly enough to make a completely accurate attribution—or perhaps it is more nearly correct to say that no situation is so simple that everyone can agree on one attribution. Nevertheless, understanding heuristics and biases can help you make more nearly accurate attributions in your daily lives. The extent to which you are correct in making attributions about the causes of your own behavior and that of others might be viewed as indices of interpersonal and intrapersonal intelligences, respectively (H. Gardner, 1983, 1999; see chapter 9).

We now broaden our scope to encompass more than just how we make causal attributions regarding the behavior of ourselves and other people. Next, we consider how people perceive and interpret a wide variety of information about other people, in order to form an impression of them. Note that *impression formation* is the impression you form regarding other people, whereas *impression management* is the impression you try to encourage others to form about you.

Impression Formation

How do people form impressions?

Forming Impressions

When you go to a party and meet new people, how do you decide what you think of them? An entire branch of social psychology devotes itself to exactly this question of how we form impressions. The study of **impression formation** is an examination of the process by which individuals form unified intuitive conceptions about other people, based on inferences from information obtained both directly and indirectly (Hamilton & Sherman, 1996).

Models of Impression Formation

A landmark study in the field of impression formation was performed by Solomon Asch (1946). Asch presented his participants with the following list of

When we form impressions of people, we make inferences about them based on direct and indirect information—what others say about them, what we know about them, how they themselves look and talk, the interests and opinions they express, and so on.

adjectives describing a person named Jim: "intelligent, skillful, industrious, . . . determined, practical, cautious." In the blank was one of these words: "warm," "cold," "polite," or "blunt." Based on these seven adjectives, participants were asked to write descriptions of their impressions of Jim and to indicate whether the adjectives *generous, wise, happy, good-natured,* or *reliable* could also describe him. Some of Asch's data appear in Table 13-1.

Asch interpreted the findings shown in Table 13-1 as indicating that the words "warm" and "cold" seemed to be **central traits,** or characteristics of a person that stand out in their importance for the personality and behavior of an individual (see chapter 15). When either of these two words appeared in the blank, there was a radical effect on the sort of person Jim was perceived to be. "Polite" or "blunt" in the blank, however, had relatively little effect on impression formation by Asch's participants.

Other investigators have criticized various aspects of Asch's study. They have pointed out, for example, that the words "warm" and "cold" are social traits, whereas the other words in the initial list given to the participants ("intelligent, skillful, industrious," etc.) are more intellectual in nature. This difference in kind may have given the social words disproportionate weight in impression formation (Zanna & Hamilton, 1972). How well the results generalize to real-world situations (their *ecological validity*) can also be questioned. Nonetheless, Asch's ideas, especially the notion of central traits around which we organize information about other personality characteristics, have had a lasting influence. Some of the early psy-

chologists studying heuristics and biases have also had a lasting effect.

Heuristics and Biases in Impression Formation

One of the reasons that people do not form uniform impressions or compute standardized impressions of other people is that almost all of us take shortcuts when we are forming impressions of people (Gigerenzer, Todd, & the ABC Research Group, 1999). Most of the time, these shortcuts save us time and give us a good enough impression to help us interact with other people appropriately. Often, however, our shortcuts are altogether too short and cut out too much important information. Research suggests that our processing of information can cause us to distort our perceptions through a variety of heuristics and biases, such as the primacy effect, confirmation bias, self-fulfilling prophecy, and person-positivity bias.

The Primacy Effect.   First impressions can be powerful. In one experiment (Asch, 1946), one group of people was told that a person was "intelligent, industrious, impulsive, critical, stubborn, and envious." A second group of participants was told that the person was "envious, stubborn, critical, impulsive, industrious, and intelligent." Notice that the second list of traits is exactly the same as the first, but in reverse order. Despite the objective similarity of the two lists, however, people who heard the first order—with positive traits first—formed a more positive impression than did those people who heard the second order—with negative traits first. Asch concluded that we

TABLE 13-1

Impression Formation   *Based on a list of adjectives, participants were asked to write descriptions of their impressions of a person and to indicate whether the adjectives* generous, wise, happy, good-natured, *or* reliable *could also describe the person. The following percentages indicate the proportion of participants, for each of the lists, who agreed that a given trait would also characterize the person described by the list of adjectives. (After Asch, 1946)*

	TRAITS INSERTED INTO LIST			
Additional Traits	*"Warm"*	*"Cold"*	*"Polite"*	*"Blunt"*
Generous	91%	8%	56%	58%
Wise	65	25	30	50
Happy	90	34	75	65
Good-natured	94	17	87	56
Reliable	94	99	95	100

demonstrate a *primacy effect* in our evaluations of people—whereby first impressions can influence subsequent ones. Thus, we give more weight to the things we learn earlier than to the things we learn later. The primacy effect causes bias in judgments of abilities as well as of personality.

One reason that the primacy effect works may be explained by our use of schemas. As we take in new information, we try to make sense of the information as quickly as possible, either by assimilating the new information into our existing schemas (e.g., our schemas about "people like that") or by creating new schemas to accommodate the new information. If we must create new schemas, we start creating them quickly, to minimize the amount of time during which we must feel the uncomfortable lack of an integrated way in which to understand the new information. As soon as we have the beginnings of a schema, we can rapidly and easily assimilate any additional information into the new schema. If the new information is sharply discrepant from the new schema, we may modify the schema to accommodate the new information but we leave the fundamental structure of the schema intact. We do not discard or even completely overhaul the schema once we create it. It is harder to correct an initial bad impression about abilities than to ruin an initial good one.

Confirmation Bias. A second reason that we tend to maintain our first impressions of people (the primacy effect) may be due to confirmation bias. *Confirmation bias* is the human tendency to seek ways to confirm rather than to refute existing beliefs (Edwards & Smith, 1996). Our confirmation biases may lead us to seek, interpret, and even distort information in ways that verify our first impressions or preexisting beliefs about a person or a group (Yzerbyt, Rocher, & Schadron, 1996). We tend to notice and to remember the events and behaviors that fit into our existing schemas, whereas we tend to ignore and to forget those that do not. Thus, we have the illusion that our preconceptions are confirmed by our experiences. Our confirmation biases can lead us to distortions that not only hinder our appreciation of others but also that hamper our full understanding of the world in which we live. We may under- or overestimate the skills, abilities, and merits of the people around us as a result of our confirmation biases.

Confirmation bias can be a reason that even flagrant examples of child abuse go unnoticed. A teacher may see possible signs of physical abuse toward a child. These signs even may be ones that, in most circumstances, would lead to strong suspicions of abuse. But the child happens to come from a family that is prominent in the community, perhaps even a family in which the parents have been outspoken in their criticisms of child abuse. The teacher, having a strong positive impression of the behavior of the parents, may interpret the signs of child abuse as signs of a propensity of the child to have accidents and thereby leave the child at risk for further harm.

Why would we persist in doing something that eventually might hurt us, as well as others? Because confirmation biases, like other heuristic shortcuts, save us time. If we took the time to get to know everyone with whom we had any contact, we would have time for little else. In our daily, transitory interactions with most people, our confirmation biases probably do us little harm, and they save us a great deal of time. On the other hand, in many situations, we would do well to consider the powerful influence of our confirmation biases.

Confirmation bias can lead to **self-fulfilling prophecy,** whereby what is believed to be true becomes true or at least is perceived to have become true. Robert Rosenthal and Leonore Jacobson (1968) pioneered the study of self-fulfilling prophecies in their landmark investigation showing the effects of teacher expectations on student performance (see chapter 2). Their particular study looked at positive self-fulfilling prophecies, but such prophecies can be negative as well (Harris, Milich, Corbitt, Hoover, & Brady, 1992). In general, people often have a certain expectation for another person. They then act in a way to make that expectation come true. Then they conclude that their original expectation was correct without acknowledging their role in making it come true.

Person-Positivity Bias. **Person-positivity bias** involves the tendency for people to evaluate individuals more positively than they evaluate groups, including the groups to which those individuals belong (Sears, 1983). Often, for example, people have a prejudice toward a group, but may have a more positive attitude toward a particular person who is a member of that group. One way of looking at this bias is that we are willing to take the time to form a rather elaborate schema for a particular individual whom we know well and with whom we interact often. When we observe an individual often, our frequent observations may so sharply conflict with our stereotype that we are forced to notice that the person defies the stereotype. Such observations would require us to make some kind of cognitive adjustment. We still try to exert as little effort as possible, however, and we try to minimize the amount of cognitive adjustment we must make. It takes less mental effort to note simply that this individual happens to deviate from the stereotype than to dismiss or to overhaul the stereotype altogether. Thus, although we may have to change our views toward individuals who happen to belong to a group, when thinking about the group of people as a whole, we may still prefer to use a nice, neat stereotype. Such a stereotype works as a convenient shortcut in place of getting to know all the possible exceptions to the rule, all the varied details of the general description, and all the contextual information that might influence how we interpret a particular characteristic.

Social Comparison

Leon Festinger (1954), noted earlier in regard to his theory of cognitive dissonance, also proposed another theory regarding how we look at ourselves. According to Festinger's **social-comparison theory,** people evaluate their own abilities and accomplishments largely by comparing these abilities and accomplishments to the abilities and accomplishments of others, particularly in novel, uncertain, or ambiguous settings for which internal standards are not yet established (Suls & Fletcher, 1983; Suls & Miller, 1977). Our self-esteem suffers when others perform better than we do (Kulik & Gump, 1997). The realism and accuracy of our self-appraisals will therefore depend in large part on whether the others with whom we compare ourselves are, in fact, appropriate bases for setting our own standards (Goethals & Darley, 1977). For example, suppose that Darrell, a sophomore in college, compares himself to a high school student in terms of academic accomplishments; he might thereby have an unrealistically positive image of what he has accomplished. In contrast, Melba—also a college sophomore—compares herself to a graduate student, and so she may end up with an unrealistically negative self-image. It is important to compare ourselves to people with whom we can make appropriate comparisons.

People use a variety of techniques to maintain their self-esteem, despite unfavorable social comparisons. For example, they may exaggerate the abilities of those who outperform them, thereby continuing to see themselves as quite able even if not quite at the superlative level (Alicke, LoSchiavo, Zerbst, & Zhang, 1997). Or they may compare themselves to others who are substantially worse than they are, again maintaining their self-esteem (Gibbons, Benhow, & Gerrard, 1994). When people make inappropriate social comparisons, they may come to form overly harsh or overly accepting attitudes toward their own behavior. In the next section, we will discuss what attitudes are, how they are formed, how they can change, and how they affect behavior.

Attraction, Liking, and Loving

In Search of...

What leads us to like and love others?

In the first part of this chapter we looked at the mental processes by which we form and change attitudes, make attributions, and form impressions. In this section, we take one step away from purely internal social processing and begin to look at what happens when the initially internal notion of attraction becomes liking or sometimes loving. First, we consider some variables that influence whether we come to like or love another person. Next we consider some theories of liking and then of loving.

Each of us needs friendship, love, and even physical attraction. Relationships, as mentioned earlier, are important to our physical and emotional well-being. Our perceptions of ourselves are partly shaped by our friendships, our loving relationships, and our feelings of attractiveness and attraction to others. We may even have ideal stories of what love should be, leading us to be attracted to people who fit those stories and not attracted to those who do not (R. J. Sternberg, 1995a, 1996a, 1998b). Social psychologists have asked: What is going on in the mind of a person who feels attracted to someone? Why are we more attracted— and more attractive—to one person rather than another?

Psychologists are not the only ones who have explored questions regarding liking and loving. Sculptors, composers, writers, artists, and philosophers have explored these same questions. While reading about the psychological perspective, bear in mind that scientific analysis of love or friendship can give us only a part of a much wider picture.

Forces Influencing Attraction

What are the forces that lead to attraction in the first place, and hence to liking and loving? Some of the underlying variables are familiarity, arousal, proximity, physical attractiveness, and similarity (Berscheid & Reis, 1997). Recall, from the discussion on persuasion, that familiarity is a factor that increases our liking for someone. That is, due to the mere exposure effect, we tend to feel stronger liking for people who are more familiar to us. The remaining four factors are described next.

Arousal

Arousal can play an important role in interpersonal attraction. The role of arousal was demonstrated in a famous and creative study (Dutton & Aron, 1974)

How Important Are Spectators to Athletes' Performance?

Bernd Strauss, *University of Muenster*

A common belief among athletes, coaches, spectators, as well as journalists is that spectators strongly influence performance in sports. When basketball players were asked to report how they perform in front of an audience, 89% reported being more strongly motivated through the support of the crowd at home games (Jurkovac, 1985). However, if we want to investigate the impact of spectators on sports performance scientifically, it is not enough to ask athletes what they think. We have to look at performance itself, and empirical research based on performance instead of self-reports often fails to support this common belief (Moore & Brylinsky, 1993).

Clearly, such differing results indicate that the impact of spectators and the size of spectator effects is not as simple and straightforward as athletes and others believe. My group's work took one of the first steps toward a more detailed analysis of this issue. First we analyzed the research findings that already existed, looking at the variety of influences studied by other researchers. Working from this knowledge, we developed our own study.

The Impact of Cheering on Football

We chose to study sports performance and spectator cheering in the "New Yorker Hurricanes," a member of the American Football premier league based in the German city of Kiel. Data were collected from four home games in 1997 that were each attended by an average of about 4,000 spectators. Team performance and spectator behavior during all four home games were videotaped and then shown to raters. These raters assessed spectator behavior ("cheering," when more than 50% of spectators exhibited support for their team, vs. "no cheering") for 15 seconds before the start of a down ("spectator behavior before Down t") and during a down ("spectator behavior during Down t"). The outcome of each down was given either a positive or negative rating (using a standardized list of items such as gaining territory, completing a touchdown, etc.) by the head coach and one other person ("performance on Down t"). These ratings were carried out before the referee made a decision.

All four games combined produced 631downs. A statistical procedure known as hierarchical log linear analysis was applied to the data on these downs. This revealed that none of the spectators' and athletes' beliefs in the positive effects of cheering on the home team could be confirmed. Although previous performance related to subsequent spectator behavior, spectator behavior did not relate to subsequent game performance. In other words, this study provides no indications that spectator behavior such as cheering before a down influences performance. On the other hand, performance certainly influences spectator behavior: Spectators—as in a theater—react to the performance.

How can this be explained? Research has shown that the presence of others enhances quantitative performance when the task involved is simple, but that when we turn to tasks that focus on the *qualitative* aspects of performance, such as those requiring stamina, speed, *and* coordination, we find that spectators seem to "interfere" with performance, and it tends to drop. Such qualitative tasks are typical for sports like soccer, handball, or American football.

This, then, would explain our earlier results. Whether performance improves, deteriorates (e.g., in the sense of choking under pressure), or even does not change at all seems to depend on the individual components involved. For example, it is plausible that spectators contribute to improving the quantitative aspects of performance (e.g., that an athlete runs more miles during a match, sprints faster, etc.). However, at the same time, spectators and their activities may have a negative effect on qualitative aspects (e.g., the same athlete makes more mistakes).

Conclusions

Hence, if we look at the available empirical research using performance measures rather than athletes' self-reports, *we can find no single study that has been able to demonstrate that cheering leads to improved global performance in team sports*. Summarizing the body of knowledge on the impact of spectators in general (beyond cheering), effects are smaller than athletes and others believe.

References

Bond, C. F., & Titus, L. J. (1983). Social facilitation: A meta-analysis of 241 studies. *Psychological Bulletin, 94,* 265–292.

Butler, J. L., & Baumeister, R. F. (1998). The trouble with friendly faces: Skilled performance with a supportive audience. *Journal of Personality and Social Psychology, 75,* 1214–1230.

Dashiell, J. F. (1935). Experimental studies of the influence of social situations on the behavior of individual human adults. In C. Murchison (Ed.), *A handbook of social psychology* (pp. 1097–1158). Worcester, MA: Clark University Press.

Heckhausen, H., & Strang, H. (1988). Efficiency under record performance demands: Exertion control—An individual difference variable? *Journal of Personality and Social Psychology, 55,* 489–498.

Jurkovac, T. (1985). *Collegiate basketball players' perceptions of the home advantage.* Unpublished master's thesis, Bowling Green State University, Bowling Green, OH.

Kluger, A. N., & DeNisi, A. (1996). The effects of feedback interventions on performance: A historical review, a meta-analysis, and a preliminary feedback intervention theory. *Psychological Bulletin, 119,* 254–284.

Moore, J. T., & Brylinsky, J. (1993). Spectator effect on team performance in college basketball. *Journal of Sport Behavior, 16,* 77–84.

Strauss, B. (1999). Die Beeinflussung sportlicher Leistungen durch Zuschauer [The impact of spectators on sports performance]. Lengerich, Germany: Pabst.

Strauss, B. (under review). The Impact of Supportive Spectator Behavior on Performance in Team Sports.

 Find out more about this topic at
www.harcourtcollege.com/psych/ishm

conducted in a scenic spot with two bridges in different places. The first bridge extended over a deep gorge and swayed precariously from side to side when people walked across it. For most people, walking across this bridge aroused fear. The second bridge was stable, solid, and near the ground. Walking across it did not arouse anxiety.

Participants (all males) were assigned to walk across one bridge or the other, and as they walked across the bridge, they were met by either a male or a female assistant of the experimenter. The assistant asked each person to answer a few questions and to write a brief story in response to a picture. After the participants wrote their stories and then finished crossing the bridge, the research assistant gave the men his or her home phone number and remarked that they should feel free to call if they would like further information about the experiment. The experimenters found that those participants who had become aroused by walking across the anxiety-evoking suspension bridge and who were met by a female assistant wrote stories containing relatively high levels of sexual imagery and were more likely than other participants to call the female research assistant at home. Of course, the fact that the participants were able even to meet the research assistant was important, which leads us to a discussion of the importance of proximity.

Proximity

We are more likely to be exposed to and to be aroused by those with whom we have the most contact. Thus, *proximity*—geographical nearness of people toward whom an individual might feel attracted—can lead to increased friendship or attraction because it facilitates the likelihood of familiarity and possibly also of arousal.

Patterns of friendship were investigated among military veterans and their spouses who lived in two married-student dormitories at the Massachusetts Institute of Technology (Festinger, Schachter, & Back, 1950). The two dormitories had different architectural designs, so it was possible to investigate the effects of proximity in two fairly different, yet confined, physical settings. The basic finding was that people who lived closer to each other were more likely to become friends than were people who lived farther apart—even though none of the distances involved was great. Moreover, people who lived in centrally located apartments were likely to form more friendships than were people who lived in apartments toward the end of a floor. Many kinds of relationships may also be enhanced if people find each other physically attractive.

Physical Attractiveness

If you are like most people—and you are honest with yourself—physical attraction is a very important component of your attraction to people in general, at least at first. One study found that more physically attractive people are judged to be kinder and stronger; to be more outgoing, nurturant, sensitive, interesting, poised, sociable, and sexually warm and responsive; to be more exciting dates; and to have better characters. More attractive people also are predicted to have greater marital happiness and competence, more prestige, more social and professional success, and more fulfillment in life than less attractive people (Dion, Berscheid, & Walster, 1972). These predictions, of course, are based on stereotypes rather than on facts. In collectivist cultures such as Taiwan and South Korea, more attractive individuals are also believed to have greater concern for others and ability to relate to others (Chen, Shaffer, & Wu, 1997; Wheeler & Kim, 1997).

We treat people differently as a function of how attractive they are to us. Indeed, Hatfield and Sprecher (1986) have shown that attractive people have superior life outcomes, and Langlois, Ritter, Casey, and Savin (1995) have shown that mothers are more affectionate and playful with attractive than with unattractive infants. But our generalized judgments solely on the basis of physical attractiveness are often overly positive and hence wrong (A. Feingold, 1992).

Another important consideration in regard to physical attractiveness is the cultural context of the beholders of beauty. Cross-cultural studies of beauty have clearly documented that different cultures can have different views of what constitutes a standard of beauty. We have known for decades that different societies have different views of physical attractiveness. An early review of more than 200 widely divergent cultures (C. S. Ford & Beach, 1951) found that societies differ not only in what they consider beautiful, but also in the parts of the body (e.g., eye shape, pelvis size, overall height and weight) they emphasize in evaluating beauty. More recent reviews (e.g., Berscheid & Walster, 1974) support this diversity of cultural views of attractiveness.

Similarity

As you might have guessed, based on the long-term benefits of having compatible values and compatible ideas about roles, evidence on interpersonal attraction suggests that the more similar individuals are, the more likely they are to be attracted to each other (E. W. Burgess & Wallin, 1953; T. L. Huston &

Levinger, 1978). Among the factors for which similarity has been shown to have a positive effect on attraction are attitudes and temperament (Byrne, 1971; Hatfield & Rapson, 1992), social and communication skills (Burleson & Denton, 1992), and even sense of humor (Murstein & Brust, 1985). In other words, the more similar people are with respect to many variables, the more likely they are to be attracted to one another. People are aware of this fact, so look for others similar to themselves (Stiles, Walz, Schroeder, Williams, & Ickes, 1996) and also expect people who are similar physically and in other ways to have more successful relationships (Garcia & Khersonsky, 1997).

Theories of Liking and Interpersonal Attraction

In general, we are more likely to be attracted to people whose presence we find to be rewarding (Clore & Byrne, 1974; Lott & Lott, 1968). The rewards we receive may be tangible, such as physical contact or gifts, or they may be intangible, as when we feel delight in another's presence. But is there more to attraction than just being rewarded?

The **equity theory** (Walster, Walster, & Berscheid, 1978) of attraction suggests that people feel more strongly attracted to those with whom they have a more equitable (fair) relationship of giving and taking. Equity theory has important implications for relationships. The first and simplest is that, over the long term, it is important that both people in a relationship

One way of viewing attraction is in terms of equity. People will be more attracted to those with whom they have an equitable relationship—that is, each partner has something of equal value to offer in the relationship. Like the Peruvians bartering in this marketplace, each partner can give something to the relationship that is equal in value to what each receives from the relationship.

feel that their benefits and costs are approximately equal. A relationship starts to deteriorate when either person feels that the relationship is one-sided in terms of sacrifices or benefits. Second, when one partner feels wronged by the other, the partners must find a way in which to restore equity as quickly as possible. If this restoration is not achieved, and one partner continually reminds the other of the inequity, the relationship may be jeopardized. If a partner feels that no matter what he or she does, equity cannot be restored, that person may lower his or her opinion of the partner and decide to give up on the relationship. A related finding is that people induced accidentally to hurt someone who are unable to remedy the hurt they have caused end up lowering their opinion not of themselves, but of their victim (Davis & Jones, 1960).

According to **balance theory** (F. Heider, 1958), people attempt to maintain a sense of give and take (*reciprocity*) in a relationship, and people tend to be drawn to friends whose attitudes toward other people are similar to their own attitudes toward those other people (*similarity*). We try to maintain consistency regarding our likes and dislikes as a means of attaining cognitive consistency. Previously, we saw that we tend to be attracted to people who are similar to ourselves. One kind of similarity is with respect to likes and dislikes. We expect our friends to like the people and things we like and to dislike those people we dislike. Similarly, we expect our friends to share our other positive and negative attitudes. When we feel positively toward something that our friends dislike (or vice versa), we feel an uncomfortable imbalance in the relationship. This imbalance tends to weaken the stability of the relationship, so we try to correct it. Maybe we change our attitude, or try to change our friends' attitude, or decide that the issue really is not an important one after all.

Consider an example of balance theory at work. Suppose you were to discover that your romantic partner, with whom you are deeply in love, is a member of the American Nazi Party. Probably you would feel very uncomfortable, and even distressed, upon hearing the news. Your positive attitude toward your partner is now out of balance with your negative attitude toward the American Nazi Party. In order to maintain cognitive consistency, you very likely would find yourself (a) trying to change your partner's attitude toward this organization, (b) changing your own attitude toward this organization, or (c) changing your attitude toward your partner.

Love

Most of us distinguish between liking and loving, but we also admit that it is difficult to define precisely all the differences between liking and loving—not to mention the difficulty in trying to define precisely the two terms themselves. Here, we assume that *love* is a deeper, stronger feeling than is liking; both are rooted in attraction, but love perhaps stems from more powerful—perhaps even instinctual—emotional and physical attractions than does liking. People further distinguish between "loving" someone and being "in love" with someone (Meyers & Berscheid, 1997). Consider some of the psychological theories that have been proposed to elucidate love—what kinds of love have been found to exist, where love comes from, and why love exists at all.

Love and Survival

One way to understand love is in evolutionary terms. According to evolutionary theory, adult love is an outgrowth of three main instincts that have proved to be evolutionarily useful by aiding in the survival of our species: (1) the need of the infant to be protected either by its parents or by parent substitutes; (2) the desire for an adult to protect and to be protected by a lover; and (3) the sexual drive (Wilson, 1981; see also Buss, 1988a, 1988b, 1994; Buss & Kenrick, 1998; Buss & Schmitt, 1993; Wright, 1994).

The ultimate function of romantic love, in the evolutionary view, is to propagate the species. Unfortunately, however, romantic love generally does not last long—sometimes just long enough to commit the procreative act. Were romantic love the only force keeping couples together, children might not be raised in a way that would enable them to form attachments and to develop their potential. Fortunately, companionate love—just plain, strong liking—often helps a couple stay together and bring up the children, even after romantic love has waned.

The evolutionary point of view suggests that females and males will value somewhat different things in love relationships (Buss & Schmitt, 1993; Kenrick & Keefe, 1992; Kenrick, Groth, Trost, & Sadalla, 1993). In particular, females, from this point of view, have more investment in their offspring because they (a) must carry the offspring during pregnancy, (b) know that the offspring they bear is their own, and (c) across species, tend to be more involved in bringing up the offspring. Because of their greater investment, they are particularly interested in males who have considerable resources to bring to the relationship. Males, on the other hand, (a) can impregnate many females in a short period of time, (b) cannot be certain the offspring is theirs, and (c) tend to be less involved, on average, in the offspring's upbringing. Evolutionarily, their best strategy is to find a female who will bear the healthiest possible offspring. As a result, males tend to be attracted to females who have signs of good health, such as youth and beauty. Across cultures, these predictors seem to hold up.

In considering these findings, there are two important things to keep in mind. First, the lower social status of women in almost all cultures may be responsible for observed differences between the sexes in mate preferences. For example, greater emphasis on finding a mate with resources may be simply a consequence of the female's not having much or even any access to those resources. Second, although men and women may not look for exactly the same things in relationships, the similarities outweigh the differences. Most people of both sexes prefer to be with someone who is physically attractive, supportive, nurturing, healthy, and so forth.

The evolutionary point of view also shows the importance of parental love. Children need their parents so that they can become independent, self-sustaining individuals. Thus, from an evolutionary point of view, parental love helps keep the parent attentive to the child long enough for the child to become self-sufficient and to survive. In this way, evolutionary theory is similar to attachment theory, described next.

Attachment Theory

Another view of love sees love as a reflection of the attachment patterns that individuals first form during infancy as they bond with their caregivers. The attachment theory of love (Hazan & Shaver, 1987, 1994; Mickelson, Kessler, & Shaver, 1997; Shaver, Collins, & Clark, 1996) uses the attachment concept of John Bowlby (1969) but extends it by showing that styles of adult romantic love correspond to

There seems to be quite a bit of support for evolutionary theory when we look at the universality of parental love, as shown by a contemporary photograph of an Ifugao father and child in the Philippines (left) and by Marie-Elisabeth-Louise Vigée-Lebrun's painting, Self-Portrait With Her Daughter.

styles of attachment among infants for their mothers (Ainsworth, 1973; see chapter 11). The Hazan–Shaver theory distinguishes among three basic types of lovers. (1) *Secure lovers* find it relatively easy to get close to others. They are comfortable depending on others and having others depend on them. They do not worry about being abandoned or about someone getting too close to them. (2) *Avoidant lovers* are uncomfortable being close to others. They find it difficult to trust others and to allow themselves to depend on others. They get nervous when anyone gets too close, and they often find that their partners in love want to become more intimate than they find comfortable. (3) *Anxious–ambivalent lovers* (analogous to infants with a resistant attachment style) find that their potential or actual partners in love are reluctant to get as close as the anxious–ambivalent lovers would like. Anxious–ambivalent lovers often worry that their partners do not really love them or want to stay with them. They want to merge completely with another person—a desire that sometimes scares potential or actual partners away.

An interesting implication of attachment theory is that people with different styles may respond differently to feelings of anxiety or stress. And indeed, Simpson, Rholes, and Nelligan (1992) found that when women become anxious, secure women sought and received more comfort and support from their partners, whereas avoidant women sought and received less comfort and support.

Types of Love

Another theory also proposes that there are multiple types of love. John Alan Lee (1977, 1988) proposed six kinds of love, each named with a Greek or Latin word, the meaning of which characterizes it. The three primary types of love are *eros*, love characterized by passion and desire; *ludus*, based on play; and *storge*, a love based in affection and friendship. Three secondary types formed by combining various aspects of the primary types are *agape*, love shown through altruistic, selfless adoration, a combination of eros and storge; *pragma*, love with a basis in practicality, a combination of ludus and storge; and *mania*, love characterized by madness and possessiveness, a combination of ludus and eros. According to Lee, the kinds of love are like colors, and different "shades" of love can be formed from their combinations. (See Figure 13-4 for definitions of the terms and descriptions of some of Lee's types of love.) Support for the existence of these six kinds of love has been found in a series of investigations using questionnaires (Hendrick & Hendrick, 1986, 1992, 1997). In particular, people seem to characterize many of their relationships in terms of these distinctive types of love.

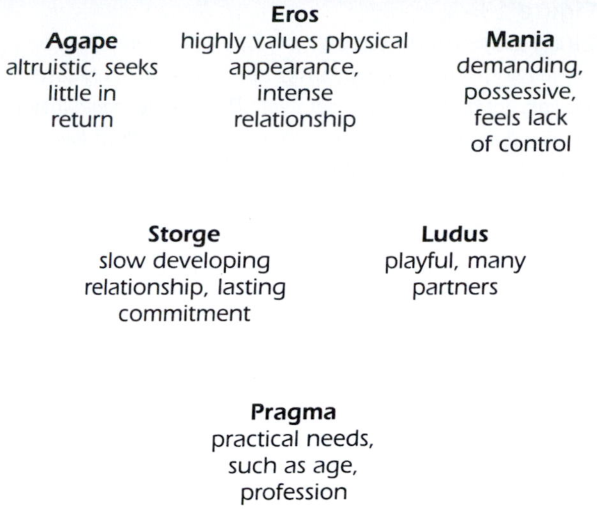

Eros
highly values physical appearance, intense relationship

Agape
altruistic, seeks little in return

Mania
demanding, possessive, feels lack of control

Storge
slow developing relationship, lasting commitment

Ludus
playful, many partners

Pragma
practical needs, such as age, profession

Figure 13–4
LEE'S SIX TYPES OF LOVE. *When John Alan Lee was formulating his three primary types of love, he looked back across the centuries of great literature for inspiration. (After Lee, 1977, 1988)*

My study of love began with the most successful teachers of romantic ideology for half a millennium—the great novelists. Then I turned to nonfictional observers of love, from Plato and Ovid to Andreas Cappellanus and Castiglione to the most recent psychologists. . . . It soon became obvious that no single set of statements would describe love. (John Alan Lee, "Love-Styles")

Triangular Theory of Love

An alternative view of love is my own **triangular theory of love** (Sternberg, 1986b, 1998a), according to which love has three basic components: (1) **intimacy,** feelings that promote closeness and connection; (2) **passion,** the intense desire for union with another person (Hatfield & Walster, 1981); and (3) **commitment,** the decision to maintain a relationship over the long term. Different combinations of these three components yield different kinds of love, as shown in Figure 13-5. For example, the combination of intimacy and passion yields romantic love, the kind immortalized by Shakespeare in *Romeo and Juliet.* The combination of intimacy and commitment yields companionate love, which is an enduring friendship (see also Berscheid & Walster, 1974, for a comparable distinction). The combination of passion plus commitment without intimacy yields foolish (or fatuous) love, the kind that is so common in Hollywood movies where people meet, fall in love in moments, and then commit themselves to each other without even really getting to know each other. The triangular theory appears to come closer than many others in capturing

Figure 13–5
THE TRIANGULAR THEORY OF LOVE. *Robert Sternberg's triangular theory of love proposes three components of love: passion, intimacy, and commitment. These components may be combined in various ways to produce various kinds of love. (After R. J. Sternberg, 1986b)*

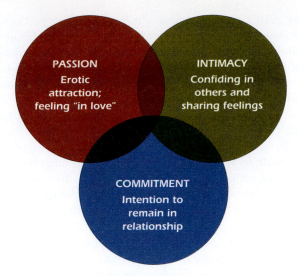

PASSION	INTIMACY	DECISION AND COMMITMENT		TYPE OF LOVE THAT RESULTS
–	–	–	=	Nonlove
+	–	–	=	Infatuated Love
–	+	–	=	Liking (Friendship)
–	–	+	=	Empty Love
+	+	–	=	Romantic Love
–	+	+	=	Companionate Love
+	–	+	=	Fatuous Love
+	+	+	=	Consummate (Complete) Love

Note: The kinds of love are typical representations; most relationships do not fit neatly and concisely within only one type. (+ = component present; – = component absent.)

people's intuitive conceptions of love (Aron & Westbay, 1996; Barnes & Sternberg, 1997). The theory also emphasizes, through the intimacy component, the importance of communication to success in close relationships.

Meaningful communication is probably essential for success in love relationships. For example, couples in happy marriages truly listen to each other and validate each other's points of view, whereas couples in unhappy marriages are less likely to listen and to cross-validate (Gottman, 1979, 1994; Gottman & Levenson, 1992). Instead, unhappy couples often *cross-complain*—each moans and whines without paying attention to what the other is saying. One complains that the other is never home, while the other complains that the one spends too much money. They talk past rather than to each other.

Other factors also contribute to unsuccessful communication in couples (Gottman, 1994; Gottman, Notarius, Gonso, & Markman, 1976). If at least one of the partners (a) feels hurt and ignored, (b) feels that the other does not see his or her point of view, (c) neglects to stay on one problem long enough to resolve the problem, (d) frequently interrupts one another, and (e) drags many irrelevant issues into the discussion, the likelihood of communication difficulties increases.

To summarize, people seek out others for many kinds of relationships: work relationships, friendships, intimate relationships, and other kinds of relationships as well. Sometimes, these relationships go beyond two people to relationships occurring in groups. Groups are considered in the next chapter.

THINK ABOUT IT

1. Many advertisers spend a lot of money to get celebrity endorsements of their products. Do you think that the advertisers' money is well-spent? Why or why not?

2. Some investigators, such as Deborah Tannen, believe that men place more emphasis on social hierarchies than women do. Do you agree? Why or why not?

3. Describe a particular conflict you have observed, first from the perspective of one participant and then from the perspective of the other. Which heuristics and biases affected the views of each participant?

4. How would you create an advertisement for a product using the principles discussed in this chapter?

5. How could you use one or more principles of persuasion, as described in this chapter, to help elect a candidate for a student-government position?

6. Give an example of a self-handicapping behavior (e.g., drug abuse). Why and how does this example show self-handicapping?

online *You can provide your own answers to these questions online at the* **Sternberg,** In Search of the Human Mind *Web site:* http://www.harcourtcollege.com/psych/ishm

SUMMARY

The Nature of Social Psychology   423

1. Social psychologists seek to understand and explain how the presence of others (actual, imagined, or implied) affects the thoughts, feelings, and behavior of the individual.

2. *Social cognition* refers to the ways in which we perceive and interpret information from others and ourselves.

The Nature and Functions of Attitudes   424

3. *Attitudes* are learned (not inborn), stable, relatively lasting evaluations of people, ideas, and things; attitudes affect our behavior.

4. Attitudes serve four functions: to get what we want and avoid what we do not want, to avoid internal conflicts and anxieties, to understand and integrate information, and to show our deeply held values.

5. Learning theories regarding attitude formation include classical conditioning, operant conditioning, and observational learning.

6. In attempting to change other people's attitudes, the following characteristics are important: characteristics of the recipient of the message (e.g., motivation and expertise), characteristics of the message itself (balance and familiarity due to repetition), and characteristics of the source of the message (the source's credibility and likability).

7. The links between attitudes and behavior are not always predictable and are influenced by characteristics of the attitude, of the attitude bearer, of the situation, and of the behavior.

Attributions: Explaining and Interpreting Behavior   433

8. One of the better known experiments in social psychology established the theory of *cognitive dissonance*, which states that when a person's behavior and cognitions do not mesh, discomfort results. To ease this discomfort, the person must justify his or her behavior. The results of a seminal experiment that studied cognitive dissonance have also been explained in other ways—by *self-perception theory*, for example.

9. *Attribution* theory deals with how we go about explaining the causes of behavior—why we do what we do, and why others act as they do. In making attributions, we look for the locus (source) of the behavior, which can be personal or situational.

10. Biases and heuristics help us to make attributions but also sometimes to distort them. We give more weight to socially undesirable behavior over its opposite. We are biased by the *fundamental attribution error*, which makes us overemphasize internal over external causes when viewing the behavior of others; and by the *actor–observer effect*, which expands this view to encompass also our own behavior, which we explain by overemphasizing situational factors. We also use (and are used by!) self-serving biases and *self-handicapping*.

Impression Formation   435

11. Biases and heuristics are also active in *impression formation*. Due to the primacy effect, we give more weight to things we learn earlier; due to

confirmation bias, we interpret new information so that it verifies beliefs we already have; due to *self-fulfilling prophecy*, we can make our expectations come true; due to *person-positivity bias*, we evaluate individuals more positively than we do groups.

12. We often judge ourselves through *social comparisons* to others.

Attraction, Liking, and Loving 438

13. Studies show that physical attraction enhances overall attraction and liking. Other important factors underlying attraction include degree of arousal, familiarity, *proximity*, and similarity.

14. Social-psychological research asks why we are attracted to some people and not to others. According to *equity theory*, attraction is a balancing act between give and take. *Cognitive-consistency* theories focus on balance.

15. Evolutionary theory deals with the genetic basis of mating behavior, as well as practical, survival-of-the-species reasons for love.

16. Attachment theory describes three styles of lovers: secure, avoidant, and anxious–ambivalent.

17. According to Lee, the six types of love are *eros*, *ludus*, *storge*, *mania*, *agape*, and *pragma*.

18. The *triangular theory of love* posits that three components—*intimacy*, *passion*, and *commitment*—are involved in love.

KEY TERMS

actor–observer effect 434
attitude 424
attribution 433
balance theory 441
central traits 436
cognitive consistency 430
cognitive dissonance 430
commitment 443
equity theory 441

fundamental attribution error
433
impression formation 435
intimacy 443
likability effect 428
mere exposure effect 427
passion 443
personal attribution 433
person-positivity bias 437

self-fulfilling prophecy 437
self-perception theory 431
situational attribution 433
social cognition 424
social-comparison theory 438
social psychology 423
triangular theory of love 443

■ THINK ABOUT IT SAMPLE RESPONSES

1. Many advertisers spend a lot of money to get celebrity endorsements of their products. Do you think that the advertisers' money is well-spent? Why or why not?

From the standpoint of selling products, celebrity endorsements often are successful. People come to associate the products with the celebrities and may use the products in order to be more like the celebrities. People also may assign greater credibility to celebrities than to other people, even though the celebrities may have no expertise in the area for which they endorse products and almost always are paid to endorse the products. At the same time, it is perhaps unfortunate that advertisers take advantage of people's gullibility through celebrity endorsements.

2. Some investigators, such as Deborah Tannen, believe that men place more emphasis on social hierarchies than women do. Do you agree? Why or why not?

Tannen may be correct, although her evidence lacks the kinds of controls for extraneous variables or even scientific evidence that most social psychologists would expect. At this time, Tannen's idea remains more an hypothesis than a well-demonstrated phenomenon.

3. Describe a particular conflict you have observed, first from the perspective of one participant and then from the perspective of the other. Which heuristics and biases affected the views of each participant?

George W. Bush and John McCain slugged it out for the Republican presidential nomination for the 2000 election. Bush and his camp seemed to view themselves as representing the true Republican mainstream and the traditional values of Republicans. They therefore believed that Bush should be nominated. McCain and his camp seemed to view themselves as representing a reform movement that would dispense with patronage politics as usual. They believed that their reforms were necessary to straighten out the government. Each side believed that what they had to offer was what the country needed. Republicans chose Bush.

4. How would you create an advertisement for a product using the principles discussed in this chapter?

There are many principles you might use to create your advertisement. One is the foot-in-the-door technique. You might advertise a magazine with a low introductory rate for subscriptions. Often these introductory rates are way below the rates for resubscriptions. The reason is that the hardest thing is to get people interested in the first place. Once people have initiated a subscription, they may continue it because they like the magazine or simply because of inertia.

5. How could you use one or more principles of persuasion, as described in this chapter, to help elect a candidate for a student-government position?

In such an election, you might decide to use the central route to persuasion, figuring that the election is important to students and that they will be at least somewhat informed about their options. In this case, you would want to give strong, solid reasons to elect your candidate. You would also want to respond to and discount arguments against your candidate.

6. Give an example of a self-handicapping behavior (e.g., drug abuse). Why and how does this example show self-handicapping?

Sometimes students are convinced that they cannot do well in a course, no matter how hard they try. They therefore do not try very hard. They then can conclude that they did not do well because they did not try to do well. But their self-handicapping may be the main reason behind their failure to do well. If they had tried harder, they might indeed have succeeded.

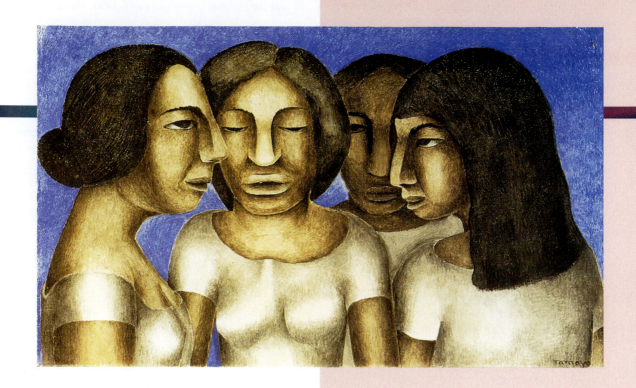

Once conform, once do what other people do because they do it, and a lethargy steals over all the finer nerves and faculty of the soul. She becomes all outer show and inward emptiness; dull, callous, and indifferent.

—Virginia Woolf, novelist (1882–1941)

14

SOCIAL PSYCHOLOGY:
INTERPERSONAL AND GROUP PERSPECTIVES

Our interactions with others reveal not only how we react to others, but also how they react to us. Sometimes the influence of others is obvious, as in the case of a performer who comes alive before an audience. Other times it is hidden. A full understanding of the topics in the last chapter requires an understanding of the topics in this chapter, namely, those relating to interpersonal and group perspectives. The reason is simple: Much of our social cognition occurs in interpersonal or group contexts.

Why do smart people, put together into a group, sometimes do stupid things? For that matter, how do groups of people reach a consensus about what they will do? What factors influence the route to consensus and the kind of consensus they achieve? What makes individuals within a group conform to a group decision, even if they do not believe in it? These are some of the questions that social psychologists consider.

Of course, as we have seen in earlier chapters, different cultures may respond differently to given situations. As you read about the studies in this chapter, be aware that most of them have been conducted in the United States, involving U.S. psychologists and research participants (Moghaddam, Taylor, & Wright, 1993; Öngel & Smith, 1994; Triandis, 1994). Many social psychologists question the generality of findings that are based on U.S. studies alone (M. H. Bond, 1988). However, although we must be wary of overgeneralizing findings from one culture to the next, most of the questions and the problems are still the same.

Groups

In Search of . . .   *How does the presence of other people affect our behavior and beliefs?*

What, exactly, is a group? As social psychologists define and study it, a **group** is a collection of individuals who *interact* with each other, usually either to accomplish work, to promote interpersonal relationships, or both. A group is sometimes distinguished from a *collective*, a set of people engaged in common activity but with minimal direct interaction. For example, if you go to a basketball game and sit in the audience, you would be part of a collective; the members of the basketball team, however, would be part of a group.

Groups typically have *roles*, or various kinds of responsibilities for their various members; a *communication structure*, which refers to who talks to whom; and a *power structure*, which determines who yields more and less influence in the group (Forsyth, 1990). They also have *norms*, or expected standards of behavior. When members depart from these norms, they may be punished by the group or by its individual members.

In some groups, such as a problem-solving group in a business, the emphasis is likely to be on accomplishing tasks. In other groups, such as a group of single parents seeking emotional support, the emphasis is likely to be on handling relationships among the group members. In still other groups, of course, there may be more of a balance between the two. As you might expect, leaders of groups also serve two key functions: to guide the group to achieve its task-oriented goals and to facilitate the group's functions of mutual support and group cohesion (Bales, 1958).

Because they view interaction as the defining feature of groups, social psychologists are interested in knowing what kinds of things happen when members of a group interact. The following sections will cover some of the effects psychologists have noted among groups of people. Note that the effects of groups are complex because these effects interact with the ways individuals in these groups respond to various kinds of group processes. Different individuals within a group may react to group processes in different ways, depending on their social cognitions and personality.

Social Facilitation and Social Inhibition

Having other people around can affect the quality of the work you do. This fact was recognized long ago by Norman Triplett (1898), who observed that bicyclists who competed against each other seemed to cycle faster than those who cycled alone against a clock. Similarly, children who were instructed to wind fishing reels as quickly as they could performed faster when

they were with others than when they were alone. **Social facilitation** is a phenomenon in which the presence of other people positively influences the performance of an individual. Those of you who have raced may have experienced the effect of social facilitation.

However, having other people around does not always improve performance. Anyone who has ever tried to give a speech, perform in a recital, or act a role in front of an audience and has been tripped up by nervousness can testify to this **social inhibition,** a phenomenon in which the presence of other people has a detrimental influence on an individual's performance. The question then becomes, when does the presence (or perceived presence) of other people facilitate performance and when does such presence interfere with it?

A widely accepted view of this phenomenon has been offered by Robert Zajonc. According to Zajonc (1965, 1980), the presence of other people is arousing. Arousal facilitates well-learned responses but inhibits newly or poorly learned responses (see Figure 14-1). Thus, to predict whether facilitation or inhibition will occur, we need to look at the individual's level of experience in the particular behavior. Suppose, for example, that Reuben is going to audition for membership

While one's performance may be facilitated by the presence of others, there are situations in which this is not always the case. Stage fright is one of the better known examples of social inhibition.

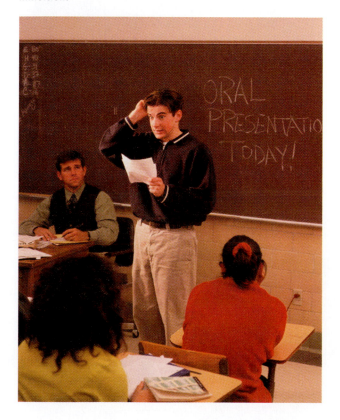

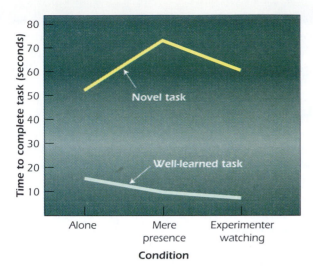

Figure 14–1

SOCIAL FACILITATION.   *According to Robert Zajonc's theory of social facilitation, the mere presence of other people causes arousal. Arousal then facilitates well-learned behavior but inhibits poorly or newly learned behavior. (After Schmitt, Gilovich, Goore, & Joseph, 1986)*

in an orchestra. He has prepared for the audition by learning a new, difficult piece. Under these circumstances, the conductor's presence is likely to inhibit Reuben's playing. Had he instead chosen a piece that he had known for a long time, the presence of the conductor probably would have facilitated his performance. Amazingly enough, social facilitation and inhibition apply not only to people but also to animals. Even cockroaches exhibit social facilitation in performing an easy, automatic task, but show inhibition in performing a difficult one (Zajonc, Heingartner, & Herman, 1969): Cockroaches running in pairs toward a goal run faster than cockroaches running alone.

What is behind these effects? **Distraction-conflict theory** holds that the effect of the presence of others is due not to the mere presence of others, or even to evaluation apprehension, but rather to the distracting effect of having other people around (R. S. Baron, 1986; R. S. Baron, Moore, & Sanders, 1978). In sum, general agreement exists that people can show either facilitation (usually of a familiar, well-learned behavior) or inhibition (usually of an unfamiliar, poorly learned behavior) through the presence of others. However, alternative explanations of exactly when and why facilitation and inhibition occur are still being considered.

Social Loafing

What happens to our performance when we cooperate with others? Have you ever worked on a task with a group and found that you (or some of your associates) did not work as hard as you (or they) would have act-

ing alone? For example, do you put in the same effort when you are a member of a chorus or a band as you do when you are singing or playing alone? As the number of people increases, the average amount of effort exerted by each individual decreases (Ringelmann, 1913). The phenomenon by which each individual member of a group puts forth less effort as the size of the group increases is termed **social loafing** (Latané, Williams, & Harkins, 1979).

Is it the actual presence of others or merely the perceived presence of others that causes social loafing? Part of the apparent social-loafing effect might be caused by other factors, such as a lack of coordination of effort. To rule out this possibility, researchers created both actual groups of individuals (varying from two to six persons) and pseudogroups of individuals (Latané, Williams, & Harkins, 1979). Participants in the *pseudogroups* were led to believe that they were participating with others, but each individual was actually alone. The participants were asked either to clap as loudly as they could or to cheer at the top of their voices.

The researchers found that people expended more effort when they were alone than when they were in either groups or pseudogroups. In addition, the investigators noted that lack of coordination of effort did contribute to a decrease in the output produced by actual groups, as opposed to pseudogroups. As the number of people in the groups or pseudogroups increased, the amount of individual effort expended decreased, as shown in Figure 14-2.

Figure 14–2

SOCIAL LOAFING.   *The social-loafing phenomenon appears to occur even when other contributing factors are separated out (Latané et al., 1979). When people believe that increasing numbers of other persons are participating in work, they exert less individual effort—even when no other persons are actually present. (After Latané et al., 1979)*

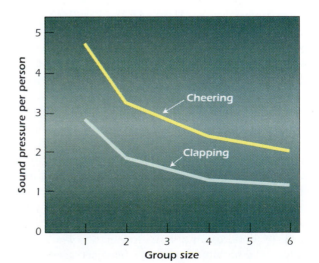

Can social loafing be discouraged or eliminated altogether? Probably the most effective method is to introduce evaluation apprehension. If members in a working group believe that their individual performance is being evaluated, social loafing can be reduced and social facilitation can be enhanced (Harkins, 1987; Harkins & Szymanski, 1987). For example, social loafing is unlikely to occur if an orchestra conductor can hear each member and makes the members aware of this fact, or if students involved in a group problem-solving task are told that their performance is being watched by teachers and that each student will be evaluated in terms of his or her contribution to the group. Social loafing is also reduced when the task is important, when the group expects to be punished as a whole if their performance is poor, or if the group is highly cohesive, so that membership is valuable to each person in the group (Karau & Williams, 1993, 1997; Sheppard, 1993).

Social loafing is affected by cultural orientation toward either *individualism* or *collectivism*. Although social loafing may commonly occur in highly individualistic societies, such as in the United States, it may be less common in societies with a more collectivistic orientation, such as China and Taiwan. For instance, studies involving Chinese participants have shown that individuals work *harder* when they are in a group than when they are alone (Early, 1989; Gabrenya, Latané, & Wang, 1983; Gabrenya, Wang, & Latané, 1985).

Group Polarization

Clearly, groups exert an influence on individual behavior, making members more or less likely to act in various ways. In certain circumstances, groups also exert an influence over members' attitudes. In some instances, groups choose riskier alternatives, but in others, they choose more conservative alternatives. The exaggeration of the initial views of members of a group through the dynamic processes of group interaction is known as **group polarization** (Moscovici & Zavalloni, 1969; D. G. Myers & Lamm, 1976). If the members of a group, on average, initially tend toward taking risks, the group will tend to exaggerate this risk-taking tendency. The group members will show what sometimes is called a *risky shift*, that is, the group shifts toward a more risky course of action. However, if the members of a group originally tend toward conservatism, the group will usually tend to make a more conservative response than that of the individual members. The decisions do not have to be major ones. Group polarization has been shown even when group members are only trying to decide what theme to use at their next party (Chandrashekaran, Walker, Ward, & Reingen, 1996).

Why does group polarization occur? Two factors appear to be responsible. First is the effect of *new infor-*

mation. People initially have a point of view that they believe. In the group, they hear new arguments supporting their point of view. They thus become even more extreme in their conviction (Burnstein & Vinokur, 1973, 1977). The more new arguments they hear, the more persuasive they believe the arguments to be and the more extreme they become in their attitudes.

The second effect is *movement toward the group norm.* As people meet other people who support their point of view, and as they receive social approval from them, they begin to move in the direction of the group norm. The group may gain more and more solidarity as their position becomes more extreme, but at the expense of rational decision making. It seems that not all people who provide information and reactions are equally effective in stimulating this process. A person will be most affected by the opinions and sentiments of those the person identifies as members of his or her respected "in group" (J. C. Turner, 1987). Thus, for example, Republicans are more likely to be influenced by Republicans than by Democrats in their group decision making, and vice versa. (Informational influence and normative influence are discussed again later, in regard to conformity.)

Resolving Conflicts in Groups

As the phenomenon of group polarization implies, groups of people are often in conflict with one another: risk takers versus risk avoiders, Democrats versus Republicans, and so on. In addition, as your own experience has probably shown, members of groups are often in conflict with one another. How do people resolve these intergroup and intragroup conflicts?

Some investigators (e.g., Kuhlman & Marshello, 1975; McClintock & Liebrand, 1988) have suggested that people have particular goals in resolving conflicts. People may have a *cooperative orientation*, seeking to maximize both their outcomes and those of others; an *individualistic orientation*, seeking to maximize only their own outcomes; a *competitive orientation*, seeking to maximize their own outcomes at the expense of others; or an *altruistic orientation*, seeking to maximize only the outcomes of others. These values appear to be relatively stable and valid predictors of people's behavior in situations involving decision making (see McClintock & Liebrand, 1988).

Groupthink

Ironically, one of the most troublesome group processes arises when there is *too little conflict* within the group. Irving Janis has given special attention to a particular kind of group process, **groupthink,** which takes place when group members focus on the goal of unanimity of opinion more than they focus on the achievement of other

Student Rating Systems and Professors' Course Objectives

A. G. Greenwald, *University of Washington*

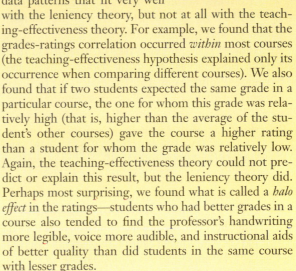

In 1989, I received extremely high student ratings for teaching a social psychology undergraduate seminar; in 1990, my ratings for teaching the same course in essentially the same fashion were extremely low. Because I had not become a different person in the interval, I assumed that things other than the quality of my teaching had influenced my ratings. But what were they? With the collaboration of a colleague at the University of Washington, educational psychologist Gerald Gillmore, I set out to analyze the rating process at that university.

Our research started by adding some questions to the ratings questionnaires used in a diverse group of about 100 courses whose instructors were willing to include the extra questions. They had to do with the amount of work a course required and the grades students' expected. We were impressed by two findings: (1) courses in which students expected high grades were also the courses that tended to get the highest ratings (this has been observed frequently and is known as the *grades-ratings correlation*); and (2) quite unexpectedly, we found that courses in which students expected high grades were also ones for which they reported doing relatively *little* work.

We needed to develop an interpretation that could account for both of these findings. We started by speculating that teachers vary in their course goals and strategies. Consider two relatively extreme types of professors: One, call him or her Dr. AllSucceed, wants to maximize the number of students who perform well, and the other, Dr. PainGain, wants to maximize the amount that students learn. Dr. AllSucceed may offer a course with an amount of material that does not overtax lower-performing students—making it possible for all to achieve a high level of mastery. Because Dr. PainGain is likely to include much more material in the course, to give more tests (to motivate students to learn more), and to have stricter grading policies, Dr. PainGain's students are likely to get lower grades than Dr. AllSucceed's less hard-working students.

We concluded that we could explain our two main findings with just two hypotheses: (1) that instructors' strategies vary between AllSucceed and Paingain, and (2) that students give high ratings because they like getting high grades (this is known as the *leniency* theory). The leniency theory is controversial. Its competitor is the *teacher-effectiveness* theory that good teachers get students to learn more. The question is: Do students who get high grades give their teachers higher ratings because they like the high grade (leniency) or because they have learned more (teacher effectiveness)? To determine the better explanation, we added our new questions to the rating forms used in *all* courses at the University of Washington, giving us a very large database. We then started to look for data patterns that might support the leniency theory in preference to the teaching-effectiveness theory, or vice versa.

Using statistical techniques known as regression analysis and structural equation modeling, we found several data patterns that fit very well with the leniency theory, but not at all with the teaching-effectiveness theory. For example, we found that the grades-ratings correlation occurred *within* most courses (the teaching-effectiveness hypothesis explained only its occurrence when comparing different courses). We also found that if two students expected the same grade in a particular course, the one for whom this grade was relatively high (that is, higher than the average of the student's other courses) gave the course a higher rating than a student for whom the grade was relatively low. Again, the teaching-effectiveness theory could not predict or explain this result, but the leniency theory did. Perhaps most surprising, we found what is called a *halo effect* in the ratings—students who had better grades in a course also tended to find the professor's handwriting more legible, voice more audible, and instructional aids of better quality than did students in the same course with lesser grades.

Despite having problems such as encouraging instructors to inflate grades or "dumb down" course content, or both, student ratings systems have three very attractive features. First, they are easy to administer. Second, they provide a simple numerical index. And third, they give students a voice in evaluating quality of instruction. With these three very desirable properties, it makes more sense to repair the student ratings system than to abandon it. This is what we have been doing at the the University of Washington. The modifications we have made include, most importantly, statistically adjusting ratings for the grade-ratings correlation (instructors who grade especially leniently now receive a downward adjustment) and including measures of course workloads in order to assess the extent to which courses challenge students.

We suspect that the ideal instructor, whom we can call Dr. AllGain, combines the positive qualities of Dr. AllSucceed and Dr. PainGain. In Dr. AllGain's courses, students work hard and learn a lot, not because they have to but because they want to.

References

Greenwald, A. G. (1997). Validity concerns and usefulness of student ratings. *American Psychologist, 52,* 1182–1186.

Greenwald, A. G., & Gillmore, G. M. (1997a). Grading leniency is a removable contaminant of student ratings. *American Psychologist, 52,* 1209–1217.

Greenwald, A. G., & Gillmore, G. M. (1997b). No pain, no gain? The importance of measuring course workload in student ratings of instruction. *Journal of Educational Psychology, 89,* 743–751.

Find out more about this topic at
www.harcourtcollege.com/psych/ishm

goals, such as realizing the purpose for which the group may have been designed in the first place (Janis, 1972). Janis analyzed a number of foreign-policy decisions he believed to reflect groupthink, including the Bay of Pigs fiasco, the failure to anticipate the invasion of Pearl Harbor, and the appeasement of Adolf Hitler by British Prime Minister Neville Chamberlain prior to World War II.

> The Kennedy administration's Bay of Pigs decision ranks among the worst fiascoes ever perpetrated by a responsible government. Planned by an overambitious, eager group of American intelligence officers who had little background or experience in military matters, the attempt to place a small brigade of Cuban exiles secretly on a beach-head in Cuba with the ultimate aim of overthrowing the government of Fidel Castro proved to be a "perfect failure." The group that made the decision to approve the invasion plan included some of the most intelligent men ever to participate in the councils of government. Yet all the major assumptions supporting the plan were so completely wrong that the venture began to founder at the outset and failed in its earliest stages. (I. L. Janis, *Victims of Groupthink*)

What conditions lead to groupthink? Janis cited three kinds: (1) an isolated, cohesive, and homogeneous group (such as a presidential advisory board) empowered to make decisions; (2) the absence of objective and impartial leadership, either within the group or outside of it; and (3) high levels of stress impinging on the group decision-making process. Not all researchers agree with the importance of these three factors (Mohamed & Wiebe, 1996; Street, 1997; Tetlock, 1998). Cohesiveness, for example, appears to have inconsistent effects, although its effects are typically negative if there is a threat that knowledge of a bad decision will leak out to the public (Turner, Pratkanis, Probasco, & Leve, 1992). Note that the groups responsible for making foreign-policy decisions are excellent candidates for groupthink. They are often like-minded and frequently isolate themselves from what is going on outside of their own group. They are generally trying to meet specific foreign-policy objectives and cannot always afford—or believe they cannot afford—to be impartial. Also, of course, they are under very high stress because the stakes involved in their decisions can be tremendous.

Six Symptoms of Groupthink

Janis further delineates six symptoms of groupthink: (1) *closed-mindedness*—the group is not open to a variety of alternative conceptualizations; (2) *rationalization*—the group goes to great lengths to justify both the process and the product of its decision making, distorting reality where necessary in order to accomplish this justification; (3) the *squelching of dissent*—those who do not agree are ignored, criticized, or even ostracized; (4) the *formation of a "mindguard"* for the group—one person who appoints himself or herself the keeper of the group norm and who makes sure that people stay in line; (5) the *feeling of invulnerability*—the group believes that it must be right, given the intelligence of and the information available to its members; and (6) the *feeling of unanimity*—the group members believe that all those in the group are unanimous in sharing the opinions expressed by the group. The result of groupthink is defective decision making due to incomplete examination of alternatives, failure to examine adequately the risks involved in following the course of the decision recommended, and an incomplete search for information about alternatives (see Figure 14-3).

Consider how groupthink might arise in a decision by college students to damage a statue on the campus of a football rival. The group has decided that it must teach a lesson to the students and faculty in the rival university. It rationalizes that damage to a statue really is no big deal. Who cares about an old ugly statue anyway? When one member dissents, other members of the group quickly make him feel disloyal and cowardly. His dissent is squelched. The group's members feel invulnerable: They are going to damage the statue under the cover of darkness, and the statue is never guarded. They are sure they will not be caught. Finally, all the members agree on the course of action. This apparent feeling of unanimity convinces the group members that far from being out of line, they are doing what needs to be done.

Antidotes for Groupthink

Janis has prescribed several antidotes for groupthink. For example, the leader of a policy-making group should encourage criticism, be impartial rather than stating preferences at the outset, and make sure that members of the group seek input from people outside the group. The group should also break down into subgroups that meet separately to consider alternative solutions to the same problem. It is important that the leader of the group needs to take responsibility for preventing the occurrence of the factors that lead to spurious conformity to a group norm.

In 1997, members of the Heaven's Gate religious sect in California committed mass suicide in the hope of meeting up with extraterrestrials in a spaceship behind a comet. Although this mass suicide is a

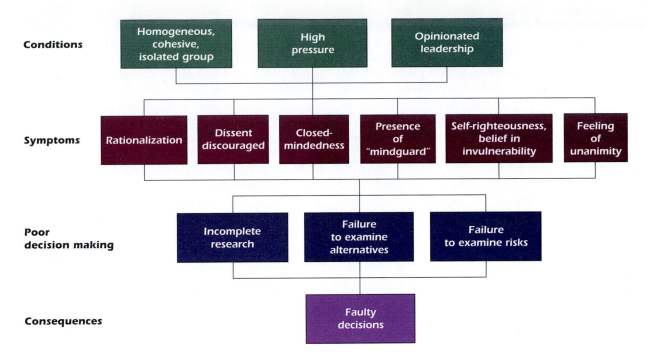

Figure 14–3
JANIS'S GROUPTHINK.   *This chart summarizes the antecedent conditions, symptoms, decision-making defects, and consequences of groupthink. (After Janis, 1972)*

striking example of conformity to a destructive group norm, numerous other astonishing examples have arisen throughout human history, such as the suicide of more than 900 members of the Jonestown, Guyana, religious cult in 1978. Worse was the murder in 2000 of hundreds of individuals in Uganda by leaders of a cult that the individuals had joined. Nazi soldiers during World War II and Serbian soldiers in the early 1990s also participated in mass killings; in these cases, the group norm was genocide rather than suicide.

Most group processes involve the pressure to conform. The next section covers in more detail the factors that lead to conformity.

Conformity, Compliance, and Obedience

In Search of . . .   *What are the factors that lead people to conform to, comply with, and obey the desires, requests, and demands of others?*

Conformity, compliance, and obedience all involve changes in one person's behavior caused by the social influence of another individual or group of persons. **Conformity** refers to the process in which an indi-

vidual shapes his or her behavior to make it consistent with the norms of a group. For example, when a gang member decides to wear green because other members of the gang wear green, the gang member is exhibiting conformity. **Compliance** refers to the process in which an individual goes along with a request made by one or more other persons. For example, if a student who skipped a lecture asks you for your notes and you give the notes to the student, you are complying with the student's request. **Obedience** refers to the process in which an individual follows the commands of an actual or perceived authority figure. For example, if a soldier fires on a group of enemy soldiers because he is instructed to do so, he is exhibiting obedience. We consider each of these three kinds of social influence in turn. For each form of social influence, the individual may experience changes both in behavior and in perceptions, beliefs, and attitudes.

Conformity

Some of the classic studies on conformity were done by Solomon Asch (1951, 1956), whose work on person perception was discussed in chapter 13. In Asch's studies, participants believed that they were participating in an experiment on perceptual judgment. Imagine that you are participating in one such experiment. You sit down in a group with six other people. You are all shown a white card containing a black line and another white card containing three other black lines of varying lengths. The task of each member of the group is simply to say which of the three black lines on the second card is of the same length as the black line on the first card. Only one of the black lines on the second card is even remotely close in length to the line on the first white card (see Figure 14-4).

Members of the group are asked to communicate their judgments in order, starting with participant number 1. As a participant, you expect the test to be a piece of cake. What could be easier? Unfortunately, however, participant number 1 gives what appears to be the wrong answer. You are surprised. Then, to your amazement, participant number 2 gives the same answer. So it goes until it is your turn, as participant number 6. What do you say? It is not easy to know

what to say, as shown by the harried and puzzled look on the face of participant number 6 from one of Asch's actual studies, seen in Figure 14-4. Of course, you do not yet realize that all of the other participants are confederates who have been instructed to lie.

Asch found that most people will go along with the majority, on average, in about one-third of the erroneous judgments. Not everyone conforms, of course. Roughly one-fourth of the participants remain true to their convictions and do not conform to any of the incorrect judgments.

Although Asch's participants frequently went along with the group, they generally did not believe the responses they announced. If participants were separated from the group and wrote down rather than orally announced the responses, conformity to the group norm dropped by about two-thirds. Also, when Asch interviewed his participants, their responses revealed that,

Figure 14-4

LINE LENGTH AND NORMATIVE INFLUENCE. *In Solomon Asch's study, participants were shown a standard line and then were asked to indicate which of the comparison lines matched the standard line. If a unanimous majority of your peers chose the first line (or third), would you agree with them? In Asch's experiment, about three-fourths of the participants agreed with a unanimous majority in more than one-third of their responses, even when the majority clearly made erroneous judgments (such as choosing either the first or third lines). Check the facial expression of participant number 6. Although he may decide to conform to the group norms in terms of his behavior—agreeing publicly that an incorrect match is correct—his own private beliefs clearly do not conform to the group norm. (After Asch, 1956)*

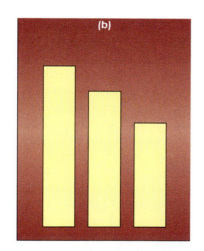

overwhelmingly, they did not believe the incorrect answers they had produced. Rather, the participants felt group pressure to conform.

Would a group member who deviated actually be ridiculed if he or she did not conform to the group norm? Asch (1952) reversed his initial procedure and placed one confederate among a group of genuine experimental participants. The confederate was instructed in advance to give wildly incorrect answers on certain trials. In fact, the others did laugh at and ridicule the confederate. People who deviate from the group norm are not only ridiculed but also are actively disliked and often rejected by the rest of the group (Schachter, 1951).

Group influences can extend to more consequential kinds of situations. Researchers asked college students to view a 1992 debate pitting three presidential candidates against one another: George Bush, Bill Clinton, and Ross Perot (Fein, Goethals, & Kassin, 1998). The task was to evaluate the performance of each of the candidates. The student participants were divided into three conditions. In one room, a group of confederates cheered for Bush. In a second room, they cheered for Clinton. In the third room, there were no confederates and there was no cheering. The investigators found that the cheering affected evaluations of debate performance by 45 points on a 100-point scale. In other words, without their realizing it, the student participants conformed to the evaluations of the cheering confederates.

What factors influence people's decisions to conform, regardless of the particular situation?

The Effects of Group Size and Cohesiveness

Several factors seem to affect the likelihood of conformity. The first is *group size*. Asch (1955) varied the number of confederates in his line-length study from as few as 1 person to as many as 15, and he found that conformity reached its greatest level with groups of roughly three to four members. Others have confirmed that, in most situations, beyond three or four members, conformity appears to level off (e.g., Latané, 1981; Tanford & Penrod, 1984). In some situations, however, much larger group sizes continue to increase the likelihood of conformity. Consider, for example, the behavior of people in elevators, of a crowd gathering on a sidewalk and looking upward, or of a rioting crowd.

A second factor that influences conformity is the *cohesiveness* of the group. A cohesive group is one in which the members feel very much a part of the group and are highly attracted to it. One of the best-known studies of group cohesiveness was conducted by Theodore Newcomb (1943) among women attending Bennington College, a small college in Vermont then well known for its liberal philosophy and social mores. Although women attending the college tended to be from families that were politically conservative (and well-to-do financially), the women's attitudes became increasingly liberal with each successive year at Bennington as they became more and more attached to their group of classmates and friends. Moreover, this liberalism remained even 20 years after graduation.

A third factor influencing conformity is simply the *perception* of what others are doing. Researchers found that most students tended to overestimate the extent to which their fellow students were comfortable with the amount of drinking that took place on a college campus (Prentice & Miller, 1996). Those students most likely to make such overestimates tended to conform in their own attitudes not to the actual perceptions of others, but to the perceived perceptions of these others.

Gender and Conformity

A third factor appears to be *gender*. However, gender-related conformity depends in part on the kind of topic being discussed and may actually illustrate the influence of other factors. For example, in one study (Sistrunk & McDavid, 1971), females tended to conform more to a majority view on topics that were stereotypically masculine, such as warfare, whereas males tended to conform more on topics that were stereotypically feminine, like family planning. On gender-neutral topics, no sex differences were observed. In 1971, the investigators concluded that gender seems to interact with the topic. The research showed that both men and women conform more when they are unfamiliar with the topic and thus more likely to believe that the group knows best. Today, we might observe that knowledge, rather than gender, seems to be the key factor.

Although many studies show that women and men are each likely to conform under different circumstances and in regard to different topics, Alice Eagly's *social-roles theory of gender* (Eagly, 1987) posits that women are generally more likely to conform than men under most circumstances. According to Eagly's view, women conform more because they perceive their gender as being of lower status, which in turn leads to feelings of reduced self-worth. Other research supports the notion that people of either gender may be more likely to conform if they feel inadequate or possess low self-esteem (Asch, 1956). For example, Birenbaum and Kraemer (1995) found greater effects of ethnic group than of sex on feelings of competence in mathematics and language examinations, and D. E. Smith and R. A. Muenchen (1995) found that age was a more powerful determinant of self-image than was sex in a group of Jamaican adolescents.

Social Status and Conformity

As suggested by Eagly's work, a fourth factor affecting conformity is *social status*. Researchers (Dittes & Kelley, 1956) addressed this question by having participants engage in group discussions and then rate each other on "desirability." Participants were next told how others had rated them, except that they received phony feedback. Participants then took part in an Asch-like experiment, in which the other members of the group were the other participants. Those who had been rated "average" in desirability were more likely to conform than those rated high, low, or very low. Those receiving the high, low, and very low ratings did not markedly differ from one another in conformity. The result makes sense: If you are high in status already, you may not need to conform because of your more exalted position. On the other hand, if you are low in status, you may feel that the situation is hopeless anyway, so why bother to conform?

The Influence of Culture

A fifth consideration is *culture*. Many researchers have tried to replicate in other cultures some of the studies on conformity and other social-psychological phenomena that have been well documented in the United States. For instance, the procedure used by Asch has been used in numerous cross-cultural studies, spanning more than 40 years. Although considerable variability has been found in these studies, a fairly clear picture has emerged: People in individualistic societies tend to conform less than do people in collectivistic societies (P. B. Smith & Bond, 1994). Actually, the extent to which people in different societies vary on many social–psychological variables can often be explained by the notions of individualism and collectivism that were described earlier and the ways that individualism and collectivism influence social behavior (Han & Shavitt, 1994; Kim, Triandis, & Kagitcibasi, 1994).

The Effects of Unanimity and Idiosyncrasy

A sixth variable affecting conformity is the *appearance of unanimity*. Conformity is much more likely when the group norm appears to be unanimous; even a single dissenter can seriously diminish conformity. Asch (1951) found that if even one of the six confederates disagreed with the group's answer in the line-length experiment, conformity was drastically reduced. Surprisingly, this effect occurred even if the dissenter offered an answer that was even further off the mark than the response of the group. Apparently, if you have a model of dissent, the model can help inoculate you against conforming to a norm established by other group members, even if the model does not agree with your point of view. Thus, another consideration in determining your degree of conformity is whether you believe your views to be in the majority, in the minority, or altogether unique within the group.

Majorities exert influence through the sheer number of people who share a given point of view. Although majorities are powerful from sheer numbers, minorities can be powerful from the style of their behavior (Moscovici, 1976, 1980). In other words, it is not just what they say, but how they say it, that determines their impact. Minorities can be powerful if they are forceful, persistent, and unflagging in support of their views. Simultaneously, they need to project an image of being flexible, as well as open-minded. In other words, they need to show that they are willing to listen to the majority.

Those in the minority who wish to lead and to change the way a group is functioning first need to accumulate *idiosyncrasy credits*, commonly known as "brownie points," among group members (Hollander, 1958, 1985). That is, they need to be willing to play the game of the group to a great enough extent so that members will come to accept them as part of the group and will then listen to them when they advocate changing the group norms. In this way, a potent minority may still influence the behavior—and perhaps the views—of the majority. Individuals operating outside of group settings may also be quite persuasive in causing others to behave as they want them to behave. Compliance with the requests made by individuals is the subject of the next section.

Compliance

Do you know somebody who always seems to get his or her way? Do you ever wonder how swindlers manage to bamboozle their "marks," the persons who are the objects of their compliance-seeking techniques? Have you ever bought something just because you were wheedled into it by a salesperson? All of these questions address the issue of *compliance*—going along with other people's requests. Some of the most common techniques for eliciting compliance are shown in Table 14-1. Sometimes, attempts to gain compliance elicit *reactance*—the unpleasant feeling of arousal we get when we believe that our freedom of choosing from a wide range of behavior is being threatened or restricted.

Each of the techniques in Table 14-1 involves having someone you consider a peer—more or less—ask you to comply with a request. Not all requests come from peers, however. At times, those who make

TABLE 14–1

Techniques for Eliciting Compliance   *How can you use these techniques to elicit compliance from another person? How can your knowledge of these techniques help you to resist complying with unwanted and unreasonable requests?*

TECHNIQUE	DESCRIPTION: YOU ARE MORE LIKELY TO GAIN COMPLIANCE IF YOU . . .
Justification	Justify your request. Even when the justification is weak, you will gain compliance more readily than if you simply make the request but do not justify it.
Reciprocity	Appear to be giving your target something, so that the target is thereby obliged to give you something in return.
Low-ball	Get the target to comply and to commit to a deal under misleadingly favorable circumstances. After obtaining the target's commitment, you add the hidden costs or reveal the hidden drawbacks.
Foot-in-the-door	Ask for compliance with a smaller request, which is designed to "soften up" the target for the big request.
Door-in-the-face	Make an outlandishly large request that is almost certain to be rejected, in the hope of getting the target to accede to a more reasonable but perhaps still quite large request.
That's-not-all	Offer something at a high price, and then, before the target has a chance to respond, you throw in something else to sweeten the deal.
Hard-to-get	Convince your target that whatever you are offering (or trying to get rid of) is very difficult to obtain.

requests of us are in a position of authority. Their authority may stem from actual or perceived greater relative power, expertise, or desirability, such as social competence or physical attractiveness. When we agree to the requests of persons who have authority over us, we are being obedient.

Obedience

Consider what you would do if you were a participant in the following experiment. An experimenter wearing a lab coat and carrying a clipboard meets you in the laboratory and tells you that you are about to participate in an experiment on the effects of punishment on learning (see chapter 6). You and another participant, Mr. Wallace (an accountant who seems average in appearance and demeanor), agree to draw lots to determine who will be the "teacher" in the experiment and who will be the "learner." You draw the "teacher" lot, so it will be your job to teach the learner a list of words that he must remember. Every time Mr. Wallace makes an error in learning, you will punish him by sending him an electric shock.

You watch the experimenter strap Mr. Wallace into a chair, roll up Mr. Wallace's sleeves, and swab electrode paste onto his arms "to avoid blisters and burns" from the shocks (Milgram, 1974, p. 19). The experimenter now mentions that the shocks may become extremely painful, but he assures Mr. Wallace that they will "cause no permanent tissue damage" (p. 19). You are then shown the machine you will use to deliver the shocks. The forbidding-looking device has a row of levers marked in increments of 15 volts from a mere 15 volts (labeled "slight shock") to a full 450 volts (labeled "XXX," beyond the setting for "danger: severe shock"; see Figure 14-5). Before beginning, the experimenter also administers to you what he describes as a mild shock, to give you an idea of what the shocks are like. The shock is rather painful.

The experiment begins. You read Mr. Wallace the words, and he must recall their paired associates (see chapter 7 for a description of paired associates). If he answers correctly you move on to the next word. If he answers incorrectly you tell him the correct answer and administer a shock. Each time Mr. Wallace makes

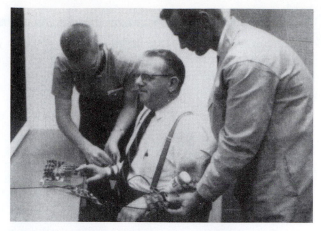
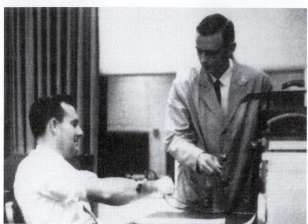

Figure 14-5
THE SHOCKING TREATMENT OF MR. WALLACE. *At the upper left is the voltmeter used by Stanley Milgram's participants for delivering shocks to Mr. Wallace. On the upper right is Mr. Wallace, pictured here as he was being strapped into the chair where he was expected to receive the shocks administered by Milgram's participants. Milgram's participants believed that Mr. Wallace was unable to escape the shocks that the participants were administering. The bottom two photos show a participant being instructed by the experimenter to continue administering shocks (bottom left) and refusing to continue (bottom right), an unfortunately rare occurrence. (After Milgram, 1974)*

a mistake you are told to increase the intensity of the shock by 15 volts. Mr. Wallace begins to make mistakes. As he makes more and more mistakes, his protestations become louder and more forceful. Eventually, there is only silence.

Would you continue administering shocks until the end—up to 450 volts? Perhaps at some point it would occur to you that something is very wrong with this experiment and that you simply do not want to continue. If you tell the experimenter your concerns, he responds, "Please continue." If you protest further, he tells you, "The experiment requires that you continue." If you continue to argue, he says, "It is absolutely essential that you continue." If you still protest, he replies, "You have no other choice, you *must* go on." What would you do? Before you read on, guess how you believe that most people would have responded to this interpersonal experiment.

Prior to conducting his experiments, psychologist Stanley Milgram had expected that very few people would completely obey the commands of the experimenter and that many might refuse to obey even the early requests of the experimenter. As he was formulating the design for the experiment, he consulted many other colleagues, all of whose expectations were similar to his (Milgram, 1974). Instead, a little more than an electrifying two-thirds of the people tested in this procedure continued up to the maximum level of 450 volts. Not one person stopped administering shocks before 300 volts, the point at which Mr. Wallace let out an agonizing scream, absolutely refused to answer any more questions, and demanded to get out, saying that the experimenter could not hold him. The results (see Figure 14-6) were even more of a shocker than the shocks administered by the machine.

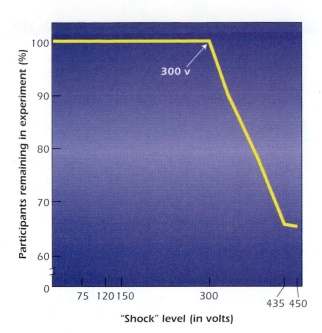

Figure 14–6
MILGRAM'S BASELINE RESULTS ON VOLTAGE LEVELS.
To Stanley Milgram's great surprise, not one participant stopped administering shocks prior to the reported level of 300 volts, and an alarming 65% of participants administered the maximum level of shock. (After Milgram, 1963)

The results so astounded Milgram that he asked members of three groups—middle-class adults with various occupations, college students, and psychiatrists—to predict what would happen. Their predictions confirmed Milgram's initial expectations that few would demonstrate much obedience in the experiment. On average, those who were surveyed estimated that the "teacher" would stop at 145 volts. Almost no one surveyed thought anyone would go up to 450 volts. The psychiatrists estimated that "only a pathological fringe, not exceeding [1% or 2% of the participants]" would go right up to the end (Milgram, 1974, p. 31). Everyone was wrong.

Of course the machine was a fake, and Mr. Wallace was a confederate of the experimenter who never received any shocks at all. Also, both lots said "teacher," so no matter which one you drew, you would have ended up being the teacher and Mr. Wallace the learner.

The experiment, as you probably have guessed, had nothing at all to do with an interest in the effect of punishment on learning. Rather, it was an experiment on obedience. The motivation for the experiment was Milgram's interest in why German soldiers during World War II had obeyed the outrageous genocidal commands of their leaders. Milgram

(1963, 1965, 1974) concluded that people in general are astonishingly capable of blind, mindless obedience. The results he obtained were even more depressing than was just indicated. For example, in Milgram's initial study, the participants were men. He thought that perhaps women would be less likely to go to the maximum in their administration of shock. However, when women participated in the same procedure, the same percentage (65%) of women as of men went to the maximum. The results that Milgram obtained have been repeated both across age groups and across cultures (Shanab & Yahya, 1977, 1978). The effect has also been replicated with the appearance of verbal rather than physical abuse (Meeus & Raaijmakers, 1995). Participants were asked verbally to abuse another person (actually, a confederate). Under the commands of an experimenter, 92% did so, no matter how abusive was what they were instructed to say.

Why are people so willing to obey the orders of people in authority, regardless of what the orders are (see Hofling, Brotzman, Dalrymple, Graves, & Pierce, 1966)? Milgram (1974) proposed several explanations, although whether any of them is adequate to describe the extremity of the findings is doubtful. One explanation is that experimenters use a procedure analogous to the successful foot-in-the-door technique; they start off asking for relatively little and later ask for much more. Along the way, people may become immune to the effects of what they are doing, or they may feel committed to complying with the demands of the situation. Moreover, people are socialized to respect authority, and this socialization seems to carry over into situations requiring obedience.

What seems to make the difference is the situation that demands and elicits obedience from a surprising array of people. Practically anybody placed in this situation acts in ways that no one would have thought possible. That is what is so stunning about the obedience research by Milgram and others.

Some people may believe that instances of blind obedience are a thing of the past. Far from it. Massacres in the 1990s in Rwanda, Burundi, Bosnia, and Kosovo all show that obedience by soldiers and civilians alike to irrational and inhuman commands to kill compatriots continues to plague the world.

It is unwise to discuss the Milgram experiment without raising the issue of experimental ethics. Although participants in the experiment were debriefed, it is not clear that any debriefing could fully counteract the effect of the realization of what the experiment was about and what their role was. There is no sure-fire way of ascertaining whether the costs to the participants justified the gains to scientific knowledge. Today, the experiment would be unlikely to pass

As the genocide in Kosovo shows, blind obedience, even to the point of killing one's fellow man, continues to this day. Here, a Kosovo Liberation Army gunman looks at a mass grave of ethnic Albanians allegedly executed by Serb troops.

an institutional review board. But experiments on behavior of another kind—prosocial behavior—typically pass review boards easily.

Prosocial Behavior

In Search of . . . *Under what circumstances do people help or not help their fellow human beings?*

Prosocial behavior involves societally approved actions that offer some benefit to society in general or to particular members of society, and that are approved of by most members of the society. In this section we deal with several aspects of prosocial behavior, particularly in terms of helping others.

Offering Help: Bystander Intervention

In 1964, Kitty Genovese, a young woman in New York City, left her night job at 3 o'clock in the morning. Before she reached home, she was repeatedly attacked for a half hour by a man who eventually killed her. Thirty-eight people living in her apartment complex in Queens heard her cries and screams. How many neighbors came to her aid? How many called the police? How many sought any assistance for her whatsoever? Not one. How could people hear someone be attacked over such a long period and do absolutely nothing? Bibb Latané and John Darley sought to answer this question in a series of studies on *bystander intervention* and helping behavior (Latané & Darley, 1968, 1970).

A common view of the Genovese case was that life in the big city had hardened people to the point where they stopped caring about others. Latané and Darley suspected, however, that what happened to Kitty Genovese in New York could have happened anywhere.

In one of the Latané and Darley experiments, a participant arrived and was taken to one of a set of small rooms. Over an intercom, the experimenter then explained that the participant and a small group of college students were to discuss some of their personal problems of college life. To protect confidentiality, the experimenter explained, conversations would take place via intercom, with each person in a separate room and without the experimenter listening. Each person was to speak separately in turn.

During the fairly routine opening of the experiment, one of the participants admitted that he sometimes had seizures triggered by the pressures of his work. When it was this person's turn to speak once again, it became clear that he was suffering a seizure. He started sounding as if he were in serious distress (Latané & Darley, 1970, p. 96).

As you may have guessed, the apparent seizure victim was not actually having a seizure. In fact, there were no participants other than the one who was placed in the room with the intercom. Although group sizes supposedly ranged from two (the participant and the seizure victim) to six (the participant, the seizure victim, and four other strangers), in fact only the one person was an actual participant, and the others were all previously recorded. The dependent variable was the percentage of participants who helped and the amount of time it took them to respond. The independent variable was the number of people that the research participants believed to be involved in the experiment. Almost 90% of the participants who thought they were the only person with whom the seizure victim was communicating left the experimental room to get help. But as the number of persons believed to be in communication with the seizure victim increased, the likelihood of a participant's seeking help decreased, going below 50% in the larger groups.

Clearly, Kitty Genovese's neighbors were not alone in being unresponsive. They illustrated what has come to be termed the **bystander effect,** the phenomenon in which the presence of increasing numbers of people available to help leads to decreasing likelihood that any given observer will help. The effect occurs in a variety of different situations. Each person involved typically experiences a **diffusion of responsibility,** an implied reduction of personal responsibility to take action due to the presence of other persons, particularly in considering how to respond to a crisis. Many other studies have revealed the same findings (see Latané, Nida, & Wilson, 1981).

In 1964, Kitty Genovese was stabbed repeatedly as 38 adults, mostly in the large apartment building nearby, watched, listened, and did nothing to help her—not even lifting a finger to call the police. After Genovese died, only one of her neighbors bothered to call the authorities to report the murder. Could this incident have happened just as easily in a suburban or a rural area as in a big city? Why or why not?

The bystander effect can be witnessed on almost any modern highway. Cars whiz by stranded motorists, some of whom may be desperately in need of help. Each driver passing by is likely to think that because there are so many people on the road, certainly help must be on its way. Often it is not.

Helping behavior seems to vary as a function of place. In one study, helping behavior was studied in different cities and regions of the United States (Levine, Martinez, Brase, & Sorenson, 1994). Cities with the most helping behavior tended to be in the South and cities with the least helping behavior tended to be in the Northeast of the country. However, the top city with helping behavior (Rochester, New York) is in the Northeast, as was the bottom city (Paterson, New Jersey). Density of population appears to be an important underlying factor.

What is really strange is that the bystander effect appears even when a person's own safety is at stake. One study (Latané & Darley, 1968) asked students to fill out a questionnaire on problems of urban life. Shortly after the students began answering the questions, smoke from a ventilator in the wall began to pour into the room where the participant was sitting.

The researchers were interested in how the number of people in the room affected the participants' decisions to report the smoke. When only one participant was in the room, half the people reported the smoke within 4 minutes, and three-quarters within 6 minutes. However, when there were three participants in the room, only 1 of 24 participants reported the smoke within the first 4 minutes, and only three did so within 6 minutes. People may fail to take action even when their own safety is in jeopardy!

Why are people so passive in the face of emergencies? According to Latané and Darley (1970), the reason is that what appears to be a simple matter—seeking help—is actually more complex than it appears. Suppose you are the bystander. To seek or provide help, you must actually take five steps, as shown in Figure 14-7. Thus, there are at least five opportunities for a bystander to do nothing.

The Effect of Others' Actions

What factors might affect whether people help in emergencies? The characteristics of the setting, the victim, and the bystander lead either to intervention

1. Notice the emergency

If yes → If no → Do nothing

2. Define it as an emergency

If yes → If no → Do nothing

3. Decide to take responsibility

If yes → If no → Do nothing

4. Decide on a way to help

If yes → If no → Do nothing

5. Implement the chosen way to help

If yes → If no → Do nothing

Help

Figure 14–7
LATANÉ AND DARLEY'S FIVE-STEP DECISION MODEL OF INTERVENTION. *According to Bibb Latané and John Darley, before you take any action to help another person, you must take the five steps shown in the figure. If you fail to complete any one of these steps, you will not take any action to provide helpful intervention. (After Latané & Darley, 1970)*

or to nonintervention. (See Table 14-2 for a summary of these factors.) One such factor is how people interpret a situation. Sometimes, nobody helps because individuals attribute other people's actions to different causes than they would attribute their own actions, despite the fact that their own actions are identical to those of the other people in the group (D. T. Miller & McFarland, 1987). For example, confronted with an emergency in which you see other people taking no action, you may assume that you are the only person confused about what to do and that the other people are doing nothing because they have somehow realized that what appears to be an emergency is not one at all. Of course, the other people are making exactly the same attribution that you are.

This misattribution applies to situations that are nonemergencies as well. Very often, students in a class are afraid to ask questions because they assume that they are the only ones who do not understand what the professor is saying, when in fact each person has exactly the same anxiety. As a result, all the students

end up confused but thinking that they are alone in their confusion.

The bystander effect applies even in unexpected populations. Students in a religious seminary were asked to give a talk, either on the parable of the Good Samaritan—a man who exhibited extraordinary helping behavior—or on jobs that seminary students enjoy (J. M. Darley & Batson, 1973). The participants were instructed to go to a university building nearby to give the talk.

On the way to the talk, each student passed an alley in which a man was sitting, moaning, slumped over, his eyes closed. Surely, if anyone would help the man, seminarians would, and especially those thinking about the Good Samaritan. However, only 40% of the students offered to help, and whether they were going to speak on the Good Samaritan or on jobs had no significant impact on whether they helped. Thus, even some of those who are giving serious thought to helping behavior, and who have, in fact, pledged to devote their lives to serving others, are often unlikely actually to help others in an ambiguous situation. Of course, the results might have been quite different for trained emergency personnel, such as rescue workers, who devote their lives to saving other people's lives.

The Effect of Time

Although the topic of the talk the seminarians were to give did not affect helping behavior, another manipulation in the experiment did. Students were told either that they were in a great hurry (they were already overdue), a medium hurry (everything was ready to go), or not really in a hurry at all (it would be a few minutes before things would even be ready). Although 63% of students who were not in a hurry helped, only 10% of those who were in a great hurry did. An intermediate percentage, 45%, helped in the medium-hurry condition.

Altruism

By now, you may be depressed or distressed at the results of the various studies on bystander intervention. Is **altruism**—a generous willingness to help another person or persons even when there is no reward or discernible benefit to the helper, which often includes some sacrifice on the part of the helper—nonexistent? Every day, parents sacrifice for children, firefighters rush into burning buildings, police risk their lives for the public, and volunteers give their time and efforts to increase the well-being of other people. Altruism has also been demonstrated in experimental circumstances.

Recent studies have focused on the motives people have for performing altruistic behavior. Are people motivated by empathy or by more egoistic concerns?

TABLE 14-2

Factors That May Influence Helping Behavior   *Several characteristics of the victim, of the situation, and of the bystander may increase or decrease the likelihood that the bystander will intervene to aid the victim.*

FACTOR	EFFECT ON LIKELIHOOD OF HELPING BEHAVIOR
Characteristics of the Victim	
Similarity to bystander (age, sex, etc.)	Increase
Relationship to bystander (if any)	Probably increase
Bleeding or bloody	Decrease
Recognizability as being a member of a stigmatized group	Decrease
Characteristics of the Situation	
Increases in the number of bystanders	Decrease
Increased time pressures on bystander	Decrease
Characteristics of the Bystander	
Similarity to victim (age, sex, etc.)	Increase
Relationship to victim (if any)	Probably increase
Negative responses to characteristics of the victim (e. g., prejudices, negative reactions to clothing, grooming, presence of blood)	Decrease
Empathy	Increase
Emotionality	Probably increase
Knowledge of how to help the victim (e. g., know CPR or have medical expertise)	Increase
Dedication to a life of serving others	No effect
Recently has given thought to helping behavior	No effect
Being in a good mood	Increase

Robert Cialdini and his associates (1987; Cialdini, Brown, Lewis, Luce, & Neuberg, 1997; Neuberg, et al., 1997) have attempted to explain altruistic behavior by arguing that empathy produces helping behavior because a person who responds empathetically to someone in distress feels saddened and is motivated to help in order to elevate his or her *own* mood. So, from this perspective, even empathy-based helping may be selfish. Daniel Batson and his colleagues (Batson, 1997; Batson, Batson, et al., 1989; Batson, Dyck, et al., 1988) disagree with this interpretation, having found that the rate of helping among high-empathy participants was no lower when they already anticipated mood enhancement than when they did not. That is,

empathetic people did not help any less in situations where they were already expecting to improve their mood soon anyway. They believe that helping behavior results from feelings of oneness with the person in need of help.

Does altruism ever make sense from an evolutionary point of view? After all, one would seem to be sacrificing one's own self-interest for the sake of others. According to George Williams (1966) and Robert Trivers (1971), it does. Williams pointed out that relationships between organisms, including humans, tend to be characterized by reciprocity. Indeed, as shown by the reciprocity technique for gaining compliance which was mentioned earlier, doing something for someone is one of the best ways to get the person to do something for you. For example, Anatol Rapaport (1960) showed that in mutual negotiations, those who reciprocate the kind behavior of others tend to fare best in the negotiation. Moreover, people who are perceived as selfish often find themselves with few friends and at risk of making enemies, which is clearly not to the individual's advantage in the struggle for survival. An implication of the evolutionary view, however, is that it is being perceived as altruistic, rather than actually being altruistic, that leads to positive outcomes for the individual (R. Wright, 1994). Nevertheless, many apparently altruistic acts, such as the hiding of Jews during the Nazi regime of terror in Germany (Oliner & Oliner, 1988), seem well characterized as genuinely altruistic. The behavior of the Nazis, on the other hand, seems well characterized as genuinely antisocial.

Antisocial Behavior

In Search of . . . *What makes behavior antisocial and what are the sources of it?*

Antisocial behavior is behavior that is harmful to a given society or to its members. Although people might disagree about which kinds of behaviors are antisocial or even are condemned by society as a whole, people generally agree that two classes of behavior are harmful to society: prejudice and aggression.

Prejudice

> For the first time I noticed that there were two lines of people at the ticket window, a "white" line and a "black" line. During my visit at Granny's a sense of the two races had been born in me with a sharp concreteness that would never die until I died. . . . I had begun to notice that my mother became irritated when I questioned her about whites and blacks, and I could not quite understand it. I wanted to understand these two sets of people who lived side by side and never touched, it seemed, except in violence. (Richard Wright, *Black Boy*)

Prejudice is a negative attitude toward groups of individuals based on limited or wrong information about those groups of individuals. Note that prejudice is an attitude toward a group, not toward an individual. Unfortunately, we tend to extend many of our attitudes toward groups to all of the individual members

of the groups as well. A negative attitude toward a group is not necessarily a prejudice. For example, if you have ample evidence that a particular group, such as a criminal gang, is responsible for numerous homicides, you would probably be entitled to have a negative attitude toward that group. An attitude involves prejudice when it is based on insufficient or incorrect information.

How can we form attitudes without enough correct information? Social categorization and stereotypes are two cognitive shortcuts that can sometimes lead us to form prejudices.

Social Categorization and Stereotypes

Social categorization is the normal human tendency to sort people into groups according to various characteristics the observer perceives to be common to the members of each group. Across cultures, we effortlessly categorize people according to their gender, occupation, age, ethnicity, and so on (see Neto, Williams, & Widner, 1991). These categories generally have particular defining characteristics (e.g., specific sexual characteristics or occupational requirements). In addition, we tend to formulate prototypes for various categories, based on what we perceive as being typical members of the categories (see chapter 8); when such prototypes are applied to people, we term them **stereotypes**, which can be thought of as perceived typical examples that illustrate the main characteristics of a particular social category, usually based on the assumption that the typical example represents *all* examples of the social category. Social categories and stereotypes help us to organize our perceptions of people and provide us with speedy access to a wealth of information (for example, regarding traits and expected behaviors) about new people whom we meet (Sherman, Judd, & Park, 1989; Srull & Wyer, 1989). Thus, stereotypes help us know what to expect from people we do not know well. The problem with categorizing people according to stereotypes is that we often overgeneralize the characteristics of the stereotype, assuming that all the typical characteristics apply to every member of a group, when they usually apply only to some or perhaps even most—but not all—members.

Ingroups and Outgroups

Actually, we are less likely to overgeneralize from stereotypes when considering our own *ingroups*—those categories of which we consider ourselves members—than when considering *outgroups*—those of which we do not see ourselves as members. This tendency to view the members of an outgroup as all being alike is **outgroup homogeneity bias.** When we fall prey to this bias, we take stereotypical characteristics or actions that apply only to a portion of a group and infer that they apply to all or almost all of the group members (Brehm & Kassin, 1990). Such bias is commonplace (Linville, 1998; Vonk & van Knippenberg, 1995). For example, it may very well be that many clerics are honest, many professors are well informed, many social workers are compassionate, and so on. However, these and other stereotypes do not necessarily apply to all members of these groups. Moreover, members of many other groups will show the same tendencies attributed to the members of the targeted group. We also exacerbate the negative effects of outgroup homogeneity bias by seeking information that bolsters our sense of being dissimilar from the outgroup and of being similar to the ingroup (Wilder & Allen, 1978).

Another source of prejudice is **illusory correlation,** an inferred perception of a relation between unrelated variables, usually arising because the instances in which the variables coincide seem more noticeable than the instances in which the variables do not coincide. For example, we are more likely to notice instances of unusual behavior in relation to a minority population than we are to notice the same unusual behaviors in members of a majority population (D. L. Hamilton & Gifford, 1976). If a member of a minority group commits a crime, we may associate members of the minority group with criminal behavior, whereas if a member of a majority group commits the same crime, we may see no such association. Indeed, newspapers sometimes even identify alleged criminals by membership in a minority group, while saying nothing about group membership if the alleged criminals are members of the majority group. Thus, we may form an illusory correlation between the unusual behavior (e.g., commission of crimes) and the minority population.

Context cues also can enhance the likelihood of using stereotypes. For example, when research participants evaluated women and men leaders, they showed greater gender stereotyping and prejudicial responses toward women leaders in particular contexts (see Eagly, Makhijani, & Klonsky, 1992): (a) those in which the leaders used leadership styles considered more stereotypically masculine (e.g., task oriented and directive, rather than interpersonally oriented and collaborative), or (b) contexts in which women were occupying roles that are male dominated in our society (e.g., athletic coaches, manufacturing supervisors, and business managers). Outgroup versus ingroup effects also influenced the results. In other words, members of another group were judged more harshly than members of one's own group. In particular, men were more likely to evaluate women negatively than were other women.

The Subtle Effects of Stereotypes

Often, stereotypes are activated in our thinking and affect our behavior without our even realizing it (Bargh, 1997; Greenwald & Banaji, 1995; Monteith, Devine, & Zuwerink, 1993). Stereotypes and the prejudices that sometimes accompany them can have stunning effects, as was shown in an experiment on subliminal exposure to faces of different colors (Chen & Bargh, 1997). White participants were shown pictures of either black male or white male faces. The exposure of the pictures was subliminal, so the participants were not even aware that they saw the faces. After being exposed to the faces, each participant played a game with another participant who had not been exposed to the faces. The interactions of the two participants were audiotaped, and judges rated the hostility shown by each game participant. The results showed that participants who had been subliminally exposed to the black faces showed more hostility in their interactions with their game partners than did the participants who had been exposed to the white faces, presumably because the black faces had triggered stereotypes about blacks among the white participants. The hostility of the participants who had been exposed to the black faces in turn triggered hostility in their game partners.

People are often motivated to categorize and stereotype others in order to maintain their perceptions of being in a powerful position (Jost & Banaji, 1994; Operario & Fiske, 1998; Pratto, Stallworth, Sidanius, & Siers, 1997). For example, people in positions of political power may suppress or even imprison rebellious elements and label their behavior as criminal, insane, or both because such labeling gives them an excuse both to maintain political power and to remove threats to this power.

Although social cognition plays a role in the formation of stereotypes, the fact that stereotypes are so remarkably resistant to change may be due to factors such as motivation and conformity rather than to cognitive variables (Rojahn & Pettigrew, 1992), as shown in the following study.

The Robber's Cave Study

What is often considered to be the classic experiment on prejudice was conducted in the summer of 1954 at the Robber's Cave State Park in Oklahoma (Sherif, Harvey, White, Hood, & Sherif, 1961/1988). At a camp were two groups of boys, all of them 11 years old, all of them white, all of them middle class, and all of them previously unknown to one another. For about a week, the boys engaged in typical camp activities, such as swimming, camping, and hiking. Each group of boys chose a name for itself, and the boys

---

Psychology in Everyday Life

Reducing Prejudice

Perhaps the first step in reducing prejudice is to *recognize* how resistant it is to change. For example, male police officers and police supervisors commonly have prejudicial attitudes against female members of the force (Balkin, 1988; Ott, 1989), despite clear research evidence documenting women's effectiveness as field patrol officers. One view of prejudice suggests that prejudicial treatment against females and minorities will decline when their numbers increase—that is, when they are in a larger minority. However, females already comprise 51% of the U.S. population, so clearly, sheer numbers alone are not enough to reduce prejudice. Although prejudicial treatment against minorities does diminish somewhat when numbers of the minorities increase, prejudicial treatment is not eliminated. In fact, minority status in itself—that is, the numeric proportion alone—does not determine whether prejudicial treatment occurs. For example, male nurses generally experience special positive—rather than negative—treatment among nurses (Ott, 1989). For negative prejudicial treatment to occur, the minority group must also be assigned a relatively lower status within the larger social context. So to reduce prejudice, steps need to be taken to raise the perceived status of the outgroup experiencing prejudice.

Another suggestion for reducing prejudice has been the **contact hypothesis,** the assumption that prejudice will be reduced simply as a result of direct contact between social groups that have prejudicial attitudes toward each other (or of one group toward the other), without any regard for the context in which such contact occurs (Allport, 1954). However, as shown by the conflicts that still exist in many desegregated school systems, as well as among Serbs, Muslims, and Croatians in the former Yugoslavia, contact in itself is not sufficient to alleviate prejudice (N. Miller & Brewer, 1984). Rather, the quality of contact, as in the cooperative tasks in the Robber's Cave study, is important to alleviating prejudice.

For exposure to reduce prejudice between groups, it needs to have the following qualities:

1. The two interacting groups must be of *equal status*.
2. The contact must involve *personal interactions* between members of the two groups.
3. The groups need to engage in *cooperative activities*.
4. The social norms must *favor reduction* of prejudice.

For example, suppose that members of one religious group in a university community realize that many of them are showing signs of prejudice against members of another religious group in the community. They decide to take affirmative steps to reduce the prejudice they have observed. The affirmative steps are more likely to be successful if the above conditions are met. In particular, members of the first religious group need to see members of the second religious group as having equal status. Positive interactions need to be established between members of the two groups, perhaps by developing cooperative activities, such as an interfaith organization to help the homeless. Finally, the group members must seriously want to reduce prejudice. This last idea suggests another tactic: If social norms that condemn prejudicial or intolerant behavior are established, this too can help reduce prejudicial attitudes.

Another consideration in reducing prejudice is to use *cognition* to reduce the use of stereotypes. Krystyna Rojahn and Thomas Pettigrew (1992) have suggested that we can change our own stereotypes by making any information that contradicts a stereotype more salient—for example, by minimizing irrelevant distracting information, by giving ourselves enough time to notice and process the relevant information that contradicts the stereotype, and by ensuring that we notice the relevance of the contradictory information to the stereotype. So by paying attention to how effective a female police officer is at gathering information and how useful her observations on the beat are, fellow officers' prejudice would be lessened.

Finally, one of the best ways of reducing or eliminating prejudice is to *experience* directly another culture, whether in a foreign country or in your own country. Learning the language of another culture, visiting that culture, and actually living as a person of that culture can help us better understand the extent to which humans are the same all over the world.

---

then printed their groups' names on their caps and T-shirts.

After about a week, the boys in each group made a discovery—the existence of the other group of boys. They also discovered that a series of athletic tournaments had been set up that would pit the two groups against each other. As the competitions took place, so did confrontations, which spread well beyond the games. After a while, the members of the two groups had become extremely antagonistic. At this point, cabins had been ransacked, food fights had broken out, and items had been stolen by members of each group.

According to social identity theory, prejudice often begins as a way of protecting one's self-esteem. To feel better about themselves, people come to believe an outgroup or groups have lower status. These youths from rival gangs were probably attracted to their gangs in part because of the social identity that membership in the gang offered.

Prejudice of the members of one group against the other group had been artificially created. Would it now be possible to reduce or eliminate this prejudice? The investigators created apparent emergencies that had to be resolved through cooperative efforts. In one emergency, the water supply for the camp was lost because of a leak in a pipe. The boys were assigned to intergroup teams to inspect the pipe and to find the leak. In another incident, a truck carrying boys to a campsite got trapped in the mud. Boys from the two teams needed to cooperate to get the truck out. By the end of the camping season, the two groups of boys were engaged in a variety of cooperative activities and were playing together peacefully. Thus, by forcing people to work together, the prejudices of the members of each group against the other largely had been eliminated.

Theories of Prejudice

How did the two groups of boys develop prejudices against one another so easily? Various theories have been proposed to account for why people have prejudices. **Realistic-conflict theory** (R. A. Levine &

Campbell, 1972) argues that competition among groups for valuable but scarce resources leads to prejudice. For example, immigrant groups are often met with hostility because they are perceived as taking jobs away from people who are already living in the country. Often, the jobs these immigrant groups take are those jobs that other people generally do not want, but even the perception of the loss of jobs can cause unwarranted prejudice. For example, some people in the United States resent various groups of illegal immigrants for taking jobs away from Americans. The fact is that the illegal immigrants typically are occupying jobs that most citizens are not filling and do not want, such as sharecropping in the fruit and vegetable fields of California. Thus, although there may be valid reasons for resenting these immigrants, taking jobs away from Americans probably is not one of them.

A second theory, **social-identity theory** (Tajfel, 1982; Tajfel & Turner, 1986), suggests that people are motivated to protect their self-esteem and that they have prejudices in order to increase their self-esteem through believing that outgroups have less status than ingroups. Part of our self-esteem derives from the social groups of which we are members. By forming prejudices against other groups in order to boost their own group's status, people increase the self-esteem they feel through membership in the group. In other words, they achieve self-esteem by denigrating others and thereby believing they look good in comparison.

A third theory (Devine, Evett, & Vasquez-Suson, 1995; Devine, Monteith, Zuwerink, & Elliot, 1991) is that people view prejudice within themselves in somewhat the way they view bad habits. They are aware that

Increasing the number of minorities in a particular job or profession, so that they are less of a minority, helps ease prejudice, but it doesn't eliminate it. One of the best ways of eliminating prejudice is to experience another culture first-hand.

they have the prejudice, and they know, consciously or not, that it affects their behavior. Where people differ, however, is in the extent to which they tolerate the behavior in themselves. Some people have high tolerance for their own prejudices, whereas others view their own prejudices as unjustifiable and not as valid bases for action. For example, some people may have a prejudice against overweight individuals, and they justify their prejudice by saying that overweight people deserve the negative reaction they get because these people lack self-discipline. Though no one theory completely explains the social phenomenon of prejudice, theories of prejudice, taken together, do suggest how prejudice might be reduced. These efforts are the topic of the Psychology in Everyday Life box in this chapter. As the box discusses, prejudices are fostered by ignorance. They can also lead to aggression.

Aggression

Aggression is behavior that is intended to cause harm or injury to another person. It should be distinguished from *assertion*, which is forceful behavior, such as arguing strongly for one's point of view, that causes neither injury nor harm. There are two main kinds of aggression: hostile and instrumental (R. A. Baron, 1977; Berkowitz, 1994; Feshbach, 1970; Geen, 1990). **Hostile aggression** is behavior that is intended to cause harm as a result of an emotional outburst, caused by pain or distress. The consequences usually lead to little gain for the aggressor and may even lead to losses for the aggressor. In fact, valuable relationships and objects may be harmed or put at risk of harm through hostile aggression, such as damaging a personal relationship, injuring ourselves or persons we love, or destroying property we cherish or must replace. People who frequently display hostile aggression are likely to perceive the world as a dangerous place and to respond to ambiguous stimuli in an aggressive way (Bushman, 1996).

In contrast, **instrumental aggression** is behavior that happens to cause harm or injury to another person, as a byproduct of trying to get something valued by the aggressor. It is often planned rather than impulsive. Assassins, bank robbers, and embezzlers are aggressive, but most of them probably feel no personal animosity toward the people they kill or injure. If they could get whatever they wanted without being aggressive, they might not bother to be aggressive. Similarly, the 2-year-old child who grabs another child's toy truck is showing instrumental aggression—nothing personal; she just wants the truck. The two kinds of aggression have somewhat different causes and therefore respond to somewhat different kinds of interventions. In a given situation, however, aggressive behavior may reflect both hostile and instrumental aspects, as when one fights for the land controlled by a hated

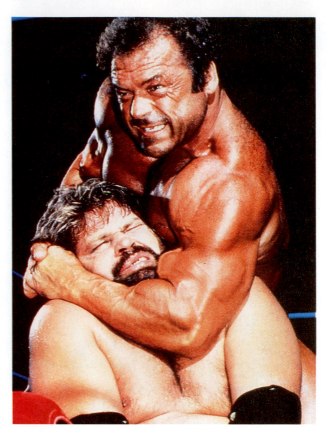

Given the importance of social learning as a contributing factor in violent behavior, we should pay attention to the kinds of role models we provide to one another.

enemy, or as when, in 1997, boxer Mike Tyson bit his opponent's ear in the misguided hope of gaining an advantage in their boxing match.

Some psychologists study aggression as a basic human motivation, as we have seen in this chapter. Others study aggression as a personality trait, looking at individual differences across people (see chapter 15). Here, we are largely interested in how social interactions, as well as other environmental events and characteristics, contribute to aggressive behavior. First, however, we briefly consider some biological factors in human aggression.

Biological Factors in Human Aggression

Although we may tend to view aggression as undesirable, it has evolved for a reason. Aggressive responses may be one means by which organisms, especially males, have warded off invasions of their territory by other males. They may also have used aggression as a means of protecting females and thereby of ensuring their own paternity for any future offspring of the female or females with whom they are residing. In contrast, a very nonaggressive male would risk losing both

"What's amazing to me is that this late in the game we <u>still</u> have to settle our differences with rocks."

his territory and his paternity, as well as his own life. The role of evolution is also suggested by the fact that stepchildren, who do not share genes with a stepparent, are much more likely to be abused and killed by their stepparents than are children who are biologically related to their parents (Daly & Wilson, 1991, 1996). The same pattern holds in species other than humans (Lore & Schultz, 1993).

Nature and nurture interact in determining the specific expression of aggression in humans (Renfrew, 1997). As in other species of animals, the neural circuitry underlying aggressive behavior is hereditary and seems to be common across humans. Research on twins suggests that a tendency toward aggression is partly heritable (Miles & Carey, 1997). In particular, both the hypothalamus and the amygdala play an important role in stimulating or inhibiting aggressive behavior (see Figure 3-11 on page 74). The amygdala is influential in our emotional responses and in our responses to odors, and this fact helps to explain the powerful interactions between odors and emotions, and between emotions and aggressive behavior. In fact, among nonhuman animals, odor plays a direct role in aggressive behavior; for example, although a male animal may attack an animal that smells like a fellow male, it will not attack an animal that smells like a female. Similarly, a mother rat may readily eat infant rats that smell strange to her, but she will not eat infant rats that she has marked with her own scent.

Aggression in other animals is subject to hormonal influence. For example, in both nonhuman male and female animals, the presence of androgens very early in development seems to influence the degree of aggressive behavior shown in adulthood. In adult animals, testosterone (a male sex hormone) seems to increase aggression in both males and females (Archer, 1991; Berman, Gladue, & Taylor, 1993; Dabbs, Carr, Frady, & Riad, 1995; Dabbs, Hargrove, & Heusel, 1996; Orengo, Kunik, Ghusn, & Yudofsky, 1997), and estradiol (a female sex hormone) seems to decrease aggression in females (Albert, Jonik, & Walsh, 1991).

In humans, hormones also may influence aggression (Delgado, 1969). In institutionalized populations, those men and women who have been identified as having higher levels of testosterone have shown a greater frequency of aggressive behavior, as well as a greater likelihood of having been convicted of violent crimes. In addition, institutionalized women seem more likely to engage in aggression just prior to menstruation and less likely to do so during ovulation.

Outside of institutions, some evidence also links hormones and aggression. For example, children who were exposed prenatally to male sex hormones, because their mothers were given a synthetic hormone to prevent miscarriage, have shown greater levels of aggression than their same-sex siblings (Reinisch, Ziemba-Davis, & Sanders, 1991). It is important to recall that we cannot predict causation based on correlation alone. Nonetheless, it is well documented that high doses of synthetic male sex hormones have been linked to extreme aggression, severe mood swings, and mental instability (Pope & Katz, 1988).

Among nonhuman animals, aggressive behavior is generally associated with certain situations, such as self-defense, predation (killing a potential food source), and reproduction (winning or keeping sexual access to a mate). Among humans, although the fundamental biochemistry underlying aggression is universal across the human species, the specific circumstances that prompt the aggressive impulses and the specific forms of expressing aggression differ across cultures (Averill, 1993) and even across individuals. One of the ways humans may determine which circumstances warrant, or permit, aggressive behavior is through watching others, or social learning.

Social Learning and Violence

Social learning plays a major role in aggressive behavior (Bandura, 1973, 1977a, 1983; R. A. Baron & Richardson, 1992). According to this view, people learn aggressive behavior by watching aggressive models (see chapters 6, 11, and 12), as shown in the Bobo-doll experiments of Bandura (see chapter 6). For example, having one or more violent parents as a role model can promote violent behavior in children (Bandura, 1973). People who do not directly show high levels of aggression themselves may enjoy watching others do so, as in movies and sports (Mustonen, 1997).

Given the importance of social learning in contributing to violent behavior, we should pay careful attention to the kinds of role models we provide to one another. Watching aggressive behavior on television also influences aggressive behavior. Children play more aggressively immediately after watching violent shows on television (Liebert & Baron, 1972; see chapter 6). Similarly, watching violent films increased the aggressiveness of juvenile delinquents, especially among those who were initially the most aggressive (Parke et al., 1977).

Significant correlations exist between the amount of television violence watched by children and the children's aggression, as rated by peers (Huesmann, Lagerspetz, & Eron, 1984; Huesmann & Miller, 1994). Moreover, these correlations appear across four countries—Australia, Finland, Poland, and the United States. In short, watching violence teaches children how to engage in violence and *desensitizes* them to its devastating consequences.

It is not just children who can become desensitized. Many studies have shown that prolonged exposure to violence desensitizes adult viewers as well; they become less affected by violence when later viewing a brawl, whether on television or in real life (Rule & Ferguson, 1986). David Linz, Edward Donnerstein, and Steven Penrod (1984) concluded that repeated exposure to filmed violence lowered participants' emotional reactions to the material and resulted in participants' rating the films less offensive by the last day of viewing.

A particular form of aggression against women is violent pornography. Male aggression toward females increases after males watch pornographic films displaying sexual violence (Donnerstein & Berkowitz, 1981). In addition, Linz, Donnerstein, and Penrod (1988) found that after viewing five sexually violent films in 10 days, men evaluated the films more positively (as less depressing, less anxiety producing, and less negatively arousing) than they had after viewing just one film. They also perceived the films as less violent and as less degrading to women. A less definitive support for the link between violent pornography and male aggression against females is a correlation between more liberal pornography laws and incidents of reported rape (Court, 1984). As mentioned, we should not infer causation from correlation because the more liberal pornography laws may, but do not necessarily, cause the incidents.

Environmental Factors Contributing to Aggression

Aggression was a problem for society long before television or movies came on the scene. Other than social learning, what factors in the environment lead to aggression? One such factor is *aggression* itself. Aggression has been found to lead to more aggression. Although some religions may teach us to turn the other cheek, in practice people are more likely to meet aggression with a counterattack (Borden, Bowen, & Tay-lor, 1971; Ohbuchi & Kambara, 1985). Often, groups end up with a chicken-and-egg problem. In 1999, a group of Serbs attacked a group of Kosovars. The Kosovars later attacked the Serbs. The Serbs originally claimed they were provoked, and the Kosovars made the same claim. Often it is hard to tell where the aggression began, and it often is difficult to stop.

Pain also can lead to aggression (Berkowitz, 1993; Berkowitz, Cochran, & Embree, 1981; Ulrich & Azrin, 1962). Hostile aggression is often provoked by feelings of pain. If you are hurt by someone, sometimes even if you were hurt accidentally, you may feel provoked to respond aggressively. If a person's aggressive act leads to a decrease in pain, aggression becomes even more likely (Azrin, 1967).

Discomfort is a further source of aggressive behavior. People become more aggressive when they are simply uncomfortable, such as when they are exposed to bad smells (Rotton, Barry, Frey, & Soler, 1978), cigarette smoke, and air pollution (Rotton & Frey, 1985). Exposure to heat above 80 degrees Fahrenheit (27°C) also increases aggression (R. A. Baron & Bell, 1975; Bell & Baron, 1976). Indeed, increased feelings of discomfort may be a reason why cities that have higher temperatures on the average also have higher average rates of violent crime compared with cities that have more moderate temperatures (C. A. Anderson, 1987). As Figure 14-8 shows, violent crimes more commonly occur on hotter days, in hotter seasons, in hotter years, and in hotter regions (C. A. Anderson, 1989).

Another influence on aggression is frustration. Indeed, some classic research (e.g., Dollard, Miller, Doob, Mowrer, & Sears, 1939) has viewed frustration as a necessary and sufficient condition for aggression. Although a clear empirical link between frustration and aggression exists (Barker, Dembo, & Lewin, 1941), we now know that frustration does not *always* lead to aggression. For example, although strong frustrations that seem to have arbitrary causes are quite likely to lead to aggression, mild frustrations are less likely to lead to aggression, especially if they are viewed as having a reasonable cause (R. A. Baron, 1977). For example, suppose that the light at an intersection turns green but you cannot move your car because you are being blocked by the car in front of you. Whether you react aggressively will probably depend on why the car in front of you stops. Your reaction will be different if the driver in front of you is engaged in a conversation than if the driver has suffered a heart attack.

We also know that individualistic cultures experience more aggressive behavior than collectivist cultures (Oatley, 1993). Further, individualistic societies themselves vary in the extent to which they accept and promote aggression (DeAngelis, 1992; Montagu, 1976). Even in collectivist cultures, aggression may be promoted. For example, aggression is viewed as a

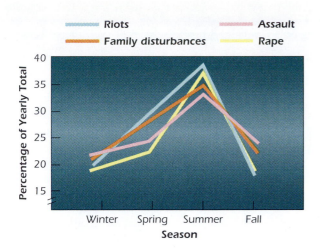

Figure 14–8

TEMPERATURE AND AGGRESSION.   *When the temperature rises, rates of violent crimes often rise as well (C. A. Anderson, 1987). Although the link between high heat and aggression is only correlational (and we therefore cannot draw any causal conclusions), the correlation is robust. (C. A. Anderson, 1989)*

desirable trait for women among the island dwellers of Margarita, Venezuela (Cook, 1992).

Another factor contributing to aggression related to culture is a *sense of honor*. According to R. E. Nisbett and D. Cohen (1996), southerners in the United States are sometimes more prone to respond aggressively and even violently to perceived insults than are northerners because southerners are more likely to see their sense of honor as having been violated. (See the Psychology in Everyday Life box in chapter 13.)

Deindividuation

What enables some of us to *dehumanize* others, to make victims feel as if they are less than human and deserving of poor treatment? A possible answer may be shown by an example. Every once in a while, you read in the newspaper or see on television how fans at an athletic contest—such as a European soccer match—lose control and riot, trampling and mutilating people and destroying everything in the path of the crowd. How does a group become an out-of-control crowd? At the end of the nineteenth century, Gustave Le Bon (1896) attempted to analyze the factors that lead to the mass hysteria of mob behavior. Le Bon contended that people in a crowd are more susceptible to mob behavior because they feel anonymous and invulnerable. They start acting more like lower animals than like people and they become highly impulsive and unreasoning in their actions.

Perhaps mob behavior can be understood in terms of the phenomenon of **deindividuation,** which is the loss of a sense of individual identity resulting in fewer controls that prevent the individual from engaging in

behavior that violates social norms and even the individual's personal moral beliefs. In a study whose findings jolted the scientific community, the basement of a building that housed the Stanford University Psychology Department was converted into a "jail" (Zimbardo, 1972). Male volunteers for the experiment were arbitrarily assigned to be either "prisoners" or "guards." Phil Zimbardo used a number of techniques to deindividuate members of both groups. The prisoners wore prisonlike uniforms and nylon stocking caps and were referred to by serial numbers instead of by names. Guards also wore uniforms and mirrored sunglasses to hide their eyes and they carried clubs.

What started off as a simulation became a nightmare. Prisoners started acting like prisoners, and guards truly acted like guards. The guards started harassing and deriding the prisoners. The guards frequently inflicted cruel treatment, apparently with little or no reason. The prisoners soon staged a revolt that was crushed. Prisoners became morose, depressed, and lethargic, and some started to experience mental breakdowns. The experiment was terminated when it became obvious that it had gotten out of control. It is important to realize that Zimbardo had assigned people arbitrarily to groups. Once deindividuated, people can act in ways they would never have thought possible, whether on the giving or the receiving end of hostile levels of aggression. Such deindividuated behavior is frequently seen in mobs.

Reducing Aggression

Can aggression be controlled or at least reduced? Based on the studies of deindividuation, we might guess that some forms of aggression might be minimized by maximizing people's (a) sense of their own individual identities as humans and (b) awareness of the humanity of their fellow humans. Several specific methods for reducing aggression also have been proposed, some of which seem to be more successful than others. As Table 14-3 shows, some methods for reducing aggression that are based on these principles and social learning, such as observing *nonaggressive modeling* and *generating incompatible responses*, can be effective.

Group behavior can be mindless, inappropriate, and even disastrous if each member of the group yields his or her individual thoughts, beliefs, and actions to the apparent consensus of the group. Mob lynchings in the United States and elsewhere have attested to this fact. Yet, when even a single individual takes the initiative and takes positive action, such as helping others or refusing to harm others, other members of the group may be motivated to reconsider their own beliefs and behavior. The personal characteristics that might enable someone to stand up for what he or she believes, despite group pressure to the contrary, are qualities considered in the next chapter.

TABLE 14–3

Methods for Reducing Aggression *Of the many methods for reducing aggression that have been proposed, some are much more effective than others. Indeed, some methods may even exacerbate aggression, increasing its likelihood.*

METHOD	DESCRIPTION
Observing nonaggressive models	Watching nonaggressive models can increase the likelihood of choosing alternatives to aggressive behavior.
Generating incompatible responses	One of the most successful techniques; empathy, humor, unexpected responses can defuse aggression.
Using cognitive strategies	A stop-and-think strategy raises alternatives to using aggression in frustrating or threatening situations; an awareness of individual people as humans and of the humanity of fellow humans reduces deindividuation; an awareness of the reasons for another person's behavior can reduce feelings of anger, frustration, hostility.

THINK ABOUT IT

1. What criteria would you propose for determining whether behavior derives from motives that are truly altruistic?

2. Some developmental psychologists have noticed that adolescents who demonstrate a high degree of conformity to their peers during adolescence are more likely to have shown a high degree of obedience to their parents during childhood. What do you believe to be the relationship between conformity and obedience, if any?

3. How might a working group avoid suffering the ill effects of groupthink?

4. How might you help people to avoid falling prey to some of the strategies for gaining compliance described in this chapter?

5. Imagine that you wished to reduce the likelihood of your own aggression or the aggression of another person. What would you do?

6. Which compliance-seeking strategy is the most likely to be effective in gaining your own compliance? Why?

 You can provide your own answers to these questions online at the **Sternberg, In Search of the Human Mind** *Web site:* **http://www.harcourtcollege.com/psych/ishm**

Summary

Groups 450

1. Researchers who study the social psychology of groups seek to understand and explain how groups reach consensus and how individuals perform in a *group*. Groups differ in the emphasis they give to task functions versus relationships among members of the group.

2. *Social-facilitation* theory and *distraction-conflict theory* offer explanations for how the presence of others affects our performance.

3. *Social loafing* occurs in groups and can be discouraged through evaluation apprehension.

4. Groups often become polarized. New arguments confirm old beliefs, and social norms emerge. Ingroup members are especially influential.

5. The resolution of intergroup and intragroup conflicts may be viewed in terms of the reasons why people resolve conflicts and the strategies they use to resolve conflicts.

6. *Groupthink* occurs when a closely knit group cares more about consensus than about honest interaction. Stress, biased leadership, and isolation compound the problem. To counter groupthink, the group needs a subgroup structure, outside input, and strong leadership.

Conformity, Compliance, and Obedience 455

7. People yield to social pressure by conforming, complying, and obeying.

8. Solomon Asch's studies showed that a member of a group may conform publicly or privately. People who deviate from the norm often are rejected by the group. Factors affecting *conformity* include group size, cohesiveness of the group, gender, social status, culture, and the appearance of unanimity. Majorities urge conformity through their large numbers; minorities, if persistent, also can influence opinion.

9. *Compliance* is encouraged through such techniques as justification, reciprocity, low-ball, that's-not-all, foot-in-the-door, door-in-the-face, and hard-to-get.

10. Stanley Milgram's experiments on *obedience* showed that most participants were willing to inflict excruciating pain on others when "under orders" to do so. Other research has replicated Milgram's surprising findings.

Prosocial Behavior 462

11. According to the *bystander effect*, the presence of others diffuses responsibility and inhibits helping behavior. Also important are the characteristics of the victim, the bystander, and the situation.

12. *Altruism* is selfless sacrifice. Psychologists agree that it exists, but disagree over how to define it.

Antisocial Behavior 466

13. *Prejudice* is based on faulty evidence, which in turn often is based on *social categorization* and on *stereotypes*. The Robber's Cave study showed how prejudice can be reduced by cooperative activities. Prejudice may develop when groups compete for scarce resources (*realistic-conflict theory*) or when people seek to increase their own self-esteem and to boost the esteem of their ingroup (*social-identity theory*). To reduce prejudice, groups must recognize that it exists, work cooperatively together, use information to counter the stereotypes, and, if possible, experience other cultures.

14. *Aggression* is *antisocial behavior* that harms another; it may be *hostile* or *instrumental*. Aggression may be prompted by hormones. People learn aggressive behavior when they see it modeled, such as on television and in the movies. Violent pornography is a strong example of modeling aggressive behavior. Pain, discomfort, and frustration also can promote aggressive behavior.

15. A group can become an unruly mob. When *deindividuation* occurs, people behave in ways they would not behave if they were alone.

16. Aggression can be reduced if we as individuals maximize our own identities as humans and our awareness of others as fellow humans.

Key Terms

■ THINK ABOUT IT SAMPLE RESPONSES

1. What criteria would you propose for determining whether behavior derives from motives that are truly altruistic?

An action is altruistic when it helps one or more persons but has no benefit to the person who has engaged in the action. One could argue that no actions are 100% altruistic, because people can gain a sense of pleasure by helping others and therefore benefit indirectly from the actions in which they engage that apparently help only others. In order to circumvent this problem, altruistic actions can be characterized in terms of material benefits. But there are clear benefits to actors that go beyond the materialistic.

2. Some developmental psychologists have noticed that adolescents who demonstrate a high degree of conformity to their peers during adolescence are more likely to have shown a high degree of obedience to their parents during childhood. What do you believe to be the relationship between conformity and obedience, if any?

Obedience requires conformity to the implicit or explicit desires of others. It therefore may in general promote a mindset toward conformity. For example, when a child is obedient to his or her parents, the child is conforming to the parents' wishes. The stage therefore may be set for other types of conformity.

3. How might a working group avoid suffering the ill effects of groupthink?

The best way for a working group to avoid suffering these ill effects is to be aware of what they are and constantly to be monitoring its own behavior in terms of whether it is showing any signs of groupthink. Ideally, an out-side consultant would also monitor the group, as those within the group may not be fully sensitive to the signs of groupthink within their own group.

4. How might you help people to avoid falling prey to some of the strategies for gaining compliance described in this chapter?

One way to help people is to point out what the strategies are, give examples, and ask learners to generate their own examples and how they might resist these techniques. It is important for the learners to be involved in generating both examples and counter-strategies so that their knowledge becomes useful, not just "book" knowledge that they are unable to translate into practice.

5. Imagine that you wished to reduce the likelihood of your own aggression or the aggression of another person. What would you do?

Aggression is most likely to occur when the only point of view you see or appreciate is your own. One way to reduce aggression, therefore, would be to try to understand the other person's point of view.

6. Which compliance-seeking strategy is the most likely to be effective in gaining your own compliance? Why?

Everyone must answer this question for himself or herself. Often people find reciprocity to be particularly effective. The reason is that it is the only technique that involves someone's first doing something explicitly for you. You are then likely to wish to repay the favor.

We lose an object if we have quarreled with the person who gave it to us and do not want to be reminded of him, or if we no longer like the object itself and want to have an excuse for getting another and better one instead. The same intention directed against an object can also play a part, of course, in cases of dropping, breaking, or destroying things.

—Sigmund Freud, Introductory Lectures on Psychoanalysis

15

PERSONALITY

Chapter Outline

Bart and Bert are brothers, but to a casual observer, they appear to have little in common. Bart is outgoing and sociable. He loves spending time with other people and going to parties. Bert is quiet, withdrawn, and even reclusive. He prefers to be by himself and is almost never to be seen at parties. How can two brothers be so different? The question we ask about the two brothers is essentially the same question psychologists ask about the intriguing phenomenon of **personality**—the enduring dispositional characteristics of an individual that hold together and explain the person's behavior. Researchers have come up with several ways to study personality. Some psychologists have conducted intensive studies of the personalities of individuals over long periods. Others have developed a wide array of means for assessing individual personalities at a single point in time. Still others have carried out empirical studies of isolated aspects or common dimensions of personality across individuals.

There are a number of alternative theories for understanding and integrating observations about personality. These various theories can be classified according to the major approaches to psychology discussed in chapter 1. The assumptions and ideas behind the major approaches to personality are quite different from one another. Some of the approaches emphasize the importance of early experience to understanding personality. Some emphasize the importance of highly stable personal characteristics that vary little over time. And some of the approaches have generated a great deal of research and rigorous testing of their ideas. What, then, are these particular approaches to understanding personality? How can we compare the theories generated by psychologists

Personality is an intriguing phenomenon, defined as the enduring dispositional characteristics of a person that hold together and explain his or her behavior. What was it about Rosa Parks's personality that enabled her to find the courage to resolve to challenge segregation on city buses and how did she come by it?

who take such different approaches? Most personality psychologists probably would agree on the importance of the following set of criteria for evaluating the various approaches:

1. *Importance to and influence on the field of psychology:* How have the development of theory and research in the field been affected by this approach at various times?

2. *Testability:* Has the approach given rise to empirically testable propositions and have these propositions, in fact, been tested?

3. *Comprehensiveness:* To what extent do the theories within the approach give a reasonably complete account of the phenomena they set out to describe or explain?

4. *Usefulness to applications in psychological assessment and psychotherapy techniques:* Can the theory be usefully employed by clinicians and other practitioners?

This chapter considers some of the principal alternative approaches to personality theory: psychodynamic, humanistic, cognitive-behavioral, trait and biological. The theories within a given approach, de-

spite their variations, share common elements, as you will see in the table that evaluates and summarizes each approach.

Psychodynamic Approaches

In Search of . . . *Why is Freud's view of personality so influential and controversial?*

The Nature of Psychodynamic Theories

While the scientific community around the beginning of the 20th century was excitedly elaborating and investigating certain laws of physics (in particular, those of thermodynamics), psychodynamic psychologists were developing theories of personality that underscored the *dynamic processes* underlying personality. Psychodynamic theories view each person as a complex system of *diverse sources of psychic energy,* each of which pushes the person in a somewhat different direction. As we observe a person's behavior, we are watching the moment-by-moment convergence of these multidirectional sources of what some psychologists call "psychic energy." For example, the son or daughter whose mother returns to work may be affected by a number of factors that may push his or her personality development in different directions. If her mother has made her feel loved and valued, she may feel fine about the return and continue to develop a sense of security and emotional stability. But if her mother has not instilled feelings of security, the daughter may feel abandoned and unloved. The daughter's reactions may also be shaped by whether the mother returns to work happily or grudgingly. At any time, it is not only the set of events, but also the constellation of feelings and thoughts surrounding those events, that can shape the personality of the young child.

Conflict and Biology

Another key commonality underlying psychodynamic theories is the importance of *conflict.* The different sources of energy tend to propel the person in conflicting directions and the behavior prompted by these multiple sources of energy usually cannot satisfy all of the conflicting psychic drives at once. Similarly, psychodynamic theorists observe conflict between individuals and the society in which they live. For example, internal psychic energy may prompt a person to desire sexual fulfillment in ways that society prohibits, such as through sexual intercourse between parents and children.

Adaptation and Development

Biological drives (especially sexual ones) and other biological forces play a key role in psychodynamic theories. Sigmund Freud, the first of the great psychodynamic thinkers, viewed his theory as *biological* in nature, in part because this theory and other psychodynamic theories have been influenced by Charles Darwin's notions of evolution through natural selection. Specifically, psychodynamic theories study how people constantly seek to adapt to the environment, even though people may not always succeed in their efforts. For example, in trying to adapt to the environment, people may attempt to put out of their minds in various ways serious problems that they urgently need to solve, such as a highly conflictual relationship with a parent. Their attempt to adapt ultimately can backfire.

What is adaptive can change with age. Psychodynamic theories thus particularly emphasize the ways in which early childhood experiences influence personality development. Psychodynamicists theorize that our early development influences the moment-to-moment dynamics of how we adapt to our external environments while responding to conflicting internal psychic forces.

The biological and developmental characteristics of psychodynamic theories suggest another of the key features of Freud's theory: **determinism**—the belief that people's behavior is ruled by forces over which the people have little or no control. Freud believed behavior is strongly influenced by often uncontrollable forces, particularly, sexual and aggressive drives. In contrast, the psychodynamically oriented theorists who followed Freud, the **neo-Freudians,** reacted against Freud's emphasis on instincts and his determinism, and generally viewed people as having somewhat more control over their own actions.

The Importance of the Unconscious

Another variable influencing our control over our actions is the role of the *unconscious,* an internal structure of the mind that is outside the grasp of our awareness. Although the various psychodynamic theories differ regarding the exact nature of this role, each theory gives the unconscious some function. The idea that much of our behavior is motivated by forces outside our conscious comprehension pervades all psychodynamic theories, although Freud emphasized the importance of the unconscious much more heavily than did the neo-Freudians.

Finally, many psychodynamic theories draw on data from *observations* of patients in clinical settings, which typically do not lend themselves readily to controlled observation or to rigorous experimentation. To

Sigmund Freud, shown here with his daughter, Anna, is the primary theorist of the psychodynamic paradigm, viewed by many as the seminal thinker in the psychology of personality.

summarize, the various psychodynamic theories share a common focus on dynamic processes, sources and transformations of psychic energy, conflicts, biological and societal adaptation, developmental changes, deterministic and unconscious forces, and clinical observations. They emphasize early experience and the biological and environmental forces that shape such experience. Next, we consider how these commonalities manifest themselves in a few of the distinct psychodynamic approaches.

Psychoanalysis: The Theory of Sigmund Freud

Sigmund Freud is considered to be one of the greatest thinkers of the 20th century. His theory is sometimes considered to be the most influential in all of psychology.

The Structure of Personality

As we have seen, Freud (1917/1963b) believed that the mind exists at two basic levels: conscious and unconscious (see chapter 5). In addition to conscious thought (of which we are aware) and unconscious thought (of which we are unaware), Freud suggested the existence of *preconscious* thought. Preconscious thought is thought of which we are not currently aware but that we can bring into awareness more readily than we can bring unconscious thought into awareness. For example, most of our memories would reside in our preconscious. Freud (1933/1964a) also believed that the mind can be divided into three basic structures: the id, the ego, and the superego. The id and the superego are largely unconscious, and the ego is largely conscious, although with some preconscious and unconscious components.

The Id.   At the most primitive level, the **id** is the personality structure that serves as the unconscious, instinctual, and irrational source of primitive impulses. The id functions by means of **primary-process thought,** a form of thought that is irrational, instinct-driven, and unrealistic. We engage in primary-process thought as infants and also later in our dreams. For example, a baby does not care that she is in a plane or a museum or a concert hall or a lecture—if she is hungry, she cries.

This mode of thought accepts both content and forms that would be unacceptable when we are thinking logically. For example, the content of primary-process thought allows us to consummate sexual desires that we would never be able to fulfill in everyday life. This wish fulfillment could occur in a dream or other fantasy. Another expression of primary-process thought can be found in Freudian slips of the tongue (which are described in chapter 8). In addition to the important functions of permitting the expression of wishes through dreams, primary-process thinking also provides a wellspring for creativity by permitting novel and even surprising connections.

The novel connections and other aspects of primary-process thinking are as unacceptable to consciousness as is the content of the thoughts. For example, primary-process thinking may include blatant contradictions. In a dream, you may be fully engaged in developing events, yet at the same time you may be observing those events as a detached nonparticipant. In conscious thought, you would need to view yourself as either participating or not participating.

Freud addressed the paradoxical nature of dreams by distinguishing between the **manifest content** of dreams (the stream of events that pass through the mind of an individual during dreams) and the **latent content** of dreams (the repressed impulses and other unconscious material expressed in dreams that give rise to the manifest content). Freud believed that the thinking we experience in dreams serves to disguise unacceptable impulses. Many elements of dreams are symbolic (e.g., a box can symbolize the womb). The manifest content of a dream might be to seek refuge from a wild animal, but the latent content of the dream might be the need to seek protection from savage impulses. People also disguise unacceptable thoughts through *condensation*, whereby several unacceptable thoughts or impulses are combined into a single dream image.

According to Freudian theory, dreams offer a way to fulfill some of the wishes that we are unable to fulfill in our daily conscious lives. Wish fulfillment via dreams is only one of many ways we immediately gratify the impulses of the id. Immediate gratification transforms the psychic energy of the id's impulses, reducing internal tension and conflict. Because the id irrationally pursues immediate gratification of urges for pleasure, regardless of the external realities that might impinge on those urges, the id is said to operate in terms of the **pleasure principle.**

The Ego.   The **ego** is a personality structure that is largely conscious and realistic in responding to events in the world. In contrast to the id, the ego operates on the basis of the **reality principle,** which responds to the real world as it is perceived to be, rather than as the person may want it to be (the province of the id) or may believe that it should be. Through the reality principle, the ego mediates between the id and the external world, deciding on the extent to which we can act on our impulses and the extent to which we must suppress them to meet the demands of reality. In other words, the ego tries to find realistic ways to gratify the id's impulses. For example, the id may be behind the idea that "I want a big piece of that cake!" while the ego may lead one to opt for a small piece of the cake.

Each person's ego originally develops from the id during infancy. Throughout life, the ego remains in contact with the id, as well as with the external world. The ego relies on **secondary-process thought,** which is basically rational and based on reality, helping the thinker make sense of the world and act in ways that make sense both to the thinker and to observers of the thinker's actions. As you read this textbook, trying to make sense of it, you are engaging in secondary-process thought.

Freud's third structure of personality, the **superego,** is unconscious and irrational, based on the rules and prohibitions we have internalized from interactions with our parents and possibly other authority figures. The superego comprises all our internalized representations of the norms and values of society. The superego emerges later than the id and the ego, around 3 to 5 years of age. To some extent, the superego is an internalized representation of our parents—the authority figures who tell us what we can and cannot do; it is based on the norms and values of society.

The Superego. The superego operates by means of the **idealistic principle,** which guides a person's actions in terms of what she or he should do as dictated by internalized authority figures without regard for rationality or even external reality. Whereas the ego is largely rational in its thinking, the superego is not. The superego checks whether we are conforming to our internalized moral authority, not whether we are behaving rationally. For example, if we are interested in having a sexual relationship with someone forbidden to us—perhaps someone else's spouse—the superego will be telling us to forsake such an unacceptable relationship. The id, however, may hold sway, and we may pursue the relationship after all.

The superego has two parts: the conscience and the ego ideal. Roughly speaking, the *conscience* arises from those experiences in which we were punished for unacceptable behavior, whereas the *ego ideal* results from those experiences in which we were rewarded for praiseworthy behavior. In other words, the conscience focuses on prohibited or other questionable behaviors, whereas the ego ideal focuses on societally (or morally) valued behaviors. Thus, the superego presents a third factor that the ego must contend with when trying to determine behavior. The relations among the id, the ego, and the superego are shown in Figure 15-1.

Defense Mechanisms

The id, ego, and superego form the structures of personality and the basis for personality development and expression, according to Freud's psychodynamic theory. How they are expressed has a good deal to do with how a person copes with the conflicts that arise among the three structures. The id's strong impulses and the superego's strong prohibitions often pose problems for the ego. Freud (see also A. Freud, 1946) suggested that in response to these problems, people use **defense mechanisms** as the ego's means of protecting itself from unacceptable thoughts and impulses. The goal of these defense mechanisms is to protect the ego from anxiety associated with the conflicting urges and prohibitions of the id and the superego, such as the case discussed above of whether to pursue a sexual relationship with a forbidden partner. The eight main defense mechanisms are *denial, repression, projection, displacement, sublimation, reaction formation, rationalization,* and *regression.* In the short term, these defense mechanisms may help us deal with the discomfort of having to deal with problems we do not wish to face. In the long term, they can be maladaptive as they prevent us from finding solutions to these problems.

1. *Denial* occurs when our mind defends itself from thinking about unpleasant, unwanted, or threatening situations. It may also screen out anxiety-provoking physical sensations in our own bodies. For instance, alcoholics may deny perceiving all the obvious signs of alcoholism surrounding them; adolescents deny that their unsafe sex practices may cause them to get sexually transmitted diseases; or someone with a possibly cancerous mole may "forget" noticing it and therefore not seek medical attention for it.

2. *Repression* is the internal counterpart to denial; we *unknowingly* exclude from consciousness any unacceptable and potentially dangerous impulses. For example, a woman may be afraid of intimate contact with men because she was sexually molested

Figure 15–1

PERSONALITY STRUCTURES OF PSYCHODYNAMIC THEORY. *The id, the ego, and the superego are believed to form the basis for personality development and expression, according to psychodynamic theory.*

Structure	Levels of thought	Operating principle	Description		
Id	Unconscious; primary process	Pleasure	Source of psychic energy and instinctual impulses	Ego	Conscious
Ego	Largely conscious; secondary process	Reality	Mediator among the id, the superego, and external reality		Preconscious
Superego	Largely unconscious	Idealistic	Comprises the *conscience* (prohibitions, based on punishments) and the *ego ideal* (ideal behaviors, based on rewards)	Id / Superego	Unconscious

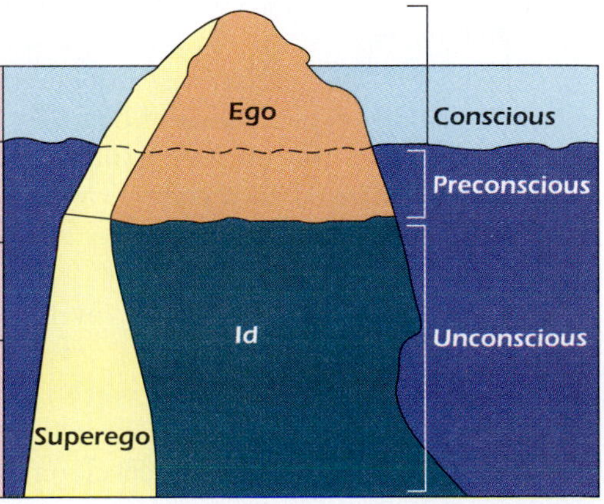

by an uncle as a child. However, she has repressed all memory of the sexual molestation and therefore can neither recall the unhappy episode nor relate it to her fear of sexual intimacy.

3. *Projection* is a defense mechanism that leads us to attribute our own unacceptable and possibly dangerous thoughts or impulses to another person. Projection allows us to be aware of the thought or impulse but to attribute it to someone else, whereas repression keeps the thought out of consciousness altogether. An illustration of projection can be found in the instance of a person who becomes obsessed with thoughts of his or her partner's infidelity as a way of defending against sexual impulses toward others that he or she finds unacceptable.

4. *Displacement* allows us to redirect an impulse away from the person who prompts it and toward another person who is a safe substitute. For example, a young boy who has been punished unfairly by his father would like to lash out vengefully against the father. However, his ego recognizes that he cannot attack such a threatening figure, so instead, he becomes a bully and attacks helpless classmates.

5. *Sublimation* is the process whereby we redirect socially unacceptable impulses, transforming the psychic energy of unacceptable impulses into acceptable and even admirable behavioral expressions. For instance, a composer or other artist may rechannel sexual energy into creative products that are valued by the society as a whole.

6. *Reaction formation* is the defense mechanism that transforms an unacceptable impulse or thought into its opposite. By unconsciously convincing ourselves that we think or feel exactly the opposite of what we actually do unconsciously think or feel, we protect our positive views of ourselves. For instance, we may be inwardly jealous of a neighbor's new luxury car and wish we had such a vehicle, but consciously we decide that spending so much on a mere car is incredibly superficial and materialistic.

7. Through *rationalization*, we can avoid threatening thoughts and explanations of behavior by replacing them with nonthreatening ones. For example, a woman married to a compulsive gambler may justify (rationalize) her husband's behavior by attributing it to his desire to win a lot of money because of his great concern for the financial well-being of the family.

8. When *regression* occurs, we revert to thinking and behaving in ways that are characteristic of an earlier stage of socioemotional development. For in-

stance, when a newborn enters the family, older siblings may start acting more like infants to attract the attention that is now being bestowed on the newborn. Adults, too, may revert to babyish or childish behaviors when they do not get what they want. In this way, we ward off the anxiety or pain that we are experiencing in our present stage of development (see chapter 11). The anxiety or pain we feel may be a function of experiences in early childhood development.

Freud's Theory of Personality Development

Freud (1905/1964b) proposed that psychosexual development (gender- and sexuality-based development, see chapter 11) begins immediately after birth and continues through adulthood. According to Freud, there are four major stages of development: oral, anal, phallic, and genital. Freud posited that a set of personality characteristics would be associated with each of his stages of psychosexual development. The **oral stage** typically occurs during the first 2 years of life, when an infant explores sucking and other oral activity, learning that such activity provides not only nourishment, but also pleasure. The **anal stage** typically occurs between the ages of 2 and 4 years, during which time the child learns to derive pleasure from urination and especially defecation. The **phallic stage** typically begins at about 4 years of age and continues until about 6 years of age. Children discover during this stage that stimulation of the genitals can feel good. This stage can also give rise to **Oedipal conflict,** in which the child starts to feel jealous and competitive with the parent of the same sex, because of romantic feelings felt for the parent of the opposite sex. In particular, boys desire their mothers but fear the powerful wrath of their fathers. The conflict is named for the Greek myth in which Oedipus, who had long been separated from his parents and therefore did not recognize them, killed his father and married his mother. Girls may desire their fathers but worry about the wrath of their mothers (sometimes called the **Electra conflict,** after the myth of Electra, who despised her mother for having cheated on and killed her husband, Electra's father).

According to Freud, the Oedipal and Electra conflicts cause great turmoil in children. To resolve these conflicts, children must accept the sexual unattainability of the parent of the opposite sex. The feelings they directed toward the opposite-sex parent become *sublimated*—redirected in a more socially acceptable fashion. Freud believed that these feelings go into **latency,** an interim period in which children repress their sexual feelings toward their parents and sublimate their sexual energy into productive fields of endeavor.

Eventually, sexual feelings reappear during adolescence, and the feelings that children once felt toward the parent of the opposite sex are now directed toward an age-mate of the opposite sex. Ultimately, the child develops a mature relationship with a partner of the opposite sex, thereby entering into the final and mature psychosexual stage, the **genital stage.**

According to Freud, at any point during psychosexual development, the child might become **fixated**—unable to resolve the relevant issues of the current stage and therefore unable to progress to the next stage. Fixation in the given stage of development would mean that the individual would show the characteristics of that stage in adulthood. (See Table 15-1.)

Evaluating Freud's Theory

Freud's theory was groundbreaking, but it generated heated debate that continues to this day. Some psychologists are concerned about the population Freud studied and upon which he based many of his theories. Many of Freud's ideas came from observations of patients in his clinical practice. Most of Freud's patients were women, many of whom were referred to his neurological practice because of *hysterical symptoms*—physical complaints for which no medical causes could be found and that are relatively rare today.

Freud's case-study approach was both intensive and qualitative. It was *intensive* in the sense that Freud would subject a single case to penetrating scrutiny. Freud's analyses were *qualitative* in the sense that Freud made no effort to quantify anything about the case studies. Others have used the case study to gain extensive and quantitative data, as well.

In addition to the concern that his theories were based on qualitative case-study analysis, many psychologists think that Freud placed too much emphasis on sex as the basis of a general theory of development. Freud clearly developed his theory within the particular

---

TABLE 15-1

Freud's Stages of Psychosexual Development   *For each of his stages of psychosexual development, Sigmund Freud posited that a set of personality characteristics would be associated with that stage of development. Fixation in the given stage of development would mean that the individual would show those characteristics in adulthood. (After Freud, 1905/1964b)*

State	Characteristics Associated With Fixation
Oral (birth to age 2)	Display many activities centered around the mouth: excessive eating, drinking; smoking, talking
Oral eroticism	Sucking and eating predominate; cheerful, dependent, and needy; expects to be taken care of by others
Oral sadism	Biting and chewing predominate; tends to be cynical and cruel
Anal (ages 2 to 4)	
Anal-retentive	Excessively neat, clean, meticulous, and obsessive
Anal-expulsive	Moody, sarcastic, biting, and often aggressive; untidy in personal habits
Phallic (age 4 to middle childhood)	Overly preoccupied with self; often vain and arrogant; unrealistic level of self-confidence and self-absorption
Latency (middle childhood)	Demonstrates sexual sublimation and repression
Genital (adolescence through adulthood)	Traditional sex roles and heterosexual orientation

context of his times, as evidenced by his traditional views of female sex roles and of sexual orientation, as well as his heavy emphasis on the role of sexual repression in normal adult feelings, thoughts, and behavior. Some of Freud's followers, discussed next, developed less sexually oriented developmental theories in part as a reaction to the sexual emphasis of Freud.

The Neo-Freudians

Freud's work inspired many to follow him and many to react against him. The sheer abundance of theories that can be viewed as reactions to different aspects of Freud's theorizing indicates the immense contribution of his work. In this way, Freud's work resembles the work of Jean Piaget (see chapter 10), whose enormous influences also have prompted many theorists to create their own theories (see, e.g., Berg & Sternberg, 1992).

The neo-Freudians emphasized more than did Freud the importance to the development of personality, throughout the lifespan, of continued interactions with others and the world. Indeed, one theorist, Henry Stack Sullivan (1953), believed that all of personality develops through interpersonal interactions. Most neo-Freudians, however, took a less extreme position.

The Individual Psychology of Alfred Adler

Alfred Adler, one of Freud's earliest students, was also one of the first to break with Freud and to disagree with many of his views. For example, Adler did not accept Freud's view that people are victimized by competing and largely instinctual forces within themselves. Instead, Adler believed that all psychological phenomena within the individual are unified and consistent among themselves. Although people may seem to behave inconsistently or unpredictably, in fact these apparently inconsistent behaviors can be understood when viewed as being consistently directed toward a single goal: *superiority.*

According to Adler, our personality results in large part from the energy behind our striving for superiority by attempting to become as competent as possible in whatever we do. Olympic athletes and famous musicians are outstanding examples of people who achieve superiority, but all of us strive for it. This striving for superiority gives meaning and coherence to our actions. Unfortunately, however, some of us feel that we cannot attain superiority. When people organize their thoughts, emotions, and behavior based on their perceived mistakes and feelings of inferiority, they develop an **inferiority complex** (Adler's coinage to describe the resulting pathology).

Alfred Adler (1870–1937) believed that all psychological phenomena are directed toward the goal of superiority, and Adler's notion of the "inferiority complex" often is used as a means of describing persons whose personality centers on feelings of inferiority.

In addition, Adler held that our actions are largely shaped by our *expectations for the future,* through the goals we set, rather than by our past experiences and development, which Freud had emphasized. Adler referred to these motivating expectations of what the future will hold as *fictions.* Thus, in Adler's view, we are motivated not by what is actually true but rather by our *subjective perceptions* of what we believe to be true. For example, if a man believes that his coworkers are putting him down behind his back, he is likely to act in ways that reflect his belief, whether or not the belief has any factual basis.

Finally, Adler believed in the importance of birth order. He suggested that first-borns are more likely than later-borns to strive toward and reach high levels of achievement.

The Analytical Psychology of Carl Jung

Like Freud, Carl Jung believed that the mind can be divided into conscious and unconscious parts. However, Jung theorized that the unconscious differed sharply from what Freud's theory had suggested. Jung referred to the first layer of the unconscious as the **personal unconscious,** the part of the unconscious mind in which is stored each person's unique personal experiences and repressed memories that are perceived below the level of consciousness. Each person's personal unconscious derives solely from his or her own experiences. Jung believed that the contents of each person's personal unconscious are organized in terms of **complexes,** which are clusters of independently functioning, emotionally tinged unconscious thoughts, as would be the case for a complex regarding the person's mother, father, or other close relation. Although Jung's view of the organization of the personal unconscious may have differed somewhat from Freud's more holistic view of the unconscious, Jung's view of another layer of the unconscious was what distinguished Jung as radically departing from Freud.

Jung referred to the second layer as the **collective unconscious.** This level contains memories and behavioral predispositions that all people have inherited from common ancestors in the distant human past. According to Jung, people have a common collective unconscious because we have the same distant ancestors; thus, our common ancestral heritage provides each of us with essentially identical shared memories and tendencies.

Carl Jung (1875–1961) believed that the unconscious comprises both a personal unconscious, distinct to each individual, and a collective unconscious, in which are stored common ancestral personality archetypes.

People across space and time tend to interpret and use experiences in similar ways because of the existence of **archetypes**—universal, inherited human tendencies to perceive and act on things in particular ways. Archetypes in the collective unconscious are roughly analogous to complexes in the personal unconscious, except that whereas complexes are individual, archetypes are shared. To Jung, the fact that myths, legends, religions, and even cultural customs bear resemblances across cultures provides evidence for the existence of archetypes within the collective unconscious.

Jung believed that certain archetypes, listed below, have evolved in ways that make them particularly important in people's lives:

1. *Persona:* The part of our personality that we show the world; the part that we are willing to share with others.

2. *Shadow:* The darker part of us, the part that embraces what we view as frightening, hateful, and even evil about ourselves; the part of us that we hide not only from others, but also from ourselves.

3. *Anima:* The feminine side of a man's personality, which shows tenderness, caring, compassion, and warmth toward others, yet which is more irrational and based on emotions.

4. *Animus:* The masculine side of a woman's personality, the more rational and logical side of the woman.

Other archetypes in our collective unconscious include the great mother, the wise old man, and the hero; many of these archetypes play major roles in fairy tales. Jung posited that men often try to hide their anima both from others and from themselves because it goes against their idealized image of what men should be. For example, a man might learn never to cry or might avoid taking care of children, assuming that women are more nurturing.

According to Jung, archetypes play a role in our interpersonal relationships. For example, the relationship between a man and a woman calls into play the archetypes in each individual's collective unconscious. The anima helps the man understand his female companion, just as the animus helps the woman understand her male companion. However, we may fall in love with our idealization of a man or a woman, based on archetypes in the collective unconscious, rather than with the other person as he or she really is. In fact, people do seem to have ideals in their relationships (R. J. Sternberg & Barnes, 1985; see chapter 13), although it is not at all clear that these ideals derive from any collective unconscious. Jung believed that the **self**—the whole of the personality, including both conscious and unconscious elements—strives for unity among often opposing parts of the personality (see Figure 15-2).

The Psychoanalytic Theory of Karen Horney

Although Karen Horney trained in the psychoanalytic tradition, she later broke with Freud in several key respects. A major contribution was her recognition that Freud's view of personality development was very male oriented and that his concepts of female development were inadequate (Horney, 1937, 1939). Perhaps most fundamentally, Horney believed that *cultural rather than biological variables* are the fundamental basis for the development of personality. She argued that the psychological differences between men and women are not the result of biology or anatomy, but rather of cultural expectations for each of the two genders. She believed that what females really want are the privileges that the culture gives only to males (Horney, 1939). Indeed, her own career was delayed until a German university was willing to admit women to study medicine.

The essential concept in Horney's theory is that of *basic anxiety* (Horney, 1950), a feeling of isolation and helplessness in a world conceived as being potentially hostile, due to the competitiveness of mod-

Karen Horney (1885–1952) believed that what females really want are the privileges that the culture gives to males but not to females (Horney, 1939). Her own career was delayed until a German university was willing to admit women to study medicine.

Figure 15-2

MANDALA SYMBOLS.   *Carl Jung symbolized the search for unity in terms of the mandala (magic circle), which often is represented as a circle containing various geometric configurations. In many cultures, in Asia and in other parts of the world, the mandala represents the universe.*

ern culture. As a result of this competitive climate, people have particularly strong needs for affection, which are not easily met by society. Horney (1937) suggested that we can protect ourselves from the discomfort of basic anxiety in three ways. We can allay anxiety by showing *affection* and *submissiveness*, which move us toward other people. Another way we can allay anxiety is by being aggressive, *striving for power*, *prestige*, or *possession*. This strategy moves against people. Also, we can allay anxiety by *withdrawing* or moving away from people and by simply avoiding them altogether.

Object-Relations Theories

A contemporary extension of psychodynamic theory is **object-relations theory.** This theory addresses how people relate to one another and how people conceptualize these relationships, largely in terms of their investment in other persons or *objects*, which are mental representations of fundamental sources of sustenance and comfort such as the mother, the father, friends, teachers, and the like. In object-relations theory, *investments* in other people are more than just outlets for the satisfaction of instincts. Some of these object relations are primary and provide structure for the self. For example, the child may become invested in receiving affection and attention from rejecting others, such as a rejecting classmate, because the child had a rejecting relationship with his or her parents. People who develop successful object relations generally become emotionally stable, whereas those who do not are at risk for mental disorders, according to object-relations theorists (Bacal & Newman, 1990; Kernberg, 1975, 1976; Klein, 1975; Kohut, 1984). For example, secure adults are able to talk easily and openly about their relationships with their parents (Main et al., 1985).

Whereas Freud particularly emphasized the Oedipal conflict, object-relations theorists look back even further, especially to the infant's attachment to the mother (see the discussion of attachment theory in chapter 11). In this way, maladaptive behavior in later life can be caused by an unsuccessful early attachment

Object-relations theory emphasizes the quality of the bond of attachment between parent and infant as crucial to personality development. It is seen as affecting a person's ability to form close relationships with others throughout life.

or an environment that provides harsh and inconsistent treatment of a young child (Ainsworth, 1989; Herman, Perry, & Van der Kolk, 1989).

Object-relations theory, then, differs from classical psychodynamic theory in several ways (Horner, 1991; Hughes, 1989). First, whereas Freud emphasized the fear of the father that develops during the Oedipal period, object-relations theorists emphasize attachment to the mother that develops during the first two years (as studied by Bowlby, 1958). Second, whereas Freud emphasized impulse gratification and the role of the unconscious in achieving it, object-relations theorists emphasize the need for attachment in human relationships, in adulthood as well as in childhood. Third, whereas Freud viewed the nature of female development as somewhat problematic and difficult to understand, object-relations theorists view male development as being somewhat puzzling (Chodorow, 1978, 1992; Dinnerstein, 1976; Sagan, 1988). In the view of these theorists, infants of both sexes initially identify with the mother, who, according to Bowlby, is the first figure to which the infant attaches himself or herself. Boys, but not girls, need to break away from this attachment to reidentify with the father. It remains an open question whether the tendency to identify initially with the mother is biologically programmed or simply a cultural convention (Chodorow, 1992).

Evaluating the Psychodynamic Approach

Table 15-2 comparatively evaluates psychodynamic research as a whole, using the criteria specified at the outset of this chapter. As this table shows, psychodynamic theories have been highly influential but have led directly to little experimental research because they are most often concerned with and based on work with individuals. The bulk of the research that has been done is relatively limited in scope. Psychodynamic theories vary in terms of their comprehensiveness. Freud's theory was rather comprehensive, but the other theories were less so. The theories have produced numerous extensive psychotherapeutic approaches and techniques.

Several other specific criticisms have been lodged against psychodynamic theory. Primarily, as suggested by the paucity of experimental research, the theory is very difficult to test.

Some theorists believed that psychodynamic theories were too deterministic and too fatalistic in their approach to human nature. The next section details for us the humanistic theories of personality, which represent a rebellion, in many respects, against the psychodynamic point of view.

TABLE 15–2

Psychodynamic Theories: A Critical Evaluation

Psychodynamic theories get high marks for influence on psychology, as well as for comprehensiveness.

CRITERIA	PSYCHODYNAMIC APPROACHES
Importance to and influence in psychology	Have spawned little research to test theories that developed within the approach, as a response to it, or as a reaction against it. Freud, the first major psychodynamic theorist, remains the most influential thinker in personality psychology. Many clinical psychologists (especially psychiatrists) today adhere to Freudian or neo-Freudian perspectives.
Testability of its propositions	Theories do not rate high for testability. Relatively small number of experiments, none of which studied the theories as a whole or fully compared and contrasted the theories. Case studies tend to be open to many interpretations; research has proven to be nondefinitive.
Comprehensiveness	Reasonably complete account of personality phenomena. Freud's theory was comprehensive, as were Adler's and Erikson's, but many other neo-Freudian theories (e.g., Horney) were much less so. Although Jung's theory was relatively comprehensive, it is in part mystical. All of the theories were derived from work with patients who presented adjustment problems and so are more descriptive of the structures and processes underlying extraordinary problems than they are of those of normal persons who have milder, more usual problems.
Parsimoniousness	Less parsimonious than some theories, but the number of constructs is not excessive.
Usefulness to applications in (a) assessment and (b) therapeutic technique	The TAT, Rorschach, and other projective tests have arisen from these theories.

The Humanistic Approach

In Search of . . . *How are the values of humanism expressed in humanistic psychology's view of personality?*

The humanistic tradition in philosophy dates back to the ancient Greeks and reflects a philosophical approach that centers on the unique character of humans and their relationship to the natural world, on human interactions, on human concerns, and on secular human values. **Humanism** emphasizes the potential of the individual for growth and change. Unlike other living organisms, humans are future-oriented and purposeful in their actions. To a large extent, people can create their own lives and determine their own destinies, rather than allowing themselves to be shaped and buffeted by inexplicable forces outside their conscious grasp. One aspect of the humanists' nondeterministic perspective is a heavy emphasis on the role of conscious rather than unconscious experience. We now consider two of the major humanistic theorists—Carl Rogers and Abraham Maslow.

The Self Theory of Carl Rogers

Carl Rogers's **person-centered approach** to personality strongly emphasizes the self and each person's perception of self. Rogers's *self theory* focuses on the way in which the individual defines reality and personality, rather than on any external, objective view of reality or of personality. Each person's conception of self begins in infancy and continues to develop throughout the life span. This *self-concept* comprises all the aspects of the self that the person perceives, whether or not these perceptions are accurate or are shared by others. In addition, each person has an *ideal self*, the personal characteristics that the person would like to embody. A major contribution of Rogers was the recognition that the greater the similarity between the self-concept and the ideal self, the better adjusted the person is in his or her life (C. R. Rogers, 1959, 1980). A good chess player who has always dreamed of becoming a great chess player and winning international tournaments may be less satisfied than a good chess player whose ideal does not include outstanding chess skills.

Rogers (1978) argued that people tend to become more and more complex as they try to fulfill their potential. To Rogers, people have within them the power to make themselves whatever they want to be, if only they choose to use this power.

Like Abraham Maslow (whose hierarchy of needs was described in chapter 12), Rogers (1961b, 1980) suggested that all people strive toward *self-actualization*—the fulfillment of their human potential—although some persons self-actualize more effectively than others. According to Rogers, self-actualizing persons have five characteristics:

1. They will constantly grow and evolve.
2. They will be open to experience, avoid defensiveness, and accept experiences as opportunities for learning.
3. They will trust themselves, and, although they will seek guidance from other people, they will make their own decisions rather than strictly following what others suggest.
4. They will have harmonious relations with other people and will realize that they do not need to be well-liked by everyone. Achieving conditional acceptance from at least some others will free them from the need to be well-liked by all.
5. They will live fully in the present rather than dwell on the past or live only for the future.

The Holistic-Dynamic Theory of Abraham Maslow

In Abraham Maslow's theory of motivation, based upon a hypothesized hierarchy of needs, the highest level is the need for self-actualization (see chapter 12 for a full description of the hierarchy). Maslow's (1970) description of self-actualized people (those who fully use all of their potentials and make the most of who they are) is similar to Rogers's: Self-actualized people are free of mental illness and have reached the top of the hierarchy of needs. They have experienced love and have a full sense of their self-worth and value. They accept both themselves and others unconditionally and accept what the world brings to them. They have a keen perception of reality and can discern genuineness in others, shunning

phoniness in themselves. They are neutral and ethical in their dealings with others. As they face the events in their lives, they are problem-centered, seeing problems for what they are, rather than seeing all problems in relation to themselves and their own needs. They are able to be alone without constantly feeling lonely, and they have the ability to map out their own paths. They have constructed their own system of beliefs and values and do not need others to agree with them in order to hold true to what they stand for. They appreciate and enjoy life and live it to its fullest.

Both Maslow's and Rogers's descriptions of self-actualization may represent more an ideal toward which we strive than a state that many of us are likely to reach. Few, if any people, meet all of the criteria for self-actualization, but many people have satisfied at least some of these criteria, for at least some of the time. These criteria are worthy of our strivings, even if we do not fully reach them.

Evaluating the Humanistic Approach

The humanistic approach has lost some popularity since its heyday during the 1960s and early 1970s. Approaches go in and out of favor, perhaps because every approach and every theory is a reflection of the time in which it is formulated, and times change. Freud's theory very much reflects Victorian thinking, and some of the conflicts that were prevalent in Victorian times are no longer common today. Indeed, some of the ailments Freud treated (e.g., those he linked to sexual repression) are rarely found in present, less prudish times. Similarly, humanism closely fit the *zeitgeist*, or intellectual climate, of the era when it was popular—the 1960s and early 1970s, when the human-potential movement was flourishing. It may fit today's *zeitgeist* less well. Moreover, empirical research in support of the approach has been scanty, at best. Still, its message regarding the importance of the individual and the opportunities for controlling our own fate and striving toward self-actualization may be as relevant today as they ever were.

Table 15-3 summarizes the evaluation of the humanistic in terms of the four criteria previously used for evaluating the psychodynamic approach. At present, the humanistic approach may not fully explain personality and its development and it may function best when used in conjunction with other views. Indeed, it often seems more to characterize what personality we can achieve than the one we have. Nonetheless, humanists encourage us to move beyond narrow views of ourselves to realize more of our great human potential.

In the next section we discuss yet a third approach, the cognitive-behavioral one.

TABLE 15–3

Humanistic Theories: A Critical Evaluation
Humanistic messages continue to relate to contemporary experience.

CRITERIA	HUMANISTIC APPROACHES
Importance to and influence in psychology	Have generated even less empirical research than psychodynamic theories; messages continue to be important, however: focus on individuals, personal choices, opportunities to control fate, striving toward self-actualization
Testability of its propositions	Almost untestable, by definition; predictions seldom operationally defined with enough precision to generate experiments
Comprehensiveness	Although theories deal with some aspects of human nature (e.g., need for self-actualization or individual potential), they leave much unsaid; theories lack comprehensiveness
Parsimoniousness	Reasonably parsimonious; do not have many terms or overwhelming constructs
Usefulness to applications in (a) assessment and (b) therapeutic technique	(a) Tend to be averse to assessment because tests focus on assigning labels to the client rather than on the person's evolving potential; (b) strongly influenced therapy during 1960s and 1970s, but less influential today

The Cognitive-Behavioral Approach

In Search of . . . *What is the cognitive-behavioral approach and how is it distinctive?*

Cognitive-behavioral approaches to personality look at how people think, how they behave, and how thinking and behaving interact.

Antecedents of Cognitive-Behavioral Approaches

Behaviorists seek to understand personality in terms of the way people act. Behavioral approaches to personality also emphasize the explanation of observable behavior in terms of environmental contingencies that shape various forms of behavior.

For example, B. F. Skinner (1974) saw people as differing in their personalities because they have been subjected to different environmental contingencies and schedules of reinforcement. Skinner did not deny that internal states might exist; he simply believed that they are not available for scientific study and therefore are not appropriate objects of psychological theory or investigation.

If people develop personalities through patterns of reinforcement contingencies in the environment, how do apparently maladjusted personalities develop? In the Skinnerian view, people can become malad-

justed in several ways. One way is through reinforcement of antisocial behaviors, such as giving extra attention to a student who is disruptive in class. Another way is through punishment of prosocial behaviors, such as punishing a child for truthfully confessing to accidentally breaking a dish.

Behavioral psychologists, therefore, have tended to emphasize responses to environmental contingencies in personality and have sought to understand how people respond to the various contingencies of their environments. For example, they might seek to understand the causes of depression in terms of low levels of reinforcing events occurring in a person's life. In contrast, cognitive psychologists are concerned with processes going on in the mind. Cognitive-behavioral psychologists are concerned with the link between mind and behavior. Two such theorists are Julian Rotter and Albert Bandura.

The Social-Learning Theory of Julian Rotter

Although Julian Rotter is behaviorally oriented, he does not believe that behavior depends solely on external stimuli and reinforcements. Rather, what is important is the meaning that the person assigns to a given external stimulus or reinforcement. If a person consistently behaves in a certain way because he or she consistently interprets situations in a certain way, those mental tendencies can be viewed as part of

Julian Rotter (b. 1916) considers some features of the behavioral perspective on personality by noting the importance of environmental events in personality development. However, Rotter believes that the importance of these events lies in the meaning that the individual assigns to these events more than in the actual stimuli or reinforcers alone.

such a person were fired due to incompetence and lack of effort, he or she would be likely still to feel as though other factors (the boss's prejudice, coworkers' conspiracies, etc.) had caused the termination. Thus, an internal believes that he or she has control of his or her own fate, whereas an external tends to see fate as controlled by luck, by others, or by destiny. Thousands of studies, including some cross-cultural studies (Dyal, 1984), have focused on Rotter's theory and his *Internal–External (I–E) Control Scale*, and have provided good support.

The Social-Cognitive Theory of Albert Bandura

Albert Bandura's theory addresses the *interaction* between how we think and how we act; it is truly a cognitive-behavioral approach. His model of **reciprocal determinism** (1986) attributes human functioning to an interaction among behavior, personal variables, and the environment (see Figure 15-3). For example, the decision to go to college will be affected by *personal variables*, such as motivation and the ability to succeed in cognitive, academic work. This decision also will be affected by *environmental events*, such as parental encouragement and the funds to enroll. The result is *behavior*—going to college—which will in turn affect the opportunities the student has later in life, such as to pursue occupations that will be unavailable to those who choose not to go to college, and which may affect personal variables as well.

personality (Rotter, 1966, 1990; Rotter & Hochreich, 1975). In other words, Rotter, unlike Skinner, is interested in cognitive aspects of personality, not just behavioral ones.

Rotter's focus on the individual's perceptions of the environment leads naturally to what may be the most important and the most widely cited aspect of his theory: his notion of internal versus external locus of control. People with an **internal locus of control** believe that the causes of behavioral consequences originate within the individual. Internals tend to take personal responsibility for what happens to them. If such a person were laid off during an economic recession, he or she would still probably feel personally responsible for the layoff. Taken to an extreme, an internal person misattributes causality to internal rather than to external causes.

People with an **external locus of control**, in contrast, tend to believe that the causes of behavioral consequences originate in the environment. Taken to an extreme, an external consistently misattributes causality to external rather than to internal causes. If

"I told him it wouldn't kill him to try to be nice once in a while, but I was wrong."

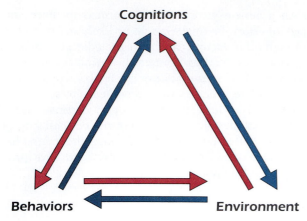

Cognitions

Behaviors   **Environment**

Figure 15–3
RECIPROCAL DETERMINISM. *Albert Bandura's social-cognitive theory emphasizes reciprocal determinism, in which thinking, behavior, and the environment reciprocally interact.*

A crucial personal variable in personality is our set of beliefs in our own *self-efficacy*—that is, our feelings of competence to do things. Feelings of self-efficacy seem actually to lead to our being better able to do those things (Bandura, 1986; Zimmerman, Bandura, & Martinez-Pons, 1992; see chapter 12). If I tell myself I cannot do something, I often will not even try it, with the result that I will never really learn how to do it. If I go ahead and try to do the thing, while constantly telling myself that I will not succeed, my negative expectations may get in the way of what I do, resulting in a negative, self-fulfilling prophecy. Self-efficacy is an excellent predictor of success in many realms (Bandura, 1986).

Other cognitive-behavioral theorists have described personality in terms of schema-based theories and in terms of social intelligence, described next.

Evaluating Cognitive-Behavioral Theories

Table 15-4 offers a brief evaluation of the cognitive-behavioral approach in terms of its influence on theory and research and its testability, comprehensiveness, and practical applicability. The cognitive-behavioral approach to personality is particularly useful in therapy for achieving behavioral change, perhaps because of its emphasis on conscious rather than unconscious function. It is much easier for us to gain access to and to change things about which we are conscious. If our behaviors and our thoughts fall outside of our awareness and cannot be brought into awareness except with great difficulty, we are hard-pressed to change them. By concentrating on the conscious, the cognitive-behavioral approach enables us to implement change more directly, and, many would argue, more effectively as well.

TABLE 15–4

Cognitive-Behavioral Theories: A Critical Evaluation *Cognitive-behavioral theories have spawned a great deal of research interest, at least partly because their propositions are highly testable.*

CRITERIA	COGNITIVE-BEHAVIORAL APPROACHES
Importance to and influence in psychology	Have generated much research by theorists in this and other areas
Testability of its propositions	More testable than psychodynamic or humanistic approaches; strong data
Comprehensiveness	Less comprehensive than other views, these theories address aspects of personality and behavior that follow from learning, but they do not specify the dimensions on which people differ; they say less than other theories about the structure of personality
Parsimoniousness	These theories rate high on parsimony, especially Bandura's because he adhered so closely to his data; Rotter's theory is only slightly less so
Usefulness to applications in (a) assessment and (b) therapeutic technique	(a) Rotter's locus of control and interpersonal trust scales widely used, but they measure narrow bands of personality, not the whole thing; (b) have generated many different methods of psychotherapy (see chapter 17) and have been very influential in health psychology (see chapter 18)

However, because cognitive-behavioral theories focus on the interactions between how people think and how they behave, these theories do not specify any particular list of distinctive traits that characterizes people and how they differ. Such lists are addressed by the trait theorists, considered next.

The Trait-Based Approach

In Search of . . . *Are our personalities based on sets of distinguishable and consistent traits?*

Trait theories emphasize **traits**—stable characteristics that distinguish each person. Is there one set of traits from which our personalities emerge or does each person possess different traits? One of the deans of personality theory, Gordon Allport, believed that much of personality is characterized by **personal dispositions**—traits that are unique to each individual (Allport, 1937, 1961). Although Allport also mentioned *common traits* (which are common across individuals), he believed that much of what makes each of us who we are can be found in the personal dispositions rather than in the common traits.

Allport also believed that each person's various traits differ in their importance for the person. For example, some people possess a **cardinal trait,** which is a single personality trait that is so salient in an individual's personality and so dominant in the person's behavior that almost everything the person does somehow relates back to this trait (Allport, 1961). Although not everyone has a cardinal trait, all people do have **central traits**—the 5 to 10 most salient traits in a person's disposition, affecting much of the person's behavior. In addition, all people have **secondary traits**—personality traits that have some bearing on a person's behavior but that are not particularly central to what the person does.

Other theorists believe that all people have essentially the same set of traits and that they differ only in terms of the extent to which they manifest each trait. Some of these theories try to specify the whole range of personality, suggesting a list of traits believed to characterize fully what people are like. Other theories deal with just a single trait, but in great depth.

The Theory of Hans Eysenck

The simplicity of this theory has been one reason for its acceptance by some researchers. An extensive research base backing up the theory is another. Hans Eysenck (1952, 1981) argued that personality comprises three major traits: extroversion, neuroticism, and psychoticism. The **extroversion** trait character-

izes people who are sociable, expansive, lively, oriented toward having fun, and have interest in interacting with other people. Introverts, in contrast, are quiet, reserved, and generally unsociable. People characterized by **neuroticism** are nervous, emotionally unstable, moody, tense, and irritable, and they frequently worry. In contrast, emotionally stable people tend to be less fretful, more uniform in their behavior, and less subject to sudden mood swings. People characterized by **psychoticism** are solitary, detached from others in their interpersonal relationships, lack feelings, and especially lack caring, empathy, and sensitivity (see Figure 15-4 and the Psychology in Everyday Life box).

The "Big Five" Personality Traits

As you may have noticed, many of the theorists, even those from different approaches, seem to mention some of the same key personality characteristics (termed *traits, factors,* etc.). The "**Big Five**" theory of personality, currently the most widely accepted trait theory, recognizes the frequent recurrence of five personality traits across studies (especially factor-analytic studies) and even across theorists. The "Big Five" traits were first proposed by Warren Norman (1963) but have since been championed by many other investigators (e.g., Costa & McCrae, 1992a, 1992b, 1995; Digman, 1990; Goldberg, 1993; Goldberg & Saucier,

Figure 15–4
EYSENCK'S PERSONALITY DIMENSIONS. *This chart illustrates two of the three personality dimensions described by Hans Eysenck and shows how they may be related to Hippocrates' four humors. (Eysenck's third dimension, psychoticism, is not shown here.)*

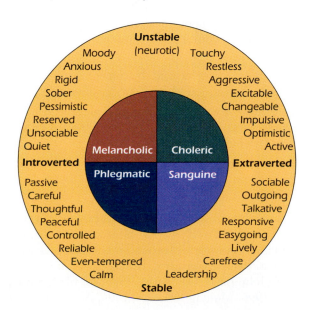

Psychology in Everyday Life

Psychoticisms in Everyday Life

Every so often, we hear about people whom we would rather not get to know: sexual predators, serial killers, terrorist bombers, and the like. Is there any personality characteristic that these twisted people who make the news have in common?

According to Hans Eysenck (1975), there is a personality characteristic that most such people have in common, namely, very high levels of what Eysenck refers to as *psychoticism*, which is a predisposition to psychosis (see also Liebert & Liebert, 1998, from which this summary is drawn). People who are very high in psy-

choticism tend to show certain common characteristics. They tend to be solitary and care little about others. They also tend to be troublesome and do not fit in with society. They have a tendency to be cruel and inhumane and to be insensitive. They lack empathy or genuine feelings for others. They also tend to be high in sensation seeking. They tend to be hostile toward others and to respond aggressively toward these others. They may be eccentric and favor odd or unusual things or patterns of behavior. They are often foolhardy and disregard obvious danger. In social situations, they tend

to be rude and may enjoy embarrassing or upsetting other people. They tend to be oppositional to accepted social customs and to avoid closer personal interactions. They are also impulsive (Roger & Morris, 1991) and to have problems in school (Furnham & Medhurst, 1995). They are likely not to hold religious beliefs (White, Joseph, & Neil, 1993) and tend to show little or no church attendance or personal prayer (Lewis & Maltby, 1995; Maltby, 1995). They are also likely to be susceptible to drug use and to engaging in risky sexual practices (Fontaine, 1994).

1995; McCrae & Costa, 1997; McCrae & John, 1992; Peabody & Goldberg, 1989; D. Watson, 1989).

Although investigators sometimes have given the "Big Five" different names, they generally have agreed on five key characteristics as a useful way to organize and describe individual differences in personality. The following descriptions paired with their characteristics depict someone rated high in these traits:

1. *Neuroticism:* characterized by nervousness, emotional instability, moodiness, tension, irritability, and a tendency to worry.

2. *Extroversion:* characterized by sociability, expansiveness, liveliness, an orientation toward having fun, and an interest in interacting with other people.

3. *Openness:* characterized by imagination, intelligence, curiosity, and aesthetic sensitivity.

4. *Agreeableness:* characterized by a pleasant disposition, a charitable nature, empathy toward others, and friendliness.

5. *Conscientiousness:* characterized by reliability, hard work, punctuality, and a concern about doing things right.

A number of studies have found evidence in support of the "Big Five," in both children and adults, and in people from countries around the world, such as in Australia, China, Germany, Israel, Japan, and South Korea (Johnson & Ostendorf, 1993; McCrae, Costa, & Yik, 1996; Montag & Levin, 1994; Noller, Law, &

Comrey, 1987; Ostendorf & Angleitner, 1994; Piedmont & Chae, 1997; Wiggins, 1996; Wiggins & Trapnell, 1997). Moreover, this set of traits appears to stick around throughout the entire life span, even up to the mid-90s, the highest ages that have been studied (Costa & McCrae, 1988). Some of the traits appear to be associated with personal feelings of well-being, in particular, openness to experience, agreeableness, and extroversion (Magnus, Diener, Fujita, & Pavot, 1993; McCrae, 1996; McCrae & Costa, 1991); whereas others, such as neuroticism, are associated with poorer life adjustment (Ormel & Wohlfarth, 1991). High scores on extroversion, and especially the aspect of it related to positive emotions, predict positive mood in everyday life (Velting & Liebert, 1997).

Some studies have looked at the relation between Eysenck's theory and five-factor theory. One study found that people high in psychoticism (a trait in Eysenck's theory) tend to be low in agreeableness and that people low in psychoticism tend to be high in conscientiousness (Goldberg & Rosolack, 1994). Another study showed that low scores on neuroticism (in Eysenck's model) tend to be associated with high scores on extroversion (in both Eysenck's model and in the five-factor model—Draycott & Kline, 1995).

Not all trait theorists agree with the "Big Five" theory, of course. For example, Block (1995) and Hogan (1996) have argued that the evidence suggests more about the way people perceive the personality traits themselves than it does about actual people, a point that itself has been disputed (Costa

& McCrae, 1995). But the "Big Five" is probably the most widely accepted trait theory of those that are currently available.

How Consistent Are Traits?

Psychologist Walter Mischel (1968) has questioned trait theories, arguing that although traits might correlate highly from one paper-and-pencil measure to another, their correlations with any meaningful kind of behavior are low, usually around 0.30. It turns out, however, that behavior across situations is no more highly correlated than are scores on personality traits. Studies of the cross-situational consistency of behavior have found correlations across situations ranging from −0.11 to 0.47 (Funder, Kolar, & Blackman, 1995; Funder & Ozer, 1983; Sneed, McCrae, & Funder, 1998). Thus, these correlations center at about .20, if anything, a bit lower than is found with personality traits. The modest correlations for personality traits may therefore reflect not limitations in trait theory, but simply limitations in how consistent human beings are in their lives.

Mischel was not stating that higher correlations are not possible or that they are never obtained. For example, he noted that correlations involving intelligence as a predictor of behavior were often higher. Still, the correlations in the personality literature were so low that he questioned whether the idea of personality traits had any basis at all. Mischel (1968; Mischel & Peake, 1983) suggested instead that personality theorists should concentrate on the relations between situations and behavior, rather than on hypothetically stable traits, which he claimed had little effect on behavior. Today, Mischel's critique is seen as less relevant than it once was (Westen, 1995). For one thing, new trait theories have had somewhat more success than many earlier ones in predicting various kinds of behavior. For another thing, psychologists have recognized the importance of how personality interacts with situations.

The Biological Approach

In *Search of . . .* *What kind of role does biology play in determining personality?*

Trait theorists diverge regarding how strongly they emphasize the lifelong stability of traits. Some theorists hold that personality traits are largely inborn and stable across the life span, whereas others believe that personality traits develop and change somewhat, although the predisposition to develop particular traits may exist at birth. Robert Plomin (1986, 1989), a developmental psychologist, has been interested in observing how both heredity and environment influence the developmental changes in our personalities. In Plomin's view, just as our physiological growth is influenced by heredity within an environmental framework, so is the growth of our personalities and their associated traits. Table 15-5 summarizes the biological approach to personality.

TABLE 15–5

Biological Theories: A Critical Evaluation
Biological theories rate high in testability, which can result in more empirical research.

CRITERIA	BIOLOGICAL APPROACHES
Importance to and influence in psychology	Have generated some empirical research
Testability of its propositions	Testable; most theories make empirically testable predictions
Comprehensiveness	These theories tend to focus on specific aspects of personality and, hence, are generally not comprehensive
Parsimoniousness	These theories generally are quite parsimonious.
Usefulness to applications in (a) assessment and (b) therapeutic technique	(a) Biological theories have not yet generated viable personality tests; (b) many biological therapies are available, but they do not derive from biologically based theories of personality

Studying Human Temperament

Jerome Kagan, *Harvard University*

Human temperaments are combinations of psychological profiles, behaviors, thoughts, and emotions, along with their presumed biological foundation. Because many of the temperamental categories are the result of distinctive neurochemical profiles in the brain, there will be a large number of temperaments that scientists will discover in future work. My laboratory has been studying two frequently occurring temperaments: inhibited and uninhibited. The former category refers to children who are shy, timid, and avoidant when they encounter unfamiliar people, places, or situations. The child classified as uninhibited approaches unfamiliar people, objects, and events without timidity and often with a great deal of excitement and enthusiasm.

Research with animals reveals that the amygdala and its connections to other places in the brain make an important contribution to the tendency to avoid or approach unfamiliar events. The amygdala contains receptors for a large number of neurotransmitters that play a part in the display of fearful behavior. Because a low threshold of excitability in the amygdala would lead to vigorous motor discharge and irritability in infants, we observed a large group of 4-month-old infants while they watched interesting visual stimuli and listened to human voices speaking short sentences. About 20% of the infants showed a great deal of vigorous motor activity and fretting or crying to these stimuli. These infants are called high reactive. By contrast, about 40% of the infants showed the opposite profile, characterized by very little motor activity and no fretting or crying. This group of infants is called low reactive. It is assumed that the high reactive infants have an excitable amygdala and, therefore, should become inhibited children, while low reactive infants should become uninhibited children.

These children were observed again in the laboratory, at 14 months and 21 months of age, where they encountered a variety of unfamiliar people, objects, and procedures. The children who had been high reactive infants were much more fearful than those who had been low reactive.

When these children were evaluated again at 4 years and 7 years of age, we once again found that those who had been high reactive as infants were more likely to be quiet, subdued, and anxious compared with children who had been low reactive infants, who were now spontaneous, sociable, and minimally anxious.

We are evaluating these children as they pass their 10th birthdays. The two groups are displaying different physiological profiles that are related to their temperaments. Other scientists, such as Richard Davidson and Nathan Fox, have suggested that children and adults who are avoidant or fearful of novelty show greater activation over the right frontal area of the brain compared with the left under resting conditions. Because neural activity in the amygdala is transmitted to the frontal lobes, it is possible that greater activation in the right frontal area reflects greater activity in the right amygdala. The 10-year-old children who had been high reactive are showing greater EEG activation on the right frontal area, compared with the left.

Another physiological measure that differentiates the groups involves the brain stem auditory evoked potential. Structures in the brain stem respond to auditory stimuli with an electrical response called an evoked potential. One of these structures is the inferior colliculus, which is responsible for a component in the evoked potential occurring between 5 and 6 milliseconds after the onset of auditory energy. The inferior colliculus is primed by the amygdala and, therefore, children with an excitable amygdala should have a larger evoked potential from the inferior colliculus than those with a less excitable amygdala.

The results reveal that children who had been high reactives have significantly larger event-related evoked potentials from the colliculus than do the low reactives. It is important to note, however, that this is not always the case. A small number of children who had been high reactive and, in addition, were fearful in the second year and had a larger evoked potential from the inferior colliculus, were not particularly shy or timid when they appeared in the laboratory at 10 years of age. Further, some of these children told an interviewer that they were neither shy nor anxious, and their parents agreed with that description. This fact suggests the possibility of a dissociation between the biological processes that form part of the foundation of a temperamental category and the contemporary behavioral phenotype. Biology is not always destiny. Or, as the cliché goes, "You can't judge a book by its cover."

It is important to appreciate that the temperamental category of high reactive is more likely to constrain the development of an uninhibited temperament than to determine a shy, timid personality. Fewer than 20% of the children who had been high reactive infants were consistently fearful, shy, and inhibited from age 1 through 7 years. However, not one high reactive infant developed the complementary profile of consistently uninhibited behavior. Because 80% of the high reactive infants did not become consistently shy, timid, and avoidant, it is misleading to suggest that a high reactive temperament determines an inhibited profile. It is more accurate to conclude that being born with a high reactive temperament limits the likelihood that the child will become a consistently enthusiastic, sociable, fearless child.

 Find out more about this topic at *www.harcourtcollege.com/psych/ishm*

The Heritability of Personality and Temperament

Research (e.g., see Loehlin, 1992a, 1992b; Plomin, 1986, 1989, 1994, 1995) indicates that both nature and nurture contribute to the development of our distinctive personality traits, usually in interaction (Lee, 1993; Lyon & Gorner, 1995). Twin studies (see chapter 9) comparing identical twins raised apart, as well as identical versus fraternal twins, have shown that about half of the individual-differences variation in many personality traits, as well as in intelligence, is inherited (Bouchard, 1997; Bouchard, Lykken, McGue, Segal, & Telegen, 1990; Loehlin, 1992a, 1992b; Loehlin, Horn, & Willerman, 1997; N. L. Pedersen, Plomin, McClearn, & Friberg, 1988; Plomin, DeFries, McClearn, & Rutter, 1997; Tellegen, Lykken, Bouchard, Wilcox, & Rich, 1988; Waller, Kojetin, Bouchard, Lykken, & Tellegen, 1990). However, heritability may differ somewhat as a function of the particular trait, as well as of the population in which it is studied. Heritability also varies as a function of age, with effects increasing as people grow older (McGue, Bouchard, Iacono, & Lykken, 1993).

Curiously, though, even certain aspects of attitudes, such as religious attitudes, and of behavior, such as watching television in childhood and, in adulthood, such as divorce, show substantial heritability (McGue et al., 1993; Waller et al., 1990; Plomin et al., 1997). How could television-watching behavior be heritable, when historically, the overwhelming majority of societies did not have television? How could divorce be heritable, when to this day it is not even permitted in some societies? Clearly, it is not the behavior itself that is inherited, but rather the personal predispositions that can lead to that behavior. For example, people who divorce may have a greater predisposition to dissatisfaction or to conflict than do those who do not.

Work by Jerome Kagan (1994) and others has indeed suggested that temperament—our relatively stable and characteristic modes of responding to people and events in the environment (see chapter 11)—may be, in part, heritable. Babies show marked differences in temperament essentially immediately after birth. Although these differences may be caused in part by differences in intra-uterine environments, it seems likely that genetic differences also have a role.

Interestingly, the variation in traits that is environmental is mostly *within* rather than *between* families (Dunn & Plomin, 1990). In other words, more important than differences between families in the way children are treated are differences within families in, say, the way earlier- and later-born children are treated. We still have much to learn, however, as to just what these differences are.

Biological Correlates of Disposition and Temperament

Some researchers look for direct biological causes or correlates of personality dispositions. One group of studies links aspects of personality to genes. For example, hyperactivity in childhood has been linked to a gene that serves as a transporter for dopamine (Cook et al., 1995) and a dopamine receptor gene has been linked to the trait of novelty seeking (Ebstein et al., 1996). Another group of studies links aspects of personality to the brain (Davidson & Sutton, 1995). For example, behavioral inhibition—the tendency to experience strong negative affect or to feel inhibited in the face of threats—has been linked to greater left-hemisphere activation of the prefrontal cortex (Sutton & Davidson, 1997; see also Davidson, 1994).

Some researchers have attempted to integrate the biological approach with the trait approach. For example, one investigator has suggested that the "Big Five" theory is useful because it represents the results of evolutionary adaptations (Buss, 1994, 1995). According to this point of view, each of the five traits in the theory represents a different kind of adaptation. For example, extroversion represents the tendency to bond with others, agreeableness an individual's willingness to cooperate with others, (low) neuroticism facility in handling stress, openness to experience the tendency to be an innovative problem solver, and conscientiousness the tendency to be reliable. It should be noted, however, that this interpretation is speculative. Moreover, trait theories deal largely with individual differences, whereas evolutionary theory deals mostly with human commonalities. It is not clear how much the study of the one is likely to illuminate the study of the other.

Interactionist Perspectives

In Search of... *Can personality be the result of an interaction of environmental, biological, and other factors?*

An *interactionist perspective* emphasizes the interaction between characteristics of the person and characteristics of the situation. Interactionist perspectives are not limited to trait theories. Indeed, Rotter's, Bandura's, and other theorists' approaches can be viewed as broadly interactionist. In fact, even Mischel, who originally took the strictly cognitive-behavioral approach, now views personality from an interactionist perspective.

The basic idea is simple: The correlations among traits, or between traits and behaviors, depend on the kinds of situations the particular person encounters. For example, to relate extroversion to happiness, the interactionist would suggest that extroverts will be happy if they are in the center of constant interactions with other people but will be unhappy if stranded on a desert island by themselves. From the interactionist point of view, then, the correlation between personality traits and various kinds of behavior, or even between one trait and another, is mediated by situations. Thus, whereas a trait theorist might look only at the trait, and a behaviorist might look only at the situation, the interactionist would look at the interaction between the personality trait and the situation (Bowers, 1973; Endler & Magnusson, 1976).

One interactionist idea is Mark Snyder's (1979, 1983) construct of *self-monitoring*—the degree to which people monitor and change their behavior in response to situational demands—some people (high self-monitors) behave very differently, depending on with whom they are associating. Such a person might act in one way in the presence of a professor but in a totally different way when the professor is not there. Other people (low self-monitors) are more consistent in their behavior, acting much the same with everyone. If we wanted to look at consistency of behavior across situations, we would want to know about people's tendency to monitor themselves because low self-monitors tend to be much more consistent than high self-monitors.

Another concept that examines how people react to various kinds of situations is the construct of *sensation seeking*, which is a generalized preference for rela-

tively higher versus lower levels of sensory stimulation (M. Zuckerman, 1979, 1990, 1994, 1998). People who are high in sensation seeking tend to show four main attributions. First, they tend to seek thrills and adventures, such as skydiving and bungee jumping. Second, they tend to seek new experiences, such as traveling to exotic places or trying out unusual foods. Third, they tend to be uninhibited, and thus are more likely to show high levels of use of alcohol or seeking of sexual satisfaction. Finally, they tend to be highly susceptible to boredom, and so often are seeking to break out of what they perceive as the monotony of life. People with higher levels of sensation seeking are more at risk for substance abuse and problems in school and at work (Horvath & Zuckerman, 1993; Zuckerman, 1990). In general, people tend to have greater levels of success with partners who match them in terms of level of sensation seeking (Schroth, 1991). Sensation seeking is supposed to have both biological and environmentally socialized aspects.

In conclusion, interactionists build on the trait-based approach by asserting that the predictive validity of personality measures for behavior can be moderated by the kinds of situations in which the behavior takes place, as well as by possible differences in intraindividual consistency in a given trait. Table 15-6 summarizes the trait-based approach to personality, and Table 15-7 summarizes all of the major approaches we have covered in this chapter.

TABLE 15–6

Trait Theories: A Critical Evaluation
Because of their foundation in factor-analytical techniques, trait theories are highly testable and have spawned a great many empirical studies.

Criteria	Trait-Based Approaches
Importance to and influence in psychology	Have generated much empirical research, like the cognitive-behavioral approach
Testability of its propositions	Highly testable: Most theories make fairly precise predictions, especially compared with psychodynamic or humanistic theories
Comprehensiveness	Those theories focusing on personality as a whole are comprehensive; those focusing on specific traits clearly are not; trait theories say less than others do about the development of personality traits
Parsimoniousness	Depends on the theory: Eysenck's theory and the "Big Five" are extremely parsimonious; Cattell's theory is not
Usefulness to applications in (a) assessment and (b) therapeutic technique	(a) Many trait theories have generated personality tests, (b) but these theories have generated far fewer therapeutic techniques than have other theories; trait theories focus more on static characteristics and less on dynamic processes

TABLE 15–7

Five Major Personality Paradigms   *The major theoretical paradigms of personality are psychoanalytic, humanistic, cognitive-behavioral, trait, and biological theories.*

	PARADIGM				
	Psychoanalytic	*Humanistic*	*Cognitive-Behavioral*	*Trait*	*Biological*
Major Theorists	Freud, Adler, Jung, Horney	Rogers, Maslow	Rotter, Bandura, Mischel (also interactionists)	Eysenck	David Buss, Marvin Zuckerman
Basis for Personality	Conflicting sources of psychic energy	The distinctive human ability to act purposefully and to shape our own destiny by being future-oriented	The interactions between thought and the environment, which influence behavior	Stable sources of individual differences that characterize an individual, based on an interaction of nature and nurture	Evolutionary adaptations/biological attributes (e.g., hormonal influences)
Key Features of Personality Theory	(a) Developmental changes across the life span, with early childhood experiences profoundly influencing adult personality (b) *Deterministic* view of personality as being largely governed by forces over which the individual has little control (c) Importance of unconscious processes in shaping personality and behavior	*Nondeterministic* view of personality as being subject to the conscious control of the individual	(a) How individuals think about and give meaning to stimuli and events in their environment, as well as to their own behavior, shapes their personality and behavior (b) People need to feel that they are competent in controlling their environment	Some theorists hold that all people have the same set of traits, but that individuals differ in the degree to which they manifest that trait. Other theorists hold that each individual has a different set of traits	Biological theorists believe that personality is best studied by understanding the brain-based bases of individual differences. These theorists may study the brain or mechanisms of the transmission of traits from one generation to the other
Basis for Theory Development	Case studies of individuals seeking help for psychological problems	Humanistic philosophy, personal experiences, and clinical practice	Experimental findings, as well as the development and use of personality tests	Trait theorists often use correlational methods and factor analysis to analyze their data	Biological theorists use a wide variety of methods, including brain scans and studies of people's genetic profiles

Now that we know some different conceptions of what personality is, let's consider some different conceptions of how to measure personality.

Measuring Personality

How is personality measured?

Projective Tests

Many assessment techniques based on psychodynamic theory have emerged from the attempt to probe the unconscious. These techniques are termed **projective tests** because it is held that the individual's unconscious conflicts may be projected (thrown forward or propelled outward) into responses to the assessments, much as an image might be projected on a screen. Several projective tests (only some of which, of course, are described here) have proven useful in the assessment of constructs from psychodynamic theory. The most well-known test based on the psychodynamic approach is the *Rorschach Inkblot Test.*

The Rorschach Inkblot Test

In 1921, Hermann Rorschach devised the *Rorschach Inkblot Test,* which is still widely used. Originally, Rorschach viewed his test as potentially useful for diagnosing psychopathology, but today it is used much

more commonly for assessing personality across a broad spectrum of individuals. Those who use the test believe it provides a means for exploring patients' needs, conflicts, and desires (Erdberg, 1990; Exner, 1978, 1985; D. Rapaport, Gill, & Schafer, 1968).

The test consists of 10 symmetrical inkblot designs, each printed on a separate card. Five of the blots are in black, white, and shades of gray, and the other five are in color. An example of what a Rorschach card might look like is shown in Figure 15-5. Rorschach intentionally created the inkblots to be nonrepresentational. Although inkblots do not look like anything in particular, people see things such as other people, insects, bats and plants in them, and typically describe several things in a single design. The examiner carefully records how the client describes each blot. Psychologists who use the Rorschach believe that people see different things in the blots because they are projecting themselves into the designs. People's answers can reveal aspects of their psychological makeup.

Although many scoring systems have been devised for the Rorschach, the most widely used at present is John Exner's (1974, 1978, 1985; Viglione & Exner, 1983) "Comprehensive System," which takes into account four factors: the *location, determinants, content,* and *popularity* of the responses.

The Thematic Apperception Test

Another widely used psychodynamic assessment tool is the **Thematic Apperception Test (TAT)** (C. D. Morgan & Murray, 1935; H. A. Murray, 1943b). In

Figure 15–5

RORSCHACH INKBLOT TEST. *One way of scoring this projective test is to consider the following four factors: location, the place on the blot where a person sees the image; determinants, the examinee's use of three principal characteristics in responding to the blot—form (F), human movement (M), and color (C); content of the descriptions, such subject matter as humans, animals, geography, sex objects or acts, and so on; and popularity, whether the individual gives responses that are unusual or otherwise outside the mainstream of responses.*

administering the TAT, the examiner presents a series of ambiguous but representationally realistic pictures. People project their feelings into these pictures by suggesting what has led up to the scene in the picture, what is happening in the picture, and what will happen. *Apperception* refers to this projection of personal information into the stimulus that is perceived. Henry Murray (1943c) suggested that the examiner must consider six things when scoring the TAT: (1) the hero of the story; (2) the hero's motives, actions, and feelings; (3) the forces in the hero's environment that act on the hero; (4) the outcomes of the story; (5) the types of environmental stimuli that impinge on the people in the story; and (6) the interests and sentiments that appear in the story (see Figure 15-6).

The TAT also may be scored for different kinds of motivation (see chapter 12), such as achievement motivation (J. W. Atkinson, 1958; McClelland et al., 1953) and power motivation (Veroff, 1957; Winter, 1973). It can also be used to assess a person's use of the psychodynamically defined defense mechanisms (Stewart, 1982; Stewart & Healy, 1985; Stewart, Sokol, Healy, & Chester, 1986).

On what bases can we appraise the various instruments used to assess people in psychodynamic terms? Some clinicians (e.g., Spangler, 1992; Stewart, 1982;

Figure 15–6

THEMATIC APPERCEPTION TEST (TAT). *In the Thematic Apperception Test, illustrations of ambiguous situations, such as this one, are used as a means of prompting test takers to project their own personalities into the situation depicted.*

Stewart & Healy, 1989) take projective tests such as the Rorschach and the TAT very seriously. Others believe that these tests lead clinicians to faulty decisions (Mischel, 1977, 1986), such as the interpretation of test data based on what the clinicians would like to see in the test data, not on what is actually implicit in the test data (see e.g., L. J. Chapman & Chapman, 1969; Dawes, 1994). The subjective nature of scoring for projective tests has led many psychologists to depend on objective personality tests.

Objective Personality Tests

Objective personality tests are administered using a standardized (i.e., *objective*) and uniform procedure for scoring the assessment instruments. Two popular tests that fall into this category are the NEO Five-Factor Inventory and the revised *Minnesota Multiphasic Personality Inventory,* or *MMPI-2.*

The NEO Personality Inventory Revised (NEO-PI-R; Costa & McCrae, 1992c) is a successor to an earlier instrument, the NEO-PI (Costa & McCrae, 1985). The NEO-PI contains 240 items that measure the five factors of "Big-Five" theory (neuroticism, extroversion, openness, agreeableness, conscientiousness). It is a self-report inventory, requiring individuals to indicate whether certain statements characterize them.

The most widely used of the objective tests for assessing abnormal behavior is the Minnesota Multiphasic Personality Inventory (MMPI) (Hathaway & McKinley, 1943). This test is not strictly based on psychodynamic theory. In fact, psychologists with a variety of perspectives have contributed to its continuing development. The MMPI consists of 550 items covering a wide range of topics. Test takers answer each of the items, such as the following, as either *true* or *false* (Hathaway & McKinley, 1951, p. 28):

I often feel as if things are not real.	T	F
Someone has it in for me.	T	F

As shown in Figure 15-7, the MMPI contains 4 validity scales and 10 clinical scales. The *validity scales* are designed to assess the extent to which the clinician can have confidence in the results for the other scales. For example, the Lie Scale (L) measures the tendency of the test-takers to try to present themselves in a way that is excessively favorable. The *clinical scales* measure 10 different forms of abnormal behavior. For example, a person with a high score on Scale 6, Paranoia, tends to have suspicious or grandiose ideas.

The MMPI has several strengths. First, the test is objectively scored, which avoids the subjectivities of scoring and interpretation that characterize projective tests. Second, the scale has been widely used, so a

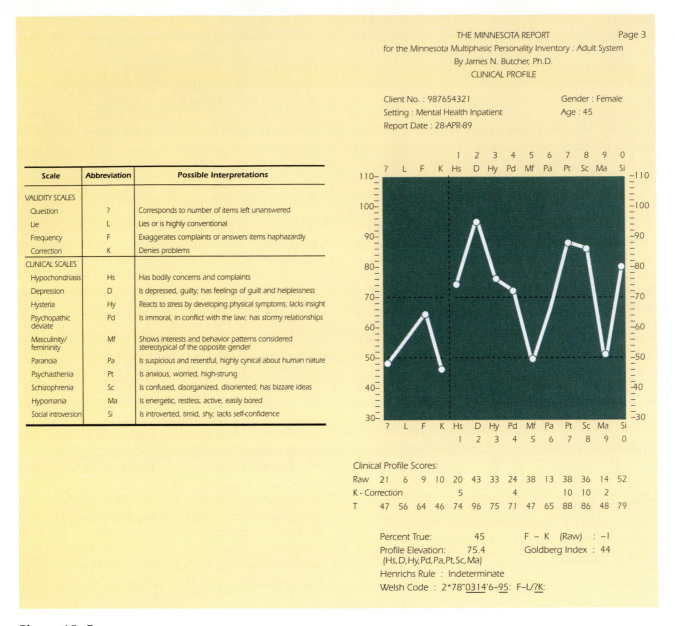

THE MINNESOTA REPORT Page 3
for the Minnesota Multiphasic Personality Inventory : Adult System
By James N. Butcher, Ph.D.
CLINICAL PROFILE

Client No. : 987654321   Gender : Female
Setting : Mental Health Inpatient   Age : 45
Report Date : 28-APR-89

Scale	Abbreviation	Possible Interpretations
VALIDITY SCALES		
Question	?	Corresponds to number of items left unanswered
Lie	L	Lies or is highly conventional
Frequency	F	Exaggerates complaints or answers items haphazardly
Correction	K	Denies problems
CLINICAL SCALES		
Hypochondriasis	Hs	Has bodily concerns and complaints
Depression	D	Is depressed, guilty; has feelings of guilt and helplessness
Hysteria	Hy	Reacts to stress by developing physical symptoms; lacks insight
Psychopathic deviate	Pd	Is immoral, in conflict with the law; has stormy relationships
Masculinity/femininity	Mf	Shows interests and behavior patterns considered stereotypical of the opposite gender
Paranoia	Pa	Is suspicious and resentful, highly cynical about human nature
Psychasthenia	Pt	Is anxious, worried, high-strung
Schizophrenia	Sc	Is confused, disorganized, disoriented; has bizzare ideas
Hypomania	Ma	Is energetic, restless, active, easily bored
Social introversion	Si	Is introverted, timid, shy; lacks self-confidence

Clinical Profile Scores:

	?	L	F	K	Hs	D	Hy	Pd	Mf	Pa	Pt	Sc	Ma	Si
Raw	21	6	9	10	20	43	33	24	38	13	38	36	14	52
K - Correction				5				4			10	10	2	
T		47	56	64	46	74	96	75	71	47	65	88	86	48	79

Percent True: 45   F – K (Raw) : –1
Profile Elevation: 75.4   Goldberg Index : 44
(Hs, D, Hy, Pd, Pa, Pt, Sc, Ma)
Henrichs Rule : Indeterminate
Welsh Code : 2*78"0314'6–95: F–L/?K:

Figure 15–7
THE MMPI PROFILE WITH AN INTERPRETATION. *This graph shows the profile of a client's responses to the MMPI. Each column indicates a separate dimension measured by the scale. The left column indicates measures of validity, such as whether the person is believed to be lying (L), and the right column indicates dimensions of personality.*

wealth of data is available for interpretation and comparison of scores and score profiles. The data suggest the scale is useful not only for understanding personality disorders (Kolotkin, Revis, Kirkley & Janick, 1987), but also for making predictions about health and welfare. For example, high scores on the depression scale are predictive of an individual's later contracting cancer (Persky, Kempthorne-Rawson, & Shekele, 1987). Third, it contains several validity scales, which help the clinician assess the extent to which the results are credible. Fourth, the scale covers a range of abnormal behavior.

The MMPI also has some problems. The primary drawback is that it is hard to know how to interpret responses to the MMPI. When test-takers are asked merely to respond "true" or "false" to a series of statements, they may find themselves interpreting the statements in ways that give a particular impression rather than answering the statements literally. Moreover, although the MMPI may adequately assess people's impressions of what they are like or of what they do with their time, these responses do not necessarily correspond to what they really like to do (see Helmes & Reddon, 1993). A new version of the MMPI (MMPI-2) was developed to deal with some of these concerns (Butcher, Dahlström, Graham, Tellegen, & Kaemmer, 1989).

The MMPI has been used extensively with ethnic minorities in the United States and elsewhere (Butcher & Pancheri, 1976). When clinicians use the MMPI with ethnic minorities in the United States, various adjustments are necessary (R. L. Greene, 1987). The main reason for this need is because ethnic and racial groups were not included—or were drastically underrepresented—in the original standardization sample used in developing the norms for the test (Butcher & Williams, 1992; J. R. Graham, 1990).

When the MMPI is used cross-culturally, other problems also must be considered. For instance, if the test is used in non-English-speaking countries, it must be carefully translated. Furthermore, people in other cultural contexts may not be as familiar with the very concept of testing devices, so they may either approach the task indifferently or misunderstand what is expected of them in order to perform the task (Lonner, 1990).

The personality theories and approaches in this chapter have focused on personality traits as they apply to the normal range of behavior. However, many psychologists interested in personality, especially those who treat patients, are interested particularly in the abnormal personality. We turn to this type of personality in the next chapter.

THINK ABOUT IT

1. Of the various theories of personality proposed in this chapter, which seems to you to be most reasonable—that is, which explains personality most effectively? Why?
2. In what ways do both humanistic and cognitive-behavioral theories view personality similarly to the psychodynamic perspective? How do these two theories differ from the psychodynamic perspective?
3. Picture yourself as a medically trained neurologist living in Victorian Vienna. Many of your patients are women and a number of them come to you to ask you to relieve their hysterical symptoms (i.e., physical complaints for which you can find no medical explanations). How might you help your patients and what theory might you propose as explaining the underlying cause of their ailments?
4. What are several ways in which you can ensure that your significant other or your child (hypothetical or real) feels sure of your unconditional positive regard?
5. What do you consider to be the essential personality characteristics, based on yourself and on the people you know?
6. In what ways might your self-schemas be limiting your flexibility? What can you do to increase your flexibility?

online *You can provide your own answers to these questions online at the Sternberg,* **In Search of the Human Mind** *Web site: http://www.harcourtcollege.com/psych/isbm*

Summary

1. *Personality* can be evaluated in terms of several criteria. Five such criteria are important in psychology: importance and influence, testability, comprehensiveness in accounting for psychological phenomena, parsimoniousness, and usefulness to applied fields.

Psychodynamic Approaches 480

2. Freud created the seminal psychodynamic theory of personality, which emphasizes dynamic, biologically oriented processes. The theory also emphasizes how early development influences a person's adaptability to environments.

3. Freud's theory underscores the role of the unconscious in the life of the mind. Freud described three components of the mind: the *id* (which is largely instinctual and impulsive and seeks immediate gratification of sexual and aggressive wishes), the *ego* (which is rational and seeks to satisfy the id in ways that adapt effectively to the real world), and the *superego* (which is irrational and seeks to avoid the punishment associated with internalized moral strictures). The id operates on the basis of the *pleasure principle*, the ego on the basis of the *reality principle*, and the superego on the basis of the *idealistic principle*.

4. Eight of Freud's *defense mechanisms* include denial, repression, projection, displacement, sublimation, reaction formation, rationalization, and regression, which Freud believed people use to protect themselves from unacceptable thoughts and impulses.

5. Freud's theory was based largely on his case studies of individual patients in his neurological/psychoanalytic practice. He also made extensive use of dream analysis, distinguishing between the *manifest content* and the *latent content* of dreams.

6. *Neo-Freudians*—such as Adler, Jung, and Horney—originally based their theories on Freud's but developed their own psychodynamic theories. Most neo-Freudian theories are less deterministic than Freud's and they give more consideration to continuing development of the personality after childhood, as well as to the broader social context within which the individual's personality operates. In particular, Alfred Adler contributed the notion of the *inferiority complex;* Carl Jung, the notion of there being various layers of the unconscious, such as the *personal unconscious* and the *collective unconscious;* and Karen Horney, the importance of *basic anxiety* in leading people to feelings of isolation.

7. More contemporary psychodynamic theories include *object-relations theories,* which consider how people conceptualize their relationships with other people.

8. Psychodynamic theories have been criticized largely in terms of their lack of empirical support.

The Humanistic Approach 490

9. *Humanistic* theory opposes the psychodynamic approach by emphasizing individual responsibility and an appreciation of human experience.

10. Rogers's *person-centered approach* to personality may be termed *self* theory. Rogers identified the self-concept (the aspects of the self that an individual perceives herself or himself to embody) and the *ideal self* (the aspects of the self that the person wishes to embody) and emphasized the importance of modifying one or the other to achieve as close a match as possible between the two.

11. Maslow emphasized the importance of self-actualization in the development of a healthy personality.

12. Humanistic theories have not been as influential as other personality theories, but their strength is in the emphasis they place on the value of each individual human being.

The Cognitive-Behavioral Approach 492

13. B. F. Skinner and other strict behaviorists have attempted to explain personality exclusively in terms of emitted behavior resulting from environmental contingencies, without reverting to mentalistic descriptions.

14. Rotter has used a cognitive-behavioral approach to explain personality. Rotter has emphasized the personality dimension of perceived *internal* versus *external* locus of control.

15. Bandura, also a cognitive-behavior theorist, has emphasized the interaction of how we think and how we act. Perceived self-efficacy is a key aspect of personality.

16. Cognitive-behavioral theories have spawned a wealth of empirical research and clinical assessment applications, partly due to the ease of testing such theories. Their parsimony varies from one theory to the next, and they are not known for great comprehensiveness.

The Trait-Based Approach 495

17. *Traits* are stable sources of individual differences that characterize a person.

18. Gordon Allport underscored the importance of conscious awareness of experience, in stark contrast to the Freudian emphasis on the role of the unconscious. Allport posited that some individuals have *cardinal traits*, which are so central that they explain almost all behavior of the individual. In addition, all people have both *central traits* (highly salient characteristics) and *secondary traits* (less salient characteristics). Their behavior is usually explained by their central traits, but in some situations their secondary traits also play a role. Other theorists have modified Allport's idiographic approach.

19. Hans Eysenck posited that personality comprises the traits of *extroversion, neuroticism,* and *psychoticism;* others have preferred the widely investigated *"Big Five"* (*neuroticism, extroversion, openness, agreeableness,* and *conscientiousness*) theory.

20. Walter Mischel has criticized nomothetic theories for inadequately considering situational factors affecting behavior. Recent advances in personality theory and measurement have tended to blunt the force of Mischel's critique.

The Biological Approach 497

21. Both nature and nurture influence personality traits and different theorists give differing emphasis to one or the other.

22. Some theorists link personality traits to brain functioning.

Interactionist Perspectives 499

23. Some contemporary theorists emphasize an *interactionist* perspective, which underscores the interaction between the individual's personality and the given situation. An example of such a notion is Mark Snyder's construct of *self-monitoring*, by which people are more or less consistent in their behavior according to their perceptions of what others would like to see and hear. Another example is Marvin Zuckerman's construct of *sensation seeking*.

Measuring Personality 502

24. *Projective tests*, which encourage individuals to project their unconscious characteristics and conflicts in response to open-ended questions, are a product of the psychodynamic tradition. These tests include the *Rorschach Inkblot Test* and the *Thematic Apperception Test (TAT)*.

25. Objective tests of personality are named for their objective methods of scoring, as opposed to the subjective ratings testers must make for projective tests. Two of the most widely used objective tests are the NEO-PI-R and the *MMPI-2*.

KEY TERMS

anal stage 484
archetypes 487
"Big Five" 495
cardinal trait 495
central traits 495
collective unconscious 487
complexes 487
defense mechanisms 483
determinism 481
ego 482
Electra conflict 484
external locus of control 493
extroversion 495
fixated 485
genital stage 485
humanism 490

id 482
idealistic principle 483
inferiority complex 486
internal locus of control 493
latency 484
latent content 482
manifest content 482
neo-Freudians 481
neuroticism 495
objective personality tests 503
object-relations theory 488
Oedipal conflict 484
oral stage 484
personal dispositions 495
personality 479
personal unconscious 486

person-centered approach 490
phallic stage 484
pleasure principle 482
primary-process thought 482
projective tests 502
psychoticism 495
reality principle 482
reciprocal determinism 493
secondary-process thought 482
secondary traits 495
self 487
superego 482
Thematic Apperception Test (TAT) 502
traits 495

■ THINK ABOUT IT SAMPLE RESPONSES

1. Of the various theories of personality proposed in this chapter, which seems to you to be most reasonable—that is, which explains personality most effectively? Why?

Everyone must answer this question for himself or herself, of course. Many trait theorists today accept five-factor theory because it seems to capture in a parsimonious fashion many of the major aspects of personality. Some researchers find other approaches to personality more useful. There is no one "right" approach to personality, and at present, there is no one theory of personality that dominates others the way Freud's theory once did.

2. In what ways do both humanistic and cognitive-behavioral theories view personality similarly to the psychodynamic perspective? How do these two theories differ from the psychodynamic perspective?

The humanistic and cognitive-behavioral perspectives share with the psychodynamic perspective an emphasis on how personality develops, in contrast, say, to trait theory. The humanistic and cognitive-behavioral approaches place much less emphasis on early experience than does the psychodynamic approach and they also are much less deterministic.

3. Picture yourself as a medically trained neurologist living in Victorian Vienna. Many of your patients are women and a number of them come to you to ask you to relieve their hysterical symptoms (i.e., physical complaints for which you can find no medical explanations). How might you help your patients and what theory might you propose as explaining the underlying cause of their ailments?

If you were a Freudian, you might try to discover some early traumatic but repressed experience that is responsible for the symptoms. You might use extensive psycho-analysis in order to try to uncover the experience and help the patient understand its significance for her life.

4. What are several ways in which you can ensure that your significant other or your child (hypothetical or real) feels sure of your unconditional positive regard?

One thing you can do is, when you criticize, to criticize actions rather than the person himself or herself. Another thing you can do is to emphasize, even when you criticize the person, the unconditional positive regard you have for the person.

5. What do you consider to be the essential personality characteristics, based on yourself and on the people you know?

Everyone must answer this question for himself or herself. Many people generate theories related to five-factor theory. The reason is that five-factor theory is based largely on analyses of people's implicit theories (conceptions) of personality.

6. In what ways might your self-schemas be limiting your flexibility? What can you do to increase your flexibility?

People all have certain ways of conceiving of themselves. They may conceive of themselves as introverts, for example, and then avoid people because they believe they are the kinds of people who avoid others. Or they may conceive of themselves as extroverts and be afraid to spend much time alone because they believe that they need others. People need constantly to be aware of the self-schemas that limit their flexibility.

Depression, like adolescence, springs at least in part from a feeling of not being quite connected, of being at some in-between stage, of being stuck in the middle, of not being able to claim an identity. Imagine Hamlet with no end, picture the Hanging Man as the only card in the tarot deck.

—Elizabeth Wurtzel, Prozac Nation

16

ABNORMAL PSYCHOLOGY

What Is Abnormal Behavior?

In Search of . . .
What makes behavior abnormal?

Abnormal behavior, like many of the psychological concepts described in this textbook, has been defined in many ways. To define abnormal behavior adequately, we need to consider several aspects of this concept, although not all of these aspects need to be present for behavior to be considered abnormal. **Abnormal behavior** is (1) statistically unusual—it deviates from statistically normal, average behavior; (2) nonadaptive—it hampers the individual's ability to function more effectively within a given context; (3) a potential threat to the self or others; (4) labeled as abnormal by the majority of persons in the given social context; and (5) characterized by some degree of perceptual or cognitive distortion. As with other definitions, it is possible to think of some exceptions in which a given abnormal behavior may not show all five aspects of the definition.

No one of these five aspects of abnormal behavior alone would suffice for a definition. For example, behavior most people would *not* consider abnormal may be statistically unusual, such as winning a Nobel Prize, saving a child from a burning building, or earning a graduate degree in nuclear engineering. Behavior that is not abnormal also may be nonadaptive, such as smoking cigarettes.

The behavior of people who are labeled as abnormal may be a challenge to other people and even disruptive of their lives. It is nevertheless important that we act with respect and compassion toward people with psychological disorders. As we come better to understand the causes of abnormal behavior, we also may better come to understand what we can do to help people with psychological disorders lead happy and productive lives that are minimally or not at all disruptive of others.

This chapter deals with problems in living that have reached the point where they are maladaptive for the individual's everyday functioning, and sometimes even survival. In some cases, though, a psychological state becomes maladaptive only when it reaches a certain degree over an extended period of time. For example, mild and temporary bouts with depression can signal to people that something is amiss in their lives and needs to be corrected. The symptoms characterizing these low periods, unpleasant though they may be, are not comparable in intensity or duration to the symptoms experienced by those with clinical depression. Thus, you should not be concerned if some of the symptoms described in this chapter seem familiar. In some cases, they become maladaptive only when they genuinely interfere with daily life.

As you might expect, whether a particular behavior is statistically unusual or maladaptive varies across cultural contexts. Behavior that is quite common and adaptive in one culture may be considered highly unusual and maladaptive in another. For example, many individuals in modern Western cultures who hear about the rituals of Yoruba or Eskimo *shamans* (religious leaders who use magical rituals to bring about therapeutic effects for individuals or for the cultural group as a whole) might deem the shamans' behavior abnormal. The Yorubas and the Eskimos, though, clearly distinguish between shamans, whose behavior is believed to be highly adaptive and appropriate, and people whose psychotic or delusional behavior is considered to be abnormal and neither adaptive nor appropriate (Davison & Neale, 1994; Matsumoto, 1994, 1996). People from other cultures might find some behavior common in American culture, such as the ritual of watching Monday Night Football, abnormal.

As these examples suggest, differences in context influence which kinds of behavior are labeled as abnormal, regardless of their statistical frequency or even their relative adaptiveness. For example, political dissidents are sometimes labeled as insane in countries governed by totalitarian rule. In Nazi-occupied lands, many heroic individuals who hid Jewish families were considered demented by those who became aware of the heroes' behavior. The labels used by psychiatrists are also sometimes subject to question. Once people's behavior has been labeled as indicative of mental illness and the people have been hospitalized for the illness, their subsequent normal behavior may be viewed largely in light of the identified mental illness (Rosenhan, 1973).

Distortion in perception and cognition may be appropriate and even normal under some circumstances. In fact, Shelley Taylor and Jonathon Brown (1988) argue that some degree of perceptual and cognitive distortion is good for our mental health. Assume that you and I are normal, mentally healthy, well-adjusted people. According to Taylor and Brown, one reason for our undisputed (at least until now) mental health is that we seem to distort our perceptions of reality through self-serving biases that inflate our positive evaluations of ourselves. We also tend to inflate our importance and our ability to control our actions and even our environments, and we tint our views of reality and of our future prospects to be far more optimistic than the objective reality would seem to justify. These self-serving distortions seem to enhance our sense of self-esteem, boost our ability to feel happy, and increase our ability to be involved in productive, creative work.

Historical Views of Abnormal Behavior

Today, we view the study of abnormal behavior as a part of psychology and psychiatry. It was not always so. In ancient times, people studied abnormal behavior under the heading of *demonology*. The reason was that they believed that a person exhibiting abnormal behavior was possessed by a supernatural force, often in the form of an evil demon. Treatment included exorcism, which might not leave the possessed individual completely whole, physically or mentally.

The first challenge to the demonological view was posed in the 5th century B.C., when Hippocrates proposed that illnesses had physiological causes and that people with mental illnesses suffered from some kind

In the past, people saw demons that caused psychological disorders as largely external, subject to extrications via exorcism. Today, we see demons as largely internal, requiring psychological treatment.

of pathology of the brain. Although Hippocrates was incorrect in his appraisal of the specific physiological causes (which he believed to be imbalances in the four humors—yellow bile, black bile, phlegm, and blood) of abnormal behavior, he changed history by recognizing the importance of scientific rather than supernatural explanations of abnormality.

Unfortunately, scientific ideas that are widely grasped at one time can recede from public consciousness when the political and intellectual climate opposes scientific explorations and embraces metaphysical ones. Demonic explanations of abnormal behavior have come back into favor periodically since the time of Hippocrates. For example, during the Middle Ages, many Europeans believed that people who acted oddly—some of whom were probably mentally ill—were witches. Suspected witches were subjected to horrendous tortures to rid them of evil spirits. In many instances they were killed. By the time of the Renaissance, mentally ill Europeans were hospitalized rather than executed, but their treatment was still far from humane or therapeutic, and many people continued to consider the mentally ill to be witches.

A famous example of assigning demonic causes for abnormal behavior happened in the 1690s, near Salem, Massachusetts, when eight girls started acting strangely—hallucinating and convulsing—but doctors could find nothing wrong with them. The girls claimed to have been bewitched, and the resulting witchcraft hysteria spread rapidly, resulting in the execution of 20 townsfolk (J. W. Davidson & Lytle, 1986). At the height of the witchcraft frenzy, a prominent Harvard-educated minister, Cotton Mather, published a work considered to offer scientific proof of the work of the devil in Salem. More reasoned explanations for the strange behavior of the accusers have since surfaced. Many scientists now believe that the girls' strange behavior may have been due in part to poisoning from the cereal-grain fungus *ergot*, which contains a precursor to lysergic acid diethylamide—LSD (Caporael, 1976). Eating food made from contaminated flour can cause hallucinations similar to those apparently experienced by the girls in Salem.

Modern Theoretical Perspectives

Once demonic interpretations of abnormal behaviors had fallen from favor, other interpretations were sought. Modern theoretical approaches to abnormal behavior closely parallel those on personality in general. These theoretical approaches have shaped research, with different kinds of research emanating from different theoretical perspectives. Because these approaches were considered in the previous chapter, they are only briefly reviewed here, as they apply specifically to the abnormal personality.

The Psychodynamic Approach

According to the psychodynamic perspective, abnormal behavior is largely a result of intrapsychic conflict. Recall that, according to Sigmund Freud, intrapsychic conflict is behind much of what we feel, think, say, and do. The ego is constantly battling the id and the superego. Because the id is governed by the pleasure principle, the ego by the reality principle, and the superego by the idealistic principle, the personality depends on which psychic force dominates. A person in whom the id dominates will be relatively unrestrained, uninhibited, and perhaps impulsive. A person in whom the ego is stronger is likely to be more restrained, more reality oriented, and more in touch with the rational thought of the self. A person dominated by the superego will be virtually immobilized by moral strictures against any behavior that might be deemed morally questionable in any way, even when such behavior is essential to the person's effective functioning in the social world (e.g., shaking hands with a person whose moral behavior is viewed as questionable). According to the psychodynamic approach, powerful intrapsychic conflict among these forces may lead to abnormal behavior. For example, a person with an overactive superego may feel compelled to wash his or her hands hundreds of times a day.

The Humanistic Approach

According to the humanistic approach to abnormal behavior, problems arise when people are overly sensitive to other people's judgments or when they are unable to accept their own nature. Often, the two problems are linked. People who have low self-regard, or who are overly critical of themselves, may not have received sufficient unconditional positive regard from parents or other significant persons. In other words, their parents or significant others may have shown positive regard toward them, but only conditionally on their acting in certain ways.

The Behavioral Approach

According to the learning perspective, abnormal behavior is the result of either classical or instrumental conditioning gone awry. A phobia, for example, might be the result of accidental pairings in which an object or set of objects that normally would not stimulate fear were paired, perhaps repeatedly, with punishment (see chapter 6). Recall, for example, Watson and Rayner's experiment in which Little Albert experienced conditioned fear as a result of his having been exposed to a neutral stimulus (a white rat) paired with a loud and frightening stimulus. According to this view, the phobic person acquires a set of responses that is involuntary and nonadaptive. Learning theorists would then use principles of learning to try to counteract the detrimental effect of the conditioning (see chapter 17).

The Cognitive Approach

According to the cognitive perspective, abnormal behavior is the result of distorted thinking. The distortions may be in the processes of thinking, the contents of thinking, or both. For example, depression tends to occur in persons who often minimize their own accomplishments or who believe that no matter what they do the result will be failure. People who irrationally believe that snakes of all kinds are capable of doing them a great deal of harm are likely to develop a phobia about snakes. In each case, the label is simply a description of a syndrome that involves distorted or erroneous thought. Therapy would be directed at changing the processes or the contents of the phobic person's thoughts.

The Biological Approach

The biological approach holds that abnormal behavior is caused by underlying biological abnormalities in the nervous system, particularly in the brain. Often, these physiological signs relate to problems in neuronal transmission (see chapter 3). For example, abnormal behavior may result from the shortage or surplus of a neurotransmitter or from problems in the passage or reuptake of the neurotransmitter. Those who maintain this point of view often treat psychological problems with drugs and with other types of biological interventions.

The Biopsychosocial Approach

The biopsychosocial approach emphasizes the interaction of biological with psychological and social factors. Most psychologists recognize that biological factors interact with the environment. A now popular theory of abnormal behavior is **diathesis-stress theory,** according to which people have differential genetic vulnerability to particular psychological disorders (indeed, *diathesis* means "predisposition"). The likelihood that people will develop these disorders increases as they are exposed to increasing amounts of stress. The disorder to which the person is vulnerable then develops if the person experiences so much stress that he or she is unable to cope with the environment. This theory has most successfully been applied to schizophrenia (Zubin, Magaziner, &

Steinhauer, 1983; Zubin & Spring, 1977), although it has been applied to other disorders as well. Because this approach combines other approaches, it will not be considered separately for each of the major disorders considered below.

Is there one right position with respect to the causes of abnormal behavior? Different approaches address different levels of a problem, with respect to both **etiology** (cause) and treatment of the problem. In the next section, we shall examine how clinicians of varying approaches classify and diagnose mental disorders with agreement.

Classifying and Diagnosing Abnormal Behavior

In *Search of . . .* *What are the criteria for classifying and diagnosing the various mental disorders?*

By the middle of the 20th century, clinicians began to reach some formalized consensus regarding psychological diagnoses. Part of diagnosis is classification of what the possible diagnoses are. In 1948, the World Health Organization published the *International Classification of Diseases (ICD)*, and 4 years later, the American Psychiatric Association published its *Diagnostic and Statistical Manual (DSM)*. The ICD-10 (1992) and DSM-IV (1994) are the current editions of these diagnostic manuals and are coordinated closely with each other. The DSM, like the ICD, is descriptive and *atheoretical*, which means that it is not based on any particular theoretical approach. It is based on clinical experience rather than any strong experimental or other rigorouly collected evidence. The DSM lists the symptoms necessary for making a diagnosis in each category, without seeking to assess the causes of the disorder. Thus, the classification system is based wholly on observable symptoms, making it usable by psychologists and psychiatrists of a wide variety of theoretical orientations (see Table 16-1).

The Five Axes of DSM-IV

Under DSM-IV, individuals are given a separate diagnosis on each of five *axes* (or dimensions). The major classifications of psychological disorders are covered by Axes I and II. The remaining three axes (III, IV, and V) are used to note other conditions that may be important to diagnosis and treatment, as well as severity of a presenting disorder.

Axis IV of the DSM addresses psychosocial stressors, such as poverty, trouble with the law, or family upheaval, that may contribute to mental disorder.

Axis I

Axis I addresses clinical syndromes and contains the major disorders, such as schizophrenia; anxiety disorders; disorders usually first diagnosed in infancy, childhood, or adolescence, which may also continue into adulthood; somatoform disorders; and sexual disorders. The first three of these are described in greater detail in the text. The latter two types of disorders, somatoform and sexual disorders, are not described in detail for lack of space. *Somatoform disorders* center on the person's relationship with her or his own body. They are relatively rare bodily symptoms or complaints of bodily symptoms for which no physiological basis can be found. In *sexual disorders*, the individual engages in sexual behavior that either distresses the individual or others or causes difficulty for the individual in other aspects of her or his life. The various sexual disorders can be mild or severe and of brief or long duration.

Axis I also includes various other disorders, such as *delirium* (a confused, disordered state of mind often

involving perceptual distortions), *amnesia* (memory loss), *dementia* (general deterioration in cognitive abilities, especially affecting memory and judgment, due to physiological changes in the brain—for example, Alzheimer's disease, stroke, or head trauma), and other cognitive disorders, which are not discussed in this chapter (see chapters 5, 7, 8, and 10). In addition, Axis I includes eating disorders (see chapters 12 and 18) and sleeping disorders (see chapter 5).

Axis II

Axis II addresses *personality disorders*, which are long-standing disturbances of personality that are disruptive of a person's functioning. The major personality disorders, such as avoidant and dependent personalities, are described in this chapter. The disorders in Axis II may coexist with those in Axis I, and people may receive diagnoses on both axes. For example, someone may have a phobia and at the same time have a narcissistic personality disorder.

Axis III

Axis III addresses physical disorders and conditions. Although such disorders can be of the brain, they can also be of any other kind as well, such as asthma, diabetes, heart problems, or physical handicaps. Physical disorders are included because they may interact with or precipitate psychological conditions. For example, fear of an asthmatic attack may provoke an anxiety attack.

Axis IV

Axis IV addresses the severity of psychosocial stressors, such as extreme poverty or conflict with the law. The diagnostician uses the information from the other axes and from the patient's (or client's) existing situation and history to determine the level of psychological stress that he or she is experiencing.

Axis V

Axis V represents a global assessment of the person's level of functioning. For example, a code of 90 would represent minimal symptoms and a code of 1 maximal danger, as in the case of someone who is extremely violent and is viewed as likely to cause harm to others.

An Example of a Multiaxial Diagnosis

Why do clinicians use five separate axes instead of just a summary diagnosis? The goal is to provide as comprehensive a portrait of abnormal functioning as

TABLE 16–1

Diagnostic and Statistical Manual (DSM-IV; Fourth Edition)   *This summary of the five axes of the DSM-IV system of classifying mental disorders illustrates the major considerations involved in diagnosing psychological disorders.*

AXIS I	AXIS II
Clinical Syndromes	*Personality Disorders*
■ Disorders usually first diagnosed in infancy, childhood, or adolescence ■ Delirium, dementia, amnesic and other cognitive disorders ■ Substance-related disorders ■ Schizophrenia and other psychotic disorders ■ Mood disorders ■ Anxiety disorders ■ Somatoform disorders ■ Factitious disorder ■ Dissociative disorders ■ Sexual and gender-identity disorders ■ Eating disorders ■ Sleep disorders ■ Impulse control disorders not elsewhere classified ■ Adjustment disorders	■ Antisocial ■ Avoidant ■ Borderline ■ Dependent ■ Histrionic ■ Narcissistic ■ Obsessive–compulsive ■ Paranoid ■ Schizoid ■ Schizotypal

AXIS III
General medical conditions

AXIS IV
Psychosocial and Environmental Problems
■ Problems with primary support group (childhood, adult, parent–child). Specify: _____ ■ Problems related to the social environment. Specify: _____ ■ Educational problem. Specify: _____ ■ Occupational problem. Specify: _____ ■ Housing problem. Specify: _____ ■ Economic problem. Specify: _____ ■ Problems with access to health care services. Specify: _____ ■ Problems related to interaction with the legal system/crime. Specify: _____ ■ Other psychosocial problem. Specify: _____

continued

possible. Consider the case of Thomas, a 9-year-old who is extremely anxious and is sweating when he enters the psychologist's office. He is diagnosed along Axis I as having an anxiety disorder. He is also observed as having an academic skill disorder: He is having difficulty in mathematics and is performing 3 years behind grade level, despite the fact that his overall intelligence is in the normal range. Along Axis II, Thomas is noted as having a paranoid personality disorder. By having separate diagnoses, the therapist is able to consider the possibility that the anxiety disorder, the personality disorder, and the problem in mathematics are related.

Along Axis III, it is noted that Thomas had mild head trauma from an automobile accident 7 years ago. It is unclear at this point whether the head injury is related to the diagnosed difficulties, but having this information might prove useful in diagnosis and treatment.

TABLE 16–1

Diagnostic and Statistical Manual (DSM-IV; Fourth Edition)   *(continued)*

AXIS V

Global Assessment of Functioning Scale (GAF Scale)

Consider psychological, social, and occupational functioning on a hypothetical continuum of mental health/illness. Do not include impairment in functioning due to physical (or environmental) limitations.

Code

100	Superior functioning in a wide range of activities
90	Absent or minimal symptoms, good functioning in all areas
80	No more than slight impairment in social, occupational, or school functioning
70	Some mild symptoms or some difficulty in social, occupational, or school functioning
60	Moderate symptoms or moderate difficulty in functioning
50	Serious symptoms or any serious impairment in functioning
40	Some impairment in reality testing or communication or major impairment in several areas
30	Behavior is considerably influenced by delusions or hallucinations, or serious impairment in communication, or judgment, or inability to function in almost all areas
20	Some danger of hurting self or others or occasionally fails to maintain minimal personal hygiene, or gross impairment in communication
10	Persistent danger of severely hurting self or others (e.g., recurrent violence), or persistent inability to maintain minimal personal hygiene
0	Inadequate information

On Axis IV, Thomas is coded as currently being subjected to severe stress in his life. His parents are going through a divorce and each wants the other parent to take custody. The parents have shown little interest in Thomas and their lack of interest is showing in the divorce proceedings as well. Finally, on Axis V, Thomas receives a rating of 55. He shows moderate symptoms, including anxiety and occasional panic attacks, especially when he needs to use mathematics or when he suspects others of plotting against him. His anxiety is interfering with his schoolwork and with his ability to form friendships and he is becoming something of a target for other children. Note that each axis gives us different but complementary information regarding the boy's psychological problems.

Evaluating DSM-IV

Any diagnostic system, including DSM-IV, is potentially problematic. First, because the system is atheoretical, it gives us no real insight into the causes of the abnormal behavior. A second problem is its subjectivity. Although the DSM-IV and the ICD-10 allow "clinicians to reach the same diagnosis in a remarkably high proportion of

Considering Culture in Clinical Assessment

James Butcher, *University of Minnesota*

I have been intrigued with the similarities and differences between people from different cultures since I was an 18-year-old soldier during the Korean War. I served in a military unit comprised of soldiers from several different countries (South Korea, Colombia, and the United States) with frequent contact with attached units from Turkey and Ethiopia. During this period, I became fascinated by the ways in which people from different cultural backgrounds viewed problems and reacted to situations that arose. When I became a psychologist after the war (even during graduate school) I began to conduct research on the possible influences of culture on personality development.

During my training in clinical psychology, I became involved in empirically based research using an objective personality assessment instrument—the Minnesota Multiphasic Personality Inventory (MMPI) (Hathaway & McKinley, 1940). This clinical personality measure, an objective self-report survey, is made up of a broad range of items that address symptoms, attitudes, beliefs, and so forth that focus on mental health adjustment. The items were simply written so that persons with a sixth-grade reading level could understand them. People taking the test are asked to respond in a "true–false" manner to the statements in the inventory, and their responses are grouped into scales that have been developed through empirical means to measure mental health problems such as depression, schizophrenia, antisocial behavior, and so forth. The items on the MMPI have been found to be effective at discriminating psychological problems in other countries.

In order to use a measuring instrument like the MMPI-2, the revised version of MMPI developed in the United States, with people in another culture, it is important to assure test equivalence—both linguistic and psychological. The items on the scale must be translated so as to assure that they are linguistically correct in each culture and that the content of the items address similar symptoms and problems. This latter requirement may involve changing a word in some items in the target language to obtain the same "psychological sense" for the particular symptoms being addressed. In some situations an entire item might need to be substituted for one that is more appropriate. For example, the item "I wish I were not so shy" measures depression in many Western countries. However, it does not work well in Japan where "shyness" is commonly held as a valued cultural characteristic. Consequently, another similar behavior thought to be more common among depressed people in Japan was substituted. Given these sorts of adjustments, interpretations of the MMPI have been found to generalize well to patients in different cultures (Butcher, Berah, Ellertsen, Miach, Lim, Nezami, Pancheri, Derksen, & Almagor, 1998).

Overall conclusions from this line of research are difficult to derive. However, one important conclusion is that the symptoms and structure of many mental disorders are universal—symptom clusters of the major mental disorders are found in all cultures studied. For example, people who are depressed tend to experience the world through "similar eyes"; people who have the serious mental disorder called schizophrenia (with hallucinations and delusions) tend to have similar personality patterns regardless of whether they live in Beijing, Calcutta, or Chicago.

This is not to say that culture is irrelevant in the development and expression of psychopathology. On the contrary, we found that though various major mental disorders produced similar general personality profiles on the MMPI, cultural differences were evident (Butcher & Pancheri, 1975). For example, Italian psychiatric patients differed from other groups in being more expressive about their symptoms.

The unique contribution of culture to the development of abnormal disorders can also be seen in what have been referred to as "culture-bound disorders." These are abnormal patterns that are only found in a particular culture. For example, the disorder referred to as "latah" is found in Malay-Indonesian culture and is characterized by an extreme, exaggerated, and involuntary response to startle. Another disorder, "running amok," involves an extreme reaction occurring in some young men in Malaysia in which the person (after sitting in a quiet state for some time) suddenly jumps up and engages in murderous aggression.

The study of psychopathology across cultures is an active research area, yet one that is still in its infancy.

References

Butcher, J. N., & Pancheri, P. (1976). *Handbook of cross-national MMPI research.* Minneapolis, MN: University of Minnesota Press.

Butcher, J. N. (1996). *International adaptations of the MMPI-2: Research and clinical applications.* Minneapolis, MN: University of Minnesota Press.

Butcher, J. N., Berah, E., Ellertsen, B., Miach, P., Lim, J., Nezami, E., Pancheri, P., Derksen, J., & Almagor, M. (1998). Objective personality assessment: Computer-based MMPI-2 interpretation in international clinical settings. In C. Belar (Ed). *Comprehensive clinical psychology: Sociocultural and individual differences* (pp. 277–312). New York: Elsevier.

Hathaway, S. R., & McKinley, J. C. (1940). A multiphasic personality schedule (Minnesota): I: Construction of the schedule. *Journal of Psychology, 10,* 249–254.

World Health Organization. (1993). *International Classification of Diseases* (CD-10). Geneva: WHO.

 Find out more about this topic at www.harcourtcollege.com/psych/ishm

cases" (Sartorius et al., 1993b, p. xvi), reliable agreement among clinicians certainly is not perfect. A third problem, common to any diagnostic system, is "mapping" behavior onto the descriptive categories. A diagnostician needs to translate or map observed behavior onto the symptoms expressed in DSM-IV and then to map those symptoms onto a diagnosis. DSM-IV is the product of outstanding efforts to achieve specificity and clarity with respect to the mapping of symptoms onto diagnoses, but practitioners still need to map the behavior they observe onto the symptoms in the DSM.

Classification in the General Population: Prevalence, Incidence, and Comorbidity

Because it is impossible to specify every possible type of behavior, there is always the potential for ambiguity in any classification system. For example, when do the quantity and character of antisocial acts lead a clinician to label an antisocial personality? DSM-IV gives guidelines, but ultimately the clinician's judgment is key in making the diagnosis. Despite the lack of a single perfect method for diagnosis, when various forms of assessment are used together, they can give clinicians a wide variety of information that the clinicians can integrate and interpret, based on their professional expertise. Some of the kinds of disorders diagnosed by clinicians are described in the following sections of this chapter. Psychologists are interested, among other things, in several key concepts.

First, psychologists are interested in prevalence. *Prevalence* is how often a given disorder occurs in the population. This statistic is important to know in order to assess the extent to which a given disorder is common.

Second, they are interested in *incidence*, which is the number of new cases of a disorder that begin during a certain period of time. This information is important to know when it is suspected that some factor newly introduced into the environment (e.g., war, a chemical agent, soaring crime) has increased or decreased the extent to which a disorder occurs in a population.

Third, psychologists are interested in *comorbidity*, which is the extent to which there is overlap in the presenting symptoms or conditions of different disorders. For example, anxiety and depression, both of which will be discussed, show a substantial degree of comorbidity. Sometimes people experience two disorders with overlapping symptoms. About half of people who qualify for a diagnosis qualify for a second diagnosis as well (Kessler, 1995). Finally, *concordance* is the degree to which various family members (often identical twins) show the same characteristic which for present purposes is a particular psychological disorder.

Concordance helps us understand the extent to which a disorder runs in families. As we shall see, the picture presented by prevalence, incidence, comorbidity, and concordance figures can provide information that is useful in considering the causes and treatment of mental disorders. The next sections look at several of the most common classifications of mental disorder.

Anxiety Disorders

In *Search of . . .* *When does fear become an anxiety disorder? What kinds of anxiety disorders do people experience?*

Anxiety is a general feeling of dread or apprehension. **Anxiety disorders** are characterized primarily by feelings of *anxiety* that are so intense or so frequent that they cause distress to or difficulty for an individual. Common symptoms are tension, nervousness, distress, or uncomfortable arousal—of varying levels of intensity, excessive worry and a concentration of thoughts on worrisome phenomena, and somatic symptoms associated with high arousal of the autonomic nervous system.

Types of Anxiety Disorders

DSM-IV divides anxiety disorders into five main categories: phobias, panic disorder, generalized anxiety disorder, stress disorders (posttraumatic stress disorder and acute stress disorder), and obsessive–compulsive disorder. These various forms of anxiety disorders differ in their population frequencies. Anxiety disorders usually first appear in the late teens or early 20s (Yonkers, Warshaw, Massion, & Keller, 1996). They are more common in people who are divorced, separated, or unemployed (Wittchen, Zhao, Kessler, & Eaton, 1994). Phobias and panic disorder are more common in women, and obsessive–compulsive disorder is more common in men (J. K. Myers et al., 1984). In particular, J. K. Myers and his colleagues found that, within the general population, 8% of women, but only 3.5% of men, are phobic. All five disorders share several common symptoms that characterize them as anxiety disorders. These disorders include the following.

Phobias

Phobias are characterized by exaggerated, persistent, irrational, and disruptive fears of a particular object, a particular event, or a particular setting, or fears of a general kind of object, event, or setting. A fear is classified as a phobia either when it is substantially greater than what seems justified or when it has no basis in reality. People with phobias are aware that their fears are irrational and would like to overcome them, but they have a great deal of difficulty doing so. About 6% of the population say that their phobias are at least somewhat disruptive of their lives (J. K. Myers et al., 1984). Phobias can be specific, social, or complex, as in agoraphobia.

Specific phobias are characterized by marked, persistent, irrational fears of objects, such as spiders, snakes, rats, high places, and darkness. About 11% of the population reports a specific phobia at some point in their lifetime (Robins & Regier, 1991).

Social phobias are characterized by extreme fear of being criticized by others, which leads to the avoidance of groups of people and the avoidance of any situations that may lead to the possibility of being criticized, of being embarrassed, or of being

Some of the common phobias include acrophobia (fear of heights), agoraphobia (fear of public settings and situations), and claustrophobia (fear of small, enclosed spaces). Unlike the fear shown in phobias, which is irrational or at least is unreasonably exaggerated, all of us experience fear in situations in which our lives, our safety, or our well-being are jeopardized, such as during the aftermath of a major disaster.

otherwise subject to ridicule, such as when meeting new people or speaking in public. Slightly under 3% of the population reports such a phobia at some point during their lifetime (Robins & Regier, 1991).

Agoraphobia is characterized by an intense fear of open spaces or of being in public places from which it might be difficult to escape in the event of a panic attack. Agoraphobia accounts for 60% of all phobias; the majority of agoraphobics are female, and the disorder usually begins to develop in adolescence or early adulthood. About 5% of the population reports experiencing agoraphobia at some point (Robins & Regier, 1991). Extreme agoraphobics are unable to leave their homes, although some will leave their home if accompanied by someone they trust (Hollander, Simeon, & Gorman, 1994). Consider the following case, in which a related anxiety disorder that usually accompanies agoraphobia, panic disorder (discussed below), has precipitated an agoraphobic response to leaving a person's house:

> Mrs. Reiss is a 48-year-old woman who recently was referred to a psychiatric clinic by her general practitioner because of her fears of going out alone. She has had these fears for 6 years, but they have intensified during the past 2 years. As a result, she has not gone out of her house unescorted. Her symptoms first appeared after an argument with her husband. She proceeded to go out to the mailbox and was then overwhelmed with feelings of dizziness and anxiety. She had to struggle back to the house. Her symptoms abated for a few years, but reappeared with greater intensity after she learned that her sister had ovarian cancer. Her symptoms often were exacerbated by frequent arguments with her husband. She began to feel increasingly apprehensive and fearful upon leaving the front door. If she did leave, she began getting panicky and dizzy after a few minutes on the street. Her heart pounded and she would start perspiring. At this point, she would turn back to her house to alleviate the anxiety. When accompanied by her husband or one of her children, she felt uneasy, but was usually able to enter crowded areas for short periods of time. (After Greenberg, Szmukler, & Tantam, 1986, pp. 148–149)

Panic Disorder

Panic disorder is characterized by brief, abrupt, and unprovoked but recurrent episodes during which a person experiences intense and uncontrollable anxiety. The person suddenly feels apprehensive or even terrified, experiencing difficulty breathing, heart palpitations, dizziness, sweating, and trembling. Persons with this disorder may fear either losing control of themselves or going crazy. They may fear they are having a heart attack. Panic attacks often lead to agoraphobia, as in the case above, because the individual is afraid that leaving his or her house will lead to a panic attack. Panic disorders afflict about 1.5% of the U.S. population (McGinn & Sanderson, 1995).

Generalized Anxiety Disorder

Generalized anxiety disorder is characterized by general, persistent, constant, and often debilitating high levels of anxiety; the anxiety is accompanied by physiological symptoms typical of a hyperactive autonomic nervous system, and that can last any length of time, from a month to years. The cause for such anxiety is difficult to identify. About 5% of people report experiencing this disorder at some point in their lives (Robins & Regier, 1991). A person with this disorder commonly experiences physical symptoms, as shown in the following example:

> A 67-year-old woman was referred to a psychiatric clinic for treatment of an anxiety state. At the interview she appeared to be tense; she sat upright and rigid in her chair and answered questions politely. She admitted that for most of her life she had been a great worrier. She said, "I'm inclined to look ahead and expect the worst to happen. I find it hard to relax, especially while lying in bed. My worst fears come to mind." In her more anxious moments, she has experienced palpitations of the heart, and often has had difficulty falling asleep due to her brooding thoughts. Although she has experienced a persistent and chronic anxiety, she has been unable to trace her anxiety to any particular problem. (After Fottrell, 1983, p. 149)

Stress Disorders

Stress disorders are characterized by an extreme reaction to a highly stressful event or situation, such as rape or combat. Stress disorders often are linked to adjustment disorders (see chapter 18). Variations include posttraumatic stress disorder and acute stress disorder.

In **posttraumatic stress disorder,** a person experiences a psychological reenactment of a past traumatic event, such as recurring nightmares or repeated wakeful resurfacing of painful memories of the event while consciously engaged in other activities. He or she may experience flashbacks that are so strong that the person believes he or she is reliving the event. The event may be participation in a war or exposure to a disaster, such as flood, fire, earthquake, tornado, or serious accident. Some victims are so plagued by these recurrences that they may become apathetic and detached.

In **acute stress disorder,** a brief mental disturbance arises in response to a traumatic event, lasting fewer than 4 weeks. Persons may experience a sense of detachment from the physical and social worlds, distortions or other changes in perceptions, and disturbances of memory.

Obsessive–Compulsive Disorder

Obsessive–compulsive anxiety disorder is characterized by unwanted, persistent thoughts and irresistible impulses to perform a ritual to relieve those thoughts. About 2.5% of the U.S. population is affected by this disorder.

An **obsession** is an unwanted, persistent thought, image, or impulse that cannot be suppressed. Obsessives are unhappy with the obsession and with being unable to keep it out of their minds. For example, one woman obsessively had thoughts that her children were being kidnapped.

A **compulsion** is an irresistible impulse to perform a relatively meaningless act repeatedly and in a stereotypical fashion. Compulsive persons are often aware of the absurdity of their behavior and yet are unable to stop it. Compulsive hand washers may wash their hands several hundred times a day. In addition to being time-consuming, compulsions can be costly to a person's well-being. Other common compulsions are counting things to make sure they are all there, checking the placement of objects, and checking that appliances are turned off. Consider the following case of a person with an obsessive–compulsive anxiety disorder:

> Ruth Langley was 30 years old when she sought help from a therapist after experiencing long-standing fears of contamination. She stated that she became intensely uncomfortable with any dirt on herself or in her immediate environment. After noticing any dirt, she felt compelled to carry out elaborate and time-consuming cleaning procedures. This usually involved thoroughly washing her hands and arms. Moreover, if she found dirt in her apartment, she was compelled to scrub her apartment methodically, in addition to showering in a very regimented manner. Her cleaning rituals have severely restricted her life. She now washes her hands at least four or five times an hour, showers six or seven times a day, and thoroughly cleans her apartment at least twice a day. (After G. R. Leon, 1974, pp. 129–130)

Symptoms of Anxiety Disorders

Anxiety disorders create mood, cognitive, somatic, and motor symptoms. *Mood symptoms* include feelings of tension, apprehension, and sometimes panic. Often, those who experience these symptoms do not know exactly why they feel the way they do. They may have a sense of foreboding or even of doom but not know why. Sometimes, anxious persons become depressed, if only because they do not see any way to alleviate the symptoms.

Cognitive symptoms may include a person's spending a lot of time trying to figure out why various mood symptoms are occurring. When unable to identify the causes, the individual may feel frustrated. Often, thinking about the problem actually worsens it, making it hard for the person to concentrate on other things.

Typical *somatic* (i.e., bodily) *symptoms* include sweating, hyperventilation, high pulse rate or blood pressure, and muscle tension. All of these symptoms are characteristic of a high level of autonomic nervous system arousal (see chapter 3). These primary

Edvard Munch (1863–1944) captured in his painting "The Cry" (sometimes translated as "The Scream") the terror often felt by persons with anxiety disorders.

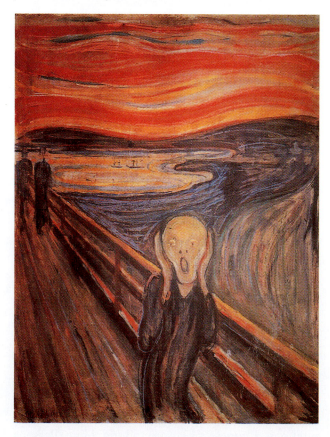

symptoms may lead to secondary ones. For example, hyperventilation may lead to feelings of lightheadedness or breathlessness. Muscular tension can lead to headaches or muscle spasms. High blood pressure can cause strokes or even cardiac problems. People who suffer anxiety disorders vary widely in the extent to which they experience somatic symptoms and also in the kinds of somatic symptoms they experience. Some people may express their anxiety in headaches, others in stomachaches, and so on.

Typical *motor symptoms* include restlessness, fidgeting, and various kinds of bodily movements that seem to have no particular purpose (such as pacing, finger tapping, tics, and the like). People are often unaware that they are doing these things. For example, they may pace around a room while others are seated, not realizing how others are perceiving their behavior.

When Does Anxiety Become a Disorder?

When is anxiety a disorder? What distinguishes the normal anxiety that everyone occasionally experiences from debilitating anxiety? Generally, three factors must be considered:

1. *Level of anxiety:* It is one thing to have a slight, occasional fear of elevators, especially overcrowded, rickety-looking ones; it is another thing to be unable to use any elevators at all even to get to a job at the top of a tall building.

2. *Source of anxiety:* It is normal to feel somewhat anxious before an important event, such as a final examination, a first date, or an important speech, but it is not normal constantly to feel that same level of anxiety when there are no precipitating stressful events (see Figure 16-1).

3. *Consequences* of the anxiety: If the anxiety leads to serious maladaptive results, such as the loss of a job because of an inability to leave home, the consequences will be sufficiently severe to lead a clinician to classify the person as having an anxiety disorder.

Cultural Influences

One factor causing anxiety may be the stress brought on by modern society. This culturally based factor is suggested by the higher rates of anxiety disorders occurring in technologically advanced societies (Carson & Butcher, 1992). The particular manifestations of symptoms and the grouping of symptoms into diagnosed disorders also varies across cultures, even modern ones. For example, in Japan, *taijin-kyofusho* (fear of humans) is a common manifestation of anxiety (Kirmayer, 1991). This condition mainly affects males,

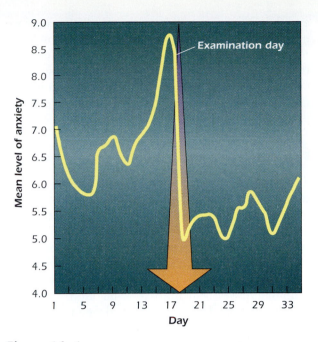

Figure 16-1
SITUATIONAL ANXIETY. *In normal individuals, levels of anxiety are situation related, such as in relation to a major examination. (After Bolger, 1990)*

and their symptoms include staring inappropriately, emitting offensive odors or flatulence, and blushing easily. The Japanese condition of *taijin-kyofusho* is significantly related to the Western condition of social phobia (Kleinknecht, Dinnel, Tanouye, & Lonner, 1993) and to the Latin American condition of *susto*, characterized by extreme anxiety, restlessness, and fear of black magic and the evil eye (*mal ojo*), although each complex of symptoms reflects characteristics and values of the respective cultures.

Quite a different anxiety disorder has been observed in Islamic societies, in which the obsessive–compulsive syndrome of *Waswas* has been linked to the Islamic ritual of cleansing and prayer. According to W. Pfeiffer (1982), the syndrome "relates to ritual cleanliness and to the validity of the ritual procedures, which are particularly important in Islam. Thus, the sufferer of *Waswas* finds it hard to terminate the ablutions because he is afraid that he is not yet clean enough to carry out his prayers in a lawful manner" (p. 213). Why do sufferers of *Waswas* or any other syndrome experience such debilitating symptoms?

Explanations of Anxiety Disorders

As you might expect, the different theoretical approaches lead to alternative explanations for the origin of anxiety disorders. Here as elsewhere, these explanations are not necessarily mutually exclusive and may even be wholly compatible, in that disorders may have multiple causes or causes that coexist at different levels of analysis. Researchers seldom find a single element that causes a psychological phenomenon. Instead, as each of several factors comes to light, each new insight contributes to an increasingly detailed picture of the phenomenon.

Psychodynamic Explanations

The emphasis in psychodynamic explanations is on internal conflict. Freud distinguished among three types of anxiety and believed that each requires a distinct explanation. The first of these three types, *objective anxiety*, derives from threats in the external world. Included here would be anxiety about realistic financial problems, failure in work or in personal relationships, serious illnesses, and the like. This kind of anxiety would correspond to *fear*, as it was defined in our previous distinction between anxiety and fear. Freud maintained that this kind of anxiety is not linked to abnormal behavior because the threat causing the anxiety is real.

The second and third types of anxiety stem from battles between the id and the superego. *Moral anxiety* derives from fear of punishment by the superego, which arises from conflict within the person over expression of impulses from the id. *After* the impulses of the id have won out and are expressed, the person experiences moral anxiety. For example, a poorly qualified, dull candidate who seeks to win an election might attempt to win by smearing an opponent. Later, this person might experience some degree of moral anxiety. By giving in to impulses to succeed at the other person's expense, the candidate creates internal conflict.

Neurotic anxiety derives from a person's fear that the superego (with the aid of the ego) will not be able to control the id and that the person may not be able to avoid engaging in unacceptable behavior. For example, a person may be afraid to go out on a date with a particularly attractive person for fear of acting in an unacceptable way, and thereby losing the potential for a relationship with the attractive person. Note that neurotic anxiety occurs *before* the impulses of the id have been expressed and while the superego is still restraining its expression.

Freud believed that phobias occur when anxiety is focused on one or more particular objects; these objects represent a conflict at a symbolic level. For example, a phobia of snakes might symbolically represent sexual conflict, whereby the snake serves as a phallic symbol to focus the anxiety. Freud believed that many anxieties originate in sexual conflicts. In contrast, many neo-Freudians believed that other important conflicts, such as those centering on feelings of inferi-

ority (Alfred Adler) or of attachment could also lead to anxiety in a number of instances. In any case, the evidence for psychodynamic interpretations of anxiety is relatively weak.

Learning Theory Explanations

The emphasis in learning-theory explanations is on conditioned fears and observational learning. Many learning (or behavioral) theorists view anxiety as being classically conditioned. According to this thinking, a fear response has been paired with a stimulus that was previously neutral. Thus, what was previously a neutral stimulus is now a fear-producing one (see chapter 6). For example, a person might have a neutral or slightly favorable attitude toward dogs. Then one day the person is seriously bitten by a dog. Through classical conditioning, the person becomes anxious in the presence of dogs or possibly even at the thought of dogs. As it turns out, about 44% of people with social phobia can identify a traumatic conditioning experience that they believe has contributed to their problem (Stemberger, Turner, Beidel, & Calhoun, 1995).

According to classical learning theory, the unpleasant experience would have to happen to the individual experiencing the anxiety for conditioning to occur. According to contemporary forms of learning theory, however, it is possible to experience *vicarious conditioning* (Bandura & Rosenthal, 1966). Simply through observational learning (see chapters 11 and 15), we can be conditioned to experience anxiety. For example, most of us, thankfully, have not contracted acquired immune deficiency syndrome (AIDS). By observing the effects of AIDS, however—on television or through friends or family—we could become anxious about AIDS and even phobic about the possibility of contracting AIDS, solely through having been vicariously conditioned.

Operant conditioning can also play a part in the development of anxiety disorders. Consider, for example, compulsive behavior. Suppose that you have an irrational fear of bacteria. Washing your hands makes you feel safer, at least temporarily. You are thereby reinforced for the hand-washing behavior, but soon the fear returns. You have learned that hand washing helps alleviate anxiety, so you wash your hands again. The anxiety is alleviated again, but not for long. In this way, you have learned to engage in the compulsive behavior because it temporarily alleviates anxiety, as a result of operant conditioning.

Cognitive Explanations

Cognitive explanations emphasize automatic self-defeating thoughts. Suppose a woman wants to ask a man out to lunch, but the thought of actually picking up the phone and calling him makes her sweat with anxiety. She starts thinking, "I know I'm going to fail. I know he's going to put me down. I'd really like to invite him, but I just can't stand being rejected again." These kinds of thoughts produce anxiety, causing people to be unable to do some of the things that they would like to do (Beck, Emery, & Greenberg, 1985). These thoughts are likely to become *automatic thoughts*—thought patterns that people seem to fall into without being aware of them and that they experience without effort (Beck, 1976). Often, such thoughts are the beginning of a self-defeating cycle. Someone who expects rejection may feel spurned when receiving neutral cues or may find seeds of repudiation even in positive things that another person says. Thus, anxiety disorders tend to be self-propagating. In general, the thoughts are not of what is happening at the moment, but of what is expected to happen (Barlow, 1988).

Humanistic Explanations

One humanistic explanation for anxiety disorders is that the person experiences a discrepancy between the perceived self and the idealized self, causing feelings of failure. These feelings of failure cause the anxiety. Anxious people tend to indicate more of a discrepancy than do confident people between the persons they believe they are and the persons they believe they should be (C. R. Rogers, 1961b). Anxious people also show lower social skills than do nonanxious people (Fischetti, Curran, & Wessberg, 1977), which may further reduce their confidence in themselves.

Biological Explanations

Several biological explanations for anxiety disorders have been proposed. One explanation suggests that inhibitory neurons that serve to reduce neurological activity may function improperly in people with anxiety disorders. For example, insufficient levels of the neurotransmitter GABA (gamma-aminobutyric acid) lower activity in the inhibitory neurons and thereby increase brain activity; the result is a high level of arousal, which can be experienced as anxiety (Lloyd, Fletcher, & Minchin, 1992). Drugs that decrease GABA activity lead to increasing anxiety (Insell, 1986). Various tranquilizers, such as diazepam (Valium), increase GABA activity and thereby decrease anxiety (Bertilsson, 1978; Enna & DeFranz, 1980; Haefely, 1977). There also appears to be a link between a gene that controls the brain's ability to use serotonin and anxiety-related behavior (Lesch et al., 1996; Stein & Uhde, 1995). Research suggests that anxiety disorders often run in families (Andreasen & Black, 1991).

Mood Disorders

In **Search of . . .** *What are mood disorders? How do they differ from the highs and lows we all experience?*

Mood disorders are psychological disorders involving periods of extremely sad, low-energy moods or swings between extremely high and extremely low moods. They involve disruptions of physical, cognitive, and social processes. The two major mood disorders are major depression (sometimes called unipolar depression) and bipolar disorder. Each of these disorders impairs function; they are more than transitory high or low moods.

Depression is relatively common. Almost 23% of men and 36% of women have reported experiencing a period of at least two weeks when they have felt very sad and blue. However, for only 4% of the men and 9% of the women would the symptoms be classified as severe enough for a diagnosis of clinical depression (Robins & Regier, 1991). Thus, depression is more common in women than in men (Shumaker & Hill, 1991) and particularly in married women (Paykel, 1991).

Depression is more likely to occur in persons of lower socioeconomic status (SES) than in those of higher SES (Hirschfield & Cross, 1982). The higher frequencies in women and in persons of lower SES suggest that situational factors may be involved. For example, Susan Nolen-Hoeksema (1990; Nolen-Hoeksema & Girgus, 1994) has found that men tend to deal with depression by trying to distract themselves, but women are more likely to ruminate on the causes and effects of their depression, a strategy that may leave them even more depressed. Depression is further associated with lack of social support or failing social relationships (Harris, 1992; Henderson, 1992).

Bipolar disorder, on the other hand, afflicts men and women of all socioeconomic classes equally (Krauthammer & Klerman, 1979; MacKinnon, Jamison, & De Paulo, 1997; Robins et al., 1984). Bipolar disorder is also much rarer than unipolar depression (occurring in only 0.75% to 1% of the population), and it appears to run in families (suggesting possible genetic and physiological aspects of the illness). Some people initially diagnosed with depression are later realized to suffer from bipolar disorder (Bowden, 1993; Winokur, Coryell, Keller, Endicott, & Leon, 1995).

Major Depression

Persons with **major depression** have persistent feelings for at least six weeks of sadness, discouragement, and hopelessness. It may seem to them that nothing is right with their lives. Famous people who have been reported to suffer from depression are William Styron, the author; Mike Wallace, the newsman; Winston Churchill, the statesman; and Abraham Lincoln, the 16th president of the United States. Typical cognitive symptoms of depression are low self-esteem, loss of motivation, and pessimism. Depressed people often generalize, so that a single failure, or an event that they interpret as indicating a failure, is assumed to foreshadow worse things. They often have a very low level of energy and may slow down their body movements and even speech. Typical somatic symptoms are difficulty in sleeping and in waking up, so that the person may have trouble falling asleep or may sleep most of the time.

> The reason I hadn't washed my clothes or my hair was because it seemed so silly.
>
> I saw the days of the year stretching ahead like a series of bright, white boxes, and separating one box from another was sleep, like a black shade. Only for me, the long perspective of shades that set off one box from the next had suddenly snapped up, and I could see day after day after day glaring ahead of me like a white, broad, infinitely desolate avenue.
>
> It seemed silly to wash one day when I would only have to wash again the next.
>
> It made me tired just to think of it.
>
> I wanted to do everything once and for all and be through with it. (Sylvia Plath, *The Bell Jar*)

There are various types and origins of depression (see Table 16-2). For example, clinicians distinguish between external, environmental variables and internal, physiological variables. Another important distinction is whether the depression is the principal

disorder or a symptom of another clinical disorder. It is essential to determine the cause of the depression in order to treat it (see chapter 17). Some kinds of depression are linked to phases of life, as shown in Table 16-2.

Recent research suggests that a cause of depression in many cases is linked to lack of exposure to sunlight. In particular, **seasonal affective disorder (SAD)** is a form of depression that typically occurs during the winter months or the months surrounding them. The fact that this form of depression is more common in the extreme north—where the winter sun may shine for just a few hours a day if at all—has suggested a link to available ambient light. Indeed, light therapy has been used to treat this form of depression (Lewy, Sack, Miller, & Hober, 1987). SAD appears to be linked to irregularities in the body's production of melatonin, which is secreted by the pineal gland and is implicated in the sleeping–waking cycle.

A large cross-national study involving more than 40,000 participants in Western and non-Western countries concluded that major depression occurs across a broad range of cultures and that more recent generations are at an increased risk of depression (Cross-National Collaborative Group, 1992). The findings of that study take on added significance because the scientists who conducted it claim that the study is the first one to use standard diagnostic criteria across all societies.

Bipolar Disorder

Bipolar disorder, or manic-depressive disorder, is a mood disorder in which the individual alternates between periods of depression and mania. Two well-known people who have suffered from bipolar disorder are actor Patty Duke and Kay Jamison, a psychiatrist at James Hopkins University who has written about the disorder. We have seen the symptoms of depression. When a person suffering from bipolar disorder swings to the manic phase, the most prominent symptom of **mania** is a mood in which a person feels highly energetic and extremely joyful. Manic persons may believe there is no limit to their possible accomplishments and may act accordingly (for example, one individual tried to climb Mount McKinley as an impromptu outing, equipped with only a cotton jacket and a pocket knife). Manic individuals often have trouble focusing their attention and may move from one activity to another in rapid succession. Occasionally, the manic person will suffer from other **delusions**—false beliefs that contradict known facts. Delusions may be the result of distorted thought processes. Manic individuals may spend money wildly, attempt to start numerous projects they cannot finish, or become hypersexual. Consequently,

Axis IV of the DSM addresses psychosocial stressors, such as poverty, trouble with the law, or family upheaval, that may contribute to mental disorder.

TABLE 16–2

Origins of Depression
In diagnosing depression, clinicians often classify depression according to its origins.

Type	Description	Cause
Exogenous depression	A reaction to external (environmental) factors	Conflict with a spouse or lover, stress on the job, failure to achieve a goal, or similar types of events
Endogenous depression	Reaction to internal (physiological) factors, such as imbalance of particular neurotransmitters	Chronic depression, without regard to what is going on around the person; may stem from a family history of depression
Primary depression	Depression is the main medical problem	Someone who is depressed over the breakup of a relationship and who feels unable to get out of bed as a result
Secondary depression	Another disorder has caused the depression	Someone who is injured and is therefore bedridden and then becomes depressed because of the physical limitations
Involutional depression	Associated with advanced age	Consequences associated with age, such as the realization that it is too late in life to achieve goals that were set at an earlier stage
Postpartum depression	Occurs after childbirth and can last anywhere from a few weeks to a year	Stress is usually the primary cause; other causes might be hormonal changes, changes in neurotransmitters, and fatigue; external locus of control, anxiety, and hostility; and lack of spousal and other social support
Seasonal affective disorder (SAD)	Typically occurs during winter months	A lack of available ambient light; irregularities in melatonin production

they may end up bankrupt, fired from their jobs, or divorced by their mates. On the other hand, persons who are experiencing mania have a greatly reduced need for sleep and tend to be immune from the fatigue that would hit most people after very strenuous periods of activity (see Figure 16-2).

Explanations of Mood Disorders

For most of the explanations in this section, we consider theories of major depression, not of bipolar depression. Research has shown that major and bipolar disorders are different disorders, with different suggested treatments (as chapter 17 shows). Bipolar disorder is definitely not unipolar depression with a dash of mania added; its origins appear to be primarily biological. In contrast, major depression has multiple possible explanations.

Psychodynamic Explanations

Psychodynamic explanations emphasize feelings of loss. The psychodynamic explanation of depression begins with an analogy that Freud observed between depression and mourning (S. Freud, 1917/1957). He noticed that in both cases there is a sense of strong and possibly overwhelming sorrow, and that people in mourning frequently become depressed. He suggested that when we lose an object of our love (any termination of a relationship, including by death), we often have ambivalent feelings about the person we have lost. We may still love the person, yet feel angry that the person has left us. We may even realize that it is irrational to feel angry toward someone who died involuntarily. According to Freud, when we lose an object of our love, we incorporate aspects of that person in a fruitless effort to regain at least parts of the person. At

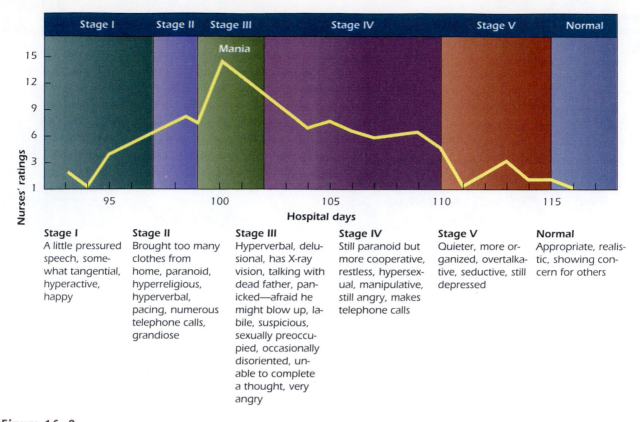

Stage I	Stage II	Stage III	Stage IV	Stage V	Normal
Stage I A little pressured speech, somewhat tangential, hyperactive, happy	**Stage II** Brought too many clothes from home, paranoid, hyperreligious, hyperverbal, pacing, numerous telephone calls, grandiose	**Stage III** Hyperverbal, delusional, has X-ray vision, talking with dead father, panicked—afraid he might blow up, labile, suspicious, sexually preoccupied, occasionally disoriented, unable to complete a thought, very angry	**Stage IV** Still paranoid but more cooperative, restless, hypersexual, manipulative, still angry, makes telephone calls	**Stage V** Quieter, more organized, overtalkative, seductive, still depressed	**Normal** Appropriate, realistic, showing concern for others

Figure 16–2
STAGES OF A MANIC EPISODE. *Case-study research often provides depth of insight not easily available through laboratory studies, as shown in this longitudinal analysis of nurses' ratings of manic behavior in a patient hospitalized for mania. (After Carlson & Goodwin, 1973)*

first glance, it seems as though incorporating aspects of that person should minimize our sense of loss and that this minimization should also reduce depressive symptoms, but Freud saw a downside to incorporation: If we are angry toward the lost person, and we have incorporated aspects of that person, then we may become angry with ourselves.

Freud suggested that this anger turned inward is the source of depression and that the precipitating event is a process of loss. As is typical of Freudian conceptualization, the emphasis is on losses that occurred during early childhood, although Freud acknowledged that losses at any time can cause depression.

Learning Theory Explanations

Learning theory explanations emphasize lack of rewards. The basic learning theory explanation of depression states that depressed people receive fewer rewards than do people who are not depressed (Ferster, 1973; A. A. Lazarus, 1968; Lewinsohn, 1974). In other words, fewer things make a depressed person happy and more things make a depressed person unhappy.

The lower level of energy and activity seen in depressed people is consistent with this explanation. Receiving little reinforcement, the depressed person has little incentive to act. A vicious cycle then ensues, whereby the individual withdraws from the kinds of activities that would provide rewards, further increasing the individual's level of depression.

Depression may be self-sustaining, especially if other people actually give the depressed person fewer rewards. One study found that when nondepressed people were interacting with depressed people, the nondepressed people smiled less, were generally less pleasant, and made more negative comments than they did when interacting with other nondepressed people (Gotlib & Robinson, 1982). Other investigations have also shown that we are less pleasant toward depressed persons than toward people who are not depressed, perhaps because the low mood of the depressed person is contagious and leaves the interacting partner at least temporarily drained as well (Coyne, 1976a; Gotlib & Robinson, 1982).

Evidence also shows that when depressed people actually receive the same amount of reward or punishment as those who are not depressed, they think that they are receiving fewer rewards and more punishments (R. E. Nelson & Craighead, 1977). Their perception of the treatment they receive is worse than the treatment they actually receive. Depressed people also appear to give themselves fewer rewards and more punishments for their own behavior (Rehm, 1977). This finding holds true whether we look at the general population or at people who are hospitalized for depression (Lobitz & Post, 1979; R. E. Nelson & Craighead, 1977, 1981).

Recall that women are more likely to be depressed than men. Although we cannot yet rule out the possibility that the higher frequency of depression in women may be due in part to hormonal differences, a more intriguing although speculative possibility is that learned helplessness (see chapter 6) may contribute to the higher rate in women (Matlin, 1993; Seligman, 1974; Strickland, 1992). According to this view, women's social roles are more likely to lead them to feel depressed. Women traditionally have been forced into roles in which they have less control over the outcomes that affect them than do men. This lack of control may cause them to depend financially and emotionally on others, usually men. This dependence may lead to a form of learned helplessness. Both frustration and helplessness are linked to depression.

Cognitive Explanations

Cognitive explanations emphasize errors in thinking and misattributions. Inappropriate attributions and inferences directly contribute to depression, according to Aaron Beck (1967, 1985, 1991, 1997), whose theory is probably the most prominent of the contemporary cognitive theories of depression. Beck suggests that depressed people are particularly susceptible to errors in thinking. In particular, depressed people are susceptible to one or more of five logical errors that lead them to see things in an unfavorable manner:

1. *Arbitrary inference* refers to drawing a conclusion even though there is little or no evidence to support it.
2. *Selective abstraction* involves focusing on an insignificant detail of a situation while ignoring the more important features.
3. *Overgeneralization* is drawing global conclusions about ability on the basis of a single fact or episode.
4. *Magnification and minimization* refer to committing gross errors of evaluation by magnifying small, unfavorable events, yet minimizing important, large, favorable events.
5. *Personalization* involves taking personal responsibility for events that are situational.

A related model, at least of a type of depression, is a model of *hopelessness depression* (Abramson, Metalsky, & Alloy, 1989). According to this model, a series of negative events in a person's life can lead that person to feel hopeless about the future. Feelings of hopelessness spark depression, which in turn spark both further negative events and further feelings of hopelessness. The cycle then continues.

Humanistic Explanations

Humanistic theorists have been less specific about depression than have others, but one significant theory was proposed by Viktor Frankl (1959). Frankl drew largely on his own experience, particularly the time he spent in Nazi concentration camps during World War II. He observed that of those individuals who were not put to death, the greatest difference between those who survived mentally intact and those who did not seemed to be in the ability to find meaning in their suffering and to relate the experience to their spiritual lives. Generalizing from this experience, Frankl suggested that depression results from a lack of purpose in living. In this view, people who are depressed will be helped if they can find meaning in their lives.

Biological Explanations

Biological explanations of depression suggest that abnormally low levels of neurotransmitters may be linked to depression. One theory focuses on norepinephrine, the other on serotonin imbalance. Both theories stem from ways in which particular drugs act on depression (see chapter 17).

Certain monoamine neurotransmitters have been suggested as playing a role in depression. These transmitters incude norepinephrine, dopamine, and serotonin. GABA and acetylcholine also may play a role. In particular, research suggests that people with depression or bipolar disorder may have a lack of receptors, or receptors lacking in sensitivity, to serotonin and norepinephrine, especially in the hypothalamus (Malone & Mann, 1993; McBride, Brown, Demeo, & Keilp, 1994).

Feelings of sadness and helplessness have been found to be associated with changes in the flow of blood in the cerebrum and in particular in the frontal-temporal areas of the cortex (Cummings, 1993; George, Ring, & Costa, 1991). It is important to remember, however, that such associations do not reveal causal direction. The changes may result from, rather than cause, clinical depression.

Recent data suggest that the causes of bipolar depression may be primarily biological. The causes of major depression may also be partly biological. Genetic factors seem to influence the development of both kinds of mood disorders (Rieder, Kaufmann, & Knowles, 1994), although bipolar disorder seems to be more strongly genetically based (Gershon & Nurnberger, 1995). For example, the norepinephrine theory of bipolar disorder postulates that the manic phase is caused by an excess of norepinephrine (Bunney, Goodwin, & Murphy, 1972; Schildkraut, 1965). Urinary levels of norepinephrine decrease during the depressive phase (Bunney, Murphy, Goodwin, & Borge, 1970). One supportive finding for considering bipolar disorder to be biologically based is that the most effective therapy for bipolar disorder so far is biochemical—namely, the administration of lithium. As mentioned earlier, the biological explanation of bipolar disorder is further supported by genetic studies showing substantially higher genetic transmission of bipolar than of major depressive disorders.

Suicide

Personality disorders and most of the other psychological disorders described in this chapter are rarely life threatening. Depression can be, however, and severe depression often precedes suicide, or at least suicide attempts, as shown in the following example:

> Mr. Wrigley was referred by his general practitioner for an outpatient assessment after suicidal thoughts resulting from depression. Mr. Wrigley recently had been forced to retire as a hospital porter because of a series of strokes that made lifting heavy equipment impossible. He felt "completely changed" after this incident. He would burst into tears over seemingly trivial events. He had to force himself to eat because he had no appetite, and his sleeping periods became shorter and shorter. His social interactions decreased, and he became more isolated and withdrawn. Mr. Wrigley reported that he made an attempt on his life while having tea with his daughter and wife. He picked up a knife from the table as if to stab himself. He was restrained by his wife, then burst into tears sobbing, "I'm sorry, I'm sorry." (After Greenberg et al., 1986, pp. 16–17)

What do we know about suicide? For one thing, suicide is in the top 10 causes of death in many countries (Diekstra, 1996). It is estimated that more than 450,000 people in the world commit suicide each year. Many Western countries have suicide rates of 20 or more per 100,000 people; in fact, Western cultures in general seem to have higher rates of suicide (Carson & Butcher, 1992)—perhaps as an outcome of their higher rates of depression. In contrast, some cultures (e.g., that of the aborigines of Australia) have no known incidence of suicide whatsoever. The rate of suicide also rises in old age (particularly among white

men), reaching a rate of more than 25 per 100,000 for people between the ages of 75 and 84 years.

Although we are not certain of the number of people who attempt suicide, estimates range roughly between 250,000 and 600,000 per year in the United States. Many attempts probably go unrecorded. These estimates imply that for every successful suicide, there are probably more than 10 unsuccessful attempts. Many people who try once will then try again and may continue until they succeed.

Men are much more likely to succeed in committing suicide than are women. Although the rate of suicide for men is almost four times that for women, the rate of suicide *attempts* is three times as great for women as for men. At least one reason for the difference is that men are more likely to shoot or hang themselves, whereas women are more likely to use drugs, such as sleeping pills. Clearly, shooting and hanging are more likely to lead to death than is an overdose of pills.

Other demographic factors also play a role. Men who are divorced are three times more likely to kill themselves than are married men. Both men and women at all socioeconomic levels commit suicide, but professionals (e.g., psychologists, psychiatrists,

Contrary to popular belief, threats of suicide should be taken very seriously. Many persons who commit suicide have threatened suicide prior to taking their own lives.

attorneys, and physicians) are especially likely to do so. Finally, although suicide ranks in general only eighth as a cause of death among adults it ranks third after accidents and homicides as a cause of death among people between the ages of 15 and 24 years. Among these young adults, whites are twice as likely as blacks to kill themselves (Bingham, Bennion, Oppenshaw, & Adams, 1994; Garland & Zigler, 1994).

The Motives for Suicide

The two main motivations for suicide appear to be surcease and manipulation. Those who seek *surcease* are people who have given up on life. They see death as the only solution to their problems and take their lives. Slightly more than half of suicides appear to be of this kind. People seeking surcease are usually depressed, hopeless, and more nearly certain that they really wish for their lives to end.

In contrast, those who view suicide as a means of *manipulation* use suicide to maneuver the world ac-

cording to their desires. They may view suicide as a way to inflict revenge on a lover who has rejected them, to gain the attention of those who have ignored them, to hurt those who have hurt them, or to have the last word in an argument. Many of those who attempt suicide in this manner are not fully committed to dying but rather are using suicide as a call for attention and help (see Myth 2 in the Psychology in Everyday Life box). Roughly 13% of suicide attempts are of this kind. Unless they receive help, people who attempt manipulative suicide often try to commit suicide again and may continue until they succeed. The following passage suggests primarily the wish for manipulation, but also the wish for surcease.

And suddenly, as she recalled the man who had been run over the day she first met Vronsky, she realized what she had to do. With a quick, light stride she descended the steps that went from the water tank to the rails and stopped next to the train that was passing right beside her. She looked

---

Myths About Suicide

Several myths surround suicide (Fremouw, Perczel, & Ellis, 1990; Pokorny, 1968; Shneidman, 1973). It is useful to know about these myths so that you or anyone can be more helpful to depressed individuals who are contemplating suicide. If you think those who consider suicide cannot be talked out of it, you are already a believer in the first myth.

Myth 1: All people who commit suicide have definitely decided that they want to die. In fact, many of those who commit suicide are not certain that they really want to die. They often take a gamble that someone will save them. Sometimes, for example, persons attempting suicide will take pills and then call someone to tell that person of the suicide attempt. If the person is not there, or if that person does not follow through quickly in response to the call, the suicide attempt may succeed.

Myth 2: People who talk about committing suicide do not actually go

ahead and do it. In fact, close to 8 out of 10 of the people who commit suicide have given some warning beforehand that they were about to do something. Often, they have given multiple warnings.

Myth 3: Suicide occurs more often among people who are wealthy. In fact, suicide is about equally prevalent at all levels of the socioeconomic spectrum.

Myth 4: People who commit suicide are always depressed beforehand. Although depression is linked with suicide, some people who take their lives show no signs of depression at all. People with terminal physical illnesses, for example, may commit suicide not because they are depressed, but to spare loved ones the suffering of having to support them, or because they have made peace with the idea of death and have decided that the time has come.

Myth 5: People who commit suicide are crazy. Although suicide is linked to depression, relatively

few of the people who commit suicide are truly out of touch with reality.

Myth 6: The risk of suicide ends when a person improves in mood following a major depression or a previous suicidal crisis. In fact, most suicides occur while an individual is still depressed but after the individual has begun to show some recovery. Often, people who are severely depressed are unable even to gather the energy to put together the means to commit suicide, so the suicide is more likely to occur as they are beginning to feel better and have the energy to do something about their wish to die.

Myth 7: Suicide is influenced by the cosmos—sun spots, phases of the moon, the position of the planets, and so on. In fact, no evidence supports any of these beliefs.

at the bottom of the freight cars, at the bolts and chains and at the great iron wheels of the first car that was slowly rolling by, and tried to measure with her eye the middle point between the front and the back wheels, and the moment that point would be opposite her.

There! she said to herself, looking at the shadow of the freight car on the mixture of sand and coal the ties were sprinkled with. There—right in the middle! I'll punish him and escape from everyone and from myself. . . . And just at this moment she was horror-struck by what she was doing. Where am I? What am I doing? Why? She tried to get up, to throw herself back, but something huge and implacable struck her on the head and dragged her down. "Lord, forgive me for everything" she murmured, feeling the impossibility of struggling. (Leo Tolstoy, *Anna Karenina*)

Schizophrenic Disorders

In Search of . . . *What is schizophrenia? What are its main symptoms and causes?*

The term **schizophrenia** refers to a class of disorders marked by disturbances of perceptual symptoms (hallucinations—perception of things in the absence of any physical presence), cognitive symptoms (delusions—false beliefs), and emotional symptoms—such as flat affect (a blunting of emotions) or inappropriate affect—and even motor behavior. These symptoms are sometimes characterized as being either *negative* or *positive*. *Negative symptoms* include deficits in behavior, such as affective flattening, language deficits, apathy, and avoidance of social activity. *Positive symptoms* include delusions, hallucinations, and bizarre behavior, such as that described in the following passage.

[Rose] had her first psychotic break when she was fifteen. She had been coming home moody and tearful, then quietly beaming, then she stopped coming home. . . .

Dinner was filled with all of our starts and stops and Rose's desperate efforts to control herself. She could barely eat and hummed the McDonald's theme song over and over again, pausing only to spill her juice down the front of her smock and begin weeping. My father looked at my mother and handed Rose his napkin. She dabbed at herself, listlessly, but the tears stopped.

"I want to go to bed. I want to go to bed and be in my head. I want to go to bed and be in my bed and in my head and just wear red. For red is

the color that my baby wore and once more, it's true, yes, it is, it's true. Please don't wear red tonight, ohh, ohh, please don't wear red tonight, for red is the color—" (Amy Bloom, "Silver Water")

To be diagnosed as schizophrenic, an individual must show (1) impairment in areas such as work, social relations, and self-care; (2) at least two of the cognitive, affective, or motor characteristics; and (3) persistence of these symptoms for at least 6 months.

The prognosis for schizophrenia is not particularly encouraging. Schizophrenia typically involves a series of acute episodes with intermittent periods of remission. In many cases, the victim's ability to function during the periods of remission declines with each successive acute episode. The consensus is that once people have a full-fledged episode of schizophrenia, they are rarely completely rid of the disorder. In other words, the disease process appears to be chronic. Despite disagreement about this prognosis, many psychologists believe that, in most cases, a number of the symptoms can be treated through psychotherapy and drugs (Dixon, Lehman, & Levine, 1995; Sartorius, Shapiro, & Jablonsky, 1974; S. C. Schultz, 1995).

Schizophrenia affects 1% to 2% of the population. The disorder tends to run in families. A review of several studies on the genetic transmission of schizophrenia found that a relative of a schizophrenic is 10 times more likely than a nonrelative to develop this disorder (Gottesman, 1991, 1994; Gottesman, McGuffin, & Farmer, 1987). Families seem to inherit a predisposition to schizophrenia. For example, among schizophrenics the prevalence rates of schizophrenia are 44% for identical twins, 12% for fraternal twins, 7% for siblings, 9% for children, and 3% for grandchildren (see Figure 16-3).

Figure 16–3
Vulnerability to Schizophrenia. *The rates of overlap in the occurrence of schizophrenia increase in relation to the closeness of the hereditary link between individuals. (After data from Gottesman, 1991; Gottesman, McGuffin, & Farmer, 1987)*

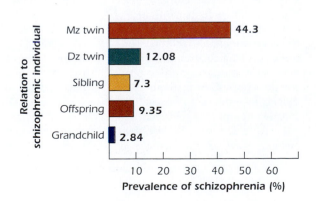

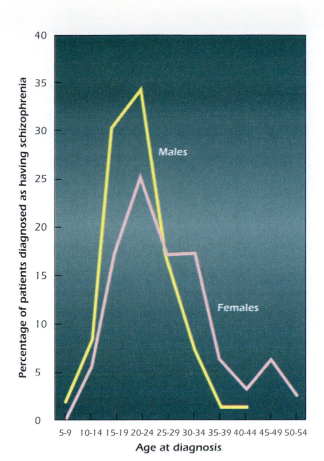

Figure 16–4

DIAGNOSIS OF SCHIZOPHRENIA. *According to A. W. Loranger, schizophrenia usually is diagnosed in males at younger ages than it is in females. (After Loranger, 1984)*

Schizophrenia is generally diagnosed in early adulthood, usually before age 45 (see Figure 16-4). Schizophrenia also has been found to vary with socioeconomic status (SES). In particular, members of the lowest SES group are roughly eight times more likely to suffer from schizophrenia than are members of the middle and upper SES groups (B. S. Dohrenwend & Dohrenwend, 1974; Strauss, Kokes, Ritzler, Harder, & Van Ord, 1978). There exist several types of schizophrenia.

Types of Schizophrenia

DSM-IV recognizes five main types of schizophrenia: disorganized schizophrenia, catatonic schizophrenia, paranoid schizophrenia, undifferentiated schizophrenia, and residual schizophrenia.

Disorganized Schizophrenia

This type of schizophrenia is characterized by profound psychological disorganization. People with this type of schizophrenia may experience hallucinations and delusions, and their speech is often incoherent. For example, when a 23-year-old schizophrenic was asked, "How have you been feeling?" he answered flatly, "I'm as sure as you can help me as I have ice cubes in my ears" (R. L. Spitzer, Skodol, Gibbon, & Williams, 1983, p. 156). People with disorganized schizophrenia show flat affect, and may grimace or have fatuous smiles for no particular reason. They may giggle in a childish manner, invent words, and experience rapid mood swings.

Catatonic Schizophrenia

People with catatonic schizophrenia experience predominantly negative symptoms. These people often exhibit stupor and immobility for long periods of time. Victims often stare into space, seemingly completely detached from the rest of the world. Because catatonics move so little, their limbs may become stiff and swollen. This form of schizophrenia is less common today than it was in the past.

Paranoid Schizophrenia

People with this kind of schizophrenia may have delusions of persecution, hearing voices criticizing or threatening them. Or they may have delusions of

Catatonic schizophrenics show waxy flexibility, assuming odd poses for long periods of time. Although this woman's arm appears frozen in place, it can be manipulated into another pose, which the woman will then continue to hold.

grandeur, hearing voices telling them how wonderful they are. Consider this example:

> A 26-year-old woman was referred to a psychiatric hospital after attempting suicide by drug overdose. Her father had been diagnosed as schizophrenic and died when she was 13 by committing suicide. She was hospitalized twice in the past year for various psychotic episodes. For the previous few weeks, she had been convinced that the Devil was persecuting her. She would lay awake at night fantasizing that the Devil was tapping on her window. She believed that other individuals were talking to her and could read her mind. Many times she felt she was under the Devil's control. He would talk through her and had the power to inflict pain. She believed the only way to avoid the Devil was to kill herself. Her mother found her on the floor and called the ambulance. At the hospital, she said that she still heard voices talking to her and that they had the power to control her thinking. (After Fottrell, 1983, p. 128)

Paranoid schizophrenics are particularly susceptible to delusions of reference, taking an insignificant event and interpreting it as though it has great personal meaning for them.

Undifferentiated Schizophrenia

This is a catchall category used for schizophrenic symptoms either that do not quite fit any of the other patterns or that fit more than one pattern.

Residual Schizophrenia

This is a diagnosis applied to persons who have had at least one schizophrenic episode and who currently show some mild symptoms but do not exhibit profoundly disturbed behavior.

Stressors Contributing to Schizophrenia

Why is there such a pronounced difference among the SES groups? According to the *social-drift hypothesis* (Myerson, 1940), those who suffer from schizophrenia tend to drift downward in SES. Their inability to hold a job, to earn a living, to relate to other people, and to function effectively leads them to successively lower SES levels until they bottom out. Evidence (R. J. Turner & Wagonfeld, 1967) shows that schizophrenics are much more likely than are others to drift downward in SES.

An alternative explanation is that the social and economic conditions a person faces in the lowest SES groups are so stressful that they tend to precipitate schizophrenia, at least more so than is the case for conditions in higher SES groups. According to the diathesis-stress theory discussed earlier, people with a genetic susceptibility to schizophrenia are more likely to display it when they are subjected to life stresses. Recent data suggest that members of groups experiencing discrimination and the stress that results from it are more prone to schizophrenia, regardless of social class (Dohrenwend et al., 1992). Still another explanation is that people with lower SES are more likely to be diagnosed as schizophrenic. That is, people with higher SES may be able to hide their symptoms better or they may have more help from others in hiding their symptoms. Also, if psychiatrically assessed, it appears that the lower SES individual is more likely to be diagnosed as schizophrenic, even if the symptoms are the same as those of someone with higher SES (Hollingshead & Redlich, 1958; M. A. Kramer, 1957). Why do people of any SES experience schizophrenia?

Explanations of Schizophrenia

The many explanations of schizophrenia are not necessarily mutually exclusive. They may simply apply to different kinds or levels of severity of schizophrenia. At present, none of the existing theories seems to account for all aspects of each of the schizophrenic disorders.

Psychodynamic Explanations

The psychodynamic paradigm has offered some explanations for schizophrenia that currently do not receive much support. The classical Freudian explanation of schizophrenia is in terms of *primary narcissism*—that is, the schizophrenic returns to very early stages of psychological development. This phase occurs early during the oral stage, before the ego has differentiated itself from the id. In this phase, reality testing suffers because the ego is undifferentiated; schizophrenics are securely wrapped up in themselves but out of touch with the world (Arieti, 1974). However, even Freud felt that his theory did not have an adequate explanation or means of treating schizophrenia.

Learning Theory Explanations

A prominent learning-based theory is known as *labeling theory* (Scheff, 1966), which holds that once people are labeled as schizophrenics, they are more likely to appear to exhibit symptoms of schizophrenia, in part because they come to feel rewarded for acting this way, or others are rewarded for labeling them this way. For one thing, persons who have been labeled schizophrenics may then feel free (or even expected) to engage in antisocial behavior that would be prohibited in so-called normal people. Also, once they begin acting abnormally, more of their actions are likely to be interpreted as being abnormal. For example, David Rosenhan (1973) observed that the behavior of patients in psychiatric wards is likely to be viewed as abnormal, even if the patients are normal, mentally healthy individuals. According to this theory, someone who begins to act strangely and is labeled a schizophrenic is susceptible to actually becoming schizophrenic merely because of the labeling process. Thus, the very fact of the label may create a self-fulfilling prophecy.

However, the preponderance of evidence does not favor labeling theory. If labeling theory were correct, one might expect, say, that in other cultures, schizophrenic behavior would be viewed as quite normal. But in both the Eskimo and Yoruba cultures, for example, the behavior labeled in our society as schizophrenic is also viewed as "crazy" (Murphy, 1976). Thus, there is at least some overlap in what is seen as nonadaptive across societies. For the most part, it would be hard to argue that the labels are extremely arbitrary.

Cognitive Explanations

Essentially, cognitive explanations of schizophrenia suggest that people who are schizophrenic have sensory experiences that differ from those of normal individuals. From this perspective, many of the symptoms of schizophrenia could be construed as attempts by people suffering from these symptoms to explain their sensory experiences to others. Unlike the other explanations of schizophrenia we have considered, cognitive explanations interpret the bizarre sensory experiences of schizophrenics as being genuine sensory experiences and as causing the disorder. According to this view, breakdowns in communication with schizophrenics often result from their attempt to explain what is happening to them. People with schizophrenia are viewed as being particularly susceptible to stimulus overload, which leads them to function in a maladaptive manner. It may be that schizophrenics lack a kind of filtering mechanism that allows most people to screen out irrelevant stimuli (Payne, Matussek, & George, 1959).

Humanistic Explanations

Humanistic psychologists usually deal with disorders that are less seriously disruptive than is schizophrenia. However, two humanistic psychologists have taken quite unorthodox views. Thomas Szasz (1961) argued that mental illness is simply a myth—that schizophrenia and other so-called mental illnesses are merely al-

ternative ways of experiencing the world. In a related vein, therapist R. D. Laing (1964) suggested that schizophrenia is not an illness but merely a label that society applies to behavior it finds problematic. According to Laing, people become schizophrenic when they live in situations that are simply not livable. No matter what they do, nothing seems to work, and they feel symbolically in a position of checkmate. Today the theories of Szasz and Laing generally are given little credence.

Biological Explanations

Biological explanations of schizophrenia emphasize neurochemical imbalances. Some of the most promising explanations of schizophrenia today are biological. One such view holds that schizophrenia results from an excess of the neurotransmitter dopamine (Seidman, 1990; Wong et al., 1986; see chapter 3), although the evidence is mixed (Heinrichs, 1993). Another biological explanation suggests structural abnormalities in the brain as the cause (Seidman, 1983). Some evidence indicates that schizophrenics have enlarged *ventricles* in the brain (Andreasen et al., 1994; Andreasen et al., 1990; Andreasen, Olsen, Dennert, & Smith, 1982a, 1982b; DeGreef et al., 1992). These ventricles—the canals through which cerebrospinal fluid (CSF) flows—generally appear enlarged when the surrounding tissue has atrophied, and additional evidence documents atrophy in portions of the brains of schizophrenics. Another intriguing finding is that in a card-sorting task, schizophrenics show less actuation of the prefrontal region of the brain than do nonschizophrenics (Berman, Torrey, Daniel, & Weinberger, 1992; Weinberger, Wagner, & Wyatt, 1983). The prefrontal cortex is generally smaller as well as showing less activation in people with schizophrenia than in those without this disorder (Andreasen, Flaum, Schultz, Duzyurek, & Miller, 1997; Buchsbaum, Haier, Potkin, & Nuechterlein, 1992).

One possible biological explanation of schizophrenia, or at least certain variants of it, is that it is primarily caused by a virus contracted by the mother during the prenatal period (and usually the second trimester, when the brain is developing most rapidly) (Torrey, 1988; Torrey, Bowler, Taylor, & Gottesman, 1994). Such an explanation might account for why mothers exposed to the influenza virus during the second trimester of pregnancy have a somewhat greater tendency to have children who later develop schizophrenia (Barr, Mednick, & Munk-Jorgensen, 1990; Mednick, Hutunen, & Machon, 1994). At the present time, though, the virus explanation must be viewed as still being rather speculative. A second and even more speculative

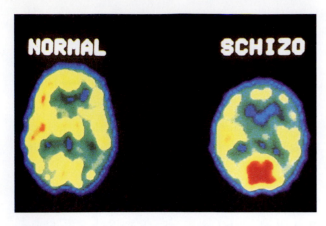

Contemporary imaging techniques offer insight into some of the cerebral processes that underlie psychological disorders. For example, these images show the differences in the patterns of activity in a normal brain, as compared with the brain of a schizophrenic.

viral explanation of schizophrenia is that it is itself caused by a slow-acting virus (see Gottesman, 1991).

Nonpsychologists confuse schizophrenia with what is popularly called "multiple personality." This disorder, formally known as dissociative identity disorder, is included in the next section.

Dissociative Disorders

In Search of ... *What are the dissociative disorders and how do they manifest themselves?*

Dissociative disorders tend to be severe but rare. There are three main **dissociative disorders:** dissociative amnesia, dissociative fugue, and dissociative identity disorder (formerly termed *multiple personality disorder*). All of these disorders involve an alteration in the normally integrative functions of consciousness, identity, or motor behavior. For some of the dissociative disorders, environmental traumas have been more strongly implicated than have been hereditary factors.

Dissociative Amnesia

Dissociative amnesia is characterized by sudden memory loss of declarative knowledge and usually affects the recollection of events that took place during and immediately after a stressful event. In addition, the person has difficulty remembering most of his or her own important details, such as name, address, and family members. The amnesic is able to function relatively normally, though. The duration of the amnesia may be from several hours to several years. Recovery of the lost information is usually as rapid as the loss was, after which the episode ends and the memory loss is not repeated.

Dissociative Fugue

When suffering from **dissociative fugue,** a person responds to severe stress by starting a whole new life and experiencing total amnesia about the past. He or she assumes a new identity, may take a new job, and behaves as though he or she were a totally different person, perhaps even with a new personality. Recovery time is variable. When a person does recover, he or she may or may not remember anything that took place during the fugue.

Dissociative Identity Disorder

Dissociative identity disorder typically arises as a result of extreme early trauma—usually severe child abuse—and is characterized by the appearance of two or more identities (*alters*) within the same individual, in which each identity is relatively independent of the others, has a stable life of its own, and occasionally takes full control of the person's behavior. One personality may know about the existence of others. Because this disorder seems to be linked to early emotional trauma, such as child abuse, it may begin early, when the child first experiences the serious emotional problem (Bliss, 1980). The disorder is more common in women than in men, perhaps because of the greater likelihood that women will have been subjected to sexual abuse as children (Boon & Draijer, 1993). Individuals with this disorder tend to have a rich fantasy life and are also susceptible to self-hypnosis (see chapter 5). Once they discover, unconsciously, that they can create another identity through self-hypnosis, they are relieved of some of the emotional burden facing the primary identity. Later, when they confront an emotional trauma that cannot readily be handled by their existing identities, they create another identity to deal with the new problem. Persons who develop multiple personalities in childhood may not know about the other personalities until adulthood. Recovery takes extensive therapy.

One of the most famous cases of dissociative identities is that of Chris Sizemore, whose case was popularized in the motion picture *The Three Faces of Eve* (see also Thigpen & Cleckley, 1957). One of the faces was "Eve White," a quiet, proper, and relatively inhibited young woman. Eve White sought psychotherapy to treat headaches and blackouts. One day, in the presence of her physician, she suddenly grasped her head as though seized by a sudden and violent headache. Shortly thereafter, she seemed to recover, but the person who recovered was not the same one who had had the headache. She identified herself as "Eve Black." Eve Black's personality was wild, promiscuous, and reckless—almost the opposite of Eve White's. Eve Black was aware of Eve White, but the reverse was not true. The third personality, Jane, was the most stable of the three and seemed to be the most well-integrated. Jane was aware of both of the other two personalities and seemed to think more highly of Eve Black than of Eve White. The case may be somewhat more complicated than it appeared. Sizemore later wrote a book claiming to have had as many as 21 separate personalities (Sizemore & Pittillo, 1977). Moreover, she claims that, contrary to the claims of C. Thigpen and H. Cleckley, who popularized her story, the therapy she received did not cure her.

There is controversy today over whether dissociative identity disorder really exists (S. D. Miller & Triggiano, 1992; Spanos, 1994). Almost certainly, some cases that have been described as presenting this order have been misdiagnosed, especially in highly suggestible people (American Psychiatric Association, 1994). It has been suggested, for example, that some clients may wish to believe they suffer from this disorder or that therapists may implant the idea of this disorder in the clients. At present, therefore, we cannot say for sure whether the disorder is a genuine one or not.

Disorders Usually First Diagnosed in Infancy, Childhood, or Adolescence

In Search of . . . *Do children have mental disorders? Are they the same as those seen in adults?*

Depression and anxiety disorders unfortunately affect children as well as adults. There are a few disorders, however, that characteristically appear before adulthood. In particular, three major disorders usually are diagnosed first in infancy, childhood, or adolescence:

Attention-Deficit Hyperactivity Disorder (ADHD)

Attention-deficit hyperactivity disorder (ADHD) is characterized by a difficulty in focusing attention for reasonable amounts of time. Children with this dis-

order tend to be impulsive and disruptive in social settings. They are often unable to sit still and constantly seem to be seeking attention. This disorder is much more common in boys than in girls and usually appears before age 7. As many as 3% to 5% of children may have this disorder (American Psychiatric Association, 1987). Psychologists do not know what causes this disorder, but it is generally believed to reflect an organic brain dysfunction. It is often treated with a stimulant called Ritalin. Because the prevalence of this disorder has grown over the last decade, some believe that the diagnosis is being abused by educators and parents who simply wish to make normally energetic and at times unruly children less troublesome.

Conduct Disorders

Conduct disorders are characterized by habitual misbehavior, such as stealing, skipping school, destroying property, fighting, being cruel both to animals and to other people, and frequently telling lies. Children with this disorder may misbehave independently or in groups or gangs. This disorder is often a precursor to antisocial personality disorder, a disorder that frequently involves unlawful behavior and is discussed below.

Pervasive Developmental Disorder (PDD)

Pervasive developmental disorder (PDD) is also known as *autism*. It is characterized by three main symptoms: (1) minimal or no responsiveness to others and seeming obliviousness to the surrounding world; (2) impairment in communication, both verbal and nonverbal; and (3) highly restricted range of interest, sitting alone for hours, immobility or rocking back and forth, and staring off into space. PDD occurs in only about 0.04% of the population and is four times as likely to occur in boys as in girls. Infants with PDD do not cry when left alone and do not smile when others smile at them. Even by age 5, many PDD children are unable to use language.

Many children with PDD show a striking lack of both intellectual development and speech development, for example:

Five-year-old Jimmy Patterson was brought to the inpatient child psychiatric unit at a large city hospital. His parents complained that he was impossible to manage, was not toilet trained, and screamed or gestured whenever he became frustrated or wanted to be noticed. He was allowed a free-play period and an interaction period involving a cooperative task with his mother. He wandered about the playroom and played by himself with a number of toys. His mother then tried to involve him in some cooperative play with wooden blocks. She spoke to Jimmy in a cheerful tone, but he seemed not to notice her and moved to an opposite part of the room. Mrs. Patterson made several comments to Jimmy, but he remained oblivious to her encouragements. She then tried to begin a jigsaw puzzle with Jimmy. She led him over to a chair, but as soon as he sat down, he got up again and continued to wander about the room. His mother then firmly, although not harshly, took Jimmy by the arm and led him over to a chair. Jimmy began to whine and scream and flail his arms about, and eventually wiggled out of his mother's grasp. (After G. R. Leon, 1974, p. 9)

Clinicians originally believed that PDD might be a childhood form of schizophrenia. They now believe that PDD and childhood schizophrenia are different disorders (American Psychiatric Association, 1994). Children with schizophrenia often show a family history of schizophrenia, but those with PDD do not. Also, the drugs that alleviate symptoms of schizophrenia are not effective with PDD (see chapter 17).

Personality Disorders

In Search of . . . *What are personality disorders and what are some of their symptoms?*

DSM-IV specifically places personality disorders on a separate axis of disorders. Personality disorders seem comparatively less tractable in terms of treatment, and our legal system is less willing to consider personality disorders when considering a plea of "not guilty by reason of insanity." What is there about personality disorders that so sharply distinguishes them from other forms of abnormal behavior?

As difficult as it may be to categorize various types of schizophrenia, it is even more difficult to differentiate the many personality disorders in DSM-IV. **Personality disorders** are psychological disorders involving exaggerated and maladaptive personality characteristics that persist over a long period of time and that cause problems in a person's adjustment to everyday situations. Although it may be possible to detect some features of personality disorders during childhood or adolescence, these disorders generally are not diagnosed until early adulthood. The major personality disorders include the following:

Paranoid Personality Disorder. The individual is suspicious of others, expects to be poorly treated, and blames others for things that happen to him or her.

Schizoid Personality Disorder. The individual has difficulty forming relationships with other people. He or she tends to be indifferent to what others think about, say about, or feel toward him or her.

Schizotypal Personality Disorder. The individual has serious problems with other people and shows eccentric or bizarre behavior. He or she is susceptible to illusions and may engage in magical thinking, believing that he or she has contact with the supernatural. This disorder may be a mild form of schizophrenia.

Borderline Personality Disorder. Victims show extreme instability in moods, self-image, and relationships with other people.

Narcissistic Personality Disorder. The individual has an inflated view of himself or herself and is intensely self-centered and selfish in his or her personal relationships. The individual lacks empathy for others and often uses others for his or her own ends. He or she often spends time fantasizing about past and future successes.

Histrionic Personality Disorder. The individual generally acts as though he or she is on stage, is very dramatic, and continually tries to draw attention to him- or herself. The individual is lavish in his or her emotional displays, but shallow in the depth of his or her emotions. He or she often has trouble in relationships and tends to be manipulative and demanding. Here is an example of histrionic personality disorder, probably with complicating factors:

A 58-year-old woman recently was brought to the hospital after police picked her up off the street where she had been shouting, crying, and banging her head against a wall. During the initial interview she recalled that, "I had my first breakdown when I learned of my husband's illness." Since then she has had 16 admissions to the hospital for a variety of reasons. She indicated that her present illness began when she was discharged to an apartment she did not like, and was upset with her son because she did not approve of the woman he had chosen to marry. During the next few days, she became depressed and began to behave in a boisterous, attention-seeking manner. She created various disturbances in her neighborhood and subsequently was brought to the hospital by police. In the hospital, she was extremely uncooperative. She kept eyes firmly shut and refused to

"Tremaine, could I see you for a moment—alone?"

open them. She would sit up on her bed only when told, and then immediately fall back under the covers. (After Fottrell, 1983, p. 122)

Avoidant Personality Disorder. The individual is reluctant to enter into close personal relationships. He or she may wish for closeness but be so sensitive to rejection that he or she becomes afraid to be close to others. This individual often has very low self-esteem and devalues much of what he or she does.

Dependent Personality Disorder. The individual lacks self-confidence and has difficulty taking personal responsibility for himself or herself. The individual subordinates his or her own needs to those of loved ones, partly in fear of losing the loved ones if the individual's needs are expressed. He or she is extremely sensitive to criticism. This disorder is more common in women than in men.

Obsessive–Compulsive Personality Disorder. The individual displays excessive concern with details, rules, and codes of behavior; the individual also tends to be perfectionistic and to require everything be done just so; the individual further tends to be highly work oriented. He or she often has trouble relating to other people and tends to be cold and distant in interpersonal relationships. The disorder

is more common in men than in women. (This disorder differs from obsessive–compulsive anxiety disorder, in which the person experiences feelings of dread if the compulsive behaviors are not performed.)

Antisocial Personality Disorder. The individual has a tendency to be superficially charming and appears to be sincere. In fact the individual is insincere, untruthful, and unreliable in relations with others. He or she has virtually no sense of responsibility and feels no shame or remorse when hurting others. The individual also tends to process information in a way that views many acts toward him or herself as aggressively motivated and in need of an aggressive response (Crick & Dodge, 1994). The person is extremely self-centered and is incapable of genuine love or affection. Typically, people with this disorder are poised, calm, and verbally facile. This disorder can run in families. The evidence shows both genetic and environmental contributory factors. People with this disorder may have low natural baseline levels of arousal and may seek stimulation through antisocial means in order to arouse themselves and thus make their lives less seemingly dull (Morey, 1993). This disorder is more common in men than in women.

People with antisocial personality disorder are prone to run into trouble with the law. Indeed, it is hard to discuss abnormal behavior without discussing matters of law. Thus, legal issues in abnormal behavior are discussed next.

Legal Issues

In Search of . . . *What are some of the major legal issues that clinical psychologists confront?*

The DSM-IV descriptions of abnormal behavior are designed to aid clinicians in diagnosing their patients and to aid psychologists in understanding such behavior. Although these descriptions are imperfect, often permitting ambiguous diagnoses and flawed understandings, they generally serve the purpose for which psychiatrists and psychologists intended them. Nonpsychologists, however, may have different requirements, which may lead to different definitions.

For example, in courtrooms and law offices, alternative definitions of abnormal behavior are required. The term *sanity*, for example, is a legal term for describing behavior, not a psychological one. Perhaps the best-known construction of the insanity defense is the *M'Naghten Rule*, formulated as the result of a murder trial in 1843 by a court in England. This rule holds that "to establish a defense on the ground of insanity, it must be clearly proved that, at the time of committing the act, the party accused was laboring under such a defect of reasoning, from disease of the mind, as not to know the nature and quality of the act he [or she] was doing, or if he [or she] did know it, that he [or she] did not know he [or she] was doing what was wrong" (*Stedman's Medical Dictionary*, 25th edition, 1990, p. 1374).

In 1962, the American Law Institute provided a set of guidelines intended to reflect the current state of the insanity defense and its legal and psychological ramifications. These guidelines state that people cannot be held responsible for criminal conduct if, as a consequence of a mental disease or defect, they lack the capacity either to appreciate the wrongness of their conduct or to conform their conduct with the requirements of the law. The guidelines exclude, however, repeated criminal actions or antisocial conduct. In other words, the intent of the guidelines is to embrace extraordinary acts, not habitual criminal behavior.

The topic remains controversial, and some psychiatrists, such as Thomas Szasz and R. D. Laing, have argued that concepts of mental illness and insanity have no place in the courtroom at all. According to Szasz, acts of violence are as rational and goal directed as any other acts, and perpetrators of such acts should be treated accordingly.

In 1981, John Hinckley, Jr., in an attempt to impress the actress Jodie Foster, tried to assassinate President Ronald Reagan. Hinckley was found not guilty by reason of insanity. Such a verdict is scarcely a "free ride." But as a result of this case and the outrage that followed, a number of states have introduced a new verdict, "guilty but mentally ill." Federal courts have also tightened up guidelines for finding a defendant not guilty by reason of insanity. The Insanity Defense Reform Act, passed by the Congress in October 1984, makes it much more difficult for a defendant to escape the punishment of the law, regardless of the defendant's mental state.

Psychology and the law are also interrelated in noncriminal matters. For example, do the mentally ill have a right to treatment? In the case of *Wyatt* v. *Stickney*, decided in Alabama in 1971, the court ruled that they do. This ruling has generally held up. However, there is always latitude in the interpretation of who is mentally ill and really needs treatment. In recent years, federal spending on mental institutions has decreased, so many patients who were formerly in psychiatric hospitals have been released. These people sometimes join the ranks of the homeless and may now be seen wandering the streets instead of the halls of mental hospitals.

People suffering from mental illnesses today also are recognized as having a right to refuse treatment unless their behavior is potentially dangerous to others. In deciding whether to require treatment or confinement, we need to consider not only the rights of the potential patient, but also the rights of persons they might harm.

Once again, we face a dilemma—trying to find the right balance between the rights of the prospective patient to be free to refuse treatment or hospitalization and the rights of other persons to be protected from any harm that the prospective patient might cause.

Just what are the options for treatment? We consider some of them in the next chapter.

THINK ABOUT IT

1. Why does science as a whole benefit when researchers conduct their studies based on explicit rather than merely implicit underlying assumptions about their theoretical perspectives?

2. Choose one of the psychological perspectives, the one which you find most suitable to your own beliefs about abnormal behavior. Compare your preferred perspective with the others, showing why yours makes better sense.

3. Suppose you are assigned to choose exactly one personality disorder to be allowed as a legal defense for a not-guilty-by-reason-of-insanity plea. Which disorder would you choose and why? If you would not be willing to make such a choice, explain why.

4. Suppose your English teacher assigns you the task of creating a believable literary character who is schizophrenic. Briefly describe that person as others view the person, then describe how that person sees the world, including other persons.

5. Suppose you are volunteering to answer telephones on a suicide hotline. What kinds of strategies would you use—and what might you actually say—to try to prevent someone from committing suicide?

6. Sometimes, it is tempting to analyze people you know in terms of the disorders they seem to show. What are the risks of assuming this kind of role as an amateur psychologist?

online *You can provide your own answers to these questions online at the* Sternberg, **In Search of the Human Mind** *Web site:* **http://www.harcourtcollege.com/psych/ishm**

SUMMARY

What Is Abnormal Behavior?   511

1. *Abnormal behavior* can be defined as statistically unusual, nonadaptive, labeled as abnormal by the surrounding society, and characterized by some degree of perceptual or cognitive distortion. There is a lack of universal consensus regarding any one definition of abnormal behavior.

2. Early explanations of abnormal behavior included witchcraft and spiritual possession by demons. More contemporary perspectives on abnormal behavior include psychodynamic, behavioral (learning), cognitive, humanistic, and biological approaches.

Classifying and Diagnosing Abnormal Behavior   514

3. In the middle of the twentieth century, clinicians began to reach formalized consensus regarding the diagnosis of mental disorders. Subsequently, clinicians have continued to refine the documents recording these consensual agreements, both in the United States (DSM-IV) and in the world community (ICD-10).

Anxiety Disorders   519

4. *Anxiety disorders* encompass the individual's feelings of anxiety—tension, nervousness, distress, or uncomfortable arousal. DSM-IV divides anxiety disorders into five main categories: phobic disorders, including *specific phobias, social phobias,* and *agoraphobia; panic disorder; generalized anxiety disorder; stress disorder,* including *posttraumatic* and *acute stress disorders;* and *obsessive-compulsive anxiety disorder.* Anxiety disorders involve mood, cognitive, somatic, and motor symptoms. There are various explanations of the disorders and the symptoms they cause. For example, psychodynamic explanations emphasize childhood events, whereas biological explanations emphasize links to neurotransmitters.

Mood Disorders   525

5. The two major *mood disorders* (extreme disturbances in a person's emotional state) are *major depression* and bipolar disorder. Depression is relatively common and is generally believed to be influenced by situational factors. *Bipolar disorder,* however, is much rarer and runs in families, suggesting a possible genetic, biological component. Both disorders probably are influenced by both biological factors and situational factors. For example, bipolar disorder may be biologically rooted, but some environments may lead to more intense expression of the disorder than do other environments.

6. Cultures vary widely in their rates of suicide.

7. Many myths surround suicide. Perhaps the most important caution is that any person, of any background or set of characteristics, may decide to commit suicide, and any threats of suicide should be considered seriously.

Schizophrenic Disorders   532

8. *Schizophrenia* refers to a set of disorders encompassing a variety of symptoms, including hallucinations, *delusions*, disturbed thought processes, and disturbed emotional responses.

9. Types of schizophrenia include disorganized schizophrenia, catatonic schizophrenia, paranoid schizophrenia, undifferentiated schizophrenia, and residual schizophrenia.

10. Of the various explanations for schizophrenia, biological explanations seem particularly interesting because they help explain the familial trends in the development of schizophrenia (as well as the positive outcomes associated with antipsychotic drugs). The specific biological causes remain unknown, however. Other explanations have different emphases. For example, a psychodynamic explanation emphasizes the role of primary narcissism—a return to a very early stage of psychological development.

Dissociative Disorders   536

11. Environmental traumas have been implicated more strongly for *dissociative disorders* than have been hereditary or biological factors.

12. There are three main dissociative disorders: *dissociative amnesia* (sudden memory loss, usually after a highly stressful life experience), *dissociative fugue* (amnesia regarding a past identity and assumption of an entirely new identity), and *dissociative identity disorder* (the occurrence of two or more distinct, independent identities within the same individual). All of these disorders involve an alteration in the normally integrative functions of consciousness, identity, or motor behavior.

Disorders Usually First Diagnosed in Infancy, Childhood, or Adolescence   537

13. Three major disorders usually are diagnosed first in infancy, childhood, or adolescence: attention-deficit hyperactivity disorder (ADHD), conduct disorder, and pervasive developmental disorder (PDD).

Personality Disorders   538

14. *Personality disorders* are consistent, long-term, extreme personality characteristics that cause great unhappiness or that seriously impair a person's ability to adjust to the demands of everyday living or to function well in her or his environment.

15. The major personality disorders are paranoid, schizoid, schizotypal, borderline, narcissistic, histrionic, avoidant, dependent, obsessive–compulsive, and antisocial disorders.

Legal Issues   540

16. The term *sanity* is a legal term for describing behavior, not a psychological one. At present, a person's sanity is an important factor in determining the adjudication of the person's criminal behavior. Just how sanity is determined and how it is considered in making legal judgments still is being evaluated in the courts.

Key Terms

abnormal behavior   511
acute stress disorder   522
agoraphobia   521
anxiety disorders   519
bipolar disorder   526
compulsion   522
delusions   526
diathesis-stress theory   514
dissociative amnesia   536
dissociative disorders   536
dissociative fugue   536

dissociative identity disorder   536
etiology   514
generalized anxiety disorder   521
major depression   525
mania   526
mood disorders   525
obsession   522
obsessive–compulsive anxiety disorder   522
panic disorder   521

personality disorders   538
phobias   519
posttraumatic stress disorder   521
schizophrenia   532
seasonal affective disorder (SAD)   526
specific phobias   520
social phobias   520
stress disorder   521

THINK ABOUT IT SAMPLE RESPONSES

1. Why does science as a whole benefit when researchers conduct their studies based on explicit rather than merely implicit underlying assumptions about their theoretical perspectives?

The problem with implicit underlying assumptions is that, because the researchers are unaware of their own assumptions, they also are unaware of how these assumptions affect their scientific work. The researchers may ask only certain questions but not others, or do only certain experiments but not others that are more important, because they are being restricted by these underlying assumptions.

2. Choose one of the psychological perspectives, the one which you find most suitable to your own beliefs about abnormal behavior. Compare your preferred perspective with the others, showing why yours makes better sense.

Everyone must choose a perspective that makes particular sense to him or her. Some people might, for example, choose the cognitive perspective. An advantage of this perspective is that it recognizes the fact that much of the reaction people have to situations is not determined by the situations, per se, but by the cognitive interpretations people give to these situations. For example, one person might interpret as depressing a certain event that another person would interpret as cheerful, such as spending a day helping people living in very poor conditions. Each perspective has its own advantages and, of course, disadvantages. The cognitive perspective at times may overemphasize the role of thought in psychological disorders.

3. Suppose you are assigned to choose exactly one personality disorder to be allowed as a legal defense for a not-guilty-by-reason-of-insanity plea. Which disorder would you choose and why? If you would not be willing to make such a choice, explain why.

Almost certainly such a choice would depend not only on the choice but also on the severity of the disorder experienced. One disorder for which such a defense might be considered is disorganized schizophrenia, which can be a particularly severe kind. Persons with severe disorganized schizophrenia may cause harm without necessarily realizing what they are doing.

4. Suppose your English teacher assigns you the task of creating a believable literary character who is schizophrenic. Briefly describe that person as others view the person, then describe how that person sees the world, including other persons.

The way the character perceives the world will depend in part upon the type of schizophrenia from which the person suffers. For example, a paranoid schizophrenic may imagine being attacked by another person whereas a catatonic schizophrenic may be oblivious to the other person.

5. Suppose you are volunteering to answer telephones on a suicide hotline. What kinds of strategies would you use—and what might you actually say—to try to prevent someone from committing suicide?

Your goal is to stop the person from committing suicide and for the person to find help. One strategy is to point out that everyone goes through bad periods but generally the periods do not last forever. Often people find that things not only get better, but even that they get much better. A second thing you might point out is how much other people depend on him or her and wish to have his or her presence in their lives. A third thing you might point out is that suicide is a final decision and that it certainly is not a decision to be made in a time of great distress. The person should wait. Another thing you can point out is that you personally care about the outcome and will do everything you can to make sure the person gets help.

6. Sometimes, it is tempting to analyze people you know in terms of the disorders they seem to show. What are the risks of assuming this kind of role as an amateur psychologist?

This kind of behavior is very risky because you are likely to make a diagnosis for which there really is no justification and then to treat the people as though the diagnosis were true. If you truly believe that someone you know needs help, you should encourage the person to seek professional help rather than giving the person amateur help that may hurt rather than help.

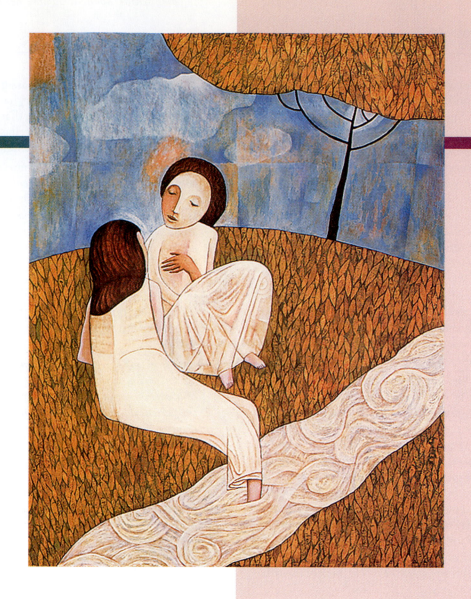

"If we are not going to talk about my toilet-training, what is the process of your treatment? Bullying and lectures?"

"If necessary. But it usually isn't necessary, and when it is, that is only a small part of the treatment."

"Then what are you going to do?"

"I am not going to do anything to you. I am going to try to help you in the process of becoming yourself."

—Robertson Davies, The Manticore

17

PSYCHOTHERAPY

Chapter Outline

Psychotherapy is an intervention that uses the principles of psychology to try to treat mental disorders and to improve the life of a person who is unhappy or disturbed. Psychotherapy takes many forms. Common to many of the therapeutic approaches and techniques, however, is the idea that by working on a problem with a trained therapist, one can improve one's life.

Early History of Psychotherapeutic Interventions

In Search of . . . *What were early methods of treating people who seemed to behave in abnormal ways?*

In ancient times, abnormal behavior was viewed as being caused by demons (see chapter 16). To an extent, this belief persists among some groups today. The treatment of persons suspected of being possessed (demoniacs) has ranged from the innocuous to the brutally homicidal. Harsher forms of exorcism included flogging, drowning, or starving the suspected demoniac in the attempt to drive out the evil spirits.

As the Middle Ages came to an end, so did the treatment of the mentally ill via exorcism (at least in most cases). During the 15th and 16th centuries, **asylums**—hospitals for the mentally ill—became a popular

During earlier eras, persons who were behaving in ways that did not conform to societal expectations often were subjected to torture techniques, such as "dunking," used for extracting confessions of witchery. The accused witch is repeatedly submerged. The longer it took her to die, the more fervently her accusers would assert that devilish powers were permitting her to survive.

means for the housing and possible rehabilitation of persons suffering from mental disorders. At that time, the definition of what constituted a disorder was flexible, and the asylums housed a diverse assortment of people, including those who were viewed as socially undesirable for one reason or another, whether or not they were truly disordered.

In 1547, King Henry VIII donated the Crown's 300-year-old asylum, St. Mary of Bethlehem (commonly known as "Bedlam"), to the city of London; the rededicated Bedlam became the first hospital devoted exclusively to serving the mentally ill. The term *bedlam* has become synonymous with uproar or confusion, which aptly describes the conditions within the original Bedlam hospital. Many inmates were chained to the walls of the cramped quarters, often in positions that did not allow them even to sleep properly. Others were chained to large iron balls, which they had to drag with them wherever they went.

Such conditions appalled Phillipe Pinel (1745–1826), first chief physician at the Parisian men's asylum, La Bicêtre, and then director of the women's asylum, Saltpêtrière. At both asylums, Pinel decided to remove the shackles and other instruments of confinement from patients. Much to the surprise of Parisian society, Pinel's crazed inmates became much calmer and more manageable.

By the end of the 18th century and into the 19th century, clinicians were attempting to treat the psychological bases of abnormal behavior. For example, neurologist Jean Martin Charcot used hypnosis as a method to cure hysteria and other mental illnesses. Later, Josef Breuer (1842–1925), a Viennese physi-

cian, also treated hysterical patients with hypnotic methods. Breuer found that if he could get his hypnotized patients to talk about their problems, especially the origins of their difficulties, the patients seemed to improve. Breuer concluded that if he could get a patient to relive and tell about the painful events that had caused some particular form of psychological damage, the patient would be freed from the shackles of these past hurts. Breuer's method became known as the **cathartic method,** in which the patient is encouraged to reveal and discuss the painful origins of a psychological problem as a means of purging the problem from the patient's mental life. Later, Charcot's student Sigmund Freud began working with Breuer, and thus began the modern history of psychotherapy.

As we will see, there are many kinds of psychotherapy available today. In most cases, no matter what his or her persuasion, the therapist begins the process by trying to figure out what the problem is. This process of diagnosis and assessment may be quite brief, as in the case of someone who wants to get over his or her fear of heights. On the other hand, it may be lengthier, as in the case of a child who is afraid to go to school. Is the issue one of separating from his parents? The behavior of schoolmates? A reaction to something going on between parents at home? Or some earlier trauma that the child may or may not recall? Whatever the process and approach of therapy, the therapist is initially trying to pinpoint the problem.

Diagnosing and Assessing Abnormal Behavior

In Search of . . . *How do therapists diagnose the individuals who come to them for treatment?*

As discussed in chapter 16, both the *Diagnostic and Statistical Manual* (DSM-IV) and the International Classification of Diseases (ICD-10) enjoy widespread acceptance. The diagnostic reliability of the clinical guidelines in the ICD-10 has been field tested in 40 countries and has yielded promising results (Sartorius et al., 1993b). The DSM-IV classification system for diagnoses, described in chapter 16, is highly compatible with the ICD classification system.

Given both clinical expertise and diagnostic tools such as the DSM-IV, a clinician must answer three questions when deciding how to respond to a new client: (1) Does the client have one or more problems? (2) If so, what are the problems? (3) Once the problems are diagnosed, how should they be treated? Clinicians use a variety of different techniques to answer these questions, such as clinical interviews and psychological tests.

Structured and Unstructured Clinical Interviews

The *clinical interview*, in which a psychotherapist asks a client a series of questions about his or her condition and surrounding circumstances, is by far the most widely used clinical assessment technique. Interviews may be structured, unstructured, or a combination of both. In a *structured interview*, the interviewer conscientiously follows a specific list of questions and rarely departs from the structured sequence of questions. The advantage of a structured interview is that the clinician can obtain a relatively large amount of information in a relatively short period of time. Moreover, by specifying the questions in advance, the clinician avoids missing pieces of information that later might be important in making a diagnosis. The main disadvantage of the structured interview is that it lacks flexibility. Structured interviews tend to emphasize breadth at the expense of depth.

In contrast, an *unstructured interview* does not involve any specific list of questions and enables the interviewer to follow rather than lead the client. Because people differ in the kinds of issues that bring them to therapy, an unstructured interview has the advantage of focusing on issues that are of particular importance for a specific client. The unstructured interview has two key potential disadvantages: The clinician might miss or forget to ask important questions, and the clinician cannot obtain comparable data from one interview to the next. Thus, responses across unstructured interviews are probably less comparable than responses across structured interviews. Unstructured interviews tend to emphasize depth at the expense of breadth. The ideal is a combination of the two techniques: Therapists have some standard questions that they make sure to ask, yet they freely pursue particular issues that appear to be important for a given client.

In a clinical interview, how clients say something is often as important as—or even more important than—what they say. For example, if a male client repeatedly emphasizes his success with women and goes to great pains to underscore that he can have any woman he wants, the therapist almost certainly would do well to be suspicious of these claims. Other aspects of behavior, such as crying while saying something or suddenly having lapses of memory or becoming fatigued while talking about a particular topic, also can be important to understanding the meaning of what is being said.

In making a diagnosis, clinicians need to be sensitive not only to what clients are saying and to how they are saying it, but also to how the clients' relationship with them may be affecting the content of the interview. They also need to realize that diagnosis is not the same as explanation (Carson, 1996). The interviewer may be able to reach a diagnosis without being able to explain why the client has the problems that present themselves. Clients react differently to different interviewers, and clinicians further need to realize that their age, gender, ethnic group, way of thinking, and even manner of dress can affect the outcome of a clinical interview. When dealing with members of another culture, clinicians have to be especially careful both to recognize and to appreciate cultural differences and to avoid attributing genuinely abnormal behavior to cultural difference (Lopez & Nuñez, 1987). For example, persistent fears of spirits might be viewed as abnormal in one culture but as perfectly normal in another one. But killing another person because of a fear that the person is harboring such a spirit needs to be viewed as abnormal, regardless of culture.

Sometimes, psychological tests are used to make accurate diagnoses, even in the face of attempts at deception by the test taker.

Psychological Testing

Some clinicians regularly use psychological testing, others never use it, and the rest fall in between. Many of those who use it would swear by its diagnostic utility, whereas most of those who do not use it would say they are confident that tests do not give them useful psychodiagnostic information.

Chief among the psychological tests used in clinical assessment are personality tests. Personality tests are either projective, such as the TAT and Rorschach tests, or objective, such as the MMPI (see chapter 15). Clinicians sometimes use intelligence tests (see chapter 9) both to assess various cognitive disorders and to observe an individual's approach to solving problems. Neuropsychological and psychophysiological tests also are used in formulating a diagnosis that can serve as the basis for treatment.

Neuropsychological Tests

Clinicians use neuropsychological tests in those cases where they suspect organic brain damage and to make other assessments on Axis III (physical disorders and conditions) of DSM-IV. The two most widely used neuropsychological tests are the *Halstead–Reitan Battery* (see Boll, 1978) and the *Luria–Nebraska Battery* (see Golden, Hammecke, & Purisch, 1978). In fact, often the Halstead–Reitan *test battery* (a series of tests given sequentially over a period of hours or days, to aid in diagnosis) is administered along with the *Wechsler Adult Intelligence Scale, 3rd ed.* (WAIS-III) and the *Minnesota Multiphasic Personality Inventory–Revised* (MMPI-R). Thus, in applied (practical) settings,

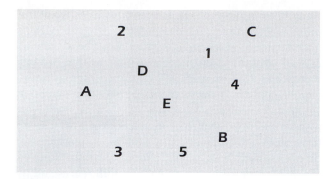

Figure 17–1

TRAIL-MAKING TEST OF THE HALSTEAD-REITAN BATTERY. *In the Trail-Making test, you are shown a page such as the one shown here, speckled with numerals and letters. You are asked to start with 1, then go to A, then to 2, then to B, and so on. In other words, the order of the paths on the trail alternates between the numerals and the letters.*

clinicians integrate information from many different types of diagnostic tools.

To get an idea of the kinds of items that appear in a neuropsychological test, suppose that a client is given two tests from the Halstead–Reitan battery. On the Tactual Performance test, the client is blindfolded and is asked to try to place blocks of various shapes into a board that has spaces corresponding to the various shapes. Because he cannot see the board, the client would have to use tactile cues to determine which blocks go into which spaces. After completing the board to the best of his ability, the client would be asked to draw what he believes the board looks like, showing the spaces in the board and the blocks that fill these spaces, all in their proper locations. A second test is Trail-Making. To see how you might perform the Trail-Making test, see Figure 17-1.

How do clinicians score the Halstead–Reitan subtests and other neuropsychological tests? The scoring draws on knowledge of the relations between performance and localization of function in different parts of the brain. For example, the Tactual Performance test draws largely on right-hemisphere functioning. Thus, for this form of assessment, the idea is to relate the functioning of the brain to behavior and to infer impairments of brain functioning from this behavior.

Biologically Based Measurements

Further aids in assessing brain function include less formal assessments of reflex functions and of sensory function. Your own physician has probably often tested your knee-jerk reflex (in response to a tap with a rubber mallet) and your pupillary reflex (in response to a bright light).

Biologically based measurement indices include heart rate, muscle tension, blood flow to various parts of the body, galvanic skin response (GSR), evoked potentials (series of electroencephalograph recordings that minimize electrical interference), CAT (computerized axial tomography) and PET (positron emission tomography) scans, and other measurements for assessing biological functioning (see chapters 3 and 12). These indices are not commonly used in clinical assessments. Clinicians have found, nevertheless, that PET scans of people with bipolar disorder show higher levels of glucose metabolism in the cerebrum during manic phases (when patients are hyperactive, expansive, and unabashedly joyful) than during depressive phases (when patients are relatively inactive and feeling low); see Figure 17-2 (Baxter et al., 1985).

To conclude, a variety of forms of assessment are now available to clinicians. No single form gives a complete picture, but used in conjunction, the various forms of assessment can give clinicians a relatively

Figure 17–2

PSYCHOPHYSIOLOGICAL INDICATIONS OF DISORDER. *Compare the CAT-scan images at the top left and the top right. Both of these images show a horizontal slice through the brain, but the brain on the left is normal, whereas the brain on the right shows a tumor exerting pressure on the other structures of the brain. The bottom two images are from PET scans, with the one on the left showing a normal brain and the one on the right showing the brain of a patient with senile dementia (possibly caused by Alzheimer's disease).*

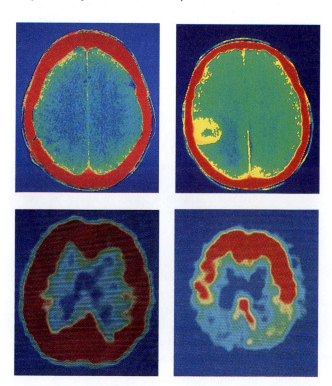

wide variety of information that they can integrate and interpret. Once the clinician has diagnosed the problem, what remains is to treat it. We now turn to some of the kinds of therapies used for treating psychological disorders.

Approaches to Psychotherapy

In Search of . . .   *How do the various theoretical perspectives on personality and abnormal behavior relate to the various approaches to psychotherapy?*

Psychotherapy may be given by clinical psychologists (who usually possess a doctor of philosophy or a doctor of psychology degree), psychiatrists (who possess a medical doctor degree), by social workers (typically possessing a master of social work degree), or by others. Psychotherapists use a variety of different approaches. Each of the many approaches to psychotherapy has accompanying advantages and disadvantages. Many of the therapies overlap, but it is still useful to consider the distinctions among the five main approaches: psychodynamic, humanistic, behavioral, cognitive, and biological. A cultural perspective can be viewed as an additional approach.

Psychodynamic Therapies

Psychodynamic therapies have in common their emphasis on gaining *insight* as the key to improvement. The basic assumption is that when patients have insight into the source or sources of their problems, they will be largely freed of their problems. Psychoanalytic therapy is a major type of psychodynamic therapy, though there are many other offshoots.

Psychoanalytic Therapy

Psychoanalytic therapists assume that disorders result from people's lack of awareness of their underlying thoughts, feelings, and, especially, motivations. According to this view, insight needs to be gained into the childhood roots of problematic feelings and patterns in relationships. Patients will improve when they become conscious of ego-threatening material that has been repressed. Thus, treatment centers on peeling away layers of self-deceit and rationalization in an attempt to discover the underlying truth. If a patient enters psychotherapy to conquer anxiety, for example, the therapist would be foolish to treat the anxiety directly because, according to this view, the anxiety is only a symptom of unconscious repressed feelings,

Psychoanalytic therapy's goal is to help patients gain insight into their defenses. The therapy is nondirective, with the therapist sitting out of sight to avoid influencing the patient's train of thought.

thoughts, and motives. The therapy is nondirective, and often the psychoanalytic therapist sits out of sight of the patient in order to avoid influencing the patient's stream of thought.

Free Association.   How does the therapist actually go about eliciting the unconscious conflicts that underlie an observable disorder? Psychoanalysts use several techniques, the most prominent of which is free association. In **free association,** the patient freely says whatever comes to mind, not censoring or otherwise editing the free flow of words before reporting them. At first, the patient may find the unedited reporting of free associations difficult, but with practice and familiarity with the analyst and the process, he or she usually improves. It is critical not to edit anything out because, according to the psychoanalytic view, chances are good that the most interesting and important details will be those that the patient reveals unconsciously. The therapist acts only as a guide and does not try to direct the course of the associations. Typically, the patient is placed in a relaxed state of mind in a comfortable setting, with only the psychotherapist present. The patient simply reports everything that comes to mind.

Analyzing Resistance. If patients could make free associations that immediately led them to repressed material, psychoanalysis would be over in short order. The actual course of therapy rarely works that way. The reason it does not, according to psychoanalytic beliefs, is the presence of resistances. **Resistances** are attempts to block therapeutic progress in psychodynamic treatment, usually as a result of unconscious conflicts. Why would any rational patients want to block progress, especially when they are paying for therapy? The reason for resistance is that dealing with the contents of the unconscious is often painful and possibly even devastating, so patients unconsciously attempt to divert the therapy from doing so. Resistances can take a variety of forms, such as remaining silent, trying to digress from unpleasant topics, making jokes, or even not attending sessions. Psychoanalysts identify and deal with resistances when they arise.

Analysis of Dreams. A second technique used in psychoanalytic therapy is the analysis of dreams (see chapters 5 and 15). According to Freud, the *manifest content* of dreams—the actual occurrences that take place within the dreams—is symbolic of the underlying, *latent content* of the dreams. Thus, the job of the analyst is to penetrate the manifest content in order to understand what lies beneath it. For example, a male patient's dream of sticking an old man with a pencil might represent an unresolved Oedipal conflict in which the dreaming patient is battling with his father for possession of his mother. Psychoanalysts believe that the dream sufficiently disguises these symbolic elements to avoid causing extreme discomfort to the dreamer.

After the patient has been in therapy for a while, the psychoanalyst increasingly interprets the content of what the patient says. Often, patients are unhappy with and may not believe what they hear. Freud believed that such attempts at denial were further ways in which patients could resist learning the truth about themselves. From the psychoanalytic standpoint, the more vigorously a patient denies a particular interpretation, the more likely the interpretation is to be true. Of course, this reasoning creates a "damned if you do, damned if you don't" kind of logic. The therapist's interpretations are difficult to disconfirm because they are accepted as true if the patient agrees and accepted even more strongly if the patient forcefully disagrees.

Analyzing the Transference. Psychoanalytic therapists remain relatively detached from their patients and avoid overt emotional signs. The therapist seems almost like a shadowy parent figure who tries to help the patient without becoming too involved in the patient's problems. Patients, however, often become quite involved with the therapist, imbuing the therapist with various kinds of qualities and thoughts that the therapist may not actually have. Indeed, patients may start viewing the therapist as the source of, or at least an active contributor to, their problems. This involvement of the patient with the therapist is referred to as transference. In **transference,** the patient projects her or his feelings and internal conflicts onto the therapist, often also projecting onto the therapist–patient relationship many aspects of the patient's early childhood relationships, such as with the patient's parents. For example, if the patient's parents were extremely concerned with his or her school performance, the patient may assume that the analyst is similarly judging the patient's performance in therapy. By staying neutral and seemingly detached, therapists actually encourage transference because patients can project onto the therapist whatever conflicts or fantasies arise during therapy. The detached therapist is something like a blank screen onto which patients can project their past relationships. According to Freud, such transference is a positive rather than a negative phenomenon. It helps the patient bring out into the open the conflicts that have been suppressed in the past.

All psychoanalysts must themselves first be psychoanalyzed to understand better their own conflicts and sources of psychological distress. This understanding is particularly important to control for **countertransference,** in which the therapist projects onto the patient the therapist's own feelings. Therapists who project their own problems onto the patient can cause the therapy to go seriously awry. Thus, it is important that psychoanalytic therapists recognize their own problems and fantasies, to deal with those issues as they arise, and to avoid projecting them onto the patient.

Modern Schools of Psychoanalytic Therapy

Psychoanalytic therapy, important both historically and in modern times, has generated a variety of offshoots. Many of these offshoots developed from the theories of personality offered by Freud's followers, neo-Freudians such as Carl Jung, Erik Erikson, and Karen Horney (described in chapter 15). The various forms of neo-Freudian therapy are sometimes termed *ego analysis* because of their common view that the ego is at least as important as is the id. In other words, conscious processing is just as important as—and possibly more important than—unconscious processing. People have purposes and goals, and to a large extent, they act to fulfill those goals. To understand the patient fully, the therapist needs to understand not only the patient's past, but also the patient's envisioned future—where the patient sees himself or herself heading.

Classical psychoanalysis can be a long process, continuing over a period of years, during which the patient and the therapist may meet as often as three to five times per week. Psychodynamic therapists, however, have placed increasing emphasis on *time-limited psychotherapy* (Mann, 1973; Strupp, 1981). The idea of such therapy is to apply the principles of psychoanalysis but to effect improvement in a relatively short time. To this end, the therapist, while guided by psychodynamic prinicples, is somewhat more directive—pointing out, for example, the patient's defenses and conflicts more readily than an analyst would.

Humanistic (Client-Centered) Therapies

Like psychoanalysis and other psychodynamic therapies, humanistic therapy emphasizes insight. Beyond this similarity, however, there are salient differences. Humanistic therapists refer to the people whom they treat as "clients," whereas traditional psychodynamically oriented therapists usually refer to them as "patients." This difference is not merely semantic. Psychodynamic therapy is based on a model of disorder that is much closer to a medical model (recall Freud's medical training), according to which an underlying disease process is the source of the patient's troubles. In contrast, the humanistic model eschews the medical model and replaces it with a model that views each person as an individual with feelings and thoughts that may come into conflict with society or with each other, thereby causing problems in living.

For psychodynamic therapists, understanding of behavior is elusive and extremely difficult to achieve for all but the most skilled psychoanalyst (much like a physician's expertise); for humanistic therapists, understanding is not that elusive. The therapist is not an authority who dictates the correct perceptions to the passive patient. Rather, the therapist is a helpful facilitator who helps the client gain his or her own insights.

In the psychodynamic view, we are deterministically ruled by unconscious forces; in the humanistic view, we have free will and are ruled by our own conscious decisions. Humanistic therapists assume that people who are mentally well are aware of and understand their behavior. People can thus change their behavior at will. Because people are free to make choices, a goal of therapy is to help people to *feel* completely free in the choices they make. Of the various forms of humanistic therapies, some are briefly described here.

All humanistic therapy is centered on the client because, according to this view, it is in the client's experience of his or her deepest needs that the power to make fulfilling choices lies. Carl Rogers (1961a) developed his particular form of **client-centered therapy** on the assumption that the client's construction of reality provides the basis for understanding the client. Thus, client-centered therapy is *nondirective*, in that the therapist is not supposed to guide the course of therapy in any particular direction. What matters are not the events that occur in people's lives, but rather the way people construe these events. Thus, client-centered therapists make little effort to impose a theoretical system (such as Freud's) onto the client; instead, they try to understand their client's view of the world.

In addition to believing in the value of a client's view of the world and in the importance of the client's free will, Rogers believed that people are basically good and adaptive both in what they do and in the goals they set for themselves. When they act otherwise, it is because of flaws that have taken place in their learning processes. For example, the clients may receive inadequate socialization or may have inappropriate role models. The goal of client-centered therapy is to help people realize their full potential.

Rogers believed there are three keys that can unlock the doors barring clients from realizing their potential. The first key is *genuineness* on the part of the therapist. Client-centered therapists need to be totally honest, both with themselves and with their clients. Whereas psychoanalysts might be viewed as having a detached objectivity, Rogerian therapists must present no detachment whatsoever. They should be as open and genuine in the expression of their feelings as they want their clients to be. In effect, they become models for their clients, showing the clients how to be open and self-disclosing in a world that often seems not to value the qualities of openness and self-disclosure.

The second key is for the therapist to give the client *unconditional positive regard*. Rogers believed that many of the problems we encounter are caused by our having received only conditional positive regard as we grew up. We were given positive regard only when we behaved in socially acceptable ways, and this positive regard was withdrawn when we behaved in less accepted ways. The result, according to Rogers, is that we develop a conditional sense of self-worth. We feel that we will be loved or appreciated only if we do those things that others have deemed acceptable. To be psychologically whole, however, we must achieve a sense of unconditional self-worth. The Rogerian therapist's unconditional positive regard helps the client achieve this state.

The third key is for the therapist to experience *accurate empathic understanding* of the client. A good therapist needs to be able to see the world in the same way that the client sees it. Without such empathy, the therapist does not truly understand the client's point of view. The result will be miscommunication, which limits the client's ability to profit from the therapy.

In client-centered, nondirective therapy, the therapist follows the client's lead; in contrast, in psychodynamic therapy, the therapist has a particular direction in mind regarding how to lead the patient—namely, toward the uncovering of unconscious conflicts. Thus, the course of client-centered therapy is likely to be quite different from that of psychodynamic therapy. Nondirective, client-centered therapists believe that by listening empathically to clients and by helping clients to clarify and explore their feelings, clients will then feel free to live as they choose. Behavior therapists use different means to achieve the same ends.

Behavior Therapy and Its Associated Techniques

Behavior therapy refers to a collection of techniques based primarily on the principles of classical conditioning or operant conditioning, as well as on observational learning from models (see chapter 6). Behavior therapy differs in several fundamental ways from all of the other kinds of therapies considered up to this point. First, behavior therapy is deliberately short term. The goal is to seek behavioral change over a brief period. Thus, whereas psychoanalysis may go on for years, behavior therapy typically lasts only months or even less.

Second, whereas psychoanalysis shuns the treatment of symptoms, behavior therapy deliberately seeks intervention to alleviate symptoms. To the behavior therapist, the symptom *is* the problem. If a person is experiencing anxiety, then the person needs to reduce that anxiety to function effectively. If a person is depressed, then the goal should be to relieve the depression. In the behaviorists' view, chasing after deep-seated causes in the murky past is essentially a waste of time. The original causes of the maladaptive behavior may not even have anything to do with the factors that currently maintain the behavior.

Third, in addition to being very direct, behavior therapy is extremely directive, in sharp contrast to humanistic therapies, which are explicitly nondirective, and to psychodynamic therapy, which is only partially directive. That is, although the behavior therapist collaborates with the client, it is the therapist who formulates an explicit treatment plan. The client follows the therapist's treatment plan, and when the implementation of the plan is completed, the therapy ends.

Fourth, as its name implies, behavior therapy concentrates on behavior, such as quitting smoking or overcoming a fear of public speaking. Whereas other techniques of therapy seek to obtain behavioral change through psychological insights and changes, behavior therapy seeks to obtain psychological changes through behavioral changes. Indeed, some behavior therapists do not even particularly concern themselves with the psychological changes. What they seek is modification of maladaptive behavior.

Finally, behavior therapists try to follow more closely the classical scientific model than do some other types of therapists. Whereas humanistic therapists often feel as though scientific analysis turns the client into an object or a depersonalized entity, behavior therapists are very concerned with taking a scientific, objective approach, both to the therapy and to the evaluation of the outcomes of the therapy. Many behaviorists have said that the precepts of psychoanalysis cannot be disconfirmed by scientific investigation. Probably no one says the same of behavior therapy.

Behavior therapy consists of a set of explicit techniques, which include counterconditioning, extinction procedures, and operant conditioning, as well as modeling.

Counterconditioning

In *counterconditioning*, a particular response to a particular stimulus is replaced by an alternative response to that stimulus. The alternative response is incompatible with the unwanted initial response. For example, suppose that before counterconditioning, a person enjoys positive feelings toward the stimulus of smoking cigarettes. Through counterconditioning, the person would learn to feel negatively about cigarettes. On the other hand, if a person became anxious when taking tests, counterconditioning would replace the negative anxiety response with a positive relaxation response that would permit the person to take tests without feeling anxiety. Two of the main techniques used to achieve counterconditioning are aversion therapy and systematic desensitization.

Aversion Therapy

In **aversion therapy,** the client is taught to experience negative feelings in the presence of a stimulus that is considered inappropriately attractive, with the aim that the client will eventually learn to feel repelled by the stimulus. For example, a *pedophiliac* (an adult who is sexually attracted to children) might seek aversion therapy to learn not to respond with sexual interest when presented with the stimulus of a little child. The client's exposure to the inappropriately attractive stimulus would be accompanied by an aversive unconditioned stimulus, such as a painful electrical shock. The pedophiliac might be exposed to a picture of an attractive child at the exact moment or immediately before being shocked. Similarly, an alcoholic might seek aversion therapy. For example, problem drinkers sometimes are given a drug that causes them to feel nauseated immediately after they have consumed any alcohol (see chapter 6). Aversion therapy seeks to foster avoidance learning and is generally used in combination with other techniques. It is often useful to substitute some other more socially desirable interest for the one that is being replaced.

Systematic Desensitization

In **systematic desensitization,** almost the antithesis of aversion therapy, the therapist seeks to help the client combat anxiety and other troublesome responses by teaching the client a set of relaxation techniques. Joseph Wolpe (1958) introduced the technique of systematic desensitization as a way of combating particular psychological problems, most notably anxiety. Wolpe's basic idea involves replacing one response with another—typically, a response of anxiety with one of relaxation. In all cases, systematic desensitization involves engaging in a response that is incompatible with the initial unwanted response.

Suppose, for instance, that you experienced such extreme anxiety about standardized admissions tests that your test anxiety threatened your ability to compete successfully for admission to graduate school. The therapist would create with you a *desensitization hierarchy*, which is a series of imagined scenes, each one more anxiety provoking than the previous one. Next, you would learn a set of techniques to achieve

For those afraid of snakes or with other phobias, behavior therapy aimed at extinguishing their fears can be helpful. Often systematic desensitization is used, with the person gradually being introduced to or imagining successively more anxiety-provoking stimuli.

deep relaxation. These techniques would involve relaxation of individual muscle groups, picturing pleasant scenes, and the like. Once you had learned how to relax deeply, the actual systematic desensitization process would begin. You would first imagine the least anxiety-provoking scene. If you were to find yourself feeling anxious, you would be reminded immediately to relax deeply. After several efforts, you would find yourself able to handle the first step of your hierarchy without feeling anxious. After you were sure of your ability to deal with that initial stimulus, you would proceed to the next step of your hierarchy, and you would continue in this manner until you had mastered each step in your hierarchy. Many studies (see Cottraux, 1993) indicate that behavior therapy is highly effective in aiding clients with simple phobias and with many other anxiety disorders.

Extinction Procedures

Extinction procedures weaken maladaptive responses, such as anxiety. Two types of extinction therapies are flooding and implosion therapy. Like systematic desensitization, **flooding** is designed to lessen anxiety by exposing a client to a carefully controlled environment in which an anxiety-provoking stimulus is presented, but the client experiences no harm from the stimulus, so the client is expected to cease to feel anxiety in response to the stimulus. In flooding, however, the client is immediately placed in a situation that causes anxiety, not just a sequence of imagined situations, and the client is not instructed in how to use relaxation techniques. The idea underlying the use of this technique is that clients who have been forced to remain in the anxiety-provoking situation will realize that nothing horrible has happened to them, so they can cope with the situation again when they face it in the future. For instance, a person with a phobia of snakes would be forced to confront snakes, or a person who is afraid of heights would be taken to the top of a high building.

Implosion is an intermediate form of therapy, including elements of both flooding and systematic desensitization. **Implosion therapy** is designed to weaken anxiety by having clients imagine as vividly as possible the unpleasant events that are causing them anxiety. Suppose, for example, that you had once almost drowned, that you now fear swimming, and that you are reluctant even to have any contact with water. Your implosion therapist might ask you to imagine placing yourself in a bottomless bathtub and then to imagine yourself starting to slip beneath the water. Of course, imagining this scene would cause you intense anxiety. Soon, however, you would realize that nothing has happened to you. You would have imagined the scene, but you would still be alive and in the therapist's office. You would then be asked to imagine this scene on an increasingly frequent basis. Eventually, the scene would lose its ability to cause you anxiety and you would stop feeling afraid.

This visualization technique is similar to systematic desensitization in that the client imagines but does not actually experience the anxiety-producing scenes. However, it differs from systematic desensitization in the method of relieving anxiety. Of the two techniques, systematic desensitization has proven to be demonstrably superior to implosion therapy (see M. L. Smith & Glass, 1977).

The techniques described up to this point have basically made use of the classical-conditioning model. However, operant conditioning has also been used for achieving behavioral change. A simple example of operant conditioning, one used by parents, is to reward their children with, say, candy or money for good grades or for going to bed early. Several methods of using operant conditioning are relevant, including the use of token economies (introduced in chapter 6) and behavioral contracting.

Token Economies

The basic principle of the **token economy** is that *tokens* (tangible objects that have no intrinsic worth) are used as a means of reinforcing for various operant behaviors. The tokens can later be exchanged for goods or services that the individuals desire. The clients are generally in an institutional setting, which allows the therapist to control the distribution of the tokens and other reinforcers. This technique has been used primarily with children who have PDD (pervasive developmental disorder, or autism), although it has been used with other populations as well (see Figure 17-3).

The use of tokens has several attractive features. First, the number of tokens can be linked directly to whether the client exhibits the desired behavior. Second, there is very little ambiguity with regard to the nature of the reward. Third, the therapist can tailor the goods or services that can be purchased in accordance with the client's needs and wants. As time goes on, the nature of the things that can be purchased with the tokens can be changed to suit the client's current desires. Fourth, the tokens can be distributed immediately as a reward for desirable behavior. Fifth, the client can choose the reward, rather than having to accept what is given. Finally, there is a touch of realism in the token economy because it resembles what happens in the world outside the institution (Carson, 1996; G. L. Paul & Lentz, 1977; G. L. Paul & Menditto, 1992). For noninstitutionalized populations, some researchers have expressed concern that these *extrinsic reinforcers* (external, material rewards, as opposed to intrinsic ones such as self-esteem and

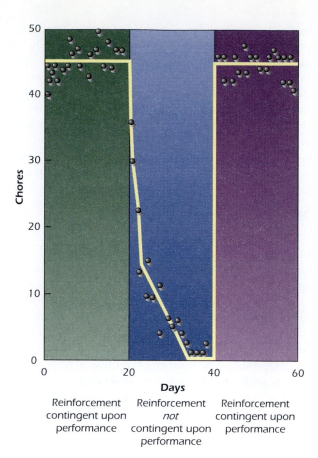

Figure 17-3
RESULTS OF A TOKEN ECONOMY. *In an institutional setting, a token economy can be highly effective in modifying the behavior of confined individuals. Positive behaviors that may be reinforced in a token economy include self-help (e.g., grooming) or chores, as shown here.*

achievement motivation) may undermine children's natural interest in performing the behaviors that are being rewarded (Deci & Ryan, 1985; Lepper et al., 1973). Psychotherapists and other clinicians must often choose from among imperfect alternatives, balancing desired benefits against possible risks.

Behavioral Contracting

Behavioral contracting also has a real-world connotation. In **behavioral contracting,** the therapist and the client draw up a contract specifying clearly the responsibilities and behavioral expectations of each party, and obligating both parties to live up to the terms of the contract. The contract requires the client to exhibit specific behaviors that are being sought as part of the therapy, in return for which the therapist will give the client particular things that the client may want, even including permission to terminate the therapy. Behavioral contracting has two key advantages: (1) The responsibilities of both the therapist and the patient are clear, and (2) the criteria for success in meeting the goals of the therapy are concretely defined. Behavioral contracting is not itself a form of therapy, but rather a supplement that can be used in conjunction with virtually any type of therapy.

A part of a contract, or simply of behaviorial therapy in general, may be self-administered rewards for self-control. In other words, when the client achieves certain clearly specified goals, he or she rewards him or herself for the achievement of these goals.

Modeling

Modeling represents a third approach to behavior therapy, beyond the approaches based on classical and operant conditioning. In this form of behaviorial therapy, clients are asked to observe persons coping effectively in situations that the clients find anxiety-provoking or that the clients respond to in other maladaptive ways. The principles of modeling derive in large part, although not exclusively, from the work of Albert Bandura (1969; see chapter 6). Bandura's basic idea is that people can change simply by watching models of other people successfully coping with the problems they face. For example, Bandura, Edward Blanchard, and Brunhilde Ritter (1969) helped people overcome snake phobias by having phobic adults watch other people confront snakes, preferably in live situations, or alternatively, on film. The clients watched as the models moved closer and closer to the snakes; with time, the clients' phobias subsided.

Modeling also has been used in a variety of other kinds of therapy, including the treatment of a variety of phobias and sexual disorders. It has been suggested that the therapeutic effects of many interventions stem largely from modeling (Braswell & Kendall, 1988). Modeling appears to be quite effective in comparison with other forms of therapy, especially if it is live modeling involving the actual confrontation of the phobia (see Figure 17-4).

Cognitive Approaches to Therapy

The modeling approach provides the transition between behaviorally and cognitively oriented approaches to psychotherapy. The thought processes that the observer uses for imitating the model are certainly cognitive ones (Bandura, 1986).

Cognitive therapists believe that clients change their behaviors by changing their thinking. If people can be made to think differently about themselves and about the phenomena they experience, then they can feel and act differently. The two most well-known cognitive approaches are probably Albert

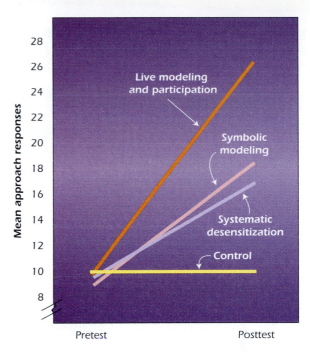

Figure 17–4
Effectiveness of Various Behavior Therapies.
Live modeling and participation appear to be much more potent in effecting behaviorial changes than are symbolic modeling or systematic desensitization.

Ellis's rational-emotive therapy and Aaron Beck's cognitive therapy (see chapter 15).

Rational-Emotive Therapy

When Albert Ellis (1962, 1973, 1989; Ellis & Dryden, 1997) formulated **rational-emotive therapy (RET)** (sometimes referred to as *rational emotive behavior therapy*), his fundamental idea was that emotional reactions occur because people internally recite sentences that express incorrect or maladaptive thoughts. For example, Ellis believes that cognition precedes emotion (in agreement with Richard Lazarus; see chapter 12). According to Ellis, the emotions we feel are caused by the thoughts we have, and we can change our emotions only by changing our thoughts. The goal of Ellis's psychotherapy, therefore, is to help people control their own maladaptive emotional reactions by helping them to correct their incorrect and maladaptive thoughts. Ellis's RET and other forms of cognitive-behavioral therapy have been particularly effective in treating anxious patients who have come to abuse antianxiety medications (Perris & Herlofson, 1993), and we may presume that this form of therapy will also be effective in persons at risk for such abuse.

Ellis (1970) has given a number of examples of the incorrect beliefs that have led people to maladjustment.

TABLE 17-1

Ellis's List of Common Irrational Beliefs
Ellis believes that false ideas, such as those listed below, lead to maladjustment in peoples' lives.

1. It is a dire necessity for an adult to be loved or approved by virtually every other significant person in his or her community.
2. One should be thoroughly competent, adequate, and achieving in all possible respects if one is to consider oneself worthwhile.
3. Certain people are bad, wicked, or villainous and should be severely blamed and punished for their villainy.
4. It is awful and catastrophic when things are not the way one would very much like them to be.
5. Human unhappiness is externally caused and people have little or no ability to control their sorrows and disturbances.
6. If something is or may be dangerous or fearsome one should be terribly concerned about it and should keep dwelling on the possibility of its occurring.
7. It is easier to avoid than to face certain life difficulties and self-responsibilities.
8. One should be dependent on others and need someone stronger than oneself on whom to rely.
9. One's past history is an all-important determiner of one's present behavior, and because something once strongly affected one's life, it should indefinitely have a similar effect.
10. One should become quite upset over other people's problems and disturbances.
11. There is invariably a right, precise, and perfect solution to human problems and it is catastrophic if this perfect solution is not found.

Some of these beliefs are listed in Table 17-1. Ellis believes that the best technique for dealing with these beliefs is to confront the client directly and to dispute the client's incorrect and maladaptive beliefs. In other words, the therapist actually attempts to show the client that these false, futile beliefs are leading the client to be unhappy and dysfunctional in everyday life. Thus, Ellis's techniques are quite different from those of humanistic therapy, in which a therapist would almost never directly confront a client. Although the method is different, the goals are similar to those of humanistic therapy: to increase a client's sense of self-worth and to facilitate the client's ability to grow and to make choices by recognizing all of the available options.

Beck's Cognitive Therapy

The **cognitive therapy** of Aaron Beck (1976, 1986, 1997) differs from Ellis's RET in both the cognitive theorizing and the form of the psychotherapy. This form of therapy focuses on developing adaptive, rather than maladaptive, thoughts and thought processes. Beck views people as being maladjusted as a result of cognitive distortion (see chapter 16). Beck has concentrated particularly on depression, and a World Health Organization report (Perris & Herlofson, 1993) on psychotherapy has indicated that the demonstrated efficacy for cognitive therapy is higher for depressive disorders than for other disorders. (See in chapter 16 Beck's list of some of the cognitive distortions that fre-

quently underlie depression.) Cognitive therapy also seems to work quite well with anxiety disorders (Hollon & Beck, 1994). Beck particularly emphasizes the importance of maladaptive schemas, such as feeling unattractive or incompetent, that lead us to feel distress (see also Young, 1990; Young & Klosko, 1993).

Biological Therapies

Biological therapies treat psychological disorders through medical or quasi-medical intervention. These therapies differ from all those we have considered up to this point because the client–therapist discourse plays no real role, or at least no more of a role than would be the case for any patient–doctor discourse. Biological therapies can be used in conjunction with more psychologically oriented ones, of course, and they often are. Let's consider briefly some of the history of biological therapies.

A History of Biological Therapies

Biological therapies date back at least to ancient Rome, where particular psychological disorders were viewed as being caused by poisons or other undesirable substances that had entered the body. As a result, laxatives and emetics were used to purge the body of these foreign substances. Such treatment continued even as recently as the 18th century (Agnew, 1985). Another way of ridding the body of unwanted substances was through selective bleeding, which also was

Aaron Beck's (1991) cognitive therapy focuses on getting people to change maladaptive cognitive schemas that lead them to believe they are incompetent or worthless.

used as recently as the 18th century. The idea was that undesirable substances were mixed with the blood, and that as the blood left the body, so would the undesirable substances. New blood created to replace the old would be free of the contamination.

Electroconvulsive Therapy

Electroconvulsive therapy (ECT)—the use of a brief but severe electrical shock—is used for the treatment of severe, unremitting depression that does not respond to psychotherapy or drugs (Bolwig, 1993). In one form of ECT, a current of about 150 volts is passed from one side of the patient's head to another for approximately 1½ seconds.

Use of ECT seems to be effective for some (Abrams, 1988; Scovern & Kilmann, 1980), but it does not work for others (Scott, 1989). In the majority of cases, depression can be treated with psychotherapy, perhaps combined with antidepressant drugs, rendering ECT unnecessary.

Psychosurgery

Another treatment, which proved to be among the most disastrous attempts of the psychiatric profession to achieve biological cures, was prefrontal lobotomy, a form of **psychosurgery,** a procedure intended to alleviate mental disorders by probing, slicing, dissecting, or removing some part of the brain. The procedure of *prefrontal lobotomy* severed the frontal lobes from the posterior portions of the brain, thereby cutting off all communication between the frontal lobes and the rest of the brain. The operation left many patients vegetative, incapable of functioning independently in any meaningful way. Even those operations that were less disastrously tragic could not be considered successful in terms of restoring mental health and normal cognitive function. Between 1935 (when the operation was first introduced) and 1955 (when antipsychotic drugs became the method of choice for treating many of the symptoms of schizophrenia and other disorders), prefrontal lobotomy is estimated to have victimized tens of thousands of patients, primarily in mental institutions (Freeman, 1959). The inventor of the operation even received the Nobel Prize in medicine for his contributions.

How could such a disaster have taken place? Elliot Valenstein (1986) has suggested several explanations. For one thing, the treatment came into prominence at a time when psychiatry was trying to gain respectability as a medical science. Psychosurgery seemed to offer such respectability because it was a medical procedure. Psychosurgery also allowed those in charge of mental hospitals to maintain control; the patients who received the operation stopped being disorderly and disruptive to the institutional regimen.

When we examine the failure of early psychosurgery, we should view it in the broader context of many other failed medical and psychological treatments. For example, heroin was introduced as an analgesic by a drug company. Countless other harmful and addictive drugs have been given to patients in the mistaken belief that the patients would benefit from using the drugs. The harm that is clearly visible retrospectively is often obscure or even invisible prospectively. Interventions introduced to help people can end up causing more harm than benefit in the long run. Therefore, we need to pay more attention to the long-term consequences of the interventions we introduce. Today, some modern forms of psychosurgery are used in extreme cases, but these uses are rare.

The next section describes some of the important drug therapies recently developed for the treatment of mental disorders.

Drug Therapies

During the second half of the 20th century, the introduction of drug therapies has unquestionably been the major advance in the biological approach to the treatment of mental disorders. Disorders that formerly were resistant to treatment now have become treatable, at least to some degree. There are four main classes of **psychotropic drugs** (i.e., affecting the individual's psychological processes or state of mind): antipsychotic drugs, antidepressant drugs, antianxiety drugs, and lithium.

Antipsychotic Drugs. Antipsychotic drugs were a breakthrough in the treatment of psychotic patients. Prior to the introduction of such drugs, wards of mental hospitals resembled many of our worst stereotypes. They were characterized by wild screaming and the always present threat of violence. Antipsychotic drugs completely changed the atmosphere in many of these wards.

The most commonly used antipsychotic drugs, introduced in the early 1950s, are *phenothiazines.* The best-known of these is also the first that was introduced: chlorpromazine, usually sold under the trade name Thorazine. Another common antipsychotic drug is haloperidol (Haldol). These antipsychotic drugs alleviate the symptoms of schizophrenia by blocking the dopamine receptors in the schizophrenic brain (see chapter 3). Although these drugs are quite successful in treating the positive symptoms of schizophrenia (see Figure 17-5), they are less successful in treating the negative symptoms (see chapter 16).

Antipsychotic drugs also have serious side effects, such as dryness of the mouth, tremors, stiffness, and involuntary jerking movements. Patients differ in the severity of their symptoms and in the length of time until symptom onset. Severe side effects can appear after prolonged use of these drugs.

Another problem of antipsychotic drugs is that not all psychotic patients respond to the traditional antipsychotic medication. Occasionally, another drug, such as clozapine, may be successful when the traditional drugs have failed. The overall success rate for treating patients who do not respond to other antipsychotic medication is about 30% (Kane et al., 1988). Clozapine can occasionally cause side effects (e.g., immune-system deficiencies), although they differ from those of the traditional antipsychotic drugs. Clearly, we are far from any panaceas in the biological treatment of psychoses. At the same time, the benefits of these drugs appear far to outweigh their costs. These potential costs pertain not only to the patient but to the world around the patient.

There are social issues with the use of antipsychotic drugs, in that the clinician is duty-bound to obtain informed consent from those who are to receive the drugs. However, one could easily argue that people suffering from psychotic episodes are in no position to give true informed consent. Nor is it clear that a patient's relatives can give true informed consent. There is no easy answer.

Figure 17–5

EFFECTIVENESS OF ANTIPSYCHOTIC MEDICATION VERSUS PLACEBO.   *The rates of symptomatic behavior are much higher for the placebo-control group than for the treatment group (receiving Mellaril, a brand name of phenothiazine). In addition, the rate of symptomatic behavior for the treatment group temporarily rose during a brief trial (observation 41–45) of placebo substitution and declined again following reinstitution of the drug treatment.*

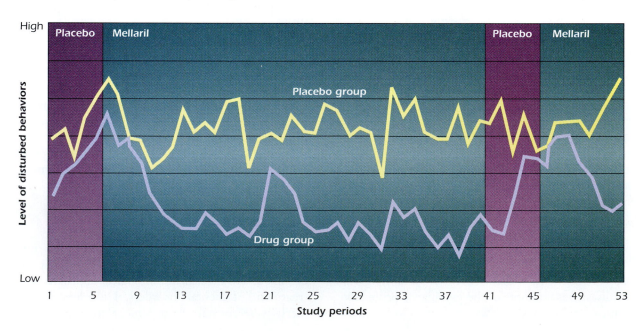

Antidepressant Drugs. Antidepressant drugs are of three main kinds: *tricyclics, monoamine oxidase (MAO) inhibitors,* and *selective serotonin reuptake inhibitors (SSRI).* MAO inhibitors are the least frequently used because they are more toxic and require adherence to a special diet. The MAO inhibitors thus tend to be used for those patients who do not respond to other drugs. MAO inhibitors include isocarboxazid (Marplan) and phenelzine (Nardil). Examples of tricyclics are imipramine (Tofranil) and amitriptyline (Elavil).

Both tricyclics and MAO inhibitors increase concentrations of two neurotransmitters, serotonin and norepinephrine, at particular synapses in the brain (see chapter 3). Concentrations of these neurotransmitters begin to increase almost immediately after patients start taking the drugs. However, the antidepressant effect does not begin immediately. It can take several weeks, and sometimes longer, before the patient starts to feel the effects.

The SSRI drugs have been introduced more recently. They work by inhibiting the reuptake of serotonin during transmission between neurons. This inhibition effectively increases the concentrations of the neurotransmitter, but it does so less directly than do the other two types of antidepressant drugs. The best known of these new drugs is fluoxetine (Prozac). Other such drugs are paroxetine (Paxil) and sertraline (Zoloft). Depressed patients typically start to show improvement after about three weeks of taking the drug. They seem to work for a wide variety of patients, but they too may have side effects, such as nausea and nervousness. These drugs even have been shown to work for obsessive-compulsive disorder, although at this point it appears that a particular tricyclic drug, Anafranil, is more effective for the treatment of this disorder (Greist, Jefferson, Koback, Katzelnick, & Serline, 1995).

From one point of view, drug treatment of depression has been considerably more successful than drug treatment of schizophrenia. Whereas antipsychotic drugs only suppress symptoms, antidepressant drugs seem to cause more lasting change. Patients who stop taking antipsychotic drugs typically return to their earlier psychotic state, whereas patients who stop taking antidepressant drugs often remain symptom free for quite some time, and possibly indefinitely.

When we consider the difference in the longer term effectiveness of antipsychotic versus antidepressant drugs, however, we must also consider the rates of spontaneous recovery. **Spontaneous recovery** is the unprompted and unaided (untreated) disappearance of maladaptive symptomatology over the course of time. The rate of spontaneous recovery for depression is much higher than that for schizophrenia and other psychoses, so an unknown proportion of the depressed patients who become better through the use of drugs or psychotherapy might have become better even if they had received no treatment at all. In addition, researchers and clinicians must consider the effects of placebos. Patients may improve simply because they believe that they are being helped, even if the treatment they receive actually has no direct effect whatsoever. To rule out both the effects of spontaneous recovery and the effects of placebos, researchers studying the effects of drugs often use both control groups that take placebos and control groups that are simply put on a waiting list for subsequent treatment. The control group taking placebos also may be studied using a *double-blind technique,* in which both the experimenter administering the treatment and the patient are blind as to whether a particular patient is receiving a placebo or an active drug.

Antianxiety Drugs. Clinicians prescribe antianxiety drugs (also called anxiolytics or tranquilizers) to alleviate their patients' feelings of tension and anxiety, to increase patients' feelings of well-being, and to counteract symptoms of insomnia. The earliest antianxiety drugs, the *barbiturates,* are rarely used today because they are highly addictive and potentially dangerous (see chapter 5). More commonly used are two classes of antianxiety drugs: muscle relaxants and benzodiazepines. Muscle relaxants cause feelings of tranquility. Two of the more frequently used drugs of this class are meprobamate drugs (Miltown and Equanil).

Benzodiazepines also cause muscle relaxation and have an additional notable tranquilizing effect. Two of the most widely used of these drugs are chlordiazepoxide (Librium) and diazepam (Valium). Two more recent such drugs are Xanax and Klonopine. Clinicians have commonly prescribed these drugs without sufficient heed of their possible consequences. The drugs can be habit forming, and their tranquilizing effect can impair attention and alertness (Schweizer, Rickels, Case, & Greenblatt, 1990). The SSRI drugs used for depression appear to work not only for depression, but for anxiety as well (Lydiard, Brawman, & Ballenger, 1996).

Lithium. In 1949, lithium was found to be effective in treating manic–depressive disorders, and it remains the drug of choice for these disorders. It is very effective, causing almost immediate alleviation of symptoms in roughly three-fourths of cases. However, it alleviates depressive symptoms only in manic–depressives (those persons with bipolar disorder), adding credence to the notion that bipolar disorder differs qualitatively from major (unipolar) depression (M. Baron, Gershon, Rudy, Jonas, & Buchsbaum, 1975). We still do not know why lithium has the effect it does (Manji et al., 1991), and the drug must be used with care because overdoses can lead to convulsions and even to death.

Psychotherapy Process and Outcome Research

Paul Crits-Christoph, *University of Pennsylvania*

How does one study psychotherapy? Psychotherapy is an intimate, subjective, evolving relationship between a therapist and a patient (or group of patients) that at first appears to defy systematic empirical investigation. A variety of strategies have been developed in our lab and others' to examine what happens during psychotherapy sessions and how psychotherapy affects patients.

Psychotherapy *outcome* research is concerned with identifying the types of psychotherapies, therapists, settings, and formats (e.g., duration, frequency of sessions) that lead to relatively better outcomes for patients. In designing such research, our initial consideration is whether the goal is primarily to establish a causal link between an independent variable (e.g., a specific treatment technique) and outcome or to answer a practical question about which treatment works best.

Psychodynamic psychotherapy, broadly defined, consists of a variety of techniques that are *supportive* in nature—they serve to foster a positive collaboration with the patient through empathy, recognizing the patient's strengths and achievements, and establishing a shared agenda for treatment and change. Psychodynamic psychotherapy also consists of a variety of *exploratory* techniques to increase patient insight about relationship patterns and feelings. The value of supportive techniques and a positive therapeutic relationship in association with outcome is one of the most robust findings in the psychotherapy research literature (Horvath & Symonds, 1991). Less clear, however, is the extent to which the exploratory, insight-oriented interventions also contribute to positive outcomes.

To address this question, we have been conducting an ongoing clinical experiment to test the potential causal link between exploratory, insight-oriented interventions and treatment outcome. Patients with generalized anxiety disorder are randomly assigned to either a full 16-week treatment package of both supportive and exploratory interventions or a treatment that contains only supportive interventions.

In conducting this form of research, it is particularly important that we attempt to standardize the treatment interventions as much as possible. Without such standardization, an investigator runs the risk of obtaining large differences between therapists that undermine the ability to sort out whether outcome effects have more to do with different therapist skills and personality rather than treatment techniques (Crits-Christoph, Baranackie, & Kurcias, et al., 1991; Crits-Christoph & Mintz, 1991).

One psychotherapy outcome study that has a practical aim was conducted involving patients with cocaine dependence (Crits-Christoph, Siqueland, & Blaine, et al., 1999). In most community substance abuse treatment facilities, services are delivered by drug counselors with bachelor's or master's degrees in addiction counseling. Their treatment usually involves monitoring drug usage, education, and facilitating abstinence.

In our study, we compared two forms of professional psychotherapy (cognitive-behavioral and psychodynamic) to standard drug counseling. The results indicated that the drug counselors produced significantly better patient outcomes (lower drug use) than did the professional psychotherapists. Based on these results, we are now turning to the question of how we can improve the treatments administered by drug counselors.

Psychotherapy *process* research takes on a different form—the interior of psychotherapy sessions. Using transcripts of audiotapes of psychotherapy sessions, we first have a set of judges, working independently, identify the central interpersonal/emotional issues for each patient. Another set of judges identifies the main therapist statements in the transcripts that attempt to provide some learning or insight to the patient. A third set of judges then evaluates the extent to which each main therapist statement does, or does not, address the central themes that our judges have identified for each patient. Using this methodology, we have found that the accuracy of therapist interventions is significantly correlated with both improvement in the quality of the therapeutic relationship over time, as well as the eventual outcome of psychodynamic psychotherapy (Crits-Christoph, Cooper, & Luborsky, 1988; Crits-Christoph, Barber, & Kurcias, 1993).

References

Crits-Christoph, P., Baranackie, K., Kurcias, J. S., Beck, A. T., Carroll, K., Perry, K., Luborsky, L., McLellan, A. T., Woody, G. E., Thompson, L., Gallagher, D., Zitrin, C. (1991). Meta-analysis of therapist effects in psychotherapy outcome studies. *Psychotherapy Research, 1*, 81–91.

Crits-Christoph, P., Barber, J., & Kurcias, J. (1993). The accuracy of therapists' interpretations and the development of the therapeutic alliance. *Psychotherapy Research, 3*, 25–35.

Crits-Christoph, P., Cooper, A., Luborsky, L. (1988). The accuracy of therapists' interpretations and the outcome of dynamic psychotherapy. *Journal of Consulting and Clinical Psychology, 56*, 490–495.

Crits-Christoph, P., & Mintz, J. (1991). Implications of therapist effects for the design and analysis of comparative studies of psychotherapies. *Journal of Consulting and Clinical Psychology, 59*, 20–26.

Crits-Christoph, P., Siqueland, L., Blaine, J., Frank, A., Luborsky, L., Onken, L. S., Muenz, L. R., Thase, M. E., Weiss, R. D., Gastfriend, D. R., Woody, G. E., Barber, J. P., Butler, S. F., Daley, D., Salloum, I., Bishop, S., Najavits, L. M., Lis, J., Mercer, D., Griffin, M. L., Moras, K., Beck, A. T. (1999). Psychosocial treatments for cocaine dependence: National Institute on Drug Abuse Collaborative Cocaine Treatment Study. *Archives of General Psychiatry, 56*, 493–502.

Horvath, A. O., & Symonds, B. D. (1991). Relation between working alliance and outcome in psychotherapy: A meta-analysis. *Journal of Counseling Psychology, 38*, 139–149.

 Find out more about this topic at *www.harcourtcollege.com/psych/ishm*

Conclusions

A 1993 World Health Organization report (Sartorius, de Girolano, Andrews, German, & Eisenberg, 1993a) indicates that the main breakthroughs in pharmacotherapy (represented by the preceding four classes of psychotropic drugs) have revolutionized the psychiatric treatment of mental illness. Subsequent developments have offered refinements that enhance the applicability of these treatments, but they have not offered additional breakthroughs. In other cultures, very different drugs, as well as other forms of therapy, may be used more generally.

Who Seeks Out Psychotherapy?

Not everyone who needs psychotherapy seeks it out (Pekarik, 1993). Indeed, it is estimated that over half of those who need psychotherapy do not seek it out (Torrey, 1997). Those who do seek it out are likely to be the more educated among the population, and also to be those with health insurance (Olfson & Pincus, 1996). Some who do not seek out psychotherapy are unable to simply because the areas in which they live have no facilities for psychotherapy, or because they lack the economic resources to use the sources of help that are available (*Mental Health, United States,* 1996). There are, as discussed in a later section, alternatives to individual psychotherapy, many of which are offered in areas which may be underserved in terms of individual psychotherapy. The people who do seek help may be suffering from a particular identifiable set of symptoms or may simply be feeling uncomfortable with the way their life is going (Strupp, 1996). The culture of the therapist and the person seeking therapy as well as that in which the therapy takes place, also affects the approach used.

Psychotherapy in a Cultural Perspective

Although the range of psychotherapies is quite broad, cross-cultural commonalities exist among the various approaches to psychotherapy. Across such diverse psychotherapists as U.S. and European clinical psychologists, psychiatrists, Native American *shamans,* Latin American *curanderos* (or *curanderas,* in Mexico and elsewhere), and Yoruban *babalawo* (in Nigeria), psychotherapy appears to have five basic components (Torrey, 1986): (1) an emphasis on construction of a shared worldview between client and therapist, including a common language and similar conceptions of causes and effects; (2) therapist characteristics such as warmth, genuineness, and empathy; (3) patient expectations that reflect the culturally relevant beliefs of the patient and the therapist; (4) a set of specific tech-

niques employed by the therapist (e.g., talking or using biological techniques such as drugs or shock therapy); and (5) a process by which the therapist enables or empowers the client to gain increased knowledge, awareness, and mastery, thereby gaining hope. According to E. Fuller Torrey, psychotherapists across various cultures "perform essentially the same function in their respective cultures. [Both Western and non-Western] therapists . . . treat patients using similar techniques; and both get similar results."

Although there are many commonalities among therapists and among clients in different cultures, there are also many differences among cultures. As any culture-rich nation becomes still more culturally diverse, it is becoming increasingly necessary for counselors and therapists to develop competence in dealing with clients who are culturally different from themselves. It is not unusual for counselors to encounter clients from diverse ethnic groups or even recent immigrants from other countries. For example, Asian American and Hispanic American therapists may well confront Haitian, Ukrainian, or Turkish clients. Therapists need to consider the various backgrounds of their clients, which may influence the process of therapy. When clients and therapists come from radically different places, in which they were socialized to have sharply different beliefs, values, expectations, or conceptions of self, significant problems can arise. These problems may result in distrust, disappointment, or failed interventions.

The need for guidance in cross-cultural psychotherapy has spawned numerous books dealing with various key issues in the field (e.g., Axelson,

The Native American shaman *or Latin American* curandero *or* curandera *shares with Western psychotherapists an emphasis on empathy, warmth, and genuineness; specialized techniques; and an interest in empowering the person seeking help to gain increased knowledge and mastery.*

1993; Ivey, Ivey, & Simek-Morgan, 1993). Many college professors and administrators are becoming aware of the need to provide courses and lectures on cross-cultural psychology. Among the many issues in cross-cultural psychotherapy addressed by such courses and books, the following questions frequently arise: (a) Are certain types of therapy more appropriate for particular ethnic groups? (b) How can mental-health programs reach out to the members of ethnic groups who typically underuse available resources? (c) How can a therapist communicate empathically with clients who have worldviews that differ from the therapist's?

Before we discuss the comparative effectiveness of the various approaches to psychotherapy, we broaden our view of psychotherapy to encompass forms of psychotherapy delivered by modes other than the interaction between one therapist and one client.

The advantages of having such a large group for psychotherapy may include reduced cost, greater social pressure to effect positive changes, and greater diversity of persons who may offer a fresh perspective on a troubling situation. The disadvantages of group therapy include the potential for dilution of the treatment and for group dynamics to take precedence over the presenting problem that stimulated the desire to obtain therapy.

Alternatives to Individual Psychotherapy

In Search of . . .

Are there alternatives to individual psychotherapy?

We have described drug therapies and the other forms of psychotherapy in terms of one psychotherapist administering treatment to one client. In some circumstances, however, various alternatives to one-on-one therapy may be more helpful. These options include group therapy, couples and family therapy, community psychology, and self-help. A 1993 World Health Organization report (Langsley, Hodes, & Grimson, 1993) indicated that these alternatives to individual psychotherapy have been widely available among many non-Western cultures.

Group Therapy

Psychotherapy can be administered either individually or in groups. Group therapy offers several distinct advantages over individual psychotherapy: (a) group therapy is almost always less expensive than individual therapy; (b) group therapy may offer greater support than individual therapy because groups usually comprise individuals with similar problems; (c) group therapy offers the potential value of social pressure to change, which may supplement (or even supplant) the authoritative pressure to change that comes from the therapist; (d) the very dynamic of group interaction may lead to therapeutic change, especially in the cases of people who have problems with interpersonal interactions.

Group therapy also has several potential disadvantages: (a) the treatment effect may be diluted by the presence of others requiring the attention of the therapist; (b) group psychotherapy may embroil the clients in so many issues related to the group interactions that the clients no longer focus on resolving the problems that prompted them to seek therapy in the first place; (c) the content of the group process may move away from the dynamics of psychotherapy, so that group members start dealing with problems that are interesting but irrelevant to the issues for which the group was formed.

Group therapy should be distinguished from "encounter groups" or "T-groups," which are formed in order to help individuals grow psychologically and sometimes to achieve spiritual fulfillment. Some of these groups subject individuals to fairly harsh psychological and even physical rigors. Although these groups may help serve people, they also seem to take a heavy toll in terms of psychological harm they can cause (M. Galanter, 1989; Mithers, 1994).

Twelve-step groups have become very popular for the treatment of addictions. Such groups typically do not use a professionally trained therapist or other group leader. The first such group was Alcoholics Anonymous (AA), which was founded in the mid-1930s. Twelve-step groups are based on developing the addicts' relationship to God, as well as to self and others. Members typically attend three to five meetings each week, and at each meeting members discuss their difficulties in overcoming their addiction. The support of other members is viewed as key to overcoming these addictions. The effectiveness of AA and similar programs is not well documented, however (see D. C. Walsh et al., 1991).

The philosophy of AA is that alcoholism is a disease that can be managed but never fully cured. AA members who are in *recovery* have acknowledged that they have the disease, that there is no cure for it, and that alcohol therefore can never again play a part in their lives. Related groups include Al-Anon (for the spouses and adult children of alcoholics), Alateen (for the adolescent children of alcoholics), and Overeaters Anonymous (for those who feel unable to control how much or what they eat). Attendance at programs such as these goes beyond mere participation in therapy. It is more of a *conversion experience*, in which a person adopts a totally new way of living. People attempt to move beyond the addiction that has ruled their lives, and they do so by participating in a group that can itself become a way of life (see Table 17-2).

Behavior therapy also can be done in groups. For example, A. A. Lazarus (1961, 1968, 1989) has used behavioral techniques in a group setting. Phobias are especially treatable in this way. In group desensitization, a single psychotherapist can teach many people at once how to relax deeply, and then can develop a common desensitization hierarchy for the alleviation of various kinds of phobias, such as fear of snakes, heights, and so on. Various behavioral techniques also have been used in other group treatment programs, such as programs to lose weight (Wollersheim, 1970).

Sometimes, instead of treating a group of unrelated people, a psychotherapist treats a group of related people, such as a couple or a family.

Couples and Family Therapy

The goal of couples and family therapy is to treat problems from the perspective of **family systems therapy**—that is, the treatment of the couple or the family unit as a whole, which involves complex internal interactions, rather than in terms of the discrete problems of distinct members of the unit. The identified problem may be centered on the family unit, such as troubled communication among family members, or it may be centered on the problem of one member. The underlying notion in this kind of therapy is that even individual problems often have roots in the family system, and to treat the problem, the whole family should be part of the solution (see Langsley et al., 1993). For example, a conduct disorder on the part of a child almost inevitably affects a whole family, not just the child who expresses the conduct disorder.

In cases of marital conflict, couples therapy is more successful than individual therapy both in holding couples together and in bringing them back together (Gurman, Kniskern, & Pinsoff, 1986). Couples therapy tends to be particularly successful for people who have had problems for only a short time before they seek therapy and when they have not yet initiated action toward divorce. One reason for the greater success of couples therapy is that the therapist can hear about reality as expressed by both members of the couple. Hearing both points of view enables the therapist to mediate more effectively than does hearing just a single point of view.

Couples therapy emphasizes communication and mutual empathy. Partners are trained to listen carefully

| **TABLE 17-2** |

The 12 Steps of Alcoholics Anonymous *These 12 steps are well-known around the world to the many members of Alcoholics Anonymous, a support group for persons struggling with problems related to alcohol abuse.*

1. We admitted we were powerless over alcohol—that our lives had become unmanageable.
2. Came to believe that a power greater than ourselves could restore us to sanity.
3. Made a decision to turn our will and our lives over to the care of God *as we understood Him.*
4. Made a searching and fearless moral inventory of ourselves.
5. Admitted to God, to ourselves, and to another human being the exact nature of our wrongs.
6. Were entirely ready to have God remove all these defects of character.
7. Humbly asked Him to remove our shortcomings.
8. Made a list of all persons we had harmed, and became willing to make amends to them all.
9. Made direct amends to such people wherever possible, except when to do so would injure them or others.
10. Continued to take personal inventory and, when we were wrong, promptly admitted it.
11. Sought through prayer and meditation to improve our conscious contact with God *as we understood Him,* praying only for knowledge of His will for us and the power to carry that out.
12. Having had a spiritual awakening as the result of these steps, we tried to carry this message to alcoholics and to practice these principles in all our affairs.

Couples therapy is highly effective in helping couples to resolve interpersonal conflict and to enhance communication, particularly if the presenting problems have been of short duration prior to treatment and the couple has not yet started divorce action.

and empathically to each other, and they learn to restate what the partner is saying, thereby confirming that they accurately understood the partner's point of view. Couples are also taught how to make requests of each other in constructive but direct ways, rather than to make indirect requests that can be confusing and at

times harmful to the relationship. Erving Goffman (1967) found that partners in unsuccessful relationships often fail to hear even the positive things that they say about each other.

Aaron Beck (1988) has emphasized the importance of having each partner understand the perspective of the other. He urges partners to clarify the differences in what each partner seeks for the relationship, noting that partners often have secret "shoulds": things that each of us believes that our partner ought to do, but which our partner may not believe to be important or worth doing. Beck believes many problems in a relationship can be attributed to the *automatic thoughts* that can rise into consciousness, and which we believe to be self-evident, whether they are or not.

Community Psychology

Community psychology views people not only as a part of a couple or a family system, but also as part of the larger system of the community. The community psychologist may intervene at any level, ranging from the individual to the community, depending on what will most effectively help the client or clients being served.

Darrel Regier, director of epidemiological studies at the National Institute of Mental Health (quoted in Goleman, 1993), studied more than 20,000 U.S. men and women, trying to determine the prevalence of

"The work being done on your marriage—are you having it done, or are you doing it yourselves?"

mental illness. Based on his representative sample, he extrapolated that 52 million Americans (one in every five) suffer from some type of psychological disorder that meaningfully impairs their functioning in some way. Of the 52 million, 20 million have phobias severe enough to cause them to limit their behavior, and another 15 million would be diagnosed as depressed. Of the 52 million Americans who are impaired, only 8% are being treated for their impairment. The best course of action, certainly, is to treat people before they even begin to show impairment—in other words, to focus on prevention.

The emphasis in community psychology is at least as much on prevention as it is on treatment. With so many members of a community at risk for psychological distress, it makes sense to try to prevent problems before they happen. Community psychologists may intervene at one or more of three levels of prevention. *Primary prevention* is aimed at preventing disorders before they happen. *Secondary prevention* is targeted toward detecting disorders early, before they become major problems. *Tertiary prevention* essentially treats disorders once they have developed more fully, and it can be considered preventive only in the sense that the continuation of the disorders may be prevented.

Whereas most traditional psychotherapists wait for clients to come to them, community psychologists often actively seek out people who have problems or who are likely to have them in the future. Moreover, community psychologists often perceive themselves to be part of the communities they serve rather than detached, outside experts. That is, community psychologists may become actively involved in the lives of people in the community.

One of the means by which community psychologists offer appropriate services to members of the community is through *community mental-health centers*. The goal of such centers is to provide outpatient mental health care to people in the community. Costs are generally lower than those of individual psychotherapy, and many centers offer 24-hour walk-in crisis services.

An outgrowth of the community-psychology movement and the related community-health movement, and one that places more emphasis on treatment than on prevention, is the hotline. *Hotlines* serve people, usually 24 hours a day, who are desperate for assistance. The most well-known of the hotlines are those dealing with suicide prevention, but hotlines also exist for potential child abusers and for people with other problems as well. People answering the phones of these hotlines are taught a series of procedures to defuse the immediate problem. For example, a person answering the phone in a suicide-prevention hotline is taught to communicate empathy to the caller, show understanding of the caller's problem, provide information regarding sources of help, and obtain the caller's verbal agreement to take actions that will lead the caller away from suicide (Speer, 1972).

Unfortunately, many communities have reduced their funding of community mental-health services. At about the same time that funding cuts were hurting community mental-health services, the need for such services increased, as many mentally ill persons who had been hospitalized were *deinstitutionalized* (released from health-care institutions and onto the streets). Although community-based outpatient treatment may be as effective as—or more effective than—inpatient treatment for many disorders, many deinstitutionalized patients receive little or no treatment whatsoever. As a result, they are left homeless on our streets, in need of appropriate treatment. The deinstitutionalization of the mentally ill in many countries around the world has created problems when there has been an associated failure to deliver appropriate community-based mental-health care (Burti & Yastrebov, 1993).

A lack of funds may be one reason many people try to improve their mental health on their own, as discussed in the Psychology in Everyday Life box on Self Help.

The previous sections describe various kinds of psychotherapy, each of which makes different assumptions about both the nature of psychological disorders and the optimal ways to treat these disorders. In light of this diversity of approaches, it seems that they cannot all be right. At some level, this perception is probably correct, but at another level, the approaches to psychotherapy may be more complementary than they initially appear.

Consider, for example, the issue of what causes mental disorders. Part of the difference in treatment procedures derives from different views about causation. Psychodynamic theories tend to focus on repressed early childhood experiences as the cause of mental disorders. Humanistic theories consider the primary cause of these disorders to be deficits either in feelings of self-worth or in feelings of unconditional acceptance by others. Behavior therapies look to faulty conditioning, whereas cognitive theories emphasize maladaptive thoughts or schemas. Biological therapies look to psychophysiological causes of distress, such as depletion of neurotransmitters. To what extent are these various causal explanations mutually exclusive?

To see the complementarity of the various approaches, we can view mental disorders as having causes at different levels of analysis. For example, traumatic experiences in early childhood may lead to or even be viewed as inappropriate forms of behavioral

Psychology in Everyday Life

Self-Help

Psychotherapy for individuals, couples, families, and even entire communities involves personal interactions between psychotherapists and the clients they serve. There is yet another alternative for people seeking psychotherapeutic assistance: self-help. Your neighborhood bookstore probably features a generously stocked self-help section, with books suggesting how to help yourself resolve almost any problem you could imagine: how to treat addiction (including many books based on Alcoholics Anonymous), how to improve your love life, how to become more assertive, and how to

overcome various forms of self-defeating behavior. Thousands of such books are published every year, some making outrageous claims (Rosen, 1987, 1993) but others offering reasonable advice. Moreover, as many as 15 million people may be involved in self-help groups (Christensen & Jacobson, 1994).

Do any of these books actually work? This is a hard question to answer because no one is monitoring the effectiveness of the various programs. There are relatively few classics in the field—books that continue to be printed long after the initial burst of sales—sug-

gesting that the large majority of these books are not so helpful that purchasers are recommending them to an ever-widening circle of buyers. Perhaps the most appropriate comment with regard to such books is "Let the buyer beware!" Some of the books may be helpful, others not. Users need to judge each book on its own merit and realize that for serious problems, no self-help book is likely to suffice. Those in need of psychotherapy might do better to choose the most appropriate means of professionally administered psychotherapy.

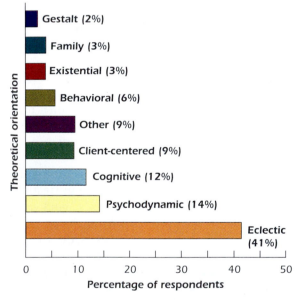

Figure 17–6
ORIENTATION OF PSYCHOTHERAPISTS. *Out of 415 clinical psychologists surveyed, almost half indicated that they followed an eclectic approach. (After D. Smith, 1982)*

conditioning. Imbalances in or lack of neurotransmitter substances may lead to maladaptive thoughts, or maladaptive thoughts may lead to low self-esteem, which may in turn affect neurotransmitter levels. Often, the causal direction of these various levels of analysis is not clear.

Some psychotherapists synthesize several therapies into a single approach. The term *eclectic therapy* describes a strategy for therapy that integrates several approaches. Indeed, many therapists today take an eclectic approach (see Figure 17-6).

Before a clinician or a consumer chooses a particular kind of psychotherapeutic technique, he or she should consider the relative effectiveness of each. We will discuss the effectiveness of psychotherapy next.

Effectiveness of Psychotherapy

In Search of . . . *How effective are the various approaches to psychotherapy?*

Does psychotherapy work? There has been a great deal of research done in attempts to answer this question. Perhaps the most striking finding is that, on average, psychotherapy seems to work (Lambert & Bergin, 1994; Lipsey & Wilson, 1993; Maling & Howard, 1994; Seligman, 1995).

In evaluating the effectiveness of psychotherapy, it is important to compare the effectiveness of a given treatment not only against alternative treatments, but against no therapy at all. Over time, some people show spontaneous remission—they simply get better of their own accord. Individual humans, like members of other species, have evolved in ways that equip them to fight off a variety of kinds of threats to their existence, ranging from large animal predators to parasitic infections to the kinds of problems in living that psychotherapy is meant to address. Thus, we can expect that some people will improve without any active intervention. The success of psychotherapy needs always to be measured against this baseline rate of improvement. At the same time, there can be ethical problems with giving a person in need no therapy at all.

Other factors also should be considered in an ideal research program—for example, the length of treatment dramatically affects therapeutic outcomes. One *meta-analytic study* (i.e., a study that analyzes a large number of other studies; K. I. Howard, Kopta, Krause, & Orlinsky, 1986) showed that when the effects of dropping out of treatment are statistically controlled, 29–38% of psychotherapy clients improve by the first 3 sessions, 48–58% improve by the first 4–7 sessions, 56–68% improve by the first 8–16 sessions, 74–81% by the first 17–52 sessions, and 85% by the first 53–100 sessions. Clearly, studies that failed to consider treatment length would obtain results that would be inconclusive. (It may be useful to point out that the average number of psychotherapy sessions for Americans receiving treatment is 14 in a given year; Goleman, 1993.)

The Impact of Managed Care

A problem in modern times is that both the initiation and duration of psychotherapy often are controlled by insurance companies under the general label of *managed care*. The problem is that sometimes the management emphasizes cost cutting more than it emphasizes high-quality service. Access to psychotherapy may be restricted or its duration curtailed. Less trained practitioners may be preferred by managed-care companies to more trained practitioners, in part because their services cost less. The issues surrounding the attainment of good psychotherapeutic care at what managed-care companies consider to be a reasonable cost are far from being resolved. The increasing dominance of decisions made by managed care is likely to increase the importance of evaluation in psychotherapy, because evaluations provide a basis for managed-care companies to decide whether or how much psychotherapy is called for (Beutler, Kim, Davison, Karno, & Fisher, 1996)

Issues in Therapy Research

Researchers should consider not only the length of treatment, but also the length of treatment for specific disorders. For example, Figure 17-7 shows the results of the meta-analytic study by Kenneth Howard and

Figure 17–7

META-ANALYSIS OF THE COURSE OF PSYCHOTHERAPY. *Although self-ratings and therapist ratings differed, and the degree of improvement differed across various diagnoses, on the whole, the data seem to show that psychotherapy is highly effective for helping persons with psychological problems. (After Howard et al., 1986)*

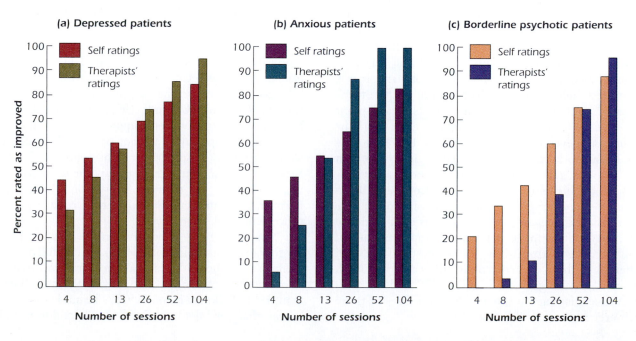

his colleagues (1986). If researchers were to determine the effectiveness of therapy for borderline psychotic patients in terms of therapist ratings at the conclusion of eight sessions, the results would be profoundly discouraging; yet if the researchers were to assess therapist ratings in these same patients at the conclusion of 104 sessions, the studies would be extremely encouraging. However, for depressed and anxious patients, therapy results would be much more positive after much shorter durations of therapy.

Additional factors to consider might be whether individual, family, couple, or group therapy would be most helpful; the relevant type of setting (e.g., inpatient or outpatient); additional characteristics of the client and of the therapist (e.g., cultural background, personality variables such as extroversion/introversion, attitudes, and values); therapeutic technique (e.g., how closely the therapist followed the approach prescribed by a particular theoretical paradigm); and so on. Although the call for this kind of research first went out decades ago (e.g., Kiesler, 1966; G. L. Paul, 1967), it has yet to materialize. Given its complexity, its failure to materialize is not surprising.

Although the ideal research that would allow perfect tailoring of psychotherapy to client diagnosis has not yet been done, meta-analytic and other research clearly shows that psychotherapy produces significant improvement in clients, above and beyond any spontaneous recovery that might have occurred (e.g., Andrews, 1993; M. L. Smith & Glass, 1977; Stiles, Shapiro, & Elliott, 1986). In particular, clients who receive psychotherapy, on average, are better off than 75% or more of research control participants who did not receive psychotherapy. Psychotherapy is especially helpful (better than for 82–83% of untreated controls) in improving clients' self-esteem and in reducing their anxiety. However, psychotherapy was less helpful (better than for only 71% of untreated controls) in increasing the level of adjustment in persons institutionalized for psychotic, alcoholic, or criminal behaviors, and it was even less helpful (better than for only 62% of untreated controls) in increasing clients' grade-point average or otherwise in enhancing their work or school achievements (Smith & Glass, 1977). In general, psychotherapy is more effective for those with less serious, rather than with more serious, psychological problems (Kopta, Howard, Lowry, & Beutler, 1994) and for people who really want to improve (Orlinsky & Howard, 1994). There is even evidence that psychotherapy can result in improved health and recovery from illness (Bennett, 1996) and thereby reduce the cost of health care (Gabbard, Lazar, Hornberger, & Spiegel, 1997). It also is perceived as playing a positive role in the lives of those who receive it (Shadish et al.,1997).

Long-Term Versus Short-Term Treatment

A study reported in *Consumer Reports* (1995) and directed in large part by psychologist Martin Seligman suggested the efficacy of psychotherapy. In particular, Seligman (1995) has reported that patients who received long-term treatment did substantially better than those who received only short-term treatment, and that patients who received both medication and psychotherapy did no better than those who received just psychotherapy. No specific type of psychotherapy was, on average, better than any other for any disorder. Psychologists, psychiatrists, and social workers did not differ, on average, in effectiveness, although all were more effective than marriage counselors and family doctors. Patients whose length of therapy or whose choice of therapist was dictated by an insurance company or a managed-care program did worse than those who had freedom of choice.

It is important in evaluating these results to take into account that the *Consumer Reports* survey was based on users' subjective impressions of the effectiveness of the therapy rather than on the basis of objective measures of therapeutic outcomes. The response rate for surveys was very low, which further leaves one somewhat skeptical of the validity of the results. The responses also were from the standpoint of the clients, and it would be interesting to compare the views regarding of the clients with those of the clients' therapists (Brock, Green, & Reich, 1998).

Moreover, not all research suggests equal effectiveness of psychotherapies. Many studies have suggested that, on average, behavior therapies and cognitive therapies may be more effective than psychodynamic therapy or no therapy at all (Chambless, 1995; Lambert & Bergin, 1994; A. A. Lazarus, 1990; Weisz, Weiss, Hun, Granger, & Morton, 1995). Moreover, some research suggests that particular therapy techniques may work especially well for particular disorders. For example, fears and phobias seem best to be treated behaviorally by exposing clients to the source of their fears (S. L. Kaplan, Randolph, & Lemli, 1991). But even the behavioral and cognitive techniques have their limitations. For example, they are not particularly effective with personality disorders or schizophrenia (L. R. Brody, 1990). Cognitive therapies appear to be particularly effective in treating depression (Robinson, Berman, & Neimeyer, 1990). There is room for improvement in all techniques.

Not everyone is as positive on the value of psychotherapy as is Seligman (1995). A carefully controlled study, the Fort Bragg Demonstration Project, also set out to test the value of psychotherapy (Bickman, 1996; Bickman et al., 1995). The study involved a unit that served more than 42,000 children and adolescent dependents for more than 5 years, from June 1990 to September 1995. This study, unlike Seligman's, evaluated treatment effectiveness rather than relying only on reports of satisfaction from clients. It looked at whether there were actual improvements in functioning. The results suggested that psychotherapy was not particularly useful and that greater length of time in psychotherapy often did not improve outcomes (see also Dineen, 1998; Hoagwood, 1997). Given the positive results of other studies, the results of this study cannot be viewed as conclusive. At the very least, they suggest the need to know better under what kinds of circumstances psychotherapy is more or less effective.

In sum, psychotherapy is often, although certainly not always, beneficial. Somewhat surprising is the finding in some studies that the positive outcomes of therapy seem to occur regardless of the type of therapy implemented. That is, when the researchers' allegiance to a particular therapy is ruled out, each type of psychotherapy seems to be just about as effective as the next. When the researchers' allegiance is not ruled out, whatever therapy program the researcher prefers seems to fare better in the comparisons across therapy programs.

Common Elements in Effective Therapy

Common Characteristics Across Therapists

Despite the variety of their therapeutic approaches, all psychotherapists seek to communicate to their clients a new perspective on the client and his or her situation. Perhaps these attributes account for the primary effects of psychotherapy of all sorts.

The therapeutic alliance forged between therapist and client appears to be important to the success of all forms of therapy.

Several meta-analytic studies have shown that despite widely divergent therapeutic techniques and approaches, two global characteristics of therapists appear across theoretical orientations: (1) their "warm involvement with the client," and (2) their "communication of a new perspective on the client's person and situation" (Stiles et al., 1986, p. 172). Thus, regardless of the therapist's theoretical orientation, all therapists try to establish *rapport* with clients, which means that they try to ensure feelings of trust and to establish ease of communication with the client. Further, the client needs to feel that the therapist genuinely cares about the outcome, or therapeutic change is much less likely to occur.

Common Characteristics Across Clients

An interesting counterpart to the hypothesized crucial importance of the role of the therapist is that the role of the client in a therapeutic relationship promotes improvement. The client's style of communication within a therapeutic context is distinctively self-disclosing, and this self-disclosing communication may in itself promote improvement. The client's desire to improve and belief in the efficacy of therapy may also facilitate the therapeutic process.

The Therapeutic Alliance

A synthesis of the preceding two approaches is that the client and the therapist form a distinctive *therapeutic alliance*, in which they are allies in the effort to help the client improve through the process of psychotherapy. William Stiles and his colleagues (1986) evaluated dozens of studies and found that the available research supported the importance of the therapeutic alliance in terms of the clients' therapeutic outcomes. Also important for success is scrupulously ethical behavior on the part of the psychotherapist.

Ethical Issues in Psychotherapy

In Search of . . . *What are the professional responsibilities and ethical obligations to which psychotherapists must commit themselves?*

In the fall of 1992, Ann Landers, an advice columnist, devoted her entire column to an exposé of a world-renowned psychiatrist who had held various prestigious positions in psychiatric associations. The disgraced psychiatrist was forced to resign from the American Psychiatric Association after losing a lawsuit brought by former patients who claimed he had abused them sexually and in other ways. This type of case is not unique, although it is rare. Psychotherapists are in a position to cause enormous harm to patients by virtue of their status and their position as dispensers of treatment; a few of them do so. Inevitably, they hurt not only their clients and themselves, but also the entire profession through their unethical behavior.

Perhaps even more than many other professionals, psychotherapists are expected to behave ethically toward clients. Psychotherapists are expected to refrain, for example, from becoming sexually involved with clients. Moreover, psychotherapists are expected to maintain the confidentiality of communications between themselves and their clients. Only in rare cases can they be required to divulge the contents of these communications. Examples of such cases occur primarily when the therapist determines that clients may be dangerous to themselves or to others. In addition, in some states, psychotherapists must breach confidentiality when a client has been accused of a crime and the records of the psychotherapist might be relevant to determining the client's sanity, when the psychotherapist has been accused of malpractice, when psychotherapy has been sought with the goal of evading the law, or when a child under age 16 has been a victim of child abuse. In most states, in cases of child abuse or of potential danger to others, therapists are legally required to take action. In other words, they cannot expose a child or other person to great risk simply to maintain confidential communications.

Sometimes the risks emanating from psychotherapy emanate from good, but misdirected intentions. In May 1994, a civil court awarded half a million dollars to a man whose adult daughter had accused him of sexually abusing her during her childhood (Berkman, 1994; LaGanga, 1994; Shuit, 1994). The award followed a verdict asserting that the daughter's therapists negligently had reinforced false memories of sexual abuse (see chapter 7). The man's 23-year-old daughter had accused him of sexually abusing her after she underwent treatment that her psychotherapists asserted was designed to "recover suppressed memories." When the daughter made those accusations, her father lost his $400,000-a-year job as a vice president of marketing for a major company and her mother divorced him.

In this case, the therapist used questionable therapeutic techniques to elicit the daughter's horrifying recollections. The daughter remains entirely sure of her memories, but many other people, including the jurors in her father's civil case, question the accuracy of the memories. Whatever the verdict in cases such as this one, it is clear that both the parent and the child will have suffered greatly. One source (described in Geyelin, 1994) estimates that thousands of parents and their adult children are confronting the heart-wrenching problems posed by trying to determine whether disturbing memories have arisen from accurate recollection, elicited by techniques that facilitate their recovery, or from inaccurate distortions, introduced by techniques that lead to their creation. Professional organizations of clinical therapists are grappling with the need to guide therapists in the treatment of people who appear to be suffering ill effects from suppressed or repressed memories of painful events.

Another ethical protection for clients demands that before clients participate in what are viewed as experimental treatments, they must first give **informed consent**—that is, experimental participants are briefed before the experiment and are fully informed of the nature of the treatment procedure and of any possible harmful side effects or consequences of the treatment, as well as of the likelihood that these consequences will occur. Also, during the experimental treatment, the psychotherapist is expected to preserve the well-being of the experimental participant to the fullest extent possible.

Although we would like to believe that ethical issues can be viewed in black and white, they often come in shades of gray. For example, in the past, homosexuality was treated as a disorder, and people with homosexual preferences were viewed as needing to change their sexual preference to restore them to full mental health. Today, homosexuals are usually viewed as requiring treatment only if they are unhappy with their sexual preference. Treatment is recommended if homosexuals want either to come to feel satisfied with this preference or to try to change it. The gray area becomes visible when we ask, "To what extent should the therapist encourage the client either to accept a homosexual preference or to try to change it?" Different therapists would approach this question with different points of view. On the one hand, it is important for psychotherapists to respect the values of their clients; on the other hand, some view psychotherapy partly as a tool for transmitting a value system from the psychotherapist to the client.

The important point is that psychotherapists need to consider ethics in their treatment of clients. They need to take into account not only their own ethical standards, but also those of the field and of the society in which it is embedded.

When psychotherapy is implemented appropriately, another benefit of psychotherapy appears to be a reduction in overall health-care costs. Thus, when companies provide mental-health counseling for their employees, they obtain not only increases in productivity and decreases in employee absenteeism and turnover, but also savings in the overall cost of health care (Docherty, 1993). Health psychology is the topic of the next—and final—chapter.

THINK ABOUT IT

1. Cognitive and behavioral therapies often are paired. What does each technique have to offer that complements the other?
2. If you were a marriage and family therapist, which two psychotherapeutic approaches might you be most likely to use? Why would you choose those two methods?
3. Suppose you were a biochemist concocting the next big breakthrough drug that would minimize the problems caused by a particular psychological disorder. If you could choose any disorder to attack and any negative side effects to tolerate, which disorder—and which symptoms of the disorder—would you wish that your drug could minimize? What modest negative side effects would you find least offensive in your new wonder drug?
4. What would you view as an ideal treatment for depression, one that perhaps combines elements of the therapies about which you have read?

5. How might a psychotherapist who has doubts about the ethics of a new treatment program go about resolving his or her doubts prior to administering the treatment?
6. If you were to have a need for psychotherapy, which method of therapy would you choose? If you were to decide to become a psychotherapist, would your choice be the same? Analyze the benefits and drawbacks of the method you would prefer in each role.

online *You can provide your own answers to these questions online at the* Sternberg, **In Search of the Human Mind** *Web site:* **http://www.harcourtcollege.com/psych/ishm**

SUMMARY

Early History of Psychotherapeutic Intervention   545

1. Early views of psychotherapy reflected the prevalent idea that persons afflicted with mental illness were possessed by demons. Subsequent treatment in *asylums* was essentially a form of warehousing mentally ill persons to keep them off the streets, with little thought given to humane treatment, let alone psychotherapy. Some early forms of treatment were bizarre and of no value. However, by the 19th century, Josef Breuer proposed a talking cure, which became the basis for Freud's psychoanalytic methods.

Diagnosing and Assessing Abnormal Behavior   546

2. More than half the people who need psychotherapy probably do not seek it out.
3. The DSM and ICD systems of diagnostic classification have helped clinicians make appropriate and consensually understood diagnoses as a basis for treatment.
4. Clinical assessment procedures include *clinical interviews*, which may be structured or unstructured; and psychological tests.
5. Psychological tests include personality tests (both objective and projective measures), intelligence

tests, neuropsychological tests, and psychophysiological tests.

Approaches to Psychotherapy   549

6. There are five main approaches to psychotherapy: psychodynamic, humanistic, behavioral, cognitive, and biological. The cultural approach can be viewed as an additional approach.
7. Psychodynamic therapies emphasize insight into underlying unconscious processes as the key to the therapeutic process. Freudian psychoanalytic therapy and neo-Freudian ego-analysis therapies are the two major types of psychodynamic therapies.
8. Humanistic therapies emphasize the therapeutic effects of the therapist's unconditional positive regard for the client, as exemplified by Carl Rogers's *client-centered therapy.*
9. Behavior therapies emphasize techniques based on principles of operant and classical conditioning. Techniques include counterconditioning, *aversion therapy, systematic desensitization,* and *extinction procedures,* such as *flooding* and *implosion therapy.* Additional techniques include the use of *token economies* and *behavioral contracting.* The use of *modeling* bridges the gap between behavioral and cognitive therapies.
10. Cognitive therapies encourage patients to change their cognitions in order to achieve therapeutic

changes in behavior and other desired outcomes. Albert Ellis's *rational-emotive behavior therapy* and Aaron Beck's *cognitive therapy* are two of the main schools of cognitive therapy.

11. Historically, biological treatments of mental illness have included a wide array of treatments, such as *electroconvulsive therapy (ECT)* and *psychosurgery.*

12. Modern biological treatments, such as the development of effective *psychotropic drugs*, have revolutionized biological treatments. Today, the four key classes of psychotropic drugs are antipsychotics, antidepressants, antianxiety drugs, and lithium. Although these drugs are certainly not cure-alls, they have been a welcome asset to the clinician's armamentarium. A cultural perspective provides an additional approach.

Alternatives to Individual Psychotherapy   562

13. Alternatives to individual psychotherapy include group therapy, couples and family therapy, community psychology, and self-help. Group therapy, couples therapy, and family therapy often address problems specific to interpersonal relationships, and they address these problems through the dynamic interplay that occurs in the group, the couple, or the family. Community psychology focuses primarily on preventive mental health; community psychologists may use several strategies, including education of all members of a community, outreach to persons experiencing stress, and treatment of persons in distress. In self-help therapies, individuals seek guidance in handling stressful situations or minor psychological difficulties through books and other informational media.

14. No single approach to psychotherapy is ideal for all persons, or in all situations or cultural settings. Rather, the various approaches to psychotherapy may be viewed as complementary alternatives for aiding persons in need of psychotherapeutic assistance. For example, drug therapy often may be combined with verbal forms of psychotherapy to achieve results neither form of therapy would yield alone.

Effectiveness of Psychotherapy   566

15. In some studies, psychotherapies of various forms have proven to be about equally effective. Several possible explanations for this paradox (i.e., different forms but similar outcomes) have been proposed. Other studies, however, have shown differential effectiveness of various kinds of psychotherapy. The effectiveness of any psychotherapy has to be evaluated against rates of *spontaneous recovery*—that is, recovery without treatment.

16. The length of treatment and other factors not specific to a particular approach may play a role in the relative effectiveness of psychotherapy.

17. Each approach to psychotherapy has distinctive advantages and disadvantages, and it may be best to view the approaches as complementary rather than competing. We have not yet reached the point at which we can prescribe a particular form of therapy for a particular type of psychological problem. Effective therapy generally requires warm involvement of the therapist with the patient and good communications. In particular, both the therapist and the client need to feel a sense of alliance in trying to overcome the client's difficulties.

Ethical Issues in Psychotherapy   569

18. Because psychotherapists have the potential to influence clients profoundly, psychotherapists must be especially mindful of ethical considerations.

KEY TERMS

asylums   545
aversion therapy   552
behavioral contracting   554
behavior therapy   552
cathartic method   546
client-centered therapy   551
cognitive therapy   556
countertransference   550
electroconvulsive therapy
   (ECT)   557

extinction procedures   553
family systems therapy   563
flooding   553
free association   549
implosion therapy   553
informed consent   570
modeling   555
psychosurgery   557
psychotropic drugs   558

rational-emotive behavior therapy
   (RET)   555
resistances   550
spontaneous recovery   559
systematic desensitization   553
token economy   554
transference   550

■ THINK ABOUT IT SAMPLE RESPONSES

1. Cognitive and behavioral therapies often are paired. What does each technique have to offer that complements the other?

Cognitive therapy focuses on how people think and behavior therapy on how people behave. The combination is often viewed as particularly useful because both thought and action are critical to psychological disorders and to curing them or at least lessening their severity.

2. If you were a marriage and family therapist, which two psychotherapeutic approaches might you be most likely to use? Why would you choose those two methods?

Each individual must answer this question for himself or herself. Some people might find cognitive and behavioral techniques particularly useful because they focus on both thought and action. Other people might prefer other combinations.

3. Suppose you were a biochemist concocting the next big breakthrough drug that would minimize the problems caused by a particular psychological disorder. If you could choose any disorder to attack and any negative side effects to tolerate, which disorder—and which symptoms of the disorder—would you wish that your drug could minimize? What modest negative side effects would you find least offensive in your new wonder drug?

Each individual must answer for himself or herself. For example, schizophrenia can severely disrupt people's lives. But depression can be very disruptive too and is far more likely to lead to suicidal behavior. Depression is also far more prevalent. Many antidepressants have side effects, but they are usually relatively mild, such as dry mouth.

4. What would you view as an ideal treatment for depression, one that perhaps combines elements of the therapies about which you have read?

An ideal treatment for some would be a combination of cognitive-behavioral therapy and some kind of drug treatment. But the ideal treatment must depend on the particular symptoms, their severity, and a constant monitoring of treatment to evaluate how it is working.

5. How might a psychotherapist who has doubts about the ethics of a new treatment program go about resolving his or her doubts prior to administering the treatment?

The psychotherapist might talk to colleagues in order to get their advice. He or she might consult the American Psychological Association for guidelines. He or she also might talk to someone who specializes in ethics.

6. If you were to have a need for psychotherapy, which method of therapy would you choose? If you were to decide to become a psychotherapist, would your choice be the same? Analyze the benefits and drawbacks of the method you would prefer in each role.

Each individual must decide for himself or herself. The author of this book would prefer an eclectic approach, trying to deal with each problem in the way that has proven most effective in the past and that works best with each client.

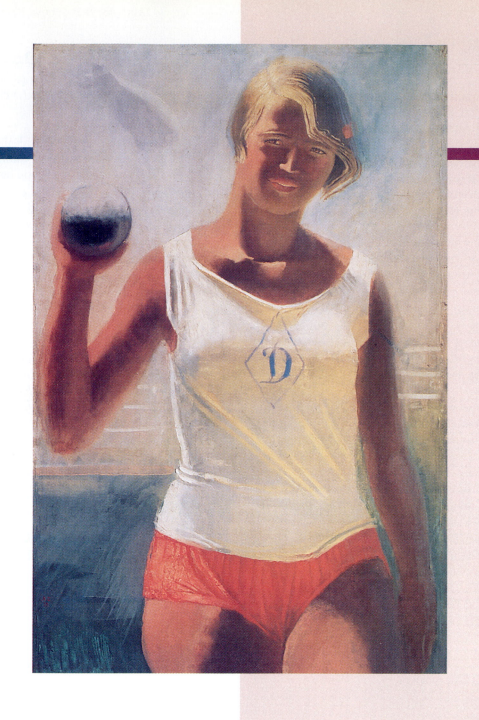

If you don't mind, it doesn't matter.

18

HEALTH PSYCHOLOGY

Chapter Outline

Psychology and Health

In Search of . . . *If our mental and physical health are related, what is the basis for this relationship and what does it mean for psychology?*

As we have seen throughout this text, the body and mind, the physical and the mental, are intimately connected. It is no surprise therefore that an entire area of psychology is devoted to the ways in which our mental state affects our health and vice versa. It's no surprise either that part of what health psychology has to tell us is (in slightly exaggerated form) that if you don't mind, it doesn't matter.

Health psychology is the study of the reciprocal interaction between psychological processes of the mind and the physical health of the body. Note that the interaction of psychological and physiological processes works both ways. Particular psychological processes can lead to either better or worse health, which in turn can lead to particular psychological processes. For example, research has shown that people under stress are more susceptible to catching colds (S. Cohen, Tyrrell, & Smith, 1993) and, of course, catching a cold can lead to further stress as one falls behind in things one had hoped to do.

Health psychologists are interested in the psychological antecedents and consequences of how people achieve health, how they become ill or prevent illness, and how they respond to illness—such as how they seek to overcome illness or how they adapt to illnesses that they are unlikely to overcome completely. Health psychologists delve into many aspects of the connection between mind and body.

A primary goal of health psychology is to promote health and health-enhancing behavior. Simple examples of such behavior are eating well, exercising, stopping smoking, and avoiding harmful drugs. Of course, health psychologists recognize that serious psychological and physiological disorders (e.g., eating disorders or cancer) can affect people's health. Nonetheless, health psychologists assume that people can influence their health through the psychological regulation of their behavior. Research supports this assumption, particularly for health-related behavior that is subject to our conscious control. For example, people can significantly reduce their risk of dying at any given age by following seven health-related practices (Belloc & Breslow, 1972; Breslow, 1983). In fact, the risk of death at a given age has been found to decrease almost linearly with the number of the following health-related practices that have been implemented:

1. sleeping 7 to 8 hours a day

2. eating breakfast almost every day

3. rarely eating between meals

4. being at a roughly appropriate weight in relation to height

5. not smoking

6. drinking alcohol in moderation or not at all

7. exercising or engaging in physical activity regularly

Note that we control many aspects of our health by *not* engaging in harmful, or at least health-compromising, behavior (such as ingesting alcohol, nicotine, or other harmful drugs; see chapters 5 and 6). In addition, we can take positive steps to enhance our health through nutrition and exercise. Health psychology is a widely encompassing field. Indeed, some of the topics frequently addressed in the field of health psychology have been covered elsewhere in this book. This chapter covers only those topics of health psychology that have not been covered elsewhere. First, we shall examine the models of health and illness, as well as the history of health psychology.

The Mind–Body Connection

Hippocrates (ca. 430 B.C.) revolutionized ancient Greek medicine with the notion that disease had specific physical origins and was not punishment inflicted by the gods (S. E. Taylor, 1999; see chapter 1). Centuries after Hippocrates described his iconoclastic views of health and well-being, Galen (who practiced medicine in Rome, ca. A.D. 129–199) suggested that illnesses are attributable to **pathogens** (specific disease-causing agents; Stone, 1979). Eventually, subsequent medical practitioners agreed with him, and Galen's views became the basis for medical treatment for many centuries. Today, of course, we have identified—and even seen, with the aid of microscopes—many more of these pathogens than Galen ever imagined possible.

The pathogenic view of illness gave rise to the biomedical model. According to the **biomedical model,** disease is caused by pathogens that have invaded the body; the focus is on the elimination of pathogens that cause diseases. The model has served people's needs relatively successfully for almost 2,000 years, providing a basis for treating and often for curing illnesses. Nonetheless, the biomedical model has not been universally accepted. Some consider it too mechanistic and too narrow in scope. Although the model centers on how to treat illness and allows for some concern as to how to prevent illness, it gives little consideration to the question of how to promote wellness. Also, the model gives little attention to psychological factors that contribute to various diseases, and it gives no heed to the psychological processes that may help promote both healing and well-being. Today, we might seek a broader model, one incorporating the biomedical model as a part of our total understanding of health.

The most widely accepted alternative model in health psychology is the **biopsychosocial model,** which has largely replaced the biomedical model, and which seeks an understanding of the psychological, social, and biological factors that contribute to illness, to the prevention of illness, to recovery from illness, and to promotion of wellness (G. L. Engel, 1977, 1980; G. E. Schwartz, 1982). Most of us seem to embrace this model intuitively, which underscores the importance of context in understanding health and illness. For example, most people believe that factors such as changes in weather, poor diet, lack of sleep, and stress (pressures or strain) can contribute to a cold (Lau & Hartman, 1983). Although a virus may be directly responsible for the cold, other factors can make it more likely that we will become susceptible to the virus. When we refer to someone as being "worried sick" or as having a "tension headache," we recognize that psychological and social factors may contribute to physiological illness. People have long recognized these connections, as is shown by the history of the field of health psychology.

Health and Behavioral Medicine

People have been trying to understand the causes of health and illness for centuries. During some eras, the mind was seen as relevant to the causes; in other times, neither the mind nor the body was considered the immediate source of illness. People believed that illness was sent by divine beings as a punishment for misbehavior or for disbelief. Ancient literature and legends describe many instances in which a punitive god caused illness or injury to smite those who mistreated believers, who disobeyed divine commandments, or who otherwise showed a lack of respect or belief. By the 21st century, however, the mind has become widely accepted as influential in both health and illness.

One of the earliest modern psychological antecedents of health psychology is the field of psychosomatic medicine, based on a psychodynamic perspective. For much of the 20th century, researchers in the field of *psychosomatic medicine* studied the psychological roots of physical illnesses, such as ulcers, asthma, and migraine headaches. Although it is arguable whether psychological factors actually *cause* any of these diseases, it is well known that such factors can worsen symptoms of these diseases.

By the 1970s, behavioral approaches to psychology became more popular than psychodynamic ones, and behavioral medicine emerged. Originally, **behavioral medicine** focused on the use of behavioral techniques to help people modify health-related problems, such as heavy smoking or overeating (see chapter 17). As the cognitive revolution began to affect all aspects of psychology, the field of health psychology began to embrace a cognitive orientation. Contemporary health psychologists often seek to know how thought processes mediate both wellness and the progression of illnesses. As the biopsychosocial model suggests, the fairly simplistic view of psychological factors "causing" disease has been replaced by a view that recognizes the complex psychological, physical, and environmental factors that interact in leading to both illness and health.

Many of the historical trends that have influenced health psychology derive from developments in the health field in general. Initially, health practitioners focused exclusively on helping people respond to illness or injury. The illnesses that received the greatest attention were acute (e.g., influenza). If the patient survived the illness—which was by no means assured—the patient required no further care from health professionals. Much less attention was given to chronic illnesses (e.g., diabetes). Most illnesses were treated in terms of discrete episodes or symptoms.

This early emphasis on treating disease was entirely appropriate, given the leading causes of death at the time. Antibiotics and a vast array of other medical treatments virtually wiped out such diseases as smallpox, which had devastated huge proportions of the world's population. Other diseases—such as influenza, diphtheria, and tuberculosis—became far less deadly (see Figure 18-1).

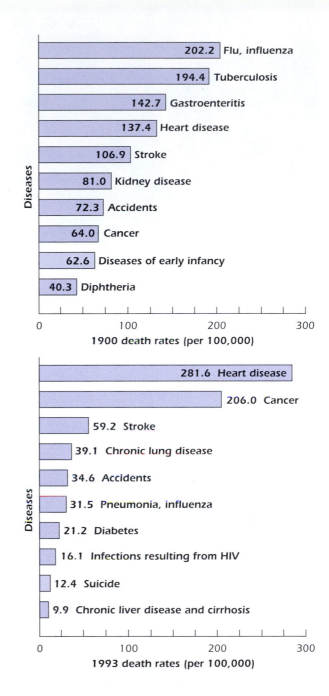

Figure 18–1
THE 10 LEADING CAUSES OF DEATH: 1900 AND 1993.
Within this century, the trend has been away from acute infectious diseases and toward chronic diseases and nonmedical causes of death, such as accidents, suicides, and homicides.

As medicine's tools for conquering illnesses—particularly acute ones—have become more powerful, health-care professionals have turned their attention to helping people prevent illness. They encourage people to watch for early symptoms (e.g., digestive difficulties), to seek medical care when warranted (including regular checkups), to avoid behaviors that compromise health

The primary goal of health psychology is to promote health and health enhancing behavior.

(e.g., using psychoactive drugs such as alcohol or nicotine), to take appropriate preventive-medicine steps (e.g., being vaccinated or otherwise immunized), and to engage in appropriate hygiene and safety practices (e.g., washing hands before eating, wearing a safety belt in a moving vehicle). More recently, health psychologists and other health practitioners have turned their attention to promoting wellness—engaging in health and safety practices that help people not only prevent illness but also promote their overall health and well-being.

Stress and Coping

In Search of . . . *What is stress? Is it different for everyone? Why do some people seem to handle it better than others?*

"I'm totally stressed out" is a sentence most of us have muttered at one time or another. What this means physically and psychologically is the subject of a rather large area of inquiry among health and behavioral psychologists and other scientists. Among them are those working in the relatively new field of psychoneuroimmunology, which examines the effects of stress at the cellular level, particulary in our immune systems.

Stress

When we think of stress, we usually think of feeling mentally and perhaps physically distressed from something external such as time pressure, work pressure, or family pressure. That implicit definition works pretty well, but it is only part of the picture. When researchers investigate stress, they define the term in a slightly dif-

ferent way. **Stress** refers to a person's response to something in the environment that challenges the person. The internal and external adaptation by an individual is known as a **stress response.** Sometimes, for example, the little hassles of everyday life may accumulate and lead to considerable stress (Pearlstone, Russell, & Wells, 1994) and even to reduced resistance to infection (Brosschot, Benschop, Godaert, & Olf, 1994) and physical ailments (P. M. Kohn, Gurevich, Pickering, & MacDonald, 1994). Sometimes, one major stressful event gives rise to a multitude of minor ones. For example, a divorce often leads to the need for an attorney, a new house, a new perspective on economic affairs, and so forth (Pillow, Zautra, & Sandler, 1996). A major move similarly can lead to many sources of stress.

Chronic or accumulated stress can harm health and well-being (House & Smith, 1985) and can lead to psychological dysfunction (Eckenrode, 1984; Eckenrode & Gore, 1990). Stress encountered on the job, for example, may ultimately lead to *burnout*—a feeling of emotional exhaustion and distance from the people whom you serve and the sense that you are no longer accomplishing anything meaningful.

Stressors

Surprisingly, stressors do not necessarily have to be things we perceive as negative. For example, having a new baby, getting married, and moving to a new home are all stressors because they require the new parent, spouse, or home dweller to adapt in many ways. Most of us would welcome certain stressors, such as outstanding personal achievement or marriage. Nevertheless, most stressors are negative events.

Stressors can also vary in their intensity. Unhappiness in a marriage as well as divorce are major stressors (Kiecolt-Glaser et al., 1993; Kiecolt-Glaser et al., 1996), as is a feeling of being imposed on by people

Stressors can be positive or negative—a vacation away from home or just the daily hassle of traffic, lines, or crowds.

(Evans & Lepore, 1993). Stressors also can be relatively minor or transient changes, such as being on vacation, going away for a weekend, or having a treasured friend or family member visit for a few days. These pleasant changes are potential stressors because they cause you to adapt in some way: In the middle of the night in your luxury hotel, you must find your way to the bathroom. Or while your best friend is visiting, you must cope with new demands on your time and on your physical space. Stressors even can be routine annoyances or challenges to your ability to cope, such as traffic hassles, disagreements with an acquaintance, disputes with a bureaucratic

functionary, getting accustomed to new equipment or appliances, rearranging items in a cabinet, or having to have a vehicle repaired.

Stress as Life Changes

Thomas Holmes and Richard Rahe designed a test to measure the amount of accumulated stress a person is experiencing. In the Social Readjustment Rating Scale (SRRS), these researchers ranked 43 stressors and assigned weights to them; for example, getting married was rated as more stressful—more challenging—than having trouble with a boss (see Table 18-1). These

TABLE 18–1

Social Readjustment Rating Scale   *Thomas Holmes and Richard Rahe analyzed the life events that lead to stress and assigned various weights to each of these potential stressors. (After Holmes & Rahe, 1967)*

RANK	LIFE EVENT	MEAN VALUE	RANK	LIFE EVENT	MEAN VALUE
1	Death of spouse	100	23	Son or daughter leaving home	29
2	Divorce	73	24	Trouble with in-laws	29
3	Marital separation	65	25	Outstanding personal achievement	28
4	Jail term	63	26	Spouse begins or stops work	26
5	Death of close family member	63	27	Begin or end school	26
6	Personal injury or illness	53	28	Change in living conditions	25
7	Marriage	50	29	Revision of personal habits	24
8	Fired at work	47	30	Trouble with boss	23
9	Marital reconciliation	45	31	Change in work hours or conditions	20
10	Retirement	45	32	Change in residence	20
11	Change in health of family member	44	33	Change in schools	20
12	Pregnancy	40	34	Change in recreation	19
13	Sex difficulties	39	35	Change in church activities	19
14	Gain of new family member	39	36	Change in social activities	18
15	Business readjustment	39	37	Mortgage or loan less than $10,000	17
16	Change in financial state	38	38	Change in sleeping habits	16
17	Death of close friend	37	39	Change in number of family get-togethers	15
18	Change to different line of work	36	40	Change in eating habits	15
19	Change in number of arguments with spouse	35	41	Vacation	13
20	Mortgage over $10,000	31	42	Christmas	12
21	Foreclosure of mortgage or loan	30	43	Minor violations of the law	11
22	Change in responsibilities at work	29			

researchers then correlated the stressors with the likelihood of becoming ill. They found that this likelihood was positively correlated with the person's increasing totals for the weighted values of these stressors. (Recall, however, the difficulties in determining causality based on correlational evidence alone.)

Shortly after the SRRS was introduced in 1967, the scale was introduced to other countries, either in its original form or in an adapted form (see, e.g., Yahiro, Inoue, & Nozawa, 1993). Research suggests that the scale has wide cross-cultural applicability, but that some of the items, some descriptions of the items, and some of the weightings and rankings given to the items may need to be adapted to suit different cultural contexts. An early study illustrates both the utility and the need for adaptation of the scale across cultures: The responses of 266 Malaysian medical students were compared with a matched sample in the Seattle, Washington, area, where the SRRS was created. Although there were many similarities in the responses, there were also significant differences, particularly on items dealing with romantic love and with infringement of laws (Woon, Masuda, Wagner, & Holmes, 1971). In a later study of Chinese citizens, events related to family and to career were rated as more stressful than were those related to personal habits, such as social activities and living conditions (Hwang, 1981).

Although the SRRS has been widely used, it has been criticized on a number of grounds (Rabkin, 1993). First, some of the terms, such as *personal injury*, can be viewed as vague (Taylor, 1999). Second, what is stressful for one person may be less stressful for another (Schroeder & Costa, 1984). Third, whether an event is stressful, or how stressful it is, may depend on how well it is resolved (Thoits, 1994). For example, one person may cope well with retirement, finding many relaxing and enjoyable activities to pursue, while another person may feel frustrated, stressed out, and unable to cope. Finally, although the SRRS includes both positive and negative events, research suggests that negative events cause considerably more stress than do positive ones (Smith, 1993; Turner & Wheaton, 1995).

A major stressor not included in the SRRS is the adjustment associated with adapting to a new culture. The technical term for stress of this kind is *acculturative stress* (J. W. Berry, 1989; Nwadiora & McAdoo, 1996). Acculturative stress can range from relatively minor (e.g., voluntary migration to be with loved ones or to seek out more desired lifestyle options) to catastrophic (e.g., totally involuntary uprooting, as in the case of religious or ethnic persecution or even threat of genocide). Such stress has particularly interested cross-cultural psychologists who live in pluralistic societies in which immigrants continue to arrive

(see J. W. Berry, 1994; J. W. Berry, Kim, Minde, & Mok, 1987).

One of the worst stressors that a person can encounter is torture, which is widely encountered in many parts of the world (Basoglu, 1997). One study of victims of torture found that nearly half suffered even many years later from nightmares and other symptoms, such as anxiety, depression, and social withdrawal (Basoglu, Paker, Paker, Ozmen, Marks, Sahin, & Sarimurat, 1994). Treating victims of torture is a major challenge for psychologists.

Physical Responses to Stress

Environmental events alone do not create stress; the individual must *perceive* the stressor and must respond to the stressor in some way. Often—initially, at least—the primary response of the individual is physiological. When we feel challenged by the need to adapt or threatened by some menace, our bodies physiologically prepare us to confront the challenge ("fight") or to escape from the threatening situation ("flight"). This fight-or-flight response probably has adaptive evolutionary origins. Those who reacted too slowly or inappropriately to mortal threats in the distant past usually became neither our ancestors nor anyone else's: They died on the spot.

The physiological fight-or-flight response was discovered by accident. Hans Selye was seeking a new sex hormone when he happened across a surprising phenomenon: When the body is attacked or is damaged, it seems to respond in the same general way, regardless of the nature of the assault (e.g., shock, extreme temperatures, or fatigue) or the target of the damage (e.g., the whole body or only a particular body part or organ). Selye soon saw the potential ramifications of this discovery, and he shifted his research to focus on this puzzling physiological response. Selye and other researchers have noted some patterns in our physiological response to relatively extreme levels of stress, which Selye (e.g., 1976) termed the **general adaptation syndrome (GAS),** in which the body initially exerts maximal effort to adapt. There appear to be three phases of response: alarm, resistance, and exhaustion (see Figure 18-2).

Alarm

The body immediately is aroused, and the sympathetic nervous system helps trigger the release of hormones from the adrenal glands—corticosteroids, epinephrine (adrenaline), and norepinephrine (noradrenaline). These hormones increase heart and respiration rate; slow down or stop the activity of the digestive tract, making more blood available to other organs; trigger biochemical reactions that create

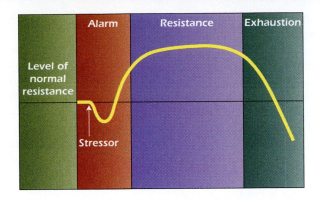

Figure 18–2

GENERAL ADAPTATION SYNDROME (GAS). *According to Hans Selye, we undergo three phases in responding to stressors: an alarm phase, in which we shift into high gear, using up our bodily resources at a rapid rate; a resistance phase, in which we shift down somewhat from using our resources in a spendthrift manner; and an exhaustion phase, in which our bodily resources are depleted.*

tension in the muscles; increase energy consumption, which produces heat; increase perspiration, which helps cool the body; and increase the release of clotting factors into the bloodstream, to minimize blood loss in case of injury. All these physiological responses go on without our ever having to initiate them consciously. The state of alarm will generally be lesser to the extent that we can predict or control potential stressors in our environment. These stressors may be particular to the individual, or they may affect a whole group, such as racism and sexism.

Resistance

The alarm state cannot continue indefinitely, and the body imposes a counterbalance to the sympathetic nervous system's plundering of the body's energy stores. Quite soon, the parasympathetic nervous system (which is involved in anabolic, energy-storing processes) calls for more prudent use of the body's reserves. For example, the demands on the heart and lungs decline. Physiological stress responses generally decrease in intensity, although they do not return to normal if the perceived stress continues.

Exhaustion

Eventually, even at the reduced rates associated with the resistance phase, the body's reserves are exhausted, and its ability to restore damaged or worn-out tissues is diminished. The individual becomes more susceptible to many health problems, including heart disease. Another outcome is that resistance to *opportunistic in-*

fections (infections that take advantage of a weakened immune system or other vulnerability, as discussed below) decreases. Stress has been linked now to a large number of infectious diseases, including various types of herpes virus infections (such as cold sores, chicken pox, mononucleosis, and genital lesions) (S. Cohen, Kaplan, Cunnick, Manuck, & Rabin, 1992; S. Cohen, Tyrell, & Smith, 1991; S. Cohen & Williamson, 1991; Jemmott & Locke, 1984; Kiecolt-Glaser & Glaser, 1987; VanderPlate, Aral, & Magder, 1988). *Chronic fatigue syndrome (CFS)*, an ailment in which a person feels tired much of the time and has trouble meeting the demands of daily life, tends to be aggravated by fatigue. The cause of this illness is unknown, and it is possible that it is not even one illness but a collection of illnesses with similar symptoms.

Not only stress itself, but even the anticipation of stress, can result in suppressed functioning of the immune system (Kemeny, Cohen, Zegans, & Conant, 1989). Researchers in the cross-disciplinary field of psychoneuroimmunology revel in the findings being discovered almost daily regarding how our psychological processes, our neural physiology, and our immune systems interact in ways we never imagined—let alone understood—previously.

Although Selye's model has helped elucidate the effects of stress, it also has been criticized on a number of grounds. For example, it assumes greater uniformity in response to stress than there probably is (Hobfoll, 1989), and it underestimates the role of psychological factors in response to stress (R. S. Lazarus & Folkman, 1984).

Perceived Stress

It is not a given set of events, per se, that results in immune-system compromise, but rather the subjectively experienced stress that results from these events that is significant. For example, one individual might feel that dealing with an extremely dependent friend is highly stressful, but another individual might perceive the same experience as an interesting challenge. Also, each of us perceives some stressors as more distressing than others. For example, suppose that you hate confrontation of any kind and find conflict extremely stressful. Someone else might feel little distress in confrontational situations or might even relish conflict. Both you and your adversarial counterpart may experience the physiological alarm phase of the stress response and even the resistance phase; but because you fret about the confrontation for a while afterward you may reach the stage of exhaustion, whereas your antagonist may forget quickly about the conflict and avoid the exhaustion phase.

Each of us also experiences different degrees of internal conflict in response to external demands (work versus family, spouse versus friend, etc.). Moreover, the very same environment can be experienced as quite different, depending on personality variables. An extrovert who works in a library serving a remote community of illiterates might be about as distressed as an introvert who leads all the recreational activities for a cruise ship. Each, however, would consider the other's job idyllic.

Susan Folkman and Richard Lazarus (Folkman & Lazarus, 1988; Folkman, Lazarus, Gruen, & DeLongis, 1986) have proposed a model for the way personality factors, stressful circumstances, and health interact. According to Folkman and Lazarus, when confronted with a potentially stressful situation, we go first through a two-step appraisal process and then a two-dimensional coping process, both of which interact with our distinctive personalities and the situation at hand (see Figure 18-3). **Primary appraisal** involves a person's determination of whether it is important even to deal with the situation, based on the significance of the situation for the person and its possible outcomes for the person as a result of dealing with versus not dealing with the situation.

Suppose that, at the end of the term, a professor unexpectedly assigns a long paper. Some students might perform a primary appraisal and immediately feel their stress level skyrocket. There are few things in their everyday world that stress them out more than writing a paper, especially one assigned at the end of the term. Other students, for whom writing a paper even at the last moment is no big deal, may hardly react. They view the assignment as just another one in a long list of things to do.

Secondary appraisal involves a person's assessment of strategies she or he can use in order to make a beneficial outcome more likely and a harmful outcome less likely. In thinking about final exams, you would probably try to assess how you could increase the probability that you would score well and decrease the possibility that you would score poorly. Reading textbooks and studying lecture notes might figure prominently in your secondary appraisal.

Figure 18–3

AN INTEGRATED MODEL OF STRESS.   *The biopsychosocial model of stress incorporates psychological factors, such as cognitive appraisal, as well as physiological mechanisms in responding to stress.*

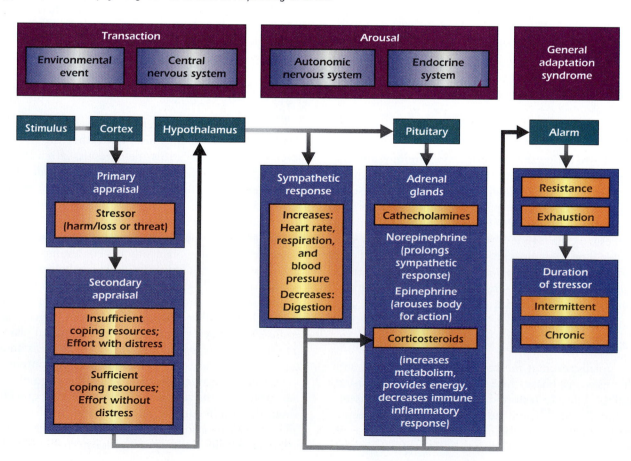

Coping Strategies and the Issue of Control

Both primary and secondary appraisal proceed at a cognitive level. At this level, you have yet to crack a book or jot down a note. Once your primary and secondary appraisals are complete, you are ready to begin **coping** with the situation—that is, the process of trying to manage the internal and external challenges posed by a troublesome situation. The two dimensions of coping serve different functions. **Problem-focused coping** involves the specific strategies used for confronting and resolving the problematic situation. For example, you would study the textbook, attend study sessions, and review your lecture notes as problem-focused coping strategies. **Emotion-focused**

coping involves handling internal emotional reactions to the situation. For example, while studying you might try to suppress your anxiety about the exams. Just before taking the exams, you might try some relaxation techniques to reduce your anxiety during the exams.

In circumstances over which we have more control (e.g., exam grades), problem-focused coping strategies are more likely to yield more satisfactory outcomes. In circumstances over which we have less control (e.g., what questions your instructor will ask), emotion-focused coping is more likely to yield more satisfactory outcomes. Myriad interactions are possible, depending on the individual's pri-

mary appraisal of what is at stake, the person's secondary appraisal of what coping options are available, and the person's implementation of those coping options. The net interaction determines the degree of stress that the individual experiences. According to Folkman and Lazarus, detrimental health consequences are associated with situations in which the person experiences greater stress, particularly if the person feels that his or her options for coping are inadequate for the situation at hand. Low self-esteem and lack of social support can also contribute to the sense of having inadequate options for coping (DeLongis, Folkman, & Lazarus, 1988).

Internal Variables and Stress: Type-A Versus Type-B Behavior Patterns

Like Selye's discovery of the physiological response to stress, a set of personality variables linked to health was discovered quite by accident. Meyer Friedman and Ray Rosenman (1974) were studying the differences in dietary cholesterol between male victims of heart disease and their wives when one of the wives commented, "If you really want to know what is giving our husbands heart attacks, I'll tell you. It's stress, the stress they receive in their work, that's what's doing it" (p. 56). This comment led the researchers to look at differences not only in levels of stress experienced by the victims of heart disease, but also in how these victims responded to stress.

Eventually, they formulated the notion of the **Type-A behavior pattern,** in which the individual demonstrates: (1) a competitive orientation toward achievement, (2) a sense of urgency about time, and (3) a strong tendency to feel anger and hostility. Type As tend to strive very hard and competitively toward achieving goals, often without feeling much enjoyment in the process; they tend constantly to be racing against the clock; and they tend to feel anger and hostility toward other people.

In contrast to the Type-A is the **Type-B behavior pattern,** in which the individual demonstrates relatively low levels of competitiveness, urgency about

time, and hostility. Type Bs tend to be more easygoing, relaxed, and willing to enjoy the process of life. Before you read on, stop for a moment to reflect on which pattern describes your own behavior. (*Clue:* If you felt angry at the suggestion to stop working toward your goal of finishing this chapter as quickly as possible, perhaps you do not need to think too much about which pattern best describes you.) If you are unsure of how you would describe yourself, think about how a family member or a close friend might describe your behavior.

A variety of methods have sprung up for measuring Type-A behavior. These measures include both structured interviews, which ask a more-or-less fixed set of questions, and paper-and-pencil questionnaires. For example, the *Jenkins Activity Survey* (JAS; Jenkins, Zyzanski, & Rosenman, 1979), a self-report questionnaire, asks questions such as these: When you listen to other people talking, do you sometimes wish that they would hurry up and say what they have to say? Do you tend to set deadlines or quotas for getting work done? Would people you know agree that you tend to be easily irritated? Do you find that you are often doing things in a hurry? In essence, Type-A people create their own stress.

Differential Reactions to Stress

Type-A individuals tend to react differently to stress than do Type-B individuals. Type-A individuals generally respond more quickly and forcefully and tend to

If you are the kind of person who is always in a hurry or trying to finish this chapter as quickly as possible, you fit the Type-A behavior pattern.

view sources of stress as threats to their personal self-control (Carver, Diamond, & Humphries, 1985; Glass, 1977). Type-A people also act in ways that increase the likelihood that they will encounter stress. In other words, they create some of the stress by seeking out demanding, competitive situations and by creating artificial deadlines for themselves (D. G. Byrne & Rosenman, 1986; T. W. Smith & Anderson, 1986).

The critical question from the standpoint of this chapter is whether Type As are more susceptible to health problems than are Type Bs. A number of studies have found a link between Type-A behavior and coronary heart disease (Booth-Kewley & Friedman, 1987; Haynes, Feinleib, & Kannel, 1980; Haynes & Matthews, 1988). Other studies have not confirmed the link (e.g., Shekelle et al., 1985).

It appears that merely linking Type-A behavior to coronary heart disease is too simplistic. For example, Suzanne Haynes and Karen Matthews (1988) found that Type-A behavior leads to increased risk of coronary heart disease for men with white-collar jobs but not for those with blue-collar jobs.

It also appears that the three components of Type-A behavior may not contribute equally to heart attack, although it may be related to generally poorer health outcomes (Adler & Matthews, 1994). Redford Williams (1986) argued that the component of anger and hostility is the most lethal (see also Ewart & Kolodner, 1994; Lassner, Matthews, & Stony, 1994; T. W. Smith, 1992; S. E. Taylor, 1999). Types of hostility can themselves be subdivided. People who are chronic complainers or who tend to be irritable much of the time are sometimes referred to as showing *neurotic hostility.* In contrast, those who seek out confrontations and conflicts with others are referred to as showing *antagonistic hostility.* This latter kind of hostility is the kind that appears to be related to heart attacks (Dembroski & Costa, 1988; Helmers & Krantz, 1996; G. N. Marshall, Wortman, Vickers, Kusulas, & Hewig, 1994). Other studies have supported this position (e.g., Barefoot, Dahlstrom, & Williams, 1983). Anger and hostility directed against the self may be especially damaging to health (Dembroski, MacDougall, Williams, Haney, & Blumenthal, 1985; R. Williams, 1986). Also, hostility characterized by suspiciousness, resentment, frequent anger, and antagonism toward others (which is sometimes referred to as *cynical hostility*) seems to be especially deleterious to health (Barefoot, Dodge, Peterson, Dahlstrom, & Williams, 1989; Dembroski & Costa, 1988; T. W. Smith, 1992; R. B. Williams & Barefoot, 1988). People who are cynically hostile are likely to have difficulty in getting social support from others (Benotsch, Christensen, & McKelvey, 1997) and they may fail to use what social supports are available (Lepore, 1995). It also appears that the overt expression of cynical hostility toward others, rather than merely feeling such hostility, may be most associated with adverse cardiovascular outcomes (Siegman & Snow, 1997).

In addition, some people who appear to be Type Bs are so only on the surface. These *phony Type Bs* (M. I. Friedman, 1991) or *defensive deniers* (Shedler, Mayman, & Manis, 1993) seem relaxed, unaggressive, and unresponsive to pressure, but deep down they are tense, hostile, and troubled. These individuals appear to be more at risk for illness than are even hostile Type As, and once they become ill, they show greater than average rates of mortality from the illness (Burgess, Morris, & Pettingale, 1988).

Possible Physiological Mechanisms for Health Effects

Researchers agree that Type-A individuals, especially hostile ones, experience more stress than do truly Type-B individuals, and greater levels of stress are linked to coronary heart disease. Although scientists are not certain of the exact physiological mechanisms that link stress to coronary heart disease, they are likely to espouse one of three major theories. One theory suggests that perceived stress causes the blood vessels to constrict while the heart rate increases. In effect, when people perceive stress, their bodies try to pump larger volumes of blood through narrower vessels. This process may wear out the coronary arteries, lead to lesions (areas of injury or disease), and eventually produce a heart attack (Eliot & Buell, 1983). Another theory suggests that hormones activated by stress may cause rapid and continual change in blood pressure, undermining the resilience of blood vessels (Glass, 1977; Haft, 1974; Herd, 1978). A third possibility is that stress may cause lipids to be released into the bloodstream, which contributes to *atherosclerosis*, a disease in which the fatty deposits constrict the blood vessels, making them rigid and hampering circulation. Of course, these possibilities are not mutually exclusive, so each may contribute to the net detrimental effect (Laragh, 1988; Parfyonova, Korichneva, Suvorov, & Krasnikova, 1988). When there is a detrimental effect, intervention is called for.

Possible Options for Intervention

Type-A behavior appears to be at least somewhat modifiable (M. Friedman et al., 1994; Levenkron & Moore, 1988). A variety of techniques have been used, including relaxation (Roskies, Spevack, Surkis, Cohen, & Gilman, 1978), aerobic exercise, weight training, and cognitive-behavioral stress management (Blumenthal et al., 1988; Roskies et al., 1986). To a certain extent, as mentioned in earlier chapters, we can influence our perceptions by changing our cognitions. Thus, interventions to increase the functioning of the immune system tend to be oriented toward improving people's reactions to events so the people feel less distressed in the face of life's challenges. In addition, lifestyle changes might be appropriate interventions. Type-A individuals tend to have very different lifestyles from those of Type-B individuals, and it may be as much the lifestyle as the personality itself that leads to coronary heart disease.

Health Care and Psychology

In Search of . . . *What implications does the relationship between mental and physical health have for the field of health care?*

Health care can be improved if providers recognize the importance of psychology to health-care outcomes. Patients also need to recognize the importance of psychology.

Recognition and Interpretation of Symptoms

What prompts people to seek health services? The first step in obtaining medical treatment for illness is to recognize and interpret symptoms. **Symptoms** are any unusual sensations or features (e.g., a queasy stomach or an itchy rash) in or on the body that a patient observes and thinks indicate some kind of pathology. Symptoms are, by definition, from the patient's point of view (in medicine, any unusual features observed by the physician are termed **signs**). For the most part, people seek health services only when they think they have symptoms.

When clinicians make diagnoses based on reported symptoms and observed signs, the clinicians use *explicit theories* for mentally representing various illnesses. Nonclinicians are not without mental models, however. Most nonphysicians have *implicit theories*—commonsense schemas—of illnesses and of the symptoms they comprise. These schemas help us to organize the information we know regarding various diseases. In addition to the identity of the illnesses, this information includes the symptoms, probable consequences, relative seriousness, and probable duration of the illnesses.

We use schemas to recognize and interpret our symptoms, matching the sensations or observations we perceive with our existing schemas for illness and wellness. If the sensations or observations seem to match our schemas for illness more closely than our schemas for wellness, we are more likely to attribute our sensations and observations to being sick (or injured), and we think of them as symptoms. If the sensations and perceptions of them more closely match our schemas for wellness, we are less likely to view the sensations as symptoms of illness.

Health psychologists have observed that people's reactions to illness are usually different when they face an illness that they believe to be **chronic**—recurrent, constant, or very long in duration, like migraine headaches or hypertension—versus when they suffer from one they believe to be **acute**—brief, usually characterized by sudden onset and intense symptomatology, but in any case not recurrent and not long in duration, such as a cold or a flu (Nerenz & Leventhal, 1983). For example, it appears that people are more likely to seek medical help if they have clear labels to attach to the symptoms that they experience and if they believe that their symptoms are treatable (Lau, Bernard, & Hartman, 1989).

Once people have decided they have symptoms, their next decision is whether or not to seek medical attention. This decision can be affected by factors other than the patient's schemas for illness and wellness.

Managed Care and Use of Health Services

One of the main challenges for health care is the growing influence of managed care. Because of the skyrocketing costs of health care and insurance, many people have joined health maintenance organizations (HMOs) and other plans that, for a fixed cost, provide reimbursement for health care as well as insurance in the case of major medical or psychological problems. These plans have the advantage of protecting people from health costs that could bankrupt them. But the drawback to the plans is that they make money the way any insurance company does—by seeking policy holders who do *not* file claims and by minimizing the payouts on claims. Many of these organizations have been quite aggressive in restricting the amount of care that they will allow to members. Moreover, health providers, including psychotherapists, who are not willing to "sign on" to these terms may be declared ineligible to be involved in the plans, resulting in a loss of patients. Typically, health providers also receive less money per patient visit when the patient is sponsored by a managed-care organization than when the patient is not so sponsored. Not only doctors, but patients as well have shown widespread dissatisfaction with HMOs (Freudenheim, 1993).

As a result of the spread of managed care, the concerns of many individuals have shifted from those of doctors who provide unnecessary services in order to increase their income to those of doctors who may be unable to provide all the services that are needed because of restrictions by managed-care companies. As the years go on, we can hope that a system will be worked out whereby patients can receive the services they need at reasonable prices.

Just what does happen when a medical practitioner and a patient finally do get together?

Interactions Between Medical Practitioners and Patients

The conversation that takes place between a doctor and patient is at once professional and personal. It may be a conversation between two strangers, or at least two individuals who need to communicate clearly in short order. A good deal of work among health psychologists has focused on answering questions such as: Which factors affect this communication, and how can it be improved?

Patient Styles

Medical schools gradually have come to appreciate a problem that patients have long recognized: The physician who received the highest grades in medical school or even who is more technically competent is not necessarily the one who interacts best with patients. To be highly effective, a medical practitioner needs to take into account not only the medical condition but also the distinctive psychological needs of the individual patient. Researchers have found that patients are more satisfied with their treatment if they are able to participate in the treatment in a way that matches their own preferences with respect to their perceived needs (Auerbach, Martelli, & Mercuri, 1983; Martelli, Auerbach, Alexander, & Mercuri, 1987). Those preferences, based on a health-opinion survey (Krantz, Baum, & Wideman, 1980), include (1) preference for information about health care, (2) preference for self-care, and (3) preference for involvement in health care. People vary in how much they need of each of these—information, self-sufficiency, and involvement with their practitioner.

Physician Styles

The regard that physicians show toward patients can substantially affect how the patient reacts not only toward the physician, but to the entire experience of health care (J. A. Hall, Epstein, DeCiantis, & McNeil, 1993). Physicians, like patients, have distinctive preferences and styles for patient–physician interactions. P. Byrne and B. Long (1976) analyzed 2,500 tape-recorded medical consultations in various countries. They found that physicians' interactions with their patients showed one of two styles. A **doctor-centered style** involves a highly directive interaction pattern, in which a physician narrowly focuses on presenting the medical problem (for which the patient has made the appointment), uses highly convergent questioning to elicit brief and targeted responses from the patient, and then formulates a diagnosis and a treatment regimen. If the patient diverged from the narrow, focused response and mentioned other problems or other symptoms, the doctor tended to ignore the further information. A **patient-centered style** is characterized by a relatively nondirective style of interaction, in which the physician asks divergent questions and allows the patient to take part in guiding the course of the interview, the diagnosis of the presenting problem, and the decision regarding the optimal treatment.

Patient-centered doctors were less likely to use medical jargon than were doctor-centered ones. Medical jargon can seriously impede communication between doctors and patients. Indeed, a number of studies have found that patients, particularly those of lower socioeconomic status, do not understand many of the terms that physicians tend to use (DiMatteo & DiNicola, 1982; McKinlay, 1975). The result of using such jargon is that a patient may not really understand the information the physician is providing.

Sometimes a patient's interaction with medical practitioners will go beyond just a visit to the doctor's office. Health psychologists have also studied the behavior of people in hospitals.

Patients in Hospitals

Roughly 33 million people are admitted every year to the more than 7,000 hospitals in the United States (American Hospital Association, 1987). Over the past three decades, hospital admissions have tended to increase, but the length of stay has tended to decrease (American Hospital Association, 1982, 1989).

Responses to the Need for Help

Although most patients feel anxious, confused, and perhaps even depressed when first admitted to the hospital, hospital staffers tend to categorize patients as either "good" or "bad." "Good" patients are fully compliant with the hospital procedures and regimens, and "bad" patients are more likely to complain, to demand attention, and to engage in behavior that is contrary to hospital policies. Hospital staff members tend to react negatively to such patients and want to have as little to do with them as possible. Ironically, the assertiveness of these patients may result in their being subjected to more risks at the hands of health professionals than are less assertive patients (Lorber, 1975). Hospital staff members are more likely to deal with such patients by medicating them, ignoring them, referring them to psychiatric care, or discharging them before they are ready.

Research has shown that increasing a hospitalized patient's sense of control, for example, by informing him or her in advance of what to expect from surgery and ways to respond to it, increases positive outcomes.

When you think about the kinds of behavior that are being fostered in this setting, you may realize that the hospital setting actually encourages patients to think and act in a manner that we described previously as demonstrating *learned helplessness* (Raps, Peterson, Jonas, & Seligman, 1982; S. E. Taylor, 1979; see chapter 6). Learned helplessness discourages patients from actively participating in their own recovery (E. Brown, 1963; S. E. Taylor, 1979). Unfortunately, although learned helplessness is adaptive for getting help from hospital staff members, this behavior can be detrimental to recovery, both in the hospital and after leaving it. Once patients leave the hospital setting, they are then expected suddenly to take full responsibility for all aspects of their recovery, despite having adaptively learned not to take any responsibility whatsoever for their in-hospital recovery.

Increasing Patients' Sense of Control

If hospitals tend to foster a lack of sense of control in the patient, and if a sense of control is important for patients' well-being and recovery, what can be done? A number of researchers have sought to figure out what hospitals could do to increase patients' psychological as well as physical well-being. Methods for increasing patients' sense of control are **control-enhancing interventions,** which increase patients' abilities to respond appropriately to illness and eventually to cope effectively with illness. In a classic, trailblazing study by Irving Janis (1958), postoperative recovery was compared in three groups—one group with a low level of fear about an impending operation, a second group with a moderate level of fear, and a third group with a high level of fear. Janis also looked at how well patients in each of the three groups understood and were able to use the information given them by the hospital about probable aftereffects of the surgery. Janis found that patients in the moderate-fear group had the best postoperative recovery.

Subsequent research has shown that what is most important is the extent to which patients process the information given to them in advance about the effects of the surgery, rather than their level of fear per se (K. O. Anderson & Masur, 1983; Johnson, Lauver, & Nail, 1989). Patients who know better what to expect during and after surgery are less emotionally upset after surgery and are also able to leave the hospital more quickly than are uninformed or less informed patients (Johnson, 1984). Other investigators have extended this work to suggest that patients who are prepared in advance regarding what to expect from a variety of medical procedures may feel a stronger sense of personal control and self-efficacy in mastering their reactions (see S. E. Taylor, 1999). This enhanced sense of control and efficacy then results in more positive outcomes.

Research further suggests that it is important to teach patients not only *what* will happen during and after surgery, but also *how* they should respond to what happens. One study showed that if patients are instructed to try to distract themselves from those aspects of surgery that are unpleasant, and to try to concentrate instead on the benefits they will receive from the surgery, the patients will need fewer *analgesics* (pain-relieving drugs) after the surgery (Langer, Janis, & Wolfer, 1975). Other effective control-enhancing interventions include learning both relaxation responses and cognitive-behavioral interventions to overcome anxiety and to adapt to the situation more effectively (Ludwick-Rosenthal & Neufeld, 1988).

Even children can benefit from the control that increased information can provide. In some ways, hospitalization is most difficult on children, because children have little idea of what is going on or of what to expect. Research suggests that giving children advance information before hospitalization or at least before they undergo surgical procedures, and even showing them films of children undergoing a similar procedure, can help the children in their adjustment to the hospital and the surgical procedures they are about to undergo (Melamed & Siegel, 1975; Pinto & Hollandsworth, 1989). Thus, we should not assume that children should be kept entirely uninformed. On the contrary, they need to be given appropriate information.

The preceding studies have shown the benefits of control-enhancing procedures. As we might expect, given the interactive dialectical evolution of scientific research, subsequent studies have shown that there are limitations on what control-enhancing procedures can provide. For one thing, people differ in their desire for control, just as they differ in most other personal attributes (Burger & Cooper, 1979). Patients who are low in their desire for control may become anxious if they are given more control than they would like. Such patients may feel a burden of responsibility or self-blame when asked to make decisions that they do not want to make in the context of a stressful situation, such as the context surrounding surgery (Burger, 1989; S. C. Thompson, Cheek, & Graham, 1988). Moreover, giving patients too much information to absorb about operative procedures and about postoperative recovery may make the patients feel even more distressed than they ordinarily would feel. Attempts to enhance patients' sense of control may boomerang and actually overwhelm them and make them feel powerless (Mills & Krantz, 1979; S. C. Thompson et al., 1988). Although a sense of enhanced control is probably good for most patients in most surgical situations, patients do best if the style of the medical worker fits their own style.

Psychological Processes and Healing

As we saw earlier, we are beginning to understand some of the ways our personalities may affect our physical health and well-being. In addition, we are beginning to recognize some of the ways psychological processes can influence physiological healing of the body, once we have become ill or injured. For example, hypnosis and meditation have been used to influence health-related practices.

Even less exotic psychological states may influence our health. Emotions may play a role in healing. Some people have suggested that laughter has a restorative effect (Restak, 1988), and others have suggested that expressing sadness (such as crying) may offer recuperative properties (Moyers, 1993). Even physicians generally acknowledge the power of a positive attitude to effect recovery and healing.

In fact, physicians and other medical care providers can influence their patients' attitudes toward recovery through their interactions with their patients. For example, it has been found that having a warm and nurturing relationship with someone such as a nurse during hospitalization can help children's adjustment (Branstetter, 1969). Indeed, all patients benefit from having warm relationships while they are confined in a hospital. Such relationships may help mitigate some of the negative aspects of hospitalization and of the illness itself.

Psychological processes even affect our perception and ability to manage pain, as discussed next.

Pain and Its Management

Pain is the intense sensory discomfort and emotional suffering associated with actual, imagined, or threatened damage to or irritation of body tissues (Sanders, 1985). It involves psychological, physiological, and behavioral components (Kroner-Herwig et al., 1996). We previously discussed the sensory aspects of pain (see chapter 4). Here, we discuss the adaptive value of pain, cognitive and emotional aspects of pain, as well as different kinds of pain, how pain is assessed, and what can be done to alleviate it.

Few people enjoy the experience of pain. Indeed, inadequate pain relief is the most common reason patients request euthanasia or commit assisted suicide (Cherny, 1996). Yet, from an evolutionary standpoint, pain has tremendous adaptive value. Why? Because it alerts us to the fact that tissue damage has been or may be taking place. Those rare individuals who do not feel pain are at great risk. By the time they discover the tissue damage taking place, as in the case of burns, it may be too late for them even to save their own lives.

Many psychologists conceptualize pain in a way very similar to the popular conception of pain. It has

Studying Stress and the Body's Ability to Fight Infection

Sheldon Cohen, *Carnegie Mellon University*

The belief that when we are under stress we are more susceptible to the common cold, influenza, and other infectious diseases is widely accepted in our culture. It is endorsed by numerous contemporary newspaper and magazine articles. It is also supported by the fact that 60% of those volunteering for our studies report that they are more likely to catch a cold during stressful than nonstressful periods.

For the last 15 years, our laboratory has studied the role of psychological stress in immunity and infectious disease. The questions we have posed include: Does psychological stress make a difference in the body's ability to fight off infections? If so, what kinds of stressful events count? Finally, how could a psychological state like stress influence how our immune systems respond?

We chose a unique experimental design to study the effects of stress on susceptibility to infectious disease. First, we measure psychological stress in healthy volunteers using questionnaires or interview techniques. After stress assessments, we intentionally expose our subjects to a virus that causes a common cold by putting nose drops with the virus into each subject's nostrils. After exposure, we follow our subjects closely (in quarantine) for five to seven days to see who among them develops infectious illness. Approximately 40% of those exposed develop a common cold. Consequently, we ask whether stress levels assessed before exposure to the virus predict who is able to resist infection and illness.

A series of these studies has led to the conclusion that people reporting higher levels of psychological stress are more likely to become ill when exposed to a virus. This association seems to occur no matter what cold virus is used. (We have used 7 so far but there are as many as 200.) Also, the more stress subjects report, the greater their susceptibility. We also learned that the longer a stressful event lasts, the greater the probability that it will influence ill health. In fact, stressful situations that lasted at least a month were most toxic. Finally, stressful events that involved conflicts with others were more powerful predictors of illness than other sources of stress.

How could a stressful experience like failing an important exam, getting divorced, or the death of a close relative or friend influence our ability to fight infection? When the demands on us are perceived to exceed our ability to cope, we label ourselves as stressed and experience negative emotional responses such as anxiety, anger, and depression. In turn, these states set into motion a series of biological and behavioral changes that alter immune function and as a consequence may put persons at higher risk for developing an infectious illness when exposed to a virus. Stress effects on immunity are probably attributable to direct (through nerves) communication between the brain and immune cells, to destructive ways we often cope with stress (e.g.,

smoking, excessive alcohol consumption, poor diet), and to the effects of hormones our brains release under stress on the function of immune cells.

Our studies attempt to identify which pathways are responsible for the associations between stress and illness susceptibility. Unfortunately, we cannot directly assess the importance of nerve fibers connecting the brain and immune system in studies of humans. We have, however, studied the roles of stress-elicited behaviors and hormones. On the one hand, we have found that stress-induced increases in destructive behaviors, such as smoking and excessive alcohol consumption, are not responsible for increased susceptibility to illness for stressed persons. On the other hand, initial evidence suggests the possibility that activation of the sympathetic nervous system, as indicated by the stress-induced increases in the hormones epinephrine and norepinephrine, may be contributing.

This work is being extended in two directions. First, we are studying the possibility that positive aspects of our social relationships *decrease* our susceptibility to disease. What are the effects of being married, having close friends and family members, and belonging to social groups on our ability to fight off infection? Second, we are concentrating on identifying the immunological pathways through which psychological stress influences immune function. That is, what specific changes in the immune system under stress can account for the association between stress and increased susceptibility to colds and influenza? We are excited about initial evidence that illness symptoms occur because people under stress cannot effectively regulate a group of molecules known as pro-inflammatory cytokines. These molecules are responsible for triggering symptoms of respiratory diseases and may be under the control of stress hormones such as epinephrine and cortisol. Our hope is that our current work will definitively establish that stress influences the release of the stress-hormones that alter the release of cytokines and consequently the expression of cold symptoms.

Our work is an example of a growing area of psychology that attempts to understand how psychological cognitions and emotions are associated with changes in our brains and bodies. As we learn more about these relationships, we will come closer to understanding the importance of psychological phenomena for health. In addition, we hope that this type of work will inform us regarding how we can intervene at a psychological level to improve our physical health.

 Find out more about this topic at
www.harcourtcollege.com/psych/ishm

both a *sensory* component (the sensations at the site where the pain originates, such as throbbing, aching, or stinging pain) and an *affective* component (the emotions that accompany the pain, such as fear, anger, or sadness). It seems that these two components are highly interactive (each profoundly affects the other), but it is possible, at least at some level, to distinguish the contribution of each (Dar, Leventhal, & Leventhal, 1993; Fernandez & Turk, 1992).

Our perceptions of pain also interact with our cognitions regarding pain. Based on our experiences with and observations of pain, we form schemas regarding it, as well as beliefs regarding our ability to control it. The interaction goes both ways. Just as our cognitions are affected by our experiences with pain, our cognitions also affect our perception of it. For example, if we believe that we will be able to overcome our pain, we may be more effective in doing so than if we believe that we will be defeated by our sensations of pain (described as *catastrophizing*, sometimes as a result of learned helplessness). In fact, self-efficacy beliefs may play an important role in pain control (Turk & Rudy, 1992).

Kinds of Pain

A distinction is sometimes made between organic pain and psychogenic pain. **Organic pain** is characterized by sensations of extreme discomfort and suffering caused by damage to bodily tissue. **Psychogenic pain** is the intense sensory discomfort and emotional suffering for which physiological origins cannot be found. We need to be careful in labeling pain "psychogenic" because even if the medical profession has been unable to find an organic source of pain, it does not therefore mean that such pain does not exist or even that no organic cause of the pain exists. The current tools for diagnosis of the sources of pain are still imprecise (see Turk & Rudy, 1992). Such a cause may exist but may simply not have been found. In most cases, the experience of pain represents an interaction between physiological and psychological factors.

The three most common kinds of psychogenic pain are neuralgia, causalgia, and phantom-limb pains. *Neuralgia* is a syndrome in which a person experiences recurrent episodes of intense shooting pain along a nerve (C. R. Chapman, 1984; Melzack & Wall, 1982). The cause of this pattern of pain remains a mystery. *Causalgia* is characterized by recurrent episodes of severe burning pain (Melzack & Wall, 1982). People experiencing causalgia may suddenly feel as though a body part or region is on fire or is being pressed against a hot oven. Often, patients experiencing this syndrome once suffered a serious wound in the place where they feel the burning pain. *Phantom-limb pain* is felt in a limb that either has been amputated or no

Pain can be acute, lasting no longer than six months, or chronic, long-term, recurring pain. Those with chronic pain are at greater risk for depression, suggesting that depression is a result rather than a cause of pain.

longer has functioning nerves (C. R. Chapman, 1984; Melzack & Wall, 1982). Many patients who have had a limb amputated report feeling this phantom-limb pain, even though they lost the limb years before.

The phenomenon of psychogenic pain shows that the link between the perception of pain and the presence of a known pathology or injury is not certain. Additional evidence of the weakness of this link is the phenomenon in which the experience of pain is delayed for a while after serious injury or is altogether absent despite extreme pathology (Melzack, Wall, & Ty, 1982; see also Fernandez & Turk, 1992).

Time Course of Pain Symptoms

Whether pain is organic or psychogenic, it can be classified as either acute or chronic. **Acute pain** is brief (lasting no longer than 6 months), intense, uncomfortable stimulation usually associated with internal or external damage of tissue. Some researchers (e.g., Turk, Meichenbaum, & Genest, 1983) have used 6 months as a somewhat arbitrary cutoff. Recurrent or constant long-term (lasting 6 months or more) discomfort, usually associated with tissue damage, is referred to as **chronic pain.** Of patients who seek treatment in pain clinics, the average amount of time they have endured chronic pain is about 7 years (Turk & Rudy, 1992).

Personality and Pain

Given the wide differences in people's thresholds and limits for pain, some investigators have sought to discover whether there is a relation between personality attributes and the experience of pain. Such research might sound relatively easy to do. You just think of a few traits that you believe might be associated with pain perceptions (e.g., perfectionism or emotional sensitivity), and then test to see whether those traits match up to measurements of people's perceptions of pain. The problem with this research is the same one that arises with most correlational studies. Finding a correlation between a personality attribute and the experiencing of pain may indicate a relationship between the two, but it does not indicate the direction or the cause of the relationship. That is, someone may be susceptible to experiencing pain because of particular personality attributes, but an equally plausible relationship is that the person acquired those attributes from having experienced the pain. For example, if we were to find a correlation between anxiety or depression and scores on a scale measuring chronic pain, we would scarcely be surprised if we were to learn that the anxiety or depression was caused by the pain, rather than vice versa. It is also possible that both the personality attribute and the experiencing of pain may depend on some higher-order third factor.

Some research has found that scales of the *Minnesota Multiphasic Personality Inventory* (*MMPI*; see chapter 15) can help identify patients who are particularly susceptible to pain. Michael Bond (1979) has found that patients who experience *acute pain* tend to score especially high on the hypochondriasis and hysteria scales of the MMPI. People high in hysteria tend to show extreme emotional behavior and also tend to exaggerate the level and seriousness of their symptoms. Similarly, Bond found that *chronic-pain* patients tend to score high on hypochondriasis and hysteria, as well as on depression. As it happens, this grouping of three attributes is sometimes referred to as the "neurotic triad" because elevated scores on these three scales are frequently associated with various types of neurotic disorders.

The fact that greater indications of depression are seen in chronic, but not in acute-pain patients, suggests that the depression is a result, rather than a cause, of the pain. However, Thomas Rudy, Robert Kerns, and Dennis Turk (1988) have found that the development of depression may be related not just to the experience of pain itself, but also to the concomitants of pain, such as the reduction in level of activity, a diminished sense of personal control, and a general sense of inability to master the environment. Some of these effects can be moderated with pain control, discussed next.

Control of Pain

How can pain be controlled? A wide variety of techniques have been used (S. E. Taylor, 1999). Some of the major methods, described in Table 18-2, include pharmacological control (including patient-controlled analgesia), surgical control, sensory control, biofeedback, hypnosis, relaxation techniques, distraction, and guided imagery. Pain-treatment centers across the country use a variety of techniques for helping patients to cope with pain. In many cases, these techniques have been quite successful. The use of these techniques becomes particularly important in cases of chronic pain related to serious illness. Pain control is one aspect of living with serious, chronic illness, which we shall examine in the following section.

Living With Serious, Chronic Health Problems

We often do not truly value our health until we no longer have it. When we recover from acute illnesses, we sometimes briefly cherish our health, only to forget about it after a little while. People with chronic illnesses do not have this luxury. The most dramatic chronic illness of our time is AIDS.

AIDS: Incidence and Prevention

Acquired immune deficiency syndrome, or AIDS, is caused by the human immunodeficiency virus (HIV). HIV attacks the immune system and especially the *T-cells*, which are specialized, relatively long-living white blood cells that protect the body at the cellular level (G. F. Solomon & Temoshok, 1987). The virus is transmitted by the exchange of bodily fluids that contain the virus, most notably blood and semen.

Being *HIV-positive* (having HIV in the blood) does not mean that the person already has developed AIDS. Individuals differ widely in the time it takes them to develop AIDS from the time they contract the virus; the latency period can be as long as 8 to 10 years. Even with full-blown AIDS, it is not the AIDS virus itself that kills people, but rather opportunistic infections that thrive in the person's impaired immune system. Common infections of this type include rare forms of pneumonia and cancer.

Despite its rapid spread, AIDS can be controlled and, in principle, eliminated through behavioral interventions. For example, people who engage in sexual relations outside of marriage should always use condoms

TABLE 18–2

Methods of Pain Control *Having available a diversity of methods for pain control increases the likelihood that both chronic and acute pain can be brought under control with a minimum of undesirable side effects. Contemporary medical investigators constantly are developing new pharmacological, technological, and psychological methods for controlling pain.*

METHOD	HOW IT CONTROLS PAIN	DRAWBACKS
Pharmacological control	The administration of drugs (e.g., aspirin, acetaminophen, or ibuprofen, or, for more extreme cases, morphine) to reduce pain	Some drugs, such as morphine, are addictive, so their administrations must be controlled carefully. Even the milder drugs can have negative consequences if used in excess or over long periods of time
Patient-controlled analgesia	Intravenous infusion of medication; the patient pushes a button that triggers a pump to release analgesic from a computer-regulated reservoir; generally used in a hospital or hospice setting when patients suffer from extreme pain	Some risks exist, but the specially selected patient populations usually minimize the likelihood of addiction
Surgical control	Surgical incision to create lesions in the fibers that carry the sensation of pain; intended to prevent or at least diminish the transmission of pain sensations	The risks associated with surgery, possible side effects, cost, and short-lived positive outcomes have made this technique less preferable
Acupuncture	Originated in Asia; involves the use of needles on particular points on the body; Western adaptation is transcutaneous electrical nerve stimulation (TENS)	Many Western physicians and patients resist its use; may not be as effective in minimizing chronic pain as acute pain
Biofeedback	Biofeedback is an operant-learning procedure (see chapter 6); feedback from a machine translates the body's responses into a form that the patient can easily observe and therefore bring under conscious control	Because the equipment is expensive and cumbersome, and the technique provides results no better than relaxation training, it may not be the treatment of choice

continued

during sexual intercourse and restrict their number of sexual contacts. People who inject themselves with drugs should not share needles. Prevention is especially important for this disease because there is no known cure. Moreover, as far as we know, the overwhelming majority of those who contract HIV eventually will develop AIDS. Particular drugs seem to postpone the development of the disease but do not head it off entirely. Tests can detect HIV antibodies in the body, indicating whether a person has been infected. Of course, the most difficult psychological phenomenon associated with AIDS is living your life as HIV-positive, knowing that you are likely to develop a disease causing intense pain and suffering and that is almost always fatal. New triple-drug therapies may re-

duce what has been a 100 percent mortality rate. Coping mechanisms are extremely important.

Psychological Models for Coping With Chronic Illness

People with chronic illnesses encounter a variety of psychological challenges usually only secondarily related to the physical cause of the illness, such as depression and anxiety. Therefore, a part of the mission of health psychology is to help people deal with their psychological reactions to serious illness, particularly if the illness has long-term repercussions.

Franklin C. Shontz (1975) proposed a stage model of how people react when they realize that they have a

Methods of Pain Control   *(continued)*

METHOD	HOW IT CONTROLS PAIN	DRAWBACKS
Hypnosis	Under hypnosis, the patient receives the suggestion that he or she is not feeling pain	Requires that the patient be susceptible to hypnosis or to self-hypnosis
Relaxation techniques	The patient enters a state of low arousal, controls his or her breathing, and relaxes his or her muscles; meditation (chapter 5) also can induce a state of relaxation	An inexpensive strategy that often proves effective; requires a modest amount of training as well as full patient participation
Guided imagery	Similar and often used as an adjunct to deep relaxation; when people are experiencing pain, they imagine scenes that help them cope with the pain; in one form, visualization, patients imagine actively confronting the pain, such as being a soldier or other fighter who ultimately conquers the pain	An inexpensive strategy that often proves effective; may require some additional training of patient; requires full patient participation, and effectiveness depends in part on patient's ability to visualize
Sensory control through counterirritation	Involves stimulating or mildly irritating a part of the body that differs from the one experiencing pain; effective in reducing the original pain, perhaps because the patient starts to concentrate on the area that is being irritated	Does not work in all cases or at all times, particularly in cases of severe pain
Distraction	Patients shift their attention away from the pain, to focus on something else; the technique has been used successfully for thousands of years	Does not work in all cases or at all times, particularly in cases of severe pain

chronic and probably life-threatening disease. The first stage is one of *shock*. People are stunned, bewildered, and often feel detached from the situation: How can this illness be happening to *me*? The second stage is *encounter*. The person gives way to feelings of despair, loss, grief, and hopelessness. During this stage, people are often unable to function effectively. They do not think well, they have difficulty in planning, and they are ineffective in solving problems. During *retreat*, the third stage, individuals often try to deny the existence of the problem or at least the implications of what the problem means for them. Eventually, however, people reach a fourth stage, *adjustment*, during which they make whatever adjustments are necessary to live with the reality of the disease.

It is important in evaluating a stage model to keep in mind that not everyone is likely to go through all the stages in the exact order specified, or to do so in a strictly linear fashion. People may enter a stage, leave it, and then return to it. Thus, stage models are useful for a general understanding of a process of coping, but only if viewed flexibly (Silver & Wortman, 1980).

Shelley Taylor (1983; Taylor & Aspinwall, 1990) proposed an alternative model that highlights the ways people adapt cognitively to serious chronic illness. Taylor views her model not as a stage model, but rather as one that specifies aspects of cognitive adaptation. According to Taylor, patients try to *find meaning* in the experience of the illness. They may try to figure out what they were doing wrong that led to the illness—and start doing whatever it is right—or they may simply rethink their own attitudes and priorities. Patients further try to *gain a sense of control* over the illness and over the rest of their lives. They may seek as much information as possible about their illness and its treatment, or they may undertake activities that they believe will help restore function and well-being or will at least inhibit the degenerative progress of their illness. Finally, patients try to *restore their self-esteem*, despite the offense of being struck by such an illness. They may compare their own situations with those of others, in ways that shed favorable light on their own situations.

Individuals differ in terms of their effectiveness in coping. Rudolf Moos (1982, 1988; 1995; Moos & Schaefer, 1986) has described a *crisis theory* (shown in Figure 18-4), which attempts to characterize individual differences in people's abilities to cope with serious health problems. According to this model, how well a person copes depends on three sets of factors:

1. *Background and personal factors* such as emotional maturity, self-esteem, religious beliefs, and age. Men are more likely to respond negatively to diseases that compromise their ability to work; older people will have to live fewer years with a chronic illness than younger ones and thus may be better able to cope with the prospects.

2. *Illness-related factors* such as how disabling, painful, or life-threatening the disease is. Unsurprisingly, the greater the disability, pain, and threat, the more difficulty people have in coping with the illness.

3. *Environmental factors* such as social supports, the ability of the person to remain financially solvent, and the kinds of conditions in which the person lives. Some factors may diminish the ability to cope, whereas others may enhance it.

According to Moos, the coping process has three main components: cognitive appraisal, the decision to adapt, and the development of coping skills. In *cognitive appraisal*, the individual assesses the meaning and significance of the health problem for his or her life.

(Note that this kind of cognitive appraisal is similar to the primary and secondary appraisals described by Folkman and Lazarus in the perception of stress and is somewhat related to the appraisals involved in symptom recognition and interpretation.) As a result of this cognitive appraisal, the person *decides* how to perform tasks in a way that is adaptive, given the illness. In this way, the person *develops coping skills* for living with the illness. The outcome of the coping process will, in turn, affect the outcome of the crisis in general—how well the person is able to live with the disabling illness.

Ultimately, the key to coping with serious chronic illness is *adaptation*. The individual will need to make changes and adjustments to live happily and effectively. On the one hand, those persons with serious chronic illnesses need to make more effort than practically anyone to adapt to the environment. On the other hand, each of us confronts situations requiring us to adapt, in varying ways and to varying degrees. We constantly need to adjust ourselves to regulate our fit to our environment. But whether we are healthy or ill, young or old, lucky or not, we can *shape* our environment, too. Just as we need to adapt ourselves to fit the environment, we can modify the environment to suit ourselves. If there is a key to psychological adjustment, perhaps it is in the balance between adaptation to and shaping of the environment, with the added option of *selection*. When we find that a particular environment simply cannot be shaped to fit us, and we cannot adapt ourselves to fit it, we can seek a more suitable environment. It is my hope that you can adapt to, shape, and select your environment, to find what you want in life, reach for it, and ultimately obtain it.

Be careful in choosing what you want in life, for it shall be yours.—Proverb

Figure 18-4

THREE SETS OF FACTORS IN COPING. *In his crisis theory, Rudolf Moos emphasizes individual differences in coping with serious illness. He has identified three sets of factors influencing each individual's response. In addition, Moos has discerned three main components of adjusting to serious illness. It is the interaction of individual differences and the coping process itself that influences the outcome of the crisis.*

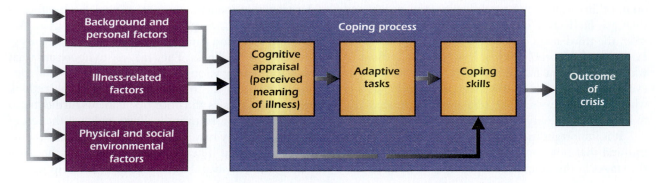

THINK ABOUT IT

1. Suppose that an instructor of student nurses invites you to discuss the patient's view of hospital care. What are the key points you would try to communicate? How would you communicate those points so that the nurses would really understand you and would not feel threatened by what you say?
2. This chapter included health recommendations regarding several aspects of lifestyle. Which recommendation do you consider the most important of these? Why?
3. What advice would you give doctors, based on your knowledge of psychology, to help them communicate with patients who have to be told that they have a life-threatening illness?
4. Choose the pain-relief or pain-control method you consider most likely to be effective in a variety of situations. Describe a situation in which pain relief or pain control would be needed and in which this technique might be effective. State how you would use it.
5. What decision criteria should you use to decide when you need to consult a physician?
6. What are some realistic things that you can do to minimize feelings of stress in your life?

online *You can provide your own answers to these questions online at the* Sternberg, **In Search of the Human Mind** *Web site:* *http://www.harcourtcollege.com/psych/ishm*

SUMMARY

Psychology and Health   575

1. *Health psychology* is the study of the interaction between mental processes and physiological health.
2. Galen is credited with being the first to suggest a *biomedical model* of illness. According to this model, disease results when disease-causing agents (*pathogens*) invade the body, and we can eliminate disease if we eliminate the causative pathogens.
3. Almost all health psychologists now embrace a more contemporary alternative model, the *biopsychosocial model*, which proposes that psychological, social, and biological factors can influence health.
4. As one of the newest fields in psychology, health psychology has roots in *psychosomatic medicine* and in *behavioral medicine*.

Stress and Coping   578

5. *Stress* is the situation in which environmental factors cause a person to feel threatened or challenged in some way.
6. Stressors (situations or events that create the stress) are environmental changes that cause the person to have to adapt to or cope with the situation, and these adaptations are *stress responses*.
7. The initial stress response is adaptive in helping the person to prepare to flee from or fight in the threatening situation. After the initial alarm phase of stress, if the perceived stressor continues to confront the individual, the body shifts down to a resistance phase and finally to an exhaustion phase.

8. Stress has been linked to many diseases, and its direct effect on the immune system is now being explored.
9. In *primary appraisal*, we analyze our stake in the outcome of handling a particular situation.
10. In *secondary appraisal*, we assess what we can do to maximize the likelihood of potentially beneficial outcomes and to minimize the likelihood of potentially harmful outcomes of a situation.
11. *Problem-focused coping* is directed at solving a problem. *Emotion-focused coping* is directed at handling the emotions you experience as a result of the problem.
12. Several personality factors influence health, particularly the personality characteristics related to competitiveness, sense of urgency, and tendency to feel anger and hostility. Persons who rate high on these three characteristics have a *Type-A* pattern of behavior; persons who rate low on these characteristics have a *Type-B* pattern of behavior. Of the three characteristics, feelings of anger and hostility seem most clearly threatening to health, particularly in terms of coronary heart disease and other stress-related illnesses. Lifestyle differences also may contribute to these effects.

Health Care and Psychology   585

13. People generally seek health services only after noticing *symptoms* of ill health. Whereas doctors use explicit theories to make diagnoses, most laypersons have an implicit theory (based on

commonsense schemas) to explain their symptoms and what might be the probable course of their illness.

14. We classify illnesses according to their duration: *acute illnesses* are relatively brief; *chronic illnesses* last for a long time, often across the entire life span.

15. Patient styles differ in terms of patients' preferences for participation in their medical care. Physician styles also differ in terms of whether they are *doctor centered* (focused on the single problem that prompted the visit) or *patient centered* (focused on serving the patients' needs even when they diverge from the identified problem). The use of medical jargon (more common in doctor-centered physicians) may impede communication with some patients.

16. Patient characteristics affect the treatment patients receive. More compliant, passive, unquestioning, and unassertive patients generally receive better treatment in the hospital, although their passivity and their lack of awareness about the treatment may impede their recovery outside the hospital setting.

17. *Organic pain* is caused by damage to bodily tissue. *Psychogenic pain* is the discomfort felt when there appears to be no physical cause of the pain, such as neuralgia (involving recurrent pain along a nerve), causalgia (involving burning pain), and phantom-limb pain (which occurs in the absence of a neurological connection to the perceived source of the pain). What may appear to be psychogenic pain, however, may be caused by unidentified organic pathology.

18. Pain may be *acute* (lasting less than 6 months) or *chronic* (lasting 6 months or more).

19. Although several personality traits have been associated with pain, it has proven difficult to determine the direction of causality for these correlations.

20. Methods for controlling pain include pharmacological control (via drugs, including patient-controlled analgesia), surgical control, sensory control (e.g., counterirritation), biofeedback, relaxation techniques, distraction, guided imagery, hypnosis, and acupuncture.

21. AIDS (acquired immune deficiency syndrome) is usually a terminal illness caused by the human immunovirus (HIV). AIDS is contracted largely through contact with the semen or blood of those who carry HIV.

22. When people recognize that they have a serious, chronic health problem, they may experience shock (stunned detachment), encounter (grief and despair), and retreat (withdrawal from the problem) before they finally make the needed adjustment. An alternative model describes cognitive adaptations to chronic illness as the needs to find meaning, to gain control, and to restore self-esteem. Factors influencing these reactions include characteristics of the individual (including experiences and background), the illness, and the environment.

23. Three adaptive ways to respond to chronic illness are to change the individual (and his or her lifestyle), to change the environment (making it fit the individual's different needs and abilities), or to select a different environment.

KEY TERMS

acute illness   585
acute pain   590
behavioral medicine   577
biomedical model   576
biopsychosocial model   576
chronic illness   585
chronic pain   591
control-enhancing interventions   587
coping   583

doctor-centered style   586
emotion-focused coping   583
general adaptation syndrome (GAS)   580
health psychology   575
organic pain   590
pain   588
pathogens   576
patient-centered style   586
primary appraisal   582

problem-focused coping   583
psychogenic pain   590
secondary appraisal   582
signs   585
stress   578
stress response   578
symptoms   585
Type-A behavior pattern   583
Type-B behavior pattern   583

THINK ABOUT IT SAMPLE RESPONSES

1. Suppose that an instructor of student nurses invites you to discuss the patient's view of hospital care. What are the key points you would try to communicate? How would you communicate those points so that the nurses would really understand you and would not feel threatened by what you say?

A patient will generally want to be treated with courtesy and respect. The patient also will wish to understand both the nature of the illness confronting him or her and the treatment options available. Patients often will have better medical outcomes if they have a feeling of some control over their treatment options.

2. This chapter included health recommendations regarding several aspects of lifestyle. Which recommendation do you consider the most important of these? Why?

Everyone must answer this question for himself or herself. Important things one can do to improve one's health are to eat well, exercise, stop smoking, and avoid use of harmful drugs.

3. What advice would you give doctors, based on your knowledge of psychology, to help them communicate with patients who have to be told that they have a life-threatening illness?

Doctors should treat patients with dignity and emphasize their compassion for their patients. They should also emphasize their own professionalism and their commitment to doing the best they can to providing optimal patient care. Where possible, they should allow patients to have some control over the situation and to participate in important treatment decisions.

4. Choose the pain-relief or pain-control method you consider most likely to be effective in a variety of situations. Describe a situation in which pain relief or pain control would be needed and in which this technique might be effective. State how you would use it.

What method of pain relief works best depends on the person, the cause of the pain, and the particular situation in which pain relief is to be administered. One particularly effective method for some people in some situations is relaxation. People can make pain worse by becoming tense. The pain causes tension, which in turn may worsen the pain, which may in turn lead to more tension, and so on. Relaxation can help break this cycle and help the individual focus to the extent possible on positive aspects of his or her life.

5. What decision criteria should you use to decide when you need to consult a physician?

You should consult a doctor if you have a fever, if you are ill for several days without signs of getting better, or if your illness notably impairs your ability to function in daily life. In cases of doubt, it is better to consult a physician than to hope that you will somehow get better.

6. What are some realistic things that you can do to minimize feelings of stress in your life?

You can ask yourself how many of the things causing you stress really will matter in the long run. Often things are stressful at the moment but are of little long-term consequence. You can also exercise as a form of stress relief. A third thing you can do is practice guided relaxation or meditation.

STATISTICAL APPENDIX

Do you ever wonder whether some groups of people are smarter, or more assertive, or more honest than others? Or whether students who earn better grades actually work more, on average, than do students who earn lower grades? Or whether, in close relationships, women feel more intimacy toward men, or men toward women? These are all questions that can be addressed by using statistics.

Although statistics can help us answer questions, they cannot themselves provide definitive answers. The answers lie not in the statistics themselves, but in how the statistics are interpreted. Statistics provide people with tools—with information to explore issues, answer questions, solve problems, and make decisions. Statistics do not actually do the exploration, question answering, problem solving, or decision making. People do.

A **statistic** is a numerical value obtained by analyzing numerical data about a representative sample of a population. For example, if you want to know how satisfied people are in their close relationships, you might give people a scale measuring relationship satisfaction and then compute various numbers summarizing their level of satisfaction. **Statistics** as a field of study involves the analysis of numerical data about representative samples of populations.

Statistics are often used in psychology, and they can also be applied to other aspects of our lives. Consider this example. Suppose you are interested in qualities of love and how they relate to satisfaction in close relationships. In particular, you decide to explore the three aspects of love incorporated in the triangular theory of love (R. J. Sternberg, 1986b, 1988c, 1998): *intimacy* (feelings of warmth, closeness, communication, and support), *passion* (feelings of intense longing and desire), and *commitment* (desire to remain in the relationship; see chapter 12). You might be interested in the relation of these aspects to each other; or of each of the aspects to overall satisfaction; or of the relative levels of each of these aspects people experience in different close relationships—for example, with lovers, friends, or parents.

In order to use statistics to assess these issues, you would first need a scale to measure them. *The Triangular Love Scale*, a version of which is shown in Table A-1, is such a scale (R. J. Sternberg, 1988c). If you wish, you can compare your data with those from a sample of 84 adults whose summary data will be presented later (R. J. Sternberg, 1997a).

Note that this version of the scale has a total of 36 items, 12 of which measure intimacy; 12, passion; and 12, commitment. Each item consists of a statement rated on a 1-to-9 scale, where 1 means that the statement does not characterize the person at all, 5 means that it is moderately characteristic of the person, and 9 means that it is extremely characteristic. Intermediate points represent intermediate levels of feelings. The final score on each of the three subscales is the average of the numbers assigned to each of the statements in that subscale (i.e., the sum of the numbers divided by 12, the number of items).

In research that uses statistics, we are interested in two kinds of variables: *independent* and *dependent* (see chapter 2). **Independent variables** are attributes that are individually manipulated by the experimenter, while other aspects of the investigation are held constant; **dependent variables** are outcome responses or attributes that vary as a consequence of variation in one or more independent variables. In an experiment, some of the independent variables are usually manipulated, and the dependent variable may change in value as a function of the manipulations. Other independent variables may be predictors but not be manipulated variables. For example, the sex of the participants may be an independent variable that predicts various aspects of love, but it is not manipulated by the experimenter. Rather, data may be separated by sex of participants if the data are expected to show different patterns for males versus females.

TABLE A–1

Triangular Love Scale *The blanks represent a person with whom you are in a close relationship. Rate on a scale of 1–9 the extent to which each statement characterizes your feelings, where 1 = not at all, 5 = moderately, 9 = extremely, and other numerals indicate levels in between.*

INTIMACY

1. I have a warm and comfortable relationship with _____.
2. I experience intimate communication with _____.
3. I strongly desire to promote the well-being of _____.
4. I have a relationship of mutual understanding with _____.
5. I receive considerable emotional support from _____.
6. I am able to count on _____ in times of need.
7. _____ is able to count on me in times of need.
8. I value _____ greatly in my life.
9. I am willing to share myself and my possessions with _____.
10. I experience great happiness with _____.
11. I feel emotionally close to _____.
12. I give considerable emotional support to _____.

PASSION

1. I cannot imagine another person making me as happy as _____ does.
2. There is nothing more important to me than my relationship with _____.
3. My relationship with _____ is very romantic.
4. I cannot imagine life without _____.
5. I adore _____.
6. I find myself thinking about _____ frequently during the day.
7. Just seeing _____ is exciting for me.
8. I find _____ very attractive physically.
9. I idealize _____.
10. There is something almost "magical" about my relationship with _____.
11. My relationship with _____ is very "alive."
12. I especially like giving presents to _____.

continued

Descriptive Statistics

Descriptive statistics are numerical analyses that summarize quantitative information about a population. They reduce a larger mass of information down to a smaller and more useful base of information.

Measures of Central Tendency

In studying love, you might be interested in typical levels of intimacy, passion, and commitment for different relationships—say, for a lover and a sibling.

There are several ways in which you might characterize the typical value, or **central tendency,** of a set of data.

The **mean** is the average score within a distribution of values, computed by adding all the scores and then dividing by the number of scores.

Another measure of central tendency is the **median,** which is the middle score or other measurement value within a distribution of values. With an odd number of values, the median is the number right in the middle. For example, if you have seven values ranked from lowest to highest, the median will be the

TABLE A–1

Triangular Love Scale *(continued)*

COMMITMENT
1. I will always feel a strong responsibility for _____.
2. I expect my love for _____ to last for the rest of my life.
3. I can't imagine ending my relationship with _____.
4. I view my relationship with _____ as permanent.
5. I would stay with _____ through the most difficult times.
6. I view my commitment to _____ as a matter of principle.
7. I am certain of my love for _____.
8. I have decided that I love _____.
9. I am committed to maintaining my relationship with _____.
10. I view my relationship with _____ as, in part, a thought-out decision.
11. I could not let anything get in the way of my commitment to _____.
12. I have confidence in the stability of my relationship with _____.

Note: Scores are obtained by adding scale values (from 1 = low to 9 = high) for each item in each subscale, and then dividing by 12 (the number of items per subscale), yielding a score for each subscale of between 1 and 9.

fourth (middle) value. With an even number of values, there is no one middle value. For example, if you have eight values ranked from lowest to highest, the median will be the number half-way between (the average) the fourth and fifth values—again, the middle.

A third measure of central tendency is the **mode,** or the most frequent score or other measurement value within a distribution of values. Obviously, the mode is useful only when there are at least some repeated values.

Consider, for example, the scores of eight individuals on the intimacy subscale, rounded to the nearest whole number and ranked from lowest to highest: 3, 4, 4, 4, 5, 5, 6, 7. In this set of numbers, the mean is 4.75, or $(3 + 4 + 4 + 4 + 5 + 5 + 6 + 7)/8$; the median is 4.5, or the middle value between the fourth and fifth values above (4 and 5); and the mode is 4, the value that occurs most frequently.

The advantage of the mean as a measure of central tendency is that it fully takes into account the information in each data point. Because of this fact, the mean is generally the preferred measure of central tendency. However, the mean is also sensitive to extremes. If just a few numbers in a distribution are extreme, the mean will be greatly affected by them. For example, if five people took the passion subscale to indicate their feelings toward their pet gerbils, and their scores were 1, 1, 1, 1, and 8, the mean of 3 would reflect a number that is higher than the rating given by four of the five people surveyed.

The advantage of the median is that it is less sensitive to extremes. In the distribution of passion scores for pet gerbils, the median is 1, better reflecting the distribution than does the mean. The median does not take into account all the information given, however. For example, the median would have been the same if the fifth score were 2 rather than 8.

The advantage of the mode is that it provides a quick index of central tendency. It is rough, though. Sometimes no number in a distribution appears more than once, and hence there is no mode. Other times, several numbers appear most often, so that the distribution is **multimodal** (characteristic of a non-normal distribution of values, in which the distribution comprises more than one mode). The mode takes into account the least information in the distribution. For these reasons, the mode is the least used of the three measures of central tendency.

Sometimes, it is useful to show values obtained via a **frequency distribution,** which shows the dispersion of values in a set of values, represented as the number, proportion, or percentage of instances of each value. We can distinguish between two kinds of numbers at each score level. The **relative frequency** represents the number of cases that received a given score or range of scores. The **cumulative frequency** represents the total number of instances of values up to a given level—that is, of that level or lower. In the case of the two distributions of numbers mentioned previously for two sets of participants in connection with the Triangular Love Scale, the frequency distributions would be as follows:

Intimacy Subscale			Passion Subscale		
Value	Relative frequency	Cumulative frequency	Value	Relative frequency	Cumulative frequency
3	1	1	1	4	4
4	3	4	8	1	5
5	2	6			
6	1	7			
7	1	8			

In these frequency distributions, relative and cumulative frequencies are represented by numbers of cases at each level. An alternative would have been to represent them by proportions or percentages. For example, expressed as a proportion, the relative frequency at score value 3 on the intimacy subscale would be .125 (1/8).

Scatter plots also can be represented graphically in various ways. Two of the main kinds of graphic representations are a **bar graph,** in which items reflecting larger numeric values are represented as longer bars on the graph, and a **line graph,** in which quantities (e.g., amounts or scores) are associated with linear information (e.g., time or age) and this association is represented by changing heights of a broken line, both of which are shown in Figure A-1 for the simple frequency distribution of intimacy scores expressed above numerically. People use graphs in order to help readers visualize the relations among numbers and to help the readers clarify just what these relations are.

Measures of Dispersion

You now know three ways to assess the central tendency of a distribution of numbers. Another question you might have about the distribution concerns *dispersion* of the distribution. How much do scores vary? You might assess dispersion in several different ways.

A first measure of dispersion is the **range,** which is the full expanse of a distribution of values, from the lowest to the highest value. For example, the range of intimacy scores represented previously is 4 (i.e., 7–3). But the range is a rough measure. For example, consider two distributions of intimacy scores: 3, 4, 5, 6, 7, and 3, 3, 3, 3, 7. Although the range is the same, the dispersion of scores seems different. Other measures take more information into account.

A second measure of variability is the **standard deviation,** which is a statistical measurement of dispersion, indicating the degree to which a set of values typically deviates from the mean value for the set. The advantage of the standard deviation over the range is that the standard deviation takes into account the full information in the distribution of scores. Researchers care about the standard deviation because it indicates how much scores group together, on the one hand, or are more dispersed, on the other. The standard deviation also is used in statistical significance testing, as discussed later.

To compute the standard deviation, you must:

1. Compute the difference between each value and the mean;

Figure A–1

GRAPHING FREQUENCY DISTRIBUTIONS. *Frequency distributions may be represented graphically either as bar graphs, showing discontinuous levels of a variable, or as line graphs, showing continuous levels of a variable.*

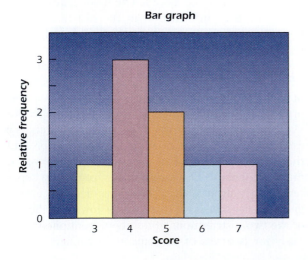

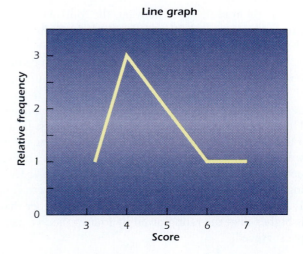

2. Square the difference between each value and the mean (to get rid of negative signs);

3. Sum the squared differences;

4. Take the average of the sum of squared differences; and

5. Take the square root of this average, in order to bring the final value back to the original scale.

Let us take the two distributions above to see whether their standard deviations are indeed different. The mean of 3, 4, 5, 6, 7 is 5. So the squared differences of each value from the mean are 4, 1, 0, 1, and 4. The sum of the squared differences is 10, and the average, 2. The square root of 2 is about 1.41, which is the standard deviation. In contrast, the mean of 3, 3, 3, 3, 7 is 3.80. So the squared differences of each value from the mean are .64, .64, .64, .64, and 10.24. The sum of the squared differences is 12.80, and the average, 2.56. The square root of 2.56 is 1.60. Thus, the second distribution has a higher standard deviation, 1.60, than the first distribution, for which the standard deviation is 1.41.

What does a standard deviation tell us? As a measure of variability, it tells us how much scores depart from the mean. At the extreme, if all values were equal to the mean, the standard deviation would be 0. At the opposite extreme, the maximum value of the standard deviation is half the value of the range (for numerical values that are very spread apart).

For typical (but not all) distributions of values, about 68% of the values fall between the mean and plus or minus one standard deviation from that mean; about 95% of the values fall between the mean and plus or minus two standard deviations from that mean. And well over 99% of the values fall between the mean and plus or minus three standard deviations. For example, the mean of the scale for intelligence quotients (IQs) is 100, and the standard deviation is typi-

cally 15 (see chapter 9). Thus, roughly two-thirds of IQs fall between 85 and 115 (plus or minus one standard deviation from the mean), and about 19 out of 20 IQs fall between 70 and 130 (plus or minus two standard deviations from the mean).

A third measure of variability is the **variance,** which is the degree to which a set of values varies from the mean of the set of values. Thus, the variances of the distributions of intimacy scores above are 2 and 2.56 (which were the values obtained before taking square roots). The variance of IQ scores is 15 squared, or 225. Variances are useful in many statistical calculations, but are not as readily interpretable as are standard deviations.

Now that you have read about measures of central tendency and dispersion, you can appreciate two of these measures—the mean and standard deviation—for the Triangular Love Scale. Table A-2 shows means and standard deviations of intimacy, passion, and commitment scores for various relationships computed from a sample of 84 adults. If you took the scale yourself, you can compare your own scores to that of our normative sample.

The Normal Distribution

In the previous discussion of the percentages of values between the mean and various numbers of standard deviations from the mean, we have been making an assumption without making that assumption explicit. The assumption is that the distribution of values is a **normal distribution**—that is, a distribution of scores or other measurement values, in which most values congregate around the median, and the measurement values rapidly decline in number on either side of the median, tailing off more slowly as scores get more extreme. The shape of the normal distribution is shown

---

TABLE A–2

Basic Statistics for the *Triangular Love Scale*   *The relative extent to which individuals indicate feelings of intimacy, passion, and commitment differ across various kinds of relationships.*

	INTIMACY		PASSION		COMMITMENT	
	Mean	*SD*	*Mean*	*SD*	*Mean*	*SD*
Mother	6.49	1.74	4.98	1.90	6.83	1.57
Father	5.17	2.10	3.99	1.84	5.82	2.22
Sibling	5.92	1.67	4.51	1.71	6.60	1.67
Lover	7.55	1.49	6.91	1.65	7.06	1.49
Friend	6.78	1.67	4.90	1.71	6.06	1.63

Note: "Friend" refers to a close friend of the same sex; "SD" refers to standard deviation. Statistics are based on a sample of 84 adults from southern Connecticut.

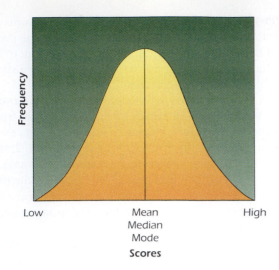

Figure A–2
NORMAL DISTRIBUTION.   *As this figure shows, in a normal distribution, the median (the middle value in the distribution), the mean (the average value in the distribution), and the mode (the most frequent value in the distribution) are the same.*

in Figure A-2. Notice that the distribution of scores is symmetrical, and that indeed, the large majority of scores fall close to the center of the distribution.

Nature seems to favor normal distributions, because the distributions of an amazing variety of attributes prove to be roughly normal. For example, heights are roughly distributed around the average, as are intelligence quotients. In a *completely normal distribution*, the mean, the median, and the mode are all exactly equal.

Not all distributions are normal. Distributions can be nonnormal in a variety of ways, but one of the most common is in terms of **skewness,** or lopsidedness, which indicates the degree to which the modal value is shifted above or below the mean and median values. Figure A-3 shows both a *negatively skewed distribution*, in which the values on the lower (left) side of the mode tail off more slowly than do the values on the right; and a *positively skewed distribution*, in which values on the upper (right) side of the mode tail off more slowly than do the values on the left.

Notice that the respective values of the mean, median, and mode are displaced in these two kinds of distributions. Why? Consider as an example a distribution that is almost always positively skewed: personal incomes. The distribution tends to rise quickly up to the mode, and then to trail off. The existence of a small number of very high-income earners creates the positive skew. What will be the effect of the small number of very high-income earners? They will tend to displace the mean upward, because as we have

seen, the mean is especially sensitive to extreme values. The median is less affected by the extreme values, and the mode is not affected at all. Thus, in this positively skewed distribution, the mean will be the highest, followed by the median and then the mode. In a negatively skewed distribution, the opposite ordering will tend to occur.

As we have seen, one way to obtain skewness is to have a distribution with a natural "tail," as is the case with high incomes. Another way to obtain such a distribution is the way something is measured. Suppose a professor gave a very easy test, with an average score of

Figure A–3
SKEWED DISTRIBUTION.   *In a skewed distribution, the mean, the median, and the mode differ. In a negatively skewed distribution (a), the values of the median and the mode are greater than the value of the mean. In a positively skewed distribution (b), the value of the mean is greater than the values of the mode and the median.*

(a) Negatively skewed distribution

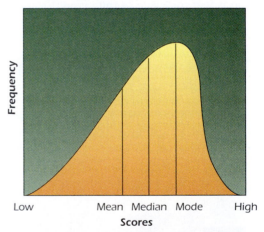

(b) Positively skewed distribution

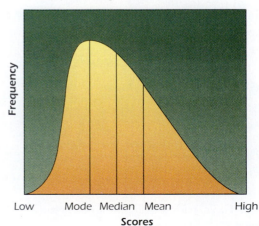

90% correct, and a range of scores from 60% to 100%. This distribution would be negatively skewed because of a ceiling effect: Many people received very high scores because the easiness of the test placed an artificial limit, or ceiling, on how well they could do on the test.

Suppose, instead, that the professor gave a very difficult test, with an average score of just 10% correct, and a range of scores from 0% to 40%. This distribution would be positively skewed because of a floor effect: Many people received very low scores because the difficulty of the test placed an artificial limit, or floor, on how poorly they could do on the test.

Fortunately, most distributions are approximately normal. The advantage of such distributions is that many of the statistics used in psychology, only a few of which are discussed here, assume a normal distribution. Other statistics do not assume a normal distribution, but are more interpretable when we have such a distribution.

Types of Scores

One such statistic is the *standard score*. The standard score is one that can be used for any distribution to equate the scores for that distribution to scores for other distributions. Standard scores, also called *z-scores*, are arbitrarily defined to have a mean of 0 and a standard deviation of 1. If the distribution of scores is normal, therefore, roughly 68% of the scores will be between −1 and 1, and roughly 95% of scores will be between −2 and 2.

Why bother to have standard scores? The advantage of standard scores is that they render comparable scores that are initially on different scales. For example, suppose two professors teaching the same course to two comparable classes of students differ in the difficulty of the tests they give. Professor A tends to give relatively difficult tests, and the mean score on his tests is 65%. Professor B, on the other hand, tends to give very easy tests, and the mean score on his tests is 80%. Yet, the difference in these two means reflects not a difference in achievement, but a difference in the difficulty of the tests the professors give. If we convert scores separately in each class to standard scores, the mean and standard deviation will be the same in the two classes (that is, a mean of 0 and a standard deviation of 1), so that it will be possible to compare achievement in the two classes in a way that corrects for the differential difficulty of the professors' tests.

Standard scores also can be applied to the distributions of love-scale scores described earlier. People who feel more intimacy, passion, or commitment toward a partner will have a higher standard score relative to the mean, and people who feel less intimacy, passion, or commitment will have a lower standard score.

The computation of standard scores is simple. Start with a **raw score,** which is simply the actual total sum of points obtained by a given test-taker for a given test, which often equals the actual number of items answered correctly on the test. Then convert the raw score to a standard score following these steps:

1. Subtract the mean raw score from the raw score of interest;
2. Divide the difference by the standard deviation of the distribution of raw scores.

You can now see why standard scores always have a mean of 0 and a standard deviation of 1. Suppose that a given raw score equals the mean. If the raw score equals the mean, when the mean is subtracted from that score, the number will be subtracted from itself, yielding a difference in the numerator (see Step 1 above) of 0. Of course, 0 divided by anything equals 0. Suppose now that the score is 1 standard deviation above the mean. When the mean is subtracted from that score, the difference will be the value of the standard deviation. When this value (the standard deviation) is divided by the standard deviation (in Step 2 above), the result is a value of 1, because any value divided by itself equals 1.

Thus, if we take our distribution of intimacy scores of 3, 4, 5, 6, 7, with a mean of 5 and a standard deviation of 1.41, the standard score for a raw score of 6 will be (6 − 5)/1.41, or .71. The standard score for a raw score of 5, which is the mean, will be (5 − 5)/1.41, or 0. The standard score for a raw score of 4 will be (4 − 5)/1.41, or −.71.

Many kinds of scores are variants of standard scores. For example, an IQ of 115, which is one standard deviation above the mean, corresponds to a z-score (standard score) of 1. An IQ of 85 corresponds to a z-score of −1, and so on. The Scholastic Assessment Test uses scores set to have a mean of 500 and a standard deviation of 100. In the verbal and mathematical parts, therefore, a score of 600 represents a score of 1 standard deviation above the mean (i.e., a z-score of 1), whereas a score of 400 represents a score of 1 standard deviation below the mean (i.e., a z-score of −1).

Another convenient kind of score is called the **percentile.** This score refers to the proportion of persons whose scores fall below a given score, multiplied by 100. Thus, if, on a test, your score is higher than that of half (50%) of the students who have taken the test (and lower than that of the other half), your percentile will be 50. If your score is higher than everyone else's (and lower than no one else's), your percentile will be 100. In the distribution 3, 4, 5, 6, 7, the score corresponding to the 50th percentile is 5 (the median), because it is higher than half the other scores and lower than half the other scores. The

100th percentile is 7, because it is higher than all the other scores and lower than none of them.

Correlation and Regression

So now you know something about central tendency and dispersion, as well as about the kinds of scores that can contribute to central tendency and dispersion. You also may be interested in a different question: How are scores on one kind of measure related to scores on another kind of measure? For example, how do people's scores on the intimacy subscale relate to their scores on the passion subscale, or to their scores on the commitment subscale? The question here would be whether people who feel more intimacy toward someone also tend to feel more passion or commitment toward that person.

The measure of statistical association, called the **correlation coefficient**, ranges from −1 (perfect inverse relation) to 0 (no relation) to +1 (perfect positive relation) and addresses the question of the degree of relation between two arrays of values. Basically, correlation expresses the degree of relation between two variables. A correlation of 0 indicates no relation at all between two variables; a correlation of 1 indicates a perfect (positive) relation between the two variables; a correlation of −1 indicates a perfect inverse relation between the two variables. Figure A-4 shows hypothetical distributions with correlations of 0, 1, and −1.

Most frequently, people use a measure of linear relation called the **Pearson product-moment correlation coefficient**. There are other correlation coefficients as well, but they go beyond the scope of this text, as do the mathematical formulas for the coefficients of correlation. The Pearson product-moment correlation coefficient expresses only the degree of **linear relation**, meaning that it considers only the association between two quantities that takes the form of a straight line, or $Y' = a + bX$, as shown in Panels B and C of Figure A-4. What this means is that you can have a perfect correlation between two variables without regard to their scale, as long as they are linearly related.

For example, suppose that in a hypothetical group of participants, the scores of five participants on the intimacy subscale were 4, 5, 6, 6, and 7, and the scores of the same participants on the passion subscale were also 4, 5, 6, 6, and 7. In other words, each participant received the same score on the passion subscale as on the intimacy scale. The correlation between the two sets of scores is 1. Now suppose that you add a constant (of 1) to the passion scores, so that instead of being 4, 5, 6, 6, and 7, they are 5, 6, 7, 7, and 8. Because correlations do not change with the addition or subtraction of a constant, the correlation would still be 1. And if instead of adding a constant, you multi-

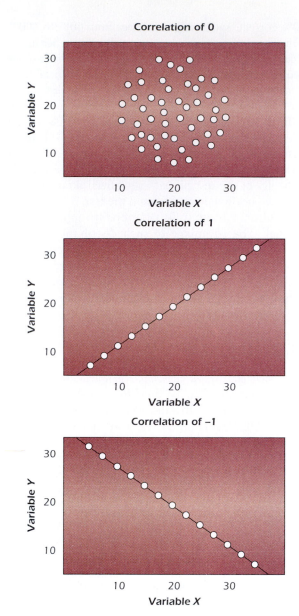

Figure A–4
CORRELATION COEFFICIENT. *When two variables show a correlation of 0, increases or decreases in the value of one variable (variable X) bear no relation to increases or decreases in the value of the other variable (variable Y). When variable X and variable Y are positively correlated, increases in X are related to increases in Y, and decreases in X are related to decreases in Y. When variable X and variable Y are negatively (inversely) correlated, increases in X are related to decreases in Y, and decreases in X are related to increases in Y.*

plied by a constant, the correlation would still be 1. Remember, then, correlation looks at degree of linear relation, regardless of the scale on which the numbers are expressed. There are other kinds of relations—

quadratic, cubic, and so on—but the Pearson coefficient does not take them into account.

The prediction of one quantified variable from one or more others, in which the two sets of variables are assumed to have a relation that takes the form of a straight line, is called **linear regression.** If the correlation is perfect, the prediction will be perfect. For example, if you predict people's height in inches from their height in centimeters, the prediction will be perfect, yielding a correlation of 1.

The predictive equation specifying the relation between predicted values of a dependent variable (Y') and one or more independent variables (X) is called a **regression equation.** In the equation, $Y' = a + bX$, *a* is called the *regression constant* and *b* is called the *regression coefficient*. Note that the regression constant is additive, whereas the regression coefficient is multiplicative. The formula, which is that of a straight line, is what relates the Y' (predicted) values to the X (predictor) values.

Well, what are the correlations among the various subscales of the Triangular Love Scale? For love of a lover, the correlations are very high: .88 between intimacy and passion, .84 between intimacy and commitment, and .85 between passion and commitment. These data suggest that if you feel high (or low) levels of one of these aspects of love toward a lover, you are likely also to feel high (or low) levels of the other two of the aspects toward your lover. However, the correlations vary somewhat with the relationship. For example, the comparable correlations for a sibling are .79, .77, and .76. Incidentally, in close relationships with a lover, the correlations between satisfaction and each of the subscales are .86 for intimacy, .77 for passion, and .75 for commitment.

So now you know that there is a strong relation between intimacy, passion, and commitment in feelings toward a lover, as well as between each of these aspects of love and satisfaction in the relationship with the lover. Can you infer anything about the causal relations from these correlations? For example, might you be able to conclude that intimacy leads to commitment? Unfortunately, you cannot infer anything for sure. Consider three alternative interpretations of the correlation between intimacy and commitment.

One possibility is that intimacy produces commitment. This interpretation makes sense. As you develop more trust, communication, and support in a relationship, you are likely to feel more committed to that relationship. However, there is a second possibility, namely, that commitment leads to intimacy. This interpretation also makes sense. You may feel that until you really commit yourself to a relationship, you do not want to trust your partner with the more intimate secrets of your life, or to communicate some of your deepest feelings about things. A third possibility exists as well—that both intimacy and commitment depend on some third factor. In this view, neither causes the other, but both are dependent on some third variable. For example, it may be that intimacy and commitment both depend on a shared sense of values. Without such shared values, it may be difficult to build a relationship based on either intimacy or commitment.

The point is simple: As is often said in statistics, *correlation does not imply causation*. You cannot infer the direction of causality without further information. Correlation indicates only that there is a relation, not how the relation came to be. You can make a guess about the direction of causal relationship, but to be certain, you would need additional data.

In the example of the correlation between intimacy and commitment, you have a problem in addition to direction of causality. How much of a correlation do you need in order to characterize a relationship between two variables as statistically meaningful? In other words, at what level is a correlation strong enough to take it as indicating a true relationship between two variables, rather than a relationship that might have occurred by chance—by a fluke? Fortunately, there are statistics that can tell us when correlations, and other indices, are statistically meaningful. These statistics are called inferential statistics.

Inferential Statistics

Inferential statistics are one of two key ways in which statistics are used, in which a researcher analyzes numerical data in order to determine the likelihood that the given findings are a result of systematic, rather than random, fluctuations or events. In order to understand how inferential statistics are used, you need to understand the concepts of a population and a sample.

Populations and Samples

A **population** is the entire set of individuals to which a generalization is to be made. Suppose a psychologist does an experiment involving feelings of love in close relationships. She tests a group of college students on the Triangular Love Scale. The psychologist is probably not interested in drawing conclusions only about the students she happened to test in a given place on a given day. Rather, she is more likely to be interested in generalizing the results obtained to college students in general, or perhaps even to adults in general. If so, then college students (or adults) in general constitute the population of interest, and the college students actually tested constitute the **sample**—that is, the subset of individuals actually tested.

In order to generalize results from the sample to college students (or adults) in general, the sample must be **representative**—that is, a subset of the population, carefully chosen to represent the proportionate diversity of the population as a whole. The less representative of the population is the sample, the harder it will be to generalize. For example, it probably would be safer to generalize the results the psychologist obtained to all college students than to all adults. However, even this generalization would be suspect, because college students differ from one college to another, and even from year to year within the same college.

Occasionally, you work with populations rather than with samples. Suppose, for example, that you are interested only in the people you have tested and no others. Then you are dealing with the population of interest, and inferential statistics do not apply. The values you obtain are for the population rather than just for a sample of the population. There is no need to generalize from sample to population, because you have the population. If, however, you view these students as only a sample of all college students, then you are working with a sample, and inferential statistics do apply.

In particular, inferential statistics indicate the probability that you can reject the **null hypothesis**—that is, a proposed expectation of no difference or relation in the population from which the tested sample or samples were drawn. Typically, the question you are asking when you use inferential statistics is whether the results you have obtained for your sample can be generalized to a population. For example, suppose you find a difference in intimacy scores between men and women in your sample. The null hypothesis would be that the difference you obtained in your sample is a result of chance variation in the data, and would not generalize to the population of all college men and women. The alternative hypothesis would be that the difference is statistically meaningful, and generalizes to the population.

Statistical Significance

When we speak of the meaningfulness of statistical results, we often use something called a test of *statistical significance*. Such a test tells us the probability that a given result would be obtained were only chance at work. A result, therefore, is statistically significant when the result is ascribed as most likely due to systematic rather than to chance factors. It is important to realize that a statistical test can show only the probability that one group differs from another in some respect. For example, you can compute the probability that a mean or a correlation is different from zero, or the probability that one mean differs meaningfully

from another mean. You cannot use statistics to estimate the probability that two samples are the same in any respect.

The distinction is an important one. Suppose you have two hypothetical individuals who are identical twins and who have always scored exactly the same on every test they have ever been given. There is no statistical way of estimating the probability that they truly are the same on every test. Some future test might always distinguish them.

Psychologists need to pay particular attention to two types of error in research. One type concerns drawing a conclusion when you should not, and the other not drawing a conclusion when you should.

The first is called **Type I error,** and refers to the belief that a finding has appeared due to systematic changes, when in fact the finding is a result of random fluctuation. In signal-detection theory (considered in chapter 4), this probability corresponds to the probability of a false alarm. For example, suppose you compare mean intimacy scores that individuals express toward mothers and fathers. The two values shown in Table A-2 are 6.49 and 5.17 for the mother and father respectively. You find that the score for the mother is higher than that for the father. A Type I error would occur if you believed that the difference was meaningful when in fact it was due just to random error of measurement.

The second type, **Type II error,** refers to the belief that a finding has appeared due to random fluctuations, when in fact the finding is a result of systematic changes. In signal-detection theory, this kind of error is called a miss. For example, if you conclude that the difference between mothers and fathers is due to chance, when in fact the difference exists in the population, you would be committing a Type II error.

Most researchers pay more attention to Type I than to Type II errors, although both are important. The reason for the greater attention to Type I errors is probably conservatism: Type I error deals with making a claim for a finding when there is none, whereas Type II error deals with failing to make a claim when there might be one to make. Researchers tend to be more concerned about investigators who make false claims than about those who fail to make claims that they might be entitled to make.

When we do psychological research, we usually compute inferential statistics that allow us to calculate the probability of a Type I error. Typically, researchers are allowed to report a result as "statistically significant" if the probability of a Type I error is less than .05. This probability is referred to as a **p-value,** the statistical quantity indicating the probability (p) that a particular outcome as extreme as that observed would have occurred as a result of random variation when the null hypothesis is true. In other words, we allow just 1 chance in 20 that we are claiming a finding when we do not have one. Investigators often report *p*-values as being either less than .05 or less than .01. A decision made with just a .01 chance of being erroneous generally is considered a very strong decision indeed. We can have a lot of confidence in that decision, although we cannot be certain of it.

The chances of finding a statistically significant result generally increase as more participants are tested, because with greater numbers of participants, random errors tend to average out. Thus, if you tested only 10 male participants and 10 female participants for their feelings of intimacy toward their partners, you probably would hesitate to draw any conclusions from this sample about whether there is a difference between men and women in general in their experiencing of intimacy toward their partners. However, if you tested 10,000 men and 10,000 women, you probably would have considerable confidence in your results, so long as your sample was representative of the population of interest.

It is important to distinguish between statistical significance and practical significance, which refers to whether a result is of any practical or everyday import. Suppose, for example, that you find that the difference between the men and the women in intimacy feelings is .07 point on a 1 to 9 scale. With a large enough sample, the result may reach statistical significance. But is this result of practical significance? Perhaps not. Remember, an inferential statistical test can merely tell you the probability that a result would occur were only chance at work. It does not tell you how large the difference is, nor whether the difference is great enough really to matter for whatever practical purposes you might wish to use the information. In research, investigators often pay primary attention to statistical significance. However, as a consumer of research, you need to pay attention to practical significance as well, whether the researchers do or not. Ultimately, in psychology, we need to concentrate on results that make a difference to us as we go about living our lives.

GLOSSARY

a posteriori knowledge. Knowledge that is acquired as a result of experience (from the Latin, meaning "from afterward")

a priori knowledge. Knowledge that exists regardless of whether an individual becomes aware of it through experience (from the Latin, meaning "from beforehand")

abnormal behavior. Behavior, inappropriate for the given social context, that is characterized by some degree of perceptual or cognitive distortion; the behavior typically is statistically unusual, nonadaptive, and readily labeled *abnormal* by the majority of persons in the given social context; although some abnormal behavior may not have all of the preceding characteristics, most abnormal behavior does

absolute refractory phase. A time following the firing of a *neuron*, during which the neuron cannot fire again regardless of the strength of the *stimulus* that reaches the neuron (cf. *relative refractory phase*)

absolute threshold. The hypothetical construct of a minimum amount of a particular form of physical energy (e.g., mechanical pressure of sounds, electrochemical scents or tastes) that reaches a sensory receptor, which is sufficient for the individual to detect that energy (stimulus); hypothetically, a person will be able to sense any stimuli that are at or above the absolute threshold, and unable to detect stimuli that are below that threshold

accessibility. The ease of gaining access to information that has been stored in long-term memory (cf. *availability*, *long-term store*)

accommodation (as a cognitive process). The process of responding to cognitively disequilibrating information about the environment by modifying relevant *schemas*, thereby adapting the schemas to fit the new information, thus reestablishing cognitive equilibrium (cf. *assimilation*; see also *equilibration*)

accommodation (as a means of adjusting the focus of the eye). The process by which curvature of the lens changes in order to focus on objects at different distances

acetylcholine (Ach). A *neurotransmitter* synthesized from choline in the diet; present in both the *central nervous system* and the *peripheral nervous system*; may affect memory function, as well as other neural processes in the brain; is involved in muscle contraction in the body and affects the muscles of the heart (see *neurotransmitter*; cf. *dopamine*, *serotonin*)

achievement. An accomplishment, an attained level of expertise on performance of a task, or an acquired base of knowledge (cf. *aptitude*)

achromatic. Lacking color; usually refers to stimuli that lack both *hue* and *saturation*, but that may differ in terms of *brightness* (from the Greek; *a-*, absence of, not; *chroma-*, color)

acquisition. The phase of *classical conditioning* during which a *conditioned response* strengthens and the occurrence of the response increases in likelihood

acronyms. See *mnemonic devices*

acrostics. See *mnemonic devices*

action potential. When an action potential occurs, the neuron is said to "fire." A change in the electrochemical balance inside and outside a neuron that occurs when positively and negatively charged ions quickly flood across the neuronal membrane; occurs when electrochemical stimulation of the neuron reaches or exceeds the neuronal *threshold of excitation*

activation–synthesis hypothesis. A proposed perspective on dreaming, which considers dreams to be the result of subjective organization and interpretation (synthesis) of neural activity (activation) that takes place during sleep; contrasting views include the Freudian view of dreams as a symbolic manifestation of wishes and the Crick–Mitchison view of dreams as "mental garbage"

active theories (of speech perception). A category of theories (e.g., *motor theory*, *phonetic-refinement theory*) that explain speech perception in terms of the active cognitive involvement of the listener; theories that consider the listener's cognitive processes, such as the listener's expectations, context, memory, and attention (cf. *passive theories*)

actor–observer effect. A psychological phenomenon in which people attribute the actions of others to the stable dispositional characteristics of those persons, but they attribute their own actions to the momentary characteristics of the situation (see also *fundamental attribution error*, *self-handicapping*)

acuity. The keenness (sharpness) of sensation in a sensory mode

acute (symptom or illness). Brief, usually characterized by sudden onset and intense symptomatology, but in any case not recurrent and not long in duration (cf. *chronic*)

acute pain. Brief (lasting no longer than six months), intense, uncomfortable stimulation usually associated with internal or external damage of tissue (cf. *chronic pain*)

acute stress disorder. A brief mental illness (lasting fewer than four months) that arises in response to a traumatic event; characterized by perceptual distortions, memory disturbances, and/or physical or social detachment (cf. *posttraumatic stress disorder*; see *anxiety disorders*)

adaptation level. The existing level of sensory stimulation (e.g., brightness or sound intensity), which an individual uses as a reference level for sensing new stimuli or changes in existing stimuli

addiction. A persistent, habitual, or compulsive physiological, or at least psychological, dependency on one or more *psychoactive* drugs (see also *tolerance*, *withdrawal*, as well as specific psychoactive drugs)

additive bilingualism. The addition of a second language to an established, well-developed primary language (see *bilingual*; cf. *subtractive bilingualism*)

additive mixture. The blending of various *wavelengths* of light (such as spotlights) which add together to produce a summative effect of the combined wavelengths which is perceived as a different color than the original lights (cf. *subtractive mixture*)

adrenal medulla. One of the two adrenal (*a-*, near or toward; *renal*, kidney [Latin]) glands, which are located above the kidneys; secretes epinephrine (*epi-*, on; *nephron*, kidney [Greek]) and norepinephrine, which act as *neurotransmitters* in the brain and as hormones elsewhere in the body, particularly aiding in *stress*-related responses, such as sudden arousal

aerial perspective. See *monocular depth cues*

aerobic exercise. Any activities that involve high-intensity, long-duration performance of motor behavior and that increase both heart rate and oxygen consumption, thereby enhancing overall health, particularly cardiovascular (heart and blood vessels) and respiratory (breathing) fitness

afferent. A neuron that brings information into a structure (see also *sensory neuron*)

aggression. A form of antisocial behavior that is directed against another person or persons, intended to cause harm or injury to the recipient of the aggression (see *hostile aggression*, *instrumental aggression*)

agnosia. A severe deficit in the ability to perceive sensory information, usually related to the visual sensory modality;

oddly, agnosics have normal sensations but lack the ability to interpret and recognize what they sense, usually as a result of lesions in the brain (*a-*, lack; *gnosis-*, knowledge [Greek])

agoraphobia. An *anxiety disorder* characterized by an intense fear (*phobia*) of open spaces or of being in public places from which it might be difficult to escape in the event of a panic attack; usually associated with panic attacks or with a fear of losing control or of some other dreaded but indistinct consequence that might occur outside the home (cf. *social phobia*)

agreeableness. See *Big Five*

algorithm. A means of solving a problem, which—if implemented correctly and appropriately—guarantees an accurate solution; generally involves successive, somewhat mechanical, repetitions of a particular strategy until the correct solution is reached; in many situations, implementation of an algorithm is either impossible or impractical as a means for solving problems (cf. *heuristics*)

alienated achievement. An alternative to the four main types of identity (cf. *foreclosure, identity achievement, identity diffusion, moratorium*), in which the individual considers the values of mainstream society to be inappropriate, or even bankrupt, and rejects identification with that society

alternate-forms reliability. See *reliability*

altruism. Selfless behavior focused on helping another person or persons, or at least behavior performed out of concern for another person or persons, regardless of whether the action has positive or negative consequences for the altruist (see also *prosocial behavior*)

amacrine cells. One of three kinds of *interneuron* cells in the middle of three layers of cells in the *retina*; the amacrine cells and the *horizontal cells* provide lateral connections, which permit lateral communication with adjacent areas of the retina in the middle layer of cells (cf. *bipolar cells*; see *ganglion cells, photoreceptors*)

amnesia. Severe loss of memory, usually affecting primarily episodic memory (see also *dissociative amnesia*); *anterograde amnesia*—inability to recall events that occur *after* whatever trauma caused the memory loss (affects the acquisition of *episodic memory*, but apparently not the acquisition of *procedural memory*); *infantile amnesia*—the inability to recall events that happened during early development of the brain (usually the first 3 to 5 years); *retrograde amnesia*—inability to recall events that occurred *before* the trauma that causes the memory loss (often, the amnesic gradually begins to recall earlier events, starting with the earliest experiences and gradually recalling events that occurred closer to the time of the trauma, perhaps eventually even recalling the traumatic episode

amphetamine. A type of synthetic *central nervous system (CNS) stimulant* that is usually either ingested orally or injected; short-term effects include increased body temperature, heart rate, and endurance, as well as reduced appetite; psychological effects include stimulation of the release of *neurotransmitters*, such as norepinephrine and *dopamine* into brain synapses, as well as inhibition of *reuptake* of neurotransmitters, leading to a sense of euphoria and increased alertness, arousal, and motor activity; long-term effects are a reduction of *serotonin* and other neurotransmitters in the brain, thereby impairing neural communication within the brain; long-term use also leads to *tolerance* and intermittent use may lead to *sensitization*

amplitude. The objective physical intensity of sound or light; when sound or light energy is displayed on an oscilloscope, higher waves correspond to greater intensity; in terms of subjective perception, greater amplitude of light is perceived as increased *brightness* and greater amplitude of sound is perceived as increased loudness

amygdala. The portion of the brain that plays a role in anger and aggression

anal stage. A stage of *psychosexual development*, which typically occurs between the ages of 2 and 4 years, during which time the child learns to derive gratification from the control over urination and especially defecation

angiograms. Essentially X-ray pictures for which the visual contrast has been enhanced by injecting special dyes into the blood vessels of the head; primarily used clinically to assess vascular diseases (diseases of the blood vessels, which may lead to strokes) and to locate particular kinds of brain tumors; also used experimentally as a means of determining which parts of the brain are active when people perform different kinds of listening, speaking, or movement tasks

anorexia nervosa. A pathological mental disorder in which an individual does not eat enough to avoid starvation, despite the availability of food

anterograde amnesia. See *amnesia*

antisocial behavior. Behavior that is harmful to a society or to its members

antithesis. A statement of opinion presenting an alternative view that differs from the opinion stated originally and may seem to contradict it (cf. *thesis*; see *dialectic*; see also *synthesis*)

anxiety. A generalized, diffused feeling of being threatened, despite the inability to pinpoint the source of the threat; tends to be more pervasive and long-lasting than fear; characterized by tension, nervousness, distress, or uncomfortable *arousal* (see also *cognitive anxiety, somatic anxiety*)

anxiety disorders. A category of psychological disorders (e.g., *generalized anxiety disorder, obsessive-compulsive disorder, panic disorder, phobia*, and stress disorders such as *acute stress disorder* and *posttraumatic stress disorder*) characterized primarily by feelings of anxiety (a mood symptom) of varying levels of intensity, excessive worry and a concentration of thoughts on worrisome phenomena (cognitive symptoms), many purposeless movements (e.g., fidgeting, pacing, motor tics, and other *motor* symptoms), and somatic symptoms associated with high *arousal* of the *autonomic nervous system* (e.g., sweating, muscle tension, high pulse and respiration rates, and high blood pressure)

aptitude. A potential ability to accomplish something, to attain a level of expertise on performance of a task or a set of tasks, or to acquire knowledge in a given domain or set of domains

arbitrary symbolic reference. A property of *language*, indicating that human language involves a shared system of symbols (images, sounds, or objects that represent or suggest other things) that are selected arbitrarily as a means of representing particular things, ideas, processes, relationships, and descriptions

archetype. A universal, inherited human tendency to perceive and act on things in particular ways, as evidenced by the similarities among various myths, legends, religions, and even customs across cultures; the most common Jungian archetypes: *anima*—the feminine side of a man's personality, which shows tenderness, caring, compassion, and warmth toward others, yet which is more irrational and based on emotions; *animus*—the masculine side of a woman's personality, the more rational and logical side of the woman; *persona*—the part of the personality that a person shows the world and that the person is willing to share with other persons; *shadow*—the part of the personality that is viewed as frightening, hateful, or even evil, and which the individual therefore hides not only from others, but also from her- or himself

arousal. A hypothetical construct representing alertness, wakefulness, and activation, caused by the activity of the *central nervous system (CNS)*

assimilation (as a cognitive process). The process of adapting to new information that conflicts with existing schemas by changing the new information to fit the existing schemas, thereby reestablishing cognitive equilibrium (cf. *accommodation*; see also *equilibration*)

association areas. Regions of the cerebral lobes that are not part of the sensory (visual, auditory, somatosensory) or motor cortices, believed to connect (associate) the activity of the sensory and motor cortices

associationism. A school of psychological thought that examines how events or ideas can become associated with one another in the mind, thereby resulting in a form of learning

associationist. Person who subscribed to *associationism* and who therefore believed that events occurring close to one another in time become associated in the mind, so that these events may later be recalled in tandem

asylum. Institution intended for housing mentally ill persons, sometimes also involving some form of rehabilitative treatment for the residents

asymptote. The most stable level of response associated with a psychological phenomenon, usually graphed as a curve on which the maximum level of stability can be observed as the region of response that shows the least variation; for learning curves, the most stable level of response appears at the high point of the curve; for habituation, the asymptote appears at a low point on the curve; for other psychological phenomena, the most stable level of response may appear at other locations of the curve

atheoretical. Not based on or guided by any particular theoretical approach (*a-*, "lacking" or "without")

attachment. A strong and relatively long-lasting emotional tie between two humans

attention. The active cognitive processing of a limited amount of information from the vast amount of information available through the senses, in memory and through cognitive processes; focus on a small subset of available stimuli

attitude. A learned (not inherited), stable (not volatile), and relatively enduring (not transitory) evaluation (positive or negative judgment) of a person, object, or idea that can affect an individual's behavior

attribution. An explanation that points to the cause of a person's behavior, including the behavior of the individual devising the explanation (see *personal attribution, situational attribution*)

attribution theory. A theory regarding the way in which people point to the causes of a person's behavior, including the behavior of the individual devising the explanation (see *attribution*; see also *actor–observer effect, fundamental attribution error, self-handicapping*)

authoritarian parents. Mothers and fathers who exhibit a style of parenting in which they tend to be firm, punitive, and generally unsympathetic to their children; who highlight their own authority, who hold exacting standards for and prize obedience in their children, and who show little praise toward and attachment to their children (cf. *permissive parents, authoritative parents*)

authoritative parents. Mothers and fathers who exhibit a style of parenting in which they tend to encourage and support responsibility and reasoning in their children, explaining their reasoning for what they do, establishing firm limits within which they encourage children to be independent, and which they enforce firmly but with understanding (cf. *authoritarian parents, permissive parents*)

automaticity. A phenomenon in which experts have so thoroughly mastered the procedures and *heuristics* in their area of expertise that their performance of these operations is virtually automatic and requires little conscious effort for implementation

autonomic nervous system. The part of the *peripheral nervous system* that controls movement of nonskeletal muscles (the heart muscle and the smooth muscles), over which people have little or no voluntary control or even conscious awareness (*autonomic* means "self-regulating"; cf. *somatic nervous system*)

availability. The existing storage of given information in long-term memory, without which it would be impossible to retrieve the information, and with which it is possible to retrieve the information if appropriate retrieval strategies can be implemented (cf. *accessibility*)

availability heuristic. An intuitive strategy for making judgments or inferences, or for solving problems, on the basis of the ease with which particular examples or ideas may be called to mind, without necessarily considering the degree to which the particular examples or ideas are relevant to or suitable for the given context (see *heuristic*)

aversion therapy. A behavioristic *counterconditioning* technique in which the client learns to experience negative feelings in the presence of a stimulus that is considered inappropriately attractive, with the aim that the client will eventually learn to feel repelled by the stimulus

aversive conditioning. A form of *operant conditioning*, in which the subject is encouraged to avoid a particular behavior or setting as a consequence of punishment in association with the given behavior or setting (see *avoidance learning*)

avoidance learning. A form of *operant conditioning*, in which the subject learns to refrain from a particular behavior or to keep away from a particular stimulus as a result of *aversive conditioning*

avoidant attachment pattern. Pattern in which a child generally ignores the mother while she is present and in which the child shows minimal distress when the mother leaves; one of three major attachment patterns observed in the *strange situation* (cf. *resistant attachment pattern, secure attachment pattern*)

axon. The long, thin, tubular part of the *neuron*, which responds to information received by the *dendrites* and some of the neuron, either ignoring or transmitting the information through the neuron until it can be transmitted to other neurons through the release of chemical substances by the axon's terminal buttons

babbling. A preferential production of distinct phonemes characteristic of the babbler's own language (cf. *cooing*)

backward conditioning. An ineffective form of *classical conditioning* in which the initiation of the *conditioned stimulus* follows rather than precedes the initiation of the *unconditioned stimulus*, thus resulting in little or no learning

balance theory. A proposed means of attaining *cognitive consistency* regarding friendships, in which it is suggested that people attempt to maintain a sense of give and take (*reciprocity*) in a relationship, and that people tend to be drawn to friends whose attitudes toward other people are similar to their own (*similarity*)

balanced presentation of viewpoints. A presentation of both favorable (pro) and unfavorable (con) perspectives on a given issue

bar graph. One of many types of graphic displays of numeric information (cf. *line graph*), in which items reflecting larger numerical values are represented as longer bars on the graph

barbiturate. The most widely used type of *sedative–hypnotic drug*; antianxiety drug prescribed to reduce *anxiety* through physiological inhibition of *arousal* (high dosages can even induce sleep), which may lead to grogginess that may impair functioning in situations requiring alertness; chronic use leads to *tolerance* and to physiological *addiction*, and high doses can lead to respiratory failure (see also *central nervous system (CNS) depressant*)

base rate. The prevalence of an event or characteristic within its population of events or characteristics (cf. *representativeness*; see *heuristic*)

basic anxiety. A feeling of isolation and helplessness in a world conceived as being potentially hostile, due to the competitiveness of modern culture

basilar membrane. One of the membranes that separates the fluid-filled canals of the *cochlea*; the physiological structure on which the *hair cells* (auditory receptors) are arranged; vibrations from the *stapes* stimulate the hair cells on the membrane in various locations, in association with differing sound frequencies

behavior therapy. A collection of techniques (see *counterconditioning, extinction procedures, modeling*) that are based at least partly on the principles of *classical conditioning* or *operant conditioning*, or on observational learning; usually involves short-term treatment in which the therapist directs the patient in techniques that focus exclusively on relieving symptoms and on changes in behavior, unconcerned with whether patients may gain insights or other nonbehavioral benefits of treatment

behavioral contracting. A behavioristic psychotherapeutic technique in which the therapist and the client draw up a contract specifying clearly the responsibilities and behavioral expectations of each party, and obligating both parties to live up to the terms of the contract

behavioral genetics. A branch of psychology that attempts to account for behavior (and often particular psychological characteristics and phenomena, such as intelligence) by attributing behavior in part to the influence of particular combinations of genes; often viewed as a marriage of psychology and genetics (see *genetics*)

behavioral medicine. A psychological approach to medicine, which focuses on the use of behavioral techniques to help people modify health-related problems (e.g., heavy smoking or overeating)

behaviorism. A school of psychology that focuses entirely on the association between an observed *stimulus* and an observed *response* and therefore may be viewed as an extreme extension of *associationism*

Big Five. The five key characteristics that are often described by various theorists as a useful way to organize and describe individual differences in personality: *agreeableness*—characterized by a pleasant disposition, a charitable nature, empathy toward others, and friendliness; *conscientiousness*—characterized by reliability, hard work, punctuality, and a concern with doing things right; *extroversion*—characterized by sociability, expansiveness, liveliness, an orientation toward having fun, and an interest in interacting with other people; *neuroticism*—characterized by nervousness, emotional instability, moodiness, tension, irritability, and frequent tendency to worry (cf. *psychoticism*); *openness*—characterized by imagination, intelligence, curiosity, and aesthetic sensitivity

bilingual. Person who can speak two languages (cf. *monolingual*; see also *additive bilingualism, subtractive bilingualism*)

binocular depth cues. One of the two chief means of judging the distances of visible objects, based on the two different angles from which each eye views a scene, which leads to a disparity of viewing angles that provides information about depth (*bi-*, "two"; *ocular*, pertaining to the eye; see *binocular disparity*; cf. *monocular depth cues*)

binocular disparity. The modest discrepancy in the viewpoint of each eye due to

the slightly different positions of each eye, which leads to slightly different sets of sensory information going to the brain from each of the two optic nerves; in the brain, the information is integrated in order to make determinations regarding depth, as well as height and width (see *binocular depth cues*)

biological psychology. A branch of psychology that attempts to understand behavior through the careful study of anatomy and physiology, especially of the brain (often considered synonymous with *physiological psychology* and *neuropsychology*)

biological trait. See *central trait*

biomedical model. A paradigm for health care, in which the focus is on the elimination of pathogens that cause diseases; serves as a basis for treating and often for curing illnesses, with little concern for preventive health practices, for health practices that promote wellness, or for psychological factors that may contribute to illness, recovery, or wellness

biopsychosocial model. A paradigm for health care, in which the focus is on an understanding of the various psychological, social, and biological factors that contribute to illness, prevention of illness, recovery from illness, and promotion of wellness

bipolar cells. One of three kinds of *interneuron* cells in the middle of three layers of cells in the *retina*; provide vertical connections, which permit communication between the *ganglion cells* in the first (outermost) layer of the retina and the *photoreceptors* in the third (innermost) of the three layers of retinal cells (cf. *amacrine cells, horizontal cells*)

bipolar disorder. A mental illness characterized by alternating extremes of depression and mania (also termed *manic-depressive disorder*)

bisexual. A person whose sexual orientation may be both heterosexual and homosexual (see *homosexuality*)

blind spot. The small area on the *retina* where the optic nerve leaves the eye, pushing aside *photoreceptors* to exit the eye

blocking effect. The failure of a second *unconditioned stimulus* to become classically conditioned because the first unconditioned stimulus blocks the effectiveness of the second one in eliciting a *conditioned response* (see *simultaneous conditioning*; see also *classical conditioning*)

bounded rationality. The limits within which humans demonstrate reasoned behavior (see also *satisficing*)

brain. The organ of the body encased in the skull that most directly controls thoughts, emotions, and motivations, as well as *motor* responses, and that responds to information it receives from elsewhere in the body, such as through sensory receptors

brain stem. The portion of the *brain* that comprises the *thalamus* and *hypothalamus*, the *midbrain*, and the *hindbrain*, and that connects the rest of the brain to the *spinal cord*; essential to the independent functioning of fundamental physiological processes (without which a physician will certify that the individual is brain dead)

brightness. The psychological perception of light intensity, rather than the actual physical quantity of light intensity, based on lightwave *amplitude*

bystander effect. A decreased likelihood that an individual will help a person or persons in distress, due to the actual or implied presence of other potential helpers (see *prosocial behavior*)

caffeine. A mild *central nervous system (CNS)* stimulant

canalization. The extent to which an ability develops independently of environmental circumstances; based on the imagery of a canal (a channel), in which abilities that are more canalized are positioned deeper in their canals, where they are less accessible to the influences of the outside world

cardinal trait. A single personality *trait* that is so salient in an individual's personality and so dominant in the person's behavior that almost everything the person does somehow relates back to this trait; although many people do not have cardinal traits, all people do have *central traits* and *secondary traits*

case study. Intensive investigation of a single individual or set of individuals, which is used as a basis for drawing general conclusions about the behavior of the individual and perhaps about other persons as well (cf. *experiment, naturalistic observation, survey, test*)

categorical clustering. See *mnemonic devices*

categorical syllogism. A deductive argument that involves drawing a conclusion regarding class or category membership, based on two premises; each of the premises contains two terms and makes assertions regarding category membership such that some, all, or none of the members of the category of one term are members of the class indicated by the other term, and one of the two terms of each premise is common to both premises (see *deductive reasoning, syllogism*); four types of statements used in categorical syllogisms: *particular affirmative statement*—assertion that *some* members of a category *are* members of another category; *particular negative statement*—assertion that *some* members of a category *are not* members of another category; *universal affirmative statement*—assertion that *all* members of a category *are* members of another category; *universal* *negative statement*—assertion that *all* members of a category *are not* members of another category

cathartic method. A psychotherapeutic technique associated with psychodynamic treatments, in which the patient is encouraged to reveal and discuss the painful origins of a psychological problem as a means of purging the problem from the patient's mental life

causal inference. A conclusion regarding one or more antecedents that are believed to have led to a given consequence; although a goal of science is to draw conclusions regarding causality, the complex interactions of multiple variables impinging on a particular phenomenon make it difficult to assert such conclusions with certainty, so scientists generally infer causality in terms of the relative likelihood that a particular variable was crucial in causing a particular phenomenon to occur (see also *inductive reasoning*)

central nervous system (CNS). The *brain* (encased in the skull) and the *spinal cord* (encased in the spinal column), including all of the *neurons* therein

central nervous system (CNS) depressant. Drug (e.g., alcohol and *sedative–hypnotic drug*) that slows the operation of the CNS and is often prescribed in low doses to reduce anxiety and in relatively higher doses to combat insomnia (see *barbiturate, tranquilizer*; cf. *narcotic*; see also *central nervous system (CNS) stimulant*)

central nervous system (CNS) stimulant. Drug (e.g., caffeine, *amphetamines*, cocaine, and nicotine—found in tobacco) that arouses and excites the CNS, either by stimulating the heart or by inhibiting the actions of natural compounds that depress brain activity (in other words, it acts as a "double-negative" on brain stimulation); short-term effects of relatively low doses include increased stamina and alertness, reduced appetite, and exuberant euphoria; stronger doses may cause anxiety and irritability; problems with *tolerance* and *addiction* are linked with long-term use, and problems with *sensitization* are tied to intermittent use (cf. *central nervous system (CNS) depressant*)

central route to persuasion. One of two routes to persuasion (cf. *peripheral route to persuasion*), which emphasizes thoughtful arguments related to the issue about which an attitude is being formed; most effective when the recipient is both motivated to think about the issue and able to do so

central tendency. The value (or values) that most commonly typifies an entire set of values (see *mean, median, mode*)

central traits affecting impression formation. Characteristics that form a basis for organizing other information in regard to forming an impression of an individual (see also *central traits of personality*)

central traits of personality. The five to ten most salient traits in a person's disposition, affecting much of the person's behavior (cf. *cardinal trait, secondary traits*; see also *central traits affecting impression formation*)

cerebellum. The part of the *brain* (*cerebellum*, "little brain" [Latin]) that controls bodily coordination, balance, and muscle tone; when damaged, subsequent movement becomes jerky and disjointed; located in the *hindbrain*

cerebral cortex. (*plural*: cortices) A highly convoluted 2-millimeter layer (give or take a millimeter) on the surface of the brain, which forms part of the *forebrain*; responsible for most high-level cognitive processes, such as planning and using language

cerebral hemispheres. The two rounded halves of the brain, on the surface of which is the *cerebral cortex* and inside which are the other structures of the brain (*hemi-*, half; *spherical*, globe-shaped)

cerebrospinal fluid. The clear, colorless fluid that circulates constantly throughout the *brain* and *spinal cord*, buffering them from shocks and minor traumas (injuries) and possibly helping in the elimination of waste products from the *central nervous system*

characteristic features. The qualities that describe a prototypical model of a word (or concept) and thereby serve as the basis for the meaning of the word, according to *prototype theory*; these qualities would characterize many or most of the instances of the word, but not necessarily all instances (cf. *defining features*)

child-directed speech. The characteristic form of speech that adults tend to use when speaking with infants and young children, which usually involves a higher pitch, exaggerated vocal inflections (i.e., more extreme raising and lowering of pitch and volume), and simpler sentence constructions; generally more effective than normal speech in gaining and keeping the attention of infants and young children (formerly termed *motherese*)

chromosome. Each of a pair of rod-shaped bodies that contain innumerable *genes*, composed largely of *deoxyribonucleic acid (DNA)*; humans have 23 chromosomal pairs

chronic (symptom or illness). Recurrent, constant, or very long in duration (cf. *acute*)

chronic pain. Recurrent or constant long-term (lasting at least six months or more) discomfort (of any level of intensity), usually associated with tissue damage (cf. *acute pain*); may be characterized as: (a) *chronic, intractable-benign pain*, which may vary in intensity but never entirely disappears, but which is not caused by an underlying fatal or injurious condition; (b) *chronic-progressive pain*, which is caused by an underlying pathology that worsens and that may eventually be fatal; or (c) *chronic-recurrent pain*, which disappears and then reappears repeatedly

chunk. A collection of separate items into a single clump, which can be more readily stored in memory and recalled later than is likely to occur if the various discrete items are stored and later retrieved as separate entities

circadian rhythm. The usual sleeping–waking pattern that corresponds roughly to the cycle of darkness and light associated with a single day (*circa*, "around"; *dies*, "day" [Latin]); many physiological changes (e.g., body temperature and hormone levels) are associated with this daily rhythmic pattern

classical conditioning. A learning process whereby an originally neutral stimulus (see *conditioned stimulus, CS*) comes to be associated with a stimulus (see *unconditioned stimulus, US*) that already produces a particular physiological or emotional response (see *unconditioned response, UR*), such that once the conditioning takes place, the physiological or emotional response (see *conditioned response, CR*) occurs as a direct result of the stimulus that was originally neutral (the CS), even in the absence of the other stimulus (the US); also termed *classically conditioned learning* (see *backward conditioning, delay conditioning, simultaneous conditioning, temporal conditioning, trace conditioning*)

classically conditioned learning. See *classical conditioning*

client-centered therapy. A form of humanistic therapy that assumes that the client's construction of reality provides the basis for understanding the client; characterized by nondirective interactions (thereby allowing the client to direct the course of therapy), genuineness (thereby offering honest communication with the client, rather than communications calculated to create a particular effect in the client), unconditional positive regard for the client (thereby encouraging the client to discontinue self-imposed conditions for positive self-regard), and accurate empathic understanding of the client (thereby helping the client to explore and to clarify her or his own worldview)

clinical. Describing a branch of psychology oriented toward the treatment of clients requiring therapeutic guidance by psychologists and psychiatrists

clinical interview. The most widely used clinical assessment technique; involves a meeting between the person seeking psychological assistance and a clinician who tries to obtain information from the client in order to diagnose the client's need for psychotherapeutic treatment (cf. *naturalistic observation, objective personality test, projective test*)

cocaine. A powerful *central nervous system (CNS) stimulant*

cochlea. The coiled and channeled main structure of the inner ear, which contains three fluid-filled canals that run along its entire convoluted length; the fluid-filled canals are separated by membranes, one of which is the *basilar membrane*, on which thousands of *hair cells* (auditory receptors) are arranged and are stimulated by the vibration of the *stapes*

cocktail party phenomenon. The process of tracking one conversation in the face of the distraction of other conversations, a phenomenon often experienced at cocktail parties

cognitive anxiety. Feelings of worry, tension, or frustration, or of being preoccupied with thoughts of impending failure (see *anxiety*; cf. *somatic anxiety*)

cognitive consistency. A match between the cognitions (thoughts) and the behaviors of a person, as perceived by the person who is thinking and behaving (cf. *cognitive dissonance*; see *self-perception theory*)

cognitive development. The study of how mental skills build and change with increasing physiological maturity and experience

cognitive dissonance. A person's disquieting perception of a mismatch between her or his attitudes (cognitions) and her or his behavior (cf. *cognitive consistency*; cf. also *self-perception theory*)

cognitive map. An internal, mental representation of a pattern (e.g., a maze or a hierarchy) or an abstraction (e.g, a concept)

cognitive therapy. *Psychotherapy* involving a cognitivistic approach to psychological problems, such as a focus on developing adaptive, rather than maladaptive, thoughts and thought processes

cognitivism. A school of psychology that underscores the importance of cognition as a basis for understanding much of human behavior

cohort effects. The distinctive effects of a particular group of participants having lived through a particular time in history, in which they experienced particular educational systems, opportunities, and values, which may affect findings based on *cross-sectional studies* (cf. *longitudinal study*)

cold fibers. Bundles of *neurons* that respond to cooling of the skin by increasing their rate of firing relative to the rate at which they fire when at rest (cf. *warm fibers*)

collective unconscious. A Jungian construct involving an aspect of the unconscious that contains memories and behavioral predispositions that all people have inherited from common ancestors in the distant human past (cf. *personal unconscious*)

commissive. See *speech acts*

commitment. One of three basic components of love, according to the *triangular theory of love* (cf. *intimacy, passion*): the decision to maintain a relationship over the long term

complex cells. One of the key physiological structures described by the *feature-detector approach* to form perception, according to which any members of a given group of *simple cells* may prompt the complex cell to fire in response to lines of particular orientations anywhere in the receptive field for the given complex cell; the particular type of light–dark contrasts of a line segment appear not to affect the firing of the complex cell as long as the line segment demonstrates the appropriate orientation; however, for some complex cells, the length of the line segments may also play a role in whether the cells fire

complexes. Clusters of independently functioning, emotionally tinged unconscious thoughts that may be found within the Jungian construct of the *personal unconscious*

compliance. The modification of behavior as a result of a request by another person or by other persons, which may involve taking an action, refraining from an action, or tailoring an action to suit another person or persons (cf. *conformity, obedience*); several techniques are often used: *door-in-the-face*—the compliance-seeker makes an outlandishly large request that is almost certain to be rejected, in the hope of getting the "target" (person whose compliance is being sought) of such efforts to accede to a more reasonable but perhaps still quite large request; *foot-in-the-door*—the compliance-seeker asks for compliance with a relatively small request, which is designed to "soften up" the target for a big request; *hard-to-get*—the compliance-seeker convinces the target that whatever the compliance-seeker is offering (or trying to get rid of) is very difficult to obtain; *justification*—the compliance-seeker justifies the request for compliance (often effective even when the justification is astonishingly weak); *low-balling*—the compliance-seeker gets the target to comply and to commit to a deal under misleadingly favorable circumstances, and then adds hidden costs or reveals hidden drawbacks only after obtaining a commitment to comply; *reciprocity*—the compliance-seeker appears to be giving something to the target, thereby obligating the target to give something in return, based on the notion that people should not receive things without giving things of comparable value in return; *that's-not-all*—the compliance-seeker offers something at a high price, and then, before the target has a chance to respond, throws in something else to sweeten the deal (or offers a discounted price on the product or service), thereby enticing the target to buy the offered product or service

componential theory. One of two primary theories of semantics, which claims that the meaning of a word (or concept) can be understood by disassembling the word into a set of *defining features*, which are essential elements of meaning that are singly necessary and jointly sufficient to define the word; that is, each defining feature is an essential element of the meaning of a concept, and the combination of those defining features uniquely defines the concept (also termed *definitional theory*; cf. *prototype theory*; cf. also *characteristic features*)

comprehension monitoring. A strategy of *verbal comprehension*, which involves watchfulness to observe whether the information being processed is being understood, contains internal contradictions, or contains other problematic features that require attention for their resolution

compulsion. An irresistible impulse to perform a relatively meaningless act repeatedly and in a stereotypical fashion; associated with feelings of *anxiety*, not joy, and often associated with *obsessions* (see also *obsessive–compulsive anxiety disorder*)

computerized axial tomogram (CAT). A highly sophisticated X-ray-based technique that produces pictures (*-gram*, "drawing" or "recording") of cross-sectional slices (*tomo-*, "slice" or "cut" [Greek]) of the living brain, derived from computer analysis of X rays that pass through the brain at various angles around a central axis in the brain (often termed *CAT scan*); usually used clinically to detect blood clots, tumors, or brain diseases, but also used experimentally to study how particular types and locations of brain damage (lesions) affect people's behavior

concentrative meditation. A form of contemplation in which the meditator focuses on an object or thought and attempts to remove all else from *consciousness* (see *meditation*)

concept. Idea to which various characteristics may be attached and to which various other ideas may be connected; may be used to describe a highly abstract idea or a concrete one

concrete operations. A stage of cognitive development in Piaget's theory of development, in which the individual can engage in mental manipulations of internal representations of tangible (concrete) objects (cf. *formal–operational stage, preoperational stage, sensorimotor stage*)

concurrent validity. An aspect of criterion-related *validity*, in which the predictor and the criterion are assessed at roughly the same time

condition (as an aspect of experimental design). A situation in an experiment in which a group of participants experience a carefully prescribed set of circumstances (see *control condition, experiment, experimental condition*)

conditional syllogism. A deductive argument that involves drawing a conclusion regarding an outcome based on contingencies or causal relationships; uses the form, "If A, then B (or 'then not B'). A (or 'not A'). Therefore, B (or 'not B')." (see *deductive reasoning, syllogism*)

conditioned emotional responses. Classically conditioned feelings (emotions) that an individual experiences in association with particular stimulus events

conditioned response (CR). A learned (classically conditioned) pattern of behavior that occurs in association with a *stimulus* that was not associated with this pattern of behavior prior to learning

conditioned stimulus (CS). A *stimulus* that initially does not lead to a particular physiological or emotional response, but that eventually does lead to the particular response, as a result of *classical conditioning*

cones. One of the two kinds of *photoreceptors* in the eye; less numerous, shorter, thicker, and more highly concentrated in the foveal region of the *retina* than in the periphery of the retina than are *rods* (the other type of photoreceptor); virtually nonfunctional in dim light, but highly effective in bright light, and essential to color vision (see *fovea*)

confirmation bias. The human tendency to seek ways in which to confirm rather than to refute existing beliefs

conformity. The modification of behavior in order to bring the behavior into line with the norms of the social group; may involve taking an action, refraining from an action, or tailoring an action to suit the social group (cf. *compliance, obedience*); also, the tendency to give up personal individuality and independent decision making, in order to become like others and to share in the power of a collectivity

conscientiousness. See *Big Five*

consciousness. The complex phenomenon of evaluating the environment and then filtering that information through the mind, with awareness of doing so; may be viewed as the mental reality created in order to adapt to the world

construct-related validity. An aspect of *validity*, in which an evaluation is made regarding the degree to which a test or other measurement actually reflects the hypothetical construct (e.g., intelligence)

that the test or other measurement is designed to assess

constructive memory. The psychological phenomenon in which an individual actually builds memories, based on prior experience and expectations, such that existing *schemas* may affect the way in which new information is stored in *memory* (cf. *reconstructive memory*)

constructive perception. Assertion that the perceiver builds the stimulus that is perceived, using sensory information as the foundation for the structure, but also considering the existing knowledge and thought processes of the individual; one of the two key views of perception (also termed *intelligent perception*; cf. *direct perception*)

contact hypothesis. The unsubstantiated assumption that *prejudice* will be reduced, simply as a result of direct contact between social groups that have prejudicial attitudes toward each other, without any regard to the context in which such contact occurs

content-related validity. An aspect of *validity*, in which experts judge the extent to which the content of a test measures all of the knowledge or skills that are supposed to be included within the domain being tested

context effects. The influences of the surrounding environment on cognition, particularly as applied to the visual perception of forms

contextualist. Psychologist who theorizes about a psychological phenomenon (e.g., intelligence) strictly in terms of the context in which an individual is observed, and who suggests that the phenomenon cannot be understood—let alone measured—outside the real-world context of the individual; particularly, a theorist who studies how intelligence relates to the external world

contingency. The dependent relationship between the occurrence of an *unconditioned stimulus* and the occurrence of a *conditioned stimulus* (cf. *temporal contiguity*)

continuous reinforcement. A pattern of *operant conditioning* in which reinforcement always and invariably follows a particular *operant* behavior (cf. *partial reinforcement*)

contour. The features of a surface that permit differentiation of one surface from another (e.g., convexity or concavity)

contralateral. Occurring or appearing on the opposite side (*contra-*, opposite; *lateral*, side); often used for describing the crossed pattern of sensory and motor connections between the physiological structures of the body and those of the brain (cf. *ipsilateral*)

control. Having power or authority over something; the ability to manage or manipulate; one of four goals of psychologi-

cal research (the other three are *description, explanation,* and *prediction*)

control condition. A situation in which a group of experimental participants experience a carefully prescribed set of circumstances, which are almost identical to the *experimental condition*, but which do not involve the *independent variable* being manipulated in the experimental treatment condition

control-enhancing interventions. Methods for increasing patients' sense of control, thereby enhancing their ability to respond appropriately to illness and eventually to cope effectively with illness; such methods may include informing patients regarding the origins of their illness, the symptoms and other consequences of their illness, and the strategies they may use for promoting their recovery from illness or at least for minimizing the negative consequences of their illness

controlled experimental design. A plan for conducting a study in which the experimenter carefully manipulates or controls one or more independent variables in order to see the effect on the dependent variable or variables; although experimental control is usually the ideal means by which to study cause–effect relations, for many phenomena, such control is either impossible or highly impractical, so other means of study must be used instead (cf. *correlational design, quasi-experimental design*)

controlling. The individual plans what to do, based on the information received from the monitoring process; one of the two main purposes of consciousness (cf. *monitoring*)

conventional morality. A phase of moral development, in which moral reasoning is guided by mutual interpersonal expectations (e.g., to be good and to show good motives) and by interpersonal conformity (e.g., obeying rules and showing respect for authority); societal rules have become internalized, and the individual conforms because it is the right thing to do

convergent thinking. A form of *critical thinking*, which involves focusing in (converging toward) on one idea from an assortment of possible ideas (cf. *divergent thinking*)

cooing. Oral expression that explores the production of all the phones that humans can possibly produce; precedes *babbling*, which precedes language articulation

cooperative principle. The principle of conversation in which it is held that people seek to communicate in ways that make it easy for a listener to understand what a speaker means, such as by following the maxims of *manner, quality, quantity,* and *relation* proposed by H. P. Grice

coping. The process of trying to manage the internal and external challenges posed by a troublesome situation; sometimes conceptualized in terms of emotion-focused coping, which involves handling internal emotional reactions to the situation, and problem-focused coping, which involves the specific strategies used for confronting and resolving the problematic situation

cornea. On the eye, the clear dome-shaped window that forms a specialized region of the sclera (the external rubbery layer that holds in the gelatinous substance of the eye), through which light passes and which serves primarily as a curved exterior surface that gathers and focuses the entering light, making gross adjustments of the curvature in order to focus the image relatively well (cf. *lens*)

corpus callosum. A dense aggregate of nerve fibers (*corpus*, "body"; *callosum*, "dense"), which connects the two cerebral hemispheres, thereby allowing easy transmission of information between the two hemispheres

correct rejection. One of the four possible combinations of stimulus and response, according to *signal-detection theory (SDT)* (cf. *false alarm, hit, miss*); the accurate recognition that a signal stimulus was not detected

correlation. The statistical relationship between two attributes (characteristics of the subjects, of a setting, or of a situation), expressed as a number on a scale that ranges from −1 (a *negative correlation*) to 0 (no correlation) to +1 (a *positive correlation*); (see also *correlational design*)

correlation coefficient. A measure of statistical association that ranges from −1 (perfect inverse relation) to 0 (no relation) to +1 (perfect positive relation)

correlational design. A plan for conducting a study in which the researchers merely observe the degree of association between two (or more) attributes that already occur naturally in the group(s) under study, and researchers do not directly manipulate the variables (cf. *controlled experimental design, quasi-experimental design*)

counterconditioning. A technique of behavioral therapy (or experimentation), in which the positive association between a given *unconditioned stimulus (US)* and a given *conditioned stimulus (CS)* is replaced with a negative one by substituting a new US, which has a different (and negative) *unconditioned response (UR)*, and in which the alternative response is incompatible with the initial response (see *classical conditioning*; see also *aversion therapy, systematic desensitization*)

countertransference. An unwanted phenomenon sometimes arising during psy-chodynamic therapy, in which the therapist projects onto the patient the therapist's own feelings (cf. *transference*)

CR. See *conditioned response*

creativity. The process of producing something that is both original and valuable; one of the fundamental processes of *thinking* (cf. *judgment and decision making, problem solving, reasoning*)

credibility. Believability

critical period. A brief period of rapid development, during which the organism is preprogrammed for learning to take place, given adequate environmental support for the learning, and after which learning is less likely to occur

critical thinking. The conscious direction of mental processes toward representing and processing information, usually in order to find thoughtful solutions to problems (see *thinking*; see also *convergent thinking, divergent thinking, synthesis*)

critical tradition. An established pattern of permitting current beliefs (*theses*) to be challenged by alternative, contrasting, and sometimes even radically (*radic-*, root) divergent views (*antitheses*), which may then lead to the origination of new ideas based on an integration of several features of the old ideas (*syntheses*; see also *dialectic*)

cross-sectional study. Research that investigates a diverse sampling of persons of various ages at a given time (cf. *longitudinal study*; see also *cohort effects*)

crystallized intelligence. One of two major subfactors of general intelligence; represents the accumulation of knowledge over the life span of the individual; may be measured by tests in areas such as vocabulary, general information, and achievement (cf. *fluid intelligence*)

CS. See *conditioned stimulus*

cued recall. Recall for which a cue, prompt, or other reminder is provided

cultural relativism. The view that assessments and even descriptions of intelligence and other psychological constructs should be based solely on indigenous (native to the cultural context) notions regarding the constructs under consideration

culture-fair test. Assessment that is equally appropriate for members of all cultures and that comprises items that are equally fair to members of all cultures; probably as elusive as a three-eyed unicorn (cf. *culture-relevant test*)

culture-relevant test. Assessment that employs skills and knowledge that relate to the cultural experiences of the test-takers, by using content and procedures that are relatively appropriate to the cultural context of the test-takers, although the test-makers' definitions of competent performance that demonstrates the hypothetical construct (e.g., intelligence) may differ from the definitions of the test-takers (cf. *culture-fair test*)

cumulative frequency. The total number of instances of values up to a given level (i.e., at or below a given level)

dark adaptation. The unconscious physiological response to a reduction of light intensity in the environment, characterized by an increase in *pupil* area by a factor of about 16, and an increase in visual sensitivity to light by a factor of as much as 100,000; usually takes about 30–40 minutes for full dark adaptation to occur (cf. *light adaptation*)

daydreaming. A state of consciousness somewhere between waking and sleeping, which permits a shift in the focus of conscious processing toward internal thoughts and images and away from external events; useful in cognitive processes that involve the generation of creative ideas, but disruptive in cognitive processes requiring focused attention on environmental events

decay. The phenomenon of memory by which simply the passage of time leads to forgetting

decay theory. The assertion that information is forgotten because it gradually disappears over time, rather than because the information is displaced by other information (cf. *interference theory*)

decibel (dB). The customary unit of measurement for the intensity of sound; 0 (zero) decibels is the absolute threshold for normal human hearing

declaration. See *speech acts*; synonym: *performative*

declarative knowledge. A recognition and understanding of factual information ("knowing that" *not* "knowing how"; cf. *procedural knowledge*)

deductive reasoning. The process of drawing conclusions from evidence involving one or more general *premises* regarding what is known, to reach a logically certain specific conclusion (see *reasoning, syllogism*; cf. *inductive reasoning*)

deductively valid. Characterized by having a conclusion follow logically from premises (see *deductive reasoning*; cf. *validity*)

deep-structure level. A level of syntactical analysis at which the underlying meanings (*deep structures*) of a sentence may be derived from a given surface structure and from which a given deep structure may be viewed as providing the basis for deriving various surface structures; a given deep structure may be expressed in more than one surface structure, and a given surface structure may serve as the basis for deriving more than one deep structure; takes into account the meanings derived from sentence structure (see *transformational grammar*)

defense mechanisms. Methods for protecting the ego from anxiety associated with the conflicting urges and prohibitions of the id and the superego; nine main defense mechanisms include *denial, displacement, fixation, projection, rationalization, reaction formation, regression, repression,* and *sublimation*

defining features. A set of component characteristics, each of which is an essential element of a given concept, and which together compose the properties that uniquely define the concept, according to *componential theory* (cf. *characteristic features, prototype theory*)

deindividuation. A loss of a sense of individual identity, associated with a reduction of internal constraints against socially unacceptable behavior

delay conditioning. A paradigm for *classical conditioning,* in which there is a long delay between the onset of the *CS* and the onset of the *US* (cf. *trace conditioning*)

delusion. Distorted thought process characterized by an erroneous belief that persists despite strong evidence to the contrary (e.g., *delusions of persecution* involve the belief that others are scheming to harm the person in some manner; *delusions of reference* involve the belief that particular chance events or appearances have special significance; *delusions of identity* involve the person's belief that she or he is somebody else, usually someone famous; other delusions involve the belief that persons can insert thoughts into the minds of others or can transmit their thoughts nonverbally); (cf. *illusion*)

dendrites. Parts of the *neuron* at the end of the *soma;* primary structures for receiving communications from other cells via distinctive receptors on their external membranes, although some communications are also received by the soma (from the Greek word for "trees," which the multibranched dendrites resemble)

deoxyribonucleic acid (DNA). The physiological material that provides the mechanism for transmission of genetic information (see also *chromosomes, genes*)

dependent variable. The outcome response or attribute that varies as a consequence of variation in one or more independent variables (cf. *independent variable*)

depth. As applied to *perception:* the perceived distance of something from the body of the perceiver (see *monocular depth cues, binocular depth cues*)

description. A goal of science in which the scientist characterizes what and how people think, feel, or act in response to various kinds of situations (other goals include explanation, prediction, and perhaps even control of phenomena)

descriptive grammar. See *grammar*

descriptive statistic. Numerical analysis that summarizes quantitative information about a population

design (of experiments). A way in which a given set of experimental variables are chosen and interrelated, as well as a plan for selecting and assigning participants to experimental and control conditions

detection. Active, usually conscious, sensing of a *stimulus,* influenced by an individual's threshold for a given sense and by confounding sensory stimuli in the surrounding environment

determinism. The belief that people's behavior is ruled by forces over which the people have little or no control

development. Qualitative changes in complexity, often accompanied by quantitative increases in size or amount (cf. *growth*)

developmental psychologists. Psychologists who study the differences and similarities among people of different ages, as well as the qualitative and quantitative psychological changes that occur across the life span

deviation IQs. A means of determining intelligence-test scores, based on deviations from an average score, calculated such that the normative equivalent for the median score is 100, about 68% of the scores are computed to fall between 85 and 115, and about 95% of the scores fall between 70 and 130; not, strictly speaking, IQs, because no quotient is involved (cf. *mental age, ratio IQ*)

dialectic. A continuing intellectual dialogue in which thinkers strive for increased understanding, first by formulating an initial *thesis,* then by considering an *antithesis* to the initial view, and finally by integrating the most insightful and well-founded aspects of each view to form a *synthesis;* because ultimate truth and understanding are ever-elusive, the dialogue never ends, and the synthesis view then serves as a new thesis for which a new antithesis may be posited, and so on

dialectical thinking. A form of thinking that characterizes a stage of mental operations hypothesized to follow the Piagetian stage of *formal operations;* such thinking recognizes that humans seldom find final, correct answers to the important questions in life, but rather pass through a progression of beliefs comprising some kind of *thesis,* a subsequent *antithesis,* and then a *synthesis,* which then serves as the new thesis for the continuing evolution of thought (see *dialectic;* cf. *problem finding, postformal thinking*)

diathesis-stress theory. According to this theory people have differential genetic vulnerability to particular psychological disorders. The likelihood that people will develop these disorders increases as they are exposed to increasing amounts of stress. The disorder to which the person is vulnerable then develops if the person experiences so much stress that he or she is unable to cope with the environment.

diffusion of responsibility. An implied reduction of personal responsibility to take action due to the presence of other persons, particularly in considering how to respond to a crisis (see also *bystander effect*)

direct perception. One of the two key views of perception (cf. *constructive perception*); asserts that the array of information in the sensory receptors, including the sensory context, is all that is needed for an individual to perceive anything; according to this view, prior knowledge or thought processes are not necessary for perception (see *feature-matching*)

directive. See *speech acts*

disconfirm. Show that a particular hypothesis is not supported by data

discourse. The most comprehensive level of linguistic analysis, which encompasses language use at the level beyond the sentence, such as in conversation, in paragraphs, articles, and chapters, and entire books (cf. *semantics, syntax*)

discrete-emotions theory. A theory of emotional development, which asserts that the human neural system is innately predisposed to feel various discrete emotions, given the appropriate situation in which to express those emotions

discrimination. The ability to ascertain the difference between one stimulus and another (see *stimulus discrimination;* cf. *stimulus generalization*)

dissociative amnesia. A *dissociative disorder* characterized by a sudden memory loss of *declarative knowledge* (e.g, difficulty or inability in recalling important personal details) and usually affecting the recollection of the events that took place during and immediately after the stressful event (see also *acute stress disorder*), but usually not affecting *procedural knowledge;* duration of the *amnesia* is variable (anywhere from several hours to several years), although recovery of the lost information is usually as rapid as was the loss of the information, after which the episode typically ends and the memory loss is not repeated

dissociative disorder. Disorder characterized by an alteration in the normally integrative functions of consciousness and identity, usually in response to a highly stressful life experience (see *dissociative amnesia, dissociative fugue, dissociative identity disorder*)

dissociative fugue. A *dissociative disorder* in which a person responds to severe stress by starting a whole new life and experiencing total *amnesia* about the past; the person moves to a new place, assumes a new identity, takes a new job, and behaves as though she or he were a completely new person, perhaps even with a new personality; duration of the fugue state is variable, but when recovery occurs it is usually total, and the individual fully remembers her or his life prior to the fugue state but completely forgets the events that took place during the fugue state

dissociative identity disorder. (Formerly termed *multiple personality disorder*) A *dissociative disorder* that typically arises as a result of extreme early trauma—usually, severe child abuse—and that is characterized by the occurrence of two or more individual identities (personalities) within the same individual, in which each identity is relatively independent of any others, has a stable life of its own, and occasionally takes full control of the person's behavior

distal stimulus. An external source of stimulation as it exists in the world, which may differ somewhat from the internal sensation of the source of stimulation that is detected in the sensory receptors (cf. *proximal stimulus;* see also *perceptual constancy*)

distraction–conflict theory. A view of *social facilitation* and social interference, in which it is held that the effect of the presence of others is due not to the mere presence of others, or even to evaluation apprehension, but rather to the distracting effect of having other people around

distributed learning. An apportionment of time spent learning a body of information by spacing the total time over various sessions, rather than consolidating the total time in a single session; generally leads to more learning than does *massed learning*

divergent production. Generation of a diverse assortment of appropriate responses to a problem, question, or task; often considered an aspect of *creativity* (see also *divergent thinking*)

divergent thinking. A form of *critical thinking*, which involves generating many ideas, and which may be considered to complement *convergent thinking*

doctor-centered style (of physician interactions). One of two basic patterns for physician–patient interactions (cf. *patient-centered style*); characterized by a highly directive interaction pattern, in which a physician narrowly focuses on the presenting medical problem, uses highly convergent questioning to elicit brief and targeted responses from the patient, and then formulates a diagnosis and a treatment regimen that is prescribed to the patient

dominant trait. The stronger genetic trait, which appears in the *phenotype* of an organism when the *genotype* comprises a dominant trait and a *recessive trait*

dopamine. A *neurotransmitter* that seems to influence several important activities, including movement, attention, and learning; deficits of the substance are linked with Parkinson's disease, but surpluses may be linked to symptoms of *schizophrenia* (cf. *acetylcholine, serotonin*)

drive. A hypothesized composite source of energy related to physiological needs, which impels people to behave in ways that reduce the given source of energy and thereby to satisfy the physiological needs

dual-system hypothesis (of bilingualism). A view of bilingualism, which suggests that the two languages are represented somehow in separate systems of the mind, and possibly even in distinct areas of the brain (cf. *single-system hypothesis;* see *bilingual*)

duplex retina theory. A widely accepted psychophysical theory that recognizes the existence of two separate visual systems, one of which is responsible for vision in dim light (which depends on the *rods*), and the other of which is responsible for vision in brighter light (which depends on the *cones*)

duplicity theory. A currently accepted view of the way in which humans sense pitch, which gives some credence to both *place theory* and *frequency theory*, but which has yet to provide a full explanation of the specific mechanisms and their interactions

dynamic assessment environment. A context for measurement of cognitive abilities, in which the interaction between the test-taker and the examiner does not end when the test-taker gives an incorrect response; rather, the examiner offers the test-taker a sequence of guided and graded hints designed to facilitate problem solving; this kind of assessment environment is oriented toward determining the test-taker's ability to use hints and to profit from opportunities to learn, not toward determining the fixed state of existing knowledge in the test-taker (cf. *static assessment environment;* see also *zone of proximal development*)

eardrum. An anatomical structure of the outer ear which vibrates in response to sound waves that have moved through the auditory canal from the *pinna;* its vibrations are passed to the middle ear, where it transfers its vibrations to a series of ossicles (see *incus, malleus, stapes*) such that higher frequencies of sound cause more rapid vibrations (also termed *tympanum*)

echoic store. A hypothesized sensory register for fleeting storage of auditory stimuli; evidence of such a register has been insubstantial to date

efferents. The *neurons* and *nerves* that transmit motor information (e.g., movements of the large and small muscles) either from the *brain* through the spinal cord to the muscles (for voluntary muscle movements) or directly from the *spinal cord* to the muscles (in the case of *reflexes*), thus controlling bodily responses (cf. *receptors;* see *motor neuron*)

ego. One of three psychodynamic concepts (cf. *id, superego*), which responds to the real world as it is perceived to be, rather than as the person may want it to be or may believe that it should be; more broadly, an individual's unique sense of her- or himself, which embraces the person's wishes and urges but tempers them with a realization of how the world works (see *reality principle*)

egocentrism. A cognitive characteristic (not a personality trait) in which mental representations are focused on the point of view and experiences of the individual thinker and in which the individual finds it difficult to grasp the viewpoint of others

Electra conflict. A conflict believed by Freudians to be characteristically experienced by girls during the *phallic stage* of *psychosexual development;* named for the Greek myth in which Electra despised her mother for having cheated on and killed her husband, Electra's father; often considered the female equivalent of the *Oedipal conflict*

electroconvulsive therapy (ECT). A psychophysiological treatment for severe, unremitting depression, in which electrical shocks are passed through the head of a patient, causing the patient to experience convulsive muscular seizures and temporary loss of consciousness; use of this treatment has been largely as a last resort

electroencephalogram (EEG). A recording (*-gram*) of the electrical activity of the living brain, as detected by various electrodes (*en-*, in, *cephlo-*, head [Greek])

electromagnetic spectrum. A range of energy of varying wavelengths, a narrow band of which is visible to the human eye

emotion. A feeling comprising physiological and behavioral (and possibly cognitive) reactions to internal (e.g., thoughts, memories) and external events

emotion-focused coping. See *coping*

emotional intelligence. The ability to perceive accurately, appraise, and express emotion; the ability to access and/or generate feelings when they facilitate thought; the ability to understand emotion and emotional knowledge; the ability to regulate emotions to promote emotional and intellectual growth

empirical method. Means of obtaining information and understanding through experience, observation, and experimentation

empiricist. Person who believes that knowledge is most effectively acquired through *empirical methods* (cf. *rationalist*)

empty-nest syndrome. Transitional period in adult social development, during which parents adjust to having their children grow up and move out of the family home

encoding. Process by which a physical, sensory input is transformed into a representation that can be stored in memory (see also *memory, rehearsal*)

encoding specificity. Phenomenon of memory in which the specific way of representing information as it is placed into memory affects the specific way in which the information may be recalled later

endocrine system. A physiological communication network that complements the *nervous system;* operates via *glands* that secrete *hormones* directly into the bloodstream; regulates the levels of hormones in the bloodstream via negative-feedback loops (*endo-*, inside; *-crine*, related to secretion [Greek])

episodic memory. Encoding, storage, and retrieval of events or episodes that the rememberer experienced personally at a particular time and place (cf. *semantic memory*)

equilibration. A process of cognitive development, in which thinkers seek a balance (equilibrium) between the information and experiences they encounter in their environments and the cognitive processes and structures they bring to the encounter, as well as among the cognitive capabilities themselves; comprises three processes: the use of existing modes of thought and existing *schemas*, the process of *assimilation*, and the process of *accommodation*

equity theory. A theory of interpersonal attraction, which holds that individuals will be attracted to persons with whom they have an equitable give-and-take relationship

ethologist. Scientist who studies the way in which different species of animals behave and how behavior has evolved within differing species

etiology. All of the causes of an abnormal condition

evoked response potentials (ERPs). *Electroencephalogram (EEG)* recordings in which at least some of the electrical interference has been averaged out of the data by means of averaging the EEG wave forms on successive EEG recordings; experimental uses have included using the recordings to map the electrical activity of various parts of the brain during various cognitive tasks or in response to various kinds of stimuli

evolutionary psychology. The branch of psychology whose goal is to explain behavior in terms of organisms' evolved adaptations to a constantly changing environment

exemplar. One of several typical representatives of a particular concept or of a class of objects; sometimes, several exemplars are used as a set of alternatives to a single prototype for deriving the meaning of a concept (see *prototype theory*)

exhaustive serial processing. A means of responding to a task involving recognition of a particular item from a list of items, in which an individual seeks to retrieve an item stored in memory by checking the item being sought against all of the possible items that are presented, even if a match is found partway through the list (cf. *self-terminating serial processing*; cf. also *parallel processing*)

experiment. An investigation of cause–effect relationships through the control of variables and the careful manipulation of one or more particular variables, to note their outcome effects on other variables (see *control condition, experimental condition;* cf. *case study, naturalistic observation, survey, test*)

experimental analysis of behavior. An extreme behavioristic view that all behavior should be studied and analyzed in terms of specific behavior emitted as a result of environmental contingencies

experimental condition. A situation in which a group of experimental participants experience a carefully prescribed set of circumstances, which are almost identical to the *control condition* but which also include the treatment involving the *independent variable* that is being manipulated in the *experiment* (also termed *treatment condition*)

experimental neurosis. Inducement of a maladjustment in behavior or cognitive processing by means of classical conditioning, in which the discriminative stimulus is so ambiguous that it is virtually impossible to discern whether a particular response is appropriate or is inappropriate

explanation. Addresses why people think, feel, or act as they do. One of four goals of psychological research (the other three are *control, description,* and *prediction*)

explicit memory. A form of memory retrieval in which an individual consciously acts to recall or recognize particular information (cf. *implicit memory*)

expressive. See *speech acts*

external locus of control. Characterized by the tendency to believe that the causes of behavioral consequences originate in the environment, sometimes involving an extreme view in which the individual consistently misattributes causality to external rather than to internal causes (cf. *internal locus of control*)

extinction (as a phase of learning). A period of time during which the probability of the occurrence of a *CR* decreases, eventually approaching zero, due to the unlinking of the *CS* with the *US;* the individual still retains some memory of the learning; however, the *CR* can be relearned very quickly if the *CS* and the *US* become paired again

extinction procedure. A *behavior therapy* technique (e.g., *flooding, implosion therapy*) that is designed to weaken maladaptive responses

extrasensory perception (ESP). Apparent perception of phenomena that cannot be explained by known sensory and perceptual processes; considered by some to be an altered state of consciousness

extrinsic motivators. One of the two primary types of sources of motivation (cf. *intrinsic motivators*); motivating forces that come from *outside* the motivated individual, which encourage the person to engage in behavior because the person either is rewarded for doing so or is threatened with punishment for not doing so; often decrease intrinsic motivation to engage in behavior, such that the individual discontinues the behavior when extrinsic motivators are removed, even though the individual may have been intrinsically motivated to engage in the behavior prior to the introduction of extrinsic motivators; decrements in intrinsic motivation are particularly likely if extrinsic motivators are expected, are perceived as relevant and important to the individual, and are tangible

extroversion. See *Big Five*

eye contact. A major source of nonverbal communication, signaling culturally determined social information about intimacy and dominance via the frequency and duration of exchanged gazes

face validity. A kind of *validity*, in which test-takers judge the extent to which the content of a test measures all of the knowledge or skills that are supposed to be included within the domain being tested

facial-feedback hypothesis. An assumption suggesting that the cognitive feedback going to the brain as a result of the stimulation of particular facial muscles associated with particular emotional expressions (e.g., a smile or a frown) causes a person to infer that she or he is feeling a particular emotion

factor analysis. A method of statistical decomposition that allows an investigator to infer distinct hypothetical constructs, elements, or structures that underlie a phenomenon

false alarm. A response in which an individual inaccurately asserts that a signal stimulus has been observed; in *signal-detection theory (SDT)*, the inaccurate belief that a signal stimulus was detected when it was actually absent (cf. *correct rejection, hit, miss*); in memory tasks, a response in which subjects indicate that they have previously seen an item in a list, even though the item was not shown previously

family systems therapy. The treatment of the couple or the family unit as a whole, which involves complex internal interactions, rather than in terms of the discrete problems of distinct members of the unit

feature-detector approach. A psychophysiological approach to form *perception*, which attempts to link the psychological perception of form to the functioning of *neurons* in the *brain*, based on single-cell (neuronal) recording techniques for tracing the route of the neurons from the *receptors* within the *retina*, through the *ganglion cells*, then the thalamic nucleus cells, to the visual cortex; these psychophysiological studies indicated that specific neurons of the visual cortex respond to various stimuli that are presented to the specific retinal regions connected to these neurons; apparently, each individual cortical neuron can be mapped to a specific receptive field on the retina (see *complex cells, simple cells*)

feature hypothesis. A view regarding the means by which children make *overextension errors*: Children form definitions that include too few features, and they therefore overextend the use of given words because they lack one or more defining features that would more narrowly constrain the application of a given word (cf. *functional hypothesis*)

feature-matching. Theories of form perception (see *direct perception*; cf. *constructive perception*), according to which people attempt to match features of an observed pattern to features stored in memory, without considering the prior experience of the perceiver or what the perceiver already knows about the context in which the form is presented

fetal alcohol syndrome. An assemblage of disorders, chief among which are permanent and irreparable mental retardation and facial deformities, which may result when pregnant mothers consume alcohol during the fetal development of their infants

field. A domain of study, centered on a set of topics that have a common sphere of related interests or a common core of related phenomena (cf. *perspective*)

figure. See *figure–ground*; cf. *ground*

figure–ground. A Gestalt principle of form perception (see *Gestalt approach*): The tendency to perceive that an object in or an aspect of a perceptual field seems prominent (termed the *figure*), whereas other aspects or objects recede into the background (termed the *ground*)

first-order conditioning. A *classical-conditioning* procedure whereby a CS is linked directly with a US (cf. *higher order conditioning*)

fixated. A phenomenon of *psychosexual development*, in which an individual is unable to resolve the relevant issues of the current stage and therefore is unable to progress to the next stage (see also *defense mechanisms*)

fixed-interval reinforcement. A schedule of *operant conditioning* in which reinforcement always occurs after the passage of a certain amount of time, as long as the *operant* response has occurred at least once during the particular period of time (see *partial reinforcement*; cf. *fixed-ratio reinforcement, variable-interval reinforcement*; cf. also *variable-ratio reinforcement*)

fixed-ratio reinforcement. An *operant-conditioning* schedule in which reinforcement always occurs after a certain number of operant responses, regardless of the amount of time it takes to produce that number of responses (see *partial reinforcement*; cf. *fixed-interval reinforcement, variable-ratio reinforcement*; cf. also *variable-interval reinforcement*)

flashbulb memory. Recollection of an event that is so emotionally powerful that the recollection is highly vivid and richly detailed, as if it were indelibly preserved on film, although the true accuracy of such recall is not as great as the rememberer might believe it to be

flooding. Extinction procedures designed to lessen anxiety by exposing a client to a carefully controlled environment in which an anxiety-provoking stimulus is presented, but the client experiences no harm from the stimulus, so the client is expected to cease to feel anxiety in response to the stimulus (cf. *implosion therapy*)

fluid intelligence. One of two major subfactors of general intelligence; represents the acquisition of new information or the grasping of new relations and abstractions regarding known information (may be measured, for example, by timed tests involving analogies, series completions, or inductive reasoning; cf. *crystallized intelligence*)

forebrain. The farthest forward (toward the face) of the three major regions of the *brain* (cf. *midbrain, hindbrain*; names correspond roughly to the front-to-back arrangement of these parts in the developing embryo): the region located toward the top and front of the brain in adults; comprises the *cerebral cortex*, the *limbic system*, the *thalamus*, and the *hypothalamus*

foreclosure. One of four main types of identity (cf. *identity achievement, identity diffusion, moratorium*; cf. also *alienated achievement*), in which an individual makes a commitment to beliefs without

ever having considered various alternatives to those beliefs

formal-operational stage. A stage of cognitive development in Piaget's theory in which the individual can engage in mental manipulations of internal representations of abstract symbols that (a) may not have specific concrete equivalents, and (b) may relate to experiences the individual may not have encountered personally (cf. *concrete operations, preoperational stage, sensorimotor stage*)

fovea. A small, central, thin region of the *retina* that has a high concentration of *cones*, each of which has its own *ganglion cell* leading to the optic nerve, thereby increasing the visual *acuity* in bright light of images within the visual field of the foveal region (in contrast, the periphery of the retina has relatively fewer cones and more *rods*, which have to share ganglion cells with other rods, thereby reducing visual acuity in the peripheral visual field and in dim light)

free association. A phenomenon of *psychodynamic therapy* in which the patient freely says whatever comes to mind, not censoring or otherwise editing the free flow of words before reporting them

free nerve endings. Sensory receptors in the skin, which lack the globular swellings that characterize some other somatosensory receptors

free recall. A type of memory task in which a participant is presented with a list of items and is asked to repeat the items in any order the participant prefers (cf. *paired-associates recall, serial recall*)

frequency. In statistical contexts, applies to the number of instances of a given attribute, phenomenon, or response; *in psychophysical*, sensory contexts, applies to the number of waves of sound or light that occur within a specified interval, usually a second; *in sound waves*, higher frequencies are associated with higher pitches of sounds; *in light waves* (which are usually measured in terms of wavelengths, which are inversely related to frequencies), various frequencies are associated with various colors in the visible electromagnetic spectrum, as well as with various other forms of radiance (e.g., microwaves or gamma waves)

frequency distribution. The dispersion of values in a set of values, represented as the number, proportion, or percentage (i.e., the frequency) of instances of each value

frequency theory. One of two views of the way in which humans sense *pitch* (cf. *place theory*); the *basilar membrane* reproduces the vibrations that enter the ear, triggering neural impulses at the same *frequency* as the original sound wave, so that the frequency of the impulses that enter the auditory nerve determines the number of electrical responses per second in the auditory nerve; these responses are then sensed as a given pitch by the brain (see also *duplicity theory, volley principle*)

frontal lobe. One of the four major regions of the *cerebral cortex* (cf. *occipital lobe, parietal lobe, temporal lobe*); generally responsible for motor processing and for higher thought processes, such as abstract reasoning

functional fixedness. A particular type of *mental set*, in which the problem solver is unable to recognize that something that is known to be used in one way, for one purpose, may also be used for performing other functions, perhaps even through use in another way

functional hypothesis. A view regarding the means by which children make *overextension errors* (cf. *feature hypothesis*); children base their initial use of words on the important purposes (functions) of the concepts represented by the words, and children then make overextension errors because of their confusion regarding the functions of the objects being identified

functionalism. A school of psychology that focuses on active psychological processes, rather than on passive psychological structures or elements; for example, functionalists were more interested in how people think than in what they think, in how people perceive rather than what they perceive, and in how and why organisms evolve as they do rather than in what particular outcomes are produced by the evolutionary process (cf. *structuralism*)

fundamental attribution error. A bias of *attribution* in which an individual tends to overemphasize internal causes and personal responsibility and to deemphasize external causes and situational influences when observing the behavior of other people (see also *actor–observer effect, self-handicapping*)

fundamental frequency. The single tone produced by a note played on a musical instrument, which may also produce a series of harmonic tones at various multiples of the fundamental frequency (see *harmonics*)

gambler's fallacy. An intuitive and fallacious inference that when a sequence of coincidental events appears to be occurring in a nonrandom pattern (e.g., a protracted series of heads in a coin toss), subsequent events are more likely to deviate from the apparent pattern (e.g., the appearance of a tail) than to continue in the apparent pattern (e.g., the appearance of another head), when actually the probability of each event continues to have the same random probability at each occurrence (see *heuristic*)

game theory. A theory regarding decision making, which suggests that the ways in which people make many decisions, especially those involving more than one person, are often characterized by properties that resemble the properties of games (cf. *satisficing, subjective-utility theory, utility maximization theory*); four of the strategies are: *maximax gain rule*—the decision-maker seeks to *maxi*mize the *maxi*mum possible gain; *maximin gain rule*—the decision-maker *maxi*mizes the *mini*mum possible gain; *minimax loss rule*—the decision-maker makes a choice that *mini*mizes the *maxi*mum possible loss; *minimin loss rule*—the decision-maker makes a choice that *mini*mizes the *mini*mum possible loss

ganglion cells. Cells that form the first of three layers of cells in the *retina*; the *axons* of these cells form the optic nerve and communicate with the *photoreceptors* (in the third layer) via the middle layer of cells in the retina (cf. *amacrine cells, bipolar cells, horizontal cells*)

gate-control theory. A theory proposing a possible mechanism by which cognition, emotion, and sensation may interact to affect pain perception, in which it is posited that (a) the *central nervous system* serves as a physiological gating mechanism which can modulate the degree to which pain is perceived, and (b) cognitions and emotions in the brain can cause the spinal cord to intensify or to inhibit pain transmission by raising or lowering the "gate" (the pain threshold that determines the amount of stimulus required to trigger the sensation of pain) for pain stimulation

gender constancy. The realization that a person's gender is stable and cannot be changed by changing superficial characteristics (e.g., hair length) or behaviors (e.g., carrying a purse); see *gender typing*

gender typing. The process of acquiring the roles and associations related to the social and psychological distinction as being masculine or feminine

gene. Each of the basic physiological building blocks for the hereditary transmission of *traits* in all life forms (see *chromosomes, deoxyribonucleic acid [DNA]*)

general adaptation syndrome (GAS). A physiological response to stress, in which the body initially exerts maximal effort to adapt; if the stressor continues to prompt a response, however, the body reduces exertion in order to conserve physiological resources until eventually the body exhausts those resources

generalized anxiety disorder. An *anxiety disorder* characterized by general, persistent, constant, and often debilitating high levels of anxiety, which are accompanied by psychophysiological symptoms typical of a hyperactive *autonomic nervous system*,

and which can last any length of time, from a month to years; such anxiety is often described as "free floating" because a cause or source is not readily available

genes. The basic building blocks of hereditary transmission of traits in all life forms

genetics. The study of genes and heredity and variations among individuals as well as their expression in the environment (see *behavioral genetics*)

genital stage. A stage of *psychosexual development*; typically starts in adolescence, continues through adulthood, and involves normal adult sexuality, as Freud defined it—i.e., the adoption of traditional sex roles and of a heterosexual orientation

genotype. The pair of genes on a given chromosome pair, which is inherited from each parent and *not* subject to environmental influence (except in cases of genetic mutation); possibilities include both *dominant traits* and *recessive traits*, either of which may be passed on to biological offspring (cf. *phenotype*)

Gestalt. The distinctive totality of an integrated whole, as opposed to merely a sum of various parts; (from the German word *Gestalt*, meaning "form, shape")

Gestalt approach. A way of studying form perception, based on the notion that the whole of the form is different than the sum of its individual parts; *Gestalt*, meaning "form, shape" [German] (see also *Gestalt psychology*)

Gestalt psychology. A school of psychological thought, which holds that psychological phenomena are best understood when viewed as organized, structured wholes, not analyzed into myriad component elements; *Gestalt*, meaning "form, shape" [German] (see also *Gestalt approach*)

gland. Group of cells that secretes chemical substances; in the *endocrine system*, glands secrete *hormones* directly into the bloodstream; in the exocrine system, glands secrete fluids (e.g., tears, sweat) into ducts that channel the fluids out of the body

glial cell. Type of structure (also termed *neuroglia*) that nourishes, supports, and positions neurons within the *central nervous system (CNS)*, functioning as a kind of glue holding the CNS together, and keeping the neurons at optimal distances from one another and from other structures in the body, thereby helping to minimize miscommunication problems among neurons; also assist in forming the **myelin sheath,** such that the gaps between glial cells form the nodes in the sheath (see *nodes of Ranvier*)

glucostatic hypothesis. One of two major alternative assumptions regarding how the body signals hunger versus satiety (cf. *lipostatic hypothesis*); suggests that the levels of glucose (a simple body sugar) in the blood signal the body regarding the need for food; glucostatic: maintaining the stability (-*static*) of glucose (*gluco-*) levels in the body and in the brain

gradient of reinforcement. An important consideration in establishing, maintaining, or extinguishing *operant conditioning*, in which the length of time that occurs between the operant *response* and the reinforcing *stimulus* affects the strength of the conditioning; the longer the interval of time, the weaker the effect of the reinforcer

grammar. The study of *language* in terms of regular patterns that relate to the functions and relationships of words in a sentence—extending as broadly as the level of discourse and as narrowly as the pronunciation and meaning of individual words; *descriptive grammar*—the description of language patterns that relate to the structures, functions, and relationships of words in a sentence (see *phrase-structure grammar; transformational grammar*); *prescriptive grammar*—the formulation of various rules dictating the preferred use of written and spoken language, such as the functions, structures, and relationships of words in a sentence

ground. See *figure–ground*

group. A collection of individuals who interact with each other, often for a common purpose or *activity*

group polarization. Exaggeration of the initial views of members of a group through the dynamic processes of group interaction

groupthink. A process of the dynamics of group interactions, in which group members focus on the goal of unanimity of opinion more than they focus on the achievement of other goals, such as the purpose for which the group may have been designed in the first place; such a process is characterized by six symptoms: (1) close-mindedness to alternative conceptualizations; (2) rationalization of both the processes and the products of group decision making; (3) the squelching of dissent through ostracism, criticism, or ignoring; (4) the inclusion of a self-appointed mindguard, who diligently upholds the group norm; (5) the feeling of invulnerability, due to special knowledge or expertise; and (6) the feeling of unanimity; the net result of this process is defective decision making

growth. Quantitative linear increases in size or amount (cf. *development*)

hair cells. The thousands of specialized hairlike appendages on the *basilar membrane*, which function as auditory *receptors*, transducing mechanical energy from the vibration of the *stapes* into electrochemical energy that goes to the sensory neurons, which carry the auditory information to the brain (see *transduce*; see also *cochlea*)

hallucinations. Perceptions of sensory stimulation (e.g., sounds, the most common hallucinated sensations; sights; smells; or tactile sensations) in the absence of any actual corresponding external sensory input from the physical world

hallucinogenic. A type of *psychoactive* drug (e.g., mescaline, LSD, and marijuana) that alters consciousness by inducing hallucinations and affecting the way the drug-takers perceive both their inner worlds and their external environments; often termed *psychotomimetics* (also known as "psychedelics") because some clinicians believe that these drugs mimic the effects produced by psychosis

haptic. Characterized by sensitivity to pressure, temperature, and pain stimulation directly on the skin

harmonics. Distinctive tones that musical instruments generate, along with the *fundamental frequency* of the note being played, which are higher multiples of the fundamental frequency (cf. *noise*); different musical instruments yield distinctive multiples of the fundamental frequencies, resulting in the distinctive tonal qualities of the instruments

health psychology. The study of the reciprocal interaction between the psychological processes of the mind and the physical health of the body

heritability. The proportion of variation among individuals that is due to genetic causes

heritability coefficient. The degree to which heredity contributes to intelligence, expressed in terms of a number on a scale from 0 to 1, such that a coefficient of 0 means that heredity has no influence on variation among people, whereas a coefficient of 1 means that heredity is the only influence on such variation

hertz (Hz). A *frequency* of one cycle per second, often applied to sound waves

heuristic. An informal, intuitive, speculative strategy (e.g., a trial-and-error heuristic) that sometimes works effectively for solving problems; cf. *algorithm*; (see *availability heuristic, gambler's fallacy, illusory correlation, representativeness heuristic*); problem-solving heuristics include the following: *generate and test*—innovative origination of a series of alternative courses of action (with no particular systematic method for producing the alternatives) and assessment of the usefulness of each course of action until an alternative is found that solves the problem; *means–ends analysis*—analysis of the problem by viewing the end—the goal being sought—and then trying to decrease the distance between the current position in the problem space and the end goal in that space, using any means available; *working backward*—problem solving that focuses on the desired end, and then works backward to the beginning from the end; *working forward*—problem solving that starts at the beginning of the problem and then solves the problem from the start to the finish; also, some heuristics serve as mental short-cuts that aid in making speedy responses, but that sometimes also lead to errors in judgment

higher order conditioning. A *classical-conditioning* procedure (e.g., *first-order conditioning*) whereby a CS is not linked directly with a US, but rather is linked to an established CS, thereby producing a weaker (more volatile and more susceptible to *extinction*) form of classical conditioning

hindbrain. The farthest back of the three major regions of the *brain* (cf. *forebrain, midbrain*), located near the back of the neck in adults; comprises the *medulla oblongata*, the *pons*, and the *cerebellum*

hippocampus. A portion of the *limbic system* (*hippocampus*, Greek for "seahorse," its approximate shape); plays an essential role in the formation of new memories

hit. One of the four possible combinations of stimulus and response described in *signal-detection theory (SDT)*; (cf. *correct rejection, false alarm, miss*); the accurate recognition that a signal stimulus was detected, which was truly present

homeostatic regulation. Process by which the body maintains a state of equilibrium, such that when the body lacks something, it sends signals that prompt the individual to seek the missing resource, whereas when the body is satiated, it sends signals to stop obtaining that resource

homosexuality. A tendency to direct sexual desire toward another person of the same (Greek, *homo-*, "same") sex; often termed *lesbianism* in women (cf. *bisexual*)

horizontal cells. One of three kinds of *interneuron* cells in the middle of three layers of cells in the *retina*; the *amacrine cells* and the horizontal cells provide lateral connections, which permit lateral communication with adjacent areas of the retina in the middle layer of cells (cf. *bipolar cells*; see *ganglion cells, photoreceptors*)

hormone. Chemical substance, secreted by one or more *glands*, which regulates many physiological processes through specific actions on cells, fosters the growth and proliferation of cells, and may affect the way a receptive cell goes about its activities (see *endocrine system*)

hostile aggression. An emotional and usually impulsive action intended to cause harm or injury to another person or persons, often provoked by feelings of pain or distress, not by a desire to gain something through the aggressive act—in fact, valuable relationships and objects may be harmed or put at risk of harm through hostile aggression (see *aggression*, cf. *instrumental aggression*)

hue. Physical properties of light waves that correspond closely to the psychological properties of color, which is the subjective interpretation of the physiological processing of various wavelengths of the narrow band of visible light within the electromagnetic spectrum

humanism. A philosophical approach that centers on the unique character of humans and their relationship to the natural world, on human interactions, on human concerns, and on secular human values, including the need for humans to treat one another humanely; arose during the Renaissance, in contrast to the prevailing philosophy, which emphasized divinely determined values and divine explanations for human behavior

humanistic. See *humanism* and *humanistic psychology*

humanistic psychology. A school of psychological thought that emphasizes (a) conscious experience in personal development rather than unconscious experience, (b) free will and the importance of human potential rather than determinism, and (c) holistic approaches to psychological phenomena rather than analytic approaches

hypnosis. An altered state of consciousness that usually involves deep relaxation and extreme sensitivity to suggestion and appears to bear some resemblance to sleep (see *posthypnotic suggestion*)

hypothalamus. Located at the base of the *forebrain*, beneath (*hypo-*, Greek, "under") the *thalamus*; controls water balance in the tissues and bloodstream; regulates internal temperature, appetite, and thirst, as well as many other functions of the *autonomic nervous system*; plays a key role in controlling the *endocrine system*; interacts with the *limbic system* for regulating behavior related to species survival (fighting, feeding, fleeing, and mating); in conjunction with the *reticular activating system*, plays a role in controlling *consciousness*; involved in regulating *emotions*, pleasure, *pain*, and *stress* reactions

hypotheses. Tentative proposals regarding expected consequences, such as the outcomes of research (singular, hypothesis)

hypothesis testing. A view of language acquisition, which asserts that children acquire *language* by mentally forming tentative *hypotheses* regarding language and then testing these hypotheses in the environment, using several operating principles for generating and testing their hypotheses; also more broadly applies to testing of scientific and other hypotheses

hypothetical construct. Abstract concept (e.g., beauty, truth, or intelligence) that is not itself directly measurable or observable but that can be presumed to give rise to responses and attributes that can be observed and measured

iconic store. A sensory register for the fleeting storage of discrete visual images in the form of icons (visual images that represent something, usually resembling whatever is being represented)

id. The most primitive of three psychodynamic concepts (cf. *ego, superego*): the unconscious, instinctual source of impulsive urges, such as sexual and aggressive impulses, as well as the source of the wishes and fantasies that derive from these impulses, without consideration for rationality or for external reality

ideal self. A person's view of the personal characteristics that the person would like to embody (cf. *self-concept*)

idealistic principle. Operating principle of the *superego*, which guides a person's actions in terms of what she or he should do, as dictated by internalized authority figures, without regard for rationality or even for external reality (cf. *pleasure principle, reality principle*)

identity achievement. One of four main types of identity (cf. *foreclosure, identity diffusion, moratorium*; cf. also *alienated achievement*), in which the individual establishes a firm and secure sense of self, following a period of questioning her or his personal values and beliefs

identity diffusion. One of four main types of identity (cf. *foreclosure, identity achievement, moratorium*; cf. also *alienated achievement*), in which the individual cannot establish a firm and secure sense of self and therefore lacks direction and commitment

idiographic personality theory. One of two basic kinds of trait theories of personality (cf. *nomothetic personality theory*); characterizing a belief that people differ in the set of personality traits they have or at least in the importance of these traits to who they are

ill-structured problem. A type of problem for which a clear path to solution is not known (cf. *well-structured problem*)

illusion. Distorted perception of objects and other external stimuli, which may be due to misleading cues in the objects themselves or due to distortions of the perceptual process, such as distortions due to altered states of consciousness or psychological disorder (see *optical illusion*; cf. *delusion*)

illusory correlation. An inferred perception of a relation between unrelated variables, usually arising because the instances in which the variables coincide seem more noticeable than the instances

in which the variables do not coincide; as applied to *prejudice*, people are more likely to notice instances of unusual behavior in relation to a minority population than to notice common behaviors in members of a minority population or unusual behaviors in members of a majority population (see *heuristic*)

imaginary audience. A form of adolescent egocentrism, in which the adolescent believes that other people are constantly watching and judging his or her behavior

implicit memory. A form of memory retrieval in which an individual uses recalled or recognized information without consciously being aware of doing so (cf. *explicit memory*)

implosion therapy. A set of *extinction procedures* designed to weaken anxiety by having clients imagine as vividly as possible the unpleasant events that are causing them anxiety; clients repeat the procedure as often as necessary to extinguish their anxiety (cf. *flooding*)

impression formation. The process by which individuals form intuitive conceptions about other people, based on inferences from information obtained both directly and indirectly (see *confirmation bias, person-positivity bias, primacy effect, self-fulfilling prophecy*)

imprinting. A form of preprogrammed learning in which a newborn individual engages in a particular behavior simply as a result of being exposed to a particular kind of stimulus, although the specific stimulus that prompts the preprogrammed behavior is learned

incubation. A process by which a problem solver discontinues intensive work on solving a problem, stops focusing conscious attention on solving the problem for a while, and permits problem solving to occur at a subconscious level for a period of time; believed to be particularly helpful in solving some insight problems

incus. One of the three bones of the middle ear (cf. *malleus, stapes*), which normally receive and amplify the vibrations transmitted by the *tympanum* (*eardrum*) and then transmit those vibrations to the *cochlea*

independent variable. An attribute that is individually manipulated by the experimenter, while other aspects of the investigation are held constant (i.e., not subject to variation; cf. *dependent variable*)

indirect request. A form of *speech act* in which the individual makes requests (see *speech acts: directives*) in an oblique, rather than a direct, manner

induced movement. The perceptual phenomenon in which individuals who are moving and are observing other objects within a stable perceptual frame (such as the side window of a car or train) perceive that the fixed objects are moving rather than that they (the observers) are moving

inductive reasoning. The process of drawing general explanatory conclusions based on evidence involving specific facts or observations; permits the reasoner to draw well-founded or probable conclusions but not logically certain conclusions (see *reasoning*; cf. *deductive reasoning*)

infantile amnesia. See *amnesia*

inferential statistics. One of two key ways in which statistics are used (cf. *descriptive statistic*), in which a researcher analyzes numerical data in order to determine the likelihood that the given findings are a result of systematic, rather than random, fluctuations or events

inferiority complex. A means by which people organize their thoughts, emotions, and behavior based on their perceived mistakes and feelings of inferiority

information processing. Operations by which people mentally manipulate what they learn and know about the world

information-processing theorists. Theorists who seek to understand the ways in which various people perform mental operations on information (i.e., decode, encode, transfer, combine, store, and retrieve information), particularly when solving challenging mental problems

informed consent. An ethical procedure of experimentation: Experimental participants are briefed prior to the implementation of the experiment and are fully informed of the nature of the treatment procedure and any possible harmful side effects or consequences of the treatment, as well as the likelihood that these consequences may take place

insight. A distinctive and apparently sudden understanding of a problem or a sudden realization of a strategy that aids in solving a problem, which is usually preceded by a great deal of prior thought and hard work; often involves reconceptualizing a problem or a strategy for its solution in a totally new way; frequently emerges by detecting and combining relevant old and new information to gain a novel view of the problem or of its solution; often associated with finding solutions to *ill-structured problems* (see *insight problem*)

insight problem. A problem that requires *insight* (novel reconceptualization of the problem) in order to reach a solution

insomnia. Any of various disturbances of sleep, which include difficulty falling asleep, waking up during the night and being unable to go back to sleep, or waking up too early in the morning, and which may vary in intensity and duration

instinct. An inherited, species-specific, stereotyped pattern of preprogrammed behavior that involves a relatively complex pattern of response (cf. *reflex*); generally characterized by less flexibility in adaptability to changes in an environment but greater assurance that a complex pattern of behavior will occur as it is preprogrammed to occur without variation

instrumental aggression. A form of *antisocial behavior* that the aggressor realizes may result in harm or injury to the recipient(s) of the *aggression* but that the aggressor pursues anyway in order to gain something of value to the aggressor; generally not as impulsive or as emotional as *hostile aggression* and often implemented without particularly malicious intentions toward the recipients of the aggression; that is, the recipients of the aggression were not seen as targets, but rather were viewed as obstacles in the way of obtaining something valuable to the aggressor

intelligence. Goal-directed adaptive behavior

intensity. The amount of physical energy that is transduced by a sensory *receptor* and then sensed in the *brain* (cf. *quality*)

interactionist approach. A theoretical approach that emphasizes the interaction between characteristics of the person and characteristics of the situation

interactive images. See *mnemonic devices*

interference. Information that competes with the information that the individual is trying to store in memory, thereby causing the individual to forget that information (cf. *decay*; see also *interference theory*)

interference theory. The assertion that information is forgotten because it is displaced by interfering information, which disrupts and displaces the information that the individual had tried to store in memory originally, rather than because the information gradually disappears over time (cf. *decay theory*)

internal-consistency reliability. See *reliability*

internal locus of control. Characterized by an individual's tendency to believe that the causes of behavioral consequences originate within the individual; sometimes involving an extreme view in which the individual misattributes causality to internal rather than to external causes (cf. *external locus of control*)

internalization. A process of cognitive development in which an individual absorbs knowledge from an external environmental context

interneuron. The most numerous type of neuron of the three main types of *neurons* in humans (cf. *motor neuron, sensory neuron*); intermediate between (*inter-*, "between") sensory and motor neurons, receiving signals from either sensory neurons or other interneurons, and then sending signals either to other interneurons or to motor neurons

interposition. See *monocular depth cues*

interrater reliability. See *reliability*

interval schedule. See *fixed-interval reinforcement; variable-interval reinforcement; see also partial reinforcement*

intimacy. One of three basic components of love, according to the *triangular theory of love* (cf. *commitment, passion*); feelings that promote closeness and connection

intoxicated. Characterized by stupefaction due to the effects of toxins such as alcohol or *sedative–hypnotic drugs*

intrinsic motivators. One of the primary two sources of motivation (cf. *extrinsic motivators*); motivating forces that come from within a motivated individual, which are at work when the person engages in behavior because the person enjoys doing so

introspection. Self-examination of inner ideas and experiences, used by early psychologists as a method of studying psychological phenomena (*intro-*, "inward, within"; *-spect*, "look")

invincibility fallacy. A form of adolescent egocentrism, in which the adolescent believes that he or she is invulnerable to harm or ill fortune

ipsilateral. Characterized as occurring or appearing on the same side (*ipsi-*, self; *lateral*, side); often used in describing physiological structures (cf. *contralateral*)

iris. A circular membrane that reflects light beams outward and away from the eye; surrounds the *pupil*, which is essentially a hole in the center of the iris

judgment and decision making. One of the fundamental kinds of thinking (cf. *creativity, problem solving, reasoning*), in which the goal is to evaluate various opportunities or to choose from among various options (see *game theory, satisficing, subjective-utility theory, utility maximization theory; see also heuristic*)

just noticeable difference (jnd). The minimum amount of difference between two sensory stimuli that a given individual can detect at a particular time and place, subject to variations that may cause measurement error, for which psychophysical psychologists often compensate by averaging data from multiple trials; operationally defined as the difference between two stimuli that can be detected 50% of the time (sometimes termed the *difference threshold*; cf. *absolute threshold*)

justification of effort. A means by which an individual rationalizes the expenditure of energy

keyword system. See *mnemonic devices*

kinesthesis. The sense that helps in ascertaining skeletal movements and positioning, via receptors in the muscles, tendons, joints, and skin; changes in position are detected by kinesthetic *receptors*, which *transduce* the mechanical energy caused by pressure into electrochemical neural energy, which codes information about the speed of the change, the angle of the bones, and the tension of the muscles, and then sends this information through the *spinal cord* to the *contralateral* region of the somatosensory cortex and to the *cerebellum*

language. An organized means of combining words in order to communicate (see *arbitrary symbolic reference*)

language-acquisition device (LAD). The hypothetical construct of an innate human predisposition to acquire language; not yet found as a specific physiological structure or function

latency. An interim period that occurs during *psychosexual development*, between the *phallic stage* and the *genital stage*, in which children repress their sexual feelings toward their parents and sublimate their sexual energy into productive fields of endeavor

latent content. The repressed impulses and other unconscious material expressed in dreams or in other primary-process thoughts, which give rise to the *manifest content* of such processes, as these processes are understood by psychodynamic psychologists

latent learning. Conditioning or acquired knowledge that is not presently reflected in performance; the learned information or response may be elicited when the individual believes that it may be rewarding to demonstrate the learning

law of effect. A behavioristic principle used for explaining *operant conditioning*, which states that over time, actions ("the effect") for which an organism is rewarded ("the satisfaction") are strengthened and are therefore more likely to occur again in the future, whereas actions that are followed by punishment tend to be weakened and are thus less likely to occur in the future

learned helplessness. A negative consequence of conditioning, particularly of *punishment*, in which an individual is conditioned to make no response, including no attempt to escape aversive conditions (e.g., after repeated trials in which the individual is unable to escape an aversive condition, the individual has so effectively learned not to attempt escape that the individual continues not to attempt escape even when a means of escape becomes available)

learning. Any relatively permanent change in the behavior, thoughts, or feelings of an organism as a consequence of prior experience (cf. *maturation*)

lens. The curved interior surface of the eye, which bends (refracts) light into the eye and complements the cornea's gross adjustments in curvature, by making fine adjustments in the amount of curvature in order to focus the image as clearly as possible (cf. *cornea*)

lesbianism. See *homosexuality*

lexicon. The entire set of morphemes in a given language or in a given person's linguistic repertoire (cf. *vocabulary*)

life-span development. The changes in characteristics that occur over the course of a lifetime

light adaptation. Unconscious physiological response to an increase in light intensity in the environment, characterized by a decrease in pupillary area (cf. *dark adaptation*)

lightness constancy. A form of *perceptual constancy* in which an individual continues to perceive a constant degree of illumination of an object, even when the actual amount of light that reaches the *retina* differs for different parts of the object

likability effect. Tendency for a recipient of a message to be persuaded more easily by messages from people whom the message recipient likes than by messages from people whom the recipient does not like

Likert scale. A type of *self-report measure* (also termed *summated rating scale*) in which a participant first is asked to review statements about his or her feelings, thoughts, attitudes, or behaviors, worded from the person's point of view (e.g., "I love psychology," "I plan to buy 10 more copies of my psychology textbook"); the participant is then asked to rate each of the statements on a numerical scale, from 0 (which means that the statement is not at all accurate) to the highest value on the scale (which means that the statement is very accurate); the person's responses are then averaged (or summed) to determine an overall rating of the participant's responses

limbic system. Comprises the *hippocampus*, the *amygdala*, and the *septum* and forms part of the *forebrain*, as does the *cerebral cortex*; important to emotion, motivation, and learning, as well as the suppression of instinctive responses, thereby enabling humans to adapt behaviors more flexibly in response to a changing environment

line graph. One of many types of graphic displays of numerical information (cf. *bar graph*), in which quantities (e.g., amounts or scores) are associated with linear information (e.g., time or age) and this association is represented by changing heights of a horizontal line

linear perspective. See *monocular depth cues*; see also *vanishing point*

linear regression. Prediction of one quantified variable from one or more

others, in which the two sets of variables are assumed to have a relation that takes the form of a straight line

linear relation. An association between two quantities that takes the form of a straight line

linguistic relativity. One of two interrelated propositions regarding the relationship between thought and language asserts that the speakers of different languages have differing cognitive systems, based on the languages they use, and that these different cognitive systems influence the ways in which people speaking the various languages think about the world

linguistic universals. Characteristic patterns of language that apply across all of the languages of various cultures

linguistics. The study of language structure and change

lipostatic hypothesis. One of two major alternative assumptions regarding how the body signals hunger versus satiety (cf. *glucostatic hypothesis*); suggests that the levels of lipids (fats) in the blood signal the body regarding the need for food; lipostatic: maintaining the stability (*-static*) of lipid (*lipo-*) levels in the body

location in the picture plane. See *monocular depth cues*

logical positivism. A philosophical belief that the only basis for knowledge is sensory perceptions, and all else is idle conjecture

long-term store. According to a three-stores theory of memory, the hypothetical construct of a long-term store has a greater capacity than both the *sensory store* and the *short-term store*, and it can store information for very long periods of time, perhaps even indefinitely

longitudinal study. Research that follows a particular group of individuals (usually selected as a sample representing a population as a whole) over the course of their life span, or at least across many years (cf. *cross-sectional study*)

magnetic resonance imaging (MRI). A sophisticated technique for revealing high-resolution images of the structure of the living brain by computing and analyzing magnetic changes in the energy of the orbits of nuclear particles in the molecules of the body (also sometimes termed *NMR*, for *nuclear magnetic resonance*); produces clearer and more detailed images than *computerized axial tomography (CAT)* scans and uses no X radiation

major depression. A mood disorder characterized by feeling down, discouraged, and hopeless. Typical cognitive symptoms of depression are low self-esteem, loss of motivation, and pessimism. A depressed person may also experience a very low energy level, slow body movements and speech, and difficulty sleeping and waking up

malleus. One of the three bones of the middle ear, which normally receive and amplify the vibrations transmitted by the *eardrum* and then transmit those vibrations to the *cochlea* (cf. *incus, stapes*)

mania. A mood of unrestrained euphoria involving high excitement, expansiveness, and often hyperactivity; often accompanied by an overinflated sense of self-esteem, grandiose illusions in regard to what the manic person can accomplish, difficulty in focusing attention on one activity, and a tendency to flit from one activity to another in rapid succession (see *bipolar disorder*)

manifest content. The stream of events that pass through the mind of an individual during dreams or other primary-process thoughts, as these processes are understood by psychodynamic psychologists (cf. *latent content*)

massed learning. Learning a body of knowledge or task all at one time rather than spacing learning over time; generally does not lead to as much learning as does *distributed learning*

maturation. One of the two key processes by which cognitive development occurs (cf. *learning*); any relatively permanent change in thought or behavior that occurs as a result of the internally (biologically) prompted processes of aging, without regard to personal experiences and subject to little environmental influence

mean. The average score within a distribution of values, computed by adding all the scores and then dividing by the number of scores (cf. *median, mode*)

median. The middle score (half of the scores fall above and half the scores fall below) or other measurement value within a distribution of values (cf. *mean, mode*)

meditation. A set of techniques used for altering consciousness through focused contemplation (see *concentrative meditation, opening-up meditation*)

medulla oblongata. An elongated interior structure of the *brain*, located at the point where the *spinal cord* enters the skull and joins with the brain; forms part of the *reticular activating system*, and thereby helps to sustain life by controlling the heartbeat and helping to control breathing, swallowing, and digestion; the location in the brain where nerves from the right side of the body cross over to the left side of the brain, and nerves from the left side of the body cross over to the right side of the brain (see *contralateral*)

memory. The means by which individuals draw on past knowledge in order to use such knowledge in the present; the dynamic mechanisms associated with the

retention and retrieval of information; the three operations through which information is processed by and for the memory are *encoding* (translating sensory information into a form that can be represented and stored in memory), *storage* (moving encoded information into a memory store and maintaining the information in storage), and *retrieval* (recovery of stored information from a memory store and moving the information into *consciousness* for use in active cognitive processing)

memory scanning. A phenomenon of memory in which an individual checks what is contained in memory, usually in short-term memory

menarche. The onset of menstruation

menopause. Signals the end of a woman's menstrual cycle

mental age. A means of indicating a person's level of intelligence (generally in reference to a child), based on the individual's performance on tests of intelligence, by indicating the chronological age of persons who typically perform at the same level of intelligence as the test-taker (cf. *deviation IQs, intelligence, ratio IQ*)

mental retardation. Low level of intelligence, usually reflected by both poor performance on tests of intelligence and poor adaptive competence (the degree to which a person functions effectively within a normal situational context)

mental set. A frame of mind in which a problem-solver is predisposed to think of a problem or a situation in a particular way (sometimes termed *entrenchment*), often leading the problem-solver to fixate on a strategy that normally works in solving some (or perhaps even most) problems, but that does not work in solving this particular problem (see also *negative transfer*; cf. *positive transfer*)

mere exposure effect. The positive effect on attitudes that results from repeated exposure to a message supporting the attitude or even just exposure to the stimulus about which the attitude is being formed or modified

metamemory. An aspect of metacognition, involving knowledge and understanding of memory abilities and ways in which to enhance memory abilities (e.g., through the use of *mnemonic devices*)

method of loci. See *mnemonic devices*

method of successive approximations. The sequence of *operant* behaviors reinforced during the shaping of a desired behavior

midbrain. Located between the *forebrain* and the *hindbrain*; comprises several cerebral structures, among which is the *reticular activating system (RAS)*, which also extends into the hindbrain

mind–body dualism. A philosophical belief that the body is separate from the mind and that the body is composed of physical substance, whereas the mind is ephemeral and is not composed of physical substance (cf. *monism*)

minimax loss rule. See *game theory*

miss. One of the four possible combinations of stimulus and response described in *signal-detection theory (SDT)* (cf. *correct rejection, false alarm, hit*): the state in which the individual did not detect a signal stimulus even though the stimulus was actually present

mnemonic devices. Specific techniques for aiding in the memorization of various isolated items, thereby adding meaning or imagery to an otherwise arbitrary listing of isolated items that may be difficult to remember; for example, *acronym*—a set of letters that forms a word or phrase, in which each letter stands for a certain other word or concept (e.g., U.S.A., IQ, and laser), and which thereby may aid in recalling the words or concepts that the letters represent; *acrostics*—the initial letters of a series of items are used in forming a sentence, such that the sentence prompts recall of the initial letters, and the letters prompt recall of each of the items; *categorical clustering*—various items are grouped into categories in order to facilitate recall of the items; *interactive images*—a means of linking a set of isolated words by creating visual representations for the words and then picturing interactions among the items (e.g., causing one item to act on or with another); *keywords*—a mnemonic strategy for learning isolated words in a foreign language by forming an interactive image that links the sound and meaning of a foreign word with the sound and meaning of a familiar word; *method of loci*—visualization of a familiar area with distinctive landmarks that can be linked (via interactive images) to specific items to be remembered; *pegword system*—memorization of a familiar list of items (e.g., in a nursery rhyme) that can then be linked (via interactive images) with unfamiliar items on a new list

mnemonist. A person who uses memory-enhancing techniques for greatly improving his or her memory or who has a distinctive sensory or cognitive ability to remember information, particularly information that is highly concrete or that can be visualized readily

mode. The most frequent score or other measurement value within a distribution of values (cf. *mean, median*)

modeling. A situation in which an individual observes another person and acts in kind; also a form of behavior therapy in which clients are asked to observe persons coping effectively in situations that the clients find anxiety provoking or that the clients respond to in other maladaptive ways

monism. A philosophical belief that the body and mind are unified, based on the belief that reality is a unified whole, existing in a single plane, rather than separated in terms of physical substance versus nonphysical mind (*mon[o]-*, one; -*ism*, set of beliefs, school of thought, or dogma [Greek]; cf. *mind–body dualism*)

monitoring. One of the two main purposes of consciousness (cf. *controlling*): The individual keeps track of internal mental processes, of personal behavior, and of the environment, in order to maintain self-awareness in relation to the surrounding environment

monocular depth cues. One of the two chief means of judging the distances of visible objects (cf. *binocular depth cues*), based on sensed information that can be represented in just two dimensions and observed with just one (*mono-*) eye (*ocular*): *aerial perspective*—the observation that nearer objects appear to be more highly resolved and more clearly distinct than farther objects, which appear to be hazier (occurs because farther objects are observed through greater numbers of moisture and dust particles, whereas closer objects are observed through fewer such particles); *interposition*—the observation that an object that appears to block or partially obstruct the view of another object is perceived as being nearer, whereas the blocked object is perceived to be farther away, such that the blocking object is perceived to be closer to the observer and in front of the blocked object; *linear perspective*—the observation that parallel lines seem to converge as they move farther into the distance; *location in the picture plane*—the observation that objects that are higher in the picture plane but are below the horizon, or at least extend below it, are perceived as being farther from the viewer, whereas objects that are entirely above the horizon and higher in the picture plane are perceived as being closer to the viewer than are objects that are lower in the picture plane (i.e., as objects converge toward the horizon line, they are perceived as being farther from the viewer); *motion parallax*—the perception of stationary objects from a moving viewpoint, such that if an observer visually fixates on a single point in the scene, the objects that are closer to the observer than is the fixation point will appear to be moving in the direction opposite to the direction in which the observer is moving, whereas objects farther from the observer than is the fixation point will appear to be moving in the same direction as the observer (also, objects closer to the observer appear to be moving more quickly than objects farther from the observer); *relative size*—the observation that things that are farther away appear to be smaller in the retina, and the farther away the object, the smaller is its image on the retina; *texture gradient*—the observation that the relative sizes of objects decrease and the densities of distribution of objects increase as objects appear farther from the observer

monolingual. Person who can speak only one language (cf. *bilingual*; see also *additive bilingualism, subtractive bilingualism*)

mood disorders. Extreme disturbances in a person's emotional state, which may involve either unipolar disorder (also termed *depression*) or bipolar disorder (also termed *manic-depressive disorder*)

moratorium. One of four main types of identity (cf. *foreclosure, identity achievement, identity diffusion*; cf. also *alienated achievement*), in which the individual is currently questioning her or his values and beliefs, prior to establishing a firm and secure sense of self

morpheme. the smallest unit of sound that denotes meaning within a particular language

motion parallax. See *monocular depth cues*

motive. A stimulus that prompts a person to act in a particular way

motor. Characterized by the movement of muscles (related to *psychomotor*—motor skills associated with psychological processes)

motor neuron. One of the three main types of *neurons* (cf. *interneuron, sensory neuron*); carries information away from the *spinal cord* and the *brain* and toward the body parts that are supposed to respond to the information in some way (see *efferents*)

motor theory. One of the *active theories (of speech perception)*; asserts that speech perception depends on both what a speaker is heard to articulate and what the listener infers to be the intended articulations of the speaker

Müller–Lyer illusion. An *optical illusion* in which two equally long line segments are perceived to differ in length because one of the line segments is braced by inward-facing, arrowhead-shaped diagonal lines, but the other line segment is braced by outward-facing, arrowhead-shaped diagonal lines; an optical illusion, which causes the observer to perceive that two equally long line segments differ in length; may be an artifact of some of the monocular depth cues with which perceivers are familiar (cf. *Ponzo illusion*)

multimodal. Characteristic of a nonnormal distribution of values, in which the distribution comprises more than one *mode* (cf. *normal distribution*)

mutation. A sudden structural change in a hereditary characteristic, which serves as a mechanism for changes in inheritance from one generation to the next and thereby permits evolutionary changes to occur (see also *behavioral genetics, genes, genetics*)

myelin sheath. A protective, insulating layer of myelin, which coats the *axons* of some *neurons*, thereby speeding up neuronal conduction and insulating and protecting the axons from electrochemical interference by nearby neurons (see *nodes of Ranvier*)

N-REM sleep. The four stages of sleep that are not characterized by rapid eye movements (hence, the acronym for **n**on**r**apid **e**ye **m**ovement) and that are less frequently associated with dreaming (cf. *REM sleep*)

narcolepsy. A disturbance of the pattern of wakefulness and sleep, in which the narcoleptic person experiences an uncontrollable urge to fall asleep periodically during the day and as a result loses consciousness for brief periods of time (usually about 10 to 15 minutes), thereby putting the narcoleptic in grave danger if the attacks occur when the person is driving or otherwise is engaged in activities for which sudden sleep might be hazardous

narcotic. Any drug in a class of drugs derived from opium (*opiates* such as heroin, morphine, or codeine) or synthetically produced to create the numbing, stuporous effects of opium (*opioids* such as meperidine or methadone) and that lead to addiction; lead to a reduction in pain and an overall sense of well-being (from the Greek term for "numbness"; see also *central nervous system (CNS) depressant*)

natural selection. Evolutionary principle describing a mechanism by which organisms have developed and changed, based on what is commonly called the "survival of the fittest," in that those organisms that are best suited for adapting to a given environment are the ones most likely to reach sexual maturity and to produce offspring; that is, the organisms that are best suited for adapting to a given environment are then selected by nature for survival and ultimately the birth of descendants

naturalistic observation. A method of scientific study in which the researcher goes out into the field (settings in the community) to record the behavior of people engaged in the normal activities of their daily lives (also termed *field study*; cf. *case study, experiment, survey, test*); also occasionally used as a clinical assessment technique (cf. *clinical interview*)

near-death experience. An experience in which an individual either comes extremely close to dying or is actually believed to be dead and is then revived before permanent brain death occurs; the unusual psychological phenomena associated with such experiences are believed to be linked to the oxygen deprivation that occurs during such experiences

negative acceleration. Gradual reduction in the amount of increase that occurs in successive conditioning trials; that is, as the strength of the conditioned association increases, subsequent conditioning trials provide smaller increases in the strength of the association

negative (inverse) correlation. A relationship between two attributes, in which an increase in either one of the attributes is associated with a decrease in the other attribute; a perfect negative correlation is indicated by -1 (also termed *inverse correlation*; see *correlation*; cf. *positive correlation*)

negative-feedback loop. A physiological mechanism whereby the body monitors a particular resource (e.g., hormones, glucose, or lipids in the blood), signaling to find a way to increase the levels of the resource when levels are low, and then signaling to find a way to decrease the levels of the resource when levels are high (e.g., by discontinuing the release of hormones or refraining from eating or drinking; see also *homeostatic regulation*)

negative punishment. The removal of a pleasant stimulus, intended to decrease the probability of a response (also called *penalty*)

negative reinforcement. The process of removing an unpleasant stimulus that results in an increased probability of response (see *negative reinforcer*)

negative reinforcer. An unpleasant stimulus (e.g., physical or psychological pain or discomfort) whose removal is welcome following an operant response; its removal strengthens the operant response (see *negative reinforcement*)

negative transfer. A situation in which prior learning may lead to greater difficulty in learning and remembering new material (see *mental set*; cf. *positive transfer*)

neodissociative theory. A view of hypnosis in which it is asserted that some individuals are capable of separating one part of their conscious minds from another part; in one part, the individual responds to the hypnotist's commands, while in the other part, the individual observes and monitors the events and actions taking place, including some of the actions that the hypnotized individual appears not to be processing in the part of the conscious mind that is engaging in the actions

neo-Freudians. The psychodynamically oriented theorists who followed Freud and who differed from Freud in some ways, but who still clung to many

Freudian principles regarding human personality development

neonate. Newborn (*neo-*, "new"; *-nate*, "born")

nerve. Bundle of neurons; many neurons can be observed as fibers extending from the *brain* down through the center of the back (in the *central nervous system*) and then out to various parts of the body (in the *peripheral nervous system*)

nervous system. Physiological network of *nerves* that form the basis of the ability to perceive, adapt to, and interact with the world; the means by which humans and other vertebrates receive, process, and then respond to messages from the environment and from inside our bodies (see *central nervous system, peripheral nervous system*; cf. *endocrine system*; see also *autonomic nervous system, parasympathetic nervous system, somatic nervous system, sympathetic nervous system*)

neuromodulator. Chemical substance released by the *terminal buttons* of some *neurons*, which serves to enhance or to diminish the responsivity of postsynaptic neurons, either by directly affecting the axons or by affecting the sensitivity of the receptor sites (cf. *neurotransmitter*)

neuron. Nerve cell, involved in neural communication within the *nervous system* (see also *interneuron, motor neuron, sensory neuron*; cf. *glial cell*)

neuroticism. See *Big Five*

neurotransmitter. Chemical messenger that is released by the *terminal buttons* on the axon of a presynaptic *neuron* and then carries the chemical messages across the *synapse* to receptor sites on the receiving *dendrites* or *soma* of the postsynaptic neuron (cf. *neuromodulator*; see also *acetylcholine, dopamine, serotonin*)

nodes of Ranvier. Small gaps in the myelin coating along the axons of myelinated neurons (see *glial cell, myelin sheath*)

noise. Confusing, nonsensical, and often unpleasant sound that results when the note of a fundamental frequency is accompanied by irregular and unrelated sound waves, rather than by multiples of the *fundamental frequency* (cf. *harmonics*)

nomothetic personality theory. One of two basic kinds of trait theories of personality (cf. *idiographic personality theory*): based on the belief that all people have essentially the same set of traits and that they differ only in terms of the extent to which they manifest each trait

normal distribution. A distribution of scores or other measurement values, in which most values congregate around the median, and the measurement values rapidly decline in number on either side of the median, tailing off more slowly as scores get more extreme; in such a distribution, the *median* is approximately the same as both the *mean* and the *mode*

normal science. Scientific work that gradually and progressively builds on an established *paradigm* (cf. *revolutionary science*)

normative scores. The set of normative equivalents for a range of raw *test* scores that represent the *normal distribution* of scores obtained by giving a test to a huge number of individuals; once a set of normative scores (also termed *norm*; for standardized tests, also termed *standard scores*) are established for a given test, the normative scores for subsequent test-takers represent a translation of *raw scores* into scaled equivalents that reflect the relative levels of performance of the various test-takers within the normal distribution of scores

null hypothesis. A proposed expectation of no difference or relation between levels of performance; may be assessed in terms of likelihood but not in terms of absolute certainty

obedience. Modification of behavior in response to the command of an actual or perceived authority; may involve taking an action, refraining from an action, or tailoring an action to suit another person or persons (cf. *compliance, conformity*)

object permanence. A cognitive realization that objects continue to exist even when the objects are not immediately perceptible

object-relations theory. A contemporary extension of Freudian theory, primarily concerned with how people relate to one another and with how people conceptualize these relationships largely in terms of their investment of libidinal energy in other persons or objects

objective personality test. A means of assessing personality by using a standardized and uniform procedure for scoring the assessment instrument; not necessarily characterized by objective means of determining what to test, how to interpret test scores, or the theory on which to base the test (cf. *projective test*)

obsession. An unwanted, persistent thought, image, or impulse that cannot be suppressed; obsessions may focus on persistent doubts regarding task completion, persistent thoughts about something, such as a person or a relationship, persistent impulses to engage in undesired behavior, persistent fears, or persistent images

obsessive–compulsive anxiety disorder. Characterized by unwanted, persistent thoughts and irresistible impulses to perform a ritual to relieve those thoughts

occipital lobe. Located at the back of the *brain*, chiefly responsible for visual processing. One of the four major regions of the *cerebral cortex* (cf. *frontal lobe, parietal lobe, temporal lobe*)

Oedipal conflict. A central issue of the *phallic stage* of *psychosexual development*, in which boys feel sexual desires toward their mothers but fear the powerful wrath of their fathers; named for the Greek myth in which Oedipus, who had long been separated from his parents and therefore did not recognize them, killed his father and married his mother; sometimes also used as a generic term to encompass both the Oedipal conflict and the analogous *Electra conflict* in girls

olfaction. Sense of smell, which is chemically activated by airborne molecules that can dissolve in either water or fat

olfactory bulb. The location, just below the *frontal lobes*, where sensory receptors receive chemical inputs and send them on to the *temporal lobe* or to the *limbic system* (especially the *hypothalamus*)

olfactory epithelium. The "smell skin" in the nasal membranes, where airborne scent molecules contact the olfactory receptor cells that detect the scent molecules and then initiate the transduction of the chemical energy of the odors into the electrochemical energy of neural transmission

opening-up meditation. One of the two main forms of contemplation, in which the meditator integrates *meditation* with the events of everyday life, seeking to expand awareness of everyday events, rather than to separate meditation from mundane existence; often involves an attempt to focus on becoming one with an ordinary activity, and on putting all other interfering thoughts out of consciousness (cf. *concentrative meditation*)

openness. See *Big Five*

operant. Active behavioral response during interactions with the environment, which may be strengthened by positive or negative reinforcement or may be weakened either by a lack of reinforcement or by *punishment* during interactions with the environment

operant conditioning. *Learning* that occurs as a result of stimuli that either strengthen (through reinforcement) or weaken (through *punishment* or through lack of reinforcement) the likelihood of a given behavioral response (an *operant*) (also termed *instrumental conditioning*)

operational definition. A specific description of one or more precise elements and procedures involved in solving a given research problem, which allows researchers to communicate clearly the means by which they conducted an experiment and reached their conclusions

opiate. *Narcotic* that is derived from the opium poppy bulb; may be injected intravenously, smoked, ingested orally, or inhaled (cf. *opioid*)

opioid. *Narcotic* that has a similar chemical structure and set of effects to those of an opiate but that is made synthetically through combinations of chemicals

opponent-process theory (of addiction and motivation). In regard to emotions, the theory posits the existence of a process whereby the body seeks to ensure motivational neutrality, such that when one process or motivational source impels the person to feel positive or negative motivations, an opposing motivational force (an opponent process) acts to bring the person back to the neutral baseline; in the case of positive motivations, the opponent process will involve negative movement back down to the baseline; in the case of negative motivations, the opponent process will involve positive movement back up to the baseline; in regard to addictions to *psychoactive* drugs, opponent processes counteract the effects of consuming the addictive substance, thus leading to or at least exacerbating the effects of *addiction*, *tolerance*, and *withdrawal*

opponent-process theory (of color vision). One of the two major theories of color vision (cf. *trichromatic theory of color vision*); based on the notion of three opposing processes in human vision, two of which contrast each of two colors with another (yielding four fundamental colors—red/green and yellow/blue), and one of which contrasts black and white as a third opposing set of achromatic primaries that are perceived in much the same way as are the other opposing pairs

optic chiasma. The place in the *occipital lobe* of the brain where neural fibers carrying visual information cross over from one side of the body to the *contralateral* hemisphere of the brain (*chiasma*, "X-shaped or crossed configuration")

optical illusion. Visual stimulus that leads to distortion in visual perception (see *Müller–Lyer illusion*, *Ponzo illusion*)

oral stage. A Freudian stage of *psychosexual development*, which typically occurs during the first 2 years, when an infant explores sucking and other oral activity, learning that such activity not only provides nourishment, but also gratification

organic pain. Sensations of extreme discomfort and suffering caused by damage to bodily tissue (cf. *psychogenic pain*; see also *pain*)

orienting reflex. A series of preprogrammed responses that are prompted by a sudden change in the environment (e.g., a flash of light or an abrupt loud noise); included among the specific preprogrammed responses are a generalized reflexive orientation toward the origin of the change, changes in brain-wave patterns (see *electroencephalogram*), dilation of the pupils, and some other physiological changes associated with stress (see also *instinct*, *reflex*)

outgroup homogeneity bias. Tendency to view the members of an outgroup (of which the individual is not a member) as all being alike, often in contrast to a tendency to view members of an ingroup (of which the individual is a member) as distinct individuals who have dissimilar characteristics, thus facilitating the ease of forming *stereotypes* regarding outgroups but not of ingroups

oval window. First part of the inner ear, at one end of which is the *cochlea* and at the other end of which is the spot where the *stapes* either rests or vibrates in response to sounds; when the stapes vibrates, the mechanical vibration is transmitted to the cochlea via the oval window

overconfidence. Excessively high evaluation of skills, knowledge, or judgment, usually applied to a person's valuation of her or his own abilities

overdose. Ingestion of a life-threatening or lethal dose of drugs, often associated with the use of *psychoactive* drugs, such as *narcotics*, *amphetamines*, or *sedative– hypnotic drugs*; although often linked to intentional suicide, overdoses commonly occur due to *tolerance* or *sensitization*, particularly when the users are also using street drugs, which contain many impurities and are not reliably controlled in regard to the concentrations of psychoactive elements in the drug compounds being sold

overextension error. Overapplication (usually by children or other persons acquiring a language) of the meaning of a given word to more things, ideas, and situations than is appropriate for the denotation and the defining features of the word; generally no longer typifies language once the vocabulary of the language user has expanded to comprise enough words to describe the meanings the individual intends to convey (see also *feature hypothesis*, *functional hypothesis*)

overregularization. An error that commonly occurs during language acquisition, in which the novice language user has gained an understanding of how a language usually works and then over applies the general rules of the language to the exceptions in which the rule does not apply

p-value. Statistical quantity indicating the probability (p) that a particular outcome may have occurred as a result of chance

pain. Intense sensory discomfort and emotional suffering associated with actual, imagined, or threatened damage to or irritation of body tissues (see *organic pain*, *psychogenic pain*)

paired-associates recall. A memory task in which the individual is presented with a list of paired (and often related) items, which the individual is asked to store in memory, then the individual is presented with one item in each pair and is asked to provide the mate of each given item (cf. *free recall, serial recall*)

panic disorder. An *anxiety disorder* characterized by brief (usually only a few minutes), abrupt, and unprovoked, but recurrent episodes during which a person experiences intense and uncontrollable anxiety; during the episodes (termed *panic attacks*), the panicked individual feels terrified and exhibits psychophysiological symptoms of heightened *arousal*, such as difficulty in breathing, heart palpitations, dizziness, sweating, and trembling; often associated with *agoraphobia* and sometimes associated with feelings of depersonalization (the feeling of being outside of the body looking in rather than on the inside looking out)

papillae. Small visible protrusions on the tongue, inside which are located thousands of taste-receptor cells (see *taste buds*)

paradigm. Theoretical system that provides an overarching model for organizing related theories for understanding a particular phenomenon such as intelligence, learning, personality, or psychological development; also used to describe a model or framework for conducting a particular type of experiment (e.g., *simulating paradigm*)

parallel processing. Cognitive manipulation of multiple operations simultaneously; as applied to short-term memory, the items stored in short-term memory would be retrieved all at once, not one at a time (cf. *serial processing*)

parapsychology. A branch of psychology concerned with phenomena that are not presently explained by the application of known psychological principles

parasympathetic nervous system. The part of the *autonomic nervous system* that is concerned primarily with anabolism (cf. *sympathetic nervous system*)

parietal lobe. One of the four major regions of the *cerebral cortex* (cf. *frontal lobe, occipital lobe, temporal lobe*): chiefly responsible for processing of somatosensory sensations that come from the skin and muscles of the body (*soma-*)

partial reinforcement. An *operant-conditioning* schedule (also termed *intermittent reinforcement*) in which a given type of *operant* response is rewarded some of the time but not all of the time; comprises two types of reinforcement schedules: *ratio schedules* (see *fixed-ratio reinforcement; variable-ratio reinforcement* and *interval schedules*, see also *fixed-interval reinforcement, variable-interval reinforcement*): such schedules are more resistant to *extinction* than is *continuous reinforcement*

passion. The intense desire for union with another person; one of three basic components of love, according to the *triangular theory of love* (cf. *commitment, intimacy*)

passive theories. A category of theories that explains speech perception exclusively in terms of the listener's passive reception of speech, without involving cognitive processes such as memory and consideration of context; according to these kinds of theories, the listener perceives speech exclusively through sensory processes such as filtering (e.g., screening out irrelevant sounds) and feature detection (e.g., matching features of speech sounds to existing *templates);* (see *feature-matching;* cf. *active theories*)

pathogen. A specific disease-causing agent (*patho-,* "suffering" or "disease"; *-gen,* "producer")

patient-centered style (of physician interactions). One of two basic patterns for physician-patient interactions (cf. *doctor-centered style*); characterized by a relatively nondirective style of interaction, in which the physician asks divergent questions and allows the patient to take part in guiding the course of the interview, the diagnosis of the presenting problem, and the decision regarding the optimal treatment for the problem

payoff matrix. Tabular display of the discrete consequences for each decision maker regarding the outcomes that would result from each of various decisions that might be made (see *game theory*)

Pearson product-moment correlation coefficient. A measure of linear relation, ranging from –1 (perfect inverse relation) to 0 (no relation) to +1 (perfect positive relation)

pegword system. See *mnemonic devices*

percentile. A value used in describing a score, indicating the proportion of persons whose scores fall below a given score, multiplied by 100

perception. The set of psychological processes by which people recognize, organize, synthesize, and give meaning (in the brain) to the sensations received from environmental stimuli by the sense organs; (cf. *sensation*)

perceptual constancy. The perception that a given object remains the same even when the immediate sensation of the object changes (see *lightness constancy, shape constancy, size constancy*)

performative. See *speech acts;* synonym: *declaration*

peripheral nervous system (PNS). One of the two main parts of the *nervous system* (cf. *central nervous system [CNS]*): comprises all of the nerve cells, including the nerves of the face and head, except the neurons of the *brain* and the *spinal cord* (the CNS); primarily relays information between the CNS and the rest of the body (including the face and the internal organs other than the brain); connects the CNS with sensory *receptors* in both external sensory organs (e.g., skin, ears, eyes) and internal body parts (e.g., stomach, muscles) and connects the CNS with motor effectors in parts of the body that produce movement, speech, and so on (*peripheral* means both "auxiliary," for the PNS assists the CNS; and "away from the center," for the peripheral nerves are external to the CNS)

peripheral route to persuasion. One of two routes to persuasion (cf. *central route to persuasion*), which emphasizes tangential, situational features of the persuasive message, such as the appeal of the message sender, the attractiveness of the message's presentation, or rewarding features of the message or its source; most effective when the recipient is not strongly interested in the issue or is unable to consider the issue carefully for various reasons

permissive parents. Mothers and fathers who exhibit a style of parenting in which they tend to give their children a great deal of freedom, possibly more than the children can handle and who tend to be lax in discipline and to let children make their own decisions about many things that other parents might find questionably appropriate (cf. *authoritarian parents, authoritative parents*)

person-centered approach. A humanistic approach to personality theory, which strongly emphasizes the *self* and each person's perception of self

person–environment interaction. The individual fit between a particular person and the environment in which the individual develops and interacts with others

person-positivity bias. A bias of *impression formation*, which involves the tendency for people to evaluate individuals more positively than they evaluate groups, including the groups to which those individuals belong

personal attribution. One of two fundamental types of *attributions* (cf. *situational attribution*): The causes of human behavior are attributed to the internal factors in the person engaging in the given behavior (also termed *dispositional attribution*)

personal dispositions. Personality *traits* that are unique to each individual and therefore may be difficult to assess via interpersonal correlational studies or standardized personality inventories

personal fable. A form of adolescent egocentrism, in which the adolescent believes that he or she is somehow unique and destined for fame and fortune

personal space. An aspect of nonverbal communication, which centers on the distance between people engaged in interactions; the specific interpersonal distance that seems comfortable for people is affected by cultural differences (e.g., Arabs vs. Canadians), status differences (e.g., supervisors vs. employees), role expectations (e.g., parents and children), degree of intimacy in the relationship (e.g., between acquaintances vs. between spouses), and other sociological considerations (e.g., settings such as elevators or crowded trains)

personal unconscious. One of two Jungian parts of the unconscious mind (cf. *collective unconscious*), in which is stored each person's unique personal experiences and repressed memories (see also *complexes*)

personality. The enduring characteristics and dispositions of a person that provide some degree of coherence across the various ways in which the person behaves

personality disorders. Psychological disorders involving a pattern of consistent, long-term, extreme personality characteristics that cause the person great unhappiness or that seriously impair the person's ability to adjust to the demands of everyday living or to function well in her or his environment, such as the following: *antisocial personality disorder*—characterized by at least average intelligence and the tendency to appear superficially charming, sincere, poised, calm, and verbally facile, as a strategy for winning the trust and cooperation of other persons despite actually being insincere, untruthful, self-centered, ungrateful, and unreliable in interpersonal relations (formerly termed *psychopathy* or *sociopathy*); *avoidant personality disorder*—characterized by reluctance to enter into close personal relationships due to an intense fear of rejection, often accompanied by self-devaluation, very low self-esteem, and a wish for unattainable closeness; *borderline personality disorder*—characterized by extreme volatility and instability in mood, self-image, and interpersonal relationships; *dependent personality disorder*—characterized by little self-confidence, extreme sensitivity to criticism, difficulty in taking personal responsibility for self-care; *histrionic personality disorder*—characterized by highly dramatic behavior and continual attempts to attract attention, such as lavish displays of emotionality and affection (despite actual shallowness of feeling), extreme volatility, great vanity, and manipulative interpersonal relationships (formerly called "hysterical personality"); *narcissistic personality disorder*—characterized by an inflated self-image, intense self-centeredness and selfishness in interpersonal relationships, lack of empathy for others, strong feelings of entitlement from others without concern for reciprocating to others; *obsessive–compulsive personality disorder*—characterized by having *obsessions* or

compulsions or both; *paranoid personality disorder*—characterized by suspiciousness of others and a tendency to suspect that others are plotting against the paranoid individual, to view other people's innocuous behavior as directed against the individual (cf. *schizophrenia* [paranoid]); *schizoid personality disorder*—characterized by difficulty in forming relationships with other people, a tendency to prefer solitude over companionship, and apparent indifference to what others think, say, or even feel about the disordered individual; *schizotypal personality disorder*—characterized by major problems in interpersonal interactions and by other attributes that tend to cause these persons to be viewed as eccentric or even bizarre, such as susceptibility to *illusions* and to *magical thinking* (e.g., believing in extrasensory perceptive powers or other supernatural phenomena for which there is little supporting evidence)

perspective. A view of psychological phenomena, which centers on a particular set of theories and beliefs (cf. *field*)

phallic stage. A Freudian stage of *psychosexual development*, which typically begins at about 4 years of age and continues until about 6 years of age; during this stage, children discover that stimulation of the genitals can be pleasurable, and they first experience either the *Oedipal conflict* (in boys) or the *Electra conflict* (in girls)

phenotype. Expression of an inherited trait, based on the dominant trait in the *genotype* and also subject to environmental influence; *dominant traits* will prevail over *recessive traits* in determining whether genotypic traits are expressed in the phenotype

pheromones. Chemical substances secreted by animals, which trigger specific kinds of reactions (largely related to reproduction, territory, or aggression) in other animals, usually of the same species

philosophy. A system of ideas or a set of fundamental beliefs; a means of seeking to explore and understand the general nature of many aspects of the world

phobia. One of five main categories of *anxiety disorders*, characterized by an exaggerated, persistent, irrational, and disruptive fear of a particular object, a particular event, or a particular setting, or a fear of a general kind of object, event, or setting (see also *agoraphobia*, *social phobia*)

phoneme. The particular speech sounds the users of a specific language can identify

phonetic-refinement theory. One of the *active theories (of speech perception)* which posits that words are identified through successive elimination of extraneous words (*refinement*) from the set of possi-

ble words that the heard word might be; elimination is based on the initial sounds of the words (*phonetics*) and the context in which the word occurs

photopigments. Chemical substances that absorb light, thereby starting the complex transduction process that transforms physical electromagnetic energy into an electrochemical neural impulse; the *rods* and the *cones* contain different types of photopigments; different types of photopigments absorb differing amounts of light, and some detect different *hues* (see *photoreceptors*)

photoreceptors. The physiological structures in the *retina* of the eye that *transduce* light energy into electrochemical energy, thus enabling the eye to see; located in the innermost layer of the retina, farthest from the light source; the two kinds of photoreceptors are the *rods* and the *cones* (see also *photopigments*)

phrase-structure grammar. A form of syntactical analysis, which analyzes sentences in terms of the superficial sequence of words in sentences, regardless of differences or similarities of meaning; analysis often centers on the analysis of noun phrases and verb phrases; also termed *surface-structured grammars* because analysis centers on syntax at a surface level of analysis (cf. *deep-structure level, transformational grammar*)

physiology. Scientific study of living organisms and of life-sustaining functions and processes (in contrast to anatomy, which studies the structures of living organisms)

pinna. Visible outer part of the ear, which collects sound waves

pitch. Sensation of how high or low a tone sounds, based on the *frequency* of the sound wave that reaches the auditory receptors

pituitary gland. An endocrine *gland* located above the mouth and underneath the *hypothalamus* (in the *forebrain*), to which it is attached and by which it is controlled; sometimes considered the master gland of the body because of its central importance to the *endocrine system*; provides a direct link from the endocrine system to the *nervous system* via the hypothalamus; secretes *hormones* that directly affect other physiological functions and that indirectly affect other functions through the release of pituitary hormones that control many other endocrine glands, stimulating those glands to release hormones that produce specific physiological effects; in particular, when stimulated by the hypothalamus, the pituitary gland plays an important role in the response to *stress*, secreting adrenocorticotropic hormone (ACTH), which is carried by the bloodstream to other organs, most notably the adrenal glands, which then release epinephrine and nor-epinephrine

place theory. One of the two alternative views of the way in which humans sense pitch (cf. *frequency theory*; see also *duplicity theory*); suggests that the sensation of *pitch* is determined by the location on the *basilar membrane* where the sound wave vibrates the *hair cells*; thus, hair cells located at various places on the basilar membrane vibrate in response to sounds of different frequencies and then stimulate different sensory neurons, which then determine the pitch that is perceived

plasticity. Modifiable, subject to being changed

pleasure principle. Operating principle by which the *id* irrationally pursues immediate gratification of libidinal urges, regardless of the external realities that might impinge on those urges (cf. *idealistic principle*, *reality principle*)

polygraph. (Referred to as a *lie detector*.) A method of assessing the truthfulness of self–report measures, by assessing the psychophysiological reactivity of various physiological processes, such as heart rate, galvanic skin response (GSR), and respiration; such measurements assess arousal, usually associated with emotional stress; thus, for persons who feel stressful arousal in association with lying, such measures indicate instances of lying; however, for persons who feel stressful arousal in association with other situations, such measures also indicate those sources of arousal; and for persons who feel no stressful arousal in association with lying, such measures do not indicate instances of lying

pons. A structure in the *hindbrain*, containing nerve cells that pass signals from one part of the brain to another, thereby serving as a kind of relay station or bridge (*pons*, Latin, "bridge"); also contains a portion of the *reticular activating system* and contains nerves serving parts of the head and face

Ponzo illusion. An *optical illusion*, in which two equally long horizontal line segments, which are framed by diagonally converging line segments, are perceived to differ in length; may be an artifact of some of the *monocular depth cues* with which perceivers are familiar (cf. *Müller–Lyer illusion*)

population. The entire set of individuals to which a generalization is to be made

population parameters. The set of numerical values that characterizes all persons in a population under investigation; under most circumstances, it is impossible or impractical to determine population parameters, so *sample statistics* are used as an indication of the population parameters (see also *representative sample*)

positive correlation. A relationship between two attributes, in which an increase in either one of the attributes is associated with an increase in the other attribute, and a decrease in either one of the attributes is associated with a decrease in the other attribute; a perfect positive correlation is indicated by +1 (see *correlation*; cf. *negative correlation*)

positive punishment. The application of an unpleasant stimulus, intended to decrease the probability of a response

positive reinforcement. The pairing of a given *operant* behavior with a stimulus that is rewarding to the organism engaged in the operant, which thereby strengthens the likelihood that the organism will produce the operant again (see *operant conditioning*, *positive reinforcer*; cf. *negative reinforcement*)

positive reinforcer. A reward (pleasant stimulus) that follows an *operant* and strengthens the associated response (see *operant conditioning*, *positive reinforcement*; cf. *negative reinforcer*; cf. also *punishment*)

positive transfer. A situation in which prior learning may lead to greater ease of learning and remembering new material (cf. *negative transfer*)

positron emission tomography (PET). A technique for creating dynamic images of the *brain* in action (thus revealing physiological processes, not just anatomical structures); involves injecting into a patient a mildly radioactive form of glucose, which is absorbed by cells of the body including the brain; the amount of glucose absorption in the brain indicates the level of metabolic activity of the cells; computer analysis of the glucose absorption thereby indicates the locations of high rates of metabolic activity during various cognitive tasks (e.g., playing computer games, speaking, moving parts of the body); largely used as a research tool, but clinical applications are forthcoming

postconventional (principled) morality. A phase of moral development in which the individual recognizes the importance of (a) social contracts (the importance of societal rules as a basis for behavior) and (b) individual rights (internal moral rights and principles that may outweigh societal rules in some situations, for example rights to life and liberty)

postformal thinking. A stage of cognitive development that may follow the stage of *formal operations*, in which individuals recognize the constant unfolding and evolution of thought (see *dialectical thinking*), and they can manipulate mentally various options for decisions and diverse alternative answers to questions, recognizing that a single ideal option or a simple unambiguous answer may not be available (cf. *problem finding*)

posthypnotic suggestion. An instruction given to an individual during *hypnosis*, which the individual is to implement after having wakened from the hypnotic state; subjects often have no recollection of having been given the instructions or even of having been hypnotized

posttraumatic stress disorder. A stress disorder (a form of *anxiety disorder*; cf. also *acute stress disorder*) characterized by the intrusive psychological reenactment of a past traumatic event, such as recurring nightmares or repeated wakeful resurfacing of painful memories of the event while consciously engaged in unrelated activities; often accompanied by difficulties in sleeping or in concentrating while awake; sometimes accompanied by an uncomfortable feeling of experiencing life in ways that other people do not, as well as by feelings of apathy and detachment

pragmatic reasoning schemas. A set of goal-related organizing principles that form cognitive frameworks for deductive reasoning regarding what to expect in various realistic situations about which an individual lacks complete information regarding what to expect

pragmatics. The study of how people use *language*, emphasizing the social contexts in which language is used, as well as the nonverbal communication that augments verbal communication

pragmatism. A school of psychological thought, which (a) asserts that knowledge is validated by its usefulness, and (b) is concerned not only with asking how and why people behave as they do but also with asking how psychologists and other people can use this knowledge

preconscious. A part of consciousness that comprises information that could become conscious readily, but that is not continuously available in awareness

preconventional morality. A phase of moral development, in which moral reasoning is guided by punishments and rewards; initially, individual moral reasoners focus on the avoidance of *punishment* and on *obedience* to authority, without concern for the interests or feelings of other persons, except as those interests or feelings may affect the likelihood of punishment; later in this phase, moral reasoners recognize the interests of others, but strictly in terms of how to strike deals in order to gain self-interested advantages (rewards)

prediction. One of four goals of psychological research (the other three are *control*, *description*, and *explanation*): a declaration or indication about the future in advance, based on observation, experience, or reasoning

predictive validity. An aspect of criterion-related *validity*, which assesses the extent to which a test or other measurement (the predictor) predicts some kind of performance outcome (the criterion), which is to be measured well after the test or other measurement has been taken

prejudice. A form of thinking, whereby an individual forms an unfavorable attitude directed toward groups of people (usually outgroups, of which they are not members), based on insufficient or incorrect evidence about these groups (see *realistic-conflict theory*; *social-identity theory*)

Premack principle. An axiom of *operant conditioning* asserting that (a) more preferred activities reinforce less preferred ones, and (b) the specific degree of preference is determined by the individual who holds the preference; to apply this principle, a person's *operant* behavior can be reinforced by offering as a reward something the person prefers more than the behavior being reinforced

premise. Statement of fact or assertion of belief, on which a deductively reasoned argument may be based (see *deductive reasoning*)

preoperational stage. Second stage of cognitive development, according to Piaget, which is characterized by the development of internal mental representations (the precursors of which actually arose at the end of the previous [sensorimotor] stage) and verbal communication (cf. *concrete operations, formal-operational stage, sensorimotor stage*)

prescriptive grammar. Rules that specify the correct ways to structure the use of written or spoken language

primacy effect. Tendency to show superior recall of words that occur at and near the beginning of a list of words (cf. *recency effect*): affects *impression formation*, such that first impressions can influence subsequent ones

primary appraisal. The first step in a two-step process of appraising a potentially stressful situation (cf. *secondary appraisal*); involves a person's determination of whether it is important to deal with the situation, based on the significance of the situation for the person and its possible outcomes for the person as a result of dealing with versus not dealing with the situation

primary colors. The three colors (red, green, and blue) that can be combined additively to form all other colors (see also *additive mixture, trichromatic theory of color vision*)

primary motor cortex. The portion of the *frontal lobe* that plans, controls, and executes movements, particularly those movements involving any kind of delayed response; this portion of the *cerebral cortex* can be mapped to show the places in the *brain* that control specific groups of muscles in the body

primary-process thought. A form of thought that is irrational, instinct driven, and out of touch with reality, often thought to be a wellspring of creativity and of dreams, as well as of symbolic expressions of sexual and aggressive urges (cf. *secondary-process thought*)

primary reinforcer. Rewarding stimulus used in *operant conditioning*, which provides immediate satisfaction to the learner (cf. *secondary reinforcer*)

primary somatosensory cortex. The portion of the *parietal lobe* (located directly behind the *primary motor cortex* in the *frontal lobe*) that receives information from the senses about pressure, texture, temperature, and *pain*; this portion of the *cerebral cortex* can be mapped to show the places in the brain that receive sensory information from precise locations on the surface of the body

priming. The activation of a node by a *prime* (activating node) to which the node is connected in a network, in the process of spreading activation, according to the network view of memory processes

proactive interference. A type of memory disruption, which occurs when interfering information is presented before, rather than after, presentation of the information that is to be remembered (also termed *proactive inhibition*; cf. *retroactive interference*)

problem finding. A stage of cognitive development that may follow the stage of *formal operations*, in which individuals become proficient in figuring out exactly what problems face them and in deciding which problems they should try most assiduously and vigorously to solve (cf. *dialectical thinking, postformal thinking*)

problem-focused coping. See *coping*

problem solving. One of the fundamental kinds of thinking, which involves the resolution of a difficulty, the overcoming of obstacles, the answering of a question, or the achievement of a goal (see *problem-solving cycle*; cf. *creativity, judgment and decision making, reasoning*)

problem-solving cycle. A sequence of steps for resolving a problematic situation: (1) identify the problem; (2) define the problem; (3) formulate a strategy; (4) represent and organize the information; (5) allocate resources; (6) monitor the problem-solving process; and (7) evaluate the solution; requires flexibility in following the various steps of the cycle to achieve effective solution (see *problem solving*)

procedural knowledge. A recognition and awareness of how to perform particular tasks, skills, or procedures ("knowing how," not "knowing that"; cf. *declarative knowledge*)

productive thinking. A form of *critical thinking*, which involves insight that goes

beyond the bounds of the existing associations identified by the thinker (cf. *reproductive thinking*)

projection areas. The areas in the cortical lobes where sensory and motor processing occurs; sensory projection areas are the locations in the *cerebral cortex* to which *sensory neurons* are projected via the *thalamus* from elsewhere in the body; motor projection areas are the regions that project *motor neurons* downward through the *spinal cord*, via the *peripheral nervous system*, to control desired movement of the appropriate muscles

projective test. Psychological assessment based on *psychodynamic theory*, in which it is held that the individual's unconscious conflicts may be projected into responses to the assessment (cf. *objective personality test*)

prosocial behavior. Societally approved actions that are seen as furthering the common good, that are at least consistent with the interests of the social group, or that help one or more other persons (cf. *antisocial behavior*)

prototype theory. One of two primary theories of semantics (cf. *componential theory*), which claims that the meaning of a word (or concept) can be understood by describing the concept in terms of a *prototype* (see also *exemplar*), which best represents a given concept and which comprises a set of *characteristic features* that tend to be typical of most examples of the concept (cf. *defining features*)

proxemics. The study of interpersonal proximity and distancing (personal space)

proximal stimulus. The internal sensation of a source of stimulation, as it is registered by the sensory *receptors*, regardless of whether the internal sensation exactly matches the external source of stimulation as it exists in the world (cf. *distal stimulus*; see also *perceptual constancy*)

proximity (as an aspect of interpersonal attraction). The geographical nearness of people toward whom an individual might feel attracted; a factor increasing the likelihood that a person may be attracted to another person, perhaps by also enhancing the probability of familiarity with or arousal by the other person

psychoactive. Characteristic of drugs that produce a *psychopharmacological* effect, thereby affecting behavior, mood, and consciousness; can be classified into four basic categories: *central nervous system (CNS) depressant, central nervous system (CNS) stimulant, hallucinogenic, narcotic*

psychoanalysis. A form of psychological treatment based on *psychodynamic theory*

psychodynamic theory. A theory of human motivations and behavior, which emphasizes the importance of conflicting unconscious mental processes and the importance of early childhood experiences in affecting adult personality

psychogenic pain. Intense sensory discomfort and emotional suffering for which physiological origins (due to injury of body tissues) cannot be found (cf. *organic pain*); three common types are: *causalgia*—characterized by recurrent episodes of severe burning pain in a body part or region (often in a location where tissue has been damaged due to a serious wound); *neuralgia*—characterized by recurrent episodes of intense shooting pain along a nerve; and *phantom-limb pain*—characterized by pain sensations in a limb that no longer has functioning nerves (e.g., due to amputation)

psychology. The study of the mind and of the behavior of people and other organisms

psychometric. Characterized by psychological measurement (*psycho-*, "pertaining to the mind or mental processes," *-metric*, "measurement")

psychopharmacological. An outcome affecting behavior, mood, and consciousness, produced by drugs (see *psychoactive*)

psychophysics. The study and measurement of the functioning of the senses, which involves the attempt to measure the relationship between a form of physical stimulation and the psychological sensations produced as a consequence

psychosexual development. An aspect of personality development that refers to the increasing self-identification with a particular gender and changing self-perception about sexuality

psychosocial theory (of personality development). A theory of *personality* development that deals with how social factors interact with personality throughout the entire life span

psychosomatic medicine. A psychodynamic view of illness, which studied the psychological roots of physical illnesses (e.g., ulcers, asthma, migraine headaches)

psychosurgery. A surgical procedure intended to alleviate mental disorders by probing, slicing, dissecting, or removing some part of the brain

psychotherapy. An intervention that uses the principles of *psychology* in order to treat mental or emotional disorders or otherwise to improve the adjustment and well-being of the person who receives the intervention

psychoticism. A personality attribute characterized by solitariness, detached interpersonal relationships, and a lack of feelings, especially a lack of caring, empathy, and sensitivity (cf. *Big Five*)

psychotropic drugs. Drugs affecting the individual's psychological processes or state of mind; four main classes of psy-

chotropic drugs include *antipsychotics*, *antidepressants*, antianxiety drugs, and lithium (see also *psychoactive*)

puberty. The stage of development at which humans become capable of reproduction

punishment. A process used in *operant conditioning*, which *decreases* the probability of an operant response, through either the application of an unpleasant stimulus or the removal of a pleasant one; an ineffective means of reducing *aggression* if physical punishment (rather than penalty) is used as a means of operant conditioning (cf. *negative reinforcer*, *positive reinforcer*)

pupil. The hole in the *iris* (roughly in its center) through which light gains access to the interior of the eye, particularly the *retina*; in dim light, the pupil reflexively expands, permitting more light to enter, but in bright light, it reflexively contracts limiting the amount of light that can enter the eye

purity (as related to color). The extent to which a *hue* cannot be analyzed in terms of a combination of other hues (see also *additive mixture, subtractive mixture*)

quality. The nature of a stimulus that reaches a sensory *receptor* and is then sensed in the *brain* (cf. *intensity*)

quasi-experimental design. A plan for conducting a study that has many of the features of a controlled experimental design but that does not ensure the random assignment of participants to the treatment and the control groups (cf. *controlled experimental design, correlational design*)

questionnaire. A set of questions used by social-science researchers for conducting a *survey* (cf. *test*; cf. also *case study, experiment, naturalistic observation*)

range. The full expanse of a distribution of values, from the lowest to the highest value

ratio IQ. A means of indicating performance on intelligence tests, based on a quotient of *mental age* divided by chronological age (cf. *deviation IQs*)

ratio schedule. A schedule of reinforcement in *operant conditioning*, in which a proportion (ratio) of *operant* responses are reinforced, regardless of the amount of time that has passed (see *fixed-ratio reinforcement, variable-ratio reinforcement*; cf. *fixed-interval reinforcement, variable-interval reinforcement*; see also *partial reinforcement, positive reinforcement*)

rational-emotive behavior therapy (REBT). A form of cognitive therapy designed to help people with their emotional reactions by helping them to rectify their incorrect or maladaptive thoughts (see *cognitivism*)

rationalist. Person who believes that knowledge is most effectively acquired through rational methods (cf. *empiricist*)

raw score. The actual total sum of points obtained by a given test-taker for a given test, which often equals the actual number of items answered correctly on the test

reaction range. The broad limits within which a particular attribute (e.g., intelligence) may be expressed in various possible ways, given the inherited potential for expression of the attribute in the particular individual

realistic-conflict theory. A theory regarding *prejudice*, which argues that competition among groups for valuable but scarce resources leads to prejudice

reality principle. The operating principle by which the ego responds as rationally as possible to the real world as it is consciously perceived to be, rather than as the person desires the world to be (cf. *pleasure principle*) or as the person believes that the world should be (cf. *idealistic principle*); mediates among the urges of the *id*, the prohibitions of the *superego*, and the realities of the external world

reasoning. One of the fundamental processes of thinking, which involves drawing conclusions from evidence; often classified as either involving *deductive reasoning* or *inductive reasoning* (cf. *creativity, judgment and decision making, problem solving*)

recall memory. A process of memory often employed in memory tasks, in which the individual is asked to produce (not just to recognize as correct) a fact, a word, or other item from memory (see also *free recall, paired-associates recall, serial recall*; cf. *recognition memory*)

recency effect. Tendency to show superior recall of words that occur at and near the end of a list of words (cf. *primacy effect*)

receptive field. The region of the external world from which a receptor cell receives sensory information

receptors. Physiological structures designed to receive something (e.g., a given substance or a particular kind of information), which may refer either to (a) the structures that receive external stimulation and *transduce* it into electrochemical sensory information, or to (b) the structures that receive electrochemical sensory information; sensory receptors are physiological structures that provide a mechanism for receiving external stimulation (from outside the body), which can then be transduced into sensation as electrochemical sensory information within the body; receptor *nerves* and *neurons* receive electrochemical sensory information (e.g., sensations in the eyes, ears, and skin) from sensory receptors or from other *sensory neurons* and then transmit that information back up through the *spinal cord* to the *brain* (cf. *interneuron, motor neuron*)

recessive trait. The weaker genetic trait in a pair of *traits*, which does not appear in the *phenotype* of an organism when the *genotype* comprises a *dominant trait* and a recessive trait

reciprocal determinism. A principle of a *personality* theory that attributes human functioning to an interaction among behavior, personal variables, and the environment

recognition memory. A process of memory often employed in memory tasks, in which the individual is asked just to recognize as correct (not to produce) a fact, a word, or other item from memory (cf. *recall memory*)

recognition task. See *recognition memory*

reconstructive memory. Psychological phenomenon in which an individual stores and then retrieves from memory some information about events or facts, almost exactly as the events or facts took place (cf. *constructive memory*)

reductionism. An extreme form of *monism*, which reduces the role of the mind to the status of a mere cog in a larger physiological machine and which reduces the vast complexity of human behavior to a mere by-product of physiological phenomena

reflex. An automatic physiological response to an external stimulus; the spinal cord transmits a message directly from receptor nerves to effector nerves, without routing the message through the brain prior to the bodily response to the sensory information (cf. *instinct, learning*)

refraction. The degree to which light waves are bent, usually by curvature of the surface of the medium (e.g., a lens) through which the light waves are passing

regions of similarity. Areas that are largely undifferentiated from each other, often mentioned in regard to *direct-perception* theories of vision

regression equation. A predictive equation specifying the relation between a dependent variable and one or more independent variables

rehearsal. Strategy for keeping information in short-term memory or for moving information into long–term memory by repeating the information over and over

reinforcer. A *stimulus* used in *operant conditioning*, which increases the probability that a given *operant* behavior associated with the stimulus (which usually has occurred immediately or almost immediately before the reinforcing stimulus) will be repeated (see *positive reinforcers, negative reinforcers*)

relative frequency. Represents the number of cases that received a given score or range of scores (see *frequency distribution;* cf. *cumulative frequency*)

relative refractory phase. A time following the firing of a neuron, during which the neuron can fire again, but only in response to a much stronger stimulus than is normally required (cf. *absolute refractory phase*)

relative size. See *monocular depth cues*

reliability. The dependability of an experimental procedure, indicating that the procedure consistently yields the same results, as long as the procedure is administered in the same way each time; the dependability of a measurement instrument (e.g., a test), indicating that the instrument consistently measures the outcome being measured; may be measured as follows: *alternate-forms reliability*—the degree of relationship between test scores when people take one form of a test and the test scores when they take an alternate, parallel form of the same test some time later; *internal-consistency reliability*—the extent to which all items on a test measure the same thing; *interrater reliability*—the extent to which two or more raters of a given response would rate the response in the same way (generally applicable to subjective measurements); *test–retest reliability*—the degree to which people's test scores when taking the test on one occasion dependably predict their test scores if they take exactly the same test again some time later (may be confounded by performance enhancement that may result from the prior experience in taking the test; cf. *validity*)

reliable. See *reliability*

REM sleep. The distinctive kind of sleep that is characterized by **r**apid **e**ye **m**ovements (REMs) and frequently—although not exclusively—associated with dreaming (cf. *N-REM sleep*)

replicate. Repeat the methods used in a previous experiment, in order to observe whether the same methods will yield the same results

representation. A means of showing information in one or more alternative forms in order to understand or to communicate the given information

representational thought. Cognitive processes involving internal representations of external stimuli

representative (as a speech act). See *speech acts*

representative (as a characteristic of a sample). See *representative sample*

representative sample. A subset of the population, carefully chosen to represent the proportionate diversity of the population as a whole; well chosen representative samples permit inferences regarding the probability that a given set of *sample statistics* accurately indicates a comparable set of *population parameters*

representativeness heuristic. A judgment regarding the probability of an uncertain event according to (a) how obviously the event is similar to or representative of the population from which it is derived, and (b) the degree to which the event reflects the salient features, such as randomness, of the process by which it is generated (see *heuristic*)

reproductive thinking. A form of *thinking*, in which the thinker makes use of existing associations involving what the thinker already knows (cf. *productive thinking*)

resistance. An attempt to block therapeutic progress in psychodynamic treatment, usually as a result of unconscious conflicts

resistant attachment pattern. One of three attachment patterns observed in the *strange situation* (cf. *avoidant attachment pattern, secure attachment pattern*): A child generally shows ambivalence toward the mother while she is present, seeking both to gain and to resist physical contact with her when the mother returns after being gone a short time

response. An action or reaction that is linked to a *stimulus*

reticular activating system (RAS). A network of *neurons* (located primarily in the *midbrain* and extending into the *hindbrain*) that is essential to the regulation of *consciousness* (sleep, wakefulness, *arousal*, and even attention, to some extent), as well as to such vital functions as heartbeat and breathing

retina. A network of *neurons* extending over most of the posterior surface of the interior of the eye, containing the *photoreceptors* responsible for transducing electromagnetic light energy into neural electrochemical impulses (see *amacrine cells, bipolar cells, ganglion cells, horizontal cells;* see also *cones, photopigments, rods*)

retrieval. See *memory retroactive interference*. A type of memory disruption, which occurs when interfering information is presented after, rather than before, presentation of the information that is to be remembered (also termed *retroactive inhibition;* cf. *proactive interference*)

retrograde amnesia. See *amnesia*

reuptake. The more common of two mechanisms by which neurotransmitters are removed from the synaptic cleft: The *terminal buttons* of an *axon* reabsorb (take up again) any remaining *neurotransmitter* or *neuromodulator* substances that had been released into the *synapse*, thereby conserving these substances and sparing the surrounding *neurons* from excessive stimulation

reversible figures. Displayed images in which each of a given pair of adjacent or even interconnecting figures can be seen as either figure or ground, although both cannot be the focus of *perception* simultaneously (see *figure–ground*)

revolutionary science. Scientific work that radically modifies or perhaps contradicts altogether the existing *paradigm*, inventing instead a new paradigm (cf. *normal science*)

rods. One of the two kinds of *photoreceptors* in the eye; more numerous, longer, thinner, and more highly concentrated in the periphery of the *retina* than in the foveal region of the retina than are *cones*, the other type of photoreceptor; function more effectively in dim light than in bright light, but incapable of color vision (see *fovea*)

sample. See *representative sample* and *sample statistics*

sample statistics. The set of numerical values that (a) characterize the sample of persons who have been measured in regard to the attributes under investigation and (b) are presumed to give some indication of the *population parameters* (see also *representative sample*)

satisficing. A strategy for making decisions, in which the decision maker considers options one by one, immediately selecting the first option that appears to be satisfactory (just good enough), rather than considering all of the possible options and then carefully computing which of the entire universe of options will maximize gains and minimize losses; that is, decision makers consider only the minimum possible number of options that are believed necessary to achieve a satisfactory decision (see *judgment and decision making*)

saturation. One of three properties of color (cf. *hue*, *brightness*): the vividness, vibrancy, or richness of the hue

savings. A phenomenon of *classical conditioning*, in which there is a period of time during which the *CS* and the *US* are not linked, and then the CS is presented again in the presence of the US; even when the CS is paired with the US only briefly, the CR returns to levels approaching those at the *asymptote* of the *acquisition* phase of conditioning (cf. *spontaneous recovery*)

schedules of reinforcement. Patterns of *operant conditioning*, which determine the timing of reinforcement following the *operant* behavior (see *continuous reinforcement*, *fixed-interval reinforcement*, *fixed-ratio reinforcement*, *partial reinforcement*, *variable-interval reinforcement*, *variable-ratio reinforcement*)

schema. A cognitive framework for organizing associated concepts, based on previous experiences

schema theory. A cognitively based theory of sex-role development, which is based on the view that organized mental systems of information (i.e., *schemas*) help people both to make sense of their experiences and to shape their interactions, particularly in terms of their gender-relevant schemes for how males and females demonstrate differing sex-role-relevant behaviors and attitudes

schizophrenia. A set of disorders that encompasses a variety of symptoms, including disturbances of perception, cognition, emotion, and even motor behavior (see *delusions*, *hallucinations*): *catatonic schizophrenia*—characterized by stupor, apparently complete detachment from the rest of the world, and long periods of immobility and of staring into space; *disorganized schizophrenia*—characterized by profound psychological disorganization, including cognitive symptoms (e.g., hallucinations, delusions, and incoherent speech such as meaningless neologisms), apparent disturbances of mood (e.g., rapid mood swings and either flat affect or inappropriate affect), and extreme neglect of self-care and self-grooming; *paranoid schizophrenia*—characterized by delusions of persecution or of grandeur, which may be accompanied by auditory hallucinations of voices telling the people either of plots against them (persecution) or of their own magnificence (grandeur), as well as by particular susceptibility to delusions of reference; *residual schizophrenia*—characterized by some mild symptoms of schizophrenia that seem to linger after the individual has experienced one or more severe episodes of one of the other forms of schizophrenia; *undifferentiated schizophrenia*—characterized by symptoms of schizophrenia that do not seem to fit neatly into one of the other patterns of schizophrenia (cf. *personality disorder* [schizoid and schizotypal personality disorders])

script(s). A shared understanding about the characteristic actors, objects, and sequence of actions in a situation being described, which facilitates interactions and conversational communication about the situation

seasonal affective disorder (SAD). A form of depression that typically occurs during the winter months or the months surrounding them

secondary appraisal. The second step in a two-step process of appraising a potentially stressful situation (cf. *primary appraisal*); involves a person's assessment of strategies she or he can use in order to maximize the likelihood of potentially beneficial outcomes and to minimize the likelihood of potentially harmful outcomes of the stressful situation

secondary-process thought. A form of thought that is basically rational and based on reality, helping the thinker to make sense of the world and to act in ways that make sense both to the thinker and to observers of the thinker's actions (cf. *primary-process thought*)

secondary reinforcer(s). Rewarding stimuli that are less immediately satisfying and perhaps also less tangible than *primary reinforcers*, but that may gain reinforcing value through association with primary reinforcers; often used during *operant conditioning* when a primary reinforcer is not immediately available or is inconvenient to administer, such that the secondary reinforcers provide sufficient reinforcement until primary reinforcers can be administered; greatly enhances the flexibility of applying operant conditioning because so many stimuli can be used as secondary reinforcers (see also *token economy*); a behavioristic theory of interpersonal attraction suggests that persons who are present in rewarding situations may acquire some of the properties of secondary reinforcers

secondary traits. Personality *traits* that have some bearing on a person's behavior but that are not particularly central to what the person does (cf. *cardinal trait*, *central traits of personality*)

secure attachment pattern. One of three attachment patterns observed in the *strange situation* (cf. *avoidant attachment pattern*, *resistant attachment pattern*), in which a child generally shows preferential interest in—but not excessive dependence on—the attention of the mother while she is present and in which the child shows some distress when the mother leaves but can be calmed and reassured by her when she returns

sedative–hypnotic drugs. One of the two primary types of *central nervous system (CNS) depressants*, used for calming anxiety and relieving insomnia (e.g., *barbiturate*, *tranquilizer*, methequalone, and chloral hydrate)

selective attention. A process by which an individual attempts to track one stimulus or one type of stimulus and to ignore another

self. The whole of the *personality*, including both conscious and unconscious elements, which is posited to strive for unity among often opposing parts of the personality (see also *ideal self*, *self-concept*, *self-esteem*, *self-understanding*)

self-concept. An individual's view of her- or himself (cf. *ideal self*), which may or may not be realistic or even perceived similarly by other persons; often believed to involve both *self-understanding* (cognitions regarding the self) and *self-esteem* (emotions and valuations regarding the self)

self-determination theory. A theory of motivation, which posits that people need to feel competent, autonomous, and securely and satisfyingly connected to other people

self-efficacy theory. A theory of motivation, which considers goal-related behavior in terms of the importance of people's belief in their ability to reach their goal

self-esteem. The degree to which a person values him- or herself (cf. *self-understanding*; see *self-concept*)

self-fulfilling prophecy. A psychological phenomenon whereby what is believed to be true becomes true or at least is perceived to have become true

self-handicapping. An *attribution* bias in which people take actions to sabotage their own performance so that they will have excuses in case they fail to perform satisfactorily (see also *actor–observer effect*; *fundamental attribution error*)

self-monitoring. (In regard to personality theory) the degree to which people monitor and change their behavior in response to situational demands, from the perspective of the degree to which individuals show consistency across various situations

self-perception theory. A theory regarding *cognitive consistency*, which suggests that when people are not sure of what they believe, they infer their beliefs from their behavior, perceiving their own actions much as an outside observer would, and thereby drawing conclusions about themselves, based on their actions (cf. *cognitive dissonance*)

self-report measure. Measure of psychological attitudes, feelings, opinions, or behaviors, which are obtained simply by asking people to state their responses to questions regarding those psychological processes and products (see also *Likert scale*)

self-schema. Cognitive framework for the way in which people organize information (thoughts, feelings, and beliefs) about themselves (see *schema*)

self-terminating serial processing. A means of responding to a task involving recognition of a particular item from a list of items, in which an individual seeks to retrieve a particular item stored in memory by checking each of the items that is presented against the item being sought until the individual reaches the item being sought, at which time the individual stops checking the other items (cf. *exhaustive serial processing*; cf. also *parallel processing*)

self theory. A *humanistic* theory of personality, which focuses on the way in which the individual defines reality and personality, not in terms of an external, objective view of reality or of personality (see *self*; see also *ideal self, self-concept*)

self-understanding. The way in which individuals comprehend themselves, including the various roles and characteris-

tics that form a part of the individual's identity (cf. *self-esteem*; see *self-concept*)

semantic memory. Encoding, storage, and retrieval of facts (e.g., *declarative knowledge* about the world) that do not describe the unique experiences of the individual recalling the facts, and that are not characterized by any particular temporal context in which the individual acquired the facts (cf. *episodic memory*)

semantics. The study of the meanings of words

sensation. The neural information that the *brain* receives from the sensory *receptors* (cf. *perception*)

sense. A physiological system that collects information from *receptors* regarding various forms of energy that are received from within the body and from the external world and that then translates the collected information into an electrochemical form that can be comprehended by the *nervous system*, particularly the *brain*

sensitization. Paradoxical phenomenon in which an intermittent user of a drug actually demonstrates heightened sensitivity to low doses of the drug

sensorimotor stage. The first stage of cognitive development in Piaget's theory, in which individuals largely develop in terms of sensory (input) and *motor* (output) abilities, beginning with reflexive responses and gradually expanding in complexity to modify reflexive *schemas* toward purposeful actions that are environmentally adaptive (cf. *concrete operations, formal–operational stage, preoperational stage*)

sensory adaptation. A temporary physiological response to a sensed change in the environment, which is generally not subject to conscious manipulation or control

sensory coding. The way in which sensory *receptors* transform a range of information about various stimuli, which arrives in a variety of forms of energy, changing that information into electrochemical representations that signify the various kinds of information

sensory neurons. Nerve cells that receive information from the environment through sensory *receptors* and then carry that information away from the sensory receptors and toward the *central nervous system* (see *neuron*; cf. *interneuron, motor neuron*)

sensory store. According to a three-stores theory of memory (cf. *long-term store, short-term store*), the hypothetical construct of a sensory store that stores relatively limited amounts of information for very brief periods of time

separation anxiety. A generalized fear of being separated from a primary caregiver (e.g., a parent) or other familiar adult

septum. The portion of the brain which is involved in anger and fear

serial-position curve. A graphic display representing the probability that each of a series of given items will be recalled, given the order in which the items were presented in a list

serial processing. The cognitive manipulation of operations in which each operation is executed one at a time, in a series; as applied to short-term memory, the items stored in short-term memory would be retrieved one at a time, not all at once (cf. *parallel processing;* see also *exhaustive serial processing, self-terminating serial processing*)

serial recall. A type of memory task in which the participant is presented with a list of items and is asked to repeat the items in the exact order in which the items were presented (cf. *free recall*)

serotonin. A *neurotransmitter* synthesized from tryptophan in the diet; appears to be related to *arousal*, sleep, and dreams, as well as to regulation of mood, appetite, and sensitivity to *pain* (cf. *acetylcholine, dopamine*)

set-point theory. A theory regarding hunger, linked to the *lipostatic hypothesis*, according to which each person has a preset body weight that is biologically determined either at birth or within the first few years following birth, based on the fat cells in the body, which may increase but not decrease in number during the course of the life span; that is, although the size of the cells may fluctuate in relation to the amount of food consumed, the number may never decrease, regardless of how little food is consumed; according to this view, people with more fat cells tend to have greater bodyweight, although the size of their fat cells may be equivalent to the fat cells in persons who are lighter in body weight

shape constancy. A form of *perceptual constancy*, in which an individual continues to perceive that an observed object retains its shape, even though the actual retinal sensations of the shape of the object change

shaping. Means of *operant conditioning* for behavior that is unlikely to be generated spontaneously by the organism; accomplished using a method of successive approximations, by which crude approximations of the desired behavior are rewarded, then when the initial approximations are fully conditioned, closer approximations are conditioned, and this process of reinforcing successive approximations continues until full performance of the desired behavior is being reinforced (see *positive reinforcement*)

short-term store. According to a three-stores theory of memory (cf. *long-term store, sensory store*), the hypothetical construct of a short-term store has the capacity to store information longer than the sensory store, but is still relatively limited

sign. In medicine, any unusual feature observed by the physician (cf. *symptom*)

signal. See *signal-detection theory* and *stimulus*

signal-detection theory (SDT). A psychophysical theory that posits four possible stimulus-response pairs: a *hit*, a *miss*, a *false alarm*, or a *correct rejection*

simple cells. One of the key physiological structures described by the *feature-detector approach* to form perception according to which primitive cortical cells provide information to adjacent simple cells regarding the features of objects in the receptive field for each simple cell; the simple cells then fire in response to lines with particular features, such as particular angular orientations, particular light/dark boundaries and contrasts, and particular locations in the receptive field of the cell, with the specifically stimulating features differing from one simple cell to another (see also *complex cells*)

simple phobia. See *phobia*

simulating paradigm. A research technique for determining the true effects of a psychological treatment (e.g., *hypnosis*), in which one group of participants is subjected to the treatment and another group (a control group) is not, but the control participants are asked to behave as though they had received the treatment; people must then try to distinguish between the behavior of the treatment group and the behavior of the control group (most effective if the persons making the distinction are blind as to which participants are in the treatment group and which are in the control group)

simultaneous conditioning. An ineffective form of *classical conditioning* in which the *CS* and the *US* occur simultaneously; produces little or no conditioning clue to the blocking effect and to overshadowing

single-cell recording. Technique for detecting the firing patterns of individual neurons in response to stimuli, used on monkeys and other animals

single-system hypothesis (of bilingualism). A view of bilingualism, which suggests that both languages are represented in just one system of the mind and in one area of the brain (cf. *dual-system hypothesis*; see *bilingual*)

situational attribution. One of two fundamental types of attributions (cf. *personal attribution*): The causes of human behavior are attributed to external factors such as the settings, events, or other people in the environment of the person engaging in the given behavior

Sixteen Personality-Factor Scale (16PF). An objective, self-report personality test designed by Raymond Cattell to obtain scores for sixteen key personality factors

size constancy. Form of *perceptual constancy* in which an individual continues to perceive that an object remains the same size despite changes in the size of the object in the *retina*

skewness. Characteristic of a distribution of values, indicating the degree to which the modal value is shifted above or below the mean and the median values; when the distribution is plotted graphically, skewness appears as a lopsidedness toward the left or the right of the middle value

Skinner box. A container in which an animal undergoes conditioning experiments, named after behaviorist B. F. Skinner

sleep apnea. A breathing disorder that occurs during sleep, in which the sleeper repeatedly (perhaps hundreds of times per night) stops breathing during sleep

slips of the tongue. Inadvertent *semantic* or articulatory (related to the production of language sounds) errors in what is said (e.g., *spoonerism*)

social categorization. The normal human tendency to sort things and people into groups, based on perceived common attributes; often leads to the formation of *stereotypes*

social cognition. The thought processes through which people perceive and interpret information from and about themselves (intrapersonal world) and other persons (interpersonal world) (see *cognitive-consistency theory, impression formation, social-comparison theory*)

social-comparison theory. A *social-cognition* theory, which suggests that people evaluate their own abilities and accomplishments largely by comparing these abilities and accomplishments to the abilities and accomplishments of others, particularly in novel, uncertain, or ambiguous settings for which internal standards are not yet established

social development. The process by which people learn to interact with other people and learn about themselves as human beings

social facilitation. The beneficial effect on performance that results from the perceived presence of other persons

social-identity theory. A theory regarding *prejudice*, which suggests that people are motivated to protect their self-esteem and that they have prejudices in order to increase their self-esteem by believing that *outgroups* (of which they are not members) have less status than *ingroups* (of which they are members)

social inhibition. The detrimental effect on performance that results from the perceived presence of other persons

social learning. A form of vicarious (rather than direct) learning that occurs as a result of observing both the behavior of others and the environmental outcomes of the behavior observed

social loafing. The phenomenon by which the average amount of effort exerted by each individual in a group decreases in association with increases in the number of people participating in a joint effort

social penetration. A pattern of communication in interpersonal relationships, in which the breadth of topics and the depth of discussions tend to increase during the course of the relationship

social phobia. An *anxiety disorder* characterized by extreme fear of being criticized by others, which leads to the avoidance of groups of people and the avoidance of any situations that may lead to the possibility of being criticized, of being embarrassed, or of being otherwise subject to ridicule (see *phobia*)

social psychology. The study of the ways in which human thoughts, emotions, and behavior are affected by other people, whose presence may be actual, imagined, or implied

soma. The part of the *neuron* that contains the nucleus (center portion, which performs metabolic and reproductive functions for the cell) and that is responsible for the life of the neuron

somatic anxiety. Feelings of anxiety manifested in bodily discomfort, such as muscular tension, restlessness, rapid heartbeat, upset stomach, or headache (cf. *cognitive anxiety*)

somatic nervous system. The portion of the *peripheral nervous system* that is in charge of quick and conscious movement of skeletal muscles, which are attached directly to bones, thereby permitting movements such as walking or typing; (cf. *autonomic nervous system*)

somnambulism. Sleepwalking, which combines aspects of waking and sleeping, with the sleepwalker able to see, walk, and perhaps even talk, but usually unable to remember the sleepwalking episodes; rarely accompanied by dreaming

source traits. One of two levels of personality *traits* (cf. *surface traits*): underlying, fundamental psychological dimensions of *personality* that generate the more numerous surface-level personality traits

specific phobias. Characterized by marked, persistent, irrational fears of objects, such as spiders, snakes, rats, high places, and darkness

speech acts. Any of five basic categories of speech, analyzed in terms of the purposes accomplished by the given act: *commissive*—a commitment by the speaker to engage in some future course of action; *declaration* (also termed *performative*)—a statement that brings about an intended new state of affairs (e.g., an announcement of resignation from employment); *directive*—an attempt by a speaker to get a listener to do something, such as supplying the answer to a question (see also *indirect requests*); *expressive*—a statement regarding the psychological state of the speaker; *representative*—an assertion of a belief that a given proposition is true, which may be characterized by any degree of veridicality or by any amount of supporting evidence (i.e., the statement of belief may be so well supported that it may be universally accepted as true, or it may be so ill supported that other persons may consider the statement a *delusion*)

spinal cord. A slender, roughly cylindrical bundle of interconnected *nerves*, which is enclosed within the spinal column and which extends through the center of the back, starting at the *brain* and ending at the branches of the *peripheral nervous system* that go to each of the two legs

spontaneous recovery. A phenomenon of *classical conditioning*, in which a *CR* reappears without any environmental prompting; the unprompted reappearance of the CR occurs after a conditioned behavior has been established and then extinguished and then the organism is allowed to rest; that is, the organism appears spontaneously to recover a modest level of response during the rest period, although the response disappears again if the *CS* is not paired with the *US* again (cf. *savings*)

spontaneous recovery (from mental illness). The unprompted and unaided (i.e., untreated) disappearance of maladaptive symptomatology over the course of time

spoonerism. A *slip of the tongue*, in which a reversal of the initial sounds of two words produces two entirely different words, usually yielding a humorous outcome (named after the Reverend William Spooner, who was famous for producing humorous instances of such reversals)

standard deviation. Statistical measurement of dispersion, indicating the degree to which a set of values typically deviates from the *mean* value for the set; calculated by determining the square root of the *variance* for the distribution of values

standardization. The administration of a test in a way that ensures that the conditions for taking the test are the same for all test-takers; also, the administration of an experimental procedure in a way that ensures that the experimental conditions are the same for all participants

stapes. The last in the series of three bones in the middle ear (cf. *incus*, *malleus*), which normally receive and amplify the vibrations transmitted by the

tympanum (*eardrum*) and then transmit those vibrations to the *cochlea*

state-dependent memory. The tendency for a person to recall learned information more easily when in the same emotional state as the state in which the information was learned

static assessment environment. A context for testing, in which an examiner asks a series of questions, offering no hints or guidance if the test-taker makes incorrect responses, and usually not even signaling whether the test-taker has answered correctly or incorrectly (cf. *dynamic assessment environment*)

statistic. A numerical value obtained by analyzing numerical data about a *representative sample* of a population (see *sample statistics*; cf. *population parameters*)

statistical significance. A degree of numerically analyzed probability suggesting the likelihood that a particular outcome may have occurred as a result of systematic factors rather than by chance

statistics. A field of study involving the analysis of numerical data about representative samples of *populations*

stereopsis. Three-dimensional perception of the world through the cognitive fusion of the visual fields seen by each of the two eyes (see *binocular depth cues*, *binocular disparity*)

stereotype. *Schema* regarding groups of persons, in which it is held that members of a group tend more or less uniformly to have particular types of characteristics (see also *outgroup homogeneity*, *prejudice*, *social categorization*)

stimulus. Something that prompts action (plural, *stimuli*; *stimulus* is Latin for the sharpened stick used by Romans for goading sluggish animals into action)

stimulus discrimination. The ability to ascertain the difference between one stimulus and another; often used in *psychophysics* experiments and assessments, as well as in behavioral experiments (cf. *stimulus generalization*)

stimulus generalization (in classical conditioning). A broadening of the conditioned response, such that stimuli that resemble a specifically *conditioned stimulus* also elicit the *conditioned response* (cf. *stimulus discrimination*)

storage. See *memory*

strange situation. An experimental technique for observing attachment in young children, conducted in a laboratory room containing various toys and some chairs; in the room is a one-way mirror, behind which an observer watches and records the behavior of the subject (usually a toddler, age 12–18 months); for the procedure, the toddler and her or his mother enter the room and the mother sits in one of the chairs; a few minutes later, an unfamiliar woman enters the room, talks to

the mother, and then tries to play with the child; while the stranger is trying to play with the child, the mother quietly walks out of the room, leaving her purse on the chair to indicate that she will return; later, the mother returns, and soon after, the stranger leaves; still later, the mother leaves the child alone in the room; soon after, she returns and sits in the chair again; finally, the toddler and mother leave the room, thus ending the experimental procedure

stress. A phenomenon in which some factor (or factors) in the environment causes a person to feel threatened or challenged in some way; usually involves some kind of environmental change that requires the person to make some kind of adaptive or *coping* response

stress disorder. An *anxiety disorder*; see *acute stress disorder* and *posttraumatic stress disorder*

stress response. Reaction to some kind of *stressor*, involving internal and external adaptation by an individual (see *stress*)

stressor. Situation or event that leads to *stress* (see *stress response*)

stroboscopic motion. The perception of movement that is produced when a stroboscope (*strobo-*, "whirling"; *-scope*, "device or means of viewing") intermittently flashes an alternating pair of lights against a dark background at appropriate distances and appropriately timed intervals (within milliseconds), such that it appears that a single light has moved forward and backward across the visual field

structuralism. The first major school of thought in psychology, which focused on analyzing the distinctive configuration of component elements of the mind, such as particular sensations or thoughts; for example, structuralists would be more interested in what people think than in how they think, in what people perceive, rather than how they perceive (cf. *functionalism*)

subconscious. A level of *consciousness* that involves less awareness than full consciousness and either is synonymous with the **unconscious** level (according to many theorists) or is slightly more accessible to consciousness than is the unconscious level (according to a few theorists)

subjective-utility theory. A theory of decision making, which acknowledges that each individual may have a distinctive understanding regarding the various utilities for a given action based on the idiosyncratic hopes, fears, and other subjective motivations of the individual (cf. *game theory*, *utility maximization theory*)

subtractive bilingualism. A form of bilingualism in which some elements of a second language replace some elements of a poorly established primary language (cf. *additive bilingualism*; see *bilingual*)

subtractive mixture. The remaining combined *wavelengths* of light that are reflected from an object after other wavelengths of light have been absorbed (subtracted from the reflected light) by the object; darker objects absorb more wavelengths of light and reflect fewer wavelengths than do brighter objects (cf. *additive mixture*)

superego. One of three psychodynamic concepts (cf. *ego*, *id*), which comprises all the internalized representations of the norms and values of society acquired during early *psychosexual development*, through interactions with the parents as figures of societal authority (see *idealistic principle*)

surface traits. One of two levels of personality *traits* (cf. *source traits*): the numerous superficial *personality* traits that vary widely across individuals and that are derived from combinations of underlying fundamental source traits

survey. A method of social-science research, in which the researcher records people's responses to questions regarding their beliefs and opinions; rarely involve answers that are scored as either right or wrong (see, e. g., *questionnaire*; cf. *test*; cf. also *case study, experiment, naturalistic observation*)

syllogism. A deductive argument that permits a conclusion to be drawn, based on two premises, in which each of the two premises contains two terms, at least one term of which is common to both premises (see also *categorical syllogism, conditional syllogism*)

sympathetic nervous system. The portion of the *autonomic nervous system* that is concerned primarily with catabolism (cf. *parasympathetic nervous system*)

symptom. Any unusual sensation in or feature on the body, and which is believed to indicate some kind of pathology (cf. *sign*)

synapse. The point of communication between two neurons; the area comprising the interneuronal gap between the *terminal buttons* of one neuron's *axon*, and the *dendrites* (or sometimes the *soma*) of the next *neuron*; the cleft into which the terminal buttons of the presynaptic neuron may release a chemical *neurotransmitter* or *neuromodulator* for receipt by the postsynaptic neuron

syntax. A level of linguistic analysis, which centers on the patterns by which users of a particular language put words together at the level of the sentence; systematic structure through which words can be combined and sequenced to make meaningful phrases and sentences (see also *grammar*)

synthesis. As an aspect of a *dialectic:* a statement of opinion that integrates

some aspects of a *thesis* and some aspects of an *antithesis*, usually based on evidence or logic that supports the aspects that have been integrated; as a process of *critical thinking:* a process that involves integrating component parts into wholes, and that may be viewed as a process that complements analysis (see also *convergent thinking, divergent thinking*)

systematic desensitization. A *counterconditioning* technique of behavioral therapy (cf. *aversion therapy*) in which the therapist seeks to help the client combat anxiety and other troublesome responses by teaching the client a set of relaxation techniques so that the client can effectively replace the troublesome responses with relaxation responses, usually in association with a *desensitization hierarchy* of stimuli that previously induced the troublesome responses

taste bud. Cluster of taste-receptor cells located inside the *papillae* of the tongue; in the center of each cluster are pores into which the molecules from foods and beverages may fall, and when moistened chemicals contact the receptor cells, the cells *transduce* the chemical energy of the tastes into the electrochemical energy of neural transmission, which involves encoding of the tastes to distinguish among particular kinds of chemicals (e.g., salts, acids, or alkalies)

telegraphic speech. Rudimentary syntactical communications of two words or more, which are characteristic of very early language acquisition, and which seem more like telegrams than like conversation because articles, prepositions, and other function morphemes are usually omitted

temperament. Individual differences in the intensity and duration of emotions, as well as the individual's characteristic disposition

template. Prototype or pattern for distinctive forms, such as distinctive shapes of odorous chemicals and smell receptors or the distinctive patterns mentioned in some *passive theories* of perception

temporal conditioning. A *classical conditioning* procedure in which the *CS* is a fixed interval of time between presentations of the *US*, so that the learner learns that the US will occur at a given, fixed time

temporal contiguity. The proximity in time between two events or stimuli; without *contingency* between the two events or stimuli, conditioning does not take place (see also *classical conditioning, operant conditioning*)

temporal lobe. On the lower portion of the sides of the *brain*, chiefly responsible for auditory processing. One of the four

major regions of the *cerebral cortex* (cf. *frontal lobe, occipital lobe, parietal lobe*)

terminal buttons. Small knobby structures located at the tips of the branches of *axons*, which release *neurotransmitters* or *neuromodulators* into a *synapse*, which borders on the *dendrites* or *somas* of nearby *neurons*

test. A research method used for measuring a given ability or attribute in a particular individual or set of individuals at a particular time and in a particular place; almost invariably involves keying the test-takers' responses as either right or wrong or at least as being better (more accurate, more appropriate, more creative, etc.) or worse; (cf. *survey*; cf. also *case study, experiment, naturalistic observation*)

test–retest reliability. See *reliability*

texture gradient. *See* monocular depth cues

thalamus. A two-lobed structure, located in about the center of the *brain*, at about the level of the eyes, which helps in the control of sleep and waking and seems to serve as a relay for sensory information; contains various nuclei (groups of neurons with a similar function) that receive assorted types of sensory input entering the brain and then transmit that input via projection fibers to the appropriate sensory regions of the *cerebral cortex*

Thematic Apperception Test (TAT). A psychodynamic personality assessment tool in which the examiner presents a series of ambiguous but representationally realistic pictures; test-takers are believed to project their feelings into their descriptions of the pictures

theory. A statement of some general principles that explains a psychological phenomenon or set of phenomena

theory of multiple intelligences. A theory of intelligence suggesting that intelligence comprises eight distinct constructs that function somewhat independently of one another, but that may interact to produce intelligent behavior: bodily–kinesthetic intelligence, interpersonal intelligence, intrapersonal intelligence, linguistic intelligence, mathematical–logical intelligence, musical intelligence, naturalist intelligence, and spatial intelligence

thesis. A statement of an opinion or of a perspective (cf. *antithesis, synthesis*; see *dialectic*)

thinking. A psychological function that involves the representation and processing of information in the mind (also termed *cognition*; see *critical thinking, creativity, judgment and decision making, problem solving, reasoning*)

threshold of excitation. The level of electrochemical stimulation, at or above which an *action potential* may be generated, but below which an action potential cannot be generated; the specific threshold required for a given neuron's action potential differs for the various neurons and depends on whether the neuron is in the midst of a refractory period (see *absolute refractory phase*, *relative refractory phase*)

thyroid gland. An endocrine *gland* located at the front of the throat, which regulates the metabolic rate of cells, thereby influencing weight gain or loss, blood pressure, muscular strength, and level of activity

timbre. A psychological quality of sound that permits detection of the difference between a note (e.g., B-flat) played on a piano and the same note played on a harmonica, based on the distinctive *harmonics* produced by each instrument rather than the *fundamental frequency* of the note

tobacco. A plant product containing nicotine, a *central nervous system (CNS) stimulant*

token economy. A system of *operant conditioning* in which tokens are used as a means of reinforcing various *operant* behaviors; most frequently used in controlled environments such as residential institutions for persons who are psychologically impaired, in order to encourage adaptive behavior and discourage maladaptive behavior; generally not used with persons for whom their natural interest in performing the operant behavior would be reduced as a result of the use of extrinsic reinforcers (see *extrinsic motivators*)

tolerance. A consequence of prolonged use of *psychoactive* drugs, in which the drug user stops feeling *psychotropic* effects of a given drug at one level of dosage and must take increasing amounts of drugs in order to achieve the effects, eventually reaching a level of nonresponse at which the current level no longer produces the desired effects, but higher levels will cause overdose—the person generally still continues taking the drugs, despite the lack of psychotropic effects, simply to avoid experiencing the unpleasant feelings associated with drug *withdrawal* (see *addiction*; see also specific drugs, e.g., *amphetamine* and *barbiturate*)

total-time hypothesis. A widely accepted assumption regarding memory, which holds that the degree to which a person is able to learn information by storing it in memory depends on the total amount of time spent studying the material in a given session, rather than on the way in which the time is apportioned within a given session

trace conditioning. A form of *classical conditioning*, in which the *CS* is terminated for a while before the *US* begins (cf. *delay conditioning*)

trait. May refer either to a personality trait or to a genetic trait; personality traits are stable sources of individual differences that characterize a person and that may originate in the person's nature (heredity) or the person's nurture (environment); genetic traits are distinctive characteristics or behavior patterns that are genetically determined

tranquilizer. One of the *sedative–hypnotic drugs* used for combating anxiety; considered to be safer than *barbiturates*, due to the lower dosages required and the reduced likelihood of drowsiness and respiratory difficulties, although the potential for *addiction* remains a problem (see *central nervous system (CNS) depressants*)

transduce. Convert energy from one form into another, such as the process that occurs in a sensory *receptor*, which converts a form of energy (mechanical, chemical, etc.) received from the environment into the electrochemical form of energy that is meaningful to the *nervous system*

transference. A phenomenon of psychodynamic therapy whereby the patient projects her or his feelings and internal conflicts onto the therapist, often also projecting onto the therapist-patient relationship many aspects of the patient's early childhood relationships, such as with parents; deemed to be an important means by which the patient can resolve some of the conflicts characterizing these early relationships (cf. *countertransference*)

transformational grammar. A form of syntactical analysis, which centers on the transformational operations used for generating surface structures from deep structures (cf. *phrase-structure grammars*; see also *deep-structure level*)

transparency. Phenomenon in which individuals see false analogies of the formal structure of problems because of the apparent similarity of attributes related to the content of the problems

triangular theory of love. A theory of love, according to which love has three basic components: *commitment*, *intimacy*, and *passion*, different combinations of which yield different kinds of love

triarchic theory of human intelligence. A theory of intelligence, which asserts that intelligence comprises three aspects, which deal with the relation of intelligence (a) to the internal world, (b) to experience, and (c) to the external world

trichromatic theory of color vision. One of two proposed mechanisms for explaining how color vision occurs (also termed *Young–Helmholtz theory*; cf. *opponent-process theory*); draws on the notion of primary colors, which can combine additively to form all other colors; according to this view, various photoreceptive *cones* are somehow attuned to each of the primary colors, such that some cones are

sensitive to red (and are therefore activated in response to the sight of red), others to green, and others to blue, and the full range of colors may be seen when various combinations of these three primary colors are sensed

two-component theory of emotion. A view of emotions positing that emotions comprise two elements: a state of physiological *arousal* and a cognitive label identifying the aroused state as signifying a particular emotion

Type-A behavior pattern. A characteristic pattern of personality and behavior, in which the individual demonstrates a competitive orientation toward achievement, a sense of urgency about time, and a strong tendency to feel anger and hostility (cf. *Type-B behavior pattern*)

Type-B behavior pattern. A characteristic pattern of personality and behavior, in which the individual demonstrates relatively low levels of competitiveness, urgency about time, and hostility (cf. *Type-A behavior pattern*)

Type I error. An error in interpreting research, which refers to the belief that a finding has appeared due to systematic changes, when in fact the finding is a result of random fluctuation

Type II error. An error in interpreting research, which refers to the belief that a finding has appeared due to random fluctuations, when in fact the finding is a result of systematic changes

UR. See *unconditioned response*

US. See *unconditioned stimulus*

unconditioned response (UR). Automatic, unlearned physiological response to a stimulus (the *unconditioned stimulus*), used in *classical conditioning* as a means of eventually teaching the learner to produce a *conditioned response*

unconditioned stimulus (US). A stimulus that automatically, without prior learning, elicits a given physiological or emotional response, used in *classical conditioning* as a means of eventually teaching the learner to respond to a *conditioned stimulus* (see also *unconditioned response*)

unconscious. A level of consciousness at which thoughts, wishes, and feelings are not accessible to conscious awareness (often considered synonymous with *subconscious*); an important construct of *psychodynamic theory*

unconscious inference. A phenomenon of *constructive perception*, according to which perceivers make correct attributions regarding their visual sensations because they engage in a process by which they assimilate information from a number of sources to create a perception, without consciously doing so; such inferences consider not only the immediate sensory information available to the perceiver, but also the prior experience and cognitive strategies of the perceiver

utility-maximization theory. A decision-making theory, according to which the goal of human action is to maximize pleasure (positive utility) and to minimize pain (negative utility); assumes that humans make decisions based on un-bounded rationality (cf. *bounded rational-ity, game theory, subjective-utility theory*)

valid. See *validity*

validity. The extent to which a given form of measurement assesses what it is sup-posed to measure (see *concurrent validity, construct-related validity, content-related va-lidity, face validity, predictive validity*); also, the extent to which a set of experimental procedures reveals what it is purported to reveal (cf. *reliability*; see also *deductively valid*)

vanishing point. A phenomenon of visual perception, in which parallel lines seem to converge as they move farther into the distance and eventually to converge en-tirely, to become indistinguishable, and then to disappear entirely at the horizon (see *monocular depth cues; linear perspective*)

variable. Attribute or characteristic of a situation, a person, or a phenomenon, which may differ or fluctuate across situ-ations, across persons, or across phe-nomena (see also *dependent variable, independent variable*)

variable-interval reinforcement. A schedule for implementing *operant condi-tioning*, in which reinforcement occurs, on average, after a certain period of time, assuming that the *operant* behavior has occurred at least once during that time period, but in which the specific amount of time preceding reinforcement changes from one reinforcement to the next (see *partial reinforcement, schedules of reinforcement*; cf. *fixed-interval reinforce-ment, variable-ratio reinforcement*)

variable-ratio reinforcement. A schedule for implementing *operant conditioning*, in which reinforcement occurs, on average, after a certain number of operant re-sponses, but in which the specific number of responses preceding reinforcement changes from one reinforcement to the next (see *partial reinforcement, schedules of reinforcement*; cf. *fixed-ratio reinforcement, variable-interval reinforcement*)

variance. Statistical measurement indicat-ing the degree to which a set of values varies from the *mean* of the set of values; the basis for determining a *standard devia-tion*, which is more commonly used in psychological research

verbal comprehension. The ability to comprehend written and spoken linguis-tic input, such as words, sentences, and paragraphs (cf. *verbal fluency*)

verbal fluency. The ability to produce written and spoken linguistic output, such as words, sentences, and paragraphs (cf. *verbal comprehension*)

verifiable. Characteristic of scientific find-ings, by which there is some means of confirming the results

vertebrae. The protective backbones that encase the *spinal cord* and that form the spinal column of vertebrates

vestibular system. The sensory system that comprises the vestibular sacs and semicircular canals in the inner ear, which contains receptors for the sensa-tions associated with equilibrium; oper-ates via movement of the head, which causes movement of fluid in the sacs and canals, which bends hairlike cells that *transduce* the mechanical energy of the various movements into the electrochem-ical energy of neural transmission; this energy travels via the auditory nerve to the *cerebellum* and to the *cerebral cortex* and is encoded as information about the direction of movement, relative orienta-tion, and rate of acceleration of the head

vibration theory. One of two theories re-garding the sensation of smell: the mole-cules of each distinctively smelled substance generate a specific vibration frequency, which specifically affects the olfactory receptors by disrupting particu-lar chemical bonds in the receptor cell membranes, and the rupture of these bonds releases the chemical energy stored in those bonds; the distinctive pat-tern of rupturing of the bonds is *trans-duced* into a characteristic pattern of electrochemical activity, which is inter-preted in the brain as specific odors

visual mask. A pattern of visual stimuli that wipes out any visual afterimage that might remain on the *retina*, but which is not distinguishable as meaningful (and thereby does not distort the perception of the image that preceded the mask)

vocabulary. A repertoire of words, formed by combining morphemes

volley principle. A hypothesis supportive of the *frequency theory* of hearing, which suggests that auditory neurons fire coop-eratively in alternating groups, such that while some neurons are resting, neigh-boring neurons are firing, thereby yield-ing a combined pattern of neural firing that can indicate high-frequency vibra-tions of sound (cf. *place theory*; see also *du-plicity theory*)

warm fibers. Bundles of *neurons* that re-spond to warming of the skin (in the range of 95–115 degrees Fahrenheit [35–46 centigrade]; cf. *cold fibers*)

wavelength. The distance from the crest of one wave to the crest of the next wave (e.g., sound waves or light waves), often used as a means of measuring a quality of sound or light; for light waves, the objective wavelength of a light wave is associated with hue, and for sound waves, the objective wavelength is asso-ciated with the sensation of *pitch* (actu-ally, for sound, frequency is the more common measurement)

Weber fraction. The value that indicates the relation between the intensity of a standard stimulus and the intensity of a stimulus required to produce a *just notice-able difference (jnd)*; this value varies for different types of sensory experiences, and smaller fractions are required for sensory modalities to which humans ex-perience greater sensitivity (e.g., the painful sensation of electric shock), whereas larger fractions are required for less sensitive modalities (e.g., the sensa-tion of taste)

Weber's law. Broadly interpreted, the law suggests that the greater the magni-tude of the stimulus, the larger the dis-tance must be in order to be detectable as a difference; a principle relating the intensity of a standard stimulus to the intensity of a stimulus required to pro-duce a *just noticeable difference (jnd)*, often expressed as an equation: $\Delta I = KI$, where K is a constant (a numerical value that does not vary, such as pi), I is the intensity of the standard stimulus, and ΔI is the increase in intensity needed to produce a jnd

well-structured problem. A type of problem for which a clear path to solu-tion is known, although it may still be very difficult to implement (cf. *ill-structured problem*)

withdrawal. The temporary discomfort (which may be extremely negative, much like a severe case of intestinal flu, accom-panied by extreme depression or *anxiety*) associated with a decrease in dosage or a discontinuation altogether of a *psychoac-tive* drug, during which the drug user's physiology and mental processes must adjust to an absence of the drug; during withdrawal from some drugs (e.g., some stimulants and some *sedative–hypnotic drugs*), the user should obtain medical su-pervision, to avoid life-threatening com-plications that may arise during the readjustment to normal physiological and mental functioning

word-superiority effect. A phenomenon of form perception in which an individual can more readily identify (discriminate) letters when they are presented in the context of words than when they are pre-sented as solitary letters

working memory. A portion of memory that may be viewed as a specialized part of long-term memory which holds only the most recently activated portion of long-term memory, and which moves these activated elements into and out of short-term memory (which may be viewed as the narrow portion of working memory that enters immediate awareness); some psychologists consider working memory to be a hypothetical construct in opposition to the three-stores view, but others consider it a complement to the three-stores view

yoga. A form of *concentrative meditation*, which comes in various forms, including active exercises as well as contemplative quiescence

Zen. A classical Buddhist form of *concentrative meditation*, which usually involves sitting in a cross-legged position but which may be practiced in many forms and during which meditators may progress through a graded series of steps, advancing from novice to expert

zero-sum game. A game in which a positive outcome for the winner is balanced by a negative outcome for the loser, which yields an outcome of zero because the net positive equals the net negative (see also *game theory*)

zone of proximal development (ZPD). The range of ability between a person's observable level of ability and the person's latent capacity, which is not directly observable, but which may be detected by providing a context in which the latent capacity may be revealed and expressed (sometimes termed the *zone of potential development*)

References

Abrams, R. (1988). *Electroconvulsive treatment: It apparently works, but how and at what risks are not yet clear*. New York: Oxford University Press.

Abramson, L. Y., Metalsky, G. I., & Alloy, L. B. (1989). Hopelessness depression: A theory-based subtype of depression. *Psychological Review, 96*, 358–372.

Achenbach, T. M. (1970). The children's associative responding test: A possible alternative to group IQ tests. *Journal of Educational Psychology, 61*, 340–348.

Adams, M. J. (Ed.). (1986). *Odyssey: A curriculum for thinking* (Vols. 1–6). Watertown, MA: Charlesbridge.

Adler, N., & Matthews, K. A. (1994). Health and psychology: Why do some people get sick and some stay well? *Annual Review of Psychology, 45*, 229–259.

Agnew, J. (1985). Man's purgative passion. *American Journal of Psychotherapy, 39*(2), 236–246.

Ahn, W.-K., Kalish, C. W., Medin, D. L., & Gelman, S. A. (1995). The role of covariation versus mechanism information in causal attribution. *Cognition, 54*, 299–352.

Ainsworth, M. D. S. (1973). The development of infant–mother attachment. In B. M. Caldwell & H. M. Ricciuti (Eds.), *Review of child development research* (Vol. 3). Chicago: University of Chicago Press.

Ainsworth, M. D. S. (1989). Attachments beyond infancy. *American Psychologist, 44*, 709–716.

Ainsworth, M. D. S., Bell, S. M., & Stayton, D. J. (1971). Individual differences in strange-situation behavior in one-year-olds. In H. R. Schaffer (Ed.), *The origins of human social relations*. London: Academic Press.

Ainsworth, M. D. S., Blehar, M., Waters, E., & Wall, S. (1978). *Patterns of attachment*. Hillsdale, NJ: Erlbaum.

Albert, D. J., Jonik, R. H., & Walsh, M. L. (1991). Hormone-dependent aggression in the female rat: Testosterone plus estradiol implants prevent the decline in aggression following ovariectomy. *Physiology & Behavior, 49*, 673–677.

Alexander, J. M., & Schwanenflugel, P. J. (1994). Strategy regulation: The role of intelligence, metacognitive attributions, and knowledge base. *Developmental Psychology, 30*, 709–723.

Alicke, M. D., LoSchiavo, F. M., Zerbst, J., & Zhang, S. (1997). The person who outperforms me is a genius: Maintaining perceived competence in upward social comparison. *Journal of Personality and Social Psychology, 73*, 781–789.

Allison, T., & Cicchetti, D. V. (1976). Sleep in mammals: Ecological and constitutional correlates. *Science, 194*, 732–734.

Allport, G. W. (1935). Attitudes. In C. M. Murchison (Ed.), *Handbook of social psychology*. Worcester, MA: Clark University Press.

Allport, G. W. (1937). *Personality: A psychological interpretation*. New York: Holt, Rinehart & Winston.

Allport, G. W. (1954). *The nature of prejudice*. Reading, MA: Addison-Wesley.

Allport, G. W. (1961). *Pattern and growth in personality*. New York: Holt, Rinehart & Winston.

Allport, G. W. (1985). The historical background of social psychology. In G. Lindzey & E. Aronson (Eds.), *Handbook of social psychology* (3rd ed., Vol. 1, pp. 1–46). New York: Random House.

Alpert, B., Field, T., Goldstein, S., & Perry, S. (1990). Aerobics enhances cardiovascular fitness and agility in preschoolers. *Health Psychology, 9*, 48–56.

Altman, I., & Taylor, D. A. (1973). *Social penetration: The development of interpersonal relationships*. New York: Holt, Rinehart & Winston.

Amabile, T. M. (1983). *The social psychology of creativity*. New York: Springer-Verlag.

Amabile, T. M. (1985). Motivation and creativity: Effects of motivational orientation on creative writers. *Journal of Personality and Social Psychology, 48*, 393–399.

Amabile, T. M. (1996). *The context of creativity*. Boulder, CO: Westview.

Amenson, C. S., & Lewinsohn, P. M. (1981). An investigation into the observed sex difference in prevalence of unipolar depression. *Journal of Abnormal Psychology, 90*, 1–3.

American Association on Mental Retardation. (1992). *Mental retardation: Definition, classification, and systems of supports*. Washington, DC: Author.

American Association of University Women Educational Foundation and the Wellesley College Center for Research on Women. (1992). *The AAUW Report: How schools shortchange girls—A study of major findings on girls and education*. Washington, DC: Author.

American Hospital Association. (1982). *Hospital statistics*. Chicago: Author.

American Hospital Association. (1987). *Hospital statistics*. Chicago: Author.

American Hospital Association. (1989). *Hospital statistics*. Chicago: Author.

American Psychiatric Association. (1987). *Diagnostic and statistical manual of mental disorders* (3rd ed.-Rev.). Washington, DC: Author.

American Psychiatric Association. (1994). *Diagnostic and statistical manual of mental disorders* (4th ed.). Washington, DC: Author.

Ames, C. (1992). Classrooms: Goals, structures, and student motivation. *Journal of Educational Psychology, 84*, 261–271.

Amoore, J. E. (1970). *Molecular basis of odor*. Springfield, IL: Thomas.

Amsel, E., & Renninger, A. K. (Eds.). (1997). *Change and development: Issues of theory, method and application*. Mahwah, NJ: Erlbaum.

Anand, B. K., & Brobeck, J. R. (1951). Hypothalamic control of food intake in rats and cats. *Yale Journal of Biology and Medicine, 24*, 123–140.

Anand, B. K., Chhina, G., & Singh, B. (1961). Some aspects of electroencephalographic studies in yogis. *Electroencephalography and Clinical Neurophysiology, 13*, 452–456.

Anand, B. K., Chhina, G. S., & Singh, B. (1962). Effect of glucose on the activity of hypothalamic "feeding centers." *Science, 138*, 597–598.

Anastasi, A. (1988). *Psychological testing* (6th ed.). New York: Macmillan.

Anastasi, A., & Urbina, S. (1997). *Psychological testing* (7th ed.). Upper Saddle River, NJ: Prentice-Hall.

Anderson, B. F. (1975). *Cognitive psychology*. New York: Academic Press.

Anderson, C. A. (1987). Temperature and aggression: Effects on quarterly, yearly, and city rates of violent and nonviolent crime. *Journal of Personality and Social Psychology, 52*, 1161–1173.

Anderson, C. A. (1989). Temperature and aggression: Ubiquitous effects of heat on occurrence of human violence. *Psychological Bulletin, 106*(1), 74–96.

Anderson, J. R. (1983). Retrieval of information from long-term memory. *Science, 220*, 25–30.

Anderson, J. R. (1985). *Cognitive psychology and its implications*. New York: Freeman.

Anderson, J. R. (1993). Problem solving and learning. *American Psychologist, 48*, 35–44.

Anderson, J. R., & Bower, G. H. (1973). *Human associative memory*. New York: Wiley.

Anderson, K. L. (1990). Arousal and the inverted-U hypothesis: A critique of Neiss's "Reconceptualizing arousal." *Psychological Bulletin, 107,* 96–100.

Anderson, K. O., & Masur, F. T., III. (1983). Psychological preparation for invasive medical and dental procedures. *Journal of Behavioral Medicine, 6,* 1–40.

Anderson, N. H. (1968). Likableness ratings of 555 personality-trait words. *Journal of Personality and Social Psychology, 9,* 272–279.

Andersson, B. E. (1989). Effects of public daycare: A longitudinal study. *Child Development, 60,* 857–866.

Andreasen, N. C., Arndt, S., Swayze, V., Cizadlo, T., et al. (1994). Thalamic abnormalities in schizophrenia visualized through magnetic resonance image averaging. *Science, 266,* 294–298.

Andreasen, N. C., & Black, D. W. (1991). *Introductory text of psychiatry.* Washington, DC: American Psychiatric Press.

Andreasen, N. C., Ehrhardt, J., Swayze, V., Alliger, R., Yuh, T., Cohen, G., & Ziebell, S. (1990). Magnetic resonance imaging of the brain in schizophrenia. *Archives of General Psychiatry, 47,* 35–44.

Andreasen, N. C., Flaum, M., Swayze, V. W., Tyrrell, G., & Arndt. S. (1990). Positive and negative symptoms in schizophrenia: A critical reappraisal. *Archives of General Psychiatry, 47,* 615–621.

Andreasen, N. C., Olsen, S. A., Dennert, J. W., & Smith, M. R. (1982a). Ventricular enlargement in schizophrenia: Definition and prevalence. *American Journal of Psychiatry, 139,* 292–296.

Andreasen, N. C., Olsen, S. A., Dennert, J. W., & Smith, M. R. (1982b). Ventricular enlargement in schizophrenia: Relationship to positive and negative symptoms. *American Journal of Psychiatry, 139,* 297–302.

Andrews, G. (1993). The benefits of psychotherapy. In N. Sartorius, G. de Girolano, G. Andrews, G. A. German, & L. Eisenberg (Eds.), *Treatment of mental disorders: A review of effectiveness.* Geneva, Switzerland, and Washington, DC: World Health Organization and American Psychiatric Press.

Angell, J. R. (1907). The province of functional psychology. *Psychological Review, 14,* 61–91.

Angier, N. (1993, April 25). "Stopit!" she said. "Nomore!" [Review of the book *Genie: An abused child's flight from silence*]. *New York Times Book Review,* p. 12.

Antrobus, J. (1991). Dreaming: Cognitive processes during cortical activation and high afferent thresholds. *Psychological Review, 98,* 69–121.

Appel, L. F., Cooper, R. G., McCarrell, N., Sims-Knight, J., Yussen, S. R., & Flavell, J. H. (1972). The development of the distinction between perceiving and memorizing. *Child Development, 43,* 1365–1381.

Archer, J. (1991). Human sociobiology: Basic concepts and limitations. *Journal of Social Issues, 47*(3), 11–26.

Archer, J., & Lloyd, B. B. (1985). *Sex and gender.* New York: Cambridge University Press.

Arendt, J., Aldhous, M., & Wright, J. (1988, April 2). Synchronization of a disturbed sleep-wake cycle in a blind man by melatonin treatment. *Lancet, 1,* (8588), 772–773.

Arieti, S. (1974). An overview of schizophrenia from a predominantly psychological approach. *American Journal of Psychiatry, 131*(3), 241–249.

Arkes, H. R., Boehm, L. E., & Xu, G. (1991). The determinants of judged validity. *Journal of Experimental Social Psychology, 27,* 576–605.

Arlin, P. K. (1975). Cognitive development in adulthood: A fifth stage? *Developmental Psychology, 11,* 602–606.

Arlin, P. K. (1990). Wisdom: The art of problem finding. In R. J. Sternberg (Ed.), *Wisdom* (pp. 230–243). New York: Cambridge University Press.

Armstrong, S. L., Gleitman, L. R., & Gleitman, H. (1983). What some concepts may not be. *Cognition, 13,* 263–308.

Arnold, M. B. (1960). *Emotion and personality* (Vols. 1–2). New York: Columbia University Press.

Arnold, M. B. (1970). Perennial problems in the field of emotion. In M. B. Arnold (Ed.), *Feelings and emotions* (pp. 169–185). New York: Academic Press.

Aron, A., & Westbay, L. (1996). Dimensions of the prototype of love. *Journal of Personality and Social Psychology, 70,* 535–551.

Aronson, E., Blaney, N., Stephan, C., Sikes, J., & Snapp, M. (1978). *The jigsaw classroom.* Beverly Hills, CA: Sage.

Asch, S. E. (1946). Forming impressions of personality. *Journal of Abnormal and Social Psychology, 41,* 258–290.

Asch, S. E. (1951). Effects of group pressure upon the modification and distortion of judgments. In H. Guetzkow (Ed.), *Groups, leadership, and men.* Pittsburgh: Carnegie.

Asch, S. E. (1952). *Social psychology.* New York: Prentice-Hall.

Asch, S. E. (1955). Opinions and social pressure. *Scientific American, 193,* 31–35.

Asch, S. E. (1956). Studies of independence and conformity: A minority of one against a unanimous majority. *Psychological Monographs, 70,* 416.

Astington, J. W. (1993). *The child's discovery of the mind.* Cambridge, MA: Harvard University Press.

Atkinson, J. W. (Ed.). (1958). *Motives in fantasy, action, and society.* Princeton, NJ: D. Van Nostrand.

Atkinson, R. C., & Shiffrin, R. M. (1968). Human memory: A proposed system and its control processes. In K. W. Spence & J. T. Spence (Eds.), *The psychology of learning and motivation: Advances in research and theory* (Vol. 2). New York: Academic Press.

Atkinson, R. C., & Shiffrin, R. M. (1971). The control of short-term memory. *Scientific American, 225,* 82–90.

Atkinson, R. L., Atkinson, R. C., Smith, E. E., & Bem, D. J. (1993). *Introduction to psychology* (11th ed.). Fort Worth, TX: Harcourt Brace Jovanovich.

Auerbach, S. M., Martelli, M. F., & Mercuri, L. G. (1983). Anxiety, information, interpersonal impacts, and adjustment to a stressful health care situation. *Journal of Personality and Social Psychology, 44,* 1284–1296.

Averill, J. R. (1980). A constructionist view of emotion. In R. Plutchik & H. Kellerman (Eds.), *Emotion: Theory, research, and experience: Vol. 1. Theories of emotion* (pp. 305–339). New York: Academic Press.

Averill, J. R. (1983). Studies on anger and aggression: Implications for theories of emotions? *American Psychologist, 38,* 1145–1160.

Averill, J. R. (1993). Putting the social in social cognition, with special reference to emotion. In R. S. Wyer & T. K. Srull (Eds.), *Toward a general theory of anger and emotional aggression: Vol. 6. Advances in social cognition.* Hillsdale, NJ: Erlbaum.

Axelson, J. A. (1993). *Counseling and development in a multicultural society* (2nd ed.). Pacific Grove, CA: Brooks/Cole.

Ayres, J. J. B., Haddad, C. L., & Albert, M. (1987). One-trial excitatory backward conditioning as assessed by suppression of licking in rats: Concurrent observations of lick suppression and defensive behaviors. *Animal Learning & Behavior, 15,* 212–217.

Azrin, N. H. (1967, May). Pain and aggression. *Psychology Today,* pp. 27–33.

Azuma, H. (1986). Why study child development in Japan? In H. Stevenson, H. Azuma, & K. Hakuta (Eds.), *Child development and education in Japan* (pp. 3–12). New York: Freeman.

Bacal, H. A., & Newman, K. M. (1990). *Theories of object relations: Bridges to self psychology.* New York: Columbia University Press.

Baddeley, A. D. (1966). Short-term memory for word sequences as function of acoustic, semantic, and formal similarity. *Quarterly Journal of Experimental Psychology, 18,* 362–365.

Baddeley, A. D. (1989). The psychology of remembering and forgetting. In T. Butler (Ed.), *Memory: History, culture and the mind.* London: Basil Blackwell.

Baddeley, A. D. (1990a). *Human memory*. Hove, England: Erlbaum.

Baddeley, A. D. (1990b). *Human memory: Theory and practice*. Needham Heights, MA: Allyn & Bacon.

Baddeley, A. D. (1992). Working memory. *Science, 255,* 356–559.

Baddeley, A., & Hitch, G. J. (1994). Developments in the concept of working memory. *Neuropsychology, 8,* 485–493.

Bahrick, H. P., Bahrick, P. O., & Wittlinger, R. P. (1975). Fifty years of memory for names and faces: A cross-sectional approach. *Journal of Experimental Psychology: General, 104,* 54–75.

Bahrick, H. P., & Phelps, E. (1987). Retention of Spanish vocabulary over eight years. *Journal of Experimental Psychology: Learning Memory and Cognition, 13,* 344–349.

Bailey, C. (1991). *The new fit or fat* (Rev. ed.). Boston: Houghton Mifflin.

Bailey, C. H., Alberini, C., Ghirardi, M., & Kandel, E. R. (1994). Molecular and structural changes underlying long-term memory storage in Aplysia. *Advances in Second Messenger and Phosphoprotein Research, 29,* 529–544.

Bailey, J. M., & Pillard, R. C. (1991). A genetic study of male sexual orientation. *Archives of General Psychiatry, 48*(N12), 1089–1096.

Baillargeon, R. (1987). Object permanence in 3½- and 4½-month-old infants. *Developmental Psychology, 23,* 655–664.

Baillargeon, R. & DeVos, J. (1991). Object permanence in young infants: Further evidence. *Child Development, 62,* 1227–1246.

Bales, R. F. (1950). *Interaction process analysis: A method for the study of small groups*. Reading, MA: Addison-Wesley.

Bales, R. F. (1958). Task roles and social roles in problem-solving groups. In E. E. Maccoby, T. M. Newcomb, & E. L. Hartley (Eds.), *Readings in social psychology*. New York: Holt, Rinehart & Winston.

Bales, R. F. (1970). *Personality and interpersonal behavior*. New York: Holt, Rinehart & Winston.

Balkin, J. (1988). Why policemen don't like policewomen. *Journal of Police Science and Administration, 16*(1), 29–38.

Balsam, P. D., & Tomie, A. (Eds.). (1985). *Context and learning*. Hillsdale, NJ: Erlbaum.

Baltes, P. B. (1997). On the incomplete architecture of human ontogeny: Selection, optimization, and compensation as foundations of developmental theory. *American Psychologist, 52,* 366–380.

Baltes, P. B., & Smith, J. (1990). Toward a psychology of wisdom and its ontogenesis. In R. J. Sternberg (Ed.), *Wisdom: Its nature, origins, and development* (pp. 87–120). New York: Cambridge University Press.

Baltes, P. B., & Staudinger, J. (in press). *Wisdom: The orchestration of mind and virtue*. Boston: Blackwell.

Baltes, P. B., & Willis, S. L. (1979). Toward psychological theories of aging and development. In J. E. Birren & K. W. Schaie (Eds.), *Handbook of the psychology of aging*. New York: Van Nostrand Reinhold.

Bandura, A. (1965). Influence of models' reinforcement contingencies on the acquisition of imitative responses. *Journal of Personality and Social Psychology, 1,* 589–595.

Bandura, A. (1969). *Principles of behavior modification*. New York: Holt, Rinehart & Winston.

Bandura, A. (1973). *Aggression: A social learning analysis*. Englewood Cliffs, NJ: Prentice-Hall.

Bandura, A. (1977a). Self-efficacy: Toward a unifying theory of behavioral change. *Psychological Review, 84,* 181–215.

Bandura, A. (1977b). *Social learning theory*. Englewood Cliffs, NJ: Prentice-Hall.

Bandura, A. (1983). Psychological mechanisms of aggression. In R. G. Geen & E. I. Donnerstein (Eds.), *Aggression: Theoretical and empirical reviews: Vol. 1. Theoretical and methodological issues* (pp. 1–40). New York: Academic Press.

Bandura, A. (1986). *Social foundations of thought and action: A social cognitive theory*. Englewood Cliffs, NJ: Prentice-Hall.

Bandura, A. (1988). Self-efficacy conception of anxiety. *Anxiety Research, 1*(2), 77–98.

Bandura, A. (1995). *Self-efficacy in changing societies*. New York: Cambridge University Press.

Bandura, A. (1996). *Self-efficacy: The exercise of control*. New York: Freeman.

Bandura, A., Blanchard, E. B., & Ritter, B. (1969). Relative efficacy of desensitization and modelling approaches for inducing behavioral, affective, and attitudinal changes. *Journal of Personality and Social Psychology, 13,* 173–199.

Bandura, A., & Rosenthal, T. (1966). Vicarious classical conditioning as a function of arousal level. *Journal of Personality and Social Psychology, 3,* 54–62.

Bandura, A., Ross, D., & Ross, S. (1961). Transmission of aggression through imitation of aggressive models. *Journal of Abnormal and Social Psychology, 63,* 575–582.

Bandura, A., Ross, D., & Ross, S. (1963). Imitation of film-mediated aggressive models. *Journal of Abnormal and Social Psychology, 66,* 3–11.

Bandura, A., & Walters, R. H. (1963). *Social learning and personality development*. New York: Ronald Press.

Banks, M. S., & Salapatek, P. (1983). Infant visual perception. In M. M. Haith & J. J. Campos (Eds.), *Handbook of child psychology: Infancy and developmental psychobiology* (4th ed., Vol. 2). New York: Wiley.

Bao, J. X., Kandel, E. R., & Hawkins, R. D. (1998). Involvement of presynaptic and postsynaptic mechanisms in a cellular analog of classical conditioning at Aplysia sensory-motor neuron synapses in isolated cell culture. *Journal of Neuroscience, 18,* 458–466.

Barber, T. X. (1964a). Hypnotic "colorblindness," "blindness," and "deafness." *Diseases of the Nervous System, 25,* 529–537.

Barber, T. X. (1964b). Toward a theory of "hypnotic" behavior: Positive visual and auditory hallucinations. *Psychological Record, 14,* 197–210.

Barber, T. X. (1979). Suggested ("hypnotic") behavior: The trance paradigm versus an alternative paradigm. In E. Fromm, & R. E. Shor (Eds.), *Hypnosis: Developments in research and new perspectives*. New York: Aldine.

Barber, T. X. (1986). Realities of stage hypnosis. In B. Zilbergeld, M. G. Edelstein, & D. L. Araoz (Eds.), *Hypnosis: Questions and answers*. New York: Norton.

Bard, P. (1934). On emotional experience after decortication with some remarks on theoretical views. *Psychological Review, 41,* 309–329.

Barefoot, J. C., Dahlstrom, W. G., & Williams, R. B. (1983). Hostility, CHD incidence and total mortality: A 25-year follow-up study of 255 physicians. *Psychosomatic Medicine, 45,* 559–563.

Barefoot, J. C., Dodge, K. A., Peterson, B. L., Dahlstrom, W. G., & Williams, R. B. (1989). The Cook-Medley hostility scale: Item content and ability to predict survival. *Psychosomatic Medicine, 51,* 46–57.

Bargh, J. A. (1997). The automaticity of everyday life. In R. S. Wyer (Ed.), *The automaticity of everyday life: Advances in social cognition* (Vol. 10, pp. 1–61). Mahwah, NJ: Erlbaum.

Barker, R. G., Dembo, T., & Lewin, K. (1941). Frustration and regression: An experiment with young children. *University of Iowa Studies in Child Welfare, 18*(1).

Barlow, D. H. (1988). *Anxiety and its disorders*. New York: Guilford Press.

Barnes, M. L., & Sternberg, R. J. (1997). A hierarchical model of love and its prediction of satisfaction in close relationships. In R. J. Sternberg & M. Hojjat (Eds.), *Satisfaction in close relationships*. New York: Guilford Press.

Baron, M., Gershon, E. S., Rudy, V., Jonas, W. Z., & Buchsbaum, M. (1975). Lithium carbonate response in depression. *Archives of General Psychiatry, 32,* 1107–1111.

Baron, R. A. (1976). The reduction of human aggression: A field study of the influence of incompatible reactions. *Journal of Applied Social Psychology, 6,* 260–274.

Baron, R. A. (1977). *Human aggression.* New York: Plenum.

Baron, R. A., & Bell, P. A. (1975). Aggression and heat: Mediating effects of prior provocation and exposure to an aggressive model. *Journal of Personality and Social Psychology, 31,* 825–832.

Baron, R. A., & Byrne, D. (1991). *Social psychology: Understanding human interaction* (6th ed.). Boston: Allyn & Bacon.

Baron, R. A., & Richardson, D. R. (1992). *Human aggression* (2nd ed.). New York: Plenum.

Baron, R. S. (1986). Distraction-conflict theory: Progress and problems. In L. Berkowitz (Ed.), *Advances in experimental social psychology.* Orlando, FL: Academic Press.

Baron, R. S., Moore, D., & Sanders, G. S. (1978). Distraction as a source of drive social facilitation. *Journal of Personality and Social Psychology, 36,* 816–824.

Barr, C. E., Mednick, S. A., & Munk-Jorgensen, P. (1990). Exposure to influenza epidemics during gestation and adult schizophrenia: A 40-year study. *Archives of General Psychiatry, 47,* 869–874.

Barrett, P. T., & Eysenck, H. J. (1992). Brain evoked potentials and intelligence: The Hendrickson paradigm. *Intelligence, 16*(3–4), 361–381.

Barron, F. (1988). Putting creativity to work. In R. J. Sternberg (Ed.), *The nature of creativity* (pp. 76–98). New York: Cambridge University Press.

Bartlett, F. C. (1932). *Remembering: A study in experimental and social psychology.* Cambridge, England: Cambridge University Press.

Bartoshuk, L. M. (1988). Taste. In R. C. Atkinson, R. J. Herrnstein, G. Lindzey, & R. D. Luce (Eds.), *Stevens handbook of experimental psychology: Perception and motivation* (Vol. 1). New York: Wiley.

Bartoshuk, L. M. (1993). The biological basis of food perception and acceptance. *Food Quality and Preference, 4,* 21–32.

Bashore, T. R., Osman, A., & Hefley, E. F. (1989). Mental slowing in elderly persons: A cognitive psychophysiological analysis. *Psychology and Aging, 4,* 235–244.

Bashore, T. R., & Rapp, P. E. (1993). Are there alternatives to traditional polygraph procedures? *Psychological Bulletin, 113*(1), 3–22.

Basoglu, M. (1997). Torture as a stressful life event: A review of the current status of knowledge. In T. W. Miller (Ed.), *Clinical disorders and stressful life events* (pp. 45–70). Madison, CT: International Universities Press.

Basoglu, M., Paker, O., Pozmen, E., Marks, I., Sahin, D., & Sarimurat, N. (1994). Psychological effects of torture: A comparison of tortured with nontortured political activists in Turkey. *American Journal of Psychiatry, 11,* 6–81.

Basow, S. A. (1986). *Gender stereotypes: Traditions and alternatives* (2nd ed.). Belmont, CA: Brooks/Cole.

Basseches, M. (1984). *Dialectical thinking and adult development.* Norwood, NJ: Ablex.

Bassok, M., Wu, L., & Olseth, K. L. (1995). Judging a book by its cover: Interpretive effects of content on problem-solving transfer. *Memory and Cognition, 23,* 354–367.

Bastik, T. (1982). *Intuition: How we think and act.* Chichester, England: Wiley.

Bateson, G., Jackson, D. D., Haley, J., & Weakland, J. (1956). Toward a theory of schizophrenia. *Behavioral Science, 1,* 251–264.

Batson, C. D. (1990). How social an animal? The human capacity for caring. *American Psychologist, 45,* 336–346.

Batson, C. D. (1997). Self-other merging and the empathy-altruism hypothesis: Reply to Neuberg et al. (1997). *Journal of Personality and Social Psychology, 73,* 517–522.

Batson, C. D., Batson, J. G., Griffitt, C. A., Barrientos, S., Brandt, J. R., Sprengelmeyer, P., & Bayly, M. J. (1989). Negative-state relief and the empathy–altruism hypothesis. *Journal of Personality and Social Psychology, 56,* 922–933.

Batson, C. D., Duncan, B. D., Ackerman, P., Buckley, T., & Birch, K. (1981). Is empathic emotion a source of altruistic motivation? *Journal of Personality and Social Psychology, 40,* 290–302.

Batson, C. D., Dyck, J. L., Brandt, J. R., Batson, J. G., Powell, A. L., McMaster, R. M., & Griffit, C. A. (1988). Five studies testing two new egoistic alternatives to the empathy-altruism hypothesis. *Journal of Personality and Social Psychology, 55,* 52–77.

Baumeister, R. F. (1982). A self-presentational view of social phenomena. *Psychological Bulletin, 91,* 3–26.

Baumeister, R. F., & Tice, D. M. (1984). Role of self-presentation and choice in cognitive dissonance under forced compliance: Necessary or sufficient causes? *Journal of Personality and Social Psychology, 46,* 5–13.

Baumrind, D. (1971). Current patterns of parental authority. *Developmental Psychology Monograph, 4*(1, Pt. 2), 79–103.

Baumrind, D. (1978). Parental disciplinary patterns and social competence in children. *Youth and Society, 9,* 239–276.

Baumrind, D. (1986). Sex differences in moral reasoning: Response to Walker's (1984) conclusion that there are none. *Child Development, 57,* 511–521.

Baumrind, D. (1991. Effective parenting during the early adolescent transition. In P. A. Cowan & E. M. Hetherington (Eds.), *Family transitions* (pp. 111–164). Hillsdale, NJ: Erlbaum.

Baxter, L. R., Phelps, M. E., Mazziotta, J. C., Schwartz, J. M., Gerner, R. H., Selin, C. E., & Sumida, R. M. (1985). Cerebral metabolic rates for glucose in mood disorders. *Archives of General Psychiatry, 42,* 441–447.

Bayley, N. (1968). Behavioral correlates of mental growth: Birth to thirty-six years. *American Psychologist, 23,* 1–17.

Bayley, N. (1993). *The Bayley Scales of Mental and Motor Development (Revised).* New York: Psychological Corporation.

Bayley, N., & Oden, M. H. (1955). The maintenance of intellectual ability in gifted adults. *Journal of Gerontology, 10,* 91–107.

Beall, A., & Sternberg, R. J. (Eds.). (1993). *Perspectives on the psychology of gender.* New York: Guilford Press.

Beall, A., & Sternberg, R. J. (1995). The social construction of love. *Journal of Personal and Social Relationships, 2*(3), 417–438.

Beck, A. T. (1967). *Depression: Causes and treatment.* Philadelphia: University of Pennsylvania Press.

Beck, A. T. (1976). *Cognitive therapy and the emotional disorders.* New York: International Universities Press.

Beck, A. T. (1985). Theoretical perspectives on clinical anxiety. In A. H. Tuma & J. D. Maser (Eds.), *Anxiety and the anxiety disorder* (pp. 183–198). Hillsdale, NJ: Erlbaum.

Beck, A. T. (1986). Cognitive therapy: A sign of retrogression of progress. *The Behavior Therapist, 9,* 2–3.

Beck, A. T. (1988). Cognitive approaches to panic disorder: Theory and therapy. In S. Rachman & J. D. Maser (Eds.), *Panic: Psychological perspectives.* Hillsdale, NJ: Erlbaum.

Beck, A. T. (1991). Cognitive therapy: A thirty-year retrospective. *American Psychologist, 46,* 368–375.

Beck, A. T. (1997). Interview. *Cognitive Therapy Today, 2,* 1–3.

Beck, A. T., & Emery, G., (with) Greenberg, R. L. (1985). *Anxiety disorders and phobias: A cognitive perspective.* New York: Basic Books.

Beck, A. T., & Ward, C. H. (1961). Dreams of depressed patients: Characteristic themes in manifest content. *Archives of General Psychiatry, 5,* 462–467.

Beeri, R., Le Novere, N., Mervis, R., Huberman, T., Grauer, E., Changeux, J. P., & Soreq, H. (1997). Enhanced hemicholinium binding and attenuated dendrite branching in cognitively impaired acetylcholinesterase-transgenic mice. *Journal of Neurochemistry, 69,* 2441–2451.

Beilin, H. (1971). The training and acquisition of logical operation. In M. Rosskopf, L. Steffe, & S. Taback (Eds.), *Piagetian cognitive development research and mathematical education.* Washington, DC: National Council of Teachers of Mathematics.

Bekerian, D. A. (1993). In search of the typical eyewitness. *American Psychologist, 48*(5), 574–576.

Békésy, G. von. (1960). *Experiments in hearing.* New York: McGraw-Hill.

Bell, P. A., & Baron, R. A. (1976). Aggression and heat: The mediating role of negative affect. *Journal of Applied Social Psychology, 6,* 18–30.

Belloc, N. D., & Breslow, L. (1972). Relationship of physical health status and family practices. *Preventive Medicine, 1,* 409–421.

Bellugi, U., Poizner, H., & Klima, E. S. (1989). Language, modality and the brain. *Trends in Neuroscience, 12*(10), 380–388.

Belmont, J. M., & Butterfield, E. C. (1971). Learning strategies as determinants of memory deficiencies. *Cognitive Psychology, 2,* 411–420.

Belsky, J. (1990). Parental and nonparental child care and children's socioemotional development: A decade in review. *Journal of Marriage and the Family, 52,* 885–903.

Belsky, J., & Rovine, M. (1988). Nonmaternal care in the first year of life and the security of infant–parent attachment. *Child Development, 59,* 157–167.

Bem, D., & Honorton, C. (1994). Does psi exist? Replicable evidence for an anomalous process of information transfer. *Psychological Bulletin, 115,* 4–18.

Bem, D. J. (1967). Self-perception: An alternative interpretation of cognitive dissonance phenomena. *Psychological Review, 74,* 183–200.

Bem, D. J. (1972). Self-perception theory. In L. Berkowitz (Ed.), *Advances in experimental social psychology* (Vol. 6). New York: Academic Press.

Bem, D. J. (1996). Exotic becomes erotic: A developmental theory of sexual orientation. *Psychological Review, 103,* 320–323.

Bem, D. J., & Allen, A. (1974). On predicting some of the people some of the time: The search for cross-situational consistencies in behavior. *Psychological Review, 81,* 506–520.

Bem, D. J., & Funder, D. C. (1978). Predicting more of the people more of the time: Assessing the personality of situations. *Psychological Review, 85,* 485–501.

Bem, S. (1993). *The lenses of gender: Transforming the debate on sexual inequality.* New Haven, CT: Yale University Press.

Bem, S. L. (1981). Gender schema theory: A cognitive account of sex typing. *Psychological Review, 88,* 354–364.

Benbow, C. P., & Stanley, J. C. (1980). Sex differences in mathematical ability: Fact or artifact? *Science, 210,* 1262–1264.

Ben-Shakhar, G., & Furedy, J. J. (1990). *Theories and applications in the detection of deception: A psychophysiological and international perspective.* New York: Springer-Verlag.

Benjamin, Jr., L. T. (1986). Why don't they understand us? A history of psychology's public image. *American Psychologist, 41,* 941–946.

Benjamin, Jr., L. T. (1988). A history of teaching machines. *American Psychologist, 43,* 703–712.

Benjamin, Jr., L. T., & Bryant, W. H. M. (1997). A history of popular psychology magazines in America. In W. G. Bringmann, H. E. Luck, R. Miller, & C. E. Early (Eds.), *A pictorial history of psychology* (pp. 585–593). Carol Stream, IL: Quintessence.

Benjamin, Jr., L. T., Bryant, W. H. M., Campbell, C., Luttrell, J., & Holtz, C. (1997). Between psoriasis and ptarmigan: American encyclopedias portray psychology, 1880–1940. *Review of General Psychology, 1,* 5–18.

Bennett, M. (1999). Introduction. In M. Bennett (Ed.), *Developmental psychology* (pp. 1–12). Philadelphia: Psychology Press.

Bennett, M. J. (1996). Is psychotherapy ever medically necessary? *Psychiatric Services, 47,* 966–970.

Benotsch, E. G., Christensen, A. J., & McKelvey, L. (1997). Hostility, social support, and ambulatory cardiovascular activity. *Journal of Behavioral Medicine, 20,* 163–182.

Benson, A. J. (1984). *Motion sickness.* In M. R. Dix, & J. D. Hood, (Eds.), *Vertigo.* New York: John Wiley & Sons, Ltd.

Benson, H. (1977). Systemic hypertension and the relaxation response. *New England Journal of Medicine, 296,* 1152–1156.

Bereiter, C., & Scardamalia, M. (1993). *Surpassing ourselves: An inquiry into the nature and implications of expertise.* Chicago: Open Court.

Berg, C. A., & Sternberg, R. J. (1992). Adults' conceptions of intelligence across the adult life span. *Psychology and Aging, 7*(2), 221–231.

Berger, K. S. (1980). *The developing person.* New York: Worth.

Berglas, S., & Jones, E. E. (1978). Drug choice as a self-handicapping strategy in response to noncontingent success. *Journal of Personality and Social Psychology, 36,* 405–417.

Bergman, E. T., & Roediger, H. L. (1999). Can Bartlett's repeated reproduction experiments be replicated? *Memory and Cognition, 27,* 937–947.

Berkman, L. (1994, May 22). "I really was hurt by the verdict." (Holly Ramona says jury's decision will undermine her attempt to recover damages from her father, Gary Ramona, who she alleges molested her.) *Los Angeles Times,* p. A3.

Berkowitz, L. (1972). Social norms, feelings, and other factors affecting helping and altruism. In L. Berkowitz (Ed.), *Advances in experimental social psychology* (Vol. 6, pp. 63–108). New York: Academic Press.

Berkowitz, L. (1993). *Aggression: Its causes, consequences, and control.* New York: McGraw-Hill.

Berkowitz, L. (1994). On the escalation of aggression. In M. Potegal & J. F. Knutson (Eds.), *The dynamics of aggression: Biological and social processes in dyads and groups* (pp. 33–41). Hillsdale, NJ: Erlbaum.

Berkowitz, L., Cochran, S., & Embree, M. (1981). Physical pain and the goal of aversively stimulated aggression. *Journal of Personality and Social Psychology, 40,* 687–700.

Berlin, B., & Kay, P. (1969). *Basic color terms: Their universality and evolution.* Los Angeles: University of California Press.

Berlyne, D. E. (1960). *Conflict, arousal, and curiosity.* New York: McGraw-Hill.

Berlyne, D. E. (1967). Arousal reinforcement. In D. Levine (Ed.), *Nebraska symposium on motivation* (pp. 1–110). Lincoln: University of Nebraska Press.

Berman, K. F., Torrey, E. F., Daniel, D. G., & Weinberger, D. R. (1992). Regional cerebral blood flow in monozygotic twins discordant and concordant for schizophrenia. *Archives for General Psychiatry, 49,* 927–934.

Berman, M., Gladue, B., & Taylor, S. (1993). The effects of hormones, Type A behavior pattern, and provocation on aggression in men. *Motivation and Emotion, 17,* 125–148.

Bernard, L. L. (1924). *Instinct.* New York: Holt, Rinehart & Winston.

Berndt, T. J. (1982). The features and effects of friendship in early adolescence. *Child Development, 53*(6), 1447–1460.

Berndt, T. J. (1986). Children's comments about their friendships. In M. Perlmutter (Ed.), *Cognitive perspectives on children's social and behavioral development: The Minnesota symposia on child psychology* (Vol. 18, pp. 189–212). Hillsdale, NJ: Erlbaum.

Berry, J. W. (1974). Radical cultural relativism and the concept of intelligence. In J. W. Berry & P. R. Dasen (Eds.), *Culture and cognition: Readings in cross-cultural psychology* (pp. 225–229). London: Methuen.

Berry, J. W. (1976). *Human ecology and cognitive style: Comparative studies in cultural and psychological adaptation.* New York: Sage/Halsted.

Berry, J. W. (1989). Psychology of acculturation. In J. Berman (Ed.), *Nebraska symposium on motivation* (Vol. 37, pp. 201–234). Lincoln, NE: University of Nebraska Press.

Berry, J. W. (1994). Acculturative stress. In W. J. Lonner & R. W. Malpass (Eds.), *Psychology and culture.* Boston: Allyn & Bacon.

Berry, J. W., Kim, U., Minde, T., & Mok, D. (1987). Comparative studies of acculturative stress. *International Migration Review, 21,* 491–511.

Berry, J. W., Poortinga, Y. H., Segall, M. H., & Dasen, P. R. (1992). *Cross-cultural psychology: Research and applications.* New York: Cambridge University Press.

Berry, S. L., Beatty, W. W., & Klesges, R. C. (1985). Sensory and social influences on ice cream consumption by males and females in a laboratory setting. *Appetite, 6,* 41–45.

Berscheid, E. (1999). Personal communication.

Berscheid, E., & Reis, H. T. (1998). Attraction and close relationships. In D. Gilbert, S. Fiske, & G. Lindzey (Eds.), *Handbook of social psychology* (4th ed.). New York: McGraw-Hill.

Berscheid, E., & Reis, N. (1997). Attraction and close relationships. In *Handbook of social psychology* (4th ed.). New York: McGraw-Hill.

Berscheid, E., & Walster, E. (1974). A little bit about love. In T. L. Huston (Ed.), *Foundations of interpersonal attraction.* New York: Academic Press.

Bersoff, D. M., & Miller, J. (1993). Culture, context, and the development of moral accountability judgments. *Developmental Psychology, 29,* 664–676.

Bertenthal, B. I., & Fischer, K. W. (1978). Development of self-recognition in the infant. *Developmental Psychology, 14,* 44–50.

Bertilsson, L. (1978). Mechanism of action of benzodiazepines: The GABA hypothesis. *Acta Psychiatrica Scandinavica, 274,* 19–26.

Bertoncini, J. (1993). Infants' perception of speech units: Primary representation capacities. In B. B. De Boysson-Bardies, S. De-Schonen, P. Jusczyk, P. MacNeilage, & J. Morton (Eds.), *Developmental neurocognition: Speech and face processing in the first year of life.* Dordrecht: Kluwer.

Beutler, L. E., Kim, E. J., Davison, E., Karno, M., & Fisher, D. (1996). Research contributions to improving managed health care outcomes. *Psychotherapy, 33,* 197–206.

Bexton, W. H., Heron, W., & Scott, T. H. (1954). Effects of decreased variation in the sensory environment. *Canadian Journal of Psychology, 8,* 70–76.

Bezooijen, R. V., Otto, S. A., & Heenan, T. A. (1983). Recognition of vocal expressions of emotion: A three nation study to identify universal characteristics. *Journal of Cross-Cultural Psychology, 14,* 387–406.

Bialystok, E., & Hakuta, K. (1994). *In other words: The science and psychology of second-language acquisition.* New York: Basic Books.

Bianchin, M., Mello E., Souza, T., Medina, J. H., & Izquierdo, I. The amygdala is involved in the modulation of long-term memory, but not in working or short-term memory. *Neurobiology of Learning & Memory, 71,* 127–131.

Bickman, L. (1996). A continuum of care: More is not always better. *American Psychologist, 51.*

Bickman, L., Guthrie, P. R., Foster, E. M., Lambert, E. W., Summerfelt, W. T., Breda, C. S., & Heflinger, C. A. (1995). *Evaluating managed mental health services: The Fort Bragg Experiment.* New York: Plenum.

Bidell, T. R., & Fischer, K. W. (1992). Beyond the stage debate: Action, structure, and variability in Piagetian theory and research. In R. J. Sternberg & C. A. Berg (Eds.), *Intellectual development* (pp. 100–140). New York: Cambridge University Press.

Biederman, I. (1987). Recognition-by-components: A theory of human image understanding. *Psychological Review, 94,* 115–147.

Biery, R. E. (1990). *Understanding homosexuality: The pride and the prejudice.* Austin, TX: Edward-William.

Billings, A. G., Cronkite, R. C., & Moos, R. H. (1983). Social-environmental factors in unipolar depression: Comparisons of depressed patients and nondepressed controls. *Journal of Abnormal Psychology, 92,* 119–133.

Binet, A., & Simon, T. (1916). *The development of intelligence in children* (E. S. Kite, Trans.). Baltimore: Williams & Wilkins.

Bingham, C. R., Bennion, L. D., Oppenshaw, D. K., & Adams, G. R. (1994). An analysis of age, gender, and racial differences in recent national trends of youth suicide. *Journal of Adolescence, 17,* 53–71.

Birenbaum, M., and Kraemer, R. (1995). Gender and ethnic group differences in causal attributions for success and failure in mathematics and language examinations. *Journal of Cross-Cultural Psychology, 26*(4), 342–359.

Bisanz, J., Bisanz, G. L., & Korpan, C. A. (1994). Inductive reasoning. In R. J. Sternberg (Ed.), *Thinking and problem solving* (pp. 181–213). San Diego: Academic Press.

Blackmore, S. J. (1993). *Dying to live: Science and the near-death experience.* London: Grafton.

Blakeslee, A. F., & Salmon, T. H. (1935). Genetics of sensory thresholds: Individual taste reactions for different substances. *Proceedings of the National Academy of Sciences of the U. S. A., 21,* 84–90.

Blasi, A. (1980). Bridging moral cognition and moral action: A critical review of the literature. *Psychological Bulletin, 88,* 1–45.

Blass, E. M. (1990). Suckling: Determinants, changes, mechanisms, and lasting impressions. *Developmental Psychology, 26,* 520–533.

Bliss, E. L. (1980). Multiple personality. *Archives of General Psychiatry, 37,* 1388–1397.

Block, J. H. (1980). From infancy to adulthood: A clarification. *Child Development, 51*(2), 622–623.

Block, J. (1981). Some enduring and consequential structures of personality. In A. I. Rabin, J. Arnoff, A. M. Barclay, & R. A. Zucker (Eds.), *Further explorations in personality.* New York: Wiley.

Block, J. (1983). Differential premises arising from differential socialization of the sexes: Some conjectures. *Child Development, 54,* 1335–1354.

Block, J. (1995). A contrarian view of the five-factor approach to personality description. *Psychological Bulletin, 117,* 187–215.

Bloom, B. S. (1964). *Stability and change in human characteristics.* New York: Wiley.

Bloom, B. S., & Broder, L. J. (1950). *Problem-solving processes of college students.* Chicago: University of Chicago Press.

Blumenthal, J. A., Emery, C. F., Walsh, M. A., Cox, D. R., Kuhn, C. M., Williams, R. B., & Williams, R. S. (1988). Exercise training in healthy Type A middle-aged men: Effects to behavioral and cardiovascular responses. *Psychosomatic Medicine, 50,* 418–433.

Bock, K. (1990). Structure in language: Creating form in talk. *American Psychologist, 45,* 1221–1236.

Bolger, N. (1990). Coping as a personality process: A prospective study. *Journal of Personality and Social Psychology, 59*(3), 531.

Boll, T. J. (1978). Diagnosing brain impairment. In B. B. Wolman (Ed.), *Clinical diagnosis of mental disorders: A handbook.* New York: Plenum.

Bolwig, T. G. (1993). Biological treatments other than drugs (electroconvulsive therapy, brain surgery, insulin therapy, and photo therapy). In N. Sartorius, G. de Girolano, G. Andrews, G. A. German, & L. Eisenberg (Eds.), *Treatment of mental disorders: A review of effectiveness.* Geneva, Switzerland, and Washington, DC: World Health Organization and American Psychiatric Press.

Bond, C. F., & Titus, L. J. (1983). Social facilitation: A meta-analysis of 241 studies. *Psychological Bulletin, 94,* 265–292.

Bond, M. H. (1986). *The psychology of the Chinese people.* Hong Kong: Oxford University Press.

Bond, M. H. (Ed.). (1988). *Cross-cultural research and methodology series: Vol. 11. The cross-cultural challenge to social psychology.* Newbury Park, CA: Sage.

Bond, M. R. (1979). *Pain: Its nature, analysis and treatment.* New York: Longman.

Bongiovanni, A. (1977). *A review of research on the effects of punishment in the schools.* Paper presented at the Conference on Child Abuse, Children's Hospital National Medical Center, Washington, DC.

Boon, S., & Draijer, N. (1993). Multiple personality disorder in The Netherlands: A clinical investigation of 71 patients. *American Journal of Psychiatry, 150,* 489–494.

Booth-Kewley, S., & Friedman, H. S. (1987). Psychological predictors of heart disease: A quantitative review. *Psychological Bulletin, 101,* 343–362.

Bootzin, R. R., Manger, R., Perlis, M. L., Salvio, M. A., & Wyatt, J. K. (1993). Sleep disorders. In P. B. Sutker & H. E. Adams (Eds.), *Comprehensive handbook of psychopathology* (2nd ed.). New York: Plenum.

Borbely, A. (1986). *Secrets of sleep.* New York: Basic Books.

Borden, R. J., Bowen, R., & Taylor, S. P. (1971). School setting as a function of physical attack and extrinsic reward. *Perceptual and Motor Skills, 33,* 563–568.

Bornstein, M. H. (1989). Information processing (habituation) in infancy and stability in cognitive development. *Human Development, 32*(3–4), 129–136.

Bornstein, M. H. (1999). Human infancy: Past, present, and future. In M. Bennett (Ed.), *Developmental psychology* (pp. 35). Philadelphia: Psychology Press.

Bornstein, M. H., & Sigman, M. D. (1986). Continuity in mental development from infancy. *Child Development, 57,* 251–274.

Bornstein, P. E., Clayton, P. J., Halikas, J. A., Maurice, W. L., & Robins, E. (1973). The depression of widowhood after thirteen months. *British Journal of Psychiatry, 122,* 561–566.

Bothwell, R. K., Brigham, J. C., & Malpass, R. S. (1989). Cross-racial identification. *Personality & Social Psychology Bulletin, 15,* 19–25.

Bouchard, T. J. (1997). IQ similarity in twins reared apart: Findings and responses to critics. In R. J. Sternberg & E. L. Grigorenko (Eds.), *Intelligence, heredity, and environment* (pp. 126–160). New York: Cambridge University Press.

Bouchard, T. J., Lykken, D. T., McGue, M., Segal, N. L., & Tellegen, A. (1990). Sources of human psychological differences. The Minnesota study of twins reared apart. *Science, 250,* 223–228.

Bouchard, T. J., & McGue, M. (1981). Familial studies of intelligence: A review. *Science, 212,* 1055–1059.

Bousfield, W. A. (1953). The occurrence of clustering in the recall of randomly arranged associates. *Journal of General Psychology, 49,* 229–240.

Bouton, M. E. (1991). Context and retrieval in extinction and in other examples of interference in simple associative learning. In L. Dachowski & C. F. Flaherty (Eds.), *Current topics in animal learning* (pp. 25–53). Hillsdale, NJ: Erlbaum.

Bouton, M. E. (1993). Context, time, and memory retrieval in the interference paradigms of Pavlovian learning. *Psychological Bulletin, 114,* 80–99.

Bowden, C. L. (1993). The clinical approach to the differential diagnosis of bipolar disorder. *Psychiatric Annals, 23,* 57–63.

Bower, B. (1993). A child's theory of mind. *Science News, 144,* 40–42.

Bower, G. H. (1981, February). Mood and memory. *American Psychologist, 36*(2), 129–148.

Bower, G. H. (1983). Affect and cognition. *Philosophical Transaction: Royal Society of London 302,* (Series B), 387–402.

Bower, G. H., Black, J. B., & Turner, T. J. (1979). Scripts in memory for texts. *Cognitive Psychology, 11,* 177–220.

Bower, G. H., Clark, M. C., Lesgold, A. M., & Winzenz, D. (1969). Hierarchical retrieval schemes in recall of categorized word lists. *Journal of Verbal Learning and Verbal Behavior, 8,* 323–343.

Bower, G. H., Karlin, M. B., & Dueck, A. (1975). Comprehension and memory for pictures. *Memory and Cognition, 3,* 216–220.

Bower, T. G. R. (1971, October). The object in the world of the infant. In *Scientific American: Mind and Behavior.* San Francisco: Freeman.

Bower, T. G. R. (1989). *The rational infant: Learning in infancy.* New York: Freeman.

Bowers, K. S. (1973). Situationism in psychology: An analysis and critique. *Psychological Review, 80,* 307–336.

Bowers, K. S. (1976). *Hypnosis for the seriously curious.* New York: Norton.

Bowers, K. S., & Farvolden, P. (1996). Revisiting a century-old Freudian slip: From suggestion disavowed to the truth repressed. *Psychological Bulletin, 119,* 355–380.

Bowlby, J. (1951). *Maternal care and mental health* (World Health Organization Monograph Series No. 2). Schocken Books, 1966. Geneva, Switzerland: World Health Organization.

Bowlby, J. (1958). The nature of the child's tie to his mother. *International Journal of Psycho-Analysis, 39,* 350–373.

Bowlby, J. (1969). *Attachment: Vol. 1. Attachment and loss.* New York: Basic Books.

Boyd, J. H., & Weissman, M. M. (1982). Epidemiology. In E. S. Paykel (Ed.), *Handbook of affective disorders.* New York: Guilford.

Bradburn, N. M. (1969). *The structure of psychological well-being.* Chicago: Aldine.

Bradburn, N. M., & Capovitz, D. (1965). *Reports on happiness.* Chicago: Aldine.

Bradley, R. H., & Caldwell, B. M. (1984). 174 Children: A study of the relationship between home environment and cognitive development during the first 5 years. In A. W. Gottfried (Ed.), *Home environment and early cognitive development: Longitudinal research.* San Diego, CA: Academic Press.

Brainerd, C. J. (1978). The stage question in cognitive-developmental theory. *Behavioral and Brain Sciences, 1,* 173–182.

Bransford, J. D. (1979). *Human cognition: Learning, understanding, and remembering.* Belmont, CA: Wadsworth.

Bransford, J. D., & Johnson, M. K. (1972). Contextual prerequisites for understanding: Some investigations of comprehension and recall. *Journal of Verbal Learning and Verbal Behavior, 11,* 717–726.

Bransford, J. D., & Johnson, M. K. (1973). Considerations of some problems of comprehension. In W. G. Chase (Ed.), *Visual information processing.* New York: Academic Press.

Bransford, J. D., & Stein, B. (1984). *The IDEAL problem solver.* New York: Freeman.

Bransford, J. D., & Stein, B. S. (1993). *The ideal problem solver: A guide for improving thinking, learning, and creativity* (2nd ed.). New York: W. H. Freeman.

Branstetter, E. (1969). The young child's response to hospitalization: Separation anxiety or lack of mothering care? *American Journal of Public Health, 59,* 92–97.

Braswell, L., & Kendall, P. C. (1988). Cognitive-behavioral methods with children. In K. S. Dobson (Ed.), *Handbook of cognitive-behavioral therapies.* New York: Guilford.

Brazelton, T. B. (1983). Precursors for the development of emotions in early infancy. In R. Plutchik & H. Kellerman (Eds.), *Emotion: Theory, research, and experience* (Vol. 2). New York: Academic Press.

Brehm, S. S., & Kassin, S. M. (1990). *Social psychology.* Boston: Houghton Mifflin.

Breslow, L. (1983). The potential of health promotion. In D. Mechanic (Ed.), *Handbook of health, health care, and the health professions.* New York: Free Press.

Bretherton, I., & Waters, E. (Eds.). (1985). Growing points of attachment theory research. *Monographs of the Society for Research in Child Development, 50*(1–2, Serial No. 209).

Breuer, J. T. (1993). *Schools for thought.* Cambridge, MA: MIT Press.

Breuer, J., & Freud, S. (1895). *Studies in hysteria* (J. Strachey, Ed. and Trans., with A. Freud). New York: Basic Books.

Bridges, L. J., Connell, J. P., & Belsky, J. (1988). Similarities and differences in infant–mother and infant–father interaction in the strange situation: A component process analysis. *Developmental Psychology, 24,* 92–100.

Brigden, R. (1933). A tachistoscopic study of the differentiation of perception. *Psychological Monographs, 44,* 153–166.

Brigham, J. C., & Malpass, R. S. (1985). The role of experience and contact in the recognition of faces of own and other-race persons. *Journal of Social Issues, 41,* 139–155.

Brislin, R. W. (1986). The wording and translation of research instruments. In W. J. Lonner & J. W. Berry (Eds.), *Field methods in cross-cultural research.* Newbury Park, CA: Sage.

Broadbent, D. (1958). *Perception and communication.* Oxford, England: Pergamon.

Broadbent, D. E., & Gregory, M. (1965). Effects of noise and of signal rate upon vigilance analyzed by means of decision theory. *Human Factors, 7,* 155–162.

Broadhurst, P. L. (1957). Emotionality and the Yerkes–Dodson law. *Journal of Experimental Psychology, 54,* 345–352.

Brock, T. C., Green, M. C., & Reich, D. A. (1998). New evidence in the *Consumer Reports* study of psychotherapy. *American Psychologist, 53,* 62–63

Brody, L. R. (1996). Gender, emotional expression, and parent-child boundaries. In R. D. Kavanaugh, B. Zimmerberg, & S. Fein (Eds.), *Emotion: Interdisciplinary perspectives.* Hillsdale, NJ: Erlbaum.

Brody, N. (2000). History of theories and measurements of intelligence. In R. J. Sternberg (Ed.), *Handbook of intelligence.* New York: Cambridge University Press.

Brosschot, J. F., Benschop, R. J., Godaert, G. L. R., & Olf, M. (1994). Influence of life stress on immunological reactivity to mild psychological stress. *Psychosomatic Medicine, 56*(3), 216–224.

Brown, A. L., Campione, J. C., Bray, N. W., & Wilcox, B. L. (1973). Keeping track of changing variables: Effects of rehearsal training and rehearsal prevention in normal and retarded adolescents. *Journal of Experimental Psychology, 101,* 123–131.

Brown, A. L., & French, A. L. (1979). The zone of potential development: Implications for intelligence testing in the year 2000. In R. J. Sternberg & D. K. Detterman (Eds.), *Human intelligence: Perspectives on its theory and measurement* (pp. 217–235). Norwood, NJ: Ablex.

Brown, A. L., & Kane, M. J. (1988). Preschool children can learn to transfer: Learning to learn and learning by example. *Cognitive Psychology, 20,* 493–523.

Brown, E. (1963). Meeting patients' psychosocial needs in the general hospital. *Annals of the American Academy of Political and Social Science, 346,* 117–122.

Brown, G. W., & Harris, T. O. (1978). *Social origins of depression.* London: Tavistock.

Brown, J. A. (1958). Some tests of the decay theory of immediate memory. *Quarterly Journal of Experimental Psychology, 10,* 12–21.

Brown, R. (1965). *Social psychology.* New York: The Free Press.

Brown, R. (1973). *A first language: The early stages.* Cambridge, MA: Harvard University Press.

Brown, R., Cazden, C. B., & Bellugi, U. (1969). The child's grammar from 1 to 3. In J. P. Hill (Ed.), *Minnesota symposium on child psychology* (Vol. 2). Minneapolis: University of Minnesota Press.

Brown, R., & Kulik, J. (1977). Flashbulb memories. *Cognition, 5,* 73–99.

Brown, R., & McNeill, D. (1966). The "tip of the tongue" phenomenon. *Journal of Verbal Learning and Verbal Behavior, 5,* 325–337.

Brownell, K. D., & Rodin, J. (1994). The dieting maelstrom: Is it possible and advisable to lose weight? *American Psychologist, 49,* 781–791.

Brownell, K. D., & Wadden, T. A. (1992). Etiology and treatment of obesity: Understanding a serious, prevalent, and refractory disorder. *Journal of Consulting and Clinical Psychology, 60,* 505–517.

Bruch, H. (1973). *Eating disorders: Obesity, anorexia nervosa, and the person within.* New York: Basic Books.

Bruer, J. T. (1993). *Schools for thought.* Cambridge, MA: MIT Press.

Brunner, D., Buhot, M. C., Hen, R., & Hofer, M. (1999). Anxiety, motor activation, and maternal-infant interactions in $5HT_{1B}$ knockout mice. *Behavioral Neuroscience, 113,* 587–601.

Bryant, P. E., & Trabasso, T. (1971). Transitive inferences and memory in young children. *Nature, 232,* 456–458.

Bryson, M., Bereiter, C., Scardamalia, M., & Joram, E. (1991). Going beyond the problem as given: Problem solving in expert and novice writers. In R. J. Sternberg & P. A. Frensch (Eds.), *Complex problem solving: Principles and mechanisms* (pp. 61–84). Hillsdale, NJ: Erlbaum.

Buchsbaum, M. S., Haier, R. J., Potkin, S. G., & Nuechterlein, K. (1992). Frontostriatal disorder of cerebral metabolism in never-medicated schizophrenics. *Archives of General Psychiatry, 49,* 935–942.

Bunney, W. E., Goodwin, F. K., & Murphy, D. L. (1972). The "switch process" in manic–depressive illness. *Archives in General Psychiatry, 27,* 312–317.

Bunney, W. E., Murphy, D. L., Goodwin, F. K., & Borge, G. F. (1970). The switch process from depression to mania: Relationship to drugs which alter brain amines. *Lancet, 1,* (1022).

Burger, J. M. (1989). Negative reactions to increases in perceived personal control. *Journal of Personality and Social Psychology, 56,* 246–256.

Burger, J. M. (1992). *Desire for control: Personality, social, and clinical perspectives.* New York: Plenum.

Burger, J. M., & Cooper, H. M. (1979). The desirability of control. *Motivation and Emotion, 3,* 381–393.

Burgess, C., Morris, T., & Pettingale, K. W. (1988). Psychological response to cancer diagnosis—II. Evidence for coping styles. *Journal of Psychosomatic Research, 32,* 263–272.

Burgess, E. W., & Wallin, P. (1953). *Engagement and marriage.* Philadelphia: Lippincott.

Burleson, B. R., & Denton, W. H. (1992). A new look at similarity and attraction in marriage: Similarities in social-cognitive and communication skills as predictors of attraction and satisfaction. *Communication Monographs, 59*(3), 268–287.

Burnstein, E., & Vinokur, A. (1973). Testing two classes of theories about group-induced shifts in individual choice. *Journal of Experimental Social Psychology, 9,* 123–137.

Burnstein, E., & Vinokur, A. (1977). Persuasive arguments and social comparison as determinates of attitude polarization. *Journal of Experimental Social Psychology, 13,* 315–332.

Burti, L., & Yastrebov, V. S. (1993). Procedures used in rehabilitation. In N. Sartorius, G. de Girolano, G. Andrews, G. A. German, & L. Eisenberg (Eds.), *Treatment of mental disorders: A review of effectiveness.* Geneva, Switzerland, and Washington, DC: World Health Organization and American Psychiatric Press.

Bushman, B. J. (1996). Individual differences in the extent and development of aggressive cognitive-associative networks. *Personality and Social Psychology Bulletin, 22,* 811–819.

Buss, D. M. (1988a). The evolution of human intrasexual competition: Tactics of mate attraction. *Journal of Personality and Social Psychology, 54,* 616–628.

Buss, D. M. (1988b). Love acts: The evolutionary biology of love. In R. J. Sternberg & M. L. Barnes (Eds.), *The psychology of love* (pp. 100–118). New Haven, CT: Yale University Press.

Buss, D. M. (1994). *The evolution of desire.* New York: Basic Books.

Buss, D. M. (1995). Evolutionary psychology: A new paradigm for psychological science. *Psychological Inquiry, 6,* 1–30.

Buss, D. M. (1996). The evolutionary psychology of human social strategies. In E. T. Higgins & A. W. Kruglanski (Eds.), *Social psychology: Handbook of basic principles.* New York; Guilford.

Buss, D. M., & Barnes, M. (1986). Preferences in human mate selection. *Journal of Personality and Social Psychology, 50,* 559–570.

Buss, D. M., & Craik, K. H. (1984). Acts, dispositions, and personality. In B. A. Maher & W. B. Maher (Eds.), *Progress in experimental personality research* (Vol. 13, pp. 241–301). Orlando, FL: Academic Press.

Buss, D. M., & Kenrick, D. T. (1998). Evolutionary social psychology. In D. T. Gilbert, S. T., Fiske, & G. Lindzey (Eds.), *The handbook of social psychology* (4th ed., Vol. 2, pp. 982–1026). New York: McGraw-Hill.

Buss, D. M., & Schmitt, D. P. (1993). Sexual strategies theory: A contextual evolutionary analysis of human mating. *Psychological Review, 100,* 204–232.

Butcher, J. N., Dahlström, W. G., Graham, J. R., Tellegen, A., & Kaemmer, B. (1989). *Minnesota Multiphasic Personality Inventory (MMPI-2): Manual for administration and scoring.* Minneapolis: University of Minnesota Press.

Butcher, J. N., & Pancheri, P. (1976). *A handbook of cross-national MMPI research.* Minneapolis: University of Minnesota Press.

Butcher, J. N., & Williams, C. L. (1992). *Essentials of MMPI-2 and MMPI-A interpretation.* Minneapolis: University of Minnesota Press.

Butler, J., & Rovee-Collier, C. (1989). Contextual gating of memory retrieval. *Developmental Psychobiology, 22,* 533–552.

Butler, J. L., & Baumeister, R. F. (1998). The trouble with friendly faces. Skilled performance with a supportive audience. *Journal of Personality and Social Psychology, 75,* 1214–1230.

Butterfield, E. C., Wambold, C., & Belmont, J. M. (1973). On the theory and practice of improving short-term memory. *American Journal of Mental Deficiency, 77,* 654–669.

Byrne, D. (1961). Anxiety and the experimental arousal of affiliation need. *Journal of Abnormal and Social Psychology, 63,* 660–662.

Byrne, D. (1971). *The attraction paradigm.* New York: Academic Press.

Byrne, D. G., & Rosenman, R. H. (1986). The Type A behaviour pattern as a precursor to stressful life-events: A confluence of coronary risks. *British Journal of Medical Psychology, 59,* 75–82.

Byrne, P. S., & Long, B. E. L. (1976). *Doctors talking to patients.* London: Her Majesty's Stationery Office.

Byrne, R. (1995). *The thinking ape: Evolutionary origins of intelligence.* Oxford: Oxford University Press.

Byrnes, J. P. (1988). Formal operations: A systematic reformulation. *Developmental Review, 8,* 66–87.

Cabeza, R., & Nyberg, L. (1997). Imaging cognition: An empirical review of PET studies with normal subjects. *Journal of Cognitive Neuroscience, 9,* 1–26.

Cacioppo, J. T., Klein, D. J., Berntson, G. G., & Hatfield, E. (1993). The psychophysiology of emotions. In M. Lewis & J. M. Haviland (Eds.), *Handbook of emotions.* New York: Guilford Press.

Cacioppo, J. T., & Petty, R. E. (1979). Effects of message repetition and position on cognitive responses, recall, and persuasion. *Journal of Personality and Social Psychology, 37,* 97–109.

Cacioppo, J. T., & Petty, R. E. (1980). Persuasiveness of commercials is affected by exposure frequency and communicator cogency: A theoretical and empirical analysis. In J. H. Leigh & C. R. Martin (Eds.), *Current issues and research in advertising.* Ann Arbor: University of Michigan Press.

Cacioppo, J. T., & Petty, R. E. (1983). *Social psychophysiology: A sourcebook.* New York: Guilford.

Cacioppo, J. T., & Petty, R. E. (1986). Social processes. In M. G. H. Coles, E. Donehin, & S. W. Porges (Eds.), *Psychophysiology.* New York: Guilford.

Cain, W. S. (1977). Differential sensitivity for smell: "Noise" at the nose. *Science, 195,* 796–798.

Cameron, J., & Pierce, W. D. (1994). Reinforcement, reward and intrinsic motivation: A meta-analysis. *Review of Educational Research, 64,* 363–423.

Calkins, S. D., & Fox, N. A. (1994). Individual differences in the biological aspects of temperament. In J. E. Bates & T. D. Wachs (Eds.), *Temperament: Individual differences at the interface of biology and behavior* (pp. 199–217). Washington, DC: American Psychological Association.

Callahan, C. (2000). Intelligence and giftedness. In R. J. Sternberg (Ed.), *Handbook of intelligence.* New York: Cambridge University Press.

Campbell, D. T. (1960). Blind variation and selective retention in creative thought as in other knowledge processes. *Psychological Review, 67,* 380–400.

Campbell, M., Rosenbloom, S., Perry, R., George, A. E., Kercheff, I. I., Anderson, L., Small, A. M., & Jennings, S. J. (1982). Computerized axial tomography in young autistic children. *American Journal of Psychiatry, 139,* 510–512.

Campione, J. C. (1989). Assisted assessments: A taxonomy of approaches and an outline of strengths and weaknesses. *Journal of Learning Disabilities, 22,* 151–165.

Campione, J. C., & Brown, A. L. (1990). Guided learning and transfer: Implications for approaches to assessment. In N. Frederiksen, R. Glaser, A. Lesgold, & M. Shafto (Eds.), *Diagnostic monitoring of skill and knowledge acquisition* (pp. 141–172). Hillsdale, NJ: Erlbaum.

Campione, J. C., Brown, A. L., & Ferrara, R. (1982). Mental retardation and intelligence. In R. J. Sternberg (Ed.), *Handbook of human intelligence* (pp. 392–490). New York: Cambridge University Press.

Campos, J. J., Barrett, K. C., Lamb, M. E., Goldsmith, H. H., & Stenberg, C. (1983). Socioemotional development. In P. H. Mussen (Ed.), *Handbook of child psychology* (4th ed., Vol. 2, pp. 783–915). New York: Wiley.

Candland, D. K. (1977). The persistent problems of emotion. In D. K. Candland, J. P. Fell, E. Keen, A. I. Leshner, R. Plutchik, & R. M. Tarpy (Eds.), *Emotion* (pp. 1–84). Monterey, CA: Brooks/Cole.

Cannon, W. B. (1927). The James–Lange theory of emotion: A critical examination and alternative theory. *American Journal of Psychology, 39,* 106–124.

Cannon, W. B. (1929). *Bodily changes in pain, hunger, fear, and rage, on account of recent researches into the function of emotional excitement* (2nd ed.). New York: Appleton.

Cannon, W. B., & Washburn, A. L. (1912). An explanation of hunger. *American Journal of Psychology, 29,* 444–454.

Cantor, J., & Engle, R. W. (1993). Working memory capacity as long-term memory activation: An individual differences approach. *Journal of Experimental Psychology: Learning, Memory, and Cognition 19,* 1101–1114.

Cantor, N., & Kihlstrom, J. F. (1987a). Social intelligence: The cognitive basis of personality. In P. Shaver (Ed.), *Review of personality and social psychology* (Vol. 6, pp. 15–34). Beverly Hills, CA: Sage.

Cantor, N., & Kihlstrom. J. F. (1987b). *Personality and social intelligence.* Englewood Cliffs, NJ: Prentice-Hall.

Cantwell, D. P., Baker, L., & Rutter, M. (1979). Families of autistic and dysphasic children: 1. Family life and interaction patterns. *Archives of General Psychiatry, 29,* 682–687.

Caplan, L. (1993). *Stroke* (2nd ed.). Stoneham, MA: Butterworth-Heineman.

Caporael, L. (1976). Ergotism: The satan loosed in Salem? *Science, 192,* 21–26.

Cappa, S. F., Perani, D., Grassli, F., Bressi, S., et al. (1997). A PET follow-up study of recovery after stroke in acute aphasics. *Brain and Language, 56,* 55–67.

Carlson, G., & Goodwin, F. K. (1973). The stages of mania: A longitudinal analysis of the manic episode. *Archives of General Psychiatry, 28*(2), 221–228.

Carlson, J. G., & Hatfield, E. (1992). *Psychology of emotion.* New York: Harcourt Brace Jovanovich.

Carraher, T. N., Carraher, D., & Schliemann, A. D. (1985). Mathematics in the streets and in the schools. *British Journal of Developmental Psychology, 3,* 21–29.

Carraher, T. N., Schliemann, A. D., & Carraher, D. W. (1988). Mathematical concepts in everyday life. In G. B. Saxe & M. Gearhart (Eds.), Children's mathematics. *New Directions in Child Development, 41,* 71–87.

Carroll, D. W. (1986). *Psychology of language.* Monterey, CA: Brooks/Cole.

Carroll, J. B. (1993). *Human cognitive abilities: A survey of factor-analytic studies.* New York: Cambridge University Press.

Carroll, L. (1946). *Alice in Wonderland and through the looking-glass.* New York: Grosset & Dunlap. (Original works published 1865, 1872)

Carson, R. C. (1996). Aristotle, Galileo, and the DSM taxonomy: The case of schizophrenia. *Journal of Consulting and Clinical Psychology, 64,* 1133–1139.

Carson, R. C., & Butcher, J. N. (1992). *Abnormal psychology and modern life* (9th ed.). New York: HarperCollins.

Cartwright, R. D. (1977). *Night life: Explorations in dreaming.* Englewood Cliffs, NJ: Prentice-Hall.

Cartwright, R. D. (1991). Dreams that work: The relation of dream incorporation to adaptation to stressful events. *Dreaming, 1,* 3–9.

Cartwright, R. D., & Lamberg, L. (1992). *Crisis dreaming.* New York: HarperCollins.

Carver, C. S., Diamond, E. L., & Humphries, C. (1985). Coronary prone behavior. In N. Schneiderman & J. T. Tapp (Eds.), *Behavioral medicine: The biopsychosocial approach.* Hillsdale, NJ: Erlbaum.

Caryl, P. G. (1994). Early event-related potentials correlate with inspection time and intelligence. *Intelligence, 18,* 15–46.

Case, R. (1985). *Intellectual development: A systematic reinterpretation.* New York: Academic Press.

Case, R. (1992). Neo-Piagetian theories of child development. In R. J. Sternberg & C. A. Berg (Eds.), *Intellectual development* (pp. 161–196). New York: Cambridge University Press.

Case, R. (1992). The role of the frontal lobes in the regulation of cognitive development. *Brain and Cognition, 20,* 51–73.

Case, R., & Okamoto, Y. (1996). The role of central conceptual structures in the development of scientific and social thought. In C. A. Hauert (Ed.), *Developmental psychology: Cognitive, perceptuo-motor and neuropsychological perspectives.* Amsterdam: North-Holland.

Caspi, A. (1998). Personality development across the life course. In W. Damon (Gen. Ed.) & N. Eisenberg (Vol. Ed.), *Handbook of child psychology* (Vol. 3): *Social, emotional, and personality development* (pp. 311–388). New York: Wiley.

Cattell, J. M. (1886). The influence of the intensity of the stimulus on the length of the reaction time. *Brain, 9,* 512–514.

Cattell, J. M. (1890). Mental tests and measurements. *Mind, 15,* 373–380.

Cattell, R. B. (1971). *Abilities: Their structure, growth, and action.* Boston: Houghton Mifflin.

Cattell, R. B. (1973, July). A 16PF profile. *Psychology Today,* pp. 40–46.

Cattell, R. B. (1979). *Personality and learning theory.* New York: Springer.

Cattell, R. B. (1982). *The inheritance of personality and ability: Research methods and findings.* New York: Academic Press.

Cattell, R. B., Eber, H. W., & Tatsuoka, M. M. (1970). *Handbook for the sixteen personality factor questionnaire.* Champaign, IL: Institute for Personality and Ability Testing.

Ceci, S. J. (1991). How much does schooling influence general intelligence and its cognitive components? A reassessment of the evidence. *Developmental Psychology, 27*(5), 703–722.

Ceci, S. J. (1996). *On intelligence.* Cambridge, MA: Cambridge University Press.

Ceci, S. J., & Bronfenbrenner, U. (1985). Don't forget to take the cupcakes out of the oven: Strategic time-monitoring, prospective memory and context. *Child Development, 56,* 175–190.

Ceci, S. J., & Bruck, M. (1993). Suggestibility of the child witness: A historical review and synthesis. *Psychological Bulletin, 113*(3), 403–439.

Ceci, S. J., & Bruck, M. (1995). *Jeopardy in the courtroom.* Washington, DC: APA Books.

Ceci, S. J., & Loftus, E. F. (1994). "Memory work": A royal road to false memories? *Applied Cognitive Psychology, 8,* 351–364.

Ceci, S. J., & Roazzi, A. (1994). The effects of context on cognition: Postcards from Brazil. In R. J. Sternberg & R. K. Wagner (Eds.), *Minds in context: Interactionist perspectives on human intelligence.* New York: Cambridge University Press.

Centers for Disease Control and Prevention (1994a). *Addressing emerging infectious disease threats: A prevention strategy for the United States.* Washington, DC: Author.

Centers for Disease Control and Prevention (1994b). *Cardiovascular disease surveillance: Stroke 1980–1989.* Washington, DC: Author.

Centers for Disease Control and Prevention (1994c). *The Center for Disease Control's heath surveillance for women, infants, and children.* Washington, DC: Author.

Cerella, J. (1985). Information processing rates in the elderly. *Psychological Bulletin, 98,* 67–83.

Cernoch, J. M., & Porter, R. H. (1985). Recognition of maternal axillary odors by infants. *Child Development, 56,* 1593–1598.

Chaiken, S., & Eagly, A. (1983). Communication modality as a determinant of persuasion: The role of communicator salience. *Journal of Personality and Social Psychology, 45,* 241–256.

Chambless, D. L. (1995). Training in and dissemination of empirically validated psychological treatments: Report and recommendations. *The Clinical Psychologist, 48,* 3–24.

Chandrashekaran, M., Walker, B. A., Ward, J. C., & Reingen, P. H. (1996). Modeling individual preference evolution and choice in a dynamic group setting. *Journal of Marketing Research, 33,* 211–223.

Chaplin, W. F., & Goldberg, L. R. (1984). A failure to replicate the Bem and Allen study of individual differences in cross-situational consistency. *Journal of Personality and Social Psychology, 47,* 1074–1090.

Chapman, C. R. (1984). New directions in the understanding and management of pain. *Social Science and Medicine, 19,* 1262–1277.

Chapman, L. J., & Chapman, J. P. (1969). Illusory correlation as an obstacle to the use of valid psycho-diagnostic signs. *Journal of Abnormal Psychology, 74,* 271–280.

Chase, W. G., & Simon, H. A. (1973). The mind's eye in chess. In W. G. Chase (Ed.), *Visual information processing* (pp. 215–281). New York: Academic Press.

Chen, M., & Bargh, J. A. (1997). Nonconscious behavioral confirmation processes: The self-fulfilling consequences of automatic stereotype activation. *Journal of Experimental Social Psychology, 33,* 541–560.

Chen, N. Y., Shaffer, D. R., & Wu, C. (1997). On physical attractiveness stereotyping in Taiwan: A revised sociocultural perspective. *Journal of Social Psychology, 137,* 117–124.

Cheng, P. W., & Holyoak, K. J. (1985). Pragmatic reasoning schemas. *Cognitive Psychology, 17,* 391–416.

Cherny, N. I. (1996). The problem of inadequately relieved suffering. *Journal of Social Issues, 52,* 13–30.

Cherry, E. C. (1953). Some experiments on the recognition of speech with one and two ears. *Journal of the Acoustical Society of America, 25,* 975–979.

Chi, M. T. H. (1978). Knowledge structures and memory development. In R. S. Siegler (Ed.), *Children's thinking: What develops?* Hillsdale, NJ: Erlbaum.

Chi, M. T. H., Feltovich, P., & Glaser, R. (1981). Categorization and representation of physics problems by experts and novices. *Cognitive Science, 5,* 121–152.

Chi, M. T. H., Glaser, R., & Farr, M. (Eds.). (1988). *The nature of expertise.* Hillsdale, NJ: Erlbaum.

Chi, M. T. H., & Koeske, R. D. (1983). Network representations of a child's dinosaur knowledge. *Developmental Psychology, 19,* 29–39.

Cialdini, R. B., Brown, S. L., Lewis, B. P., Luce, C., & Neuberg, S. L. (1997). Reinterpreting the empathy-altruism relationship: When one into one equals oneness. *Journal of Personality and Social Psychology, 73,* 481–494.

Chodorow, N. (1978). *The reproduction of mothering.* Berkeley: University of California Press.

Chodorow, N. (1992). *Feminism and psychoanalytic theory.* New Haven, CT: Yale University Press.

Chomsky, N. (1957). *Syntactic structures.* The Hague, Netherlands: Mouton.

Chomsky, N. (1965). *Aspects of the theory of syntax.* Cambridge, MA: MIT Press.

Chomsky, N. (1972). *Language and mind* (2nd ed.). New York: Harcourt Brace Jovanovich.

Chomsky, N. (1980). *Rules and representations.* New York: Columbia University Press.

Chomsky, N. (1991, March). [Quoted in] *Discover, 12*(3), 20.

Christensen, A., & Jacobsen, N. S. (1994). Who (or what) can do psychotherapy: The status and challenge of nonprofessional therapies. *Psychological Science, 5*, 8–14.

Cialdini, R. B. (1984). *Influence*. New York: Quill.

Cialdini, R. B. (1988). *Influence: Science and practice* (2nd ed.). Glenview, IL: Scott, Foresman/Little, Brown.

Cialdini, R. B., Petty, R. E., & Cacioppo, J. T. (1981). Attitude and attitude change. *Annual Review of Psychology, 32*, 357–404.

Cialdini, R. B., Schaller, M., Houlihan, D., Arps, K., Fultz, J., & Beaman, A. L. (1987). Empathy-based helping: Is it selflessly or selfishly motivated? *Journal of Personality and Social Psychology, 52*, 599–604.

Cimbalo, R. S., Faling, V., & Mousaw, P. (1976). The course of love: A cross-sectional design. *Psychological Reports, 38*, 1292–1294.

Clark, E. V. (1973). What's in a word? On the child's acquisition of semantics in his first language. In T. E. Moore (Ed.), *Cognitive development and the acquisition of language.* New York: Academic Press.

Clark, H. H. (1969). Linguistic processes in deductive reasoning. *Psychological Review, 76*, 387–404.

Clark, H. H., & Chase, W. G. (1972). On the process of comparing sentences against pictures. *Cognitive Psychology, 3*, 472–517.

Clark, H. H., & Clark, E. V. (1977). *Psychology and language: An introduction to psycholinguistics.* New York: Harcourt Brace Jovanovich.

Clarke-Stewart, K. A. (1978). And daddy makes three: The father's impact on mother and young child. *Child Development, 49*, 466–478.

Clarke-Stewart, K. A. (1989). Infant day care: Maligned or malignant? *American Psychologist, 44*, 266–273.

Clarke-Stewart, K. A. (1993). *Daycare* (rev. ed.). Cambridge, MA: Harvard University Press.

Clarke-Stewart, K. A., Perlmutter, M., & Friedman, S. (1988). *Lifelong human development.* New York: Wiley.

Clayton, P., Desmarais, L., & Winokur, G. (1968). A study of normal bereavement. *American Journal of Psychiatry, 125*, 168–178.

Clayton, I. C., Richards, J. C., & Edwards, C. J. (1999). Selective attention in obsessive-compulsive disorder. *Journal of Abnormal Psychology, 108*, 171–175.

Clore, G. L., & Byrne, D. (1974). A reinforcement-affect model of attraction. In T. L. Huston (Ed.), *Foundations of interpersonal attraction* (pp. 143–170). New York: Academic Press.

Coates, J. B., & Wortman, C. B. (1980). Depression maintenance and interpersonal control. In A. Baum & J. E. Singer (Eds.), *Advances in environmental psychology: Applications of personal control* (Vol. 2). Hillsdale, NJ: Erlbaum.

Cofer, C. N., & Appley, M. H. (1964). *Motivation: Theory and research.* New York: Wiley.

Cohen, D., Nisbett, R. E., Bowdle, B. F., & Schwarz, N. (1996). Insult, aggression, and the southern culture of honor: An "experimental ethnography." *Journal of Personality and Social Psychology, 70*, 945–960.

Cohen, J. (1981). Can human irrationality be experimentally demonstrated? *Behavioral and Brain Sciences, 4*, 317–331.

Cohen, J. D., Forman, S. D., Braver, T. S., Casey, B. J., Servan-Schreiber, D., & Noll, D. C. (1994). Activation of prefrontal cortex in a non-spatial working memory task with functional MRI. *Human Brain Mapping, 1*, 293–304.

Cohen, J. D., Romero, R. D., Servan-Schreiber, D., & Farah, M. J. (1994). Mechanisms of spatial attention: The relation of macrostructure to microstructure in parietal neglect. *Journal of Cognitive Neuroscience, 6*, 377–387.

Cohen, S. (1981). *The substance abuse problems.* New York: Haworth Press.

Cohen, S., Kaplan, J. R., Cunnick, J. E., Manuck, S. B., & Rabin, B. S. (1992). Chronic social stress, affiliation, and cellular immune response in nonhuman primates. *Psychological Science, 3*, 301–304.

Cohen, S., Tyrell, D., & Smith, A. (1991). Psychological stress and susceptibility to the common cold. *The New England Journal of Medicine, 235*, 606–612.

Cohen, S., Tyrrell, D. A. J., & Smith, A. P. (1993). Negative life events, perceive stress, negative affect, and susceptibility to the common cold. *Journal of Personality and Social Psychology, 64*, 131–140.

Cohen, S., & Williamson, G. (1991). Stress and infectious disease. *Psychological Bulletin, 109*, 5–24.

Colby, A., Kohlberg, L., Gibbs, J., & Lieberman, M. (1983). A longitudinal study of moral judgment. *Monographs of the Society for Research in Child Development, 48*(1–2), 124.

Cole, J. O., & Bodkin, J. A. (1990). Antidepressant drug side effects. *Journal of Clinical Psychiatry, 51*, 21–26.

Cole, M., Gay, J., Glick, J., & Sharp, D. W. (1971). *The cultural context of learning and thinking.* New York: Basic Books.

Cole, M., & Scribner, S. (1974). *Culture and thought: A psychological introduction.* New York: Wiley.

Coleman, P. D., & Flood, D. G. (1986). Dendritic proliferation in the aging brain as a compensatory repair mechanism. In D. F. Swaab, E. Fliers, M. Mirmiram, W. A. Van Gool, & F. Van Haaren (Eds.), *Progress in brain research* (Vol. 20). New York: Elsevier.

Colin, V. L. (1996). *Human attachment.* New York: McGraw-Hill.

Collins, A. M., & Loftus, E. F. (1975). A spreading-activation theory of semantic processing. *Psychological Review, 82*, 407–429.

Collins, A. M., & Quillian, M. R. (1969). Retrieval time from semantic memory. *Journal of Verbal Learning and Verbal Behavior, 8*, 240–248.

Colombo, J. (1993). *Infant cognition: Predicting childhood intellectual function.* Newbury Park, CA: Sage.

Colwell, C. S., Ralph, M. R., & Menaker, M. (1990). Do NMDA receptors mediate the effects of light on circadian behavior? *Brain Research, 523*(1), 117–120.

Colwill, R. M., & Delamater, B. A. (1995). An associative analysis of instrumental biconditional discrimination learning. *Animal Learning & Behavior, 22*, 384–394.

Condry, J. (1977). Enemies of exploration: Self-initiated versus other-initiated learning. *Journal of Personality and Social Psychology, 18*, 105–115.

Conrad, R. (1964). Acoustic confusions in immediate memory. *British Journal of Psychology, 55*, 75–84.

Cook, B. H., Stein, M. A., Krasowski, M. D., Cox, N. J., Olkon, D. M., Keiffer, J. E., & Leventhal, B. L. (1995). Association of attention-deficit disorder and the dopamine transporter gene. *American Journal of Human Genetics, 86*, 993–998.

Cook, H. B. K. (1992). Matrilocality and female aggression in Margariteño society. In K. Björkqvist & P. Niemelä (Es.), *Of mice and women: Aspects of female aggression* (pp. 149–162). San Diego, CA: Harcourt Brace.

Cook, M., & Mineka, S. (1990). Selective associations in the observational conditioning of fear in rhesus monkeys. *Journal of Experimental Psychology: Animal Behavior Processes, 16*, 372–389.

Cooley, C. H. (1982). *Human nature and the social order.* New York: Scribners. (Original work published 1902)

Cooper, E. H., & Pantle, A. J. (1967). The total-time hypothesis in verbal learning. *Psychological Bulletin, 68*(4), 221–234.

Cooper, J., Zanna, M. P., & Taves, P. A. (1978). Arousal as a necessary condition for attitude change following induced compliance. *Journal of Personality and Social Psychology, 36*, 1101–1106.

Corbetta, M., Miezin, F. M., Dobmeyer, S., Shulman, G. L., & Petersen, S. E. (1991). Selective and divided attention during visual discriminations of shape, color and speed: Functional anatomy by positron emission tomography. *Journal of Neuroscience, 11*, 2383–2402.

Corbetta, M., Miezin, F. M., Shulman, G. L., & Petersen, S. E. (1993). A PET study of visuospatial attention. *Journal of Neuroscience, 13*, 1202–1226.

Coren, S. (1994). *Intelligence in dogs.* New York: Macmillan.

Coren, S., & Girgus, J. S. (1978). *Seeing is deceiving: The psychology of visual illusions.* Hillsdale, NJ: Erlbaum.

Coren, S., & Ward, L. M. (1989). *Sensation and perception* (3rd ed.). San Diego, CA: Harcourt Brace Jovanovich.

Coren, S., Ward, L. M., & Enns, J. T. (1994). *Sensation and perception* (4th ed.). Orlando, FL: Harcourt Brace.

Corina, D. P., Poizner, H., Bellugi, U., Feinberg, T., et al. (1992a). Dissociation between linguistic and nonlinguistic gestural systems: A case for compositionality. *Brain & Language, 43*(3), 414–447.

Corina, D. P., Vaid, J., Bellugi, U. (1992b). The linguistic basis of left hemisphere specialization. *Science 255*(5049), 1258–1260.

Cornsweet, T. N. (1985). Prentice Award Lecture: A simple retinal mechanism that has complex and profound effects on perception. *American Journal of Optometry and Physiological Optics, 62,* 427–438.

Cosmides, L. (1989). The logic of social exchange: Has natural selection shaped how humans reason? Studies with the selection task. *Cognition, 31,* 187–276.

Cosmides, L., & Tooby, J. (1987). From evolution to behavior: Evolutionary psychology as the missing link. In J. Dupre (Ed.), *The latest on the best: Essays on evolution and optimality* (pp. 277–306). Cambridge, MA: MIT Press.

Cosmides, L., & Tooby, J. (1992). Cognitive adaptations for social exchange. In J. H. Barkow, L. Cosmides, & J. Tooby (Eds.), *The adapted mind: Evolutionary psychology and the generation of culture.* Oxford: Oxford University Press.

Costa, P. T., Jr., & McCrae, R. (1985). *NEO Personality Inventory.* Odessa, FL: Psychological Assessment Resources.

Costa, P. T., & McCrae, R. R. (1988). Personality in adulthood: A six-year longitudinal study of self-reports and spouse ratings on the NEO personality inventory. *Journal of Personality and Social Psychology, 54,* 853–863.

Costa, P. T., & McCrae, R. R. (1992a). "Four ways five factors are not basic": Reply. *Personality & Individual Differences, 13*(8), 861–865.

Costa, P. T., & McCrae, R. R. (1992b). Four ways five factors are basic. *Personality & Individual Differences, 13*(6), 653–665.

Costa, P. T., Jr., & McCrae, R. (1992c). Normal personality assessment in clinical practice: The NEO Personality Inventory. *Psychological Assessment: A Journal of Consulting and Clinical Psychology, 4,* 5–13.

Costa, P. T., & McCrae, R. R. (1995). Domains and facets: Hierarchical personality assessment using the revised NEO personality inventory. *Journal of Personality Assessment, 64,* 21–50.

Costa, P. T., & McCrae, R. R. (1995). Solid ground in the wetlands of personality: A reply to Block. *Psychological Bulletin, 117,* 216–220.

Cotman, C. W., & McGaugh, J. L. (1980). *Behavioral neuroscience: An introduction.* New York: Academic Press.

Cottraux, J. (1993). Behavior therapy. In N. Sartorius, G. de Girolano, G. Andrews, G. A. German, & L. Eisenberg (Eds.), *Treatment of mental disorders: A review of effectiveness.* Geneva, Switzerland, and Washington, DC: World Health Organization and American Psychiatric Press.

Courchesne, E., Yeung-Courchesne, R., Press, G. A., Hesselink, J. R., & Jernigan, T. L. (1988). Hypoplasia of cerebellar vermal lobules VI and VII autism. *New England Journal of Medicine, 318,* 1349–1354.

Court, J. H. (1984). Sex and violence: A ripple effect. In N. M. Malamuth & E. Donnerstein (Eds.), *Pornography and social aggression.* Orlando, FL: Academic Press.

Cox, D. J., Freundlich, A., & Meyer, R. G. (1975). Differential effectiveness of electromyographic feedback, verbal relaxation instructions, and medication placebo with tension headaches. *Journal of Consulting and Clinical Psychology, 43,* 892–898.

Cox, V. C., Paulus, P. B., & McCain, G. (1984). Prison crowding research: The relevance for prison housing standards and a general approach regarding crowding phenomena. *American Psychologist, 39,* 1148–1160.

Coyne, J. C. (1976a). Depression and the response of others. *Journal of Abnormal Psychology, 55*(2), 186–193.

Coyne, J. C. (1976b). Toward an interactional description of depression. *Psychiatry, 39,* 14–27.

Craik, F. I. M., & Lockhart, R. S. (1972). Levels of processing: A framework for memory research. *Journal of Verbal Learning and Verbal Behavior, 11,* 671–684.

Craik, F. I. M., & Tulving, E. (1975). Depth of processing and the retention of words in episodic memory. *Journal of Experimental Psychology: General, 104,* 268–294.

Crick, F., & Mitchison, G. (1983). The function of dream sleep. *Nature, 304,* 111–114.

Crick, N. R., & Dodge, K. A. (1994). A review and reformulation of social information-processing mechanisms in children's social adjustment. *Psychological Bulletin, 115,* 74–101.

Crook, C. (1987). Taste and olfaction. In P. Salapatek & L. Cohen (Eds.), *Handbook of infant perception: Vol. 1. From sensation to perception* (pp. 237–264). Orlando, FL: Academic Press.

Cross-National Collaborative Group. (1992). The changing rate of major depression. *Journal of the American Medical Association, 268*(21), 3098–3105.

Crowder, R. G. (1976). *Principles of learning and memory.* Hillsdale, NJ: Erlbaum.

Crutchfield, R. (1962). Conformity and creative thinking. In H. Gruber, G. Terrell, & M. Wertheimer (Eds.), *Contemporary approaches to creative thinking* (pp. 120–140). New York: Atherton.

Csikszentmihalyi, M. (1988). Society, culture, and person: A systems view of creativity. In R. J. Sternberg (Ed.), *The nature of creativity* (pp. 325–339). New York: Cambridge University Press.

Csikszentmihalyi, M. (1996). *Creativity: Flow and the psychology of discovery and invention.* New York: HarperCollins.

Csikszentmihalyi, M. (1999). Implications of a systems perspective for the study of creativity. In R. J. Sternberg (Ed.), *Handbook of creativity* (pp. 313–335). New York: Cambridge University Press.

Cummings, J. L. (1993). The neuroanatomy of depression. *Journal of Clinical Psychiatry, 54: 11* (Suppl.), 14–20.

Cummins, J. (1976). The influence of bilingualism on cognitive growth: A synthesis of research findings and explanatory hypothesis. *Working Papers on Bilingualism, 9,* 1–43.

Curtiss, S. (1977). *Genie: A linguistic study of a modern-day wild child.* New York: Academic Press.

Cutler, B. L., & Penrod, S. D. (1995). *Mistaken identification: The eyewitness, psychology, and the law.* New York: Cambridge University Press.

Cutler, W. B., Preti, G., Krieger, A., Huggins, G. R., Garcia, C. R., & Lawley, H. J. (1986). Human axillary secretions influence women's menstrual cycles: The role of donor extract from men. *Hormones and Behavior, 20,* 463–473.

Cutting, J. E., Proffitt, D. R., & Kozlowski, L. T. (1978). A biomechanical invariant for gait perception. *Journal of Experimental Psychology: Human Perception and Performance, 4,* 357–372.

Dabbs, J. M., Jr., Carr, T. S., Frady, R. L., & Riad, J. K. (1995). Testosterone, crime, and misbehavior among 692 male prison inmates. *Personality and Individual Differences, 18,* 627–633.

Dabbs, J. M., Jr., Hargrove, M. F., & Heusel, C. (1996). Testosterone differences among college fraternities: Well-behaved vs. rambunctious. *Personality and Individual Differences, 20,* 157–161.

Daly, M., & Wilson, M. I. (1991). A reply to Gelles: Stepchildren are disproportionately abused, and diverse forms of violence can share causal factors. *Human Nature, 2,* 419–426.

Daly, M., & Wilson, M. I. (1996). Violence against stepchildren. *Current Directions in Psychological Science, 5,* 77–81.

Damasio, A. R. (1985). Prosopagnosia. *Trends in Neurosciences, 8,* 132–135.

Damon, W., & Hart, D. (1982). The development of self-understanding from childhood to adolescence. *Child Development, 53,* 841–864.

Damon, W., & Hart, D. (1992). Self-understanding and its role in social and moral development. In M. H. Bornstein & M. E. Lamb (Eds.), *Developmental psychology: An advanced textbook* (3rd ed., pp. 421–464). Hillsdale, NJ: Erlbaum.

Daneman, M., & Carpenter, P. A. (1980). Individual differences in working memory and reading. *Journal of Verbal Learning and Verbal Behavior, 19,* 450–466.

Daneman, M., & Tardif, T. (1987). Working memory and reading skill re-examined. In M. Coltheart (Ed.), *Attention and performance: Vol. 12. The psychology of reading* (pp. 491–508). Hove, England: Erlbaum.

Daniel, M. (1997). Intelligence testing: Status and trends. *American Psychologist, 52,* 1038–1045.

Daniel, M. (2000). Interpretation of intelligence test scores. In R. J. Sternberg (Ed.), *Handbook of intelligence.* New York: Cambridge University Press.

Dar, R., Leventhal, E. A., & Leventhal, H. (1993). Schematic processes in pain perception. *Cognitive Therapy and Research, 17,* 341–357.

Darley, C. F., Tinklenberg, J. R., Roth, W. T., Hollister, L. E., & Atkinson, R. C. (1973). Influence of marijuana on storage and retrieval processes in memory. *Memory and Cognition, 1,* 196–200.

Darley, J. M., & Batson, C. D. (1973). From Jerusalem to Jericho: A study of situational and dispositional variables in helping behavior. *Journal of Personality and Social Psychology, 27,* 100–108.

Darwin, C. (1859). *Origin of species.* London: John Murray.

Darwin, C. (1965). *The expression of the emotions in man and animals.* Chicago: University of Chicago Press. (Original work published 1872)

Darwin, C. J., Turvey, M. T., & Crowder, R. G. (1972). An auditory analogue of the Sperling partial report procedure: Evidence for brief auditory storage. *Cognitive Psychology, 3,* 255–267.

Dasen, P. R., & Heron, A. (1981). Cross-cultural tests of Piaget's theory. In H. C. Triandis & A. Heron (Eds.), *Handbook of cross-cultural psychology* (Vol. 4). Boston: Allyn & Bacon.

Dashiell, J. F. (1935). Experimental studies of the influence of social situations on the behavior of individual human adults. In C. Murchison (Ed.), *A handbook of social psychology* (pp. 1097–1158). Worcester, MA: Clark University Press.

Davidson, J. E. (1986). The role of insight in giftedness. In R. J. Sternberg & J. E. Davidson (Eds.), *Conceptions of giftedness* (pp. 201–222). New York: Cambridge University Press.

Davidson, J. E. (1995). The suddenness of insight. In R. J. Sternberg & J. E. Davidson (Eds.), *The nature of insight* (pp. 125–155). Cambridge, MA: MIT Press.

Davidson, J. E., & Downing, C. L. (2000). Contemporary models of intelligence. In R. J. Sternberg (Ed.), *Handbook of intelligence.* New York: Cambridge University Press.

Davidson, J. E., & Sternberg, R. J. (1984). The role of insight in intellectual giftedness. *Gifted Child Quarterly, 28,* 58–64.

Davidson, J. W., & Lytle, M. H. (1986). *After the fact: The art of historical detection* (2nd ed.). New York: Knopf.

Davidson, R. J. (1994). The role of prefrontal activation in the inhibition of negative affect. *Psychophysiology, 31,* S7.

Davidson, R. J., & Sutton, S. K. (1995). Affective neuroscience: The emergence of a discipline. *Current Opinion in Neurobiology, 5,* 217–224.

Davies, I. (1998). A study of colour grouping in three languages: A test of the linguistic relativity hypothesis. *British Journal of Psychology, 89,* 433–452.

Davies, I., & Corbett, G. G. (1997). A cross-cultural study of colour grouping: Evidence for a weak linguistic relativity. *British Journal of Psychology, 88,* 493–517.

Davies, M., Stankov, L., & Roberts, R. D. (1998). Emotional intelligence: In search of an elusive construct. *Journal of Personality and Social Psychology, 75,* 985–1015.

Davis, K., & Jones, E. E. (1960). Changes in interpersonal perception as a means of reducing cognitive dissonance. *Journal of Abnormal and Social Psychology, 61,* 402–410.

Davison, G. C., & Neale, J. M. (1994). *Abnormal psychology* (6th ed.). New York: Wiley.

Dawes, R. M. (1994). *House of cards.* New York: The Free Press.

Dawkins, R. (1989). *The selfish gene* (New ed.). New York: Oxford University Press.

Dawson, D., Lack, L., & Morris, M. (1993). Phase resetting of the human circadian pacemaker with use of a single use of bright light. *Chronobiology International, 10,* 94–102.

Dawson, J. L. (1977). Alaskan Eskimo hand, eye, auditory dominance and cognitive style. *Psychologia: An International Journal of Psychology in the Orient, 20*(3), 121–135.

DeAngelis, T. (1992, May). Senate seeks answers to rising tide of violence. *APA Monitor,* p. 11.

Deary, I. (2000). Simple information processing and intelligence. In R. J. Sternberg (Ed.), *Handbook of intelligence.* New York: Cambridge University Press.

Deary, I. J., & Stough, L. (1996). Intelligence and inspection time: Achievements, prospects, and problems. *American Psychologist, 51,* 599–608.

DeCasper, A. J., & Fifer, W. P. (1980). Of human bonding: Newborns prefer their mothers' voices. *Science, 208,* 1174–1176.

DeCasper, A. J., & Prescott, P. A. (1983). Human newborns' perception of male voices: Preference, discrimination, and reinforcing value. *Developmental Psychobiology, 17,* 481–491.

DeCasper, A. J., & Spence, M. J. (1986). Prenatal maternal speech influences newborns' perception of speech sounds. *Infant Behavior and Development, 9,* 133–150.

deCastro, J. M., & Brewer, E. M. (1992). The amount eaten in meals by humans is a power function of the number of people present. *Physiology and Behavior, 51,* 121–125.

deCharms, R. (1968). *Personal causation: The internal affective determinants of behavior.* New York: Academic Press.

De Yoe, E. A., & Van Essen, D. C. (1988). Concurrent processing streams in monkey visual cortex. *Trends in Neurosciences, 11,* 219–226.

Deci, E. L. (1971). Effects of externally mediated rewards on intrinsic motivation. *Journal of Personality and Social Psychology, 18,* 105–115.

Deci, E. L. (1972). Intrinsic motivation, extrinsic reinforcement, and inequity. *Journal of Personality and Social Psychology, 22,* 113–120.

Deci, E. L., Koestner, R., & Ryan, R. M. (1999b). The undermining effect is a reality after all—extrinsic rewards, task interest, and self-determination: Reply to Eisenberger, Pierce, and Cameron (1999) and Lepper, Henderlong, and Gingras (1999). *Psychological Bulletin, 125,* 692–700.

Deci, E. L., & Ryan, R. M. (1985). *Intrinsic motivation and self-determination in human behavior.* New York: Plenum.

Deci, E. L., & Ryan, R. M. (1995). Human autonomy: The basis for true self-esteem. In M. Kernis (Ed.), *Efficacy, agency, and self-esteem* (pp. 31–49). New York: Plenum.

Deci, E. L., Vallerand, R. J., Pelletier, L. G., & Ryan, R. M. (1991). Motivation and education: The self-determination perspective. *Educational Psychologist, 26*(3–4), 325–346.

Deffenbacher, J. L. (1994, August). Anger and diagnosis: Where has all the anger gone? Paper presented at the meeting of the American Psychological Association, Los Angeles, CA.

DeGreef, G., Ashari, M., Bogerts, B., Bilder, R. M., Jody, D. N., Alvir, J. M. J., & Lieberman, J. A. (1992). Volumes of ventricular system subdivisions measured from magnetic resonance images in first-episode schizophrenic patients. *Archives of General Psychiatry, 49,* 531–537.

de Groot, A. D. (1965). *Thought and choice in chess.* The Hague, Netherlands: Mouton.

de la Croix, H., Tansey, R. G., & Kirkpatrick, D. (1991). *Gardner's art through the ages* (9th ed.). New York: Harcourt Brace Jovanovich.

Delgado, J. M. R. (1969). *Physical control of the mind: Toward a psychocivilized society.* New York: Harper & Row.

Delgado, J. M. R., Roberts, W. W., & Miller, N. E. (1954). Learning motivated by electrical stimulation of the brain. *American Journal of Physiology, 179,* 587–593.

DeLoache, J. S. (1987). Rapid change in the symbolic functioning of young children. *Science, 9238,* 1556–1557.

DeLoache, J. S. (1991). Symbolic functioning in very young children: Understanding of pictures and models. *Child Development, 62,* 736–752.

DeLoache, J. S. (1995). Early understanding and use of symbols: The model model. *Current Directions in Psychological Science, 4,* 109–113.

DeLongis, A., Folkman, S., & Lazarus, R. S. (1988). The impact of daily stress on health and mood: Psychological and social resources as mediators. *Journal of Personality and Social Psychology, 54(3),* 486–495.

Dembroski, T. M., & Costa, P. T. (1988). Assessment of coronary-prone behavior: A current overview. *Annals of Behavioral Medicine, 10,* 60–63.

Dembroski, T. M., MacDougall, J. M., Williams, R. B., Haney, T. L., & Blumenthal, J. A. (1985). Components of Type A, hostility, and anger in relationship to angiographic findings. *Psychosomatic Medicine, 47,* 219–233.

Dement, W. C. (1976). *Some must watch while some must sleep.* New York: Norton.

Dement, W. C., & Kleitman, N. (1957). The relation of eye movements during sleep to dream activity: An objective method for the study of dreaming. *Journal of Experimental Psychology, 55,* 543–553.

Demetriou, A., Efklides, A., & Platsidou, M. (1993). The architecture and dynamics of developing mind. *Monographs of the Society for Research in Child Development, 58* (5–6), Serial No. 234.

Dennett, D. (1991). *Consciousness explained.* Boston: Little, Brown.

Dennett, D. C. (1995). *Darwin's dangerous idea.* New York: Simon & Schuster.

Denny, N. W. (1980). Task demands and problem-solving strategies in middle-age and older adults. *Journal of Gerontology, 35,* 559–564.

Derryberry, D., & Rothbart, M. K. (1988). Arousal, affect, and attention as components of temperament. *Journal of Personality and Social Psychology, 55,* 958–966.

Derryberry, D., & Tucker, D. M. (1992). Neural mechanisms of emotion. *Journal of Consulting and Clinical Psychology, 60,* 329–338.

Descartes, R. (1972). *The treatise of man.* Cambridge, MA: Harvard University Press. (Original work published 1662)

DeSoto, C. B., London, M., & Handel, S. (1965). Social reasoning and spatial paralogic. *Journal of Personality and Social Psychology, 2,* 513–521.

Detterman, D. K., Gabriel, L., & Ruthsatz, J. (2000). Intelligence and mental retardation. In R. J. Sternberg (Ed.), *Handbook of intelligence.* New York: Cambridge University Press.

Detterman, D. K., & Sternberg, R. J. (Eds.). (1982). *How and how much can intelligence be increased?* Norwood, NJ: Ablex.

Detterman, D. K., & Sternberg, R. J. (Eds.). (1993). *Transfer on trial: Intelligence, cognition, and instruction.* Norwood, NJ: Ablex.

Detterman, D. K., & Thompson, L. A. (1997). What is so special about special education? *American Psychologist, 52,* 1082–1090.

Deutsch, J. A., & Deutsch, D. (1963). Attention: Some theoretical considerations. *Psychological Review, 70,* 80–90.

Deutsch, M. (1968). The effects of cooperation and competition upon group process. In D. Cartwright & A. Zander (Eds.), *Group dynamics: Research and theory* (3rd ed.). New York: Harper & Row.

DeValois, R. L., & DeValois, K. K. (1980). Spatial vision. *Annual Review of Psychology, 31,* 309–341.

Devine, P. G., Evett, S. R., & Vasquez-Suson, K. A. (1995). Exploring the interpersonal dynamics of intergroup contact. In R. Sorrentino & E. T. Higgins (Eds.), *Handbook of motivation and cognition: The interpersonal context* (Vol. 3). New York: Guilford.

Devine, P. G., Monteith, M. J., Zuwerink, J. R., & Elliot, A. J. (1991). Prejudice with and without compunction. *Journal of Personality and Social Psychology, 60(6),* 817–830.

Dewey, J. (1910). *How we think.* Boston: Heath.

Dewey, J. (1913). *Interest and effort in education.* New York: Houghton Mifflin.

Dewey, J. (1922). *Human nature and conduct: An introduction to social psychology.* New York: Holt.

Diamond, I. T. (1979). The subdivisions of neocortex: A proposal to revise the traditional view of sensory, motor, and association areas. *Progress in Psychobiology and Physiological Psychology, 8,* 1–43.

Diamond, I. T. (1983). Parallel pathways in the auditory, visual, and somatic systems. In G. Macchi, R. Rustioni, & R. Spreafico (Eds.), *Somatosensory integration in the thalamus* (pp. 251–272). Amsterdam: Elsevier.

Dichgans, J., & Brandt, T. (1973). Optokinetic motion sickness and pseudo-Coriolis effects induced by moving visual stimuli. *Acta Otolaryngology – Stockholm, 76(5),* 339–348.

Diekstra, R. F. W. (1996). The epidemiology of suicide and parasuicide. *Archives of Suicide Research, 2,* 1–29.

Diener, E. (1979). Deindividuation, self-awareness, and disinhibition. *Journal of Personality and Social Psychology, 37(7),* 1160–1171.

Diener, E. (1980). Deindividuation: The absence of self-awareness and self-regulation in group members. In P. B. Paulus (Ed.), *The psychology of group influence.* Hillsdale, NJ: Erlbaum.

Differential aptitudes test (4th ed.). (1982). Austin, TX: Psychological Corporation. (Original work published 1972)

Digman, J. M. (1990). Personality structure: Emergence of the five-factor model. *Annual Review of Psychology, 41,* 417–440.

DiMatteo, M. R., & DiNicola, D. D. (1982). *Achieving patient compliance: The psychology of the medical practitioner's role.* New York: Pergamon.

Dineen, T. (1998). Psychotherapy: The snake oil of the 90s? *Skeptic, 6(3),* 54–63.

Dinnerstein, D. (1976). *The mermaid and the minotaur: Sexual arrangements and human malise.* New York: Harper & Row.

Dion, K. K., Berscheid, E., & Walster, E. (1972). What is beautiful is good. *Journal of Personality and Social Psychology, 24,* 285–290.

Dion, K. L., & Dion, K. K. (1976). Love, liking, and trust in heterosexual relationships. *Personality and Social Psychology Bulletin, 2,* 191–206.

Dittes, J. E., & Kelley, H. H. (1956). Effects of different conditions of acceptance upon conformity to group norms. *Journal of Abnormal and Social Psychology, 53,* 100–107.

Dixon, L. B., Lehman, A. F., & Levine, J. (1995). Conventional antipsychotic medications for schizophrenia. *Schizophrenia Bulletin, 21,* 567–577.

Dixon, R. A., & Baltes, P. B. (1986). Toward life-span research on the functions and pragmatics of intelligence. In R. J. Sternberg & R. K. Wagner (Eds.), *Practical intelligence: Nature and origins of competence in the everyday world* (pp. 203–235). New York: Cambridge University Press.

Docherty, J. (1993, May 23). Pay for mental health care—and save. *New York Times,* Sect. 3, p. 13.

Dohrenwend, B. P., Levav, I., Schwartz, S., Naveh, G., Link, B. G., Skodol, A. G., & Stueve, A. (1992). Socioeconomic status and psychiatric disorders: The causation–selection issue. *Science, 255,* 946–952.

Dohrenwend, B. S., & Dohrenwend, B. P. (1974). *Stressful life events.* New York: Wiley.

Dolan, M. (1995, February 11). When the mind's eye blinks. *Los Angeles Times*, 114, pp. A1, A24, A25.

Dollard, J., Miller, N., Doob, L., Mowrer, O. H., & Sears, R. R. (1939). *Frustration and aggression*. New Haven, CT: Institute of Human Relations, Yale University Press.

Domjan, M. (1997). Behavior systems and the demise of equipotentiality: Historical antecedents and evidence from sexual conditioning. In M. E. Bouton & M. S. Fanselow (Eds.), *Learning, motivation, and cognition* (pp. 31–51). Washington, DC: American Psychological Association.

Donnerstein, E., & Berkowitz, L. (1981). Victim reaction in aggressive erotic films as a factor in violence against women. *Journal of Personality and Social Psychology*, 41, 710–724.

Douglas, J. D. (1967). *The social meanings of suicide*. Princeton, NJ: Princeton University Press.

Douvan, E., & Adelson, J. (1966). *The adolescent experience*. New York: Wiley.

Dovidio, J. F., Allen, J. L., & Schroeder, D. A. (1990). Specificity of empathy-induced helping: Evidence for altruistic motivation. *Journal of Personality and Social Psychology*, 59, 249–260.

Dowling, W. J., & Harwood, D. L. (1986). *Music cognition*. Orlando, FL: Academic Press.

Dozier, M., & Kobak, R. R. (1992). Psychophysiology in attachment interviews: Converging evidence for deactivating strategies. *Child Development*, 63, 1473–1480.

Draycock, S. G., & Kline, R. P. (1995). The Big Three or the Big Five—the EPQ-R vs the NEO-PI: A research note, replication and elaboration. *Personality and Individual Differences*, 18, 801–804.

Dubbert, P. (1992). Exercise in behavioral medicine. *Journal of Consulting and Clinical Psychology*, 60, 613–618.

Duncker, K. (1929). Über induzierte Bewegung (ein Beitrag zur Theorie optisch wahrgenommener Bewegung). *Psychologische Forschung*, 2, 180–259.

Duncker, K. (1945). On problem-solving. *Psychological Monographs*, 58(5, Whole No. 270).

Dunn, J., & Plomin, R. (1990) *Separate lives: Why siblings are so different*. New York: Basic Books.

Durlach, N. I., & Colburn, H. S. (1978). Binaural phenomenon. In E. C. Carterette & M. P. Friedman (Eds.), *Handbook of perception* (Vol. 4). New York: Academic Press.

Dutton, D. G., & Aron, A. P. (1974). Some evidence for heightened sexual attraction under conditions of high anxiety. *Journal of Personality and Social Psychology*, 30, 510–517.

Dweck, C. S. (1992). The study of goals in human behavior. *Psychological Science*, 3, 165–167.

Dweck, C. S. (1999). *Self-theories: Their role in motivation, personality, and development*. Philadelphia, PA: Psychology Press.

Dyal, J. A. (1984). Cross-cultural research with the locus of control concept. In H. Lefcourt (Ed.), *Research with the locus of control construct: Vol. 3. Extensions and limitations*. San Diego, CA: Academic Press.

D'Zurilla, T. J. (1986). *Problem-solving therapy: A social competence approach to clinical intervention*. New York: Springer.

D'Zurilla, T. J. (1990). Problem-solving training for effective stress management and prevention. *Journal of Cognitive Psychotherapy: An International Quarterly*, 4, 327–355.

D'Zurilla, T. J., & Goldfried, M. R. (1971). Problem solving and behavior modification. *Journal of Abnormal Psychology*, 78(1), 107–126.

Eagly, A. H. (1987). *Sex differences and social behavior: A social-role interpretation*. Hillsdale, NJ: Erlbaum.

Eagly, A. H., & Chaiken, S. (1975). An attribution analysis of communicator attractiveness. *Journal of Personality and Social Psychology*, 32, 136–144.

Eagly, A. H., & Chaiken, S. (1992). *The psychology of attitudes*. San Diego: Harcourt Brace.

Eagly, A. H., & Chaiken, S. (1998). Attitude structure and function. In D. Gilbert, S. Fiske, & G. Lindzey (Eds.), *The handbook of social psychology* (4th ed.). New York: McGraw-Hill.

Eagly, A. H., Makhijani, M. G., & Klonsky, B. G. (1992). Gender and the evaluation of leaders: A meta-analysis. *Psychological Bulletin*, 111(1), 3–22.

Eals, M., & Silverman, I. (1992). The hunter-gatherer theory of spatial sex differences: Proximate factors mediating the female advantage in recall of object arrays. *Ethology and Sociobiology*, 15(2), 95–105.

Early, P. C. (1989). Social loafing and collectivism: A comparison of the United States and the People's Republic of China. *Administrative Science Quarterly*, 34, 565–581.

Ebbinghaus, H. E. (1902). *Grundzuge der psychologie*. Leipzig, Germany: Von Veit.

Ebbinghaus, H. E. (1964). *Memory: A contribution to experimental psychology*. New York: Dover. (Original work published 1885)

Ebenholtz, S. M., Cohen, M. M., & Linder, B. J. (1994). The possible role of nystagmus in motion sickness: a hypothesis. *Aviation, Space and Environmental Medicine*, 65(11), 1032–1035.

Ebstein, R. P., Novick, O., Umansky, R., Priel, B., Osher, Y., Blaine, D., Bennett, E. R., Nemanov, L., Katz, M., & Belmaker, R. H. (1996). Dopamine D4 receptor (D4DR) exon III polymorphism associated with human personality trait of novelty seeking. *Nature Genetics*, 12, 78–80.

Eccles, J. S., Jacobs, J., Harold, R., Yoon, K. S., Abreton, A., & Freedman-Doan, C. (1993). Parents' and gender-role socialization during the middle childhood and adolescent years. In S. Oskamp & M. Costanzo (Eds.), *Gender issues in contemporary society* (pp. 59–83). Newbury Park, CA: Sage.

Eccles, J. S., Wigfield, A., Harold, R. D., & Blumenfield, P. (1993). Age and gender differences in children's self- and task perceptions during elementary school. *Child Development*, 64, 830–847.

Eccles, J. S., Wigfield, A., & Schiefele, U. (1998). Motivation to succeed. In W. Damon (Gen. Ed.), & N. Eisenberg (Vol. Ed.), *Handbook of child psychology* (Vol. 3): *Social, emotional, and personality development*. New York: Wiley.

Eckenrode, J. (1984). Impact of chronic and acute stressors on daily reports of mood. *Journal of Personality and Social Psychology*, 46, 907–918.

Eckenrode, J., & Gore, S. (Eds.). (1990). *Stress between work and family*. New York: Plenum Press.

Edgerton, R. (1967). *The cloak of competence*. Berkeley: University of California Press.

Edmonston, W. E., Jr. (1981). *Hypnosis and relaxation*. New York: Wiley.

Edwards, K., & Smith, E. E. (1996). A disconfirmation bias in the evaluation of arguments. *Journal of Personality and Social Psychology*, 71, 5–24.

Egeland, B., & Sroufe, L. A. (1981). Attachment and early maltreatment. *Child Development*, 52, 44–52.

Egeth, H. E. (1993). What do we not know about eyewitness identification? *American Psychologist*, 48(5), 577–580.

Eimas, P. D. (1985). The perception of speech in early infancy. *Scientific American*, 252, 46–52.

Eisenberg, M. (1991). Meta-analytic contributions to the literature on prosocial behavior. *Personality and Social Psychology Bulletin*, 17, 273–282.

Eisenberg, N., & Fabes, R. A. (1998). Prosocial development. In W. Damon (Gen. Ed.) & N. Eisenberg (Vol. Ed.), *Handbook of child psychology* (Vol. 3): *Social, emotional, and personality development* (pp. 701–778). New York: Wiley.

Eisenberger, R., & Armeli, S. (1997). Can salient reward increase creative performance without reducing intrinsic creative interest? *Journal of Personality and Social Psychology*, 72, 652–663.

Eisenberger, R., & Cameron, J. (1996). Detrimental effects of reward: Reality or myth? *American Psychologist*, 51, 1153–1166.

Eisenstock, B. (1984). Sex-role differences in children's identification with counterstereotypical televised portrayals. *Sex Roles, 10*(5–6), 417–430.

Ekman, P. (1971). Universals and cultural differences in the facial expression of emotion. In J. Cole (Ed.), *Nebraska Symposium on Motivation* (Vol. 19, pp. 207–284). Lincoln: University of Nebraska Press.

Ekman, P. (1973). *Darwin and facial expression: A century of research in review.* New York: Academic Press.

Ekman, P. (1984). Expression and the nature of emotion. In P. Ekman & K. Scherer (Eds.), *Approaches to emotion* (pp. 319–343). Hillsdale, NJ: Erlbaum.

Ekman, P. (1992a). *Telling lies.* New York: Norton.

Ekman, P. (1992b). Facial expressions of emotion: New findings, new questions. *Psychological Science, 3,* 34–38.

Ekman, P. (1993). Facial expression and emotion. *American Psychologist, 48,* 384–392.

Ekman, P. (1994). Strong evidence of universals in facial expressions: A reply to Russell's mistaken critique. *Psychological Bulletin, 115,* 268–287.

Ekman, P., & Davidson, R. J. (Eds.). (1994). *The nature of emotion: Fundamental questions.* New York: Oxford University Press.

Ekman, P., & Friesen, W. V. (1971). Constants across cultures in the face and emotion. *Journal of Personality and Social Psychology, 17,* 124–129.

Ekman, P., & Friesen, W. V. (1975). *Unmasking the face.* Englewood Cliffs, NJ: Prentice-Hall.

Ekman, P., & Friesen, W. V. (1984). *Unmasking the face* (2nd ed.). Palo Alto, CA: Consulting Psychologists Press.

Ekman, P., Friesen, W. V., & O'Sullivan, M. (1988). Smiles when lying. *Journal of Personality and Social Psychology, 54,* 414–420.

Ekman, P., Levenson, R. W., & Friesen, W. V. (1983). Autonomic nervous system activity distinguishes among emotions. *Science, 221,* 1208–1210.

Ekman, P., & Oster, H. (1979). Facial expression of emotion. *Annual Review of Psychology, 30,* 527–554.

Elashoff, J. R., & Snow, R. E. (1971). *Pygmalion reconsidered.* Worthington, OH: Charles A. Jones.

Eliot, R. S., & Buell, J. C. (1983). The role of the central nervous system in sudden cardiac death. In T. M. Dembroski, T. Schmidt, & G. Blunchen (Eds.), *Biobehavioral bases of coronary-prone behavior.* New York: Plenum.

Elkind, D. (1967). Egocentrism in adolescence. *Child Development, 38,* 1025–1034.

Elkind, D. (1985). Egocentrism redux. *Developmental Review, 5,* 218–226.

Ellis, A. (1962). *Reason and emotion in psychotherapy.* Secaucus, NJ: Lyle Stuart.

Ellis, A. (1970). *Reason and emotion in psychotherapy.* New York: Lyle Stuart.

Ellis, A. (1973). Rational-emotive therapy. In R. J. Corsini (Ed.), *Current psychotherapies.* Itasca, IL: Peacock.

Ellis, A. (1989). The history of cognition in psychotherapy. In A. Freeman, K. M. Simon, L. E. Beutler, & H. Arkowitz (Eds.), *Comprehensive handbook of cognitive therapy* (pp. 5–19). New York: Plenum.

Ellis, A., & Dryden, W. (1997). *The practice of rational-emotive behavior therapy* (2nd ed.). New York: Springer.

Embretson, S., & McCollam, K. (2000). Psychometric approaches to the understanding of intelligence. In R. J. Sternberg (Ed.), *Handbook of intelligence.* New York: Cambridge University Press.

Endler, N. S., & Magnusson, D. (1976). Toward an interactional psychology of personality. *Psychological Bulletin, 83,* 956–974.

Engel, A. S., Rumelhart, D. E., Wandell, B. A., Lee A. T., Gover, G. H., Chichilisky, E. J., & Shadlen, M. S. (1994). MRI measurement of language lateralization in Wada-tested patients. *Brain, 118,* 1411–1419.

Engel, G. L. (1977). The need for a new medical model: A challenge for biomedicine. *Science, 196,* 129–136.

Engel, G. L. (1980). The clincial application of the biopsychosocial model. *American Journal of Psychiatry, 137,* 535–544.

Engle, R. W. (1994). Memory. In R. J. Sternberg (Ed.), *Encyclopedia of intelligence* (Vol. 2, pp. 700–704). New York: Macmillan.

Engle, R. W., Cantor, J., & Carullo, J. J. (1992). Individual differences in working memory and comprehension: A test of four hypotheses. *Journal of Experimental Psychology: Learning, Memory, & Cognition, 18*(5), 972–992.

Engle, R. W., Carullo, J. J., & Collins, K. W. (1992). Individual differences in working memory for comprehension and following directions. *Journal of Educational Research, 84*(5), 253–262.

Enna, S. J., & DeFranz, J. F. (1980). Glycine, GABA and benzodiazepine receptors. In S. J. Enna & H. I. Yamamura (Eds.), *Neurotransmitter receptors (Part 1).* London: Chapman & Hall.

Entwistle, D. R., & Baker, D. P. (1983). Gender and young children's expectations for performance in arithmetic. *Developmental Psychology, 19,* 200–209.

Epstein, R. (1991). Skinner, creativity, and the problem of spontaneous behavior. *Psychological Science, 2,* 362–370.

Epstein, S. (1992). Coping ability, negative self-evaluation, and overgeneralization: Experiment and theory. *Journal of Personality and Social Psychology, 62,* 826–836.

Erdberg, P. (1990). Rorschach assessment. In G. Goldstein & M. Hersen (Eds.), *Psychological assessment* (2nd ed.). New York: Pergamon.

Ericsson, K. A. (1996). *The road to excellence.* Mahwah, NJ: Lawrence Erlbaum.

Ericsson, K. A., & Charness, N. (1994). Expert performance: Its structure and acquisition. *American Psychologist, 49,* 725–747.

Ericsson, K. A., Chase, W. G., & Faloon, S. (1980). Acquisition of a memory skill. *Science, 208,* 1181–1182.

Ericsson, K. A., & Simon, H. A. (1980). Verbal reports as data. *Psychological Review, 87,* 215–251.

Erikson, E. H. (1950). *Childhood and society.* New York: Norton.

Erikson, E. H. (1963). *Childhood and society* (2nd ed.). New York: Norton.

Erikson, E. H. (1968). *Identity, youth, and crisis.* New York: Norton.

Erickson, M. A., & Kruschke, J. K. (1998). Rules and exemplars in category learning. *Journal of Experimental Psychology: General, 127,* 107–140.

Estes, W. K. (1982). Learning, memory, and intelligence. In R. J. Sternberg (Ed.), *Handbook of intelligence* (pp. 170–224). New York: Cambridge University Press.

Evans, G. W., & Lepore, S. J. (1993). Household crowding and social support: A quasiexperimental analysis. *Journal of Personality and Social Psychology, 65,* 308–316.

Ewart, C. K., & Kolodner, K. B. (1994). Negative affect, gender, and expressive style predict elevated ambulatory blood pressure in adolescents. *Journal of Personality and Social Psychology, 66,* 596–605.

Exline, R. V. (1962). Need affiliation and initial communication behavior in problem solving groups characterized by low interpersonal visibility. *Psychological Reports, 10,* 405–411.

Exline, R. V. (1972). Visual interaction: The glances of power and preference. In J. Cole (Ed.), *Nebraska Symposium on Motivation, 1971.* Lincoln: University of Nebraska Press.

Exner, J. E. (1974). *The Rorschach: A comprehensive system (Vol. 1).* New York: Wiley.

Exner, J. E. (1978). *The Rorschach: A comprehensive system. (Vol. 2). Current research and advanced interpretation.* New York: Wiley.

Exner, J. E. (1985). *The Rorschach: A comprehensive system (Vol. 1)* (2nd ed.). New York: Wiley.

Eyferth, K. (1961). Leistungen verschiedener Gruppen von Besatzungskindern in Hamburg—Weschler Intelligenztest für kinder (HAWIK). *Archiv für die gesamte Psychologie, 113,* 222–241.

Eysenck, H. (1975). *The inequality of man.* San Diego: EdITS/Educational & Industrial Testing Service.

Eysenck, H. J. (1952). *The scientific study of personality.* London: Routledge & Kegan Paul.

Eysenck, H. J. (1967). Intelligence assessment: A theoretical and experimental approach. *British Journal of Educational Psychology, 37,* 81–98.

Eysenck, H. J. (1971). *Readings in extraversion-introversion: II. Fields of application.* London: Staples.

Eysenck, H. J. (Ed.). (1981). *A model for personality.* New York: Springer.

Eysenck, H. J., & Kamin, L. (1981). *The intelligence controversy: H. J. Eysenck vs. Leon Kamin.* New York: Wiley.

Fagan, J. F. (1984). The intelligent infant: Theoretical implications. *Intelligence, 8,* 1–9.

Fagan, J. F. (1985). A new look at infant intelligence. In D. K. Detterman (Ed.), *Current topics in human intelligence: Vol. 1. Research methodology.* Norwood, NJ: Ablex.

Fagan, J. F., III, & Montie, J. E. (1988). Behavioral assessment of cognitive well-being in the infant. In J. Kavanagh (Ed.), *Understanding mental retardation: Research accomplishments and new frontiers.* Baltimore: Brookes.

Fanselow, M., & Lester, L. (1988). A functional behavioristic approach to aversively motivated behavior: Predatory imminence as a determinant of the topography of defensive behavior. In R. C. Bolles & M. D. Beecher (Eds.), *Evolution and learning* (pp. 185–212). Hillsdale, NJ: Erlbaum.

Fantz, R. L. (1958). Pattern vision in young infants. *Psychological Record, 8,* 43–47.

Fantz, R. L. (1961). The origin of form perception. *Scientific American, 204,* 66–72.

Farah, M. J. (1988a). Is visual imagery really visual? Overlooked evidence from neuropsychology. *Psychological Review, 95*(3), 307–317.

Farah, M. J. (1988b). The neuropsychology of mental imagery: Converging evidence from brain-damaged and normal subjects. In J. Stiles-Davis, M. Kritchevsky, & U. Bellugi (Eds.), *Spatial cognition: Brain bases and development* (pp. 33–56). Hillsdale, NJ: Erlbaum.

Farah, M. J. (1994). Neuropsychological inference with an interactive brain: A critique of the "locality" assumption. *Behavioral and Brain Sciences, 17,* 43–104.

Farah, M. J., Levinson, K. L., & Klein, K. L. (1995). Face perception and within category discrimination in prosopagnosia. *Neuropsychologia, 33,* 661–674.

Farah, M. J., Wilson, K. D., Drain, H. M., & Tanaka, J. R. (1995). The inverted face inversion effect in prosopagnosia: Evidence for mandatory, face-specific, perceptual mechanisms. *Vision Research, 35,* 2089–2093.

Farne, M. A., Boni, P., Corallo, A., Gnugnoli, D. (1994). Personality variables as moderators between hassles and objective indications of distress (S-IgA). *Stress Medicine, 10*(1), 15–20.

Faust, I. M., Johnson, P. R., & Hirsch, J. (1977a). Adipose tissue regeneration following lipectomy. *Science, 197,* 391–393.

Faust, I. M., Johnson, P. R., & Hirsch, J. (1977b). Surgical removal of adipose tissue alters feeding behavior and the development of obesity in rats. *Science, 197,* 393–396.

Fay, R. E., Turner, C. F., Klassen, A. D., & Gagnon, J. H. (1989). Prevalence and patterns of same-gender sexual contact among men. *Science, 243,* 338–348.

Fazio, R. H., Zanna, M. P., & Cooper, J. (1977). Dissonance and self perception: An integrative view of each theory's proper domain of application. *Journal of Experimental Social Psychology, 13,* 464–479.

Fechner, G. T. (1966). *Elements of psychophysics* (H. E. Adler, Trans.). New York: Holt, Rinehart & Winston. (Original work published 1860)

Federal Bureau of Investigation. (1992). *1991 Uniform Crime Reports.* Washington, DC: U. S. Government Printing Office.

Feeney, J. A., & Noller, P. (1990). Attachment style as a predictor of adult romantic relationships. *Journal of Personality and Social Psychology, 58,* 284–291.

Fein, S., Goethals, G. R., & Kassin, S. M. (1998). *Social influence and presidential debates.* Manuscript submitted for publication.

Feingold, A. (1988). Cognitive gender differences are disappearing. *American Psychologist, 43,* 95–103.

Feingold, A. (1992). Good-looking people are not what we think. *Psychological Bulletin, 111*(2), 304–341.

Feingold, R. (1988). Cognitive gender differences are disappearing. *American Psychologist, 43,* 95–103.

Feist, J. (1990). *Theories of personality* (3rd ed.). Fort Worth, TX: Holt, Rinehart & Winston.

Feldhusen, J. F. (1986). A conception of giftedness. In R. J. Sternberg & J. E. Davidson (Eds.), *Conceptions of giftedness* (pp. 112–127). New York: Cambridge University Press.

Feldman, D. H. (1986). *Nature's gambit: Child prodigies and the development of human potential.* New York: Basic Books.

Feldman, D. H. (1988). Creativity: Dreams, insights, and transformations. In R. J. Sternberg (Ed.), *The nature of creativity* (pp. 271–297). New York: Cambridge University Press.

Feldman, D. H. (1999). The development of creativity. In R. J. Sternberg (Ed.), *Handbook of creativity* (pp. 169–186). New York: Cambridge University Press.

Fenigstein, A., Scheier, M. F., & Buss, A. H. (1975). Public and private self-consciousness: Assessment and theory. *Journal of Consulting and Clinical Psychology, 43,* 522–527.

Fenwick, P. (1987). Meditation and the EEG. In M. A. West (Ed.), *The psychology of meditation.* Oxford, England: Clarendon Press.

Fernald, A. (1985). Four-month-old infants prefer to listen to motherese. *Infant Behavior and Development, 8,* 118–195.

Fernald, A., Taeschner, T., Dunn, J., Papousek, M., De Boysson-Bardies, B., & Fukui, I. (1989). A cross-cultural study of prosodic modification in mothers' and fathers' speech to preverbal infants. *Journal of Child Language, 16,* 477–501.

Fernandez, E., & Turk, D. C. (1992). Sensory and affective components of pain: Separation and synthesis. *Psychological Bulletin, 112*(2), 205–217.

Ferster, C. B. (1961). Positive reinforcement and behavioral deficits of autistic children. *Child Development, 32,* 437–456.

Ferster, C. B. (1973). A functional analysis of depression. *American Psychology, 28*(110), 857–870.

Feshbach, S. (1970). Aggression. In P. H. Mussen (Ed.), *Carmichael's manual of child psychology.* New York: Wiley.

Festinger, L. (1954). A theory of social comparison processes. *Human Relations, 7,* 117–140.

Festinger, L. (1957). *A theory of cognitive dissonance.* Evanston, IL: Row, Peterson.

Festinger, L., & Carlsmith, J. M. (1959). Cognitive consequences of forced compliance. *Journal of Abnormal and Social Psychology, 58,* 203–210.

Festinger, L., Schachter, S., & Back, K. (1950). *Social pressures in informal groups: A study of human factors in housing.* New York: Harper & Brothers.

Feuerstein, R. (1979). *The dynamic assessment of retarded performers: The learning potential assessment device, theory, instruments, and techniques.* Baltimore: University Park Press.

Feuerstein, R. (1980). *Instrumental enrichment: An intervention program for cognitive modifiability.* Baltimore: University Park Press.

Feynman, R. (1985). *Surely you're joking, Mr. Feynman.* New York: Norton.

Field, T. M. (1978). Interaction behaviors of primary versus secondary caregiver fathers. *Developmental Psychology, 14,* 183–184.

Field, T. M. (1989). Individual and maturational differences in infant expressivity. In N. Eisenberg (Ed.), *Empathy and related responses.* San Francisco: Jossey-Bass.

Field, T. M. (1990). Infant daycare has positive effects on grade school behavior and performance. Unpublished manuscript. University of Miami, Coral Gables, FL.

Figlewicz, D. P., Schwartz, M. W., Seeley, R. J., Chavez, M., Baskin, D. G., Woods, S. C., & Porte, D. (1996). Endocrine regulation of food intake and body weight. *Journal of Laboratory and Clinical Medicine, 127,* 328–332.

Finger, W. J., Borduin, C. M., & Baumstark, K. E. (1992). Correlates of moral judgment development in college students. *Journal of Genetic Psychology, 153*(2), 221–223.

Fiore, E. (1989). *Encounters: A psychologist reveals case studies of abductions by extraterrestrials.* New York: Doubleday.

Fischer, C. S., Hout, M., Jankowski, M. S., Lucas, S. R., Swidler, A., & Voss, K. (1996). *Inequality by design.* Princeton: Princeton University Press.

Fischer, K. W., & Grannott, N. (1995). Beyond one-dimensional change: Parallel, concurrent, socially distributed processes in learning and development. *Human Development, 38,* 302–314.

Fischetti, M., Curran, S. P., & Wessberg, H. W. (1977). Sense of timing. *Behavior Modification, 1,* 179–194.

Fischhoff, B. (1988). Judgment and decision making. In R. J. Sternberg & E. E. Smith (Eds.), *The psychology of human thought* (pp. 153–187). New York: Cambridge University Press.

Fischhoff, B., Slovic, P., & Lichtenstein, S. (1977). Knowing with certainty: The appropriateness of extreme confidence. *Journal of Experimental Psychology: Human Perception and Performance, 3,* 552–564.

Fisher, R., & Ury, W. (1981). *Getting to yes.* Boston: Houghton Mifflin.

Fisk, A. D., & Schneider, W. (1981). Control and automatic processing during tasks requiring sustained attention: A new approach to vigilance. *Human Factors, 23,* 737–750.

Fiske, S. (1995). Social cognition. In A. Tesser (Ed.), *Constructing social psychology.* New York: McGraw Hill.

Fiske, S., & Taylor, S. E. (1991). *Social cognition.* New York: McGraw-Hill.

Fivush, R., & Hamond, N. R. (1991). Autobiographical memory across the preschool years: Toward reconceptualizing childhood memory. In R. Fivush & N. R. Hamond (Eds.), *Knowing and remembering in young children.* New York: Cambridge University Press.

Flatow, I. (1993). *They all laughed . . . from light bulbs to lasers: The fascinating stories behind the great inventions that have changed our lives.* New York: HarperCollins.

Flavell, J. H. (1971). Stage-related properties of cognitive development. *Cognitive Psychology, 2,* 421–453.

Flavell, J. H. (1976). Metacognitive aspects of problem solving. In L. Resnick (Ed.), *The nature of intelligence.* Hillsdale, NJ: Erlbaum.

Flavell, J. H. (1981). Cognitive monitoring. In W. P. Dickson (Ed.), *Children's oral communication skills* (pp. 35–60). New York: Academic Press.

Flavell, J. H. (1985). *Cognitive development* (2nd ed.). Englewood Cliffs, NJ: Prentice-Hall.

Flavell, J. H., Flavell, E. R., & Green, F. L. (1983). Development of the appearance–reality distinction. *Cognitive Psychology, 15,* 95–120.

Flavell, J. H., Green, F. L., & Flavell, E. R. (1995). Young children's knowledge about thinking. *Monographs of the Society for Research in Child Development, 60* (1, Serial No. 243).

Flavell, J. H., & Wellman, H. M. (1977). Metamemory. In R. V. Kail, Jr., & J. W. Hagen (Eds.), *Perspectives on the development of memory and cognition* (pp. 3–33). Hillsdale, NJ: Erlbaum.

Floody, O. R. (1983). Hormones and aggression in female mammals. In B. B. Svare (Ed.), *Hormones and aggressive behavior* (pp. 39–89). New York: Plenum.

Flynn, J. R. (1987). Massive IQ gains in 14 nations: What IQ tests really measure. *Psychological Bulletin, 95,* 29–51.

Fodor, J. A. (1975). *The language of thought.* New York: Crowell.

Fogel, A. (1991). *Infancy: Infant, family, and society* (2nd ed.). St. Paul, MN: West.

Fogel, A. (1992). Movement and communication in human infancy: The social dynamics of development. *Human Movement Science, 11*(4), 387–423.

Folkman, S., & Lazarus, R. S. (1988). *Manual for the ways of coping questionnaire.* Palo Alto, CA: Consulting Psychologists Press.

Folkman, S., Lazarus, R. S., Gruen, R. J., & DeLongis, A. (1986). Appraisal, coping, health status, and psychological symptoms. *Journal of Personality and Social Psychology, 50*(3), 571–579.

Fontaine, K. R. (1994). Personality correlates of sexual risk-taking among men. *Personality and Individual Differences, 17,* 693–694.

Forbes, M. S. (1990). *Women who made a difference.* New York: Simon & Schuster.

Ford, C. S., & Beach, F. A. (1951). *Patterns of sexual behavior.* New York: Harper & Row.

Ford, M. E. (1994). Social intelligence. In R. J. Sternberg (Ed.), *Encyclopedia of human intelligence* (Vol. 2, pp. 974–978). New York: Macmillan.

Forsyth, D. R. (1990). *An introduction to group dynamics.* Pacific Grove, CA: Brooks/Cole.

Fottrell, E. (1983). *Case histories in psychiatry.* New York: Churchill Livingston.

Foulke, E., & Sticht, T. (1969). Review of research on the intelligibility and comprehension of accelerated speech. *Psychological Bulletin, 72,* 50–62.

Foulkes, D. (1985). *Dreaming: A cognitive psychological analysis.* Hillsdale, NJ: Erlbaum.

Foulkes, D. (1990). Dreaming and consciousness. *European Journal of Cognitive Psychology, 2,* 39–55.

Frankl, V. (1959). *From death camp to existentialism.* Boston: Beacon.

Fraser, S. (Ed.). (1995). *The bell curve wars: Race, intelligence, and the future of America.* New York: Basic Books.

Freeman, A. W., & Badcock, D. R. (1999). Visual sensitivity in the presence of a patterned background. *Journal of the Optical Society of America, 16,* 979–986.

Freeman, W. (1959). Psychosurgery. In S. Arieti (Ed.), *American handbook of psychiatry* (Vol. 2, pp. 1521–1540). New York: Basic Books.

Fremouw, W. J., Perczel, W. J., & Ellis, T. E. (1990). *Suicide risk: Assessment and response guidelines.* Elmsford, NY: Pergamon.

Frensch, P. A., & Buchner, A. (1999). Domain-generality versus domain-specificity in cognition. In R. J. Sternberg (Ed.), *The nature of cognition* (pp. 137–172). Cambridge, MA: MIT Press.

Frensch, P. A., & Funke, J. (1995). *Complex problem solving: European perspectives.* Hillsdale, NJ: Lawrence Erlbaum Associates.

Frensch, P. A., & Sternberg, R. J. (1989). Expertise and intelligent thinking: When is it worse to know better? In R. J. Sternberg (Ed.), *Advances in the psychology of human intelligence.* Hillsdale, NJ: Erlbaum.

Freud, A. (1946). *The ego and the mechanisms of defense.* New York: International Universities Press.

Freud, S. (1922). Certain neurotic mechanisms in jealousy, paranoia, and homosexuality. In *Collected Papers* (Vol. 2). London: Hogarth Press.

Freud, S. (1949). *A general introduction to psychoanalysis.* New York: Penguin.

Freud, S. (1953). *An aphasia.* London: Imago.

Freud, S. (1954). *Interpretation of dreams.* London: Allen & Unwin. (Original work published 1900)

Freud, S. (1957). Mourning and melancholia. In *Standard edition of the complete psychological works of Sigmund Freud* (Vol. 14). London: Hogarth. (Original work published 1917)

Freud, S. (1963a). *Dora: An analysis of a case of hysteria.* New York: Macmillan. (Original work published 1905)

Freud, S. (1963b). Introductory lectures on psychoanalysis. In *Standard edition of the complete psychological works of Sigmund Freud* (Vols. 15, 16). (Original work published 1917)

Freud, S. (1963). Introductory lectures on psychoanalysis. In J. Strachey (Ed. and Trans.), *The standard edition of the complete psychological works of Sigmund Freud* (Vol. 9). London: Hogarth. (Original work published 1908)

Freud, S. (1964a). New introductory lectures. In *Standard edition of the complete psychological works of Sigmund Freud* (Vol. 21). London: Hogarth. (Original work published 1933)

Freud, S. (1964b). Three essays on the theory of sexuality. In *Standard edition of the complete psychological works of Sigmund Freud* (Vol. 7). London: Hogarth Press—Institute of Psychological Analysis. (Original work published 1905)

Freudenheim, M. (1993, August 18). Many patients unhappy with H. M. O.'s. *New York Times*, pp. 5,16.

Frey, K. S., & Ruble, D. N. (1987). Social comparison and self-evaluation in the classroom: Developmental changes in knowledge and function. In J. C. Masters & W. S. Smith (Eds.), *Social comparisons, social justice, and relative deprivation* (pp. 81–104). Hillsdale, NJ: Erlbaum.

Friedman, M., & Rosenman, R. H. (1974). *Type A behavior and your heart.* New York: Knopf.

Friedman, M., Thoresen, C. E., Gill, J. J., Ulmer, D., et al. (1994). Alteration of Type A behavior and its effect on cardiac recurrences in post myocardial infarction patients: Summary results of the recurrent coronary prevention project. In A. Steptoe & J. Wardle (Eds.), *Psychosocial processes and health: A reader* (pp. 478–506). Cambridge, England: Cambridge University Press.

Friedman, M. I. (1991). Metabolic control of calorie intake. In M. I. Friedman, M. G. Tordoff, & M. R. Kare (Eds.), *Chemical senses: Vol. 4. Appetite and Nutrition* (pp. 19–38). New York: Marcel Dekker.

Friedman, M. I., & Stricker, E. M. (1976). The physiological psychology of hunger: A physiological perspective. *Psychological Review, 83,* 409–431.

Friedrich-Cofer, L., & Huston, A. C. (1986). Television violence and aggression: The debate continues. *Psychological Bulletin, 100*(3), 364–371.

Frith, U., & Baron-Cohen, S. (1987). Perception in autistic children. In D. J. Cohen & A. M. Donnellan (Eds.), *Handbook of autism and pervasive developmental disorders* (pp. 55–102). New York: Wiley.

Fromkin, V. A. (1973). *Speech errors as linguistic evidence.* The Hague, Netherlands: Mouton.

Fromm, E. (1941). *Escape from freedom.* New York: Farrar & Rinehart.

Fromm, E. (1947). *Man for himself.* Greenwich, CT: Fawcett.

Fromm, E. (1955). *The sane society.* Greenwich, CT: Fawcett.

Fromm-Reichmann, F. (1948). Notes on the development of treatment of schizophrenics by psychoanalytic psychotherapy. *Psychiatry, 11,* 263–273.

Frost, N. (1972). Encoding and retrieval in visual memory tasks. *Journal of Experimental Psychology, 95,* 317–326.

Fuchs, J., Levinson, R., Stoddard, R., Mullet, M., & Jones, D. (1990). Health risk factors among the Amish: Results of a survey. *Health Education Quarterly, 17,* 197–211.

Funder, D. C., Kolar, D. C., & Blackman, M. C. (1995). Agreement among judges of personality: Interpersonal relations, similarity, and acquaintanceship. *Journal of Personality and Social Psychology, 69,* 656–672.

Funder, D. C., & Ozer, D. J. (1983). Behavior as a function of the situation. *Journal of Personality & Social Psychology, 44*(1), 107–112.

Furnham, A., & Medhurst, S. (1995). Personality correlates of academic seminar behaviour: A study of four instruments. *Personality and Individual Differences, 19,* 197–208.

Furnham, A., & Skae, E. (1997). Changes in the stereotypical portrayal of men and women in British television advertisements. *European Psychologist, 2,* 44–51.

Furomoto, L., & Scarborough, E. (1986). Placing women in the history of psychology: The first American women psychologists. *American Psychologist, 41*(1), 35–42.

Gabbard, G. O., Lazar, S. G., Hornberger, J., & Spiegel, D. (1997). The economic impact of psychotherapy: A review. *American Journal of Psychiatry, 154,* 147–155.

Gabrenya, W. K., Latané, B., & Wang, Y. E. (1983). Social loafing in cross-cultural perspective: Chinese in Taiwan. *Journal of Cross-Cultural Psychology, 14,* 368–384.

Gabrenya, W. K., Wang, Y. E., & Latané, B. (1985). Social loafing on an optimizing task: Cross-cultural differences among Chinese and Americans. *Journal of Cross-Cultural Psychology, 16,* 223–242.

Gabrieli, J. D. E., Desmond, J. E., Demb, J. B., Wagner, A. D., Stone, M. V., Vaidya, C. J., & Glover, G. H. (1996). Functional magnetic resonance imaging of semantic memory processes in the frontal lobes. *Psychological Science, 7,* 278–283.

Gagnon, J. H. (1973). Scripts and the coordination of sexual conduct. In J. K. Cole & R. Riensteiber (Eds.), *Nebraska Symposium on Motivation* (Vol. 21, pp. 27–59). Lincoln: University of Nebraska Press.

Galanter, E. (1962). Contemporary psychophysics. In R. Brown et al. (Eds.), *New directions in psychology* (Vol. 1). New York: Holt, Rinehart & Winston.

Galanter, M., (1989). *Cults: Faith, healing, and coercion.* New York: Oxford University Press.

Galef, B. G., Jr., & Whiskin, E. E. (1998). Limits on social influence on food choices of Norway rats. *Animal Behavior, 56,* 1015–1020.

Galef, B. G., Jr., Whiskin, E. E., & Bielvaska, E. (1997). Interaction with demonstrator rats changes observer rats' affective responses to flavors. *Journal of Comparative Psychology, 111,* 393–398.

Galton, F. (1883). *Inquiry into human faculty and its development.* London: Macmillan.

Gan, S., Zillmann, D., & Mitrook, M. (1997). Stereotyping effect of Black women's sexual rap on White audiences. *Basic and Applied Social Psychology, 19,* 381–399.

Gara, M. A., Woolfolk, R. L., Cohen, B. D., Goldston, R. B., Allen, L. A., & Novalany, J. (1993). Perception of self and other in major depression. *Journal of Abnormal Psychology, 102,* 93–100.

Garcia, J., & Koelling, R. A. (1966). The relation of cue to consequence in avoidance learning. *Psychonomic Science, 4,* 123–124.

Garcia, L. D., & Khersonsky, D. (1997). "They are a lovely couple": Further examination of perceptions of couple attractiveness. *Journal of Social Behavior and Personality, 12,* 367–380.

Gardner, H. (1983). *Frames of mind: The theory of multiple intelligences.* New York: Basic Books.

Gardner, H. (1988). Creative lives and creative works: A synthetic scientific approach. In R. J. Sternberg (Ed.), *The nature of creativity.* New York: Cambridge University Press.

Gardner, H. (1993a). Intelligence and intelligences: Universal principles and differences. *Archives de Psychologie, 61*(238), 169–172.

Gardner, H. (1993b). *Multiple intelligences: The theory in practice.* New York: Basic Books.

Gardner, H. (1999). Are there additional intelligences? The case for naturalist, spiritual, and existential intelligences. In J. Kane (Ed.), *Education, information, and transformation* (pp. 111–131). Upper Saddle River, NJ: Prentice-Hall.

Gardner, R. A., & Gardner, B. T. (1969). Teaching sign language to a chimpanzee. *Science, 165,* 664–672.

Garland, A. F., & Zigler, E. (1994). Adolescent suicide prevention: Current research and social policy implications. *American Psychologist, 48,* 169–182.

Garn, S. M. (1980). Human growth. *Annual Review of Anthropology, 9,* 275–292.

Garner, W. R., Hake, H. W., & Eriksen, C. W. (1956). Operationism and the concept of perception. *Psychological Review, 63,* 149–159.

Garrett, M. F. (1992). Disorders of lexical selection. *Cognition, 42,* 143–180.

Garro, L. C. (1986). Language, memory, and focality: A reexamination. *American Anthropologist, 88,* 128–136.

Gazzaniga, M. S. (1970). *The bisected brain.* New York: Appleton-Century-Crofts.

Gazzaniga, M. S. (1985). *The social brain: Discovering the networks of the mind.* New York: Basic Books.

Gazzaniga, M. S., Ivry, R. B., & Mangun, G. R. (1998). *Cognitive neuroscience: The biology of the mind.* New York: Norton.

Gazzaniga, M. S., & LeDoux, J. E. (1978). *The integrated mind.* New York: Plenum.

Geen, R. G. (1990). *Human aggression.* Stony Stratford, UK: Open University Press.

Gegenfurtner, K. R., Mayser, H., & Sharpe, L. T. (1999). Seeing movement in the dark. *Nature, 398,* 475–476.

Geiselman, R. E., Fisher, R. P., MacKinnon, P. P., & Holland, H. L. (1985). Eyewitness memory enhancement in the police interview: Cognitive retrieval mnemonics versus hypnosis. *Journal of Applied Psychology, 70,* 401–412.

Gelman, R., & Baillargeon, R. (1983). A review of some Piagetian concepts. In P. H. Mussen (Series Ed.), J. Flavell & E. Markman (Vol. Eds.), *Handbook of child psychology: Vol. 3. Cognitive development* (4th ed., pp. 167–230). New York: Wiley.

Gelman, R., & Gallistel, C. R. (1978). *The child's understanding of number.* Cambridge, MA: Harvard University Press.

Gelman, S. A. (1985). Children's inductive inferences from natural kind and artifact categories (Doctoral dissertation, Stanford University, 1984). *Dissertation Abstracts International, 45*(10–B), 3351–3352.

Gelman, S. A., & Kremer, K. E. (1991). Understanding natural causes: Children's explanations of how objects and their properties originate. *Child Development, 62*(2), 396–414.

Gelman, S. A., & Markman, E. M. (1987). Young children's inductions from natural kinds: The role of categories and appearances. *Child Development, 58*(6), 1532–1541.

Gelman, S. A., & Wellman, H. M. (1991). Insides and essence: Early understandings of the non-obvious. *Cognition, 38,* 213–244.

Gentner, D. (1983). Structure-mapping: A theoretical framework for analogy. *Cognitive Science, 7,* 155–170.

George, M. S., Ring, H. A., & Costa, D. C. (1991). *Neuroactivation and neuroimaging with SPECT.* London: Springer-Verlag.

Gerrig, R. J., & Banaji, M. R. (1994). Language and thought. In R. J. Sternberg (Ed.), *Handbook of perception and cognition: Thinking and problem solving.* New York: Academic Press.

Gesell, A. L. (1928). *Infancy and human growth.* New York: Macmillan.

Gesell, A. L., & Ilg, F. L. (1949). *Child development.* New York: Harper.

Geyelin, M. (1994, May 15). Lawsuits over false memories face hurdles. *Wall Street Journal,* p. 10(N).

Gibbons, F. X., Benhow, C. P., & Gerrard, M. (1994). From top dog to bottom half: Social comparison strategies in response to poor performance. *Journal of Personality and Social Psychology, 67,* 638–652.

Gibbs, J. (Ed.). (1968). *Suicide.* New York: Harper & Row.

Gibbs, J. C., Arnold, K. D., Ahlborn, H. H., & Cheesman, F. L. (1984). Facilitation of sociomoral reasoning in delinquents. *Journal of Consulting and Clinical Psychology, 52,* 37–45.

Gibson, J. J. (1950). *The perception of the visual world.* Boston: Houghton Mifflin.

Gibson, J. J. (1979). *The ecological approach to visual perception.* Boston: Houghton Mifflin.

Gick, M. L., & Holyoak, K. J. (1980). Analogical problem solving. *Cognitive Psychology, 12,* 306–355.

Gick, M. L., & Holyoak, K. J. (1983). Schema induction and analogical transfer. *Cognitive Psychology, 15,* 1–38.

Gigerenzer, G., Todd, P. M., & the ABC Research Group (1999). *Simple heuristics that make us smart.* New York: Oxford University Press.

Gilbert, E., & DeBlassie, R. (1984). Anorexia nervosa: Adolescent starvation by choice. *Adolescence, 19,* 840–846.

Gill, M. M. (1972). Hypnosis as an altered and regressed state. *International Journal of Clinical and Experimental Hypnosis, 20,* 224–337.

Gilligan, C. (1982). *In a different voice: Psychological theory and women's development.* Cambridge, MA: Harvard University Press.

Gilligan, C., & Attanucci, J. (1988). Two moral orientations: Gender differences and similarities. *Merrill-Palmer Quarterly, 34,* 223–237.

Gilligan, C., Hamner, T., & Lyons, N. (1990). *Making connections.* Cambridge, MA: Harvard University Press.

Gilly, M. C. (1988). Sex roles in advertising: A comparison of television advertisements in Australia, Mexico, and the United States. *Journal of Marketing, 52*(2), 75–85.

Gladwin, T. (1970). *East is a big bird.* Cambridge, MA: Belknap Press.

Glaser, R., & Chi, M. T. H. (1988). Overview. In M. T. H. Chi, R. Glaser, & M. Farr (Eds.), *The nature of expertise* (pp. xv–xxxvi). Hillsdale, NJ: Erlbaum.

Glass, D. C. (1977). *Behavior patterns, stress, and coronary heart disease.* Hillsdale, NJ: Erlbaum.

Glick, J. (1975). Cognitive development in cross-cultural perspective. In T. D. Horowitz (Ed.), *Review of child development research.* Chicago: University of Chicago Press.

Glucksberg, S., & Danks, J. H. (1975). *Experimental psycholinguistics.* Hillsdale, NJ: Erlbaum.

Glueck, B. C., & Stroebel, C. F. (1975). Biofeedback and meditation in the treatment of psychiatric illness. *Comprehensive Psychiatry, 16,* 302–321.

Goddard, H. H. (1917). Mental tests and immigrants. *Journal of Delinquency, 2,* 243–277.

Godden, D. R., & Baddeley, A. D. (1975). Context-dependent memory in two natural environments: On land and underwater. *British Journal of Psychology, 66,* 325–331.

Goertzel, M. G., Goertzel, V., & Goertzel, T. G. (1978). *Three hundred eminent personalities.* San Francisco: Jossey-Bass.

Goethals, G. R., & Darley, J. M. (1977). Social comparison theory: An attributional approach. In J. M. Suls & R. L. Miller (Eds.), *Social comparison processes: Theoretical and empirical perspectives* (pp. 259–278). Washington, DC: Hemisphere.

Goff, L. M., & Roediger, H. L. (1998). Imagination inflation for action events: Repeated imaginings lead to illusory recollections. *Memory and Cognition, 26,* 20–33.

Goffman, E. (1967). *Interaction ritual.* New York: Doubleday.

Goldberg, L. R. (1993). The structure of phenotypic personality traits. *American Psychologist, 48,* 26–34.

Goldberg, L. R., & Rosolack, T. K. (1994). The Big Five factor structure as an integrative framework: An empirical comparison with Eysenck's P-E-N model. In C. F. Halverson, Jr., G. A. Kohnstamm, & R. P. Martin (Eds.), *The developing structure of temperament and personality from infancy to adulthood.* Hillsdale, NJ: Erlbaum.

Goldberg, L. R., & Saucier, G. (1995). So what do you propose we use instead? A reply to Block. *Psychological Bulletin, 117,* 221–225.

Golden, C. J., Hammecke, T., & Purisch, A. (1978). Diagnostic validity of a standardized neuropsychological battery derived from Luria's neuropsychological test. *Journal of Consulting and Clinical Psychology, 46,* 1258–1265.

Goldfried, M. R. (1969). Prediction of improvement in an alcoholism outpatient clinic. *Quarterly Journal of Studies on Alcohol, 30*(1–A), 129–139.

Goleman, D. (1993, April 18). When a long therapy goes a little way. *New York Times,* Sect. 4, p. 6.

Goleman, D. (1995). *Emotional intelligence.* New York: Bantam.

Gordon, D., & Lakoff, G. (1971). Conversational postulates. In *Papers from the Seventh Regional Meeting, Chicago Linguistic Society* (pp. 63–84).

Gorman, M. E. (1992). *Simulating science: Heuristics, mental models, and technoscientific thinking.* Bloomington: Indiana University Press.

Gotlib, I. H., & Robinson, L. A. (1982). Responses to depressed individuals: Discrepancies between self-report and observer-rated behavior. *Journal of Abnormal Psychology, 91,* 231–240.

Gottesman, I. I. (1991). *Schizophrenia genesis: The origins of madness.* New York: Freeman.

Gottesman, I. I. (1994). Perils and pleasures of genetic psychopathology. Distinguished Scientist Award address presented at the annual meeting of the American Psychological Association, Los Angeles.

Gottesman, I. I., McGuffin, P., & Farmer, A. E. (1987). Clinical genetics as clues to the "real" genetics of schizophrenia. *Schizophrenia Bulletin, 13,* 23–47.

Gottfried, A. E., & Gottfried, A. W. (Eds.). (1988). *Maternal employment and children's development.* New York: Plenum.

Gottman, J. M. (1979). *Marital interaction.* New York: Academic Press.

Gottman, J. M. (1983). How children become friends. *Monographs of the Society for Research in Child Development, 48*(Serial No. 201).

Gottman, J. M. (1986). The world of coordinated play: Same- and cross-sex friendship in young children. In J. M. Gottman & J. G. Parker (Eds.), *Conversations of friends: Speculations on affective development* (pp. 139–191). Cambridge, England: Cambridge University Press.

Gottman, J. M. (1994). *Why marriages succeed or fail.* New York: Simon & Schuster.

Gottman, J. M., & Levenson, R. W. (1992). Marital processes predictive of later dissolution: Behavior, physiology, and health. *Journal of Personality and Social Psychology, 63,* 221–233.

Gottman, J. M., Notarius, C., Gonso, J., & Markman, H. J. (1976). *A couple's guide to communication.* Champaign, IL: Research Press.

Gottschalk, L. A., Buchsbaum, M. S., Gillin, J. C., Wu, J. C., et al. (1991). Anxiety levels in dreams: Relation to localized cerebral glucose metabolic rate. *Brain Research, 538*(1), 107–110.

Gould, S. J. (1981). *The mismeasure of man.* New York: Norton.

Graf, P. (1990). Life-span changes in implicit and explicit memory. *Bulletin of the Psychonomic Society, 28,* 353–358.

Graf, P., & Schacter, D. L. (1985). Implicit and explicit memory for new associations in normal and amnesic subjects. *Journal of Experimental Psychology: Learning, Memory, and Cognition, 11,* 501–518.

Graham, C. H., & Hsia, Y. (1954). Luminosity curves for normal and dichromatic subjects including a case of unilateral color blindness. *Science, 120,* 780.

Graham, J. R. (1990). *MMPI-2: Assessing personality and psychopathology.* New York: Oxford University Press.

Gray, A. L., Bowers, K. S., & Fenz, W. D. (1970). Heart rate in anticipation of and during a negative visual hallucination. *International Journal of Clinical and Experimental Hypnosis, 18,* 41–51.

Green, D. M., & Swets, J. A. (1966). *Signal detection theory and psychophysics.* Reprint. New York: Krieger.

Greenberg, M., Szmukler, G., & Tantam, D. (1986). *Making sense of psychiatric cases.* New York: Oxford University Press.

Greenberg, R., & Underwood, B. J. (1950). Retention as a function of stage of practice. *Journal of Experimental Psychology, 40,* 452–457.

Greene, D., & Lepper, M. R. (1974). Effects of extrinsic rewards on children's subsequent intrinsic interest. *Child Development, 45,* 1141–1145.

Greene, R. L. (1987). Ethnicity and MMPI performance: A review. *Journal of Consulting and Clinical Psychology, 55,* 497–512.

Greene, R. L. (1990). Stability of MMPI scale scores with four codetypes across forty years. *Journal of Personality Assessment, 55*(1–2), 1–6.

Greene, R. L., & Crowder, R. G. (1984). Modality and suffix effects in the absence of auditory stimulation. *Journal of Verbal Learning and Verbal Behavior, 23,* 371–382.

Greenfield, P. M. (1997). You can't take it with you: Why ability assessments don't cross cultures. *American Psychologist, 52,* 1115–1124.

Greenfield, P. M., & Savage-Rumbaugh, S. (1990). Grammatical combination in Pan paniscus: Processes of learning and invention in the evolution and development of language. In S. Parker & K. Gibson (Eds.), *"Language" and intelligence in monkeys and apes: Comparative developmental perspectives.* New York: Cambridge University Press.

Greeno, J. G. (1974). Hobbits and orcs: Acquisition of a sequential concept. *Cognitive Psychology, 6,* 270–292.

Greeno, J. G., & Simon, H. A. (1988). Problem solving and reasoning. In R. C. Atkinson, R. Herrnstein, G. Lindzey, & R. D. Luce (Eds.), *Stevens' handbook of experimental psychology* (Rev. ed.). New York: Wiley.

Greenwald, A. G., & Banaji, M. R. (1995). Implicit social cognition: Attitudes, self-esteem, and stereotypes. *Psychological Review, 102,* 4–27.

Greenwald, A. G., Pratkanis, A. R., Leippe, M. R., & Baumgardner, M. H. (1986). Under what conditions does theory obstruct research progress? *Psychological Review, 93,* 216–229.

Greenwald, A. G., Spangenberg, E. R., Pratkanis, A. R., & Eskenazi, J. (1991). Double-blind tests of subliminal self-help audiotapes. *Psychological Science, 2,* 119–122.

Gregory, R. L. (1966). *Eye and brain.* New York: World University Library.

Greist, J. H., Jefferson, J. W., Kobak, K. A., Katzelnick, D. J., & Serline, R. C. (1995). Efficacy and tolerability of serotonin transport inhibitors in obsessive–compulsive disorder: A meta-analysis. *Archives of General Psychiatry, 21,* 53–60.

Greyson, B. (1990). Near-death encounters with and without near-death experiences: Comparative NDE scale profiles. *Journal of Near-Death Studies, 8,* 151–161.

Grice, H. P. (1967). William James Lectures, Harvard University, published in part as "Logic and conversation." In P. Cole & J. L. Morgan (Eds.), *Syntax and semantics: Speech acts* (Vol. 3, pp. 41–58). New York: Seminar Press.

Griffith, D. R., Azuma, S. D., & Chasnoff, I. J. (1994). Three-year outcome of children exposed prenatally to drugs. Special section: Cocaine babies. *Journal of the American Academy of Child and Adolescent Psychiatry, 33,* 20–27.

Griffith, R. M., Miyago, M., & Tago, A. (1958). The universality of typical dreams: Japanese vs. Americans. *American Anthropologist, 60,* 1173–1179.

Griffitt, W. & Veitch, R. (1971). Hot and crowded: Influences of population density and temperature on interpersonal affective behavior. *Journal of Personality and Social Psychology, 17,* 92–98.

Grigorenko, E. L. (1999). Heredity versus environment as the basis of cognitive abilities. In R. J. Sternberg (Ed.), *The nature of cognition* (pp. 665–696). Cambridge, MA: MIT Press.

Grigorenko, E. L. (2000). Genes, environment, and intelligence. In R. J. Sternberg (Ed.), *Handbook of intelligence.* New York: Cambridge University Press.

Grigorenko, E. L. & Sternberg, R. J. (1998). Dynamic testing. *Psychological Bulletin, 24,* 75–111.

Grilo, C. M., & Pogue-Geile, M. F. (1991). The nature of environmental influences on weight and obesity: A behavior genetic analysis. *Psychological Bulletin, 110,* 520–537.

Grossman, L., & Eagle, M. (1970). Synonymity, antonymity, and association in false recognition responses. *Journal of Experimental Psychology, 83,* 244–248.

Grossman, M. I., & Stein, I. F. (1948). Vagotomy and the hunger producing action of insulin in man. *Journal of Applied Physiology, 1,* 263–269.

Grossman, S. P., & Grossman, L. (1963). Food and water intake following lesions or electrical stimulation of the amygdala. *American Journal of Physiology, 205,* 761–765.

Grotzer, T., & Perkins, D. (2000). Teaching of intelligence. In R. J. Sternberg (Ed.), *Handbook of intelligence.* New York: Cambridge University Press.

Groves, P. M., & Rebec, G. V. (1976). Biochemistry and behavior: Some central actions of amphetamine and antipsychotic drugs. *Annual Review of Psychology, 27,* 97–128.

Groves, P. M., & Rebec, G. V. (1988). *Introduction to biological psychology* (3rd ed.). Dubuque, IA: William C. Brown.

Gruber, H. E. (1981). *Darwin on man: A psychological study of scientific creativity* (2nd ed.). Chicago: University of Chicago Press. (Original work published 1974)

Gruber, H. E., & Davis, S. N. (1988). Inching our way up Mount Olympus: The evolving-systems approach to creative thinking. In R. J. Sternberg (Ed.), *The nature of creativity* (pp. 243–270). New York: Cambridge University Press.

Gruder, C. L., Cook, T. D., Hennigan, K. M., Flay, B. R., Alessis, C., & Halamaj, J. (1978). Empirical tests of the absolute sleeper effect predicted from the discounting cue hypothesis. *Journal of Personality and Social Psychology, 36,* 1061–1074.

Guha, D., Dutta, S. N., & Pradhan, S. N. (1974). Conditioning of gastric secretion by epinephrine in rats. *Proceedings of the Society for Experimental Biology and Medicine, 147,* 817–819.

Guilford, J. P. (1950). Creativity. *American Psychologist, 5*(9), 444–454.

Guilford, J. P. (1967). *The nature of human intelligence.* New York: McGraw-Hill.

Guilford, J. P. (1982). Cognitive psychology's ambiguities: Some suggested remedies. *Psychological Review, 89,* 48–59.

Gurman, A. S., Kniskern, D. P., & Pinsoff, W. M. (1986). Research on the process and outcome of marital and family therapy. In S. L. Garfield & A. E. Bergin (Eds.), *Handbook of psychotherapy and behavior change* (3rd ed.). New York: Wiley.

Guyote, M. J., & Sternberg, R. J. (1981). A transitive-chain theory of syllogistic reasoning. *Cognitive Psychology, 13,* 461–525.

Guzman, A. (1971). *Analysis of curved line drawings using context and global information. Machine intelligence* (Vol. 6, pp. 325–375). Edinburgh, Scotland: Edinburgh University Press.

Gwirtsman, H. E., & Germer, R. H. (1981). Abnormalities of dexamethasone suppression test and urinary MHPG in anorexia nervosa. *American Journal of Psychiatry, 138,* 650–653.

Haaga, D., Dyck, M., & Ernst, D. (1991). Empirical status of the cognitive theory of depression. *Psychological Bulletin, 110,* 215–236.

Haefely, W. E. (1977). Synaptic pharmacology of barbiturates and benzodiazepines. *Agents and Actions, 713,* 353–359.

Haft, J. I. (1974). Cardiovascular injury induced by sympathetic catecholamines. *Progress in Cardiovascular Disease, 17,* 73.

Haglund, M. M., Ojemann, G. A., Lettich, E., Bellugi, U., et al. (1993). Dissociation of cortical and single unit activity in spoken and signed languages. *Brain & Language, 44*(1), 19–27.

Haier, R. J., Siegel, B. V., Nuechterlein, K. H., Hazlett, E., Wu, J. C., Pack, J., Browning, H. L., & Buchsbaum, M. S. (1988). Cortical glucose metabolic rate correlates of abstract reasoning and attention studied with positron emission tomography. *Intelligence, 12,* 199–217.

Haier, R. J., Siegel, B., Tang, C., Abel, L., & Buchsbaum, M. S. (1992). Intelligence and changes in regional cerebral glucose metabolic rate following learning. *Intelligence, 16*(3–4), 415–426.

Haith, M. M. (1979). Visual cognition in early infancy. In R. B. Kearsley & I. E. Sigel (Eds.), *Infants at risk: Assessment of cognitive functioning.* Hillsdale, NJ: Erlbaum.

Haith, M. M. (1994). Visual expectations as the first step toward the development of future-oriented processes. In M. M. Haith, J. B. Benseon, R. J. Roberts, Jr., & B. F. Pennington (Eds.), *The development of future-oriented processes.* Chicago: University of Chicago Press.

Hakuta, K. (1986). *Mirror of language.* New York: Basic Books.

Halford, G. S. (1995). Learning processes in cognitive development A reassessment with some unexpected implications. *Child Development, 38,* 295–301.

Hall, E. T. (1966). *The hidden dimension.* New York: Doubleday.

Hall, J. A., Epstein, A. M., DeCiantis, M. L., & McNeil, B. (1993). Physician's liking for their patients: More evidence for the role of affect in medical care. *Health Psychology, 12,* 140–146.

Halpern, A. R. (1986). Memory for tune titles after organized or unorganized presentation. *American Journal of Psychology, 49,* 57–70.

Halpern, A. R. (1989). Disappearance of cognitive gender differences: What you see depends on where you look. *American Psychologist, 44,* 1156–1158.

Halpern, D. F. (1995). *Thought and knowledge: An introduction to critical thinking* (3rd ed.). Hillsdale, NJ: Erlbaum.

Halpern, D. F. (1996). *Thinking critically about critical thinking.* Mahwah, NJ: Erlbaum.

Halpern, D. F. (1997). Sex differences in intelligence. *American Psychologist, 52,* 1091–1102.

Hameroff, S. R. (1994). Quantum coherence in microtubules: a neural basis for emergent consciousness. *Journal of Consciousness Studies, 1,* 91–118.

Hameroff, S., & Penrose, R. (1995). Orchestrated reduction of quantum coherence in brain microtubules: a model for consciousness. In J. King & K. H. Pribram (Eds.), *Scale in conscious experience: Is the brain too important to be left to specialists to study?* (pp. 243–274). Mahwah, NJ: Erlbaum.

Hamilton, D. L., & Gifford, R. K. (1976). Illusory correlation in interpersonal perception: A cognitive basis of stereotypic judgments. *Journal of Experimental Social Psychology, 12,* 392–407.

Hamilton, D. L., & Sherman, S. J. (1996). Perceiving persons and groups. *Psychological Review, 103,* 336–355.

Hamilton, E. (1942). *Cupid and Psyche in Mythology* (pp. 92–100). New York: Penguin.

Han, S., & Shavitt, S. (1994). Persuasion and culture: Advertising appeals in individualistic and collectivistic societies. *Journal of Experimental Social Psychology, 30,* 326–350.

Harkins, S. G. (1987). Social loafing and social facilitation. *Journal of Experimental Social Psychology, 23,* 1–18.

Harkins, S. G., & Szymanski, K. (1987). Social loafing and social facilitation: New wine in old bottles. In C. Hendrick (Ed.), *Review of personality and social psychology: Group processes and intergroup relations* (Vol. 9, pp. 167–188). Beverly Hills, CA: Sage.

Harlow, H. F. (1949). The formation of learning sets. *Psychological Review, 56,* 51–65.

Harlow, H. F. (1958). The nature of love. *American Psychologist, 13,* 673–685.

Harlow, H. F. (1962). Heterosexual affectional system in monkeys. *American Psychologist, 17,* 1–9.

Harlow, H. F., & Harlow, M. K. (1965). The affectional systems. In A. M. Schrier, H. F. Harlow, & F. Stollnitz (Eds.), *Behavior of nonhuman primates* (Vol. 2, pp. 287–334). New York: Academic Press.

Harlow, H. F., & Harlow, M. K. (1966). Learning to love. *American Scientist, 54,* 244–272.

Harlow, H. F., Harlow, M. K., & Meyer, D. R. (1950). Learning motivated by a manipulation drive. *Journal of Experimental Psychology, 40,* 228–234.

Harman, G. (1995). Rationality. In E. E. Smith & D. N. Osherson (Eds.), *An invitation to cognitive science: Vol. 3. Thinking* (pp. 175–211). Cambridge, MA: MIT Press.

Harris, M. J., Millich, R., Corbitt, E. M., Hoover, D. W., & Brady, M. (1992). Self-fulfilling effects of stigmatizing information on children's social interactions. *Journal of Personality and Social Psychology, 63,* 41–50.

Harris, T. O. (1992). Social support and unsupportive behaviors. In H. O. F. Veiel & U. Baumann (Eds.), *The meaning and measurement of social support* (pp. 171–192). New York: Hemisphere.

Harte, J. L., Eifert, G. H., & Smith, R. (1995). The effects of running and meditation on beta-endorphin, corticotropin-releasing hormone and cortisol in plasma, and on mood. *Biological Psychology, 40,* 251–265.

Harter, S. (1983). Developmental perspectives on the self-system. In P. H. Mussen (Ed.), *Handbook of child psychology* (4th ed., Vol. 4, pp. 275–385). New York: Wiley.

Harter, S. (1985). Competence as a dimension of self-evaluation: Toward a comprehensive model of self-worth. In R. Leahy (Ed.), *The development of the self* (pp. 55–118). New York: Academic Press.

Harter, S. (1990). Causes, correlates, and the functional role of global self-worth: A life-span perspective. In R. J. Sternberg & J. Kolligian, Jr. (Eds.), *Competence considered* (pp. 67–97). New Haven, CT: Yale University Press.

Harter, S. (1998). The development of self-representations. In W. Damon (Gen. Ed.), & N. Eisenberg (Vol. Ed.), *Handbook of child psychology* (Vol. 3): *Social, emotional, and personality development* (pp. 553–618). New York: Wiley.

Harter, S., & Pike, R. (1984). The pictorial perceived competence scale for young children. *Child Development, 55,* 1969–1982.

Hartmann, E. (1968). The 90-minute sleep–dream cycle. *Archives of General Psychiatry, 18*(3), 280–286.

Hartshorne, H., & May, M. A. (1928). *Studies in the nature of character: Vol. 1. Studies in deceit.* New York: Macmillan.

Hartup, W. W. (1996). The company they keep: Friendships and their developmental significance. *Child Development, 67,* 1–13.

Hasselhorn, M. (1990). The emergence of strategic knowledge activation in categorical clustering during retrieval. *Journal of Experimental Child Psychology, 50,* 59–80.

Hastings, E. H., & Hastings, P. K. (Eds.). (1982). *Index to international public opinion, 1980–81.* Westport, CT: Greenwood Press.

Hatfield, E., & Rapson, R. L. (1992). Similarity and attraction in close relationships. *Communication Monographs, 59*(2), 209–212.

Hatfield, E., & Sprecher, S. (1986). Measuring passionate love in intimate relationships. *Journal of Adolescence, 9,* 383–410.

Hatfield, E., & Walster, G. W. (1981). *A new look at love.* Reading, MA: Addison-Wesley.

Hathaway, S. R., & McKinley, J. C. (1943). *Manual for the Minnesota Multiphasic Personality Inventory.* New York: Psychological Corporation.

Hathaway, S. R., & McKinley, J. C. (1951). *The Minnesota Multiphasic Personality Inventory* (Rev. ed.). New York: Psychological Corporation.

Hauri, P. (1994). Primary insomnia. In M. H. Kryger, T. Roth, & W. C. Dement (Eds.), *Principles and practice of sleep medicine* (2nd ed.). Philadelphia: Saunders.

Hawkins, R. D., Greene, W., & Kandel, E. R. (1998). Classical conditioning, differential conditioning, and second-order conditioning of the Aplysia gill-withdrawal reflex in a simplified mantle organ preparation. *Behavioral Neuroscience, 112,* 636–645.

Hawkins, R. D., Kandel, E. R., & Siegelbaum, S. A. (1993). Learning to modulate transmitter release: Themes and variations in synaptic plasticity. *Annual Review of Neuroscience, 16,* 625–665.

Haxby, J. V., Ungerleider, L. G., Horwitz, B., Maisog, J. M., Rappaport, S. L., & Grady, C. L. (1995). Hemispheric differences in neural systems for face working memory: A PET-rCBF study. *Human Brain Mapping, 3,* 68–82.

Haxby, J. V., Ungerleider, L. G., Horwitz, B., Maisog, J. M., Rappaport, W. L., & Grady, C. L. (1996). Face encoding and recognition in the human brain. *Proceedings of the National Academy of Sciences USA, 98,* 922–927.

Hayes, C. (1951). *The ape in our house.* New York: Harper & Row.

Hayes, D., & Ross, C. E. (1986). Body and mind: The effect of exercise, overweight, and physical health on psychological well-being. *Journal of Health and Social Behavior, 27,* 387–400.

Haynes, S. G., Feinleib, M., & Kannel, W. B. (1980). The relationship of psychosocial factors to coronary heart disease in the Framingham Study: III. Eight-year incidence of coronary heart disease. *American Journal of Epidemiology, 111,* 37–58.

Haynes, S. G., & Matthews, K. A. (1988). Review and methodological critique of recent studies on Type A behavior and cardiovascular disease. *Annals of Behavioral Medicine, 10,* 47–59.

Hazan, C., & Shaver, P. (1987). Romantic love conceptualized as an attachment process. *Journal of Personality and Social Psychology, 52,* 511–524.

Hazan, C., & Shaver, P. (1994). Attachment as an organizational framework for research or close relationship. *Psychological Inquiry, 5,* 1–22.

Hearst, E. (1989). Backward associations: Differential learning about stimuli that follow the presence versus the absence of food in pigeons. *Animal Learning & Behavior, 17,* 280–290.

Heath, S. B. (1983). *Ways with words.* New York: Cambridge University Press.

Heath, S. B., & McLaughlin, M. W. (Eds.). (1993). *Identity and inner-city youth.* New York: Teachers College Press.

Heaton, J. M. (1968). *The eye: Phenomenology and psychology of function and disorder.* London: Tavistock.

Heckhausen, H., & Strang, H. (1988). Efficiency under record performance demands: Exertion control—An individual difference variable? *Journal of Personality and Social Psychology, 55,* 489–498.

Hegel, G. W. F. (1931). *The phenomenology of mind* (2nd ed., J. B. Baillie, Trans.). London: Allen & Unwin. (Original work published 1807)

Heider, E. R., & Olivier, D. C. (1972). The structure of color space in naming and memory for two languages. *Cognitive Psychology, 3,* 337–354.

Heider, F. (1958). *The psychology of interpersonal relations.* New York: Wiley.

Heilbrun, A. B., & Witt, N. (1990). Distorted body image as a risk factor in anorexia nervosa: Replication and clarification. *Psychological Reports, 66,* 407–416.

Heinrichs, R. W. (1993). Schizophrenia and the brain: Conditions for a neuropsychology of madness. *American Psychologist, 48,* 221–233.

Helmers, K. F., & Krantz, D. S. (1996). Defensive hostility, gender and cardiovascular levels and responses to stress. *Annals of Behavioral Medicine, 18,* 246–254.

Helmes, E., & Reddon, J. R. (1993). A perspective on developments in assessing psychopathology: A critical review of the MMPI and MMPI-2. *Psychological Bulletin, 113*(3), 453–471.

Helmholtz, H. L. F. von. (1896). *Vorträge und Reden.* Braunschweig, Germany: Vieweg und Sohn.

Helmholtz, H. L. F. von. (1930). *The sensations of tone* (A. J. Ellis, Trans.). New York: Longmans, Green. (Original work published 1863)

Helmholtz, H. L. F. von. (1962). *Treatise on physiological optics* (3rd ed., J. P. C. Southall, Ed. and Trans.). New York: Dover. (Original work published 1909)

Helson, H. (1964). *Adaptation level theory: An experimental and systematic approach to behavior.* New York: Harper.

Helwig, C. C. (1995). Adolescents' and young adults' conceptions of civil liberties: Freedom of speech and religion. *Child Development, 66,* 152–166.

Henderson, A. S. (1992). Social support and depression. In H. O. F. Veiel & U. Baumann (Eds.), *The meaning and measurement of social support* (pp. 85–92). New York: Hemisphere.

Hendrick, C., & Hendrick, S. (1986). A theory and method of love. *Journal of Personality and Social Psychology, 50,* 392–402.

Hendrick, S. S., & Hendrick, C. (1992). *Romantic love.* Newbury Park, CA: Sage.

Hendrick, S. S., & Hendrick, C. (1997). Love and satisfaction. In R. J. Sternberg & M. Hojjat (Eds.), *Satisfaction in close relationships* (pp. 56–78). New York: Guilford.

Henley, N. M. (1969). A psychological study of the semantics of animal terms. *Journal of Verbal Learning and Verbal Behavior, 8,* 176–184.

Hennessey, B. A., & Amabile, T. M. (1988). The conditions of creativity. In R. J. Sternberg (Ed.), *The nature of creativity* (pp. 11–38). New York: Cambridge University Press.

Henning, F. (1915). *Die Grundlagen, Methoden und Ergebnisse der Temperaturmessung.* Braunschweig, Germany: Vieweg und Sohn.

Henry, J. P., & Stephens, P. M. (1977). *Stress, health, and the social environment: A sociobiologic approach to medicine.* New York: Springer-Verlag.

Hensel, H. (1981). *Thermoreception and temperature regulation.* London: Academic Press.

Herd, J. A. (1978). Physiological correlates of coronary-prone behavior. In T. Dembroski, S. Weiss, J. Shields, S. Haynes, & M. Feinleib (Eds.), *Coronary-prone behavior.* New York: Springer.

Hering, E. (1964). *Outlines of a theory of the light sense* (L. M. Hurvich & D. Jameson, Trans.). Cambridge, MA: Harvard University Press. (Original work published in 1878)

Herity, B., Moriarty, M., Daly, L., Dunn, J., & Bourke, G. J. (1982). The role of tobacco and alcohol in the aetiology of lung and larynx cancer. *British Journal of Cancer, 46,* 961–964.

Herman, J. L., Perry, J. C., & Van der Kolk, B. A. (1989). Childhood trauma in borderline personality disorder. *American Journal of Psychiatry, 146*(4), 490–495.

Herrnstein, R. J. (1973). *IQ in the meritocracy.* Boston: Atlantic Monthly Press.

Herrnstein, R. J., & Murray, C. (1994). *The bell curve.* New York: The Free Press.

Hetherington, A. W., & Ranson, S. W. (1940). Hypothalamic lesions and adiposity in the rat. *Anatomical Record, 78,* 149–172.

Heuch, I., Kvale, G., Jacobsen, B. K., & Bjelke, E. (1983). Use of alcohol, tobacco and coffee, and risk of pancreatic cancer. *British Journal of Cancer, 48,* 637–643.

Heyduk, R. G., & Bahrick, L. E. (1977). Complexity, response competition, and preference implications for affective consequences of repeated exposure. *Motivation and Emotion, 1,* 249–259.

Hilgard, E. R. (1965). *Hypnotic susceptibility.* New York: Harcourt, Brace & World.

Hilgard, E. R. (1977). *Divided consciousness: Multiple controls in human thought and action.* New York: Wiley.

Hilgard, E. R. (1987). *Psychology in America.* Orlando, FL: Harcourt Brace Jovanovich.

Hintzman, D. L. (1978). *The psychology of learning and memory.* San Francisco: Freeman.

Hirschfield, R. A., & Cross, C. K. (1982). Epidemiology of affective disorders. *Archives of General Psychiatry, 39,* 35–46.

Hittner, J. B. (1997). Alcohol-related outcome expectancies: Construct overview and implications for primary and secondary prevention. *Journal of Primary Prevention, 17,* 297–314.

Ho, D. Y. F. (1986). Chinese patterns of socialization. In M. H. Bond (Ed.), *The psychology of the Chinese people.* Hong Kong: Oxford University Press.

Hoagwood, K. (1997). Interpreting nullity: The Fort Bragg Experiment—a comparative success or failure? *American Psychologist, 52,* 548.

Hobfoll, S. E. (1989). Conservation of resources: A new attempt at conceptualizing stress. *American Psychologist, 44,* 513–524.

Hobson, J. A. (1989). *Sleep.* New York: Scientific American Library.

Hochberg, J. (1978). *Perception* (2nd ed.). Englewood Cliffs, NJ: Prentice-Hall.

Hodapp, R. N. (1994). Mental retardation: Cultural-familial. In R. J. Sternberg (Ed.), *Encyclopedia of human intelligence* (Vol. 2, pp. 711–717). New York: Macmillan.

Hoebel, B. G., & Teitelbaum, G. (1966). Weight regulation in normal and hypothalamic hyperphagic rats. *Journal of Comparative and Physiological Psychology, 61,* 189–193.

Hoffding, H. (1891). *Outlines of psychology.* New York: Macmillan.

Hoffman, C., Lau, I., & Johnson, D. R. (1986). The linguistic relativity of person cognition: An English–Chinese comparison. *Journal of Personality and Social Psychology, 51,* 1097–1105.

Hoffman, L. W. (1989). Effects of maternal employment in the two-parent family. *American Psychologist, 44,* 283–292.

Hofling, C. K., Brotzman, E., Dalrymple, S., Graves, N., & Pierce, C. (1966). An experimental study of nurse–physician relations. *Journal of Nervous and Mental Disease, 143,* 171–180.

Hogan, R. (1996). A socioanalytic perspective on the five-factor model. In J. S. Wiggins (Ed.), *The five-factor model of personality: Theoretical perspectives* (pp. 163–179). New York: Guilford.

Hogan, R., DeSoto, C. B., & Solano, C. (1977). Traits, tests, and personality research. *American Psychologist, 32,* 255–264.

Holinger, P. C. (1987). *Violent deaths in the United States.* New York: Guilford.

Holland, J., Holyoak, K. J., Nisbett, R. E., & Thagard, P. (1986). *Induction: Processes of inference, learning, and discovery.* Cambridge, MA: MIT Press.

Holland, P. C. (1992). Occasion setting in Pavlovian conditioning. In D. L. Medin (Ed.), *The psychology of learning and motivation* (Vol. 28, pp. 69–125). San Diego, CA: Academic Press.

Hollander, E., Simeon, D., & Gorman, J. M. (1994). Anxiety disorders. In R. E. Hales, S. C., Yudofsky, & J. A. Talbott (Eds.), *The American Psychiatric Press textbook of psychiatry* (2nd ed.). Washington, DC: American Psychiatric Press.

Hollander, E. P. (1958). Conformity, status, and idiosyncrasy credit. *Psychological Review, 65,* 117–127.

Hollander, E. P. (1985). Leadership and power. In G. Lindzey & E. Aronson (Eds.), *Handbook of social psychology* (3rd ed., Vol. 2, pp. 485–537). New York: Random House.

Hollingshead, A. B., & Redlich, F. C. (1958). *Social class and mental illness.* New York: Wiley.

Hollon, S. D., & Beck, A. T. (1994). Cognitive and cognitive-behavioral therapies. In A. E. Bergin & S. L. Garfield (Eds.), *Handbook of psychotherapy and behavior change* (4th ed.) pp. 428–466). New York: Wiley.

Hollon, S. D., & Kendall, P. C. (1980). Cognitive self-statements in depression: Development of an automatic thoughts questionnaire. *Cognitive Therapy and Research, 4,* 383–395.

Holmes, D. S., & Roth, D. L. (1989). *The measurement of cognitive and somatic anxiety.* Manuscript in preparation.

Holmes, T., & Rahe, R. (1967). The social readjustment rating scale. *Journal of Psychosomatic Research, 11,* 213–218.

Holstein, C. B. (1976). Irreversible, stepwise sequence in the development of moral judgment: A longitudinal study of males and females. *Child Development, 47,* 51–61.

Holyoak, K. J. (1984). Analogical thinking and human intelligence. In R. J. Sternberg (Ed.), *Advances in the psychology of human intelligence* (Vol. 2, pp. 199–230). Hillsdale, NJ: Erlbaum.

Holyoak, K. J. (1995). Problem solving. In E. E. Smith & D. N. Osherson (Eds.), *An invitation to cognitive science: Vol. 3. Thinking* (pp. 267–296). Cambridge, MA: MIT Press.

Homans, G. C. (1974). *Social behavior: Its elementary forms.* New York: Harcourt Brace Jovanovich.

Honsberger, R. W., & Wilson, A. F. (1973). Transcendental meditation in treating asthma. *Respiratory Therapy: The Journal of Inhalation Technology, 3,* 79–80.

Hooker, E. (1993). Reflections of a 40-year exploration: A scientific view on homosexuality. *American Psychologist, 48*(4), 450–453.

Hoosain, R., & Salili, F. (1987). Language differences in pronunciation speed for numbers, digit span, and mathematics ability. *Psychologia: An International Journal of Psychology in the Orient, 30*(1), 34–38.

Horn, J. L. (1994). Theory of fluid and crystallized intelligence. In R. J. Sternberg (Ed.), *The encyclopedia of human intelligence* (Vol. 1, pp. 443–451). New York: Macmillan.

Horn, J. L., & Cattell, R. B. (1966). Refinement and test of the theory of fluid and crystallized ability intelligences. *Journal of Educational Psychology, 57,* 253–270.

Horn, J. L., & Hofer, S. M. (1992). Major abilities and development in the adult period. In R. J. Sternberg and C. A. Berg (Eds.), *Intellectual development* (pp. 44–99). New York: Cambridge University Press.

Horn, J. L., & Knapp, J. R. (1973). On the subjective character of the empirical base of Guilford's structure-of-intellect model. *Psychological Bulletin, 80,* 33–43.

Horner, A. J. (1991). *Psychoanalytic object relations therapy.* New York: Jason Aronson.

Horney, K. (1937). *The neurotic personality of our time.* New York: Norton.

Horney, K. (1939). *New ways in psychoanalysis.* New York: Norton.

Horney, K. (1950). *Neurosis and human growth: The struggle toward self-realization.* New York: Norton.

Horvath, P., & Zuckerman, M. (1993). Sensation seeking, risk appraisal, and risky behavior. *Personality and Individual Differences, 14,* 41–52.

Houpt, T. A., Boulos, Z., & Moore-Ede, M. C. (1996). MidnightSun: Software for determining light exposure and phase-shifting schedules during global travel. *Physiology & Behavior, 59,* 561–568.

House, J. S., & Smith, D. A. (1985). Evaluating the health effects of demanding work on and off the job. In T. F. Drury (Ed.), *Assessing physical fitness and physical activity in population-base surveys* (pp. 481–508). Hyattsville, MD: National Center for Health Statistics.

Houston, J. P. (1985). *Motivation.* New York: Macmillan.

Hovland, C. I., Janis, I. L., & Kelley, H. H. (1953). *Communication and persuasion: Psychological studies of opinion change.* New Haven, CT: Yale University Press.

Hovland, C. I., & Weiss, W. (1951). The influences of source credibility on communication effectiveness. *Public Opinion Quarterly, 15,* 635–650.

Howard, A., Pion, G. M., Gottfredson, G. D., Flattau, P. E., Oskamp, S., Pfafflin, S. M., Bray, D. W., & Burstein, A. G. (1986). The changing face of American psychology: A report from the committee on employment and human resources. *American Psychologist, 41*(12), 1311–1327.

Howard, K. I., Kopta, S. M., Krause, M. S., & Orlinsky, D. E. (1986). The dose–effect relationship in psychotherapy. *American Psychologist, 41*(2), 159–164.

Howes, C. (1988). Peer interaction of young children. *Monographs of the Society for Research in Child Development, 53*(1, Serial No. 217).

Howes, C. (1990). Can the age of entry into childcare and the quality of childcare predict adjustment in kindergarten? *Developmental Psychology, 26,* 292–303.

Hubel, D. H., & Wiesel, T. N. (1967). Cortical and callosal connections concerned with the vertical meridian of visual fields in the cat. *Journal of Neurophysiology, 30*(6), 1561–1573.

Hubel, D. H., & Wiesel, T. N. (1979). Brain mechanisms of vision. *Scientific American, 241,* 150–162.

Huebner, R. R., & Izard, C. E. (1988). Mothers' responses to infants' facial expressions of sadness, anger, and physical distress. *Motivation and Emotion, 12,* 185–196.

Huesmann, L. R., Lagerspetz, K., & Eron, L. D. (1984). Intervening variable in the TV violence-aggression relation: Evidence from two countries. *Developmental Psychology, 20,* 746–775.

Huesmann, L. R., & Miller, L. S. (1994). Long-term effects of repeated exposure to media violence in childhood. In L. R Huesmann (Ed.), *Aggressive behavior: Current perspectives* (pp. 153–186). New York: Plenum.

Hughes, J. M. (1989). *Reshaping the psychoanalytic domain: The work of Melanie Klein, W. R. D. Fairburn, and D. W. Winnicott.* Berkeley: University of California Press.

Hull, C. L. (1943). *Principles of behavior.* New York: Appleton-Century-Crofts.

Hull, C. L. (1952). *A behavior system: An introduction to behavior theory concerning the individual organism.* New Haven, CT: Yale University Press.

Hultsch, D. F., & Dixon, R. A. (1990). Learning and memory in aging. In J. E. Birren & K. W. Schaie (Eds.), *Handbook of the psychology of aging: The handbooks of aging* (3rd ed.). San Diego, CA: Academic Press.

Humphreys, L. G., & Davey, T. C. (1988). Continuity in intellectual growth from 12 months to 9 years. *Intelligence, 12,* 183–197.

Hunt, E. (1999). What is a theory of thought? In R. J. Sternberg (Ed.), *The nature of cognition* (pp. 3–49). Cambridge, MA: MIT Press.

Hunt, E. B. (1978). Mechanics of verbal ability. *Psychological Review, 85,* 109–130.

Hunt, E. B., Lunneberg, C., & Lewis, J. (1975). What does it mean to be high verbal? *Cognitive Psychology, 7,* 194–227.

Hunt, E. B., Streissguth, A. P., Kerr, B., & Olsen, H. C. (1995). Mothers' alcohol consumption during pregnancy: Effects on spatial-visual reasoning in 14-year-old children. *Psychological Science, 6,* 339–342.

Hurvich, L. M. (1981). *Color vision.* Sunderland, MA: Sinnauer Associates.

Hurvich, L., & Jameson, D. (1957). An opponent-process theory of color vision. *Psychological Review, 64,* 384–404.

Huston, A. C. (1983). Sex-typing. In P. H. Mussen (Series Ed.) & E. M. Hetherington (Vol. Ed.), *Handbook of child psychology:* Vol. 4. Socialization, personality, and social development (4th ed., pp. 387–467). New York: Wiley.

Huston, A. C., Carpenter, C. J., Atwater, J. B., & Johnson, L. M. (1986). Gender, adult structuring of activities, and social behavior in middle childhood. *Child Development, 57*(5), 1200–1209.

Huston, T. L., & Levinger, G. (1978). Interpersonal attraction and relationships. *Annual Review of Psychology, 29,* 115–156.

Huttenlocher, J. (1968). Constructing spatial images: A strategy in reasoning. *Psychological Review, 75,* 550–560.

Huttenlocher, J., Newcombe, N., & Sandberg, E. H. (1994). The coding of spatial location in young children. *Cognitive Psychology, 27,* 115–147.

Huttenlocher, J., & Presson, C. C. (1973). Mental rotation and the perspective problem. *Cognitive Psychology, 4,* 277–299.

Hwang, K. K. (1981). Perception of life events: The application of nonmetric multidimensional scaling. *Acta Psychologica Taiwanica, 22,* 22–32.

Hyman, R. (1994). Anomaly or artifact? Comments on Bem and Honorton. *Psychological Bulletin, 115,* 25–27.

Inhelder, B., & Piaget, J. (1958). *The growth of logical thinking from childhood to adolescence.* New York: Basic Books.

Inoue, S., Uchizono, K., & Nagasaki, H. (1982). Endogenous sleep-promoting factors. *Trends in Neurosciences, 5,* 218–220.

Insell, T. R. (1986). The neurobiology of anxiety. In B. F. Shaw, Z. V. Segal, T. M. Wallis, & F. E. Cashman (Eds.), *Anxiety disorders.* New York: Plenum.

Insko, C. A. (1965). Verbal reinforcement of attitude. *Journal of Personality and Social Psychology, 21,* 621–623.

Intelligence and its measurement: A symposium. (1921). *Journal of Educational Psychology, 12,* 123–147, 195–216, 271–275.

Isen, A. M. (1987). Passive affect, cognitive processes, and social behavior. In L. Berkowitz (Ed.), *Advances in experimental social psychology* (Vol. 20, pp. 203–253). New York: Academic Press.

Islam, M. R., & Hewstone, M. (1993). Intergroup attributions and affective consequences in majority and minority groups. *Journal of Personality and Social Psychology, 64,* 936–950.

Ivey, A. E., Ivey, M. B., & Simek-Morgan, L. (1993). *Counseling and psychotherapy: A multicultural perspective.* Boston: Allyn & Bacon.

Izard, C. E. (1977). *Human emotions.* New York: Plenum.

Izard, C. E. (1989). The structure and functions of emotions: Implications for cognition, motivation, and personality. In I. S. Cohen (Ed.), *The G. Stanley Hall lecture series* (Vol. 9, pp. 39–73). Washington, DC: American Psychological Association.

Izard, C. E. (1991). *The psychology of emotions.* New York: Plenum.

Izard, C. E. (1993). Four systems for emotional activation: Cognitive and noncognitive development. *Psychological Review, 100,* 69–90.

Izard, C. E. (1994). Innate and universal facial expressions: Evidence from developmental and cross-cultural research. *Psychological Bulletin, 115,* 288–299.

Izard, C. E., Fantauzzo, C. A., Castle, J. M., Haynes, O. M., & Slomine, B. S. (1995). *The morphological stability and social validity of infants' facial expression.* Unpublished manuscript, University of Delaware.

Izard, C. E., Kagan, J., & Zajonc, R. B. (1984). *Emotions, cognition, and behavior.* New York: Cambridge University Press.

Jackendoff, R. (1991). Parts and boundaries. *Cognition, 41,* 9–45.

Jacobs, B. L. (1987). How hallucinogenic drugs work. *American Scientist, 75,* 386–392.

Jacobs, B. L., & Trulson, M. E. (1979). Mechanisms of action of LSD. *American Scientist, 67,* 396–404.

Jacobson, J. L., Jacobson, S. W., & Humphrey, H. E. (1990). Effects of exposure to PCBs and related compounds on growth and activity in children. *Neurotoxicology & Teratology, 12*(4), 319–326.

Jacobson, J. L., Jacobson, S. W., Padgett, R. J., Brunitt, G. A., & Billings, R. L. (1992). Effects of prenatal PCB exposure on cognitive processing efficiency and sustained attention. *Developmental Psychology, 28*(2), 297–306.

Jacoby, R., & Glauberman, N. (1995). *The bell curve debate: History, documents, opinions.* New York: Times Books.

James, W. (1890a). *Psychology.* New York: Holt.

James, W. (1890b). *Principles of psychology* (Vol. 1). New York: Holt. (Reprinted 1983, Cambridge, MA: Harvard University Press)

James, W. (1970). *The principles of psychology* (Vol. 1). New York: Holt. (Original work published 1890)

Janis, I. L. (1958). *Psychological stress.* New York: Wiley.

Janis, I. L. (1972). *Victims of groupthink.* Boston: Houghton Mifflin.

Janis, I. L., Kaye, D., & Kirschner, P. (1965). Facilitating effects of "eating while reading" on responsiveness to persuasive communications. *Journal of Personality and Social Psychology, 1,* 17–27.

Janos, P. M. (1990). The self-perception of uncommonly bright youngsters. In R. J. Sternberg & J. Kolligian (Eds.), *Competence considered* (pp. 98–116). New Haven, CT: Yale University Press.

Janowitz, H. D. (1967). Role of gastrointestinal tract in the regulation of food intake. In C. F. Code (Ed.), *Handbook of physiology: Alimentary canal 1.* Washington, DC: American Physiological Society.

Jemmott, J. B. III, & Locke, S. E. (1984). Psychosocial factors, immunologic mediation, and human susceptibility to infectious diseases: How much do we know? *Psychological Bulletin, 95,* 78–108.

Jenkins, C. D., Zyzanski, S. J., & Rosenman, R. H. (1979). *Jenkins Activity Survey.* Cleveland, OH: Psychological Corporation.

Jensen, A. R. (1980). *Bias in mental testing.* New York: The Free Press.

Jensen, A. R. (1993). *Structure in American life.* New York: The Free Press.

Jensen, A. R. (1997). The puzzle of nongenetic variance. In R. J. Sternberg & E. L. Grigorenko (Eds.), *Intelligence, heredity, and environment* (pp. 42–88.) NY: Cambridge University Press.

Jensen, A. R. (1998). *The g factor.* Westport, CT: Praeger.

Jerison, H. (2000). The evolution of intelligence. In R. J. Sternberg (Ed.), *Handbook of intelligence.* New York: Cambridge University Press.

Jha, A. P., Kroll, N. E. A., Baynes, K., & Gazzaniga, M. S. (1997). Memory encoding following complete callostomy. *Journal of Cognitive Neuroscience, 9,* 143–159.

Johanssen, G. (1975, June). Visual motion perception. *Scientific American,* 76–87.

Johnson, J. A., & Osterdorf, F. (1993). Clarification of the five-factor model with the abridged Big Five dimensional circumflex. *Journal of Personality and Social Psychology, 65,* 563–576.

Johnson, J. E. (1984). Psychological interventions and coping with surgery. In A. Baum, S. E. Taylor, & J. E. Singer (Eds.), *Handbook of psychology and health* (Vol. 4, pp. 167–188). Hillsdale, NJ: Erlbaum.

Johnson, J. E., Lauver, D. R., & Nail, L. M. (1989). Process of coping with radiation therapy. *Journal of Consulting and Clinical Psychology, 57,* 358–364.

Johnson, M. H. (1997). *Developmental cognitive neuroscience: An introduction.* Oxford, UK: Oxford University Press.

Johnson, M. H. (1999). Developmental cognitive neuroscience. In M. Bennett (Ed.), *Developmental psychology* (pp. 147–164). Philadelphia: Psychology Press.

Johnson, M. K. (1996). Fact, fantasy, and public policy. In D. J. Herrmann, C. McEvoy, C. Hertzog, P. Hertel, & M. K. Johnson (Eds.), *Basic and applied memory research: Theory in context* (Vol. 1). Mahwah, NJ: Erlbaum.

Johnson, M. K., Hashtroudi, S., & Lindsay, D. S. (1993). Source monitoring. *Psychological Bulletin, 114,* 3–28.

Johnson-Laird, P. N. (1988). *The computer and the mind.* Cambridge, MA: Harvard University Press.

Johnson-Laird, P. N. (1999). Formal rules versus mental models in reasoning. In R. J. Sternberg (Ed.), *The nature of cognition* (pp. 587–624). Cambridge, MA: MIT Press.

Johnson-Laird, P. N., & Byrne, R. M. J. (1991). *Deduction.* Hillsdale, NJ: Erlbaum.

Johnson-Laird, P. N., & Steedman, M. (1978). The psychology of syllogisms. *Cognitive Psychology, 10,* 64–99.

Johnston, J. C., & McClelland, J. L. (1973). Visual factors in word perception. *Perception & Psychophysics, 14,* 365–370.

Johnston, T. D. & Pietrewica, A. T. (Eds.). (1985) *Issues in the ecological study of learning.* Hillsdale, NJ: Erlbaum.

Jones, B. E. (1994). Basic mechanisms of sleep-wake states. In M. H. Kryger, T. Roth, & W. C. Dement (Eds.), *Principles and practice of sleep medicine* (2nd ed.). Philadelphia: Saunders.

Jones, E. E., (1964). *Ingratiation: A social psychological analysis.* New York: Appleton-Century-Crofts.

Jones, E. E., & Davis, K. E. (1965). From acts to dispositions: The attribution process in person perception. In L. Berkowitz (Ed.), *Advances in experimental social psychology* (Vol. 2). New York: Academic Press.

Jones, E. E., & Harris, V. W. (1967). The attribution of attitudes. *Journal of Experimental Social Psychology, 3,* 1–24.

Jones, E. E., & Nisbett, R. (1971). *The actor and the observer: Divergent perceptions of the causes of behavior.* Morristown, NJ: General Learning Press.

Jones, E. E., & Nisbett, R. E. (1987). The actor and the observer: Divergent perceptions of causality. In E. E. Jones, D. E. Kanouse, H. H. Kelley, & R. E. Nisbett (Eds.), *Attribution: Perceiving the causes of behavior* (pp. 79–94). Morristown, NJ: General Learning Press.

Jones, E. E., Rock, L., Shaver, K. G., Goethals, G. R., & Ward, L. M. (1968). Pattern of performance and ability attribution: An unexpected primary effect. *Journal of Personality and Social Psychology, 10,* 317–340.

Jones, E. E., & Wortman, C. (1973). *Ingratiation: An attributional approach.* Morristown, NJ: General Learning Press.

Jost, J. T., & Banaji, M. R. (1994). The role of stereotyping in system justification and the production of false consciousness. *British Journal of Social Psychology, 33,* 1–27.

Juel-Nielsen, N. (1965). Individual and environment: A psychiatric-psychological investigation of monozygous twins reared apart.

Acta Psychiatrica et Neurologica Scandinavica (Monograph Supplement, 183).

Julien, R. M. (1995). *A primer of drug action.* New York: Freeman.

Jurkovac, T. (1985). *Collegiate basketball players' perceptions of the home advantage.* Unpublished master's thesis, Bowling Green State University, Bowling Green, OH.

Jusczyk, P. W. (1997). *The discovery of spoken language.* Cambridge, MA: MIT Press.

Kagan, J. (1981). *The second year: The emergence of self-awareness.* Cambridge, MA: Harvard University Press.

Kagan, J. (1982). *Psychological research on the infant: An evaluative summary.* New York: W. T. Grant Foundation.

Kagan, J. (1984). *The nature of the child.* New York: Basic Books.

Kagan, J. (1986). *Psychological research on the human infant: An evaluative summary.* New York: W. T. Grant Foundation.

Kagan, J. (1989a). Commentary [Special topic: Continuity in early cognitive development—conceptual and methodological challenges]. *Human Development, 32,* 172–176.

Kagan, J. (1989b). Temperamental contributions to social behavior. *American Psychologist, 44,* 668–674.

Kagan, J. (1994). *Galen's prophecy: Temperament in human nature.* New York: Basic Books.

Kagan, J., Kearsley, R., & Zelazo P. (1978). *Infancy: Its place in human development.* Cambridge, MA: Harvard University Press.

Kagan, J., & Moss, H. A. (1962). *From birth to maturity.* New York: Wiley.

Kagan, J., Reznick, R. J., Clarke, C., Snidman, N., & Garcia-Coll, C. (1984). Behavioral inhibition to the unfamiliar. *Child Development, 55,* 2212–2225.

Kahneman, D. (1973). *Attention and effort.* Englewood Cliffs, NJ: Prentice-Hall.

Kahneman, D., & Tversky, A. (1971). Subjective probability: A judgment of representativeness. *Cognitive Psychology, 3,* 430–454.

Kahneman, D., & Tversky, A. (1973). On the psychology of prediction. *Psychological Review, 80,* 237.

Kahneman, D., & Tversky, A. (1979). Intuitive prediction: Biases and corrective procedures. *Management Science, 12,* 313–327.

Kail, R. V. (1990). *The development of memory in children* (3rd ed.). New York: Freeman.

Kail, R. V., Pellegrino, J. W., & Carter, P. (1980). Developmental changes in mental rotation. *Journal of Experimental Child Psychology, 29,* 102–116.

Kalin, N. H. (1993, May). The neurobiology of fear. *Scientific American,* 94–101.

Kalmar, D. A., & Sternberg, R. J. (1988). Theory knitting: An integrative approach to theory development. *Philosophical Psychology, 1,* 153–170.

Kalsner, S. (1990). Heteroreceptors, autoreceptors, and other terminal sites. *Annals of the New York Academy of Sciences, 604,* 1–6.

Kamin, L. J. (1969). Predictability, surprise, attention, and conditioning. In B. A. Campbell & R. M. Church (Eds.), *Punishment and aversive behavior* (pp. 279–296). New York: Appleton-Century-Crofts.

Kandel, E. (1991). Cellular mechanisms of learning and the biological basis of individuality. In E. R. Kandel, J. H. Schwartz, & T. M. Jessell (Eds.), *Principles of neural science* (3rd ed.). New York: Elsevier.

Kane, J., Honigfeld, G., Singer, J., Meltzer, H., et al. (1988). Clozapine for treatment of resistant schizophrenics. *Archives of General Psychiatry, 45,* 789–796.

Kanner, L. (1943). Autistic disturbances of effective content. *Nervous Child, 2,* 217–240.

Kant, I. (1987). The critique of pure reason. In *Great books of the Western world: Vol. 42. Kant.* Chicago: Encyclopaedia Britannica.

Kaplan, C. A., & Davidson, J. E. (1989). *Incubation effects in problem solving.* Unpublished manuscript.

Kaplan, S. L., Randolph, S. W., & Lemli, J. M. (1991). *Treatment outcomes in the reduction of fear: A meta-analysis.* Paper presented at the annual meeting of the American Psychological Association, San Francisco.

Karau, S. J., & Williams, K. D. (1993). Social loafing: A meta-analytic review and theoretical integration. *Journal of Personality and Social Psychology, 65,* 681–706.

Karau, S. J., & Williams, K. D. (1997). The effects of group cohesiveness on social loafing and social compensation. *Group Dynamics, 1,* 156–168.

Kass-Simon, G., & Farnes, P. (Eds.). (1990). *Women of science: Righting the record.* Bloomington: Indiana University Press.

Katz, D. (1960). The functional approach to the study of attitudes. *Public Opinion Quarterly, 24,* 163–204.

Katz, D., & Stotland, E. (1959). A preliminary statement to a theory of attitude structure and change. In S. Koch (Ed.), *Psychology: A study of a science* (Vol. 3, pp. 423–475). New York: McGraw-Hill.

Katz, J. J. (1972). *Semantic theory.* New York: Harper & Row.

Katz, J. J., & Fodor, J. A. (1963). The structure of a semantic theory. *Language, 39,* 170–210.

Kaufman, A. (2000). Tests of intelligence. In R. J. Sternberg (Ed.), *Handbook of intelligence.* New York: Cambridge University Press.

Kauffman, S. (1995). *At home in the universe.* New York: Oxford.

Kay, P. (1975). Synchronic variability and diachronic changes in basic color terms. *Language in Society, 4,* 257–270.

Kay, P., & Kempton, W. (1984). What is the Sapir–Whorf hypothesis? *American Anthropologist, 86,* 65–79.

Kearins, J. M. (1981). Visual spatial memory in Australian aboriginal children of desert regions. *Cognitive Psychology, 13*(3), 434–460.

Keating, D. P., & Bobbitt, B. L. (1978). Individual and developmental differences in cognitive-processing components of mental ability. *Child Development, 49,* 155–167.

Keesey, R. E. (1980). A set point analysis of the regulation of body weight. In A. J. Stunkard (Ed.), *Obesity.* Philadelphia: W. B. Saunders.

Keesey, R. E., Boyle, P. C., Kemnitz, J. W., & Mitchell, J. J. (1976). The role of the lateral hypothalamus in determining the body weight set point. In D. Novin, W. Wyrwicka, & G. A. Bray (Eds.), *Hunger: Basic mechanisms and clinical implications.* New York: Raven Press.

Keesey, R. E., & Powley, T. L. (1975). Hypothalamic regulation of body weight. *American Scientist, 63,* 558–565.

Keesey, R. E., & Powley, T. L. (1986). The regulation of body weight. *Annual Review of Psychology, 37,* 109–133.

Keil, F. C. (1981). Constraints on knowledge and cognitive development. *Psychological Review, 88,* 197–227.

Keil, F. C. (1989). *Concepts, kinds, and cognitive development.* Cambridge, MA: MIT Press.

Keil, F. C. (1999). Cognition, content, and development. In M. Bennett (Ed.), *Developmental psychology* (pp. 165–184). Philadelphia: Psychology Press.

Keller, M., Eckensberger, L. H., & von Rosen, K. (1989). A critical note on the conception of preconventional morality: The case of stage 2 in Kohlberg's theory. *International Journal of Behavioral Development, 12*(1), 57–69.

Kellogg, W. N., & Kellogg, L. A. (1933). *The ape and the child.* New York: McGraw-Hill.

Kelly, G. (1955). *The psychology of personal constructs.* New York: Norton.

Kelly, H. H. (1967). Attribution theory in social psychology. In D. L. Vine (Ed.), *Nebraska symposium on motivation.* Lincoln: University of Nebraska Press.

Kemeny, M. E., Cohen, R., Zegans, L. S., & Conant, M. A. (1989). Psychological and immunological predictors of genital herpes recurrence. *Psychosomatic Medicine, 51,* 195–208.

Kennedy, R. S., Lanham, D. S., Drexler, J. M., & Massey, C. J. (1997). A comparison of cybersickness incidences, symptom profiles, measurement technique, and suggestions for further research. *Presence, 6,* 638–644.

Kenny, D. (1994). *Interpersonal perception: A social relations analysis.* New York: Guilford.

Kenny, D., & DePaulo, B. M. (1993). Do people know how others view them? An empirical and theoretical account. *Psychological Bulletin, 114,* 145–161.

Kenrick, D. T., Groth, G. E., Trost, M. R., & Sadalla, E. K. (1993). Integrating evolutionary and social exchange perspective on relationships: Effects of gender, self-appraisal, and involvement level on mate selection criteria. *Journal of Personality and Social Psychology, 64,* 951–969.

Kenrick, D. T., & Keefe, R. C. (1992). Age preferences in mates reflect sex differences in human reproductive strategies. *Behavioral and Brain Sciences, 15,* 75–133.

Kenrick, D. T., & Stringfield, D. O. (1980). Personality traits and the eye of the beholder: Crossing some traditional philosophical boundaries in the search for consistency in all the people. *Psychological Review, 87,* 88–104.

Kenrick, D. T., & Trost, M. R. (1993). The evolutionary perspective. In A. Beall & R. J. Sternberg (Eds.), *Perspectives on the psychology of gender.* New York: Guilford.

Kenshalo, D. R., Nafe, J. P., & Brooks, B. (1961). Variations in thermal sensitivity. *Science, 134,* 104–105.

Keppel, G., & Underwood, B. J. (1962). Proactive inhibition in short-term retention of single items. *Journal of Verbal Learning and Verbal Behavior, 1,* 153–161.

Kernberg, O. F. (1975). Transference and countertransference in the treatment of borderline patients. *Journal of the National Association of Private Psychiatric Hospitals, 7*(2), 14–24.

Kernberg, O. F. (1976). *Objects relations theory and clinical psychoanalysis.* New York: Jason Aronsen.

Kessler, R. C. (1995). Epidemiology of psychiatric comorbidity. In M. T. Tsuang, M. Tohen, & G. E. P. Zahner (Eds.), *Textbook in psychiatric epidemiology.* New York: Wiley.

Kiecolt, J. & Glaser, R. (1989). Behavioral influences on immune function: Evidence for the interplay between stress and health. In J. Field, P. McCabe, & N. Schneiderman (Eds.), *Stress and coping* (Vol. 2). Hillsdale, NJ: Erlbaum.

Kiecolt-Glaser, J. K., & Glaser, R. (1987). Psychosocial influences on herpes virus latency. In E. Kurstak, Z. J. Lipowski, & P. V. Morozov (Eds.), *Viruses, immunity, and mental disorders* (pp. 403–412). New York: Plenum.

Kiecolt-Glaser, J. K., Malarkey, W. B., Chee, M., & Newton, T., et al. (1993). Negative behavior during marital conflict is associated with immunological down-regulation. *Psychosomatic Medicine, 55,* 395–404.

Kiecolt-Glaser, J. K., Newton, T., Cacioppo, J. T., MacCallum, R. C., Glaser, R., & Malarkey, W. B. (1996). Marital conflict and endocrine function: Are men really more psychologically affected than women? *Journal of Consulting and Clinical Psychology, 64,* 324–332.

Kiesler, D. J. (1966). Some myths of psychotherapy research and the search for a paradigm. *Psychological Bulletin, 65,* 110–136.

Kihlstrom, J. F. (1984). Conscious, subconscious, unconscious: A cognitive view. In K. S. Bowers & D. Meichenbaum (Eds.), *The unconscious: Reconsidered.* New York: Wiley.

Kihlstrom, J. F. (1985). Hypnosis. *Annual Review of Psychology, 36,* 385–418.

Kihlstrom, J., & Cantor, N. (2000). Social intelligence. In R. J. Sternberg (Ed.), *Handbook of intelligence.* New York: Cambridge University Press.

Kim, S. G., Ashe, J., Hendrick, K., Ellermann, J. M., Merkle, H., Ugurbil, K., & Georgopolus, A. P. (1993). Functional magnetic resonance imaging of motor cortex: Hemispheric asymmetry and handedness. *Science, 161,* 615–617.

Kim, U., Triandis, H. C., & Kagitcibasi, C. (Eds.). (1994). *Individualism and collectivism: Theory and applications.* Newbury Park, CA: Sage.

Kimura, D. (1983). Sex differences in cerebral organization for speech and praxic functions. *Canadian Journal of Psychology, 37(1),* 19–35.

Kimura, D. (1987). Are men's and women's brains really different? *Canadian Psychology, 28*(2), 133–147.

Kinnunen, T., Zamansky, H. B., & Block, M. L. (1994). Is the hypnotized subject lying? *Journal of Abnormal Psychology, 103,* 184–191.

Kirmayer, L. (1991). The place of culture in psychiatric nosology: Taijin-kyofusho and the DSM-III-R. *Journal of Nervous and Mental Disease, 179,* 19–28.

Kite, K. E., & Deaux, D. (1986). Sample Likert scale. *Basic and Applied Social Psychology, 7,* 137–162.

Klahr, D., Fay, A. L., & Dunbar, K. (1993). Heuristics for scientific experimentation: A developmental study. *Cognitive Psychology, 25,* 111–145.

Klein, M. (1975). *The writings of Melanie Klein* (Vol. 3). London: Hogarth Press.

Kleinknecht, R. A., Dinnel, D. L., Tanouye, S., & Lonner, W. (1993). The relationship between symptoms of taijin-kyofusho and social phobia among Japanese-Americans in Hawaii. Manuscript submitted for publication, Department of Psychology, Western Washington University, Bellingham, WA.

Kleinmuntz, B., & Szucko, J. J. (1984). A field study of the fallibility of polygraphic lie detection. *Nature, 308,* 449–450.

Kleitman, N. (1963). *Sleep and wakefulness* (2nd ed.). Chicago: University of Chicago Press.

Klivington, K. A. (1989). *The science of mind.* Cambridge, MA: MIT Press.

Kluger, A. N., & DeNisi, A. (1996). The effects of feedback interventions on performance: A historical review, a meta-analysis, and a preliminary feedback intervention theory. *Psychological Bulletin, 119,* 254–284.

Knox, V. J., Crutchfield, L., & Hilgard, E. R. (1975). The nature of task interference in hypnotic dissociation: An investigation of hypnotic behavior. *International Journal of Clinical and Experimental Hypnosis, 23,* 305–323.

Koegel, R. L., Schreibman, L., O'Neill, R. E., & Burke, J. C. (1983). The personality and family-interaction characteristics of parents of autistic children. *Journal of Consulting and Clinical Psychology, 51,* 683–692.

Kohlberg, L. (1963). The development of children's orientations toward a moral order: Pt. 1. Sequence in the development of moral thought. *Vita Humana, 6,* 11–33.

Kohlberg, L. (1984). *The psychology of moral development: The nature and validity of moral stages. In Essays on moral development* (Vol. 2). New York: Harper & Row.

Kohlberg, L., & Kramer, R. (1969). Continuities and discontinuities in childhood and adult moral development. *Human Development, 12,* 93–120.

Köhler, W. (1927). *The mentality of apes.* New York: Harcourt Brace.

Köhler, W. (1940). *Dynamics in psychology.* New York: Liveright.

Köhler, W., Kapur, S., Moscovitch, M., Winocur, G., & Houle, S. (1995). Dissociation of pathways for object and spatial vision in the intact human brain. *Neuroreport, 6,* 1865–1868.

Kohn, A. (1993). *Punished by rewards: The trouble with gold stars, incentive plans, A's, praise, and other bribes.* Boston: Houghton-Mifflin.

Kohn, M. L. (1976). Social class and parental values: Another confirmation of the relationship. *American Sociological Review, 41,* 538–545.

Kohn, P. M., Gurevich, M., Pickering, D. I., & MacDonald, J. E. (1994). Alexithymia, reactivity, and the adverse impact of hassles-based stress. *Personality & Individual Differences, 16*(6), 805–812.

Kohnstamm, G. A. (1989). Temperament in childhood: Cross-cultural and sex differences. In G. A. Kohnstamm, J. E. Bates, & M. K. Rothbart (Eds.), *Temperament in childhood* (pp. 483–508). West Sussex, UK: Wiley.

Kohut, H. (1984). Selected problems of self-psychological theory. In J. D. Lichtenberg & S. Kaplan (Eds.), *Reflection on self psychology* (pp. 387–416). Hillsdale, NJ: Erlbaum.

Kolb, B., & Whishaw, I. Q. (1990). *Fundamentals of human neuropsychology* (3rd ed.). New York: Freeman.

Kolers, P. A. (1966a). Interlingual facilitation of short-term memory. *Journal of Verbal Learning and Verbal Behavior, 5*, 314–319.

Kolers, P. A. (1966b). Reading and talking bilingually. *American Journal of Psychology, 79*, 357–376.

Kolotkin, R. L., Revis, E. S., Kirkley, B. G., & Janick, L. (1987). Binge eating and obesity: Associated with MMPI characteristics. *Journal of Consulting and Clinical Psychology, 55*, 872–876.

Koob, G. F. & Bloom, F. E. (1988). Cellular and molecular mechanisms of drug dependence. *Science, 242*, 715–723.

Kopta, S. M., Howard, K. I., Lowry, J. L., & Beutler, L. E. (1994). Patterns of symptomatic recovery in psychotherapy. *Journal of Consulting and Clinical Psychology, 62*, 1009–1016.

Kosslyn, S. M. (1988). Aspects of a cognitive neuroscience of mental imagery. *Science, 240*, 1621–1626.

Kosslyn, S. M., Ball, T. M., & Reiser, B. J. (1978). Visual images preserve metric spatial information: Evidence from studies of image scanning. *Journal of Experimental Psychology: Human Perception and Performance, 4*, 47–60.

Kosslyn, S. M., & Koenig, O. (1992). *Wet mind: The new cognitive neuroscience*. New York: The Free Press.

Kosslyn, S. M., & Koenig, O. (1995). *Wet mind: The new cognitive neuroscience*. (Paperback). New York: The Free Press.

Kotovsky, K., Hayes, J. R., & Simon, H. A. (1985). Why are some problems hard? Evidence from the tower of Hanoi. *Cognitive Psychology, 17*, 248–294.

Kotovsky, L., & Baillargeon, R. (1994). Calibration-based reasoning about collision events in 11-month-old infants. *Cognition, 51*, 107–129.

Kraemer, G. (1992). A psychobiological theory of attachment. *Behavioral and Brain Sciences, 15*, 493–541.

Kramer, D. A. (1990). Conceptualizing wisdom: The primacy of affect-cognition relations. In R. J. Sternberg (Ed.), *Wisdom: Its nature, origins, and development* (pp. 279–313). New York: Cambridge University Press.

Kramer, M. A. (1957). A discussion of the concepts of incidence and prevalence as related to epidemiologic studies of mental disorders. *American Journal of Public Health, 47*, 826–840.

Krantz, D. S., Baum, A., & Wideman, M. V. (1980). Assessment for preferences for self-treatment and information in health care. *Journal of Personality and Social Psychology, 39*, 977–990.

Krantz, L. (1992). *What the odds are: A-to-Z odds on everything you hoped or feared could happen*. New York: Harper Perennial.

Krantz, S., & Hammen, C. L. (1979). Assessment of cognitive bias in depression. *Journal of Abnormal Psychology, 88*, 611–619.

Krauthammer, C., & Klerman, G. L. (1979). The epidemiology of mania. In B. Shopsin (Ed.), *Manic illness* (pp. 11–28). New York: Raven Press.

Krech, D., & Crutchfield, R. (1958). *Elements of psychology*. New York: Knopf.

Kries, J. A. von (1895). Ueber die Natur gewisser mit den psychischen Vorgangen verknupfter Gehirnzustande. *Zeitschrift fur Psychologie, 8*, 1–33.

Kroner-Herwig, B., Jakle, C., Frettloh, J., Peters, K., Seemann, H., Franz, C., & Basler, H. D. (1996). Predicting subjective disability in chronic pain patients. *International Journal of Behavioral Medicine, 3*, 30–41.

Krosnick, J. A., Betz, A. I., Jussim, L. J., & Lynn, A. R. (1992). Subliminal conditioning of attitudes. *Personality and Social Psychology Bulletin, 18*, 152–162.

Kuhlman, D. M., & Marshello, A. F. J. (1975). Individual differences in game motivation as moderators of pre-programmed strategy effects in prisoner's dilemma. *Journal of Personality and Social Psychology, 32*, 922–931.

Kuhn, D., Garcia-Mila, M., Zohar, A., & Andersen, C. (1995). Strategies of knowledge acquisition. *Monographs of the Society for Research in Child Development, 60*, Serial No. 245.

Kuhn, D., Schauble, L., & Garcia-Mila, M. (1992). Cross-domain development of scientific reasoning. *Cognition and Instruction, 9*, 285–327.

Kuhn, T. S. (1970). *The structure of scientific revolutions* (2nd ed.). Chicago: University of Chicago Press.

Kulik, J. A., Mahler, H. I. M., & Moore, P. J. (1996). Social comparison and affiliation under threat: Effects on recovery from major surgery. *Journal of Personality and Social Psychology, 71*, 967–979.

Kulkarni, S. S., & Puhan, B. N. (1988). Psychological assessment: Its present and future trends. In J. Pandey (Ed.), *Psychology in India: The state of the art: Vol. 1. Personality and mental processes*. New Delhi: Sage.

Kunda, Z. (1987). Motivated inference: Self-serving generation and evaluation of causal theories. *Journal of Personality and Social Psychology, 45*, 763–771.

Kuo, Z. Y. (1921). Giving up instincts in psychology. *Journal of Philosophy, 17*, 645–664.

Kurtines, W., & Greif, E. B. (1974). The development of moral thought: Review and evaluation of Kohlberg's approach. *Psychological Bulletin, 81*, 453–470.

Labouvie-Vief, G. (1980). Beyond formal operations: Uses and limits of pure logic in life span development. *Human Development, 23*, 141–161.

Labouvie-Vief, G. (1990). Wisdom as integrated thought: Historical and developmental perspectives. In R. J. Sternberg (Ed.), *Wisdom: Its nature, origins, and development* (pp. 52–83). New York: Cambridge University Press.

Labouvie-Vief, G., & Schell, D. A. (1982). Learning and memory in later life. In B. B. Wolman (Ed.), *Handbook of developmental psychology*. Englewood Cliffs, NJ: Prentice-Hall.

Lachman, M. E. (1986). Locus of control in aging research: A case for multi-dimensional and domain-specific assessment. *Psychology and Aging, 1*, 34–40.

Ladefoged, P., & Maddieson, I. (1996). *The sounds of the world's languages*. Cambridge: Blackwell.

LaFraniere, S. (1992, August 27). Identifying 'Ivan': Does memory mislead? *Washington Post, 115*, p. A29.

La Ganga, M. L. (1994, May 14). Father wins in "false memory" case. *Los Angeles Times*, p. A1.

Laing, R. D. (1964). Is schizophrenia a disease? *International Journal of Social Psychiatry, 10*, 184–193.

Lamb, M. E. (1977a). The development of mother–infant and father–infant attachments in the second year of life. *Developmental Psychology, 13*, 637–648.

Lamb, M. E. (1977b). Father–infant and mother–infant interactions in the first year of life. *Child Development, 48*, 167–181.

Lamb, M. E. (1979). Separation and reunion behaviors as criteria of attachment to mothers and fathers. *Early Human Development, 3/4*, 329–339.

Lamb, M. E. (1996). *The role of the father in child development* (3rd ed.). New York: Wiley.

Lambert, M. J., & Bergin, A. E. (1994). The effectiveness of psychotherapy. In A. E. Bergin and S. L. Garfield (Eds.), *Handbook of psychotherapy and behavior change* (4th ed.), pp. 143–189. New York: Wiley.

Lane, J. D., & Williams, R. B. (1987). Cardiovascular effects of caffeine and stress in regular coffee drinkers. *Psychophysiology, 24,* 157–164.

Lange, R. D., & James, W. (1922). *The emotions.* Baltimore: Williams & Wilkins.

Langer, E. J. (1989). *Mindfulness.* New York: Addison-Wesley.

Langer, E. J. (1997). *The power of mindful learning.* Needham Heights, MA: Addison-Wesley.

Langer, E. J., Janis, I. L., & Wolfer, J. A. (1975). Reduction of psychological stress in surgical patients. *Journal of Experimental Social Psychology, 11,* 155–165.

Langley, P., & Jones, R. (1988). A computational model of scientific insight. In R. J. Sternberg (Ed.), *The nature of creativity* (pp. 177–201). New York: Cambridge University Press.

Langley, P., Simon, H. A., Bradshaw, G. L., & Zytkow, J. M. (1986). *Scientific discovery: Computational explorations of the creative processes.* Cambridge, MA: MIT Press.

Langlois, J. H., Ritter, J. M., Casey, R. J., and Savin, D. B. (1995). Infant attractiveness predicts maternal behaviors and attitudes. *Developmental Psychology, 31,* 164–472.

Langsley, D. G., Hodes, M., & Grimson, W. R. (1993). In N. Sartorius, H. de Girolano, G. Andrews, G. A. German, & L. Eisenberg (Eds.), *Treatment of mental disorders: A review of effectiveness.* Geneva, Switzerland, and Washington, DC: World Health Organization and American Psychiatric Press.

Laragh, J. H. (1988). Pathophysiology of diastolic hypertension. *Health Psychology, 7*(Suppl.), 15–31.

Larkin, J. H., McDermott, J., Simon, D. P., & Simon, H. A. (1980). Expert and novice performance in solving physics problems. *Science, 208,* 1335–1342.

Lashley, K. S. (1950). In search of the engram. *Symposia of the Society for Experimental Biology, 4,* 454–482.

Lassner, J. B., Matthews, K. A., & Stony, C. M. (1994). Are cardiovascular reactors to asocial stress also reactors to social stress? *Journal Personality and Social Psychology, 66,* 69–77.

Latané, B. (1981). The psychology of social impact. *American Psychologist, 36,* 343–356.

Latané, B., & Darley, J. M. (1968). Group inhibition of bystander intervention. *Journal of Personality and Social Psychology, 10,* 215–221.

Latané, B., & Darley, J. M. (1970). *The unresponsive bystander: Why doesn't he help?* New York: Appleton-Century-Crofts.

Latané, B., Nida, S. A., & Wilson, D. W. (1981). The effects of a group size on helping behavior. In J. P. Rushton & R. M. Sorrentino (Eds.), *Altruism and helping behavior: Social, personality, and developmental perspectives.* Hillsdale, NJ: Erlbaum.

Latané, B., Williams, K., & Harkins, S. (1979). Many hands make light the work: The causes and consequences of social loafing. *Journal of Personality and Social Psychology, 37,* 822–832.

Lau, R. R., Bernard, T. M., & Hartman, K. A. (1989). Further explorations of commonsense representations of common illness. *Health Psychology, 8,* 195–219.

Lau, R. R., & Hartman, K. A. (1983). Commonsense representations of common illnesses. *Health Psychology, 2,* 167–185.

Lazar, I., & Darlington, R. (1982). Lasting effects of early education: A report from the consortium for longitudinal studies. *Monographs of the Society for Research in Child Development, 47*(2–3, Serial No. 195).

Lazarus, A. A. (1961). Group therapy of phobic disorders by systematic desensitization. *Journal of Abnormal and Social Psychology, 63,* 504–510.

Lazarus, A. A. (1968). Learning theory and the treatment of depression. *Behaviour Research and Therapy, 6,* 83–89.

Lazarus, A. A. (1989). *The practice of multimodal therapy.* Baltimore: Johns Hopkins University Press.

Lazarus, A. A. (1990). If this be research... *American Psychologist, 58,* 670–671.

Lazarus, R. S. (1977). A cognitive analysis of biofeedback control. In G. E. Schwartz & J. Beatty (Eds.), *Biofeedback: Theory and research* (pp. 69–71). New York: Academic Press.

Lazarus, R. S. (1982). Thoughts on the relations between emotion and cognition. *American Psychologist, 37*(9), 1019–1024.

Lazarus, R. S. (1984). On the primacy of cognition. *American Psychologist, 39,* 124–129.

Lazarus, R. S. (1991). *Emotion and adaptation.* New York: Oxford University Press.

Lazarus, R. S. (1993). From psychological stress to the emotions: A history of changing outlooks. *Annual Review of Psychology, 44,* 1–21.

Lazarus, R. S., & Folkman, S. (1984). *Stress, appraisal, and coping.* New York: Springer.

Lazarus, R. S., Kanner, A., & Folkman, F. (1980). Emotions: a cognitive-phenomenological analysis. In R. Plutchik & H. Kellerman (Eds.), *Emotion: Theory, research and experience: Vol. 1. Theories of emotion.* New York: Academic Press.

Le Bon, G. (1896). *The crowd: A study of the popular mind.* New York: Macmillan.

Lederer, R. (1987). *Anguished English.* New York: Pocket Books.

Lederer, R. (1991). *The miracle of language.* New York: Pocket Books.

LeDoux, J. E. (1986). The neurobiology of emotion. In J. E. LeDoux & W. Hirst (Eds.), *Mind and brain: Dialogues in cognitive neuroscience* (pp. 301–354). Cambridge, England: Cambridge University Press.

LeDoux, J. E. (1992). Emotional memory systems in the brain. *Behavioural Brain Research, 58,* 69–79.

LeDoux, J. E. (1993). Emotional networks in the brain. In M. Lewis & J. M. Haviland (Eds.), *Handbook of emotions.* New York: Guilford Press.

LeDoux, J. E. (1995). Emotion: Clues from the brain. *Annual Review of Psychology, 46,* 209–235.

LeDoux, J. E., Romanski, L., & Xagoraris, A. (1989). Indelibility of subcortical emotional memories. *Journal of Cognitive Neuroscience, 1,* 238–243.

Lee, J. A. (1977). A typology of styles of loving. *Personality and Social Psychology Bulletin, 3,* 173–182.

Lee, J. A. (1988). Love-styles. In R. J. Sternberg & M. L. Barnes (Eds.), *The psychology of love* (pp. 38–67). New Haven, CT: Yale University Press.

Lee, T. F. (1993. *Gene future: The promise and perils of the new biology.* New York; Plenum.

Leon, A. S. (1983). Exercise and coronary heart disease. *Hospital Medicine, 19,* 38–59.

Leon, A. S., & Fox, S. M. III. (1981). Physical fitness. In E. L. Wynder (Ed.), *The book of health* (pp. 283–341). New York: Franklin Watts.

Leon, G. R. (1974). *Case histories of deviant behavior: A social learning analysis.* Boston: Holbrook Press.

Lepore, S. J. (1995). Cynicism, social support, and cardiovascular reactivity. *Health Psychology, 14,* 210–216.

Lepper, M. R. (1998). A whole much less than the sum of its parts. *American Psychologist, 53,* 675–676.

Lepper, M. R., Greene, D., & Nisbett, R. E. (1973). Undermining children's intrinsic interest with extrinsic rewards: A test of the "overjustification" hypothesis. *Journal of Personality and Social Psychology, 28,* 129–137.

Lepper, M. R., & Henderlong, J. (in press). Turning "play" into "work" and "work" into "play": 25 years of research on intrinsic versus extrinsic motivation. In C. Sansone & J. M. Harackiewicz (Eds.), *Intrinsic motivation: Controversies and new directions.* New York: Academic Press.

Lepper, M. R., Henderlong, J., & Gingras, I. (1999). Understanding the effects of extrinsic rewards on intrinsic motivation—Uses and abuses of meta-analysis: Comment on Deci, Koestner, and Ryan (1999). *Psychological Bulletin, 125,* 669–676.

Lepper, M. R., Keavney, M., & Drake, M. (1996). Instrinsic motivation and extrinsic rewards: A commentary on Cameron and Pierce's meta-analysis. *Review of Educational Research, 66,* 5–32.

Lerner, M. J. (1970). The desire for justice and reactions to victims. In J. R. Macaulty & L. Berkowitz (Eds.), *Altruism and helping behavior* (pp. 205–229). New York: Academic Press.

Lerner, M. J. (1980). *The belief in a just world: A fundamental delusion.* New York: Plenum.

Lerner, M. J., & Meindl, J. R. (1981). Justice and altruism. In J. P. Rushton & R. M. Sorrentino (Eds.), *Altruism and helping behavior: Social, personality, and developmental perspectives* (pp. 213–232). Hillsdale, NJ: Erlbaum.

Lesch, K. P., Bengel, D., Heils, A., Sabol, S. Z., Greenberg, B. D., Petri, S., Benjamin, J., Muelller, C. R., Hamer, D. H., & Murphy, D. (1996). Association of anxiety-related traits with a polymorphism in the serotonin transporter gene regulatory region. *Science, 274,* 1527–1531.

Lesgold, A. M. (1988). Problem solving. In R. J. Sternberg & E. E. Smith (Eds.), *The psychology of human thought* (pp. 188–213). New York: Cambridge University Press.

Lesgold, A. M., Rubinson, H., Feltovich, P., Glaser, R., Klopfer, D., & Wang, Y. (1988). Expertise in a complex skill: Diagnosing X-ray pictures. In M. T. H. Chi, R. Glaser, & M. Farr (Eds.), *The nature of expertise.* Hillsdale, NJ: Erlbaum.

Lester, B. M., Corwin, M. J., Sepkoski, C., Seifer, R., Peuker, McLauglin, & Golub. (1991). Neurobehavioral syndromes in cocaine-exposed newborn infants. *Child Development, 62,* 694–705.

LeVay, S. (1991). A difference in hypothalamic structure between heterosexual and homosexual men. *Science, 253,* 1034–1037.

Levenkron, J. C., & Moore, L. G. (1988). The Type A behavior pattern: Issues for intervention research. *Annals of Behavioral Medicine, 10,* 78–83.

Levenson, R. W., Ekman, P., & Friesen, W. V. (1990). Voluntary facial action generates emotion specific autonomic nervous system activity. *Psychophysiology, 27*(4), 363–384.

Leventhal, H., & Tomarken, A. J. (1986). Emotion: Today's problems. *Annual Review of Psychology, 37,* 565–610.

Levine, L. E. (1983). Mine: Self-definition in 2-year-old boys. *Developmental Psychology, 19,* 544–549.

Levine, R. A., & Campbell, D. T. (1972). *Ethnocentrism: Theories of conflict, ethnic attitudes, and group behavior.* New York: Wiley.

Levine, R. V., & Bartlett, K. (1984). Pace of life, punctuality, and coronary heart disease in six countries. *Journal of Cross-Cultural Psychology, 15*(2), 233–255.

Levine, R. V., Martinez, T. S., Brase, G., & Sorenson, K. (1994). Helping in 36 U.S. cities. *Journal of Personality and Social Psychology, 67,* 69–82.

Levinson, D. J. (1978). *The seasons of a man's life.* New York: Ballantine.

Levinson, D. J. (1986). A conception of adult development. *American Psychologist, 41,* 3–13.

Levi-Strauss, C. (1966). *The savage mind.* Chicago: University of Chicago Press.

Levy, J. (1974). Cerebral asymmetries as manifested in split-brain man. In M. Kinsbourne & W. L. Smith (Eds.), *Hemispheric disconnection and cerebral function.* Springfield, IL: Charles C. Thomas.

Levy, J., Trevarthen, C., & Sperry, R. W. (1972). Perception of bilateral chimeric figures following hemispheric deconnexion. *Brain, 95*(1), 61–78.

Lewey, A. J., Ahmed, S., Jackson, J. L., & Sack, R. L. (1992). Melatonin shifts human circadian ryhthms according to a phase-response curve. *Chronobiology International, 9,* 380–392.

Lewin, K. (1948). *Resolving social conflicts: Selected papers on group dynamics.* New York: Harper.

Lewin, K. (1951). *Field theory in social science: Selected theoretical papers.* New York: Harper. (Original work published 1935)

Lewinsohn, P. M. (1974). A behavioral approach to depression. In R. J. Friedman & M. M. Katz (Eds.), *The psychology of depression: Contemporary theory and research.* New York: Halstead Press.

Lewinsohn, P. M., Steinmetz, J. L., Larson, D. W., & Franklin, J. (1981). Depression-related cognitions: Antecedent or consequence? *Journal of Abnormal Psychiatry, 136,* 231–233.

Lewis, C. A., & Maltby, J. (1995). Religiosity and personality among U.S. adults. *Personality and Individual Differences, 18,* 293–295.

Lewis, M., & Brooks, J. (1974). Self, other and fear: Infants' reactions to people. In M. Lewis & L. A. Rosenblum (Eds.), *The origins of fear.* New York: Wiley.

Lewis, M., & Brooks-Gunn, J. (1981). Visual attention at three months as a predictor of cognitive functioning at two years of age. *Intelligence, 5,* 131–140.

Lewontin, R. C. (1975). Genetic aspects of intelligence. *Annual Review of Genetics, 9,* 387–405.

Lewy, A., Sack, L., Miller, S., & Itoban, T. M. (1987). Anti-depressant and circadian-phase shifting effects of light. *Science, 235,* 352–367.

Li, P. (1975). *Path analysis: A primer.* Pacific Grove, CA: Boxwood Press.

Liberman, A. M., Cooper, F. S., Shankweiler, D. P., & Studdert-Kennedy, M. (1967). Perception of the speech code. *Psychological Review, 74,* 431–461.

Liberman, A. M., & Mattingly, I. G. (1985). The motor theory of speech perception revised. *Cognition, 21,* 1–36.

Liebert, R. M., & Baron, R. A. (1972). Some immediate effects of televised violence on children's behavior. *Developmental Psychology, 6,* 469–475.

Liebert, R. M., & Liebert, L. L. (1998). *Liebert & Spiegler's Personality: Strategies and issues* (8th ed.). Pacific Grove, CA: Brooks/Cole.

Lindsay, D. S., & Johnson, M. K. (1991). Recognition memory and source monitoring. *Bulletin of the Psychonomic Society, 29,* 203–205.

Lindsay, D. S., & Read, J. D. (1994). Psychotherapy and memories of childhood sexual abuse: A cognitive perspective. *Applied Cognitive Psychology, 8,* 281–338.

Linville, P. (1998). The heterogeneity of homogeneity. In J. Cooper & J. Darley (Eds.), *Attribution processes, person perception, and social interaction: The legacy of Ned Jones.* Washington, D. C.: American Psychological Association.

Linz, D., Donnerstein, E., & Penrod, S. (1984). The effects of multiple exposures to filmed violence against women. *Journal of Communication, 43,* 130–147.

Linz, D., Donnerstein, E., & Penrod, S. (1988). Effects of long-term exposure to violent and sexually degrading depictions of women. *Journal of Personality and Social Psychology, 55,* 758–768.

Lipman, M. (1982). *Harry Stottlemeier's discovery.* Upper Montclair, NJ: First Mountain Foundation.

Lippa, R. A. (1990). *Introduction to social psychology.* Belmont, CA: Wadsworth.

Lipsey, M. W., & Wilson, D. B. (1993). The efficacy of psychological, educational, and behavioral treatment: Confirmation from meta-analysis. *American Psychologist, 48,* 1181–1209.

Lissner, L., Odell, P. M., D'Agostino, R. B., Stokes, J., Kreger, B. E., Belanger, A. J., & Brownell, K. D. (1991). Variability of body weight and health outcomes in the Framingham population. *New England Journal of Medicine, 324,* 1839–1844.

Lloyd, G. K., Fletcher, A., & Minchin, M. C. W. (1992). GABA agonists as potential anxiolytics. In G. D. Burrows, S. GM. Roth, & R. Noyes, Jr. (Eds.), *Handbook of anxiety* (Vol. 5). Oxford, England: Elsevier.

Lobitz, W. C., & Post, R. D. (1979). Parameters of self-reinforcement and depression. *Journal of Abnormal Psychology, 88,* 33–41.

Locke, E. A., & Latham, G. P. (1985). The application of goal setting to sports. *Journal of Sport Psychology, 7,* 205–222.

Locke, E. A., & Latham, G. P. (1990). *A theory of goal-setting and task performance.* Englewood Cliffs, NJ: Prentice-Hall.

Locke, E. A., Shaw, K. N., Saari, L. M., & Latham, G. P. (1981). Goal setting and task performance: 1969–1980. *Psychological Bulletin, 90,* 125–152.

Locke, J. (1961). An essay concerning human understanding. In *Great books of the Western world: Vol. 35. Locke, Berkeley, Hume.* Chicago: Encyclopaedia Britannica. (Original work published 1690)

Locke, J. L. (1994). Phases in the child's development of language. *American Scientist, 82,* 436–445.

Loehlin, J. C. (1992). *Genes and environment in personality development.* Newbury Park, CA: Sage.

Loehlin, J. C. (1992). Using EQs for a simple analysis of the Colorado Adoption Project data on height and intelligence. *Behavior Genetics, 22,* 234–245.

Loehlin, J. C, (2000). Group differences in intelligence. In R. J. Sternberg (Ed.), *Handbook of intelligence.* New York: Cambridge University Press.

Loehlin, J. C., Horn, J. M., & Willerman, L. (1997). Heredity, environment, and IQ in the Texas Adoption Project. In R. J. Sternberg & E. L. Grigorenko (Eds.), *Intelligence, heredity, and environment* (pp. 105–125). New York: Cambridge University Press.

Loewenstein, G. (1994). The psychology of curiosity: A review and reinterpretation. *Psychological Bulletin, 116,* 75–98.

Loftus, E. F. (1975). Leading questions and the eyewitness report. *Cognitive Psychology, 7,* 560–572.

Loftus, E. F. (1977). Shifting human color memory. *Memory and Cognition, 5,* 696–699.

Loftus, E. F. (1993a). Psychologists in the eyewitness world. *American Psychologist, 48*(5), 550–552.

Loftus, E. F. (1993b). The reality of repressed memories. *American Psychologist, 48*(5), 518–537.

Loftus, E. F., & Ketcham, K. (1991). *Witness for the defense: The accused, the eyewitness, and the expert who puts memory on trial.* New York: St. Martin's Press.

Loftus, E. F., & Loftus, G. R. (1980). On the permanence of stored information in the human brain. *American Psychologist, 35,* 409–420.

Loftus, E. F., Miller, D. G., & Burns, H. J. (1978). Semantic integration of verbal information into a visual memory. *Journal of Experimental Psychology: Human Learning and Memory, 4,* 19–31.

Lohman, D. (2000). Complex information processing and intelligence. In R. J. Sternberg (Ed.), *Handbook of intelligence.* New York: Cambridge University Press.

Lonner, W. J. (1989). The introductory psychology text: Beyond Ekman, Whorf, and biased IQ tests. In D. M. Keats, D. Munro, & L. Mann (Eds.), *Heterogeneity in cross-cultural psychology.* Amsterdam: Swets & Zeitlinger.

Lonner, W. J. (1990). An overview of cross-cultural testing and assessment. In R. W. Brislin (Ed.), *Applied cross-cultural psychology.* Newbury Park, CA: Sage.

Lonner, W. J., & Berry, J. W. (1986). Sampling and surveying. In W. J. Lonner & J. W. Berry (Eds.), *Field methods in cross-cultural research: Vol. 8. Cross-cultural research and methodology series.* Beverly Hills, CA: Sage.

Lopez, S., & Nuñez, J. A. (1987). Cultural factors considered in selected diagnostic criteria and interview schedules. *Journal of Abnormal Psychology, 96,* 270–272.

Loranger, A. W. (1984). Sex differences in age of onset of schizophrenia. *Archives of General Psychiatry, 41,* 157–161.

Lorber, J. (1975). Good patients and problem patients: Conformity and deviance in a general hospital. *Journal of Health and Social Behavior, 16,* 213–225.

Lore, R., & Schultz, L. A. (1993). Control of human aggression: A comparative perspective. *American Psychologist, 48,* 16–25.

Lorenz, K. (1937). The companion in the bird's world. *Auk, 54,* 245–273.

Lorenz, K. (1950). The comparative method in studying innate behavior patterns. *Symposium for the Society for Experimental Biology, 4,* 221–268.

Lott, A., & Lott, B. (1968). A learning theory approach to interpersonal attitudes. In A. G. Greenwald, T. C. Brock, & T. M. Ostrom (Eds.), *Psychological foundations of attitude.* New York: Academic Press.

Lovaas, O. I. (1968). Learning theory approach to the treatment of childhood schizophrenia. In *California Mental Health Research Symposium: No. 2. Behavior theory and therapy.* Sacramento: California Department of Mental Hygiene.

Lovaas, O. I. (1977). *The autistic child.* New York: Wiley.

Lovaas, O. I., Koegel, R., Simmons, J. Q., & Long, J. S. (1973). Some generalization and follow-up measures on autistic children in behavior therapy. *Journal of Applied Behavior Analysis, 6,* 131–166.

Luce, R. D., & Raiffa, H. (1957). *Games and decisions.* New York: Wiley.

Luchins, A. S. (1942). Mechanization in problem solving. *Psychological Monographs, 54*(6, Whole No. 248).

Lucy, J. A. (1997). Linguistic relativity. *Annual review of anthropology, 26,* 291–312.

Lucy, J. A., & Schweder, R. A. (1979). Whorf and his critics: Linguistic and nonlinguistic influences on color memory. *American Anthropologist, 81,* 581–615.

Lucy, J. A., & Schweder, R. A. (1988). The effect of incidental conversation on memory for focal colors. *American Anthropologist, 90,* 923–931.

Ludwick-Rosenthal, R., & Neufeld, R. W. J. (1988). Stress management during noxious medical procedures: An evaluative review of outcome studies. *Psychological Bulletin, 104,* 326–342.

Lumsdaine, A. A., & Janis, I. L. (1953). Resistance to "counterpropaganda" produced by one-sided and two-sided "propaganda" presentation. *Public Opinion Quarterly, 17,* 311–318.

Lumsden, C. J. (1998). Evolving creative minds: Stories and mechanisms. In R. J. Sternberg (Ed.), *Handbook of creativity* (pp. 153–168). New York: Cambridge University Press.

Lundberg, U. (1976). Urban commuting: Crowdedness and catecholamine excretion. *Journal of Human Stress, 2,* 26–32.

Luria, A. R. (1968). *The mind of a mnemonist.* New York: Basic Books.

Luria, A. R. (1973). *The working brain.* London: Penguin.

Luria, A. R. (1976). *Cognitive development: Its cultural and social foundations.* Cambridge, MA: Harvard University Press.

Luria, A. R. (1984). *The working brain: An introduction to neuropsychology* (B. Haigh, Trans.). Harmondsworth, England: Penguin. (Original work published 1973)

Lutz, D., & Sternberg, R. J. (1999). Cognitive development. In M. H. Bornstein & M. E. Lamb (Eds.), *Developmental psychology: An advanced textbook* (4th ed.) (pp. 275–311). Mahwah, NJ: Lawrence Erlbaum Associates.

Lydiard, L. R., Brawman, M. O., & Ballenger, J. C. (1996). Recent developments in the psychopharmacology of anxiety disorders. *Journal of Consulting and Clinical Psychology, 64,* 660–668.

Lykken, D. (1998). *A tremor in the blood.* New York: Plenum.

Lyon, J., & Gorner, P. (1995). *Altered fates: Gene therapy and the retooling of human life.* New York: Norton.

Ma, H. K. (1988). The Chinese perspectives on moral judgment development. *International Journal of Psychology, 23*(2), 201–227.

Maccini, C. A. (1989). *Life scientists.* Baltimore: Media Materials.

MacFarlane, A. (1975). Olfaction in the development of social preferences in the human neonate. *Ciba Foundation Symposium, 33,* 103–117.

MacKinnon, D., Jamison, R., & DePaulo, J. R. (1997). Genetics of manic depressive illness. *Annual Review of Neuroscience, 20,* 355–373.

Mackintosh, N. (1998). *IQ and intelligence.* New York: Oxford University Press.

Mackworth, N. H. (1948). The breakdown of vigilance during prolonged visual search. *Quarterly Journal of Experimental Psychology, 1,* 6–21.

MacLeod, C. M., Hunt, E. B., & Mathews, N. N. (1978). Individual differences in the verification of sentence-picture relationships. *Journal of Verbal Learning and Verbal Behavior, 17,* 493–507.

Maehr, M., & Nicholls, J. (1980). Culture and achievement motivation: A second look. In N. Warren (Ed.), *Studies in cross-cultural psychology* (Vol. 2). London: Academic Press.

Magnus, K., Diener, E., Fujita, F., & Pavot, W. (1993). Extraversion and neuroticism as predictors of objective life events: A longitudinal analysis. *Journal of Personality and Social Psychology, 65,* 1046–1053.

Maher, B. A. (1972). The language of schizophrenia: A review and interpretation. *British Journal of Psychiatry, 120,* 4–17.

Maher, B. A. (1983). A tentative theory of schizophrenic utterance. In B. A. Maher & W. Maher (Eds.), *Progress in experimental personality research* (Vol. 12, pp. 1–52). Orlando, FL: Academic Press.

Maier, S. F., Rapaport, P., & Wheatley, K. L. (1976). Conditioned inhibition and the UCS-CS interval. *Animal Learning & Behavior, 4,* 217–220.

Main, M., Kaplan, N., & Cassidy, J. (1985). Security in infancy, childhood, and adulthood: A move to the level of representation. In I. Bretherton and E. Waters (Eds.), Growing points of attachment theory and research: *Monographs of the Society for Research in Child Development, 50,* (Nos. 1–2), 67–104.

Main, M., & Solomon, J. (1990). Procedures for identifying infants as disorganized/disoriented during the Ainsworth strange situation. In M. Greenberg, D. Cicchetti, & E. M. Cummings (Eds.), *Attachment in the preschool years: Theory, research and intervention* (pp. 121–160). Chicago: University of Chicago Press.

Malamuth, N. M., & Check, J. V. P. (1981). The effects of mass media exposure on acceptance of violence against women: A field experiment. *Journal of Research in Personality, 15,* 436–446.

Maling, M. S., & Howard, K. I. (1994). From research to practice to research to . . . . In P. F. Talley, H. H. Strupp, and S. F. Butler (Eds.), *Psychotherapy research and practice: Bridging the gap.* New York: Basic Books.

Malone, K. Y., Mann, J. J. (1993). Serotonin and major depression. In J. J. Mann & D. J. Kupfer (Eds.), *Biology of depressive disorders: Part A. A systems perspective* (pp. 29–49). New York: Plenum.

Maltby, J. (1995). Personality, prayer, and church attendance among U.S. female adults. *Journal of Social Psychology, 135,* 529–531.

Mandler, G. (1980). The generation of emotion: A psychological theory. In R. Plutchik & H. Kellerman (Eds.), *Emotion: Theory, research, and experience* (Vol. 1). New York: Academic Press.

Mangelsdorf, S. C., Shapiro, J. R., & Marzolf, D. (1995). Developmental and temperamental differences in emotion regulation in infancy. *Child Development, 66,* 1817–1828.

Manji, H. K., Hsiao, J. K., Risby, E. D., et al. (1991). The mechanisms of action of lithium: I. Effects on serotonergic and noradrenergic systems in normal subjects. *Archives of General Psychiatry, 48,* 505–512.

Mann, J. (1973). *Time-dated psychotherapy.* Cambridge, MA: Harvard University Press.

Mantyla, T. (1986). Optimizing cue effectiveness: Recall of 500 and 600 incidentally learned words. *Journal of Experimental Psychology: Learning, Memory, and Cognition, 12,* 66–71.

Maqsud, M., & Rouhani, S. (1990). Self-concept and moral reasoning among Batswana adolescents. *Journal of Social Psychology, 130*(6), 829–830.

Marcel, A. J. (1983). Conscious and unconscious perception: An approach to the relations between phenomenal experience and perceptual processes. *Cognitive Psychology, 15,* 238–300.

Marcia, J. E. (1966). Development and validation of ego identity status. *Journal of Personality and Social Psychology, 3*(5), 551–558.

Marcia, J. E. (1980). Identity in adolescence. In J. Adelson (Ed.), *Handbook of adolescent psychology* (pp. 159–187). New York: Wiley.

Markman, E. M. (1977). Realizing that you don't understand: A preliminary investigation. *Child Development, 48,* 986–992.

Markman, E. M. (1979). Realizing that you don't understand: Elementary school children's awareness of inconsistencies. *Child Development, 50,* 643–655.

Markman, E. M. (1992). Constraints on word learning: Speculation about their nature, origins and domain specificity. In M. R. Gunner & M. P. Maratsos (Eds.), *Modularity and constraints in language and cognition: The Minnesota symposium on child psychology.* Hillsdale, NJ: Erlbaum.

Markman, H. J. (1981). Prediction of marital distress: A 5-year follow-up. *Journal of Consulting and Clinical Psychology, 49,* 760–762.

Marks, I. M., & Gelder, M. G. (1967). Transvestism and fetishism: Clinical and psychological changes during faradic aversion. *British Journal of Psychiatry, 113,* 711–729.

Markus, H. (1977). Self-schemata and processing information about the self. *Journal of Personality and Social Psychology, 35,* 63–78.

Markus, H., Cross, S., & Wurt, E. (1990). The role of the self-system in competence. In R. J. Sternberg & J. Kolligan (Eds.), *Competence considered* (pp. 205–226). New Haven, CT: Yale University Press.

Markus, H., & Kitayama, S. (1991). Culture and the self: Implications for cognition, emotion, and motivation. *Psychological Review, 98*(2), 224–253.

Markus, H. R., & Kitayama, S. (1994). The cultural construction of self and emotion: Implications for social behavior. In S. Kitayama & H. R. Markus (Eds.), *Emotions and culture: Empirical studies of mutual influence.* Washington, DC: American Psychological Association.

Markus, H. R., Kitayama, S., & Heiman, R. J. (1996). Culture and "basic" psychological principles. In E. T. Higgins & A. W. Kruglanski (Eds.), *Social psychology: Handbook of basic principles* (pp. 857–913). New York: Guilford Press.

Markus, H., & Smith, J. (1981). The influence of self-schema on the perception of others. In N. Cantor & J. F. Kihlstrom (Eds.), *Personality, cognition, and social interaction* (pp. 233–262). Hillsdale, NJ: Erlbaum.

Marmor, G. S. (1975). Development of kinetic images: When does the child first represent movement in mental images? *Cognitive Psychology, 7,* 548–559.

Marmor, G. S. (1977). Mental rotation and number conservation: Are they related? *Developmental Psychology, 13,* 320–325.

Marr, D. (1982). *Vision.* San Francisco: Freeman.

Marshall, G. D., & Zimbardo, P. G. (1979). Affective consequences of inadequately explained arousal. *Journal of Personality and Social Psychology, 37,* 970–985.

Marshall, G. N., Wortman, C. B., Vickers, R. R., Kusulas, J. W., & Hewig, L. K. (1994). The five-factor model of personality as a framework for personality-health research. *Journal of Personality and Social Psychology, 48,* 278–286.

Marslen-Wilson, W. D. (1980). Speech understanding as a psychological process. In J. C. Simon (Ed.), *Spoken language generation and understanding* (pp. 39–67). Dordrecht, Netherlands: Reidel.

Martelli, M. F., Auerbach, S. M., Alexander, J., & Mercuri, L. G. (1987). Stress management in the health care setting: Matching interventions with patient coping styles. *Journal of Consulting and Clinical Psychology, 55,* 201–207.

Martin, F. E. (1985). The treatment and outcome of anorexia nervosa in adolescents: A prospective study and five year follow-up. *Journal of Psychiatric Research, 19,* 509–514.

Martin, J. A. (1981). A longitudinal study of the consequences of early mother–infant interaction: A microanalytic approach. *Monographs of the Society for Research in Child Development, 46*(203, Serial No. 190).

Martin, L. (1986). Eskimo words for snow: A case study in the genesis and decay of an anthropological example. *American Psychologist, 88,* 418–423.

Martin, M. (1979). Local and global processing: The role of sparsity. *Memory and Cognition, 7,* 476–484.

Martindale, C. (1981). *Cognition and consciousness.* Homewood, IL: Dorsey Press.

Maslow, A. H. (1943). A theory of human motivation. *Psychological Review, 50,* 370–396.

Maslow, A. H. (1954). *Motivation and personality.* New York: Harper & Row.

Maslow, A. H. (1970). *Motivation and personality* (2nd ed.). New York: Harper.

Massaro, D. W. (1987). *Speech perception by ear and eye: A paradigm for psychological inquiry.* Hillsdale, NJ: Erlbaum.

Masters, W. H., & Johnson, V. E. (1966). *Human sexual response.* Boston: Little, Brown.

Matarazzo, J. D. (1992). Biological and physiological correlates of intelligence. *Intelligence, 16*(3–4), 257–258.

Matas, L., Arend, R., & Sroufe, L. A. (1978). Continuity of adaptation in the second year: The relationship between quality of attachment and later competence. *Child Development, 49,* 547–556.

Mathur, M., & Chattopadhyay, A. (1991). The impact of moods generated by TV programs on responses to advertising. *Psychology and Marketing, 8,* 59–77.

Matlin, M. (1993). *The psychology of women* (2nd ed.). Fort Worth, TX: Harcourt Brace Jovanovich.

Matsumoto, D. (1994). *People: Psychology from a cross-cultural perspective.* Belmont, CA: Brooks/Cole.

Matsumoto, D. (1996). *Culture and psychology.* Belmont, CA: Brooks/Cole.

Maurer, D., & Adams, R. J. (1987). Emergence of the ability to discriminate a blue from a gray at one month of age. *Journal of Experimental Child Psychology, 44,* 147–156.

Maurer, D., & Maurer, C. (1988). *The world of the newborn.* New York: Basic Books.

May, R. (1969). *Love and will.* New York: Norton.

Mayer, D. J. (1952). The glucostatic theory of regulation of food intake and the problem of obesity. *Bulletin of the New England Medical Center, 14,* 43.

Mayer, D. J. (1953). Glucostatic mechanism of regulation of food intake. *New England Journal of Medicine, 249,* 13–16.

Mayer, J. D., & Gehr, G. (1996). Emotional intelligence and the identification of emotion. *Intelligence, 22,* 89–114.

Mayer, J. D., & Salovey, P. (1993). The intelligence of emotional intelligence. *Intelligence, 197,* 433–442.

Mayer, J. D., & Salovey, P. (1995). Emotional intelligence and the construction and regulation of feelings. *Applied and Preventive Psychology, 4,* 197–208.

Mayer, J., Salovey, P., & Caruso, D. (2000). Models of emotional intelligence. In R. J. Sternberg (Ed.), *Handbook of intelligence,* (pp. 396–421). New York: Cambridge University Press.

Mayer, R. (2000). Intelligence and education. In R. J. Sternberg (Ed.), *Handbook of intelligence.* New York: Cambridge University Press.

McAdams, D. P. (1990). *The person: An introduction to personality psychology.* New York: Harcourt Brace Jovanovich.

McBride, P., Brown, R. P., Demeo, M., & Deilp, J. (1994). The relationship of platelet 5-HT-sub-2 receptor indices to major depressive disorder, personality traits, and suicidal behavior. *Biological Psychiatry, 35,* 295–308.

McCall, R. B. (1989). The development of intellectual functioning in infancy and the prediction of later IQ. In S. D. Osofsky (Ed.), *The handbook of infant development* (pp. 707–741). New York: Wiley.

McCall, R. B., & Carriger, M. S. (1993). A meta-analysis of infant habituation and recognition memory performance as predictors of later IQ. *Child Development, 64,* 57–79.

McCall, R. B., Kennedy, C. B., & Appelbaum, M. I. (1977). Magnitude of discrepancy and the distribution of attention in infants. *Child Development, 48,* 772–786.

McCarley, R. W., & Hobson, J. A. (1981). REM sleep dreams and the activation-synthesis hypothesis. *American Journal of Psychiatry, 138,* 904–912.

McCarthy, G., Blamire, A. M., Puce, A., Nobe, A. C., Bloch, G., Hyder, F., Goldman-Rakic, P., & Shulman, R. G. (1994). Functional magentic resonance imaging of human prefrontal cortex activation during a spatial working memory task. *Proceedings of the National Academy of Sciences, USA, 91,* 8690–8694.

McCarthy, G., Blamire, A. M., Rothman, D. L., Gruetter, R., & Shulman, R. G. (1993). Echo-planar magnetic resonance imaging studies of frontal cortex activation during word generation in humans. *Proceedings of the National Academy of Sciences, USA, 90,* 4952–4956.

McClelland, D. C. (1961). *The achieving society.* Princeton, NJ: Van Nostrand.

McClelland, D. C. (1985). *Human motivation.* New York: Scott, Foresman.

McClelland, D. C., Atkinson, J. W., Clark, R. A., & Lowell, E. L. (1953). *The achievement motive.* New York: Appleton-Century-Crofts.

McClelland, D. C., Atkinson, J. W., Clark, R. A., & Lowell, E. L. (1976). *The achievement motive.* New York: Irvington.

McClelland, D. C., & Franz, C. E. (1992). Motivational and other sources of work accomplishments in mid-life: A longitudinal study. *Journey of Personality, 60,* 679–707.

McClelland, D. C., & Koestner, R. (1992). The achievement motive. In C. P. Smith (Ed.), *Motivation and personality: Handbook of thematic content analysis.* New York: Cambridge University Press.

McClelland, D. C., Koestner, R., & Weinberger, J. (1992). How do self-attributed and implicit motives differ? In C. P. Smith (Ed.), *Motivation and personality: Handbook of thematic content analysis.* New York: Cambridge University Press.

McClelland, D. C., & Teague, G. (1975). Predicting risk preferences among power-related tasks. *Journal of Personality, 43,* 266–285.

McClelland, D. C., & Winter, D. G. (1969). *Motivating economic achievement.* New York: Free Press.

McClintock, C. G., & Liebrand, W. B. G. (1988). Role of interdependence structure, individual value orientation, and another's strategy in social decision making: A transformational analysis. *Journal of Personality and Social Psychology, 55*(3), 396–409.

McCormick, D. A., & Thompson, R. F. (1984). Cerebellum: Essential involvement in the classically conditioned eyelid response. *Science, 223,* 296–299.

McCrae, R. R. (1996). Social consequences of experiential openness. *Psychological Bulletin, 120,* 323–337.

McCrae, R. R., & Costa, P. T., (1987). Validation of the five-factor model of personality across instruments and observers. *Journal of Personality and Social Psychology, 52,* 81–90.

McCrae, R. R., & Costa, P. T., (1991). Adding *Liebe und Arbeit:* The full five-factor model and well-being. *Personality and Social Psychology Bulletin, 17,* 227–232.

McCrae, R. R., & Costa, P. T. (1997). Personality trait structure as a human universal. *American Psychologist, 5,* 509–516.

McCrae, R. R., Costa, P. T., Jr., & Yik, M. S. M. (1996). Universal aspects of Chinese personality structure. In M. H. Bond (Ed.), *The handbook of Chinese psychology* (pp. 189–207). Hong Kong: Oxford University Press.

McCrae, R. R., & John, O. (1992). An introduction to the five-factor model and its applications. *Journal of Personality, 60,* 175–215.

McCutcheon, M. (1989). *The compass in your nose and other astonishing facts about humans.* Los Angeles: Tarcher.

McDermott, K. B. (1996). The persistence of false memories in list recall. *Journal of Memory and Language, 35,* 212–230.

McDougall, W. (1908). *An introduction to social psychology.* London: Methuen.

McGarry-Roberts, P. A., Stelmack, R. M., & Campbell, K. B. (1992). Intelligence, reaction time, and event-related potentials. *Intelligence, 16*(3–4), 289–313.

McGinn, L. K., & Sanderson, W. C. (1995). The nature of panic disorder. *In Session: Psychotherapy in Practice, 1,* 7–19.

McGue, M., Bouchard, T. J., Jr., Iacono, W. G., & Lykken, D. T. (1993). Behavioral genetics of cognitive ability: A life-span perspective. In R. Plomin & G. E. McClearn (Eds.), *Nature, nurture, and psychology* (pp. 59–76). Washington, DC: American Psychological Association.

McGuire, W. J. (1983). A contextualist theory of knowledge: Its implications for innovation and reform in psychological research. In L. Berkowitz (Ed.), *Advances in experimental social psychology* (Vol. 16, pp. 1–47). New York: Academic Press.

McGurk, H., & MacDonald, J. (1976). Hearing lips and seeing voices. *Nature, 264,* 746–748.

McHugh, P. R., & Moran, T. H. (1985). The stomach: A conception of its dynamic role in satiety. In J. M. Sprague & A. N. Epstein (Eds.), *Progress in psychobiology and physiological psychology* (Vol. 11, pp. 197–232). Orlando, FL: Academic Press.

McKenna, J., Treadway, M., & McCloskey, M. E. (1992). Expert psychological testimony on eyewitness reliability: Selling psychology before its time. In P. Suedfeld & P. E. Tetlock (Eds.), *Psychology and social policy* (pp. 283–293). New York: Hemisphere.

McKinlay, J. B. (1975). Who is really ignorant—Physician or patient? *Journal of Health and Social Behavior, 16,* 3–11.

McKoon, G., & Ratcliff, R. (1980). Priming in item recognition: The organization of propositions in memory for text. *Journal of Verbal Learning and Verbal Behavior, 19,* 369–386.

Meacham, J. A. (1983). Wisdom and the context of knowledge: Knowing that one doesn't know. In D. Kuhn & J. A. Meacham (Eds.), *On the development of developmental psychology* (pp. 111–134). Basel, Switzerland: Karger.

Meacham, J. A. (1990). The loss of wisdom. In R. J. Sternberg (Ed.), *Wisdom: Its nature, origins, and development* (pp. 181–211). New York: Cambridge University Press.

Mednick, S. A., Hutunen, M. O., & Machon, R. (1994). Prenatal influenza infections and adult schizophrenia. *Schizophrenia Bulletin, 20,* 263–267.

Meece, J. L., & Holt, K. (1993). A pattern analysis of students' achievement goals. *Journal of Educational Psychology, 85,* 582–590.

Meeker, W. B., & Barber, T. X. (1971). Toward an explanation of stage hypnosis. *Journal of Abnormal Psychology, 77,* 61–70.

Meeus, W. H., & Raaijmakers, Q. A. (1986). Administrative obedience: Carrying out orders to use psychological-administrative violence. *European Journal of Social Psychology, 16*(4), 311–324.

Meeus, W. H. J., & Raaijmakers, Q. A. W. (1995). Obedience in modern society: The Utrecht studies. *Journal of Social Issues, 51,* 155–175.

Mehler, J., Dupoux, E., Nazzi, T., & Dehaene-Lambertz, G. (1996). Coping with linguistic diversity: The infant's viewpoint. In J. L. Morgan & K. Demuth (Eds.), *Signal to syntax: Bootstrapping from speech to grammar in early acquisition* (pp. 101–116). Mahwah, NJ: Erlbaum.

Meichenbaum, D., & Cameron, R. (1982). Cognitive behavior therapy. In G. T. Wilson & C. M. Franks (Eds.), *Contemporary behavior therapy: Conceptual and empirical foundations.* New York: Guilford.

Meier, R. P. (1991). Language acquisition by deaf children. *American Scientist, 79,* 60–76.

Melamed, B. G., & Siegel, L. (1975). Reduction of anxiety in children facing hospitalization and surgery by use of filmed modeling. *Journal of Consulting and Clinical Psychology, 43,* 511–521.

The melting of a mighty myth: Guess what—Eskimos don't have 23 words for snow. (1991, July 22). *Newsweek, 118*(4), 63.

Mellinger, G. D., Balter, M. B., & Uhlenhuth, E. H. (1985). Insomnia and its treatment: Prevalence and correlations. *Archives of General Psychiatry, 42,* 225–232.

Meltzoff, A. N., & Borton, R. W. (1979). Intermodal matching by human neonates. *Nature, 282,* 403–404.

Meltzoff, A. N., & Moore, M. K. (1989). Imitation in newborn infants: Exploring the range of gestures imitated and the underlying mechanisms. *Developmental Psychology, 25*(6), 954–962.

Melzack, R. (Ed.). (1983). *Pain measurement and assessment.* New York: Raven Press.

Melzack, R., & Wall, P. D. (1965). Pain mechanisms: A new theory. *Science, 150,* 971–979.

Melzack, R., & Wall, P. D. (1982). *The challenge of pain.* New York: Basic Books.

Melzack, R., Wall, P. D., & Ty, T. C. (1982). Acute pain in an emergency clinic: Latency of onset and descriptor patterns related to different injuries. *Pain, 14*(1), 33–43.

Mental Health, United States, 1996–1997. Washington, DC: Substance Abuse and Mental Health Services Administration.

Merton, R. K. (1973). Behavior patterns of scientists. In *The Sociology of Science.* Chicago: University of Chicago Press.

Mesquita, B., & Frijda, N. H. (1992). Cultural variations in emotions: A review. *Psychological Bulletin, 112*(3), 179–204.

Messadié, G. (1991a). *Great inventions through history.* New York: Chambers.

Messadié, G. (1991b). *Great modern inventions.* New York: Chambers.

Messadié, G. (1991c). *Great scientific discoveries.* New York: Chambers.

Messer, B., & Harter, S. (1985). *The self-perception scale for adults.* Unpublished manuscript, University of Denver.

Messick S. (1984). The nature of cognitive styles: Problems and promises in educational practice. *Educational Psychologist, 19,* 59–74.

Messick, S. (1995). Validity of psychological assessment: Validation of inferences from persons' responses and performances as scientific inquiry into score meaning. *American Psychologist, 50,* 741–749.

Messick, S., Jungeblut, A. (1981). Time and method in coaching for the SAT. *Psychological Bulletin, 89,* 191–216.

Meyers, S. A., & Berscheid, E. (1997). The language of love: The difference a preposition makes. *Personality and Social Psychology Bulletin, 23,* 347–362.

Michael, R. T., Gagnon, J. H., Laumann, E. O., & Kolatu, G. (1994). *Sex in America: A definitive survey.* Boston: Little, Brown.

Michotte, A. (1963). *The perception of causality.* New York: Basic Books.

Mickelson, K. D., Kessler, R. C., & Shaver, P. R. (1997). Adult attachment in a nationally representative sample. *Journal of Personality and Social Psychology, 73,* 1092–1106.

Miles, D. R., & Carey, G. (1997). Genetic and environmental architecture of human aggression. *Journal of Personality and Social Psychology, 72,* 207–217.

Milgram, S. (1963). Behavioral study of obedience. *Journal of Abnormal and Social Psychology, 67,* 371–378.

Milgram, S. (1965). Some conditions of obedience and disobedience to authority. *Human Relations, 18,* 57–76.

Milgram, S. (1974). *Obedience to authority: An experimental view.* New York: Harper & Row.

Mill, J. S. (1843). *A system of logic, ratiocinative and inductive.* London: J. W. Parker.

Mill, J. S. (1887). *A system of logic.* New York: Harper & Brothers.

Miller, D. T., & McFarland, C. (1987). Pluralistic ignorance: When similarity is interpreted as dissimilarity. *Journal of Personality and Social Psychology, 53,* 298–305.

Miller, G. A. (1956). The magical number seven, plus or minus two: Some limits on our capacity for processing information. *Psychological Review, 63,* 81–97.

Miller, G. A. (1990). *The science of words.* New York: Scientific American Library.

Miller, G. A., Galanter, E. H., & Pribram, K. H. (1960). *Plans and the structure of behavior.* New York: Holt, Rinehart & Winston.

Miller, N., & Brewer, M. B. (Eds.). (1984). *Groups in contact: The psychology of desegregation.* New York: Academic Press.

Miller, S. D., Triggiano, P. J. (1992). The psychophysiological investigation of multiple personality disorder: Review and update. *American Journal of Clinical Hypnosis, 35,* 47–61.

Mills, R. T., & Krantz, D. S. (1979). Information, choice, and reactions to stress: A field experiment in a blood bank with laboratory analogue. *Journal of Personality and Social Psychology, 4,* 608–620.

Millsap, R. E. (1994). Psychometrics. In R. J. Sternberg (Ed.), *Encyclopedia of human intelligence* (Vol. 2, pp. 866–868). New York: Macmillan.

Milner, B., Corkin, S., & Teuber, H. L. (1968). Further analysis of the hippocampal amnesic syndrome: 14-year follow-up study of H. M. *Neuropsychologia, 6,* 215–234.

Mischel, W. (1968). *Personality and assessment.* New York: Wiley.

Mischel, W. (1973). Toward a social learning reconceptualization of personality. *Psychological Review, 80,* 252–283.

Mischel, W. (1977). On the future of personality measurement. *American Psychologist, 32,* 246–254.

Mischel, W. (1986). *Introduction to personality* (4th ed.). New York: Holt, Rinehart & Winston.

Mischel, W., & Peake, P. K. (1982). Beyond deja vu in the search for cross-situational consistency. *Psychological Review, 89*(6), 730–755.

Mischel, W., & Peake, P. K. (1983). Some facets of consistency: Replies to Epstein, Funder, and Bem. *Psychological Review, 90,* 394–402.

Mishkin, M., & Petri, H. L. (1984). Memories and habits: Some implications for the analysis of learning and retention. In L. R. Squire & N. Butters (Eds.), *Neurophysiology of memory* (pp. 287–296). New York: Guilford.

Mistlberger, R. E., & Rusak, B. (1999). Circadian rhythms in mammmals: Formal properties and environmental influences. In M. H. Kryger, T. Roth, & W. C. Dement (Eds.), *Principles and practice of sleep medicine* (2nd ed.). Philadelphia: Saunders.

Mithers, C. L. (1994). *Reasonable insanity: A true story of the seventies.* Reading, MA: Addison-Wesley.

Miyake, K., Chen, S., & Campos, J. J. (1985). Infant temperament, mother's mode of interaction, and attachment in Japan: An interim report. In I. Bretherton & E. Waters (Eds.), *Growing points of attachment in theory and research* (Reprinted from *Monographs of the Society for Research in Child Development 50,* 1–2, Serial No. 209).

Moghaddam, F. M., Taylor, D. M., & Wright, S. C. (1993). *Social psychology in cross-cultural perspective.* New York: Freeman.

Mohamed, A., A., & Wiebe, F. A. (1996). Toward a process theory of groupthink. *Small Group Research, 27,* 416–430.

Money, J., Wiedeking, C., Walker, P. A., & Gain, D. (1976). Combined antiandrogenic and counseling program for treatment of 46 XY and 47 XYY sex offenders. *Hormones, behavior, and psychopathology, 66,* 105–109.

Montag, I., & Levin, J. (1994). The five-factor personality model in applied settings. *European Journal of Personality, 8,* 1–11.

Montagu, A. (1976). *The nature of human aggression.* New York: Oxford University Press.

Monteith, M. J., Devine, P. G., & Zuwerink, J. R. (1993). Self-directed versus other-directed affect as a consequence of prejudice-related discrepancies. *Journal of Personality and Social Psychology, 64,* 198–210.

Moore, E. G. J. (1986). Family socialization and the IQ test performance of traditionally and transracially adopted black children. *Developmental Psychology, 22,* 317–326.

Moore, J. T., & Brylinsky, J. (1993). Spectator effect on team performance in college basketball. *Journal of Sport Behavior, 16,* 77–84.

Moos, R. H. (1982). Coping with acute health crises. In T. Millon, C. Green, & R. Meagher (Eds.), *Handbook of clinical health psychology.* New York: Plenum.

Moos, R. H. (1988). Life stressors and coping resources influence health and well-being. *Psychological Assessment, 4,* 133–158.

Moos, R. H. (1995). Development and applications of new measures of life stressors, social resources, and coping responses. *European Journal of Psychological Assessment, 11,* 1–13.

Moos, R. H., & Schaefer, J. A. (1986). Life transitions and crises: A conceptual overview. In R. H. Moos (Ed.), *Coping with life crises: An integrated approach.* New York: Plenum.

Moray, N. (1959). Attention in dichotic listening: Affective cues and the influence of instructions. *Quarterly Journal of Experimental Psychology, 11,* 56–60.

Morelli, G. A., Rogoff, B., Oppenheim, D., & Goldsmith, D. (1992). Cultural variations in infants' sleeping arrangements: Questions of independence. *Developmental Psychology, 28,* 604–613.

Morey, L. C. (1993). Psychological correlates of personality disorder. *Journal of Personality Disorders* (suppl.), 149–166.

Morgan, C. D., & Murray, H. A. (1935). A method for investigating fantasy: The Thematic Apperception Test. *Archives of Neurology and Psychiatry, 34,* 289–306.

Morgan, C. T., & Morgan, J. T. (1940). Studies in hunger II: The relation of gastric denervation and dietary sugar to the effect of insulin upon food-intake in the rat. *Journal of Genetic Psychology, 57,* 153–163.

Morris, M. W., & Larrick, R. P. (1995). When one cause casts doubt on another: A normative analysis of discounting in causal attribution. *Psychological Review, 102,* 331–355.

Morton, T. U. (1978). Intimacy and reciprocity of exchange: A comparison of spouses and strangers. *Journal of Personality and Social Psychology, 36,* 72–81.

Moscovici, S. (1976). *Social influence and social change.* London: Academic Press.

Moscovici, S. (1980). Toward a theory of conversion behavior. In L. Berkowitz (Ed.), *Advances in Experimental Social Psychology, 6,* 149–202.

Moscovici, S., & Zavalloni, M. (1969). The group as a polarizer of attitudes. *Journal of Personality and Social Psychology, 12,* 125–135.

Moss, P. A. (1994). Validity. In R. J. Sternberg (Ed.), *Encyclopedia of human intelligence* (Vol. 2, pp. 1101–1106). New York: Macmillan.

Moyers, B. D. (1993). *Healing and the mind.* New York: Doubleday.

Murdock, B. B., Jr. (1961). Short-term retention of single paired-associates. *Psychological Reports, 8,* 280.

Murnen, S. K., Peroit, A., & Byrne, D. (1989). Coping with unwanted sexual activity: Normative responses, situational determinants, and individual differences. *Journal of Sex Research, 26,* 85–106.

Murphy, J. (1976). Psychiatric labeling in cross-cultural perspective. *Science, 191,* 1019–1028.

Murray, H. A. (1938). *Explorations in personality.* New York: Oxford University Press.

Murray, H. A. (1943a). *Explorations in personality.* New York: Oxford University Press.

Murray, H. A. (1943b). *Thematic apperception test.* Cambridge, MA: Harvard University Press.

Murray, H. A. (1943c). *The Thematic Apperception Test: Manual.* Cambridge, MA: Harvard University Press.

Murray, K. (1993, May 9). When the therapist is a computer. *New York Times,* Sect. 3, p. 25.

Murstein, B. I. (1986). *Paths to marriage.* Beverly Hills, CA: Sage.

Murstein, B. I. (1988). A taxonomy of love. In R. J. Sternberg & M. L. Barnes (Eds.), *Psychology of love* (pp. 13–37). New Haven, CT: Yale University Press.

Murstein, B. I., & Brust, R. G. (1985). Humor and interpersonal attraction. *Journal of Personality Assessment, 49*(6), 637–640.

Mustonen, A. (1997). Nature of screen violence and its relation to program popularity. *Aggressive Behavior, 23,* 281–292.

Muzur, A., Fabbro, F., Clarici, A., Braun, S., & Bava, A. (1998). Encoding and recall of parsed stories in hypnosis. *Perceptual & Motor Skills 87,* 963–971.

Mwangi, M. W. (1996). Gender roles portrayed in Kenyan television commericals. *Sex Roles, 34,* 205–214.

Myers, B. J. (1984a). Mother–infant bonding: Rejoinder to Kennell and Klaus. *Developmental Review, 4,* 283–288.

Myers, B. J. (1984b). Mother–infant bonding: The status of this critical-period hypothesis. *Developmental Review, 4,* 240–274.

Myers, D., & Diener, E. (1995). Who is happy? *Psychological Science, 6,* 10–19.

Myers, D. G., & Bishop, G. D. (1970). Discussion effects on racial attitudes. *Science, 169,* 778–789.

Myers, D. G., & Lamm, H. (1976). The group polarization phenomenon. *Psychological Bulletin, 83,* 602–627.

Myers, J. K., Weissman, M. M., Tischler, G. L., Holzer, C. E., Leaf, P. J., & Stoltzman, R. (1984). Six-month prevalence of psychiatric disorders in three communities: 1980 to 1982. *Archives of General Psychiatry, 41,* 959–967.

Myerson, A. (1940). Review of *Mental disorders in urban areas: An ecological study of schizophrenia and other psychoses. American Journal of Psychiatry, 96,* 995–997.

Nairne, J. S., & Crowder, R. G. (1982). On the locus of the stimulus suffix effect. *Memory and Cognition, 10,* 350–357.

Nasby, W. (1985). Private self-consciousness, articulation of the self-schema, and the recognition memory of trait adjectives. *Journal of Personality and Social Psychology, 49,* 704–709.

Nathans, J., Thomas, D., & Hogness, D. S. (1986). Molecular genetics of human color vision: The genes encoding blue, green, and red pigments. *Science, 232*(47), 193–202.

National Center for Health Statistics. (1988). Advance report of final mortality statistics, 1986. *NCHS Monthly Vital Statistics Report, 37*(Suppl. 6).

National Center for Health Statistics. (1993). *Advance data from vital and health statistics* (U. S. Department of Health and Human Services, Public Health Service, Centers for Disease Control, National Center for Health Statistics). Washington, DC: U.S. Government Printing Office.

National Institute of Child Health and Human Development (1996), Early Child Care Research Network. (1996, Spring). Child care and the family: An opportunity to study development in context. *Society for Research in Child Development Newsletter,* Ann Arbor, MI: SRCD.

Navon, D. (1977). Forest before trees: The precedence of global features in visual perception. *Cognitive Psychology, 9,* 353–383.

Navon, D., & Gopher, D. (1979). On the economy of the human-processing system. *Psychological Review, 86,* 214–255.

Neimark, E. D. (1975). Intellectual development during adolescence. In F. D. Horowitz (Ed.), *Review of child development research* (Vol. 4). Chicago: University of Chicago Press.

Neisser, U. (1967). *Cognitive psychology.* New York: Appleton-Century-Crofts.

Neisser, U. (1982). Snapshots or benchmarks? In U. Neisser (Ed.), *Memory observed: Remembering in natural contexts.* San Francisco: Freeman.

Neisser, U. (Ed.). (1998). *The rising curve.* Washington, DC: American Psychological Association.

Nelson, C. (1990). *Gender and the social studies: Training preservice secondary social studies teachers.* Doctoral dissertation, University of Minnesota.

Nelson, C. A., & Bloom, F. E. (1997). Child development and neuroscience. *Child Development, 68,* 970–987.

Nelson, K. (1973). Structure and strategy in learning to talk. *Monograph of the Society for Research in Child Development, 38*(149).

Nelson, K. (1999). The developmental psychology of language and thought. In M. Bennett (Ed.), *Developmental psychology* (pp. 185–204). Philadelphia: Psychology Press.

Nelson, R. E., & Craighead, W. E. (1977). Selective recall of positive and negative feedback, self-control behaviors and depression. *Journal of Abnormal Psychology, 86,* 379–388.

Nelson, R. E., & Craighead, W. E. (1981). Tests of a self-control model of depression. *Behavior Therapy, 12,* 123–129.

Nelson, T. O. (1996). Consciousness and metacognition. *American Psychologist, 51,* 102–116.

Nelson, T. O. (1999). Cognition versus metacognition. In R. J. Sternberg (Ed.), *The nature of cognition* (pp. 625–641).

Nelson, T. O., & Rothbart, R. (1972). Acoustic savings for items forgotten from long-term memory. *Journal of Experimental Psychology, 93,* 357–360.

Nerenz, D. R., & Leventhal, H. (1983). Self-regulation theory in chronic illness. In T. G. Burish & L. A. Bradley (Eds.), *Coping with chronic disease: Research and applications* (pp. 13–38). New York: Academic Press.

Neto, F., Williams, J. E., & Widner, S. C. (1991). Portuguese children's knowledge of sex stereotypes: Effects of age, gender, and socioeconomic status. *Journal of Cross-Cultural Psychology, 22*(3), 376–388.

Nettelbeck T., & Lally, M. (1976). Inspection time and measured intelligence. *British Journal of Psychology, 67,* 17–22.

Neuberg, S. L., Cialdini, R. B., Brown, S. L., Luce, C., Sagarin, B. J., & Lewis, B. P. (1997). Does empathy lead to anything more than superficial helping? Comment on Batson et al., (1997). *Journal of Personality and Social Psychology, 73,* 510–516.

Neville, H. J. (1998). An interview with Helen J. Neville, Ph.D. In M. S. Gazzaniga, R. B. Ivry, & G. R. Mangun (Eds.), *Cognitive neuroscience* (pp. 492–493). New York: Norton.

Newcomb, A. F., & Bagwell, C. (1995). Children's friendship relations: A meta-analytic review. *Psychological Bulletin, 117,* 306–347.

Newcomb, T. M. (1943). *Personality and social change.* New York: Dryden.

Newcomb, T. M. (1957). Social psychological theory. In J. H. Roher & M. Sherif (Eds.), *Social psychology at the crossroads.* New York: Harper.

Newell, A. (1990). *Unified theories of cognition.* Cambridge, MA: Harvard University Press.

Newell, A., & Simon, H. A. (1972). *Human problem solving.* Englewood Cliffs, NJ: Prentice-Hall.

Newman, H. H., Freeman, F. N., & Holzinger, K. J. (1937). *Twins: A study of heredity and environment.* Chicago: University of Chicago Press.

Newman, L. S. & Baumeister, R. F. (1994, August). *"Who would wish for the trauma?" Explaining UFO Abductions.* Paper presented at the meeting of the American Psychological Association, Los Angeles, CA.

Newport, E. L. (1990). Maturational constraints on language learning. *Cognitive Science, 14,* 11–28.

Newsome, W. T., Britten, K. H., & Moushon, J. A. (1989). Neuronal correlates of a perceptual decision. *Nature, 341,* 52–54.

Nielsen, S. (1990). Epidemiology of anorexia nervosa in Denmark from 1983–1987: A nationwide register study of psychiatric admission. *Acta Psychiatricia Scandinavica, 81,* 507–514.

Niemczynski, A., Czyzowska, D., Pourkos, M., & Mirski, A. (1988). The Cracow study with Kohlberg's Moral Judgment Interview: Data pertaining to the assumption of cross-cultural validity. *Polish Psychological Bulletin, 19*(1), 43–53.

Nisan, M., & Kohlberg, L. (1982). Universality and variation in moral judgment: A longitudinal and cross-sectional study in Turkey. *Child Development, 53,* 865–876.

Nisbett, R. E. (1972). Hunger, obesity, and the ventromedial hypothalamus. *Psychological Review, 79,* 433–453.

Nisbett, R. E. (Ed.). (1993). *Rules for reasoning.* Hillsdale, NJ: Erlbaum.

Nisbett, R. E. (1995). Dangerous, but important. In R. Jacoby & N. Glauberman (Eds.). *The bell curve debate.* New York: Times Books.

Nisbett, R. E., Caputo, C., Legant, P., & Maracek, J. (1973). Behavior as seen by the actor and as seen by the observer. *Journal of Personality and Social Psychology, 27,* 154–164.

Nisbett, R. E. & Cohen, D. (1996). *Culture of honor: The psychology of violence in the south.* Boulder, CO: Westview Press.

Nisbett, R. E., & Wilson, T. D. (1977). Telling more than we can know: Verbal reports on mental processes. *Psychological Review, 84,* 231–259.

Noesjirwan, J. (1977). Contrasting cultural patterns on interpersonal closeness in doctors' waiting rooms in Sydney and Jakarta. *Journal of Cross-Cultural Psychology, 8*(3), 357–368.

Nolen-Hoeksema, S. (1990). *Sex differences in depression.* Stanford, CA: Stanford University Press.

Nolen-Hoeksema, S., & Girgus, J. S. (1994). The emergence of gender differences in depression during adolescence. *Psychological Bulletin, 115,* 424–443.

Noller, P., Law, H., & Comrey, A. L. (1987). Cattell, Comrey, and Eysenck personality factors compared: More evidence for the five robust factors? *Journal of Personality and Social Psychology, 53,* 775–782.

Norman, D. A. (1968). Toward a theory of memory and attention. *Psychological Review, 75,* 522–536.

Norman, D. A., & Rumelhart, D. E. (1975). *Explorations in cognition.* San Francisco: Freeman.

Norman, W. T. (1963). Toward an adequate taxonomy of personality attributes: Replicated factor structure in peer nomination personality ratings. *Journal of Abnormal and Social Psychology, 66,* 574–583.

Notarius, C., & Markman, H. (1993). *We can work it out.* New York: Putnam.

Nucci, L. P., & Weber, E. (1995). Social interactions in the home and the development of young children's conceptions of the personal. *Child Development, 66,* 1438–1452.

Nuñes, T. (1994). Street intelligence. In R. J. Sternberg (Ed.), *Encyclopedia of human intelligence* (pp. 1045–1049). New York: Macmillan.

Nuñes, T., Schliemann, A. D., & Carraher, D. W. (1993). *Street mathematics and school mathematics.* New York: Cambridge University Press.

Nurnberger, J. I., Jr., & Gershon, E. S. (1992). Genetics. In E. S. Paykel (Eds.), *Handbook of affective disorders* (2nd ed.). New York: Guilford.

Nwadiora, E., & McAdoo, H. (1996). Acculturative stress among Amerasian refugees: Gender and racial differences. *Adolescence, 31,* 477–487.

Oakes, L. M., & Cohen, L. B. (1995). Infant causal perception. In C. Rovee-Collier & L. P. Lipsitt (Eds.), *Advances in infancy research* (Vol. 9). Norwood, NJ: Ablex.

Oatley, K. (1993). Those to whom evil is done. In R. S. Wyer & T. K Srull (Eds.), *Perspectives on anger and emotion: Advances in social cognition* (Vol. 6, pp. 159–165). Hillsdale, NJ: Erlbaum.

Ochse, R. (1990). *Before the gates of excellence: The determinants of creative genius.* New York: Cambridge University Press.

Ogawa, S., Lee, T. M., Nayak, A. S., & Glynn, P. (1990). Oxygenation-sensitive contrast in magnetic resonance image of rodent brain at high magnetic fields. *Magnetic Resonance in Medicine, 14,* 68–78.

Ohbuchi, K., & Kambara, T. (1985). Attacker's intent and awareness of outcome, impression management, and retaliation. *Journal of Experimental Social Psychology, 2,* 321–330.

Ojemann, G. A. (1982). Models of the brain organization for higher integrative functions derived with electrical stimulation techniques. *Human Neurobiology, 1,* 243–250.

Ojemann, G. A., & Mateer, C. (1979). Human language cortex: Localization of memory, syntax, and sequential motor–phoneme identification systems. *Science, 205,* 1401–1403.

Ojemann, G. A., & Whitaker, H. A. (1978). The bilingual brain. *Archives of Neurology, 35,* 409–412.

Olds, J., & Milner, P. (1954). Positive reinforcement produced by electrical stimulation of septal area and other regions of the rat brain. *Journal of Comparative and Physiological Psychology, 47,* 419–427.

Olfson, M., & Pincus, H. J. A. (1996). Outpatient mental health care in nonhospital settings: Distribution of patients across provider groups. *American Journal of Psychiatry, 153,* 1353–1356.

Oliner, S. P., & Oliner, P. M. (1988). *The altruistic personality: Rescuers of Jews in Nazi Europe.* New York: The Free Press.

Olson, H. C. (1994). Fetal alcohol syndrome. In R. J. Sternberg (Ed.), *Encyclopedia of human intelligence* (Vol. 1, pp. 439–443). New York: Macmillan.

Öngel, U., & Smith, P. B. (1994). Who are we and where are we going? JCCP approaches its 100th issue. *Journal of Cross-Cultural Psychology, 25*(1), 25–54.

Oomara, Y. (1976). Significance of glucose insulin and free fatty acid on the hypothalamic feeding and satiety neurons. In D. Novin, W. Wyrwicka, & G. Bray (Eds.), *Hunger: Basic mechanisms and clinical implications.* New York: Raven Press.

Operario, D., & Fiske, S. (1998). Power plus prejudice: Sociocultural and psychological foundations of racial oppression. In J. L. Eberhardt & S. T. Fiske (Eds.), *Racism: The problem and the response.* Thousand Oaks, CA: Sage.

Orengo, C. A., Kunik, M. E., Ghusn, H., & Yudofsky, S. C. (1997). Correlation of testosterone with aggression in demented elderly men. *Journal of Nervous and Mental Disease, 185,* 349–351.

Orlinsky, D. E., & Howard, K. I. (1994). Unity and diversity among psychotherapies: A comparative perspective. In B. Bonger & L. E. Beutler (Eds.), *Foundations of psychotherapy: Theory, research, and practice.* New York: Basic Books.

Ormel, J., & Wohlfarth, T. (1991). How neuroticism, long-term difficulties, and life situation change influence psychological distress: A longitudinal model. *Journal of Personality and Social Psychology, 60,* 744–755.

Orne, M. T. (1959). Hypnosis: Artifact and essence. *Journal of Abnormal Psychology, 58,* 277–299.

Ornstein, R. (1977). *The psychology of consciousness* (2nd ed.). New York: Harcourt Brace Jovanovich.

Ornstein, R. (1986). *The psychology of consciousness.* (2nd rev. ed.). New York: Pelican Books.

Osherson, D. N. (1995). Probability judgment. In E. E. Smith & D. N. Osherson (Eds.), *An invitation to cognitive science: Vol. 3. Thinking* (pp. 35–75). Cambridge, MA: MIT Press.

Ostendorf, F., & Angleitner, A. (1994, July). *Psychometric properties of the German translation of the NEO Personality Inventory (NEO-PI-R).* Poster session presented at the Seventh Conference of the European Association for Personality Psychology, Madrid, Spain.

Otis, L. S. (1984). The adverse effects of meditation. In D. H. Shapiro & R. N. Walsh (Eds.), *Meditation: Classical and contemporary perspectives.* New York: Aldine.

Ott, E. M. (1989). Effects of male–female ratio at work: Policewomen and male nurses. *Psychology of Women Quarterly, 13*(1), 41–57.

Paivio, A. (1971). *Imagery and verbal processes.* New York: Holt, Rinehart & Winston.

Paivio, A. (1986). *Mental representations: A dual coding approach.* New York: Oxford University Press.

Palmer, S. E. (1975). The effects of contextual scenes on the identification of objects. *Memory and Cognition, 3,* 519–526.

Palmer, S. E. (1992). Modern theories of Gestalt perception. In G. W. Humphreys (Ed.), *Understanding vision: An interdisciplinary perspective—Readings in mind and language* (pp. 39–72). Oxford, England. Blackwell.

Papp, L., & Gorman, J. M. (1990). Suicidal preoccupation during fluoxetine treatment. *American Journal of Psychiatry, 147,* 1380.

Pappenheimer, J. R., Koski, G., Fencl, V., Karnovsky, M. L., & Krueger, J. (1975). Extraction of sleep-promoting factors from cerebrospinal fluid and from brains of sleep-deprived animals. *Journal of Neurophysiology, 38,* 1299–1311.

Paradis, M. (1977). Bilingualism and aphasia. In H. A. Whitaker & H. Whitaker (Eds.), *Studies in neurolinguistics* (Vol. 3). New York: Academic Press.

Paradis, M. (1981). Neurolinguistic organization of a bilingual's two languages. In J. E. Copeland & P. W. Davis (Eds.), *The seventh LACUS forum.* Columbia, SC: Hornbeam Press.

Parfyonova, G. V., Korichneva, I. L., Suvorov, Y. I., & Krasnikova, T. L. (1988). Characteristics of lymphocyte b-adrenoreceptors in essential hypertension: Effects of propranolol treatment and dynamic exercise. *Health Psychology, 7*(Suppl.), 33–52.

Parke, R. D. (1981). *Fathers.* Cambridge, MA: Harvard University Press.

Parke, R. D. (1996). *Fatherhood.* Cambridge, MA: Harvard University Press.

Parke, R. D., & Asher, S. R. (1983). Social and personality development. In M. R. Rosenzweig & L. W. Porter (Eds.), *Annual Review of Psychology, 34,* 465–509.

Parke, R. D., Berkowitz, L., Leyens, J. P., West, S. G., & Sebastian, R. J. (1977). Some effects of violent and nonviolent movies on the behavior of juvenile delinquents. In L. Berkowitz (Ed.), *Advances in experimental social psychology* (Vol. 10). New York: Academic Press.

Parke, R. D., & O'Neil, R. (1997). The influence of significant others on learning about relationships. In S. Duck (Ed.), *Handbook of personal relationships* (2nd ed., pp. 29–60). New York: Wiley.

Parke, R. D., & O'Neil, R. (1998). Social relationships across contexts: Family-peer linkages. In W. A. Collins & B. Laursen (Eds.), *Minnesota symposium on child psychology* (Vol. 3). Mahwah, NJ: Erlbaum.

Parke, R. D., & Sawin, D. B. (1980). The family in early infancy: Social interaction and attitudinal analyses. In F. A. Pederson (Ed.), *The father–infant relationship: Observational studies in a family context.* New York: Praeger.

Parke, R. D., & Tinsley, B. J. (1987). Family interaction in infancy. In J. D. Osofsky (Ed.), *Handbook of infant development* (pp. 579–641). New York: Wiley.

Parke, R. D., & Walters, R. H. (1967). Some factors influencing the efficacy of punishment training for inducing response inhibition. *Monographs of the Society for Research in Child Development, 32*(1, Whole No. 109).

Parten, M. (1932). Social participation among pre-school children. *Journal of Abnormal and Social Psychology, 27,* 243–269.

Pascual-Leone, J. (1984). Attentional, dialectic, and mental effort. In M. L. Commons, F. A. Richards, & C. Armon (Eds.), *Beyond formal operations.* New York: Plenum.

Pascual-Leone, J. (1990). An essay on wisdom: Toward organismic processes that make it possible. In R. J. Sternberg (Ed.), *Wisdom: Its nature, origins, and development* (pp. 244–278). New York: Cambridge University Press.

Paul, G. L. (1966). *Insight vs. desensitization in psychotherapy.* Stanford, CA: Stanford University Press.

Paul, G. L. (1967). Strategy of outcome research in psychotherapy. *Journal of Consulting Psychology, 31,* 109–118.

Paul, G. L., & Lentz, R. J. (1977). *Psychosocial treatment of chronic mental patients: Milieu versus social learning programs.* Cambridge, MA: Harvard University Press.

Paul, G. L., & Menditto, A. A. (1992). Effectiveness of inpatient treatment programs for mentally ill adults in public psychiatric facilities. *Applied and Preventive Psychology: Current Scientific Perspectives, 1,* 41–63.

Paul, R. (1990). *Critical thinking: What every person needs to survive in a rapidly changing world.* Rohnert Park, CA: Center for Critical Thinking and Moral Critique.

Pavlov, I. P. (1928). *Lectures on conditioned reflexes: The higher nervous activity of animals* (Vol. 1, H. Gantt, Trans.). London: Lawrence & Wishart.

Pavlov, I. P. (1955). *Selected works.* Moscow: Foreign Languages Publishing House.

Paykel, E. S. (1991). Depression in women. *British Journal of Psychiatry, 158,* 22–29.

Paykel, E. S., & Tanner, J. (1976). Life events, depressive relapse and maintenance treatment. *Psychological Medicine, 6,* 481–485.

Payne, R. W., Matussek, P., & George, E. I. (1959). An experimental study of schizophrenic thought disorder. *Journal of Mental Science, 105,* 627–652.

Peabody, D., & Goldberg, L. R. (1989). Some determinants of factor structures from personality-trait descriptors. *Journal of Personality and Social Psychology, 57*(3), 552–567.

Pearlstone, A., Russell, R. J. H., & Wells, P. A. (1994). A re-examination of the stress/illness relationship: How useful is the concept of stress? *Personality & Individual Differences, 17*(4), 577–580.

Pedersen, P. B., Draguns, J. G., Lonner, W. J., & Trimble, J. E. (Eds.). (1996). *Counseling across cultures* (4th ed.). Newbury Park, CA: Sage.

Pederson, N. L., Plomin, R., McClearn, G. E., & Friberg, L. (1988). Neuroticism, extraversion, and related traits in adult twins reared apart and reared together. *Journal of Personality and Social Psychology, 55,* 950–957.

Pellegrino, J. W., & Glaser, R. (1980). Components of inductive reasoning. In R. E. Snow, P.-A. Federico, & W. E. Montague (Eds.), *Aptitude, learning, and instruction: Vol 1. Cognitive process analyses of aptitude.* Hillsdale, NJ: Lawrence Erlbaum Associates.

Penfield, W. (1955). The permanent record of the stream of consciousness. *Acta Psychologica, 11,* 47–69.

Penfield, W. (1969). Consciousness, memory, and man's conditioned reflexes. In K. H. Pribram (Ed.), *On the biology of learning.* New York: Harcourt, Brace & World.

Penfield, W., & Roberts, L. (1959). *Speech and brain mechanisms.* Princeton, NJ: Princeton University Press.

Pennebaker, J. W., & Memon, A. (1996). Recovered memories in context: Thoughts and elaborations on Bowers and Farvolden (1996). *Psychological Bulletin, 119,* 381–385.

Penrose, R. (1989). *The emperor's new mind: Concerning computers, minds, and the laws of physics.* New York: Oxford University Press.

Penrose, R. (1994). *Shadows of the mind: A search for the missing science of consciousness.* Oxford: Oxford University Press.

Peplau, L. A. (1983). Roles and gender. In H. H. Kelley (Ed.), *Close relationships.* New York: Freeman.

Perkarik, G. (1993). Beyond effectiveness: Uses of consumer-oriented criteria in defining treatment success. In T. R. Giles (Ed.), *Handbook of effective psychotherapy.* New York: Plenum.

Perkins, D. N. (1981). *The mind's best work.* Cambridge, MA: Harvard University Press.

Perkins, D. N. (1988). The possibility of invention. In R. J. Sternberg (Ed.), *The nature of creativity* (pp. 362–385). New York: Cambridge University Press.

Perkins, D. N. (1995a). *Outsmarting IQ.* New York: The Free Press.

Perkins, D. N. (1995b). Insight in minds and genes. In R. J. Sternberg & J. E. Davidson (Eds.), *The nature of insight* (pp. 495–533). Cambridge, MA: MIT Press.

Perkins, D. N., & Grotzer, T. A. (1997). Teaching intelligence. *American Psychologist, 52,* 1125–1133.

Perlmutter, M. (1983). Learning and memory through adulthood. In M. W. Riley, B. B. Hess, & K. Bond (Eds.), *Aging in society: Selected reviews of recent research.* Hillsdale, NJ: Erlbaum.

Perlmutter, M., & Lange, G. (1978). A developmental analysis of recall–recognition distinctions. In P. A. Ornstein (Ed.), *Memory development in children.* Hillsdale, NJ: Erlbaum.

Perner, J. (1999). Theory of mind. In M. Bennett (Ed.), *Developmental psychology* (pp. 205–230). Philadelphia: Psychology Press.

Perris, C., & Herlofson, J. (1993). Cognitive therapy. In N. Sartorius, G. de Girolano, G. Andrews, G. A. German, & L. Eisenberg (Eds.), *Treatment of mental disorders: A review of effectiveness.* Geneva, Switzerland, and Washington, DC: World Health Organization and American Psychiatric Press.

Perry, J., & Bratman, M. (1986). *Introduction to philosophy: Classical and contemporary readings.* New York: Oxford University Press.

Persinger, M. A. (1999). Near-death experiences and ecstasy: a product of the organization of the human brain? In S. Della Salla (Ed.), *Mind myths: Exploring popular assumptions about the mind and brain* (pp. 85–99). New York: Wiley.

Persinger, M. A., & Richards, P. M. (1995). Vestibular experiences during brief periods of partial sensory deprivation are enhanced when daily geomagnetic activity exceeds 15–20 nT. *Neuroscience Letters, 194,* 169–172.

Persky, V. M., Kempthorne-Rawson, J., & Shekele, R. B. (1987). Personality and the risk of cancer: 20-year follow-up of the Western Electric Study. *Psychosomatic Medicine, 49,* 435–449.

Pervin, L. A. (1985). Personality: Current controversies, issues, and directions. *Annual Review of Psychology, 36,* 83–114.

Petersen, S., Fox, P. T., Posner, M. I., Mintun, M., & Raichle, M. E. (1988). Positron-emission tomographic studies of the cortical anatomy of single-word processing. *Nature, 331*(6157), 585–589.

Peterson, C., Maier, S. F., & Seligman, M. E. P. (1993). *Learned helplessness: A theory for the age of personal control.* New York: Oxford University Press.

Peterson, L. R., & Peterson, M. J. (1959). Short-term retention of individual verbal items. *Journal of Experimental Psychology, 58,* 193–198.

Petitto, L., & Marentette, P. F. (1991). Babbling in the manual mode: Evidence for the ontogeny of language. *Science, 251,* 1493–1499.

Petty, R. E., & Cacioppo, J. T. (1981). *Attitudes and persuasion: Classic and contemporary approaches.* Dubuque, IA: William C. Brown.

Petty, R. E., & Wegener, D. T. (1998). Attitude change: Multiple roles for persuasion variables. In D. Gilbert, S. Fiske, & G. Lindzey (Eds.), *The handbook of social psychology* (4th ed., pp. 323–390). New York: McGraw-Hill.

Pfaffman, C. (1974). Specificity of the sweet receptors of the squirrel monkey. *Chemical Senses and Flavor, 1,* 61–67.

Pfaffman, C. (1978). The vertebrate phylogeny, neural code, and integrative process of taste. In E. Carterette & M. P. Friedman (Eds.), *Handbook of perception* (Vol. 6A). San Diego: Academic Press.

Pfeiffer, W. M. (1982). Culture-bound syndromes. In I. Al-Issa (Ed.), *Culture and psychopathology.* Baltimore: University Park Press.

Phares, E. J. (1988). *Introduction to personality* (2nd ed.). Glenview, IL: Scott, Foresman.

Phares, E. J. (1991). *Introduction to personality* (3rd ed.). New York: HarperCollins.

Phillips, D. A. (1984). The illusion of incompetence among academically competent children. *Child Development, 55,* 2000–2016.

Phillips, D. A. (1987). Socialization of perceived academic competence among highly competent children. *Child Development, 58,* 1308–1320.

Phillips, D. A., & Zimmerman, M. (1990). The developmental course of perceived competence and incompetence among competent children. In R. J. Sternberg & J. Kolligian, Jr. (Eds.), *Competence considered* (pp. 41–66). New Haven, CT: Yale University Press.

Piaget, J. (1928). *Judgment and reasoning in the child.* London: Routledge & Kegan Paul.

Piaget, J. (1952). *The origins of intelligence in children.* New York: International Universities Press.

Piaget, J. (1954). *The construction of reality in the child.* New York: Basic Books.

Piaget, J. (1955). *The language and thought of the child.* New York: Meridian Books.

Piaget, J. (1965). *The moral judgment of the child* (M. Gabain, Trans.). New York: Harcourt. (Original work published 1932)

Piaget, J. (1969). *The child's conception of physical causality.* Totowa, NJ: Littlefield, Adams.

Piaget, J. (1972). *The psychology of intelligence.* Totowa, NJ: Littlefield, Adams.

Piedmont, R. L., & Chae, J. H. (1997). Cross-cultural generalizability of the Five-Factor Model of personality: Development and validation of the NEO-PI-R for Koreans. *Journal of Cross-Cultural Psychology, 28,* 131–155.

Piliavin, J. A., Dovidio, J. F., Gaertner, S. S., & Clark, R. D., III. (1981). *Emergency intervention.* New York: Academic Press.

Pillow, D. R., Zautra, A. J., Sandler, I. (1996). Major life events and minor stressors: identifying mediational links in the stress process. *Journal of Personality and Social Psychology, 70,* 381–394.

Pinker, S. (1994) *The language instinct.* New York: William Morrow.

Pinker, S. (1998). *How the mind works.* New York: Norton.

Pinto, R. P., & Hollandsworth, J. G., Jr. (1989). Using videotape modeling to prepare children psychologically for surgery: Influence of parents and costs versus benefits of providing preparation services. *Health Psychology, 8,* 79–95.

Pisoni, D. B., Nusbaum, H. C., Luce, P. A., & Slowiaczek, L. M. (1985). Speech perception, word recognition and the structure of the lexicon. *Speech Communication, 4,* 75–95.

Pizzagalli, D., Koenig, T., Regard, M., & Lehmann, D. (1999). Affective attitudes to face images associated with intracerebral EEG source location before face viewing. *Cognitive Brain Research, 7,* 371–377.

Plomin, R. (1986). *Development, genetics, and psychology.* Hillsdale, NJ: Erlbaum.

Plomin, R. (1989). Environment and games: Determinants of behavior. *American Psychologist, 44,* 105–111.

Plomin, R. (1994). *Genetics and experience: The interplay between nature and nurture.* Thousand Oaks, CA: Sage.

Plomin, R. (1995). Molecular genetics and psychology. *Current Directions in Psychological Science, 4,* 114–177.

Plomin, R. (1997). Identifying genes for cognitive abilities and disabilities. In R. J. Sternberg & E. L. Grigorenko (Eds.), *Intelligence, heredity and environment* (pp. 89–104). New York: Cambridge University Press.

Plomin, R. (1999). Behavioral genetics. In M. Bennett (Ed.), *Developmental psychology* (pp. 231–252). Philadelphia: Psychology Press.

Plomin, R., DeFries, J. C., McClearn, G. E., & Rutter, M. (1997). *Behavioral genetics* (3rd ed.). New York: Freeman.

Plomin, R., Fulker, D. W., Corley, R., & DeFries, J. C. (1997). Nature, nurture and cognitive development from 1 to 16 years: A parent-offspring adoption study. *Psychological Science, 8,* 442–447.

Plutchik, R. (1980). *Emotion: A psychoevolutionary analysis.* New York: Harper & Row.

Plutchik, R. (1983). Emotions in early development: A psychoevolutionary approach. In R. Plutchik & H. Kellerman (Eds.), *Emotion: Theory, research, and experience: Vol. 2. Emotions in early development.* New York: Academic Press.

Plutchik, R., & Kellerman, H. (1974). *Emotions Profile Index manual.* Los Angeles: Western Psychological Services.

Plutchik, R., & Kellerman, H. (Eds.). (1983). *Emotion: Theory, research, and experience: Vol. 2. Emotions in early development.* New York: Academic Press.

Poincaré, H. (1913). *The foundations of science.* New York: Science Press.

Poizner, H., Bellugi, U., & Klima, E. S. (1990). Biological foundations of language: Clues from sign language. *Annual Review of Neuroscience, 13,* 282–307.

Poizner, H., Kaplan, E., Bellugi, U., & Padden, C. A. (1984). Visualspatial processing in deaf brain-damaged signers. *Brain & Cognition, 3*(3), 281–306.

Pokorny, A. D. (1968). Myths about suicide. In H. Resnik (Ed.), *Suicidal behaviors.* Boston: Little, Brown.

Polanyi, M. (1976). Tacit knowing. In M. Marx & F. Goodson (Eds.), *Theories in contemporary psychology.* New York: Macmillan.

Policastro, E., & Gardner, H. (1999). From case studies to robust generalizations: An approach to the study of creativity. In R. J. Sternberg (Ed.), *Handbook of creativity* (pp. 213–225). New York: Cambridge University Press.

Polivy, J., & Herman, C. P. (1983). *Breaking the diet habit.* New York: Basic Books.

Polivy, J., & Herman, C. P. (1985). Dieting and binging. *American Psychologist, 40,* 193–201.

Polivy, J., & Herman, C. P. (1993). Etiology of binge eating: Psychological mechanisms. In C. E. Fairburn & G. T. Wilson (Eds.), *Binge eating: Nature, assessment, and treatment.* New York: Guilford.

Polivy, J., Herman, C. P., & McFarlane, T. (1994). Effects of anxiety on eating: Does palatability moderate distress-induced overeating in dieters? *Journal of Abnormal Psychology, 103,* 505–510.

Pomerantz, J. R. (1981). Perceptual organization in information processing. In M. Kubovy & J. R. Pomerantz (Eds.), *Perceptual organization* (pp. 141–180). Hillsdale, NJ: Erlbaum.

Poon, L. W. (1987). *Myths and truisms: Beyond extant analyses of speed of behavior and age.* Address to the Eastern Psychological Association Convention.

Poortinga, Y. H., Kop, P. F. M., & van de Vijver, F. J. R. (1990). Differences between psychological domains in the range of cross-cultural variation. In P. J. D. Drenth, J. A. Sergeant, & R. J. Takens (Eds.), *European perspectives in psychology: Vol. 3. Work and organizational, social and economic, cross-cultural* (pp. 355–376). Chichester, England: Wiley.

Pope, H. G., & Katz, D. L. (1988). Affective and psychotic symptoms associated with anabolic steroid use. *American Journal of Psychiatry, 145*(4), 487–490.

Popper, K. R. (1959). *The logic of scientific discovery.* London: Hutchinson.

Porter, C. A., & Suedfeld, P. (1981). Integrative complexity in the correspondence of literary figures: Effects of personal and societal stress. *Journal of Personality and Social Psychology, 40,* 321–330.

Posner, M. I. (1995). Attention in cognitive neuroscience: An overview. In M. Gazzaniga (Ed.), *The cognitive neurosciences* (pp. 615–624). Cambridge, MA: MIT Press.

Posner, M. I., & Mitchell, R. F. (1967). Chronometric analysis of classification. *Psychological Review, 74,* 392–409.

Pratto, F., Stallworth, L. M., Sidanius, J., & Siers, B. (1997). The gender gap in occupational attainment: A social dominance approach. *Journal of Personality and Social Psychology, 72,* 37–53.

Premack, D. (1959). Toward empirical behavior laws: I. Positive reinforcement. *Psychological Review, 66,* 219–233.

Premack, D. (1971). Language in chimpanzees? *Science, 172,* 808–822.

Prentice, D. A., & Miller, D. T. (1996). Pluralistic ignorance and the perpetuation of social norms by unwitting actors. *Advances in Experimental Social Psychology, 28,* 161–209.

Preston, G. A. N. (1986). Dementia in elderly adults: Prevalence and institutionalization. *Journal of Gerontology, 41,* 261–267.

Pullum, G. K. (1991). *The great Eskimo vocabulary hoax and other irreverent essays on the study of language.* Chicago: University of Chicago Press.

Pylyshyn, Z. W. (1973). What the mind's eye tells the mind's brain: A critique of mental imagery. *Psychological Bulletin, 80,* 1–24.

Quadagno, D. M. (1987). Pheromones and human sexuality. *Medical Aspects of Human Sexuality, 21,* 149–154.

Rabin, M. D., & Cain, W. S. (1986). Determinants of measured olfactory sensitivity. *Perception and Psychophysics, 39,* 361–373.

Rabkin, J. G. (1993). Stress and psychiatric disorders. In L. Goldberger & S. Breznitz (Eds.), *Handbook of stress: Theoretical and clinical aspects* (2nd ed.). New York: Free Press.

Ralph, M. R., Foster, R. G., Davis, F. C., & Menaker, M. (1990). Transplanted suprachiasmatic nucleus determines circadian period. *Science, 247,* 975–978.

Ramey, C. (2000). Intelligence and public policy. In R. J. Sternberg (Ed.), *Handbook of intelligence.* New York: Cambridge University Press.

Rapaport, A. (1960). *Fights, games, and debates.* Ann Arbor, MI: University of Michigan Press.

Rapaport, D., Gill, M. M., & Schafer, R. (1968). *Diagnostic psychological testing.* New York: International Universities Press.

Raps, C. S., Peterson, C., Jonas, M., & Seligman, M. E. P. (1982). Patient behavior in hospitals: Helplessness, reactance, or both? *Journal of Personality and Social Psychology, 42,* 1036–1041.

Ray, O., & Ksir, C. (1990). *Drugs, society, & human behavior.* St. Louis: Times Mirror/Mosby.

Reed, T. E., & Jensen, A. R. (1992). Conduction velocity in a brain nerve pathway of normal adults correlates with intelligence level. *Intelligence, 16*(3–4), 259–272.

Reep, D. C., & Dambrot, F. H. (1988). In the eye of the beholder: Viewer perceptions of TV's male/female working partners. *Communication Research, 15*(1), 51–69.

Reeve, J., & Deci, E. L. (1996). Elements of the competitive situation that affect intrinsic motivation. *Personality and Social Psychology Bulletin, 22,* 24–33.

Rehm, L. P. (1977). A self-control model of depression. *Behavior Therapy, 8,* 787–804.

Reicher, G. M. (1969). Perceptual recognition as a function of meaningfulness of stimulus material. *Journal of Experimental Psychology, 81,* 275–280.

Reinisch, J. M., Ziemba-Davis, M., & Sanders, S. A. (1991). Hormonal contributions to sexually dimorphic behavioral development in humans: Neuroendocrine effects on brain development and cognition [Special issue]. *Psychoneuroendocrinology, 16*(1–3), 213–278.

Reis, H., Collins, A., & Berscheid, E. (in press). Relationships as the context for behavior and development. *Psychological Bulletin.*

Reissland, N. (1988). Neonatal imitation in the first hour of life: Observations in rural Nepal. *Developmental Psychology, 24,* 464–469.

Reitman, J. S. (1971). Mechanisms of forgetting in short-term memory. *Cognitive Psychology, 2,* 185–195.

Reitman, J. S. (1974). Without surreptitious rehearsal, information in short-term memory decays. *Journal of Verbal Learning and Verbal Behavior, 13,* 365–377.

Renfrew, J. W. (1997). *Aggression and its causes: A biopsychosocial approach.* New York: Oxford University Press.

Renzulli, J. S. (1986). The three ring conception of giftedness: A developmental model for creative productivity. In R. J. Sternberg & J. E. Davidson (Eds.), *Conceptions of giftedness* (pp. 53–92). New York: Cambridge University Press.

Reppert, S. M., Weaver, D. R., Rivkees, S. A., & Stopa, E. G. (1988). Putative melatonin receptors in a human biological clock. *Science, 242,* 78–81.

Rescorla, R. A. (1967). Pavlovian conditioning and its proper control procedures. *Psychological Review, 74,* 71–80.

Rescorla, R. A. (1985). Conditioned inhibition and facilitation. In R. R. Miller & N. E. Spear (Eds.), *Information processing in animals: Conditioned inhibition* (pp. 299–326). Hillsdale, NJ; Erlbaum.

Rescorla, R. A. (1988). Pavlovian conditioning: It's not what you think it is. *American Psychologist, 43,* 151–160.

Rescorla, R. A., & Wagner, A. R. (1972). A theory of Pavlovian conditioning: Variations in the effectiveness of reinforcement and non-reinforcement. In A. H. Black & W. F. Prokasy (Eds.), *Classical conditioning: Vol. 2. Current research and theory.* New York: Appleton-Century-Crofts.

Resnick, H. L. P. (Ed.). (1968). *Suicidal behaviors.* Boston: Little, Brown.

Resnick, L. B. (1989). Developing mathematical knowledge. *American Psychologist, 44,* 162–169.

Rest, J. R. (1975). Longitudinal study of the Defining Issues Test of moral judgment: A strategy for analyzing developmental change. *Developmental Psychology, 11*(6), 738–748.

Rest, J. R. (1979). *Development in judging moral issues.* Minneapolis: University of Minnesota Press.

Rest, J. R. (1983). Moral development. In P. H. Mussen (Ed.), *Handbook of child psychology* (4th ed., Vol. 3, pp. 556–629). New York: Wiley.

Rest, J. R., & Thoma, S. J. (1985). Relation of moral judgment development to formal education. *Developmental Psychology, 21*(4), 709–714.

Restak, R. (1984). *The brain.* New York: Bantam.

Restak, R. (1988). *The mind.* New York: Bantam.

Restle, F. (1970). Moon illusion explained on the basis of relative size. *Science, 167,* 1092–1096.

Reynolds, C. R. (1994). Bias in testing. In R. J. Sternberg (Ed.), *Encyclopedia of human intelligence* (Vol. 1, pp. 175–178). New York: Macmillan.

Rholes, W. S., Jones, M., & Wade, C. (1980). A developmental study of learned helplessness. *Developmental Psychology, 16,* 616–624.

Richards, D. D., & Siegler, R. S. (1984). The effects of task requirements on children's life judgments. *Child Development, 55,* 1687–1696.

Ricks, S. S. (1985). Father–infant interaction: A review of empirical research. *Family Relations, 34,* 505–511.

Rieder, R. O., Kaufmann, C. A., & Knowles, J. A. (1994). Genetics. In R. E. Hales, S. C. Yudofsky, & J. A. Talbott (Eds.), *The American Psychiatric Press textbook of psychiatry* (2nd ed.). Washington, DC: American Psychiatric Press.

Riegel, K. F. (1973). Dialectical operations: The final period of cognitive development. *Human Development, 16,* 346–370.

Rieser, J., Yonas, A., & Wilkner, K. (1976). Radial localization of odors by human newborns. *Child Development, 47,* 856–859.

Rigby, C. S., Deci, E. L., Patrick, B. P., & Ryan, R. M. (1992). Beyond the intrinsic-extrinsic dichotomy: Self-determination in motivation and learning. *Motivation and Emotion, 16,* 165–185.

Ring, K. (1980). *Life at death: A scientific investigation of the near-death experience.* New York: Coward-McCann.

Ringelman, M. (1913). Recherches sur les moteurs animés: Travail de l'homme. *Annales de l'Institut National Agronomique, 2s série, tom XII,* 1–40.

Rips, L. J. (1994). Deduction and its cognitive basis. In R. J. Sternberg (Ed.), *Thinking and problem solving* (pp. 150–178). San Diego: Academic Press.

Rips, L. J. (1995). Deduction and cognition. In E. E. Smith & D. N. Osherson (Eds.), *An invitation to cognitive science: Vol. 3. Thinking* (pp. 297–343). Cambridge, MA: MIT Press.

Roberts, A. C., Robbins, T. W., & Weiskrantz, L. (1996). Executive and cognitive functions of the pre-frontal cortex. *Philosophical Transactions of the Royal Society (London), B, 351,* 1346.

Roberts, G., & Owen, J. (1988). The near-death experience. *British Journal of Psychiatry, 153,* 607–617.

Robertson, L. C. (1986). From Gestalt to neo-Gestalt. In T. J. Knapp & L. C. Robertson (Eds.), *Approaches to cognition: Contrasts and controversies* (pp. 159–188). Hillsdale, NJ: Erlbaum.

Robertson, L. S. (1986). Behavioral and environmental interventions for reducing motor vehicle trauma. In L. Breslow, J. E. Fielding, & L. B. Lave (Eds.), *Annual review of public health* (Vol. 7). Palo Alto, CA: Annual Reviews.

Robins, L. N., Helzer, J. E., Weissman, M. M., Orvaschel, H., Gruenberg, E., Burke, J. D., & Regier, D. (1984). Lifetime prevalence of specific psychiatric disorders in three sites. *Archives of General Psychiatry, 41,* 949–958.

Robins, L. N., & Regier, D. A. (1991). *Psychiatric disorders in America: The epidemiological catchment area.* New York: Free Press.

Robinson, D. N. (1986). *An intellectual history of psychology.* Madison, WI: University of Wisconsin Press.

Robinson, D. N. (1995). *An intellectual history of psychology* (3rd ed.). Madison, WI: University of Wisconsin Press.

Robinson, L. A., Berman, J. S., & Neimeyer, R. A. (1990). Psychotherapy for the treatment of depression: A comprehensive review of controlled outcome research. *Psychological Bulletin, 108*(1), 30–49.

Rock, I. (1983). *The logic of perception.* Cambridge, MA: MIT Press.

Rodin, J. (1981). Current status of the external-internal hypothalamus for obesity. *American Psychologist, 36,* 361–372.

Rodin, J., & Plante, T. (1989). The psychological effects of exercise. In R. S. Williams & A. Wellece (Eds.), *Biological effects of physical activity* (pp. 127–137). Champaign, IL: Human Kinetics.

Roediger, H. L., III. (1980). Memory metaphors in cognitive psychology. *Memory and Cognition, 8*(3), 231–246.

Roediger, H. L., III., & McDermott, K. B. (1995). Creating false memories: Remembering words not presented in lists. *Journal of Experimental Psychology: Learning, Memory, and Cognition, 21,* 803–814.

Roger, D., & Morris, J. (1991). The internal structure of the EPQ scales. *Personality and Individual Differences, 12,* 759–764.

Rogers, A., & Gilligan, C. (1988). Translating girls' voices: Two languages of development (pp. 42–43). Harvard University Graduate School of Education, Harvard Project on the Psychology of Women and the Development of Girls.

Rogers, C. R. (1959). A theory of therapy, personality, and interpersonal relationships, as developed in the client-centered framework. In S. Koch (Ed.), *Psychology: A study of a science* (Vol. 3). New York: McGraw-Hill.

Rogers, C. R. (1961a). *On becoming a person: A client's view of psychotherapy.* Boston: Houghton Mifflin.

Rogers, C. R. (1961b). *On becoming a person: A therapist's view of psychotherapy.* Boston: Houghton Mifflin.

Rogers, C. R. (1978). The formative tendency. *Journal of Humanistic Psychology, 18*(1), 23–26.

Rogers, C. R. (1980). *A way of being.* Boston: Houghton Mifflin.

Rogers, S. M., & Turner, C. F. (1991). Male–male sexual contact in the U.S.A.: Findings from five sample surveys, 1970–1990. *Journal of Sex Research, 28*(4), 491–519.

Rogoff, B. (1986). The development of strategic use of context in spatial memory. In M. Perlmutter (Ed.), *Perspectives on intellectual development.* Hillsdale, NJ: Erlbaum.

Rogoff, B. (1990). *Apprenticeship in thinking.* New York: Oxford University Press.

Rogoff, B., Mistry, J., Goncu, A., & Mosler, C. (1993). Guided participation in cultural activity by toddlers and caregivers. *Monographs of the Society for Research in Child Development, 58* (8, Serial No. 236).

Rohner-Jeanrenaud, F., Cusin, I., Sainsbury, A., Zakrzewska, K. E., & Jeanrenaud, B. (1996). The loop system between neuropeptide Y and leptin in normal and obese rodents. *Hormone and Metabolic Research, 28,* 642–648.

Rohner, R. P., & Rohner, E. C. (1981). Assessing interrater influence in holocultural research: A methodological note. *Behavior Science Research, 16*(3–4), 341–351.

Roitblat, H. L., & Fersen, L. von (1992). Comparative cognition: Representations and processes in learning and memory. *Annual Review of Psychology, 43,* 671–710.

Rojahn, K., & Pettigrew, T. F. (1992). Memory for schema-relevant information: A meta-analytic resolution. *British Journal of Social Psychology, 31*(2), 81–109.

Rolls, B. J. (1979). How variety and palatability can stimulate appetite. *Nutrition Bulletin, 5,* 78–86.

Rolls, B. J., Rowe, E. T., & Rolls, E. T. (1982). How sensory properties of food affect human feeding behavior. *Physiology and Behavior, 29,* 409–417.

Rolls, B. J., Wood, R. J., & Rolls, E. T. (1980). Thirst: The initiation, maintenance, and termination of drinking. In J. M. Sprague & A. N. Epstein (Eds.), *Progress in psychobiology and physiological psychology* (Vol. 9, pp. 263–321). New York: Academic Press.

Rosch, E. H. (1973). On the internal structure of perceptual and semantic categories. In T. E. Moore (Ed.), *Cognitive development and the acquisition of language.* New York: Academic Press.

Rosch, E. H., & Mervis, C. B. (1975). Family resemblances: Studies in the internal structure of categories. *Cognitive Psychology, 7,* 573–605.

Rose, S. A, & Feldman, J. F. (1995). Prediction of IQ and specific cognitive abilities at 11 years from infancy measures. *Developmental Psychology, 31,* 685–696.

Rosen, G. M. (1976). *Don't be afraid.* Englewood Cliffs, NJ: Prentice-Hall.

Rosen, G. M. (1987). Self-help treatment books and the commercialization of psychotherapy. *American Psychologist, 42*(1), 46–51.

Rosen, G. M. (1993). Self-help or hype? Comments on psychology's failure to advance self-care. *Professional Psychology: Research and Practice, 24,* 340–345.

Rosenhan, D. L. (1973). On being sane in insane places. *Science, 179,* 250–258.

Rosenthal, R., & Jacobson, L. (1968). *Pygmalion in the classroom: Teacher expectation and pupils' intellectual development.* New York: Holt, Rinehart & Winston.

Rosenthal, R., & Rubin, D. B. (1982). A simple, general purpose display of magnitude of experimental effect. *Journal of Educational Psychology, 74,* 166–169.

Roskies, E., Seraganian, R., Hanley, J. A., Collu, R., Martin, N., & Smilga, C. (1986). The Montreal Type A intervention project: Major findings. *Health Psychology, 5,* 45–69.

Roskies, E., Spevack, M., Surkis, A., Cohen, C., & Gilman, S. (1978). Changing the coronary-prone (Type A) behavior pattern in a nonclinical population. *Journal of Behavioral Medicine, 1,* 201–216.

Ross, B. H., & Makin, V. S. (1999). Prototype versus exemplar models in cognition. In R. J. Sternberg (Ed.), *The nature of cognition* (pp. 205–241). Cambridge, MA: MIT Press.

Ross, B. H., & Spalding, T. L. (1994). Concepts and categories. In R. J. Sternberg (Ed.), *Handbook of perception and cognition: Thinking and problem solving.* (pp. 119–148). San Francisco: Academic Press.

Ross, L. (1977). The intuitive psychologist and his shortcomings: Distortions in the attribution process. In L. Berkowitz (Ed.), *Advances in experimental social psychology* (Vol. 10). New York: Academic Press.

Ross, R. (1975). Salience of reward and intrinsic motivation. *Journal of Personality and Social Psychology, 32,* 245–254.

Ross, R. T. (1983). Relationships between the determinants of performance in serial feature-positive discriminations. *Journal of Experimental Psychology: Animal Behavior Processes, 9,* 349–373.

Ross, R. T., & Holland, P. C. (1981). Conditioning of simultaneous and serial feature-positive discriminations. *Animal Learning & Behavior, 9,* 293–303.

Roth, D., & Rehm, L. P. (1980). Relationships among self-monitoring processes, memory, and depression. *Cognitive Therapy and Research, 4,* 149–157.

Rothbart, M. K., & Bates, J. E. (1998). Temperament. In W. Damon (Gen. Ed.) & N. Eisenberg (Vol. Ed.), *Handbook of child psychology* (Vol. 3): *Social, emotional, and personality development* (pp. 37–86). New York: Wiley.

Rothenberg, A. (1979). *The emerging goddess.* Chicago: University of Chicago Press.

Rotter, J. B. (1966). Generalized expectancies for internal versus external control of reinforcement. *Psychological Monographs, 80*(1, Whole No. 609).

Rotter, J. B. (1990). Internal versus external control of reinforcement: A case history of a variable. *American Psychologist, 45,* 489–493.

Rotter, J. B., & Hochreich, D. J. (1975). *Personality.* Glenview, IL: Scott, Foresman.

Rotton, J., Barry, T., Frey, J., & Soler, E. (1978). Air pollution and interpersonal attraction. *Journal of Applied Social Psychology, 8,* 57–71.

Rotton, J., & Frey, J. (1985). Air pollution, weather, and violent crimes: Concomitant time-series analysis of archival data. *Journal of Personality and Social Psychology, 49*(5), 1207–1220.

Rovee-Collier, C., Borza, M. A., Adler, S. A., & Boller, K. (1993). Infants' eyewitness testimony: Effects of postevent information on a prior memory representation. *Memory & Cognition, 21,* 267–279.

Rovee-Collier, C., Evancio, S., & Earley, L. A. (1995). The time window hypothesis: Spacing effects. *Infant Behavior & Development, 18,* 69–78.

Rozin, P. (1996). Towards a psychology of food and eating: From motivation to module to model to marker, morality, meaning, and metaphor. *Current Directions in Psychological Science, 5,* 18–24.

Rozin, P., & Fallon, A. (1987). A perspective on disgust. *Psychological Review, 94,* 23–41.

Rozin, P., Millman, L., & Nemeroff, C. (1986). Operation of the laws of sympathetic magic in disgust and other domains. *Journal of Personality and Social Psychology, 50,* 703–712.

Rubin, K. H. (1980). Fantasy play: Its role in the development of social skills and social cognition. In K. H. Rubin (Ed.), *Children's play: New directions for child development.* San Francisco: Jossey-Bass.

Rubin, K. H., Bukowski, W., & Parker, J. (1998). Peer interactions, relationships, and groups. In W. Damon (Gen. Ed.) & N. Eisenberg (Vol. Ed.), *Handbook of child psychology* (Vol. 3): *Social, emotional, and personality development* (pp. 619–700). New York: Wiley.

Rubin, K. H., Coplan, R. J., Nelson, L. J., Cheah, C. S. L., & Lagace-Seguin, D. G. (1999). Peer relationships in childhood. In M. H. Bornstein & M. E. Lamb (Eds.), *Developmental psychology: An advanced textbook* (4th ed., pp. 451–501). Mahwah, NJ: Erlbaum.

Rubin, V., & Comitas, L. (1974). *Ganja in Jamaica: A medical anthropological study of chronic marijuana use.* The Hague, Netherlands: Mouton.

Rubin, Z. (1970). Measurement of romantic love. *Journal of Personality and Social Psychology, 16,* 265–273.

Rubin, Z. (1973). *Liking and loving: An invitation to social psychology.* New York: Holt, Rinehart & Winston.

Rubin, Z., Hill, C. T., Peplau, L. A., & Dunkel-Schetter, C. (1980). Self-disclosure in dating couples: Sex roles and the ethic of openness. *Journal of Marriage and the Family, 42,* 305–317.

Ruble, D. N., & Martin, C. L. (1998). Gender development. In W. Damon (Gen. Ed.) & N. Eisenberg (Vol. Ed.), *Handbook of child psychology* (Vol. 3, pp. 933–1016). New York: Wiley.

Ruch, J. C. (1975). Self-hypnosis: The result of heterohypnosis or vice versa? *International Journal of Clinical and Experimental Hypnosis, 23,* 282–304.

Rudy, T. E., Kerns, R. D., & Turk, D. C. (1988). Chronic pain and depression: Toward a cognitive-behavioral mediation model. *Pain, 35,* 129–140.

Rule, S. R., & Ferguson, T. J. (1986). The effects of media violence on attitudes, emotions, and cognitions. *Journal of Social Issues, 42*(3), 29–50.

Rumelhart, D. E., & McClelland, J. L. (1981). Interactive processing through spreading activation. In A. M. Lesgold & C. A. Perfetti (Eds.), *Interactive processes in reading* (pp. 37–60). Hillsdale, NJ: Erlbaum.

Rumelhart, D. E., & McClelland, J. L. (1982). An interactive activation model of context effects in letter perception: Part 2. The contextual enhancement effect and some tests and extensions of the model. *Psychological Review, 9,* 60–94.

Rumelhart, D. E., McClelland, J. L., & the PDP Research Group. (1986). *Parallel distributed processing. Explorations in the microstructure of cognition: Vol. 1. Foundations.* Cambridge, MA: MIT Press.

Runeson, S., & Frykholm, G. (1986). Kinematic specification of gender and gender expression. In V. McCabe and G. J. Balzano (Eds.), *Event cognition: An ecological perspective*. Hillsdale, NJ: Erlbaum.

Russell, J. A. (1991). Culture and categorization of emotions. *Psychological Bulletin, 110*(3), 426–450.

Russell, J. A. (1994). Is there universal recognition of emotion from facial expression? A review of the cross-cultural studies. *Psychological Bulletin, 115*, 102–141.

Russell, M. J. (1976). Human olfactory communication. *Nature, 260*, 520–522.

Russell, W. R., & Nathan, P. W. (1946). Traumatic amnesia. *Brain, 69*, 280–300.

Rymer, R. (1993). *Genie: An abused child's flight from silence*. New York: HarperCollins.

Sadker, M., & Sadker, D. (1984). *Year three: Final report, promoting effectiveness in classroom instruction*. Washington, DC: National Institute of Education.

Safer, D. J. (1991). Diet, behavior modification, and exercise: A review of obesity treatments from a long-term perspective. *Southern Medical Journal, 84*, 1470–1474.

Sagan, E. (1988). *Freud, women, and morality: The psychology of good and evil*. New York: Basic Books.

Salovey, P., & Mayer, J. D. (1990). Emotional intelligence. *Imagination, Cognition, and Personality, 9*, 185–211.

Salthouse, T. A. (1992). The information-processing perspective on cognitive aging. In R. J. Sternberg & C. A. Berg (Eds.), *Intellectual Development* (pp. 261–277). New York: Cambridge University Press.

Salthouse, T. A. (1996). The processing-speed theory of adult age differences in cognition. *Psychological Review, 103*, 403–428.

Salthouse, T. A., & Somberg, B. L. (1982). Skilled performance: Effects of adult age and experience on elementary processes. *Journal of Experimental Psychology: General, 111*(2), 176–207.

Sanders, S. H. (1985). Chronic pain: Conceptualization and epidemiology. *Annals of Behavioral Medicine, 7*(3), 3–5.

Sapir, E. (1964). *Culture, language and personality*. Berkeley: University of California Press. (Original work published 1941)

Sarason, S. B., & Doris, J. (1979). *Educational handicap, public policy, and social history*. New York: The Free Press.

Sartorius, N., de Girolano, G., Andrews, G., German, G. A., & Eisenberg, L. (Eds.). (1993a). *Treatment of mental disorders: A review of effectiveness*. Geneva, Switzerland, and Washington, DC: World Health Organization and American Psychiatric Press.

Sartorius, N., Kaelber, C., Cooper, J. E., Roper, M. T., et al. (1993b). Progress toward achieving a common language in psychiatry: Results from the field trial of the clinical guidelines accompanying the WHO classification of mental and behavioral disorders in ICD-10. *Archives of General Psychiatry, 50*(2), 115–124.

Sartorius, N., Shapiro, R., & Jablonsky, A. (1974). The international pilot study of schizophrenia. *Schizophrenia Bulletin, 2*, 21–35.

Savage-Rumbaugh, S., McDonald, K., Sevcik, R. A., Hopkins, W. D., & Rubert, E. (1986). Spontaneous symbol acquisition and communicative use by pygmy chimpanzees (Pan paniscus). *Journal of Experimental Psychology: General, 112*, 211–235.

Savage-Rumbaugh, S., Murphy, J., Sevcik, R., Brakke, K., Wiliams, S., & Rumbaugh, D. M. (1993). Language comprehension in ape and child. *Monographs of the Society for Research in Child Development, 58* (3–4, Serial No. 233).

Saxe, L., Dougherty, D., & Cross, T. (1985). The validity of polygraph testing: Scientific analysis and public controversy. *American Psychologist, 40*, 355–366.

Scarr, H. A. (1994). United States population: A typical American as seen through the eyes of the Census Bureau. In *The World Almanac and Book of Facts, 1994*. Mahwah, NJ: Funk & Wagnalls.

Scarr, S. (1997). Behavior-genetic and socialization theories of intelligence: truce and reconciliation. In R. J. Sternberg & E. L. Grigorenko (Eds.), *Intelligence, heredity, and environment* (pp. 3–41). New York: Cambridge University Press.

Scarr, S., Phillips, D., & McCartney, K. (1990). Facts, fantasies, and the future of child care in the United States. *Psychological Science, 1*, 26–35.

Scarr, S., & Weinberg, R. A. (1976). I.Q. test performance of black children adopted by white families. *American Psychologist, 31*, 726–739.

Scarr, S., & Weinberg, R. A., & Waldman, I. D. (1993). IQ correlations in transracial adoptive families. *Intelligence, 17*, 541–555.

Schacter, D. L. (1996). *Searching for memory: The brain, the mind, and the past*. New York: Basic Books.

Schacter, D. L., & Graf, P. (1986a). Effects of elaborative processing on implicit and explicit memory for new associations. *Journal of Experimental Psychology: Learning, Memory, & Cognition, 12*(3), 432–444.

Schacter, D. L., & Graf, P. (1986b). Preserved learning in amnesic patients: Perspectives from research on direct priming. *Journal of Clinical & Experimental Neuropsychology, 8*(6), 727–743.

Schacter, D. L., Verfaellie, M., & Pradere, D. (1996). The neuropsychology of memory illusions: False recall and recognition in amnesic patients. *Journal of Memory and Language, 35*, 319–334.

Schachter, S. (1951). Deviation, rejection, and communication. *Journal of Abnormal Social Psychology, 46*, 190–207.

Schachter, S. (1968). Obesity and eating. *Science, 161*, 751–756.

Schachter, S. (1971a). *Emotion, obesity, and crime*. New York: Academic Press.

Schachter, S. (1971b). Some extraordinary facts about obese humans and rats. *American Psychologist, 26*, 129–144.

Schachter, S., & Gross, L. (1968). Manipulated time and eating behavior. *Journal of Personality and Social Psychology, 10*, 98–106.

Schachter, S., & Rodin, J. (1974). *Obese humans and rats*. Hillsdale, NJ: Erlbaum.

Schachter, S., & Singer, J. (1962). Cognitive, social, and physiological determinants of emotional state. *Psychological Review, 69*, 379–399.

Schafer, R. (1982). The relevance of the "here and now" transference interpretation to the reconstruction of early development. *International Journal of Psycho-Analysis, 63*(1), 77–82.

Schaffer, H. R. (1977). *Mothering*. Cambridge, MA: Harvard University Press.

Schaie, K. W. (1974). Translations in gerontology—from lab to life. *American Psychologist, 29*, 802–807.

Schaie, K. W. (1989). Perceptual speed in adulthood: Cross-sectional and longitudinal studies. *Psychology and Aging, 4*, 443–453.

Schaie, K. W. (1995). *Intellectual development in adulthood*. New York: Cambridge University Press.

Schaie, K. W., & Willis, S. L. (1986). Can decline in intellectual functioning in the elderly be reversed? *Developmental Psychology, 22*, 223–232.

Schank, R. C. (1972). Conceptual dependency: A theory of natural language understanding. *Cognitive Psychology, 3*, 552–631.

Schank, R. C. (1988). Creativity as a mechanical process. In R. J. Sternberg (Ed.), *The nature of creativity* (pp. 220–238). New York: Cambridge University Press.

Schank, R. C., & Abelson, R. P. (1977). *Scripts, plans, goals, and understanding*. Hillsdale. NJ: Erlbaum.

Scharfe, E., & Bartholomew, K. (1994). Reliability and stability of adult attachment patterns. *Personal Relationships, 1*, 23–43.

Scheff, T. J. (1966). *Being mentally ill: A sociological theory*. Chicago: Aldine.

Schiffer, F., Zaidel, E., Bogen, J., & Chasan-Taber, S. (1998). Different psychological status in the two hemispheres of two split-brain patients. *Neuropsychiatry, Neuropsychology, & Behavioral Neurology, 11*(3), 151–156.

Schildkraut, J. J. (1965). The catecholamine hypothesis of affective disorders: A review of supporting evidence. *American Journal of Psychiatry, 122,* 509–522.

Schlaefli, A., Rest, J. R., & Thoma, S. J. (1985). Does moral education improve moral judgment? A meta-analysis of intervention studies using the Defining Issues Test. *Review of Educational Research, 55*(3), 319–352.

Schliemann, A. D., & Magalhües, V. P. (1990). Proportional reasoning: From shops, to kitchens, laboratories, and, hopefully, schools. Proceedings of the Fourteenth International Conference for the Psychology of Mathematics Education, Oaxtepec, Mexico.

Schmidt, F. L., Ones, D. S., & Hunter, J. E. (1992). Personnel selection. *Annual Review of psychology, 43,* 627–670.

Schmitt, B. H., Gilovich, T., Goore, N., & Joseph, L. (1986). Mere exposure and social facilitation: One more time. *Journal of Experimental and Social Psychology, 22,* 242–248.

Schnapf, J. L., & Baylor, D. A. (1987). How photoreceptor cells respond to light. *Scientific American, 256,* 40–47.

Schonfield, D., & Robertson, D. A. (1966). Memory storage and aging. *Canadian Journal of Psychology, 20,* 228–236.

Schroder, H. M., Driver, M. J., & Streufert, S. (1967). *Human information processing.* New York: Holt, Rinehart & Winston.

Schroeder, D. H., & Costa, P. T., Jr. (1984). Influence of life event stress on physical illness: Substantive effects or methodological flaws? *Journal of Personality and Social Psychology, 46,* 853–863.

Schroeder-Helmert, D. (1985). Clinical evaluation of DSIP. In A. Wauquier, J. M. Gaillard, J. M. Monti, & M. Radulovacki (Eds.), *Sleep: Neurotransmitters and neuromodulators* (pp. 279–291). New York: Raven Press.

Schroth, M. L. (1991). Dyadic adjustment and sensation seeking compatibility. *Personality and Individual Differences, 12,* 467–471.

Schulman, H. G. (1970). Encoding and retention of semantic and phonemic information in short-term memory. *Journal of Verbal Learning and Verbal Behavior, 9,* 499–508.

Schultz, D. (1981). *A history of modern psychology* (3rd ed.). New York: Academic Press.

Schultz, T. R., Wright, K., & Schleifer, M. (1986). Assignment of moral responsibility and punishment. *Child Development, 57,* 177–184.

Schulz, S. C. (1995). Schizophrenia: Somatic treatment. In H. I. Kaplan & B. J. Sadock (Eds.), *Comprehensive textbook of psychiatry* (6th ed., pp. 987–998). Baltimore: Williams & Wilkins.

Schustack, M. W., & Sternberg, R. J. (1981). Evaluation of evidence in causal inference. *Journal of Experimental Psychology: General, 110,* 101–120.

Schwartz, B. (1989). *Psychology of learning and behavior* (3rd ed.). New York: Norton.

Schwartz, C. S., Scarr, S., and McCartney, K. (1983). Center, sitter, and home care before age two: A report on the first Bermuda infant care study. Paper presented at the meeting of the American Psychological Association, Los Angeles, CA.

Schwartz, G., & Weinberger, D. (1980). Patterns of emotional responses to affective situations: Relations among happiness, sadness, anger, fear, depression, and anxiety. *Motivation and Emotion, 4,* 175–191.

Schwartz, G. E. (1982). Testing the biopsychosocial model: The ultimate challenge facing behavioral medicine. *Journal of Consulting and Clinical Psychology, 50,* 1040–1053.

Schwartz, W. (1990). Experimental and theoretical results for some models of random-dot-pattern discrimination. *Psychological Research, 52*(4), 299–305.

Schweizer, E., Rickels, K., Case, G., & Greenblatt, D. J. (1990). Long-term therapeutic use of benzodiazepines: II. Effects of gradual taper. *Archives of General Psychiatry, 47*(10), 908–915.

Scott, A. I. F. (1989). Which depressed patients will respond to electroconvulsive therapy? The search for biological predictors of recovery. *British Journal of Psychiatry, 154,* 8–17.

Scovern, A. W., & Kilmann, P. R. (1980). Status of electroconvulsive therapy: Review of the outcome literature. *Psychological Bulletin, 87,* 260–303.

Scoville, W. B., & Milner, B. (1957). Loss of recent memory after bilateral hippocampal lesions. *Journal of Neurology, Neurosurgery, and Psychiatry, 20,* 11–19.

Searle, J. R. (1975a). Indirect speech acts. In P. Cole & J. L. Morgan (Eds.), *Syntax and semantics: Speech acts* (Vol. 3, pp. 59–82). New York: Seminar Press.

Searle, J. R. (1975b). A taxonomy of elocutionary acts. In K. Gunderson (Ed.), *Minnesota studies in the philosophy of language* (pp. 344–369). Minneapolis: University of Minnesota Press.

Sears, D. O. (1983). The person-positivity bias. *Journal of Personality and Social Psychology, 44,* 233–250.

Segal, B. (1988). *Drugs and behavior.* New York: Gardner Press.

Segall, M. H., Campbell, D. T., & Herskovits, M. J. (1966). *The influence of culture on visual perception.* New York: Bobbs-Merrill.

Seiden, R. H. (1974). Suicide: Preventable death. *Public Affairs Report, 15*(4), 1–5.

Seidenberg, M. S. (1993). Connectionist models and cognitive theory. *Psychological Science, 4,* 228–235.

Seidman, L. J. (1983). Schizophrenia and brain dysfunction: An integration of recent neurodiagnostic findings. *Psychological Bulletin, 94,* 195–238.

Seidman, L. J. (1990). The neuropsychology of schizophrenia: A neurodevelopmental and case study approach. *Journal of Neuropsychiatry and Clinical Neuroscience, 2,* 301–312.

Seifert, C. M., Meyer, D. E., Davidson, N., Patalano, A. L., & Yaniv, I. (1995). Demystification of cognitive insight: Opportunistic assimilation and the prepared-mind perspective. In R. J. Sternberg & J. E. Davidson (Eds.), *The nature of insight* (pp. 65–124). Cambridge, MA: MIT Press.

Sekuler, R., & Blake, R. (1985). *Perception.* New York: Knopf.

Selfridge, O. G. (1959). Pandemonium: A paradigm for learning. In D. V. Blake & A. M. Uttley (Eds.), *Proceedings of the symposium on the mechanization of thought processes* (pp. 511–529). London: Her Majesty's Stationery Office.

Selfridge, O. G., & Neisser, U. (1960). Pattern recognition by machine. *Scientific American, 203,* 60–68.

Seligman, M. E. P. (1971). Phobias and preparedness. *Behavior Therapy, 193,* 323–325.

Seligman, M. E. P. (1974). Depression and learned helplessness. In R. J. Friedman & M. M. Katz (Eds.), *The psychology of depression: Contemporary theory and research.* Washington, DC: Winston-Wiley.

Seligman, M. E. P. (1975). *Helplessness.* San Francisco: Freeman.

Seligman, M. E. P. (1991). *Learned optimism.* New York: Norton.

Seligman, M. E. P. (1995). The effectiveness of psychotherapy: The consumer reports study. *American Psychologist, 50*(12), 965–983.

Seligman, M. E. P., & Maier, S. F. (1967). Failure to escape traumatic shock. *Journal of Experimental Psychology, 74,* 1–9.

Selye, H. (1974). *Stress without distress.* Philadelphia: Lippincott.

Selye, H. (1976). *The stress of life* (Rev. ed.). New York: McGraw-Hill.

Sepple, C. P., & Read, N. W. (1989). Gastrointestinal correlates of the development of hunger in man. *Appetite, 13,* 183–191.

Sera, M. D. (1992). To be or not to be: Use and acquisition of the Spanish copulas. *Journal of Memory and Language, 31,* 408–427.

Seraganian, P. (Ed.). (1993). *Exercise psychology: The influence of physical exercise on psychological processes.* New York: Wiley.

Serdahely, W. J. (1990). Pediatric near-death experiences. *Journal of Near-Death Studies, 9,* 33–39.

Serpell, R. (1993). *The significance of schooling: Life journeys in an African society.* Cambridge, England: University of Cambridge Press.

Serpell, R. (1994). The cultural construction of intelligence. In W. J. Lonner & R. S. Malpass (Eds.), *Psychology and culture.* Boston: Allyn & Bacon.

Serpell, R. (2000). Intelligence and culture. In R. J. Sternberg (Ed.), *Handbook of intelligence*. New York: Cambridge University Press.

Sexton, M. M. (1979). Behavioral epidemiology. In O. F. Pomerleau & J. P. Brady (Eds.), *Behavioral medicine: Theory and practice* (pp. 3–22). Baltimore: Williams & Wilkins.

Seymour, R. B., & Smith, D. E. (1987). *Guide to psychoactive drugs: An up-to-the-minute reference to mind-altering substances.* New York: Harrington Park Press.

Shadish, W. R., Navarro, A. M., Crits-Cristoph, P., Jorm, A. F., Nietzel, M. T., Robinson, L., Svartberg, M., Matt, G. E., Siegle, G., Hazelrigg, M. D. Lyons, L. C., Prout, H. T., Smith, M. L., & Weiss, B. (1997). Evidence that therapy works in clinically representative conditions. *Journal of Consulting and Clinical Psychology, 65*, 355–365.

Shafir, E., & Tversky, A. (1995). Decision making. In E. E. Smith & D. N. Osherson (Eds.), *An invitation to cognitive science: Vol. 3. Thinking* (pp. 77–100). Cambridge, MA: MIT Press.

Shanab, M. E., & Yahya, K. A. (1977). A behavioral study of obedience in children. *Journal of Personality and Social Psychology, 35,* 530–536.

Shanab, M. E., & Yahya, K. A. (1978). A cross-cultural study of obedience. *Bulletin of the Psychonomic Society, 11,* 267–269.

Shapiro, D. H., & Giber, D. (1978). Meditation and psychotherapeutic effects: Self-regulation strategy and altered states of consciousness. *Archives of General Psychiatry, 35,* 294–302.

Shapiro, D., Lane, J. D., & Henry, J. P. (1986). Caffeine, cardiovascular reactivity, and cardiovascular disease. In K. A. Matthews, S. M. Weiss, T. Detre, T. M. Dembroski, B. Falkner, S. B. Manuck, & R. B. Williams (Eds.), *Handbook of stress, reactivity, and cardiovascular disease.* New York: Wiley.

Shapiro, P., & Penrod, S. (1986). Meta-analysis of facial identification studies. *Psychological Bulletin, 100,* 139–156.

Shapley, R., & Lennie, P. (1985). Spatial frequency analysis in the visual system. *Annual Review of Neuroscience, 8,* 547–583.

Shaver, P. R., Collins, N., & Clark, C. (1996). Attachment styles and internal working models of self and relationship partners. In G. J. O. Fletcher & J. Fitness (Eds.). *Knowledge structures in close relationships: A social psychological approach.* Mahwah, NJ: Erlbaum.

Shaver, P., Schwartz, J., Krison, D., & O'Connor, C. (1987). Emotion knowledge: Further exploration of a prototype approach. *Journal of Personality and Social Psychology, 52,* 1061–1086.

Shaver, P., Wu, S., & Schwartz, J. (1992). Cross-cultural similarities and differences in emotion and its representation: A prototype approach. In M. S. Clark (Ed.), *Review of personality and social psychology* (Vol. 13). Newbury Park, CA: Sage.

Shaywitz, B. A., Pugh, K. R., Constable, R. T., Skudlarski, P., Fulbright, R. K., Bronen, R. A., Fletcher, J. M., Shankweiler, P., Katz, L., & Gore, J. L. (1995). Sex differences in the functional organization of the brain for language. *Nature, 373,* 607–609.

Shedler, J., Mayman, M., & Manis, M. (1993). The illusion of mental health. *American Psychologist, 48,* 1117–1131.

Shekelle, R. B., Hulley, S. B., Neaton, J. D., Billings, J. H., Borhani, N. O., Gerace, T. A., Jacobs, D. R., Lasser, N. L., Mittelmark, M. B., & Stamler, J. (1985). The MRFIT behavior pattern study: II. Type A behavior and incidence of coronary heart disease. *American Journal of Epidemiology, 122,* 559–570.

Sheppard, J. A. (1993). Productivity loss in performance groups: A motivation analysis. *Psychological Bulletin, 114,* 67–81.

Sheppard, J. A., & Arkin, R. M. (1989). Self-handicapping: The moderating role of public self-consciousness and task importance. *Personality and Social Psychology Bulletin, 15,* 252–265.

Sherif, M., Harvey, L. J., White, B. J., Hood, W. R., & Sherif, C. W. (1988). *The Robber's Cave experiment: Intergroup conflict and cooperation.* Middletown, CT: Wesleyan University Press. (Original work published 1961)

Sherman, S. J., Judd, C. M., & Park, B. (1989). Social cognition. *Annual Review of Psychology, 40,* 281–326.

Shibazaki, M. (1983). Development of hemispheric function in hiragana, kanji, and figure processing for normal children and mentally retarded children. *Japanese Journal of Special Education, 21*(3), 1–9.

Shields, J. (1962). Monozygotic twins brought up apart and brought up together. London: Oxford University Press.

Shiffrin, R. M. (1973). Information persistence in short-term memory. *Journal of Experimental Psychology, 100,* 39–49.

Shiffrin, R. M. (1996). Laboratory experimentation on the genesis of expertise. In K. A. Ericsson (Ed.), *The road to excellence* (pp. 337–347). Mahwah, NJ: Erlbaum.

Shimada, M., & Otsuka, A. (1981). Functional hemispheric differences in kanji processing in Japanese. *Japanese Psychological Review, 24*(4), 472–489.

Shneidman, E. S. (1973). Suicide. In *Encyclopedia Britannica.* Chicago: Encyclopedia Britanica.

Shontz, F. C. (1975). *The psychological aspects of physical illness and disability.* New York: Macmillan.

Shook, M. D., & Shook, R. L. (1991). *The book of odds.* New York: Penguin.

Shuit, D. P. (1994, May 22). Verdict heats up memory debate. *Los Angeles Times,* p. A3.

Shulman, H. G. (1970). Encoding and retention of semantic and phonemic information in short-term memory. *Journal of Verbal Learning and Verbal Behavior, 9,* 499–508.

Shumaker, S. A., & Hill, D. R. (1991). Gender differences in social support and physical health. *Health Psychology, 10,* 102–111.

Sibitani, A. (1980). The Japanese brain. *Science, 80,* 22–26.

Siegel, S. (1977). A Pavlovian conditioning analysis of morphine tolerance (and opiate dependence). In N. A. Krasnegor (Ed.), *Behavioral tolerance: Research and treatment implications.* National Institute for Drug Abuse, Monograph No. 18. Government Printing Office Stock N1. 017-024-00699-8. Washington, DC: Government Printing Office.

Siegel, S. (1989). Pharmacological conditioning and drug effects. In A. J. Goudie & M. W. Emmett-Oglesby (Eds.), *Psychoactive drugs: Tolerance and sensitization* (pp. 115–180). Clifton, NJ: Humana Press.

Siegler, R. S. (1976). Three aspects of cognitive development. *Cognitive Psychology, 8,* 481–520.

Siegler, R. S. (1978). The origins of scientific reasoning. In R. S. Siegler (Ed.), *Children's thinking: What develops?* (pp. 109–149). Hillsdale, NJ: Erlbaum.

Siegler, R. S. (1984). Mechanisms of cognitive growth: Variation and selection. In R. J. Sternberg (Ed.), *Mechanisms of cognitive development* (pp. 142–162). New York: Freeman.

Siegler, R. S. (1986). *Children's thinking.* Englewood Cliffs, NJ: Prentice-Hall.

Siegler, R. S. (1996). *Emerging minds: The process of change in children's thinking.* New York: Oxford University Press.

Siegler, R. S. (1998). *Children's thinking* (3rd ed.). Upper Saddle River, NJ: Prentice-Hall.

Siegman, A. W., & Snow, S. C. (1997). The outward expression of anger, the inward experience of anger, and CVR: The role of vocal expression. *Journal of Behavioral Medicine, 20,* 29–46.

Signorielli, N., McLeod, D., & Healy, E. (1994). Gender stereotypes in MTV commercials: The beat goes on. *Journal of Broadcasting and Electronic Media, 38,* 91–101.

Silver, R. L., & Wortman, C. B. (1980). Coping with undesirable life events. In J. Garber & M. E. P. Seligman (Eds.), *Human helplessness: Theory and applications.* New York: Academic Press.

Silverman, I., & Eals, M. (1992). Sex differences in spatial abilities: Evolutionary theory and data. In J. Barkow, L. Cosmides, & J. Tooby (Eds.), *The adapted mind.* (pp. 533–549). New York: Oxford University Press.

Silverstein, B., Peterson, B., & Perdue, L. (1986). Some correlates of the thin standard of bodily attractiveness in women. *International Journal of Eating Disorders, 5,* 145–155.

Simon, B., & Hamilton, D. L. (1994). Self-stereotyping and social context: The effects of relative in-group size and in-group status. *Journal of Personality & Social Psychology, 66*(4), 699–711.

Simon, H. A. (1957). Administrative behavior (2nd ed.). Totowa, NJ: Littlefield, Adams.

Simon, H. A. (1976). Identifying basic abilities underlying intelligent performance of complex tasks. In L. B. Resnick (Ed.), *The nature of intelligence* (pp. 65–98). Hillsdale, NJ: Erlbaum.

Simon, H. A., & Reed, S. K. (1976). Modeling strategy shifts in a problem-solving task. *Cognitive Psychology, 8,* 86–97.

Simon, W. H., & Gagnon, J. H. (1986). Sexual scripts: Permanence and change. *Archives of Sexual Behavior, 15*(2), 97–120.

Simonton, D. K. (1975). Age and literary creativity: A cross-cultural and transhistorical survey. *Journal of Cross-Cultural Psychology, 6*(3), 259–277.

Simonton, D. K. (1988). Creativity, leadership, and chance. In R. J. Sternberg (Ed.), *The nature of creativity* (pp. 386–426). New York: Cambridge University Press.

Simonton, D. K. (1995). Foresight in insight: A Darwinian answer. In R. J. Sternberg & J. E. Davidson (Eds.), *The nature of insight* (pp. 495–534). Cambridge, MA: MIT Press.

Simonton, D. K. (1999). Creativity from a historiometric perspective. In R. J. Sternberg (Ed.), *Handbook of creativity* (pp. 116–133). New York: Cambridge University Press.

Simpson, J. A., Rholes. W. S., & Nelligan. J. S. (1992). Support-seeking and support-giving within couple members in an anxiety-provoking situation: The role of attachment styles. *Journal of Personality and Social Psychology, 62,* 434–446.

Sincoff, J. B., & Sternberg, R. J. (1988). The development of verbal fluency abilities and strategies in elementary-school-aged children. *Developmental Psychology, 24,* 646–653.

Singer, J. L. (1984). *The human personality.* San Diego, CA: Harcourt Brace Jovanovich.

Sistrunk, F., & McDavid, J. W. (1971). Sex variables in conforming behavior. *Journal of Personality and Social Psychology, 17,* 200–207.

Sizemore, C. C., & Pittillo, E. S. (1977). *I'm Eve.* Garden City, NY: Doubleday.

Skinner, B. F. (1948). *Walden II.* New York: Macmillan.

Skinner, B. F. (1953). *Science and human behavior.* New York: Macmillan.

Skinner, B. F. (1974). *About behaviorism.* New York: Knopf.

Slobin, D. I. (1971). Cognitive prerequisites for the acquisition of grammar. In C. A. Ferguson & D. I. Slobin (Eds.), *Studies of child language development.* New York: Holt, Rinehart & Winston.

Slobin, D. I. (Ed.). (1985). *The cross-linguistic study of language acquisition.* Hillsdale, NJ: Erlbaum.

Sloboda, J. A. (1985). *The musical mind: The cognitive psychology of music.* Oxford, England: Oxford University Press.

Sloman, S. A. (1996). The empirical case for two systems of reasoning. *Psychological Bulletin, 199,* 3–22.

Sloman, S. A. (1999). Rational versus arational models of thought. In R. J. Sternberg (Ed.), *The nature of cognition* (pp. 557–585). Cambridge, MA: MIT Press.

Smetana, J. G. (1995). Morality in context: Abstractions, ambiguities, and applications. In R. Vasta (Ed.), *Annals of child development* (Vol. 10, pp. 83–130). London: Jessica Kingsley.

Smetana, J. G. (1997). Parenting and the development of social knowledge reconceptualized: A social domain analysis. N J. E. Grusec & L. Kuczynski (Eds.), *Parenting and children's internalization of values* (pp. 162–192). New York: Wiley.

Smetana, J. G., & Asquith, P. (1994). Adolescents' and parents' conceptions of parental authority and adolescent autonomy. *Child Development, 65,*1147–1162.

Smith, D. (1982). Trends in counseling and psychotherapy. *American Psychologist, 37*(7), 802–809.

Smith, D. E., & Gay, G. R. (1972). *It's so good, don't even try it once: Heroin in perspective.* Englewood Cliffs, NJ: Prentice-Hall.

Smith, D. E., & Muenchen, R. A. (1995). Gender and age variations in the self-image of Jamaican adolescents. *Adolescence, 30*(119), 643–654.

Smith, E. E., & Medin, D. L. (1981). *Categories and concepts.* Cambridge, MA: Harvard University Press.

Smith, E. E., Patalano, A. L., & Jonides, J. (1998). Alternative strategies of categorization. *Cognition, 65,* 167–196.

Smith, E. E., Shoben, E. J., & Ripps, L. J. (1974). Structure and process in semantic memory: A featural model for semantic decisions. *Psychological Review, 81,* 214–241.

Smith, J. C. (1993). *Understanding stress and coping.* New York: Macmillan.

Smith, M. E., McEvoy, L. K., & Gevins, A. (1999). Neurophysiological indices of strategy development and skill acquisition. *Cognitive Brain Research, 7,* 389–404.

Smith, M. L., & Glass, G. V. (1977). Meta-analysis of psychotherapy outcome studies. *American Psychologist (November),* 752–760.

Smith, P. B., & Bond, M. H. (1994). *Social psychology across cultures: Analysis and perspectives.* Boston: Allyn & Bacon.

Smith, T. W. (1992). Hostility and health: Current status of a psychosomatic hypothesis. *Health Psychology, 11,* 139–150.

Smith, T. W., & Anderson, N. B. (1986). Models of personality and disease: An interactional approach to Type A behavior and cardiovascular risk. *Journal of Personality and Social Psychology, 50*(6), 1166–1173.

Snarey, J. R. (1985). Cross-cultural universality of social-moral development: A critical review of Kohlbergian research. *Psychological Bulletin, 97,* 202–232.

Snarey, J. R., Reimer, J., & Kohlberg, L. (1985a). Development of social-moral reasoning among kibbutz adolescents: A longitudinal cross-cultural study. *Developmental Psychology, 21,* 3–17.

Snarey, J. R., Reimer, J., & Kohlberg, L. (1985b). The kibbutz as a model for moral education: A longitudinal cross-cultural study. *Journal of Applied Developmental Psychology, 6,* 151–172.

Sneed, C. D., McCrae, R. R., & Funder, D. C. (1998). Lay conceptions of the Five-Factor Model and its indicators. *Personality and Social Psychology Bulletin, 24,* 115–126.

Snow, C. E. (1977). The development of conversation between mothers and babies. *Journal of Child Language, 4,* 1–22.

Snow, R. E. (1980). Aptitude processes. In R. E. Snow, P.-A. Federico, & W. E. Montague (Eds.), *Aptitude, learning, and instruction: Cognitive process analyses.* (Vol. 1). Hillsdale, NJ: Erlbaum.

Snow, R. E. (1994). Aptitude-treatment interaction. In R. J. Sternberg (Ed.), *Encyclopedia of human intelligence* (Vol. 1, pp. 117–121). New York: Macmillan.

Snow, R. E. (1995). Pygmalion and intelligence? *Current Directions in Psychological Science, 4,* 169–171.

Snyder, M. (1979). Self-monitoring processes. In L. Berkowitz (Ed.), *Advances in experimental social psychology* (Vol. 12). New York: Academic Press.

Snyder, M. (1983). The influence of individuals on situations: Implications for understanding the links between personality and social behavior. *Journal of Personality, 51,* 497–516.

Snyder, M., & Swann, W. B., Jr. (1978). Behavioral confirmation in social interaction: From social perception to social reality. *Journal of Personality and Social Psychology, 36,* 1202–1212.

Solomon, G. F., & Temoshok, L. (1987). A psychoneuroimmunologic perspective on AIDS research: Questions, preliminary findings, and suggestions. *Journal of Applied Social Psychology, 17,* 286–308.

Solomon, R. L. (1980). The opponent-process theory of motivation: The costs of pleasure and the benefits of pain. *American Psychologist, 35,* 681–712.

Solomon, R. L., & Corbit, J. D. (1974). An opponent-process theory of motivation: I. Temporal dynamics of affect. *Psychological Review, 81,* 119–145.

Sommer, R. (1969). *Personal space.* Englewood Cliffs, NJ: Prentice-Hall.

Spangler, W. (1992). Validity of questionnaire and TAT measures of need for achievement: Two meta-analyses. *Psychological Bulletin, 112,* 140–154.

Spanos, N. P. (1986). Hypnotic behavior: A social-psychological interpretation of amnesia, analgesia, and "trance logic." *Behavioral and Brain Sciences, 9,* 449–467.

Spanos, N. P. (1994). Multiple identity enactments and multiple personality disorder: A socio-cognitive perspective. *Psychological Bulletin, 116,* 143–165.

Spanos, N. P., Burgess, C. A., Roncon, V., Wallace-Capretta, S., & Cross, P. (1993). Surreptitiously observed hypnotic responding in simulators and in skill-trained and untrained high hypnotizables. *Journal of Personality and Social Psychology, 65,* 391–398.

Spanos, N. P., & Coe, W. C. (1992). A social-psychological approach to hypnosis. In E. Fromm & M. R. Nash (Eds.), *Contemporary hypnosis research.* New York: Guilford Press.

Spanos, N. P., DuBreuil, S. C., & Gabora, N. J. (1991). Four month follow-up of skill training induced enhancements in hypnotizability. *Contemporary Hypnosis, 8,* 25–32.

Spear, N. E. (1979). Experimental analysis of infantile amnesia. In J. E. Kihlstrom & F. J. Evans (Eds.), *Functional disorders of memory.* Hillsdale, NJ: Erlbaum.

Spearman, C. (1927). *The abilities of man.* New York: Macmillan.

Speer, D. C. (1972). Inventory commitment: Some considerations for crisis intervention outreach workers. *Crisis Intervention, 4*(4), 112–116.

Spelke, E. (1976). Infant's intermodal perception of events. *Cognitive Psychology, 8,* 553–560.

Spence, J. T., & Helmreich, R. L. (1983). Achievement-related motives and behavior. In J. T. Spence (Ed.), *Achievement and achievement motives: Psychological and sociological approaches.* New York: Freeman.

Sperling, G. (1960). The information available in brief visual presentations. *Psychological Monographs: General and Applied, 74,* 1–28.

Sperry, R. W. (1964a). The great cerebral commissure. *Scientific American, 210*(1), 42–52.

Sperry, R. W. (1964b). *Problems outstanding in the evolution of brain function.* New York: American Museum of Natural History.

Spielberger, C. D., Gorsuch, R. L., & Lushene, R. E. (1983). *Manual for the State-Trait Anxiety Inventory (STAI).* Palo Alto, CA: Consulting Psychologists Press.

Spitzer, L., & Rodin, J. (1981). Human eating behavior: A critical review of studies in normal weight and overweight individuals. *Appetite, 2,* 293–329.

Spitzer, R. L., Skodol, A. E., Gibbon, M., & Williams, J. B. W. (1983). *Psychopathology: A case book.* New York: McGraw-Hill.

Spoehr, K. T., & Corin, W. J. (1978). The stimulus suffix effect as a memory coding phenomenon. *Memory and Cognition, 6,* 583–589.

Sporakowski, M. J. (1988). A therapist's views on the consequences of change for the contemporary family. *Family Relations, 37,* 373–378.

Springer, S. P., & Deutsch, G. (1985). *Left brain, right brain.* New York: Freeman.

Squire, L. R. (1987). *Memory and the brain.* New York: Oxford University Press.

Squire, L. R., Cohen, N. J., & Nadel, L. (1984). The medial temporal region and memory consolidations: A new hypothesis. In H. Weingardner & E. Parker (Eds.), *Memory consolidation.* Hillsdale, NJ: Erlbaum.

Squire, L. R., Ojeman, J. G., Miezin, F. M., Petersen, S. E., Videen, T. O., & Raichle, M. E., (1992). Activation of the hippocampus in normal humans: A functional neuroanatomical study of memory. *Proceedings of the National Academy of Sciences, USA, 89,* 1837–1841.

Sroufe, L. A. (1979). Socioemotional development. In J. D. Osofsky (Ed.), *Handbook of infant development.* New York: Wiley.

Sroufe, L. A. (1996). *Emotional development: The organization of emotional life in the early years.* New York: Cambridge University Press.

Srull, T. K., & Wyer, R. S., Jr. (1989). Person memory and judgment. *Psychological Review, 96*(1), 58–83.

Staats, A. W., & Staats, C. K. (1958). Attitudes established by classical conditioning. *Journal of Abnormal and Social Psychology, 57,* 37–40.

Staddon, J. E. R., & Ettinger, R. H. (1989). *Learning: An introduction to the principles of adaptive behavior.* San Diego, CA: Harcourt Brace Jovanovich.

Standing, L., Conezio, J., & Haber, R. N. (1970). Perception and memory for pictures: Single-trial learning of 2500 visual stimuli. *Psychonomic Science, 19,* 73–74.

Stanovich, K. E. (1994). Reconceptualizing intelligence: Dysrationalia as an intuition pump. *Educational Researcher, 23*(4), 11–22.

Stanovich, K. E. (1996). *How to think straight about psychology* (4th ed.). New York: HarperCollins.

Starr, R. H., Dietrich, K. N., Fischoff, J., Ceresnie, S., & Zweier, D. (1984). The contribution of handicapping conditions to child abuse. *Topics in Early Childhood Special Education, 4*(1), 59–69.

Steele, C. M. (1997). A threat in the air: How stereotypes shape intellectual identity and performance. *American Psychologist, 52,* 613–629.

Steele, C. M., & Aronson, J. (1995). Stereotype threats and the intellectual test performance of African Americans. *Journal of Personality and Social Psychology, 69,* 797–811.

Steenland, K., & Deddens, J. A. (1997). Effects of travel and rest on performance of professional basketball players. *Sleep, 20,* 366–369.

Stein, M. B., & Uhde, T. W. (1995). Biology of anxiety disorders. In A. F. Schatzberg & C. B. Nemeroff (Eds.), *The American Psychiatric Press textbook of psychopharmacology.* Washington, DC: American Psychiatric Press.

Steiner, J. E. (1979). Human facial expressions in response to taste and smell stimulation. In H. Reese & L. P. Lipsitt (Eds.), *Advances in child development and behavior* (Vol. 13, pp. 257–293). New York: Academic Press.

Steinhausen, H. C., Willms, J., & Spohr, H. L. (1993). Long-term psychopathological and cognitive outcome of children with fetal alcohol syndrome. *Journal of the American Academy of Child and Adolescent Psychology, 32,* 990–994.

Stemberger, R. T., Turner, S. M., Beidel, D. C., & Calhoun, K. S. (1995). Social phobia: An analysis of possible developmental factors. *Journal of Abnormal Psychology, 104,* 526–531.

Stern, D. (1977). *The first relationship: Mother and infant.* Cambridge, MA: Harvard University Press.

Stern, W. (1912). *Psychologische Methoden der Intelligenz-Prüfung.* Leipzig, Germany: Barth.

Sternbach, R. A. (1963). Congenital insensitivity to pain: A review. *Psychological Bulletin, 60,* 252–264.

Sternberg, R. J. (1977). *Intelligence, information processing, and analogical reasoning: The componential analysis of human abilities.* Hillsdale, NJ: Erlbaum.

Sternberg, R. J. (1979, September). Beyond IQ: Stalking the IQ quark. *Psychology Today,* 42–54.

Sternberg, R. J. (1980). Representation and process in linear syllogistic reasoning. *Journal of Experimental Psychology: General, 109,* 119–159.

Sternberg, R. J. (1981a). Intelligence and nonentrenchment. *Journal of Educational Psychology, 73,* 1–16.

Sternberg, R. J. (1981b). Novelty-seeking, novelty-finding, and the developmental continuity of intelligence. *Intelligence, 5,* 149–155.

Sternberg, R. J. (Ed.). (1982). *Handbook of human intelligence.* New York: Cambridge University Press.

Sternberg, R. J. (Ed.). (1984). *Human abilities: An information-processing approach.* San Francisco, CA: Freeman.

Sternberg, R. J. (1985a). *Beyond IQ: A triarchic theory of human intelligence.* New York: Cambridge University Press.

Sternberg, R. J. (1985b). Implicit theories of intelligence, creativity, and wisdom. *Journal of Personality and Social Psychology, 49,* 607–627.

Sternberg, R. J. (1986a). *Intelligence applied: Understanding and increasing your intellectual skills.* San Diego, CA: Harcourt Brace Jovanovich.

Sternberg, R. J. (1986b). A triangular theory of love. *Psychological Review, 93,* 119–135.

Sternberg, R. J. (1986c). A triarchic theory of intellectual giftedness. In R. J. Sternberg & J. E. Davidson (Eds.), *Conceptions of giftedness* (pp. 223–243). New York: Cambridge University Press.

Sternberg, R. J. (Ed.). (1988a). *The nature of creativity.* New York: Cambridge University Press.

Sternberg, R. J. (1988b). A three-facet model of creativity. In R. J. Sternberg (Ed.), *The nature of creativity* (pp. 125–147). New York: Cambridge University Press.

Sternberg, R. J. (1988c). Triangulating love. In R. J. Sternberg & M. L. Barnes (Eds.), *The psychology of love* (pp. 119–138). New Haven, CT: Yale University Press.

Sternberg, R. J. (1988d). *The triarchic mind.* New York: Viking.

Sternberg, R. J. (1990a). *Metaphors of mind.* New York: Cambridge University Press.

Sternberg, R. J. (Ed.). (1990b). *Wisdom: Its nature, origins, and development.* New York: Cambridge University Press.

Sternberg, R. J. (1994a). Human intelligence: Its nature, use, and interaction with context. In D. K. Detterman (Ed.), *Current topics in human intelligence* (Vol. 4, pp. 361–407). Norwood, NJ: Ablex.

Sternberg, R. J. (1994b). PRSVL: An integrative framework for understanding mind in context. In R. J. Sternberg & R. K. Wagner (Eds.), *Mind in context: Interactionist perspectives on human intelligence* (pp. 218–232). New York: Cambridge University Press.

Sternberg, R. J. (1994c). Thinking styles: Theory and assessment of the interface between intelligence and personality. In R. J. Sternberg & P. Ruzgis (Eds.), *Personality and intelligence* (pp. 169–187). New York: Cambridge University Press.

Sternberg, R. J. (1995a). Love as a story. *Journal of Social and Personal Relationships, 12*(4), 541–546.

Sternberg, R. J. (1995b). Theory and measurement of tacit knowledge as a part of practical intelligence. *Zeitschrift fur Psychologie, 203,* 319–334. Leipzig: Johann Ambrosius Barth.

Sternberg, R. J. (1995c). What it means to be intelligent: The triarchic theory of human intelligence. In W. Tomic (Ed.), *Textbook for undergraduate intelligence course.* The Netherlands: The Open University.

Sternberg, R. J. (1996a). Love stories. *Personal Relationships, 3,* 1359–1379.

Sternberg, R. J. (1996b). *Successful intelligence.* New York: Simon & Schuster.

Sternberg, R. J. (Ed.). (1997a). *Career paths in psychology.* Washington, DC: APA Books.

Sternberg, R. J. (1997b). What does it mean to be smart? *Educational Leadership, 54,* 20–24.

Sternberg, R. J. (1997c). Construct validation of a triangular love scale. *European Journal of Social Psychology, 27,* 313–335.

Sternberg, R. J. (1998). A balance theory of wisdom. *Review of General Psychology, 2,* 347–365.

Sternberg, R. J. (1998a). *Cupid's arrow.* New York: Cambridge University Press.

Sternberg, R. J. (1998b). *Love is a story.* New York: Oxford University Press.

Sternberg, R. J. (1999). Successful intelligence: Finding a balance. *Trends in Cognitive Sciences, 3,* 436–442.

Sternberg, R. J. (2000). The concept of intelligence. In R. J. Sternberg (Ed.), *Handbook of intelligence.* New York: Cambridge University Press.

Sternberg, R. J., & Barnes, M. L. (1985). Real and ideal others in romantic relationships: Is four a crowd? *Journal of Personality and Social Psychology, 49,* 1586–1608.

Sternberg, R. J., & Barnes, M. L. (Eds.). (1988). *The psychology of love.* New Haven, CT: Yale University Press.

Sternberg, R. J., & Ben-Zeev, T. (2001). *Complex cognition.* New York: Oxford University Press.

Sternberg, R. J., & Berg, C. A. (Eds.). (1992). *Intellectual development.* New York: Cambridge University Press.

Sternberg, R. J., & Clinkenbeard, P. R. (1995). A triarchic view of identifying, teaching, and assessing gifted children. *Roeper Review, 17*(4), 255–260.

Sternberg, R. J., & Davidson, J. E. (Eds.). (1986). *Conceptions of giftedness.* New York: Cambridge University Press.

Sternberg, R. J., & Detterman, D. K. (Eds.). (1986). *What is intelligence? Contemporary viewpoints on its nature and definition.* Norwood, NJ: Ablex.

Sternberg, R. J., & Dobson, D. M. (1987). Resolving interpersonal conflicts: An analysis of stylistic consistency. *Journal of Personality and Social Psychology, 52,* 794–812.

Sternberg, R. J., Ferrari, M., Clinkenbeard, P. R., & Grigorenko, E. L. (1996). Identification, instruction, and assessment of gifted children: A construct validation of a triarchic model. *Gifted Child Quarterly, 40*(3), 129–137.

Sternberg, R. J., Forsythe, G. B., Hedlund, J., Horvath, J., Snook, S., Williiams, W. M., Wagner, R. K., & Grigorenko, E. L. (2000). *Practical intelligence in everyday life.* New York: Cambridge University Press.

Sternberg, R. J., & Frensch, P. A. (Eds.). (1991). *Complex problem solving: Principles and mechanisms.* Hillsdale, NJ: Erlbaum.

Sternberg, R. J., & Grajek, S. (1984). The nature of love. *Journal of Personality and Social Psychology, 47,* 312–329.

Sternberg, R. J., & Grigorenko, E. L. (Eds.). (1997). *Intelligence, heredity, and environment.* New York: Cambridge University Press.

Sternberg, R. J., & Grigorenko, E. L. (1999). Myths in psychology and education regarding the gene environment debate. *Teachers College Record, 100,* 536–553.

Sternberg, R. J., & Grigorenko, E. L. (in press). *Intelligence applied* (2nd ed.). New York: Oxford University Press.

Sternberg, R. J., Grigorenko, E. L., Ferrari, M., & Clinkenbeard, P. (1999). A triarchic analysis of an aptitude-treatment interaction. *European Journal of Psychological Assessment, 15,* 1–11.

Sternberg, R. J., & Kaufman, (1998). Human abilities. *Annual Review of Psychology, 49,* 479–502.

Sternberg, R. J., & Lubart, T. I. (1991a, April). Creating creative minds. *Phi Delta Kappan,* pp. 608–614.

Sternberg, R. J., & Lubart, T. I. (1991b). An investment theory of creativity and its development. *Human Development, 34,* 1–31.

Sternberg, R. J., & Lubart, T. I. (1993). Investing in creativity. *Psychological Inquiry, 4*(3), 229–232.

Sternberg, R. J., & Lubart, T. I. (1995). *Defying the crowd: Cultivating creativity in a culture of conformity.* New York: The Free Press.

Sternberg, R. J., & Lubart, T. I. (1996). Investing in creativity. *American Psychologist, 51*(7), 677–688.

Sternberg, R. J., & Lubart, T. I. (1999). The concept of creativity: Prospects and paradigms. In R. J. Sternberg (Ed.), *Handbook of creativity* (pp. 3–15). New York: Cambridge University Press.

Sternberg, R. J., & Nigro, G. (1980). Development patterns in the solution of verbal analogies. *Child Development, 51,* 27–38.

Sternberg, R. J., & Okagaki, L. (1989). Continuity and discontinuity in intellectual development are not a matter of "either–or." *Human Development, 32,* 158–166.

Sternberg, R. J., & Powell, J. S. (1983). Comprehending verbal comprehension. *American Psychologist, 38,* 878–893.

Sternberg, R. J., & Soriano, L. J. (1984). Styles of conflict resolution. *Journal of Personality and Social Psychology, 47,* 115–126.

Sternberg, R. J., Torff, B., & Grigorenko, E. L. (1998). Teaching triarchically improves school achievement. *Journal of Educational Psychology, 90,* 374–384.

Sternberg, R. J., & Weil, E. M. (1980). An aptitude-strategy interaction in linear syllogistic reasoning. *Journal of Educational Psychology, 72,* 226–234.

Sternberg, R. J., & Williams, W. (1997). Does the Graduate Record Examination predict meaningful success in the graduate training of psychologists? A case study. *American Psychologist, 52,* 630–641.

Sternberg, S. (1966). High-speed memory scanning in human memory. *Science, 153,* 652–654.

Sternberg, S. (1969). Memory-scanning: Mental processes revealed by reaction-time experiments. *American Scientist, 4,* 421–457.

Stevens, A., & Coupe, P. (1978). Distortions in judged spatial relations. *Cognitive Psychology, 10,* 422–437.

Stewart, A. J. (1982). The course of individual adaptation to life changes. *Journal of Personality and Social Psychology, 42,* 1100–1113.

Stewart, A. J., & Healy, J. M., Jr. (1985). Personality and adaptation to change. In R. Hogan & W. H. Jones (Eds.), *Perspectives in personality* (Vol. 1, pp. 117–144). Greenwich, CT: JAI Press.

Stewart, A. J., & Healy, J. M. (1989). Linking individual development and social changes. *American Psychologist, 44*(1), 30–42.

Stewart, A. J., Sokol, M., Healy, J. M., & Chester, N. L. (1986). Longitudinal studies of psychological consequences of life changes in children and adults. *Journal of Personality and Social Psychology, 50,* 143–151.

Stiles, W. B., Shapiro, D. A., & Elliott, R. (1986). Are all psychotherapies equivalent? *American Psychologist, 41*(2), 165–180.

Stiles, W. B., Walz, N. C., Schroeder, M. A. B., Williams, L. L., & Ickes, W. (1996). Attractiveness and disclosure in initial encounters of mixed-sex dyads. *Journal of Social and Personal Relationships, 13,* 303–312.

Stipek, D. J. (1984). Young children's performance expectations: Logical analysis or wishful thinking? In J. G. Nicholls (Ed.), *Advances in motivation and achievement: Vol 3. The development of achievement motivation* (pp. 33–56). Greenwich, CT: JAI Press.

Stone, G. C. (1979). Health and the health system: A historical overview and conceptual framework. In G. C. Stone, F. Cohen, & N. E. Adler (Eds.), *Health psychology–A handbook* (pp. 1–17). San Francisco: Jossey-Bass.

Strauss, B. (1999). Die Beeinflussung sportlicher Leistungen durch Zuschauer [The impact of spectators on sports performance]. Lengerich, Germany: Pabst.

Strauss, B. (under review). The Impact of Supportive Spectator Behavior On Performance in Team Sports.

Strauss, J. S., Kokes, F. R., Ritzler, B. A., Harder, D. W., & Van Ord, A. (1978). Patterns of disorder in first admission psychiatric patients. *Journal of Nervous and Mental Disease, 166,* 611–623.

Street, M. D. (1997). Groupthink: An examination of theoretical issues, implications, and future research suggestions. *Small Group Research, 28,* 72–93.

Streissguth, A. P., Barr, H. M., Sampson, P. D., Darby, B. L., & Martin, D. C. (1989). IQ at age four in relation to maternal alcohol use and smoking during pregnancy. *Developmental Psychology, 25,* 3–11.

Streissguth, A. P., Martin, D. C., Barr, H. M., Sandman, B. M., Kirchner, G. L., & Darby, B. L. (1984). Intrauterine alcohol and nicotine exposure. Attention and reaction time in 4-year-old children. *Developmental Psychology, 20,* 533–541.

Streissguth, A. P., Sampson, P. D., & Barr, H. M. (1989). Neurobehavioral dose-response effects of prenatal alcohol exposure in humans from infancy to adulthood. Conference of the Behav-ioral Teratology Society, the National Institute on Drug Abuse, and the New York Academy of Sciences: Prenatal abuse of licit and illicit drugs (1988, Bethesda, Maryland). *Annals of the New York Academy of Sciences, 562,* 145–158.

Streufert, S., & Swezey, R. W. (1986). *Complexity, managers, and organizations.* Orlando, FL: Academic Press.

Stricker, E. M., & Zigmond, M. J. (1976). Brain catecholamines and the lateral hypothalamic syndrome. In D. Novin, W. Wyrwicka, & G. Bray (Eds.), *Hunger: Basic mechanisms and clinical implications.* New York: Raven Press.

Strickland, B. (1992). Women and depression. *Current Directions in Psychological Science, 1,* 132–135.

Striegel-Moore, R. H., Silberstein, L. R., & Rodin, J. (1993). The social self in bulimia nervosa: Public self-consciousness, social anxiety, and perceived fraudulence. *Journal of Abnormal Psychology, 102,* 297–303.

Stroop, J. (1935). Studies of interference in serial verbal reactions. *Journal of Experimental Psychology, 18,* 624–643.

Strupp, H. H. (1981). Toward a refinement of time-limited dynamic psychotherapy. In S. H. Budman (Ed.), *Forms of brief therapy.* New York: Guilford.

Strupp, H. H. (1996). The tripartite model and the *Consumer Reports* study. *American Psychologist, 51,* 1017–1024.

Suedfeld, P., & Piedrahita, L. E. (1984). Intimations of mortality: Integrative simplification as a precursor of death. *Journal of Personality and Social Psychology, 47*(4), 848–852.

Suematsu, H., Ishikawa, H., Kuboki, T., & Ito, T. (1985). Statistical studies on anorexia nervosa in Japan: Detailed clinical data on 1,011 patients. *Psychotherapy and Psychosomatics, 43,* 96–103.

Sullivan, H. S. (1953). *The interpersonal theory of psychiatry.* New York: Norton.

Suls, J., & Fletcher, R. L. (1983). Social comparison in the social and physical sciences: An archival study. *Journal of Personality and Social Psychology, 44,* 575–580.

Suls, J. M., & Miller, R. L. (Eds.). (1977). *Social comparison processes: Theoretical and empirical perspectives.* Washington, DC: Hemisphere.

Summers, G., & Feldman, N. S. (1984). Blaming the victim versus blaming the perpetrator: An attributional analysis of spouse abuse. *Journal of Social and Clinical Psychology, 2,* 339–347.

Super, D. E. (1985). Career and life development. In D. Brown & L. Brooks (Eds.), *Career choice and development.* San Francisco: Jossey-Bass.

Sutton, S. K., & Davidson, R. J. (1997). Prefrontal brain asymmetry: A biological substrate of the behavioral approach and inhibition systems. *Psychological Science, 8,* 204–210.

Suzuki, L. A., & Valencia, R. R. (1997). Race-ethnicity and measured intelligence: Educational implications. *American Psychologist, 52,* 1103–1114.

Swann, W. B., Jr., & Pittman, T. S. (1977). Initiating play activity in children: The moderating influence of verbal cues on intrinsic motivation. *Child Development, 48,* 1125–1132.

Swets, J. A., Tanner, W. P., Jr., & Birdsall, T. G. (1961). Decision processes in perception. *Psychological Review, 68,* 301–340.

Szasz, T. S. (1961). *The myth of mental illness.* New York: Harper & Row.

Szmukler, G. I., & Russell, G. F. M. (1986). Outcome and prognosis of anorexia nervosa. In K. D. Brownell & J. P. Foreyt (Eds.), *Handbook of eating disorders.* New York: Basic Books.

Tajfel, H. (Ed.). (1982). *Social identity and intergroup relations.* London: Cambridge University Press.

Tajfel, H., & Turner, J. C. (1986). The social identity theory of intergroup behavior. In S. Worchel & W. G. Austin (Eds.), *The psychology of intergroup relations* (2nd ed., pp. 7–24). Chicago: Nelson Hall.

Tait, R. W., & Saladin, M. E. (1986). Concurrent development of excitatory and inhibitory associations during backward conditioning. *Animal Learning and Behavior, 14,* 133–137.

Tanford, S., & Penrod, S. (1984). Social influence model: A formal integration of research on majority and minority influence processes. *Psychological Bulletin, 95,* 189–225.

Tang, S. H., & Hall, V. C. (1995). The overjustification effect: A meta-analysis. *Applied Cognitive Psychology, 9,* 365–404.

Tannen, D. (1986). *That's not what I meant! How conversational style makes or breaks relationships.* New York: Ballantine.

Tannen, D. (1990). *You just don't understand: Women and men in conversation.* New York: Ballantine.

Tannen, D. (1994). *Talking from 9 to 5: How women's and men's conversational styles affect who gets heard, who gets credit, and what gets done at work.* New York: Morrow.

Taub, J. M. (1971). The sleep–wakefulness cycle in Mexican adults. *Journal of Cross-Cultural Psychology, 2*(4), 353–363.

Tavris, C. (1989) *Anger: The misunderstood emotion* (2nd ed.). New York: Simon & Schuster/Touchstone.

Taylor, C. W. (1988). Various approaches to and definitions of creativity. In R. J. Sternberg (Ed.), *The nature of creativity* (pp. 99–121). New York: Cambridge University Press.

Taylor, J. A., & Sanderson, M. (1995). A reexamination of the risk factors for the sudden infant death syndrome. *Journal of Pediatrics, 126*(6), 887–891.

Taylor, S. E. (1979). Hospital patient behavior: Reactance, helplessness, or control? *Journal of Social Issues, 35,* 156–184.

Taylor, S. E. (1983). Adjustment to threatening events: A theory of cognitive adaptation. *American Psychologist, 38,* 1161–1173.

Taylor, S. E. (1990). Health psychology: The science and the field. *American Psychologist, 45*(1), 40–50.

Taylor, S. E. (1991). *Health psychology* (2nd ed.). New York: McGraw-Hill.

Taylor, S. E., & Aspinwall, L. G. (1990). Psychological aspects of chronic illness. In G. R. Van den Bos & P. T. Costa, Jr. (Eds.), *Psychological apects of serious illness.* Washington, DC: American Psychological Association.

Taylor, S. E., & Brown, J. D. (1988). Illusion and well-being: A social psychological perspective on mental health. *Psychological Bulletin, 103*(2), 193–210.

Tedeschi, J. T., Schlenker, B. R., & Bonoma, T. V. (1971). Cognitive dissonance: Private ratiocination or public spectacle? *American Psychologist, 26,* 685–695.

Teghtsoonian, R. (1971). On the exponents in Stevens' law and the constant in Ekman's law. *Psychological Review, 78*(1), 71–80.

Teitelbaum, P. (1961). Disturbances in feeding and drinking behavior after hypothalamic lesions. In M. R. Jones (Ed.), *Nebraska Symposium on Motivation.* Lincoln: University of Nebraska Press.

Tellegen, A., Lykken, D. T., Bouchard, T. J., Jr., Wilcox, K. J., & Rich, S. (1988). Personality similarity in twins reared apart and together. *Journal of Personality and Social Psychology, 54,* 1031–1039.

Teller, D. Y., & Bornstein, M. H. (1987). Infant color vision and color perception. In P. Salapatek & L. Cohen (Eds.), *Handbook of infant perception: Vol. 1. From sensation to perception* (pp. 185–236). Orlando, FL: Academic Press.

Teller, D. Y., & Movshon, J. A. (1986). Visual development. *Vision Research, 26,* 1483–1506.

Terhune, K. W. (1968). Studies of motives, cooperation, and conflict within laboratory microcosms. In G. H. Snyder (Ed.), *Studies in international conflict* (Vol. 4, pp. 29–58). Buffalo, NY: State University of New York at Buffalo, Council on International Studies.

Terman, L. M. (1925). *Genetic studies of genius: Mental and physical traits of a thousand gifted children* (Vol. 1). Stanford, CA: Stanford University Press.

Terman, L. M., & Merrill, M. A. (1937). *Measuring intelligence.* Boston: Houghton Mifflin.

Terman, L. M., & Merrill, M. A. (1973). *Stanford-Binet Intelligence Scale: Manual for the third revision.* Boston: Houghton Mifflin.

Terman, L. M., & Oden, M. H. (1959). *Genetic studies of genius: The gifted group at midlife* (Vol. 4). Stanford, CA: Stanford University Press.

Terrace, H. S. (1979). *Nim.* New York: Knopf.

Tetlock, P. E. (1998). Social psychology and world politics. In D. T. Gilbert, S. T. Fiske, & G. Lindzey (Eds.), *The handbook of social psychology* (4th ed., Vol. 2, pp. 868–912). New York: McGraw-Hill.

Thatcher, R. W. (1992). Development as a dynamic system. *Current Directions in Psychological Science, 1,* 189–193.

Thatcher, R. W., Walker, R. A., & Giudice, S. (1987). Human cerebral hemispheres develop at different rates and ages. *Science, 236,* 1110–1113.

Thelen, E. (1995). Motor development: A new synthesis. *American Psychologist, 50,* 79–95.

Thigpen, C. H., & Cleckley, H. M. (1957). *The three faces of Eve.* New York: Fawcett.

Thoits, P. A. (1994). Stressors and problem solving: The individual as psychological activist. *Journal of Health and Social Behavior, 35,* 143–159.

Thomas, A., & Chess, S. (1977). *Temperament and development.* New York: Brunner/Mazel.

Thomas, A., & Chess, S. (1987). Commentary. In H. Goldsmith, A. Buss, R. Plomin, M. Rothbart, A. Thomas, S. Chess, R. Hinde, & R. McCall, Roundtable: What is temperament? Four approaches. *Child Development, 58,* 505–529.

Thomas, A., Chess, S., & Birch, H. G. (1970). The origin of personality. *Scientific American, 223*(2).

Thomas, J. C., Jr. (1974). An analysis of behavior in the hobbits-orcs problem. *Cognitive Psychology, 6,* 257–269.

Thomas, V. J., & Rose, F. D. (1991). Ethnic differences in the experience of pain. *Social Science and Medicine, 32,* 1063–1066.

Thompson, R. A. (1998). Early sociopersonality development. In W. Damon (Gen. Ed.) & N. Eisenberg (Vol. Ed.), *Handbook of child psychology* (Vol. 3): *Social, emotional, and personality development* (pp. 25–104). New York: Wiley.

Thompson, R. A. (1999). The individual child: Temperament, emotion, self, and personality. In M. H. Bornstein & M. E. Lamb (Eds.), *Developmental psychology: An advanced textbook* (pp. 377–409). Mahwah, NJ: Erlbaum.

Thompson, R. A., Lamb, M. E., & Estes, D. (1982). Stability of infant–mother attachment and its relationship to changing life circumstances in an unselected middle class sample. *Child Development, 53,* 144–148.

Thompson, R. F. (1975). *Introduction to physiological psychology.* New York: Harper & Row.

Thompson, R. F. (1987). The cerebellum and memory storage: A response to Bloedel. *Science, 238,* 1729–1730.

Thompson, S. C., Cheek, P. R., & Graham, M. A. (1988). The other side of perceived control: Disadvantages and negative effects. In S. Spacapan & S. Oskamp (Eds.), *The social psychology of health: The Claremont Applied Social Psychology Conference* (Vol. 2, pp. 69–94). Beverly Hills, CA: Sage.

Thompson, S. K. (1975). Gender labels and early sex role development. *Child Development, 46,* 339–347.

Thompson, W. R. (1954). The inheritance and development of intelligence. *Proceedings of the Association for Research on Nervous and Mental Disease, 33,* 209–231.

Thorndike, E. L. (1898). Animal intelligence: An experimental study of the associative processes in animals. *Psychological Monographs, 2*(Whole No. 8).

Thorndike, E. L. (1905). *The elements of psychology.* New York: Seiler.

Thorndike, E. L. (1911). *Animal intelligence: Experimental studies.* New York: Macmillan.

Thorndike, R. L., Hagen, E. P., & Sattler, J. M. (1986). *Stanford-Binet Intelligence Scale: Guide for administering and scoring the fourth edition.* Chicago: Riverside.

Thurstone, L. L. (1924). *The nature of intelligence.* New York: Harcourt Brace.

Thurstone, L. L. (1938). *Primary mental abilities.* Chicago: University of Chicago Press.

Tillich, P. (1952). *Courage to be.* New Haven, CT: Yale University Press.

Timberlake, W. T. (1993). Behavior systems and reinforcement: An integrative approach. *Journal of the Experimental Analysis of Behavior, 60,* 105–128.

Tinbergen, N. (1951). *The study of instinct.* Oxford, England: Clarendon.

Titchener, E. B. (1910). *A textbook of psychology.* New York: Macmillan.

Tolman, E. C. (1932). *Purposive behavior in animals and men.* New York: Appleton-Century-Crofts.

Tolman, E. C. (1959). Principles of purposive behavior. In S. Koch (Ed.), *Psychology: A study of science* (Vol. 2, pp. 92–157). New York: McGraw-Hill.

Tolman, E. C., & Honzik, C. H. (1930). "Insight" in rats. *University of California Publications in Psychology, 4,* 215–232.

Tomaszuk, A., Simpson, C., & Williams, G. (1996). Neuropeptide Y, the hypothalamus and the regulation of energy homeostasis. *Hormone Research, 46,* 53–58.

Tomkins, S. S. (1962). *Affect, imagery, and consciousness: Vol. 1. The positive affects.* New York: Springer.

Tomkins, S. S. (1963). *Affect, imagery, and consciousness: Vol. 2. The negative affects.* New York: Springer.

Torrance, E. P. (1974). *The Torrance tests of creative thinking: Technical-norms manual.* Bensenville, IL: Scholastic Testing Services.

Torrance, E. P. (1984). *Torrance tests of creative thinking: Streamlined (revised) manual, Figural A and B.* Bensenville, IL: Scholastic Testing Services.

Torrance, E. P. (1988). The nature of creativity as manifest in its testing. In R. J. Sternberg (Ed.), *The nature of creativity* (pp. 43–75). New York: Cambridge University Press.

Torrey, E. F. (1986). *Witchdoctors and psychiatrists: The common roots of psychotherapy and its future.* New York: Harper & Row.

Torrey, E. F. (1988). Stalking the schizovirus. *Schizophrenia Bulletin, 14,* 223–229.

Torrey, E. F. (1997). *Out of the shadows: Confronting America's mental illness crisis.* New York: Wiley.

Torrey, E. F., Bowler, A. E., Taylor, E. H., & Gottesman, I. I. (1994). *Schizophrenia and manic–depressive disorder.* New York: Basic Books.

Tourangeau, R., & Ellsworth, P. C. (1979). The role of facial response in the experience of emotion. *Journal of Personality and Social Psychology, 37,* 1519–1531.

Townsend, J. T. (1971). A note on the identifiability of parallel and serial processes. *Perception and Psychophysics, 10,* 161–163.

Trager, J. (1992). *The people's chronology.* New York: Holt.

Treisman, A. M. (1964a). Monitoring and storage of irrelevant messages in selective attention. *Journal of Verbal Learning and Verbal Behavior, 3,* 449–459.

Treisman, A. M. (1964b). Selective attention in man. *British Medical Bulletin, 20,* 12–16.

Triandis, H. (1990). Cross-cultural studies of individualism and collectivism. In J. Berman (Ed.), *Nebraska Symposium on Motivation, 1989* (pp. 41–133). Lincoln, NE: University of Nebraska Press.

Triandis, H. C. (1994). Culture and social behavior. In W. J. Lonner & R. S. Malpass (Eds.), *Psychology and culture.* Boston: Allyn & Bacon.

Tripathi, A. N. (1979). Memory for meaning and grammatical structure: An experiment on retention of a story. *Psychological Studies, 24*(2), 136–145.

Triplett, N. (1898). The dynamogenic factors in pacemaking and competition. *American Journal of Psychology, 9,* 507–533.

Trivers, R. L. (1971). The evolution of reciprocal altruism. *Quarterly Review of Biology, 46,* 35–57.

Truman, M. (1977). *Women of courage.* New York: William Morrow.

Tryon, R. (1940). Genetic differences in maze-learning ability in rats. In the *39th yearbook of the National Society for the Study of Education.* Chicago: University of Chicago Press.

Tsunoda, T. (1979). Difference in the mechanism of emotion in Japanese and Westerner. *Psychotherapy and Psychosomatics, 31*(1–4), 367–372.

Tulving, E. (1962). Subjective organization in free recall of "unrelated" words. *Psychological Review, 69,* 344–354.

Tulving, E. (1966). Subjective organization and effects of repetition in multi-trial free-recall learning. *Journal of Verbal Learning and Verbal Behavior, 5,* 193–197.

Tulving, E. (1972). Episodic and semantic memory. In E. Tulving & W. Donaldson (Eds.), *Organization of memory.* New York: Academic Press.

Tulving, E., Kapur, S., Markowitsch, H. J., Craik, F. I. M., Habib, R., & Houle, S. (1994). Neuroanatomical correlates of retrieval in episodic memory: Auditory sentence recognition. *Proceedings of the National Academy of Sciences, USA, 91,* 2012–2015.

Tulving, E., & Pearlstone, Z. (1966). Availability versus accessibility of information in memory for words. *Journal of Verbal Learning and Verbal Behavior, 5,* 381–391.

Tulving, E., & Thomson, D. M. (1973). Encoding specificity and retrieval processes in episodic memory. *Psychological Review, 80,* 352–373.

Turiel, E. (1998). The development of morality. In W. Damon (Gen. Ed.) & N. Eisenberg (Vol. Ed.), *Handbook of child psychology: Social, emotional, and personality development* (Vol. 3, pp. 863–932). New York: Wiley.

Turk, D. C., Meichenbaum, D., & Genest, M. (1983). *Pain and behavioral medicine: A cognitive behavioral perspective.* New York: Guilford.

Turk, D. C., & Rudy, T. E. (1992). Cognitive factors and persistent pain: A glimpse into Pandora's box. *Cognitive Therapy and Research, 16*(2), 99–122.

Turnbull, C. (1961). *The forest people: A study of pygmies of the Congo.* New York: Simon & Schuster.

Turner, J. C. (1987). *Rediscovering the social group: A self-categorization theory.* Oxford, England: Basil Blackwell.

Turner, J. R., & Wheaton, B. (1995). Checklist measurement of stressful life events. In S. Cohen, R. C. Kessler, & L. U. Gordon (Eds.), *Measuring stress: A guide for health and social scientists.* New York: Oxford University Press.

Turner, M. E., Pratkanis, A. R., Probasco, P., & Leve, C. (1992). Threat, cohesion, and group effectiveness: Testing a social identity maintenance perspective on groupthink. *Journal of Personality and Social Psychology, 63,* 781–796.

Turner, R. J., & Wagonfeld, M. O. (1967). Occupational mobility and schizophrenia: An assessment of the social causation and the social selection hypothesis. *American Sociological Review, 32,* 104–113.

Tversky, A., & Kahneman, D. (1973). Availability: A heuristic for judging frequency and probability. *Cognitive Psychology, 5,* 207–232.

Tzischinsky, O., Pal, I., Epstein, R., Dagan, Y., & Lavie, P. (1992). The importance of timing in melatonin administration in a blind man. *Journal of Pineal Research, 12,* 105–108.

Ulrich, R., & Azrin, N. H. (1962). Reflexive fighting in response to aversive stimulation. *Journal of the Experimental Analysis of Behavior, 5,* 511–520.

Underwood, B. J. (1957). Interference and forgetting. *Psychological Review, 64,* 49–60.

United States Department of Labor, Bureau of Labor Statistics. (1987). *Statistical Abstract of the United States* (107th ed.). Washington, DC: U. S. Department of Commerce.

Urdan, T. C., & Maehr, M. L. (1995). Beyond a two-goal theory of motivation and achievement: A case for social goals. *Review of Educational Research, 65,* 213–243.

Valenstein, E. S. (1986). *Great and desperate cures.* New York: Basic Books.

Valenstein, E. S. (1973). *Brain control.* New York: Wiley.

Vallerand, R. J., Fortier, M. S., & Guay, F. (1997). Self-determination and persistence in a real-life setting: Toward a motivational model of high school dropout. *Journal of Personality and Social Psychology, 72,* 1161–1176.

Van Bezooijen, R., Otto, S. A., & Heenan, T. A. (1983). Recognition of vocal expressions of emotion: A three-nation study to identify universal characteristics. *Journal of Cross-Cultural Psychology, 14*(4), 387–406.

Van Hoesen, G. W. (1993). The modern concept of association cortex. *Current Opinion in Neurobiology, 3,* 150–154.

Van Wieringen, J. C. (1978). Secular growth changes. In F. Falkner & J. M. Tanner (Eds.), *Human growth* (Vol. 2). New York: Plenum.

Vandell, D., & Mueller, E. C. (1980). Peer play and friendships during the first two years. In H. C. Foot, A. J. Chapman, & J. R. Smith (Eds.), *Friendship and social relations in children.* New York: Wiley.

VanderPlate, C., Aral, S. O., & Magder, L. (1988). The relationship among genital herpes simplex virus, stress, and social support. *Health Psychology, 7,* 159–168.

Vaughan, D. (1986). *Uncoupling.* New York: Vintage Books.

Vaughn, B. E., Gove, F. L., & Egeland, B. (1980). The relationship between out-of-home care and the quality of infant–mother attachment in an economically disadvantaged population. *Child Development, 51,* 1203–1214.

Velting, D. M., & Liebert, R. M. (1997). Predicting three mood phenomena from factors and facets of the NEO-PI. *Journal of Personaltiy Assessment, 68,* 164–171.

Vernon, P. A., & Mori, M. (1992). Intelligence, reaction times, and peripheral nerve conduction velocity. *Intelligence, 16*(3–4), 273–288.

Vernon, P. A., Wickett. J., Bazana, P. G., & Stelmack, R. (2000). The neuropsychology and psychophysiology of intelligence. In R. J. Sternberg (Ed.), *Handbook of intelligence.* New York: Cambridge University Press.

Vernon, P. E. (1971). *The structure of human abilities.* London: Methuen.

Veroff, J. (1957). Development and validation of a projective measure of power motivation. *Journal of Abnormal and Social Psychology, 54,* 1–8.

Viglione, D. J., & Exner, J. E. (1983). Current research in the comprehensive Rorschach system. In J. N. Butcher & C. D. Spielberger (Eds.), *Advances in personality assessment* (Vol. 2, pp. 13–40). Hillsdale, NJ: Erlbaum.

Viney, W. (1993). *A history of psychology: Ideas and context.* Needham Heights, MA: Allyn & Bacon.

Vokey, J. R., & Read, J. D. (1985). Subliminal messages: Between the devil and the media. *American Psychologist, 40,* 1231–1239.

Vonk, R., & van-Knippenberg, A. (1995). Processing attitude statements from in-group and out-group members: Effects of within-group and within-person inconsistencies on reading times. *Journal of Personality and Social Psychology, 68,* 215–227.

Vygotsky, L. S. (1962). *Thought and language.* Cambridge, MA: MIT Press. (Original work published 1934)

Vygotsky, L. S. (1978). *Mind in society: The development of higher psychological processes.* Cambridge, MA: Harvard University Press.

Waddington, C. H. (1956). *Principles of embryology.* London: Macmillan.

Wade, C., & Cirese, S. (1991). *Human sexuality* (2nd ed.). New York: Harcourt Brace Jovanovich.

Wagner, A. R., & Larew, M. B. (1985). Opponent processes and Pavlovian inhibition. In R. R. Miller & N. E. Spear (Eds.), *Information processing in animals: Conditioned inhibition* (pp. 233–265). Hillsdale, NJ: Erlbaum.

Wagner, A. R., & Rescorla, R. A. (1972). Inhibition in Pavlovian conditioning: Application of a theory. In R. A. Boakes & M. S. Halliday (Eds.), *Inhibition and learning.* New York: Academic Press.

Wagner, D. A. (1978). Memories of Morocco: The influence of age, schooling, and environment on memory. *Cognitive Psychology, 10,* 1–28.

Wagner, R. K. (1997). Intelligence, training, and employment. *American Psychologist, 52,* 1059–1069.

Wagner, R. K. (2000). Practical intelligence. In R. J. Sternberg (Ed.), *Handbook of intelligence.* New York: Cambridge University Press.

Wagner, R. K., & Stanovich, K. E. (1996). Expertise in reading. In K. A. Ericsson (Eds.), *The road to excellence* (pp. 159–227). Mahwah, NJ: Erlbaum.

Wagner, R. K., & Sternberg, R. J. (1985). Practical intelligence in real-world pursuits: The role of tacit knowledge. *Journal of Personality and Social Psychology, 49,* 436–458.

Wahlsten, D., & Gottlieb, G. (1997). The invalid separation of effects of nature and nurture: Lessons from animal experimentation. In R. J. Sternberg & E. L. Grigorenko (Eds.), *Intelligence, heredity, and environment* (pp. 163–192). New York: Cambridge University Press.

Walberg, H. J. (1988). Creativity and talent as learning. In R. J. Sternberg (Ed.), *The nature of creativity* (pp. 340–361). New York: Cambridge University Press.

Wald, G., & Brown, P. K. (1965). Human color vision and color blindness. *Cold Spring Harbor Symposia on Quantitative Biology, 30,* 345–359.

Walker, L. J. (1989). A longitudinal study of moral reasoning. *Child Development, 60,* 157–166.

Wallace, B. (1993). Day persons, night persons, and variability in hypnotic susceptibility. *Journal of Personality and Social Psychology, 64,* 827–833.

Wallace, R. K., & Benson, H. (1972). The physiology of meditation. *Scientific American,* 84–90.

Waller, N. G., Kojetin, B. A., Bouchard, T. J., Lykken, D. T., & Tellegen, A. (1990). Genetic and environmental influences on religious interests, attitudes, and values: A study of twins reared apart and together. *Psychological Science, 1,* 138–142.

Walsh, D. C., Hingson, R. W., Merrigan, D. M., Levenson, S. M., et al. (1991). A randomized trial of treatment for alcohol abusing workers. *New England Journal of Medicine, 325,* 775–782.

Walsh, W. (1997). When stereotypes get applied to the self: The role of perceived ingroup variability in self-stereotyping. Unpublished doctoral dissertation, Yale University, New Haven, CT.

Walster, E., Aronson, E., Abrahams, D., & Rottman, L. (1966). The importance of physical attractiveness in dating behavior. *Journal of Personality and Social Psychology, 4,* 508–516.

Walster, E., & Berscheid, E. (1974). A little bit about love: A minor essay on a major topic. In T. L. Huston (Ed.), *Foundations of interpersonal attraction.* New York: Academic Press.

Walster, E., Walster, G. W., & Berscheid, E. (1978). *Equity: Theory and research.* Boston: Allyn & Bacon.

Walters, G. C., & Grusec, J. F. (1977). *Punishment.* San Francisco: Freeman.

Walters, J. M., & Gardner, H. (1986). The theory of multiple intelligences: Some issues and answers. In R. J. Sternberg & R. K. Wagner (Eds.), *Practical intelligence: Nature and origins of competence in the everyday world* (pp. 163–182). New York: Cambridge University Press.

Wangensteen, O. H., & Carlson, A. J. (1931). Hunger sensation after total gastrectomy. *Proceedings of the Society for Experimental Biology, 28,* 545–547.

Warren, L. W., & McEachren, L. (1983). Psychosocial correlates of depressive symptomatology in adult women. *Journal of Abnormal Psychology, 92,* 151–160.

Warren, R. M., Obusek, C. J., Farmer, R. M., & Warren, R. P. (1969). Auditory sequence: Confusion of patterns other than speech or music. *Science, 164,* 586–587.

Wason, P. C., & Johnson-Laird, P. N. (1972). *Psychology of reasoning: Structure and content.* London: B. T. Batsford.

Wasserman, R., DiBasio, C. M., Bond, L. A., Young P., & Collett, R. (1990). Infant temperament and school age behavior: A pediatric practice. *Pediatrics, 85,* 801–807.

Waters, E., Wippman, J., & Sroufe, L. A. (1979). Attachment, positive affect, and competence in the peer group: Two studies in construct validation. *Child Development, 50,* 821–829.

Watkins, M. J., & Tulving, E. (1975). Episodic memory: When recognition fails. *Journal of Experimental Psychology: General, 104,* 5–29.

Watson, D. (1989). Strangers' ratings of the five robust personality factors: Evidence of a surprising convergence with self-report. *Journal of Personality and Social Psychology, 57*(1), 120–128.

Watson, J. B. (1928). *Psychological care of infant and child.* New York: Norton.

Watson, J. B. (1930). *Behaviorism* (Rev. ed.). New York: Norton.

Watson, J. B., & McDougall, W. (1929). *The battle of behaviorism.* New York: Norton.

Watson, J. B., & Rayner, R. (1920). Conditioned emotional reactions. *Journal of Experimental Psychology, 3,* 1–14.

Watson, O. M. (1970). *Proxemic behavior: A cross-cultural study.* The Hague, Netherlands: Mouton.

Waugh, N. C., & Norman, D. A. (1965). Primary memory. *Psychological Review, 72,* 89–104.

Weale, R. A. (1986). Aging and vision. *Vision Research, 26,* 1507–1512.

Webb, W. B. (1982). Some theories about sleep and their clinical applications. *Psychiatric Annals, 11,* 415–422.

Weber, E. H. (1834). *De pulen, resorptione, auditu et tactu: Annotationes anatomicae et physiologicae.* Leipzig, Germany: Koehler.

Wechsler, D. (1974). *The measurement and appraisal of adult intelligence.* Baltimore: Williams & Wilkins.

Weiller, C., Isansee, C., Rijntgis, M., Huber, W., et al., (1996). Recovery from Wernicke's aphasia: A positron emission tomography study. *Annals of Neurology, 37,* 723–732.

Weinberg, M. K. (1992). Boys and girls: Sex differences in emotional expressivity and self-regulation during early infancy. Paper presented in L. J. Bridges (Chair), *Early emotional self-regulation: New approaches to understanding developmental change and individual differences.* Symposium presented at the International Conference on Infant Studies (ICIS), Miami, Florida.

Weinberg, R. A., Scarr, S., & Waldman, I. D. (1992). The Minnesota transracial adoption study: A follow-up of IQ test performance at adolescence. *Intelligence, 16,* 117–135.

Weinberger, D. R., Wagner, R. L., & Wyatt, R. J. (1983). Neuropathological studies of schizophrenia: A selective review. *Schizophrenia Bulletin, 9,* 193–212.

Weiner, B. (1986). *An attributional theory of motivation and emotion.* New York: Springer-Verlag.

Weingartner, H., Rudorfer, M. V., Buchsbaum, M. S., & Linnoila, M. (1983). Effects of serotonin on memory impairments produced by ethanol. *Science, 221,* 442–473.

Weinstein, S. (1968). Intensive and extensive aspects of tactile sensitivity as a function of body part, sex, and laterality. In D. R. Renshalo (Ed.), *The skin senses* (pp. 195–218). Springfield, IL: Thomas.

Weisberg, R. W. (1986). *Creativity: Genius and other myths.* New York: Freeman.

Weisberg, R. W. (1988). Problem solving and creativity. In R. J. Sternberg (Ed.), *The nature of creativity.* New York: Cambridge University Press.

Weisberg, R. W. (1992). *Creativity: Beyond the myth of genius.* New York: Freeman.

Weiss, R. S. (1975). *Marital separation.* New York: Basic Books.

Weiss, R. S. (1982). Attachment in adult life. In C. M. Parkes & J. Stevenson-Hinde (Eds.), *The place of attachment in human behavior.* New York: Basic Books.

Weissman, M. M., & Klerman, G. L. (1977). Sex differences in the epidemiology of depression. *Archives of General Psychiatry, 36,* 98–111.

Weissman, M. M., Klerman, G. L., & Paykel, E. S. (1971). Clinical evaluation of hostility in depression. *American Journal of Psychiatry, 128,* 261–266.

Weissman, M. M., & Myers, J. K. (1978). Affective disorders in a United States urban community: The use of research diagnostic criteria in an epidemiologic survey. *Archives of General Psychiatry, 35,* 1304–1311.

Weisz, J. R., Weiss, B., Hun, S. S., Granger D. A., & Morton, T. (1995). Effects of psychotherapy with children and adolescents revisited: A meta-analysis of treatment outcome studies. *Psychological Bulletin, 117,* 450–468.

Weizenbaum, J. (1966). ELIZA—A computer program for the study of natural language communication between man and machine. *Communications of the Association for Computing Machinery, 9,* 36–45.

Wells, G. L. (1993). What do we know about eyewitness identification? *American Psychologist, 48*(5), 553–571.

Welsh, D. K. (1993). Timing of sleep and wakefulness. In M. A. Carskadon (Ed.), *Encyclopedia of sleep and dreaming.* New York: Macmillan.

Werner, E. E. (1972). Infants around the world. *Journal of Cross-Cultural Psychology, 3*(2), 111–134.

Wertheimer, M. (1912). Experimentelle Studien uber das Sehen von Bewegung. *Zeitschrift fur Psychologie, 61,* 161–165.

Wertheimer, M. (1959). *Productive thinking* (Rev. ed.). New York: Harper & Row. (Original work published 1945)

Wesman, A. E., & Ricks, D. F. (1966). *Mood and personality.* New York: Holt, Rinehart & Winston.

West, R. L. (1986). Everyday memory and aging. *Developmental Neuropsychology, 2*(4), 323–344.

Westen, D. (1995). A clinical-empirical model of personality: Life after the Mischellian Ice Age and the NEO-Lithic Era. *Journal of Personality, 63,* 495–524.

Wever, E. G. (1970). *Theory of hearing.* New York: Wiley.

Wever, R. A. (1979). *The circadian system of man.* Heidelberg, West Germany: Springer-Verlag.

Wheeler, D. D. (1970). Processes in word recognition. *Cognitive Psychology, 1,* 59–85.

Wheeler, L., & Kim. Y. (1997). What is beautiful is culturally good: The physical attractiveness stereotype has different content in collectivist cultures. *Personality and Social Psychology Bulletin, 23,* 795–800.

White, B. W., & Martin, R. J. (1997). Evidence for a central mechanism of obesity in the Zucker rat: Role of neuropeptide Y and leptin. *Proceedings of the Society for Experimental Biology and Medicine, 214,* 222–232.

White, J., Joseph, S., & Neil, A. (1993). Religiosity, psychoticism, and schizotypal traits. *Personality and Individual Differences, 19,* 847–851.

White, R. W. (1959). Motivation reconsidered: The concept of competence. *Psychological Review, 66,* 297–333.

Whitley, B. E., Jr., & Frieze, I. H. (1985). Children's causal attributions for success and failure in achievement settings: A meta-analysis. *Journal of Educational Psychology, 77,* 608–616.

Whorf, B. L. (1956). In J. B. Carroll (Ed.), *Language, thought and reality: Selected writings of Benjamin Lee Whorf.* Cambridge, MA: MIT Press.

Wiesel, T. N., & Hubel, D. H. (1966). Spatial and chromatic interactions in the lateral geniculate body of the rhesus monkey. *Journal of Neurophysiology, 29*(6), 1115–1156.

Wiggins, J. S. (Ed.). (1996). *The Five-Factor Model of personality: Theoretical perspectives.* New York: Guilford Press.

Wiggins, J. S., & Trapnell, P. D. (1997). Personality structure: The return of the big five. In R. Hogan, J. Johnson, & S. R. Briggs (Eds.), *Handbook of personality psychology* (pp. 737–765). San Diego, CA: Academic Press.

Wilder, D. A., & Allen, V. L. (1978). Group membership and preference for information about others. *Personality and Social Psychology Bulletin, 4*(1), 106–110.

Williams, G. C. (1966). *Adaptation and natural selection.* Princeton, NJ: Princeton University Press.

Williams, M. (1970). *Brain damage and the mind.* London: Penguin.

Williams, R. (1986). An untrusting heart. In M. G. Walraven & H. E. Fitzgerald (Eds.), *Annuals editions: Human development 86/87.* Guilford, CT: Dushkin.

Williams, R. B., Jr. (1989*). The trusting heart.* New York: Random House.

Williams, R. B., Jr., & Barefoot, J. C. (1988). Coronary-prone behavior: The emerging role of the hostility complex. In B. K. Houston & C. R. Snyder (Eds.), *Type A behavior pattern: Current trends and future directions* (pp. 189–211). New York: Wiley.

Williams, W., Blythe, T., White, N., Li, J., Sternberg, R. J., & Gardner, H. (1996). *Practical intelligence for school.* New York: HarperCollins.

Willis, S. L. (1985). Towards an educational psychology of the older adult learner: Intellectual and cognitive bases. In J. E. Birren & K. W. Schaie (Eds.), *Handbook of the psychology of aging* (2nd ed.). New York: Van Nostrand Reinhold.

Wilson, D. W. (1981). Is helping a laughing matter? *Psychology, 18,* 6–9.

Wingert, P., & Kantrowitz, B. (1990). The day care generation. *Newsweek special edition: The 21st century family,* 86–92.

Winner, E. (1996). *Gifted children.* New York: Basic Books.

Winner, E. (1997). Exceptionally high intelligence and schooling. *American Psychologist, 52,* 1070–1081.

Winokur, G., Coryll, W., Keller, M., Endicott, J., & Leon, A. (1995). A family study of manic-depressive (Bipolar I) disease. *Archives of General Psychiatry, 52,* 367–373.

Winter, D. G. (1973). *The power motive.* New York: The Free Press.

Winter, D. G. (1992). Content analysis of archival materials, personal documents, and everyday verbal productions. In C. P. Smith (Ed.), *Motivation and personality: Handbook of thematic content analysis.* New York: Cambridge University Press.

Winter, D. G. (1993). Power, affiliation, and war: Three tests of a motivational model. *Journal of Personality and Social Psychology, 65,* 532–545.

Winter, D. G., & Stewart, A. J. (1978). Power motivation. In H. London & J. Exner (Eds.), *Dimensions of personality.* New York: Wiley.

Wissler, C. (1901). The correlation of mental and physical tests. *Psychological Review, Monograph Supplement 3*(6).

Witkin, H. A., & Berry, J. W. (1975). Psychological differentiation in cross-cultural perspective. *Journal of Cross-Cultural Psychology, 6*(1), 4–87.

Witkin, H. A., & Goodenough, D. (1981). Cognitive styles: Essence and origins. In *Psychological Monographs* (Vol. 51). New York: International Universities Press.

Wittchen, H. U., Zhao, S., Kessler, R. C., & Eaton, W. W. (1994). DSM-III-R generalized anxiety disorder in the National Comorbidity Survey. *Archives of General Psychiatry, 51,* 355–364.

Wollersheim, J. P. (1970). Effectiveness of group therapy based upon learning principles in the treatment of overweight women. *Journal of Abnormal Psychology, 76*(3, Pt. 1), 462–474.

Wolpe, J. (1958). *Psychotherapy by reciprocal inhibition.* Stanford, CA: Stanford University Press.

Woolf, N. J. (1998). A structural basis for memory storage in mammals. *Progress in Neurobiology, 55,* 59–77.

Wong, D. F., Wagner, H. N., Tune, L. E., Dannals, R. F., Pearlson, G. D., Links, J. M., Tamminga, C. A., Broussolle, E. P., Ravert, H. T., Wilson, A. A., Toung, J. K. T., Malat, J., Williams, J. A.,

O'Tuma, L. A., Snyder, S. H., Kuhar, M. J., & Gjedde, A. (1986). Positron emission tomography reveals elevated D2 dopamine receptors in drug-naive schizophrenics. *Science, 234,* 1558–1563.

Wood, W., Jones, M., & Benjamin, Jr., L. T. (1986). Surveying psychology's public image. *American Psychologist, 41,* 947–953.

Woodruff, R. A., Goodwin, D. W., & Guze, S. B. (1974). *Psychiatric diagnosis.* New York: Oxford University Press.

Woodworth, R. S. (1918). *Dynamic psychology.* New York: Columbia University Press.

Woolfolk, R. L., Carr-Kaffashan, K., McNulty, T. F., & Lehrer P. M. (1976). Meditation training as a treatment for insomnia. *Behavior Therapy, 7,* 359–365.

Woon, T., Masuda, M., Wagner, N. N., & Holmes, T. H. (1971). The *Social Readjustment Rating Scale:* A cross-cultural study of Malaysians and Americans. *Journal of Cross-Cultural Psychology, 2,* 373–386.

World Health Organization. (1992). *International classification of diseases* (10th ed.). Geneva: Author.

Wright, R. (1994). *The moral animal.* New York: Vintage.

Wright, R. H. (1977). Odor and molecular vibration: Neural coding of olfactory information. *Journal of Theoretical Biology, 64,* 473–502.

Wright, R. H. (1982). *The sense of smell.* Boca Raton, FL: CRC Press.

Wynn, K. (1995). Infants possess a system of numerical knowledge. *Current Directions in Psychological Science, 4,* 172–177.

Yahiro, K., Inoue, M., & Nozawa, Y. (1993). An examination on the *Social Readjustment Rating Scale* (Holmes et al.) by Japanese subjects. *Japanese Journal of Health Psychology, 6*(1), 18–32.

Yalom, I. D. (1992). *When Nietzsche wept.* New York: Basic Books.

Yamamoto, T., Yuyama, N., & Kawamura, Y. (1981a). Central processing of taste perception. In Y. Katsuki, R. Norgren, & M. Sato (Eds.), *Brain mechanisms of sensation.* New York: Wiley.

Yamamoto, T., Yuyama, N., & Kawamura, Y. (1981b). Cortical neurons responding to tactile, thermal and taste stimulations of the rat's tongue. *Brain Research, 221*(1), 202–206.

Yang, K. (1986). Chinese personality and its change. In M. H. Bond (Ed.), *The psychology of the Chinese people.* Hong Kong: Oxford University Press.

Yaniv, I., & Meyer, D. E. (1987). Activation and metacognition of inaccessible stored information: Potential bases of incubation effects in problem solving. *Journal of Experimental Psychology: Learning, Memory, and Cognition, 13,* 187–205.

Yerkes, R. M., & Dodson, J. B. (1908). The relation of strength of stimulus to rapidity of habit formation. *Journal of Comparative Neurology and Psychology, 18,* 459–482.

Yonkers, K. A., Warshaw, M. G., Massion, A. O., & Keller, M. B. (1996). Phenomenology and course of generalized anxiety disorder. *British Journal of Psychiatry, 168,* 308–313.

Young, J., & Klosko, J. (1993). *Reinventing your life.* New York: St. Martin's Press.

Young, J. E. (1990). *Cognitive therapy for personality disorders: A schema-focused approach.* Sarasota, FL: Professional Resource Exchange.

Young, T. (1948). Observations on vision. In W. Dennis (Ed.), *Readings in the history of psychology* (pp. 96–101). New York: Appleton-Century-Crofts. (Original work published 1901)

Yuille, J. C. (1993). We must study forensic eyewitnesses to know about them. *American Psychologist, 48*(5), 572–573.

Yussen, S. R. (1977). Characteristics of moral dilemmas written by adolescents. *Developmental Psychology, 13,* 162–163.

Yzerbyt, V. Y., Rocher, S., & Schadron, G. (1996). Stereotypes as explanations: A subjective essentialistic view of group perception. In R. Spears, P. J. Oakes, N. Ellemers, & S. A. Haslam (Eds.), *The social psychology of stereotyping and group life.* Cambridge: Blackwell.

Zaidel, E. (1983). A response to Gazzaniga: Language in the right hemisphere, convergent perspectives. *American Psychologist, 38*(5), 542–546.

Zajonc, R. B. (1965). Social facilitation. *Science, 149,* 269–274.

Zajonc, R. B. (1968). Attitudinal effects of mere exposure. *Journal of Personality and Social Psychology Monograph Supplement, 9*(2), 1–27.

Zajonc, R. B. (1980). Compliance. In P. B. Paulus (Ed.), *Psychology of group influence* (pp. 35–60). Hillsdale, NJ: Erlbaum.

Zajonc, R. B. (1984). On the primacy of affect. *American Psychologist, 39,* 117–129.

Zajonc, R. B. (1998). Emotions. In D. T. Gilbert, S. T. Fiske, & G. Lindzey (Eds.), *The handbook of social psychology* (4th ed., Vol. 2, pp. 591–632). New York: McGraw-Hill.

Zajonc, R. B., Heingartner, A., & Herman, E. M. (1969). Social enhancement and impairment of performance in the cockroach. *Journal of Personality and Social Psychology, 22,* 242–248.

Zajonc, R. B., Pietromonaco, P., & Bargh, J. (1982). Independence and interaction of affect and cognition. In M. S. Clark & S. T. Fiske (Eds.), *Affect and cognition* (pp. 211–227). Hillsdale, NJ: LEA Publications.

Zaleski, C. (1987). *Otherworld journeys: Accounts of near-death experience in medieval and modern times.* Oxford, England: Oxford University Press.

Zamansky, H. S., & Bartis, S. P. (1985). The dissociation of an experience: The hidden observer observed. *Journal of Abnormal Psychology, 94,* 243–248.

Zanna, M. P., & Hamilton, D. L. (1972). Attribute dimension and patterns of trait inferences. *Psychonomic Science, 27,* 353–354.

Zanna, M. P., & Hamilton, D. L. (1977). Further evidence for meaning change in impression formation. *Journal of Experimental Social Psychology, 13,* 224–238.

Zaragoza, M. S., McCloskey, M., & Jamis, M. (1987). Misleading postevent information and recall of the original event: Further evidence against the memory impairment hypothesis. *Journal of Experimental Psychology: Learning, Memory, and Cognition, 13,* 36–44.

Zentall, T. (2000). Animal intelligence. In R. J. Sternberg (Ed.), *Handbook of intelligence.* New York: Cambridge University Press.

Zigler, E. (1982). Development versus difference theories of mental retardation and the problem of motivation. In E. Zigler & D. Balla (Eds.), *Mental retardation: The developmental-difference controversy.* Hillsdale, NJ: Erlbaum.

Zigler, E., & Berman, W. (1983). Discerning the future of early childhood intervention. *American Psychologist, 38,* 894–906.

Zimbardo, P. G. (1972, April). Psychology of imprisonment. *Transition/Society,* pp. 4–8.

Zimbardo, P. G., Weisenberg, M., Firestone, I., & Levy, B. (1965). Communicator effectiveness in producing public conformity and private attitude change. *Journal of Personality, 33,* 233–255.

Zimmerman, B. J., Bandura, A., & Martinez-Pons, M. (1992). Self-motivation for academic attainment: The role of self-efficacy beliefs and personal goal setting. *American Educational Research Journal, 29,* 663–676.

Zola-Morgan, S. M., & Squire, L. R. (1990). The primate hippocampal formation: Evidence for a time-limited role in memory storage. *Science, 250,* 228–290.

Zubin, J., Magaziner, J., & Steinhauer, S. R. (1983). The metamorphosis of schizophrenia: From chronicity to vulnerability. *Psychological Medicine, 13,* 551–571.

Zubin, J., & Spring, B. (1977). Vulnerability—a new view of schizophrenia. *Journal of Abnormal Psychology, 86,* 103–126.

Zuckerman, H. (1983). The scientific elite: Nobel laureates' mutual influences. In R. S. Albert (Ed.), *Genius and eminence: The social psychology of creativity and exceptional achievement* (Vol. 5, pp. 241–252). New York: Pergamon.

Zuckerman, M. (1969). Response set in Check List Test: A sometimes thing. *Psychological Reports, 25*(3), 773–774.

Zuckerman, M. (1978). Sensation seeking. In H. London & J. E. Exner (Eds.), *Dimensions of personality* (pp. 487–560). New York: Wiley.

Zuckerman, M. (1979). *Sensation seeking: Beyond the optimal level of arousal.* Hillsdale, NJ: Erlbaum.

Zuckerman, M. (1985). Biological foundations of the sensation-seeking temperament. In J. Strelau, F. H. Farley, & A. Gale (Eds.), *The biological bases of personality and behavior: Vol. 1. Theories, measurement techniques, and development.* Washington, DC: Hemisphere.

Zuckerman, M. (1990). The psychophysiology of sensation seeking. *Journal of Personality, 58,* 313–345.

Zuckerman, M. (1994). *Behavioral expressions and biosocial bases of sensation seeking.* New York: Cambridge University Press.

Zuckerman, M. (1998). Psychobiological theories of personality. In D. F. Barone, M. Hersen, & V. B. Van Hasselt (Eds.), *Advanced personality* (pp. 123–154).

Zuckerman, M., Klorman, R., Larrance, D. T., & Speigel, N. H. (1981). Facial, autonomic, and subjective components of emotion: The facial feedback hypothesis versus the externalizer-internalizer distinction. *Journal of Personality and Social Psychology, 41,* 929–944.

CREDITS

ILLUSTRATION AND LITERARY

Chapter 3
Opener, Reprinted with the permission of Simon & Schuster from THE MAN WHO MISTOOK HIS WIFE FOR A HAT AND OTHER CLINICAL TALES by Oliver Sacks. Copyright © 1970, 1981, 1983, 1984, 1985 by Oliver Sacks.

Chapter 4
Opener, Excerpt from Tom Clancy THE CARDINAL OF THE KREMLIN; Table 4-1, p. 109, Galanter, Eugene. (1962). Contemporary psychophysics. In R. Brown et al., (Eds.), *New Directions in Psychology*, New York: Holt, Rinehart & Winston, p. 97. Reprinted by permission; Figure 4-24, p. 128, James J. Gibson, "Shape Constancy Illusion—Door," from *The Ecological Approach to Visual Perception*. Copyright © 1979 James J. Gibson. Reprinted by permission; Figure 4-35, p. 127, "Biederman's Geons" in "Geons" by I. Biederman from *Computer Vision, Graphics, and Image Processing*, 1985, No.32. Copyright © 1985 Academic Press, Inc. Reprinted by permission; Figure 4-46, p. 153, "Average Absolute Thresholds for Different Regions of the Female and Male Skin," from Weinstein and Kenshalo, *The Skin Senses*, 1968, pp. 195–218. Courtesy of Charles C. Thomas, Publisher, Ltd., Springfield, IL.

Chapter 5
Opener and p. xiv, Excerpt from SONG OF SOLOMON by Toni Morrison. Reprinted by permission of International Creative Management, Inc. Copyright © 1977 Alfred A. Knopf, Inc.; Table 5-2, p. 178, From "The University of Typical Dreams: Japanese vs. Americans" by R.M. Griffith et al., *American Anthropologist*, Vol. 60, 1958, pp. 1173–1179. Copyright © 1958 by the American Anthropological Association. Reproduced by permission of the American Anthropological Association. Not for further sale or reproduction; Figure 5-3, p. 175, From Hartmann, THE BIOLOGY OF DREAMING, 1967. Courtesy of Charles C. Thomas, Publisher, Ltd., Springfield, Illinois.

Chapter 7
Opener, Reprinted by permission of the publishers and the Trustees of Amherst College from THE POEMS OF EMILY DICKINSON, Ralph W. Franklin, ed., Cambridge, Mass.: The Belknap Press of Harvard University Press. Copyright © 1998 by the President and Fellows of Harvard College. Copyright © 1951, 1955, 1979 by the President and Fellows of Harvard College; Figure 7-1, p. 232, From "The Control of Short-term Memory" by Atkinson & Shiffrin, August 1971, *Scientific American*. Artwork by Allen Beechel; Figure 7-6, p. 240, "Visual Images Preserve Metric Spatial Information" by Kosslyn et al., *Journal of Experimental Psychology*, No. 4, pp. 47–60, 1978. Copyright © 1978 by the American Psychological Association. Reprinted with permission; Figure 7-9, p. 246, Bartlett, Sir Frederic C., "The War of the Ghosts'" from REMEMBERING, p. 65. Copyright Cambridge University Press. Reprinted by permission of the publisher; p. 250, Poem #1273 from *The Poems of Emily Dickinson*. Reprinted by permission of the publishers and the Trustees of Amherst College from *The Poems of Emily Dickinson*, Thomas H. Johnson, ed., Cambridge, MA: The Belknap Press of Harvard University Press, Copyright © 1951, 1955, 1979, 1983 by the President and Fellows of Harvard College.

Chapter 8
Table 8-2, p. 281, Luchins, A. S., "Water Jar Problems" from "Mechanization in Problem Solving: The Effect of Einstellung," *Psychological Monographs*, Vol. 54, No. 6, 1942, p. 1. Reprinted by permission of the author.

Chapter 12
Figure 12-2, p. 396, "Acquired Motivation" by R. Solomon & Corbitt, *Psychological Review*, No. 81, pp. 119–145, 1974. Copyright © 1974 by the American Psychological Association. Reprinted with permission; Figure 12-5, p. 410, R. Plutchik "A Language for the Emotions," *Psychology Today*, February 1980. Reprinted with permission from *Psychology Today* Magazine. Copyright © 1980 Sussex Publishers, Inc.; Figure 12-6, p. 413, Figure from UNMASKING THE FACE, 2nd edition, by Ekman & Friesen. Copyright © 1984. Reprinted by permission of the author; Figure 12-7, p. 414, from Levenson, Ekman, & Friesen, 1990. Reprinted by permission of the author.

Chapter 13
Opener, Reprinted with the permission of Simon & Schuster from THE MAN WHO MISTOOK HIS WIFE FOR A HAT AND OTHER CLINICAL TALES by Oliver Sacks. Copyright © 1970, 1981, 1983, 1984, 1985 by Oliver Sacks; Figure 13-3, p. 432, "Qualifying Conditions for Cognitive Dissonance" from INTRODUCTION TO SOCIAL PSYCHOLOGY, R. A. Lippa. Copyright © 1990, 1994. Reprinted by permission of the author; Table 13-1, p. 436, "Trait Data/Impression Formation," S. E. Asch, *Journal of Abnormal and Social Psychology*, Vol. 41, 1946, pp. 258–290. Reprinted by permission of the author.

Chapter 14
Figure 14-2, p. 451, "Social Loafing," Latané et al., *Journal of Personality and Social Psychology*, Vol. 37, 1979, pp. 822–832. Copyright © 1974 by the American Psychological Association. Reprinted with permission; Figure 14-4, p. 456, "Line Length and Group Influence" by Solomon Asch, 1956. Reprinted by permission of Solomon Asch; Figure 14-6, p. 461, "Milgram's Results on Voltage Levels," from OBEDIENCE TO AUTHORITY by Stanley Milgram. Copyright © 1974 by Stanley Milgram. Reprinted by permission of HarperCollins Publishers, Inc.; Figure 14-8, p. 473, C. Anderson, "Temperature and Aggression" *Psychological Bulletin*, Vol. 106, 1989, pp. 74–96. Reprinted by permission of the author.

Chapter 15
Figure 15-7, p. 504, Minnesota Multiphasic Personality Inventory (MMPI). Copyright © the University of Minnesota 1943 (renewed 1970). This report 1983. Reprinted by permission of the University of Minnesota Press.

Chapter 16
Table 16-1, p. 516, "DSM-IV Axes" reprinted with permission from the DIAGNOSTIC AND STATISTICAL MANUAL OF MENTAL DISORDERS, Fourth Edition. Copyright © 1994 American Psychiatric Association; Figure 16-1, p. 523, "Anxiety and Exams" by N. Bolger, *Journal of Personality and Social Psychology*, Vol. 59, No. 3, p. 531, 1990. Copyright © 1990 by the American Psychological Association. Reprinted with permission.

Chapter 17
Figure 17-4, p. 555, "Effectiveness of Various Therapies," Bandura et al., *Journal of Personality and Social Psychology*, Vol. 13, 1969,

pp. 173–199. Copyright © 1969 by the American Psychological Association. Reprinted with permission; Table 17-1, p. 556, "List of Common Irrational Beliefs." Reprinted by permission of Albert Ellis, Institute for Rational Emotive Behavior Therapy; Table 17-2, p. 563, The Twelve Steps are reprinted with permission of Alcoholics Anonymous World Services, Inc. (A.A.W.S.). Permission to reprint the Twelve Steps does not mean that A.A.W.S. has reviewed or approved the contents of this publication, or that A.A.W.S. necessarily agrees with the view expressed herein. A.A. is a program of recovery from alcoholism *only*—use of the Twelve Steps in connection with programs and activities that are patterned after A.A., but which address other problems, or in any other non-A.A. context, does not imply otherwise.

Chapter 18
Figure 18-2, p. 581, GENERAL ADAPTATION SYNDROME from STRESS WITHOUT DISTRESS by Hans Selye, M.D. Copyright © 1974 by Hans Selye, M.D. Reprinted by permission of HarperCollins Publishers, Inc.

PHOTOS

Chapter 1
p. 2, Jean-Pierre Stora "Les Flaneurs" 1995. The Grand Design/SuperStock; p. 4, left, © Charles Gupton/Stock Boston; p. 4, right, PhotoEdit; p. 7, Vatican Museums and Galleries/Scala/SuperStock; p. 8, Archives of the History of American Psychology, University of Akron; p. 9, Archives of the History of American Psychology, University of Akron; p. 11, Archives of the History of American Psychology, University of Akron; p. 13, Culver Pictures; p. 15, top, CORBIS/Bettmann; p. 15, bottom, Archives of the History of American Psychology, University of Akron; p. 18, Chris J. Johnson/Stock Boston; p. 19, top (both), Georges Seurat, French, 1859–1891. A Sunday on La Grande Jatte–1884, oil on canvas, 1884–86, 207.6 x 308 cm, Helen Birch Bartlett memorial Collections, 1926.224, photograph © 1997, Art Institute of Chicago; p. 19, bottom, Courtesy of Wellesley College Archives; p. 20, © The New Yorker Collection 1993 Tom Cheney from cartoonbank.com. All rights reserved; p. 22, top, The Granger Collection, New York; p. 22, bottom, © William Carter/Brooks Cole Publishing; p. 23, Courtesy of Dr. Natalie Rogers.

Chapter 2
p. 30, Henri Martin, "A Couple." Study for the decoration of City Hall in the 5th arondissement, Paris. 1932–1935. Oil on canvas. Musee du Petit Palais, Paris, France. Giraudon/Art Resource. © 2001 Artists Rights Society (ARS), New York/ADAGP, Paris; p. 35, © Christiana Dittmann/Rainbow; p. 38, Archives of the History of American Psychology, University of Akron; p. 39, © Bob Daemmrich/Stock Boston; p. 43, Photo by Ken Regan/ Courtesy of the Jane Goodall Institute; p. 44, top, © Michael Newman/PhotoEdit; p. 44, bottom, © The New Yorker Collection 1975 Robert Weber from cartoonbank.com. All right reserved; p. 47, AP/Wide World Photos; p. 49, © David Young–Wolff/PhotoEdit.

Chapter 3
pp. xxvi, 58, © SuperStock; p. 60, © Jeff Greenberg/The Image Works; p. 62, ©Alfred Pasieka/ SPL/Photo Researchers; p. 65, © Quest/SPL/Photo Researchers; p. 66, © Alexander Tsiaras/Stock Boston; p. 67, Custom Medical Stock Photo; p. 71, ©Secch-Lecaque/Roussell-UCLAF/SPL/Photo Researchers; p. 74, © Manfred Kage/ Peter Arnold, Inc.; p. 81, © J. Croyle/Custom Medical Stock Photo; p. 82 (all) Kobal Collection; p. 83, © Karen Kas-

mauski/Woodfin Camp & Associates/PictureQuest; p. 86, © Biophoto Associates/Science Source/Photo Researchers; p. 87, © Biophoto Associates/Science Source/Photo Researchers; p. 88, Larry Mulvehill/Photo Researchers; p. 89, © M. Romine/SuperStock; p. 90, top, © CNRI/SPL/Photo Researchers; p. 90, center top, © Ohio Nuclear Corporation/Photo Researchers; p. 90, center bottom, CNRI/SPL/Photo Researchers; p. 90, bottom, © Spencer Grant/Stock Boston; p. 92, left, © John C. Mazziotte/PhotoEdit; p. 92, right, NIH/Science Source/Photo Researchers; p. 95, AP/Wide World Photos; p. 100 CNRI/SPl/Photo Researchers.

Chapter 4
pp. xxvii, 106, Rene Magritte "La Belle Captive" 1947. Christie's Images/SuperStock. © 2001 Artists Rights Society (ARS), New York; p. 109, © Janet Fries/Photo 20–20; p. 112, © Owen Franken/Stock Boston; p. 113, © Johnny Crawford/The Image Works; p. 117, © Ralph C. Eagle, Jr. M.D./Photo Researchers; p. 119, left, © T. J. Florian/Rainbow; p. 119, right, © Michael J. Howell/Rainbow; p. 121, both, © Leonard Lessin/Peter Arnold, Inc.; p. 122, Courtesy of Macbeth/Munsell Color, New Windsor, New York; p. 123 (both); Fritz Goro, Life © Time Warner; p. 125, top, © Anestis Diakopoulos/Stock Boston; p. 125, bottom, © Erich Lessing/Art Resource, NY; p. 126 (both), © Norman Snyder 1987; p. 128, Johannes Vermeer, WOMAN HOLDING A BALANCE, Widener Colleciton, © 2000 Board of Trustees, National Gallery of Art, Washington, c. 1664; p. 129, top, The Granger Collection, New York; p. 129, bottom, © CORBIS/Bettmann; p. 133, Kaiser Porcelain Ltd. London, England; p. 141, © Biophoto Associates/Science Source/Photo Researchers; p. 142, Dr. J. E. Hawkins, Kresge Hearing Research Institute; p. 144, © David Young–Wolff/PhotoEdit; p. 152, © Ed Reschke/Peter Arnold, Inc.; p. 153, © Claus Meyer/Black Star; p. 154, © Jean Yves Roszniewski/Photo Researchers; p. 155, top, © Tony Savino/The Image Works; p. 155, bottom, © Biophoto Associates/Science Source/Photo Researchers.

Chapter 5
pp. xxviii, 162, John S. Bunker "In the Sky with Diamonds" 1997. © John Bunker/SuperStock; p. 166, © Cynthia S. Eiler/Stock Boston; p. 169, © SuperStock; p. 171, © Phyllis Picardi/Stock Boston; p. 172, Michel Siffre, © National Geographic; p. 173, © Kathy Ferguson/PhotoEdit; p. 175, ©Philippe Plailly/Photo Researchers; p. 176 © Greig Cranna/Stock Boston; p. 177, © 2000 Joe Dator from cartoonbank.com. All right reserved; p. 179, © Will and Deni McIntyre/Photo Researchers; p. 180, © National Library of Medicine/Peter Arnold, Inc.; p. 181, Stanford University Press; p. 186, © Robert E. Daemmrich/STONE; p. 190, © Alex Farnsworth/Stock Boston; p. 191, © The New Yorker Collection 1958 Garrett Price from cartoonbank.com. All rights reserved.

Chapter 6
p. 196, Jean Puy "Study" or "The Schoolgirl" c. 1933–34. Oil on canvas. Musee d'Art Moderne de la Ville de Paris, Paris, France. Giraudon/Art Resource, NY. © 2001 Artists Rights Society (ARS) New York, ADAGP, Paris199, © CORBIS/Bettmann; p. 202, © The New Yorker Collection 1995 Gahan Wilson from cartoonbank.com. All right reserved; p. 208, Courtesy of Dr. John Garcia; p. 209, © David Young–Wolff/PhotoEdit; p. 213, © 2000 Joe Dator from cartoonbank.com. All rights reserved; p. 215, left, © Kim Massie/Rainbow; page 215, right, © Martha Cooper/Peter Arnold, Inc.; p. 217, © Bill Greene/Liaison Agency; p. 222, (all), Dr. Albert Bandura.

Chapter 7
pp. xxix, 228, G. G. Kopilak "To Bill." Private Collection/GG Kopilak/SuperStock; p. 231, © T. Rosenthal/SuperStock; p. 233, © Pat Murray/Animals Animals; p. 234, © Jeffry W. Myers/Stock Boston; p. 235, © Lee Snider/The Image Works; p. 239, © Jim

Cartier/Photo Researchers; p. 243, top, © The New Yorker Collection 1992 Robert Mankoff from cartoonbank.com. All rights reserved; p. 243, bottom, © Gale Zucker/Stock Boston; p. 247, top, © Michael Newman/PhotoEdit; p. 247, bottom, © Billy e. Barnes/Stock Boston; p. 248, © AP/Wide World Photos; p. 254, © Cecil Fox/Science Source/Photo Researchers.

Chapter 8
pp. xxx, 260, Jacob Lawrence "The Library" 1960. Tempera on fiberboard. National Museum of American Art, Washington DC/Art Resource, NY; p. 263, © Paul Fusco/Magnum Photos; p. 264, © Wellcome Department of Cognitive Neurology/SPL/Photo Researchers; p. 271, © David Young–Wolff/PhotoEdit; p. 274, © Will and Deni McIntyre/Photo Researchers; p. 276, © The New Yorker Collection 1976 James Stevenson from cartoonbank.com. All rights reserved; p. 280, (all), © SuperStock; p. 281, left, © Scala/Art Resource, NY; p. 281, right, Paul Cezanne, *Mont Sainte–Victoire*, Philadelphia Museum of Art; George W. Elkins Collection; p. 282, © T. Michaels/The Image Works; p. 285, left, © Michael Grecco/Stock Boston; p. 285, right, © David G. Curran/Rainbow; p. 289, left, © Giraudon/Art Resource, NY; p. 289, right, Rijks Museum Kroller–Muller Otterlo/A.K.G. Berlin/SuperStock; p. 291, © Christiana Dittmann/Rainbow.

Chapter 9
p. 296, Tsing-Fang Chen "Human Achievement." Lucia Gallery, New York City/TF Chen/SuperStock; p. 299, © Rollie McKenna/Photo Researchers; p. 300, © The New Yorker Collection 1998 J. B. Handelsman from cartoonbank.com. All rights reserved; p. 302, left, © Mimi Forsyth/Monkmeyer; p. 302, right, © Bob Daemmrich/The Image Works; p. 311, Courtesy of Dr. Michael Cole; p. 312, © Tom McCarthy/Rainbow; p. 314, © CORBIS/Bettmann; p. 320, © T. K. Wanstal/The Image Works; p. 321, © Dan McCoy/Rainbow.

Chapter 10
pp. xxxi, 326, Kitagawa Utamaro "Yamauba and Kintoki." Engraving. Galerie Janette Ostier, Paris, France. Giraudon/Art Resource, NY; p. 329, © The New Yorker Collection 1999 Bruce Eric Kaplan from cartoonbank.com. All rights reserved; p. 330, (all), © B. D. Lanphere/Stock Boston; p. 334, © Publiphoto/Explorer/Photo Researchers; p. 337, top and top center, © Myrleen Ferguson Cate/PhotoEdit; p. 337, bottom center, © Michael Newman/PhotoEdit; p. 337, bottom, © Tom McCarthy/PhotoEdit; p. 339, © Bill Anderson/Monkmeyer; p. 341, both, © Goodman/Monkmeyer; p. 342, (all), © Tony Freeman/PhotoEdit; p. 345, top, © Christiana Dittmann/Rainbow; p. 345, bottom, © Charles D. Winters/Stock Boston; p. 346, © Mark Antman/The Image Works; p. 347, Archives of the History of American Psychology, University of Akron; p. 353, © Bill Bachmann/Stock Boston.

Chapter 11
pp. xxxii, 358, Christian Pierre "All Sorts" 1996. Private Collection/Christian Pierre/SuperStock; p. 360, top left, © George Chan/Photo Researchers; p. 360, top center, © Tom Prettyman/PhotoEdit; p. 360, top right, © Myrleen Ferguson Cate/PhotoEdit; p. 360, bottom, © David Young–Wolff/PhotoEdit; p. 362, © Michael Newman/PhotoEdit; p. 367, © Chris Rogers/Rainbow; p. 369, © Sue Ann Miller/STONE; p. 371, Courtesy of Dr. Mary Strange; p. 373, © Bill Lai/Rainbow; p. 374, both, Harlow Primate Lab, University of Wisconsin; p. 384, © Steven D. Starr/Stock Boston.

Chapter 12
p. 392, Albert Bloch "Ragtime." Christie's Images/SuperStock; p. 394, © The New Yorker Collection 1991 Edward Frascino from cartoonbank.com. All rights reserved; p. 397, © Peter Gregoire/

Index Stock Imagery/PictureQuest; p. 402, Harlow Primate Lab, University of Wisconsin; p. 404, © Richard Howard; p. 406 (both), © William Thompson/Index Stock Imagery; p. 411, © Nita Winter/The Image Works; p. 412, © Tom Walker/Stock Boston; p. 415, (all), Ekman, P., Friesen, W. V., & O'Sullivan, M. (1988). Smiles: "Genuine" and "Fake." *Journal of Personality and Social Psychology; 54*, 414–420; p. 418, © Jerry Millevoi/Stock Boston.

Chapter 13
pp. xxxiii, 422, Romare Bearden "The Family" 1988. Collage on wood. National Museum of American Art, Washington DC/Art Resource, NY. © Romare Bearden Foundation/Licensed by VAGA, New York, NY; p. 424, © Jeff Greenberg/PhotoEdit; p. 426, © CORBIS/Bettmann; p. 430, © Joe Sohm/The Image Works; p. 435, © Michael Newman/PhotoEdit; p. 441, © Christiana Dittmann/Rainbow; p. 442, left, © Martha Cooper/Peter Arnold, Inc.; p. 442, right, © Kavaler/Art Resource, NY.

Chapter 14
p. 448, "Mujeres Conversando" by Rufino Tamayo. Christie's Images/SuperStock. Authorized reproduction by the inheritors of the artist in support of the Fundación Olga y Rufino Tamayo, A.C.; p. 450, © Eric O'Connell/FPG International/PictureQuest; p. 456, all, Dr. Solomon Asch; p. 460, all, Copyright 1965 by Stanley Milgram. From the film OBEDIENCE distributed by the Pennsylvania State University Media Sales; p. 462, © Reuters Newsmedia Inc./CORBIS; p. 463, both, © AP/Wide World Photos; p. 469, top, © Mark Richards/PhotoEdit; p. 469, bottom, © A. Ramey/Stock Boston; p. 470, © Bob Daemmrich/Stock Boston; p. 471, © The New Yorker Collection 1993 Jack Ziegler from cartoonbank.com. All rights reserved.

Chapter 15
pp. xxxiv, 478, Andy Warhol, Four Marilyns, c. 1962. Synthetic polymer paint and silkscreen ink on canvas. The Andy Warhol Foundation, Inc./Art Resource, NY. © Andy Warhol Foundation for the Visual Arts/ARS, New York; p. 480, © Reuters News Media Inc./CORBIS; p. 481, © Hulton-Deutsch Collection/CORBIS; p. 486, © UPI/Bettmann/CORBIS; p. 487, © Bettmann/Corbis; p. 488, top, National Library of Medicine; p. 488, bottom, © The Granger Collection, New York; p. 489, © Myrleen Ferguson/PhotoEdit; p. 493, top, Courtesy of Dr. Julian Rotter; p. 493, bottom, © The New Yorker Collection 1988 Robert Weber from cartoonbank.com. All rights reserved.

Chapter 16
pp. xxxv, 510, Egon Schiele "Male Nude with Red Cloth." Graphische Sammlung Albertina, Vienna, Austria. Copyright Nimatallah/Art Resource, NY; p. 512, © The Granger Collection, New York; p. 515, © Joseph Sohm/Chromosohm Inc./CORBIS; p. 520, left, © Bill Horsman/Stock Boston; p. 520, top right, © Bernard Gerard/Explorer/Photo Researchers; p. 520, bottom left, © J. Griffin/The Image Works; p. 520, bottom right, G Marc Deville/Liaison Agency; p. 522, National Gallery, Oslo, Norway/Bridgeman Art Library, London/SuperStock; p. 526, © Bill Aron/PhotoEdit; p. 530, © Nancy Hayes/Monkmeyer; p. 533, © Grunnitus/Monkmeyer; p. 536, © NIH/Science Source/Photo Researchers; p. 539, © The New Yorker Collection 1955 Richard Taylor from cartoonbank.com. All rights reserved.

Chapter 17
pp. xxxvi, 544, Daniel Nevins "Conversation" © Daniel Nevins/SuperStock; p. 546, © CORBIS/Bettmann; p. 548, all, © Dan McCoy/Rainbow; p. 549, G Rhoda Sidney/Stock Boston; p. 553, © Michael Newman/PhotoEdit; p. 557, Courtesy of Aaron Beck; p. 561, © Martin Rogers/Stock Boston; p. 562, © Jim Pickerell/Stock Boston; p. 564, top, Zigy Kaluzny/STONE; p. 564, bottom,

Chapter 18
p. 574, Aleksandr N. Samokvalov "The Sportswoman," Tretyakov Gallery, Moscow, Russia/SuperStock. © Estate of Aleksandr Samokhvalov/Licensed by VAGA, New York, NY; p. 578, top, © Nik Wheeler/CORBIS; p. 578, bottom, © Robert Brenner/PhotoEdit; p. 584, G Myrleen Ferguson/PhotoEdit; p. 587, © Guycali/Stock Connection/PictureQuest; p. 590, © Bob Daemmrich/Stock Boston.

Name Index

Abel, L., 309
Abelson, R. P., 268
Abrams, R., 557
Abramson, L. Y., 529
Adams, G. R., 531
Adams, M. J., 322
Adelson, J., 377
Adler, A., 486, 501, 524
Adler, N., 584
Adler, S. A., 248
Agnew, J., 556
Ahlborn, H. H., 384
Ahmed, S., 173
Ahn, W.-K., 345
Ainsworth, M. D. S., 371–372, 385, 443, 489
Alberini, C., 221
Albert, D. J., 471
Aldhous, M., 173
Alexander, J., 586
Alexander, J. M., 349
Alicke, M. D., 438
Allen, R., 263
Allen, V. L., 467
Allison, T., 171
Alloy, L. B., 529
Allport, G. W., 424, 468, 495, 506
Almagor, M., 518
Amabile, T. M., 289, 400
Ames, C., 402
Amsel, E., 329
Anand, B. K., 403
Anastasi, A., 304
Andersen, C., 345, 350
Anderson, C. A., 472, 473
Anderson, J. R., 20, 240
Anderson, K. O., 587
Anderson, N. B., 584
Andersson, B. E., 376
Andreasen, N. C., 525, 535
Andrews, G., 561, 568
Angelou, M., 290
Angleitner, A., 496
Antrobus, J., 171
Appelbaum, M. I., 339
Aral, S. O., 581
Archer, J., 370, 471
Arend, R., 372
Arendt, J., 173
Arieti, S., 534
Aristotle, 6–7, 7–8, 14, 27
Arkes, H. R., 427
Armeli, S., 401
Armor, D. A., 31
Arnold, K. D., 384
Arnold, M. B., 418
Aron, A. P., 438, 444
Aronson, J., 46
Asch, S. E., 435–436, 436–437, 455–457, 458, 475
Asher, S. R., 373
Aspinwall, L. G., 593
Asquith, P., 380
Astington, J. W., 349
Atkinson, J. W., 398, 503
Atkinson, R. C., 176, 192, 232
Atkinson, R. L., 176
Attanucci, J., 384
Atwater, J. B., 370
Auerbach, S. M., 586
Averill, J. R., 410, 471
Axelson, J. A., 561
Azrin, N. H., 472
Azuma, S. D., 334

Bacal, H. A., 489
Back, K., 440
Bacon, F., 8
Baddeley, A. D., 234, 244, 245, 249, 250, 251
Bagwell, C., 376
Bahrick, H. P., 242, 243, 351
Bahrick, L. E., 401
Bahrick, P. O., 243, 351
Bailey, C., 338
Bailey, C. H., 221
Bailey, J. M., 408
Baillargeon, R., 345
Baker, D. P., 367
Bales, R. F., 450
Balkin, J., 468
Ball, T. M., 240
Ballenger, J. C., 559
Balter, M. B., 176
Baltes, P. B., 351, 352, 353
Banaji, M. R., 269, 467
Bandura, A., 222, 370, 402, 471, 492, 493–494, 501, 524, 555
Banks, M. S., 335
Bao, J. X., 221
Barber, J. P., 560
Barber, T. X., 181
Bard, P., 415, 420
Barefoot, J. C., 584
Bargh, J. A., 418, 467
Barker, R. G., 472
Barlow, D. H., 525
Barnackie, K., 560
Barnes, M. L., 30, 444, 487
Baron, M., 559
Baron, R. A., 470, 471, 472
Baron, R. S., 451
Barr, C. E., 535
Barr, H. M., 334
Barrett, K. C., 363
Barrett, P. T., 309
Barry, T., 472
Bartholomew, K., 373
Bartis, S. P., 182

Bartlett, F. C., 245
Bartlett, K., 429
Bartoshuk, L. M., 145, 146
Bashore, T. R., 351
Basoglu, M., 580
Basow, S. A., 425
Bassok, M., 287
Bastik, T., 282
Bates, J. E., 368
Batson, C. D., 464, 465
Batson, J. G., 465
Baum, A., 586
Baumeister, R. F., 182, 439
Baumrind, D., 375, 384
Baumstark, K. E., 381
Bava, A., 182
Baxter, L. R., 548
Bayley, N., 332, 335
Baynes, K., 79
Bazana, P. G., 309
Beach, F. A., 440
Beall, A., 370
Beatty, W. W., 405
Beck, A. T., 525, 529, 555, 556, 557, 560, 564, 572
Beeri, R., 254
Beidel, D. C., 524
Beilin, H., 330
Bekerian, D. A., 249
Békésy, G. von, 143
Bell, P. A., 472
Bell, S. M., 371
Belloc, N. D., 576
Bellugi, U., 273
Belsky, J., 373, 376
Bem, D. J., 176, 408, 431, 432
Bem, S. L., 370
Benbow, C. P., 369, 438
Benjamin, L. T., Jr., 10, 11
Bennett, M., 329
Bennett, M. J., 568
Bennion, L. D., 531
Benotsch, E. G., 584
Benschop, R. J., 578
Ben-Shakhar, G., 413
Benson, A. J., 156
Benson, H., 183
Ben-Zeev, T., 34, 37
Berah, E., 518
Berg, C. A., 486
Berger, K. S., 171
Bergin, A. E., 566, 568
Berglas, S., 435
Berieter, C., 39
Berkman, L., 570
Berkowitz, L., 223, 470, 472
Berlin, B., 270
Berlyne, D. E., 396, 401
Berman, J. S., 568
Berman, K. F., 535

Berman, M., 471
Berman, W., 322
Bernard, T. M., 585
Berndt, T. J., 377
Bernston, G. G., 415
Berry, J. W., 48, 101, 311, 580
Berry, S. L., 405
Berscheid, E., 424, 425, 438, 440, 441, 442, 443
Bersoff, D. M., 379
Bertenthal, B. I., 366
Bertilsson, L., 525
Bertoncini, J., 270
Betz, A. I., 169
Beutler, L. E., 567, 568
Bexton, W. H., 396
Bezooijen, R. V., 419
Bianchin, M., 76
Bickman, L., 568
Biederman, I., 136, 137
Bielavska, E., 203
Biery, R. E., 408
Billings, R. L., 334
Binet, A., 298, 299, 301, 302, 323
Bingham, C. R., 531
Birch, H. G., 368
Birdsall, T. G., 110
Birenbaum, M., 457
Bisanz, G. L., 288
Bisanz, J., 288
Bishop, S., 560
Bjelke, E., 187
Black, D. W., 525
Black, J. B., 268
Blackman, M. C., 497
Blackmore, S. J., 170
Blaine, J., 560
Blamire, A. M., 91
Blanchard, E. B., 555
Blasi, A., 384
Blehar, M., 371
Bliss, E. L., 536
Block, J., 370, 496
Block, M. L., 181
Bloom, A., 532
Bloom, B. S., 39, 322
Bloom, F. E., 185, 332
Blumenfeld, P., 367
Blumenthal, J. A., 584, 585
Bly, N., 290
Bobbitt, B. L., 349
Bock, K., 267
Boehm, L. E., 427
Bogen, J., 81
Bohn, H. G., 221
Bolger, N., 523
Boll, T. J., 547
Boller, K., 248
Bolwig, T. G., 557

SUBJECT INDEX